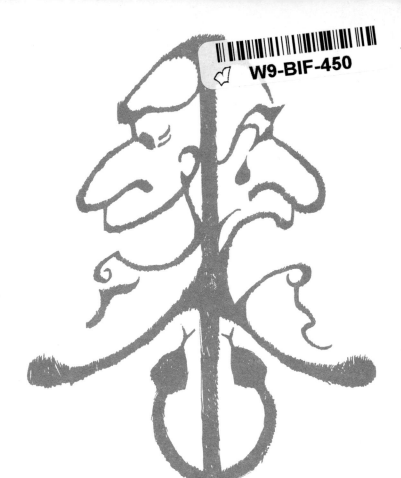

Joanne Trautmann
Associate Professor of Humanities
and
Carol Pollard
Curriculum Research Assistant

LITERATURE AND MEDICINE
Topics, Titles & Notes

Department of Humanities
The Milton S. Hershey Medical Center
The Pennsylvania State University
Hershey, Pennsylvania 17033

Published by:

Society for Health and Human Values
723 Witherspoon Building
Philadelphia, Pennsylvania 19107

Funds for the research and publication
of this volume were provided in part by
the National Endowment for the
Humanities under Grant EO 4579-71-197,
and by the Society for Health and
Human Values.

Contents

Introduction

Ever since the formal introduction several years ago of humanistic disciplines into the curriculum of a few medical colleges, creative literature has been a presence. Here and there a professor whose chief interest was perhaps in religion or in history used works of literature to make his students better able to understand life, or better to enjoy it. What was in the beginning simply a presence has become in the last four years a movement, slow at first, but assuredly gaining force. Literature courses for medical and pre-medical students and for practicing professionals are now under way at several institutions. At the same time, the medical journals are taking more interest in literature. There have always been a few short articles on, say, William Carlos Williams, or Anton Chekhov, contributed by M.D.'s who have been instructively side-tracked by the two great physician-writers. But recently there have also been articles by literary professionals who explore less obvious subjects. And C. P. Snow has told medical people that there should be a literary component throughout medical education, that this was, indeed, one practical solution to the problems he raised in his Two Cultures discussions. Furthermore, the Institute on Human Values in Medicine, since its inception attracted to the idea of literary study in medical education, has commissioned a group of medical and literary people to set up a dialogue between the disciplines.

Some of the people involved in this movement seek only to bring a pure literary experience into the medical environment. They know that _any_ first-rate poem or play or fiction, if taught with competence and received with pleasure, will be generally life-enhancing and therefore potentially conducive to that humanistically active physician they seek. But others feel that in some pedagogical and clinical circumstances it might be beneficial to isolate certain medical themes in literature so that their study promotes both the general goals of all literature and the specific goals of medicine.

For this second group, for those with a good deal of literary training and those with a little, we offer our annotated bibliography. In essence the bibliography is an attempted definition of a new discipline, which is not medicine through literature, but something of a parallel to medical history or medical ethics. Our bibliography should ultimately raise questions proper to this discipline, questions about the nature of objectivity in art as compared to medicine, for instance, or about the aesthetics of the body, or the nature of the dramatic role in a health care situation. But more immediately the bibliography provides titles of works of imaginative literature, and some information about those works, for people who want to teach or write or simply think about medical themes.

One chief principle of selection was that a literary work should be first-rate, or if not, then capable of illuminating in some special way one or more of our directly medical topics. So readers will find poems by interesting but minor doctor-writers, slim novels on V.D. and Abortion, and a somewhat relaxed Science Fiction category. They will not find, however, Christiaan Barnard's novel or Physician Extraordinary, the recent novel about William Harvey. There we drew our lines with some haughtiness. Our commitment has been first to literature written in English, second--the Classical section apart--to literature of France, Germany, and Russia, and only third to that of Italy and Spain. There are, in addition, a few capricious selections. I can think of one Polish novel, for instance, a Japanese one, and some short stories by Jorge Luis Borges. We have chosen representative works, and readers can normally assume that our authors have written other worthwhile pieces on the topics listed under their names. Thus Emily Dickinson has written several brilliant poems on Grief, though only one is part of the bibliography.

This work can be used in two ways. If readers have a topic

in mind--chosen from the thirty-nine listed on the contents page--they can go to the "Topics" section at the back of the book, and find there, in a sort of index, an alphabetical listing of works which deal with the subject. Each entry provides author, title, genre, and time period. The first entry under "Age," for instance, reads: "Amis, Kingsley. Ending Up. Novel. 20th." For further information on this novel, one may turn to the 20th Century section of the chronological list, seek out "Amis" in its alphabetical slot, and discover what we thought were the medically relevant aspects of the novel--in this case, not only Age, but also Alcoholism, Death, Disease and Health, Doctors, Dying, and Homosexuality--together with our brief summary/interpretation and full bibliographic information. Such information is given for all but the most readily available works. The date of first publication--or, in the case of plays, first performance--is given only for twentieth century works. A second method would provide aid for people who have a particular literary work in mind, know the author and period, and want some suggestions about its relationship to medicine. In that circumstance, they would go directly to the chronological list, hoping to find the work there. This method would also answer a question like, "What did Walt Whitman have to say about medical matters?" The absence of certain authors, especially in the 19th and 20th Century sections, which we have allowed to expand to two-thirds of the total entries, could be as significant as their presence.

The list of topics began with the subjects of importance to us and to our colleagues here in the Department of Humanities, grew with our consideration of what might be of interest to physicians in Family Medicine, Psychiatry, Pediatrics, Obstetrics/ Gynecology, Surgery, and Medicine, and took final shape in response to what we gradually learned about the way literature treated medical subjects. In this way it became apparent that Sexuality would have to be divided into one category for Sexual Roles and another for more general matters of human physiology and passion. When we got into the 19th Century section, it became clear that

Surgery would be a helpful topic and that Children was beginning
in this same century to be important enough to separate out from
The Family. We feel that sometimes our method results in new
insights into a work simply because we have labeled the medical
topics, and worked our interpretations around them. At the
same time, we have tried always to be just to the work as a
whole. We would be horrified to be seen as in any way encouraging the treatment of King Lear as a study in Geriatrics.

Some of the topics need further explanation. Physicians
in literature are covered in three different ways, at least.
The Evil Doctors category is probably self-explanatory (it
tends, by the way, to taper off in the 20th century, but to
return then from time to time with nightmarish intensity). We
were cautious about calling someone "evil," so most of the portraits of physicians will be found in the Doctors category.
Statements about the profession in general--as opposed to
images and portraits--will be found under Medical Profession.
Medical Ethics is covered not only by its own general topic,
but also in the specifically named Abortion and Euthanasia.
So too does the Women as Patients topic overlap with Abortion
and with Pregnancy and Childbirth. We would have preferred to
include works about Sexuality in that one category, making no
distinctions among kinds of sexuality--straight or gay or bi-
sexual--both because of our own principles and because in many
instances such demarcations are hard to identify. But we
recognized that a Homosexual category would be very useful.
Sexual Roles and the two women's topics (Women as Healers,
Women as Patients) are also responses to the current interests
of our potential readers, and in this case to our own principles
as well. We have taken Madness to mean behavior ranging from
clear psychosis to heavy neurosis. Sometimes what seemed at
first to be mad behavior, we have ultimately assigned to another
topic--often Grief--or ignored it. The Drugs topic usually refers
to the addictive sort, but in a few instances we have used the
topic to call attention to literary statements about conventional
medication. The Children and Age topics cannot be assumed to

signal characters who are, say, under eighteen or over seventy, for writers recognize that we are children whenever we are seen in relation to our parents and that we begin some part of the aging process as soon as we are aware of it.

The following works are offered as references for further sources about certain of our topics. For literary treatments of Age, see Simone de Beauvoir's The Coming of Age, New York, G. P. Putnam's Sons, 1972; for doctor-writers (the By Doctors category), see John D. Gordon, Doctors as Men of Letters: English and American Writers of Medical Background: An Exhibition in the Berg Collection, New York, The New York Public Library, 1964; for Children, The Child Study Association of America, Insights: a Selection of Creative Literature About Children, New York, Jason Aronson, 1973; for Death, Frederick Hoffman, The Mortal No: Death and the Modern Imagination, Princeton, Princeton University Press, 1964; for Disease and Health, Henry E. Sigerist, Civilization and Disease, Chicago, University of Chicago Press, 1965, and Gian-Paolo Biasin, Literary Diseases: Theme and Metaphor in the Italian Novel, Austin, University of Texas Press, 1975; for Drugs, Alethea Hayter, Opium and the Romantic Imagination, Berkeley, University of California Press, 1970; for The Family, Sven Armens, Archetypes of the Family in Literature, Seattle, University of Washington Press, 1966; for Homosexuality, Brian Reade, Male Homosexuality in English Literature from 1850 to 1900, New York, Coward-McCann, 1971; for Madness, Alan A. Stone and Sue Smart Stone, The Abnormal Personality Through Literature, Englewood Cliffs, New Jersey, Prentice-Hall, 1966; for Sexuality, James L. Malfetti and Elizabeth M. Eidlitz, Perspectives on Sexuality: a Literary Collection, New York, Holt, Rinehart and Winston, 1972; for Suicide, Seymour Perlin, A Handbook for the Study of Suicide, New York, Oxford University Press, 1974; for Women as Healers, Barbara Ehrenreich and Deirdre English, Witches, Midwives, and Nurses, Old Westbury, N. Y., The Feminist Press, 1972.

We want to thank our co-workers Alice Lundquist, Gwendolyn W. Pierce, June Watson, and Debra Weaver for their help in preparing the manuscript; Judy Bowes for designing the cover; Richard Kirby and Martin Pernick for suggesting bibliographic entries; and Joel Farber and Fred Oppenheimer for providing scholarly assistance with Greek and German poems.

This work is dedicated with respect, gratitude, and affection to June Watson.

J.T.

Classical

Aeschylus. Agamemnon. Drama.

Death   Dying   The Family
Madness   Sexuality   Sexual Roles

The first play in the Oresteia, a trilogy exploring
violence within the family. Agamemnon had sacrificed
his daughter, Iphigenia, in order to retrieve Helen,
his brother's errant wife. While he was away at Troy, his
wife, Clytemnestra, and her lover, Aegisthus, had seized
control of Argos. Now peace at Troy reopens the battle
within the family. Agamemnon returns with his concubine,
the mad Cassandra, who foretells vividly the butchery
that awaits her and Agamemnon at the hands of Clytemnestra and Aegisthus. Although the exaggerated luxury
and solicitude of Clytemnestra's welcome should warn
him, Agamemnon accepts her obsequiousness at face
value and goes to his death. Clytemnestra thereby
avenges Iphigenia and establishes female rule, seconded
by a male lover, in place of male rule, solaced by a
wife and concubine.

Aeschylus. The Eumenides. Drama.

Death   The Family   Grief
Sexual Roles

This third play of the Oresteia advocates the replace-
ment of revenge and guilt by a system of justice without
guilt. In the second play of the trilogy, The Libation
Bearers, Orestes, urged by Apollo, had murdered his
mother in revenge for his father. As The Eumenides
opens, Orestes seeks relief from guilt, personified by
the Eumenides, hideous women who pursue those who murder-
ously violate blood-ties. Apollo sends him to Athena,
who transfers judgment from the individual to the society.
The Athenian jury, not the forces of unreason or the
unconscious--not the Eumenides, in short--now decides
Orestes' guilt or innocence. Athena then placates the
Eumenides by offering them rites of worship and a role
in Athenian life. The once-destructive forces of grief
and guilt will now become beneficial to the individual
and the society. But the jury takes a strange way to
remove Orestes' guilt for his mother's murder. He has
not, as it turns out, shed his own blood because the
mother makes no contribution to her offspring. (The
deciding vote is cast by Athena, who was born, fully
armed, from her father's head.) The human mother is
only an incubator. Thus Clytemnestra, once ruler of
Argos, is reduced to a nurse tending an alien child.
The Eumenides advocates the transfer of authority from
the family to the society and so encourages the growth
of civilization--but that civilization is without women
citizens.

Apuleius. The Golden Ass. Tale.

Sexuality   Suffering   Women as Healers

A series of sketches about the humorous sufferings of a
man transformed into an ass. Lucius, drawn to amorous
witches by his lust, desires to use their shape-changing
ability to pursue his voluptuous enterprises. He tries
to be the mysterious owl, but becomes instead an ass,
driven by human cruelty and lust from misery to misery.
This human brutality is set against ideal human love:
the story of Cupid and Psyche told in the middle two
chapters. Psyche, or the Self, is content with blind
love, isolated from all nature, until she is persuaded
to see her husband, Cupid, or Love. Cupid then flees,
and the pregnant Psyche must be helped by stone, reed,
and bird before she can find her husband. The Self must
realize that communion with natural things is the way to
gain love. Psyche's story is echoed in the main tale,
for Lucius gains human shape when he prays to Ceres, the
goddess of fruitful nature, who restores his body and
leads him into the spiritual mysteries.

Aristophanes. Lysistrata. Drama.

Age   Sexuality   Sexual Roles

By boycotting the marriage bed, the women of Athens and
Sparta force their men to stop fighting and make peace.
Along the way there are some hilarious moments: the
younger men are sexually frustrated, sometimes pointedly
so; the women are tempted to weaken; the elderly men and
women fight a mock-heroic battle. To a modern reader
other readings might occur. The play could be seen,
and has, as the glorification of a woman's leadership
ability and general good sense, as opposed to her male
counterpart. But the play might also be read in an anti-
feminist way, i.e., the women are only able to unite
across battle lines because they are not members of the
two warring societies, not Athenians or Spartans, but
simply sexual objects.

The Bible. Apochrypha. Daniel and Susanna.

Age   Sexuality

A classic story of lecherous, old, socially-powerful men
and an innocent young woman. The elders threaten to
accuse Susanna falsely if she resists them. She does

resist; they do accuse. As she is sentenced to be stoned
to death, Daniel intervenes, exposes the elders' lies,
and vindicates Susanna.

The Bible. Apocrypha. Judith.

Sexual Roles

Judith seduces the besieging general, Holofernes, cuts
off his head as he sleeps in bed, and returns to the
Israelite city to direct the counter-attack upon Holofernes' demoralized army. "No one dared to threaten the
Israelites again in Judith's lifetime, or for a long time
after her death" (The New English Bible).

The Bible. Apochrypha. Tobit.

Handicaps   Sexuality

Tobit, made blind by sparrow droppings, continues to
govern his household in spite of some errors in judgment.
An angel instructs his son, Tobias, in the use of fish
parts to cure the blindness. The angel also instructs
Tobias in the use of cooked fish to drive away the demon
that has killed his bride's seven previous husbands on
seven previous wedding nights. Despite the rather ludicrous nature of their rescue, one is still moved by
Tobias and Sarah's beautiful prayer for their married
life.

The Bible. I Corinthians.

The Body   Death   Sexuality

In this famous discussion of sexuality and marriage
(Chapter VII), Paul favors chastity, but says that it
is better to marry than to burn. After a couple is
married, each has power over the body of the other.
In Chapter XV, these magnificent lines follow a discussion of the resurrection of the body: "O death
where is thy sting? O grave, where is thy victory?"

The Bible. Ecclesiastes.

Age   Death

The meaninglessness of death causes an exhortation to
enjoy life. "Wherefore I perceive that there is nothing
better, than that a man should rejoice in his own works;
for that is his portion: for who shall bring him to see
what shall be after him?" The final chapter contains
this allegory of age. "In the day when the keepers of
the house shall tremble, and the strong men shall bow
themselves, and the grinders cease because they are few,
and those that look out of the windows be darkened . . .
because man goeth to his long home."

The Bible. Esther.

Sexual Roles

King Ahasurus' first wife refuses to parade her beauty
at his command. He divorces her and looks for a replace-
ment. Esther submits to the year-long preparation of her
body and pleases the king with her charm and acquiescence.
But her submissiveness means that she is able to be controlled by other men as well. Fortunately for Ahasurus,
it is good counsel she follows as, led by her uncle
Mordeccai, she saves the Jews from Haman's wicked plots.

The Bible. Exodus.

Plague

Chapters VII - XII tell of the plagues sent by God upon
Egypt to force Pharaoh to let the Israelites go: rivers
turned to blood, frogs, lice, flies, murrain on cattle,
hail, and the death of the firstborn children. The
archetypal story of the plague as the instrument of God.

The Bible. Genesis.

Age   Children   The Family
Homosexuality Preg. & Childbirth Sexuality
Sexual Roles

The two stories of the Creation are found in Chapters
I - III. The more famous is the version wherein Eve
is created from Adam's rib, and this act is followed
by the temptation and fall. Childbirth pains are
imposed upon women as punishment for Eve's sin. Woman
as temptress is again portrayed through Potiphar's wife
(Chapter XXXIX), who attempts to seduce Joseph, imprisoning him in rage when he rejects her. Cain and Abel
(Chapter IV) are the first sibling rivals. Their rivalry
is continued by Jacob and Esau (Chapter XXVII) and the
brothers of Joseph (Chapters XXXVII, XLII - XLV).
Methusaleh (Chapter V) is our exemplus of extreme old
age. Age and sexuality are discussed together in
Chapters XVI, XVIII, and XXI, when Sarah laments her
barrenness, now assumed to be permanent because of her
age. Then she hears an angel promising Abraham a son
by her. "Therefore Sarah laughed within herself saying
'After I am waxed old shall I have pleasure, my lord being
old also?'" But she does have a son; age seems no barrier
to sexuality. Rachel also laments the humiliation of her
barrenness and then rejoices in her pregnancies, even

though she dies giving birth to her second child (Chapter XXX). Within the family, a father is seen as having a prophetic blessing--hence the need for Jacob's trickery. Further, the father's line must be maintained at all costs--as in the curious story of Lot's daughters who, to preserve his seed, make him drunk and sleep with him (Chapter XIX). In contrast to the sexual tension of Electra, this action is considered acceptable. However, the homosexuality of Sodom, told in the same chapter, is not acceptable. Onan's spilling of his seed (Chapter XXXVIII) is also an immoral act. Children are important--hence the magnitude of Abraham's grieving acceptance of Isaac's sacrifice (Chapter XXII).

The Bible. Job.

Death   Disease & Health   Suffering

Unparalled in its attempts to find some justification for suffering. Suffering is seen in all its aspects: physical, in disease; psychological, in grief for loss of family and possessions; and spiritual, through lack of understanding of God's purpose. Death is blackened emptiness--but a welcome relief from torment. God answers Job's demands for meaning by overwhelming Job with the unsearchable wonders of the universe. Job humbles himself and is silent.

The Bible. John.

Death

Chapter XI - the raising of Lazarus from the dead.

The Bible. Judges.

Handicaps   Preg. & Childbirth   Sexuality
Sexual Roles

The strong women--Deborah, the leader-judge of Israel, and Jael, who kills the enemy Sisera in his sleep (Chapters III and IV)--contrast sharply with Delilah who acts as a tool of the Philistines. These militant Israelite women also contrast with Manoah's wife, who exults upon learning of her pregnancy and the dietary precautions she must take to bring forth Samson as Nazarite (Chapter XIII). The purity of his diet does not save Samson from Delilah's temptation, but neither does his blindness prevent him from destroying the Philistines.

The Bible. Leviticus.

Disease & Health

Leprosy is the disease most described and cured in the Bible. Chapter XIII contains the elaborate tests for leprosy and the descriptions of those sores that are and those that are not signs of the disease. The priests decide who must be exiled from the community, a determination now made by doctors.

The Bible. Luke.

By Doctors   Doctors   The Family
Poverty & Health   Preg. & Childbirth   Sexual Roles
Suffering

By tradition (Paul to the Colossians IV, 14), Luke was a physician. In Chapters I and II he writes of the pregnancies of Elizabeth, who was formerly barren, and of Mary. He records there the great Magnificat and the birth of Jesus in the stable. The single line of Chapter IV, 23 is one with tremendous reverberations: "Physician, heal thyself." In Chapter X is the parable of the Good Samaritan, and in XV the parable of the Prodigal Son. Luke writes in Chapter XVI of Dives and Lazarus, not the story of Lazarus raised from the dead, but of the rich man, Dives, and the poor sick Lazarus, who lay at Dives' gate while dogs licked his sores. Lazarus goes to heaven, and Dives to hell. Chapter X, 38-42 pits Martha, who defines a woman's role as servant, against Mary, who chooses to meditate on Christ's words. Christ speaks in favor of Mary. Finally, in Chapter XXII Luke recounts Christ's agony at Gethsemane.

The Bible. Mark.

Madness

In Chapter V, Christ heals the lunatic by driving the devil, Legion, into a herd of swine.

The Bible. Matthew.

Children   The Family   Sexuality
Suicide

Jesus places the value of the family below the value of religion (Chapter X), although he elevates the value of children and childhood (Chapter XIX). In Chapter XIV we meet the perverted family of Herod, Herodias, and Salome, who uses her body, at her mother's direction, to please her stepfather and to demand in return the death of John the Baptist. The despairing suicide of Judas is mentioned in Chapter XXVII.

The Bible. New Testament.

Doctors   Dying

Christ as Physician. Although the Old Testament contains instances of miraculous cures, the New Testament shows Christ the Healer (he compares himself to a physician, e.g. Mark II, 17) faced with some of a doctor's problems: the training of subordinates (Matthew XVII), the inter-

mixture of sin and sickness, in which he feels that cure of the soul is more important than cure of the body (Matthew IX), the drain upon his strength (Mark V), and the question of heredity vs. environment as a cause for disease (John IX).

No death has been so intensely explored as the crucifixion of Jesus, and any reader seeking literary representation of the process of dying should consult the Bible.

The Bible. Proverbs.

Children   Sexual Roles

The need for the training and correction of children. "Spare the rod and spoil the child" comes from Chapter XIII. Proverbs tells of the joy brought by a virtuous child to his parents and the pains caused by a troublesome child. After diatribes against strange women and scolding women, the book ends with the portrait of the virtuous wife.

The Bible. Psalms, nos. VI, XXIII, and CXXXVII.

Death   Disease & Health   Grief

Psalm VI is the cry of a man tormented in body and soul. He is vexed in his bones with disease and in his soul with his enemies. Psalm XXIII is the grand confidence of "The Lord is my shepherd." Psalm CXXXVII is the angry lament of exiles, grieving for their country, "By the rivers of Babylon, there we sat down, yea, we wept, when we remembered Zion."

The Bible. Revelations.

Death   Plague

The four horsemen of the Apocalypse, including Death, on his pale horse, are found in Chapter VI. The apocalyptic vision of worldwide destruction is an archetype of plague.

The Bible. Ruth.

The Family

An astonishingly strong attachment between daughter-in-law and mother-in-law. Ruth supports her mother-in-law, Naomi, until her unassuming efforts capture the attention of a kinsman of Naomi's, Boaz. Following Naomi's advice, Ruth wins Boaz in marriage, thus preserving her first husband's family. The book ends with a celebration of this unique daughter worth more than seven sons.

The Bible. I Samuel, Chapters XVI, XVIII, and XIX.

Madness

The spirit of brooding madness haunts the sinning Saul. We observe the purgation of that spirit by David and his harp--and also the fear and resentment that prompt Saul to attack this young rival who preserves his sanity. Interesting model for psychiatrists.

The Bible. II Samuel.

The Family   Grief   Sexuality

This book includes the moving laments of David for Jonathan and Saul (Chapter I) and for his son Absolom (Chapter XVIII). David's family can be revealingly contrasted with the family of Oedipus. In Chapter XIII, Ammon rapes his sister Tamar, then throws her out in revulsion. Absolom kills his brother in retaliation and goes to war against his father, seeking to replace him as king. In a temporary victory, he captures and sleeps with his father's concubines. Here intra-family sexuality and warfare are, in contrast to Oedipus, vigorously expressed. In Chapter XI is the story of David's lust for Bathsheba, his murder of her husband, and his punishment through loss of their child.

The Bible. The Song of Solomon.

The Body   Sexuality

Lyric sexuality. Celebration of the beloved, especially the body of the beloved, both male and female. The beloved is compared to the most beautiful objects of nature: "A garden enclosed is my sister, my spouse; a spring shut up, a fountain sealed."

Catullus, C. Valerius. Carmina, no. 23. Poem.

The Body   Poverty & Health

An ironic description of poverty's medicinal improvement of the body. "Besides, what with heat, cold and near-starvation/Your bodies are as dry as bone . . . . You're free from sweat/And slobber and catarrah and running-wet/Noses" (James Michie, trans.).

Catullus, C. Valerius. Carmina, no. 56. Poem.

Homosexuality

The poet invites a friend to laugh at him. Coming upon a young couple making love, the poet has chosen to rape the boy. The implication is that the boy has gotten his fit reward--what he did to the girl is now done to him. But the equation between the freely given vagina and the forced anus seems questionable even to the poet, and his insistence upon laughter betrays his uneasiness with the choice.

Catullus, C. Valerius. _Carmina_, no. 63. Poem.

| Madness | Sexuality | Sexual Roles |

Attis, seized with madness, castrates himself and takes part in the rites of Cybele, leading the delirious dance. Then, recovered, Attis, now "she," mourns for her lost manhood, which for Attis means sports and social position. Castration is not terrible for its loss of sexual potency or of procreative ability, but rather for loss of country, family, admiring friends, possessions--and wrestling ground, running track, and race course. She laments that she must remain in woman's shape (thus a woman is seen solely as a man without a penis) in the wilderness, but Cybele sends a lion to terrify her into insane acceptance. The poet prays to Cybele to spare him such fury and madness. Unlike the terrible female madness in Euripides' _Bacchants_ which drives the women to mutilate men, Cybele's female madness attacks men through themselves, perhaps a more terrifying version.

Catullus, C. Valerius. _Carmina_, no. 71. Poem.

| Disease & Health | Sexuality |

Consolation for a rejected lover. The smelly armpits of his successful rival pain the lady. At the same time, the rival's attempts to please her arouse his painful gout. There is an implication that the lady passed on the gout from the rejected lover to his rival (a most terrible revenge!).

Cicero, Marcus Tullius. "On the Art of Growing Old," from _On Old Age and On Friendship_, trans. F. O. Copley. Ann Arbor: University of Michigan Press, 1967. Essay.

| Age | The Body |

By disparaging the body, Cicero is able to praise old age. He speaks of many vigorous and accomplished old men to prove that old age need not be miserable. On the contrary, by taking away pleasures of the body, old age removes the distractions of passion and vice, permitting a man to enjoy studying and farming. Cicero becomes poetic when he defends old age against the charge that death lies too near for comfort. Young and old, we are all near death, which is not an end, but an entrance to further life.

Euripides. _Alcestis_. Drama.

| Age | Death | Dying |
| Grief | Medical Ethics | |

Poses questions about the value of life and the meaning of death. Alcestis has agreed to die so that her husband, Admetus, may live. She bids an aching farewell to life, and dies. Admetus then begins to suffer under his grief. In his guilt he attacks his old father for refusing to die for him. But his father replies that life is sweet, regardless of how much remains, and that Alcestis died by her own choice and responsibility. The play thus deals with issues central to medical ethics: who shall live, and who shall die, and what sort of life is worth fighting to save. Hercules, learning of his host's loss, goes to Alcestis' tomb, wrestles with death, and brings her back to Admetus. Though she requires purification and is not yet able to speak, her return brings on the rejoicing with which the play ends.

Euripides. _The Bacchants_. Drama.

| Madness | Sexuality | Sexual Roles |

The havoc created by sexual madness. Dionysius (Bacchus), the god of wine and wild ecstasy, revenges himself upon a community which condemned his mother for adultery and so denied his divinity. He proves his godhood by unleashing the repressed sexuality in the community. The women run mad in bacchic revels--destroying cattle, performing miracles, and successfully defeating the men who attack them. The ruler, Pentheus, first proposes military action against the bacchants, but a follower of Dionysius persuades him to go alone, in women's dress, so that he, Pentheus, may spy upon the women's revels, which he imagines to be drunken orgies. The bacchants, led by his mother and his aunts, tear him into pieces, believing him to be a lion. The play ends with their horrified return to sanity. The women have unleashed great violence, while Pentheus, who "thinks his violence can master the Invincible," becomes the passive voyeur. Of the two forms of madness, that of women joined in ecstatic destruction is the one which most haunts western civilization.

Euripides. _Electra_. Drama.

| Children | The Family | Sexuality |

An exploration of feminine roles, maternal roles, and the tensions between mother and children. Clytemnestra at once fears and loves her children, but her maternal feelings are swamped by her feminism and her egotism. She attacks the double standard for men and women in sexual affairs, tacitly defending her affair with Aegisthus, and claims that Iphigenia died because she was a girl--that Agamemnon would have refused to sacrifice a son. In contrast, Electra, the daughter she has forced into a demeaning marriage, rejects all feminism for femininity coupled with reason. But Electra has her mother's desire for revenge. Orestes kills Aegisthus in revenge for his father's death, but wavers at the thought of murdering his mother. His rationalizations are ruthlessly cut short by Electra, and Clytemnestra is killed by her children. The play lacks the high solemnity of Sophocles' and Aeschylus' versions of the story, but has a realism and a light touch of its own.

Euripides. _Hippolytus_. Drama.

| The Family | Sexuality | Suicide |

An inverse Oedipal situation. Aphrodite causes the stepmother, Phaedra, granddaughter of Europa and daughter of the infamous Pasiphae, to fall in love with her stepson, Hippolytus. Hippolytus' mother was an Amazon, a warrior woman devoted to Artemis, and Hippolytus has inherited her stern chastity and devotion to blood sport. Roughly rejected by Hippolytus, Phaedra accuses him of her rape and commits suicide. Deceived, Theseus curses his son, causing Hippolytus to die under the hooves of his own mares.

Euripides. _Medea_. Drama.

| Children | Dying | Preg. & Childbirth |
| Sexuality | Sexual Roles | Suffering |

The destructiveness of passion and the manipulation of the family to cause agony. Medea loves her husband, Jason, with a passion he does not return. Instead, he arranges to marry the ruler's, Creon's, daughter, rationalizing that social advancement will aid the children he had with the now-exiled Medea. Jason forgets that Medea is a noble, powerful witch, and sees only the dismissable woman. To Medea, her children and childbirth pains are labors done for Jason. She tricks Jason's intended bride into a hideous death, described by messenger, a death that engulfs Creon as well. Having caused the daughter to kill the father, Medea then kills her own children, the children to whom Jason has shown indifference, turning the affection underlying his careless inattention to torment. In a final irony, this play, full of the mutual destruction of parent and child, ends with Medea finding refuge with Aegisthus because she has promised him children.

Euripides. _The Trojan Women_ (_Troades_). Drama.

| Age | The Family | Grief |
| Sexual Roles | Suffering | |

Dramatizes the suffering of the Trojan women as they watch the victorious Greeks exterminate the Trojan people by razing the city and destroying the last remnants of Trojan family structure. Not only are the women forced to witness the deaths of their husbands and sons, but they are themselves deprived of all recognition as wives and mothers, except for the brief moment given Andromache to mourn for Hector's son. (She is then sent as concubine to the son of the man who killed Hector.) The Greek Helen, the supreme sexual object, goes home regally with her weak husband, while the aged Hecuba, once queen of Troy, goes as cleaning woman to the household of Ulysses, the man who destroyed her family and city. The women are passive objects--they offer no resistance and do not attempt suicide--but they are feeling objects. The play, charged with grief and unrelieved by any meaning given to the suffering and death, is only for the sturdy reader.

Hesiod. _Theogony_, ed. M. L. West. Oxford: Clarendon Press, 1966. Long Poem.

| Children | The Family | Sexual Roles |

Three different roles for women. First, the muses who sing to please the heart of Zeus, aid the wise governor in his rule, and ease the griefs of men. The second is Aphrodite, lover of smiles, who is born from the sperm spilled from Cronos' castration of his father. Finally, there is woman as scourge (elsewhere called Pandora), created by Zeus to counterbalance the benefits of Prometheus' gift of fire. Zeus himself plays a rather odd family role. The early gods carry rivalry between father and son to an extreme. Because he is afraid of them, Night hides his children, until his consort, Earth, helps her son Cronos to castrate his father and take his place. To prevent a similar overthrow, Cronos eats his children. But the pattern repeats. His consort, Rhea, helps her son Zeus to escape, and Zeus overthrows his father to become ruler of the gods.

Homer. _Iliad_. Epic Poem.

| Age | Death | Grief |

In Book I, old, wise Nestor endeavors to heal the crippling quarrel between Agamemnon and Achilles. He argues from the position of respected old age--unsuccessfully. Throughout the poem, death and life are mingled as part of one whole: Achilles' shield serves as an emblem of this mixture; a marriage followed by a dispute about blood money; wives and children on the city wall are set against the strife and death of an ambush; rich fields and vineyards are followed by the lion amid the cattle. So when the poet describes a man dying with his guts spattered on the plain, he also gives some fact about the man's life, his family or wife. The epic of death ends with an outburst of grief, not victory. The two enemies unite in grief when Priam comes to Achilles, the murderer of his son, and begs for his son's body. His speech arouses Achilles' tears for Patroklos and for his father; Priam, Achilles, and the audience are drawn together by their losses.

Homer. _The Odyssey_. Epic Poem.

| Drugs | The Family | Sexuality |

Throughout _The Odyssey_ runs the theme of the family steadfast against disruptive forces, especially the forces of possessive sexuality and of unlawful greed. Agamemnon's family with its murders and betrayals is contrasted with the besieged unity of Ulysses' family. In Ithaca, Ulysses' faithful wife and loyal son resist the unruly, unwanted suitors for her hand and property. And during his voyage back to his family, Ulysses is enticed by the Sirens, held back by the magic of the sexually dehumanizing Circe, and entrapped by the possessive Calypso. He is further delayed by the crew's disregard for the rules governing the cattle of the sun and by Polyphemus' disregard for the guest laws. The oblivion induced by drugs is also a threat, as seen in the contented lassitude of the Lotus Eaters. At last Ulysses' return is expedited by Nausicaa and her family, and he is gradually recognized and re- united with his family: the loyal shepherd, his son, his dog, his nurse, his wife and, finally, his father.

Horace (Quintus Horatius Flaccus). Odes, Book I, no. XXV. Poem.

Age   Sexuality

His mistress having rebuffed him, the poet takes mali- cious delight in foreseeing the sexual frustrations awaiting her in her old age.

Horace (Quintus Horatius Flaccus). Satires, Book II, no. III. Poem.

Madness

A little dialogue proving that all men are mad, if folly and bad judgment are madness. He attacks covetousness, superstition, and ambition.

Juvenal (Decimus Iunius Iuvenalis). Satires, no. II. Poem.

Homosexuality

An attack upon two aspects of homosexuality--first, upon the hypocritical homosexual (whose sexual practices are known to the "pile doctor") who attacks the vices of women while secretly indulging in orgies himself, and second, upon the weak and base behavior that re- sults from the homosexual vice. Juvenal also derides the homosexual relationship because it is sterile: there are no children. "You rail at foul practices, do you/When you're the ditch where they dig, the Socratic buggering perverts?/Hairy parts, to be sure, and arms all covered with bristles/Promise a rough tough guy, but the pile doctor smiles; he knows better/ seeing that smooth behind, prepared for the "operation" (trans. R. Humphries).

Juvenal (Decimus Iunius Iuvenalis). Satires, no. VI. Poem.

Abortion   Sexual Roles

His lengthy diatribe against women. He is especially insistent upon their lecherous, luxurious, and per- verse natures. If a woman is not lecherous, she may be a learned woman who parades her knowledge, or a muscle-bound sort who goes in for gladiatorial-style workouts, or one who is conspicuously political. He also attacks the prevailing practice of abortion among the rich (poor women don't because they can't afford it).

Juvenal (Decimus Iunius Iuvenalis). Satires, no. X. Poem.

Age   The Body

The horrors of age. Juvenal attacks the folly of those who wish for long life, when long life means only a long old age. He paints a savage portrait of a senile mind in a senile body.

Lucian of Samosata. "Death of Peregrine," Works, trans. A. M. Haman. Cambridge: Harvard University Press, 1936. Vol. 5. Essay.

Suicide

Mockery of a suicide. Peregrine, an unsuccessful seeker of fame, ends a series of attempts to win recognition by throwing himself into a fiery pit. The narrator mocks his heroics and the folly of those who expect to see him rise from the flames.

Lucian of Samosata. "The Disowned," Works, trans. A. M. Haman. Cambridge: Harvard University Press, 1936. Vol. 5. Essay.

Doctors   Madness   Med. Ethics
Med. Profession   Sexual Roles

Conflict between the doctor as professional and the doctor as son and heir. A youth, disinherited by his father, studied medicine and became a good doctor. When his father went mad, the son cured him and so was restored as heir. Later his father's wife also went mad; the son refused to cure her and was again disinherited. This essay is his protest to a jury. The doctor argues that his profession directs that he not treat hopeless cases, that disease attacks the sexes differently (women are more prone to madness), and that he could cure his father but not his stepmother. He asserts that the profession alone should judge a doctor's actions.

Lucian of Samosata. "On Funerals," Works, trans. A. M. Haman. Cambridge: Harvard University Press, 1936. Vol. 4. Essay.

Death   Grief

The writer attacks absurd beliefs about the underworld and especially ridicules those who believe in the horrors of death. It is such beliefs that cause excesses of grief, when the dead may well be more comfortable than in life.

Martial (Marcus Valerius Martialis). Epigram, Book V, no. 9. From The Epigrams of Martial. London: G. Bell and Sons, 1914. Poem.

Disease & Health   Med. Students

A witty version of contemporary complaints--the inunda- tion of the patient by hordes of medical students and the diagnosis that creates new illness.

Old Women as Prophets.

Sexual Roles

One role associated with old women in classical times is that of foretelling and, in part, controlling the future. The Cumean sibyl and the three fates are famous examples here. Although Apollo, a young god, confers power of prophecy, it is women who are the vehicles for this power--e.g. Cassandra and the priestess at the Delphic oracle.

Ovid (Publius Ovidius Naso). Amores, Book I, Elegy VII. Poem.

Sexuality

Delightful advice given by a lover to his mistress before going to a banquet. He tells her how to avoid her husband's playful advances while dallying with the lover. His advice becomes more and more lively, until he realizes that the husband will enjoy the climax. He then begs his mistress to be an unwilling wife that night, or, at least, to tell him that she was so.

Ovid (Publius Ovidius Naso). Amores, Book II, Elegy IV. Poem.

Sexuality

A joyous rationalization of his love for every woman, whether tall, short, learned, ignorant, graceful, awk- ward, young or old.

Ovid (Publius Ovidius Naso). Amores, Book II, Elegies XIII and XIV. Poems.

Abortion

The first poem is the prayer of a lover whose mistress, without telling him, tried to terminate her pregnancy leaving her in the throes of a botched abortion. The lover attempts to convince Lucina, goddess of child- birth, that his mistress still has many virtues and so should be helped in her labor. He seems also to be convincing himself that she is not a target for his angry reprisals. The second poem deals more directly with this anger. He condemns women as murderers. Why should women, who do not take part in combat, inflict wounds on themselves? What would have happened to the great heroes, or the women themselves, if women in the past had committed such crimes. The poet works him- self into a frenzy of condemnation--and then breaks off in prayer for his mistress, cured of his resentment.

Ovid (Publius Ovidius Naso). Amores, Book III, Elegy VII. Poem.

The Body   Sexuality

The humiliations of impotence. The poet's pen gives just due to his lady's body and amorous skill. Yet his penis can do nothing. He attempts to justify himself by boasting of the other women he has had, by accusing the forces of witchcraft, and by boasting of his poetical power. His organ remains recalcitrant. His mistress finally leaves him, employing a little duplicity to conceal his deficiency from her maids.

Ovid (Publius Ovidius Naso). Metamorphoses, Books III, IV, and VIII, lines 427-642, 346-481, and 800-909. Epic Poem.

Age   The Body   Sexuality

Ovid's myths of transformations, beginning with the creation of order from chaos and ending with the exal- tation of society under the rule of Augustus, move through transmutations of the individual to transmuta- tions of a whole society. Among the myths are two that have great meaning in accounts of human psychology: the myth of Narcissus and the myth of Hermaphroditus. The first is a double story of Echo, cursed to mirror the words of others, and her beloved, Narcissus, who falls in love with his mirrored image. Narcissus dies of frustrated self-love, and Echo withers away to a voice. The myth of Hermaphroditus begins with a water nymph, passionately in love with a young boy whose beautiful body is described with loving detail. The nymph tries to rape the carefree boy, he resists, and she prays that the two will never be separated. Cruelly, the gods join them into one body, forming the Hermaphrodite. Since his strength has been cut in half, the half-man prays that all who drink of the spring may be so weakened. The predatory female deprives the young male of his strength. In contrast, the union of Philemon and Baucis, two old people famous for their simplicity and righteousness, is a source of comfort to them both. When they are rewarded for their piety, they ask only to serve the gods and to die together. They are allowed to live out their old age together, until death trans- forms them into entwined trees.

Petronius Arbiter. Satyricon. Satiric sketches.

Homosexuality   Sexuality

One of the funniest sketches is a delighted exploration of the tangles possible when several shallow, egotistical people, capable of being aroused by either sex, give free rein to their lust. Another sketch portrays the despair of impotence and the eager grasping at any possible cure: charms, diets, or thrashings by the old hags at the temple of Priapus. In a nicely decadent ending, the narrator's potency is restored by the prospect of corrupting two young children given to his patron by their greedy parents.

Pindar. "Nemea VI: For Alcimidas of Aegina: Victory in Wrestling, Boys' Division." Available in Pindar: Selected Odes, trans. C. A. P. Ruck and W. H. Matheson. Ann Arbor: University of Michigan Press, 1968. Poem.

The Body

The first strophe celebrates the body as divine and as equal to a creative mind. Although the gods alone are eternal and secure, "nonetheless, the poet's mind some way,/The athlete's body--these approximate divinity."

Pindar. "Pythia III: For Hieron of Syracuse: On the Occasion of His Illness." Available in Pindar: Selected Odes, trans. C. A. P. Ruck and W. H. Matheson. Ann Arbor: University of Michigan Press, 1968. Poem.

Disease & Health   Doctors   Med. Profession

The poet uses his poetry as medicine. At first, in his desire to cure his sick patron, he recounts the story of Asclepios--unwittingly he also describes how good is consumed by evil. The fire which consumed Asclepios' mother destroys many people; her son cures many more until, bribed, he raises a man from the dead. The gods promptly destroy both doctor and patient. The poet wishes in vain that he could find a greater, living Asclepios whom he could lure to Hieron with his musical verse. Poetry, however, can relieve suffering. The poet can help his patron to bear his ills by reminding Hieron of his good fortunes, that have called forth the balancing evil from the gods, and by urging Hieron to wait patiently for the redressing good. "We fashion with our wits the fortune that befalls us,/Doctoring it according to our art."

Plato. Apology and Phaedo. Dialogues.

Death   Dying

At the end of the Apology, Socrates rebukes the judges who have condemned him in a speech that is a powerful, reasoned acceptance of death. In the Phaedo he expands his arguments, proving that the soul is immortal and that death is not to be feared. He then acts upon his beliefs. After questioning the executioner about the best way to aid the poison in its work, he drinks the hemlock, gives consoling advice to his friends, asks Crito to sacrifice the customary cock to Asclepius in gratitude for a cure, and dies.

Plato. The Republic, Books I, III, and the Appendix to Book IV. Dialogues.

Age   The Body   Body/Mind
Med. Ethics   Med. Profession   Sexual Roles

In the first book, Cephalus draws a picture of the serene and respected old age that may be achieved by those who have trained the mind to rule over the body. Without a contented mind, youth and age are both intolerable. In the third book, Plato argues that more emphasis should be placed upon training the mind than the body, since the trained mind can perceive how to maintain a healthy body while the reverse is not true. He then limits the function of doctors to the treatment of healthy people with a temporary ailment. If a man is old, chronically disabled, or not disabled enough to stop work, he should not be treated. To do otherwise is to produce weak citizens and hypochondria. The Appendix to Book IV argues for equality in the training of women and men, since women must be healthy and educated to raise good children, and some women will help govern society.

Plato. Symposium. Dialogue.

The Body   Doctors   Homosexuality
Med. Profession   Sexuality

The Symposium is a source for many metaphors used to explain and explore human sexuality. Each speaker sets forth his concept of Love, and the images move from the purely physical to the highly spiritual. The first speaker describes two Aphrodites: one earthly and physical, the other heavenly and homosexual. The physician, Eryximachus, believes that Love reconciles warring elements in nature--and so underlies the medical profession. A good physician can provide the body with the requisite Love and so cure it. Another speaker envisions a third, hermaphrodite, sex of great power, which arrogantly attacked the gods and was, in punishment, split into two sexes. Now each half seeks the other. A fourth speaker sees Love as the source of creative power. Socrates concludes the series with the ladder of Love, which raises man from love of the beautiful object to worship of the source of all beauty and good.

Plautus. Pseudolus. Available in Six Plays of Plautus, trans. Lionel Casson. Garden City: Doubleday, 1963. Drama.

Sexuality   Suffering

Human cruelty and sexuality made comic by burlesque and witty dialogue. Unlike Terence, who is at once

more realistic and more romantic, Plautus was fantastic and hardboiled. His pimp, Ballio, is grotesquely funny as he relishes the miseries he inflicts upon his whores and his servants in his greed. The young, languishing hero desires possession of his love, one of Ballio's stable, and she desires the hero, in part as deliverance from the pimp. Her rescue is accomplished by the theatrical trickery of the hero's slave, who gets money for his success. All motives are base, all sufferings, commonplace.

Sappho. On Death. Fragments.

Death

Even the fragments of Sappho's poetry are worth consideration, as shown by these two taken from Barnstone's edition. "Death is our evil. The gods believe this,/ or else by now they would be dead." "It would be wrong for us. It is not right/for mourning to enter a home of poetry."

Sappho. On old age and sexuality (B134, D32, E42, LP21).* Poem.

Age   The Body   Sexuality

Her aging, post-menopausal body is a barrier both to marriage and the pains of love. Yet, she still can celebrate the violet-scented body of a young girl.

*Because Sappho's writings have survived only in fragments, they vary from translator to translator more than the works of other classical poets. So expect variation. Since her poems are untitled, they are identified by their numbers in principal editions of her work (Barnstone, Diehl, Edmonds, Lobel and Page).

Sappho. To Brachea (B9, D2, E2, LP31).* Short Poem.

The Body   Homosexuality

A body in sexual torment. Extraordinary images recreate the poet's response to a young girl. "my tongue is broken and thin fire/runs like a thief through my body . . . . I am paler than grass" (trans. Barnstone).

*See Sappho. On old age and sexuality.

Seneca, Lucius Annaeus. Epistles, nos. XXII and XXVI, "On Old Age" and "On Old Age and Death." Available in Seneca, trans. Richard Grummere. Cambridge, Massachusetts: Harvard University Press, 1967. Vol. I. Essays.

Age   Death

The first essay urges us to "cherish and love old age; for it is full of pleasure if one knows how to use it." Death is close to young and old alike, Seneca maintains. The second essay carries that theme further. Each of us is so close to death that we must prepare to do easily what we all must do inevitably.

Seneca, Lucius Annaeus. Epistles, no. XXIV, "On Despising Death." Available in Seneca, trans. Richard Grummere. Cambridge, Massachusetts: Harvard University Press, 1967. Vol. I. Essay.

Death

The mystique surrounding death creates needless fear. Common people face and despise death while a sick stomach, gout, and childbirth pains inflict greater suffering than death can muster. Only the fear of death is fearful.

Seneca, Lucius Annaeus. Epistles, no. LIV, "On Asthma and Death." Available in Seneca, trans. Richard Grummere. Cambridge, Massachusetts: Harvard University Press, 1967. Vol. I. Essay.

Death   Disease & Health

An asthma attack because it is a continued "last gasp" is a practice death; and recovered health gives little pleasure because it never lasts. Still, by cheerful encouragement, the writer prepares himself to make death a smooth removal, rather than a rough expulsion from life.

Seneca, Lucius Annaeus. Hercules Furens. Available in Three Tragedies, ed. H. M. Kingery. Norman: University of Oklahoma Press, 1966. Drama.

Death   The Family   Grief
Madness

A rhetorical play arguing that life is more terrible than death. Hercules completes the Labor of drawing Cerebus from Hades into the sunlight. His wife and friends rejoice at his victory over death, comparing him to a successful Orpheus. Yet the goddess Juno, his bitter enemy, drives him mad, transforming the conqueror of death into a bringer of death, who kills his own wife and children under the illusion that they are his enemies. Recovered, he wishes to escape his guilt by a return to madness or by death, but his father dissuades him.

Sophocles. Ajax. Drama.

Madness   Suicide

Madness and subsequent sanity as a punishment from the gods. As in Hercules, newly recovered sanity is more terrible than the madness. Because Ajax has asserted that he is independent of the gods, he is made mad.

Raging at a supposed slight, he storms off to kill the
Greek leaders, but kills a flock of sheep instead. Recovering his sanity, he recognizes his helplessness and
his dishonor--and so commits suicide.

Sophocles. _Antigone_. Drama.

Death	The Family	Grief
Suicide		

Battle of wills over who controls administration of burial
rites. Antigone is barred by Creon, her fiance's father,
from giving burial to her traitor-brother; but, defying
the death-penalty, she sprinkles dust on the decaying
corpse. Her motive is mixed. Love, loyalty, family pride,
perverseness, and love of death may all play a part. For
that powdering of dust, she disgraces her sister, kills
her betrothed, and loses her own life. Creon, alarmed
by his son's fatal grief and desiring to save his family
from harm, tries to rescue Antigone before the sentence
of starvation has been carried out, but she has antici-
pated both death by starvation--and life--by suicide.

Sophocles. _Electra_. Drama.

Children	The Family	Grief
Sexuality		

Sophocles' play is the source of the "Electra complex."
More than Aeschylus or Euripides, Sophocles portrays
Electra as obsessive in her love for her murdered father
and in her hatred for her mother. He contrasts her
aggressive lamentations with the resignation of her
sister, Chrysothemis, and has the chorus tinge its
sympathy with criticism of her excesses. Electra sees
herself as the mother of her brother, Orestes. Clytemnestra is greatly troubled by Electra, rejoicing at the
false news of Orestes' death because now she can eliminate
Electra. The sexual, as opposed to maternal, tensions
underlying the family are symbolized by Clytemnestra's
dream. In Aeschylus' version she is troubled by a
suckling snake. In Sophocles' version, she is troubled
by Agamemnon's scepter growing into a branch on the
hearth. Although the play conforms to myth by naming
Apollo as the force moving Orestes to vengeance against
his mother, the intensity of Electra's grief for the
lost Phallus, for her own humiliation and childlessness,
make one accept the daughter's sexuality as a major
force driving Orestes' vengeance upon the mother.

Sophocles. _Oedipus at Colonus_. Drama.

Age	Children	Death
Dying	Grief	Handicaps

The needs of old age compensated by the mysterious
power of incipient death. Oedipus, guided by Antigone,
seeks a resting place to await death. Blind, old--and
alive--he is powerless. Yet his death can confer great
power if he chooses. Both his son and the ruler who
exiled him demand that power. His son, Polyneices, who
is in a doomed rush to his own death, fails to evoke pity.
The ex-ruler Creon unsuccessfully tries force. Theseus
of Athens uses kindness and respect to win Oedipus' blessing for his city. Oedipus lovingly restrains his grieving
daughters and goes to his mysterious death and the grave
which has been predestined by the gods.

Sophocles. _Oedipus Rex_. Drama.

The Family	Grief	Handicaps
Plague	Sexuality	Suffering
Suicide		

A powerful poetic statement that a man is his own worst
enemy because he is blind to his own nature. Injured in
his feet by his true parents' attempt to kill him, Oedipus
flees his supposed parents because of a prophecy that he
will kill his father and marry his mother. Passing through
a strange land, he kills a wrathful stranger. Then, at
Thebes, he overcomes the Sphinx and her riddle: what goes
on four legs, two legs, and three legs. He answers, "man."
This recognition of man's changing nature saves the city,
but completes Oedipus' doom, for he marries Jocasta, the
widowed queen of Thebes, and settles down to be a good
ruler to the city. A plague forces him to investigate
the murder of Jocasta's first husband; the investigation
soon becomes combined with a search into his own past.
With help forced from his servants and the blind seer,
Tiresias, Oedipus learns that he is the parricide, the
husband of his mother and father of his siblings. Jocasta
kills herself in horror. Oedipus blinds himself with her
pins because he has seen that which he should not have
seen. He seeks further punishment for his guilt, punishment that is cruelly withheld by Creon, his wife's brother.

Sophocles. _Philoctetes_. Drama.

Disease & Health	Suffering

Men's desire to avoid agony and disease until forced, by
their own needs, to confront them. Philoctetes, having
inadvertently violated the shrine of a goddess, was
bitten by a serpent and is periodically tormented by the
goddess. His foot is badly ulcerated, his pain acute.
Wearied by his shrieks and the stink from his running
sores, the Greeks abandoned him on an inhospitable island,
where he survives only by use of Heracles' bow. Now the
Greeks have learned that they need the bow to conquer Troy
and have returned to steal both the bow and Philoctetes.
Neoptolemus tricks him into giving up the bow, but is
softened by the man's suffering, and, despite recriminations from Odysseus and the Greeks, returns the bow. The

resulting stalemate is broken by Heracles, who appears to
Philoctetes in a vision, urging him to go. Neoptolemus
adds the arguments that at Troy he will find both a cure
by Asclepius and great honor. Such persuasion is successful, and he goes.

Virgil (Publius Vergilius Maro). _Aeneid_. Epic Poem.

The Family	Grief	Madness
Sexuality		

Aeneas' journey from Troy and his efforts to found the
greater civilization of Rome in Italy. Rome springs from
the family. Aeneas escapes from Troy with his father and
son, losing only his wife. He then meets Dido, who is
also endeavoring to found a new city. Aeneas' goddess-
mother, Venus, disguises her son Cupid as Aeneas' son,
Ascanius, so that with his arrows he may enflame Dido
with love for Aeneas. However, in his desire for Dido,
Aeneas abandons his destined journey. Mercury must order
him to leave her, before Aeneas can conquer his passion.
He flees, using the ships she has equipped and leaving
Dido to commit suicide in her grief (Books I - IV). By
his flight, Aeneas, who has been called Father Aeneas
throughout the poem, is free to join Trojans with Latins
through his marriage to Lavinia, a marriage enforced by
his real son's arrows of warfare. The union with Lavinia
assures procreation for a future society--rather than
individual passion. But Aeneas is not able to form the
new family without purging himself of the old. Aeneas
has mourned his dead father, and, after the Cumean Sybil
has prophesied of Latium, he persuades her to take him
to the Underworld--to Dido, to the fallen Trojan warriors,
and to his father, who tells him of the cycle binding all
souls and of the future awaiting Rome. It is as though
Aeneas must feel that his dead have a future of their own
before he can abandon them to found the new family of
Rome (Book VI). The major obstacle to the new society
lies in Juno, whose hatred for Trojans remains after Troy
is gutted. She infects Lavinia's mother with a madness,
a passionate hatred akin to Dido's passionate love aroused
by Venus. The slow spread of the insanity through Amata's
body is described in vivid detail (Book VIII).

Medieval

Anonymous. <u>Aucassin and Nicolete</u>. <u>Medieval Romances</u>, eds. Roger Sherman Loomis and Laura Hibbard Loomis. New York: Modern Library, 1957. Tale.

The Family   Preg. & Childbirth   Sexuality
Sexual Roles   Women as Healers

An episodic romance concerned with many matters, but highlighting a delightful pair of lovers. Aucassin loves the apparently low-born Nicolete. His parents disapprove, pressuring him to give her up and effectively declaring war on their son. But the lovers manage to escape the prisons of the parents. Nicolete heals Aucassin's injured shoulder and provides medicine for his suffering love. They flee to Torelore, where Aucassin restores proper sexual roles by taking the king of Torelore from childbed (a version of couvade?) and the queen away from her generalship of the army (even though the ammunition is, in this case, food). After several years, the lovers return to the old world, where order has been restored by the death of the parents. Since there is no longer any opposition to their perfect marriage, Nicolete, after a series of disguises, proves that she is of noble birth, and the two live happily ever after.

Anonymous. "Bede's Death Song." Old English versions in <u>Medieval English</u>, ed. Rolf Kaiser. Berlin: Rolf Kaiser, 1961. Translation in <u>A Literary History of England</u>, ed. Albert C. Baugh. New York: Appleton-Century-Crofts, 1948. Poem: 5 lines.

Death

Cautionary advice to the learned man: no one becomes too wise to consider the judgment awaiting his soul after death.

Anonymous. <u>Beowulf</u>. Epic Poem.

Age   Death   Grief
Plague   Suffering

In the first part of this long poem, Beowulf, alone, overcomes the monster Grendel and Grendel's mother, who seem to be mysterious "plagues" of nature. They are, at any rate, destructive forces preventing the spread of civilization. In the second part, Beowulf becomes what some today might call a contradiction in terms--an aged hero. His country is threatened this time with devastation by a fiery dragon, who has terrified all the young warriors. So the hero pulls together his waning strength for a single combat, sure to be fatal. Although his energy grows with the rage of the battle, he is victorious only because he is able to create in one of his warriors a loyalty greater than fear; Beowulf's physical strength, no longer sufficient, must be supplemented by this younger man, bound to him in love. As he lies dying, Beowulf is eased by memories of his blameless life and by the sight of the dragon's treasure. And he suffers less from his wounds than from fear for his soon-to-be leaderless people. For their part, they purge their grief for the dead king and erect a temporary barrier against anxiety through the ceremonial construction of an elaborate funeral pyre.

Anonymous. "Between March and April." <u>Medieval English Verse</u>, trans. Brian Stone. Baltimore, Maryland: Penguin, 1964. Poem: 48 lines.

The Body   Sexuality

The lover celebrates his mistress' body, while lamenting the effects of desire on his own body: "I weary like milling water,/With sleepless longing sore." Yet he rejoices because "My love has left all womankind,/And lights on Alison."

Anonymous. <u>The Castle of Perseverance</u>. <u>English Morality Plays and Moral Interludes</u>, eds. Edgar T. Schell and J. D. Schuchter. New York: Holt, Rinehart and Winston, 1969. Drama: lines 2415-3008.

Age   The Body   Death

Throughout the medieval and Renaissance periods, age was associated with avarice. When age enters this play, Mankind, Humanum Genus, has reformed and is safely within the Castle of Perseverance, from which he is then lured by Covetousness, offering security for his old age. Mankind has begun to feel age twisting his body: "I gynne to waxy hory and colde,/my bake gynnth to bowe and bende." Money does provide protection--until death approaches, boasting that he can surprise men, for men are so covetous nowadays that they forget about him. When Mankind feels that he is dying, "myn eyelids may I not lyfte;/myn braynys waxyn al emptye," the world deserts him, refusing to solace his pain and taking away his goods. The play differs from <u>Everyman</u> in its warnings about age and covetousness and in its portrayal of the body's devastation by age and death.

Anonymous. "Charm for a Sudden Stitch." <u>An Anthology of Old English Poetry</u>, trans. Charles W. Kennedy. New York: Oxford University Press, 1960. Poem: 26 lines.

Disease & Health   Science & Poetry   Sexual Roles

One way of combining poetry and medicine. The use of charms to supplement medication (here feverfew, red nettle, and plantain boiled in butter) was a workable combination of psychological and chemical courses of treatment. Also, this particular charm emphatically illustrates the reverse of women as healers -- women as injurious witches. "Out little spear, if in here it be!/ I lifted up linden, my shining shield,/When the mighty women mustered their strength,/And sped against me their screaming spears."

Anonymous. "Child Waters" and "Fair Mary of Wallington" (Child, 63 & 91), <u>English and Scottish Popular Ballads</u>, eds. Helen Child Sargent and George Lyman Kittredge. Cambridge, Mass.: Riverside Press, 1932 (see Anonymous, "Robin Hood's Death"). Ballads.

Preg. & Childbirth

There are a number of ballads touching upon pregnancy and labor. A changed shape is the common means by which vengeful fathers and brothers learn of the heroine's true state of affairs. But pregnancy is also seen as a test of love, as in "Child Waters," whose hero forces the heroine in the last hours of her pregnancy to run beside his horse, to swim a raging stream, and to care for his horse instead of herself. Her loyalty and physical strength endure, so he marries her. "Fair Mary of Wallington" is a grim ballad about seven sisters forced by a cruel mother into marriages, which end with seven deaths in childbed. Finally, there is a curious set of ballads (Child, 100-103) in which a wife enters labor in the woods and sends her husband out to hunt deer, despite his desire to stay and help her.

Anonymous. <u>Everyman</u>. <u>English Morality Plays and Moral Interludes</u>, eds. Edgar T. Schell and J. D. Schuchter. New York: Holt, Rinehart and Winston, 1969. Drama.

The Body   Death   Dying

Allegorical drama demonstrating the way to meet death. Everyman, arrested by Death, is deserted by Fellowship, Kindred, and Worldly Goods. Only his woeful Good Deeds and his body (Beauty, Five Wits, Strength, and Discretion) remain with him. With the aid of Knowledge and Confession, Mankind improves his Good Deeds, so that he may face calmly the grave into which he must crawl, even though his body rudely fails him. (Strength leaves him with these words: "Thou art but a fool to complain./ You spend your speech and waste your brain;/ Go, thrust thee into the ground.") But Everyman no longer needs a healthy body, for his reliance is now upon God.

Anonymous. "I sing of a maiden." <u>Medieval English Verse</u>, trans. Brian Stone. Baltimore, Maryland: Penguin, 1964. Poem: 20 lines.

The Family   Sexuality

Jesus as both lover and son to the Virgin. He comes to her in her bower, getting her with child (with himself), as gently as the dew revives the flower. "In quiet he drew/Towards her bower,/As the April dew/Falls on the flower . . . Both mother and maiden/Was none but she:/ Well may such a lady/God's mother be."

Anonymous. "The life of this world." <u>Medieval English Verse</u>, trans. Brian Stone. Baltimore, Maryland: Penguin, 1964. Poem: 12 lines.

Death   Suffering

The poem is a disturbing one, for its strong imagery and evocative language are used to convey a clinically-detached assertion that life and death cause equal suffering. "Wind-blown we bloom,/ Wind-blown decay;/ With weeping we come/ And so pass away."

Anonymous. "Look on your Lord, Man, hanging on the Rood." <u>Medieval English Verse</u>, trans. Brian Stone. Baltimore, Maryland: Penguin, 1964. Poem: 12 lines.

The Body   Death   Suffering

A common theme in medieval religious poetry was a vivid, detailed description of Christ's anguished, crucified body, a description designed to evoke pity and guilt in the reader: "Now droops on the Cross his body bright/His naked breast glistens, now bleeds his side/And stiff grow his arms extended wide."

Anonymous. The Magi, Herod, and the Slaughter of the Innocents. (Coventry) Chief Pre-Shakespearean Dramas, ed. Joseph Quincy Adams. Cambridge, Mass.: Riverside Press, 1952. Drama: lines 777-900.

Children

The slaughter of the children by Herod is an early use of children as a stereotype of helpless innocence slaughtered to further some large scheme. (The lovely Coventry Carol is found here.) But the play also has a rather odd attitude toward the mothers who try to protect their children. In both the Coventry and the Chester cycles, the mothers' attempts at defence are funny as they threaten the soldiers with comic bluster: "Sytt he neyuer soo hy in saddull,/But I schall make his braynis addull./And here with my pott-ladull/With hym woll I fyght." Apparently maternal feelings were not yet an object for reverence.

Anonymous. "Maiden on the moor lay" and "All night by the rose, rose." Medieval English Verse, trans. Brian Stone. Baltimore, Maryland: Penguin, 1964. Poems: 26 & 4 lines.

Sexuality

Medieval lyrics invested human sexuality with great naturalness and beauty, by using flowers, birds, and other natural objects to represent aspects of sexual intercourse. (An allegorical process still found in bawdy ballads.) Knowing that the primrose, the violet, and the rose are at once flowers of Venus and medicinal herbs and that a flower may represent the hymen, a reader may translate the poems into a ritual account of a young girl's healthy initiation into sexual intercourse and a lover's account of his first night with his mistress. Yet, at the same time, the poems offer beauty, mystical overtones, and a certain ambiguity.

Anonymous. "Now fade the rose and lily-flower." Medieval English Verse, trans. Brian Stone. Baltimore, Maryland: Penguin, 1964. Poem: 60 lines.

Body/Mind   Disease & Health   Women as Healers

Fleshly lust leads to sin, which causes sickness of both body and soul. The diseased man is cured by casting off vice; and the Virgin Mary is the gentlest and the best doctor for such a course of treatment. "Better is her medicine/Than my meat or wine; . . . No doctor is so skilled and fine/at curing discontent."

Anonymous. The Owl and the Nightingale, trans. Graydon Eggers. Duke University Press, 1955. Poem: 1794 lines.

The Body   Sexuality

A lively debate between the joyous little nightingale and the lugubrious, bullying owl. Unconsciously, both birds derive their values from their own bodies: the small, spring-singer asserting that spring, love, and wisdom are most important; the night-predator claiming that reminders of sin and attacks on small vermin are of greatest importance. Each condemns the other's influence on human sexuality: the nightingale arouses love (blaming men for any misuse of desire) while the owl attacks lust and consoles the victims of love. The two birds unite in a condemnation of adultery and a celebration of married love.

Anonymous. Pearl (esp. stanzas 1-35) Medieval English Verse, trans. Brian Stone. Baltimore, Maryland: Penguin, 1964. Poem: 1212 lines.

Grief

In this elaborately rhymed and structured poem, the narrator's grief is allayed by a fantastically rich vision of his lost Pearl in heaven. He goes to the flowery patch about his Pearl's grave and swoons with grief. His soul is granted a vision of a marvelous landscape. At the foot of a "glittering cliff of crystal kind" he finds a maiden, his Pearl, who reproves him for lamenting her loss, since only the casket has been lost, not the Pearl. Also, she says, grief accomplishes nothing. He should seek God's comfort for himself since she is blissful in Paradise. She explains how the Lamb has earned her honors in heaven otherwise undeserved by her. The narrator sees the Celestial Jerusalem, tries to reach the Pearl, and awakens contrite, instructed, and consoled on her grave.

Anonymous. "Robin Hood's Death." (Child, 120) English and Scottish Popular Ballads, eds. Helen Child Sargent and George Lyman Kittredge. Cambridge, Mass.: Riverside Press, 1932.* Ballad.

Dying   Women as Healers

Robin Hood is the most famous ballad hero to be murdered by subtle craft (others are Lord Randall and, perhaps, Bonnie George Campbell). Entrusting himself to a woman healer with a grudge against him, Robin Hood is locked in a room to bleed to death. Struggling to freedom and the green woods, he dies nobly, forbidding vengeance because his slayer is a woman. As in King Arthur's case, Robin Hood's death and grave are enveloped in mystery, as though to permit everyday, doomed

mortals to hope that some men can escape the final, inevitable enemy.

*Although Child collected his ballads in the nineteenth century, their roots go back to the middle ages; many are handed down unchanged by the oral tradition. This edition contains all of his ballads, but drastically reduces the critical apparatus for each one.

Anonymous. St. George Plays. Chief Pre-Shakespearean Dramas, ed. Joseph Quincy Adams. Cambridge, Mass.: Riverside Press, 1924. Dramas.

Death   Doctors

The age of these plays is unknown. They were taken down from village performances in the 19th century, but it is generally felt that they represent corrupt survivals of the medieval folk plays. In the Oxfordshire St. George Play, the Doctor resurrects the King, the Bride, the Fool, and St. George, after which the Doctor kills the dragon with his pills. In the Lutterworth play, the doctor, having first settled his fee, cures the champion who then kills the dragon. These plays associating the physician with ritual rebirth are an exception in medieval literature, which generally insisted that the doctor (as opposed to a saint, magician, or mystic maiden) was helpless in the combat with death.

Anonymous. The Second Shepherds' Play (Wakefield). Everyman and Other Interludes, ed. Ernest Rhys. New York: E. P. Dutton, 1950. Drama.

Children   Preg. & Childbirth

In the first half of the play, Mak, forced into theft by the needs of his children, hides a stolen sheep in a cradle while his wife pretends to be recovering from labor; but the kindness of the shepherds to the supposed child leads to the sheep's comic discovery. This lambchild is an inversion of the Christ Child worshipped by the shepherds in the second half of the play.

Anonymous. Sir Gawain and the Green Knight. Poem: 2530 lines.

Death   Sexuality

An alliterative poem, at once symbolic and vividly real, about man's fear of death and unknown natural forces. To keep his oath to the Green Knight, Gawain, the perfect knight, must find the Green Chapel of his magical opponent and let him strike at Gawain's neck with an axe. Near his quest's end, he is tempted by his host's wife. He refuses sexual temptation, but is unable to resist his fear of death. He accepts a girdle of invulnerability from the lady, relying on the alien powers of magic rather than his Christian faith, and breaking an oath to his host. Gawain survives the stroke, but is conquered when the Green Knight unmasks as his host, claiming the girdle. Nature, in its various guises, had triumphed, and Gawain rides back, ashamed, to Arthur's court wearing the green girdle (as opposed to his earlier, five-point armor of perfection) as a sign of his disgrace.

Anonymous. Sir Orfeo. Medieval English Verse, trans. Brian Stone. Baltimore, Maryland: Penguin, 1964. Poem: ca. 575 lines.

Death

Medieval romance, derived, somewhat remotely, from the Orpheus legend. King Orfeo's wife is magically removed from their garden, despite the protection provided by Orfeo and a thousand knights. He wanders in search of her until he reaches a castle inhabited by people alive but with bodies mutilated by death: headless, in childbed, or insane. Like his predecessor, Orfeo wins back his wife with his music. Unlike his predecessor, he returns with his wife to his kingdom and lives happily ever after.

Anonymous. The Wanderer. An Anthology of Old English Poetry, trans. Charles W. Kennedy. New York: Oxford University Press, 1960. Poem: ca. 100 lines.

Age   Grief   Suffering

The old wanderer's grief is increased by his dreaming memories of lost friends and kinsmen. From dreams of his lord and warm halls, he awakes to the cries of gulls and the snow driving into the dark sea.

Anonymous. "Western Wind." Medieval English Lyrics: A Critical Anthology, ed. R. T. Davies. London: Faber and Faber, 1963. Poem: 4 lines.

Sexuality

An English version of a lyric found in many medieval languages, "Western Wind" is famous as a very simple, very beautiful cry of longing for reunion and love-making with an absent lover.

Anonymous. "When My Eyes are Fogged." Medieval English Verse, trans. Brian Stone. Baltimore, Maryland: Penguin, 1964. Poem: 22 lines.

The Body   Death

Grim humor derived from the repulsive nature of the dying body, as the poet foresees his own death: "And my cheeks slacken/And my lips blacken/And my mouth

blubbers/And my spittle slobbers . . . . Then I shall
go . . . From bier to pit/And be shut in it./Then lies
my house upon my nose,/And all my care for this world
goes."

Anonymous. "The Wife of Usher's Well." (Child, 79) English and
Scottish Popular Ballads, eds. Helen Child Sargent and George
Lyman Kittredge. Cambridge, Mass.: Riverside Press, 1932.
(see Anonymous, "Robin Hood's Death"). Ballad.

    Grief

    Excessive grief pulls back the dead for one night. In
    this ballad a mother calls back her three sons; in others,
    a woman calls her lover (e.g., Child, 77). All of the
    ballads of this type end with the dead breaking away by
    emphasizing their alienated condition, sometimes by stat-
    ing the terms governing their visit (as here), sometimes
    by emphasizing the calamities that would result if their
    bodies were touched.

Anonymous. "The Wife's Lament." An Anthology of Old English
Poetry, trans. Charles W. Kennedy. New York: Oxford
University Press, 1960. Poem: 58 lines.

    Grief   Suffering

    Lament of a wife separated from her husband, first by
    the sea, then by his kinsmen, and finally by his hate.
    She tries to find some relief by recalling their past
    love and then by picturing her husband as her counter-
    part, exiled in a wretched cell mourning her loss.
    However, this image leads her back to her own unhappy
    loneliness, and the poem ends.

Anonymous. "Wulf and Eadwacer" or "Eadwacer." Anglo-Saxon Poetry,
trans. Robert Kay Gordon. New York: E. P. Dutton, 1930.
Poem: 19 lines.

    Sexuality   Suffering

    A wife sickens with worry for her lover, off in the
    wilderness. Will he be fed? She has food but is
    sick, remembering her pleasure in his arms. She
    taunts Eadwacer, presumably her husband, with Wulf's
    physical strength and the strength of the love be-
    tween them.

Boccaccio, Giovanni. The Decameron: Day 1, Prologue. Sketch.

    Death   Disease & Health   Plague
    Science & Poetry   Women as Patients

    The irresistible violence of the Black Death and the
    variety of reactions to it: temperance, riot, isola-
    tion, men doctoring women, and indifference to death
    and the dead. Although the narrator has condemned those
    who flee plague-stricken Florence, he sends his seven
    young women and three young men into the countryside,
    where they live chastely and devoutly. On a beautiful
    estate, they create a new world and social order, crown-
    ing one person king or queen each day, to give orders--
    and order-- to that day. Their world is completely
    artistic: they shut out the Black Death with their
    own creations: instrumental music, dance, song, and,
    of course, the hundred marvelous stories.

Boccaccio, Giovanni. The Decameron: Day 1, Tale 5. Tale.

    Sexuality

    A short statement of a common Decameron theme: women
    are alike in bed (although vary considerably in
    their ability to please them). A faithful wife, pur-
    sued by the king, wittily rebukes him by serving him
    a lavish banquet of chicken--roasted, boiled, fried,
    stewed, etc. He takes her moral, that underneath the
    dressing all meat is chicken, and then takes his leave
    of the unsullied lady.

Boccaccio, Giovanni. The Decameron: Day 2, Tale 10. Tale.

    Age   Sexuality

    Witty handling of the conventional bawdy criticism
    of old men who egotistically overestimate their sexual
    prowess. An old man covers his deficiency with his
    young wife by expanding the custom of sexual absti-
    nence on major religious holidays to include every
    possible holiday in the calendar. He loses his wife
    to a pirate ravisher, for "the vile thief has no
    holidays."

Boccaccio, Giovanni. The Decameron: Day 3, Tales 1 & 10. Tales.

    Handicaps   Sexuality

    Two tales of man's inadequacy before female desire.
    In the first, a man pretends to be deaf and dumb so
    that he may become gardener in a small convent and
    till the young nuns. However, the nuns enjoy his
    ploughing so much that he must speak up and schedule
    activities to prevent his wasting away. The second
    tale describes the education of a young, naive girl
    who goes to a desert ascetic to learn how to be holy.
    Aroused, he teaches holiness by putting his devil in
    her hell. However, his meager diet prevents him from
    satisfying her desires to be holy, and she leaves--to
    be disabused and happily married by her family.

Boccaccio, Giovanni. The Decameron: Day 4, Tale 5. Tale.

    Grief

    A young girl hides the head of her murdered lover in
    a pot of basil, watering it with her tears until her

death from grief. A famous story of morbid, but beautiful, grief. John Keats calls his poetic version of
this tale "Isabella."

Boccaccio, Giovanni. The Decameron: Day 9, Tale 3. Tale.

    Doctors   Preg. & Childbirth   Sexuality

    Stupid Caladrino is the butt of many tales. In this
    one, his friends and their doctor accomplice, con-
    vince him that he is pregnant. He accepts this diag-
    nosis, blaming the trouble on his wife, who insists
    on being on top. He doesn't want the pain--and where
    would it come out? They sell him expensive medicine
    for a cure, ending his pregnancy and their con game.

Chaucer, Geoffrey. The Book of the Duchess. Chaucer's Major
Poetry, ed. Albert C. Baugh. New York: Appleton-Century-
Crofts, 1963. Poem: 1334 lines.

    Grief

    Level upon level of grief. It begins with the grief-
    stricken narrator. He cannot sleep, and so reads a
    story about a young wife who learns the location of
    her husband's corpse in a dream. Then falling asleep
    himself, the narrator dreams that he is in a beautiful
    chamber. A dog leads him from there to a man in black,
    who is lamenting the loss of his queen. The narrator
    presses the man to accept her death by forcing him
    first to praise her beauty, grace, and kindness, then
    to state that he cannot repent loving her, even though
    he is pained by her loss, and finally to say "she ys
    ded," words which snap the spell, sending the man back
    to his castle and the narrator to his reading. The
    dream permits the narrator to separate himself from
    his grief, to stalk it as an observer, and so to reach,
    gradually and harmlessly, a cathartic acknowledgment
    of his loss.

Chaucer, Geoffrey. The Canterbury Tales, "The General Prologue,"
lines 411-444. Sketch.

    Doctors

    A physician is among the pilgrims satirized in the
    Prologue. The "Doctour of Phisik" is learned in
    astrology, causes of disease, and drugs, as well as
    being familiar with the writings of Galen and other
    early medical authorities. He is temperate in his
    diet, but from prudence, not morality, since "his
    studie was but litel on the Bible." However, he is
    not so temperate in his love of money: "And yet he
    was but esy of dispence./He kepte that he wan in
    pestilence,/For gold in phisik is a cordial,/There-
    fore he lovede gold in special." "The Physician's
    Tale," the story he tells, is the grim moral of
    Virginia's death at her father's hand to forestall
    her dishonor by a corrupt judge. It has no obvious
    relation to the teller's profession.

Chaucer, Geoffrey. The Canterbury Tales, The Marriage Group: "The
Wife of Bath's Tale," "The Clerk's Tale," "The Merchant's Tale,"
and "The Franklin's Tale." Tales.

    Sexuality   Sexual Roles

    Although some critics deny the existence of a marriage
    group and others would include more tales than the four
    above, there does seem to be a series of tales concerned
    with domination in marriage. They range from "The Wife
    of Bath's Tale," in which the woman has her will (al-
    though the Wife herself prefers her fifth husband who
    subjugated her with beatings out of bed and pleasure in
    it) to "The Clerk's Tale" of meek Griseylde who submits
    to years of torture by her husband. The Merchant
    attacks marriage by contrasting old January's egotisti-
    cal, idealized vision of marriage with his ludicrous
    efforts to please his young wife, who finally cuckolds
    him. The question of dominance seems to be solved in
    the tempered male superiority of "The Franklin's Tale."
    Averargus and his wife both act unnaturally: he gives
    her complete freedom and she believes that she will
    never do wrong. As a result, she rashly vows to sleep
    with the lover who will remove the rocks which are par-
    tially barring her husband's return. When the rocks are
    in fact removed, Averargus prevents his wife from com-
    mitting suicide to protect her honor, saying that truth
    to her oath is more important than her honor, and sends
    her, weeping but obedient, to the triumphant lover.
    Stunned by the husband's action, the lover releases
    her, and the husband and wife live happily ever after.

Chaucer, Geoffrey. The Canterbury Tales, "The Miller's Tale."
Tale.

    Age   The Body   Sexuality

    A variety of approaches to the body, favoring the
    crude. The old, superstitious carpenter is blind
    to the beautiful body of Alisoun, his wife. He is
    easily tricked into praying in a washtub to prevent
    a second flood so that Nicholas and Alisoun can do
    full justice to their bodies. Another lover, Absolon,
    approaches her window, so full of reverence for Alisoun's
    body that he combs his hair and sweetens his breath with
    licorice. Alisoun allows him to kiss her--on the ass.
    Revolted, he returns with a glib speech and a hot iron,
    so that when Nicholas, believing that Absolon is still
    fooled, presents his ass for embracing, he gets the hot
    iron. His cries for water overturn the foolish husband,
    whose account of the affair leads his neighbors to call
    him mad. Ignorance, reverence, misuse--all attitudes
    toward the body cause difficulties.

Chaucer, Geoffrey. <u>The Canterbury Tales</u>, "The Nun's Priest's Tale."
    Tale.

Poverty & Health   Women as Healers

This delightful beast fable opens with a poor widow who
is healthy just because she is poor. But her chickens
are not so fortunate. The royal cock Chauntecleer is
troubled by dreams that are explained away by his debo-
nair wife Pertelote as fumes from indigestion. She
discourses at length on purgatives and laxatives. But
this medical approach is incorrect, for Chauntecleer
is nearly dethroned and eaten by the fox of his dreams.
Even a chicken-physician should look for distempers in
the environment as well as distempers of the body.

Chaucer, Geoffrey. <u>The Canterbury Tales</u>, "The Pardoner's Tale."
    Tale.

Age   Death   Plague

The Pardoner's Tale is designed to reprove covetousness
and evoke lucrative repentence in his audience by showing how three young wastrels, seeking to overcome death,
are directed by an old man to him. The men don't find
death <u>per se</u>, but rather death in the form of a treasure
which <u>kills</u> all three as each murders to be sole owner
of the money. But the tale is more than a moral lesson,
especially through the old man, who may or may not be
death. Moving through the plague-decimated countryside,
mocked by the three rioters, he says "Thus walke I, lyk
a resteles kaityf,/And on the ground, which is my moodres
gate,/I knokke with my staf, bothe erly and late,/And
seye, 'Leeve mooder, leet me in!/Lo, how I vanysshe,
flessh, and blood, and skyn!'" Death or Age, he grotesquely
attracts our sympathy, forfeited by the young men.

Chaucer, Geoffrey. <u>The Canterbury Tales</u>, "The Reeve's Prologue."
    Sketch.

Age   Sexuality

The Reeve claims that he cannot top the Miller's grossly
bawdy tale because he is old--then digresses on the
lecherousness of old age before telling an extremely
bawdy tale.

Chaucer, Geoffrey. <u>Troilus and Criseyde</u>. <u>Chaucer's Major Poetry</u>,
    ed. Albert C. Baugh. New York: Appleton-Century-Crofts,
    1963. Long Poem.

Sexuality

A light, elegant retelling of the Troilus story (previously
told by Boccaccio in <u>Filostrato</u>), which gently mocks the
courtly love tradition. During the first three Books,
set in Troy, Troilus is smitten by Cupid and the Greek
hostage, Criseyde. This he reluctantly tells Pandarus,
his friend and Criseyde's uncle, who persuades his niece
to listen to Troilus' suit. In a lengthy, internal
debate, Criseyde weighs reasons for and against receiving
Troilus as her lover--deciding to accept him as servant.
But Pandarus arranges an assignation for the two, an
assignation he must help consummate, for Troilus has
swooned in joyous expectancy and must be thrown onto
Criseyde. The affair is cut short by the Trojan war:
Criseyde is traded back to the Greeks. The lovers' laments fill Book IV. Then, in a few lines of the last
book, the Greek Diomed, with bald urgings, accomplishes
in a few days what took Troilus weeks of humble servitude.
Criseyde's earlier, elaborate reasoning is replaced by a
few weak objections. Courtly love is thus seen to be an
elaborate farce, motivated by, and cloaking, human desire.
Troilus' grief comes because he accepts the elaborate
rituals as real and necessary. Enraged, he tries to kill
his Greek rival, but is slain by another Greek. As his
soul climbs through the spheres, he laments this blinding
lust that gives so little and takes so much, by depriving
men of heaven.

<u>The Dance of Death</u>, eds. Florence Warren and Beatrice White.
    London: Early English Text Society, 1931. Long Poems.

Death   Doctors

A powerful image of death's omnipotence first found in
medieval painting and poetry. Death, a rotting corpse
or skeleton, leads a dancing line of kings, popes,
lords, ladies, knights, priests, peasants, doctors,
lawyers, and merchants--all the men and women in his
power. The two versions of the dance in this book
differ slightly, as illustrated by the stanzas on
death and the physician. In the Ellesmere version,
Death tells the physician that there is no cure for
death, and "the Phecissian" ruefully agrees that, despite his research, "A-yens dethe/is worth no medicyne."
In the Landsowne ms., the narrator warns physicians to
prepare for their own deaths, and his warning is illustrated by a doctor who laments that he spent too much
time getting money from his practice, taking no heed to
his spiritual health. "Wher-fore shal helpe/nother herbe
nor roote/Nor no medicyne/sauff goddis goodnesse/For a-
gens deth/is fynaly no boote."

Dante Alighieri. <u>The Divine Comedy</u>: <u>The Inferno</u>; <u>Purgatorio</u>,
Canto XXV; <u>Paradisio</u>, Canto VIII. Long Poem.

The Body   Children   Disease & Health
Homosexuality   Med. Ethics   Preg. & Childbirth
Sexuality   Suffering

The entire <u>Inferno</u> consists of bodily suffering, to
which the narrator responds at times with pity, at
times with curiosity, and at times with disgust. The

punishments translate abstract sins into bodily terms,
while the sinner's mind remains free. The sufferers
often pause in their pain to chat with Dante about the
future of Italy. Flatterers are thrust upside down in
excrement, heretics imprisoned in fiery tombs, swindlers
sunk in boiling pitch and evil counselors consumed in
flames. In an unusual twist, Alchemists and imposters,
who have sinned against nature, are punished by her
diseases. Canto V includes the beautiful story of
Paolo and Francesca who sinned through carnal passion.
Heterosexual sinners are kept quite separate from homosexual sinners, who are punished farther down in the
inferno by forced marches through fire. None of the
sins are irretrievably deadly, for both kinds of lovers
are found with the other sinners in Purgatory, again
paying for sin with their bodies (the proud carry weights
on their neck). In Canto XXV of the <u>Purgatorio</u> occurs
a rather murky passage on the conception and growth of
the child, with a discussion of the moment at which the
rational soul enters the fetus. Also, in Canto VIII of
the <u>Paradisio</u>, is a curious section dealing with genetics,
explaining why children don't always resemble their parents. Beatrice links all three sections of the <u>Comedy</u>,
representing the ideal combination of earthly and heavenly
love. Dante strives for this ideal, but tends to pause
whenever he meets another unhappy lover. Beatrice is the
channel for heavenly grace and her beautiful, but bodiless
form is an inspiration in itself for Dante to seek heaven.
(A beautiful image, but a terrible role model for women.)

Dante Alighieri. <u>La Vita Nuova</u> (The New Life). Poems in a prose
    framework.

Grief   Sexuality

One of the best and most beautiful transformations of
grief and loss into a mystic understanding that one's
loss is really gain. The poet first grieves because
his lady denies him physical consummation of his love.
This grief is intensified by the loss of the lady herself to death. But reflection on the merits of the
lady brings the poet to an intense love of God and
mankind. He is rewarded by a vision of the true and
glorified Beatrice.

Gottfried von Strassburg. <u>Tristan and Isolt</u>. <u>Medieval Romances</u>,
    eds. Roger Sherman Loomis and Laura Hibbard Loomis. New York:
    Modern Library, 1957. Tale.

Disease & Health   Sexuality   Women as Healers

The chaste love between Tristan and Isolt is transformed
by a love potion into a blazing, glorious passion, which
elevates the lovers beyond their already heroic status.
Although their countries are enemies, Tristan and Isolt
are drawn together, as though by fate. Tristan, defending his uncle's country against Morolt, Isolt's uncle,
receives a poisoned wound which only Morolt's sister, the
Queen of Ireland, can cure. Disguised as a harper, Tristan tricks the Queen into curing him, but in repaying her
by teaching music to her niece, Isolt, is struck by the
first influence of love. Like a man reborn, he returns
to King Mark, his uncle, praising Isolt. As a result of
these praises, Mark chooses Isolt for his queen. Loyally,
Tristan wins her for his uncle, but the two lovers unknowingly drink a love potion meant for Mark and Isolt,
and the two set out on a course of secret love, alter-
nately allaying and re-awakening Mark's suspicions. The
author emphasizes the beauty and benefits of the secret
love: "but his life kept her in life." This original
version of Tristan and Isolt may startle those who are
familiar with the myth through Wagner's powerful transmutation of consummated passion into a passion that can
survive only in death. In addition to the lasting images
of sexuality, the story of Tristan and Isolt provides us
with one of literature's diseased society metaphors. The
hero with a mystic thigh wound is a common motif in medieval literature. Often the man is a king, whose country
becomes sterile until the wound is cured. Although Tristan's wound is healed, his country is not; for Mark, not
Tristan, is king. Therefore, barrenness and strife result
because Isolt avoids having a child by Mark. Use of the
wounded king motif heightens the tension between the
<u>natural</u> forces that should push Tristan, the natural
ruler, to kill Mark and restore harmony, and the <u>social</u>
forces of loyalty and kinship that restrain him.

Heloise. <u>The Letters of Abelard and Heloise</u>, trans. Betty Radice,
    letter no. 3. Baltimore, Maryland: Penguin, 1974. Letter.

Grief   Sexuality   Sexual Roles
Suffering

One of the most famous and tragic of medieval romances
was the love between Heloise and Abelard, the cleric-
philosopher. Taking advantage of his position as her
tutor, they enjoyed an affair for several months until
she became pregnant. Against her wishes they married,
but in secret, to allow him to advance his career in
the church. Enraged at the secrecy, her uncle and his
friends castrated Abelard, whereupon both lovers retired
into a religious life. Despite his impotence and their
separation the love remained, and the letters between
the two, works of art in themselves, have inspired
writers ever since (see Pope's "Eloisa to Abelard").
In letter number 3 of this edition, Heloise, with great
openness and accurate self-observation, pours out her
grief and guilt. She angrily attacks Abelard for looking
ahead to his own death, then tries to force herself into
the conventional role of woman as temptress, only to recover her pride and attack the church, recognizing how

ill-fitted she is to play the hypocritical nun despite
her love for God. She begs Abelard not to praise her,
but to help her, asking him to see beyond her assumed
strength to her sexual desires, now without an outlet,
and her rebellion against the nun's role.

Henryson, Robert. _The Testament of Cresseid_. _The Poems and Fables
of Robert Henryson_, ed. H. Harvey Wood. London: Oliver and
Boyd, 1965. Poem: 616 lines.

    The Body   Disease & Health   Sexuality

    An infamous continuation of Chaucer's story of Troilus
and Criseyde, giving Cressid her proper punishment.
After she is thrown out by Diomed, who had seduced her
away from faithful Troilus, Cupid and Venus beg the
Gods to punish her for "leving unclene and Lecherous."
(The ludicrousness of such an appeal seems uninten-
tional.) Saturn destroys her beauty with foul ugliness, so that she appears to be a leper. Her father
maintains her in a hospital, or spittal house, while
she laments her hideous face and voice. A cautionary
tale for ladies, by a classically-oriented, medieval
puritan, for whom disease is a heavenly judgment.

Jean de Meun. _The Romance of the Rose_ (lines 4059-21780).
Guillaume de Lorris and Jean de Meun, _The Romance of the Rose_,
trans. Harry W. Robbins. New York: E. P. Dutton, 1962. Long
Poem.

    The Body   Death   Sexuality

    Jean de Meun's lengthy, sometimes bawdy, addition to
The Romance of the Rose is quite different in tone from
Lorris' delicate courtly love poem. Although delighting
in digressions, such as the dissertation on mirrors,
Jean de Meun steadily defends sexuality as a blessing,
condemning prudish periphrasis while directly naming the
genitals and advocating fecundity as a defense against
death. Although individual men must die (despite the
efforts of doctors), Mankind may outstrip Death's gluttonous pursuit (lines 15891-16004 & 19505-19906). The
lover takes this advice and, in a lengthy metaphor of
intercourse, plucks his rose.

Langland, William. _Piers Plowman_ (B-Text), Book 20. (There are 3
versions of the poem: the 9-book A-Text, the 21-book B-Text,
and the 24-book C-Text) _Piers The Ploughman_, trans. J. F.
Goodridge. Baltimore, Maryland: Penguin, 1959. Long Poem.

    Age   Death   Disease & Health
    Doctors   Plague

    Allegorical, alliterative poem attacking the folly and
hypocrisy of mankind and his institutions. In Book 20,
the population is attacked by the vanguard of Old Age
and Death: fevers and fluxes, catarrhs and cataracts
and other foul complaints. Life promptly rushes to a
doctor who, for gold, gives him a thin glass helmet for
defense. The doctor is accidently slain by Old Age, and
Life goes off to revel since Medicine and Surgery are
powerless against Death. Old Age then pursues the narrator, boxing his ears so he's deaf, knocking the teeth out
of his mouth, crippling him with gout, and immobilizing
his wife's favorite member of his body. The only advice
Nature offers is: "Learn to love and give up everything
else." Scattered through the whole poem are references
to the economic dislocations caused by the Black Death.

Lydgate, John. "Dietarium" ("A Dietary"). _Medieval English_, ed.
Rolf Kaiser. Berlin: Rolf Kaiser, 1961. (Also available in
Henry N. MacCracken's _Minor Poems of John Lydgate_.) Poem:
24 lines.

    Disease & Health

    An instance of the poet substituting for the unavailable
doctor. The poem consists of moralistic, rhymed advice
to rich and poor. Both are to be temperate. The poor
are to be merry within their "degree," and the rich are
to avoid anger and violence to the poor. "And yff so be,
that leches don the faile,/Than take hede to vse thynges
thre:/Temperat diet, temperat trauayle,/Not malicious, for
non aduerstie." (The poem is difficult to find in translation. This is a rough paraphrase of this passage: If
doctors fail thee, take heed to use three things: temperate diet, temperate labor, and don't bear malice against
adversity.)

Malory, Thomas. _The Book of Sir Launcelot and Queen Guinevere_ and
The Most Piteous Tale of the Morte Arthur. _Works_, ed. Eugene
Vinaver. London: Oxford University Press, n.d. Tales.

    Death   Doctors   The Family
    Sexuality

    The first set of stories follows Launcelot, who is caught
between his knightly loyalty and honor (epitomized by the
search for the Holy Grail) and his passionate love for
Guinevere, the wife of his king. In _The Book of Sir
Launcelot_ the only casualty is Elaine, who dies of unrequited love for Launcelot. And he, as the sole perfect
knight, is still the only one able to cure a brother
knight of his wounds. But the adulterous love between
Launcelot and Guinevere becomes the center of destructive
forces in the _Morte D'Arthur_. Here Launcelot the healer
destroys Camelot. Mordred, the bastard son of an incestuous affair between Arthur and his sister, seeks to overthrow his royal father-uncle, attacking him indirectly
through the queen. He forces Arthur, who loves Launcelot,
to condemn the unfaithful Guinevere and make war on his
best, most perfect knight and friend. Mordred then seizes
the kingdom <u>and</u> Guinevere. Arthur turns on his son and

destroys him, but in so doing, Arthur, together with all
his Round Table, are destroyed too. The king's sister
carries him off to her hidden realm, and the story ends
with accounts of Launcelot's and Guinevere's repentance,
and, as always, their great love.

The Paston Letters, ed. James Gairdner. Westminster: A. Constable,
1896. Vol. 2. Letters.

    Doctors

    These business and domestic letters of the active and
wide-spread Paston Family make two mentions of doctors.
Number 432 (1461) includes: "Mastres, my Lady sent to
Cawnbrygg for a doctour of fesyk. If ye wyll ony thyng
with hym, he xal abyde this daye and to morowe. He is
ryght a konnyng man and gentyll." And in 490, Margaret
Paston writes what must have been a common warning, considering the state of medicine in fifteenth-century
England. "Also for Goddys sake be war what medesyns ye
take of any fysissyans of London; I schal never trust to
hem be cause of your fadr and myn onkl, whoys sowlys God
assoyle." (Rough paraphrases of these passages go as
follows: Mistress, my Lady sent to Cambridge for a doctor of physic. If you want any thing from him, he shall
abide this day and tomorrow. He is a right cunning man
and gentle.--Also, for God's sake beware what medicines
you take of any London physicians; I shall never trust
them because of your father and my uncle, whose souls God
absolve.)

Petrarch (Francesco Petrarca). _Canzoniere_, no. CLIX (sonnet no.
126), trans. Thomas G. Bergin. _Selected Sonnets, Odes and
Letters_, ed. Thomas G. Bergin. New York: Appleton-Century-
Crofts, 1966. Sonnet.

    The Body   Sexuality

    The glorious body as expression of a glorious soul.
Laura's divine face is proof of her heavenly origins
and power. And yet, this divine, virtuous, beauty be-
guiles the heart of the narrator, killing and healing
at once. "In what divine ideal, what lofty sphere/Is
found the pattern from which Nature made/That face so
fair?"

Petrarch (Francesco Petrarca). _Canzoniere_, no. CXCV (sonnet no.
162), trans. R. G. MacGregor. _Selected Sonnets, Odes and
Letters_, ed. Thomas G. Bergin. New York: Appleton-Century-
Crofts, 1966. Sonnet.

    The Body   Sexuality

    The other side of Petrarchan love: lust for the beauti-
ful soul's container: the beautiful body. The aging
poet laments his body's continuing desire--and its pain.
Although he condemns his lustful flesh, he also implies
that it would be nice if the lady eased the demands of
this loathsome, importunate body. "For never hope I
respite from my pain/From bones and nerves and flesh till
I am free, . . . None but herself or death the blow can
heal/Which lover from her bright eyes has left my heart
to feel."

Petrarch (Francesco Petrarca). _Canzoniere_, no. CCLXXII (sonnet
no. 231), trans. Morris Bishop. _Selected Sonnets, Odes and
Letters_, ed. Thomas G. Bergin. New York: Appleton-Century-
Crofts, 1966. Sonnet.

    Grief

    One of the best of Petrarch's despairing laments for him-
self after Laura's death. "Life hurries on, a frantic
refugee,/And Death, with great forced marches, follows
fast;/And all the present leagues with all the past/And
all the future to make war on me."

Petrarch (Francesco Petrarca). _Canzoniere_, no. CCCXLIX (sonnet
no. 303), trans. Joseph Auslander. _Selected Sonnets, Odes
and Letters_, ed. Thomas G. Bergin. New York: Appleton-
Century-Crofts, 1966. Sonnet.

    The Body   Grief   Suffering

    A beautiful poem of depression and grief. Decayed in body
and fatigued with dancing "in this unholy jest with phantoms brawling," the poet longs for the day of deliverance,
when he will shed his onerous flesh and soar like an eagle
"To where my Lord and Lady walk together."

Villon, Francois. _The Testament_. _The Complete Works of Francois
Villon_, trans. Anthony Bonner. New York: Bantam Books, 1960.
Poem: 2023 lines.

    Age   The Body   Death
    Sexuality

    A glorious gallimaufry made from Villon's life. He
blends irony and sincerity in this collection of mock
legacies, voices from his past, and philosophic musings.
The first five hundred lines of the poem linger over the
horrors of age and death, slipping into the lament for
beautiful women of the past with its refrain "Mais ou
sont les neiges d'antan?" It is followed by two descriptions of old people: the portrait of the heart-sick,
begging old man, who's condemned as senile if he's silent
and as a driveler if he speaks, and the Lament of the Belle
Heaulmiere, a prostitute, contrasting her grotesque, aged
body with her youthful pleasures. Villon then wanders
onto a discussion of the women he has loved and so returns
to his testament with its evocation of the rogue's life in
the Paris underworld. The harshest self-loathing is found
in the poet-pimp's love-making with his fat whore: "Then
we make up in bed, and she, more bloated/than a poisonous
dung-hill beetle, farts . . . . Bad rat, bad cat./We both
love filth and filth pursues us."

Renaissance

Anonymous. The Celestina, trans. Lesley Byrd Simpson. Berkeley and
Los Angeles: University of California Press, 1962. Drama.

Age   Grief   Sexuality
Women as Healers

   This sixteen-act "drama" (Lesley Simpson calls it a novel
in dialogue form) combines the underworld chicanery of
Lazarillo de Tormes with Ariosto's attack upon egotistical
courtly love. The go-between who unites the worlds of the
cheating servants and the lovesick young nobleman, Calisto,
is the old--but dexterous, insidious, and lecherous--
procuress, Celestina. This bawd "had six trades, to wit:
laundress, perfumer, a master hand at making cosmetics and
replacing maidenheads, procuress, and something of a witch
. . . . For the repair of maidenheads she used bladders, or
she stitched them up." She plays upon Calisto's extravagant
despair, obtaining a meeting between Calisto and Melibea,
only child and heiress of a noble family. Although the
reader marvels at Celestina's clever seduction of Melibea
and her equally clever milking of Calisto for every penny
while out-maneuvering his greedy servants, the results of
her cunning are disasterous: Calisto dies of a fall, Melibea
commits suicide, Celestina is murdered, and Calisto's servants
are executed. The work ends with the grief of Melibea's
parents. "Oh love, love! . . . . In my youth it wounded me
and burned me with its fires. Did it free me then only to
collect its debt in my old age? . . . . Oh my good companion,
my broken daughter! . . . . Why had you no pity for your well
loved mother? Why such cruelty for your aged father?"

Anonymous. Nice Wanton. Chief Pre-Shakespearean Dramas, ed. Joseph
Quincy Adams. Cambridge, Mass.: Riverside Press, 1952. Drama.

   Children   Suicide   V.D.

   This morality play is very representative of a common
Renaissance concern: the need for strict education of
children. The plays, poems, and treatises on this subject
all foreshadow a modern extension of Freud: the problems
of the child are the fault of the parent. This play is
extreme in its condemnation of indulgent parent and un-
disciplined child. A mother spoils two of her three
children, with the result that the spoiled girl becomes
a whore and the spoiled boy a thief. The third child, who
escaped from her maternal concern by God's Grace, becomes
a saved prig. The girl dies of V.D. after repenting to
her charitable, but reproving, brother. Her thief-brother
is hung. The mother prepares to commit suicide, but is
saved by the sermons of her remaining child.

Anonymous. Tales and Quick Answers, nos. 38, 50 & 80. A Hundred
Merry Tales and Other Jestbooks of the Fifteenth and Sixteenth
Centuries, ed. P. M. Zall. Lincoln: University of Nebraska
Press, 1963. Tales.

Disease & Health   Doctors

   This is perhaps the most erudite of the Renaissance English
jestbooks, drawing upon Erasmus' aphorisms and tales by the
other Renaissance humanists. Although these tales attack
both physicians and patients, the weight of the criticism
falls upon physicians who use tricks to hide their ignorance,
such as the doctor who blames all ills on misdiet, deducing
the guilty foods by the garbage on the floor, or the doctor
who puts the names of medicines in a grab bag and cures his
patients by chance. In one instance a patient is also
mocked for ignorance. When a rich man was told to take an
enema, he arose in fury crying "Out-a-doors with those physicians! They be mad. For whereas my pain is in my head,
they would heal me in mine arse."

Anonymous. Wealth and Health. "Lost" Tudor Plays: 1460-1566, ed.
John S. Farmer. London: Early English Drama Society, 1907;
rpt. New York: Barnes and Noble, 1966. Drama.

Disease & Health

   This morality play is by no means good drama, but it is
interesting for its lengthy allegory of England as a body
losing and gaining social health. The play opens with a
debate between Health and Wealth, in which the two act as
qualities of an individual, not of a society. Wealth finally
concedes that Health is more important (there is no suggestion that wealth can buy health--probably couldn't then).
Health is defined as absence of pain. Then the two become
social symbols. They are deceived by Shrewd Wit and Ill-
Will, so that England is overrun by foreign forces. The
Wealth of the country is wasted, and England becomes sick.
Wealth and Health are cured by the vigorous social purges
of the authoritarian Good Remedy, a representative of government agents who remove those sinful tendencies that waste a
country's health and wealth.

Aretino, Pietro. Dialogues. Aretino's Dialogues, trans. Raymond
Rosenthal. New York: Stein and Day, 1971. Dialogues.

   Sexuality

   Aretino was an extremely complex figure; infamous for his
licentious paintings and blackmailing articles, he also
wrote histories and penitential psalms that influenced
Wyatt. These titillating dialogues, almost an inversion
of The Symposium, take place between two whores who gen-
teelly discuss the condition of nuns, wives, and whores.
The question is not whether two people will act upon their

desire (all people are motivated by lust) but rather which
of the two sexual partners will manage to humiliate the
other. Sexuality is merely a vehicle for exploitation
and humiliation. To be a whore is preferable to being a
wife because a whore's career imposes the least hypocrisy
and offers the greatest opportunity for a woman to gratify
her lust and satisfy her desire to humiliate and cheat men.
However, she must be clever enough to detect and avoid men's
attempts to cheat and prey upon women.

Ariosto, Ludovico. Orlando Furioso, trans. Sir John Harington, ed.
Robert McNulty. Oxford: Clarendon Press, 1972. Cantos VI-
VIII,XIX, XXIII, XXIX, XXXIV, XXXVII, XXXIX. Poem: 46 Cantos.

Madness   Sexuality   Sexual Roles
Women as Healers

   Ariosto's gently satiric romance weaves together many
stories of quests and courtly romance. One story line
relates the cautionary tale of the knight Orlando, who
goes mad (Cantos XXIII, XXIX) when he learns that Angelica,
his ladylove, has given herself to another. He goes into
a lasting frenzy which takes the form of stealing horses,
often killing their owners to get them, and then riding
the horses to death. Since the horse was a common Renaissance emblem for lust, his actions become a form of revenge
upon the worthless Angelica and, perhaps, an attempt to
cure himself. In Canto XXXIV we are told that Orlando's
madness is God's punishment for abandoning himself to love
for a heathen. Astolfo, Orlando's friend, who was himself
punished for unreasonable love, retrieves Orlando's wits
from the circle of the moon, the cosmic lost-and-found.
Astolfo is horrified to discover how much wit is lost without a person's knowledge. All diseases are found in this
circle--except for folly, which belongs to earth alone. In
Canto XXXIX Orlando is cured by Astolfo. The poem manages
to be anti-love without being anti-woman. It contains the
first of the three enchanted bowers found in the great
sixteenth-century epic romances: Alcina's bower, Arminda's
garden in Tasso's epic, and the Bower of Bliss in Spenser's
Fairie Queene. The three bowers represent three different
condemnations of uncontrolled sexuality. In Ariosto's work,
Alcina (Cantos VI-VIII) represents the quintessence of
irrational sexuality. She is opposed to her sister Logistilla
and unmasked by the ring of reason. Alcina is another version
of the infatuation that plunged the great Orlando into madness.
Yet, the poem also contains several strong, good women--
notably the warrior-woman Brandamante who goes on a quest
for her love, Rogero, and the warrior-woman Marphisa, who
joins Brandamante in battling the Saracens. Canto XXXVII
opens with a discussion of how women are handicapped, for
envious male writers deprive them of their due fame. The
Canto then continues with an account of Marphisa's restoration of order in a country in which women are ill-treated.
Even the weak Angelica is able to save her love with herbs
and simples, because she has studied medicine (Canto XIX).
In short, love leading to fame, honor, and offspring is
good. Love that is merely lust, without a social function,
is contemptible.

Bacon, Francis. The Advancement of Learning, Book II, Parts IX & X.
Selected Writings of Francis Bacon, ed. H. G. Dick. New York:
Modern Library, 1955. Treatise.

Body/Mind   Euthanasia   Med. Ethics
Med. Profession   Suffering   Women as Healers

   In Book II of The Advancement of Learning, Bacon points out
the gaps in early seventeenth-century learning. In Part IX
he advocates further study of relationships between the body
and the mind. In Part X he analyzes the medical profession.
He sympathizes with doctors who must become like charlatans
in order to compete with quacks and empirics (a sympathy also
found in early 20th-century American Literature). However,
he criticizes the profession for its lack of research, particularly in physiology. He calls for more complete case
histories, citing the example of Hippocrates. He also criticizes practitioners for neglecting dying patients: "Nay further,
I esteem it the office of a physician not only to restore
health, but to mitigate pain and dolors; and not only when
such mitigation may conduce to recovery, but when it may serve
to make a fair and easy passage . . . . they ought both to
enquire the skill and to give the attendances for the facili-
tating and assuaging of the pains and agonies of death."
Finally, Bacon censures doctors for tinkering haphazardly
with their medicines, when they should be imitating their
more successful rivals, old women and empirics, who seek out
and employ specific medicines for specific diseases.

Bacon, Francis. New Atlantis. Selected Writings of Francis Bacon, ed.
H. G. Dick. New York: The Modern Library, 1955. Treatise.

   The Family

   Bacon's treatment of the family in this Utopian work is both
like and unlike his treatment in his essays. The family is
still completely structured about the pater familias, the
one dominant male, with children and women completely subor-
dinate. However, the family is now extremely important to
the social system because it is both a means for social order
(correction of behaviour takes place within the family) and a
means for providing future subjects for the prince. Although
the work is incomplete, the New Atlantis is remarkable for

giving its attention to only two aspects of Utopian society (aside from their treatment of strangers): the family and scientific research. It is an unusual combination.

Bacon, Francis. "Of Death" (1625 ed.). Essay.

Death   Dying

Rational approach to the fear of dying. "Men fear Death, as children fear to go in the dark; and as that natural fear in children is increased by tales, so is the other . . . . Groans and convulsions, and a discolored face, and friends weeping, and blacks, and obsequies, and the like show death terrible. It is worthy the observing, that there is no passion in the mind of man so weak, but it mates and masters the fear of death . . . . It is as natural to die as to be born; and to a little infant, perhaps, the one is as painful as the other."

Bacon, Francis. "Of Deformity" (1625 ed.). Essay.

Handicaps

Bacon perpetuates the Renaissance distrust of ugly people as evil people. Yet he does believe that a misformed person can overcome his deformity by strength of will, citing cases such as those of Aesop and Socrates.

Bacon, Francis. "Of Parents and Children," and "Of Marriage and the Single Life" (1625 ed.). Essays.

Children   Sexuality

Bacon has no sense of a family unit: the only point of view discussed is that of the husband or father. On the whole, Bacon is wary of marriage because it diverts love and care from all of mankind to a few people. He opens "Of Parents and Children" with "the joys of parents are secret; and so are their griefs and fears . . . . Children sweeten labours; but they make misfortunes more bitter. They increase the cares of life; but they mitigate the remembrance of death . . . . And surely a man shall see the noblest works and foundations have proceeded from childless men." "Of Marriage and the Single Life" opens with the famous lines, "He that hath wife and children hath given hostages to fortune; for they are impediments to great enterprises, either of virtue or mischief . . . . Wives are young men's mistresses; companions for middle age; and old men's nurses."

Bacon, Francis. "Of Regiment of Health" (1625 ed.). Essay.

Disease & Health   Doctors   Drugs

Advocates a larger role for the patient and a greater attention to preventive medicine, which for the Renaissance meant adoption of a healthful life-style. Bacon also advocates caution in the use of medicines. "There is a wisdom in this beyond the rules of physic: a man's own observation, what he finds good of, and what he finds hurt of, is the best physic to preserve health . . . . To be free-minded and cheerfully disposed at hours of meat and of sleep and of exercise is one of the best precepts of long lasting . . . . If you fly physic in health altogether, it will be too strange for your body when you shall need it. If you make it too familiar, it will work no extraordinary effect when sickness cometh . . . . Despise no new accident in your body, but ask opinion of it . . . . Physicians are some of them so pleasing and conformable to the humour of the patient, as they press not the true cure of the disease; and some other are so regular in proceeding . . . as they respect not the condition of the patient. Take one of middle temper."

Bacon, Francis. "Of Youth and Age" (1625 ed.). Essay.

Age

The advantages and disadvantages of both stages of life. "Generally, youth is like the first cogitations, not so wise as the second . . . . And yet the invention of young men is more lively than that of old; and imaginations stream into their minds better, and as it were more divinely . . . . Certainly it is good to compound employments of both; for that will be good for the present, because the virtues of either age may correct the defects of both; and good for succession, that young men may be learners, while men in age are actors; and lastly, good for extern accidents, because authority followeth old men, and favour and popularity youth."

Barclay, Alexander. Ship of Fools. New York: D. Appleton & Co., 1874; rpt. New York: AMS Press, 1966. Poems.

Alcoholism   Children   Disease & Health
Doctors   Med. Profession   Women as Healers

Barclay "translates" Sebastian Brandt's fanciful satire, Narrenschiffen, into his own castigation of English sins and follies. He uses the woodcuts which accompanied Brandt's poem, but explicates the pictures after his own fashion. (Harsher than Brandt's original, Barclay's work still does not approach the subtle savagery of Katherine Anne Porter's Ship of Fools.) Barclay is representative of the early English Humanists in his concern for proper instruction of children: "Two dyuers sortes of these foles may we fynde./By whome theyr chyldren ar brought to confusion./The one is neglygent. the other is starke blynde . . . . A yonge hert is as apt to take wysdome/As is an olde . . . But fyll an erthen pot first withyll lycoure/And euer after it shall smell somewhat soure." ("Of the erudicion of neglygent faders anenst theyr chyldren") His "Of glotons and droncardes" is characteristic of the time before distilled liquors. Drunkenness is a sin which leads to yet more sin, but it is chiefly to be condemned for

being antithetical to reason, not because it is a disease or a social problem. Barclay is unusually favorable to the medical profession. He satirizes foolish patients who do not obey their wise physicians and patients who do not seek medical aid in the first, curable, stages of a disease. The latter fool is like a sinner who will not go to confession ("Of them that be diseasyd and seke ar impacient and inobedyent to the phesycan"). Barclay also attacks ignorant quacks who haven't studied the classical medical writers. He is particularly vicious toward women doctors, calling them witches, especially attacking them for giving the same medicine to different sexes and ages. ("Of folysshe Fesycyans.") Barclay rebukes only the physicians who stretch the cure to last as long as the patient's money.

Beaumont, Francis and John Fletcher. Thierry and Theodoret. Works. London: Edward Moxon, 1839. Vol. 2. Drama.

Evil Doctors   Madness   Sexuality
Suicide

Although Thierry and Theodoret shows Beaumont and Fletcher at their worst (ranting speeches and the complete sacrifice of logic and consistency for dramatic effect), it does have the interesting evil physician, Lecure, who aids the evil queen by increasing the sexual potency of her lover and by depriving her son of all sexual potency so that his marriage cannot be consummated. Her daughter-in-law is so virtuous that she does not miss sexual pleasures, but the son goes mad. The physician arranges a "cure" which involves the son murdering the first woman he sees. Of course, Lecure also arranges that the daughter-in-law be that first woman. However, the son refuses to kill his wife—to her disappointment. The play ends with an orgy of murder and suicide. Death replaces sexuality as a means of pleasurable excitement: there are four suicides and one murder in the last act. It is interesting that, although Lecure can manipulate sexual potency, increasing or decreasing it at will, in the long run sexual impotency is not as important as the will to death, which is incurably endemic in the population. Lecure, himself a suicide, cannot redirect the desire to lie with death, which has supplanted normal sexual desire.

Brome, Richard. The Antipodes, ed. Ann Haker. Lincoln: University of Nebraska Press, 1966. Drama.

Body/Mind   Doctors   Madness
Sexuality   Sexual Roles

The play is organized about three cures: the cure of a young man's disinterest in sexual intercourse, the cure of the young man's virgin wife who has gone mad with sexual frustration, and the cure of an old man's jealousy of his young wife. The young man is obsessed with travel to far away countries, so Doctor Hughbal, with the aid of local actors, transports the young man to "The Antipodes," a country in which all of the normal Jacobean social roles are reversed. Although much of the social satire is now outdated, a modern reader would still find the sexual role reversals interesting because so many of the "absurdities" are becoming commonplace today. As in the medieval romance, Aucassin and Nicolette, the sight of the reversed roles becomes too much for the young man, who intervenes to restore "normalcy," which includes bedding his wife, thus curing both young people. The cure of the jealous husband is both conventional and fantastic (the husband's rival turns out to be the lady's long-lost noble father). Although the manipulator-doctor who cures by non-chemical methods is not unusual in Renaissance literature, Doctor Hughball is one of the best and the most imaginative.

Browne, Thomas. A Letter to a Friend, Upon Occasion of the Death of his Intimate Friend. Selected Writings, ed. Geoffrey Keynes. London: Faber and Faber, 1970. Essay.

By Doctors   Death   Disease & Health
Dying

According to Sir Geoffrey Keynes, this is a philosophic essay based upon a case history of one of Browne's patients. The narration of the patient's death from consumption moves slowly, for Browne continually pauses to ruminate upon statements by earlier writers about the various aspects of dying. No matter if the topic is loss of weight or the influence of the stars upon health, Browne considers the past. "Some think there were few Consumptions in the Old World, when Men lived much upon Milk; and that the ancient Inhabitants of this Island were less troubled with Coughs when they went naked, and slept in Caves and Woods, than Men now in Chambers and Feather-beds. Plato will tell us, that there was no such Disease as a Catarrh in Homer's time . . . . New Discoveries of the Earth discover new Diseases: for besides the common swarm, there are endemial and local Infirmities proper unto certain regions . . . and if Asia, Africa, and America should bring in their List, Pandoras Box would swell, and there must be a strange Pathology."

Browne, Thomas. Religio Medici. Treatise.

By Doctors   Death   Euthanasia
Med. Profession   Preg. & Childbirth

A rationalist's uneasy acceptance of irrationality. Browne prides himself upon his religious toleration, and yet perhaps it is uneasily bought; for Browne is really ahead of his time, looking to the future when, not Roman Catholicism, but science, is considered the threat to an Englishman's faith. Browne lists the many contradictions between common sense and the Bible—only to welcome these contradictions, for "This I think no vulgar part of faith to believe a

thing not only above, but contrary to reason, and against
the argument of our proper senses." One of the more
horrifying examples of this abdication of reason is the
statement: "Experience, and History informe me, that not
onely many particular women, but likewise whole nations,
have escaped the curse of childbed, which God seemes to
pronounce upon the whole Sex; yet doe I beleeve that all
this is true, which indeed my reason would perswade me to
be false." Browne discusses death at length, noting that
dissection tends to make one contemptuous of death. He
finds death both shameful ("in a moment it can so dis-
figure us that our nearest friends, wives, and Children
stand afraid and start at us") and desirable ("There is
therefore but one comfort left, that though it be in the
power of the weakest arme to take away life, it is not
in the strongest to deprive us of death: God would not
exempt himself from that"). Browne feels that his faith
sets him apart from his profession. He is exempt from
the common trait of physicians--wishing illness upon his
patients to get business--and "I cannot goe to cure the
body of my Patient, butI forget my profession and call
unto God for his soule."

Bullein, William. _A Dialogue Against the Fever Pestilence_, eds.
Mark W. Bullen and A. H. Bullen. London: Early English Text
Society, 1888. Dialogues.

    Death   Doctors   Plague

To Bullein, the plague is not a social disaster, something
to be met with united effort by a community; rather, it is
a symbol of the death awaiting all men, and Bullein is
full of advice about the ways to approach that death. The
book is loosely structured about two dying men. One is
the wealthy, sinful Antonius, who clings to life with the
aid of the money-hungry Doctor Tocrub. Bullein creates
confusion by using the greedy, amoral doctor as his mouth-
piece for instructing his reader about temperance, the
soul, free will, as well as the causes of and cures for
the plague. However, Tocrub reverts to character as he
leaves the dying patient. "He loued me as I loued hym,
He me for healthe, and I hym for money; And thei whiche
are preseruers of the life of manne, ought not to be present at the death or buriall of the same man, therefore I
haue taken my leave, I warrante you, . . . I will retourne
to hym no more." Civis, the middle-class burgher fares
better in his death. As he flees London to escape the
plague, he is caught by death and abandoned by his wife
and servants. Fortunately, he finds a doctor of theology
who aids him to an easy and righteous death. Thus, in
this work, Bullein provides double-barrelled advice to
his readers: he gives medical advice to avoid dying of
plague, but, should that advice fail, the reader still
has the prescription for a good death.

Buonarroti, Michel Angelo. "I feel constrained and blocked as is
the marrow," in _The Complete Poems of Michelangelo_, trans.
Joseph Tusiani. New York: The Noonday Press, 1960. Poem:
55 lines.

    Age   The Body   Disease & Health

Extravagant view of the ill effects of age upon the body.
Yet the poem's absurdity and imagination cannot mask the
poet's bitterness: "My cough and cold, I gather, cannot
quench it;/But, if they do, it must escape through the
rear,/Since through the mouth my breath can hardly ven-
ture . . . . My eyes are sand which has been ground of
stones,/My teeth are keys of some old instrument/Which,
as they move, make jarring sounds and drones . . . . A
spider, in one ear, has spun a thick/Web; in the other
sings a cricket all night;/No sleep, no snore, but a
cararrhous trick . . . . Ah, I am finished, if I don't
die soon."

Buonarroti, Michel Angelo. "Just as a silkworm with much selfless
pain," in _The Complete Poems of Michelangelo_, trans. Joseph
Tusiani. New York: The Noonday Press, 1960. Poem: 14 lines.

    Homosexuality

Blissful abasement before his beloved: "Would that I were--
my hairy skin alone--/The skin that makes with its soft
hairs a plate/(O happy dress!) around his handsome breast/
All day!"

Buonarroti, Michel Angelo. "Lady, through long experience we see,"
in _The Complete Poems of Michelangelo_, trans. Joseph Tusiani.
New York: The Noonday Press, 1960. Poem: Sonnet.

    The Body   Death

Like Shakespeare's use of art for immortality, a bulwark
against death. "Believe me, what I sculpted in the past/
Is not afraid of time and death, like me./Then a long life
to both of us I'll give/In color or in stone, as you prefer
. . . . They will see how beautiful you were/And how in
loving you I was most right."

Buonarroti, Michel Angelo. "Sculpture, the first of arts, delights a
taste," in _The Complete Poems of Michelangelo_, trans. Joseph
Tusiani. New York: The Noonday Press, 1960. Poem: 8 lines.

    The Body

Unusual twist to the theme that art outlives man: in this
case, the human species outlives art. "But oh, if time's
inclement rage should waste,/Or maim, the statue that man
builds alone,/Its beauty still remains, and can be traced/
Back to the source that claims it as its own."

Buonarroti, Michel Angelo. "This new, singular beauty," in _The
Complete Poems of Michelangelo_, trans. Joseph Tusiani. New
York: The Noonday Press, 1960. Poem: 16 lines.

    Age   Sexuality

The white-haired poet is near his death and believes that
he no longer need pray for aid against sexual temptation.
He finds that he is wrong.

Buonarroti, Michel Angelo. "To Giovanni, the one from Pistoia," in
The Complete Poems of Michelangelo (no.9), trans. Joseph
Tusiani. New York: The Noonday Press, 1960. Poem: 20 lines.

    The Body   Disease & Health

Working conditions and health: his body after he has
worked on his back, painting the Sistine Chapel. "Beard
to the stars, and a nape that I pin/On the shoulders, a
harpy's breast--that's me;/And, dripping still, the brush
as you can see,/Has made my face a floor stained out and
in./Into the belly have entered my hips . . . . In front,
my skin is taut, and almost flips,/But in the back the
wrinkles make a bunch,/And I am bent like an Assyrian
arch . . . . Defend my painting dead,/Giovanni, and my
honor which grows fainter:/This place is bad; besides,
I am no painter."

Buonarroti, Michel Angelo. "When contracting, the lash seems not to
cause," in _The Complete Poems of Michelangelo_, trans. Joseph
Tusiani. New York: The Noonday Press, 1960. Poem: 14 lines.

    The Body

Although this fragment's purpose appears to be accurate
description of the eye's appearance, it still imposes the
artist's view of the body in motion, though stationary.
Michelangelo sculptures the eye in verse.

Buonarroti, Michel Angelo. "Youth, in its greenness, cannot know,
O Lord," in _The Complete Poems of Michelangelo_, trans. Joseph
Tusiani. New York: The Noonday Press, 1960. Poem: 6 lines.

    Death

The artist and the man caught in conflict. The fragment
is not entirely clear, but it seems to be the internal
struggles of an artist, fearing death, who believes that
his soul gains as it leaves the world, and yet who is
drawn to the world by his art. His only solution is a
helpless cry to God.

Burton, Robert. _The Anatomy of Melancholy_. New York: Dutton, 1968.
3 Vols. Treatise.

Age	The Body	Body/Mind
Children	Death	Disease & Health
Doctors	Grief	Handicaps
Madness	Med. Instit.	Med. Profession
Poverty & Health	Preg. & Childbirth	Sexuality
Suffering	Suicide	Women as Healers
(among others!)		

"The Compleat Madman."--for all physicians (especially for
all psychiatrists)--a thought-provoking, mirth-provoking
work touching upon the uncertainties underlying medical
practice and theory. He has caught the difficulties of
defining both disease and madness (Pt. 1. Sect. 1. Mem. 1.
Sub. 2.), of diagnosing individual cases (1. 1. 3. 4.),
and of finding entry points into curing a disease influenced by both body and mind. Ostensibly Burton is discussing types of madness, particularly melancholy or
depression; however, he manages to cover all learning
before the early seventeenth-century--on all topics.
Burton presents contradictory points of view, unifying
them by his inimitable style and his gentle humor. (He
warns the reader susceptible to melancholy to avoid reading
the list of symptoms, putting the warning at the end of the
list of symptoms.) He does seem to favor a medical theory
that accepts the interaction of body and mind and a medical
practice that unites prayer and physic. He is not entirely
friendly to doctors, describing their folly and excessive
use of medication (2. 1. 4. 2.) and writing a semi-humorous,
semi-satirical history of the corrupt profession of physic
(2. 4. 1. 1.). Yet he also praises physicians, particularly
those who work with ministers, and advises patients to
assist their doctors. He ends his condemnation of physic
with "But I will urge these cavilling and contumelious
arguments no farther, lest some physician should mistake
me, and deny me physic when I am sick." He praises herb
women. His preface describes an encounter between Hippocrates,
the practitioner, and Democritus, the researcher, with
honors given to Democritus, who rebukes Hippocrates for his
conscientiousness, saying "So if men would attempt no more
than what they can bear, they should lead contented lives
and, learning to know themselves, would limit their ambition."
His treatment for melancholy is interesting, offering cures
for both body and mind. He particularly urges activity and
supervision for the afflicted person. Burton comments on
Age (1. 1. 2. 5.--increases melancholy); The Body (1. 1.
2.--Summarizes anatomy but urges holistic view and 1. 2.
4. 3.--a woman, told of her animal and excremental interior
by a physician, dies); Children (1. 2. 1. 6.--genetic and
prenatal influences, 1. 2. 4. 1. & 2.--wet-nursing and
education as sources of melancholy); Death (2. 3. 5.--
frightful, but so is life); Disease and Health (1. 1. 1.
2.--all men have disease); Grief (1. 1. 3. 1.; 2. 3.
5.--cause of melancholy, should be eased by reason or
diversion); Handicaps (2. 3. 2.--may have ill body but
can have healthy mind); Med. Institutions (Preface--wrong
for hospitals to rely on dying, repentant sinner for
endowments); Poverty and Health (1. 2. 4. 6.--poverty
cause of melancholy; 2. 3. 3.--wealth can't buy the con-

tented mind that leads to health); Sexuality (first half
of the third book describes how sexual problems lead to
melancholy); Suffering (l. l. l.--sent by God); Suicide
(l. 4. l.--only God knows if it's lawful). Burton is
also interested in religious despair as a cause of melancholy.

Campanella, Tomaso. <u>City of the Sun</u>. Available in <u>Famous Utopias of
the Renaissance</u>, ed. Frederic R. White. Hendricks House, 1955,
or <u>Ideal Commonwealths</u>. Kennikat, 1967. rpt: 1901 ed.
Treatise.

   Disease & Health   Sci Fi   Sexual Roles

    A seventeenth-century Utopian work interesting for its
optimistic ideas. More extreme than Sir Thomas More,
Campanella asserts that a social system can prevent
disease: frugality, exercise, fresh air, bathing,
prayers, acids, cheese-bread and wheaten corn eliminate
ill-health. (However children are still instructed in
medicines and medicinal plants.) Women are equal in
status with men, although men do the more vigorous tasks
and women the more passive. Women are trained as warriors,
scientists, and governors.

Campion, Thomas. "If any hath the heart to kill," from <u>The Fourth
Book of Ayres</u> in <u>The Works of Thomas Campion</u>, ed. Walter R.
Davis. Garden City, New York: Doubleday, 1967. Song: 24
lines.

   By Doctors   Sexuality

    A physician, a controversial musical and literary theorist,
a composer, and a poet, Campion certainly qualifies as a
"Renaissance Man." Although his efforts to promulgate a
new style of lyric patterned by vowel length did not found
a new school of poetry and music, they did create poetry
and music of lasting beauty. One can best enjoy his lyrics
by hearing them sung to Campion's music. Yet they are
magnificent pieces of music in themselves, even when depicting healthy impotence, as in this lyric. The poet
has been well in body and mind--and yet could not arouse
himself to please his fair, sweet lady. Recovered, he
cannot win her to a second interview. "Now shee rejects
me as one weake,/Yet am I all compos'd of steele./Ah, this
is it my heart doth grieve:/Now though shee sees, shee'le
not believe!"

Campion, Thomas. "It fell on a sommers day," from <u>A Book of Ayres</u>
in <u>The Works of Thomas Campion</u>, ed. Walter R. Davis. Garden
City, New York: Doubleday, 1967. Song: 24 lines.

   By Doctors   Sexuality

    A light, bawdy poem illustrating Bessie's great power of
self-control. It is set to a very catchy tune. Jamy
comes upon his love, Bessie, who lies half-asleep in her
bower. Obstinately, she refuses to speak to him, pretending sleep. He resolves to make her talk to him, so
he kisses and embraces her--she remains asleep. "Jamy
then began to play,/Bessie as one buried lay,/Gladly still
through this sleight/Deceiv'd in her owne deceit/And,
since this traunce begoon,/She sleepes ev'rie afternoone."
(For additional information on Campion, see "If any hath
the heart to kill.")

Campion, Thomas. "The Sypres curten of the night is spread," from
<u>A Book of Ayres</u> in <u>The Works of Thomas Campion</u>, ed. Walter R.
Davis. Garden City, New York: Doubleday, 1967. Song: 18
lines.

   By Doctors   Grief

    Beautiful description of insomniac depression. "The Sypres
curten of the night is spread,/And over all a silent dewe
is cast./The weaker cares by sleepe are conquered;/But I
alone, with hideous griefe agast,/In spite of Morpheus
charmes a watch doe keepe/Over mine eies, to banish carelesse sleepe."

Campion, Thomas. "There is a Garden in her face," from <u>The Fourth
Book of Ayres</u> in <u>The Works of Thomas Campion</u>, ed. Walter R.
Davis. Garden City, New York: Doubleday, 1967. Song: 18
lines.

   By Doctors   Sexuality

    A charming and delicate portrait of his mistress--raised
from the commonplace by the music of his verse. "There
is a Garden in her face,/Where Roses and white Lilies
grow;/A heav'nly paradice is that place,/Wherein all
pleasant fruits doe flow./There Cherries grow, which
none may buy/Till Cherry ripe themselves doe cry." (For
additional information on Campion, see "If any hath the
heart to kill.")

Campion, Thomas. "Though you are yoong and I am olde," from <u>A Book
of Ayres</u> in <u>The Works of Thomas Campion</u>, ed. Walter R. Davis.
Garden City, New York: Doubleday, 1967. Song: 12 lines.

   Age   The Body   By Doctors
   Death

    A commonplace defense of age as sturdy and youth as close
to death as age. "You are more fresh and faire then I,/
Yet stubs doe live, when flowers doe die." The poem is
interesting for its use of the theory of humours. It was
a medical commonplace during the Renaissance, that the
body (as well as the emotions)was governed by four elements.
Health resulted from the balance of moist, hot blood and
cold phlem; of dry hot choler and dry cold melancholy.
This medical theory appealed to Renaissance writers, and
it underlies many literary works, as in the first verse
of this song. "Though you are yoong and I am olde,/Though
your vaines hot and my bloud colde,/Though youth is moist
and age is drie,/Yet embers live when flames doe die."

(Burton has an excellent summary of the humours in <u>The
Anatomy of Melancholy</u>.) (For additional information on
Campion, see "If any hath the heart to kill.")

Castiglione, Baldesar. <u>The Book of the Courtier</u>, trans. Charles S.
Singleton. Garden City, New York: Doubleday, 1959. Dialogues.

   Age   The Body   Sexuality
   Sexual Roles

    One of the clearest and most enjoyable statements of
Renaissance neoplatonism, especially as applied to court
life. Arguing among themselves, and arguing from theory,
the courtiers serving the Duchess of Urbino, try to
determine the qualifications for the ideal courtier--
perfect in birth, in body, in training, in emotions, and
in virtue. The courtier, whether male or female, must be
beautiful, for beauty is the sign of goodness. "I say
that beauty springs from God and is like a circle, the
center of which is goodness. And hence, as there can be
no circle without a center, there can be no beauty without
goodness . . . . Therefore beauty is the true trophy of
the soul's victory, when with divine power she holds sway
over material nature, and by her light conquers the darkness of the body" (Book IV). This insistence upon the
lovely body may explain the contemptuous description of
age which begins Book II and the scorn for sexual desire
in old people (found in Book IV). Sexuality is a youthful
pleasure, a union of two incomplete sexes, and a means of
propagating the noble human species (Book III). The
courtiers' attitude toward sexual roles is rather confusing.
Book II ends with a number of <u>Decameron</u> tales of trickery
between the sexes. But Book III begins with Magnifico
Giuliano's defense of women, which includes a list of good
women reminiscent of Boccaccio's <u>De Claris Mulieribus</u> (Concerning Famous Women-104 biographies of women) or Chaucer's
<u>The Legend of Good Women</u>. Magnifico Giuliano has the per-
ception to see "The poor creatures do not desire to be men
in order to become more perfect, but in order to gain freedom and to escape that rule over them which man has arrogated
to himself by his own authority . . . . But woman does not
receive her being from man; on the contrary, even as she is
perfected by him, she also perfects him." Yet, when theory
is translated into practice, one finds that the ideal court
lady should not serve the Lady of the Court (even though
this debate took place before the Duchess of Urbino) but
the male courtiers. A lame conclusion to such a promising
start.

Cellini, Benvenuto. <u>Autobiography</u>, trans. John Addington Symonds.
New York: The Modern Library, n.d. Autobiography.

   Children   Disease & Health   Doctors
   Suffering   V.D.

    In his autobiography, as well as in his life, Cellini
creates what has come to be the stereotype of the Renaissance artist: a man self-assertive, egotistical, apolitical,
amoral--and driven to create forms of great beauty and
power. Cellini has several encounters with physicians.
His friends deceive a doctor into treating him for the
plague (Book I, Ch. 29). He makes a sharp scalpel to reduce the pain of an operation upon a friend's child (Book
I, Ch. 46); he describes his encounter with venereal disease,
pluming himself on his self-cure--despite the physicians
(Book I, Ch. 59); and he describes a fever that nearly
killed him (Book I, Ch. 85). He had an ambiguous relationship with his father, who wanted him to be a musician
instead of a sculptor. Throughout his life, noticeably in
dreams and delirium (from suffering or fever), one can see
his guilt for disappointing his father. At the end of Book
I, Cellini describes his sufferings in prison. He relates
his ill-treatment in great detail, in part to evoke indig-
nation against his enemies, and in part to evoke admiration
for his steadfast endurance. He seems compelled to prove
that no suffering could shake him, e.g. "Thus, then, I continued to exist in misery upon that rotten mattress, which
in three days soaked up water like a sponge. I could hardly
stir because of my broken leg; and when I had to get out of
bed to obey a call of nature, I crawled on all fours with
extreme distress . . . . Nevertheless, as well as I was able,
I comforted my soul by calling to mind how much more painful
it would have been, on passing from this life . . . . Little
by little I felt my vital forces waning, until at last my
vigorous temperament had become adapted to that purgatory.
When I felt it quite acclimatised, I resolved to put up
with all those indescribable discomforts so long as it
held out."

Cervantes Saavedra, Miguel de. <u>Don Quixote</u>. Tale.

   Age   Madness   Sexual Roles

    The hilarious and touching madness of the aged romantic,
Don Quixote. The story touches upon the ambiguities
involved in defining madness. Don Quixote, charging
sheep and windmills, is clearly not in touch with reality.
Yet there are degrees of madness beyond his--especially
that of the lunatic lover, the furious insanity which
Don Quixote vainly tries to emulate and with which
Cerdenio is truly afflicted. Further, the tale raises
uneasy questions: is Quixote mad for wresting reality
to conform to his beloved medieval romances, or is he
mad for trying to relieve suffering and injustice? The
tale does mock the romantic view of women, contrasting
Don Quixote's noble Lady Dulcinea del Toboso with the
true Aldonza Lorenzo (I, xi; II, iv). "The same, answer'd
Don Quixote; and 'tis she that merits to be the Sovereign
Mistress of the Universe. Udsdiggers, quoth Sancho, I
know her full well; 'tis a strapping Wench, I'faith, and
pitches the Bar with e'er a lusty young Fellow in our
Parish" (trans. Motteux and Ozell).

The Commedia dell'Arte.   Dramas.

Doctors

The source of the comic doctor in drama. The stock figure of the blundering, old, lawyer-physician, made so vivid by Molière, was derived from the Commedia dell'Arte, Italian improvisational drama. The physician nearly always appears as a short-sighted, short-tempered parent--the only exceptions being a brief appearance by a doctor to sell a magic potion or a longer appearance by the lover disguised as a doctor. There are a number of collections of Commedia dell'Arte scenarios, but a summary of the character types might be more useful (e.g. Giacomo Oreglia's The Commedia dell'Arte. New York: Hill and Wang, 1968).

Copland, Robert. The Highway to the Spital-house, in The Elizabethan Underworld, ed. Arthur V. Judges. New York: Octagon Books, 1965. Dialogues in Verse.

Med. Instit.   Poverty & Health

Early 16th-century discussion of who should and should not be admitted to charitable care. "Copland" asks the spital-house (combination hospital, old-age home, and poor-house) porter: "which ye leave and which ye do succor?" Copland is worried that beggars will fake illnesses and so get in, but the porter assures him that it is only open to "old people, sick and impotent,/Poor women in childbed, have here easement,/Weak men sore wounded by great violence,/And sore men eaten with pox and pestilence,/And honest folk fallen in great poverty." Copland and the porter then discuss at length all the various cheats and disguises used to gain charity--but the petty criminals seem honest by contrast with the sinners and fools whose way of living must bring them to the spital-house. The porter has a long diatribe asserting that sin and folly lead inevitably to poverty and disease. His list of sins and follies is so long, that it seems as if England herself were one large spital-house.

Cowley, Abraham. "Ode: Upon Dr. Harvey." Poems, ed. A. R. Waller. Cambridge: Cambridge University Press, 1905. Poem: 91 lines.

The Body   Death   Doctors

The researcher as rapist. Cowley was quite interested in contemporary science. He even drew up an elaborate plan for housing scientists and laboratories for the Royal Society. Yet he could find no poetic language for his new science. At first he seems to have done quite well, comparing Harvey to Apollo, god of wisdom and medicine. But then, the only analogy to research on the human body that he can find is that of rape. Harvey ravishes Nature even more thoroughly than Apollo did Daphne. "Coy Nature . . . When Harveys violent passion she did see,/Began to tremble, and to flee . . . But Harvey our Apollo, stopt not so, Into the Bark, and root he after her did goe." She hides in the human heart, "but e're she was aware,/Harvey was with her there,/And held this slippery Proteus in a chain,/Till all her mighty Mysteries she descry'd." Cowley does praise Harvey as a true doctor of medicine: "Thus Harvey sought for Truth in Truth's own Book . . . . Great Doctor! Th'Art of Curing's cur'd by thee." Yet his body must ultimately give in to age, and Nature "Will sure have her revenge on him at last."

Cowley, Abraham. "To Dr. Scarborough." Poems, ed. A. R. Waller. Cambridge: Cambridge University Press, 1905. Poem: 111 lines.

Death   Disease & Health   Doctors
V.D.

Unusual in its unqualified praise of a doctor, and rather medieval in its conclusion that even the doctor must die. Dr. Scarborough can cure everything, including dropsie, ague, and plague. He treats V.D. so well that "thy Patients seem to be/Restor'ed not to Health onely, but Virginitie." He knows all herbs, all medicines, all anatomy. "Nor does this Science make thy Crown alone,/But whole Apollo is thine owne./His gentler Arts, belov'ed in vain by Mee,/Are wedded and enjoy'd by Thee./Thou'rt by this noble Mixture free/From the Physitians frequent Maladie,/Fantastick Incivilitie." Yet even this medical paragon must die. "Let Nature, and let Art do what they please,/When all's done, Life is an Incurable Disease."

Crashaw, Richard. "Epithalamium." The Complete Poetry of Richard Crashaw, ed. George Walton Williams. New York: New York University Press, 1972. Poem: 144 lines.

Sexuality

A curiosity--mourning the death of a maidenhead. Using the Renaissance equation between dying and sexual intercourse, Crashaw transforms the wedding into a funeral, with such relish that the concluding blessings upon the couple ring false. "Yet love in death did wayte upon her,/granting leave she should expire/in her fumes, and have the honour/t'exhale in flames of his owne fire;/her funerall pyle/the marriage bedd . . . . Twixt the pretty twylight strife/of dying maide and dawning wife;/twixt raine, and sun-shine, this sweet maydenhead alas is dead."

Crashaw, Richard. "The Flaming Heart Upon the Book and Picture of the seraphicall saint Teresa, (as she is usually expressed with a seraphim biside her)." The Complete Poetry of Richard Crashaw, ed. George Walton Williams. New York: New York University Press, 1972. Poem: 108 lines.

Sexuality

The most extreme expression of the Renaissance and Baroque fusion of religion and sexuality. Crashaw combines extravagant images, which require interpretation by the intellect,

with a nervous sensuality which elicits a sexual response. His praise of St. Teresa is almost indistinguishable from praise of a sexually-fulfilled woman. "For in love's feild was never found/A nobler weapon than a WOUND./Love's passives are his activ'st part./The wounded is the wounding heart . . . . By all thy brim-fill'd Bowles of feirce desire/By thy last Morning's draught of liquid fire;/By the full kingdome of that finall kisse/That seiz'd thy parting Soul, and seal'd thee his . . . . By all of HIM we have in THEE;/Leave nothing of my SELF in me."

Crashaw, Richard. "In praise of Lessius: Temperance, or the cheap physitian upon the translation of Lessius." The Complete Poetry of Richard Crashaw, ed. George Walton Williams. New York: New York University Press, 1972. Poem: 52 lines.

Age   Disease & Health

The extravagant Crashaw praises temperance! This poem was written as a commendatory verse for Lessius' treatise advising how to live to a ripe old age. The poem show us the radiant, healthy, temperate old man, then ends "In summe, wouldst see a man that can/Live to be old, and still a man?/Whose latest and most leaden houres/Fall with soft wings, stuck with soft flowers . . . . This rare one, reader, wouldst thou see?/Hark hither; and thy self be HE."

Crashaw, Richard. "On the Wounds of our Crucified Lord." The Complete Poetry of Richard Crashaw, ed. George Walton Williams. New York: New York University Press, 1972. Poem: 20 lines.

Suffering

Complete intellectualizing of Christ's suffering (compare with the anonymous medieval poems). This is very immediate and grotesquely violent. "O these wakefull wounds of thine!/Are they Mouthes? or are they eyes?/Be they Mouthes, or be they eyne,/Each bleeding part some one supplies./Lo! a mouth, whose full-bloom'd lips/At too deare a rate are roses./Lo! a blood-shot eye! that weepes/And many a cruell teare discloses."

Daniel, Samuel. "Care-charmer sleep." Available in most anthologies of English Renaissance poetry, such as Poetry of the English Renaissance, eds. J. W. Hebel and H. H. Hudson. New York: Appleton-Century-Crofts, 1957. Sonnet.

Grief   Suffering

Balanced and beautiful appeal to sleep, the reliever of woes. Curious interplay between the controlled verse and the sorrowful despair of the speaker, who ends pleading for eternal, rather than temporary, surcease from pain. "Care-charmer sleep, son of the sable night,/Brother to death, in silent darkness born,/Relieve my languish and restore the light,/With dark forgetting of my care, return . . . . Still let me sleep, embracing clouds in vain,/And never wake to feel the day's disdain."

Daniel, Samuel. "When Winter snows upon the golden heares (hairs)." Available in Poems and a Defence of Ryme, ed. A. C. Sprague. Chicago: University of Chicago Press, 1965. Sonnet.

Age   Sexuality

A gentle affirmation of the power of poetry to triumph over the horrors of age, by preserving the memory of youthful beauty and power. "When Winter snowes vpon thy golden heares,/And frost of age hath nipt thy flowers neere:/When darke shall seeme thy day that neuer cleares,/And all lyes withred that was held so deere./Then take this picture which I heere present thee . . . Heere see the giftes that God and nature lent thee;/Heere read thy selfe, and what I suffred for thee."

Dekker, Thomas. The Honest Whore, Pt. I. Available in many anthologies of late Tudor-Stuart Drama, such as Elizabethan and Stuart Plays, eds. Baskervill, Heltzel, and Nethercot. New York: Holt Rinehart and Winston, 1963. Drama.

Doctors   Grief   Madness
Med. Ethics   Med. Instit.   Sexuality

Three plots united by the interaction of morality and madness with sexual relationships. On the highest social level, two lovers, Hippolito and Infeliche, are separated by the wicked Duke, who has caused his physician to give Infeliche, his daughter, the potion, the drug so loved by story-tellers, the potion which creates the semblance of death. In his grief at her supposed demise, Hippolito rejects all women, converting a whore, who was supposed to solace him, to repentence and honest living. The physician also repents. He tricks the Duke into a belief that Hippolito is dead and helps the lovers to hide in Bethlehem madhouse (Bedlam) until they can marry. The repentent whore resists all efforts of her pimp (her first seducer) to force her to return to business. She ends up in Bethlehem madhouse, where she assists the noble lovers. In a third plot, a citizen's wife is so irked by her husband's placid nature, that she stages a series of calamities designed to enrage him. Failing to anger him, she declares him mad and sends him--to Bethlehem madhouse. Dekker, having sent all of his frustrated people to the madhouse, resolves all tangles there. The Duke, after laughing at the madmen, is reconciled to his married daughter; the whore is married to her pimp; and the citizen is restored to his repentent, resigned wife. All characters are sane when they go to the asylum; it is their situation that is insane. The physician is correct when he cures Hippolito's and Infeliche's tangled affairs, instead of employing yet more drugs.

Dekker, Thomas. _That Wonderful Year_. In _Three Elizabethan Pamphlets_, ed. G. R. Hibbard. London: George G. Harrap & Co., 1951. Treatise in Prose and Poetry.

Med. Profession   Plague

Although this pamphlet relates other events of 1603, it is most famous for its depiction of plague-stricken London. It is a source for many later stories and novels, especially Defoe's _Journal of the Plague Year_. Dekker deliberately mixes mirth with his disease: "If you read, you may happily laugh; 'tis my desire you should, because mirth is both physical and wholesome against the plague." He interpolates a poem on the horrors of war, which ends with these curious lines: "Physicians turn to patients, their art's dry,/For then our fat men without physic die./And to conclude, against all art and good,/War taints the doctor, lets the surgeon blood." The plague is seen as an attacking army. "The Plague is muster-master and marshall of the field; burning fevers, boils, blains, and carbuncles, the leaders, lieutenants, sergeants, and corporals; the main army consisting . . . [of] dumpish mourners, merry sextons, hungry coffin-sellers, scrubbing bearers, and nasty grave-makers." He notes the defection of the helpless physicians. "They hid their synodical heads as well as the proudest. And I cannot blame them, for their phlebotomies, lozenges, and electuaries, with their diacatholicons, diacodions, amulets, and antidotes, had not so much strength to hold life and soul together, as a pot of Pinder's ale and a nutmeg."

Donne, John. "Batter my heart, three person'd God" (Holy Sonnet XIV), _The Complete Poetry and Selected Prose of John Donne_, ed. John Hayward. New York: Modern Library, 1941. Sonnet.

Sexuality   Sexual Roles

Religious fervor in terms of sexual passion: God as the aggressor, the poet as his submissive . . . "bride" seems the closest word. Donne first asks God to batter his heart, and not remain (coyly) knocking at it. Then he wants to be taken by force because, though he tries to admit God, he cannot, being involved with another, presumably that old foe, Sin. The poem concludes with these lines, in the multiple paradoxical language of love, marriage, and sexual intercourse: "Yet dearely' I love you,' and would be loved faine,/But am betroth'd unto your enemy:/Divorce mee,/'untie, or break that knot againe,/Take mee to you, imprison mee, for I/Except you enthrall mee, never shall be free,/Nor ever chast, except you ravish mee."

Donne, John. _Bianthanatos_. 1644(46?). New York: The Facsimile Text Society, 1930. Treatise.

Suicide

Elaborate justification for suicide, especially as escape from sins of the flesh: if merchants cast away precious goods during a storm at sea, "how much more may I, when I am weather-beaten and in danger of betraying that precious soule which God hath embarqued in me, put off this burdenous flesh, till his pleasure be that I shall resume it." The work is carefully divided into sections and is composed of examples of justified suicides and examinations of proscriptions against suicide. Donne expends a good deal of effort disproving prohibitions derived from natural or civil law, by discrediting such "laws" as moral standards. Without examining the reason for this death wish, Donne assumes that many people have a drive to death: "that in all ages, in all places, upon all occasions, men of all conditions, have affected it, and inclin'd to doe it."

Donne, John. "The Comparison" (Elegy VIII), _The Complete Poetry and Selected Prose of John Donne_, ed. John Hayward. New York: Modern Library, 1941. Poem: 54 lines.

The Body   Disease & Health   Doctors
Sexuality

"Comparisons are odious": that often-quoted line ends this bizarre poem, in which the poet compares his lovely mistress with another's vile lady. Seldom has the body been seen as so repulsive: "Ranke sweaty froth thy Mistresse's brow defiles,/Like spermatique issue of ripe menstruous boiles." The lady's breast is "like worme eaten trunkes . . . . And like a bunch of ragged carrets stand/The short swolne fingers of thy gouty hand." And so on down the body till he comes to the "best lov'd part" in his own mistress, which in the other is "like the dread mouth of a fired gunne,/Or like hot liquid metals newly runne/Into clay moulds, or like to that Aetna/Where round the grasse is burnt away." The poet then imagines that sex with this creature must be "harsh, and violent,/As when a Plough a stony field doth rent." On the other hand, the poet and his mistress, when they embrace, search each other out as intimately as the Surgeon does when he is searching wounds. Presented as a comparison, the poem seems, rather, a statement of Donne's (passing?) ambivalence towards female bodies and sexuality.

Donne, John. "Death be not proud" (Holy Sonnet X), _The Complete Poetry and Selected Prose of John Donne_, ed. John Hayward. New York: Modern Library, 1941. Sonnet.

Death

A confrontation with the person of Death. Taken by many to be a fearsome, powerful thing, here Death is bravely addressed. The poet, in the first place, gets pleasure from sleep, which is a foreshadowing of death, and expects, therefore, to get even more from Death itself. Far from being powerful, Donne says, Death is at the whim of Fate and kings and illness. What's more, Death is only a short sleep, from which we wake to eternal life, "And death shall be no more; death, thou shalt die." An unusually effective poem, not for its ideas--perhaps there aren't, after all, very many ways to face death--but for its language, and rhythms, which are themselves triumphant.

Donne, John. _Devotions_, from _The Complete Poetry and Selected Prose of John Donne_, ed. John Hayward. New York: Modern Library, 1941. Essays.

Age   Death   Disease & Health
Med. Profession

Essays upon one man's illness, but also upon illness in the body politic, the microcosm, and the soul. All the medical terms have metaphorical as well as literal meanings: Physicians are healers in some larger sense; relapse is emotional and spiritual as well as medical; and so on. But the literal level is memorable enough on its own. The author (who was in fact a sickly man) complains first that as if death were not enough, we must die slowly through the torment of illness. A sick-bed is a grave--no, worse; since in the grave one may at least speak through the voices of one's friends. But in the physician we have a "Hercules against these Gyants, these Monsters," these diseases, which are so many we cannot even name them all. Every other kind of creature, Donne complains, can cure himself, but not man. As for him, "His diseases are his owne, but the Phisician is not." The worse part of serious illness is solitude, for "A long illness will weary friends at last, but a pestilentiall sicknes averts them from the beginning." Even the physician may not come for fear of infection. For that matter, fear of a different sort operates in both doctor and patient: "I observe the Phisician with the same diligence, as hee the disease; I see hee feares, and I feare with him: I overtake him, I overrun him in his feare, and I go the faster, because he disguises his fear, and I see it with the more sharpnesse, because hee would not have me see it. He knowes that his feare shall not disorder the practise, and exercise of his Art, but he knows that my fear may disorder the effect, and working of his practice." We need many physicians, Donne advises, so there must be consultations. Diseases consult with each other--why shouldn't doctors? "Age is a sicknesse, and youth is an ambush; and we need so many Phisicians, as may make up a Watch." Thus consulting is good; so is prescribing, for in writing things down, physicians are behaving openly. At last Donne must consider more fully one possible result of illness, death. And here he is most eloquent--and most familiar: "No man is an Iland . . . any mans death diminishes me . . . and therefore never send to know for whom the bell tolls; It tolls for thee."

Donne, John. "The Extasie," _The Complete Poetry and Selected Prose of John Donne_, ed. John Hayward. New York: Modern Library, 1941. Poem: 76 lines.

Body/Mind   Sexuality

One of Donne's finest poems on Platonic love, sex, and their intermingling. The poet and his mistress lie side by side, their souls gone out of their bodies to hang between them and negotiate their love. Though there is some physical contact from the beginning--their "eye-beames" are twisted up together (a marvelous Renaissance explanation for the recognizable lovers' stare)--throughout most of the poem, the contact remains spiritual. Love mixes the elements of the lovers' souls till it produces "an abler soule, which . . . Defects of loneliness controles." Finally, however, Donne must return to the body, the source of the soul, and now so mixed with the soul in the poet's mind that they cannot be separated. "To our bodies turne wee then, that so/Weake men on love reveal'd may look;/Loves mysteries in soules do grow, But yet the body is his booke." Someone once said that Donne climbs the Platonic ladder of love, but he always keeps one foot firmly planted on the bottom rung.

Donne, John. "The First Anniversary," _The Complete Poetry and Selected Prose of John Donne_, ed. John Hayward. New York: Modern Library, 1941. Poem: ca. 600 lines.

Death   Disease & Health

An analytical and occasionally preachy poem inspired by the anniversary of a virtuous woman's death. Donne seizes this occasion to describe the decay of the world, for "her death hath taught us clearly, that thou art/Corrupt and mortall in thy purest part." He then proceeds to dissect the world's anatomy, playing repeatedly upon the medical meanings of dissection, and expanding his metaphor into a general consideration of the world as sick. In the process he defines the state of health: "There is no health. Phisitians say that wee/At best, enjoy but a neutralitie./And can there be worse sicknesse than to know/That we are never well, nor can be so?" He claims that the world brought "new diseases" on itself, that its heart is dead, that it is crippled, infected, wounded, and barren. Donne knows that, like some patients, the world may deny his news: "Nor smels it well to hearers, if one tell/Them their disease, who faine would think they're well." But death--of the woman; of the world too--is "medicinall" and can act as a mid-wife, delivering us into new life.

Donne, John. "The Flea," _The Complete Poetry and Selected Prose of John Donne_, ed. John Hayward. New York: Modern Library, 1941. Poem: 27 lines.

Sexuality

Once again a poet tries to tease his mistress out of her virginity, this time doing it so ingeniously. You think it so dreadful to mingle flesh? he asks. Why, then, just look at this flea: it first sucks you, then it sucks me; and thereby swells with our two bloods. Surely, the poet protests, this is innocence itself, just as intercourse

would be. But the lady, a wit herself, is not moved by
the poet's argument, and indeed kills the flea, though
he pleads that it represents the two of them embracing.
When she mockingly retorts that neither of them is the
weaker for her "murder," the poet has yet another comeback: "'Tis true, then learne how false feares be;/Just
so much honor, when thou yeeld'st to mee,/Will wast, as
this flea's death took life from thee."

Donne, John. "Hymne to God my God in my Sicknesse," The Complete
Poetry and Selected Prose of John Donne, ed. John Hayward.
New York: Modern Library, 1941. Poem: 30 lines.

Death   Disease & Health   Doctors

The poet-cleric lies ill, perhaps dying, and so prepares
himself to meet his God. Yet even in extremis there is
clever wit--the ill man's physicians are so in love with
disease that they have become cosmographers who map out
their territory, his body. Meanwhile he lies "Flat on
this bed, that by them may be showne/That this is my
South-West discoverie/Per fretum febris, by these streights
to die." Donne expands this metaphor for several lines,
and fears not his West (i.e., his death), for just as in
flat maps--and he is one--West and East meet, so shall
Death meet with Resurrection. The poem concludes with
another version of the same idea. The poet, who has
preached to many others, now preaches to himself this
sermon on death: "Therefore that he may raise the Lord
throws down."

Donne, John. "A Nocturnall Upon S. Lucies Day: Being the Shortest
Day," The Complete Poetry and Selected Prose of John Donne, ed.
John Hayward. New York: Modern Library, 1941. Poem: 45 lines.

Grief   Madness   Sexuality

The poet is seriously depressed by the death of his beloved
(or perhaps, knowing Donne, of his love itself). As elegists
often have, he sees a parallel to his grief in nature. St.
Lucie's Day is "Both the yeares, and the dayes deep midnight." But the truly astonishing thing about the poem is
that it gives such moving utterance to a grief so profound
that one would normally expect it to run to either raving
or silence. Over and over the poet insists that he is
entirely dead, that he has no properties whatever, and for
this he blames love: "For his art did expresse/A quintessence even from nothingnesse,/From dull privations, and
lean emptinesse: He ruin'd mee, and I am re-begot/Of
absence, darknesse, death; things which are not." He himself is the epitaph of the world. What he seems to miss
most of all is his beloved's physical presence, for at
one point he remembers that sometimes they seemed only
bodies, not souls at all; and at another, he advises all
lovers to enjoy their summer lust.

Donne, John. "Sapho to Philaenis," The Complete Poetry and Selected
Prose of John Donne. New York: Modern
Library, 1941. Poem: 64 lines.

Grief   Homosexuality   Women as Healers

A sympathetic and erotic poem by a man about lesbian love.
Here Sappho addresses her absent lover, yet dares not
grieve too much, "lest Griefe remove/My beauty, and make
me' unworthy of thy love." She goes on to imagine her
lady sleeping with men, and asks: "why shouldst thou
then/Admit the tillage of a harsh rough man?/Men leave
behind them that which their sin shows./But of our dallyance
no more signes there are/Than fishes leave in streams, or
Birds in aire." Donne next makes Sappho the lesbian as
narcissist: "the likenesse being such,/Why should they
not alike in all parts touch? . . . . Likenesse begets
such strange selfe flatterie,/That touching my selfe, all
seems done to thee." The poem ends with Sappho's feeling
that her friend has restorative powers, and that merely by
coming back could prevent sickness as well.

Donne, John. "Thou hast made me" and "Oh my blacke Soule!" (Holy
Sonnets I and IV), The Complete Poetry and Selected Prose of
John Donne, ed. John Hayward. New York: Modern Library,
1941. Sonnets.

Death   Disease & Health

Two examples of Donne's despairing moods--and they were
apparently terrible indeed. Most often Donne despaired
of God's mercy and feared death, which in these two poems
he briefly represents in the language of health. In the
first sonnet, e.g., as he and death run towards each other,
the poet's eyes are dim, and his "feeble flesh doth waste/
by Sinne in it." The idea of sin as illness is found even
more explicitly in the second sonnet, where it calls out
its superior ally, death, just as physical illness does:
"Oh my blacke Soule, now thou art summoned/By sicknesse,
deaths herald, and champion." In both poems he feels
trapped by his "diseased" situation: in the first, "Des-
paire behind, and death before doth cast/Such terror"; and
in the second he feels like the prisoner awaiting execution--
he would like to be freed, but the only way out leads to
death. In both poems too he turns to God as healer, but
in neither is there much hope. Compare the later, prevailing, "Death be not proud."

Donne, John. "To His Mistris Going to Bed" (Elegy XIX), The Complete
Poetry and Selected Prose of John Donne, ed. John Hayward. New
York: Modern Library, 1941. Poem: 48 lines.

The Body   Sexuality   Sexual Roles

One of the most erotic poems in the language. The poet
instructs his mistress to undress, describing as she does
so each article of clothing she discards, and each part
of her anatomy she reveals. As he watches, his "flesh

upright," he compares her body to a new land of which he
is king, and which he must duly explore--"Before, behind,
between, above, below./O my America!" He tells his mistress to be unafraid of full nakedness, to reveal herself,
in fact, as she would to a midwife. Both sexes must be
equally naked, equally innocent, equally revealed: "To
teach thee, I am naked first; why then/What needst thou
have more covering than a man."

Donne, John. "A Valediction Forbidding Mourning," The Complete
Poetry and Selected Prose of John Donne, ed. John Hayward.
New York: Modern Library, 1941. Poem: 36 lines.

Body/Mind   Grief   Sexuality

The grief here is not a response to physical death--though
the same prescription could probably be applied--it is
grief in response to the parting of lovers. The poet
assures his lady that only those lovers who rely solely
on the body to express their love cannot abide separation.
The poet and his beloved, on the other hand, have also
intermingled their souls, and soul is a substance that
can stretch to cover distance. Donne uses his famous
analogy with a geometric compass to illustrate this concept. The lady is the fixed foot of the compass; he, as
the other foot, may make wide circles, but he will always
return where he began.

Donne, John. "Why Doth the Poxe Soe Much Affect to Undermine the
Nose?," The Complete Poetry and Selected Prose of John Donne,
ed. John Hayward. New York: Modern Library, 1941. Essay.

V.D.

A minor piece of prose from a great poet, in which he
explores a seeming paradox and wittily resolves it, much
as he does in his poetry. Here the comic question is as
the title asks it. At first, Donne suggests that one
loses one's nose through syphilis because it is a merciful
disease, and one will thereby not smell one's own stink.
Then he decides that the nose looks most like the part of
the body through which one gets the disease in the first
place. He concludes that "this Disease in particular should
affect the most eminent and perspicuous part, which in
general doth affect to take hold of the most eminent and
conspicuous men."

Dowland, John. "Flow my tears" and "I saw my Lady weep." From The
Second Book of Songs or Airs, in Shorter Elizabethan Poems, ed.
A. H. Bullen. New York: E. P. Dutton, n.d. Songs: 18 & 16
lines.

Grief   Suffering

"Flow my tears" or "Lacrimae" was one of the most popular
late-Elizabethan and Jacobean songs. Dowland's work is
the best illustration of the age's relish for grieving,
but beautiful, melancholy, a relish not to be equaled
until Poe. "Flow my tears" revels in suffering: "Down
vain lights! Shine you no more,/No nights are dark enough
for those,/That in despair, their last fortunes deplore./
Light doth but shame disclose." "I saw my Lady weep" asks
the lady not to grieve, while extravagantly praising her
sorrowing beauty: "Sorrow was there made fair,/And Passion,
wise;/Tears, a delightful thing;/Silence, beyond all speech,
a wisdom rare;/She made her sighs to sing."

Dunbar, William. "Lament for the Makers, Qwhen he wes sek" (Lament
for the poets, when he was sick). Available in Medieval and
Renaissance Poets, ed. E. Talbot Donaldson. New York: The
Viking Press, 1950. Poem: 100 lines.

Death   Disease & Health

Bleak fear created by the driving beat of death's conquests.
Dunbar begins with the dance of death (including, of course,
the physician), but shifts into an account of death's
relentless destruction of poets, ending each stanza with
the refrain, "Timor mortis conturbat me." (The fear of
death confounds me). The effect is that of a dirge, or,
in every sense of the word, a death march, as the reader
(or, even better, the listener) is battered by the rhythmical,
measured, almost mechanical progress of death. "He has done
petuously devour/The noble Chaucer, of makaris flowr,/The
Monk of Bery, and Gower, all thre:/Timor mortis conturbat me
. . . . In Dumfermeline he hes done roune/With Maister Robert
Henrysoun;/Schir Johne the Ros enbrast hes he;/Timor mortis
conturbat me . . . . Sen hes all my brether tane,/He will
nocht lat me lif alane,/On forse I man his nixt pray be;/
Timor mortis conturbat me." (A very rough translation: He
has pitilessly devoured the noble Chaucer, of poets' flower,
The Monk of Bery, and Gower all three. In Dumfermeline he
has whispered with Master Robert Henryson; Sir John the
Rose embraced has he. Since he has all my brothers taken,
he will not let me live alone. Perforce I must his next
prey be. Timor mortis conturbat me.)

Dyer, Edward. "My mind to me a kingdom is." Available in most anthol
ogies of English Renaissance poetry, such as Poetry of the Englis
Renaissance, eds. J. W. Hebel and H. H. Hudson. New York:
Appleton-Century-Crofts, 1957. Poem: 36 lines.

Body/Mind

The benefit of possessing a perfectly controlled and completely content mind. Only the inner life has meaning.
"My mind to me a kingdom is;/Such perfect joy therein I
find/That it excels all other bliss/Which God or nature
hath assigned."

Earle, John. Micro-cosmographie, 6th ed. "A Childe," "A Young-Man," "A Drunkard," "A meere dull Physitian," and "A Surgeon," in English Reprints, ed. Edward Arber. London: Alex Murray & Son, 1868. Sketches.

Adolescence   Alcoholism   Children
Doctors

In language and in observation of human nature, one of the best of the "character" books. Interesting when set next to the Barclay. The child, instead of being an object for instruction, now becomes a tabula rasa, blackened by adult experience--an early instance of the romanticized view of the child. A Child "is a Man in a small Letter, yet the best Copie of Adam before hee tasted of Eve, or the Apple; and hee is happy whose small practice in the World can only write this Character." Earle also furnishes one of the first descriptions of the adolescent in "A Young-Man." "Hee is now out of Natures protection, though not yet able to guide himselfe: But left loose to the World and Fortune, from which the weaknesse of his Childhood preserv'd him: and now his strength exposes him." "A Drunkard" shows some interesting changes from Barclay's satire written over a hundred years earlier. Drunkenness is no longer a sin leading to other sins, but a state harmful to a man's body, friends, and business. In this time, after the discovery of brandy but before the discovery of gin, drunkness has begun to be a social, rather than an individual problem. "Hee is the greatest enemy to himselfe, and the next to his friend . . . and men come from him as from a battel, wounded and bound up. Nothing takes a man off more from his credit, and businesse, and makes him more retchlesly carelesse, what becomes of all." Earle attacks the greedy, unlearned physician in "A meere dull Phisitian": "he is a sucking consumption, and a very brother to the wormes, for they are both ingendred out of mans corruption." He also satirizes the malice of the surgeon, who longs for duels or wars. "Hee deales most with broken Commodities, as a broken Head, or a mangled face, and his gaines are very ill got, for he lives by the hurt of the Common-wealth." Like lawyers and usurers, doctors are associated with the problem rather than with the cure they provide.

Elyot, Thomas. The Castle of Health (1541). New York: Scholars' facsimiles & reprints, 1936. Treatise.

Disease & Health   Med. Profession

First layman's guide to medicine in English. Elyot is best known for The Book of the Govenour, his contribution to educational reform. His second most famous work was not literary, but this layman's guide to medicine, which went through 15 editions before 1610. It drew upon him the attacks of the medical profession for opening their secrets to the public instead of hiding them in the Latin language. Elyot counterattacked by noting that Greek physicians wrote in Greek, Roman physicians in Latin, so why shouldn't English physicians write in English? He also noted that the Castle was designed to supplement the work of the physician and to enable the patient to describe quickly and accurately what was wrong. Also, Elyot defends himself to his literary and social peers for taking up the lowly occupation of physician, claiming that he only does so for the good of his country.

Erasmus, Desiderius. The Praise of Folly, trans. H. H. Hudson. Princeton: Princeton University Press, 1941. Treatise.

The Family   Madness   Med. Profession
Mental Retardation

A gentle, witty satire defending man's irrationality. Marriage cannot survive, and children cannot be born, without folly: "Or what Woman is there would ever go't [Wedlock] did she seriously consider either the peril of Child-bearing or the trouble of bringing them up?" It is folly that supports old age: "By how much the less reason they have to live, by so much the more they desire it; so far are they from being sensible of the least wearisomeness of life." It is folly that makes successful physicians: "For Physick, especially as it is now profest by most men, is nothing but a branch of Flattery." Erasmus separates folly (which verges upon what we call mental retardation) from madness (unlawful lust: Ambition, Incest, Parricide) or guilt. Folly is a blessing, a "pleasing dotage, And trust me, I think they were the madder o'th' two, and had the greater need of Hellebore, that should offer to look upon so pleasant a madness as an evil to be remov'd by Physick."

Fletcher, John. The Faithful Shepherdess. Available in Elizabethan and Stuart Plays, eds. Baskervill, Heltzel, and Nethercot. New York: Holt, Rinehart and Winston, 1963.

Sexuality   Women as Healers

Hysterical morality upon virginity. The play presents a range of sexual types. At one end is the virgin, Clorin, the Faithful Shepherdess, who is faithful to the memory of her dead fiancé. She is loved, platonically--and perversely--by Thenot, who loves her because she is faithful to the dead. Perigot and Amoret are the types of virtuous, but physical, lovers. Amarillis and the Sullen Shepherd are the types of vicious lust. Chloe, the nymphomaniac, the type of mindless lust. The satyr, once the symbol of insatiate lust, is here a type of natural lust--awed by the power of the virgin Clorin. Clorin solves all troubles, in part because of her mystic powers of healing, given her because she is a virgin.

Ford, John. The Broken Heart, ed. D. K. Anderson. Lincoln, Nebraska: University of Nebraska Press, 1968. Drama.
Disease & Health   Madness   Sexuality
Suicide

A society gone mad with intense, frustrated anger. The main characters all have an obsessive fixation upon a forbidden sexual object. All die: some by elaborate murder and some by elaborately staged suicide. Penthea forces her anger inward until it kills her; her lover, Orgilius, turns anger outward until he is condemned to die for murder. The play is full of references to incurable wounds and diseases--imagery that reinforces the idea of a society so diseased that it can only be cured by drastic amputations.

Ford, John. The Lover's Melancholy. Available in John Ford, ed. Havelock Ellis. New York: Hill and Wang, 1957. Drama.

Doctors   Grief   Madness

Unusual instance of an effective and professional physician. The play has an incredibly involved plot. The king's father had attempted to rape the daughter of his chief nobleman, Meleander. In consequence, the daughter supposedly died, the king's son, now ruler, is paralyzed with depression, Meleander has gone mad with grief, and the kingdom decays. However, Meleander's daughter turns up disguised as a boy, and all ends happily. It is only the physician, Corax, that might be of interest. He cures the king by parading true madmen before him, and he cures Meleander by a combination of drugs and news of his lost daughter. Corax is a professional. When the king disregards his prescriptions, Corax begs permission to leave the court for the university.

Ford, John. 'Tis Pity She's a Whore, ed. N. W. Bawcutt. Lincoln, Nebraska: University of Nebraska Press, 1966.

Doctors   Dying   The Family
Preg. & Childbirth   Sexuality

Rich, black meaninglessness. Lust is an innate disease; all people are reduced to sexual objects or objects of revenge. Giovanni's incestuous love for his sister, Annabella, sets off the disasters. He begins his courtship by praising her as a goddess--and ends by treating her as an anatomy, waving her heart about on his sword. The sibling lovers do go undiscovered for some time, their pleasure marred only by Giovanni's jealousy and growing instability. Finally, Annabella becomes pregnant, and her morning sickness arouses attention. Ironically, her father, the play's one rational and kindly man, mistakes the sickness for a menstrual disorder (the supposed physician treating her confirms this diagnosis), a disorder which Renaissance medical authorities cured by marriage and intercourse. Annabella is hurriedly married off to Soranzo, who has vowed passionate love to her. However, when Soranzo discovers she's pregnant, his sole desire is to kill both Annabella and her lover. Giovanni forestalls Soranzo, rushing into a birthday celebration with her heart on his sword. The shock kills his father. Giovanni kills Soranzo and is killed by Soranzo's servants. One of the subplots follows Richardetto, supposedly killed by his wife so that she could marry Soranzo. Richardetto survives, returning disguised as a physician. His bumbling efforts include the incorrect diagnosis of Annabella's trouble and the murder of a retarded suitor of Annabella. His wife is killed by the betrayal of Soranzo's servant, who gives her back the poisoned drink she intended for Soranzo. There is also a Cardinal who protects a murderer because the murderer is kinsman to one of the Cardinal's men. Amid all of this violence and betrayal, it is the passive Annabella who is condemned by the Cardinal (who has just confiscated everybody's estates). "Of one so young, so rich in nature's store,/Who could not say, 'TIS PITY SHE'S A WHORE?"

Fracastorius, Hieronymus. Hieronymus Fracastorius and his Poetical and Prose Works on Syphilis, with a full glossary of medical and other terms employed by him; and a comparison with earlier, contemporary and later medicine, ed. William R. Riddell. Toronto: The Canadian Social Hygiene Council, 1928. Poem: 3 Books (in prose translation).

By Doctors   Science & Poetry   V.D.

Poem discussing the epidemiology of, and cures for, syphilis --using all of the goddesses, sacrifices, and floral meadows of pastoral poetry. Fracastorius was a mid-sixteenth-century physician who, by this poem, gave the name syphilis to the disease. He describes the onset of the disease in this manner: "This disease did not infect the voiceless denizens of the sea, the natant throng, not the birds, not the brutes wandering in deep woods, not the droves of cattle, or the herds or the horses--but only one kind out of all living creatures, humankind, the one with the active mind; and it ate itself deep within our members . . . . Little by little was produced on the polluted pudenda a caries and, this, unconquered, eroded the parts here and there and the thigh-- then the symptoms of the evil showed themselves more openly, for when the benign light of the pure day ceased in its flight and brought in the gloomy shades of night, . . . then the joints, the arms, the shoulders, the calves, were racked with severe pains." He discusses whether or not the disease came from America on Spanish ships. He does not connect the disease with intercourse--one can avoid the disease by fresh air, temperate diet, ease of mind, and exercise. The discovery of two important cures for the disease, mercury and guiacum, are told as Ovidian legends. Mercury is found by a shepherd guided by a goddess through the regions of night, where "not far away the Cyclopes of Aetna have their dwelling with fuming furnaces and turn and melt at Vulcan's shrieked command . . . that to the right leads thee to a flood, a flood flowing with silver and living metal, from which salvation is to be hoped for." Guiacum is given by Juno to cure a country stricken by Apollo, who was offended by the shepherd, Syphilus. The nymph Ammerice instructs the king to "sacrifice a snowy heifer to mighty Juno, slay a black heifer to the Earth--she will give happy seeds from above: she will evolve from a fortunate seed, a green tree from which salvation cometh." It is interesting that both Fracastorius and Cowley ("Ode: Upon Dr. Harvey") adopt the pastoral conventions popular among their contemporaries --but do not adapt these conventions to the subject matter. Scientific and medical topics call for the same treatment as courtly love topics.

Fulke Greville, Lord Brooke. "Ah, silly Cupid, do you make it coy," Caelica, no. 19. Available in Five Courtier Poets, ed. R. M. Bender. New York: Washington Square Press, 1969. Sonnet.

Age   Sexuality

An unusual plea for acceptance of sexuality in old women. "Ah, silly Cupid, do you make it coy/To keep your seat in Cala's furrowed face?/Think in her beauty what you did enjoy,/And do not service done you so disgrace . . . . Good archers ever have two bows at least;/With beauty faded shoot the elder sort,/For though all be not to shoot at the best,/Yet archers with their butting-bows make sport./The glory that men in good kingdoms see/Is when both young and old in traffic be."

Fulke Greville, Lord Brooke. "The golden age was when the world was young." Caelica, no. 44. Available in Five Courtier Poets, ed. R. M. Bender. New York: Washington Square Press, 1969. Poem: 18 lines.

Disease & Health   Sexuality

A nice statement of a common late sixteenth- and early seventeenth-century belief that the world was decayed and sick, as compared to a golden age of individual and social health. "Desire was free and beauty's first-begotten;/ Beauty then neither net, nor made by art,/Words out of thought brought forth, and not forgotten,/The laws were inward that did rule the heart./The brazen age is now, when earth is worn,/Beauty grown sick, nature corrupt and nought,/ Pleasure untimely dead as soon as born,/Both words and kind-ness strangers to our thought."

Fulke Greville, Lord Brooke. A Treatie of Human Learning, stanzas 96 & 97. Available in Five Courtier Poets of the English Renaissance, ed. R. M. Bender. New York: Washington Square Press, 1969. Poem: 151 stanzas.

The Body   Disease & Health   Med. Profession

The poem as a whole sets forth the limits of human knowledge and the false purposes to which our partial truths have been applied. Two stanzas deal directly with medicine. He feels that physicians are doomed to uncertainty before the myster-ious body and that experience makes the best doctor.

Glissenti, F. "Death and the Anatomical Lecture," in Aldred Scott Warthin, The Physician of the Dance of Death; a Historical Survey of the Dance of Death Mythus in Art. New York: P. B. Haber, 1931. Poem and Woodcuts.

The Body   Death   Doctors
Med. Students

Death bursts in upon the dissection of a young woman in the anatomical theater at Padua. He points out how putrefaction has made repulsive the once beautiful body and its parts of love. Death is trying to drive a medical student to suicide, with only limited success. The student does give up medicine, but retires to live on an inherited income. The woodcuts are striking, but the text is long and full of moralizing.

Herbert, George. "The Collar." Available in Works, ed. F. E. Hutchinson. Oxford: The Clarendon Press, 1941. Poem: 36 lines.

Death   Grief

Answer to carpe diem. Repenting the years he spent in fasting grief, the poet resolves to recover his "sigh-blown age/On double pleasures" and to repress all fear of death. He grows wilder and wilder in his scornful rejection of restraints, until that growth is placed in true religious perspective: "But as I rav'd and grew more fierce and wilde/At every word,/Me thoughts I heard one calling, Child!/ And I replyd, My Lord."

Herbert, George. "Confession." Available in Works, ed. F. E. Hutchinson. Oxford: The Clarendon Press, 1941. Poem: 30 lines.

Grief

Self-knowledge (and mental health in our terms) as a result of God's intervention, grief as God's instrument, forcing the self-deceiving heart to speak. Grief enters the heart, no matter how well it is guarded, for pains sent by God are subtle and persistent, "and fall like rheumes, upon the tendrest parts." Openness alone shuts them out: "Smooth open hearts no fastning have: but fiction/Doth give a hold and handle to affliction."

Herbert, George. "Death." Available in Works, ed. F. E. Hutchinson. Oxford: The Clarendon Press, 1941. Poem: 24 lines.

Age   Death

Death transformed by Christ (and Herbert) into a beautiful, welcome good. The poem's tranquility contrasts with Donne's uneasy vehemence in "Death be not proud." Death was once "an uncouth hideous thing . . . the sad effect of sadder grones:/Thy mouth was open, but thou couldst not sing." Men thought of death as an event always six or ten years off: "After the losse of life and sense,/Flesh being turn'd to dust, and bones to sticks . . . . But since our Saviours death did put some bloud/Into thy face,/Thou art grown fair and full of grace,/Much in request, much sought for as a good."

Herbert, George. "The Flower." Available in Works, ed. F. E. Hutchinson. Oxford: The Clarendon Press, 1941. Poem: 49 lines.

Grief

The exuberance of a writer who has been freed from grief, with its quenching of creativity, and yet who has also understood and accepted the meaning of that grief. As God returns, "Grief melts away/Like Snow in May,/As if there were no such cold thing . . . . And now in age I bud again,/After so many deaths I live and write;/I once more smell the dew and rain,/And relish versing." Grief teaches us our insignificance, "Which when we once can finde and prove,/Thou hast a garden for us, where to bide."

Herbert, George. "The Pulley." Available in Works, ed. F. E. Hutchinson. Oxford: The Clarendon Press, 1941. Poem: 20 lines.

Suffering

A simple and witty explanation for human suffering. As God creates man, he bestows upon him all of the world's riches contracted into a span--except for rest. God fears that with too much content, man would adore Nature in place of God. "Yet let him keep the rest,/But keep them with repining restlessnesse:/Let him be rich and wearie, that at least,/If goodnesse leade him not, yet wearinesse/May tosse him to my breast."

Herrick, Robert. "To Musique, to becalme his Fever." Available in The Complete Poetry of Robert Herrick, ed. J. M. Patrick. New York: New York University Press, 1963. Poem: 33 lines.

Disease & Health   Sexuality

Perhaps the wittiest and most enticing extended analogy between sexual desire and fever, the tenor of the "musique" metaphor being left to the reader. "Thou [musique] sweetly canst convert the same/From a consuming fire,/Into a gentle-licking flame,/And make it thus expire./Then make me weep/My paines asleep;/And give me such reposes,/That I, poore I,/ May think, thereby,/I live and die/'Mongst Roses."

Herrick, Robert. "To Perilla." Available in The Complete Poetry of Robert Herrick, ed. J. M. Patrick. New York: New York Universit: Press, 1963. Poem: 18 lines.

Age   Death   Sexuality

The need for sexuality through age and death. The poet confesses that he is old and near the time when he will give his love "the supremest kisse." He requests her to prepare his body for burial, needing that final sexual caress to his body before he can rest in death. "Wash my hands and feet;/That done, then wind me in that very sheet/ Which wrapt thy smooth limbs (when thou didst implore/The Gods protection, but the night before) . . . Then shall my Ghost not walk about, but keep/Still in the coole, and silent shades of sleep."

Herrick, Robert. "To the Virgins." Available in The Complete Poetry of Robert Herrick, ed. J. M. Patrick. New York: New York University Press, 1963. Poem: 16 lines.

Death   Sexuality

Classic carpe diem (seize the day). Enjoy your youth, for age and death inevitably await you--soon. "Gather ye Rose-buds while ye may,/Old Time is still a flying:/And this same flower that smiles today,/To morrow will be dying . . . . That Age is best, which is the first,/When Youth and Blood are warmer;/But being spent, the worse and worst/Times, still succeed the former."

Herrick, Robert. "Upon Julia's Clothes." Available in The Complete Poetry of Robert Herrick, ed. J. M. Patrick. New York: New York University Press, 1963. Poem: 6 lines.

The Body   Sexuality

In "Delight in Disorder" and in the first stanza of this poem, the clothes become more than a symbol--almost a replacement--for the body and spirit. In the first sees his love's naked body, freed from the clothes. The body's natural movement does more than seize his mind ("me thinks"); it seizes upon his self. "When as in silks my Julia goes,/ Then, then (me thinks) how sweetly flowes/That liquefaction of her clothes./Next, when I cast mine eyes and see/That brave Vibration each way free;/O how that glittering taketh me!"

James I. A Counterblaste to Tobacco. In English Reprints, ed. Edward Arber. London: 1869. rpt: New York: AMS Press, 1966. Vol. 5. Treatise.

The Body   Disease & Health   V.D.

Although he prided himself upon his literary accomplish-ments, imaginative prose was not King James' forte. However, this treatise by a ruler desiring to improve his subjects' health might interest a reader for its association of tobacco with the American Indian's cure for V.D.; its refu-tation of claims that tobacco was a medicine; and its vehement condemnation of tobacco smokers.

Jonson, Benjamin. "Another in Defence of Their Inconstancie."
From Under-wood; in The Complete Poetry of Ben Jonson, ed.
W. B. Hunter. New York: New York University Press, 1963.
Poem: 24 lines.

Sexuality

Assertion of women's right to be unfaithful: "Hang up
those dull, and envious fooles/That talke abroad of Womans
change,/We were not bred to sit on stooles,/Our proper
vertue is to range . . . . For were the worthiest woman
curst/To love one man, hee'd leave her first."

Jonson, Benjamin. Bartholomew Fair, ed. E. B. Partridge. Lincoln:
University of Nebraska Press, 1964. Drama.

The Body   Madness   Mental Retardation
Preg. & Childbirth Sexuality

Play has no plot, but it is not missed in the enjoyment
of the circus-full of characters: Cokes, the happy idiot;
Wasp, his pugnacious guardian; Adam Overdo, the foolish
reformer; Zeal-of-the-Land Busy, the gluttonous Puritan
reformer; Dame Purecraft, another hypocritical Puritan
reformer; Ursula, the monstrously fat purveyor of roast
pig, chamber pots, and rooms for whores; Quarlous and
Winwife, gallants stalking rich wives; Grace Wellborn, a
rich ward and resigned sexual object; Trouble-All, the
madman; John Littlewit, the punster and terrible playwright; and his wife, Win-The-Fight, who learns how to
exploit her pregnancy to outwit her Puritan repressors.
The play exposes the folly of those who would try to curb,
rather than to enjoy or exploit, the frailties of mankind.
The thieves escape punishment; it is the reformers, Wasp,
Justice Overdo, and Zeal-of-the-Land Busy who end up in
the stocks. Justice Overdo disguises himself as the madman,
Trouble-All, to help reform the fair--he is beaten as a
pickpocket. Quarlous dons the same disguise, and exploits
it to learn who has won the rich ward and then further
exploits the pickpocket to gain the upperhand of his rival.
The weight of human flesh, magnificently embodied in Ursula,
overthrows the foolish, genteel pretentions of the Overdos
and the Littlewits. The women must beg Ursula for the use
of a chamber pot. The men's triumphs are overturned by the
drunken vomiting of their wives, who have been persuaded to
turn whore. The play also contains a puppet-play-within-a-
play, a marvelous travesty of Hero and Leander.

Jonson, Benjamin. "An Elegie on the Lady Jane Pawlet Marchion: of
Winton." Poem: 100 lines. See Milton, John. "An Epitaph on
the Marchioness of Winchester."

Jonson, Benjamin. Epigram XIII, "To Doctor Empirick," in The Complete
Poetry of Ben Jonson, ed. W. B. Hunter. New York: New York
University Press, 1963. Poem: 4 lines.

Doctors

Standard Renaissance charge against the physician-murderer.
"When men a dangerous disease did scape,/Of old, they gave
a cock to Aesculape:/Let me give two: that doubly am got
free,/From my diseases danger, and from thee." (And yet
the poet went to him!)

Jonson, Benjamin. Epigram XLI, "On Gypsee," in The Complete Poetry
of Ben Jonson. New York: New York University
Press, 1963. Poem: 4 lines.

V.D.   Women as Healers

Women as cause and cure of venereal disease. "Gypsee, new
baud, is turn'd physitian,/And get more gold, then all the
colledge can:/Such her quaint practise is, so it allures,/
For what shee gave, a whore; a baud, shee cures."

Jonson, Benjamin. Epigram XLV, "On My First Sonne," in The Complete
Poetry of Ben Jonson, ed. W. B. Hunter. New York: New York
University Press, 1963. Poem: 12 lines.

Children   Death   Grief

One of the most moving laments ever written. It is very
personal and natural, as though Jonson, the poet and drama-
tizer of grief, has been overwhelmed by Jonson, the grieving
father. (For the first, see Epigram XXII, "On My First
Daughter." "Yet, all heavens gifts, being heavens due,/
It makes the father, lesse, to rue./At six moneths end,
shee parted hence/With safetie of her innocence.") "Farewell
thou child of my right hand, and joy;/My sinne was too much
hope of thee, lov'd boy,/Seven yeeres tho'wert lent to me,
and I thee pay,/Exacted by thy fate, on the just day . . . .
Rest in soft peace, and, ask'd, say here doth lye/Ben Jonson
his best piece of poetrie./For whose sake, hence-forth, all
his vowes be such,/As what he loves may never like too much."

Jonson, Benjamin. Epigram LXII, "To Fine Lady Would-Bee," in The
Complete Poetry of Ben Jonson, ed. W. B. Hunter. New York:
New York University Press, 1963. Poem: 12 lines.

Abortion   Preg. & Childbirth

Why do you keep having abortions and avoiding childbirth?
Pain?--"that's soone forgot." Loss of complexion?--
cosmetics restore that. Oh, pregnancy causes loss of time
and sport! "Write, then on thy wombe,/Of the not borne,
yet buried, here's the tombe."

Jonson, Benjamin. "An Epitaph," from Under-wood; in The Complete
Poetry of Ben Jonson, ed. W. B. Hunter. New York: New York
University Press, 1963. Poem: 6 lines.

Children   Death   Grief

Jonson wrote a number of epitaphs for his friends. The
high mortality rate for young children explains the relatively large number written for children. This, for a

3½-year-old girl, exemplifies his gentle, witty praise.
"What Beautie would have lovely stilde,/What manners
prettie, Nature milde,/What wonder perfect, all were
fil'd,/Upon record in this blest child./And, till the
comming of the Soule/To fetch the flesh, we keepe the
Rowle."

Jonson, Benjamin. Sejanus, ed. J. A. Barish. New Haven: Yale
University Press, 1965. Drama.

Children   Death   Evil Doctors
The Family   Suffering

Dull as a whole, brilliant in parts, Sejanus depicts the
perversion of Roman society by an evil ruler and an ambitious
man. One example of degenerate Rome is the degenerate physician, Eudemus. He is actually a Renaissance "woman-
surgeon," a cosmetician--concerned with appearance, not
health. He is suborned by the ambitious Sejanus to be a
go-between with the emperor's married daughter, Livia.
Sejanus baits him with this speech, which anticipates Swift:
"Why,sir, I do not ask you of their urines,/Whose smell's
most violet, or whose seige is best,/Or who makes hardest
faces on her stool?" Eudemus later poisons Livia's husband to make way for Sejanus, a poisoning which illustrates
the downfall of the family--a husband poisoned, and families
rooted out for being of noble, and so potentially ambitious,
blood. But Sejanus' attempt to marry into Tiberius' family
brings about his own death--and the death of his family.
His young children are also executed. It is painful to read
about the death of his little daughter who must be raped
before she was strangled because Roman law forbad execution
of a virgin. "The girl so simple, as she often asked:/'Where
they would lead her? for what cause they dragged her?'/Cried,
'She would do no more:' that she could take/'Warning with
beating.' And because our laws/Admit no virgin immature to
die,/The wittily and strangely cruel Macro,/Delivered her
to be deflowered and spoiled,/By the rude lust of the licentious hangman,/Then to be strangled with her harmless brother."

Jonson, Benjamin. "Slow, slow, fresh fount, keepe time with my salt
teares," in The Complete Poetry of Ben Jonson, ed. W. B. Hunter.
New York: New York University Press, 1963. Song: 11 lines.

Grief

Transmutation of grief by a controlled, musical outburst.
"Slow, slow, fresh fount, keepe time with my salt teares;/
Yet slower, yet, ô faintly gentle springs:/List to the
heavy part the musique beares,/'Woe weepes out her division,
when shee sings . . . . O, I could still/(Like melting snow
upon some craggie hill,)/drop, drop, drop, drop,/Since
natures pride is, now, a wither'd Daffodill."

Jonson, Benjamin. "Still to be neat," in The Complete Poetry of Ben
Jonson, ed. W. B. Hunter. New York: New York University Press,
1963. Song: 12 lines.

The Body   Disease & Health   Sexuality

Praise for the natural body and simple clothing, since
primping implies concealment of disease. Contrast with
Herrick, who simply prefers the naked body, and with the
late-nineteenth-century Beerbohm, who prefers the artificially-
enhanced body. "Still to be neat, still to be drest,/As you
were going to a feast;/Still to be pou'dred, still perfum'd:/
Lady, it is to be presum'd/Though arts hid causes are not
found,/All is not sweet, all is not sound."

Jonson, Benjamin. "To Celia" (Drink to me only), from The Forrest;
in The Complete Poetry of Ben Jonson, ed. W. B. Hunter. New
York: New York University Press, 1963. Song: 16 lines.

Sexuality

The neoplatonic view of the woman as nourishment for the
soul and a divine inspiration (or, here, exhalation). A
beautiful song. "Drinke to me, onely, with thine eyes,/
And I will pledge with mine;/Or leave a kisse but in the
cup,/And Ile not looke for wine."

Jonson, Benjamin. "To Sickness," from The Forrest and "An Epigram.
To the Small Poxe," from Under-wood, in The Complete Poetry of
Ben Jonson, ed. W. B. Hunter. New York: New York University
Press, 1963. Poems: 44 & 18 lines.

Disease & Health   Poverty & Health   Women as Patients

Basis for his satire--disease is a scourge for immorality--
especially the sin of primping the body for pleasure and
vanity. "To Sickness" suggests that, since disease cannot
be satisfied with the current glut of sick men, disease
should prey upon those women who seek sickness by wasting
their husbands' money on cosmetics, empiricks, and pleasure,
"That distill their husbands land/In decoctions; and are
mann'd/With ten Emp'ricks, in their chamber,/Lying for the
spirit of amber." And in "An Epigram," Jonson chastizes
the smallpox for seizing a woman who never used cosmetics:
"were there not store/Of those that set by their false faces
more/Then this did by her true? . . . . Shee ne're had, nor
hath/Any beliefe, in Madam Baud-bees bath,/Or Turners oyle
of Talck. Nor ever got/Spanish receipt, to make her teeth
to rot." Fortunately, the woman's natural beauty prevailed
over the malicious disease.

Jonson, Benjamin. "To the Memory of My Beloved, the Author Mr.
William Shakespeare: and What He hath Left Us," in The
Complete Poetry of Ben Jonson, ed. W. B. Hunter. New York:
New York University Press, 1963. Poem: 80 lines.

Death   Grief

Less famous as an elegy than as one of the first and one
of the most interesting criticisms of Shakespeare's work.
Yet, in this, it is a typical Renaissance verse tribute,

for these poems were written as a mark of respect for the
dead and as an illustration of the writer's art. It was
not uncommon for a family to commission such verse (Ronsard
wrote several on one person--for pay) because the verse
itself was both a tribute and a way of immortalizing the
dead, a way of alleviating grief (see also current memorial
poems in small town newspapers). The poems dwell less upon
grief than upon the creations and virtues of the dead person, for it is through these creations and these virtues
that people escape death. It is particularly interesting
when one great poet writes about another poet (e.g. "Lycidas";
"Adonais"), for added to the poem is the writer's tension
about his own immortality. Jonson here seems serene (as
opposed to Milton in "Lycidas") ending with the true elegy
consolation: "Shine forth, thou starre of Poets, and with
rage,/Or influence, chide, or cheere the drooping Stage;/
Which, since thy flight from hence, hath mourn'd like night,/
And despaires day, but for thy Volumes light."

Jonson, Benjamin. Volpone, ed. A. B. Kernan. New Haven: Yale
University Press, 1962. Drama.

Age	Disease & Health	Doctors
Dying	Handicaps	Sexuality

Illness infests the play. Volpone pretends to be a wealthy
dying man. With the aid of his crafty servant, Mosca, he
inveigles large gifts from those who hope to be his heir,
including an old man a few days from death himself. His
"illness" and the callous reactions of the greedy "heirs"
to it form a large part of the play. But Volpone not only
disguises himself as an ill man, he also disguises himself
as a healer in order to woo the beautiful Celia. He makes
a magnificent speech as a traveling quack doctor, but finds
that his prospective death is a better lever to move her
jealous husband. This man, who does not want even the
light to touch her, offers her as a solace to the "feeble,"
"harmless," "dying" Volpone. For, on another level, the
play depicts a society full of mentally-ill people, people
so warped with greed that they cannot see themselves. With
the exception of Bonario and Celia (who prays for disease
to save her from Volpone's rape), all of the characters see
themselves as better than they really are, and so deserving
of more, and yet more--without knowing why they want more.
Representative of the ill society are Volpone's three
"children": a dwarf, a hermaphrodite, and a eunuch. Even
Volpone, when he comes to desire Celia, cannot see her as
she is--he must see her surrounded by jewels and transformed
into legendary women--never as herself. It is fitting that
he try to escape punishment by faking impotence. He really
is impotent. At the play's end, the judges sentence each
warped fool to the reward he truly deserved but could not
see. Volpone is diseased, Mosca crippled, the lawyer banished, the aged, harsh father of Bonario forced to give his
goods to his son and to enter a monastery to learn how to
die, and Celia's husband is exposed as a fool and divorced
from her, giving her a triple dowry. One of the judges
states the play's theme: "These possess wealth, as sick
men possess fevers,/Which trulier may be said to possess
them."

Kyd, Thomas. The Spanish Tragedy. Available in most Renaissance
drama anthologies, such as Elizabethan and Stuart Plays, eds.
Baskervill, Heltzel, and Nethercot. New York: Holt, Rinehart
and Winston, 1962. Drama.

Children	Family	Grief
Madness	Sexuality	Suicide

The hysterical, inflated language may prevent some readers
from appreciating this tragic universe in which people are
bound together by love and in which each person is
irretrievably alone. Hieronimo is driven to the border
of madness by the murder of his son, Horatio. His grief
is intense. "O eyes! No eyes, but fountains fraught with
tears!/O Life! No life, but lively form of death!" He
makes a long speech about the meaning of a son. "A thing
begot within a pair of minutes--therabout;/A lump bred up
in darkness, and doth serve/To ballace these light creatures
we call women . . . . Being born, it pouts, cries, breeds
teeth . . . . The more he grows in stature and in years,/
The more unsquared, unbeveled he appears,/Reckons his
parents among the rank of fools . . . . O, but my Horatio
grew out of reach of these insatiate humors." Yet he was
not close enough to his son to know that Horatio had taken
the dangerous step of wooing Bel-Imperia, the lover of a
dead friend, a noblewoman beloved by the prince of Portugal,
and a sister protected by an ambitious brother. Hieronimo
grieves, yet shows no sympathy, only madness, to two fathers
who come to him for justice upon their sons' murderers. He
grieves, yet gives no comfort or sympathy to his mourning
wife, who commits suicide in her mad loneliness. Hieronimo's
loving isolation is reflected many times throughout the
play: the king of Portugal goes mad for the supposed death
of his beloved son; the father of Bel-Imperia and Lorenzo
does not know that Lorenzo has kidnapped Bel-Imperia to
force her into marriage (and is also ignorant of Lorenzo's
share in Horatio's murder and Lorenzo's subtle murder of
his own two servants); the king of Spain does not know that
Horatio, his great soldier, is dead. The final statement
of man's isolation is made in a play-within-a-play, spoken
in many languages, during which Bel-Imperia kills the prince
of Portugal and herself; Hieronimo kills Lorenzo and unveils
the dead body of Horatio while the fathers and their courts
applaud and praise the acting. Desire, ambition, and revenge
are the only bridges between people.

Lodge, Thomas. A Treatise of the Plague, in The Works of Thomas
Lodge. New York: Russell and Russell, 1963. Vol. IV.
Treatise.

By Doctors	Disease & Health	Plague

One of many anti-plague handbooks for laymen. This, by
the physician Lodge, who was also a prolific poet, romancer,
and playwright, does not differ from those by physicians
who were not imaginative authors. In his address to the
reader, Lodge says that he writes the book, not because
he is both a skilled author and physician, but because he
is charitable and able to impose order and authority in
place of the confusion and deception of other plague pam-
phlets. In a play written with Greene, A Looking Glass
for London and England, Lodge shows Nineveh, a symbol for
London, threatened with Plagues. He is capable of both
the factual description of a disease and its cures--and
an imaginative description of a disease as god's scourge.
Lodge permits no cross-over between the two. His physician-
self and his poet-self are kept quite separate.

Lovelace, Richard. "To Althea, from Prison," from Lucasta; in
Poetry of the English Renaissance, eds. J. W. Hebel and H. H.
Hudson. New York: Appleton-Century-Crofts, 1957. Poem:
32 lines.

Body/Mind	Sexuality

Like Dyer's poem, a strong affirmation of the powers of
the mind. The poet, imprisoned in his love, is free--
even though his body is in prison. "When Love with un-
confined wings/Hovers within my gates,/And my divine Althea
brings/To whisper at the grates;/When I lie tangled in her
hair,/And fettered to her eye,/The gods that wanton in the
air/Know no such liberty . . . . Stone walls do not a prison make,/Nor iron bars a cage."

Love's Cure; or The Martial Maid, variously attributed to Beaumont
and Fletcher, Massinger etc. Available in The Works of
Beaumont and Fletcher, ed. George Darley. London: Edward
Moxon, 1840. Vol. 2. Drama.

Sexuality	Sexual Roles

Interactions of social conditioning, sexuality and social
roles. Because their family was disgraced, young Clara
was hidden in boy's guise and young Lucio in girl's. They
spend twenty years in their reversed roles, until Clara's
skill and bravery on the battlefield win a pardon for the
family. The play describes the parents' efforts to restore
sexual order. At first the parents expect nature to take
over immediately: the son will lose his cowardice and preoccupation with dress while the daughter will lose her
belligerence and love of battle. Nature doesn't take
effect, and the parents are exasperated. Their ideals of
female meekness and male pugnacity are contrasted with
the false images of female and male: The whore Malroda
who uses her sexuality for a living and her boastful and
lustful pimp, Alguazier. Lucio refuses to fight or for-
nicate without a good reason and is about to be disowned,
when his father is attacked by footpads and Lucio charges
to the rescue. Lucio then falls in love with the sister
of Vitelli, his father's enemy, and from her learns both
valor and the desire to propagate the species. His sister,
Clara, to complete the parallel, falls in love with Vitelli
and becomes more feminine because her beloved, a courageous
soldier, is afraid she'll dominate the household with her
martial airs (a surprising admission that "femininity" is
a response to male feelings of inadequacy--a contrast to
The Taming of the Shrew.) The sexuality of Vitelli and his
sister evokes sexuality in Clara and Lucio and so enable the
inverted siblings to mould themselves into the social roles
that will gain them their desired sexual objects, Vitelli
and his sister.

Lyly, John. Endymion. Available in most Renaissance drama anthologies, such as Elizabethan and Stuart Plays, eds. Baskervill,
Heltzel, and Nethercot. New York: Holt, Rinehart, and Winston,
1962. Drama.

The Body	Sexuality

Lengthy allegorical drama, in which the characters stand
for several types of love and lovers. Cynthia can, and
does, represent the moon, Queen Elizabeth, the soul of the
world, and the perfect object for sexual love purified of
the body. The shifting meanings add to the complexity and
the beauty of the play. Endymion is the lover who needs
only one stage of purification to become the perfect lover
(but always at a distance) of Cynthia. Tellus is both the
earth and tainted earthly love, Corsites the warrior and
earthly lover. Sir Tophas is foolish lust, for he loves
the aged, ugly, evil Dipsas, who is also still loved by
her faithful husband Geron, even though she now looks like
this: "What a pretty, low forehead! What a tall and
stately nose! What little, hollow eyes! . . . . In how
sweet a perportion her cheeks hang down to her breasts
like dugs and her paps to her waist like bags!" The jealous
Tellus bribes Dipsas into dosing Endymion with a potion to
make him sleep away his youth, to awake in age. Endymion
is cured with the aid of Eumenides, the true earthly lover,
for he places his friend above his lady. "The love of men
to women is a thing common and of course; the friendship
of man to man infinite and immortal." Cynthia completes
the cure with a kiss. She then solves all other problems,
uniting Eumenides and his love, restoring the repentant
Dipsas to her husband, and consoling Tellus with Corsites.
Sir Topas is left to find himself another ugly old woman.

Lyly, John. Midas. Available in Gallathea and Midas, ed. A. B.
Lancashire. Lincoln, Nebraska: University of Nebraska Press,
1969. Drama.

Doctors	Med. Ethics

The play is a collection of incidents, unified in part by
the story of Midas and in part by an attack on the ambitious
Phillip of Spain. One sub-plot consists of the rivalry

between a barber-surgeon and two court pages for a beard of gold. The barber-surgeon, Motto, wins a temporary victory by taking advantage of a toothache in one of the pages. He offers to relieve the pain, but, instead, rubs the page's gums with a leaf that loosens the teeth, and then holds out for the golden beard before he will repair the damage. But what Motto wins as a surgeon, he loses as a barber. For he tells of Midas' asses ears, and the pages blackmail the beard back from him.

Machiavelli, Niccolo. <u>Mandragola</u>, trans. Anne and Henry Paolucci. New York: Bobbs-Merrill, 1957. Drama.

Abortion   Doctors   Sexuality

Exploitation of a husband's weakness to consummate an affair. Messer Nicia, husband of the beautiful, but childless, Lucrezia, wants an heir. So, the lover, Callimaco, disguises himself as a physician, imposing upon the husband with Latin quotations and a logical approach to the problem of childlessness. The lover/physician tells Messer Nicia that a potion of Mandragola will cure the lady--but the next man to sleep with her will die. Therefore, a substitute must sleep with the lady for one night. The husband readily accepts this, but the lover must work frantically to get Lucrezia to agree. The lover's servant first persuades a friar to aid in an abortion ("the offense is only to piece of unborn, senseless flesh that might well be lost in a thousand ways"), making the friar's mouth water by the size of the proposed bribe. Then, having taken the friar's measure, he blithely asserts that the girl miscarried anyway, <u>but</u>, there was another, trifling matter the friar could still be paid for. The friar throws himself into the work, using a combination of authority and persuasion to corrupt Lucrezia. She will certainly become pregnant with a soul for God, while the death of the man is only uncertain--and it is sinful to displease her husband. A servant reminds her of the horrors of being a childless widow. Pressured by her husband, her mother, and her friar, Donna Lucrezia agrees. The plan succeeds, and Lucrezia, after tasting the difference between her husband (who seems to lean to homosexuality, judging by the way he examines the lover) and the vigorous Callimaco, proves that she has learned her lesson well. "Since your cunning, my husband's stupidity, my mother's foolishness, and the wickedness of my confessor have led me to do what I would never have done of myself, I'm ready to believe it was heaven's will . . . and I don't have it in me to reject what heaven wants me to accept." She blossoms into a healthy, assertive woman.

Marlowe, Christopher and George Chapman. <u>Hero and Leander</u>, available in <u>Christopher Marlowe: The Complete Poems and Translations</u>, ed. Stephen Orgel. Baltimore, Maryland: Penguin, 1971. Poem: 6 "sestiads" (ca. 2,300 lines.).

Homosexuality   Sexuality

Contrasts in eroticism. The first two sestiads, by Marlowe, are a delightful burlesque of the classical story. Hero wears a kirtle "whereon was many a stain,/Made with the blood of wretched lovers slain . . . . Buskins of shells all silvered used she,/And branched with blushing coral to the knee,/Where sparrows perched, of hollow pearl and gold . . . . Those with sweet water oft her handmaid fills,/Which as she went would chirrup through the bills." When the lovers first meet, they are so innocent that they don't know what else to do but hug and kiss, although "he suspected/Some amorous rites or others were neglected." The greatest danger in Leander's brave swim across the Hellespont comes from Neptune, who thinks Leander is Ganymede: "He clapped his plump cheek, with his tresses played . . . . He watched his arms, and as they opened wide/At every stroke, betwixt them would be slide/And steal a kiss . . . and there pry/Upon his breast, his thighs, and every limb." The lovers do finally reach a blissful, heterosexual consummation. "She trembling strove; this strife of hers (like that/Which made the world) another world begat/Of unknown joy . . . . Leander now, like Theban Hercules,/Entered the orchard of th' Hesperides,/Whose fruit none rightly can describe but he/That pulls or shakes it from the golden tree." Then, Marlowe ends and Chapman finishes the poem. The next four sestiads are full of moralized erotic woe. Leander has offended against ceremony; Hero is left lamenting for her lost maidenhead, knowing that she has offended Venus. "Her virgin waist/The wealthy girdle of the sea embraced;/Till our Leander, that made Mars his Cupid,/For soft love-suits, with iron thunders chid,/Swum to her towers, dissolved her virgin zone,/Led in his power, and made Confusion/Run through her streets amazed." Venus sees to it that Leander drowns, and Hero dies upon his body.

Marlowe, Christopher and Walter Raleigh. "The Passionate Shepherd to His Love," and "The Nymph's Reply." Available in <u>Christopher Marlowe: The Complete Poems and Translations</u>, ed. Stephen Orgel. Baltimore, Maryland: Penguin, 1971. Poems: 25 & 25 lines.

Sexuality

Marlowe's poem is famous for the beauty of idealized pastoral love. "Come live with me, and be my love,/And we will all the pleasures prove/That valleys, groves, hills and fields,/Woods, or steepy mountian yields./And we will sit upon the rocks,/Seeing the shepherds feed their flocks/By shallow rivers, to whose falls/Melodious birds sing madrigals." Sir Walter's poem is famous for the beauty of its realistic response. "But Time drives flocks from field to fold,/When rivers rage and rocks grow cold,/And Philomel becometh dumb;/The rest complain of cares to come . . . . But could youth last and love still breed,/Had joys no date, nor age no need,/Then these delights my mind might move/To live with thee and be thy love."

Marlowe, Christopher. <u>Tamburlaine: Part Two</u>. Available in <u>The Complete Plays of Christopher Marlowe</u>, ed. Irving Ribner. New York: Odyssey Press, 1963. Drama.

Age	Children	Death
Doctors	Dying	Euthanasia
Grief	Suicide	

In <u>Tamburlaine: Part One</u>, Tamburlaine, the scourge of God, tramples all opposition to win lands and love. In <u>Part Two</u>, Tamburlaine takes on the enemies of humanity: age, grief, and death. Age he disregards. Grief slows him momentarily when his wife dies. She begs him to survive but to permit her to die: "But let me die, my love; yet let me die,/With love and patience let your true love die." He rages, but conquers his grief by embalming her body and carrying it along on his campaigns, burning towns in her honor. His men receive one of their first defeats. They capture a new-made widow, who has just killed her son to prevent his suffering and who is about to commit suicide on her husband's body. Tamburlaine's lieutenants assume that gold and the sight of Tamburlaine will change grief to joy, so she manages to trick them into killing her. One of Tamburlaine's sons, his extensions of himself, proves cowardly, so Tamburlaine kills him. He harnesses conquered kings to his chariot (driving them with the infamous lines: "Holla, ye pampered jades of Asia!/What, can ye draw but twenty miles a day.") He causes more and more carnage until his final battle with sickness and death: "See where my slave, the ugly Monster Death,/Shaking and quivering, pale and wan for fear,/Stands aiming at me with his murdering dart,/Who flies away at every glance I give,/And when I look away, comes stealing on." His physicians warn him to rest and recover, or he'll die. However, his enemies offer battle and he gleefully accepts. He dies in consequence (unusual, the physicians were correct), but is comforted by leaving his sons who "shall still retain my spirit, though I die,/And live in all your seeds immortally." Death will survive death.

Marlowe, Christopher. <u>The Tragical History of Doctor Faustus</u>. Drama.

| Doctors | Dying | Med. Profession |
| Sexuality | Suffering | |

When we first see Faustus--lawyer, doctor, and divine--he appears to have a deservedly high opinion of himself. But his true weakness appears in this speech on the medical profession. "'The end of physic is our body's health.'/Why, Faustus, hast Thou not attained that end?/Is not thy common talk sound aphorisms?/Are not thy bills hung up as monuments/Whereby whole cities have escaped the plague,/And thousand desperate maladies been eased?/Yet art thou still but Faustus, and a man./Wouldst thou make man to live eternally,/Or, being dead, raise them to life again,/Then this profession were to be esteemed./Physic, farewell." This superman is afraid of death. While entertaining grandiloquent ideas of what man can do, Faustus still cannot believe that he can win salvation and immortality. Further, after conversing with Mephistophilis and after visiting Hell, Faustus refuses to believe in Hell, although believing that the devil can make him a spirit and so immortal. His capacity for self-deception is immense. He can correct Mephistophilis' description of the universe, but he does not see or understand himself. He retreats into pleasure to escape pain and the knowledge of ever-approaching death: "Was this the face that launched a thousand ships,/And burnt the topless towers of Ilium?/Sweet Helen, make me immortal with a kiss./Her lips sucks forth my soul; see where it flies!--/Come, Helen, come, give me my soul again./Here will I dwell, for heaven be in these lips,/And all is dross that is not Helena." Yet, he has, in his humanity, the means to reach God and salvation, with its true, heavenly immortality. He cannot accept this. The fear that Faustus has repressed throughout the play breaks out in his terrible, final speech, a masterpiece. His fear and agony are painful to read or hear--and yet he has still learned nothing. He ends, still trying to bargain: "I'll burn my books!--Ah, Mephistophilis!"

Marlowe, Christopher. <u>The Troublesome Reign and Lamentable Death of Edward the Second</u>. Available in most anthologies of Renaissance drama, such as <u>Elizabethan and Stuart Plays</u>, eds. Baskervill, Heltzel and Nethercot. New York: Holt, Rinehart and Winston, 1962. Drama.

Dying   Homosexuality   Suffering

Edward's reign is troublesome because he neglects the duties of a king for his homosexual love for the commoner, Gaveston. This love is explicitly homosexual and underlies one of the play's few lyric speeches. "Sometime a lovely boy in Dian's shape/With hair that gilds the water as it glides, . . . and in his sportful hands an olive tree,/To hide those parts which men delight to see . . . . Such things best please his majesty." Apparently (although the play is ambiguous) this homosexuality causes Edward's wife to turn from him and join forces with the principal rebel. Edward is overthrown and imprisoned in a way that contrasts vividly with the earlier speech. "This dungeon where they keep me is the sink/Wherein the filth of all the castle falls . . . . and, lest that I should sleep,/One plays continually upon a drum./They give me bread and water, being a king . . . And whether I have limbs or no I know not." Edward is murdered, on stage, by being pressed to death on a bed while a red-hot poker is thrust up his ass. Fortunately, Edward's young son rejects all cover-ups, executing the rebel and sending his mother to imprisonment and death.

Marston, John. <u>The Fawn</u>, ed. G. A. Smith. Lincoln, Nebraska: University of Nebraska Press, 1965. Drama.

| Age | The Body | Preg. & Childbirth |
| Sexuality | | |

A quilt of scraps from earlier authors, but united and made
original by Marston's contempt for the body and for sexual
hypocrisy. The play is an elaborate unmasking of those who
abuse their own nature. The first to suffer unmasking is the
Duke of Ferrara, Hercules. Troubled by his son's indifference
to women, the widowed Hercules sends Tiberio as a go-between
to the beautiful young daughter of the Duke of Urbin, hoping
that by making the lady forbidden she may become more desirable. Hercules then follows in disguise. In Urbin he hears
himself described without flattery, his age mercilessly
detailed. It is a rude shock. "I never knew 'till now how
old I was." In revenge, he flatters everyone: Don Herod,
who lives upon the wife of his impotent brother; Nymphadoro,
who writes the same love letter to many women; Don Zuccone,
who is insanely jealous of his wife, and the Duke Gonzago,
who is proud of his efforts to keep the prince Tiberio away
from his daughter Dulcimel. All are then unmasked by him.
Don Herod disinherits himself. Nymphadoro is rejected by
all the ladies. Don Zuccone divorces his wife for pregnancy
(he has not slept with her for months) only to learn that
the "child" was a pillow--her trick to divorce him. Of
course, he now ardently desires her. Dulcimel employs her
forbidding father as a go-between to Tiberio, whom she wins.
In general, women are the true sexual aggressors. The play
gets its character from such speeches as these: "Now, heaven
bless me, as it is pity that every knave is not a fool, so it
is shame that every old man is not and resteth not a widower.
They say in China, when women are past child-bearing, they
are all burnt to make gunpowder. I wonder what men shall be
done withal, when they are past child-getting?"

Marston, John. _The Metamorphosis of Pigmalions Image_. Available in
  Elizabethan Minor Epics, ed. E. S. Donno. New York: Columbia
  University Press, 1963. Poem: 39 verses.

The Body   Sexuality

There were a number of erotic epyllions written in the 1590's
(e.g. Marlowe's lighthearted _Hero and Leander_, Shakespeare's
grotesque _Venus and Adonis_). This, by Marston, combines
eroticism with satire in a very nastily titillating combination. Marston describes Pygmalion's hands, running over the
various parts of the statue--then jumps to a generality about
lovers or about ladies. The result is a coy strip-tease.
There is no discussion of art and nature. Pygmalion is just
a man in love with a woman's body--without the woman. "Untill
his eye discended so farre downe/That it discried Loves
pavillion:/Where Cupid doth enjoy his onely crowne,/And
Venus hath her chiefest mantion:/There would he winke, and
winking looke againe,/Both eies and thoughts would gladly
there remaine./Who ever saw the subtile Citty-dame/In
sacred church, when her pure thoughts shold pray,/Peire
through her fingers, so to hide her shame,/When that her
eye her mind would faine bewray./So would he view, and
winke, and view againe,/A chaster thought could not his
eyes retaine."

Marvell, Andrew. "A Dialogue between the Soul and the Body."
  Available in most anthologies of seventeenth-century poetry,
  such as _Poetry of the English Renaissance_, eds. J. W. Hebel
  and H. H. Hudson. New York: Appleton-Century-Crofts, 1957.
  Poem: 44 lines.

The Body   Body/Mind   Disease & Health

Completely dualistic view of the body and the mind, in which
each sees the other as a disease. The Soul complains that
it "fettered stands/In feet, and manacled in hands;/Here
blinded with an eye, and there/Deaf with the drumming of
an ear;/A soul hung up, as 'twere, in chains/Of nerves and
arteries and veins." The body, in turn, compares the soul
to a fever which "warms and moves this needless frame,/A
fever could but do the same./And, wanting where its spite
to try,/Has made me live to let me die." The soul desires
death. It endures diseases, "but, what's worse, the cure;/
And ready oft the port to gain,/Am shipwrecked into health
again." But the body has the last word: it is the soul
that is the source of sin. "But physic yet could never
reach/The maladies thou me dost teach . . . . What but a
soul could have the wit/To build me up for sin so fit?"
The desire for death and the desire for life competing for
one being.

Marvell, Andrew. "The Nymph complaining for the Death of her Fawn."
  Available in most anthologies of seventeenth-century poetry,
  such as _Poetry of the English Renaissance_, eds. J. W. Hebel
  and H. H. Hudson. New York: Appleton-Century-Crofts, 1957.
  Poem: 122 lines.

Grief   Sexuality

Murky but beautiful lament for a fawn, which has taken the
place of the nymph's lover. The fawn, shot by "the wanton
troopers," was a gift from Sylvio. "But Sylvio soon had me
beguiled./This waxed tame, while he grew wild." The fawn is
an image of chaste love. "Upon the roses it would feed/Until
its lips ev'n seemed to bleed,/And then to me 'twould boldly
trip/And print those roses on my lip./But all its chief
delight was still/On roses thus itself to fill,/And its
pure virgin limbs to fold/In whitest sheets of lilies cold./
Had it lived long it would have been/Lilies without, roses
within." But the animal does not only seem to be a kind of
pure love, it seems also to be Christ-like, dying "as calmly
as a saint." Thus, the nymph's extravagant grief, envisioning
herself as a Niobe-like statue, wearing a path down her bosom
with her tears, is not unwarranted. She has lost a sexually-
appealing innocence, a miraculous love.

Marvell, Andrew. "To His Coy Mistress." Available in most antholo-
  gies of seventeenth-century poetry, such as _Poetry of the
  English Renaissance_, eds. J. W. Hebel and H. H. Hudson. New
  York: Appleton-Century-Crofts, 1957. Poem: 46 lines.

Death   Sexuality

Death as an impelling motive for intercourse, and intercourse as an answer to death's emptiness. The poet urges
his reluctant mistress: "The grave's a fine and private
place,/But none, I think, do there embrace . . . . Let us
roll all our strength, and all/Our sweetness, up into one
ball;/And tear our pleasures with rough strife/Thorough the
iron gates of life./Thus, though we cannot make our sun/
Stand still, yet we will make him run."

Massinger, Philip. _The Unnatural Combat_, ed. R. S. Telfer (Princeton
  Studies in English, 7). Princeton: Princeton University Press,
  1932. Drama.

Children   Death   Sexuality

An extreme example of late Jacobean and early Carolinean
interest in incest (e.g. _Duchess of Malfi_, _'Tis Pity She's
a Whore_, _A King and No King_). Interfamilial warfare carried
to an extreme. Malefort hastens the death of his wife because he has conceived a passion for their daughter. His
son discovers this, declares war upon his father, and is
killed by Malefort in single combat. Malefort fights his
passion for his daughter, giving her to a friend for safe-
keeping; the friend rapes her and throws her out on the
street, where she dies. The ravisher is killed by a soldier,
and Malefort is destroyed by a lightening bolt (on stage!).
Malefort stands firmly upon his rights as a father when confronting his son: "Have I so far lost/A fathers power, that
I must give account/Of my actions to my sonne? or must I
plead/As a fearefull Prisioner at the bar, while he/That
owes his being to me sits a Judge/To censure that, which
onely by my selfe/Ought to be question'd?" However, he
then finds that his rights as a father are a barrier to his
desires: "by my crosse fates it is determined/That I am
both waies wretched." Malefort is caught in the trap of
his own nature.

Middleton, Thomas. _The Changeling_. Available in most anthologies
  of Renaissance drama, such as _Elizabethan and Stuart Plays_,
  eds. Baskervill, Heltzel, and Nethercot. New York: Holt,
  Rinehart and Winston, 1962. Drama.

Disease & Health   Madness   Med. Instit.
Mental Retardation   Sexuality

A play unified by metaphors of disease and health, of physic
and poisons. In the main plot, Beatrice-Joanna begins her
long fall from physician to poison. Although betrothed to
Alonzo, she falls in love with Alsemero. To gain Alsemero,
she employs DeFlores, a servant whom, up to this time, she
has loathed with an unreasonable passion which he has returned
as unreasonable love. She initiates the interview by offering
to act as a physician to DeFlores, to clear up his complexion.
Yet she still thinks of him as a poison, rationalizing the
murder in terms of medicine. "Why, men of art make much of
poison,/Keep one to expel another." Beatrice-Joanna thinks
to pay DeFlores with money--he expects, and takes, her maidenhead. This rape binds the two together, and Alsemero, her
reason for the crime, loses his charm as a sexual object.
In turn, she becomes less attractive to him, and his suspicions become aroused. He tests her virginity with a potion
out of his physician's chest, but she escapes, only to fall
into yet more murder and deception. When the two murderers
are finally discovered, Beatrice-Joanna recognizes her
poisonous condition. Dying, she tells her father--"O, come
not near me, sir; I shall defile you!/I am that of your blood
was taken from you/For your better health . . . . Let the
common sewer take it from distinction." The fallen Beatrice-
Joanna is set against Isabella, whose jealous husband is
keeper of the madhouse. Her husband locks her there, closely
watched by a whip-wielding servant who desires the kind of
pay DeFlores got. Two young noblemen make their way to her,
one disguised as an idiot and one as a madman. She tests
one, by appearing as a madwoman. Her lover backs off in
fright, and she rejects him in scorn, as loving only her
clothes. Isabella keeps out of the power of her servant--
and of her own sexual desires--and so escapes Beatrice-
Joanna's fate.

Middleton, Thomas. _A Chaste Maid in Cheapside_, ed. Alan Brissenden.
  London: Ernest Benn Ltd., 1968. Drama.

The Body   Children   Preg. & Childbirth
Sexuality

A number of plots united by the problems posed by children.
In all but two of the plots, sexuality is seen as an appetite,
the body itself literally food for others. The play sets the
barren Sir Oliver Kix and his discontented wife against the
over-fecund Touchwood Seniors, who must separate, even though
they love each other, because they are too fertile. The play
also sets the elaborate Christening ceremony of the Allwits,
with all its food and drunkenness, against the desperate
maneuvers of the Country Wench to get rid of her child.
Mrs. Allwit is kept by Sir Walter Whorehound; her husband
acts as Sir Walter's guardian. The new child is but one
of many by Sir Walter, all carefully raised by Allwit on
Sir Walter's money. This new child has a wet nurse, a dry
nurse, godparents, and presents. The Country Wench, got
with child by the impoverished Touchwood Senior, palms her
child off as meat upon the corrupt officers searching for
violaters of the laws prohibiting meat in Lent. The play
ends happily for all but Sir Walter. Touchwood Senior gets
the barren Lady Kix with child, and Sir Oliver is so grateful that he agrees to support Touchwood Senior and all his
family--past and future. Sir Walter loses his inheritance

by Lady Kix's pregnancy, and so is turned out by the Allwits, who use the household goods he has provided to set up a brothel. The Chaste Maid of the title, a City girl courted by Sir Walter, finally gets her City lover by pretending to die of grief, escaping from her parents in her coffin. Her foolish, educated brother, is married to Sir Walter's whore. The play seems to argue that children are best supported by sexual immorality.

Middleton, Thomas. A Fair Quarrel. Available in Thomas Middleton, ed. Havelock Ellis. New York: Charles Scribner's, n.d. Vol. II. Drama.

Children   Evil Doctors   Preg & Childbirth
Sexual Roles

Play has a double plot--both halves illustrating the near-disasterous results of short-sighted parental care and of falsely defining one's sexual role. The main plot opens with a quarrel between two soldiers and friends, the young Captain Ager and The Colonel. The quarrel turns ugly when The Colonel calls Captain Ager "boy," and ends in a challenge when The Colonel further calls the Captain "son of a whore." Lady Ager calls herself a whore to keep her son from danger. Her son backs down from the duel until he is called "coward," at which point he joyfully returns to fight, seriously wounding The Colonel. It is here that a surgeon muddles affairs, surrounding his treatment with so much jargon that all believe The Colonel to be dying. He then reconsiders his actions and tries for reconciliation, leaving his fortune and his sister to Captain Ager. Lady Ager clears herself of her own charge, The Colonel regains his health, and Captain Ager, who has thought of women, even his mother, in terms of derogatory sexual stereotypes, is forced to admit that The Colonel's sister is unique. The heroine of the subplot has secretly betrothed herself to a poor, honest gentleman and is about to have his child. However, her father wants her to marry a rich fool. Jane's honor and "womanhood" are saved by a doctor ("Your secrecy keeps me in the state of woman"), who enables her to have the child discreetly, but the doctor then meddles, demanding that she sleep with him. She indignantly refuses. He tells the rich fool about her baby; the rich fool cruelly and publicly breaks off the marriage. In desperation, Jane's father bribes the child's father to marry her, and all ends well. Both Captain Ager and Jane have false ideas of their sexual roles. Captain Ager thinks that manhood consists of fighting, and Jane that womanhood consists of a good public image. These notions are burlesqued by the rich fool, who learns how to quarrel and defend a whore's honor. In the end, both the Captain and Jane accept marriage as a proper definition of their roles--and harmony is restored to both worlds.

Middleton, Thomas and Thomas Dekker. The Roaring Girl. Available in Thomas Middleton, ed. Havelock Ellis. New York: Charles Scribner's, n.d. Vol. II. Drama.

Sexual Roles

Popular exploitation of the notorious Moll Frith, or Moll Cut-purse, who swaggered about early seventeenth-century London. She is here portrayed as a lower-class knight-errant, assisting parent-crossed lovers, rebuking City wives, fighting with bullies and lechers, and unmasking petty cheaters. Moll dresses as a man or a woman, according to her plans for the day. She is described by an unfriendly character as "a thing/One knows not how to name: her birth began/Ere she was all made: 'tis woman more than man,/Man more than woman." She says of herself: "Base is that mind that kneels unto her body,/As if a husband stood in awe on's wife!/My spirit shall be mistress of this house/As long as I have time in't."

Milton, John. "L'Allegro" and "Il Penseroso." Available in John Milton: Complete Poems and Major Prose, ed. M. Y. Hughes. New York: Odyssey Press, 1957. Poems: 152 and 176 lines.

Disease & Health

The first is the quintessence of the Renaissance belief that mirth was healthful and medicinal. Euphrosyne displaces harmful melancholy and offers the poet great pleasures to watch. The poet and the reader see and hear the English countryside in harmonized motion, see and hear the songs and fairy tales of a wedding, plays, music and poetry. All are distractions against that melancholy, anatomized by Burton. "And ever against eating Cares,/Lap me in soft Lydian Airs." "Il Penseroso" goes beyond the spectator. Its contemplation of more than nature and man in harmony leads to action--the creation of poetry. "Dissolve me into ecstasies,/And bring all Heav'n before mine eyes . . . Till old experience do attain/To something like Prophetic strain."

Milton, John. "Epitaph on the Marchioness of Winchester." Available in John Milton: The Complete Poems and Major Prose, ed. M. Y. Hughes. New York: Odyssey Press, 1957, and Ben Jonson, "An Elegie on the Lady Pawlet Marchion: of Winton." Available in The Complete Poetry of Ben Jonson, ed. W. B. Hunter. New York: New York University Press, 1963. Poems: 74 & 100 lines.

Death   Grief   Preg. & Childbirth

An interesting study of the epitaph. Both Jonson and Milton wrote epitaphs for the Marchioness, who died in childbirth. Milton's is much more remote, more general, and more beautiful, full of flowers. He laments the substitution of Atropos for Lucina and compares the lady to Rachel, who also died in her second childbed. The Lady died in a good cause. "After this thy travail sore/Sweet rest seize thee evermore,/That to give the world increase,/Short'ned hast thy own life's lease . . . . Whilst thou, bright Saint, high sitt'st in

glory. . . With thee there clad in radiant sheen,/No Marchioness, but now a Queen." Jonson makes no mention of childbirth. Instead, he praises the lady's efforts to comfort her husband, son, sisters, and parents as she was dying. At first the poet enters into their grief: "Stay, stay, I feele/A horrour in mee!All my blood is steele!" Then, as he considers the lady and her virtues, he becomes calmer: "And now, through circumfused light, she lookes,/On Natures secrets, there, as her owne bookes." Finally, Jonson's speaker adopts the stance which Milton uses throughout his poem: that of moral commentator, comforting the parents ("If you can envie your owne Daughters blisse,/And wish her state lesse happie then it is!") and reflecting upon immortality as a consolation for all dying Christians. Jonson tries to ease grief by sharing it and only then slipping into the role of counselor. Milton grapples directly with the emotions surrounding the cause of death and then moves into the traditional consolation of special status in heaven.

Milton, John. Comus: A Mask Presented at Ludlow Castle. Available in John Milton: The Complete Poems and Major Prose, ed. M. Y. Hughes. New York: Odyssey Press, 1957. Poem: 1023 lines.

The Body   Sexuality   Women as Healers

Mask in praise of Virginity. Comus, reveler and smooth-tongued defender of intemperance, captures the virgin Lady, lost on her way home. Her brothers worry about her, but are convinced her chastity will guard her from harm. "So dear to Heav'n is Saintly chastity,/That when a soul is found sincerely so,/A thousand liveried Angels lackey her,/Driving far off each thing of sin and guilt." But, although the Lady's mind remains free, her body is held paralyzed by Comus. She vigorously defends temperance, countering Comus' arguments of carpe diem, until her brothers chase away the enchanter. However, they cannot free her body. So, their guardian spirit calls upon the spirit, Sabrina, for aid. Sabrina, a virgin who chose death over dishonor, is able to release the Lady and send the three siblings homeward.

Milton, John. "In Obitum Procancellarii Medici" (On the Death of the Vice-Chancellor, A Physician). Available in John Milton: The Complete Poems and Major Prose, ed. M. Y. Hughes. New York: Odyssey Press, 1957. Poem, in Latin: 48 lines.

Death   Doctors

Unusual in its praise of physicians. Death has taken Dr. Gostlin because he has snatched so many victims from the jaws of death. The poem is almost a parody of the Renaissance commonplace that physicians are spared because they provide death with so many victims.

Milton, John. "Lycidas." Available in John Milton: The Complete Poems and Major Prose, ed. M. Y. Hughes. New York: Odyssey Press, 1957. Poem: 193 lines.

Death   Grief

Grief for the dead mingled with grief for himself. The poem, unlike Jonson's tribute to Shakespeare, is full of tension and works upon several levels. For the loss of Lycidas is not only the loss of King, the poet and good clergyman, but also the loss of great poetry and of poetry able to assist a clergyman in his pastoral duty. Milton is striving to become the elevating poet represented by Lycidas, so that grief for Lycidas is also grief for Milton's own deficiencies and doubts. He emphasizes the likeness between himself and King; he sings so that he may himself receive an elegy. The death of King the poet leads Milton to question the value of poetry, especially since death can cut short the poet's art. Then, he laments the loss of the true shepherd-clergyman, who is now replaced by those whose "lean and flashy songs/Grate on their scrannel Pipes of wretched straw." He tries to assuage this grief with the beautiful flower dirge over Lycidas' hearse, only to recognize that this is "false surmise." The truth is that the location of Lycidas' body is unknown--except to St. Michael. And, with Michael in place of the Muses, the poem moves toward resurrection, not only of Lycidas, but of the poet, who appears in the poem for the first time. The poet is not only consolation for others, but also for himself. He may be an uncouth Swain, but, instead of plucking the berries with "forc'd fingers," he is now able to watch the sun drop into the bay and to rise as poet and shepherd, "Tomorrow to fresh Woods, and Pastures new."

Milton, John. "Methought I saw." Available in John Milton: The Complete Poems and Major Prose, ed. M. Y. Hughes. New York: Odyssey Press, 1957. Sonnet.

Grief

The imagination recreating the loss of the poet's wife, and so bringing renewal of grief: "Methought I saw my late espoused Saint/Brought to me like Alcestis from the grave . . . . Mine as whom washt from spot of child-bed taint/Purification in the old Law did save . . . Her face was veil'd, yet to my fancied sight,/Love, sweetness, goodness, in her person shin'd/So clear, as in no face with more delight./But O, as to embrace me she inclin'd,/I wak'd, she fled, and day brought back my night."

Milton, John. "On the Death of a Fair Infant Dying of a Cough." Available in John Milton: The Complete Poems and Major Prose, ed. M. Y. Hughes. New York: Odyssey Press, 1957. Poem: 77 lines.

Children   Death   Grief

Curious comfort for grief. Your child has not really died because the infant, obviously divine, was not a child--but a star, or Astrae, or an angel temporarily misplaced from heaven. The last stanza, with its implicit bribery for denying the child's existence, ends a selection of beautiful conceits with cruel superiority to the grieving mother whom the poem is supposedly consoling. "Then thou the mother of so sweet a child/Her false imagin'd loss cease to lament,/And wisely learn to curb thy sorrows wild;/Think what a present thou to God has sent,/And render him with patience what he lent;/This if thou do, he will an offspring give/That till the world's last end shall make thy name to live." (Compare with Ben Jonson "On My First Son" or Molière's "Sonnet À M. La Mothe-le-Vayer" or Dylan Thomas' "A Refusal to Mourn the Death, by Fire, of a Child in London.")

Milton, John. "On the University Carrier, Who Sicken'd in the Time of his Vacancy, Being Forbid to go to London, By Reason of the Plague," and "Another on the Same." Available in John Milton: The Complete Poems and Major Prose, ed. M. Y. Hughes. New York: Odyssey Press, 1957. Poems: 18 and 34 lines.

Death

Witty toying with the idea that work defends against death. "Merely to drive the time away he sick'n'd,/Fainted, and died, nor would with Ale be quick'n'd . . . . Ease was his chief disease, and to judge right,/He died for heaviness that his Cart went light./His leisure told him that his time was come,/And lack of load made his life burdensome."

Milton, John. Paradise Lost. Epic Poem.

Age	Death	Disease & Health
The Family	Grief	Sexuality
Sexual Roles	Suffering	Suicide

Milton compels admiration as he justifies God's creation or toleration of mankind's suffering. Age (Book XI, 534-546) helps man to accept death, which comes as a welcome release. But Death is not always the end of suffering. It may appear as the terrible figure in Book II. "Black it stood as Night,/Fierce as ten Furies, terrible as Hell,/And shook a dreadful Dart; what seem'd his head/The likeness of a Kingly Crown had on" (670-673). To Adam and Eve, death is an unknown quality, a punishment of some undetermined sort. It is Adam who realizes that true death is more than cessation of life--it is a state of imperfection. (Books IX and X contain their musings on death.) "But say/That Death be not one stroke, as I suppos'd,/Bereaving sense, but endless misery . . . both Death and I/Am found Eternal, and incorporate both" (807-816). Disease is another consequence of this imperfection (Book XI, 472-495): "By Intemperance . . . which on the Earth shall bring/Diseases dire . . . that thou may'st know/What misery th'inabstinence of Eve/Shall bring on men . . . . Convulsions, Epilepsies, fierce Catarrhs,/Intestine Stone and Ulcer . . . Dropsies, and Asthmas, and Joint-racking Rheums." But the Family is a good. God has Christ as son, and Mankind as his youngest children. Satan produces a ghastly parody of this--creating Sin out of his own thoughts, mating with her in lust to produce Death, who in turn rapes his mother to produce little gnawing miseries. Adam and Eve will create a version of God's family. They are called Father Adam and Mother Eve. Although at one point, after the Fall, Eve considers having no children to prevent their misery (Book X, 967-end), Adam talks her out of it, looking ahead to revenge on Satan and applying to God for ways to meet their suffering--God's family continues. Grief is a good. Satan suffers, but he does not grieve, for he is incapable of admitting guilt. Adam and Eve, who are capable of grief for their sin and for what they have done to each other, are able to return to God and to achieve a new worth. Sexuality is also a good. The poem is a celebration of true sexual delight. Book IV, which includes the beautiful hymn to Wedded Love, and Book VIII with its account of angelic intercourse (lines 620-629) all praise this union between the sexes. But, with the Fall, sex degenerates to lust. The intercourse of Adam and Eve after the Fall (Book IX, 736-775) is that of two inflamed beasts, not two rational beings illumined by love. Appetite replaces true sexuality. Milton never notices that he has not really justified God's creation of women. Adam wanted an equal with whom to converse. God gives him a brainless beauty: "Not equal, as thir sex not equal seem'd;/For contemplation hee and valor form'd,/For softness shee and sweet attractive Grace,/Hee for God only, shee for God in him" (Book IV, 296-299). Adam gets a listener, not a companion. It is significant that their first communion appears to be intercourse, rather than conversation (Book VIII, 500-520). Both Adam and Eve consider suicide (Book X, 773-815;1000-1006). Both reject the idea, from fear and from faith in God. For, as the whole poem shows, true suffering is found only in the sinful; God supports those who turn to, and trust in, Him.

Milton, John. Samson Agonistes. Available in John Milton: The Complete Poems and Major Prose, ed. M. Y. Hughes. New York: Odyssey Press, 1957. Poem: 1758 lines.

Death	Grief	Handicaps
Sexuality	Suffering	

Moving drama of a blind, captive man discovering that he has lost nothing by his handicap or his imprisonment. Samson begins by disclaiming all identity, all responsibility, and all opportunity for action. Because he is blind, all that he can do is suffer. "Myself my Sepulcher, a moving Grave,/Buried, yet not exempt/By privilege of death and burial/From worst of other evils, pains,/and wrongs." However, as he is confronted with a series of friends and enemies who see him as a helpless object, he rejects

their pity or scorn, slowly climbing back to joyous potency. He easily sets aside the pity and hope for ease offered by his fellow Israelites and his father. His most severe temptation comes from his wife, Dalila, who offers him a life of sensual luxury, if he will abandon himself to her-- a sin, for woman was meant to be guided by man. He resists her, and from then on begins his return to the service of God, seeking ways to serve Him despite his blindness. His father and the chorus end the poem with two beautiful speeches accepting loss or death. "Nothing is here for tears, nothing to wail/Or knock the breast, no weakness, no contempt,/Dispraise, or blame, nothing but well and fair,/And what may quiet us in a death so noble . . . . His servants he with new acquist/Of true experience from this great event/With peace and consolation hath dismist,/And calm of mind, all passion spent."

Milton, John. "To Mr. Cyriak Skinner Upon His Blindness." Available in John Milton: The Complete Poems and Major Prose, ed. M. Y. Hughes. New York: Odyssey Press, 1957. Sonnet.

Handicaps

Interesting to some for Milton's description of his blind eyes ("these eyes, though clear/To outward view of blemish or of spot,/Bereft of light thir seeing have forgot."). More interesting for his account of the means by which he lost his sight and how he is able to bear its loss. "What supports me, dost thou ask?/The conscience, Friend, to have lost them overplied/In liberty's defense . . . . This thought might lead me through the world's vain mask/Content though blind, had I no better guide."

Milton, John. "When I Consider How My Light Is Spent." Available in John Milton: The Complete Poems and Major Prose, ed. M. Y. Hughes. New York: Odyssey Press, 1957. Sonnet.

Handicaps   Suffering

Fascinating because it is not certain that Milton was blind when he wrote the poem. For Milton, inner (creative and spiritual) light was infinitely more important than physical vision. Therefore, this poem could be confronting the loss of inner, or outer, vision--or both. "When I consider how my light is spent,/Ere half my days, in this dark world and wide,/And that one Talent which is death to hide,/Lodg'd with me useless . . . 'Doth God exact day-labor, light denied,'/I fondly ask . . . 'God doth not need/Either man's work or his own gifts . . . . Thousands at his bidding speed/And post o'er Land and Ocean without rest:/They also serve who only stand and wait.'"

Montaigne, Michel Eyquem de. "Of The Resemblance Betweene Children and Fathers" (Book II, xxxvii). Available in The Essayes of Montaigne, trans. John Florio. New York: The Modern Library, 1933. Essay.

Disease & Health	Doctors	Med. Profession
Surgery		

Not a study of genetics (although he notes his inheritance of his father's good health), but an examination of disease, health, and medicine. He notes that fear of pain is often worse than the pain itself, and that the pain he suffered from the stone in the bladder has reduced his fear of death. But the pains have not reduced his loathing for physicians: "So likewise in physicke, I know her glorious name, her proposition, and her promise, so profitable to mankinde: but . . . . experience makes me feare it, for of all I know, I see no kinde of men so soone sicke, nor so late cured, as those who are under the jurisdiction of Physicke . . . . Physitians are not contented to have the government over sicknesses, but they make Health to be slaves, lest a man should at any time escape their authority." He is most critical of the mystery surrounding and within the profession. He notes the constant changes and confusions in medical theory. He lists the requirements for a physician, e.g. "He ought to know the sicke mans complexion, his temper, his humours, his inclinations, his actions, his thoughts and his imaginations . . . . In drugges he should understand their weight, their vertue and their operation, the country, the figure, the age, the dispensation." He then states how difficult it is to meet any one of the requirements. He is particularly troubled by conflicting diagnoses and courses of treatment. Surgery is better off, "For it seeth and handleth what it doth: and therin is lesse conjecture and divination." Like Bacon, he chides physicians for not keeping records of their experiments and, hopefully, cures. However, "for me, I honour Physitians, not according to the common-receiv'd rule, for necessitie sake . . . but rather for the love I beare unto themselves . . . . It is not them I blame, but their Arte; yet doe I not greatly condemne them for seeking to profit by our foolishnese (for most men do so) and it is a thing common to all worldlings . . . . I send for them when I am sicke . . . and love to be entertained by them . . . . I give them authority to enjoyne me to keep my selfe warme, if I love it better so than otherwise."

Montaigne, Michel Eyquem de. "A Custome of the Ile of Cea" (Book II, iii). Available in The Essayes of Montaigne, trans. John Florio. New York: The Modern Library, 1933. Essay.

Death   Suffering   Suicide

"The wiseman liveth as long as he ought, and not so long as he can. And that is the favourablest gift, nature hath bequeathed us, and which removeth all meanes from us to complaine of our condition, is, that she hath left us the key of the fields. She hath appointed but one entrance unto life, but many a thousand wayes out of it . . . . Life dependeth on the will of others, death on ours."

Montaigne then discusses reasons others have given to
justify suicide--sickness, disturbance of the mind, or
avoidance of a worse death--and lists famous suicides.
He concludes: "Grieving smart, and a worse death seeme
to me the most excusable incitations."

Montaigne, Michel Eyquem de. "Of Age" (Book I, lvii). Available
in The Essayes of Montaigne, trans. John Florio. New York:
The Modern Library, 1933. Essay.

Age

"To die of age, is a rare, singular, and extraordinarie
death, and so much lesse naturall than others: It is the
last and extremest kind of dying." He complains less of
laws that govern old age and work, than of those that
prevent young men from employing themselves. "As for my
part, I thinke our minds are as full growne and perfectly
joynted at twentie yeares, as they should be." Since life
is so uncertain, and old age so infirm (the mind often
weakening before the body), we should set young men to
work instead of allotting "unprofitable wantonnesse in
youth, il-breeding idlenesse, and slow-learning prentissage."

Montaigne, Michel Eyquem de. "On the Force of the Imagination"
(Book I, xx). Available in The Essayes of Montaigne, trans.
John Florio. New York: The Modern Library, 1933. Essay.

Body/Mind   Disease & Health   Doctors
Sexuality

Power of mind over body, both for sickness and for health.
He cites numerous examples of the mind's power, including
the case of Marie, who, at 22, became a man. He is particularly interested in the effect of the mind upon sexual
potency and in the use of illusions by physicians, in order
to expedite cures.

Montaigne, Michel Eyquem de. "Upon Some Verses of Virgil" (Book
III, v). Available in The Essayes of Montaigne, trans. John
Florio. New York: The Modern Library, 1933. Essay.

Age   Sexuality   Sexual Roles

This long essay opens with a discussion of emotions and
old age, which leads him onto the topic of sexuality and old
age, which leads him onto the topic of sexuality, especially
in marriage. "I see no mariages faile sooner, or more
troubled, then suche as are concluded for beauties sake,
and hudled up for amorous desires. There are required
more solide foundations, and more constant grounds, and
a more warie marching to it: this earnest youthly heate
serveth to no purpose." He notes the contradictory education of women, who are instructed only in the sports of
love, and yet who are denied the opportunities for intercourse open to their husbands. He condemns sexual prudish-
ness, arguing that it too often arouses sexual prurience.
He condemns the notions of wifely chastity, and then digresses onto how to conduct yourself as a cuckold. He notes
of intercourse: "On the one side nature urgeth us into it:
having thereunto combined, yea fastned, the most noble, the
most profitable, and the most sensually-pleasing of all her
functions: and on the other suffereth us to accuse, to
condemne and to shunne it." He finds sexual intercourse to
be a bulwark against age. "I would prescribe the same unto
a man of my complexion and forme . . . to keepe him awake
and in strength, when he is well in yeares; and delay him
from the gripings of old age." He concludes: "I say, that
both male and female, are cast in one same moulde; instruction and custome excepted, there is no great difference
betweene them . . . . It is much more easie to accuse the
one sexe, then to excuse the other. It is that which some
say proverbially, 'Ill may the Kill call the Oven burnt
taile.'"

More, Thomas. A Dialogue of Comfort Against Tribulation. Available
in abridged form edited by Leland Miles. Bloomington, Indiana:
Indiana University Press, 1965. Dialogues.

Disease & Health   Dying   Suffering
Suicide

A Christian using writing to solve his problem of suffering.
More wrote these dialogues in the Tower, at first while undergoing examination, and then while awaiting death. Much of
the writing was done without books or ink (he used coals).
He discusses classical writers on suffering, the reactions
of different types of people to suffering (those who bear
it, those who complain, those who turn to God), the medicinal value of suffering ("both a cure of the sin passed
and a preservative from the sin that is to come"), the
kinds of mental suffering (unseen battle against desire
may be as painful as physical suffering), the use of re-
creation and fantasy to refresh sufferers (good, but employ
sparingly), the temptation to suicide to avoid suffering
(from the devil), and the prevention of a friend's suicide
by removing his despair. More is writing himself into an
acceptance of his own suffering. He was terribly afraid
of pain, and yet was faced with the prospect of the extremely
painful and degrading traitor's death. He therefore reasons
through, under cover of a man resisting persecution by the
Turks, ways to resist persecution in the forms of pain,
imprisonment, and shameful death. From the humor and dignity
with which he faced the block, it would seem that this therapy
was successful.

More, Thomas. Utopia, Book II. Trans. Paul Turner. Baltimore:
Penguin, 1965. Treatise.

Age   Death   Disease & Health
Euthanasia   Grief   Med. Instit.
Science & Poetry Sci Fi   Suicide

The result of an imaginative, rational, laughing man's
speculations upon the ideal society. His Utopians are
concerned about health care because they consider health
to be a positive pleasure. Therefore, their hospitals are
very carefully established and run: "These hospitals are
so well run, and so well supplied with all types of medical
equipment, the nurses are so sympathetic and conscientious,
and there are so many experienced doctors constantly available, that, though nobody's forced to go there, practically
everyone would rather be ill in a hospital than at home."
Further, since the Utopians believe in an immortal soul,
"they always mourn for an illness, they never mourn for a
death." This sympathy for illness more than death is extended to euthanasia. If someone is incurably ill and in
excruciating pain, he is visited by government officials
who argue with him, with more toughness than we would find
today: "'Let's face it, you'll never be able to live a
normal life. You're just a nuisance to other people and a
burden to yourself--in fact you're really leading a sort of
posthumous existence. So why go on feeding germs?' . . . .
If the patient finds these arguments convincing, he either
starves himself to death, or is given a soporific and put
painlessly out of his misery. But this is strictly voluntary . . . Officially sanctioned euthanasia is regarded as
an honourable death--but if you commit suicide for reasons
which the priests and the Bencheaters do not consider adequate . . . your body is just thrown unceremoniously into a
pond." Speech is an important method of shaping behavior.
In the communal dining halls, the age groups are carefully
mixed, so that the older people can restrain and instruct
younger ones, while listening to what the young people have
to say. Finally, the Utopians have a rather unusual view
of the scientific researcher--as art critic! "The scientific
investigation of nature is not only a most enjoyable process,
but also the best possible method of pleasing the Creator.
For they assume that He has the normal reactions of an
artist. Having put the marvellous system of the universe on
show for human beings to look at . . . He must prefer the
type of person who examines it carefully, and really admires
His work."

Nashe, Thomas. The Unfortunate Traveler. Available in Elizabethan
Fiction, eds. R. Ashley and E. N. Moseley. New York: Rinehart
& Co., 1960. Tale.

The Body   Disease & Health   Doctors
Plague   Sexuality   Suffering

A description of the sweating sickness, an account of looting and rape during a plague outbreak, a sale of a living
man to serve as a physician's "anatomy," and two terrible
executions are among the short sketches making up this
picaresque "novel." Nashe creates distance between subject and reader by his energetic, grotesque descriptions:
"This sweating sickness was a disease that a man then
might catch and never go to a hothouse . . . . It was
enough if a fat man did but truss his points, to turn him
over the perch . . . . I have seen an old woman at that
season, having three chins, wipe them all away one after
another, as they melted to water, and left herself nothing
of a mouth but an upper chap . . . . Galen might go shoe
the gander for any good he could do; his secretaries had
so long called him divine, that now he had lost all his
virtue upon earth." Of the plague he says: "Physicians'
greediness of gold made them greedy of their destiny.
They would come to visit those with whose infirmity their
art had no affinity; and even as a man with a fee should
be hired to hang himself, so would they quietly go home
and die presently after they had been with their patients."
Jack Wilton describes his fear when he was about to be sold
as a body for dissection: "Not a drop of sweat trickled
down my breast and sides, but I dreamt it was a smooth-
edged razor tenderly slicing down my breast and sides."
He criticizes the doctor for selling false medicines:
"His snot and spittle a hundred times he hath put over
to his apothecary for snow water. Any spider he would
temper to perfect mithridate." He describes, rather tri-
umphantly, the execution of the Jew who both sold him to
the physician and indulged in rather unusual sexual practices with his woman. But this horror is soon followed by
another: the execution of a murderer. Again, the style
tries to force distance--but thoughts of the murder and the
execution work upon Wilton, reforming him and sending him
back to England. The sight of suffering--not by an evil
man, but a man who has done evil--evokes reform of oneself,
rather than pity for the sufferer.

The Old Law. (Attributed to P. Massinger, T. Middleton, and W.
Rowley.) Available in Thomas Middleton, Works, ed. A. H.
Bullen. Boston: Houghton, Mifflin, 1885. Vol. 2. Drama.

Age   Children   Euthanasia
Sexual Roles

Unusual to find euthanasia of old people made the subject
of an early seventeenth-century play. A law has been
passed ordering that all men over eighty and all women
over sixty must be killed. The reasons are as follows:
the men are old, unable to defend the country, to beget
children, or to govern the country; and they prevent the
young people from using their inheritance while they're
young. Women are only useful for bearing young, and at
sixty they are incapable of doing so. The play really is
an attack upon such stereotypes of the sexual roles. Men
are more than warriors and women more than breeders. The
older people, with their wisdom, are able to keep the young
men under control until the younger ones have learned wisdom.
Now that this law has been made, the young men, released
from supervision and supplied with money, plunge into wasteful riot. Some marry old, rich women, knowing they can plan

on inheriting soon. One even forges an entry in the parish register, to speed his wife's demise. Other youths flock about Eugenia, the wife of an old rich man, knowing that he will be dead soon. The old man reacts by imitating youth--dying his hair, wearing new fashions, and dancing about--but able still to respond with instant courage, discomfiting the youth who challenged him to fight. One young man, Cleanthes, and his wife, Hippolita, hide his parents, but the couple are betrayed by Eugenia, angered when Hippolita chides her for disrespect to her old husband. The old man, who aped youth, returns to his proper age before his supposed death, for, having learned the art of dying, he has learned.to accept his erring wife and to lose his jealousy of the health and strength of young men. However, the law turns out to be a test by the young prince. The old men are restored to power, Hippolita and Cleanthes are honored, and those who have married old women are left to mourn.

Rabelais, Francois. Gargantua and Pantagruel. Works, trans. Urquart and Motteux. London: Bohn, 1864. 2 Vols. Tales.

The Body	By Doctors	Children
Doctors	Preg. & Childbirth	Sexuality
Women as Healers		

The most fantastical fecal, fart-ical, and funny pair of books ever written by a physician. Gargantua has an unusual birth because his mother, having earlier stuffed herself with "sixteen quarters, two bushels, three pecks, and a pipkin" of tripe, lets loose with so much shit that the midwife gives her a restrictive and binding medicine, forcing the child to climb up a hollow vein to be born out of his mother's left ear (Gargantua: Book I, ii & iv). Gargantua's childhood is consonant with his birth. "He pissed in his shoes, shit in his shirt, and wiped his nose on his sleeve; he did let his snot and snivel fall in his pottage, and dabbled and paddled and slobbered everywhere." He also "was groping his nurses and governesses, upside down, arsiversy, topsiturvy, harri bourriquet, with a Yacco haick, hyck gio!" (Gargantua: Book I, xi). Gargantua's son, Pantagruel, is more restrained. He presides over an advisory panel of a doctor, a lawyer, and a philosopher who are helping Panurge decide whether or not to marry, for he desires a wife, but fears being cuckolded. The physician's advice consists of five ways to cool lust, e.g. "for by intemperance proceeding from the excessive drinking of strong liquor, there is brought upon the body of such a swill-down bouser, a chillness in the blood, a slackening in the sinews, a dissipation of the generative seed, a numbness and hebetation of the sense, with a perversive wryness and convulsion of the muscles." However, the physician has a low opinion of women. "For nature hath posited in a privy, secret, and intestine place of their bodies, a sort of member . . . . Therin sometimes are engendered certain humours . . . their whole body is shaken and ebrangled, their senses totally ravished and transported" (Pantagruel: Book III, xxxi, xxxii). Rabelais gives a conventional defense for his writing: "But what shall I say of those poor men that are plagued with the pox and the gout? . . . . All their consolation was to have some page of the said jolly book read unto them" (Preface to Pantagruel). For the Renaissance, writing was practicing medicine.

Raleigh, Walter. "Nymph's Reply." See Marlowe, Christopher. "The Passionate Shepherd to His Love."

Raleigh, Walter. "To His Son." Available in most anthologies of Renaissance poetry, such as Five Courtier Poets, ed. R. M. Bender. New York: Washington Square Press, 1969. Sonnet.

Children

Implies a remarkable father-son relationship. Raleigh wittily threatens his son with hanging, if the son does not reform. The poem is written as though by someone remote from the youth, and yet it is incredibly menacing. "Three things there be that prosper us apace/And flourish, whilst they grow asunder far . . . . The wag, my pretty knave,* betokeneth thee./Mark well, dear boy: whilst these assemble not,/Green springs the tree, hemp grows, the wag is wild;/But when they meet, it makes the timber rot,/It frets the halter, and it chokes the child./Then bless thee, and beware, and let us pray/We part not with thee at this meeting day." *(Knave also meant a young male.)

Ronsard, Pierre de. "Double-winged monster" ("Cusin, monstre à double aile, au mufle Elephantin"). Available in free translation in Pierre de Ronsard, trans. H. Wolfe. London: George Allen and Unwin, 1972. Sonnet.

The Body	Sexuality

Equal to Donne's later "The Flea." By suddenly juxtaposing the mosquito's view of the body next to the lady's idea of virginity, the poet manages a nice disparagement of the latter. Ronsard spends twelve lines of the sonnet on the insect--its appearance, the lover's request that he be bitten instead of his love so that she may sleep, the lover's wish that the mosquito may bring him a drop of her blood to taste, and his regret that he was not a mosquito. The last two lines turn this against the lady. If he were a mosquito, the lady would know how an invisible nothing can often cause great trouble.

Ronsard, Pierre de. "Seated beside the hearth" ("La mois d'Augst bouillonnoit d'une chaleur esprise"). Available in free translation in Pierre de Ronsard, trans. H. Wolfe. London: George Allen and Unwin, 1972. Sonnet.

Disease & Health	Sexuality

The lady's sickness gives the lover hope. The sight of his pale lady, sitting before a fire in August, only sets his body to sick trembling. However, since the heat and the fire cannot warm her blood, how can the lover strike flames from a soul so cold? Ah, but her sick body, perhaps, may be a sign that she has been infected by his disease.

Ronsard, Pierre de. "These sonnets of love" ("Je chantois ces sonnets, amoureux d'une Helene"). Available in free translation in Pierre de Ronsard, trans. H. Wolfe. London: George Allen and Unwin, 1972. Sonnet.

Death	Grief	Sexuality

Grief for his mistress' cruelty confounded and combined with grief for his King's death: "These two opposed pains my soul did harrow--/my lady's cruelty and his lost years,/whose worth my praise as it my love surpassed./She living and he dead divide all sorrow,/she vain regrets, as he all hopeless tears./For love and death, it seems, are one at last."

Ronsard, Pierre de. "When you are old" ("Quand vous serez bien vielle, au soir, à la chandelle"). Available in free translation in Pierre de Ronsard, trans. H. Wolfe. London: George Allen and Unwin, 1972. Sonnet.

Age	Sexuality

When his lady is old, sitting and knitting before the fire, she will chant his verses and marvel that she was so loved, and her servant will awake and bless her name so preserved by Ronsard. He will be a boneless ghost, sleeping quietly while she remains an old hag, regretting her lost opportunities. Therefore, lady, take your opportunities now: "Cuillez dès aujourd'huy les roses de la vie."

Shakespeare, William. All's Well That Ends Well. Drama.

Adolescence	Age	Disease & Health
Sexuality	Sexual Roles	Women as Healers

A tangled play, entwining the relationships between the generations and the relationships between the sexes, with the question of personal worth. Helena, of low caste because she is a physician's daughter, falls in love with Bertram, of noble parentage. She becomes his equal by curing the dying King of France with her father's secret medicine and her own heavenly virtues. The King promises her money and the husband of her choice who is, of course, Bertram. The young noble rejects her indignantly, even though the old King asserts that he can make Helena's worth equal to his. Finally, the King must force her upon the sulky adolescent. Bertram goes through the marriage ceremony, but vows never to take her as his wife until she can present him with a child of his begetting and his ancestral ring from off his finger. Helena has really won Bertram as a "daughter" rather than a woman: she has the support of the old King, his wise counselor Lafeu, and Bertram's mother. She has been rejected by Bertram's peers, the young court nobles, and Parolles, Bertram's servant and image of manhood. It is no wonder that Bertram follows Parolles' advice ("To th' wars . . . . A young man married is a man that's marr'd") and slips off to a neighboring battlefield--only to learn there of Parolles' cowardice "and [to] take a measure of his own judgements." Meanwhile, Helena is taking Parolles' advice. She had asked in jest: "Is there no military policy, how virgins might blow up men?" He replied: "Virginity being blown down, man will quicklier be blown up." She uses Bertram's sexuality to restore both of them to their proper roles--as marital partners instead of overly dutiful or overly rebellious children. She exploits his seduction of a virtuous young woman to pull the "bed-trick," substitution of wife for lover in bed--unnoticed by the man. She trades the King's ring and her "ring" for his ancestral ring, bears him a child, and claims him before the court. Adolescence and age are reconciled, true sexual roles are restored; but, Bertram, although an attractive sexual object, is still a worthless young man, lying and weaseling up to the last revelation. She has proved her worth; he, his worthlessness. One is left wondering if Helena, gripped by her own sexual desires, has failed to choose her ends well.

Shakespeare, William. Antony and Cleopatra. Drama.

Dying	Grief	Sexuality
Suicide		

Death as consummation of, and justification for, love. On one level, the victory of rulers as politicians over rulers as sensualists. (Octavius over Antony, Rome over Egypt.) On another level, it is a victory of warmth and unchecked feeling over cold repression. (Cleopatra over Octavia.) Cleopatra prepares for death with these words: "Give me my robe, put on my crown; I have/Immortal longings in me . . . . Husband, I come!/Now to that name my courage prove my title!/I am fire and air; my other elements/I give to baser life." Octavius, the victor, enters: "Bravest at the last,/She levell'd at our purposes, and, being royal/Took her own way. The manner of their deaths?/I do not see them bleed." The controlled, analytical Octavius is victor, but it is not certain but that he has lost too much of himself to say that he has won. Antony and Cleopatra play games with each other, work behind each other's back, and increase their worth with extravagant words. And yet these double dealers are able to command the admiration and loyalty to the death of their followers. (It is the disapproving Roman, Enobarbus, who so lavishly describes Cleopatra's entrance on her barge and who speaks of her, "Age cannot wither her, nor custom stale/Her infinite variety.Other women cloy/The appetites they feed, but she makes hungry/Where most she satisfies." However, the lovers are doomed, for they love each other for qualities that their love will destroy. Their deaths are good emblems of this. Antony, the greatest soldier of the world, dies by falling on his sword (although he bungles the suicide so that his death is a lingering one). "So it should be, that none but Antony/Should conquer Antony;but woe 'tis so!" Cleopatra, the royal queen and serpent of the Nile, takes death in the form of offspring. "Peace, peace!/Dost thou not see my baby at my breast,/That sucks the nurse asleep?" Yet for all their trickery and failings, they create the feeling that, although Octavius shall create the Roman Empire, Cleopatra's grieving speech is right: "The crown o' th' earth doth melt.My lord!/O, wither'd is the garland of the war,/The soldier's pole is fall'n!Young boys and girls/Are level now with men;the odds is gone,/And there is nothing left remarkable/Beneath the visiting moon."

Shakespeare, William. _As You Like It_. Drama.

Age   Sexuality

This play is famous for Jacques' Seven-Ages-of-Man speech, Touchstone's "foolish" wit, and Rosalind's witty courtship of her Orlando. The play itself implies that the melancholy Jacques, in this speech, is more of a fool than Touchstone, the official court jester. Jacques' speech fills the time during which Orlando goes to retrieve Adam, his old servant who has saved him from the machinations of his younger brother, Oliver. Adam may be "sans teeth, sans eyes, sans taste," but he is not "sans everything;" for he has the Orlando which his integrity has earned. Throughout the play Shakespeare constructs elaborate rhetorical castles, which he then blows up with laughter. Formal love speeches from the courtly love tradition are made--and then mocked, as the true sexuality or the true absurdity of the words appears. Rosalind, dressed as a boy, Ganymede, is wooing Orlando by persuading him to woo Ganymede as Rosalind. Meanwhile Phebe, loved by Silvius, has fallen in love with the appearance of Ganymede. In one scene, there appears a most artificial discourse upon love. Silvius propounds one characteristic of love: "It is to be made of all sighs and tears, and so am I for Phebe." He is then echoed by his audience: "'And I for Ganymede.' 'And I for Rosalind.' 'And I for no woman.'" This tender responsive reading continues until Rosalind breaks it off: "'tis like the howling of Irish wolves against the moon." In another instance, Rosalind is astonished to find poems praising her, e.g. "From the east to western Ind,/No jewel is like Rosalind./Her worth, being mounted on the wind,/Through all the world bears Rosalind." Touchstone criticizes the poems and their motivation in this marvelous burlesque: "If a hart do lack a hind,/Let him seek out Rosalind./If the cat will after kind./ So be sure will Rosalind." Rosalind contents herself with criticizing the meter. So much for poetry and words as a way of courtship. But, for words gently mocking the absurdity of extravagant courtship, the play is unparalleled. When Orlando, in play, claims that he will die if Rosalind should reject him, she, as Ganymede, responds "No, faith, die by attorney . . . . Leander, he would have/liv'd many a fair year though Hero had turn'd nun,/if it had not been for a hot mid-summer night;for,/good youth, he went but forth to wash him in the/Hellespont and being taken with the cramp was/drown'd;and the foolish chroniclers of that age/found it was--Hero of Sestos.But these are all/lies. Men have died from time to time and worms/have eaten them, but not for love."

Shakespeare, William. _Comedy of Errors_. Drama.

The Family   Madness

The misfortunes suffered by members of a separated family and the restoration of prosperity by reuniting the family. Shakespeare uses this theme in a number of his plays, especially his romances (e.g. _Pericles_, _Winter's Tale_). He stretches the idea beyond the common practice of his fellow playwrights (whose characters often lost a sweetheart, husband, or daughter), scattering whole families. The delightful _Comedy of Errors_ carries the device to the extreme. Aegon, the father, is condemned to death for seeking a lost son in an enemy town. Antipholus of Syracuse comes looking for his brother: "I to the world am like a drop of water/That in the ocean seeks another drop,/Who, falling there to find his fellow forth./Unseen, inquisitive, confounds himself./So I, to find a mother and a brother,/ In quest of them, unhappy, lose myself." His twin Antipholus of Ephesus is accused, first of failure to pay his debts, then of madness, while Antipholus of Syracuse becomes bewildered and then frightened by a town that forces a wife, gold, and jewelry upon him. The two twin servants, the Dromio's, are soundly beaten in the resulting hilarious confusion. It is not until Antipholus of Syracuse takes sanctuary with a prioress, who is his lost mother, that the family members move toward the reunion that brings sanity, life, and content to them all. Madness is dealt with according to Renaissance medical practice. Antipholus of Ephesus is apparently behaving immorally, irresponsibly, and irrationally. Therefore, on the authority of his wife, he is delivered into the custody of a schoolmaster/charlatan, not a regular physician, to be imprisoned in a dark room and beaten. Antipholus escapes and takes a vengeance that is also a commentary on the medical practice. "My master and his man are both broke loose,/Beaten the maids a-row and bound the doctor,/Whose beard they have sing'd off with brands/of fire;/And ever, as it blaz'd, they threw on him/Great pails of puddled mire to quench the hair./My master preaches patience to him and the while/His man with scissors nicks him like a fool."

Shakespeare, William. _Coriolanus_. Drama.

The Body   The Family   Sexual Roles

Conflict of biological metaphors. Rome's citizens see the city as a body (this image is set forth at length in Menenius' fable of the body in rebellion against the stomach). They view Coriolanus as a diseased limb that must be amputated. Coriolanus sees only the stereotype of manhood thrust upon him, and his son, by his mother. "If my son were my/husband, I should freelier rejoice in that absence/wherein he won honour than in the embracements/of his bed where he would show most love." Every wound is proof he is a man. As a result, when Coriolanus is asked to make a political compromise, he responds as though such a compromise would castrate him. After his angry pride causes his exile, he joins Rome's enemies, Aufidius and his Volscians, but is persuaded to a peace by his family. The embassy consists of wife, son, mother, and friend, but it is his mother who undoes him by arguing that he is rejecting her by attacking Rome. She returns to Rome in triumph, while Coriolanus, deliberately provoked by Aufidius' term "boy," turns on his ally and is killed by the Volscian people.

Shakespeare, William. _Cymbeline_. Drama.

Doctors   The Family   Grief
Med. Ethics

The jumbled incidents in this romance are united by the themes of the disordered family and the working out of grief. The King of England, having lost his two sons, is well on the way to alienating his remaining child, Imogen, because of the evil influence of his second wife who is scheming to make her stupid son heir to the throne. Imogen moves from haven to haven. Secretly married to Posthumous, a worthy young man, she is separated from him by a malicious Italian who slanders her, turning Posthumous' affection to deadly hate. Dressed as a boy, she escapes Posthumous' plots and takes refuge with two mountaineers, who are, unknowingly, her missing brothers. She is driven from them by a delayed-action plot of her stepmother, who has given her pills that simulate death. Her brothers' grief is expressed in the beautiful dirge, "Fear no more the heat o' the sun." "Thou thy worldly task hast done,/Home art gone, and ta'en thy wages./Golden lads and girls all must,/As chimney-sweepers, come to dust." and "Quiet consummation have,/And renowned be thy grave!" (IV, ii). Imogen finds the body of the Queen's stupid son and takes it for the body of Posthumous. "I know the shape of 's leg;this is his hand,/His foot Mercurial, his Martial thigh." She grieves for him and then takes service with the commander of the Romans, who are invading England. Posthumous, although without further evidence, becomes convinced of Imogen's innocence. In his grief for her supposed death, he seeks his own death in the battle against the Romans. The King, learning of his queen's malice against Imogen, weeps for his daughter and favors the boy who resembles her (of course, Imogen herself), beginning the process of unification that brings the family together. Instrumental in bringing harmony is the physician, Cornelius. The Queen asks him for poisons for animal experimentation. He does not approve of such research ("Your Highness/Shall from this practice but make hard your heart"), and he does not approve of the Queen. Therefore, he gives her the death-simulating pills--thereby saving Imogen and the kingdom.

Shakespeare, William. "Th' expense of spirit in a waste of shame." Sonnet.

Sexuality

A bitter palinode that, unlike Sidney's, sees no way out. Sexuality is baited with an irresistible lure; there is no way to shun it. "Th' expense of spirit in a waste of shame/ Is lust in action;and till action, lust/Is perjur'd, murd'rous, bloody, full of blame . . . Had, having, and in quest to have, extreme;/A bliss in proof, and prov'd, a very woe;/Before, a joy propos'd;behind, a dream./All this the world well knows;yet none knows well/To shun the heaven that leads men to this hell."

Shakespeare, William. _Hamlet_. Drama.

Age   Death   Disease & Health
Dying   The Family   Grief
Sexuality   Suicide

Recall--the aging Polonius with his long-winded advice to Laertes and his complete misreading of Hamlet; the sense of death that permeates the play, from the ghost, through Hamlet's soliloquy on death and the scene with the grave-diggers to the pile of bodies that litters the stage at the end, with Horatio enjoin'd "Absent thee from felicity a while/And in this harsh world draw thy breath in pain," the beautiful account of Ophelia's death, and the noble and acquiescing deaths of Laertes and Hamlet; the diseased and corrupt State of Denmark; the two families who interact to destroy each other and themselves--the father, son, and daughter. (Polonius, Laertes, and Ophelia) and King, brother, wife, and son-nephew (the murdered King, Claudius, Gertrude, and Hamlet); the brooding grief of Hamlet for his father, the violent grief of Laertes for his father and sister and the self-destructive, mad grief of Ophelia for her father and his murderer; the complex sexual relationships between Hamlet and Ophelia, and Hamlet and his mother; Hamlet's musings on suicide, Ophelia's beautiful suicide, and perhaps Hamlet's unconscious seeking for death, his procrastination as suicidal.

Shakespeare, William. 2 Henry IV and Henry V (II, iii). Drama.

Age   Children   Death
Disease & Health   Dying

Two views of age. In 2 Henry IV, Falstaff changes (from
the cowardly, witty, life-loving foil to the valiant, vault-
ing, honor-loving Hotspur) into a diseased old man, foil to
the wise old Chief Justice. Prince Hal faces a variety of
father-figures. His true father--the usurper, Henry IV--
the Chief Justice with his strict adherence to the law, and
the riotous Falstaff. Falstaff is troubled with "the disease
of not listening, the malady of not marking." When the Chief
Justice reminds him, "Is not your voice broken, your wind
short, your chin double, your wit single, and every part
about you blasted with antiquity," Falstaff replies with a
jest, planning "to turn diseases to commodity." But he
doesn't mark the fact that the Prince is turning to him
only for respite from grief: "My heart bleeds inwardly
that my father is so sick;and keeping such vile company
as thou art hath in reason taken from me all ostentation of
sorrow." Falstaff is still able to captivate the Hostess
and Doll Tearsheet, but he has a certain resemblance to the
aging Justice Shallow (III, ii) who looks back on all his
dead friends: "Certain, 'tis certain;very sure, very sure.
Death, as the Psalmist saith, is certain to all;all shall
die.How a good yoke of bullocks at Stamford fair?" After
Henry IV dies, having been reconciled to his son, Hal, now
Henry V, takes the Chief Justice as his father and exiles
Falstaff with those infamously cruel words, "I know thee
not, old man;fall to thy prayers./How ill white hairs become
a fool and jester! . . . Make less thy body hence, and more
thy grace." Falstaff's death is reported by the Hostess in
Henry V. He may not have died with grace but, "A parted even
just between twelve and one, even at the turning o' th' tide:
for after I saw him fumble with the sheets, and play with
flowers, and smile upon his fingers' ends, I knew there was
but one way;for his nose was as sharp as a pen, and 'a
babbled of green fields."

Shakespeare, William. Julius Caesar. Drama.

| Death | Disease & Health | Dying |
| Preg. & Childbirth | Suicide | |

A play of sickness and death, of political manipulation.
Caesar is physically ill: he has an epileptic seizure and
asks Antony to shift sides because his left ear is deaf.
The conspirators against him are mentally ill, unreasonably
discontent. Portia chides her husband, Brutus: "It will
not let you eat, nor talk, nor sleep,/And could it work so
much upon your shape/As it hath much prevail'd on your condition,/I should not know you, Brutus." Both illnesses end in
death. All meet it with the stoicism of Caesar: "It seems
to me most strange that men should fear,/Seeing that death,
a necessary end,/Will come when it will come." However, it
is fitting that the conspirators suicide (and Portia, Brutus'
wife goes mad and dies by swallowing hot coals), for their
illness is caused by themselves. Calpurnia, Caesar's wife,
is barren, and Caesar tries to cure her by superstition,
having her touched in "this holy chase." Yet he will not
save himself by listening to the warning omens. He rejects
his cure.

Shakespeare, William. King Lear. Drama.

Age	Body/Mind	Children
Doctors	Dying	Family
Grief	Handicaps	Madness
Sexuality	Sexual Roles	Suicide

A richly poetic examination of age, madness, manhood, and
the interplay between the sovereign and the man--made challenging to the mind through the resonating parallels between
the two unhappy families of Lear and Gloucester, and made
challenging to the emotions through the intensity with which
we suffer with Lear. Every quality is seen from a number of
different viewpoints. At first, to Lear, age is a rationalization for shrugging off the burdens of sovereignty while re-
taining its perogatives and privileges. He comes to accept
age as weakness and dependence, largely through his two
daughters, Regan and Goneril, for whom age is an excuse for
confining their father because it has weakened his judgment
and increased his rage. For Gloucester, age is a barrier
that should save him from the depredations of Regan and her
husband, Cornwall. For Edmund, age is an excuse for killing
Lear because his "age had charms in it." Children are both
a blessing (Cordelia, Edgar) and a curse (Regan, Goneril,
Edmund); just as fathers are both sinned against and sinning.
Grief dominates the play, driving Lear to madness, Gloucester
to attempted suicide, Cordelia to incoherent tears and warfare,
and Edgar to tears and sanity (for he cannot play the madman
in his grief). Joy finally kills Gloucester (when he learns
that his wronged son, Edgar, is alive), as grief for the dead
Cordelia kills Lear. Handicaps are both physical and metaphysical. Gloucester is blinded because he was too late loyal
to his king and too trusting of his false son, Edmund. He
accepts this punishment: "I have no way, and therefore want
no eyes;/I stumbled when I saw." Lear loses the light of
his reason because he surrendered his sovereignty and trusted
his false daughters. Yet, the insights from these punishments
are lost in the handicap of being human: "As flies to wanton
boys, are we to th' gods,/They kill us for their sport." Madness is a response to mental suffering compounded by bodily
stress: "We are not ourselves/When nature, being oppress'd,
commands the mind/To suffer with the body." It seems to be
a response to strong emotion confined to inactivity. Gloucester
craves it as release from his helpless, blind sorrow. The Fool,
deprived of reason, understands more than Lear before his madness. For insanity is the means by which Lear uncovers the
truths which he has hidden from himself. Yet madness is a
cover and a protection to the fugitive Edgar. Lear's insanity
is cured by the Doctor, one of the few effective people in
the play. He uses potions to induce sleep, music, and the
comfort of Cordelia, Lear's loyal and loving daughter. Despite

Cordelia's marriage with the King of France, sexuality is
portrayed as a destructive force. Gloucester begets his
bastard Edmund and so begets his downfall. Goneril and
Regan deny their sexuality in their protestations of love
to their father--a denial immediately seized upon by
Cordelia--why then have they husbands? For they are
clearly ruled by animal sexuality in their lust for Edmund,
who seems to desire only power. Lear's diatribes against
women seem correct: "But to the girdle do the gods inherit,/
Beneath is all the fiends'." The play raises questions about
manhood and womanhood. Kent, who forces us to see Lear as
private person, is very concerned with manhood. He proudly
defines himself as "a man." He acts in rage against an
insolent servant of Lear's daughters "having more man than
wit about me." But the power to act is also destructive.
The murderer of Cordelia is able to kill her because it
is "man's work." Lear fears his daughters will "shake his
manhood." As well they might. When Albany refrains from
attacking his wife, Goneril: "Howe'er thou art a fiend,/
A woman's shape doth shield thee." She responds: "Marry,
your manhood--Mew!" Regan so dominates her husband that a
servant cries out: "If she live long . . . Women will all
turn monsters." Reason does little in the play; it is the
heart that drives the man. Gloucester, saved from suicide
by his son, dies of a cracked heart when he learns that his
son is alive. When Lear, mad once more, crouches above
Cordelia's body, Kent tries to prevent Edgar from saving
this old man too: "Break, heart;I prithee, break . . . .
Vex not his ghost;O, let him pass!He hates him/That would
upon the rack of this tough world/Stretch him out longer."
Suffering teaches and then destroys. "Men must endure/
Their going hence even as their coming hither./Ripeness
is all."

Shakespeare, William. "Let me not to the marriage of true minds
admit impediments." Sonnet.

Sexuality

Love as more than a physical link between two bodies--it
is a tie between two minds that lasts even though the
bodies of the lovers are separated or withered by age.
"Let me not to the marriage of true minds/Admit impediments. Love is not love/Which alters when it alteration
finds,/Or bends with the remover to remove . . . . Love's
not Time's fool, though rosy lips and cheeks/Within his
bending sickle's compass come;/Love alters not with his
brief hours and weeks,/But bears it out even to the edge of
doom./If this be error and upon me proved,/I never writ, nor
no man ever loved."

Shakespeare, William. "Like as the waves make towards the pebbled
shore." Sonnet.

Age

A more diffident use of his verse--it is a defense, not a
triumphant means of attack, against defacing Time. "Like
as the waves make towards the pebbled shore,/So do our
minutes hasten to their end . . . . Time doth transfix the
flourish set on youth/And delves the parallels in beauty's
brow,/Feeds on the rarities of nature's truth,/And nothing
stands but for his scythe to mow;/And yet to times in hope
my verse shall stand,/Praising thy worth, despite his cruel
hand."

Shakespeare, William. Love's Labours Lost, Act V, scene ii. Drama.

Sexuality   Suffering

The play itself is an elaborate dance of lovers, full of
artificial song. Although Ferdinand, King of Navarre, and
three of his nobles have sworn to live an ascetic, celibate
scholar's life for three years, the Princess of France and
three of her ladies soon bring out their true nature. The
men court them in an elaborate ritual of poetry, dance, and
masking. Yet, when the eight seem to be in accord, news
arrives that the Princess' father is dead, and the dance stops,
and each of the women imposes a real, not romantic, year's
task upon her lover. The lively Biron is purged of his
false wit: "'You shall this twelvemonth term from day to
day/Visit the speechless sick and still converse/With groan-
ing wretches;and your task shall be,/With all the fierce
endeavour of your wit/To enforce the pained impotent to
smile,'/'To move wild laughter in the throat of death?/It
cannot be;it is impossible;/Mirth cannot move a soul in
agony.'/'Why, that's the way to choke a gibing spirit,/
Whose influence is begot of that loose grace/Which shallow
laughing hearers give to fools.'"

Shakespeare, William. Macbeth. Drama.

Age	Children	Doctors
Grief	Madness	Preg. & Childbirth
Sexuality	Sexual Roles	Suicide

Age appears in two forms: personified in the withered
witches and idealized in Macbeth's speech on age. The
weird sisters continue the tradition of old woman as
prophetess, a tradition going back to the Three Fates.
Macbeth idealizes the old man: "And that which should
accompany old age,/As honour, love, obedience, troops of
friends,/I must not look to have." Children, especially
bloody children, are found throughout the play. Macbeth
kills for himself, but rationalizes that he has done this
for children that he does not yet have. He becomes obsessed
with children, trying to kill Banquo and his son Fleance,
then gratuitously butchering Macduff's wife and children,
and feeling safe because no man born of woman can harm him.
Of course, Fleance escapes, Macduff becomes his enemy, and
Macduff was born by Caesarean operation and so not "of woman
born." Macbeth's obsession destroys him. The play shows

guilt working into madness in two ways. Guilt leads Macbeth
to see invisible daggers but to avoid seeing himself: "To
know my deed, 'twere best not know myself." He strikes out
in a defensive panic until, paralyzed within Dunsinane, he
falls into a depression: "It [life] is a tale/Told by an
idiot, full of sound and fury,/Signifying nothing." Lady
Macbeth constantly tries to repress her guilt: "Things
without all remedy/Should be without regard;what's done is
done." The consequences are her sleepwalking and suicide.
The doctor, called in to prevent her decline, is an unusual
Renaissance physician. He is a perceptive psychologist:
"Infected minds/To their deaf pillows will discharge their
secrets./More needs she the divine than the physician."
When Macbeth asks the doctor for an antidote to "minister
to a mind diseas'd,/Pluck from the memory a rooted sorrow,/
Raze out the written troubles of the brain," the doctor
succinctly replies: "Therein the patient/Must minister to
himself." Malcolm, the rightful heir to Scotland, also
proves a good physician. He may not possess the touch for
the king's evil that the play gives to the English King (a
compliment to James I), but he can reach Macduff's grief.
When Macduff learns of his slaughtered family, he first is
silent. Malcolm urges, "Give sorrow words. The grief that
does not speak/Whispers the o'er-fraught heart and bids it
break." Then Macduff has difficulty accepting the news.
"All my pretty ones?/Did you say all? O hell-kite! All?"
Then he blames himself. "Sinful Macduff,/They were all
struck for thee!" But Malcolm encourages him "Let grief/
Convert to anger;blunt not the heart, enrage it." And
Macduff moves on to attack Macbeth. Macduff is a contrast
to Macbeth in his concept of manhood. Lady Macbeth is secure
in her womanhood, enough to desire to be unsexed, to give
milk to murder and to have given suck to child. But Macbeth
is not secure in his manhood, and she uses this constantly
against him. When Malcolm urges Macduff to "dispute it
[his grief] like a man," Macduff replies by including tears
in manhood: "But I must also feel it like a man." Macbeth
lacks the security to make a defense against his wife's constant admonitions to be a man. Manhood is courage to him.
When Banquo's ghost finally vanishes, "Being gone, I am a
man again." And when he learns of Macduff's birth, it "cows
my better part of man." This false idea of bloody manhood
acts like a disease upon Scotland, until purged by Macduff.

Shakespeare, William. Measure for Measure. Drama.

Death   Disease & Health   Preg. & Childbirth
Sexuality   V.D.

A dark play in which sexuality is inextricably entwined
with disease and death. V.D. accompanies sexuality: "I
have purchas'd as many diseases under her roof as come to--
. . . . To three thousand dolours a year . . . . A French
crown more . . . . Thy bones are hollow;impiety has made a
feast of thee." But undiseased sex can lead to death.
Claudio is sentenced to death for getting his fiancée,
Juliet, with child. Those three characters who puritani-
cally avoid sexuality, the Duke, his deputy Angelo, and
Isabella, Claudio's sister, do not fare much better. The
Duke resigns power to Angelo, hears himself slandered by
scum, fails in his plots because he overestimates Angelo,
and falls in love with rigid Isabella. Angelo also falls
for Isabella, who remains sternly cold, even after Angelo
offers to save her brother in return for her favors. Death,
for someone else, is preferable to sexual activity. (Just
as Pompey, the bawd, is made respectable by becoming assistant to Abhorson, the executioner.) The disguised Duke, in
a lengthy speech, persuades Claudio to accept death: "Thou
hast nor youth nor age,/But, as it were, an after-dinner's
sleep,/Dreaming on both." But as soon as Claudio learns
there's hope, even by his sister's dishonor, he does a
sharp turn about: "Ay, but to die, and go we know not
where;/To lie in cold obstruction and to rot;/This sensible
warm motion to become/A kneaded clod . . . . Sweet sister,
let me live." The Duke plans to save Claudio by the "bed-
trick," substituting Mariana, formerly betrothed to Angelo,
for Isabella. But Angelo does as one might expect, sleeps
with the supposed Isabella and goes ahead with the execution. So, the Duke plans to substitute Barnardine, a
criminal who does not fear death, "A man that apprehends
death no more dreadfully but as a drunken sleep." But even
he balks: "I have been drinking hard all night, and I will
have more time to prepare me, or they shall beat out my
brains with billets. I will not consent to die this day,
that's certain." So, the head of a man dead from fever is
substituted for Claudio's. Angelo's guilt is unmasked,
Isabella becomes human enough to beg forgiveness for him,
and he is saved to be Mariana's husband. The Duke proposes
to Isabella, and all, perhaps, live happily ever after.

Shakespeare, William. The Merchant of Venice. Drama.

Age   The Body   Children
Handicaps   Madness   Sexuality
Sexual Roles

An uneasy play, with great poetry creating a surface comedy
over tragic depths. Shylock and Old Gobbo are two old men
tricked by their children. Old Gobbo, blind in his old age,
is tricked by his son, Launcelot, into weeping for his son's
death, before Launcelot discloses himself. Shylock, blind
in his resentment of Christians, is tricked and robbed by
his daughter, Jessica. As in Lear, physical blindness is
paralleled by (what was to Shakespeare's audience) mental
and spiritual blindness. Not only does Shylock not see his
daughter's sexuality, he also does not fully see the body--
being deprived of his enemy's flesh because he has failed
to take into account the blood as well. Antonio's unaccount-
able depression comes close to a form of madness: "In sooth,
I know not why I am so sad./It wearies me;you say it wearies

you . . . And such a want-wit sadness makes of me,/That I
have much ado to know myself." The play also contains a
rather curious tug-of-war between Antonio and Portia for
Bassanio. Antonio has funded Bassanio's courtship of
Portia with money borrowed from his enemy, Shylock.
Bassanio wins Portia, but before the marriage is consummated, he must rush back to save Antonio from Shylock--the
only proof of his commitment to her, the ring she gave him.
Bassanio cannot save his friend, but Portia takes on the
male role saving Antonio by her wit. However, she discovers
that Bassanio loves Antonio more than her, for at Antonio's
urging, "Let his deservings and my love withal/Be valued
'gainst your wife's commandment," Bassanio gives up his
wife's ring. As a result, in the haven of sexuality at
Belmont, she leads Bassanio through hoops until Antonio releases him to her: "I dare be bound again,/My soul upon the
forfeit, that your lord/Will never more break faith advisedly."

Shakespeare, William. The Merry Wives of Windsor. Drama.

Doctors

Dr. Caius, the French physician, is one of the comic suitors
for a young girl. However, although his profession has made
him wealthy enough to win support from the girl's mother, it
is not stressed, except for its savor of urine. Dr. Caius
is noted for his personal characteristics, his excitability
and French accent, rather than his professional capabilities
or qualities.

Shakespeare, William. A Midsummer-Night's Dream. Drama.

Children   Disease & Health   Madness
Preg. & Childbirth Sexuality   Sexual Roles

The irrationality of sexuality and the relationship between proper sexual roles and both fertility and health.
On the noblest level of society, Theseus and his conquered
Amazon bride await their wedding day with love and control.
On the next level are the four interchangeable lovers, who
seem to choose their loves, and yet who are controlled by
forces beyond them. They really see each other as sexual
objects, comparable to the way Helena's father considers
her a sexual object he owns. On the lowest level, the
mechanicals see women as stereotypes taken from the romances
they are unconsciously parodying. They worry about affright-
ing the ladies with a stage lion--this is in a play before
the Amazon Hippolita and two women who have chased and been
chased through the forest and who have fought each other
with fist and fingernail. Titania deservedly falls in love
with the leading ass from this group. She has quarreled
with her lord, Oberon, bringing disease and sterility on the
land: "Therefore the winds, piping to us in vain,/As in
revenge, have suck'd up from the sea/Contagious fogs . . . .
The ploughman lost his sweat, and the green corn/Hath rotted
ere his youth attain'd a beard./Therefore the moon, the
governess of floods,/Pale in her anger, washes all the air,/
That rheumatic diseases do abound." The cause of the quarrel
is a boy that Titania wants to keep among her women because
she loved the boy's mother. When the boy is transferred to
Oberon's band of henchmen, Titania is returned to normal and
the lovers are content. When the fairies bless the palace
after the multiple marriages, they mention children, something the lovers overlooked at first. Sexuality was for
satisfaction, not progeny. There is a lovely speech by
Titania, making beautiful the body of a pregnant woman:
"When we have laugh'd to see the sails conceive/And grow
big-bellied with the wanton wind;/Which she with pretty and
with swimming gait/Following, her womb then rich with my
young squire,/Would imitate, and sail upon the land/To fetch
me trifles."

Shakespeare, William. Much Ado About Nothing. Drama.

Sexuality

The "merry wars" of Beatrice and Benedict, who first clash
with witty insults which barely disguise proud sexual interest
and who end happily and wittily in marriage: "'Come, I will
have thee;but, by this light, I take thee for pity.' 'I would
not deny you;but, by this good day, I yield upon great persuasion;and partly to save your life, for I was told you
were in a consumption.'"

Shakespeare, William. "My love is as a fever, longing still."
Sonnet.

Disease & Health   Doctors   Madness
Sexuality

An extension of the common Renaissance metaphor of desire
as disease, reason as physician. His reason acts like a
doctor abandoning a disobedient patient, leaving the poet
to a belated recognition that his physician, reason, now
beyond reach, was right: "Past cure I am, now reason is
past care,/And frantic-mad with evermore unrest;/My thoughts
and my discourse as madmen's are,/At random from the truth
vainly express'd;/For I have sworn thee fair and thought thee
bright,/Who art as black as hell, as dark as night."

Shakespeare, William. "My mistress' eyes are nothing like the sun."
Sonnet.

The Body   Sexuality

A parody of the Petrarchian ideal mistress; the real body is
equal to the ideal. "My mistress' eyes are nothing like the
sun;/Coral is far more red than her lips' red;/If snow be
white, why then her breasts are dun;/If hairs be wires,
black wires grow on her head . . . . I grant I never saw a
goddess go;/My mistress, when she walks, treads on the
ground;/And yet, by heaven, I think my love as rare/As
any she beli'd with false compare."

Shakespeare, William. "Not marble nor the gilded monuments."
Sonnet.

The Body	Death

Interesting next to Michelangelo, who saw art as re-creating
the body in the minds of future generations. Here, art re-
creates memory within the body (the eyes) of posterity:
"Not marble nor the gilded monuments/Of princes shall outlive this pow'rful rhyme;/But you shall shine more bright
in these contents/Than unswept stone besmear'd with sluttish
time . . . . The living record of your memory./'Gainst death
and all-oblivious enmity/Shall you pace forth;your praise
shall still find room/Even in the eyes of all posterity/
That wear this world out to the ending doom./So, till the
Judgement that yourself arise,/You live in this, and dwell
in lovers' eyes."

Shakespeare, William. Othello. Drama.

Age	Alcoholism	Body/Mind
Disease & Health	Grief	Madness
Sexuality	Suicide	

Like Julius Caesar, Othello shows the diseased in mind prey-
ing upon the diseased in body. Iago, malignant without
motive, uses Cassio's alcoholism to drive him temporarily
mad with drunkenness and uses the epileptic Othello's
innocence and trust, to drive him mad with jealousy. Iago
has a consistently debased view of women: he informs
Desdemona's father of her elopement with the Moor thusly,
"an old black ram/Is tupping your white ewe." (Yet all
three women in the play, Desdemona, Emilia, and Bianca, are
passionately loyal to their men.) Othello is open to in-
sinuations from Iago because the love between Desdemona and
Othello is of the mind, created by words. "I saw Othello's
visage in his mind." Othello is conscious of his inferiority
as a bodily lover, "Haply, for I am black/And have not those
soft parts of conversation/That chamberers have, or for I
am declin'd/Into the vale of years," and so is open to
"puddling" suspicions of Desdemona's bodily needs that drive
him to madness, to murder, and to grieving suicide.

Shakespeare, William. Pericles, Prince of Tyre. Drama.

Doctors	The Family	Sexuality
Women as Healers		

Cerimon the physician saves the life of Thaisa, wife of
Pericles (III, ii). He is cited in the epilogue as a
figure of learned charity. The play also contrasts two
families--the close-knit family of Antiochus, whose daughter
is his wife, and the scattered family of Pericles, who has
lost both his wife and his daughter while fleeing from
Antiochus, whose secret he has uncovered. Mariana, Pericles'
daughter, saves her father and her family by preserving her
virginity, despite being sold to a brothel. Having preserved her self, she is able to cure others, including her father,
deep in depression. The union of father and daughter provokes the vision that enables the wife to be found. The
daughter, betrothed herself, restores the mother/wife.

Shakespeare, William. "Poor soul, the centre of my sinful earth."
Sonnet.

The Body	Death

The theme of this sonnet, the overpowering of death by undervaluing the body, is an unusual one for Shakespeare. Its
grotesque images are like Donne's, and its triumphant closing
approaches the flourish that ends "Death Be Not Proud." Why
spend the soul's worth upon the body, which is only destined
for worms. Let the soul eat the body first. "Then, soul,
live thou upon thy servant's loss,/And let that pine to
aggravate thy store;/Buy terms divine in selling hours of
dross;/Within be fed, without be rich no more./So shalt
thou feed on Death that feeds on men,/And Death once dead,
there's no more dying then."

Shakespeare, William. Richard III. Drama.

Body/Mind	Children	Death
Disease & Health	The Family	Grief
Handicaps	Madness	Sexuality

It is sad that the grotesque, hunchbacked Richard of
Gloucester was in part created by Shakespeare as an emblem
for the diseased mind that had infected England. For Shakespeare's Richard has such vigorous villainy that Shakespeare's
device to identify a political evil has intensified belief
that the deformed body carries deformed mind. Richard himself traces his evil to his body. Since he is so unattractive
(unformed for love) he will compensate by becoming King. He
is just sane enough to carry out his plots and just insane
enough to overlook the fact that these plots of his will
ultimately be leveled at himself. He perceives this at
the end: "What! do I fear myself? There's none else by
. . . . Alack, I love myself. Wherefore? For any good/That
I myself have done unto myself?/O, no! alas, I rather hate
myself/For hateful deeds committed by myself." Shakespeare's
children are precocious, like the children of Clarence who
(like Macduff's children) wisely examine their elders' grief.
York and the Young Prince also speak wisely and frankly in
the poisoned air of Richard's England--they quickly die for
it. Family relationships are most complex, as politics
infuses all ties of kinship. Clarence, brother to the late
King Edward, has both supported him loyally and deserted
him like a traitor. The Queen's kin is watched by the King's
kin. The Duchess of York must stand aside and watch her
deformed, unloved son destroy all the rest of her children
and grandchildren. The play piles death on death and grief
on grief. The Body of the deposed King Henry VI (murdered
by Richard) appears in bleeding accusation in its coffin.

Clarence is stabbed and drowned in a butt of malmsy. King
Edward dies of ill health brought on by an ill-advised way
of living. Hastings, Rivers, Grey, Vaughan, and Buckingham
die in "legal" executions. The two young princes are
smothered in the Tower. As the men die, their women are
left to form a ritual chorus of hatred. Throughout the
play, curses come true; and Richard faces a growing number
of grieving queens, who will his destruction. It is as
though evil creates the grief which will ultimately expel it.

Shakespeare, William. Romeo and Juliet. Drama.

Adolescence	Children	Death
Doctors	Drugs	Dying
The Family	Grief	Sexuality

Juliet is thirteen and Romeo "young" when they meet. They
are young enough to be dominated by their parents and feuding families and old enough to love despite their families.
However, although they are mature enough to consummate their
marriage, they are not mature enough to make that passion
last. Those extravagant, passionate, enchanting speeches
in Juliet's garden are laden with metaphor and far removed
from reality. They lack Mercutio's bawdy earthiness, which
underlies his fantastical webs of words. Romeo's and
Juliet's thwarted sexuality is just as harmful as Tybalt's
violence. Romeo and Tybalt are two deadly adolescents.
Old Capulet, believing Juliet to be dead, correctly cries
out to her second bridegroom, Paris, "O son! the night
before thy wedding-day/Hath Death lain with thy wife."
Romeo is death. He and Tybalt together slay Mercutio,
whose death speech is immortal: "No, 'tis not so deep as
a well, nor so wide as a church-door;but 'tis enough, 'twill
serve . . . . A plague o'both your houses." Both Romeo and
Juliet surrender to despair, both threatening suicide before
the scene in the tomb. It is remarkable that the advice of
the father-figure, Friar Lawrence, preserves them for as
long as it does; their drive to death is so strong. It is
fitting that it is Juliet's uncontrollable grief at Romeo's
absence that leads her parents to console her as best they
know--with the impossible marriage to Paris. The one medical
figure, that of the Apothecary, is of no avail. For famine
forces him to ignore the legal restrictions on the sale of
poisons and so furnish Romeo--and Juliet--with death. However, the passion of their dying kisses, given amidst the
horrors of the charnel house (next to the bodies of Paris
and Tybalt) transcends terror. The poetry transmutes the
grotesque tragedy to enchanted grief, which unites the two
warring families in a "glooming peace."

Shakespeare, William. "Shall I compare thee to a summer's day?"
Sonnet.

Death	Sexuality

The imperfections of nature and conventional poetry are
set against the perfections of his love and the eternal
lines of Shakespeare's poetry. His love's eternal summer
will be preserved from death, growing to time in Shakespeare's
verse: "Shall I compare thee to a summer's day?/Thou art
more lovely and more temperate:/Rough winds do shake the
darling buds of May,/And summer's lease hath all too short
a date . . . And every fair from fair sometime declines,/
By chance or nature's changing course untrimm'd:/But thy
eternal summer shall not fade/Nor lose possession of that
fair thou ow'st;/Nor shall Death brag thou wand'rest in
his shade,/When in eternal lines to time thou grow'st;/
So long as men can breathe or eyes can see,/So long lives
this, and this gives life to thee."

Shakespeare, William. The Taming of the Shrew. Drama.

Sexuality	Sexual Roles

The shrewish Kate, the bane of her troubled father and
beautiful sister, Bianca, is tamed by the energetic
Petruchio, who outdoes her in curses and freakish behavior and who clearly establishes her dependence upon
him for bed, board and dress. Petruchio acts the strong
male and so brings his wife to contented obedience.
Lucentio and Hortensio, who act mildly to their gentle-
seeming brides, find themselves with contrary women on
their hands. The weak male creates the strong female. The
play ends with Katherina's long sermon to the other two
women, advocating male supremacy: "Why are our bodies soft
and weak and smooth./Unapt to toil and trouble in the world,/
But that our soft conditions and our hearts/Should well agree
with our external parts?"

Shakespeare, William. The Tempest. Drama.

Age	Children	Death
Disease & Health	The Family	Grief
Sexuality	Suffering	

Wisdom and a tendency to manipulate people are the traits
of old Prospero and Gonzalo. It is a sign of this wisdom
that Prospero ends the play with this picture of his age,
"where/Every third thought shall be my grave." He has
gained both self-control and insight into his own nature,
and so is worthy of the manipulative control he exerts over
others. Even to those he cannot change, he is forgiving.
Caliban is a "type" of lust, desiring always to rape Miranda,
Prospero's daughter. Yet, although Caliban is rendered harmless by diseases and other torments, he is also rewarded by
dreams of preternatural sweetness. Caliban is unchanging.
The humans are not so. And it is, in part, by teaching
that Prospero gains reparation for his exile by his usurp-
ing brother, Antonio, and for the wrongful aid given that
usurper by Alonso, King of Naples. Prospero works in two
ways: through grief and through sexuality. Alonso grieves
for the supposed loss of his son, Ferdinand, just as

Ferdinand grieves, at first, for the supposed loss of his father. Ferdinand's grief is cut short by the sight of Miranda, but his father's grief is overwhelming. He would soon suffer Prospero's loss of political rule (Prospero had abandoned sovereignty for personal pursuits), were he not protected from his brother's ambitious plots so that he can continue as father and as ruler. On this enchanted isle, Death is an illusion, a loss of the self that leads to re-birth, as in Ariel's song to the grieving Ferdinand. "Full fathom five thy father lies;/Of his bones are coral made;/Those are pearls that were his eyes:/Nothing of him that doth fade/But doth suffer a sea-change/Into something rich and strange." The sea-change extends to a sexual transfor-mation of political relationships. The family is here a political unit, ravaged at first by the ambitious brothers, but increased to a more procreative and sacred union by the marriage of Ferdinand and Miranda. The sexual relationship between the two child/lovers helps to wind up the charm; but it is clear from Prospero's rough admonitions to his daughter and Ferdinand, that this sexual relationship must be without lust. It must have only Ceres, not Venus or Caliban. Not lustful revenge, but creative forgiveness.

Shakespeare, William. "That time of year thou mayst in me behold." Sonnet.

    Age

A compliment to a lover who loves the aging poet. "That time of year thou mayst in me behold/When yellow leaves, or none, or few, do hang/Upon those boughs which shake against the cold,/Bare ruin'd choirs where late the sweet birds sang . . . . In me thou see'st the glowing of such fire/That on the ashes of his youth doth lie,/As the death-bed whereon it must expire,/Consum'd with that which it was nourish'd by./This thou perceiv'st, which makes thy love more strong,/To love that well which thou must leave ere long."

Shakespeare, William. "Those hours that with gentle work did frame." Sonnet.

    Age   Sexuality

One of the "marriage" group, urging a young man to marry. Age is countered by reproduction of oneself in children, rather than in works of art. "Those hours, that with gentle work did frame/The lovely gaze where every eye doth dwell,/Will play the tyrants to the very same/And that unfair which fairly doth excel;/For never-resting time leads summer on/To hideous winter and confounds him there,/Sap check'd with frost and lusty leaves quite gone,/Beauty o'ersnow'd and bareness everywhere . . . But flowers distill'd, though they with winter meet,/Leese but their show; their substance still lives sweet."

Shakespeare, William. Timon of Athens. Drama.

    Disease & Health   V.D.

Timon goes from unrealistically overvaluing to unrealistically undervaluing the human race. We feel sympathy for him in neither state. In his desire for revenge against his un-grateful friends, he prays for disease and disorder to strike men: "Son of sixteen,/Pluck the lin'd crutch from thy old limping sire;/With it beat out his brains!" He gives money to the rebel Alcibiades on condition that he will decimate Athens and money to whores on condition that they will sow disease among men. He describes with mad relish, the symp-toms of venereal disease. "Crack the lawyer's voice,/That he may never more false title plead . . . . Down with the nose,/Down with it flat;take the bridge quite away . . . . Plague all,/That your activity may defeat and quell/The source of all erection."

Shakespeare, William. Troilus and Cressida. Drama.

    The Body   Disease & Health   Homosexuality
    Sexuality   Suffering

One of the blackest views of humanity. The Greeks and Trojans have been fighting for ten years over a woman's body. The play debates the value of that body. When the Trojan nobles discuss the possibility of returning Helen and so ending the war, the debaters divide into those who value things accord-ing to their nature and those who value things according to their artificial, mercantile value. The latter wins. Women are commodities. Troilus sees his beloved Cressida as a commercial object: "there she lies, a pearl . . . Ourself the merchant, and this sailing Pandar/Our doubtful hope, our convoy, and our bark." The play implies that both the Trojans and Greeks have been swindled. Ulysses is full of rational medicine to cure the sick Gercian enterprise. His wily medi-cines are ineffective. Achilles, like Troilus, is kept from the war by love of a Trojan maiden. Like Troilus, he is returned to the war by the loss of his love, his true love--his "masculine whore," Patroclus. This play of confused values has no real end. Troilus laments Hector's death and dashes off to the war for brutal revenge, having finally perceived the harsh reality under all ideals: "words, words, mere words, no matter from the heart;/Th' effect doth operate another way." Yet, after Troilus has feelingly portrayed the effect of grief upon Hector's family, Pandarus saunters onto the stage to be reviled by Troilus, whom he answers with his disease: "A goodly med'cine for mine aching bones! O world! world! world! thus is the poor agent despis'd!" He ends with a plea for tears from V.D.-stricken prostitutes and bawds. The world is diseased, and there is no cure.

Shakespeare, William. Twelfth Night. Drama.

    The Body   Death   The Family
    Grief   Madness   Med. Instit.
    Sexuality   Sexual Roles

At the beginning of this golden comedy, three characters have chosen isolation from their peers. The Duke Orsino isolates himself in a self-induced, self-dramatized passion for the Lady Olivia, whom he courts by proxy. The Lady Olivia plans to isolate herself for seven years, to mourn a dead brother. Malvolio, her steward, isolates himself out of pride and ambition, convinced he has no peers. The artificial nature of both the Duke's love and Olivia's grief is epitomized in the song "Come away, come away death," in which a lover languidly, but so beautifully, plans a funeral for himself that will adequately match his grief and woe. Into this dream-ing Illyria, bursts the truly alive Viola. Separated from a twin brother during a storm at sea, she grieves for him, hopes for his safety, and turns to her own life. Dressed as a boy (and experiencing some difficulty crossing the sexual roles) she serves the Duke with whom she falls in love. However, the Duke uses her to court Olivia, who falls in love with Viola. The play gracefully and hilariously exploits this ludicrous triangle, creating further confusion and then eliminating all frustrations by the arrival of Viola's twin brother, Sebastian, who marries Olivia and restores order to her household--freeing the Duke to marry Viola. Malvolio's cure is not as successful. His "doctors" are Olivia's uncle and his follower (Sir Toby Belch and Sir Andrew Auguecheek) and Olivia's maid, Maria, three whose fellowship is based on the body. The trio act from pique, angered by Malvolio's pride and self-righteous efforts to halt Sir Toby's continual revelry. By a forged letter, Malvolio is deceived into con-firmation of his belief that the Lady Olivia loves him. The letter asks him to show his love by drastically altering his behavior. Malvolio does so and is believed mad by Olivia, who delegates Sir Toby to deal with this "madman." Sir Toby locks him up in a dark place (accepted treatment for madness) and sends Olivia's Fool, who also has a grudge against Malvolio, to torment him further. The Fool toys with him, but feels pity for him and helps him to get free. This "cure" sends Malvolio into further isolation, and the play ends with the united lovers seeking some way to reconcile him.

Shakespeare, William. "Two loves I have of comfort and despair." Sonnet.

    Homosexuality   Sexuality

This poem summarizes the triangle which governs Shakespeare's sonnets: the dark lady (so praised in "my mistress' eyes are nothing like the sun"), the fair young man, and the poet. "Two loves I have of comfort and despair,/Which like two spirits do suggest me still:/The better angel is a man right fair,/The worser spirit a woman colour'd ill./To win me soon to hell, my female evil/Tempteth my better angel from my side,/And would corrupt my saint to be a devil,/Wooing his purity with her foul pride./And whether that my angel be turn'd fiend/Suspect I may, yet not directly tell;/But being both from me, both to each friend,/I guess one angel in another's hell./Yet this shall I ne'er know, but live in doubt,/Till my bad angel fire my good one out."

Shakespeare, William. Venus and Adonis. Poem: 1194 lines.

    The Body   Death   Grief
    Homosexuality   Sexuality   Sexual Roles

Ludicrously disordered sexuality, delight in the erotic con-sequences of role reversal. Venus woos the young Adonis with the entire courtly-love repetoire of a poet. Her range of voice is remarkable. But the narrator provides a running commentary on this courtship, in the form of far-fetched similes pointing out the extreme reversal of sexual roles. "Even as an empty eagle, sharp by fast,/Tires with her beak on feathers, flesh, and bone,/Shaking her wings, devouring all in haste,/Till either gorge be stuff'd or prey be gone;/Even so she kiss'd his brow, his cheek, his chin." The Queen of Love, flushed and sweaty, fails to win over the sulky boy, who refuses to profit by the example given by his stallion upon a mare. Adonis rejects Venus as too wanton and lustful and goes off to hunt the wild boar. She foresees her defeat, pleads unsuccessfully with Death for his life, and passes through the stages of grief to resignation. Adonis dies because he seems to seek a homosexual encounter. "'Tis true, 'tis true;thus was Adonis slain;/He ran upon the boar with his sharp spear,/Who did not whet his teeth at him again,/But by a kiss thought to persuade him there;/And nuzzling in his flank, the loving swine/Sheath'd unaware the tusk in his soft groin." However, Adonis does beget one off-spring--a flower, which Venus plucks to die in her bosom.

Shakespeare, William. "When my love swears that she is made of truth." Sonnet.

    Age   Sexuality

Complex relationship between age and sexuality, made more complex by reaching puns. The "old" poet accepts his love's flatteries about his age to make her believe he is young. And the times she "lies" with other men are balanced by the verbal lies between her and the poet. And the verbal lies are masked as the poet lies with her. "When my love swears that she is made of truth,/I do believe her, though I know she lies,/That she might think me some untutor'd youth,/Unlearned in the world's false subtleties . . . . But where-fore says she not she is unjust?/And wherefore say not I that I am old?/O, love's best habit is in seeming trust,/And age in love loves not to have years told;/Therefore I lie with her and she with me,/And in our faults by lies we flattered be."

Shakespeare, William. The Winter's Tale. Drama.

    Adolescence   Age   Children
    The Family   Grief   Preg. & Childbirth
    Sexuality

Effect of parents' sexuality upon children and the effect of the children's sexuality upon the parents. Leontes, King of Sicilia, becomes unreasonably jealous of his childhood friend, Polixenes, the King of Bohemia. He unsuccessfully tries to murder his friend and imprisons the pregnant Hermione, Queen of Sicilia. The harsh behavior of his father and the separation from his mother kills the precocious Mamillius, the heir to the throne. Hermione gives premature birth to a daughter, whom Leontes orders destroyed as a bastard. From childbed, the Queen is brought to trial. Hearing the news of Mamillius' death, she swoons and apparently dies. Leontes recovers his sanity only to plunge into unending grief for his wife and children. Then, the movement of the play turns: "thou met'st with things dying, I with things new-born." The daughter is saved by a shepherd and lives to fall in love with Florizel, the Prince of Bohemia. Again, the parent drives away the child. Polixenes forbids his son to marry the low-born shepherd's daughter and threatens the old shepherd with death. The lovers flee to Sicilia, where Leontes gives them warm welcome, falling a bit in love with his daughter. Polixenes follows, the shepherd discloses the birth tokens which prove Perdita's birth to equal her worth, the lovers are betrothed and the friends reconciled. But the climax of the play is the "statue scene." Pauline, a lady of the court and friend to Hermione, offers to show Leontes a statue of Hermione, aged as though she had lived. The statue is, of course, the real Hermione. The parents and children are united together. The play contains an early reference to adolescence; the old shepherd grumbles about his son: "I would there were no age between ten and three-and-twenty, or that youth would sleep out the rest; for there is nothing in the between but getting wenches with child, wronging the ancientry, stealing, fighting."

Shakespeare, William. "A woman's face with Nature's own hand painted." Sonnet.

Homosexuality

This sonnet has been cited as evidence for, and against, Shakespeare's homosexuality. Since his lover's prick is both "to my purpose nothing" and "for women's pleasure," it would appear that the relationship stopped short of the physical. "A woman's face with Nature's own hand painted/Hast thou, the master-mistress of my passion . . . . An eye more bright than theirs, less false in rolling,/Gilding the object whereupon it gazeth . . . . Till Nature, as she wrought thee, fell a-doting,/And by addition me of thee defeated/By adding one thing to my purpose nothing./But since she prick'd thee out for women's pleasure,/Mine be thy love, and thy love's use their treasure."

Sidney, Philip. Arcadia, ed. Albert Feuillerat. Cambridge: Cambridge University Press, 1965. 2 Vols. Tales and Poems.

The Family   Grief   Sexuality
Sexual Roles   Women as Healers

A tangle of tales and poetry. The heroic past of two young knights is interwoven with their pastoral adventures. In the past they met with violence: kings and queens suspected them of treason and misdeeds; they aided distressed lovers and overthrew giants; they rescued each other like faithful friends; they met a king deposed by one son and restored by the other; they watched as two lovers, Argalus and Parthenia, were separated by a rejected suitor who throws a defacing potion at the lady's face; then they rejoiced when Queen Helen of Corinth cured the lady and reunited the lovers (Book I). But love has transformed the heroes into ludicrous forms. King Basilius has gone into seclusion with his wife and two daughters. One lover follows, disguised as a peasant, and humbly woos his love. The other lover is less fortunate. He disguises himself as a noble Amazon and becomes a guest in the King's household. But his love persists in regarding him as girl friend, King Basilius pursues him, believing him a woman, and Queen Gynecia, more clear-sighted than her husband and daughter, pursues him as a man. So, he must court his love, who believes him a woman, while dodging her jealous mother and besotted father. The lure of the unmarried princesses brings violence to this pastoral retreat. In the battles that follow, many lovers are killed, including Argalus and Parthenia; King Basilius and his wife are apparently killed; and the lovers are accused of murder. But all ends happily. The prevailing tone is that of distanced melancholy, beautifully embodied in the eclogues that end each book. One of the best of these is "You Goatherd Gods," in which two shepherds strive to outdo each other in portraying the devastation of their grief upon the countryside: "'I, that was once free burgess of the forests,/Where shade from sun, and sport I sought in evening,/I that was once esteemed for pleasant music,/Am banished now among the monstrous mountains/Of huge despair, and foul affliction's valleys,/Am grown a screech owl to myself each morning.'/'I, that was once delighted every morning,/Hunting the wild inhabiters of forests,/I, that was once the music of these valleys,/So darkened am that all my day is evening,/Heartbroken so that molehills seem high mountains,/And fill the vales with cries instead of music.'"

Sidney, Philip. Four Sonnets Made when his Lady had Pain in her Face: "The scourge of life, and death's extreme disgrace," "Woe, woe to me, on me return the smart," "Thou pain, the only guest of loathed constraint," and "And have I heard her say, 'O cruel pain!'" Available in Five Courtier Poets, ed. R. M. Bender. New York: Washington Square Press, 1969. Sonnets.

Disease & Health   Sexuality   Suffering

Pain from disease is set against the pains of frustrated desire. Sidney uses his lady's suffering as another approach to the courtly love tradition. The first three sonnets

provide witty solutions to the problem of pain, here expressed as the problem of how perfection, supposedly incorruptible, is afflicted with imperfection in the form of pain. The poet claims that the imperfection is not in his lady, but in pain ("He hopes for some small praise since she hath great") or in the poet who praised her so much that "her face, this age's praise, the thief doth kiss." The first sonnet contains only sympathy with the lady's pain. But in this mini-sequence, the poet draws farther and farther away from pitying the lady and more and more into pitying himself. In the second sonnet, he only praises the lady to ease his pain, and in the third, the poet proposes an alliance with pain: "So stay her tongue, that she no more say no." By the end of the sequence, the poet is attacking the lady for thinking her self above pain ("Or doth she think all pain the mind forbears?/That heavy earth, not fiery sprites may plain?") and for feeling that the pain which she causes others is justified, while that she suffers is not.

Sidney, Philip. "Grief, find the words, for thou hast made my brain," from Astrophil and Stella. Available in Five Courtier Poets, ed. R. M. Bender. New York: Washington Square Press, 1969. Sonnet.

Grief

Grief was usually associated with sexual frustration in the courtly love tradition. The portraits of grief seem highly exaggerated and artificial, and yet they do furnish interesting descriptions of depression, a fashionable Elizabethan state of mind. "Grief, find the words, for thou hast made my brain/So dark with misty vapors, which arise/From out thy heavy mold, that inbent eyes/Can scarce discern the shape of mine own pain . . . . Which even to sense, sense of itself denies,/Though harbingers of death lodge there his train."

Sidney, Philip. "Thou blind man's mark, thou fool's self-chosen snare," and "Leave me, O love which reachest but to dust." Available in Five Courtier Poets, ed. R. M. Bender. New York: Washington Square Press, 1969. Sonnets.

Sexuality

Two great palinodes. Earthly love is worthless; it is scum, dregs, a barrier to advancement in this world and achievement of heaven in the next. The two poems are full of confidence and self-congratulation that the poet has been able to conquer his own desires. The two have an impersonal beauty when set next to Shakespeare's bitter condemnation of hideous, unavoidable desire. "Desire, desire. I have too dearly bought,/With price of mangled mind, thy worthless ware . . . But yet in vain thou hast my ruin sought./In vain thou madest me to vain things aspire./In vain thou kindlest all thy smoky fire;/For virtue hath this better lesson taught:/Within myself to seek my only hire,/Desiring nought but how to kill desire."

Sidney, Philip. "Who will in fairest book of nature know," from Astrophil and Stella. Available in Five Courtier Poets, ed. R. M. Bender. New York: Washington Square Press, 1969. Sonnet.

The Body   Sexuality

Stella is first seen as composed of abstractions: virtue, beauty, reason, a force to good. And yet, abstractions are not enough: "So while thy beauty draws the heart to love,/As fast thy virtue bends that love to good;/But ah, desire still cries, give me some food."

Skelton, John. Philip Sparrow. Available in The Complete Poetry of John Skelton, ed. Philip Henderson. New York: E. P. Dutton, 1964. Poem: ca. 1350 lines.

Adolescence   Grief   Sexuality

A unique poem. The lament of a young girl for her dead sparrow (a symbol of lechery) that is both praise for her innocent grief and a gentle satire upon her innocent ignorance. She employs a variety of ways to express her grief, using lines from the Office for the Dead, shivering and wringing her hands, calling upon Jesus and the ancient Greeks to help her, cursing Gib the cat who killed her Philip, and calling upon the birds to assist his funeral. Her view of sexuality is both innocent and titillating. She describes Philip's wanderings under her clothes, picking up all the fleas he may, and she ends the account of his funeral: "Oremus,/Deus, cui proprium est misereri et parcere,/On Philip's soul have pity!/For he was a pretty cock,/And came of a gentle stock,/And wrapt in a maiden's smock,/And cherished full daintily,/Till cruel fate made him to die:/Alas, for doleful destiny!/But whereto should I/Longer mourn or cry?/To Jupiter I call,/Of heaven imperial,/That Philip may fly/Above the starry sky,/To tread the pretty wren,/That is our Lady's hen./Amen, amen, amen!"

Skelton, John. "To Mistress Margaret Hussey," in The Garland of Laurel. Available in The Complete Poems of John Skelton, ed. Philip Henderson. New York: E. P. Dutton, 1964. Poem: 34 lines.

Sexual Roles

Skelton's version of The Legend of Good Women. Occupation tells the poet of all the ladies working to crown him with laurel and suggests that he thank them in poetry. What follows is a collection of poems to Skelton's friends and patrons. They are delightful, like this, "To Mistress Margaret Hussey": (Remember that "gentle" often meant noble, and falcons were noble birds. This is not a satire.) "Merry Margaret,/As midsummer flower,/Gentle as falcon/Or hawk of the tower:/With solace and gladness,/Much mirth and no madness,/All good and no badness;/So joyously,/So maidenly,/

So womanly/Her demeaning/In every thing . . . ./Steadfast of thought,/Well made, well wrought,/Far may be sought/Ere that ye can find/So courteous, so kind/As Merry Margaret,/This midsummer flower./Gentle as falcon/Or hawk of the tower."

Skelton, John. _The Tunning of Elinour Rumming_. Available in _The Complete Poetry of John Skelton_, ed. Philip Henderson. New York: E. P. Dutton, 1964. Poem: ca. 650 lines.

Alcoholism   The Body   Sexuality

An early fifteenth-century description of alcoholic house-wives. Skelton avoids any moral condemnations. He concentrates on only two points: these women have become so physically grotesque that no man would want them, and they are so driven to the ale, that they will sell anything, including their means of livelihood, to get that drink. "Some housewives come unbraced,/With their naked pappes,/That flippes and flappes,/That wigges and wagges/Like tawny saffron bagges." Elinour, who has been described as a greasy, snotty, old hag, sells her ale as a cosmetic: "It shall make you look/Younger than ye be/Yeares two or three,/For ye may prove it by me." But here is a description of one customer: "With that her head shaked,/And her handes quaked,/One's head would have ached/To see her naked . . . . The dropsy was in her legges;/Her face glistering like glass,/All foggy fat she was./She had also the gout/In all her joints about;/Her breath was sour and stale,/And smelled all of ale:/Such a bedfellow/Would make one cast his craw." The women pay for their drinks with their wedding rings, husband's clothes, poultry from the farmyard, or their tools for spinning yarn, a major source of household money. There is no comradeship in Elinour's ale-house, only grotesque ugliness and disorder.

Skelton, John. "Womanhood, Wanton, Ye Want." Available in _The Complete Poetry of John Skelton_, ed. Philip Henderson. New York: E. P. Dutton, 1964. Poem: 30 lines.

Sexuality

Use of poetry for revenge upon a woman who has rejected him. In the infamous last stanza, he reduces the scornful woman to a well-used vagina. "Your key is meet for every lock,/Your key is common and hangeth out;/Your key is ready, we need not knock,/Nor stand ye wresting there about;/of your door-gate ye have no doubt . . . . To Mistress Anne, that farly sweet,/That wones at The Key in Thames Street."

Spenser, Edmund. _Epithalamion_. Available in _The Shepherd's Calendar and Other Poems_, ed. Philip Henderson. New York: E. P. Dutton, 1965. Poem: 433 lines.

Sexuality

Celebration of one-sided sexuality: Spenser's wedding day as envisioned by the poetic bridegroom. He calls on the muses and the wood nymphs to awaken and escort his bride; he asks fair Hours and Venus' attendants to adorn her. When she appears, he praises her body and, even more, her modest mind and inward beauty. He watches her during the sacred ceremonies (while she watches the ground), then calls for a boisterous feast in celebration: "Pour not by cups, but by the bellyful." He warns away all harmful spirits of the night and then, unlike Donne who rapturously describes the bridal bed, jumps to prayers for children. Beautiful, but perhaps the proposed marriage of desire and chastity was rightly doomed. The poem ends with the bridegroom's complaint that his bride has rejected him: "Song! made in lieu of many ornaments,/With which my love should duly have been deckt . . . Be unto her a goodly ornament,/And for short time an endless monument."

Spenser, Edmund. _The Faerie Queene_. Books II-V. Poems.

The Body   Homosexuality   Sexuality
Sexual Roles   Women as Healers

Book II, Cantos IX and XI, show the body in health and in peril. The House of Alma (Temperance) is an elaborate image of the well-regulated body of a temperate man. The image not only includes a description of the mind (including reason, imagination, and memory), it also includes the Kitchen (cooled by the bellows/lungs) and "all the rest, that noyous was and nought . . . Was close convaid, and to the backgate brought . . . whereby/It was avoided quite, and throwne out privily." However, this wonderful, well-ordered body is under constant attack by Passionate Living and the Seven Deadly Sins. Passionate Living includes any extreme, whether of impotence or impatience.

Books III-V explore sexuality and sexual roles, their allegories masking a most realistic assessment of the complexities of human sexuality. _The Faerie Queene_ has a number of places symbolizing aspects of sexual life: The Bower of Bliss with its destructive excess; The Garden of Adonis, in which the genitals are linked to the mysterious process whereby a soul is clad in flesh; The Temple of Venus, inhabited by Shamefastness, Cheerfulness, Modesty Curtesy, Silence, and Obedience who surround Womanhood, the place from which Scudamour carries off Amoret; and the church of Isis, an image of wedded love. Books III and IV ostensibly deal with Chastity and Friendship, but they also examine a variety of sexual relationships--usually not in two's, but in three's, as though a perfect relationship is an association of two discordant forces held in stasis by the mediation of a third. Britomart, who searches for her male counterpart, Artegall, throughout the two books, actually serves as a hermaphrodite, capable of joining triads with either sex and capable of destroying enemies of either sex (the vanquished are usually a part of the victor). The Books are unusual in that destruction of harmful sexual forces is not portrayed as the way to sexual balance; rather, the destructive powers usually have a productive role to play.

For example, Britomart can overthrow the sorcerer Busirane, whose house is an emblem of lust. She can force him to free Amoret and to remove the sword from Amoret's heart. (It is fitting that it is the chaste, but sexually-driven Britomart, who saves Amoret, the fearful bride forcibly stolen by her bridegroom and then forcibly stolen by lust--or fear of lust--from that bridegroom.) But Britomart cannot destroy Busirane, for Amoret's life depends upon his continued existence. The union of opposites is also illustrated in Belphoebe. She cures a wounded squire by means of herbs and divine grace. However, he falls desperately in love with this woman committed to virginity. She has cured his thigh injury while wounding his heart. She heals and injures at one time.

Book V discusses sexual roles and political power. Not surprisingly in a literature dominated by Queen Elizabeth, there are several women rulers--ranging from the strong Mercilla, through the flawed Radigund, to the weak Irena. Artegall fights with Radigund, is overcome by her beauty (as he was by the beauty of Britomart) and surrenders to her. He is thereupon forced to act the role of a woman, until Britomart comes to his rescue.

These brief notes only begin to cover the range and depth of psychology explored in _The Faerie Queene_.

Spenser, Edmund. "Februarie," from _The Shepheardes Calender_. Available in _The Shepherd's Calendar and Other Poems_, ed. Philip Henderson. New York: E. P. Dutton, 1965. Poem: 246 lines.

Age   Sexuality

Dialogue between youth and age, in which neither really listens to the other. Young Cuddie refuses to admit that Old Thenot was ever young or that he himself will be old. Cuddie rejoices in his own lustiness and that of his flocks, making snide remarks at Thenot's sexuality: "Thy flock's father his corage hath lost./Thy ewes, that want to have blowen bags,/Like wailful widows hangen their crags . . . All for their master is lustless and old." But old Thenot keeps up a steady attack on Cuddie: he's weak to complain of the cold; in his age he'll repent the folly of his youth; and tells him the long story of the old Oak and foolish Briar, who wants the hindering old Oak cut down. When the Oak falls, the Briar loses his protection and is trampled. Cuddie's response is not encouraging: "Here is a long tale, and little worth./So long have I listened to thy speech,/that graffed to the ground is my breech."

Spenser, Edmund. "Like as a huntsman after weary chase." _Amoretti_, No. LXVII. Available in _The Shepherd's Calendar and Other Poems_, ed. Philip Henderson. New York: E. P. Dutton, 1965. Sonnet.

Sexuality

Unlike most other Neoplatonist poets, Spenser was able to write about consummated love. He could maintain the pose of the unworthy lover while rejoicing in possession of the lady, an awkward position that he conveys most gracefully. "So, after long pursuit and vain assay,/When I all weary had the chase forsook,/The gentle deer returned the self-same way . . . . Till I in hand her yet half trembling took,/And with her own good-will her firmly tied./Strange thing, meseemed, to see a beast so wild,/So goodly won, with her own will beguiled."

Spenser, Edmund. "Men call you fayre, and you doe credit it." _Amoretti_, No. LXXIX. Available in _The Shepherd's Calendar and Other Poems_, ed. Philip Henderson. New York: E. P. Dutton, 1965. Sonnet.

Body/Mind   Death

His lady's mind and virtue are most to be praised: "But the true fair, that is the gentle wit,/And virtuous mind, is much more praised of me." A beautiful body is still subject to decay; true beauty lies in the mind and is derived from the creator of all beauty. "But only that is permanent, and free/From frail corruption, that doth flesh ensue./That is true beauty: that doth argue you/To be divine, and born of heavenly seed,/Derived from that fair Spirit from whom all true/And perfect beauty did at first proceed."

Spenser, Edmund. "One day I wrote her name upon the strand." _Amoretti_, No. LXXV. Available in _The Shepherd's Calendar and Other Poems_, ed. Philip Henderson. New York: E. P. Dutton, 1965. Sonnet.

Death   Sexuality

Just as his poetry combined with her virtues shall preserve her name in the heavens, so their mutual love shall preserve the two of them after death: Waves may wash away her name written in sand, but "My verse your virtues rare shall eternize,/And in the heavens write your glorious name./Where, whenas death shall all the world subdue,/Our love shall live, and later life renew."

Stevenson, William (?) ("Mr. S."). "Back and Side Go Bare," from the play _Gammer Gurton's Needle_. Available in _Elizabethan and Stuart Plays_, eds. Baskervill, Heltzel, and Nethercot. New York: Holt, Rinehart and Winston, 1962. Song: ca. 40 lines.

The Body

Exuberant praise of the ale-filled belly. Set to lively music, the song is a beautiful but pathetic defiance by the poor. The belly defends the body against illness, cold, and hunger while keeping husband and wife happy. "I cannot eat but little meat,/My stomach is not good;/But sure I think that I can drink/With him that wears a hood . . . . Back and side go bare, go bare,/Both foot and hand go cold;/But, belly, God send thee good ale enough,/ Whether it be new or old."

Suckling, John. "A Ballade. Upon a Wedding." Available in most anthologies of 17th-century verse, such as Seventeenth-Century Verse and Prose, eds. White, Wallerstein, and Quintana. New York: Macmillan, 1963. Poem: 132 lines.

   Sexuality

   Contrast between the sophistication of the narrator and the simplicity of the young bride he so admires--the perfect sexual object. "Her feet beneath her Petticoat,/Like little mice stole in and out,/As if they fear'd the light . . . . Her lips were red, and one was thin,/Compar'd to that was next her chin;/(Some Bee had stung it newly.)/But (Dick) her eyes so guard her face;/I durst no more upon them gaze,/Then on the Sun in July."

Suckling, John. "The Deformed Mistress." Works, ed. Thomas Clayton. Oxford: Clarendon Press, 1971. Vol. 1. Poem: 42 lines.

   Age   The Body   Disease & Health
   Sexuality

   One of the most grotesque of the Renaissance ugly old women. The poets delighted in creating the opposite to ideal beauty-- the nadir of sexual objects. This person was female, old, and, usually, diseased: "But soft, where am I now! here I should stride,/Lest I fall in, the place must be so wide;/ And pass unto her Thighs, which shall be just/Like to an Ants that's scraping in the dust:/Into her Legs I'de have Loves issues fall,/And all her Calf into a gouty small."

Suckling, John. "Sir J. S." ("Out upon it"). Available in most anthologies of 17th-century verse, such as Seventeenth-Century Verse and Prose, eds. White, Wallerstein, and Quintana. New York: Macmillan, 1963. Poem: 16 lines.

   Sexuality

   Archetype of rake--the blasé rover: "Out upon it, I have lov'd/Three whole days together;/And am like to love three more,/If it prove fair weather."

Suckling, John. "Upon T. C. having the Pox." Works, ed. Thomas Clayton. Oxford: Clarendon Press, 1971. Vol. 1. Poem: 12 lines.

   The Body   Sexuality   V.D.

   A flippant, witty discourse "upon Thomas Carew's having 'The French disease.'" "Troth, Tom, I must confess I much admire/Thy water should find passage through the fire:/For fire and water never could agree . . . for all know/The French ne'r grants a passage to his foe . . . . And wish that to his valor he had strength,/That he might drive the fire quite out at length:/For (troth) as yet the fire gets the day,/For evermore the water runs away."

Suckling, John. "Why so pale and wan fond Lover?" Available in most anthologies of 17th-century verse, such as Seventeenth-Century Verse and Prose, eds. White, Wallerstein, and Quintana. New York: Macmillan, 1963. Poem: 15 lines.

   Sexuality

   Perfect tone of expert, cynical sexuality. Why bother courting your love? If her own sexuality doesn't move her, nothing else will. "Will, when looking wel can't move her/ looking ill prevail?/prethee why so pale? . . . . Quit, quit for shame, this will not move,/this cannot take her;/If of her self she will not love,/nothing can make her:/the divel take her."

Tasso, Torquato. Jerusalem Delivered (Gerusalemme Liberata). Books XVI, XIX, XX. Trans. Edward Fairfax. New York: Capricorn, n.d. Epic Poem.

   Sexuality   Sexual Roles   Women as Healers

   Armida has been called "the greatest feminine creation in European literature since Dante's Francesca da Rimini" (The Continental Renaissance, ed. Krailsheimer). Armida begins as a magician-temptress, but is herself caught by love. Unlike the bowers by Ariosto or Spenser, Armida's lovely Castle of False Pleasure ensnares the temptress, Armida, as well as the tempted, Rinaldo, the Christian Knight she has spirited away from the seige of Jerusalem. Further, when his fellow knights come to rescue Rinaldo, they do not have to destroy the Castle to save him, they merely show him his effeminate image in a mirror. Rinaldo immediately flees, followed by the pleading Armida, who destroys the Castle herself when her laments fail to weaken the knight. She recognizes that she has stepped outside of her proper role, blaming her uncle who "most deserves the blame;/My heart and sex (that weak and tender be)/He bent to deeds that maidens ill became" (Book XVI). She tries to kill Rinaldo or to have him killed. When she fails and the Christian victory removes all further hope, she tries to kill herself but is stopped by Rinaldo who, his duties done, can now love her. Armida is not really condemned for aggressive violence, but aggressive sexuality: "Your love was too hot." The Christian woman, Gildippes, takes to the field with her husband and is praised for her slaughter of the enemy. Women also serve as effective healers. On the battlefield, when Ermina laments over her fallen Tancred, his friend rebukes her: "Cure him first and then complain,/ Med'cine is life's chief friend, plaint her worst foe." She is so skillful and so self-sacrificing (she uses her long hair to bind his wounds) that she cures him (Book XIX).

Tourneur, Cyril. The Atheist's Tragedy. Available in Webster and Tourneur, ed. J. A. Symonds. New York: Charles Scribner's, n.d. Drama.

   Children   Death   Disease & Health
   Doctors   Grief   Madness
   Sexuality

   An extravagant morbid-moral play. D'Amville, to increase wealth for himself and his children, kills his brother, disinherits his nephew, Charlemont, and marries Charlemont's wealthy fiancée to his own sickly son, Rousard. The play heavy-handedly sets up two contrasts. D'Amville, atheist, follower of nature and his own appetite, is set against the religious Charlemont. The topic on which they differ most is death. D'Amville fears it. Charlemont loves it. He and Castabella sleep in the graveyard with two skulls for pillows. They refuse to defend themselves against murder charges--Charlemont even leaps upon the scaffold to prove his indifference to death. Castabella's love of death is partially understandable. Married to an impotent husband, she claims deep content in her peaceful nights in bed. In the second major contrast of the play, this cold Castabella is set against the nymphomaniac Levidulche. After D'Amville loses both his sons (one from sickness, one in a duel over the worthless Levidulche), he goes mad with grief--incensed against Nature and Charlemont, but now triply terrified by death. In one of the most unusual death scenes on the stage, D'Amville, in the act of executing his nephew, dashes out his own brains with the axe. The play also contains a most unusual doctor. Called in to treat D'Amville's sons (one already dead and one close to it), he refuses to act because there is nothing effective he can do. When D'Amville persists in his entreaties, the doctor literally laughs at him, then concludes with a lecture on the insufficiency of nature: "For Nature never did bring forth/A man without a man . . . . So of necessity there must/Be a superior power to Nature." A curious moral play, in which the virtuous, with their death wishes and frigidity, seem as mad as the distracted villain.

Tourneur, Cyril. The Revenger's Tragedy, ed. L. J. Ross. Lincoln: University of Nebraska Press, 1966. Drama.

   Age   The Family   Sexuality

   The family and sexuality totally perverted. Castiza is enticed to be a whore by her brother and her mother. In the Duke's family, brother schemes to kill stepbrother, the Duchess sleeps with the Duke's bastard son, and the aged Duke pursues and murders chaste women. Sex is either forced (rape of Antonio's wife by the Duchess' younger son, the Duke's pursuit of Vindice's fiancée, Lussurioso's pursuit of Vindice's chaste sister) or unnatural (the Duchess and her stepson). The virtuous are not much better than the villains. Vindice and his brother, Hippolito, can think only of violence as a response to vice. They kill and kill. They are most ingenious, poisoning the Duke with a salve smeared on the lips of the skull of Vindice's fiancée, whom the Duke had poisoned, and keeping him alive long enough to overhear his wife making love with his son. When the two brothers reform their mother (whom Vindice had corrupted), they threaten her with daggers. The tone of the play is set by Vindice, who enters with the skull of his mistress: "O, that marrowless age/Should stuff the hollow bones with damn'd desires,/And 'stead of heat kindle infernal fires/Within the spendthrift veins of a dry duke,/ A parch'd and juiceless luxur. O God! one/That has scarce blood enough to live upon,/And he to riot it like a son and heir?"

Vaughan, Henry. "They are All Gone into the World of Light!" Available in Seventeenth-Century Verse and Prose, eds. White, Wallerstein, and Quintana. Vol. 1. New York: Macmillan, 1963. Poem: 40 lines.

   Death   Grief

   The poet grieves for his loneliness: "They are all gone into the world of light!/And I alone sit lingring here." He sees his friends in "an air of glory" which tramples on his days which are "Meer glimmering and decays." Death offers him the hope of such a beauteous shining--and yet its mysteries still tantalize him: "Either disperse these mists, which blot and fill/My perspective (still) as they pass,/Or else remove me hence unto that hill,/Where I shall need no glass."

Walton, Izaak. The Compleat Angler, ed. John Major. London, 1925. Treatise.

   Disease & Health

   One of the sanest books in the English language. Not only does it describe every aspect of stream fishing, it radiates healthful content. The fisherman must be a quiet, temperate man, who can enjoy and appreciate the glories of the outdoors, the simple pleasures of country living, and inexpensive and tranquil relaxation. Over and over, Walton urges thankfulness for whatever health we have. "And, in the next place, look to your health: and if you have it, praise God, and value it next to a good conscience; for health is the second blessing that we mortals are capable of . . . . What would a blind man give to see the pleasant rivers, and meadows, and flowers, and fountains, that we have met with since we met together? . . . And for most of them, because they be so common, most men forget to pay their praises; but let not us; because it is a sacrifice so pleasing to Him that made that sun, and us, and still protects us, and gives us flowers, and showers, and stomachs, and meat, and content, and leisure to go a-fishing" (Day V, Chapter XXI).

Webster, John. <u>The Duchess of Malfi</u>, ed. J. R. Brown. New York:
Barnes and Noble, 1969. Drama.

Death	Doctors	The Family
Madness	Sexuality	Suffering

Study in sexual repression and madness. Two unmarried
brothers, the Duke Ferdinand and the Cardinal, wish to
prevent their sister from remarrying. She circumvents
them by secretly wooing and wedding her capable steward,
Antonio. The Duchess successfully hides her marriage and
two consequent pregnancies. But, on the birth of the third
child, Antonio carelessly drops the child's horoscope where
the brothers' spy, Bosola, finds <u>it</u>. And the suffering
begins. The Duchess retreats from preserving her sexuality
to preserving herself. She is cut off from her family,
tortured in the dark with a dead man's hand, and tortured
in the light by wax figures of her murdered husband and
children. She is imprisoned next to the madhouse with its
continual noise and confusion. Ferdinand even brings in the
madmen for "entertainment." She remains steadfast and sane
amid Ferdinand's insane hell. When Bosola taunts her with
her helplessness, she responds with the famous "I am Duchess
of Malfi still!" She accepts death. When Bosola says that
the strangler's cord should terrify her, she responds, "Not
a whit./What would it pleasure me to have my throat cut/
With diamonds? Or to be smothered/With cassia? Or to be
shot to death with pearls? . . . . Tell my brothers/That
I perceive death . . . Best gift is they can give or I can
take." Her waiting woman is not as resigned and unsuccessfully pleads for life. Two of the children are killed. The
death of the Duchess sends Ferdinand into complete insanity
in the form of lycanthropy. In a comic episode a doctor
tries to cure him by outranting his madness to establish
authority over him. However, Ferdinand establishes authority
over the doctor. In an incredible fifth act, the Cardinal
kills his mistress, Bosola (reformed by Ferdinand's ingrati-
tude and the Duchess' death) kills Antonio in mistake for
Ferdinand, kills the Cardinal, and is fatally wounded while
killing Ferdinand. The oldest child of the Duchess and
Antonio is left as heir to Malfi. The strong, sane, living
force of the Duchess has been strangled by the stronger,
insane, and deadly force of her brothers.

Webster, John. <u>The White Devil</u>, ed. J. R. Mulryne. Lincoln:
University of Nebraska Press, 1970. Drama.

Dying	Evil Doctors	The Family
Grief	Madness	Sexuality
Sexual Roles		

Passion, murder, and intrigue as two Renaissance families
clash--ingenious death after ingenious death. The Duke of
Brachiano, married to Isabella, falls in love with the strong,
powerfully-attractive Vittoria, wife of Camillo. The Duchess'
two powerful brothers take exception to the Duke's affair,
urging him to pay attention to affairs of state and his
promising young son. However, one of Vittoria's two brothers,
Flamineo, is doing all he can to promote the affair in hope
of advancement. Vittoria's mother is vigorously critical
of her daughter who goes her way smoothly to destruction.
She artfully (through a "dream") incites Brachiano to murder
the Duchess and Camillo. Flamineo kills Vittoria's husband
and tries to make it look like an accident. But the powerful family moves against the less powerful. Brachiano is
not arraigned, but Vittoria and her two brothers are brought
to trial, where she boldly and intelligently defends herself
by condemning her accusing judges. She wins some sympathy
from the trial audience but is sentenced to a house of correction. Her brothers are freed. Then word comes that the
Duchess is dead. (Brachiano hired a doctor to poison his
picture, which his still-loving wife kissed every night.)
The powerful brothers debate murdering him. Meanwhile, the
two poorer brothers are quarreling. Vittoria's mother,
Cornelia, and Marcello violently criticize Flamineo for
proposing to marry the Moor, Zarche. Flamineo murders his
brother. Cornelia lies to protect him and then goes mad
with grief. One of the Duchess' brothers takes revenge,
poisoning Brachiano with a poisoned hat and visiting the
dying Brachiano as a confessor, torturing him with his sins
before strangling him. Flamineo, now going mad with disappointment and guilt, applies to his sister for money. She
refuses. He tries to kill her. She circumvents him once,
trampling on his supposedly dead body with triumphant malice.
However, her victory is not long-lived, for more murderers
enter to kill both siblings. The resolution with which she
faces death restores the admiration of Flamineo: "I love
thee now; if woman do breed man,/She ought to teach him manhood. Fare thee well./Know many glorious women that are
fam'd/For masculine virtue have been vicious . . . She hath
no faults who hath the art to hide them." Vittoria's only
response is: "My soul, like to a ship in a black storm,/
Is driven I know not whither."

Wyatt, Thomas. "My galley charged with forgetfulness." Available
in <u>Five Courtier Poets</u>, ed. R. M. Bender. New York: Washington Square Press, 1969. Sonnet.

Sexuality

Wyatt could endow the Petrarchan lament--the lady's cruelty
and the lover's helpless passion--with a rugged wistfulness
that is unique to him. "My galley charged with forgetfulness/
Thorough sharp seas in winter nights doth pass/Tween rock and
rock, and eke mine enemy, alas,/That is my lord, steereth
with cruelness . . . . The stars be hid that led me to this
pain,/Drowned is reason that should me consort,/And I remain
despairing of the port."

Wyatt, Thomas. "They flee from me, that sometime did me seek."
Available in <u>Five Courtier Poets</u>, ed. R. M. Bender. New York:
Washington Square Press, 1969. Poem: 21 lines.

Sexuality

An early statement of a theme now associated with D. H.
Lawrence. The poet complains that he has lost his lady
"thorough my gentleness." "I have seen them gentle, tame,
and meek,/That now are wild and do not remember/That sometime they put themself in danger/To take bread at my hand
. . . . Thanked be fortune it hath been otherwise . . .
When her loose gown from her shoulders did fall,/And she
me caught in her arms long and small;/Therewithal sweetly
did me kiss,/And softly said, 'Dear heart, how like you
this?'"

18th Century

Akenside, Mark. "Hymn to Science." From The Poetical Works of Akenside and Beattie. Cambridge: The Riverside Press, 1864. Poem: 42 lines.

By Doctors   Science & Poetry

According to the 19th-century editor, Alexander Dyce, Akenside is the physician/poet satirized in Dr. Smollett's novel Peregrine Pickle, for the physician/poet recites lines from Akenside's "Ode to the Earl of Huntington." "Hymn to Science" is cited here for its curious definition of science. In this poem, the word still retains its Renaissance meaning of all advanced knowledge but also has our more limited meaning of advanced knowledge acquired by scientific methods. Akenside praises the wisdom of those who study astronomy and the laws of motion; he praises those who study the human mind; and those who study social ties; he nowhere mentions any knowledge relevant to medicine. It is a curious omission. Akenside was well-known within the medical profession and prospered in it. Yet it was poetry that furnished him with his "science."

Akenside, Mark. "Hymn to the Naiads," especially lines 165-235. From The Poetical Works of Akenside and Beattie. Cambridge: The Riverside Press, 1864. Poem: 330 lines.

By Doctors   Disease & Health   Poverty & Health

Akenside has chosen an unusually effective subject: the water nymphs represent nature, power (commercial and military), health, and poetry. Lines 165-235 praise the health-giving powers of water. The simple outdoor life of Hygeia is celebrated by a feast crowned by water, which "washeth off/The dregs of luxury, the lurking seeds/Of crude disease; and through the abodes of life/Sends vigour, sends repose." Further, the metallic salt water of spas aids the patient uncurable by herbs and drops of balm. Yet it is the naiads that the Muses dwell and inspire men, despite the rude clamor of Bacchus' followers.

Akenside, Mark. "Ode XII, On Recovering From a Fit of Sickness, in the Country. 1768." From Odes. Book II. In The Poetical Works of Akenside and Beattie. Cambridge: The Riverside Press, 1864. Poem: 80 lines.

By Doctors   Disease & Health

For the doctor/poet, the countryside is medicine: "O Goulder's Hill . . . . O faithful core of oft-returning ill,/Now call thy sprightly breezes round,/Dissolve this rigid cough profound,/And bid the springs of life with gentler movement play." Health then restores poetic inspiration, lost in sickness. The Muses aid him as he celebrates a friend's country wedding.

Akenside, Mark. "Ode XVI, To Caleb Hardinge, M.D.," lines 41-50. From Odes. Book I. In The Poetical Works of Akenside and Beattie. Cambridge: The Riverside Press, 1864. Poem: 50 lines.

By Doctors   Science & Poetry

A beautiful description of science and poetry. The first 40 lines are Akenside's lengthy invitation to another physician/humanist to join him in a session with the Muse. The last stanza is his vision of the session, in which Akenside's poetic fancy is shaped by his friend's "Grecian purity," and Plato, in turn, is tamed by Francis Bacon: "O vers'd in all the human frame,/Lead thou where'er my labour lies,/And English fancy's eager flame/To Grecian purity chastise,/While hand in hand, at Wisdom's shrine,/Beauty with truth I strive to join,/And grave assent with glad applause;/To paint the story of the soul,/And Plato's visions to control/By Verulamian* laws." (*One of Bacon's titles was Baron Verulam.)

Arbuthnot, John. "Know Yourself." Available in The Penguin Book of Eighteenth-Century English Verse, ed. Dennis Davison. Baltimore: Penguin, 1973.* Poem: ca. 136 lines.

The Body   By Doctors

Dr. Arbuthnot was Physician Extraordinary to Queen Anne and friend to Swift and Pope (who praised him in "An Epistle from Mr. Pope to Dr. Arbuthnot"). In this poem he tries to reconcile the dichotomy of body and soul. The question, "Am I the abandoned orphan of blind chance,/Dropped by wild atoms in disordered dance?" is answered: "This frame, compacted, with transcendent skill . . . I call it mine, not me." Yet the body is able to "erase the new-born image from my mind." Only God is able to reconcile the two elements into one, humble, being.

*This Penguin Book of Eighteenth-Century English Verse contains several selections from poet-physicians whose work is not otherwise readily available (e.g. Arbuthnot, Samuel Garth, and Nathaniel Cotton--who kept an insane asylum in which William Cowper was a patient). Brief biographical notes are given for each author.

Armstrong, John. "The Art of Preserving Health." From The Poetical Works of Armstrong, Dyer and Green, ed. George Gilfillan. Edinburgh: James Nichol, 1858. Poem: 516 lines.

Age   Body/Mind   By Doctors
Disease & Health   Madness   Plague

The poet advocates temperance as preventive medicine. One should avoid polluted city air (this in 1744) and choose a countryside home where it is neither too hot, cold, wet or dry (Book I). One should eat temperately and drink frugally (Book II), exercising and exerting oneself constantly (Book III). However, one must accept the onset of old age: "there is a point,/By nature fixed, whence life must downward tend . . . . these strength'ning by degrees/To hard unyielding unelastic bone,/Through tedious channels the congealing flood/Crawls lazily . . . thus (so Heaven ordain'd it) life/Destroys itself." He describes the effect of plague on a city and then moves onto the more devastating effect of passions upon the body (Book IV). Virtue is necessary for health. The poem ends with the use of music to calm the emotions, thus seeing music as medicine: "And hence the wise of ancient days adored/One power of physic, melody, and song."

Behn, Aphra. Sir Patient Fancy. Available in Works, ed. Montague Summers. 1915 ed.; rpt. New York: B. Blom, 1967. Vol. 4. Drama.

Disease & Health   Med. Profession

One of several 18th-century, English adaptations of Molière's La Malade Imaginaire. Behn keeps Molière's ridicule of hypochondria and doctors' conclaves, but dilutes the satire by adding more lovers to the plot, turning attention to frustrated love rather than hypocritical medicine. Further, Behn adds more criticism of foreign doctors, again diluting Molière's universal satire upon the profession. However, Mrs. Behn does not dilute the Molière as much as Lacy does; and the last major 18th-century writer to adapt the plot, Henry Fielding, retains only mockery of the jargon. He laughs at the absurdity of the false doctor's cures rather than the absurdities in the profession his character is mimicking. Fielding's farce, The Mock Doctor: or, The Dumb Lady Cured, is more a vehicle for songs than a satire.

Bernardin de Saint Pierre. Paul and Virginia. From Vicar of Wakefield: Paul and Virginia. Philadelphia: Porter & Coates, n.d. Novel.

Children   Sexuality

This charming French novel seems to be strongly influenced by Rousseau. Two women, wronged by society, take refuge in a West Indian paradise where, with the help of two loyal slaves, they raise their two children, Paul and Virginia. Uncorrupted by society, these children grow up innocent, modest, loving, kind, and open to the world. The description of their initiation into their own sexuality, which takes place in this glorious natural retreat is enchantingly beautiful--as unreal and as beautiful as the landscape. However, their idyllic love is broken by demands of such reality as this paradise affords. The two slaves are growing old; replacements are needed and the four hermits have no money. Then, an aunt of Virginia appears on the far horizon--France; she will care for and educate Virginia, finally making Virginia an heiress, if Virginia is sent to France. Reluctantly Virginia leaves, her only motive to provide money for the little colony. Her aunt becomes disgusted with her refined simplicity and her refusal to wed an old nobleman; Virginia is sent back during the hurricane season; the ship is wrecked; she refuses rescue because it entails removing her clothes; she drowns, and Paul dies of grief.

Blackmore, Richard. Creation, Books V & VI. From "Blackmore's Creation," ed. M. M. Lovejoy. M.A. Thesis, The Pennsylvania State University, 1952. Poem: 7 Books.

The Body   By Doctors   Disease & Health
Suffering

Will be more interesting to those curious about content (i.e. which conventional ideas are chosen) than those who seek good poetry. The poet extrapolates the necessity of God's existence from various aspects of the world. For example, Book V states that human suffering is intense--whether from war, grief or disease (described in some detail); therefore, there must be a God for human consolation. Book VI extolls the work of art that is the human body: "Of every part due observation make;/All which such art disclose, so conduce/To beauty, vigour, and each destined use;/The atheist . . . May in himself his full conviction find,/And from his body teach his erring mind." (These ideas are also to be found in The Spectator, no. 543, which cites Creation.) In the poem the body is rather ludicrously anthropomorphized: "As it [the gastrointestinal tract] descends, it bores the midriff through;/The large receiver, for concoction made,/Behold amidst, the warmest bowels laid;/The spleen to this, this to the adverse side/The glowing liver's comfort is applied;/Beneath, the pancreas has its proper seat,/To cheer its neighbour, and augment its heat."

Boswell, James. The Life of Samuel Johnson. Biography.

Age   The Body   Death
Disease & Health   Dying   Grief
Madness   Sexual Roles

Johnson was in his early fifties when he first met Boswell
so, although The Life does cover Johnson's earlier years,
it is most vivid on Johnson's middle years and old age.
Johnson resisted the idea that he was old. In 1778
(he was born in 1709), he had tiffs with Boswell and
another friend who referred to him as old. However,
in a letter written December 7, 1782, he regretfully
notes the changed definition of health in old age.
Johnson was never particularly healthy. Spastic and
scarred from scrofula, he was a victim to asthma, dropsy
and gout. For 1782 there are many entries about deaths
of his friends and descriptions of his own ill health.
Letters in 1783 describe a stroke and his efforts to
cure himself. Johnson was terrified of death, and
knew it. On October 19, 1769, to Boswell's "But is
not the fear of death natural to man?" Johnson replied
"So much so, Sir, that the whole of life is but keeping
away the thoughts of it." A week later, Boswell's
efforts to persuade Johnson out of his fear of death
so infuriated the great Lexicographer, that he sent
Boswell away. Boswell's account of Johnson's death resembles Richardson's account of his heroine's death in
Clarissa. Johnson used companionship and conversation
as medicines, overcoming his almost grotesque body with
his brilliant mind. Although people kept him from dwelling on his ill health and his fear of death, they were
most useful in overcoming his lifelong affliction of
acute depression. Johnson feared that this depression
bordered on madness, but he was able to visit Bedlam and
to discuss calmly the causes of insanity on April 18,
1783, citing Bedlam as a reminder of madness occasioned
by over-indulgence of the imagination. Johnson's relationships with women are not clear. He married an un-
gainly widow, twenty years older than Johnson, who
brought her poor bridegroom a dowry of 700 pounds. He
escaped from her during her life and mourned her after
her death. He found great comfort in the company of
the blind Anna Williams and the lively Mrs. Thrale. He
subscribed to the double standard of his contemporaries.
In the spring of 1768, Boswell said that it was hard that
one slip should ruin a young woman. Johnson replied:
"Why, no, Sir: It is the great principle which she is
taught. When she has given up that principle, she has
given up every notion of female honour and virtue, which
are all included in chastity." However, he favored
learning in a wife. A complex man whose great mind
triumphed over the immense handicaps of poor physical
and mental health, coupled with a poor purse.

Bradstreet, Anne. "Before the Birth of One of her Children."
Available in The Works of Anne Bradstreet, ed. Jeannine
Hensley. Cambridge, Massachusetts: Belknap Press, 1967.
Poem: 28 lines.

Death   Grief   Preg. & Childbirth

A simple, affectionate letter to her husband, anticipating the all-too-common fate of 17th-century mothers:
death in childbed. "If any worth or virtue were in me,/
Let that live freshly in thy memory/And when thou feel'st
no grief, as I no harms,/Yet love thy dead, who long lay
in thine arms."

Bradstreet, Anne. "For Deliverance from a Fever." Available in
The Works of Anne Bradstreet, ed. Jeannine Hensley. Cambridge,
Massachusetts: Belknap Press, 1967. Poem: 28 lines.

Disease & Health

The close correspondence between the body and soul. When
she is ill with a fever ("My burning flesh in sweat did
boil,/My aching head did break"), she fears God's displeasure and cries out, "O heal my soul." When her
prayers are answered and God has "spared my body frail,"
she praises her mighty God "who hath redeemed my soul
from pit." Physical disease is spiritual disease.

Bradstreet, Anne. "In Memory of My Dear Grandchild Elizabeth Brad-
street, Who Deceased August, 1665, Being a Year and Half Old."
Available in The Works of Anne Bradstreet, ed. Jeannine
Hensley. Cambridge, Massachusetts: Belknap Press, 1967.
Poem: 14 lines.

Children   Death   Grief

Anne Bradstreet wrote several elegies for infant grandchildren (a reflection of the high infant mortality in
17th-century New England). This is one of the best,
especially the last stanza which opens with the death
of ripe plants ("plums and apples thoroughly ripe do
fall"), but closes with the faith that this early death
is not an act of nature, but a special act of God. "But
plants new set to be eradicate,/And buds new blown to
have so short a date,/Is by His hand alone that guides
nature and fate."

Bradstreet, Anne. "In Reference to her Children, 23 June, 1659."
Available in The Works of Anne Bradstreet, ed. Jeannine
Hensley. Cambridge, Massachusetts: Belknap Press, 1967.
Poem: 94 lines.

Children

This famous description of her children as "eight birds
hatched in one nest," the lengthy analogy of Bradstreet
and her children as a songbird and her young is an ingenious praise of maternal care, that will let go of

the children while still full of maternal fears, concerns
and protectiveness. "My fifth, whose down is yet scarce
gone,/Is 'mongst the shrubs and bushes flown,/And as his
wings increase in strength,/On higher boughs he'll perch
at length."

Burney, Fanny (Mme. D'Arblay). Evelina. London: G. Bell & Sons,
1927. Novel.

Age   Children   Sexuality
Sexual Roles

A witty novel of upper-class manners in late 18th-century
London, Evelina also demonstrates the numerous social
restrictions hedging women. Evelina is poor and must
marry to support herself when her guardian dies; she is
cruelly mocked for her ignorance of the conventions
governing polite society; she must answer politely the
rude remarks made by any man who chooses to harass her
on the street; she may save a young man (who, of course,
turns out to be her brother) from suicide, but she may
not write to find out how he has made his way on the
money she gave him nor make any agreement to meet him
privately. Her role is set in contrast to the witty--
and so unpleasantly masculine--Mrs. Selwyn and the languishing Lady Louisa Larpent who translates the injunction
to ladies to "be soft" into being physically soft and
languid. The different standards for men and women can
be seen in this interchange in letter LXXVII. Lord Morton
who has rudely pursued Evelina before the eyes of his
fiancée, states that a woman needs only beauty and good
nature. "For my part, deuce take me if ever I wish to
hear a word of sense from a woman as long as I live!"
Mrs. Selwyn replies, that since a man should have more
sense than his wife, the present company cannot be
accommodated "unless we should choose subjects from
Swift's hospital of idiots." Evelina's immediate reaction is: "How many enemies, my dear Sir, does this
unbounded severity excite!" But Evelina is very bound
by convention. Her noble father abandoned her mother
and the infant Evelina, who was raised by a friend of
her mother. This father has rejected Evelina's appeal
for recognition because an imposter has been foisted upon
him. However, just as Evelina is to be united with her
conventional Lord Orville, the confusion is disspelled,
and Evelina is introduced, panting and fainting, to her
distracted father. Always she has conventional attitudes
before her, and when he kneels to her, she cries "reverse
not the law of nature; rise yourself, and bless your
kneeling daughter!" Fatherhood is sacred. Evelina is
one of the first of many novels about trapped women, who
have no money and no occupation, who are totally dependent on men for survival and yet forced to restrict their
sexual appeals (otherwise the novel becomes Moll Flanders)
within a rigid social code that compels complacent acceptance of all male admiration, however rude or dishonorable,
while rejecting any advances on the part of the woman.
The helpless woman, tacitly praised by the novelist for
accepting the conventions that make her helpless, becomes
the popular subject of women's novels--appearing in such
guises as Mrs. Radcliffe's heroines or Jane Austen's
Elinor (Sense and Sensibility).

Burns, Robert. "Address to the Toothache," The Complete Poetical
Works of Burns. Cambridge: The Riverside Press, n.d. Poem:
36 lines.

Disease & Health   Suffering

The miseries of a pain that elicits no sympathy, but
rather laughter: "When fevers burn, or ague freezes,/
Rheumatics gnaw, or colic squeezes,/Our neebors sympa-
thise to ease us/Wi' pitying moan;/But thee!--thou hell
o' a' diseases,/They mock our groan!"

Burns, Robert. "Death and Doctor Hornbook," The Complete Poetical
Works of Burns. Cambridge: The Riverside Press, n.d. Poem:
31 stanzas.

Abortion   Death   Doctors

With his Latin, his instruments, and his impudence,
Doctor Hornbook kills twenty for Death's one. Death
laments: "Thus does he poison, kill, an' slay,/An's
weel paid for't;/Yet stops me o' my lawfu' prey/Wi'
his damn'd dirt." Among the Doctor's victims is a girl
seeking an abortion: "Some ill-brewn drink had hov'd
her wame [womb];/She trusts hersel, to hide the same,/
In Hornbook's care;/Horn sent her aff to her lang hame/
To hide it there."

Burns, Robert. "The Deuk's Dang O'er my Daddie" ("The Duck's
knocked over my Daddy"), Works, ed. W. E. Henley and T. F.
Henderson. Edinburgh and London, 1896-97; rpt. New York:
AMS Press, 1970. Poem: 16 lines.

Age   Sexuality

When the children shout that the duck has knocked over
their daddy, the lusty old wife grumbles that she
doesn't care: "'The fien-ma-care,' quo' the feirrie
[lusty] auld wife,/'He was but a paidling [a week action
in walking due to muscular weakness] body, O!/He paidles
out, and he paidies in,/An' he paidies late and early,
O!/This seven lang years I hae lien by his side,/An' he
is but a fusionless carlie, O! [a sapless old manikin]."
He loudly claims that he was not always this way: "I've
seen the day ye butter'd my brose,/And cuddl'd me late
and early, O/But downa-do's come o'er me now,/And och,
I find it sairly, O!"

Burns, Robert. "John Anderson My Jo," The Complete Poetical Works of Burns. Cambridge: The Riverside Press, n.d. and "John Anderson, My Jo," The Merry Muses of Caledonia: Collected and in Part Written by Robert Burns. New Hyde Park, New York: University Books, 1965. Poems: 16 & 48 lines.

Age   Death   Sexuality

The first version listed is the sentimental version proper for 18th-century publication. Old age is tolerable because the old couple have loved, and still love, each other: "Now we maun totter down, John,/And hand in hand we'll go,/And sleep thegither at the foot,/John Anderson my jo! [sweetheart]" The second version (from Burns' collection of bawdy folksongs) is the original, the complaint of the old wife: "John Anderson, my jo, John,/When first that ye began,/Ye had as good a tail-tree/As ony ither man;/But now its waxen wan, John,/And wrinkles to and fro;/I've twa gae-ups for ae gae-down,/John Anderson, my jo."

Burns, Robert. "A Poet's Welcome to His Love-Begotten Daughter. The first instance that entitled him to the venerable apellation of father." Available in The Complete Poetical Works of Burns. Cambridge: The Riverside Press, n.d. Poem: 8 stanzas.

Children   Preg. & Childbirth   Sexuality

A very paternal poem with pleasant reminiscences of the child's begetting--obviously without any attempt at birth control: "Welcome, my bonie, sweet, wee dochter!/ Tho' ye come here a wee unsought for,/And tho' your comin I hae fought for/Baith kirk and queir;/Yet, by my faith, ye're no unwrought for--/That I shall swear!"

Burns, Robert. "The Rights of Women." Available in The Complete Poetical Works of Burns. Cambridge: The Riverside Press, n.d. Poem: 5 stanzas.

Sexual Roles

This address for Miss Fontenelle on her benefit night was supposed to be flattering to women. Their rights are Protection, Decorum, and Admiration: "First, in the sexes' intermixed connexion/One sacred right of Woman is Protection:/The tender flower, that lifts its head elate,/Helpless must fall before the blasts of fate,/Sunk on the earth, defac'd its lovely form,/Unless your shelter ward th' impending storm." The poem also illustrates the opposite side of such stereotyping; men's roles are equally restricted: "A time, when rough rude man had naughty ways:/Would swagger, swear, get drunk, kick up a riot,/Nay, even thus invade a lady's quiet!"

Butler, Samuel. Hudibras, ed. John Wilders. Oxford: Clarendon Press, 1967. Long Poem.

Doctors   Euthanasia   Preg. & Childbirth
Sexuality   Sexual Roles   Suffering

This crude but hilarious anti-Puritan satire makes a passing reference to the evil practice of life-prolonging by physicians: "Not for the sickly Patients sake,/Nor what to give, but what to take./To feel the Pulses of their Fees,/More wise than fumbling Arteries:/Prolong the snuff of Life in pain,/And from the Grave Recover--Gain" (Third Part, Canto II, ll. 345-350). The Puritan Quixote, having failed in his attempts to permanently overthrow the ungodly fiddler, Crowdero, is placed in the stocks where he is visited by his lady, the widow. He constructs one of his elaborate--and false--logical arguments to defend the lie that he can control his pain: "this thing call'd Pain,/Is (as the Learned Stoicks maintain)/Not bad simpliciter, nor good,/But meerly as 'tis understood./Sense is Deceitful, and may feign,/As well in counterfeiting Pain/As other gross Phaenomena's . . . . It follows, we can ne'er be sure,/Whether we pain or not endure,/And just so far are sore and griev'd,/As by the Fancy is believ'd" (Second Part, Canto I, ll. 183-189, 197-200). Hudibras' first courting speech to his mistress, praising marriage, contains this description of pregnancy as a reason for man's greater sexual freedom: "And if the Indulgent Law allows,/A greater freedom, to the Spouse;/The reason is, because the Wife/Runs greater hazards of her Life./Is trusted with the Form, and Matter/Of all Mankind, by careful Nature;/Where Man brings nothing, but the Stuff,/She frames the wondrous Fabrick of" (Third Part, Canto I, ll. 875-882). However, after he has been frightened, beaten, and mocked by the lady whose wealth he loves so dearly, he sends her "An Heroical Epistle of Hudibras to his Lady" in which he demands that she submit to him because women are made to submit to men by Law of Nature. She replies in "The Ladies Answer to the Knight," asserting that money, not woman, is man's true love and that women have since taken over men--their management, their estates' management, and the decision as to who shall father their husband's children. Women are not about to give in to terrified men and "Let Men usurp Th' unjust Dominion,/As if they were the Better Women."

Chatterton, Thomas. "Sentiment." Available in The Complete Works of Thomas Chatterton: A Bicentenary Edition, ed. D. S. Taylor in association with B. B. Hoover. Oxford: Clarendon Press, 1971. 2 Vols. Vol. 1. Poem: 7 lines.

Death   Suicide

The adolescent poet Chatterton, who committed suicide at age 17, became a symbol of tragic, young genius. He is best known for his archaic, "medieval" verse, but this fragment written in the year he killed himself offers a

glimpse of self-dramatizing despair: "Since we can die but once what matters it/If Rope or Garter Poison Pistol Sword/Slow Wasting Sickness or the sudden burst/Of Valve Arterial in the noble Parts/Curtail the Miserys of human life/Tho' varied is the Cause the Effect's the same/All to one common Dissolution tends."

Cleland, John. Memoirs of Fanny Hill. New York: The New American Library, 1965. Novel.

Homosexuality   Sexuality

Sexuality--complete and unexpurgated, and usually joyously guiltless, even when one element is flagellation. The sole exception is male homosexuality, which fills the heroine with disgust. She regards it as "not only universally odious but absurd, and impossible to gratify." Furthermore, the madam of Fanny's brothel believes that such men are always visibly marked with a plague-spot, and have all the worst follies of women, and none of the best attributes of men. Lesbianism, however, is seen more sympathetically when an experienced prostitute initiates the young Fanny Hill, newly arrived in London from the country. Still Fanny's sexuality is overwhelmingly heterosexual. She is, in fact, a man's sexual fantasy come true, for she is pleasantly obsessed with his sexual organ and deliciously easy to gratify. Over and over she describes her ecstasy: "the magic touch took instant effect, quickened, and brought on upon the spur the symptoms of that sweet agony, the melting moment of dissolution, when pleasure dies by pleasure, and the mysterious engine of it overcomes the titillation it has raised in those parts, by plying them with the stream of a warm fluid that is itself the highest of titillations." There are no menses, no pregnancies, no impotence, save in the old, and no venereal disease. There is only climax after climax in this erotic classic, which has survived for over 200 years.

Congreve, William. The Way of the World. Available in Twelve Famous Plays of the Restoration and Eighteenth Century. New York: Modern Library, c. 1960. Drama.

Preg. & Childbirth   Sexuality   Sexual Roles

In this play of dazzling wit, sexuality is limited to the intelligent. The Fools--Witwoud, Petulant, and Sir Wilful Witwoud--are not really interested in women, although Petulant hires women to give him the appearance of an attractive man--to his male friends. Furthermore, some of the more intelligent members of society (Fainall, Marwood) combine lust with cupidity or malice--with the result that they gratify none of their desires. Lady Wishfort is the stereotype of the sex-starved, middle-aged woman, who mistakes her needs for pleasing charms. The jesting contracts between the lovers, Mirabell and Millamant, although parodying the elaborate financial contracts of the day, also foreshadow present-day wedding contracts which specify behavior and duties rather than monetary transfers (IV.i.). Interestingly, it is the prospective husband who makes conditions about pregnancy: "I denounce against all strait lacing, squeezing for a shape, till you mould my boy's head like a sugar-loaf, and instead of a man child, make me father to a crooked billet."

Cowper, William. Memoir. Available in Proc. Amer. Phil. Society. XCVII (1953). 359-82. Treatise.

Madness

The poet describes the onset of his insanity, ostensibly demonstrating that his suffering and madness were a purification sent by God. But, according to B. J. Mandel ("Artistry and Psychology in William Cowper's Memoir." Texas Studies in Language and Literature, 12:431-42.), Cowper longs for insanity before God inflicts it; and his emotionally charged descriptions after his cure indicate that he has not undergone a radical change; he has only found a new outlet for his feelings.

Crabbe, George. The Borough, Letters vii, xvii, xviii, & xxii. Available in Life and Poetical Works of George Crabbe. London: J. Murray, 1901. Long Poem.

Age   By Doctors   Children
Drugs   Madness   Med. Ethics
Med. Instit   Med. Profession   Poverty & Health
Suffering

The subject of Letter vii (296 lines) is the medical profession. The poet praises those physicians who can maintain self-control without becoming insensitive to the patient's suffering: "Men who suppress their feelings, but who feel/The painful symptoms they delight to heal;/Patient in all their trials, they sustain/The starts of passion, the reproach of pain." But such doctors are few: the profession is full of those who write treatises to get fame, those who rely on friends and fashion to get a place, quacks who use the stage and a zany to get patients, and, worst of all, doctors who indiscriminately give out drugs (here drugs begin to have the connotation of addictive medicine). Three-quarters of Letter vii is devoted to an attack on this practice, which wastes time, raises false hopes, and creates addictions. Such drugs are particularly abused in the treatment of women's diseases and in their use to keep children sedated and quiet. Only pride and avarice would bring a doctor to increase his money--and the number of dead patients-- by such means. Letter xvii (277 lines) portrays the ideal hospital, "Where love and science every aid apply," and satirizes the motivations of hospital governing boards--some members led by virtue, but more by remorse, cold wisdom, or mercantile charity. Letter xviii (408 lines) compares the poorhouse and the private houses of the poor as homes for the aged. At first it seems to condemn the poorhouse which, for all its food, airy rooms, and decent beds, is still a prison run by strangers. There are no griefs--and no joys. However, the private houses of the poor are surrounded by polluted paths, ashy heaps, and evil plants. The air is putrefied, the building has tumbled down, naked children run about, sexes, families, and ages are all mixed--and the inhabitants don't try to improve but turn to liquor. The reason Crabbe gives for aiding virtuous old people is rather frightening: we pension out our old horses, so why not old laborers and seamen. Letter xxii (375 lines) is not a treatise but a story of child abuse and madness. When a boy, Peter Grimes rebelled against his father and struck him to the ground; as an adult he takes on apprentice boys whom he tortures to death. He kills four boys before his fellow townspeople take strong action--they won't let him acquire a fifth apprentice! Isolated, Peter gradually goes mad, seeing visions of his father and the murdered boys. Finally, with "Again they come," he mutters and dies.

Crabbe, George. "Fragment, Written at Midnight." Available in Poems, ed. A. W. Ward. Cambridge: University Press, 1905. Poem: 40 lines.

| By Doctors | Drugs | Science & Poetry |

This confused poem seems to have been written under the influence of drugs (Crabbe was a heavy user of opium); it appears to be a struggle between the doctor and the poet. The poem consists of several different voices. There is a speaker who evokes Apollo, "by whose equal aid/The verse is written and the med'cine made." This first speaker orders a quack, whose "fourfold powers,/In triumph scorn this sacred art of ours," to go on his way to "land the stranger in this world of woe." The next (?) speaker passes on and sees the moonlit, restless ocean as an image of his troubled mind, comforted by the Muse "in a flood of light." Then another speaker breaks in: "Why in such haste? . . . If thou 'rt a poet, now indulge the flight/Of thy fine fancy in this dubious light." However, this speaker is denied. "Shall I, preserver deem'd around the place,/With abject rhymes a doctor's name disgrace?" The concluding speaker then takes 14 lines to sing his own praises as a doctor and surgeon and druggist.

Crabbe, George. Inebrity, Parts I & III. Available in The Life and Poetical Works of George Crabbe. London: J. Murray, 1901. Long Poem.

| Alcoholism | By Doctors | Poverty & Health |
| Sexual Roles | | |

Part I (ca. 730 lines) compares the rich, gouty drinker of strong liquor with the poor, healthy drinker of ale. Beer and ale may be vulgar, windy, and heavy--but more sophisticated imbibing causes pain of gout and gravel: "Laugh at poor sots with insolent pretence,/Yet cry when tortured, where is Providence?" Part III (333 lines) asserts that women-drinkers become uncertain about their true sexual role, which is implicitly defined as a proper relationship with men: "How should we tell, when thus you love and hate,/Who acts the Man, and who's effeminate?" Woman's dilemma is set forth in this reworking of Pope's Essay on Man. "Woman's a Being, dubiously great,/Never contented with a passive state;/With too much Knowledge to give Man the sway,/With too much Pride his humours to obey."

Crabbe, George. "The Library," lines 347-418. Available in The Life and Poetical Works of George Crabbe. London: J. Murray, 1901. Poem: 692 lines.

| By Doctors | Med. Profession |

At first the poet describes the medical profession in glowing terms: "Glorious their aim--to ease his labouring heart;/To war with death, and stop his flying dart;/To trace the source whence the fierce contest grew,/And life's short lease on easier terms renew." Then he turns to the deaths caused by the "cures." "For grave deceivers lodge their labours here,/And cloud the science they pretend to clear." Theoreticians and past writers of medical theory mislead the practitioner: "Ye first seducers of my easy heart,/Who promised knowledge ye could not impart."

Crabbe, George. The Parish Register, "Marriages," lines 358-384, 461-499; "Burials," lines 635-730. Available in The Life and Poetical Works of George Crabbe. London: J. Murray, 1901. Long Poem.

Age	The Body	By Doctors
Doctors	Med. Profession	Preg. & Childbirth
Sexuality	Women as Healers	

"Marriages," lines 358-384, is a satirical portrait of two old people, twice married before, who again marry for sex. The description of the two becomes more and more grotesque until they are seen as corpses twitched by an electric shock: "So two cold limbs, touch'd by Galvani's wire,/Move with new life, and feel awaken'd fire;/Quivering awhile, their flaccid forms remain,/Then turn to cold torpidity again." The ideal old couple is found in lines 461-499. Abandoned by their children, they exist to die: "Their graves before

them and their griefs behind,/Have each a med'cine for the rustic mind." In short, death is respectable; sex is not. "Burials," lines 635-730, depicts the triumph of the doctor over the midwife. The woman argues that experience is on her side--look at all the healthy children and adults she has delivered. But the doctor responds that she goes by luck whereas he can alter nature. He gets the custom; she loses income, turns to drink, and dies.

Crabbe, George. "Sir Eustace Grey." Available in The Life and Poetical Works of George Crabbe. London: J. Murray, 1901. Poem: 437 lines.

| By Doctors | Doctors | Madness |

Sir Eustace, who murdered his wife and best friend when he caught them in adultery, has gone mad and is confined in a madhouse, where he is shown to a visitor by a physician-guide. The visitor at first recoils from all this grief, which he cannot heal, but stops to listen to Sir Eustace as he relives the stages of his madness. The physician closes the poem with the reminder that our sanity is worth suffering pain and grief. Therefore, we must stay pure, restrain our fancy's flights, and pray to God.

Crabbe, George. The Village, Book I. Available in The Life and Poetical Works of George Crabbe. London: J. Murray, 1901. Long Poem.

| Age | By Doctors | Doctors |
| Med. Instit. | Poverty & Health | Suffering |

Gone is Goldsmith's respected old countryman: "For now he journeys to his grave in pain;/The rich disdain him, nay, the poor disdain;/Alternate masters now their slave command,/Urge the weak efforts of his feeble hand." The aged poor are found in the workhouse, separated from their spouses and children, visited by the contemptuous parish doctor: "In haste he seeks the bed where Misery lies,/Impatience mark'd in his averted eyes;/And, some habitual queries hurried o'er,/Without reply, he rushes on the door."

Defoe, Daniel. A Journal of the Plague Year. Treatise.

| Death | Med. Instit. | Plague |
| Poverty & Health | Suffering | |

Written in 1721, in part to justify government restrictions on trade aimed at preventing infection from the bubonic plague on the continent. Not surprisingly, therefore, this account of the 1665 plague in London emphasizes loss of property and the efforts of people to escape the city regulations designed to limit the spread of the disease. Defoe's narrator does describe the stages of people's reactions to so much death, and he does react to the sufferings about him. But he is entirely rationalistic and scientific, factually reporting the increases and decreases in the weekly bills of mortality and quoting verbatim from council regulations. One of his recurring concerns is to determine the cause of the contagion, whether by natural means or as God's judgment. Another concern is the greater misery of the poor, deprived of work and the ability to leave the city. But the narrator is always detached, even when recounting the worst sufferings: "It was indeed a lamentable thing to hear the miserable lamentations of poor dying creatures calling out for ministers to comfort them and pray with them, to counsel them . . . . I wish I could repeat the very sound of those groans and of those exclamations that I heard from some poor dying creatures when in the height of their agonies and distress."

Defoe, Daniel. Moll Flanders. Available in Moll Flanders. New York: The Modern Library, 1950. Novel.

| Abortion | Children | Preg. & Childbirth |
| Sexuality | Sexual Roles | |

Moll Flanders (along with Roxanna, another of Defoe's heroines) makes her way in life by marriages (mostly bigamous, one incestuous), prostitution (a little), and theft. She is a strong woman, helping (or completely directing) her husbands' businesses. Her pride at increasing the estate of her Lancashire husband is not only commercial, but sexual self-esteem, for in Moll's world, sexual drives are completely fused with monetary desires. Marriage is both a sexual and a commercial union. In all of these transactions, women have the edge in sexual matters because men have more sexual desire; but men have the edge in commercial matters because women need the security. Children are an indifferent side product of this union. Although Moll falls into tearful ecstasies over her son (by her brother) who holds an estate in trust for her, she abandons other children with small sums given for their maintenance. It is no wonder that a flourishing business can be made in ridding women of unwanted children, by abortion or by farming out the new-born infants. The middle of the novel describes such a business. The pregnant Moll must be credited with indignant rejection of any suggestion of an abortion, and she does insure that her child is not murdered by neglect. It is appropriate that she take greater steps to care for this bastard (though she never fetches the child when she is reunited with its father) than the children of her more "regular" husbands, for six-month-old Moll was abandoned in Newgate prison when her mother was transported for theft.

Dryden, John. <u>All for Love</u>. Available in <u>Six Restoration Plays</u>,
    ed. John Harold Wilson. Boston: Houghton Mifflin, 1959.
    Drama.

| Dying | Sexuality | Sexual Roles |
| Suicide | | |

A dignified, neo-classical vision of Shakespeare's <u>Antony
and Cleopatra</u>, which may lack some of the power of the
earlier play, and certainly lacks some of its glorious
poetry, but nonetheless skillfully uncovers the nature
of the famous lovers' sexuality. It has, of course,
been their undoing. The Egyptian queen proclaims that
passion has made her lose sight of reason, become, in
fact, quite mad, but she is proud of it. Antony has
suffered more, for he, according to the honorable
Ventidius, has been enslaved and therefore unmanned by
his sexual passions; and even seems to be in his dotage,
since he should be by middle age beyond desire. The
bitchy side of sexuality is wittily enacted in an encounter between jealous Cleopatra and Antony's wronged
wife, Octavia. Still there almost seems more passion
in Dryden's death scenes than his love scenes. Cleopatra proclaims, "'Tis sweet to die when they would
force life on me,/To rush into the dark abode of
death,/And seize him first. If he be like my love,/
He is not frightful, sure." The double suicide makes
the second half, at least, of the play's closing line
seem accurate: "No lovers lived so great or died so
well."

Dryden, John. "To Dr. Charleton." Available in <u>Selected Works
    of John Dryden</u>. New York: Holt, Rinehart, & Winston, 1953.
    Poem: 58 lines.

Doctors

This poem reveals the young Dryden's interest in science
and scientists. The man named in the title is not only
a medical practitioner, but also a scientific theoretician: "Such is the healing virtue of your pen,/To perfect cures in books, as well as men." Other English
researchers are praised by the poet for asserting modern
scientific truth against Aristotle's long and erroneous
reign, among them William Harvey, who discovered blood
circulation.

Dryden, John. "To John Driden," especially lines 71-116. Avail-
    able in <u>Selected Works of John Dryden</u>. New York: Holt,
    Rinehart, & Winston, 1953. Poem: 209 lines.

| Age | Disease & Health | Doctors |
| Med. Profession | Sexuality | Sexual Roles |

In this homage to his elderly kinsman, Dryden praises
country life for its natural health-giving attributes,
and denounces both physicians--he names, among others,
"Maurus" (Richard Blackmore), bad poet and bad doctor--
and their underlings, the apothecaries. These last,
mostly unlike Samuel Garth, the poet-physician who
"prescribes and gives," sell their wares and live off
others' destruction. The physicians are no better
than murderers. They are lazy and opposed to the pursuit of life-saving knowledge. Therefore, "He scapes
the best, who, nature to repair,/Draws physic from the
fields, in draughts of vital air." This has Dryden's
kinsman done, and so has survived to a healthy old age,
when he dispenses wisdom and generosity, and, as for
his own needs, now only "tastes of pleasure," whereas
"youth devours." A further reason for his delightful
old age is that he never married one of that weaker
sex ("He to God's image, she to his was made;/So
farther from the fount, the stream at random stray'd");
he knew, so the poet feels, that sexual passion is short-
lived--"a year, a month, perhaps a night"--and is followed by long penitence.

Edwards, Jonathan. "Phebe Bartlet," from <u>Narrative of Surpris-
    ing Conversions</u>. Available in <u>American Literature:
    Tradition and Innovation</u>, Vol. I, eds. Harrison T. Meserole,
    Walter Sutton, and Brom Weber. Lexington, Mass.: D. C.
    Heath, 1969. Essay.

| Children. | Death |

Perhaps the best intellect in 18th-century America,
Jonathan Edwards was also attracted to emotional, even
sentimental, matters. Here, for instance, he details
the religious conversion of a 4-year-old child, whose
most admirable quality seems to be that she weeps
regularly, out of compassion for her fellows and fear
of God. For Edwards little Phebe is also the more
admirable when she is the more precocious: she loves
to go to church; she speaks in a rather mature style;
she even contemplates death, always aware of the short
time one has to live. Her parents, in fact, frequently
ask her--she is 4, recall--whether she is prepared to
die, and usually she answers "yes, without hesitation."

Edwards, Jonathan. "Sinners in the Hands of an Angry God." From
    <u>The American Tradition in Literature</u>, eds. S. Bradley, R. C.
    Beatty, and E. H. Long. 3rd ed. New York: W. W. Norton
    & Co., 1967. 2 Vols. Vol. 1. Treatise.

| Death | Disease & Health | Suffering |

Revival sermon calling on the audience to accept Christ,
for only the will of a wrathful God stands between the
unregenerate and the everlasting pains of hell. The
precariousness of life made terrifyingly vivid. Death
or Health--they lie in His power, not ours: "There is
the dreadful pit of the glowing flames of the wrath of
God; there is Hell's wide gaping mouth open; and you

have nothing to stand upon, nor any thing to take hold
of: there is nothing between you and Hell but the air;
'tis only the power and mere pleasure of God that holds
you up. You . . . look at other things, as the good
state of your bodily constitution, your care of your
own life, and the means you use for your own preservation. But indeed these things are nothing; if God
should withdraw his hand."

Farquhar, George. <u>The Beaux' Stratagem</u>. Available in <u>Plays of
    the Restoration and Eighteenth Century</u>, eds. Dougald Mac-
    Millan and H. M. Jones. New York: Henry Holt & Co., 1931.
    Drama.

| Sexuality | Women as Healers |

The play's plot is highly complex, involving a wife's
attempt to divorce her boorish husband without forfeiting her dowry, the courtship of two impecunious gentlemen trying to recoup their fortunes by marriage, a
delightful catechism of love between the disguised
Archer and Cherry, the innkeeper's daughter, and a
robbery--plus several other confusions. The mother
of the boorish husband, Lady Bountiful, acts as physician to the local country people. The landlord praises
her ("She has cured more People . . . within Ten Years
than the Doctors have kill'd in Twenty; and that's a
bold Word."); the gentlemen laugh at her. She can
listen to a woman's garbled account of her husband's
illness and immediately prescribe the proper cure,
denying her daughter-in-law's mocking assertion that
the cure lies in the patient's faith rather than her
nostrums. Lady Bountiful is used by the lovers to gain
entrance to the ladies. One fakes a "fit" that deceives
no one but the "physician," who takes him into her house
(and the company of the young women) as a patient. The
wife is separated from her husband, but not her dowry,
one gentleman gains his mistress and money, and both
gentlemen gain the favor of their ladies--and the
prospect of the innkeeper's daughter to supplement
their more socially-elevated sexual pleasures.

Fielding, Henry. <u>Amelia</u>, Book III, chapter viii; Book V, i;
    Book VII, viii & ix. Available with original first chapter
    of Book V in <u>The Complete Works</u>, ed. W. E. Henley. New
    York: Barnes & Noble, 1967. Vols. 6 & 7 (<u>Amelia</u>, Vols.
    1 & 2). Novel.

| Doctors | Nurses | Preg. & Childbirth |
| Sexual Roles | V.D. | |

Book III, chapter viii describes two men caring for
two ill women dependent upon them. Colonel Bath is
ashamed when his efforts to nurse his sister are exposed, for he believes that such efforts are unmanly--
until Captain Booth cites cases of famous soldiers who
grieved for their women. Captain Booth is proud of
assisting his wife during her labor; he tells the cynical Miss Mathews "in defiance of your laughter, I lay
behind her bolster, and supported her in my arms; and,
upon my soul, I believe I felt more pain in my mind
than she underwent in her body . . . . do you really
think it a proper time for mirth, when the creature
one loves to distraction is undergoing the most racking
torments, as well as in the most imminent dangers?"
Book V, chapter i appeared only in the first edition.
It compares an apothecary, who frightens Amelia about
the seriousness of her child's disease and who prescribes many drugs, with a physician, who calmly and
simply prescribes a blooding, a clyster, and cooling
physic, which treatment cures the child in three days.
The chapter ends with this curious remark: "Some
readers will, perhaps, think this whole chapter might
have been omitted; but though it contains no great
matter of amusement, it may at least serve to inform
posterity concerning the present state of physic."
Chapters viii and ix of Book VII tell the pathetic
story of a wife, half-seduced and half-raped while
under the influence of drugs and alcohol. Her libertine seducer (who later dies of V.D.) gives her the
disease which she, unknowingly, gives to her husband.
He goes insane with jealousy, but is reconciled to her.
However, the husband dies soon after, and the wife
collapses because she believes the cause of his death
to be the injuries self-inflicted in his insane jealousy.
The surgeon calms her by insisting that his death was
unrelated to those injuries, that her husband died of
a polyp in his heart.

Fielding, Henry. <u>Joseph Andrews</u>. Novel.

| Doctors | Sexuality | Sexual Roles |
| V.D. | | |

The novel begins (Book I, chapters iv-viii) as a
parody of the mercenary female "virtue" (which is
solely chastity) so feelingly set forth in Richardson's <u>Pamela</u>. Fielding invents Joseph, Pamela's
brother, whose chastity is assaulted by Lady Booby
and her maid, Mrs. Slipslop. When he demurs, citing
his virtue, "'I am out of patience,' cries the lady:
'did ever mortal hear of a man's virtue!'" However,
the novel drops this parody, taking up the adventures
of Joseph, his true love, Fanny, and their friends,
the incomparable Parson Adams. There is the usual
Fielding satire upon the doctor who starts out of
bed to rush to an accident victim--until he learns
the victim is poor, when he turns back to sleep again
(Book I, chapter xii) and the surgeon who makes the
wound seem worse than it really is, to gain more fame
and pay (Book I, chapter xv). This surgeon disputes

with Parson Adams, supporting his professional mystique with two Latin tags from Homer and the names of Galen and Hippocrates, while Adams claims that his reading of modern authors has made him acquainted with medicine and surgery. Since the surgeon's diagnosis is proved incorrect, it would seem that the honors go to Adams (Book I, chapter xiv). V.D. causes Betty the Chambermaid to live a moral life: "At length, having perfectly recovered the effect of her first unhappy passion, she seemed to have vowed a state of perpetual chastity. She was long deaf to all the sufferings of her lovers, till one day . . . . " (Book I, chapter xviii). Wilson, the hero of a subplot, has three encounters with V.D., each time worse than the one before. He becomes a misogynist, until he meets the woman he makes his wife and is overcome by her intelligence, her sweetness, her loyalty, and drawn into a friendship closer than any male alliance, by their children. They have an ideal marriage.

Fielding, Henry. A Journey From This World To The Next, Chapters I-III. From The History of the Life of the Late Jonathan Wild The Great and A Journey From This World To The Next. London: Hutchinson & Co., n.d. Sketches.

Death   Disease & Health   V.D.

Satiric nonsense. The author dies, and his spirit boards a coach for the other world. One of his fellow passengers was killed by a doctor's efforts to cure his smallpox, and another, convinced her innoculation will preserve her against the pox, danced all night and died of a fever; a third spent his life in fear of smallpox, only to die of a surfeit of mussels. Prevention is more deadly than the disease. The coach stops off in the city of Disease, and the author goes looking for the disease, Fever on the Spirits, which had killed him. He is led to Consumption, Dropsy, Rheumatism, Intemperance, and Misfortune before he learns that the disease is the Maladie Alamode, who lives in a most pleasant house. It becomes clear from the symptoms (the lady has no nose and many pimples) that the illness in question is V.D. The lady praises those who try to extirpate religion and virtue and those parents who marry their children very young and without love between the proposed husband and wife: "if these fashions continued to spread, she doubted not but she should shortly be the only disease who would ever receive a visit from any person of considerable rank."

Fielding, Henry. "An Old Man Taught Wisdom or, The Virgin Unmasked. A Farce." Available in The Complete Works, ed. W. E. Henley. New York: Barnes & Noble, 1967. Vol. 10 ("Plays & Poems," Vol. 3). Drama.

Doctors   Sexuality

Whether or not medical training adversely affects sexuality, Fielding (and Molière and Swift) here implies that it does. An old man decides to give his lovely young daughter--and his fortune--to whichever of his poor relations she likes best. She is interviewed by the apothecary, Blister, a dancing master, a singing master, and a lawyer. All use professional jargon in their courtship, but the last three do so with some feeling and polish. Blister is incapable of going beyond his profession. "'How do you do? Let me feel your pulse. How do you sleep o' nights?' 'How? why, upon my back generally' . . . . 'Hum! Pray, how long do you usually sleep?' 'About ten or eleven hours.' 'Is your stomach good? Do you eat with an appetite? How often do you find in a day any inclination to eat?'"

Fielding, Henry. Tom Jones. Novel.

Adolescence   Children   Death
Doctors   Sexuality   Sexual Roles

In Book I, chapter iii, the infant Tom, through his innocence and helplessness, captures the goodwill of Mr. Allworthy, despite the handicap of bastardy. Book III contrasts the childhood and adolescence of the open, good-hearted, naive Tom and the cold, designing Blifil. Although the two youths indulge in the activities of childhood and adolescence--school, catching birds, discovering the opposite sex--they seem more like miniature adults than children. The ignorant and irascible Squire Western asserts authority over his beloved daughter, Sophia, because she is his child: "Did not I beget her? did not I beget her? . . . . But I believe you will allow me to be her father, and if I be, am I not to govern my own child? I ask you that, am I not to govern my own child?" (Book XVII, chapter iii). Sophia's lover, Tom, also falls afoul of proper parent-child relationships, when he, as he believes, inadvertently goes to bed with his own mother. However, Fielding finally relieves Tom of the sin of incest. There are a number of greedy and meddlesome doctors in the novel. A pair of doctors treat the dead Captain Blifil and his widow, overcome with "grief." "So little then did our doctors delight in death, that they discharged the corpse after a single fee; but they were not so disgusted with their living patient; concerning whose case they immediately agreed, and fell to prescribing with great diligence" (Book II, chapter ix). A surgeon gives a painful and incoherent lecture on broken limbs while setting Tom's arm (Book IV, chapter xiv). The doctors treating the grievously ill Allworthy are more sensible, one even endeavoring to prevent young Blifil from giving Allworthy harmful news (Book V, chapters vii & viii).

However, a surgeon treating Tom's head injury toadies to the landlady, prescribing a diet most profitable to her, only to abandon Tom's case when he hears that he is poor and refuses to be bled (Book VII, chapter xiii; Book VIII, chapter iii). Tom's treatment is taken over by Partridge, the barber-surgeon, who insists on mimicking the absurd manners of the medical profession while caring for Tom in his capacity as surgeon, but is better than the surgeon who abandoned Tom. Finally, Tom is once more injured by a surgeon who exaggerates the extent of Mr. Fitzpatrick's wounds to make his cure the more astounding and profitable--thereby enabling Tom's enemies to imprison him for Fitzpatrick's murder (Book XVI, chapter x). Tom faces all of his troubles with some of the calm intrepidity with which Mr. Allworthy faces death: "this unwillingness to quit our friends is the most amiable motive from which we can derive the fear of death . . . . But, alas! he who escapes from death is not pardoned; he is only reprieved, and reprieved to a short day" (Book V, chapter vii). Both Tom and Sophia are treated as sexual objects during the novel--Tom rather more than Sophia, for whereas Sophia's money and virtues raise the appetites of young Blifil and Lord Fellamar, it is Tom's person alone that arouses appetites like that of Mrs. Waters, as seen in the delightful gastronomic-amorous attack unleased in the Upton tavern (Book IX, chapters v & vi). Although Sophia defers constantly to the men about her (Fielding praises her for this), she is unique in the novel. Most of the women are aggressive (the mock epic battle of women in the churchyard, Book IV, chapter viii, is a good example), and it is a woman who argues in favor of a rape (Book XV, chapter iv). Fielding further plays with our stereotypes of women, causing us to laugh at the prudish behavior of the old maid, Mrs. Brigit, who makes so valiant a defense of an undesired citadel-- only to turn the tables on the reader by proving Mrs. Brigit to be Tom's mother. Ugly old maids may have bastards too.

Fielding, Henry. Voyage to Lisbon. Available in Jonathan Wild; The Journal of a Voyage to Lisbon. New York: Dutton, 1964. Journal.

Disease & Health   Dying   Suffering

A record of Henry Fielding's voyage to death. His own introduction self-pityingly notes his great physical deterioration, the result of his extraordinary efforts to introduce preventive (as opposed to punitive) crime control in London. (The novelist and his blind brother, "The Blind Beak," were very conscientious and useful magistrates.) Having extirpated the gangs of cutthroats responsible for street-robberies, he retired into the country "in a very weak and deplorable condition, with no fewer or less diseases than a jaundice, a dropsy, and an asthma, altogether uniting their forces in the destruction of a body so entirely emaciated that it had lost all its muscular flesh." Fielding is sent to Lisbon to recover in the warm climate; he died soon after he arrived, soon after he finished this journal. He knew that he was close to death, that warm Lisbon would only give him that chance for life, which a cold English winter would certainly deny him. He had to be continually "tapped" for his dropsy, and he records the number of quarts released with a sort of pride in the amount. One of the reasons he so fretted at the captain's delays in London was that he feared the accumulation of liquid in his tissues on the voyage would kill him before he could reach a doctor in Lisbon. The journal is one stream of outrage at rude customs officials, greedy and rude innkeepers, the captain with his rude contempt for passengers and his continual delays, the boatsmen who rudely demand inordinate fees for bringing fresh produce to the boat, and his wife and daughter whose sea-sickness prevents them from providing him with the companionship he constantly required. He fusses about his wife's toothache, which began in London where she was kept from treatment by the pilot's refusal to hold up the ship. At Gravesend, she was persuaded that the tooth was too awkwardly placed to be drawn, only to be forced by pain to try another toothdrawer farther along the coast who tries unsuccessfully to remove the tooth. Then Fielding, who has recounted how he suffered along with his wife, drops the subject, and we never know how she managed. The journal is full of witty sarcasms and keen observations, tempered by a fretful temper. Yet even this peevishness is suspect as a mask, for Fielding occasionally breaks out from under the complaints. For example, on July 21 (July 26 Journal time) he has a shouting dispute with the captain, whose rage he subdues with greater rage on his own part. The captain begs forgiveness on his knees, and Fielding forgives him--not, as he says, as a Christian but "To speak truth, I forgave him from a motive which would make men much more forgiving if they were much wiser than they are, because it was convenient for me to do so."

Franklin, Benjamin. Autobiography. Autobiography.

Disease & Health   Dying   V.D.

Three short entries may be of interest: he speaks of a brush with death, his fear of V.D., and his regret that he had not innoculated one of his sons: 1) "My Distemper was a Pleurisy, which very nearly carried me off: I suffered a good deal, gave up the Point in my own mind, & was rather disappointed when I found my Self recovering; regretting in some degree

that I must now some time or other have all that disagreeable Work to do over again" (February, 1726);
2) "In the mean time, that hard-to-be-governed Passion
of Youth, had hurried me frequently into Intrigues with
low Women that fell in my Way, which were attended with
some Expence & great Inconvenience, besides a continual
Risque to my Health by a Distemper which of all Things
I dreaded, tho' by great good Luck I escaped it" (Part I);
3) "In 1736 I lost one of my Sons, a fine Boy of 4 Years
old, by the Small Pox taken in the common way. I long
regretted bitterly & still regret that I had not given
it to him by Innoculation; This I mention for the Sake
of Parents, who omit that Operation on the Supposition
that they should never forgive themselves if a Child
died under it; my Example showing that the Regret may
be the same either way, and that therefore the safer
should be chosen" (Part II).

Franklin, Benjamin. "Dialogue Between the Gout and M. Franklin."
Available in translation in Benjamin Franklin, ed. F. L.
Mott and C. E. Jorgenson. New York: American Book Co.,
1936. Essay.

   Disease & Health   Doctors

   This charming piece was a reply, written in French, to
a verse fable, La Sage et la Goutte, sent to Franklin
by Mme. Billon. In La Sage et la Goutte, the Gout
accuses the Sage of gluttony, adultery, and excessive
chess playing. (The Sage responds that one should enjoy
heaven's gifts--and he doesn't always win at chess.)
Franklin's gout makes the same sort of accusations,
accompanying them with twinges of pain, but adds the
accusation that Franklin doesn't exercise enough, giving
a very professional explanation of the need for exercise.
"The heat produced in any given time depends on the
degree of this acceleration [of the blood stream]; the
fluids are shaken, the humours are attenuated, the
secretions facilitated, and all goes well; the cheeks
are ruddy, and health is established." "M. Franklin"
finds the discourse tedious; but twinges in his foot
restore his attention, and he finally admits to neglecting exercise. The disease claims to be his physician.
"Is it not I who, in the character of your physician,
have saved you from the palsy, dropsy, and apoplexy?
One or the other of which would have done for you long
ago but for me." Franklin claims that he's been a
friend to the disease: "Permit to hint that I have
also not been unfriendly to you. I never feed physician or quack of any kind." The Gout replies that the
physicians are finally convinced that, for such a man
as "M. Franklin," the gout isn't a disease, but a
remedy: "and wherefore cure a remedy?"

Franklin, Benjamin. Poor Richard: The Almanacks for the Years
1733-1758. New York: The Heritage Press, 1964. Treatise.

   Death   Disease & Health   Doctors
   Suicide   V.D.   Women as Healers

   The Almanacs contain a good deal of commentary on medical care and prescribe a temperate and rational life
style as preventive medicine. There is no feeling
that a rich, temperate life style is healthier than
a poor one. Medicine was not believed to prolong life:
"Can those [Heaps of Gold] (when tortur'd by Disease)/
Chear our sick Heart, or purchase Ease?/Can those prolong one Gasp of Breath,/Or calm the troubled Hour of
Death?" (June, 1740). "Death takes no bribes" (July,
1742). However, the Almanacs were full of advice on
ways to cope with or avoid disease: "When you are
sick, what you like best is to be chosen for a Medicine in the first Place; what Experience tells you is
best, is to be chosen in the second Place; what Reason
(i.e. Theory) says is best, is to be chosen in the last
Place. But if you can get Dr. Inclination, Dr. Experience and Dr. Reason to hold a Consultation together,
they will give you the best Advice that can be given"
(November, 1736). The December 1742 issue gave three
pages of advice about how to adapt your diet to your
way of life and how to live temperately and long. It
is not unexpected that a belief in life style as medicine should be accompanied by a distrust of physicians:
"Beware of the young Doctor & the old Barber" (May,
1773). "He's the best physician that knows the worthlessness of the most medicines" (September, 1733). "God
heals, and the Doctor takes the Fees" (November, 1736).
But Franklin does give this advice: "To Friend, Lawyer,
Doctor, tell plain your whole Case;/Nor think on bad
Matters to put a good Face;/How can they advise, if they
see but a Part?/'Tis very ill driving black Hogs in the
dark" (July, 1748). He also quotes Dr. Rabelais: "There's
more old Drunkards than old Doctors" (April, 1736). The
Almanac makes this cryptic reference to suicide: "9 Men
in 10 are suicides" (October, 1749). It makes a jest
about V.D.: "Some of our Sparks to London town do go/
Fashions to see, and learn the World to know;/Who at
Return have nought but these to show,/New Wig above, and
new Disease below . . . . But home returned, Fashions he
had none,/Only his Main and Tail were larger grown." Perhaps most interesting are the praises of women as nurses
(September & October, 1748). However, their nursing care
is dispensed as a charity; women ought to acquire medical
skills, but, the implication is, not as professionals.
"Cordials and Med'cines gratis to dispense,/A beauteous
Instrument of Providence;/Plaisters, and Salves, and
Sores, to understand,/The Surgeon's Art befits a tender
Hand."

Freneau, Philip. "The Blessings of the Poppy." Available in The
Poems of Philip Freneau, ed. F. L. Pattee. New York: Russell
& Russell, 1963. 3 Vols. Poem: 24 lines.

   Drugs   Suffering

   Pre-romantic view of opium--as relief from pain rather
than a door to new insights. "Conscious of pains they
knew not how to cure,/In vain they sighed, and sighing
begged relief,/No druggist came, by art or reason
taught/With strength of potent herbs, to calm their
grief./From other worlds . . . Receive a gift, all
worthy of a god,/Since pain, when hushed to sleep,--
is pain no more."

Freneau, Philip. "The British Prison Ship." Available in
A Freneau Sampler, ed. P. M. Marsh. New York: Scarecrow
Press, 1963. Poem: ca. 200 lines.

   Doctors   Suffering

   Partisan piece relating the sufferings of American
prisoners of war. (Freneau was imprisoned on such a
ship during the revolutionary war.) He seems to be
blaming the British for doing unto the prisoners what
he would like to do unto the British. One of the torments of the ship is the incompetent Hessian doctor who
experiments with and takes out his rage upon the inmates:
"Till the lean patient at the potion frown'd,/And swore
that hemlock, death, or what you will,/Were nonsense to
the drugs that stuff'd his bill./On those refusing he
bestow'd a kick . . . Here uncontroul'd he exercis'd
his trade,/And grew experienced by the deaths he made."

Freneau, Philip. Expedition of Timothy Taurus. Available in
The Poems of Philip Freneau, ed. F. L. Pattee. New York:
Russell & Russell, 1963. Vol. 1. Poem: ca. 400 lines.

   Doctors

   One section criticizes a doctor who haunts the health
spa trying to create business: "Here was Doctor Sangrado, with potion and pill,/And his prize was the
same, to recover or kill./He waddled about, and was
vext to the soul/To see so much health in this horrible
hole." He tries to persuade the landlord's son that he
feels ill, but is scornfully rejected. Late 18th-century
literature contains a number of Dr. Sangrados, continually
concerned with drumming up business, while incompetently
bleeding and slaughtering those patients in their care.
The immediate source of these death-bringers is LeSage's
bloody theorist in Gil Blas.

Freneau, Philip. The House of Night. Available in A Freneau
Sampler, ed. P. M. Marsh. New York: Scarecrow Press, 1963.
Poem: 136 stanzas.

   Death   Sexuality

   The death pangs of Death, who is portrayed as a human--
raging at his physicians, taking pills, suffering from
loneliness, crying for drink, dickering with an undertaker, and cursing his fate. Death is consoled by
memory of all his victories and the reminder that the
British will carry on his work, and then: "'All hell
demands me hence,' he said, and threw/The red lamp
hissing through the midnight air." The poem as a
whole is not good. It tries to do too much--burlesque
on death, outrage at the British, satire on the hypocritical church and on undertakers, and a Moral Message
to the reader. However, individual stanzas are intriguing, such as this forerunner of Poe spoken by
Death's nurse, a lover who has lost his lady to Death:
"Yet stranger, hold--her charms are so divine,/Such
tints of life still on her visage glow,/That even in
death this slumbering bride of mine/May seize thy heart,
and make thee wretched too."

Freneau, Philip. "The Indian Burying Ground." Available in
A Freneau Sampler, ed. P. M. Marsh. New York: Scarecrow
Press, 1963. Poem: 40 lines.

   Death

   More archeological musings on death in the tradition of
Thomas Browne's Urn-Burial. This is interesting for
its implication that the body, even after death, affects
the soul: "I still my old opinion keep;/The posture
that we give the dead,/Points out the soul's eternal
sleep." The grave itself confers a sort of immortality:
"His bow, for action ready bent,/And arrows with a head
of stone,/Can only mean that life is spent,/And not the
old ideas are gone."

Freneau, Philip. "Ode XI, To the Philadelphia Doctors" and "On
the Free Use of the Lancet." Available in The Poems of
Philip Freneau, ed. F. L. Pattee. New York: Russell &
Russell, 1963. Vol. 3. Poems: 32 & 30 lines.

   Doctors   Med. Profession   Women as Healers

   Each poem attacks the medical profession for insisting
upon bleeding as obligatory treatment. Each poem ends
with the herb woman who saves where the doctor kills:
"The secret has leak'd out--be cautious doctors/(The
whole shall be disclos'd in room with lock'd doors)/
Old women, with their simple herbs and teas/(And asking hardly two-pence for their fees)/Disarm this
dreadful epidemic fever;/Make it as tame and innocent,/
(Whether home-bred or from West Indies sent)/As Continental soldier, turn'd to Weaver" ("Ode XI").

Freneau, Philip. "On Dr. Sangrado's Flight." Available in The
Poems of Philip Freneau, ed. F. L. Pattee. New York: Russell
& Russell, 1963. Vol. 3. Poem: 30 lines.

Doctors   Med. Ethics   Plague

This poem, in its 1797 form, criticizes Dr. Sangrado,
who fled from the Philadelphia Yellow Fever epidemic.
However, the original poem (1793), entitled "Orlando's
Flight," satirizes a politician who fled the city to
the comforts of the country, instead of remaining to
govern the plague-stricken city. Freneau makes very
few changes in the poem--the doctor and the politician
are apparently equally culpable in deserting their posts.

Garth, Samuel. The Dispensary. From The Poems of Garth and
Tickell. Chiswick: C. Whittingham, 1822. Poem: ca. 2,000
lines.

By Doctors   Disease & Health   Doctors
Drugs   Dying   Evil Doctors
Med. Ethics   Med. Profession   Poverty & Health

Poetry as propaganda for fighting within the medical profession. In the late 17th century, some London physicians
wanted to provide free health care for the poor. They
found their efforts frustrated by the high cost of medicines and so tried to open a dispensary for the poor.
The Apothecaries objected and fomented discord among
the physicians in an attempt, which finally proved
successful, to close the dispensary. This satire on
the venial doctors and apothecaries opposed to the dispensary appeared in the middle of the controversy. The
poem is somewhat confused, with several Furies interfering in the action and with lengthy digressions on the
merits of literary authors, past and present. However,
the poem does contain some insights and a good deal of
medical vituperation. Canto I lauds true medicine, which
learns from nature: "Why bilious juice a golden light
puts on,/And floods of chyle in silver currents run;/
How the dim speck of entity began/To' extend its recent
form, and stretch to man . . . . Hence 'tis we wait the
wondrous cause to find,/How body acts upon impassive
mind." Canto II attacks the apothecaries, particularly
"Colon" (Birch) and "Horoscope" (Houghton). "Colon"
"Murders with jargon where medicine fails." "Horoscope"
supplements his astrology with drugs, primarily for
illicit purposes: "Some by what means they may redress
their wrong,/When fathers the possession keep too long
. . . . Poor pregnant Lais his advice would have,/To
lose by art what fruitful nature gave . . . . Young
Hylas, botch'd with stains too foul to name,/In cradle
here renews his youthful frame." The apothecaries fear
that the physicians will reveal the truths about them:
"If they should once unmask our mystery,/Each nurse, ere
long, would be as learn'd as we;/Our art exposed to
every vulgar eye,/And none, in complaisance to us, would
die . . . . Nay, they discover too, their spite is such,/
That health, than crowns more valued, costs not much."
Canto III continues the satire upon the apothecaries,
but has an invocation to Disease that represents the
18th-century belief that poverty was healthy: "Begot
by Sloth, maintain'd by Luxury,/In gilded palaces thy
prowess reigns,/But flies the humble sheds of cottage
swains." The apothecaries lament the passing of those
golden days "When, dear as Burgundy, ptisans were sold;/
When patients chose to die with better will/Than breathe,
and pay the' apothecary's bill." One apothecary advocates union with the physicians, but is attacked by
another who notes that fear of dying sends them many
customers: "The wise through thought the' insults of
death defy;/The fools, through bless'd insensibility./
'Tis what the guilty fear, the pious crave;/Sought by
the wretch, and vanquish'd by the brave." The apothecaries find allies among the evil doctors (Canto IV).
"Mirmillo" (Dr. Gibbons) boasts: "Whilst others meanly
ask'd whole months to slay,/I oft dispatch'd the patient
in a day . . . . Some fell by laudanum, and some by
steel,/And death in ambush lay in every pill." Dr. Richard Blackmore (author of Creation) endeavors to invoke
the Sibyl, Disease, with his verse; she does appear--
to make pungent comment on his verse, advising him to
take the works of Wycherley and Dryden for models.
Disease sends "Horoscope" to Fortune. Meanwhile, Discord incites "Mirmillo" to battle. The physicians
boast among themselves about their abilities and then
fall into battle: "The piercing caustics ply their
spiteful power;/Emetics ranch, and keen cathartics
scour:/The deadly drugs in double doses fly;/And
pestles peal a martial symphony." Ironically, it is
Health that ends the battle (Canto VI), ordering the
doctors to seek Harvey in the Elysian fields. The
doctors descend through the earth, passing the worst
diseases, until they reach Harvey who condemns 17th-
century medicine: "With just resentment and contempt
you see/The foul dissensions of the Faculty:/How your
sad sickening art now hangs her head,/And, once a
science, is become a trade." Harvey advises them to
seek the patronage of Lord Somers, whose virtues are
listed at length to end the poem.

Goldsmith, Oliver. "The Deserted Village," lines 85-140. Available in Goldsmith's Poems and Plays. New York: E. P. Dutton,
1966. Poem: 55 lines.

Age   By Doctors   Dying

In the past, the little community provided a respected
place for the old and comfort for the dying. Now, with
the coming of the industrial age, the community is
deserted except for "yon widow'd, solitary thing,/That

feebly bends beside the plashy spring;/She, wretched matron,
forc'd in age, for bread,/To strip the brook with mantling
cresses spread . . . To seek her nightly shed, and weep
till morn."

Goldsmith, Oliver. She Stoops to Conquer. Available in Eighteenth-
Century Plays, ed. Ricardo Quintana. New York: Modern Library,
1952. Drama.

By Doctors   Children   Disease & Health
Sexuality

In the prologue, Goldsmith has himself proclaimed as a
doctor, not for the body but for the comic muse, who is
ill, through being sentimentalized by some of Goldsmith's
contemporaries. He extends the metaphor in this way:
"This truth he boasts, will boast it while he lives,/No
pois'nous drugs are mix'd in what gives./Should he succeed,
you'll give him his degree;/If not, within he will receive
no fee!/The college you, must his pretensions try,/Pro-
nounce him regular, or dub him quack." Goldsmith continues his satirical attack on sentimental comedy in the
character of Mrs. Hardcastle's son, Tony Lumpkin, who
looks the healthy opposite of a conventionally sentimental
son, though his mother persists in thinking him consumptive.
Furthermore, he is hardly devoted to his mother in the
sentimental fashion, but contrives instead to deceive her
and make her look the fool. Goldsmith is also more realistic than sentimental in his treatment of sexuality, for
his hero, Marlow, finds that he is·shy before women of
his own station, but easily amorous with women of a lower
rank.

Goldsmith, Oliver. The Vicar of Wakefield. Novel.

By Doctors   Dying   Sexual Roles
Suffering

The book follows the ever-increasing misfortunes of a
country parson and his family. Just before the de-
nouement, he is in prison for debt, accompanied by
his family (except for a son imprisoned for murder
and a daughter mysteriously abducted), with his other
daughter seduced and betrayed and his house burned to
the ground. The parson meets his troubles with calm fortitude, preaching a sermon to his fellow prisoners: "Thus
providence has given the wretched two advantages over
the happy in this life, greater felicity in dying ["for
after a certain degree of pain, every new breach that
death opens in the constitution, nature kindly covers
with insensibility"], and in heaven all that superiority
of pleasure which arises from contrasted enjoyment." A
Deus ex machina called Sir William Thornhill then saves
the family. Olivia, the daughter who was seduced and
abandoned, is persuaded (by her mother to please her
father!) to sing the following beautiful song on the
ugly theme that, for a woman, a premarital affair means
death (the novel does not implement the song): "When
lovely woman stoops to folly,/And finds too late that
men betray,/What charm can soothe her melancholy,/What
art can wash her guilt away?/The only art her guilt to
cover,/To hide her shame from every eye,/To give repentance to her lover,/And wring his bosom--is to die."

Gray, Thomas. "Elegy Written in a Country Church Yard." Available in The Complete Poems of Thomas Gray, eds. H. W. Starr
and J. R. Hendrickson. Oxford: Clarendon Press, 1966.
Poem: 128 lines.

Death   Grief

It is not fame enblazoned in "storied urn or animated
bust" that gives solace to the dead and to the living
who must face death, for fame does not truly represent
worth. These simple country people have been denied
knowledge and have been repressed by want, so that
this country churchyard may harbor "Some mute inglorious
Milton" or "Some Cromwell guiltless of his country's
blood." It is grief, not fame, that consoles: "On
some fond breast the parting soul relies,/Some pious
drops the closing eye requires;/Ev'n from the tomb
the voice of Nature cries,/Ev'n in our Ashes live
their wonted Fires." The fame of kindly remembrance
by "some hoary-headed Swain" is sufficient memorial
for the poet.

Gray, Thomas. "Ode on a Distant Prospect of Eton College." Available in The Complete Poems of Thomas Gray, eds. H. W. Starr
and J. R. Hendrickson. Oxford: Clarendon Press, 1966. Poem:
100 lines.

Children   Suffering

Childhood as free from pain, a happy prelude to a manhood full of physical and emotional suffering. "Alas,
regardless of their doom,/The little victims play! . . .
Ah, shew them where in ambush stand/To seize their prey
the murth'rous band!/Ah, tell them, they are men! . . .
where ignorance is bliss,/'Tis folly to be wise."

Green, Matthew. "The Spleen." From The Poetical Works of Armstrong, Dyer and Green, ed. George Gilfillan. Edinburgh:
James Nichol, 1858. Poem: 835 lines.

Disease & Health   Madness

A second-rate cross between Burton's Anatomy of Melancholy and any early 18th-century satire. The poem sets
out to describe the means by which the poet keeps free
of "The Spleen," here a synonym for depression. His
life follows common 18th-century rules of preventive
medicine: it is a temperate, country life, free from
harmful passion. The poem also describes, in some detail, the follies of others that the poet complacently
avoids.

Johnson, Samuel. "The Death of Friends," from The Idler (No. 41, 27 January 1759). Available in Rasselas, Poems, and Selected Prose, ed. Bertrand H. Bronson. New York: Holt, Rinehart, & Winston, 1958. Essay.

Death   Grief

Occasioned by the death of Dr. Johnson's mother, this short essay is a simple, direct, and moving statement of grief. Johnson speculates, as many have before and since, that the death of a friend is a calamity that we cannot adequately prepare for, and that every man thinks, in the face of all evidence, that he may live on and on. But Johnson becomes more original when he suggests that the speculative reasoner, "whose eye wanders over life," is perhaps the least prepared for disasters at the doorstep. And he becomes sublime when he writes lines like these: "The life which made my own life pleasant is at an end, and the gates of death are shut upon my prospects. The loss of a friend upon whom the heart was fixed, to whom every wish and endeavour tended, is a state of dreary desolation in which the mind looks abroad impatient of itself, and finds nothing but emptiness and horror. The blameless life, the artless tenderness, the pious simplicity, the modest resignation, the patient sickness, and the quiet death, are remembered only to add value to the loss, to aggravate regret for what cannot be amended, to deepen sorrow for what cannot be recalled." Johnson turns, therefore, away from Epicurus and Zeno, and towards God, for "Philosophy may infuse stubbornness, but Religion only can give patience."

Johnson, Samuel. A Dictionary of the English Language. London, 1755. Available in a facsimile edition from AMS Press, New York. Dictionary.

Abortion   Disease & Health   Grief
Med. Profession   Sexuality   Suffering

It is interesting to see the differences time and the medical profession have made in the definitions of these words. Medicine and language interact. For Johnson, an abortion is "The act of bringing forth untimely; The produce of untimely birth." Webster's Third International Dictionary adds "non viable fetus," "12 weeks of gestation," and "criminal expulsion" to his simple definition. For Johnson, disease and health are moral as well as physical states; the body barely enters the definition. Health is defined as "Freedom from bodily pain or sickness; Welfare of mind, purity, goodness, principle of salvation; Salvation, spiritual and temporal, Wish of happiness in drinking." His idea of "doctor" is colored by the earlier use of the term for divines, but even his definition of "physician" lacks our professionalism. "Doctor" is "One that has taken the highest degree in the faculties of divinity, law, or physick; A man skilled in any profession; A physician, one who undertakes the cure of diseases; Any able or learned man." "A physician is "One who professes the art of healing." Johnson's definitions of grief, pain, and suffering are much shorter than ours with a greater separation between the pain and the body or person suffering. "Grief" is "Sorrow, trouble for something past; Grievance, harm; Pain, disease." "Pain" has several definitions: "Punishment denounced; Penalty, punishment; Sensation of uneasiness; Labour, work, toil; Labour, talk; Uneasiness of mind; The throws of childbirth." "Suffering" is simply "pain suffered."

Johnson, Samuel. "On the Death of Mr. Robert Levet." Available in The Poems of Samuel Johnson, eds. D. N. Smith and E. L. McAdam. 2nd ed. Oxford: Clarendon Press, 1974. Poem: 36 lines.

Doctors   Dying

Old Doctor Levet (he was in his eighties when he died) served as a sort of personal physician--and friend-- to Johnson and his household. In this poem Johnson praises Levet's unaffected, kindly, and skillful medical practice: "When fainting nature call'd for aid,/ And hov'ring death prepar'd the blow,/His vig'rous remedy display'd/The power of art without the show." Levet's swift and unexpected death is enviable: "Then with no throbbing fiery pain,/No cold gradations of decay,/Death broke at once the vital chain,/And free'd his soul the nearest way."

Johnson, Samuel. Rasselas, eds. Geoffrey Tillotson and Brian Jenkins. London: Oxford University Press, 1971. Tale.

The Family   Grief   Madness
Suffering

A mild Candide. Discontent and injustice are inescapable and irradicable--they are inherent in the human race. No matter how well a man knows how to withstand grief, he is helpless when he feels it, as in the case of the wise man made inconsolable by his daughter's death (Book I, chapter xviii). However, time works as well as wisdom in reducing grief, as the Princess finds when she mourns for the loss of Pekuah (Book II, chapter xxxv). Although the mad astronomer appears a special case, he illustrates the dangers of the imagination--the madness that awaits all men, whether as a limited seizure or as continual irrationality in a few affairs. Insanity is often cured by the company of others. (For Johnson, isolation was a major cause of madness. Perhaps his gregariousness was self-therapy.) Although in Rasselas the family is disordered by tensions

between the old and the young, the single person also suffers by wasting time in dreams and by becoming peevish. Unlike Voltaire's Candide in which social systems cause much of the suffering, Rasselas shows all social organization helpless before man's restlessness and insatiable desire.

Lacy, John. The Dumb Lady. Available in The Dramatic Works of John Lacy. Edinburgh: W. Paterson, 1975. Drama.

Disease & Health   Med. Instit.   Med. Profession

An adaptation from Molière's Médicin Malgré Lui. Lacy places more emphasis upon the farrier training of the man forced to play doctor, making it seem as though a veterinarian plays physician. Again, as in Aphra Behn's adaptation of Molière, the satire is diluted by the addition of lovers. However, the fifth act does mock methods used to gain a large practice (be called out of Church, treat bawds), medical jargon, and the blind belief in the authority of the doctor which enables the "physician" to persuade a man that his heart lies on his right side. Also, Lacy has added the easy commitment to Bedlam, with the attendant's grim assertion that Bedlam contains only mad people--the whips, bread, and straw insure insanity.

LeSage, Alain René. The Adventures of Gil Blas of Santillane. New York: E. P. Dutton & Co., 1910. Tale.

Doctors   Evil Doctors   Med. Profession

The wandering servant, Gil Blas, encounters many doctors in the course of his adventures--all but two of the doctors being charlatans and killers. The main butt is Dr. Sangrado, whom we first meet in Book II, chapter ii. He is pompous and firmly dedicated to the theory that warm water, bleeding, and dieting cure all ills. The doctor sets up Gil Blas as his fellow "doctor," serving the middle-class while Sangrado limits his practice to the clergy and nobility. Sangrado does not keep up his belief in his theory, but has too much pride to make a public retraction. In Book IV, chapter i, the conscience of this trickster and thief, Gil Blas, reproaches him mainly for being a physician. Don Vincent was killed "Because his physician did not understand Greek" (Book IV, chapter iii). Don Alphonso becomes ill; luckily there are no doctors in the place (Book VI, chapter iii). Gil Blas becomes ill and notes that we may laugh at doctors when we're well, but we obey them when we're ill. He is ruined by their exaggerated fees (Book VII, chapter xvi). He becomes ill again, and being suicidal, is grateful when a friend sends for a physician. After this doctor abandons Gil Blas for his poverty, nature takes over and he lives (Book IX, chapter viii). The two doctors exempt from criticism are Dr. Cuchillo (knife) who is not jealous because he's too tired from rounds (Book II, chapter iv) and a surgeon who dresses wounds and correctly predicts which will be the worst wound (Book XI, chapter xiii).

Mackenzie, Henry. The Man of Feeling. Novel.

Death   Madness   Sexuality
Suffering

The sentimental novel carried to the extreme: the hero is merely a passive surface on which the sufferings of others are registered. Harley is a sensitive young gentleman who goes to London to seek much-needed money, fails, loses money to sharpers, rescues a prostitute, visits Bedlam, and listens to a beggar and a returning soldier whose family was decimated in his absence. The young man feels--but without the consciousness of self (in contrast to Sterne's hero in A Sentimental Journey). He protests visiting Bedlam: "I think it an inhuman practice to expose the greatest misery with which our nature is afflicted, to every idle visitant who can afford a trifling perquisite to the keeper; especially as it is a distress, that it is not in their power to alleviate it." The insane are all genteel; he reacts with tears and guineas to their keeper. Harley pines away for love of a wealthy young lady; she learns that he is dying, runs to him with professions of love, whereupon he dies. It is as though he could exist by pitying, but not by being pitied. The narrator says of Harley's grave: "It is worth a thousand homilies! every nobler feeling rises within me! every beat of my heart awakens a virtue!-- but it will make you hate the world . . . . I pity the men of it." This excess of sensibility in the 18th-century sentimental novel found its opposite in its near contemporary, the Gothic novel Vathek, by William Beckford, in which the protagonist gleefully piles death on death, cruelty on cruelty. And Mackenzie's protagonist could not survive for two minutes the terrors inflicted on Mrs. Radcliffe's heroines. Pity was changed to terror.

Mather, Cotton. The Angel of Bethesda: An Essay Upon the Common Maladies of Mankind, ed. G. W. Jones, M.D. Barre, Mass.: American Antiquarian Society and Barre Publishers, 1972. Treatise.

Body/Mind   Disease & Health   Drugs
Preg. & Childbirth   V.D.

A cross between a layman's guide to medicine and Donne's Devotions. Mather studied medical literature in college, but he did not, unlike his fellow-minister, Edward Taylor, practice upon his parishioners. Still, his strong interest in science and medicine is evidenced in this guide by a lengthy dissertation upon germs ("animaculae") as a cause of disease, and an explanation of innoculation for small-pox. The minister in him comes to the fore when he asserts that sin, from the time of Adam until today, is responsible for sickness, for sin causes sickness of the spirit which, in turn, causes sickness of the body. Because he believed that the body was a machine directed by the spirit, he was alert to psychosomatic illness, urging doctors to determine and remove causes of anxiety, for instance, in patients with stomach disease. He praises the use of opiates to remove pain. And he offers good advice to women in childbed: bear the pain, think about the Christian soul being born, be ready to die, and avoid rash vows. He also lists a variety of obstetrical medications. The general pattern of each short section in this book is an opening description of the cause of a certain disease, its spiritual applications (toothache, e.g., is indicative of sins committed with the teeth), and finally a list of physical cures. There is one notable exception: he refuses to give cures for V.D., sending the sinner instead to a common surgeon and a good dose of repentance. He reminds his readers of the contradictory advice given by doctors and the uncertainty of their cures, advising patients to put their trust in God. Considering the amount of dung--goat's, cow's, horse's--in Mather's suggested cures, God would appear to be the safest physician.

Mercier, Louis Sebastian. Memoirs of the Year Two Thousand Five Hundred (original title: The Year Two Thousand Four Hundred and Forty), trans. W. Hooper. Philadelphia: T. Dobson, 1795. From University Microfilms. American Culture II, 5th year. Reel 194. II. History: Utopian and Reform Movements. Treatise.

| Disease & Health | Med. Instit. | Med. Profession |
| Sci Fi | Sexual Roles | Surgery |

Science fiction used for satire upon eighteenth-century practices and customs. In the far future, disease will be uncommon because the citizenry will be temperate and will know their own temperament. Moreover, all citizens will have access to rational medical care: the physicians, who will be honored as the first of citizens, will examine each patient as a special case rather than dispensing general precepts; surgery and physic will be united into one art; obituaries will list the name of the attending physician; and all physicians will be required to account for their prescriptions and treatment. Hospitals will be divided into small units (so that foul air will not collect), distributed about the city, and patients will enter them, not for burial but to receive better care. Mercier's proposed reforms of medical care reflect his ingenuity; his depiction of the ideal sexual role for women reflects the 18th-century preoccupation with the role of women. In the 26th-century, women will carry no dowry (i.e. money belonging to the wife) because it will be recognized that women are by nature dependent on that sex from which they derive their strength and glory. Women will be taught more than music and dancing--they will learn economy, methods of pleasing their husband, and knowledge for education of their children. Divorce will be permitted, so that if a man should be unhappy under these conditions, it will be his own fault.

Molière (Jean-Baptiste Poquelin). L'Amour Médecin (Love's the Best Doctor). Available in Dramatic Works, trans. C. H. Wall. London: G. Bell, 1913-14. Vol. 2. Drama.

Med. Profession

A daughter is depressed, so her father sends for several doctors to insure a cure. Her lover disguises himself as a doctor and joins the crowd. There is a long consultation scene, that ends in complete disagreement among the doctors, even though they have discussed the distance a mule has covered, approved a cure which killed a patient because a senior physician insisted on overruling a junior, and have used every type of jargon and absurd style. The lover-"physician" claims that all the girl needs is the appearance of a husband and, with the father, arranges a "mock" wedding in which the "parson" will be an apothecary. Of course the lover marries her before a real parson, and all ends happily.

Molière (Jean-Baptiste Poquelin). La Malade Imaginaire (The Imaginary Invalid). Available in Misanthrope and Other Plays, trans. John Wood. Baltimore: Penguin, 1959. Drama.

| Death | Disease & Health | Doctors |
| The Family | Med. Ethics | Med. Profession |

The best-known, and funniest, literary attack upon the medical profession. Argan is an odd combination of miser-hypochondriac. He rejoices in the flowery, "literary" descriptions of purges and enemas while writhing at the rich fees accompanying the rich prose. He decides to get professional courtesy by marrying his daughter to a doctor. However, his daughter prefers the gallant Cleante to the boorish Dr. Thomas who is a mere puppet of M. Diaforus, his doctor-father. Despite the encouragement of his second wife, Argan is cured of his extreme hypochondria by a female servant who disguises herself as a physician and outjargons M. Diaforus, who retreats in defeat, shouting out predictions of M. Argan's imminent death. The servant then cures Argan of uxoriousness at the expense of fatherliness, by persuading him to fake death and listen to the reactions of his family. His wife rejoices, and his daughter weeps. Finally, Argan listens to his brother, a firm opponent of the medical

profession. Nothing is more ridiculous than a man who professes to cure another--our bodies are too mysterious. Doctors' "medicines" are words and promises, and, in addition, doctors see only rules, not the patient. The principles of your life are within you. Argan's real cure is completed by his induction into the "medical profession" by actors hired by his brother for the purpose. They perform a satiric song and dance, asserting that the answer to all illness is--a clyster, and only those remedies approved by the medical faculty can effect a cure.

Molière (Jean-Baptiste Poquelin). Le Médecin Malgré Lui (The Physician In Spite of Himself). Available in Misanthrope and Other Plays, trans. John Wood. Baltimore: Penguin, 1959. Drama.

| Doctors | Med. Profession |

Sganarelle beats his wife. In revenge, she tells men seeking a good doctor to cure the mute daughter of a wealthy man that her husband is the great doctor they seek, but he is so modest that he must be beaten into admitting his profession. Sganarelle is beaten, does "admit" his medical skill, and then acts the doctor to perfection, using doggerel Latin and the name of Hippocrates to beat down common sense objections of the wealthy father. He discovers that the daughter's loss of speech is caused by an unwelcome fiancé forced upon her by her father. Doctor Sganarelle, in Latin, recommends flight with her lover as a cure--a course of treatment which she successfully follows. Sganarelle also mocks the credulity of patients. When a man seeks a medicine for his wife's dropsy, Doctor Sganarelle gives him a piece of cheese, in return for a sizeable fee.

Molière (Jean-Baptiste Poquelin). Le Médecin Volant (The Flying Doctor). Available in Dramatic Works, trans. C. H. Wall. London: G. Bell, 1913-14. Vol. 1. Drama.

Doctors

A farce in which a servant pretends to be a doctor in order to further a romantic intrigue. Criticisms of the medical profession are similar to those in La Malade Imaginaire, but are much less harsh in tone. The play's title comes from the speed with which the servant shifts from one identity to another to sustain the illusion of two men being present.

Molière (Jean-Baptiste Poquelin). "A Monsieur de la Mothe Le Vayer." Available, in French, in Oeuvres de Molière, ed. Jacques Copeau. Paris: La Cité des Livres, 1929. Vol. 10. Sonnet.

| Children | Death | Grief |

A very moving attempt to comfort his friend. Cry, my friend; when one has lost forever what you have lost, even Wisdom would cry. People offer precepts to prevent tears when one whom you love dies. That is barbarous and more brutal than supreme virtue. Of course your tears won't bring him back, but you have lost a strong heart, a great spirit, and a beautiful soul and these are subjects which always cause tears. "On sait bien que les pleurs ne ramèneront pas/Ce cher fils que t'enlève un imprévu trepas;/Mais la perte par là n'en est pas moins cruelle:/Ses vertus de chacun le faisaient révérer,/Il avait le coeur grand, l'esprit beau, l'âme belle,/Et ce sont des sujets à toujours le pleurer."

Parnell, Thomas. "On a Lady with Foul Breath." From The Poetical Works of Thomas Parnell, ed. G. A. Aitken. London: George Bell & Sons, 1894. Poem: 32 lines.

| The Body | Death | Sexuality |

A morbid intermixture of disease, sexuality, and death. "Dying" has none of the Renaissance playful punning on death and intercourse; instead, the pun becomes literal unity: death and intercourse are one. The lady of the title must be dead: "Think not you live because you speak,/For graves such hollow sounds can make . . . From thee such noisome stenches come,/Thy mouth betrays thy breast a tomb./Thy body is a corpse that goes,/By magic rais'd from its repose!/A pestilence, that walks by day,/But falls at night to worms and clay." This reminds the poet of his sweet-breathed Chloris, whose lip offers him healing nectar. However, if he approaches Chloris too closely, she will cause him to burn with inward flame and so gain a new "disease" from his cure. "I'll go where passion bids me fly,/And choose my death, since I must die."

Pepys, Samuel. The Diary: Selections, ed. O. F. Morshead. New York: Harper, 1960. (For the hardy or the true Pepys-lover, R. C. Latam and W. Mathews are preparing a multi-volume edition of the diary for the University of California Press--over seven volumes are already published.) Diary.

| Disease & Health | Plague | Sexuality |
| Surgery | | |

Although Pepys does not describe his operation for "the stone," it is obvious that it was a traumatic event for him. He celebrates the anniversary of the occasion, attends with interest a Royal Society lecture on kidneys, and constantly refers to his stone. Pepys was an interested member of the Royal Society, giving a detailed account of experiments with transfusions. His account of the London plague of 1665 is matter-of-fact. He has a fascinating attitude toward sexual matters. He believed in maintaining a firm control over his wife, of whom he was quite fond, and seemed to have a rather low opinion of women in general. Yet he was very attracted to beautiful women, causing nice domestic entanglements as he tries to allay his wife's jealousy--while being at the same time jealous of his wife.

Pope, Alexander. "Eloisa to Abelard." Available in The Poems of Alexander Pope, ed. John Butt. New Haven: Yale University Press, 1963. Poem: 366 lines.

   Sexuality

   Passionate lament of Heloise (here Eloisa) for her lost love. A soul in torment, yet strangely relishing her torment. For when she speaks of her Abelard, spared all longing by his castration, her tone takes on a tinge of contempt: "Thy life a long, dead calm of fix'd repose;/No pulse that riots, and no blood that glows." Her grief leads to ecstasy: "While prostrate here in humble grief I lie,/Kind virtuous drops just gath'ring in my eye,/While praying, trembling, in the dust I roll,/And dawning grace is opening on my soul:/Come, thou dar'st, all charming as thou art!"

Pope, Alexander. "An Epistle from Mr. Pope, to Dr. Arbuthnot." Available in The Poems of Alexander Pope, ed. John Butt. New Haven: Yale University Press, 1963. Poem: 419 lines.

   Age   Doctors   Dying

   A very curious and complex poem addressed to the doctor/ poet Dr. Arbuthnot. Pope speaks to Arbuthnot only in the role of his personal physician. He decries the scribblers, poetasters, and critics who beset him [Pope] and who misuse the art of letters. In contrast, Pope uses his poetry as medicine: "The Muse but serv'd to ease some Friend, not Wife,/To help me thro' this long Disease, my Life,/To second, ARBUTHNOT! thy Art and Care,/And teach, the Being you preserv'd, to bear." Then, having denounced those unprincipled "satirists" who attack the home life of others (particularly Pope's), the poem ends with the simple honesty of Pope's father, who died easily and Pope's wish that he may assist his mother in her age and dying moments: "With lenient Arts extend a Mother's breath,/Make Languor smile, and smooth the Bed of Death,/Explore the Thought, explain the asking Eye,/And keep a while one Parent from the Sky!" These are the proper cares for the poet and the physician: "On Cares like these if Length of days attend,/ May Heav'n, to bless those days, preserve my Friend,/ Preserve him social, chearful, and serene,/And just as rich as when he serv'd a QUEEN!"

Pope, Alexander. An Essay on Man. Poem: 4 Epistles.

   The Body   Suffering

   The poet answers the eternal search for the meaning of pain--with the assertion that "whatever is, is right." He attacks those who question Providence, who "Say, here he gives too little, there too much;/Destroy all creatures for thy sport or gust,/Yet cry, If Man's unhappy, God's unjust." The second Epistle, especially, portrays man as unfit judge of his own state--and yet as noble in his own knowledge and in his potential for rising above his own body. "Know then thyself, presume not God to scan;/ The proper study of Mankind is Man . . . . In doubt to deem himself a God, or Beast;/In doubt his Mind or Body to prefer,/Born but to die, and reas'ning but to err . . . Sole judge of truth, in endless Error hurl'd:/ The glory, jest, and riddle of the world!" Yet, this knowledge so necessary to man is not the information provided by science: "Go, wond'rous creature! mount where Science guides . . . . Go, teach Eternal Wisdom how to rule--/Then drop into thyself, and be a fool!" Even the great Newton, "whose rules the rapid Comet bind," could not "Describe or fix one movement of his Mind." Science is limited by man's nature: "But when his own great work is but begun,/What Reason weaves, by Passion is undone."

Pope, Alexander. "On Queen Caroline's Death-Bed," Epigrams 1738- 1741, no. 1. Available in The Poems of Alexander Pope, ed. John Butt. New Haven: Yale University Press, 1963. Poem: 2 lines.

   The Body

   This attack on the Hanoverian monarchy exploits the genteel fiction that a woman's body ceases to exist in public--and exploits it with the savagery of Swift: "Here lies wrapt up in forty thousand towels/The only proof that C*** had bowels."

Pope, Alexander. The Rape of the Lock. Available in The Poems of Alexander Pope, ed. John Butt. New Haven: Yale University Press, 1963. Poem: 5 Cantos.

   Disease & Health   Sexuality   Sexual Roles

   The classic mock-epic: a gentle, very witty mockery of the ignorance, the vanity, the artificiality, and the triviality of women who refuse to acknowledge the reality of sickness or old age. In Canto IV Pope describes the Cave of Spleen, inhabited by Pain and Megrim. Here, "Spleen" appears to be a hypochondriac hysteria, whose foundation lies in sexual frustration-- especially, although not always, in females. "Men prove with Child, as pow'rful Fancy works,/And Maids turn'd Bottels, call aloud for Corks . . . . Parent of Vapours and of Female Wit,/Who give th' Hysteric or Poetic Fit . . . Make some take Physick, others scribble Plays."

Racine, Jean. Phaedra. Available in Six Plays by Corneille and Racine, ed. Paul Landis. New York: Modern Library, 1959. Drama.

   Children   Madness   Sexuality

   A much more complex play than Euripides' Hippolytus. Phaedra's mad passion for her stepson, Hippolytus, burns through a web of politics, of Hippolytus' love for the true heiress to the throne, Theseus' supposed death, and the debate whether Hippolytus or Phaedra's son will succeed Theseus. Yet Phaedra's attempts to control--and then to consummate--her passion dominate the play, as though demonstrating that personal motives overwhelm political ones. The play's language is highly charged: "I see already, through a gathering mist,/ The husband whom I outrage with my presence./Death veils the light of Heaven from mine eyes,/And gives it back its purity, defiled."

Richardson, Samuel. Clarissa. Pressured students may prefer the abridged version, available edited by George Sherburn. Boston: Houghton Mifflin, 1962. More leisured readers will want the 4-volume edition. New York: Dutton, 1932. Novel.

   Death   Dying   The Family
   Sexuality   Sexual Roles

   A fascinating, perverse version of the battle between the sexes. Clarissa Harlowe is lured from her family, imprisoned, and raped by her lover-seducer, Lovelace. Clarissa is forced to yield her body to Lovelace, but she wins the victory by giving herself and her body to Lovelace's true rival, death. Lovelace, driven mad by guilt, meets his death for her sake. The sexual battle is complicated by their different economic, social, and family backgrounds, and made fascinating to the reader by the differing points-of-view presented by the letter-format of the novel, which allows a variety of characters to comment on the action. It is as though various stereotypes, such as rich, powerful seducer and poor, helpless maiden, are foisted upon the two, distorting the relationship between the vacillating Lovelace and the strong-willed Clarissa. Clarissa's death (from unspecified causes) is long and drawn-out, giving her time to prepare for death and her funeral as though for a wedding, specifying even the smallest details. Her death not only destroys Lovelace, it reconciles her to her family and fixes her importance. This is not a uniquely early version of the persecuted-woman novel; this is a very perceptive study of two sexual natures, meant to complement each other, but forced by personalities to grind each other to dust.

Rochester, Earl of (John Wilmot). "The Imperfect Enjoyment." Available in The Complete Poems of John Wilmot, Earl of Rochester, ed. D. M. Vieth. New Haven: Yale University Press, 1974. Poem: 72 lines.

   Sexuality

   A sophisticated and ironic erotic poem about premature ejaculation and impotence. The poet is briskly making love with his mistress and, at the moment when her hand "would guide that part/Which should convey my soul up to her heart,/In liquid raptures I dissolve all o'er." He then cannot play his part further: "Eager desires confound my first intent,/Succeeding shame does more success prevent,/And rage at last confirms me impotent." He scolds his wilting tool for bravely assaulting every whore in town, but failing "when great Love the onset does command." Then, having assumed the role of lover abashed by his noble lady, he gleefully throws aside the whole charade: "May'st thou [this prick] ne'er piss, who didst refuse to spend/When all my joys did on false thee depend./ And may ten thousand abler pricks agree/To do the wronged Corinna right for thee."

Rochester, Earl of (John Wilmot). "Song" ("By all love's soft, yet mighty powers"). Available in The Complete Poems of John Wilmot, Earl of Rochester, ed. D. M. Vieth. New Haven: Yale University Press, 1974. Poem: 12 lines.

   The Body   Sexuality

   A gentler, more urbane version of the theme in Swift's "Caelia shits." Nothing is more repelling than the female body menstruating or covered by shitty clothing. Men prefer "cleanly sinning." "By all love's soft, yet mighty powers,/It is a thing unfit/That men should fuck in time of flowers,/Or when the smock's beshit."

Rochester, Earl of (John Wilmot). "Song" ("Love a woman? You're an ass!"). Available in The Complete Poems of John Wilmot, Earl of Rochester, ed. D. M. Vieth. New Haven: Yale University Press, 1974. Poem: 16 lines.

   Homosexuality   Sexuality

   Sophisticated dismissal of heterosexual intercourse as lower-class drudgery: "Let the porter and the groom,/ Things designed for dirty slaves,/Drudge in fair Aurelia's womb/To get supplies for age and graves." The poet intends to use his nights for drink, mirth, and wit. "And, if busy love entrenches,/There's a sweet, soft page of mine/Does the trick worth forty wenches."

Rochester, Earl of (John Wilmot). "Signior Dildo." Available in
The Complete Poems of John Wilmot, Earl of Rochester, ed. D. M.
Vieth. New Haven: Yale University Press, 1974. Poem: 92 lines.

Sexuality

A satire written on the occasion of the proxy wedding
of James, Duke of York (brother to Charles II, and
later James II). In a time when political and sexual
affairs were often synonymous, it is not surprising
to find this bawdy satire on contemporary court ladies,
celebrating the insatiable lust of women, whether for
man or leather aid to masturbation: "That pattern of
virtue, Her Grace of Cleveland,/Has swallowed more
pricks than the ocean has sand;/But by rubbing and
scrubbing so large it does grow,/It is fit for just
nothing but Signior Dildo."

Sedley, Charles. "The Doctor and his Patients." Available in
The Poetical and Dramatic Works of Sir Charles Sedley, ed.
V. de Sola Pinto. London: Constable & Co., 1928. 2 Vols.
Vol. 1. Poem: 30 lines.

Doctors   Poverty & Health

A flippant satire upon mankind as a patient, who sees
his cure--and rejects it. "There was a prudent grave
Physician,/Careful of Patients as you'd wish one."
The doctor successfully wields his purge and glister,
"But still his Patients came again,/And most of their
old Ills complain;/The Drunkards drank, and spoil'd
their Liver:/Beaux ply'd the Smock as much as ever,/
And got the high Veneral Feaver." So, the doctor
assembles all of his patients, asks them each if a
reasonable diet and sober life would not permanently
cure them. "They all agreed that his Advice/Was honest,
wholsom, grave and wise;/But not one Man wou'd quit
his Vice;/For after all his vain Attacks,/They rose
and din'd well at Pontack's."

Shadwell, Thomas. The Virtuoso, especially Act II, scene ii;
Act IV, scene v, eds. M. H. Nicolson and D. S. Rodes.
Lincoln: University of Nebraska Press, 1966. Drama.

Doctors   Sexuality

Primarily a satire on researchers, especially those who
seek knowledge for its own sake--as in the Royal Society.
Shadwell makes the same sort of criticisms as Swift
makes through his Laputans and Lagadons in Gulliver.
The Virtuoso seeks theoretical knowledge (he learns
how to swim by mimicking a frog, even though he can't
abide water); but he does so at the expense of human
knowledge: his uncle disinherits him, his nieces
escape with their dowries, his wife cuckolds him, his
mistress leaves him, and he is left alone in debt.
The Virtuoso performs transfusions, studies spiders,
weighs air samples from locations throughout England,
and examines a variety of creatures through the microscope. In Act V, scene v he assembles all the sick
and calls out the various diseases: Gout, dropsy,
consumption, stone. He then gives each class a hand-
out with their cure (there is a mob to be cured of the
pox). However, because he is all theory, without appli-
cation, he is thoroughly credulous, unable to separate
truth from lie. Ironically, his house is nearly destroyed because his vengeful uncle tells the ribbon
weavers that The Virtuoso has successfully designed a
machine that will throw them out of work. His pleas
of ineffectuality go unheard. This malicious uncle,
Snarl, is unusual in embodying a sexual perversion on
stage. In fact, the play is generally quite free in
its treatment of sex: every character lusts after
someone, and the young heroines accept quite easily
the fact that their lovers detour from pursuit of
them to take a quick pleasure with their mother-in-
law. Still, Snarl, who cannot enjoy his mistress
without being beaten, is unusual. He says that he
got into the habit when a boy at Westminster School
and has never been able to quit the exercise. The
other characters ridicule him for the rods, calling
his mistress a schoolmistress, but their scorn is
principally retaliation for his diatribes against
the inferior, immoral younger generation.

Smart, Christopher. "Hymn to the Supreme Being on Recovery from
a Dangerous Fit of Illness." Available in Poems by Christopher Smart, ed. Robert Brittain. Princeton: Princeton
University Press, 1950. Poem: 108 lines.

Disease & Health   Madness

Smart is best known for his religious verse and his
Jubilate Agno (Rejoice in the Lamb), a long "poem"
written during his confinement for madness. "Hymn
to the Supreme Being" celebrates his recovery from
one of the fits of fever and madness that preceded
his long illness. The poem is dedicated to Doctor
James, to whose Fever Powder Smart attributed his
cure. His account of his physical and mental suffering is feelingly set forth: "My feeble feet refus'd
my body's weight,/Nor wou'd my eyes admit the glorious
light,/My nerves convuls'd shook fearful of their fate,/
My mind lay open to the powers of night./He pitying
did a second birth bestow/A birth of joy--not like the
first of tears and woe."

Smollett, Tobias. The Adventures of Ferdinand, Count Fathom.
London: Hutchinson, n.d. Novel.

By Doctors   Doctors   Med. Profession
Suffering

Most of this novel portrays the sufferings inflicted
upon others by the adventurer Ferdinand through his
cheating and impositions. However, one section centers
on the medical profession, as Ferdinand tries to make
his way by posing as a doctor. Earlier, in Chapter
XXXV Smollett notes the handicaps a physician has in
disputes about medical matters: the ignorant seek to
level the reputations of their superiors, medical
terminology obscures the argument, and the multitude
love to see "an artist foiled at his own weapons, by
one who engages him only for amusement." Chapters L
to LIV describe the difficulties encountered by the
one who engaged for amusement, Ferdinand, when he
tries to set up as a doctor in earnest. He finds
this situation in London: "In his researches, he
found that the great world was wholly engrossed by
a few practitioners who had arrived at the summit of
reputation, consequently were no longer obliged to
cultivate those arts by which they rose; and that the
rest of the business was parcelled out into small en-
closures, occupied by different groups of personages,
male and female, who stood in rings, and tossed the
ball from one to another . . . . Every knot was composed of a waiting-woman, nurse, apothecary, surgeon,
and physician, and sometimes a midwife was admitted
into the party."

Smollett, Tobias. The Adventures of Peregrine Pickle. London:
Hutchinson & Co., n.d. 2 Vols. Novel.

By Doctors   Doctors   Med. Instit.
V.D.

The main object of medical satire is a "young man, in
whose air and countenance appeared all the gravity and
supercilious self-conceit of a physician piping hot
from his studies." This young doctor has a passionate
attachment to the ancient Greeks and Romans, totally
rejecting any modern work of art or idea. He gives a
"Roman" banquet in which he substitutes gastronomic
horrors for the original Roman delicacies, while maintaining he is faithful to his classical model. He
defends dining upon cats and other flesh eaters and
adds that he has tried human flesh and found it preferable to pork: "for, in the course of his studies, he
had for the experiment's sake eaten a steak cut from
the buttock of a person who had been hanged" (Book I,
chapter xliv; Book I, chapter xlviii). In Book I,
chapter lxx, Peregrine plays a joke upon the gossipy
Bath (health spa) physicians. In Book I, chapter
lxxxiii, a usurer harangues a physician for giving
him false information: the physician said that a
client was sure to die soon of the pox, but it turns
out that the client was born with the disease, has a
strong resistance to it, and the usurer will not
collect for years. In Book II, chapter xcv, we meet
a sensible young physician who, when Peregrine is
overcome with his studies, does not dose him with
medicine but weans him from his bad habits and forces him to take early morning exercise.

Smollett, Tobias. The Adventures of Roderick Random. London:
Hutchinson & Co., n.d. Novel.

Abortion   By Doctors   Disease & Health
Doctors   Evil Doctors   Homosexuality
Med. Ethics   Med. Profession   Suffering
V.D.   Women as Patients

The hero of the book is a doctor who finds himself
surrounded by evil incompetents. He is apprenticed
to Launcelot Crab, one of the first drinking physicians in literature. When a girl claims Dr. Crab
made her pregnant, he tells her it's only a "female
disorder"--and gives her pills which he hopes will
cause an abortion, without telling her the purpose
of the pills. Dr. Random goes to London to seek advancement; he finds a patient with V.D.--himself. He
retires into cheap lodgings for a cure and meets a
woman he had once planned to marry until he discovered
she was a whore. This woman "found herself dangerously
infected with a distemper to which all of her class
are particularly subject; that her malady gaining
ground every day, she became loathsome to herself,
and offensive to others . . . that she had accordingly
chosen this place of retreat, and put herself into
the hands of an advertising doctor, who, having fleeced
her of all the money she had, or could procure, left
her three days ago in a worse condition than that in
which he found her" (Chapter XXI). Roderick goes
through the ludicrous and lucrative (to the examiners
and their flunkies) examinations for confirmation as a
naval surgeon. He passes, but does not get a berth
until he is "pressed" on board ship and rescued from
the ranks of common seamen. From Chapter XXIV to
XXXVII, Roderick tries to insure decent treatment for
himself, other low-ranking medical personnel, and his
patients. At first he serves under a capable and
compassionate chief surgeon, who is unfortunately replaced by a malicious incompetent, supported by a
brutal and ignorant captain. This Captain Oakum,
offended by the large number of sick men on board,
instead of reforming the ship's hospital, sends the
sick and injured men back to work (with the aid of
the surgeon) and so kills off most of the sick, reducing the numbers of disabled men on board. The chief
surgeon, Dr. Mackshane, hates Dr. Random, who cured a
limb the surgeon said must be amputated. Roderick and
a friend are falsely accused of treason by Dr. Mackshane and are imprisoned by the captain until they

insist upon a court martial and so are released. Captain Oakum is replaced by Captain Whiffle, whose chief surgeon, Mr. Simper, may be the first homosexual physician in literature: "a young man gaily dressed, of a very delicate complexion, with a kind of languid smile on his face, which seemed to have been rendered habitual by a long course of affection. The captain no sooner perceiving him, than, rising hastily, he flew into his arms." Roderick's fortunes swing up and down, but eventually, by the aid of a long-lost father and uncle, he becomes wealthy and married to his true-love.

Smollett, Tobias. The Expedition of Humphry Clinker, ed. R. G. Davis. New York: Holt, Rinehart & Winston, 1960. Novel.

Body/Mind	By Doctors	Disease & Health
Doctors	Grief	Sexual Roles
Suffering		

The most delightful of Dr. Smollett's books is this account of Matt Bramble's peregrinations about England and Scotland in pursuit of health (he has the gout and GI upsets) and entertainment. The novel is a collection of letters from Bramble's entourage, giving an account of their travels to various friends and acquaintances. Matt Bramble's correspondent is Dr. Lewis, his physician, friend, and common-sense advisor. Bramble visits Bath, Harrogate, and Scarborough, but is quite disgusted by the mineral water provided for drinking and bathing. He sees a child with scrofulous ulcers being carried into the King's Bath: "Good Heaven, the very thought makes my blood run cold! we know not what sores may be running into the water while we are bathing, and what sort of matter we may thus imbibe; the king's-evil, the scurvy, the cancer, and the pox; and, no doubt, the heat will render the virus the more volatile and penetrating" (April 26). Although Bramble has a goodly amount of common sense and refutes a doctor who offers to cure him of dropsy--a disease he indignantly disclaims; nevertheless, he writes off to Dr. Lewis for advice, while carefully measuring the size of his ankles with a pack thread! Spas and doctors don't help him, but he does come closer to health, for he perceives: "I find my spirits and my health affect each other reciprocally--that is to say, every thing that discomposes my mind, produces a correspondent disorder in my body; and my bodily complaints are remarkably mitigated by those considerations that dissipate the clouds of mental chagrin," although he still credits Dr. Lewis' tincture of ginseng for some of his relief (June 11). The novel has a rather contradictory approach to suffering: if it's justified, we'll pity and help; if it's unjustified we will not pity. A number of instances of suffering are presented to the reader so that he may add his or her tears to those of the characters: an old man forced to hard work in his age, a woman mad with grief for her dead husband, and crippled veterans eking out existence on half-pay. But when Baynard, who is being ruined by his beloved wife's coldhearted extravagance, expresses violent grief at her death, he is met by a dry-eyed Matt Bramble: "In a few hours [after her death], he was calm enough to hear reason, and even to own that Heaven could not have interposed more effectually to rescue him from disgrace and ruin" (October 14). Tabitha Bramble is the archetype of an old maid seeking a man, any man--even though he possess, as Lieutenant Lismahago does, the body of a plucked crow.

Smollett, Tobias. Sir Launcelot Greaves. From The Adventures of Sir Launcelot Greaves and the Adventures of an Atom. London: Hutchinson & Co., n.d. Novel.

By Doctors	Doctors	Grief
Madness	Med. Instit.	

A trifling tale of an 18th-century Don Quixote, Launcelot Greaves, who, however, relies more upon money and influence to rescue the distressed than did his Renaissance predecessor. There are a number of physicians who appear in minor roles: Mr. Fillet, the practical joker (Books VI & VII); an apothecary who prescribes expensive and debilitating treatment and is recommended over a sensible, effective physician, by a landlord who likes the apothecary for not condemning ale-drinking (Book XVI); there is a physician who takes on a brewer in a hand-to-hand combat in Kings Bench Prison (Book XX); and there is the stupid doctor who refuses to recognize sanity (Book XXIII). Madness runs through the novel. A woman, persecuted by her landlord, goes mad with grief for the supposed loss of her son. Her neighbors note that she is usually quite reasonable: "they likewise imputed a great part of the disorder to the want of quiet, proper food, and necessaries, with which she was but poorly supplied by the cold hand of chance charity" (Book XI). Both Launcelot and his love suffer from the ease with which people may be called mad. They are both illegally imprisoned in a house for lunatics, and find that the word "mad" applied to them is enough to make them be mad in the eyes of their servants and keepers. Launcelot appeals to the madhouse doctor in reasonable terms; he first praises the medical profession and then continues "The character of a physician, therefore, not only supposes natural sagacity, and acquired erudition, but also it implies every delicacy of sentiment, every tenderness of nature, and every virtue of humanity." After more flattery and a clear statement of his name and position, Launcelot ends with a statement of those legal rights that have been violated in his case. The

doctor does, indeed, follow his profession: "The doctor seemed to be a little disconcerted; but, after some recollection, resumed his air of sufficiency and importance, and assured our adventurer he would do him all the service in his power; but in the meantime advised him to take the potion he had prescribed."

The Spectator, no. 25 (attributed to Joseph Addison). From The Spectator. Philadelphia: J. J. Woodward, 1832. 2 Vols. bound in one. Essay.

Disease & Health	Med. Students

The extreme of hypochondria, in which the means employed to avoid sickness insure ill-health. The hypothetical writer of this letter to "The Spectator" was once a medical student. "I first contracted this ill habit of body, or rather of mind, by the study of physic." Studying "phthisical distempers," this valetudinarian "fell into a consumption; till at length, growing very fat, I was in a manner shamed out of that imagination. Not long after this I found in myself all the symptoms of the gout, except pain." The writer takes to living in a chair which measures his weight, regulating his existence by the chair. "And yet, sir, notwithstanding this my great care to ballast myself equally every day, and to keep my body in its proper poise, so it is, that I find myself in a sick and languishing condition."

The Spectator, nos. 115 & 195 (both attributed to Joseph Addison). From The Spectator. Philadelphia: J. J. Woodward, 1832. 2 Vols. bound in one. Essays.

The Body	Body/Mind	Disease & Health

Both essays urge bodily exercise. The first essay postulates that the body, that "system of tubes and glands" is "a proper engine for the soul to work with . . . . Labour or exercise ferments the humours . . . and helps nature in those secret distributions, without which the body cannot subsist in its vigour, nor the soul act with cheerfulness." Without exercise, the mind becomes troubled, which is why "men of studious and sedentary tempers" and women are so often troubled with the spleen and the vapors. The second essay argues that "physic, for the most part, is nothing else but the substitute of exercise and temperance . . . . The apothecary is perpetually employed in countermining the cook and the vintner . . . . It is impossible to lay down any determinate rule for temperance, because what is luxury in one may be temperance in another."

The Spectator, nos. 246 & 263 (both attributed to Richard Steele). From The Spectator. Philadelphia: J. J. Woodward, 1832. 2 Vols. bound in one. Essays.

Children	Poverty & Health	Preg. & Childbirth

The first essay urges that the upper-class mother breastfeed her child, and includes an unconsciously terrible description of the health of poor mothers. "It is unmerciful to see, that a woman endowed with all the perfections of nature, can, as soon as she is delivered, turn off her innocent, tender, and helpless infant, and give it up to a woman that is (ten thousand to one), neither in health nor good condition, neither sound in mind nor body, that has neither honour nor reputation, neither love nor pity for the poor babe, but more regard for the money than for the whole child." The second essay contains a "letter" that is a fascinating opposite to the present trend criticizing parents. The "letter-writer," watching his son grow, becomes more and more aware of the ways in which he had unconsciously pained his own parents. "There are numberless little crimes which children take no notice of while they are doing, which, upon reflection, when they shall themselves become fathers, they will look upon with the utmost sorrow and contrition, that they did not regard before those whom they offended were to be no more seen." The writer urges the strength of love to bind families, concluding with a pair of letters from a loveless family, in which the mother and son exist in a state of economic warfare.

The Spectator, no. 431 (of unknown attribution). From The Spectator. Philadelphia: J. J. Woodward, 1832. 2 Vols. bound in one. Essay.

Adolescence	Children	Sexuality
Women as Patients		

Two grotesque "letters" from children badly raised by their parents. "Richard Rentfree" was oppressed by his parents and kept in great poverty until his marriage. "Sabina Green" was given complete freedom and, contracting "the green-sickness" (a menstrual disorder), she wanders about eating oatmeal, used tobacco-pipes, chalk, wax, and the garden-wall. She is married to Richard, and the two married children are both very content.

The Spectator, no. 435 (of unknown attribution). From The Spectator. Philadelphia: J. J. Woodward, 1832. 2 Vols. bound in one. Essay.

Sexual Roles

The 18th-century was preoccupied with social roles, so it is not surprising that it gave a good deal of public attention to sexual roles. This usually took the form of criticizing the behavior of women, although the effeminate dress of foppish men was also a popular target. The Spectator papers are full of references to--

and criticisms of--feminine behavior. This sample was chosen because it is the most explicit in its support of clearly divided sexual roles. "The Spectator" is bothered by female equestrians who wear a hat, periwig, and riding coat over their petticoats. He laments the appearance of these "female cavaliers," these "herma- phrodites." "For my own part, I am for treating the sex with greater tenderness, and have all along made use of the most gentle methods to bring them off from any little extravagance into which they have sometimes unwarily fallen. I think it however absolutely neces- sary to keep up the partition between the two sexes, and to take notice of the smallest encroachments which the one makes upon the other."

The Spectator, nos. 444 & 572 (the first attributed to anon. and the second to Pearce). From The Spectator. Philadelphia: J. J. Woodward, 1832. 2 Vols. bound in one. Essays.

Doctors

In the first essay, the writer derides the tricks used by quacks to gain patients. Amazingly, they are most successful in attracting customers when they advertise traits most irrelevant--or most harmful--to their practice (e.g. the quack's father and brother both suffered from the disease that is his specialty). The writer of the second essay continues the exposure of quackery, but moves on to marvel at people's predis- position to believe in such quacks. The essay ends with a passage from the Aeneid in which a doctor at first believes a cure to be his, only to be perceptive and honest enough to recognize and extol the aid of some divine agent.

Sterne, Laurence. The Life and Opinions of Tristram Shandy, Gent. Novel.

Doctors   Grief   Med. Profession
Preg. & Childbirth   Sexuality   Women as Healers

Books I to III of this whimsical "autobiography" de- scribe the conception and birth of its author. The marriage contract provides money for Mrs. Shandy to "lie in" at London. However, she has taken her hus- band to London on a false alarm, so he requires her to remain in the country. Yet he feels guilty and so tries to force upon her the attendance of Doctor Slop, the male-midwife. Mr. Shandy is the more concerned because he believes that "by force of the woman's efforts, which, in strong labour-pains, was equal, upon an average, to the weight of 470 pounds avoirdupos acting perpendicularly upon it," the child's cerebellum, which he holds to be the seat of the soul, will be crushed and the child injured for life. Labor is protracted, the midwife is bruised upon the fender, Dr. Slop in- sists on his medical prerogatives--and crushes the child's nose with his forceps. Poor Tristram also suffers from accidental circumcision by a window sash (Book V, chapter 18). The parents are bothered by the rumors of extensive damage done by the sash, for they cannot find a way to disprove them. Mr. Shandy may, in his middle age, discharge his clock-winding and marital duties on the first of the month, without dis- quieting Mrs. Shandy. But Uncle Toby nearly loses the Widow Wadman because she is not certain of the loca- tion and effect of his wound in his groin, and he does not perceive the true motive for her solicitous in- quiries about his injuries (Book IX). The Shandy family differs widely in its reaction to the death of Bobby, the eldest son. Mr. Shandy endeavors to talk out his grief, imitating the Romans in their stoicism. Unfortunately he imitates them too closely, his wife overhears him speaking of his three children and bursts in upon him, to be informed of her loss in the following interchange: "'"I have friends--I have re- lations,--I have three desolate children,"--says Socrates.--' --'Then,' cried my mother, opening the door,--'you have one more, Mr. Shandy, than I know of.' 'By heaven! I have one less,'--said my father, getting up and walking out of the room." The servants show much more feeling--conventional lament coupled with relish in the death (Book V, chapters 1-15).

Sterne, Laurence. A Sentimental Journey. Novel.

Grief   Madness   Suffering

The book is filled with the pathetic: beggars, the stunted poor of Paris, the caged starling, etc. The most famous episode is that of poor, mad, young Maria. She lost both her lover and her pet goat, and sub- sequently went mad--thereby causing her father to die of grief. The pitiful girl is less important than her effect upon the narrator; the feelings she raises in him are like virtues: "Dear sensibility! source inexhausted of all that's precious in our joys, or costly in our sorrows! thou chainest thy martyr down upon his bed of straw--and 'tis thou who lifts him up to HEAVEN--eternal fountain of our feel- ings!--'tis here I trace thee--and this is thy divinity which stirs within me."

Swift, Jonathan. "Cassinus and Peter. A Tragical Elegy." Avail- able in Poetical Works, ed. Herbert Davis. New York: Oxford University Press, 1967. Poem: 118 lines.

The Body   Sexuality

The famous "Caelia Shits." A lover may be aware of his mistress's vagina and its diseases but never her anus and its products. The student Cassinus sits in

tragic despair: "His Breeches torn exposing wide/A ragged Shirt, and tawny Hyde./Scorcht were his Shins, his Legs were bare,/But, well embrown'd with Dirt and Hair . . . . His Jordan stood in Manner fitting/Be- tween his Legs to spew or spit in." Peter tries to discover the cause of his friend's grief--is Caelia dead? or about to lose her nose from V.D.? or in love with the Barber's Boy? No, it's worse than that: "A Crime that shocks all human Kind;/A Deed unknown to Female Race,/At which the Sun should hide his Face . . . . Nor wonder how I lost my Wits;/Oh! Caelia, Caelia, Caelia shits."

Swift, Jonathan. "The Furniture of a Woman's Mind." Available in Poetical Works, ed. Herbert Davis. New York: Oxford University Press, 1967. Poem: 64 lines.

Sexual Roles   Women as Patients

Woman as an empty-headed, vain talker who manipulates her health for her own ends: "A set of phrases learn'd by rote;/A passion for a scarlet coat . . . Never to hold her tongue a minute,/While all she prates has nothing in it . . . . Can dextrously her husband tease/By taking fits when e'er she please;/By frequent practice learns the trick/At proper seasons to be sick;/ Thinks nothing gives one airs so pretty,/At once creat- ing love and pity."

Swift, Jonathan. "In Sickness." Available in Poetical Works, ed. Herbert Davis. New York: Oxford University Press, 1967. Poem: 28 lines.

Disease & Health   Doctors   Med. Profession

A bitter poem. Having moved back to Ireland, the ill Swift finds that his "friends" give him the sympathy expected from a paid professional, and he misses Dr. Arbuthnot (the writer/physician), who was more of a friend than a professional. No, if writes about that: "Remov'd from kind Arbuthnot's Aid,/Who knows his Art but not the Trade;/ Preferring his Regard for me/Before his Credit or his Fee."

Swift, Jonathan. Gulliver's Travels. Satiric Tales.

Age   The Body   Children
Disease & Health   Doctors   Med. Profession
Sexual Roles

Gulliver was trained as a surgeon and began practice on land, but failed, "for my conscience would not suffer me to imitate the bad practice of too many among my brethren." In Lilliput, he observes children reared by people who believe that, since children are begotten in lust, they have no obligations to their parents, who are held to be "the last of all others to be trusted with the education of their own children." Each social rank and each sex receives different train- ing--the girls receiving less physical training and less learning, and more rules for domestic life, so that they are reasonable and agreeable wives. In Brobdingnag, Gulliver is exposed to the horrors of the female body: the nursing mother's breast in Chapter I, the breast cancer in Chapter IV (one of a number of references to this disease in 18th-century literature), and the naked maids of honor in VI, who cause Gulliver to frolic about their bodies. In Laputa, Gulliver observes the theoreticians, cut off from reality on their flying island. In Lagado he observes the projectors who try to impose absurd schemes upon reality. He marvels at the physician who "cures" a colicky dog by blowing wind up its anus (Shadwell, in The Virtuoso makes a similar attack upon Hooke's successful experiment with a bellows temporarily replacing the diaphragm of a dog). He learns the folly of wishing for immortality when he sees the eternal, diseased old age of the Struldbruggs. He gives the Houyhnhnms one of his naive-satiric sketches of the medical profession. He mocks the theory of evacuation which holds that cures come from feeding the anus and evacuating the mouth (glisters and purges). "But besides real dis- eases we are subject to many that are only imaginary, for which the physicians have invented imaginary cures; these have their several names, and so have the drugs that are proper for them, and with these our female yahoos [humans] are always infested." Gulliver takes on the body-image of his superiors. He imagines him- self to be larger than other humans when he returns from Brobdingnag, and after living with the Houyhnhnms he becomes incurably convinced of the superiority of the horses and so of their bodies: "At the time I am writing it is five years since my last return to England: during the first year I could not endure my wife and children in my presence, the very smell of them was in- tolerable . . . . To this hour . . . neither was I ever able to let one of them take me by the hand."

Swift, Jonathan. "The Lady's Dressing Room." Available in Poeti- cal Works, ed. Herbert Davis. New York: Oxford University Press, 1967. Poem: 142 lines.

The Body   Sexuality

To put it mildly, Swift had difficulty with women's bodies. In part, this may be the satirist's disgust at the polite, social convention that decreed that ladies were to be held as beautiful, unreal goddesses. But Swift sees their physicality in terms of stinking excretions from the body, and he always compares the filthy, female reality to the polite fiction rather

than to the male body, with its excrements. "Hard by a
filthy Bason stands,/Fowl'd with the Scouring of her
Hands;/The Bason takes whatever comes/The Scrapings of
her Teeth and Gums,/A nasty Compound of all Hues . . . .
A Glass that can to Sight disclose,/The smallest Worm in
Celia's Nose, and faithfully direct her Nail/To squeeze
it out from Head to Tail." The chamber pot may not evoke
such forcible disgust as in "Cassinus and Peter," but
its effect is discussed at greater length: "So Things,
which must not be exprest,/When plumpt into the reeking
Chest;/Send up an excremental Smell/To taint the Parts
from whence they fell./The Pettycoats and Gown perfume,/
And waft a Stink round every Room." The effect of this
close examination of the body, stripped of all illusion,
is to inhibit seeing women as sexual objects--to the
narrator's amusement: "I pity wretched Strephon blind/
To all the Charms of Woman Kind;/Should I the Queen of
Love refuse,/Because she rose from stinking Ooze? . . . .
If Strephon would but stop his Nose . . . He soon would
learn to think like me,/And bless his ravisht Eyes to
see/Such Order from Confusion sprung,/Such gaudy Tulips
rais'd from Dung."

Swift, Jonathan (?). "A Love Poem. From a Physician to his Mistress. Written at London." From The Choice Works of Dean
Swift. London: Chatto and Windus, 1876. Poem: 34 lines.

Doctors   Sexuality

An extreme example of the physician's handicap--he is
so immersed in his profession (and his body) that he
cannot woo his lady normally: "When pity in those
eyes I view,/My bowels wambling make me spew . . . .
How have you torn my heart to pieces/With maggots,
humours and caprices!/By which I got the hemorrhoids;/
And loathsome worms my anus voids."

Swift, Jonathan. "A Modest Proposal." Available in Gulliver's
Travels and Other Writings, ed. Louis A. Landa. Cambridge:
The Riverside Press, 1960. Essay.

The Body   Children   The Family
Suffering

An enraged bellow against the sufferings caused by
human stupidity--phrased in the coldest, most "scientific" language. The writer of the proposal begins
with a brief description of the poor, overburdened
with children, then states the benefits of his proposal
expressed in commercial mathematics, and then makes his
proposal: "I have been assured by a very knowing American of my acquaintance in London, that a young healthy
child well nursed is at a year old a most delicious,
nourishing and wholesome food, whether stewed, roasted,
baked, or boiled." He proposes keeping a small number,
of which one-quarter will be males, for breeding purposes and then takes off in a fanciful flight on ways
to profitably manage the sale and slaughter, interpo-
lating yet more benefits that would accrue to the
wealthy Irish from his plan. Of course, the purpose
of the essay is to shock the reader into exclaiming,
but these are humans! The human body isn't food, nor
can the human family be broken up for breeding purposes!
The essay closes with rational reforms that have been
continually rejected and concludes with the final twist:
"I profess in the sincerity of my heart that I have not
the least personal interest in endeavouring to promote
this necessary work, having no other motive than the
public good of my country, by advancing our trade,
providing for infants, relieving the poor, and giving
some pleasure to the rich. I have no children by
which I can propose to get a single penny; the youngest being nine years old, and my wife past child-bearing."

Swift, Jonathan. "Stella's Birth-day: March 13, 1726/7." Available in Poetical Works, ed. Herbert Davis. New York: Oxford
University Press, 1967. Poem: 88 lines.

Disease & Health   Dying   Suffering

This gentle poem was written when Stella was in pain
and dying (although she lasted for 10 more months).
The poet begins: "This Day then, let us not be told,/
That you are sick, and I grown old,/Nor think on our
approaching Ills,/And talk of Spectacles and Pills."
Yet the poet continues praising her for a well-spent
life, asking her to take comfort from her Virtues as
her body has taken comfort from food. Above all, the
poet asks that she not reject her friends in her
suffering: "Oh then, whatever Heav'n intends,/Take
Pity on your pitying Friends;/Nor let your Ills affect
your Mind,/To fancy they can be unkind./Me, surely me,
you ought to spare,/Who gladly would your Suff'rings
share; . . . You, to whose Care so oft I owe,/That
I'm alive to tell you so."

Swift, Jonathan. "Strephon and Chloe." Available in Poetical
Works, ed. Herbert Davis. New York: Oxford University Press,
1967. Poem: 314 lines.

The Body   Sexuality

Chloe is so genteel, "No noisom Whiffs, or sweaty
Streams,/Before, behind, above, below,/Could from
her taintless Body flow." Strephon gains her from
her father with a large marriage settlement and, carefully washing himself, prepares to bed her on their
wedding night, approaching his goddess with timorous
reverence. But Chloe rejects him fiercely until the
twelve cups of tea she has drunk force her to the
chamber pot. Strephon rejoices that she is mortal,
uses the pot himself, and splashes her. The two are

now freed from Constraint and live happy stinking lives
together. However, the narrator continues on--if
Strephon had seen her straining on the chamber pot, he
would have remained heart free. Therefore, men should
choose their wives for sense, decency, prudence and
good nature in order "to keep Esteem and Love alive."
The most beautiful woman will be ugly behind her chamber
door.

Swift, Jonathan. "Verses on the Death of Dr. Swift, D.S.P.D.
Occasioned by reading a Maxim in Rochefoucalt . . . In the
adversity of our best friends, we find something that doth
not displease us." Available in Gulliver's Travels and
Other Writings, ed. Louis A. Landa. Cambridge: The Riverside Press, 1960. Poem: ca. 494 lines.

Age   Death   Doctors
Grief   Suffering

To prove that "In all distresses of our friends/We
first consult our private ends," Swift writes this
account of his friends' responses to his illness and
death (ending with a fervid elegy to himself). His
friends tell over his illness: "'See, how the Dean
begins to break:/Poor gentleman, he droops apace,/You
plainly find it in his face:/That old vertigo in his
head,/Will never leave him, till he's dead:/Besides,
his memory decays,/He recollects not what he says'
. . . . Then hug themselves, and reason thus;/'It is
not yet so bad with us.'" The only people to take a
deep interest in his illness are those with similar
ailments. When Swift "dies," the gossip begins. The
doctors blame Swift for his death: "Had he been rul'd,
for ought appears,/He might have liv'd these twenty
years:/For when we opened him we found,/That all his
vital parts were sound." A few writers grieve a short
while for him; the ladies of his acquaintance grieve
between the fall of the cards at quadrille. His printed
verse soon goes to line pie tins. Then, "one indiff'rent
in the cause,/My character impartial draws," giving a
glowing elegy upon the persecuted, virtuous patriotic
poet now lost to the Kingdom. Sadly, this poem written
fourteen years before his death is not an inaccurate
description of the event.

Taylor, Edward. "Meditation. Col. 1.18. That in all things he
might have the Preheminence." From Preparatory Meditations,
Second Series. Available in The Poems of Edward Taylor, ed.
D. E. Stanford. New Haven: Yale University Press, 1960.
Poem: 42 lines.

By Doctors   Children   Death
Grief

Although Taylor was chiefly a minister, he also func-
tioned as a physician. Louis Martz' introduction to
The Poems of Edward Taylor cites a statement of his
grandson, Ezra Stiles: "'He was physician for the town
all his life.'" This poem, written upon the death of
Taylor's son, James, might be interesting set next to
Ben Jonson's "On My First Sonne." James' death was a
punishment for his father, a punishment that leads him
back to contemplation of God's Preeminence. "But
doth my sickness want such remedies,/As Mummy draind
out of that Body spun/Out of my bowells first? Must
th' Cure arise/Out of the coffin of a pious son? . . . .
Yet let the Rose of Sharon spring up cleare,/Out of my
James his ashes unto mee . . . . Let thy Preheminence
which, Lord, indeed/Ore all things is, me help in time
of need."

Taylor, Edward. "Meditation. 1 Cor. 3.22. Death is Yours." From
Preparatory Meditations, First Series. Available in The
Poems of Edward Taylor, ed. D. E. Stanford. New Haven:
Yale University Press, 1960. Poem: 42 lines.

By Doctors   Death

To praise God, it is only necessary to tell of His
transformation of Death. "The Painter lies who pen-
sills death's Face grim/With White bare butter Teeth,
bare staring bones . . . . Say I am thine, My Lord:
Make me thy bell/To ring thy Praise. Then Death is
mine indeed/A Hift to Grace, a Spur to Duty; Spell/To
Fear; a Frost to nip each naughty Weede./A Golden doore
to Glory. Oh I'le sing/This Triumph o're the Grave!
Death where's thy Sting?"

Taylor, Edward. "Meditation. Mal. 4.2. With Healing in His Wings."
From Preparatory Meditations, Second Series. Available in
The Poems of Edward Taylor, ed. D. E. Stanford. New Haven:
Yale University Press, 1960. Poem: 72 lines.

The Body   By Doctors   Disease & Health

As in the poems of that other famous 17th-century New
England Poet, Anne Bradstreet, it is often impossible
to separate diseases of the body from diseases of the
soul. For Taylor, Christ was medicine, but nowhere is
he so specific about bodily disease as a metaphor for
(or a result of) sin, as in this poem: "His Aire
[Satan's] I breath in, poison doth my Lungs./Hence
come Consumptions, Fevers, Head pains: Turns . . .
Ill Tongue, Mouth Ulcers, Frog, the Quinsie Throate
. . . Heart Ach, the Syncopee, bad stomach tricks/
Gaul Tumors, Liver grown; spleen evills Cricks . . .
The Kidny toucht, the Iliak, Colick Griefe . . . the
Scurvy, Sore/The Miserere Mei." He asks Christ for
purges, "Cordiall powders," rheum-caps, Light, fresh
spirits, "Pledgets," and plasters. For Christ is "O!
Sun of Righteousness Thy Beams bright, Hot/Rafter a
Doctors, and a Surgeons Shop."

Taylor, Edward. "Meditation. Phil. 3. ult. Our Vile Bodie."
   From Preparatory Meditations, Second Series. Available in
   The Poems of Edward Taylor, ed. D. E. Stanford. New Haven:
   Yale University Press, 1960. Poem: 60 lines.

The Body   By Doctors

   The body, the house defiled by garbage, is made the
   cabinet to hold the gem that is the soul. But the body
   defiles the soul. Only Grace can clean and make glorious both--a sign of the magnitude of God's power, for
   the body is portrayed as a vile thing indeed! "Guts,
   Garbage, Rotteness./And all its pipes but Sincks of
   nasty ware/That foule Earths face, and do defile the
   aire./A varnisht pot of putrid excrements,/And quickly
   turns to excrements itselfe,/By natures Law."

Taylor, Edward. "Upon Wedlock, and Death of Children." Available
   in The Poems of Edward Taylor, ed. D. E. Stanford. New
   Haven: Yale University Press, 1960. Poem: 42 lines.

By Doctors   Children   Death
Grief

   More personal than "Meditation. Col. 1.18. That in all
   things he might have the Preheminence." Marriage is
   a knot-garden (here a "True-Love-Knot" garden) that
   sends up flowers of his stock. But God crops two of
   the flowers. The first loss is accepted as a flowery
   pledge to God, now glorified with him. However, the
   second loss almost brings on the sin of repining
   against God's Will. "But oh! the tortures, Vomit,
   screechings, groans,/And six weeks Fever would pierce
   hearts like stones./Griefe o're doth flow: and nature
   fault would finde/Were not thy Will, my Spell Charm,
   Joy, and Gem . . . . I joy, may I sweet Flowers for
   Glory breed,/Whether thou getst them green, or lets
   them seed." Children as mere extensions of himself
   (not even of wife).

Voltaire, Francois-Marie Arouet. Candide. Tale.

Doctors   Plague   Sexuality
Suffering   V.D.

   Voltaire demonstrates that suffering is purposeless,
   without meaning to the sufferer or to the universe.
   Although social evils (purposeless war, religious
   persecution) cause much suffering, they are only
   part of a creation that is not "the best of all possible worlds." V.D. is one instance of the cruelty of
   existence. Although sexual intercourse is one of the
   few cooperative and pleasurable relationships between
   humans, even this blessing is cursed by the vicious
   penalty of V.D. The noseless Pangloss illustrates
   the destructiveness of the disease. Doctors are of
   little avail against disease in general, being greedy
   and ignorant (Chapters XIX and XX). Survival in this
   our world of earthquakes, disease, and human cruelty
   requires attention to the nearest duty, constant
   effort, fast feet, and good luck.

Wigglesworth, Michael. The Day of Doom, ed. K. B. Murdoch. New
   York: Russell & Russell, 1966. Poem: 224 stanzas.

By Doctors   Children   Suffering

   This 17th-century New England minister also practiced
   medicine, becoming involved in the controversy over
   smallpox innoculation. He is most famous for this
   "poem," which was very popular in its day. It depicts and justifies the suffering of sinners on the
   Judgment Day, showing how all family ties fall before
   the acceptance or rejection of Christ: "The tender
   Mother will own no other of all her tender brood,/
   But such as stand at Christ's right hand acquitted
   through his Blood./The pious Father had now much
   rather his graceless Son should ly/In Hell with Devils
   for all his evils burning eternally."

Winchilsea, Countess of (Anne Finch). "Fragment at Tunbridge
   Wells." Available in The Poems of Anne Countess of Win-
   chilsea, ed. Myra Reynolds. Chicago: University of
   Chicago Press, 1903. Poem: 18 lines.

Disease & Health

   Light-hearted contradiction of her poem "To Dr. Waldron,"
   which extolled the healing powers of poetry. "For He,
   that made, must new create us,/Ere Seneca, or Epictetus,/
   With all their serious Admonitions,/Can, for the Spleen,
   prove good Physicians . . . . At Tunbridge [health spa]
   let us still be Drinking,/Though 'tis th' Antipodes
   to Thinking: . . . Yet these, and not sententious
   Papers,/Must brighten Life, and cure the Vapours,&c."

Winchilsea, Countess of (Anne Finch). "The Spleen." Available in
   The Poems of Anne Countess of Winchilsea, ed. Myra Reynolds.
   Chicago: University of Chicago Press, 1903. Poem: 150
   lines.

Body/Mind   Disease & Health   Doctors
Madness   Women as Patients

   "The Spleen" is used as a catch-all term to cover all
   harmful interactions between the mind and the body:
   "Now a Dead Sea thou'lt represent,/A Calm of stupid
   Discontent,/Then, dashing on the Rocks wilt rage into
   a Storm." Although primarily a woman's disease (it
   can cause a wife to browbeat her husband), the spleen
   is also held responsible for sullen, tavern-haunting
   husbands and quibbles about religion. The disease
   defies the anatomist; it is profitable to physicians
   but may be infectious. "Tho' the Physicians greatest

Gains,/Altho' his growing Wealth he sees/Daily increas'd
by Ladies Fees,/Yet dost thou baffle all his studious
Pains./Not skilful Lower thy Source cou'd find,/Or
thro' the well-dissected Body trace . . . . With unsuccessful Toil he wrought,/'Till thinking Thee to've
catch'd, Himself by thee was caught . . . And sunk beneath thy Chain to a lamented Grave."

Winchilsea, Countess of (Anne Finch). "To Death." Available in
   The Poems of Anne Countess of Winchilsea, ed. Myra Reynolds.
   Chicago: University of Chicago Press, 1903. Poem: 16
   lines.

Death

   For the most part this poem is very conventional: Death
   is the "King of Terrors" who summons all ranks of men.
   The means by which he works are fearful--"thy Swords,
   thy Racks, thy Wheels;/Thy scorching Fevers, which
   distract the Sense." However, the last three lines
   create a fascinating combination of Death the business-
   man and Death the lover. "My Bus'ness is to Dye, and
   Thine to Kill./Gently thy fatal Sceptre on me lay,/
   And take to thy cold Arms, insensibly, thy Prey."

Winchilsea, Countess of (Anne Finch). "To Dr. Waldron." Avail-
   able in The Poems of Anne Countess of Winchilsea, ed. Myra
   Reynolds. Chicago: University of Chicago Press, 1903.
   Poem: 55 lines.

Doctors   Med. Profession   Science & Poetry

   According to the head-note, this poem was addressed
   to "A Fellow of All Souls Colledge in OXFORD, Who in
   a Letter acknowledg'd his mistake in having lefte
   that Society & the Muses to follow the Pratise of
   Phisck." The poet assumes that practicing medicine
   destroys poetic ability. She is very confident that
   a creative mind is true medicine, whereas the profession of medicine is merely the piling up of money.
   "'Tis true Mirtillo 'twa a fault/T' have been by
   glittering proffit wrought/To quit that seat of
   thoughts refined/That Eden to the fruitfull mind
   . . . . Why shou'd that Herb which cur'd our spleen/
   When from thy Pen so fresh so green . . . It in th'
   inliven'd Fancy sprung/Grow useless by o're labour'd
   skill . . . Why shou'd thy time and sence be Lost/
   In saving those not worth the cost."

Wycherley, William. The Country Wife. Available in Twelve Famous
   Plays of the Restoration and Eighteenth Century. New York:
   The Modern Library, c. 1960. Drama.

Doctors   Sexuality   V.D.

   Farcical treatment of the ways men and women circum-
   vent social restrictions upon free gratification of
   their sexual desires. Horner, with the aid of an
   unscrupulous doctor, gives out that he is a eunuch
   as a result of an unfortunate encounter with "The
   French Disease." As a result, husbands permit him
   to run tame with their wives, and the wives believe
   that they can indulge their appetites while preserving their reputations. "The Country Wife," totally
   ignorant of sexual matters and totally without sexual
   sophistication, rapidly learns how to hold and keep a
   lover, with the aid of her jealous husband and her own
   instincts. Her sister-in-law learns that her honor is
   worthless unless her chosen husband has enough wit, and
   desire for her, to appreciate it. V.D. is merely a
   mild penalty for pursuing one's inclinations, women's
   reputations the only bar (and a very weak one) to satisfied sexual anarchy.

Young, Edward. Night Thoughts, "The Complaint." From The Poetical Works of Edward Young. Cambridge: The Riverside Press,
   n.d. 2 Vols. in 1. Long Poem.

Death   Disease & Health   Grief

   Young lost his wife, stepdaughter, and son-in-law within
   a short period of time. He suffered from insomnia for
   years afterwards. The nine-poem work, Night Thoughts,
   begins with death, grief, and moralistic advice and
   ends with Christian consolation and moralistic advice.
   The death of friends prepares us for our own deaths
   and the eternity which awaits us. Life is powerless
   before death, whose gloomy strength is portrayed in
   striking images: "This is the desert, this the solitude:/How populous, how vital, is the grave! . . . .
   Strong death, alone can heave the massy bar,/This
   gross impediment of clay remove,/And make us embryos
   of existence free."

Young, Edward. "On Michael Angelo's Famous Piece of the Crucifixion; Who is said to have Stabbed a Person that He might
   Draw it More Naturally." From The Poetical Works of Edward
   Young. Cambridge: The Riverside Press, n.d. 2 Vols. bound
   in one. Vol. 2. Poem: 14 lines.

The Body   Science & Poetry   Suffering

   The artist as medical researcher--adopting "medical"
   detachment, draining the body of life, creating tor-
   ment--to produce a spiritual masterpiece: "The daring
   artist, cruelly serene,/Views the pale cheek and the
   distorted mien;/He drains off life by drops, and,
   deaf to cries,/Examines every spirit as it flies . . .
   Each rising agony, each dreadful grace,/Yet warm transplanting to his Saviour's Face./Oh glorious theft! oh
   nobly wicked draught!/With its full charge of death
   each feature fraught,/Such wondrous force the magic
   colours boast,/From his own skill he starts in horror
   lost."

Young, Edward. "Satire V, Characters of Women." Selections avail-
    able in <u>The Penguin Book of Eighteenth-Century English Verse</u>,
    ed. Dennis Davison. Baltimore: Penguin, 1973. Poem: ca.
    84 lines.

The Body   Women as Patients

    "Lemira" is a very early literary instance of the bored,
    hypochondriac woman: "'Though sick to death, abroad
    they safely roam,/But droop and die, in perfect health,
    at home:/For want--but not of health, are ladies ill;/
    And tickets cure beyond the doctor's bill.'" "Rosalinda"
    is so languid that she cannot move her own body: "And
    help! oh help! her spirits are so dead,/One hand scarce
    lifts the other to her head . . . . But chew she must
    herself; ah cruel fate!/That Rosalinda can't by proxy
    eat."

19th Century

Adams, Henry. The Education of Henry Adams. Boston: Houghton Mifflin, 1961. Autobiography.

Children   The Family   Sexuality

The first three chapters are a detached, brilliant recollection of the author's childhood and the forces which shaped him. The whole Autobiography analyzes the influence of being an Adams upon his preconceptions about himself and his world. The last fourteen chapters are more philosophical--an aging man's assessment of the value of his "education" and of trends for the future. One of the greatest of these assessments is "The Dynamo and the Virgin" in which he notes that the force of sexuality, loosely represented by The Virgin, which once unified the world, has been replaced in America by a sexless society, receptive to the power of the dynamo and so open to multiplicity. "The Woman had once been supreme . . . . When she was a true force, she was ignorant of fig leaves, but the monthly-magazine-made American female had not a feature that would have been recognized by Adam . . . . In any previous age, sex was strength . . . . She was goddess because of her force; she was the animated dynamo; she was reproduction--the greatest and most mysterious of energies . . . . All this was to American thought as though it had never existed."

Alcott, Louisa May. Hospital Sketches, ed. B. Z. Jones. Cambridge, Mass.: Belknap Press, 1960. Sketches.

Doctors   Dying   Grief
Med. Profession Nurses   Sexual Roles
Suffering   Surgery   Women as healers

During the Civil War, Alcott went south to nurse wounded soldiers. She lasted only a short time, part of which she was sick with typhoid, but she saw enough to write these descriptions of hospital life as viewed by a naive but sensitive amateur. She writes as an optimistic observer for "it is a part of my religion to look well after the cheerfulnesses of life, and let the dismals shift for themselves; believing, with good Sir Thomas More, that it is wise to 'be merrie in God'." She seems to have experienced two kinds of feelings about being a woman. Her nursing activities consisted of providing water and linen, of writing and reading letters, of bandaging minor wounds and administering medicine, and of feeding and washing the men. This last horrified her when she began work: "but to scrub some dozen lords of creation at a moment's notice, was really--really--. However, there was no time for nonsense . . . I drowned my scruples in a wash-bowl, clutched my soap manfully . . . ." ("A Day"). But when duties included emotional situations, she was useful. She admires Dr. P. with horrified fascination; he "seemed to regard a dilapidated body very much as I should have regarded a damaged garment." Dr. P. tells the patients, in scientific terms, what he is doing to their bodies, but he leaves it to Alcott to tell the truth to a dying patient because, as he says, "women have a way of doing such things comfortably." The patient helps her to tell him, and she offers him the opportunity to cry and visibly suffer without losing his manhood ("A Night"). She is distressed by the absence of comforters for the dying and the grieving, criticizing the chaplain for ignoring the hospitals and describing how her sympathetic tears aided a grieving sister ("A Postscript"). She is very critical of the callous and inept orderlies and supply clerks. She is also critical of those surgeons who, as one doctor admits, become blunted in feeling and insensible to pain. She praises Dr. Z. who, in addition to trying to avoid giving pain, also tries to give the patient the positive comforts of distractions and sympathy. Alcott is not aware of any professionalism in nursing; she complains of the excessive work demanded from women who must respond as compliant angels, but it is women, not nurses, whom she is defending.

Anonymous. Teleny. Excerpted in Sexual Heretics, ed. Brian Reade. New York: Coward-McCann, 1970. Novel.

The Body   Homosexuality

Excerpts are really all that are needed. Vivid descriptions of perfect bodies in perfect homosexual intercourse in perfect surroundings. The men exist only in their relationships to each other. Society never intrudes. Might be interesting set next to Fanny Hill or Genet's work. "The fumes of the smoke and those of the wine rose up to our heads, and in our re-awakened sensuality we soon had between our lips a far more fleshy mouth-piece than the amber one of the Turkish pipe. Our heads were again soon lost between each other's thighs."

Arnold, Matthew. Empedocles on Etna. Available in The Poetical Works of Matthew Arnold, eds. C. B. Tinker and H. F. Lowry. London: Oxford University Press, 1950. Dramatic Poem: ca. 1100 lines.

Age   Madness   Suicide

Philosophical poem, with some lyrical interludes. The great philosopher Empedocles, replaced in popularity by the Sophists, comes to Mt. Etna in great depression. He has lost that nice balance between the life of thought and the life of the senses that he had in his youth. He can find happiness neither in the society of men, where the mediocre now prevail

and he has outlived his time, nor in solitude. He has, like many intellectuals, been too much alone with his never-satisfied mind. At last, he takes the only course left to him; he leaps into the crater, hoping to be united with the elements and thus ease his restless mind in something physical. Compare Byron's Manfred.

Arnold, Matthew. "Growing Old." Available in The Poems of Matthew Arnold, ed. Kenneth Allott. New York: Barnes & Noble, 1965. Poem: 35 lines.

Age

A bitter poem in which age is seen as an uncompensated deterioration of the body and the ability to feel. It is "to feel each limb/Grow stiffer, every function less exact,/Each nerve more loosely strung . . . . It is to suffer this,/And feel but half, and feebly, what we feel./Deep in our hidden heart/Festers the dull remembrance of a change,/But no emotion--none." And the world will now "applaud the hollow ghost/Which blamed the living man."

Arnold, Matthew. "Haworth Churchyard." Available in The Poems of Matthew Arnold, ed. Kenneth Allott. New York: Barnes & Noble, 1965. Poem: 138 lines.

Death

An extrapolation of Wuthering Heights applied to the death-haunted Brontës themselves. The poet envisions them as sleeping as peacefully as the dying Earnshaw Heathcliff saw the moor: "The drowsy bee, as of old,/Hum o'er the thyme,/the grouse/Call from the heather in bloom!/Sleep, or only for this/Break your united repose." But the Muse interrupts as Kathy might, lashing the graves with an April rain: "Unquiet souls!/In the dark fermentation of earth,/In the never idle work shop of nature,/In the eternal movement,/Ye shall find yourselves again!"

Arnold, Matthew. "Literature and Science." In Philistinism in England and America. Available in The Complete Works of Matthew Arnold, Vol. X. ed. R. H. Super. Ann Arbor: The University of Michigan Press, 1974. Essay.

Science & Poetry

A stirring defense of humane letters (not belles lettres) against those (especially Professor Huxley) who argue for a purely natural science education. He argues that medieval education could do without both natural science and literature because its knowledge supplied the people's needs for conduct and beauty. Now, natural science is giving us new conceptions of the universe, therefore "the need of humane letters, to establish a relation between the new conceptions, and our instinct for beauty, our instinct for conduct, is only the more visible." Humane letters can engage the emotions. "We shall find that the art and poetry and eloquence of men who . . . had the most limited natural knowledge . . . have a fortifying, and elevating, and quickening, and suggestive power, capable of wonderfully helping us to relate the results of modern science to our need for conduct, our need for beauty."

Arnold, Matthew. "Thyrsis." Available in The Poetical Works of Matthew Arnold, eds. C. B. Tinker and H. F. Lowry. London: Oxford University Press, 1950. Poem: 240 lines.

Death   Grief

One of the greatest elegies, "Thyrsis" commemorates Arnold's close friend, the poet Clough, q.v., with whom he shared his student days at Oxford. Now, after Clough's death, Arnold returns to the University, following the walk they used to take together, thinking of Clough's poetic and personal traits, and mournfully regretting that everything is changed--the Oxford hills no longer look the same, and Thyrsis (Clough) is dead. Arnold remembers the legend of the Scholar Gypsy (see his poem by the same name), which supposed that while a certain elm tree stood, that single quester forever wandered the hills. The poem's mood changes abruptly when Arnold spots the tree: "Despair I will not, while I yet descry/'Neath the mild canopy of English air/That lonely tree against the western sky." He must return to the city, but he invokes the voice of Clough to follow him, and in the last lines, Clough's spirit returns, speaking these words: "Why faintest thou? I wander'd till I died./Roam on! The light we sought is shining still."

Arnold, Matthew. "A Wish." Available in The Poems of Matthew Arnold, ed. Kenneth Allott. New York: Barnes & Noble, 1965. Poem: 52 lines.

Dying

The poet asks that his deathbed be free of doctors trying to label his disease or parsons canvassing for religion. Instead, he wants to see "the wide aërial landscape," which will prepare him for death. "There let me gaze, till I become/In soul, with what I gaze on, wed!/To feel the universe my home;/To have before my mind--instead of/The sick room, the mortal strife,/The turmoil for a little breath--/The pure eternal course of life,/Not human combatings with death!"

Austen, Jane. Emma. Novel.

Children   Disease & Health   Doctors
The Family   Sexuality

Young Emma, tied to a hypochondriac father (In a funny conversation in Chapter XII, Mr. Woodhouse and his married daughter turn every topic onto illness, despite Emma's attempts to prevent them), entertains herself with prejudiced and condescending attempts at matchmaking, which have painful consequences for herself and her compliant friend, the illegitimate and stupid Miss Smith. Emma's blunders appear the more inept when placed next to the skillful intrigues of Frank Churchill, who is hiding his engagement to Jane Fairfax. Further, the marriages (and the birth of a child to her closest woman friend) that appear despite her efforts only isolate Emma from the village community she has dominated so long. She had seen marriage in terms of social status, convenience to herself, and an unreal, exciting game, rather than in terms of a close union between two people and a link to the community. A rival forces the already chastened Emma to acknowledge to herself that she is as ignorant of herself as of others. But all ends well; Emma weds her fatherly mentor, Mr. Knightly (whose Christian name she playfully refuses to use until their wedding) and settles down to design realistically a married life that would permit continuous attention from her husband and continuous attention to her querulous, but loving, father. Although the busy apothecary, Mr. Perry, never appears in person in the novel, he appears to have achieved a soothing omnipresence among the hypochondriacs and too-solicitous parents of Highbury. Mr. Perry is of great use to Emma's father, who attributes all of his own opinions to Mr. Perry, in order to endow them with medical authority.

Austen, Jane. Mansfield Park. Novel.

Children   Disease & Health   The Family
Sexuality   Sexual Roles

Effect of parental models upon children's behavior, especially sexual behavior, in three closely connected families. The irascible Admiral Crawford and his wretched wife provide poor models for their nephew and niece; the younger Crawfords, spoiled by one relation and disdained by the other, grow up without principles, living for their own gratification. Henry Crawford and his sister act as a touchstone upon the Bertram family which has suffered from similar disparity of parental models--the children have been spoiled by their Aunt Norris and reproved by their father. As a result, when sexuality contends against morality, sexuality wins handily--both the Miss Bertrams compete for the favor of Henry Crawford and even Edmund, the principled young clergyman, falls under the spell of the worldly Miss Crawford. Only their cousin, the timid Fanny Price, who is doubly shielded by her harsh upbringing and her love for Edmund, is able to see the ambition and vanity of the Crawfords. As a result, she refuses the marriage proposal of Henry Crawford, who has courted her out of pique at her coldness, and is sent by Sir Thomas Bertram to her own, poor family in Portsmith to be subdued into acceptance of the promising Crawford match. In Portsmith, Fanny experiences the horrors of a family without consideration and affection--in which the father cares only for his own comfort and the mother for her sons and one daughter, in which sibling rivalry is noisy and continuous, and in which there is no order or management. Fanny is rescued from her immediate family by Henry Crawford's adulterous elopement with her eldest cousin Maria, now Mrs. Rushworth. Fanny is recalled to comfort her aunt and uncle, sunk under the triple tragedy of Maria's adultery, her cousin Julia's elopement with a worthless young man, and Tom Bertram's illness, the result of dissipated living. She also must comfort Edmund who has been able to overlook Miss Crawford's slighting remarks about her uncle, the Admiral, who despised her (he is her uncle, he supported her, and so must be treated with respect even though the Admiral's mistress occasioned Miss Crawford's removal from his house), but Edmund cannot overlook Miss Crawford's lack of misery and shame at her brother's adultery. She doesn't feel sunk beyond reproach and does feel that she and Edmund will continue their relationship--therefore Edmund feels he must break the relationship. However, the Bertram family survives the crises fairly well: as a result of his illness, Tom discovers the value of his family; Julia turns to her father for advice and reconciliation; Edmund and Fanny marry; and Mrs. Norris and Maria go off together. Those family members who truly care for one another live happily ever after.

Austen, Jane. Persuasion. Novel.

Body/Mind   Disease & Health   The Family
Grief   Sexuality   Sexual Roles

Like Sense and Sensibility, Persuasion discusses the effect of character upon health. Mary Musgrove is doomed to chronic hypochondria because of her egotism and dependence upon others; she is content only when amused, and amused only by the constant efforts of other people. In contrast, Mrs. Smith, poor and paralyzed, is happy because she has a strong and resilient spirit. Not only the ability to bear discomfort, but health itself is affected by character: Louisa Musgrove is injured because her obstinacy causes her an unnecessary fall. Grief is not only influenced by personality, but also by the sex of the grieving person. Mrs. Musgrove may be ludicrously pathetic in her grief for a worthless son, but she mourns longer than the grief-stricken Benbow who worries his friends with his agony on the death of his fiancée and then surprises them with his sudden engagement to the interesting invalid, Louisa Musgrove. Discussing Benbow's sudden recovery, the novel's heroine, Anne Elliott, claims that men do not mourn as long as women when the object of their affection is totally lost to them. Her argument is based on analogies between the body and the emotions: "Man is more robust than woman, but he is not longer lived; which exactly explains my view of the nature of their attachments . . . . You are always laboring and toiling, exposed to every risk and hardship . . . . It would be too hard indeed . . . if woman's feelings were to be added to this." She finally agrees that every person is so biased in favor of his or her own sex that no impartial judgment can be given--although she first persuades her male opponent that he cannot use literary works as authorities because most of them were written by men. Persuasion, like all of Jane Austen's novels, is full of sexuality-- carefully buried under lively, perfect prose. Captain Wentworth is nearly trapped by his pursuit of Louisa Musgrove; Captain Benbow is seeking feminine consolation; William Elliott's efforts to prevent Mrs. Clay's wheedling herself into marriage with his uncle only lead him into her trap; and Anne Elliott is harassed by the need, first to conceal, and then to display her love for Captain Wentworth, hampered in both cases by social conventions and self-centered companions--among whom are the other members of her family. Although the exploration of the family is not as great as in Mansfield Park, Persuasion does again contain three quite different families: the isolated members of Sir Walter Elliott's falsely proud family, the cheerful, child-dominated, loving family of the Musgroves, and the quiet warmth of the Crofts and Wentworths. Admiral Croft and his wife exemplify the perfect couple--inseparable, equal but not alike, kindly, out-going, and lacking all self-consciousness--they are the ideal seen by Anne Elliott as she marries Mrs. Croft's brother.

Austen, Jane. Sense and Sensibility. Novel.

Body/Mind   Disease & Health

The novel clearly, and delightfully, hammers home the message that uncontrolled sensibility is harmful both to the person enjoying being overly emotional and any unfortunate people in his or her vicinity. "Sensibility" is embodied in Marianne, who invites pain and death in her determined pursuit of full self-expression. She first meets Willoughby, her lover, when she insists upon running headlong down a grassy hill in the rain and finds herself with the only-to-be expected twisted ankle. The book implies that she runs so wildly because the attractive Willoughby was only a few yards away. Marianne throws herself into her affair with Willoughby with the same energy and openness with which she praises gothic ruins, plays romantic music on the piano, and snubs people who bore her. When Willoughby is forced to throw her over, she becomes seriously ill because she refuses to restrain her grief. She invites death by taking long walks in the cold rain to avoid boring company--and her own feelings. Her emotions nearly kill her. In contrast, her sister Elinor is "Sense" and so is able to support both herself and Marianne. When she loses her lover, she hides her grief. When her successful rival gloats over her, Elinor baffles the woman by her calm discussion of family and financial problems affecting her lover's marriage with that rival. When Marianne loses control, Elinor does not helplessly sympathize (or offer food as consolation as does Mrs. Jennings), but instead tries to teach her how to calm herself. As a result, she can save Marianne--and marry her own lover after all. The mind is working with the emotions.

Balzac, Honoré de. Béatrix, trans. K. P. Wormeley. Boston: Hardy, Pratt & Co., 1904. Novel.

The Family   Sexuality   Sexual Roles

Interesting for two sections, both in the first half of the novel. The first is the description of Camille Maupin, a version of George Sand, a woman who escaped the normal conditioning of women as a child and so was able to express her genius. However, this description is somewhat tarnished because the woman is judged on some odd standard of "purity." Her reading as a child had this result: "She thus obtained a knowledge of life in theory, and had no innocence of mind, though virgin personally. Her intellect floated on the impurities of knowledge while her heart was pure." She falls in love with the beautiful young hero of the novel and assists him maternally in his disasterous affair with the mercenary, but enchanting, Beatrix. Her destiny is the convent which she enters on the day of the hero's marriage. The section is a grim evaluation of woman's intellect. However, the passage is lightened by the amusing conflict of ages and cultures. The hero is the spoiled center of a provincial, noble family whose incomprehension of the sophisticated Parisian games of Beatrix and Camille is ludicrous, even though their attentions are most loving and kind.

Balzac, Honoré de. The Country Doctor, trans. Ellen Marriage. New York: E. P. Dutton, 1911; rpt. 1961. Novel.

Death   Disease & Health   Doctors
Grief   Med. Profession   Mental Retardation
Sexual Roles

This "novel" is really a collection of sketches demonstrating the elevating effect of a determined, intelligent man upon a poor village. The novel's hero is a repentant man who decides to dedicate his life to helping country people. Although he has studied medicine, he debates "whether to become a curé, a country doctor, or a justice of the peace."

He decides that a doctor has the most influence: "When a peasant is ill, when he is forced to lie on his pallet, and while he is recovering, he cannot help himself, he is forced to listen to logical reasoning, which he can understand quite well if it is put clearly before him. This thought made a doctor of me." The first sketch, "The countryside and the man," shows how he forcibly removed a dozen cretins to an asylum to prevent their breeding and growing in numbers and how he pacified their neighbors by giving them the "cretins'" land! He is rather high-handed. However, he gives careful medical attention to the last, dying idiot who is described at some length: "At the sight of the deep, circular folds of the skin on the forehead, the sodden, fish-like eyes, and the head, with its short, coarse, scantily growing hair . . . Who would not have experienced, as Genestas did, an instinctive feeling of repulsion for a being that had neither the physical beauty of an animal nor the mental endowments of man, who was possessed of neither instinct nor reason, and who had never heard nor spoken any kind of articulate speech?" The doctor uses the peasants' greed to stimulate economic growth; he encourages the industrious. But he is very male-oriented in his search for the industrious. He praises a tile-worker who has created a flourishing business from a decaying one, but all his praise goes for the male head of the household who taught his wife, mother, and mother-in-law to make bricks, they working for him in rags. The need to embody the household in one figure is seen even in the treatment of grief. Earlier in "A Doctor's Round," the doctor compares the way two households grieve for the death of the master--one with violent laments, the other with stoical mourning. He approves of the first, not because it vents emotion, but because proper laments for the head of the household keep the inferiors in order. He describes the violent eulogies by the wife; however, "if the widow could reproach herself with the smallest of shortcomings, she would not dare to utter a word; for if she did, she would pronounce her own condemnation, she would be at the same time her own accuser and judge. Is there not something sublime in this custom which thus judges the living and the dead?" Dr. Genestas, the hero, enriches the countryside by generating new articles of trade and trade routes, cures the stout old veteran's son, and dies amid the universal lamentations of the country people, his "children."

Balzac, Honoré de. Cousin Pons. Poor Relations, Part II, trans. H. J. Hunt. Baltimore, Maryland: Penguin, 1968. Novel.

Death   Dying   Evil Doctors
Med. Ethics

Balzac has several cases of sensitive, aesthetically-aware individuals hounded to death by avaricious friends. Daughters bleed Père Goriot dry; a wife is barely prevented by a conscientious doctor from incarcerating her husband (A Commission in Lunacy); and monstrous inferiors haunt the deathbed of the little collector, Pons, making him miserable and robbing the only friend he loved. A coalition of a concierge, a greedy lawyer, a monomaniacal collector, a wealthy relative, and a poor, ambitious doctor destroy the two friends. The inveigling of the doctor into the plot is recounted in Chapter 17. The concierge visits him with an imaginary disease which he "cures" with great difficulty and great publicity. Now she has him for accepting a fee for a fictitious ailment. A small bribe in addition, and the doctor is ready to bend his medical ethics, recommending the callous and cruel concierge as a nurse. When she is unmasked, the doctor merely manipulates the honest priest into recommending another tool of the conspirators in her place.

Balzac, Honoré de. Père Goriot, trans. J. M. Sedgwick. New York: Dodd, Mead & Co., 1954. Novel.

Children   Dying   Med. Students
Sexuality

Classic story of excessive paternal love. Goriot, after his wife died, turned all of his love to his daughters, channeling sexual and paternal drives in one direction. He divided his fortune between his two daughters so that they might marry brilliantly. Unfortunately the daughters chose their husbands for wealth and rank, rather than sexual appeal. As a result, they both turn to lovers who drain their fortunes and so cause the daughters to drain the remnants of their father's annuity in order to keep both their lovers and their social position. The old man gives everything, which is not nearly enough, and dies of a stroke caused by the sisters' squabbling. His death-bed is attended by two "sons," the law student Rastignac (a second lover of one daughter) and the medical student, Bianchon. These young men become important characters in La Comédie humaine, both noted for their common sense and humanity. This mix is best seen in Bianchon's activities around the dying man--he scrounges for firewood and medicine, he arranges for someone to watch over the man, he listens to Père Goriot's delirious cries for his daughters and is close to tears; but he can also instruct Rastignac to note the old man's mutterings: are they the result of memory or judgment, fact or feelings. "'Oh! a scientific fact is at stake,' returned the medical student with all the ardor of a neophyte. 'Then,' said Eugène, 'I am the only one who takes care of the poor old men out of affection.' 'If you had seen me this morning, you would not say that,' answered Bianchon, without taking offense. 'Doctors who have been long in practice think of nothing but the case, but I still think of the patient, my dear boy.'"

Baudelaire, Charles Pierre. Artificial Paradise: On Hashish and Wine as Means of Expanding Individuality, trans. Ellen Fox. New York: Herder and Herder, 1971. Essays.

Alcoholism   Drugs

Baudelaire rises into poetic prose (hard to feel in translation) when he speaks of wine: "I sometimes seem to hear the wine; it speaks with its soul, in the spirit voice heard only by spirits, and says, 'Man, my beloved creature, even through my prison of glass and bolts of cork, I want to send you a song filled with good-fellowship, a song of joy and light and hope.' Even drunks overflow with goodwill. Hashish, however, is to be condemned because it saps the will, isolating and making suicidal its user. To corrupt its subjects, a government need only encourage the use of hashish. Both wine and hashish cause a poetic evolvement; both attest to Man's great desire to excite his individuality. Nevertheless, "wine is useful, it yields fruitful results. Hashish is useless and dangerous." Baudelaire's work on opium combines a summary of, translation of, and brief commentary upon De Quincey's opium essays.

Baudelaire, Charles Pierre. "The Dance of Death" ("Danse Macabre"), trans. Roy Campbell. Available in The Flowers of Evil (Les Fleurs du Mal), eds. Marthiel and Jackson Mathews, rev. ed. New York: New Directions, 1962. Poem: 60 lines.

Death

Death as a woman's skeleton come to a ball and ignored. The skeleton on the festive scene becomes the butt of grotesque comedy until the full discharge of contempt falls upon those living humans who adopt the skeleton's coquetery while ignoring her existence. "The pits of your dark eyes dread fancies breathe,/And vertigo. Among the dancers prudent,/Hope not your sixteen pairs of smiling teeth/Will ever find a contemplative student./Yet who's not squeezed a skeleton with passion?/Nor ravened with his kisses on the meat/Of charnels . . . . In every clime, Death, studies your devices/And vain contortions, laughable Humanity,/And oft, like you, perfumes herself with spices/Mixing her irony with your insanity!"

Baudelaire, Charles Pierre. "Jewels" ("Les Bijoux"), trans. David Paul. Available in The Flowers of Evil (Les Fleurs du Mal), eds. Marthiel and Jackson Mathews, rev. ed. New York: New Directions, 1962. Poem: 32 lines.

The Body   Homosexuality   Sexuality

His mistress' body, combined with her sensual artifice and arts, becomes the essence of erotic power, able to evoke both hetero- and homosexual desire. "Her long legs, her hips, shining smooth as oil,/Her arms and her thighs, undulant as a swan,/Lured my serene, clairvoyant gaze to travel/To her belly, and breasts, the grapes of my vine . . . . With the hips of Antiope, the torso of a boy,/ So deeply was the one form sprung into the other/It seemed as if desire had fashioned a new toy./Her faded, fawn-brown skin was perfection to either!"

Baudelaire, Charles Pierre. "The Little Old Women" ("Les Petites Vielles"), trans. Roy Campbell. Available in The Flowers of Evil (Les Fleurs du Mal), eds. Marthiel and Jackson Mathews, rev. ed. New York: New Directions, 1962. Poem: 84 lines.

Age   Sexuality

The poet is fascinated by the contrast between the shrivelled, disrespected bodies of the old women and their passionate souls. "They crawl: a vicious wind their carrion rides;/ From the deep roar of traffic see them cower . . . . Cracked though they are, their eyes are sharp as drills/And shine, like pools of water in the night. . . ."

Baudelaire, Charles Pierre. "The Metamorphoses of a Vampire" ("Les Metamorphoses du Vampire"), trans. Jackson Mathews. Available in The Flowers of Evil (Les Fleurs du Mal), eds. Marthiel and Jackson Mathews, rev. ed. New York: New Directions, 1962. Poem: 28 lines.

The Body   Sexuality

Post-coital depression and revulsion--with a vengeance. Before, the woman praises her body as able to bury conscience, to enliven old men, to damn angels; and the poet lets her suck the marrow from his bone. Afterwards, when he turns to kiss her, he first sees "A slimy wineskin, full of pus," and then "the cold ruins of a skeleton/Shivered, creaking like a weather vane/or like a sign hung out on an iron arm/Swinging through long winter nights in the storm."

Baudelaire, Charles Pierre. "On Delacroix's Picture of Tasso in Prison" ("Sur Le Tasse en Prison d'Eugène Delacroix"), trans. Roy Campbell. From Les Épaves. Available in The Flowers of Evil, eds. Marthiel and Jackson Mathews, rev. ed. New York: New Directions, 1962. Sonnet.

Madness   Med. Instit.

The renaissance poet Tasso (who wrote the great epic Gerusalemme liberata) was confined to a madhouse for a large portion of his life, whether entirely for medicinal or partly for political reasons is not known. In Baudelaire's poem, Tasso becomes an image of all poets forced into madness by reality. "The poet, sick, and with his chest half bare/Tramples a manuscript in his dark stall,/Gazing with terror at the yawning stair/ Down which his spirit finally must fall."

Baudelaire, Charles Pierre. "Skeletons Digging" ("Le Squelette
laboureur"), trans. Roy Campbell and Yvor Winters. Available
in The Flowers of Evil (Les Fleurs du Mal), eds. Marthiel and
Jackson Mathews, rev. ed. New York: New Directions, 1962.
Poem: 32 lines.

Death

A set of anatomical drawings are given beauty by the crafts-
man's skill, but they are invested with a mysterious horror
by having the peeled bodies depicted as plowing and digging.
The translation is a nice parody of Whitman's "Out of the
Cradle Endlessly Rocking." "Out of the earth at which you
spade,/Funereal laborers, tired and done,/Out of your straining naked bone,/Out of your muscles bare and frayed,/Tell
me, what harvest do you win? . . . That the end has betrayed
us here,/That even death himself has lied?/That though
eternity betide,/Alas! we have again to fear/That in some
unknown land we'll meet/A knotted earth that needs be flayed--/
To drive again the heavy spade/Beneath our bleeding naked
feet?"

Beddoes, Thomas Lovell. Death's Jest-Book. From Complete Works,
ed. Sir Edmund Gosse. London: Fanfrolico Press, n.d.
2 Vols. Vol. 1. Poetic drama.

By Doctors   Death   Madness
Suicide

The mentally unstable Thomas Beddoes was a doctor and
medical researcher--and poet. This closet drama, apparently
influenced by Jacobean and German Romantic playwrights, is
his most famous work. It contains magic and revenge,
innocent young women and jealous lovers, tombs and extravagant feasts, sons rebelling against their father (who is,
in disguise, a leader in the rebellion), brothers murdering
each other in rivalry, and several suicides. The elaborate
plot follows the downfall of Duke Melveric, who has stolen
away Agnes, the sister of his best friend, Wolfram, and
then murdered that friend in rivalry over another young
lady--after Wolfram has saved Melveric's life and forgiven
him for an earlier poisoning attempt! Wolfram's brother
Isbrand tries to destroy everything about Melveric, and,
with the help of Wolfram's ghost whom Melveric raises in
mistake for Agnes, he does bring down Melveric in an
incredibly complicated set of plots, counter-plots, and
sub-plots. All of this is of little interest--it is the
surreal atmosphere of death (twice the figures from a
Dance of Death mural come out from the wall and dance or
comment on the action) that is unique. For example, the
poisoner Arab, Ziba, derives his ancestry from a virgin
young boy who slept with a pale maiden who came to him at
night. The maiden vanishes, and, in his search for her,
the boy passes "a new-dug grave gaped wide for food,/'Who
was she?' cried he, and the earthy mouth/Did move its
nettle-bearded lips together,/And said, 'Twas I--I,
Death: behold our child!' . . . From that infant/My race,
the death-begotten, draw their blood:/Our prayer for the
diseased works more than medicine." The ghost of Wolfram
speculates upon life: "Or do you owe your life, not to
this body,/But to the sparks of spirit that fly off,/Each
instant disengaged and hurrying/From little particles of
flesh that die?/If so, perhaps you are the dead yourselves."
Isbrand counsels: "If you would wound your foe,/Get
swords that pierce the mind: a bodily slice/Is cured by
surgeon's butter." The play's attitude toward death is
ambiguous. On the one hand the dead seem to possess an
energetic content that the confused earthly plotters and
lovers lack. On the other hand Wolfram's ghost, who has
just persuaded his Lady Love to commit that lingering
suicide so popular in the 19th century, rebels against
his task in an aside and a plea to the maiden: "Snake
Death,/Sweet as the cowslip's honey is thy whisper:/O
let this dove escape thee! I'll not plead,/I will not
be thy suitor to this innocent:/Open thy craggy jaws;
speak, coffin-tongued,/Persuasions through the dancing
of the yew-bough/And the crow's nest upon it . . . .
You're moved to wildness, maiden. Beg not of me./I can
grant nothing good! Quiet thyself,/And seek heaven's
help."

Beerbohm, Max. "A Defense of Cosmetics." Available in Aesthetes
and Decadents of the 1890's, ed. Karl Beckson. New York:
Vintage Books, 1966. Essay.

The Body   Sexual Roles

Women are objects that can regain power by regaining
mystery. They must create beautiful masks, behind which
their minds may play unseen. "Natural" women are not
respected. Men, by beards and mustaches, have such masks
and also avoid the facial monotony of women. Quite
opposite in feeling to Ben Jonson's "Still to Be Neat."
"This greater swiftness and less erring subtlety of mind,
their forte and privilege, justifies the painted mask
that Artifice bids them wear. Behind it their minds can
play without let . . . . Yet do not their faces become
lined with thought; beautiful and without meaning are
their faces. And, truly, of all the good things that
will happen with the full renascence of cosmetics, one
of the best is that surface will finally be severed from
soul." The body will become the medium on which Art is
created.

Bellamy, Edward. Looking Backward, 2000-1887, ed. J. L. Thomas.
Cambridge, Mass.: Belknap Press, 1967. Novel.

Med. Instit.   Sci Fi   Sexual Roles

A vision of a socialistic future meant to embody paradise
but actually an embodiment of limbo. A 19th-century man
awakens in the 21st century. All people, sick and insane

included, must work up until age 45. After they are 45,
people can use their leisure for whatever interests them.
Medicine is completely socialized: the State pays for
the education of doctors and then finds work for them.
Doctors have little to do since insanity and suicide,
produced by a non-socialistic way of life, have been
eliminated and since the human race has been improved
because women choose their mates according to physical
rather than emotional, social, or financial attributes.
Women are a part of the work force, but have a lighter
load and shorter hours because "the beauty and grace of
women give greatest zest to men." Women do not vote.
The book, like Skinner's Walden II, presents controversial
ideas in a manner designed to allay all excitement and
interest in the controversy.

Bennett, Arnold. Riceyman Steps. London: Cassell, 1959. Novel.

Death   Disease & Health   Doctors
Dying   Madness   Med. Instit.

Bennett hides information from us for greater shock
value. At first we see the Earlforwards engaged in what
seems a battle of wills: she seems determined to feed
him and so stop him from losing weight; he seems determined to save money on food in addition to every other
item in his life. It is not until we are well into the
battle that we see them with the outsider's, Dr. Raste's,
eyes. The combatants become "a shrunken woman, subject
to some kind of neurosis which he could not diagnose"
and a man "emaciated: his jaws were hollowed, his little
eyes had receded, his complexion was greyish, his lips
were pale and dry . . . his ears were nearly white"
(Part IV, Chapter iii). Henry Earlforward claims that
he is dying, ostensibly to frighten his exploited servant
Elsie out of nibbling at the food, but in actuality he
is telling the truth. He vomits, is obviously ill, is
told by the doctor that he is seriously ill and that
he must go to the hospital for tests. He refuses. At
this his wife rebels, refusing to have added work placed
on her when she is not well herself. She harangues him
into agreeing to go to the hospital, only to collapse
herself and be carried off before she can tell Dr. Raste
of Henry's consent. Henry now refuses to go. It is at
this point that we see that to busy Dr. Raste, these
people are trivia. Only his daughter matters to him.
(In a short story "Elsie and the Child" which primarily
concentrates on a tense relationship in which Elsie finds
herself standing between Dr. Raste's wife and Dr. Raste's
child, while the child stands between Elsie and her
husband Joe, we catch a glimpse of Dr. Raste's work
pattern--he overworks himself to a physical and mental
collapse, takes a several-month vacation, and starts
over again.) Henry is nursed by Elsie who is also,
secretly, his lover Joe, seriously ill with
malaria. Henry is terrified of the hospital: "The
vision of the huge long, bare room, with its rows of
beds and serried pain and distress . . . the semi-
miliary bearing of the nurses, the wholesaleness of the
affair, the absence of privacy, the complete subjection
of the helpless patients, the inelasticity of regulations,
the crushing of individuality: this dreadful vision
had ineffaceably impressed itself on his imagination--
the imagination of an extreme individualist with a
passion for living his own life free of the obligation
to justify or explain it" (Part V, Chapter vi). Yet
this individualist is now dependent on Elsie and has
forgotten his wife, who is scheduled for an operation
to remove fibroids from her uterus. The grand battle
of wills that obscured the physical deterioration is
now forgotten in the need to rationalize away the
illness. At this point, Bennett gives us our greatest
shock. The wife dies of the operation because she's
undernourished. The little battles over food are now
seen to be Henry's desire to hide his illness and his
wife's attempts to get the food she needs for survival.
Henry too dies when he learns that Elsie has stolen a
small sum from his large horde to pay a messenger to
learn about his wife's condition. The property goes to
someone else, but Elsie has what matters--Joe.

Bierce, Ambrose. "A Tough Tussle." From Can Such Things Be?
Available in The Collected Writings of Ambrose Bierce. New
York: The Citadel Press, 1970. Short Story.

Death

Bierce was haunted by death. One of his best-known stories
"An Occurrence at Owl Creek Bridge" describes a man's
dream-escape as he is being hanged. Through his writings
runs one very common motif--the strong man facing his death
externalized in some object and being killed by his fear of
death. The object may be an army, a stuffed snake, a
rifle muzzle, or a dead man; but the death it only represents as fatal. In this story, death is embodied in a
dead soldier. Union Lieutenant Byring is stationed near
a dead Confederate soldier at night. He starts to think
about death, and once a Bierce character takes up such
thoughts he is doomed. He becomes so hypnotized by the
body that he begins to imagine it moves. He is found
the next morning, dead of a sword-thrust through the
heart by his own sword; his opponent is fearfully gashed.
The discoverers, a surgeon and a captain, try to move
the stiff foe. The story ends: "In the effort the body
was displaced. The dead do not wish to be moved--it
protested with a faint, sickening odor. Where it had
lain were a few maggots, manifesting an imbecile activity.
The surgeon looked at the captain. The captain looked
at the surgeon."

Blake, William. "Infant Joy," from Songs of Innocence and "Infant Sorrow," from Songs of Experience. Available in The Poetry and Prose of William Blake, ed. D. V. Erdman. Garden City, New York: Doubleday & Co., 1970. Poems: 12 & 8 lines.

The Body   Children   Preg. & Childbirth

The child's emotions as a reflection of those around him. In "Infant Joy" child and speaker become blurred together in their happiness. Note that the speaker is not labeled as parent but is simply a voice external to the child. "Pretty joy!/Sweet joy but two days old./Sweet joy I call thee./Thou dost smile./I sing the while/Sweet joy befall thee." One must not confuse this rather cloying sweetness with the later Victorian baby worship. The newborn child can also become a terror: "My mother ground . . . . Helpless, naked, piping loud;/Like a fiend hid in a cloud./ Struggling in my fathers hands:/Striving against my swaddling bands:/Bound and weary I thought best/To sulk upon my mothers breast.: Now parents are differentiated from the speaker; now the child's body is an issue. It is fiendlike in its clouds of linen and must be bound and swaddled.

Blake, William. The Island in the Moon, Chapter VI. Available in The Poetry and Prose of William Blake, ed. D. V. Erdman. Garden City, New York: Doubleday & Co., 1970. Sketches & Poems.

Disease & Health   Med. Profession   Suffering
Surgery   Women as Patients

The Island in the Moon is a series of satirical sketches upon Blake's ex-patrons. Chapter VI contains Sipsop's panegyric upon the surgeon's Jack Tearguts, who "does not mind their crying--tho they cry ever so hell Swear at them & keep them down with his fist & tell them that hell scrape their bones if they dont lay still & be quiet--What the devil should the people in the hospital that have it done for nothing, make such a piece of work for." Also, Sipsop sings a nine verse song on the indecent origins of surgery and the joys of finding/ creating new diseases. Sipsop ends the chapter rather inconclusively: "I am always unhappy too. when I think of Surgery--I don't know   I do it because I like it . . . . I think some how Ill leave it off   there was a woman having her cancer cut & she shriekd so, that I was quite sick."

Blake, William. "The Little Boy Lost" and "The Little Boy Found." From Songs of Innocence. "The Little Girl Lost," "The Little Girl Found," "A Little BOY Lost," and "A Little GIRL Lost." From Songs of Experience. Available in The Poetry and Prose of William Blake, ed. D. V. Erdman. Garden City, New York: Doubleday & Co., 1970. Short Poems.

The Family   Sexuality

Complex views of the family in apparently simple verse. In "The Little Boy Lost" and "The Little Boy Found" the boy is abandoned by his father ("Speak father, speak to your little boy/Or else I shall be lost,/The night was dark no father was there"), but he is found by "God ever nigh" and restored to his mother "Who in sorrow pale, thro' the lonely dale/Her little boy weeping sought." In the poems "The Little Girl Lost" and "The Little Girl Found" there is an ideal family. The parents are not divided. Lyca wanders in the desert and finally sleeps, despite her parents' pain. She is found by beasts of prey who gambol about her, while the old lion licks her bosom and neck. The lioness loosens her dress "And naked they convey'd/To caves the sleeping maid." The parents seek her arm in arm until they find a lion in their path who licks their hands and allays their fears. "They look upon his eyes/Fill'd with deep surprise:/ And wondering behold,/A spirit arm'd in gold." They follow this vision to Lyca and "To this day they dwell/ In a lonely dell/Nor fear the wolvish howl,/Nor the lions growl." But reality is not so kind. That glorious spirit in the animal body is not acceptable. In "A Little BOY Lost," a child says "Nought loves another as itself/Nor venerates another so./Nor is it possible to Thought/A greater than itself to know:/And Father, how can I love you,/Or any of my brothers more?/I love you like the little bird/That picks up crumbs around the door." A priest overhears and tries the child for applying reason to "our most holy Mystery." The child is then burned, despite his weeping parents. In "A Little GIRL Lost," a youthful couple frolic naked in the holy light. "And the maiden soon forgot her fear./ Tired with kisses sweet/They agree to meet,/When the silent keep/Waves o'er the heavens deep;/And the weary tired wanderers weep." But when the maiden comes to her "father white," "his loving look,/Like the holy book,/ All her tender limbs with terror shook." And he himself speaks in fear: "O the trembling fear!/O the dismal care!/That shakes the blossoms of my hoary hair." Holy, blooming, free-from-fear nature is over-ridden by the fears created from the holy book and the blossoming white hairs of the father.

Blake, William. "London." From Songs of Experience. Available in The Poetry and Prose of William Blake, ed. D. V. Erdman. Garden City, New York: Doubleday & Co., 1970. Poem: 16 lines.

Poverty & Health   Sexuality   V.D.

The diseased, repressive mind creates a mentally diseased society which, in turn, produces a physically blighted society. London is a nightmare city because "In every

voice; in every ban,/The mind-forg'd manacles I hear." Every level and aspect of society is affected, "But most thro' midnight streets I hear/How the youthful Harlots curse/Blasts the new-born Infants tear/And blights with plagues the Marriage hearse."

Blake, William. "Nurse's Song" and "Nurses Song." From Songs of Innocence and Songs of Experience. Available in The Poetry and Prose of William Blake, ed. D. V. Erdman. Garden City, New York: Doubleday & Co., 1970. Poems: 16 & 8 lines.

Children

Songs of Innocence and Songs of Experience contrast "two states of the human soul": How does "innocence" view children; how does "experience" view children. The contrast is most explicit in the two nurses' songs. In Songs of Innocence, children provide a peaceful delight: "When the voices of children are heard on the green/And laughing is heard on the hill,/My heart is at rest within my breast/And every thing else is still." When the children beg for more play time with nature, the nurse permits it. "The little ones leaped & shouted & laugh'd/ And all the hills echoed." In Songs of Experience, children and adults are seen as victims of repression and hypocrisy. "When the voices of children, are heard on the green . . . The days of my youth rise fresh in my mind,/My face turns green and pale./Then come home my children . . . Your spring & your day, are wasted in play/And your winter and night in disguise."

Blake, William. Paintings, Especially Those Accompanying Songs of Innocence and Experience. Available in facsimile ed. Paris: Trianon Press, 1967.

The Body   Children   Death
Sexuality   Suffering

Blake's art is inextricably bound up with his poetry, and so deserves mention here. His portrayal of the body (especially the manly body) as gloriously divine is better seen in his religious paintings; but the "Songs" etchings are the best place to see his visual depictions of children and perhaps suffering. Like the poems, the art first shows people, especially children, in radiant simplicity, and afterwards in more unattractive shapes: bending, turned inward, vulnerably naked. Innocent nakedness is replaced by sexual nudity. Suffering and dead bodies are strewn about.

Blake, William. "The Sick Rose." From Songs of Experience. Available in The Poetry and Prose of William Blake, ed. D. V. Erdman. Garden City, New York: Doubleday & Co., 1970. Poem: 8 lines.

Sexuality

Eight short lines convey an overwhelming feeling of diseased sexuality--the destruction of what should be naturally beautiful by a loving, unnatural horror. "O Rose, thou art sick!/The invisible worm,/That flies in the night,/In the howling storm,/Has found out thy bed/Of crimson joy;/And his dark secret love/Does thy life destroy."

Brontë, Anne. The Tenant of Wildfell Hall. New York: Harcourt, Brace, & World, 1962. Novel.

Alcoholism   Dying

A rather mediocre novel made interesting by the alcoholic Arthur Huntington, who seems to have been modeled on Bramwell Brontë, her alcoholic brother and black sheep of the Brontë family. Arthur's downfall and death, accelerated by lack of self-control and an abundance of evil companions, are feelingly portrayed, as well as the heroine's desperate attempts to prevent her son from following his father. She turns to mixing an emetic with alcohol and using wine as a punishment to wean the child from a relish for drink fostered by her father. However, what the novel also portrays is the self-complacent vacuum about the alcoholic. The wife wants to lure her active husband from his dissolute companions. She offers him books. She wants to keep him from alcohol. She lectures him. She cries out that her virtue torments him. She has no response. Bramwell's life must have been grim.

Brontë, Charlotte. Jane Eyre. Novel.

Children   Death   Disease & Health
Dying   Grief   Madness
Sexuality   Suffering

The novel consists of four sections, which fall into two pairs contrasting passion and control. The first section shows Jane's passionate childhood--her relatively warm relationship with Bessie, her persecution by her cousins and aunt, her fear of death and the dead which causes her to fall into a fit, her rebellion against her aunt, and her acceptance of her own wickedness. The second section shows Jane's controlled childhood. She falls under the influence of passionless Helen Burns, who is reasonable and reconciled to persecution by inferiors. Their school is swept by a typhus epidemic, caused by the school's location and Mr. Brocklehurt's parsimony and sadism. Amid all the deaths from typhus, Helen goes uncomplaining to her death from T.B. In Chapter 9 Jane awakens to one of the meanings of death--the loss of a friend. She tries to understand her new perceptions by talking with the dying Helen, but arrives at awareness only in time to sleep next to the now dead Helen. In the third section, it appears as though Helen will be replaced by Mr. Rochester. Jane once again abandons herself to her passions, although she does maintain enough control to avoid premarital sex and the swamping of her ego by his financial and emotional strength. The wedding is broken off because it is discovered that the madwoman living in Mr. Rochester's attic is really his wife, Bertha, who had so given way to her passions that hereditary madness soon conquered her. Jane then leaves Mr. Rochester. Because the fourth section lacks the passion and sexual games-playing of the Rochester-section, it is often overlooked. But the balancing section is needed. St. John has the controlled passion of Helen Burns and offers Jane the same result--death. His passionate, sexless wooing and his attempts to dominate through love and piety have a repelling virtuousness. St. John and Helen Burns represent the forces of saintly control; they offer only a dull and unattractive alternative to passion. The novel never reconciles passion with this kind of control. Jane, wealthy by means of a dead rich uncle, is matched with a properly diminished Mr. Rochester (he loses a hand and his eyesight), and the two live happily ever after. But the novel does not end with them. It ends with St. John dying gloriously for ever after. Passion and control are never reconciled.

Brontë, Charlotte. _Villette_. Novel.

Children   Disease & Health   Doctors
Mental Retardation Sexuality   Sexual Roles

A complex, confused, and fascinating partially-auto-biographical novel of a woman trying to find her true sexual role amid her confusion about male sexual desires. Poor, plain Lucy Snowe comes to Villette, in Belgium, seeking a job. On her arrival she meets the three kinds of men that will confront her: Dr. John (another St. John from _Jane Eyre_), rational, egotistical, domineering, cold and charming; Professor Paul Emmanuel, irrational, egotistical, domineering, passionate and infuriating; and the fashionable scholars who harass her as a lone woman in the streets. Lucy becomes first a nursemaid, and then a teacher, in Madame Beck's school for girls--the closest Lucy, for all her sexuality, will get to children she so coolly appraises. All the other women--the fleshy Ginevra, the charming, passionate Polly, the controlled, passionate Madame Beck--have children by the novel's end. Lucy has pupils. Lucy struggles to understand men's attitudes toward women. She falls in love with the benevolent, perceptive, attractive Dr. John, an old play fellow who does not recognize her. However, Dr. John is apparently in love with the body of Ginevra Fanshawe, a selfish, stupid pupil, who prefers the simpering, effeminate Alfred de Hamal. While suffering from this love, Lucy finds herself in the role of a hermaphrodite, literally acting the part of a male fop to Ginevra's sexual object in a play. She finds that Ginevra is playing to Dr. John in the audience, and so acts to win Ginevra from Dr. John. An extraordinary scene! It is followed by the vacation in which Lucy is left to care for the young cretin, a truly mindless female body. She becomes severely mentally and physically depressed, saved from death only by Dr. John and his mother, whom he adores. Under the leadership of Dr. John, who does not see her as possessing a sexual nature, Lucy learns more about men--she watches mindless, effeminate men ogling a very fleshy Cleopatra in an art gallery (Professor Emmanuel tries to persuade her to look at unaesthetic moralistic paintings) and watches the stage performance of the truly passionate woman, Vashti, whose performance is fittingly interrupted by a fire and the arrival of Polly Bassompierre, the submissive, passionate, intelligent girl-woman who is Dr. John's true mate. Lucy destroys her letters and her love for Dr. John, only to find that her daily battles with her fellow-teacher Paul Emmanuel have turned into love. She wins Paul despite some incredible Catholic plots, but loses him to the West Indies before their marriage. The novel ends ambiguously--he may have been drowned on his return journey, or the reader may believe in a happy ending.

Brontë, Emily Jane. "Ah, why, because the dazzling sun." Available in _Gondal's Queen_, ed. F. E. Ratchford. New York: McGraw-Hill, 1964. Poem: 48 lines.

Sexuality

Ostensibly a preference for the night-sky over the sun. In effect, the longing for a beloved somebody or something dispelled by day. Sexual passion without a human object. The sun breaks the spell, but the poet turns back to her pillow to recapture her world of night. "It would not do--the pillow glowed/And glowed both roof and floor,/And birds sang loudly in the wood,/And fresh winds shook the door . . . . O Stars and Dreams and Gentle Night;/O Night and Stars return!/And hide me from the hostile light/That does not warm, but burn--/That drains the blood of suffering men;/Drinks tears, instead of dew:/Let me sleep through his blinding reign,/And only wake with you!"

Brontë, Emily Jane. "A Farewell to Alexandria." Available in _Gondal's Queen_, ed. F. E. Ratchford. New York: McGraw-Hill, 1964. Poem: 36 lines.

Children   Death

A mother is forced to abandon her child, thereby killing it; and her lament is that nature keeps her from any illusion that the child might live. "I've seen this dell in July's shine/As lovely as an angel's dream . . . . Then, then I might have laid thee down . . . And thought thy God was guarding thee! . . . Wakes up the storm more madly wild,/The mountain drifts are tossed on high--/Farewell, unblessed, unfriended child,/I cannot bear to watch thee die!"

Brontë, Emily Jane. "The linnet in the rocky dells." Available in _Gondal's Queen_, ed. F. E. Ratchford. New York: McGraw-Hill, 1964. Poem: 28 lines.

Death   Grief

Begins with the conventional--the dead lover is abandoned by those who first thought their grief would flow unchecked forever. But the poem twists--well, the dead also abandon the living. "And if their eyes should watch and weep/Till sorrow's source were dry,/She would not, in her tranquil sleep,/Return a single sigh./Blow, west wind, by the lonely mound,/And murmur, summer streams,/There is no need of other sound/To soothe my Lady's dreams."

Brontë, Emily Jane. _Wuthering Heights_. Novel.

Children   Death   Disease & Health
Doctors   Dying   The Family
Grief   Preg. & Childbirth Sexuality
Suffering

Children, death, grief, and passion all intertwined. It is as though Catherine's and Heathcliff's drive to death as a means of consummating their passion infects and destroys the Linton and Earnshaw families. Until Heath-cliff dies, no life can flourish. It is not clear whether Heathcliff becomes evil because of his upbringing in the Earnshaw family and his rejection by Catherine in favor of the wealthier and more sophisticated Edgar Linton or whether Heathcliff is innately as amoral and cruel as the heaths about Wuthering Heights. Certainly he has the vitality that Edgar lacks; indeed, sensitivity and physical weakness are linked. The doctor plays an ambiguous role. On the one hand, his indifference to human emotion adds to the tragedy. He tells Henley that Henley's consumptive wife, who has just given birth, is dying of that birth--before Henley has accepted his son. As a result, the grieving Henley blames his son for his wife's death and becomes open to Heathcliff's snares. On the other hand, the doctor opposes Nelly's moralistic diagnosis of Catherine's fits; he orders that Catherine must not be emotionally disturbed. Nelly disobeys this by causing Edgar and Heathcliff to quarrel about Catherine, and Catherine dies. This death is interesting. The narrator implies that her decline is the result of her emotional storms; it is not until after her death that we learn of her pregnancy. "About twelve o'clock that night, was born the Catherine you saw at Wuthering Heights: a puny, seven months' child; and two hours after the mother died, having never recovered sufficient consciousness to miss Heathcliff or to know Edgar." Young Linton, who marries the younger Catherine, is a dying consumptive, a fretting invalid. Illness seems to be caused by personality and events rather than microorganisms. Illness, death, grief, and passion pervade the novel--but there is always a younger generation tumbling about in the kitchen, and death is a return to a beautiful earth. "I lingered around them, under that benign sky: watched the moths fluttering among the heath and hare-bells; listened to the soft wind breathing through the grass; and wondered how any one could ever imagine unquiet slumbers for the sleepers in that quiet earth."

Brown, Charles Brockden. _Arthur Mervyn_, ed. Warner Berthoff. New York: Holt, Rinehart & Winston, 1962. Novel.

Madness   Med. Instit.   Plague

This book is often cited for its depiction of the 1793 yellow fever epidemic. Defoe's plague book could well serve as a source for the solitude, the difficulty of getting horses and the horrors of being encoffined alive because about to die. What Defoe does not provide in his plague book is Brown's nightmare city, abandoned by the virtuous and left to the heartless--not the frightened and numb, as in Defoe--but those as malignant as the disease. It is in the midst of the city that Arthur is abandoned by his false friends and brought into contact with Walbeck's evil nature and evil human nature, as seen in this brief description of the fever hospital: "The atmosphere was loaded by mortal stenches. A vapour, suffocating and malignant, scarcely allowed me to breathe. No suitable receptacle was provided for the evacuations produced by medicine or disease. My nearest neighbour was struggling with death, and my bed, casually extended, was moist with the detestable matter which had flowed from his stomach. You will scarcely believe that, in this scene of horrors, the sound of laughter should be overheard . . . . The wretches who are hired, at enormous wages, to tend the sick and convey away the dead, neglect their duty and consume the cordials, which are provided for the patients, in debauchery and riot" (Part I, Chapter 18).

Brown, Charles Brockden. <u>Wieland, or the Transformation</u>.
Available edited by Fred Lewis Pattee. New York: Harcourt,
Brace and World, 1926. Novel.

The Family   Madness

One of the earliest American novels, <u>Wieland</u> appears
modern, its curious blend of the domestic and Gothic
novels producing an effective psychological study of
Wieland's madness and the destruction of his sister
Clara's ego. Their upright and pious father, noted
for the fervor of his unorthodox religious beliefs,
becomes convinced that he is condemned by some force
for leaving a duty undone and so bound to die soon.
His restlessness is ended by a blow accompanied by a
flash of light which burns his clothing--in an
inaccessible house on a cloudless day. His children
are left with uncertainty--was the interference by
a Divine Ruler or the result of some irregular but
explicable physical causes. Wieland marries and is,
like his father, known for his piety. His sister,
the narrator, becomes known as an upright, strong
woman, in love with Pleyel who loves some mysterious
foreign woman. Then enters Carwin, a mysterious
ventriloquist, who becomes piqued by Clara's strong-
mindedness and tries to shake her composure. He succeeds
too well, not perceiving how he and Wieland have become
confused in her mind and how she projects her growing
fears of Wieland onto Carwin. Carwin becomes enmeshed
in the family; and, inadvertently, by his ventriloquism,
he sends Wieland over the line into homicidal mania.
Wieland kills his wife and children and then tries to
kill his sister. Clara feels more and more bewildered
and guilty--nearly committing suicide. After the
nightmare confrontation with the homicidal--sane and
aghast--then homicidal Wieland, she does go insane
herself--saved only by a mysterious fire and a dream.
The atmosphere of mystery and uncertainty permeating
the commonplace town and characters become the mystery
of the human mind.

Browning, Elizabeth Barrett. <u>Aurora Leigh</u>. Available in <u>The
Complete Poetical Works of Mrs. Browning</u>. Cambridge, Mass.:
The Riverside Press, 1900. Poem: 9 Books (over 10,000 lines).

Med. Instit.   Science & Poetry   Sexuality
Sexual Roles

Her poem of women's liberation--wordy, but full of
interesting passages. Throughout the convoluted plot,
Romney, a wealthy philanthropist, and Aurora, a budding
writer, learn about their own natures and roles, growing
mature enough to form the perfect couple. In Book I
(which contains criticism of the narrow education for
women), Aurora rejects Romney's proposal because she
feels he is condescending to her and mocking her ambitions
to be a poet. In Book II, Romney criticizes women for
being too concerned with the particular case, instead of
the general rule. She counters that he expects his wife
to be a helpmate only to his own ends, not a woman with
interests of her own: "Women of a softer mood,/Surprised
by men when scarcely awake to life,/Will sometimes only
hear the first word, love,/And catch up with it any kind
of work,/Indifferent, so that dear love go with it./I
do not blame such women, though, for love,/They pick
much oakum" (Book II, lines 443-449). In Book III,
Aurora faces the difficulties of an apprentice writer,
of coming to terms with what it means to be a poet. She
is further troubled by Lady Waldemar who tells her that
Romney is to be married to a young girl whom in the
course of his philanthropic efforts he has saved from a
life of sin. Lady Waldemar wants to break off the marriage
so that she can have a chance at Romney. Aurora visits
Marian Erle, who was beaten by her father and sold to
the squire by her mother. Lines 1106-1149 describe
Marian's wonderful life in the hospital and her fear at
having nowhere to go when she was released. (Dickens
has a similar situation in <u>Little Dorrit</u>: the high point
of Maggie's life is her stay in the hospital. Once she
is released from the hospital, she returns to her old
environment where her condition rapidly deteriorates to
a miserable imbecility.) Marian meets Romney while
nursing a friend, worships him like a dog, and agrees to
marry him even though he is marrying according to his
principles rather than his emotions. However, the
villainess, Lady Waldemar, convinces Marian that she is
unworthy of Romney. She flees, is raped, and abandoned.
By Book V, Aurora begins to accept some of Romney's
descriptions of women as too concerned with the particular,
but his acceptance is soon swallowed up in her musings
about the task of the modern writer and the nature of
poetry. These musings are continued into Book VI, where
they turn to medicine and poetry: "How is this,/That
men of science, osteologists/And surgeons, beat some
poets in respect/For nature,--count nought common or
unclean,/Spend raptures on perfect specimens/Of indurated
veins, distorted joints,/Or beautiful new cases of curved
spine,/While we, we are shocked at nature's falling off,/
We dare to shrink back from her warts and blains . . . .
For that, she will not trust us often with/Her larger
sense of beauty and desire" (Book VI, lines 171-179, 182-
183). Aurora finds Marian, abandoned but passionately
in love with her child. Books VII-VIII cover Aurora's
attempts to discover whether or not Romney has married
Lady Waldemar. In Book IX, Marian discovers that she
has grown enough to refuse Romney's offer of marriage:

she loves her child more than Romney. Also, Aurora has
discovered that Romney has grown enough to marry her.
The two end the poem with their vows of a passionate
union that seems to be equally a physical union and a
union of their different professions.

Browning, Elizabeth Barrett. "The Cry of the Children." Available
in <u>The Complete Poetical Works of Mrs. Browning</u>. Cambridge,
Mass.: The Riverside Press, 1900. Poem: 159 lines.

Children   Suffering

A response to a report on the employment of children in
mines and factories, this poem wavers back and forth
across the boundary line between realism and sentimentality:
"For all day the wheels are droning, turning . . . Till
our hearts turn, our heads with pulses burning,/And the
walls turn in their places . . . . Still, all day, the
iron wheels go onward,/Grinding life down from its mark;/
And the children's souls, which God is calling sunward,/
Spin on blindly in the dark."

Browning, Elizabeth Barrett. "Grief." Available in <u>The Complete
Poetical Works of Mrs. Browning</u>. Cambridge, Mass.: The
Riverside Press, 1900. Sonnet.

Grief

The paralysis of grief unable to find an outlet. Emily
Dickinson's "formal feeling"--without the letting go.
"Full desertness,/In souls as well as countries, lieth
silent-bare/Under the blanching, vertical eye-glare/Of
the absolute Heavens . . . . Most like a monumental
statue set/In everlasting watch and moveless woe . . .
If it could weep, it could arise and go."

Browning, Elizabeth Barrett. "Isobel's Child." Available in <u>The
Complete Poetical Works of Mrs. Browning</u>. Cambridge, Mass.:
The Riverside Press, 1900. Poem: 550 lines.

Children   Death

This poem has two of the themes that run through all of
Elizabeth Browning's poetry: the mother-son relationship
and the blessing of death (strongly stated in "A Vision
of Life and Death"). A mother thanks God for answering
her prayers by saving her son from a serious illness.
The child then reproaches her for tearing him away from
paradise; her maternal love is sinning, earthly, dreary
love. The child dies, and Isobel prepares his corpse
for burial, content: "And a sense of tune,/A satisfièd
love meanwhile/Which nothing earthly could despoil,/Sang
on within her soul."

Browning, Elizabeth Barrett. <u>Sonnets from the Portuguese</u>, no. 1.
Sonnet.

Death   Sexuality

In opposition to many Renaissance works in which sexuality
and death are confounded or in which love can only be
consummated by death, <u>Sonnets from the Portuguese</u> sets
the two in battle for the poet's body. The note is
struck in this opening sonnet. "Straightway I was
'ware,/So weeping, how a mystic Shape did move/Behind
me, and drew me backward by the hair:/And a voice said
in mastery, while I strove,--/'Guess now who holds
thee?'--'Death,' I said. But there,/The silver answer
rang,--'Not Death, but Love.'"

Browning, Elizabeth Barrett. <u>Sonnets from the Portuguese</u>, no. 5.
Sonnet.

Children   Grief   Sexuality

Extremely rich and complicated poem, whose overtones
seem limitless. The poet is at once warning her lover
that her relationship with her father must be crushed
or he, the lover, will be destroyed, and at the same
saying that her flaming passion will flare out from the
ashes of her grief. "I lift my heavy heart up solemnly,/
As once Electra her sepulchral urn . . . . Behold and
see/What a great heap of grief lay hid in me,/And how
the red wild sparkles dimly burn/Through the ashen
grayness. If thy foot in scorn/Could tread them out to
darkness utterly,/It might be well perhaps. But if
instead/Thou wait beside me for the wind to blow/The
gray dust up, . . . those laurels on thine head . . .
will not shield thee so . . . . Stand farther off then!
go."

Browning, Elizabeth Barrett. <u>Sonnets from the Portuguese</u>, nos. 10
& 11. Sonnets.

The Body   Sexuality

These sonnets are full of the poet's sense of her body's
unworthiness, which is only just counter-balanced by her
blazing passion. Interestingly, she rarely mentions his
body, only his fame. "And when I say at need/I love thee
. . . mark! . . . I love thee--in thy sight/I stand
transfigured, glorified aright . . . . And what I feel,
across the inferior features/Of what I am, doth flash
itself, and show/How that great work of Love enhances
Nature's" (no. 10). "Cheeks as pale/As these you see,
and trembling knees that fail/To bear the burden of a
heavy heart . . . why advert/To these things? O Belovèd,
it is plain/I am not of thy worth nor for thy place!"
(no. 11).

Browning, Elizabeth Barrett. <u>Sonnets from the Portuguese</u>, no. 22. Sonnet.

Death   Sexuality

Tremendous <u>carpe diem</u>--a lovely twist to the theme of Donne's "Extasy." Although our souls will flame with passion after death, our spirits will meet best on earth where they will be isolated from angelic interruptions. "When our two souls stand up erect and strong,/Face to face, silent, drawing nigh and nigher,/Until the lengthening wings break into fire . . . . The angels would press on us and aspire/To drop some golden orb of perfect song/Into our deep, dear silence. Let us stay/Rather on earth . . . [where men] isolate pure spirits, and permit/A place to stand and love in for a day,/With darkness and the death-hour rounding it."

Browning, Robert. "Apparent Failure." Available in <u>The Complete Poetic and Dramatic Works of Robert Browning</u>. Cambridge, Mass.: The Riverside Press, 1895. Poem: 63 lines.

Suicide

Ostensibly a protest against a proposal to close the Paris Morgue, in which the dead were exhibited to the public. With a light, savage tone, Browning discusses three suicides: "What fancy was it, turned your brain? . . . Money gets women, cards and dice/Get money, and ill-luck gets just/The copper couch and one clear nice/Cool squirt of water o'er your bust,/The right things to extinguish lust!" He ends with a pious hope that human life will never deteriorate so: "My own hope is, a sun will pierce/The thickest cloud earth ever stretched . . . That what began best, can't end worst,/Nor what God blessed once, prove accurst."

Browning, Robert. "Beside the Drawing Board," no. VIII of "James Lee's Wife." From <u>The Complete Poetic and Dramatic Works of Robert Browning</u>, ed. H. E. Scudder. Cambridge, Mass.: The Riverside Press, 1895. Poem: ca. 80 lines.

The Body

The artist as aesthetician rebuked by the artist as anatomist. In the first two stanzas, an artist becomes ecstatic over the skill and beauty of a model hand which he is drawing: "Its beauty mounted into my brain,/And a fancy seized me;/I was fain/To efface my work, begin anew,/Kiss what before I only drew." However, in stanza three, the poet turns aside to the poor coarse hand of a little girl and hears Da Vinci "laugh my woes to scorn," who thought no real beauty equal to the past model. "'If haply I might reproduce/One motive of the powers profuse,/Flesh and bone and nerve that make/The poorest coarsest human hand/An object worthy to be scanned/A whole life long for its sole sake . . . . This peasant hand that spins the wool/And bakes the bread, why lives it on,/Poor and coarse with beauty gone,--/What use survives the beauty?' Fool!"

Browning, Robert. "The Bishop Orders His Tomb at Saint Praxed's Church." Available in <u>The Complete Poetic and Dramatic Works of Robert Browning</u>, ed. H. E. Scudder. Cambridge, Mass.: The Riverside Press, 1895. Poem: ca. 120 lines.

Children   Death   Sexuality

As the Bishop orders an elaborate tomb to outshine his dead rival's, Gandolf's, tomb, we gradually see that this monument in which he will continue living ("but thence/One sees the pulpit o' the epistle-side") has become his answer to an unsatisfactory life, his means of facing death. At first the Bishop seems complacently gathering his obedient sons about his death bed, happily reminiscing about how he stole his woman from his rival, but as he continues talking to his sons, his uneasiness appears. He begins to bargain: his tomb built by his heirs in return for his prayers from beyond the grave for horses and mistresses. He begins to mix his past with future, and his source for uneasiness appears: "Saint Praxed at his sermon on the mount,/Your tall pale mother with her talking eyes,/And new-found agate urns as fresh as day." He finally breaks out in fear against his sons: "Will ye ever eat my heart?/Ever your eyes were as a lizard's quick,/They glitter like your mother's for my soul" and they will deprive him of his soul by depriving him of his tomb. But he slowly sinks back into complacency, mumbling over his defeat of Gandolf "As still he envied me, so fair she was!"

Browning, Robert. "Childe Roland to the Dark Tower Came." In <u>Dramatic Romances</u>. From <u>The Complete Poetic and Dramatic Works of Robert Browning</u>, ed. H. E. Scudder. Cambridge, Mass.: The Riverside Press, 1895. Poem: 34 stanzas.

Death   Dying

A nightmare journey to death. A Knight, long on an unsuccessful quest for the Dark Tower, feels like a dying man who hears those by his deathbed discussing means for his funeral "and only craves/He may not shame such tender love and stay." He is guided by a malevolent cripple and soon finds himself in a meaningless, diseased wasteland. "As for the grass, it grew as scant as hair/In leprosy; thin dry blades pricked the mud/Which underneath looked kneaded up with blood." The Knight tries to combat his depression with happy memories, but the fond memories of a friend are supplanted by recollection of that friend's death as a traitor. The landscape is actively hostile: "So petty yet so spiteful." He crosses a river, fearing

to tread on a dead man's face, spearing an animal that gives a baby's shriek. The ground is trampled, and his mind now can only conjure up horrors to account for it: "Mad brewage set to work/Their brains, no doubt, like galley-slaves the Turk/Pits for his pastime, Christians against Jews . . . . What bad use was that engine for . . . that harrow fit to reel/Men's bodies out like silk." Then, the hellish landscape moves. Noise tolls in his ears the names of his peers, strong or bold or fortunate, who all are lost to the Tower. "There they stood, ranged along the hillsides, met/To view the last of me, a living frame/For one more picture! in a sheet of flame/I saw them and I knew them all. And yet/Dauntless the slug-horn to my lips I set,/And blew. '<u>Childe Roland to the Dark Tower Came</u>.'" As Lear's heath (<u>the title comes from Lear</u>) reduces him to "the thing itself," and Eliot's Wasteland reduces modern man to a meaningless, parched traveler, so Browning's ever-more-horrifying landscape reduces the Knight to a helpless opponent before hellish forces. The path to the Tower, one of whose meanings is death, is desolate and belittling; the task is to survive the dying with enough strength to face the end with courage.

Browning, Robert. "Epilogue." To Asolando. From <u>The Complete Poetic and Dramatic Works of Robert Browning</u>, ed. H. E. Scudder. Cambridge, Mass.: The Riverside Press, 1895. Poem: 20 lines.

Death

Written just before his fatal illness, this "Epilogue" is his not-unflattering evaluation of his life at its end. "At the midnight in the silence of the sleep-time,/When you set your fancies free,/Will they pass to where--by death, fools think, imprisoned--Low he lies who once so loved you, whom you loved so,/--Pity me?" The answer seems to be that they should not pity such an optimistic fighter. "No, at noonday in the bustle of man's work-time/Greet the unseen with a cheer!/Bid him forward, breast and back as either should be,/'Strive and thrive!' cry 'Speed,--fight on, fare ever/There as here!'"

Browning, Robert. "An Epistle: Containing the Strange Medical Experience of Karshish, the Arab Physician." Available in <u>The Complete Poetic and Dramatic Works of Robert Browning</u>, ed. H. E. Scudder. Cambridge, Mass.: The Riverside Press, 1895. Poem: ca. 300 lines.

Death   Doctors   Med. Profession

An Arab physician discusses the case of Lazarus, which troubles him as a professional. He takes great pains to establish his medical credentials in this letter, discussing minerals and herbs and diseases endemic in various populations. Then he discusses this man: "'T is but a case of mania--subinduced/By epilepsy, at the turning point/Of trance prolonged unduly some three days." Christ is a physician "the learned leech/Perished in a tumult many years ago,/Accused--our learning's fate--of wizardry." But this neat professional judgment does not satisfy his personal judgment. He is troubled by Lazarus' serenity and his love for everyone and everything. He shrugs off Lazarus' assertion that Christ was God as a sign of mania. And yet he is troubled, trying to put the responsibility on his tiredness--anything but his personal uncertainty, which he tries to hide behind his medical competence.

Browning, Robert. "The Family." No. IV of "Ferishtah's Fancies." From <u>The Complete Poetic and Dramatic Works of Robert Browning</u>, ed. H. E. Scudder. Cambridge, Mass.: The Riverside Press, 1895. Poem: 74 lines.

Doctors   Med. Ethics   Suffering

These "Fancies" all deal with relationships between God and Man. Number four discusses suffering. A woman is bitten by a snake, and the doctor says that her leg must be amputated immediately. The husband says "so be it." The eldest son says "Think first." The second says "Save the leg." The third says "The doctor must be right." It is the third son who is criticized. If God is the doctor, the husband gave angelic acquiescence. The first two sons were wrong but human and kind. "Last comes the cackler of the brood, our chit/Who, aping wisdom all beyond his years,/Thinks to discard humanity itself . . . No, be man and nothing more--/Man who . . . hopes and fears . . . And bids God help him, till death touch his eyes/And show God granted most, denying all." Acquiesce to God, not to suffering.

Browning, Robert. "Fra Lippo Lippi." In Men and Women. From <u>The Complete Poetic and Dramatic Works of Robert Browning</u>, ed. H. E. Scudder. Cambridge, Mass.: The Riverside Press, 1895. Poem: ca. 370 lines.

The Body

The painter, who renounced his body as a monk (at eight years old) to save that body from starving, is caught in a bind because as an artist he sees meaning in the world as it is--but his patrons and superiors don't want that meaning: "Make them forget there's such a thing as flesh./Your business is to paint the souls of men . . . . Give us no more of body than shows soul! . . . . Now, is this sense, I ask?/A fine way to paint soul, by painting body/

So ill, the eye can't stop there." So, he must break
out, rebel. "I always see the garden and God there/
A-making man's wife: and, my lesson learned,/The value
and significance of flesh, I can't unlearn ten minutes
afterwards . . . . we're made so that we love/First
when we see them painted, things we have passed/Perhaps
a hundred times nor cared to see."

Browning, Robert. "A Grammarian's Funeral." In Dramatic Romances.
From The Complete Poetic and Dramatic Works of Robert Browning,
ed. H. E. Scudder. Cambridge, Mass.: The Riverside Press,
1895. Poem: 146 lines.

Age   Death

The funeral of a man who would not let age or death
prevent him from preparing for life all his life. "Till
lo, the little touch, and youth was gone!/Cramped and
diminished,/Moaned he, 'New measures, other feet anon!/
My dance is finished'?/No, that's the world's way . . .
He knew the signal, and stepped on with pride/Over men's
pity;/Left play for work, and grappled with the world/
Bent on escaping."

Browning, Robert. Paracelsus. From The Complete Poetical Works
of Robert Browning. New York: Macmillan, 1927. Poem: Long
Closet Drama.

Doctors   Science & Poetry

Based on the life of Paracelsus, chemist and quack, this
explores the relationship of scientific research to the
researcher's personal life, to love, and to aesthetics.
Paracelsus dreams of finding some way to elevate mankind
by his findings, but in the second part, "Paracelsus
Attains" he meets Aprile who seeks infinite love as
Paracelsus sought infinite knowledge. In his madness he
seeks to create a perfect setting for love. He dies,
despite pleas: "Die not, Aprile! We must never part./
Are we not halves of one dissevered world . . . . Part?
never!/Till thou the lover, know; and I, the Knower,/
Love--until both are saved." For the next three acts
Paracelsus seems to seesaw back and forth next to his
unambitious friend married to the woman Paracelsus now
discovers he loves. Paracelsus is rejected by the
faculty where he gives his bitter lectures, and dies with
only his childhood friend nearby. And yet he dies
triumphant. This last section is also headed "Paracelsus
Attains." He now sees why he could not achieve the
needed synthesis, but can look back on his life and say
"I have done well." He dies in splendid egotism, anticipating his resurrection.

Browning, Robert. "Prospice," In Dramatis Personae. From The
Complete Poetic and Dramatic Works of Robert Browning, ed.
H. E. Scudder. Cambridge, Mass.: The Riverside Press,
1895. Poem: 28 lines.

Death   Dying

In this poem, written after Mrs. Browning's death, death
ennobles the dying man by providing him with a last,
glorious battle and a glorious reunion with his love.
The poem ends with a marvelous pun. "Fear death?--to
feel the fog in my throat,/The mist in my face . . . I
am nearing the place . . . Where he stands, the Arch
Fear in a visible form,/Yet the strong man must go . .
. . I was ever a fighter, so--one fight more,/The best
and the last!/I would hate that death bandaged my eyes,
and forbore,/And bade me creep past./No! let me taste
the whole of it . . . Bear the brunt, in a minute pay
glad life's arrears/Of pain, darkness and cold . . . .
The black minute's at end . . . shall become first a
peace out of pain,/Then a light, then thy breast,/O
thou soul of my soul! I shall clasp thee again,/And with
God be the rest!"

Browning, Robert. "Rabbi Ben Ezra." In Dramatis Personae. From
The Complete Poetic and Dramatic Works of Robert Browning,
ed. H. E. Scudder. Cambridge, Mass.: The Riverside Press,
1895. Poem: 32 stanzas.

Age   Death

Better than the well-known opening lines on age would
imply: "Grow old along with me!/The best is yet to be,/
The last of life, for which the first was made . . .
Youth shows but half; trust God: see all, nor be afraid."
Suffering teaches and is for a purpose: "What I aspired
to be,/And was not, comforts me." Age permits assessment: "And I shall weigh the same,/Give life its praise
or blame/Young, all lay in dispute; I shall know, being
old." Then, knowing, a man may face the future and death
with calm: "The Future I may face now I have proved the
Past." Yet there is dispute over the evaluation of
things; the poet is valued little by the world. "Fool!
All that is, at all,/Lasts ever, past recall;/Earth
changes, but thy soul and God stand sure." God moulded
the poet on the potter's wheel. And though, unlike the
laughing base, the rim is decorated with "skull-things
in order grim," it is God who uses the cup. "My times
be in thy hand!/Perfect the cup as planned!/Let age
approve of youth, and death complete the same!"

Browning, Robert. The Ring and the Book. From The Complete
Poetic and Dramatic Works of Robert Browning, ed. H. E. Scudder.
Cambridge, Mass.: The Riverside Press, 1895. Novel in Verse.

The Family   Sexuality   Sexual Roles

Complex poem exemplifying "that Art remains the only way
possible/Of speaking truth." Browning takes accounts of
a Renaissance trial bound together in a book, and creates

a work of art from them. The facts in the somewhat
complicated case run as follows: Pietro and his wife
Violante have financial difficulties because they have
no heir. The aging Violante passes off a whore's new-
born girl as their child, unknown to Pietro, who, through
love of his "child," leaves his wasteful course of
living and becomes moderately wealthy. The beautiful
thirteen-year-old Pompilia is seen by the priest, Abate
Paolo, who wins her for his noble, impoverished elder
brother, Guido, who wants her "parents'" money. Guido
becomes angry with her innocence and close relationship
with her "parents" at his expense. He drives Pietro and
Violante away with harshness, drives his wife to plead
with his family, local government, and the Church to
stop his cruelty, and finally drives the impoverished
Violante to admit Pompilia's true parentage and consequent ineligibility for a dowry, forcing a return of
the marriage money to Violante and Pietro. Pompilia,
who has not known of the deception, goes into shock at
her "parents'" rejection, made worse by her rough
initiation to sexual intercourse (she also claims brother
Paolo pursues her). Her passive obedience further
infuriates Guido, who arranges an affair between
Pompilia and a young priest, Caponsacchi, writing letters
for the illiterate Pompilia. A manipulator, Guido calls
this an incomplete work of art, which is incomplete only
because he could not force Pompilia and Caponsacchi into
bed to be found by him. Pompilia does run to her parents
in Rome with Caponsacchi; the two do share a very passionate, but nonphysical love for each other. Guido catches
them, but in separate rooms, and instead of killing them,
is attacked by Pompilia with his own sword. Caponsacchi
appeals to the Church, which does not clear Pompilia,
placing her in a convent, but which does call Guido
guilty. Pompilia returns to her "parents" to give birth
to Guido's son; Guido and four murderers gain entrance
to the house, using Caponsacchi's name, killing Pietro
and Violante, and fatally wounding Pompilia who lives
long enough to accuse and forgive him. The Book gives
accounts of public opinions, statements by Pompilia
and Guido, arguments by the lawyers in his trial, and
the Pope's decision to condemn Guido to death. Browning
gives us these different points-of-view, each claiming
to be the truth, on which judgment depends. But where
should the guilt go? To the chicanery of Violante? To
the society which told Guido he was superior but which
prevented him from gaining the money to sustain that
superiority? To the society which gave both Guido and
Pompilia false stereotypes of husband and wife? To the
male society which refused protection to Pompilia for
fear of undermining a husband's authority? To Caponsacchi who was blind to the odd caritas underlying his
charity? To the lawyers and Romans who create works of
art from facts for their own gain or satisfaction of
prejudice? Browning answers--to all. Further, he
endeavors to show the "British Public" that it is only
the poet (to this reader, a poet very like a scientist)
who has the ability to transcend gain-controlled, or
"incomplete" art and who therefore has the only art that
tells the truth.

Bryant, William Cullen. "Thanatopsis." From The American Tradition
in Literature, ed. Sculley Bradley, R. C. Beatty, E. H. Long.
3rd ed. New York: W. W. Norton & Co., 1967. Poem: 81 lines.

Death

The poem at first forces his or her own death upon the
reader: "And, lost each human trace, surrendering up/
Thine individual being, shalt thou go/To mix forever
with the elements." But the poem offers beautiful,
albeit grim, consolation in the remainder that you will
lie with great men in great beauty, and the living who
will pass unheeding over your grave will, nevertheless,
inevitably join you. "So live, that when thy summons
comes to join/The innumerable caravan . . . sustained
and soothed . . . approach thy grave,/Like one who wraps
the drapery of his couch/About him, and lies down to
pleasant dreams."

Büchner, Georg. Woyzeck. New York: Avon, 1969. Drama.

The Body   Doctors   Madness
Med. Ethics   Poverty & Health   Sexuality

A short play written in 1833 but nonetheless often considered the forerunner of most of the major modern
theatrical movements, especially the theatre of the
absurd and the naturalistic movement, for the hero is a
common man controlled by irrational social and, seemingly,
cosmic forces. The son of a rationalist doctor, Büchner
studied medicine for a time himself, and the results of
his experience might be seen in his rather unflinching,
bare recording of Woyzeck's suffering. Because he is
poor and has to support his mistress and their son,
Woyzeck sells himself as a guinea pig to a frighteningly
comic medical experimenter who feeds him nothing but
peas for 30 days and watches with pseudo-scientific glee
the resulting madness. In this state Woyzeck cannot
handle reports of his woman's infidelity, and amidst
Othello-like musings on the specific nature of her
sexuality, he murders her. Bodies become all lips and
thighs. Man becomes all fragmented body: as Woyzeck
puts it, just sand and dirt and dung.

Butler, Samuel. Erewhon. New York: Signet, 1961. Novel.

The Body   Body/Mind   Children
Death   Disease & Health   Doctors
Med. Ethics   Preg. & Childbirth

Although the satire of Erewhon attacks far more than the
medical profession, its criticism of society's attitude
toward disease is so far-reaching and complex that the
medical passages should be read by every doctor. Erewhon
("no where" backwards) society is, in many ways, the
reverse of nineteenth-century society and a frighteningly
close image of our own. People are sentenced to hard
labor for bronchitis and typhoid fever (Butler does cite
our milder uses of quarantine), but are sent to
"straighteners" (our psychiatrists) for moral or legal
crimes. People trust these "straighteners" implicitly,
following courses of treatment (such as fasting and
flogging) that are physically debilitating (and thus
tending to criminal prosecution) without questioning the
straightener's judgment. The narrator notes the existence of illegal doctors who treat the body and wishes
they would become more respectable in order to end the
painful hypocrisy. Butler is, of course, satirizing the
folly of the English penal system--but he has hit on a
very uncomfortable vehicle for his criticism. A later
section explains the Erewhon prohibition of machines--
an early thinker observed the rapid evolution of machines
and postulated that a supermachine would supersede
humanity. But the mockery of Darwinism is also uncomfortable. If our bodies are machines for which we are
responsible (we are held responsible for smoking,
drinking, drugging and over-eating), then we should be
held responsible for any accidents to the machine.
Butler plays with the medically reversed society:
Pregnancy is hidden because it is unhealthy; children
are not wanted and are made to sign a certificate of
responsibility for thrusting themselves on their
parents; death is less feared than disease; and grief
is a sign of misfortune. Since all men are responsible
for their misfortunes, grief is punished. Butler muddles
his point of view toward all the major issues, forcing
the reader to reconsider his or her own position.

Butler, Samuel. The Way of All Flesh. Novel.

Adolescence   Alcoholism   The Family
Sexuality

Although largely concerned with criticism of the Church
of England, the novel also shows the way in which a
harsh, repressive, sadistic father trains his meek son
to become another harsh repressive, sadistic father.
The principal grandson of this series, repressed and
subtly tortured by hypocritical parents and siblings,
is saved while a schoolboy by the intervention of an
aunt and by a later, disasterous, experience as a new
clergyman. Heavily under the influence of a young,
fellow clergyman, Ernest becomes so wrought up in his
evangelism that it becomes confused with sexuality and,
as a result of his endeavors to convert a respectable
young lady he believes to be a fallen woman, Ernest is
taken to court for assault and sentenced to prison.
On his release, he meets Ellen, a housemaid dismissed
for being pregnant, and marries her. She is an alcoholic and leads Ernest to great degradation before a
timely, earlier husband and a delayed legacy from his
aunt finish Ernest's salvation.

Byron, George Gordon, Lord. Childe Harold's Pilgrimage, Canto III.
Available in The Complete Poetical Works of Byron. Boston:
Houghton Mifflin, 1933. Long Poem.

Children   Madness   Sexual Roles

Among other topics, Canto III covers the links between
poetry and madness and sexual roles. It opens and closes
with lines to his daughter. The beginning wanders onto
the imagination and the madness which liesin wait for
those who live the intense creative life. Byron then
turns to another kind of intense life: the manly heroism
of the soldiers (who include his ancestor) at Waterloo
and the sweet and sacred life of Julia who broke her
heart on her father's grave. Byron seems to have
rewritten Milton: "He for Country alone, and she for
God in him." But the poet stands outside the warrior-
man, worshipper-woman duality. He is such a one as
Rousseau who could "make madness beautiful," create a
passion for Julia, and destroy old things and opinions
(LXXVI-LXXXIII). The poet-narrator finds his inspiration
in nature--"this is Love's recess"--and in heroic,
historical places, only to return to his discontent with
people and bitter consolation in his absent daughter.

Byron, George Gordon, Lord. "The Destruction of Sennacherib."
From Hebrew Melodies. Available in The Complete Poetical Works
of Byron. Boston: Houghton Mifflin, 1933. Poem: 24 lines.

Death   Plague

The power of death. Not only does the plague destroy the
countless hosts of Sennacherib, the imagery and the energy
of the anapests imply that death has power over all living
things, waiting to reduce beauty and power to desolation.

Byron, George Gordon, Lord. Don Juan. Available in The Complete
Poetical Works of Byron. Boston: Houghton Mifflin, 1933.
Poem: 16 cantos.

Adolescence   Sexuality   Sexual Roles

Byron accomplishes, in a much finer and more sophisticated
version, the inversion of sexual roles that opens Fielding's
Joseph Andrews. Don Juan's childhood and youth are very
repressed, as his mother endeavors, for some reprehensible
motive, to keep him pure. But this repression only makes
him interesting, and the hero embarks on a series of
seductions--women, who always hold some power or advantage

over him, seduce him. The pattern is repeated from
Spain to Russia, where it climaxes in the affair between
Juan and Empress Catherine. Then, the poem trails off
inconclusively, with the hero a Lion in English society,
followed by his faithful Leila, but also a prey to
English women who are severely satirized. The complexity
and the satire of the whole poem add many dimensions to
this tale of sexual reversal.

Byron, George Gordon, Lord. "Lines On Hearing That Lady Byron Was
Ill." Available in The Complete Poetical Works of Byron.
Boston: Houghton Mifflin, 1933. Poem: 60 lines.

Disease & Health   Sexual Roles

A bitter attack upon the poet's separated wife. He
marvels that she is sick: "and yet I was not near:/
Methought that joy and health alone could be/Where I
was not." He then attacks her for taking advantage
of her weakness and her love to destroy him, his
bitterness, his hurt, his deflated expectations of
proper female behavior lending savagery to his accusations.

Byron, George Gordon, Lord. Manfred. Available in The Complete
Poetical Works of Byron. Boston: Houghton Mifflin, 1933.
Dramatic Poem: ca. 925 lines.

Grief   Madness   Sexuality
Suicide

Psychological study of a man accursed and haunted by an
unknown sin (which most critics name as incest). Isolated
from his fellow human beings by agony and guilt and grief
for Astarte's death, which he has caused, he is also
unable to respond to the natural or the spiritual world.
Because he has been such a committed searcher after
intellectual knowledge (like Faust), he is now unable to
achieve a balance between a life of thought and emotion.
At the same time, Manfred is further isolated because of
his excesses of sensitivity. He longs for self-oblivion,
which he seeks in imagination, madness, and, finally,
death. Feeling at last some calm descend upon him, he
chooses to die as he has lived--alone. His last words:
"Old man! 'tis not so difficult to die." Compare
Arnold's Empedocles on Etna.

Byron, George Gordon, Lord. "She Walks in Beauty." From Hebrew
Melodies. Available in The Complete Poetical Works of Byron.
Boston: Houghton Mifflin, 1933. Poem: 18 lines.

Grief   Sexuality

The attraction of a woman in mourning, mysterious and
lovely. "And all that's best of dark and bright/Meet
in her aspect and her eyes:/Thus mellow'd to that tender
light/Which heaven to gaudy day denies."

Byron, George Gordon, Lord. "Stanzas to Augusta." Available in
The Complete Poetical Works of Byron. Boston: Houghton
Mifflin, 1933. Poem: 44 lines.

Sexual Roles

Byron's half-sister came to represent the nauseating
ideal woman by whom he judged--and so of course found
wanting--all other women. She is the "unbroken light,/
That watch'd me as a seraph's eye." A tree "devoted in
the stormiest hour/To shed my weeping leaves o'er me."
"Thy heart can feel--but will not move;/Thy soul, though
soft, will never shake." She is a comforting extension
of himself.

Cable, George Washington. Dr. Sevier. New York: Charles
Scribner's Sons, 1911. Novel.

Disease & Health   Doctors   Med. Instit.
Med. Profession   Poverty & Health   Preg. & Childbirth
Sexuality

This book manages to cover, superficially, a number of
medical topics. Dr. Sevier, an obstetrician in pre-Civil
War New Orleans, believes that doctors should work to
remove causes of disease, such as malaria-breeding
swamps, rather than simply treating individual cases.
He begins by condemning the poor for their poverty, but
comes to see how ill-health and poverty intermix. His
attention is caught by a poor, proud young married couple
who go through a number of difficulties because the
husband cannot find work and the wife has miscarriage
after miscarriage--principally caused by exertions made
unavoidable by poverty. The young man is thrown into
prison, an excuse for Dr. Sevier to discover how bad
prison life is and how bad prison medical care is--the
prison "doctor" is a poisoner in for murder. As the
doctor leaves, the prison guards laugh "'I say, Cap',
what d'you reckon he'd a' said if he'd 'a' seen the
women's department?'" The wife has yet another miscarriage in the Charity Hospital, whose chief horrors
appear to be the public examination before the crude
medical students and the label of being a charity case.
The doctor finally persuades the young man to send his
wife back to her mother while he gets a job. This plan,
however, is bad because the young man becomes obsessed,
putting his sexual drive into his work until he becomes
run down. He succeeds in his work, but his health
deteriorates so badly that the doctor persuades him to
send for his wife. However, the Civil War intervenes.
The plot then degenerates into an account of her
attempts to reach him, a gratuitous insanity on the
part of the young man's employer, the young man's death

on the night his wife reaches his side, and the wife's
decision to become a social worker under the doctor's
direction. Cable must employ circumlocution, but he
does deal with issues honestly. It is a pity that he
does so cursorily as well.

Carlyle, Thomas. "The Everlasting No," "The Center of Indifference,"
and "The Everlasting Yea." From Sartor Resartus. Available
in A Carlyle Reader. New York: Modern Library, 1969. Essays.

Death   Madness   Suicide

These three essays, which can be read separately from
the work as a whole, concern the efforts of Carlyle's
imaginary "Wanderer," Professor Teufelsdröckh, to get
himself through a period of existential depression. The
Wanderer has lost his religious faith ("Doubt had
darkened into unbelief") and before he can find something to replace it, must go through hopelessness, pain,
and even physical illness ("Such transitions are ever
full of pain"). From suicide he is restrained "by a
certain aftershine of Christianity." After a while he
names Death as something he fears, and by naming it, he
feels a little better. When he enters the numb period
he calls the "Center of Indifference," the Wanderer discovers that his depression begins to lift when he
concentrates on the "Not-me," the world of objective
fact. At last he recognizes in man a grace greater than
happiness, and that is blessedness. In a new kind of
spirituality (akin to Voltaire's in Candide), the
Wanderer determines to work: "Be no longer a Chaos, but
a World, or even Worldkin--Produce! Produce!"

Carroll, Lewis (Charles L. Dodgson). Alice's Adventures in
Wonderland. Available in The Annotated Alice, ed. Martin
Gardner. Harmondsworth, Middlesex: Penguin, 1960. Tale.

Age   The Body   Children
Death

Although Alice appears to be a simple tale which inadvertently inspires overanalysis, in fact, close reading
of Alice usually does reward the analyzer. It is
particularly interesting as a "fun-house" looking-glass
of childhood, although one must also note the marvelous
parody of Southey's "You are Old, Father William," in
which the old man defends his superior strength and
silliness until his patience runs out and he threatens
to kick the inquisitive youth down stairs. Alice's
startling changes in body size (but not shape) seem
appropriate to a child who must expect constant changes
in size--and so in body image. Alice's one stable
point is her social role; she is a "little girl,"
regardless of her size. She encounters a number of
unusual figures who all tell her extraneous facts (or
works of art) or set forth social rules, with no context provided for either facts (or works of art) or
rules. Alice breaks out of this world by assuming the
role of adult: imposing her social rules on those about
her. Among the many other non-mathematical aspects of
the book is the problem of death. Alice faces it many
times, notably in the first chapter, where, after
shrinking she wonders: "'for it might end . . . in my
going out altogether, like a candle. I wonder what I
should be like then?' And she tried to fancy what the
flame of a candle looks like after the candle is blown
out."

Chekhov, Anton. "An Attack of Nerves." Available in The Portable
Chekhov, ed. Avrahm Yarmolinsky. New York: Viking Press,
1965. Short Story.

By Doctors   Doctors   Madness
Med. Students   Suffering

This man, Anton Chekhov, easily the greatest of the
doctor-writers, wrote some 800 short stories, so many
of them eligible on all counts for this bibliography
that the choice has been made largely on the basis of
personal preference. "An Attack of Nerves" is a good
place to begin. Like all successful Chekhov stories,
this one lyrically evokes a realistic setting--the
street of prostitution in Moscow--and a realistic
problem--a law student's anguish over the morality of
dealing with "fallen women." But this story is also
something of an allegory. There are three main characters, all students, and each represents the way that
his discipline goes about solving problems: there is
a medical student, an art student, and the law student,
whose talent is not for science or art, but for
"humanity." "He possessed an extraordinarily fine
delicate scent for pain in general" (trans. Constance
Garnett). After a visit to the brothels, where the law
student has discovered not awareness of sin and hope of
salvation, but only vulgar taste, he castigates his two
friends for acting neither on medical knowledge ("your
medical books tell you that every one of these women
dies prematurely of consumption of something") nor on
artistic ("art tells you that morally they are dead even
earlier"). The student of art, speaking representatively,
one supposes, replies that this sort of viciousness
between friends is more immoral. And the student of
medicine, again typically, tries to maintain what he calls
an "objective" view of the whole matter. Later, when
the law student experiences first a mania of excitement
about saving all fallen women through a kind of mission-
ary work, and then falls into a suicidal despair, the
medical student rushes him to a nerve specialist, who
gives him a thorough examination, to which we as readers
are privy. The "attack of nerves" passes alright, with

the help of the doctor's routine, but the law student
has earlier made his point (and Chekhov's): "That I
should have taken my degree in faculties you look upon
as a great achievement; because I have written a thesis
which in three years will be thrown aside and forgotten,
I am praised up to the skies; but because I cannot
speak of fallen women as unconcernedly as of these chairs,
I am being examined by a doctor, I am called mad, I am
pitied!"

Chekhov, Anton. "Gusev." Available in The Portable Chekhov, ed.
Avrahm Yarmolinsky. New York: Viking Press, 1965. Short
Story.

The Body   By Doctors   Death
Disease & Health   Dying   Med. Instit.
Med. Profession   Poverty & Health

A remarkable story whose implications radiate out from
its central event: the slow dying from consumption of
a poor, delirious sailor. Lying in the ship's infirmary
with several other sick men--including the educated and
bitter Pavel Ivanych--Gusev drifts in and out of feverish memories of his family. Gusev cannot understand
Pavel Ivanych's cynical statements about the diseased
poor: "The doctors put you on the steamer to get rid
of you. They got tired of bothering with you, cattle .
. . You don't pay them any money, you are a nuisance,
and you spoil their statistics with your deaths" (trans.
Yarmolinsky). But he does register the dying bodies
around him, first a soldier, then Pavel Ivanych, then
Gusev himself. Gusev's death occurs almost unnoticeably,
with hardly a break in the narrative, and with no
obvious changing in point of view. The result is that
when Chekhov follows Gusev's funeral details, we have
the sense that he is still somehow alive--still real,
certainly. So it is with increasing horror and fascination that we follow Gusev's besacked body down, down
into the sea, until it encounters a shark. Directly
above this action, the sky is glorious with colors, and
somehow Chekhov's great humanity encompasses the two
normally disjunctive scenes, making each more vivid.
(The story knocked out Stephen Berg, inspiring his poem
"Why Are We Here?"--see the 20th century section.)

Chekhov, Anton. The Island: A Journey to Sakhalin. New York:
Washington Square Press, 1967. Nonfiction.

Age   By Doctors   Death
Disease & Health   Doctors   Madness
Med. Instit.   Poverty & Health   Suffering

It's hard to know how to describe this book--it is,
among other things, a sociological and medical study of
penology, a portrait of a depressed people, and a travel
diary--but this much is certain: it is a valuable
complement to the work of Chekhov the artist. Like the
law student in "An Attack of Nerves" (q.v.), Chekhov
felt that the artist and the medical person should have
a social conscience. When he was 30 years old, he
exercised his most obviously in this journey across
Siberia to Sakhalin, site of several penal colonies.
In his study he comments on the topics noted above.
About madness, for instance, he concludes that though
there is an inevitable lunacy among the sick and suffering prisoners, there is an avoidable madness among the
bureaucrats who mistreat them. His description of the
Hospital in Alexandrovsk (Chapter XXIII) could be
profitably compared with Orwell's "How the Poor Die"
(q.v.). And his description of some pathetic prisoners
trying to get across through mime the nature of their
illness (Chapter IX) is profoundly effective. About
this scene and about Chekhov's particular distancing from
his subjects, the book's introducer, Robert Payne, has
this to say: "He had studied human degradation and knew
it well. Acutely sensitive to suffering, he was equally
sensitive to the degradation of the human spirit. In
his book he describes a flogging with an almost clinical
detachment, but there was no detachment when he spoke
about the strange miming in the rain-swept courtyard."
Chapter XXIII, the last, is Chekhov's partial repayment
to the medical profession he had neglected: here he
studies--again with an interesting combination of scientific detachment and artistic rendering--the diseases of
the population and the island's hopeless medical organization.

Chekhov, Anton. Ivanov. Available in Chekhov: the Major Plays.
New York: New American Library, 1964. Drama.

By Doctors   Disease & Health   Doctors
Med. Ethics   Suicide

Chiefly a study of Ivanov, a disillusioned, middle-aged
man, who does not know why he lives. Plagued by guilt--
he has, for one thing, contributed to his wife's suffering
with tuberculosis--and the general meaninglessness of
his life, he eventually ends it. The chief moral
commentator on his life is the local physician, who
despises his callousness and egotism, as the doctor sees
it, and feels obliged to denounce Ivanov everywhere, even
to Ivanov's own wife. Everywhere too the doctor proclaims
his own honesty. He refuses at one point to treat people
who not only cannot pay him, but also don't follow his
orders. But, as Ivanov points out, "It is possible to be
an excellent doctor--and at the same time to know absolutely nothing about people" (trans. Ann Dunnigan).
Finally the doctor's "honest" interfering causes a great
deal of harm.

Chekhov, Anton. Letter to Alexey N. Pleshcheyev, October 1889.
     Available in The Portable Chekhov, ed. Avrahm Yarmolinsky.
     New York: Viking Press, 1965. Letter.

The Body   By Doctors   Disease & Health

     The Chekhov letter most often quoted, the letter most
     useful to people interested in literature and medicine,
     the one to compare with autobiographical statements by
     William Carlos Williams: "My holy of holies is the human
     body, health, intelligence, talent, inspiration, love,
     and absolute freedom--freedom from violence and falsehood,
     no matter how the last two manifest themselves" (trans.
     Yarmolinsky).

Chekhov, Anton. "Misery." Available in Great Stories by Chekhov,
     ed. David H. Greene. New York: Dell, 1959. Short Story.

By Doctors   Children   Grief
Handicaps   Poverty & Health   Suffering

     A brief story about the effects of grief unuttered. A
     poor old sledge driver sits for much of this narrative
     exposed to the snow (he and his horse look white like
     ghosts) and also to the cruelty of his young son's
     recent death. The man tries to talk about it with his
     fares, but they are indifferent, even in one case
     (someone called simply "the hunchback"), malicious.
     The old man imagines for a moment that his suffering is
     due to his poverty--he is starving; so is his horse--
     but soon comes back to his unexpressed grief: "He wants
     to talk of it properly, with deliberation . . . . He
     wants to tell how his son was taken ill, how he suffered,
     what he said before he died, how he died . . . . He wants
     to describe the funeral . . . . His listener ought to
     sigh and exclaim and lament" (trans. Constance Garnett).
     At last the bereaved father eases himself by telling the
     whole thing to his horse. A wrenching story.

Chekhov, Anton. "Peasants." Available in The Portable Chekhov,
     ed. Avrahm Yarmolinsky. New York: Viking Press, 1965.
     Short Story.

Age   Alcoholism   By Doctors
Children   Death   Disease & Health
The Family   Med. Profession   Poverty & Health
Suffering

     Chekhov's range of knowledge and compassion was enormous,
     and this story illustrates that they included the peasant
     class, living in remote Russian villages. As they are
     depicted here (seen chiefly through the eyes of Nikolay
     and Olga, the Moscow part of the family), the peasants
     are for the most part greedy, superstitious, cowardly,
     cruel, and drunken. But they are also human beings who
     suffer, and they have therefore all Chekhov's sympathetic
     concern. The whole family, from Granny through the six
     little granddaughters under eight, live together in a
     poor cabin. Granny is perhaps the meanest, but even she
     seems human during a scene in which she and some other
     old people remember their youth. Kiryak is a drunkard
     who beats his wife and causes all the children to scream
     with terror at his approach. To this suffering hole
     comes Nikolay who has fallen ill and finds it necessary
     to return home with his wife and daughter. One of the
     scenes in this rather long story depicts the bleeding of
     Nikolay by a retired surgeon's assistant. Granny is
     said to scorn most of the medical profession and is
     something of a hypochondriac. The poor peasants, Chekhov
     writes, do not fear death--many even long for it to
     relieve their suffering--but to a person they fear
     disease. A trifle--a stomach ache, a cold--sends them
     into exaggerated terror. Soon after the bleeding, Niko-
     lay dies, reducing his once proud wife and daughter to
     begging--but they are, at least, one feels, freed from
     the peasants' claustrophic existence.

Chekhov, Anton. The Seagull. Available in Chekhov: the Major
     Plays. New York: New American Library, 1964. Drama.

By Doctors   Doctors

     A play about artistic creativity, and so about Chekhov's
     beloved avocation--literature--rather than about his
     vocation--medicine. But for perspective there is a
     physician character, less important than in other Chekhov
     plays, but interesting nonetheless. Yevgeny Dorn has,
     he maintains, lived a diverse and satisfying life, but
     he claims that he would have given all that up for a
     taste of the creative life. At 50 plus, he has had many
     women fall in love with him because he was an excellent
     obstetrician, but now he finds people tiresome.

Chekhov, Anton. Three Sisters. Available in Chekhov: the Major
     Plays. New York: New American Library, 1964. Drama.

Age   Alcoholism   By Doctors
Doctors   The Family   Sexuality
Suffering

     Probably Chekhov's finest play. It is a play with several
     heroines and heroes--or perhaps none at all, nor any
     villains either, a condition that some might associate
     with the playwright's profession. This subtle exploration
     of the huge gap between people's ambitions and their
     abilities to live them includes several images of trapped,
     suffering humanity, only partly to blame for their
     situations. One of this sort is the physician Chebutykin,
     an aging man whose devotion to the sisters wins him some
     affection, but whose general uselessness in life is

obvious. When a fire breaks out and he is needed, he
must get drunk to escape his guilty awareness that he
has lost all his medical knowledge. And he compensates
for this with the half-hearted assertion that we do not
really exist, and therefore nothing matters. It is
known that Chekhov felt guilty because he often neglected
medicine for literature. The play is also valuable for
its portrayal of the relationship among the sisters,
dramatically different but showing common creative and
destructive traits; for the relationship between the
women and their ineffectual brother, who has married a
vulgar but effective wife; for its study of two adul-
teries, one (between Masha and Vershinin) romantic; the
other (between Natasha and Protopopov) simply efficient;
and for its demonstration of general malaise, psychological and metaphysical in origin, but sometimes
physical in manifestation.

Chekhov, Anton. Uncle Vanya. Available in Chekhov: the Major
     Plays. New York: New American Library, 1964. Drama.

Age   By Doctors   Disease & Health
Doctors   The Family   Madness
Sexuality   Suffering

     A household dominated by a retired professor, long
     esteemed and sacrificed for by the family, but in fact
     a self-centered old pedant. His illnesses, chiefly
     gout and rheumatism, rule everyone's existence,
     especially the doctor's, who is summoned tyrannically,
     then sent away. Dr. Askov is a pivotal character, a
     man who has turned indifferent and cranky (though most
     wonderfully wordy!), due to overwork among dull and
     mediocre people. Life in this family is made uneasy
     too by the arrival of the professor's second wife, a
     beautiful 27-year-old woman, whose unhappiness in her
     marriage, combined with her beauty, sets off sexual
     tensions within the family (the middle-aged Vanya) and
     the extended family (Doctor Askov). Moreover, the
     professor has a daughter who is about the same age as
     his young wife, though rather plain and a victim of
     unrequired love for the doctor. All this suffering is
     capped by Vanya's ineffectual attempt to murder the
     professor. He is not arrested because everyone con-
     siders the act one of insanity. He says bitterly:
     "I am insane, but those who conceal their lack of
     talent, their stupidity, their utter heartlessness
     under the guise of a professor, a learned sage--they
     are not insane. People are not insane who marry old
     men and then openly deceive them" (trans. Ann Dunnigan).

Chekhov, Anton. "Ward 6." Available in Great Stories by Chekhov,
     ed. David H. Greene. New York: Dell, 1959. Short Story.

Body/Mind   By Doctors   Disease & Health
Doctors   Dying   Madness
Med. Instit.   Poverty & Health   Suffering

     Chekhov's fullest statement about medical matters, and
     therefore of enormous importance to the whole endeavor
     of literature and medicine. The central figure is the
     director of a provincial Russian hospital. Both
     institution and town are vulgar, nasty places, and the
     doctor (like most similarly situated members of Chekhov's
     intelligentsia) despises them accordingly. He denies
     them too, denies pain even, feeling that the only true
     life is that lived in the sensitive mind. Ivan Dmitritch,
     one of his patients--a paranoid confined to the filthy,
     isolated, neglected and just generally infamous public
     Ward 6--opposes this view out of the experience of his
     own degradation. Eventually, the doctor comes to view
     the mad ward as just another prison, and the question
     of who's in and who's out as just one of chance. That
     philosophical position prepares the way for the story's
     final twist, in which the doctor, done in by what he
     sees as life's essential triviality, ends as a brutalized
     patient in his own ward. Then he realizes with terrible
     vision precisely what suffering had been endured under
     his doctor's nose for twenty years. Everything now
     blends into sameness for him, that is, into nothingness,
     and he soon dies of an apoplectic stroke, and finds
     oblivion. "Ward 6" is a story in which the author has
     equal knowledge of and equal tolerance and affection for
     the patient and the doctor.

Clare, John. "Don Juan" and "Child Harold." Available in Poems
     of John Clare's Madness, ed. Geoffrey Grigson. London:
     Routledge and Kegan Paul, Ltd., 1949. Poems: 150 & 700
     lines.

Madness   Sexual Roles

     Most of Clare's poems, whether written in or out of the
     asylum, are soft pastorals, gentle love poems, or rural
     ballads. However, these two poems, apparently written
     in one of his delusions (here that he was Lord Byron),
     are interesting for their treatment of women. The first
     imitates Byron's satiric attacks upon lecherous women,
     although it is at once more bawdy, more confused and
     saner than Byron's in that the male also has sexual
     desires. He is freer to speak than he could be, sane.
     "Children are fond of sucking sugar candy/And maids of
     sausages--larger the better./Shopmen are fond of good
     cigars and brandy,/And I of blunt--and if you change
     the letter . . . ." This poem also makes a reference
     to his madness: "Lord Byron . . . who has been dead,
     so fools their lies are giving,/And's still in Allen's
     madhouse caged and living." "Child Harold" catches
     Byron's other attitude toward women as consolers; they
     become a part of the beautiful countryside.

Clough, Arthur Hugh. "Bethesda: a Sequel." Available in The Victorian Age, 2nd ed., eds. John Wilson Bowyer and John Lee Brooks. New York: Appleton-Century-Crofts, 1954. Poem: 37 lines.

Disease & Health   Madness

Set at the Jerusalem pool said to have curative powers, this poem uses the figure of the ill and maimed person as representative of the universal human condition. The poet has a vision of all these poor, diseased spirits gathered together, seeking psychological health. In the preceding poem ("The Questioning Spirit") one man had responded to the general unknowability of life by saying that he would just do his duty. But in this poem the same man is as sick and depressed as the others. The poet wonders what will become of him: will he seek the forgetful waters of Lethe? find comfort in philosophy? turn to religion? But before an answer comes, the vision ends. So, like every other person, the poet "knows not."

Coleridge, Samuel Taylor. "Christabel." Available in The Portable Coleridge, ed. I. A. Richards. New York: The Viking Press, 1965. Poem: 677 lines.

Homosexuality   Sexuality

This unfinished poem of sweet evil derives much of its horror from the female incubus, Geraldine, who commits a "homosexual" rape upon Christabel. This rape is quite definitely physical, as well as spiritual. The sense of perversion permeates the work; from the moment that Christabel, praying under the heathen Oak (not a cross) for her lover, finds Geraldine instead, to the period of Geraldine's soft seduction of Christabel's ailing father, unnatural sexuality reigns.

Coleridge, Samuel Taylor. "Dejection: An Ode." Available in The Portable Coleridge, ed. I. A. Richards. New York: The Viking Press, 1965. Poem: 139 lines.

Grief   Suffering

One of the most vivid descriptions of a dull state: depression. The nameless grief escalates as the poet's depression blocks his ability to write and so raises the grief another level: "And those thin clouds above, in flakes and bars,/That give away their motion to the stars . . . I see them all so excellently fair,/I see, not feel, how beautiful they are!" He realizes that it is the self which must cure itself: "And from the soul itself must there be sent,/A sweet and potent voice, of its own birth." But, like an aeolian harp, the soul's sound depends upon some outside wind; the gales must fall before the wind harp ends its screams of agony. The closest the poem offers to such a breeze is the poet's friend; thoughts of her bring the poem to a quiet close.

Coleridge, Samuel Taylor. "Kubla Khan." Available in The Portable Coleridge, ed. I. A. Richards. New York: Viking Press, 1965. Poem: 54 lines.

Drugs

Whether considered as a description of creative labor or of the movement to death or as beauty crystalized, "Kubla Khan" is still best known as the poem created in an opium trance. It is the opposite side of the drug from that portrayed in "The Pains of Sleep."

Coleridge, Samual Taylor. "The Pains of Sleep." Available in The Portable Coleridge, ed. I. A. Richards. New York: Viking Press, 1965. Poem: 52 lines.

Drugs   Suffering

Aletha Hayter (Opium and the Romantic Imagination) feels that this poem was influenced by Coleridge's use of opium. It conveys the impression of an oppressive nightmare: "Deeds to be hid which were not hid,/Which all confused I could not know/Whether I suffered, or I did:/For all seemed guilt, remorse or woe,/My own or others' still the same/Life-stifling fear, soul-stifling shame."

Coleridge, Samuel Taylor. "The Rime of the Ancient Mariner." Available in The Portable Coleridge, ed. I. A. Richards. New York: Viking Press, 1965. Poem: 625 lines.

Death   Grief   Madness
Suffering

The intense suffering from thirst in parts two and three is overmatched by the grief and guilt of Life-in-Death. The mariner must live among the dead bodies of his companions, pursued by the terrible curse in their eyes, his guilt symbolized by the albatross about his neck. His release from guilt occurs when he is able to love another living creature, the water snake. However, his release from guilt does not mean release from expiation or from the consequences of his murder--he still "stoppeth one in three," compulsively retelling his tale.

Coleridge, Samuel Taylor. "Youth and Age." Available in The Portable Coleridge, ed. I. A. Richards. New York: Viking Press, 1963. Poem: 48 lines.

Age   The Body

Although most of the poem is not Coleridge's best, there is one beautiful passage in which age looks back on his youthful body: "This breathing house not built with hands,/This body that does me grievous wrong,/O'er aery cliffs and glittering sands,/How lightly then it flashed along . . . . Nought cared this body for wind or weather/When Youth and I lived in 't together . . . . What strange disguise hast now put on,/To make believe, that thou art gone?"

Collins, Wilkie. Hide and Seek and Poor Miss Finch. From Works. New York: Peter Fenelon Collier, n.d. Vols. XI & XV. Novels.

Disease & Health   Doctors   Handicaps

Wilkie Collins has an unusually high number of handicapped heroes and heroines in his novels and stories. In Hide and Seek he defends his deaf and mute heroine as a new addition to English fiction and as a demonstration of how patiently and cheerfully the afflicted bear their ailments. Poor Miss Finch multiplies handicaps by having a blind heroine and an epileptic hero whose skin turns blue as a side effect of his medicine. The plot is complicated by a villanous, non-blue, twin brother and an operation on the heroine. The novel also has the odd "nervous disease." The patient must not be upset, or she will lose her newly-regained sight. The doctor persists in keeping all disagreeable truths from the girl, at a terrible emotional price. Collins liked to write about the tortuous ways Secrets are inevitably disclosed; he had contempt for those who tried to hush up other people's scandals, and doctors almost invariably try to hush things up in his novels. Two exceptions are the doctor who makes a brief appearance in Hide and Seek and the interesting doctor in Man and Wife who warns against heavy physical training of athletes as deadly to the young men and as harmful to the nation because it produces strong, amoral animals.

Collins, Wilkie. The Moonstone. Novel.

Doctors   Drugs   Med. Ethics

The recognition received by The Moonstone as an originator of the detective novel has perhaps obscured two rather interesting portraits of physicians. The first, to be found in Chapter 10 of Gabriel Betteredge's first narrative, is that of Dr. Candy, the irascible physician, who, after offending Mrs. Threadgall by references to her dead husband, goes on to quarrel with Franklin Blake who maintains that medicine is worthless. We later learn that Dr. Candy decides to prove his point by dosing Franklin (suffering from insomnia because he has given up tobacco and is worried about the Moonstone) with opium to cure his insomnia, without Franklin's knowledge, expecting to crow over him the next morning. Unfortunately the doctor himself becomes ill and cannot tell Franklin the important news about the dose. The second physician is the mysterious Ezra Jennings, a hopeless opium addict as a result of a chronic painful illness. In Chapters 9 and 10 of Franklin Blake's third narrative, Ezra describes his progress from use to abuse. Yet, in Chapter 10, he can say: "Every medical man commits that act of treachery, Mr. Blake, in the course of his practice. The ignorant distrust of opium (in England) is by no means confined to the lower and less cultivated classes. Every doctor in large practice finds himself, every now and then, obliged to deceive his patients, as Mr. Candy deceived you."

Collins, Wilkie. The Woman in White. Garden City, N. Y.: Garden City Publishers, 1948. Novel.

Med. Instit.   Mental Retardation   Sexual Roles

A theme that haunts all of Wilkie Collins' work is the fragility of identity. Social and institutional forces have great power to create and destroy, not just social position, but personality as well. Wealthy Laura Fairlie bears a strange resemblance to the mentally retarded Anne Catherick, an illegitimate cousin. She is married against her desires to an unscrupulous lord who has a deadly Secret and an urgent need for money. She is the perfect woman--beautiful, honest, innocent, submissive, and rather stupid. However, when her husband scourges her with her innocent love for the artist, Walter Hartright, she turns against him, i.e. she refuses to help him illegally plunder her property. To get that property, her husband and his evil mentor, Count Fosco, arrange to substitute her for Anne Catherick in the asylum and to substitute the fatally ill Anne Catherick for "Lady Glyde" so that the husband may inherit without worrying about an inquest. Laura is freed by Walter and her mannish half-sister--the ugly, strong and intelligent Marion Halcombe, who is doomed by her mannishness to assist Laura for life. Laura is freed, but incarceration has turned her into a retarded person, the image of Anne Catherick. However, eventually, plot machinations uncover the truth, kill off the husband, and restore Laura to position and health.

Cooper, James Fenimore. The Last of the Mohicans. Novel.

Children   Death   Grief
Sexual Roles

This will prove enjoyable to those who have not read Twain's essays on Cooper. Chasing each other across New York State are two partial families, a hero, a villain, and a comic musician. The more noble "family" is Chingachook and his son Uncas; the more interesting family is Munro and his two daughters, Cora and Alice. The two are half-sisters, and represent a curious sexual duality in 19th-century literature, especially in Cooper and Hawthorne. Cora is dark haired (black ancestry is implied), strong, courageous and a sexual object to Uncas and the villain, Magua. She, for all her strength, dies. Alice is blond, weak, and honorably loved by Hayward; she faints whenever physical exertion is necessary. She survives and, presumably, marries Hayward. This death of the strong, dark sexually attractive woman and survival of the weak blond is typical. Both Uncas and Cora die by the hand of Magua. Alice and her worthy, but less woods-wise, soldier survive. Cooper reaches some ludicrous heights (or depths) in this novel, but the scene in which the tribe mourns the death of Uncas, the next-to-last of the Mohicans, is full of power and dignity. The grief of his father is well done.

Cooper, James Fenimore. The Prairie. New York: Signet, 1964. Novel.

Age   Doctors   Dying

Dr. Battius, physician and absurd naturalist, has become infamous. Cooper hammers ad nausem on the contrast between the common sense of practical Natty Bumppo (The Trapper) and the foolish theoretician, Dr. Battius. The fact that Battius is a competent physician does not affect the humor of his mistaken classification of his own donkey as Vespertilio horribilis, the monster of the plains. The contrast is all the sharper because The Trapper feels less worthy and more expendible than the young. Age has taken away his powers--and so his value-- but he accepts this because it is natural. The Trapper also accepts death as natural. He awaits it seated in the open among his friends. He rises suddenly and "looked about him as if to invite all in the presence to listen (the lingering remnant of human frailty), and then . . . with a voice that might be heard in every part of that numerous assembly, he pronounced the word 'here' and died." Dignity and honor in death.

Crane, Stephen. Maggie. From Maggie and Other Stories, ed. Austin McC.Fox. New York: Washington Square Press, 1966. Novella.

Alcoholism   Children   Sexual Roles

The loss of social concepts by the poor. Maggie, her brother, and her mother have lost all norms except the primitive one that a woman should not sleep with a man not her husband if that woman is your daughter or sister (your mistress is, of course, excepted). Her mother is an alcoholic virago who batters the furniture and her children with equal vigor. Her brother is a violent loafer. Yet both are able to assume self-righteous virtue when Maggie is seduced and then abandoned by a friend of his. Maggie dies as a result. The seduction is not really the point of the story which is, instead, the brutal life of the poor and their dim strugglings after honor, decency, and beauty in an environment totally lacking all three.

Crane, Stephen. "The Monster." Available in The Complete Short Stories and Sketches of Stephen Crane, ed. T. A. Gullason. Garden City, New York: Doubleday & Co., 1963. Short Story.

The Body   Doctors   Handicaps
Med. Ethics   Mental Retardation

Core of the story is the impossible predicament of Dr. Trescott, whose servant, Henry Johnson, is badly mutilated by exploding chemicals in the doctor's home laboratory while saving the doctor's son. Dr. Trescott successfully saves Henry Johnson's life--against the advice of his friend the judge: "He is purely your creation. Nature has very evidently given him up. He is dead. You are restoring him to life. You are making him, and he will be a monster with no mind." Henry is hideous to look at and is mentally retarded. Unaware of his condition, he keeps trying to return to the neighborhood he awed with his fine body and clothes. The town is terrified of him. No one will keep him, and yet the doctor does not want to institutionalize him. The town transfers its horror of Henry to the doctor, refusing to be treated by him and shrinking from him in fear. They even ostracize his wife, who took gentle pride in being a great social leader. He has paid for his son's life with the quality of life of his family and his profession. As the judge said, "It is hard for a man to know what to do."

Crane, Stephen. The Red Badge of Courage. Novel.

Adolescence   The Body   Death
Dying   Suffering

A complex novel about an idealistic adolescent's growth to assured, but still idealistic, manhood. Henry holds firm in the first battle, only to run in the second, conquered by a sudden return of his self-doubts masked as doubts about his regiment's position. Away from the front lines, Henry finds himself in the narrator's world, in which all men are only bodies. Henry may call a man "Jim Conklin" but to the narrator that man is only "a tall man." Henry looks closely into the putrefying eyes of a dead soldier, marches with the wounded, and watches his friend, Jim Conklin--who goes from "the spectral soldier" to the "tall soldier" after Henry recognizes him--choose his place of dying. Jim

dies his own hard death, despite the solicitous protests of his companions who persist as seeing him as a man who has a life: "Jim--what are you doing--what makes you do this way--you'll hurt yerself." Jim's response is monotonous: "He protested in a dulled way, keeping his eyes fastened on the mystic place of his intentions. 'No--no--don't tech me--leave me be--leave me be--.'" Henry is wounded by another fugitive, returns to the front lines where his bravery makes his name known to the generals and regains enough self-approbation to cover his guilt, even to himself. "He had been to touch the great death, and found that, after all, it was but the great death. He was a man."

Crane, Stephen. "The trees in the garden rained flowers." Available in The Complete Poems of Stephen Crane, ed. Joseph Katz. Ithaca: Cornell University Press, 1972. Poem: 28 lines.

Handicaps

Like all of Crane's poems, full of powerful ambiguity. Seemingly, the weak tutor accepts the father's claim that natural beauty belongs to the strong--only his acceptance is so phrased that it denies the father's claim: "The trees in the garden rained flowers./ Children ran there joyously . . . . Now there were some/ Who gathered great heaps . . . Until, behold, only chance blossoms/Remained for the feeble./Then a little spindling tutor/Ran importantly to the father," crying injustice. But the father rebukes him: "'Why should the strong--/--The beautiful strong--/Why should they not have the flowers?'/Upon reflection, the tutor bowed to the ground./'My Lord,' he said,/'The stars are displaced/By this towering wisdom.'"

Crane, Stephen. "When a Man Falls a Crowd Gathers (A Street Scene in New York)." Available in The Complete Short Stories and Sketches of Stephen Crane, ed. T. A. Gullason. Garden City, New York: Doubleday & Co., 1963. Sketch.

Disease & Health   Suffering

The reactions of people on the street to a man having some sort of seizure. Mindless enjoyment in viewing his predicament; a sense of possessing a right to view his sufferings. A few shout suggestions, but when authorities (a policeman, and then a doctor) come, the crowd resumes its curious pressure: "the doctor felt the skull of the prostrate man carefully . . . . The crowd pressed and crushed again. It was as if they fully expected to see blood by the light of the match, and the desire made them appear almost insane."

De Forest, John William. Miss Ravenal's Conversion from Secession to Loyalty, ed. G. S. Haight. New York: Holt, Rinehart and Winston, 1968. Novel.

Alcoholism   Children   Doctors
Med. Instit.   Preg. & Childbirth   Sexual Roles

De Forest's civil war novel offers a little bit of everything. The action is loosely connected to five characters: Doctor-geologist Ravenal, his daughter, the loose-living Colonel Carter who marries Miss Ravenal, the virtuous Captain Colbourne who unsuccessfully woos Miss Ravenal but who finally wins the widowed Mrs. Carter, and the shady lady, Mrs. Larue who seduces Colonel Carter. Around this rather fatuous fivesome are many delightful and interesting vignettes. Alcoholism is treated with a heavy hand. The reason for Carter's over-indulgence is melodramatic: Colonel Carter belongs to a set of southern men whose way of life (i.e. as slave owner) predisposes them to drink. However, the Colonel's alcoholism is described fairly straightforwardly: "His appetite was poor, especially at breakfast. His face was constantly flushed, his body had an appearance of being bloated, and his hands were tremulous. Nevertheless, obedient to a delusion common to men of his habits, he did not consider himself a hard drinker" (Chapter XXV). The doctor, who earned a living by research before the war, is very little of a physician. When Carter wants to provide for his prospective father-in-law, he offers him a sugar speculation and position as a colonel before he obtains for him the superintendency of a New Orleans hospital (Chapter XII). The wounded Captain Carter who passes through a field hospital and an understaffed military hospital sees more of sickness and the medical profession (Chapter XXI). The novel is preoccupied with three different women's roles: there is the role of sheltered innocent which prevents Lillie from understanding her father's warnings about Colonel Carter, there is the type of cruel southern woman who ostracizes Lillie and who reviles the nothern wounded as they move from the battlefield to the hospital, and there is the role of woman as mother which is explored at some length: "Woman is more intimately and irresponsibly a child of Nature than man. She comes oftener, more completely, and more evidently under the power of influences which she can neither direct nor resist . . . . Her part then is passive obedience and uncomplaining suffering, while through her the ends of life are accomplished" (Chapter XXIX). The pains of childbirth unite Lillie and Mrs. Larue, while Colonel Carter resolves to reform at the sight of her suffering. But the baby introduces a new complication. Nineteenth-century male writers often show a great ambivalence towards children. A woman should be a mother rather than a lover ("Each passion [father, husband] had been stronger than its predecessor;

but now she had reached the culminating point of her womanhood: higher than Baby it was impossible for her to go"), but then, a mother neglects her husband for her children. There are many instances of mockery of excessive maternal solicitude that causes the following result: "Lillie was amazed and shocked at discovering how little she missed him [her husband] . . . . Still, she could not be miserable; she was almost always happy with her child." Fortunately, although her maternal egotism slows down Captain Carter's courtship, Lillie does marry him and return to some sort of balance.

De L'Isle-Adam, Villiers. "The Doctor's Heroism." Available in Seventy-five Short Masterpieces, ed. Roger B. Goodman. New York: Bantam Books, 1961. Short Story.

Disease & Health   Doctors   Med. Ethics
Med. Profession

A funny little piece about one Dr. Hallidonhill, but really about medical researchers as a group. The point is simple enough and told amusingly. What happens is this: the renowned specialist is seeing patients on an assembly line basis when there appears before him a skeleton of a man with such an advanced case of t.b. that the doctor grumbles "What do you think I am--a coroner?" He gives the patient a week to live, but then, discovering that he is rich, sends him off on an absurd trip to the Riviera to eat nothing but watercress for six months, thinking never to see him again of course. But when six months later the patient returns roaring with health, the doctor takes out a pistol and shoots him on the spot, afterwards claiming to the court, with complete success, that an immediate autopsy was necessary to discover the cause of the astonishing cure. The author concludes sarcastically, "the exclusive love of the Humanity of the Future without any regard for the individual of the Present is, in our own time, the one whole motive that ought to justify the acquittal under any circumstances, of the magnanimous Extremists of Science."

De Quincey, Thomas. Confessions of an English Opium-Eater and Suspiria de Profundis. Boston: Ticknor and Fields, 1855. Essays.

The Body   Children   Death
Doctors   Drugs   Grief
Suffering

Confessions was written in 1821-22 and enlarged in 1856, so it embodies both the first flush of opium pleasure and the later disillusionment after he had cured himself of addiction--several times. The first part of Confessions, "Preliminary Confessions" and "The Pleasures of Opium," gives De Quincey's account of the childhood miseries and the months of starvation in London that he holds responsible for the stomach trouble that made him a regular opium user. He is critical of doctors' ignorance about opium and very favorable to the effects of opium. The second part, "The Pains of Opium," has a very different tone. He is incapable of mental effort, although he still desires to. He describes his dreams and his lassitude. In the appendix (usually not separated from the essay), he gives more physical symptoms and concludes by abusing his body for the suffering it has caused him, offering it to the anatomists to revenge himself upon it. De Quincey had ended this section with his "cure." In Suspiria de Profundis (1845), he admits the cure was unsuccessful and comes up with a two-part defense. In his discursive, digressive, allusive manner, he traces his attraction to opium to his childhood grief over the death of his 6-year-old sister. Although no specific connection is made, De Quincey's placement and repetition of the incident implies some responsibility for this pain by the surgeons who did an autopsy on the child to determine cause of death. He experiences a vision by her bedside that he attributes to his grief and then compares it with his later opium visions. Then, having performed a subtle transfer of his guilt for opium-taking to grief and doctors, he then goes on to show the creativity of the drug in his dream of the three ladies of Sorrows. Yet De Quincey is always aware of the dark side of the drug he is tacitly defending: "As in dreams always there is a power not contented with reproduction, but which absolutely creates or transforms. This dark being the reader will see again in a further stage of my opium experience; and I warn him that he will not always be found sitting inside my dreams, but at times outside, and in open daylight."

De Quincey, Thomas. "The English Mail Coach." From The Collected Writings of Thomas De Quincey, ed. David Masson. Edinburgh: Adam and Charles Black, 1890; rpt. New York: AMS Press, 1968. Vol. XIII. Essay.

Death   Drugs   Dying

The beautiful, deadly speed of the Mail coach nearly kills a young, courting couple, De Quincey describes his sensations as he sees the little carriage ahead of the gigantic Mail, his efforts to wake the Mail driver and to warn the couple, the boy's slow efforts to evade this sudden death, and the young girl's screaming terror as she perceives, amid the safe wreckage, how close she was to death. This episode follows a

reasoned discussion upon interpreting "sudden" death as instantaneous death. The episode is followed by a "Dream Fugue," De Quincey's emotional "dream" reactions (He says that he had taken several drops of laudanum). The episode is repeated over and over in different contexts with different emotional colors. In these variations the narrator tries to prevent death, but his efforts may provoke it. For the reader to move from the rational discourse to the vivid identification with death to the irrational "Dream Fugue" is an intense experience.

De Quincey, Thomas. "Murder as One of the Fine Arts." From The Collected Writings of Thomas De Quincey, ed. David Masson. Edinburgh: Adam and Charles Black, 1890; rpt. New York: AMS Press, 1968. Vol. XIII. Essay.

Med. Profession

The murderous means by which Burke and Hare supplied material for anatomy classes made quite an impact on 19th-century literature. The minor poet, Thomas Hood, wrote several comic poems on the subject. Stevenson used it in "The Body Snatchers." De Quincey was attracted to it also (not surprisingly, considering his heightened interest in the macabre) and facetiously recounts the activities of an ancient Roman doctor and "undertaker" engaged in a similar relationship as the climax of part 2 of this essay, full of death. Perhaps the great horror of Burke and Hare lay in their exposure of people's fear of doctors. "Life and death" are linked together so often in one phrase (and, considering the medical practices in the first part of the 19th century, more the latter than the former) that it is not surprising that "the healer," "the bringer of life," is also associated with death.

Dickens, Charles. Bleak House. Novel.

Children   Death   Disease & Health
Doctors   Drugs   The Family
Madness   Med. Students   Mental Retardation
Poverty & Health   Sexual Roles

Concentrates on disease and children. Its focus is on Chancery, which creates individuals who create disease. This is symbolized by the slum, "Tom-All-Alone," which festers as a result of the hereditary lawsuit, Jarndyce vs. Jarndyce. This place becomes a harbor for the poor, the desperate, and the sick, harboring disease as well. When the police harry the vagabonds to "move along," particularly the sick, stunted Jo, they harry the diseases of the slums into the country where they strike Charley and Esther. In addition, Chancery is directly responsible for the deaths of Richard, Tom Jarndyce, and Gridley and for Miss Flite's madness. Death is less an experience than example. Gridley dies as a victim of Chancery. Jo dies to illustrate the folly of those who seek to reform foreign heathens when there are dirty and ignorant souls in England. Krook's fantastic death by spontaneous combustion is a foretaste of Chancery's fate. Nemo dies of an opium overdose as the victim of Lady Deadlock's effort to bury her past in oblivion. Nemo is treated by the charitable doctor, Allan Woodcourt. The book also has Dr. Badger who briefly teaches medicine to Richard Carstone. However, Harold Skimpole, the destructive "child," was trained as a physician. Dickens has no condemnation for Dr. Woodcourt's furnishing Nemo with opium. He has strong condemnation for Harold Skimpole, who has a self-induced oblivion to all pains but his own. Dickens' determinism is very strong in this novel--particularly in his treatment of children. Richard is doomed to madness and death because he was born into the Jarndyce vs. Jarndyce suit. Jo's poverty has made him less intelligent than a sheep dog (Dickens drives this home by a sermon given by the hypocritical Chadband on the joys of being a human boy-- to Jo who suffers in incomprehending resentment). Esther is doomed to trouble by her hidden illegitimacy. The children of Mrs. Jellyby and Mrs. Pardiggle, who neglect their families for foreign charities, are doomed to disease and trouble. No child escapes unscathed. Presumably the next generation will be better, but since the only representative we see is the deaf-and-dumb child of two dancing instructors, Dickens does not appear hopeful.

Dickens, Charles. David Copperfield. Novel.

Adolescence   Alcoholism   Children
Death   Doctors   The Family
Grief   Handicaps   Mental Retardation
Preg. & Childbirth   Sexuality   Sexual Roles
Suffering

Out of the list above, the two main topics are grief and, of course, children. The description of childhood seems less theoretical and more indignant here, although there is still the contrast between Creaker's hideous school and Dr. Strong's fine academy. The descriptions of adolescent puppy love are amusing and portrayed straightforwardly. However, the novel as a whole seems structured about griefs and the ways of bearing them: the patient grief of Dr. Strong's wife under unjust suspicion; the alcoholic grief of Mr. Wickfield for his dead wife that leads him into the wet hands of Uriah Heep; the grief of Betsey Trotwood for her lost

illusions about men (her sufferings with her husband
apparently bring on Mr. Dick's retardation) which
causes her to hate men; the violent grief of Ham for
the fallen Emily, the selfish "grief" of the Crewlers
for the "loss" of their helpful daughter to her beloved
Traddles; the whining grief of Mrs. Gummidge which
vanishes in the presence of real grief about her; the
morbid griefs of Rosa Dartle and Mrs. Steerforth that
express themselves in hatred of each other and the
world; and the near fatal grief of David for Dora.
Dickens did not attack alcoholism very strongly; his
sense of social outrage was not aroused by liquor--
one is more likely to find pleasant scenes of convivial
drinking. However, there are, in his works, Mr. Wickfield; the degraded, alcoholic white who ruins Stephen
Blackpool in Hard Times; and, most miserable of all,
the alcoholic "child" of the crippled seamstress in
Our Mutual Friend, her sodden father whom she painfully supports. In contrast to Bleak House, in which
family is a mesh sucking in characters, the family is
supportive here. Although David's stepfather drives
him out, his aunt takes her in. Ham's family helps
him--and then themselves--through their double tragedy.
However, there are a number of perverted families as
well--Steerforth's two women are a grim counterpart of
David's aunt and his Agnes. In Hard Times, Gradgrind's
theories warp his family. The Micawber family seems
to hold together out of necessity, despite the periods
of their famous optimism. In Little Dorrit, prison
warps the Dorrit family. Yet, in Nicholas Nickleby,
Nicholas, his mother, sister and cousin form the nucleus
of a "family" which grows throughout the novel. Little
Miss Mowcher, the dwarf, who finally brings down Steerforth's oily accomplice, was apparently portrayed
unsympathetically at first. The original reportedly
complained, and the character became more sympathetic.
This is interesting because Miss Mowcher is one of the
few cases of a sympathetic handicapped adult in
Dickens. Jenny Wren in Our Mutual Friend and Tiny Tim
in A Christmas Carol are both pathetic children. Silas
Wegg, in Our Mutual Friend, with his wooden leg, and
Quilp are villains. For Dickens, mental retardation,
like madness, was the result of psychic shock. Maggy,
the woman "child" in Little Dorrit was made so by abuse
by her drunken grandmother. Barnaby Rudge becomes an
idiot as a result of shock to his pregnant mother, who
sees the bloody hands of his murderer-father, and
Guster, the servant prone to fits at the Snagsbys, in
Bleak House, was made so by her "charitable" upbringing.
Dickens devotes a rather unpleasant section to Dora's
miscarriage which leads to her death. David is suffering because the cute sexual object-"child" he married
cannot change into a proper wife. "I had hoped that
some lighter hands than mine would help to mold her
character, and that a baby-smile upon her breast might
change my child-wife to a woman. It was not to be.
The spirit fluttered for a moment on the threshold of
its little prison, and, unconscious of captivity, took
wing." She neatly dies, leaving David to his asexual
"angel," Agnes Wickfield, who does make him a good wife.
Throughout David's first marriage, he is influenced by
his grief for his childlike mother, "killed" by the
Murdstones. One must also note the gentle obstetrician
who delivers David and his ill-fated stepbrother and
who suffers Betsey Trotwood's wrath when the expected
"Betsey" is born as David.

Dickens, Charles. Dombey and Son. Novel.

Age   Children   Dying
Grief   Sexuality

The death of Paul Dombey almost ranks with the death of
little Nell as a tear jerker. Dickens seems to have
three kinds of death in his novels: the pathetic,
beautiful--and lengthy--deaths of children; the repentant
deaths of sinners; and the horrible deaths of murderers
(the ones who don't commit suicide)--Orlick, Bradley
Headstone, Rigaud and Rudge all die amid some of Dickens'
most overworked prose. Death is associated with water.
Paul Dombey goes in harmony with the sea that so
fascinated him. Barkis dies with the tide. Steerforth
and Ham, Quilp, Headstone and Riderhood (Our Mutual
Friend) drown. Martha goes to commit suicide by drowning. Hexam has a marvelous recovery from drowning in
Our Mutual Friend: while his acquaintances labor over
his body to resuscitate him, he is treated with respect;
when he recovers consciousness, he immediately returns
to his original status of pariah. Other remarkable
treatments of death are Fagin's last night in the death
cell and Oliver's observations on death as an undertaker's helper in Oliver Twist and Sidney Carton's "It
is a far, far better thing that I do, than I have done;
it is a far, far better rest that I go to, than I have
ever known" that ends A Tale of Two Cities. Dombey and
Son also contains one of Dickens' attacks on education.
Mr. Blimber's forcing hothouse for young minds may not
equal the sadism of Dotheboys Hall in Nicholas Nickleby
or the school in Hard Times which teaches facts and no
fancy (and so no morality or love) or the school in
Dombey which crushes Rob the Grinder into hypocrisy
(as Uriah Heep was crushed), but it is more insidious
because it appears to have good results; the dying Paul
Dombey and the retarded genius, Tootles, are not
considered as true consequences. Dombey and Son has
an unusual parent-child relationship as its core.
Dombey neglects his daughter in favor of his son, who
is destined to succeed him in his business. But

Florence gives her brother, Paul, love while his father
gives him only ambitions that seem foreign to the weak
boy. So, the boy loves his sister. The father is
jealous. The boy dies as a result of forcing him
through childhood too fast (and perhaps an innate weakness). In his grief, the father shuns Florence, whom
he hates for living while Paul is dead, and marries a
woman for her value as a commodity. Again, his wife
gives love to his daughter and not to him, and his
jealousy of Florence increases. When his pride and
resentment drive away his wife, he vents his anger on
the still-clinging Florence, driving her out of the
house. The novel declines into sentiment or melodrama
from this point. The only other object of interest is
the grotesque old "Cleopatra," Mrs. Skewton, who
fights off death and clings to the myth of continued
sexual attractions. Like Dombey, she erects her imposing
appearance at the cost of family love and harmony.

Dickens, Charles. Great Expectations. Novel.

Children   Disease & Health   Dying
Madness

Great Expectations has both of Dickens' attitudes toward
children. Children are formed by adults--training
determines character. In this novel, training on the
one hand and great expectations on the other ruin both
Estella and Pip. The other attitude is the unsentimental
record of the cruelties of children towards other
children. Although childhood is a great good (the
Smallweeds of Bleak House are to be pitied because they
have adults, not children), he shows Pip's patronizing
of Joe and Estella's carefully instructed wounding of
Pip. Noah Claypole is the rule that proves Oliver's
uniqueness in Oliver Twist. Madness here exemplifies
the treatment of insanity throughout Dickens' work,
including Barnaby Rudge, Nicholas Nickleby, and A Tale
of Two Cities. Madness is a response to external
pressure. Miss Haversham is driven mad by her abandonment. John Willet, in Barnaby Rudge, is driven mad by
the vandalization of his beloved inn. Dr. Manette in
A Tale of Two Cities is driven back to purposeless
shoemaking by long imprisonment and the troubles of his
son-in-law. It is true that there are several cases of
unprovoked madness: the hereditary lunatic in Pickwick
Papers, the historical figure of George Gordon in
Barnaby Rudge, and the minor character of the amorous
neighbor in smalls and grey worsted in Nicholas Nickleby
who seems insane to make Mrs. Nickleby look even more
ridiculous. Great Expectations does show the partial
purgation of madness and "childish" cruelty. Miss
Haversham is jerked back to painful reality at the sight
of the sufferings inflicted and felt by Estella. Pip
is cured of his expectations by the appearance of his
true sponsor, the convict Magwich, whose deathbed he
consoles before he falls into near fatal delirium
himself.

Dickens, Charles. Martin Chuzzlewit. Novel.

Disease & Health   Dying   Evil Doctors
The Family   Nurses   Sexual Roles
Suicide

This book is the most medical of Dickens' novels. Among
his criticisms of America, the fever-wracked community
of Eden is the harshest condemnation of the reality
behind American boasting and advertising. However,
equally harsh is the pathetic deathbed of Anthony
Chuzzlewit, made hideous by the son he has raised to
be hideous. The book contains the only two evil (as
opposed to callous or foolish) doctors in Dickens' work:
Lewsome and Jobling. In debt to Jonas Chuzzlewit,
Lewsome gives him poison for "rats," even though he
knows that Jonas really wants it for his father. A
fever deprives him of an overseas job, and he falls
into the "nursing care" of Sairey Gamp and Mrs. Prig
who bring him so far down that he repents and confesses.
Jobling serves as a doctor and a shill for the Anglo-
Bengalee insurance racket. Like Lewsome, he presents
Jonas with a good way to kill, even though he knows
Jonas is an evil man, perhaps already a murderer.
There are really two forms of families in this book:
the "natural" extended Chuzzlewit family, whose members
render each other miserable and the extended family
created by Martin Chuzzlewit and Tom Pinch, of loving
friends. The two alcohol-and-comfort-loving (and
misery-creating) nurses, Sairey Gamp (and Mrs. Harris?)
and Mrs. Prig need no further commentary. Someone with
a strong stomach might like to use the degraded portrait (supposedly flattering) of the "cute" child-
woman, Tom's sister (and the reformed Bella in Our
Mutual Friend). They bustle and blunder about the
kitchen, playing at being self-important and so enter-
tain their men. It is Dickens' laudatory patronizing
that is so irritating. Dickens has one comic treatment
of suicide; in Nicholas Nickleby a traveler tells the
story of the Baron of Grogzwig, visited by the Genius
of Despair and Suicide as he is on the verge of suicide,
who is overcome with laughter at the motives for other
men's suicides and who so is saved himself. But in
general, in Dickens' works, suicide is for murderers:
Ralph Nickleby, who hounded his own son to death; Bill
Sykes in Oliver Twist; and Jonas Chuzzlewit, for the
supposed murder of his father and his murder of Tigg.

Dickens, Charles. The Old Curiosity Shop. Novel.

Age   Children   Death
Disease & Health   Dying   Handicaps
Madness   Suffering

The main theme is Nell's encounter with an acceptance of
death. Led about England by her senile grandfather, mad
with gambling fever (which he rationalizes as a way to
enrich Nell) and fearful of incarceration in an asylum,
Nell moves on a nightmare journey from her old home,
driven by Quilp, to her death. One of her first encounters is with an old cottager who points out the grave of
a dead child. The old live while the young die. Then
she meets an old woman who mourns the sweetheart lost in
her youth. Death does not change a person more than life.
Mr. Vuffin discusses the fate of old giants and dwarves,
workers refuse bread to Nell and her grandfather because
their third child has just died of starvation, and the
death of the boy scholar brings home to her the fact that
she will die, which she does, although no cause is
apparent for her death. It may be that she dies because
the world is horrible, dominated by the sadistic dwarf
Quilp, who terrorizes his wife with the same joy with
which he abuses his serving boy and persecutes Kit.
Quilp seems to duplicate himself in the Punch and Judy
operators that try to betray Nell and her grandfather,
in the trainer who uses cruelty to teach his dogs, in
the physical and moral wrecks who attend the "fair," in
the drunken canalers who offer Nell and her grandfather
a ride, but force her to sing all night to treat and in
the men who rob her grandfather at cards and persuade
him to rob Nell and Mrs. Jarley. Disease, however, can
be beneficial. The confused Dick Swiveler, who serves
in the same office as mannish Sally Brass, is fired and
falls ill, only to be rescued by the nameless servant,
whom he nicknames "the marchioness."

Dickens, Charles. The Pickwick Papers. Novel.

Age   Children   Death
Disease & Health   Madness   Med. Students
Poverty & Health   Sexual Roles

In Dickens' work, age is not a problem, but a natural
extension of life. Pickwick and Tupman may quarrel over
whether he's too old to wear a fancy costume to a party,
but age does not stop the bewildered Mr. Pickwick from
being a sexual threat to the lady in curl papers and a
sexual object to Mrs. Bardell. Mr. Weller, Sr. is
constantly dodging predatory widows. The close relationship between Weller, Sr. and Weller, Jr. is unusual in
Dickens; for all their criticisms, father and son exist
together in hilarious, but touching, harmony. Mr. Pickwick, although quite robust for his years, has a
crippling bout of rheumatism after spending the night
in a damp apple tree. However, he wishes to accompany
his friends on their hunting party, so he is trundled
along in a wheelbarrow with further comic results.
However, what is not so comic is his stay in Debtors
prison as a result of the suit for breach of promise.
His health fails. Dickens was very concerned with the
debilitating effect of prison life, and, in Pickwick as
in the later Little Dorrit, he shows unrelieved misery
and death. The ill-health resulting from poverty in
Dickens is nearly always associated with some institution: Chancery in Bleak House; the Workhouse in Oliver
Twist (and as a specter in Our Mutual Friend); and
Dotheboys Hall in Nicholas Nickleby. It is true that
Pickwick also has the death of the poor clown, and there
are the poor workers in Hard Times and in Old Curiosity
Shop. But his most vicious attacks were on institutional
poverty—except in hospitals. One of the inserted
stories is that of the violent, homicidal maniac. More
interesting are the drunken med. students, Bob Sawyer
and Ben Allen (Chapters 30, 32, 38, and 50) who delight
in shocking acquaintances with ghoulish medical anec-
dotes but whose life is first a struggle against poverty
in school and then against poverty while trying to
establish a practice in a small town.

Dickens, Charles. "A Small Star in the East." In The Uncommercial
Traveler. From Works. New York: Peter Fenelon Collier, n.d.
Vol. 24. Sketch.

Children   Med. Instit.   Poverty & Health
Women as Healers

Opens with the double miseries of the poor: Starvation
without work and disease with work in the lead-mills.
Then, it goes on to describe the East London Children's
Hospital. Dickens was always full of praise for the
children's hospitals in London: A young child dies
beautifully in one in Our Mutual Friend; Maggie, in
Little Dorrit, remembers her stay in the hospital resulting from abuse by her drunken grandmother, as the high
point of her life. Dickens implies but does not discuss
the weakness of such institutions: they provide a bit
of comfort and then send the patient back into the
environment that caused the problem in the first place.
However, this East London Children's Hospital is remarkable. It is run by a husband-wife team. "Both have had
considerable practical experience of medicine and
surgery: he as house surgeon of a great London hospital;
she as a very earnest student, tested by severe examination, and also as a nurse of the sick poor during the
prevalence of cholera." The extremely dedicated staff
live in the hospital and try, with extremely limited
resources, to help the poor children.

Dickens, Charles. "Wapping Workhouse." In The Uncommercial
Traveler. From Works. New York: Peter Fenelon Collier,
n.d. Vol. 24. Sketch.

Madness   Med. Instit.   Women as Patients

Dickens looks at the mad women and his immediate response
is in terms of sexual roles: do they ever think of a
young woman "who is courted, and caressed, and loved, and
has a husband, and bears children, and lives in a home,
and who never knows what it is to have this lashing and
tearing come upon her." However, after he has covered
the full range of the workhouse, from children to old
women, he experiences a loss of stereotypes: "I had
ceased to believe in such fables of a golden time as
youth, the prime of life, or a hale old age. In ten
minutes all the lights of womankind seemed to have been
blown out."

Dickinson, Emily. "After great pain, a formal feeling comes—."
Available in Final Harvest: Emily Dickinson's Poems, ed.
T. H. Johnson. Boston: Little, Brown & Co., 1962. Poem:
13 lines.

Grief   Suffering

Although the opening line only mentions pain, the shock
seems to be emotional, not physical; it is a strong portrayal of the early hours of grief: "After great pain,
a formal feeling comes—/The Nerves sit ceremonious, like
Tombs . . . . This is the Hour of Lead—/Remembered, if
outlived,/As Freezing persons, recollect the Snow—/
First—Chill—then Stupor—then the letting go—."

Dickinson, Emily. "As One does Sickness over." Available in The
Poems of Emily Dickinson, ed. T. H. Johnson. Cambridge, Mass.:
Harvard University Press, 1963. 3 Vols. Vol. 2. Poem:
12 lines.

Disease & Health   Suffering

Sickness, as with great danger and suffering, later
causes one to question identity. The poem is ambiguous
as to whether it is the identity of sickness, one's own
identity, or (as this reader prefers) the combined
identity of both that is questioned: "As One does
Sickness over/In convalescent Mind,/His scrutiny of
Chances/By blessed Health obscured— . . . A Custom of
the Soul/Far after suffering/Identity to question/For
evidence't has been."

Dickinson, Emily. "Death is like the insect." Available in Final
Harvest: Emily Dickinson's Poems, ed. T. H. Johnson. Boston:
Little, Brown & Co., 1962. Poem: 12 lines.

Death   Euthanasia

A surgeon trying to save a patient from death is like a
gardener trying to save a tree from an insect. He must
fight "if it cost you/Everything you are"; but if the
insect has taken over the tree, the gardener/Surgeon
must destroy it: "Then, if it have burrowed/Out of
reach of skill—/Wring the tree and leave it,/'Tis the
vermin's will."

Dickinson, Emily. "The Heart asks Pleasure—first—." Available
in Final Harvest: Emily Dickinson's Poems, ed. T. H. Johnson.
Boston: Little, Brown & Co., 1962. Poem: 8 lines.

Death   Euthanasia   Suffering

Under some outside influence, regression from asking for
liberty to the submissive request for death: "The
Heart asks Pleasure—first—/And then—Excuse from Pain—/
And then—those little Anodynes/That deaden suffering—/
And then—to go to sleep—/And then—if it should be/The
will of its Inquisitor/The privilege to die—."

Dickinson, Emily. "I felt a Cleaving in my Mind." Available in
The Poems of Emily Dickinson, ed. T. H. Johnson. Cambridge,
Mass.: Harvard University Press, 1963. 3 Vols. Vol. 2.
Poem: 8 lines.

Madness

A vivid description of a state of madness: "I felt a
Cleaving in my Mind—/As if my Brain had split . . . .
The thought behind, I strove to join/Unto the thought
before—/But Sequence ravelled out of Sound/Like Balls—
upon a Floor."

Dickinson, Emily. "I heard a Fly buzz—when I died—." Available
in Final Harvest: Emily Dickinson's Poems, ed. T. H. Johnson.
Boston: Little, Brown & Co., 1962. Poem: 16 lines.

Dying

Astonishing poem on the interpolation of trivial, natural
disorder, or death, into the formally organized preparations for conventional death. "And Breaths were gathering
firm/For that last Onset—when the King/Be witnessed—
in the Room— . . . and then it was/There interposed a
Fly—/With Blue—uncertain stumbling Buzz—/Between the
Light—and me—/And then the Windows failed—and then/I
could not see to see."

Dickinson, Emily. "I noticed People disappeared." Available in
The Poems of Emily Dickinson, ed. T. H. Johnson. Cambridge,
Mass.: Harvard University Press, 1963. 3 Vols. Vol. 2.
Poem: 8 lines.

Children   Death

Although Death is concealed from children, the innocent
young narrator discovers the right answer: "I noticed
People disappeared/When but a little child—/Supposed

they visited remote/Or settled Rgions wild--/Now know
I--They both visited/And settled Regions wild/But did
because they died/A Fact withheld the little Child."

Dickinson, Emily. "It Knew no Medicine--." Available in The
Poems of Emily Dickinson, ed. T. H. Johnson. Cambridge,
Mass.: Harvard University Press, 1963. 3 Vols. Vol 2.
Poem: 16 lines.

Disease & Health   Suffering

Rejection of defining pain as physical pain, of considering someone not sick if there is no pain. Disease caused
by a vision of Paradise. "It Knew no Medicine--It was
not Sickness--then--/Nor any need of Surgery--/And
therefore--'twas not Pain--/It moved away the Cheeks--/
A Dimple at a time . . . . Temerity--drew near--And
sickened--ever afterward/For Somewhat that it saw?"

Dickinson, Emily. "Much Madness is divinest Sense--." Available
in Final Harvest: Emily Dickinson's Poems, ed. T. H. Johnson.
Boston: Little, Brown & Co., 1962. Poem: 8 lines.

Madness

Nicely phrased version of a somewhat trite theme--the
relative definitions of insanity: "Much Madness is
divinest Sense--/To a discerning Eye--/Much Sense--the
starkest Madness--/'Tis the Majority/In this, as All,
prevail--/Assent--and you are sane--/Demur--you're
straightway dangerous--/And handled with a Chain--."

Dickinson, Emily. "My first well Day--since many ill." Available
in The Poems of Emily Dickinson, ed. T. H. Johnson. Cambridge,
Mass.: Harvard University Press, 1963. 3 Vols. Vol. 2.
Poem: 28 lines.

Death   Disease & Health

Coming outside after a summer spent fighting death, she
notices that autumn's bright colors are only Summer's
cheat, to hide the sepulchre by a rainbow--her way "to
hide her parting Grace/From our unfitted eyes." With
typical ambiguity, Dickinson leaves us uncertain as to
whether her loss teaches her to value the Sun--or the
Grave. "My loss, by Sickness--Was it Loss?/Or that
Etherial Gain/One earns by measuring the Grave--/Then--
measuring the Sun--."

Dickinson, Emily. "Pain--has an Element of Blank--." Available in
Final Harvest: Emily Dickinson's Poems, ed. T. H. Johnson.
Boston: Little, Brown & Co., 1962. Poem: 8 lines.

Suffering

Pain blots out even the hope of anything other than pain.
"It has no Future--but itself--/Its Infinite contain/Its
Past--enlightened to perceive/New Periods--of Pain."

Dickinson, Emily. "Still own thee--still thou art." Available in
The Poems of Emily Dickinson, ed. T. H. Johnson. Cambridge,
Mass.: Harvard University Press, 1963. 3 Vols. Vol. 3.
Poem: 8 lines.

Dying   Med. Ethics

Although the patient meets the surgeons' criterion of
life, he/she is close enough to death so that questioning
of the patient (about life? about death?) becomes
imperative: "Still own thee--still thou art/What surgeons
call alive--/Though slipping--slipping I perceive/To
thy reportless Grave--/Which question shall I clutch--/
What answer wrest from thee/Before thou dost exude
away/In the recallless sea?"

Dickinson, Emily. "Surgeons must be very careful." Available in
The Poems of Emily Dickinson, ed. T. H. Johnson. Cambridge,
Mass.: Harvard University Press, 1963. 3 Vols. Vol. 1.
Poem: 4 lines.

Surgery

This playful poem can be taken as life causing disease
or as life causing trouble to surgeons or as life as a
criminal requiring medical care or--"Surgeons must be
very careful/When they take the Knife!/Underneath their
fine incisions/Stirs the culprit,--Life!"

Dostoevsky, Fyodor. The Brothers Karamazov. New York: New
American Library, 1957. Novel.

The Body   Death   Disease & Health
Dying   The Family   Grief
Madness   Med. Instit.   Sexuality
Suicide   Suffering

The classic Russian family novel, long and passionate
and profound. Fyodor Karamazov has three sons, each
interesting as individuals but each also representing
an aspect of the human personality. Dmitri is reckless;
Ivan, atheist, haunted, intellectual, and cynical;
Alyosha, saintly. But all are descended from a sensual
father and share in his mad nature (though Alyosha's
wild side doesn't appear in this novel; there was to be
a sequel). A fourth son, the bastard Smerdyakov,
manipulates everyone, and his mad mental contortions
(symbolically paralleled by his epilepsy) end in his
murdering Fyodor, then killing himself. Physical illness also visits Dmitri, who is hospitalized with a
fever, and Ivan, whose delirious fever is accompanied
by hallucinations of the devil. (Compare Crime and
Punishment, where psychological and physical torment
are also mixed.) Death hovers over the Karamozovs'

story. Father Zossima, Alyosha's beloved mentor is
dying: After his death, contrary to the expectations of
his disciples, his body decomposes like everyone else's,
and the stench permeates the monastery. The novel ends
with Alyosha at a young boy's funeral, mourning for the
boy, the Karamazovs, and the world.

Dostoevsky, Fyodor. Crime and Punishment. New York: Bantam, 1958.
Novel.

Alcoholism   Body/Mind   Death
Disease & Health   Doctors   Dying
The Family   Grief   Madness
Mental Retardation   Poverty & Health   Sexuality
Suffering

A favorite among psychiatrists (as indeed all the works
of the great 19th century Russian writers could be).
The hero's, Raskolnikov's, symptoms include delusions
of grandeur, anxiety, sleeplessness, hysteria, depression,
suicidal thoughts, and guilt: all of them were presumably present, at least in incipient form, even before
he murders the old pawnbroker and her pathetic, slightly
retarded stepsister. Physical illness is here too--
Raskolnikov's feverish state after the crime, for
instance, when he is visited by Dr. Zossimov, who says
the patient just isn't eating well enough; the consumption of the dying Katerina Ivanovna; and later in the
Siberian prison camp to which he is sent, the hero's
recurrent fever, brought on not by the deprived conditions, he believes, but by mental anguish, which is in
turn the result of his being unable to repent. He
theorizes that a man of extraordinary abilities (and
sometimes he thinks himself one) is not bound by the
ordinary moral code and might be allowed to attempt the
perfect crime, as he has done. Exactly why he committed
the murder, readers have long debated, but this much we
know: young Raskolnikov was ill, poverty-stricken,
living in urban claustrophobia, and had a troubled
relationship with his mother and sister. There is, of
course, a great deal of other suffering in this novel--
people die, they drink too much (Marmeladov), children
are orphaned, women are sexually abused (Dounia). Only
the sometime prostitute Sonia remains saintly amidst all
this. Through his love for her, Raskolnikov begins at
last to throw off some of the torment of his dual nature
(he is both kind and cruel; cf. Dostoevsky's analysis
of the paranoid clerk in The Double) and to be spiritually
regenerated. Dostoevsky, by the way, is part of that
perhaps significant number of writers whose fathers were
physicians.

Dostoevsky, Fyodor. The Idiot. Harmondsworth, England: Penguin
Books, 1955. Novel.

Disease & Health   Madness   Mental Retardation

Like all Dostoevsky's major fiction, The Idiot is partly
a study of mental illness. Here, e.g., Natasha is a
frenzied neurotic, debasing herself before the shameless
Rogozhin, who ultimately murders her. But the chief
contribution of this novel to medicine derives from its
hero, Prince Myshkin. Called "the idiot" by his friends
because of his naiveté and peculiar habits, Myshkin is
also an epileptic (like Dostoevsky himself). As a result
of all these qualities, people think him odd and make
fun of him. But they are nonetheless drawn to him because
unlike them, he is a truly innocent, even saintly, man,
full of generosity for all who help or hurt him. There
is some question about his mind, though: is he naive
and good, or is he sometimes foolish to the point of
simple-mindedness? At the beginning of the novel,
Myshkin is coming home from a sanatorium; at the end, he
returns to it, probably to stay for the rest of his life.

Dostoevsky, Fyodor. Notes From the Underground. New York: New
American Library, 1961. Novella.

Disease & Health   Madness   Med. Profession
Suffering

The narrator has gone underground, i.e., he has withdrawn
into complete isolation in a little room from which he
talks obsessively about his (and by extension modern man's)
ills. These are chiefly psychological/spiritual, but
Dostoevsky is, as usual, also interested in physical
disease. The two are intertwined. The Underground Man
claims that his liver is diseased and that he is certainly
superstitious enough to respect medicine. But he won't
go to doctors out of spite. At one point he discusses
toothache, asserting that when an educated man moans in
pain, it is for all of modern civilization. He actually
enjoys suffering, the Underground Man believes. He
summarizes his particular neurosis by saying that he
cannot feel, cannot decide anything, cannot act, because
he's too conscious, which is itself an illness. Furthermore, no matter what he learns, man will sometimes act in
opposition to all reason.

Douglas, Alfred. "Two Loves." Available in Aesthetes and Decadents
of the 1890's, ed. Karl Beckson. New York: Vintage Books,
1966. Poem: 74 lines.

Homosexuality

A homosexual extension of the "courtly love" medieval dream
vision. The narrator dreams of a "waste garden" with
"curious flowers, before unknown,/Flowers that were stained
with moonlight." He is met by a beautiful, naked youth,
with flowers in his hair and bursting grapes in his hand

(what an image of homosexual love!), who kisses the narrator and shows him "images of life": two boys, a joyous one who sings of pretty maids, and a sad sweet boy, whose appearance causes the narrator to weep and ask his name. "'My name is Love!/Then straight the first did turn himself to me/And cried, 'He lieth, for his name is Shame,/But I am Love, and I was wont to be/Alone in this fair garden, till he came/Unasked by night' . . . Then sighing, said the other, 'Have thy will,/I am the love that dare not speak its name.'"

Dowson, Ernest. "Non Sum Qualis Eram Bonae Sub Regno Cynarae." Available in Aesthetes and Decadents of the 1890's, ed. Karl Beckson. New York: Vintage Books, 1966. Poem: 24 lines.

    Sexuality

    This poem upon the line of Horace, "I am not what once I was in kind Cynara's day," shows an old passion crossing the present, leaving the narrator--not regretful or resentful--but, what is worse, jaded. The poem is famous for its refrain. "Last night, ah, yesternight, betwixt her lips and mine/There fell thy shadow, Cynara! thy breath was shed/Upon my soul between the kisses and the wine;/And I was desolate and sick of an old passion,/Yea, I was desolate and bowed my head:/I have been faithful to thee, Cynara! in my fashion."

Doyle, Arthur Conan. "The Croxley Master." From The Croxley Master and Other Tales of the Ring and Camp. New York: George H. Doran Co., 1919. Short Story.

    By Doctors   Doctors   Med. Students

    Wish-fulfillment for medical students. A poor student spends the vacation working for an indifferent (in both senses of the word) doctor in a coal-mining town; he is worried because he lacks the tuition for the next semester. He asks the doctor for a loan but is indignantly refused because the doctor hopes to keep him on as good, cheap labor. In his rage, the student knocks down and temporarily disables a husband who obstinately demands that his wife's prescription be filled immediately. The husband was the local boxing champion; someone is needed to replace him in the local tournament that is the miners' one sport, their one relief in life; the prize money is great; the student trains in secret; and wins the match. His good training and good living win over brawn and experience. Doyle's substitution of good living for brains in the usual brains vs. brawn is characteristic.

Doyle, Arthur Conan. "The Curse of Eve." From Round the Red Lamp; Being Facts and Fancies of Medical Life. Freeport, New York: Books for Libraries Press, 1969. Short Story.

    By Doctors   Doctors   Preg. & Childbirth
    Suffering

    Doyle's collection of stories about doctors, Round the Red Lamp, is well worth exploring. This sketch of a husband's experiences during his wife's labor is not the best but shows Doyle's range. The husband has trouble finding the doctor, chasing him about on his rounds until he catches up with the doctor at dinner which the doctor, for his own self-preservation, refuses to leave. When the husband finally does get the doctor to his wife, he is tormented by the sense of his helplessness and the doctor's references to leases when he wants to know about his wife. Then, complications take over; the doctor is transformed into a fighter, working with a specialist, sending the husband on a quest for an A.C.E. mixture because the woman's heart is too weak for chloroform. The doctors save the woman and leave, making a mild jest about the fee; but the husband remains, changed by his sufferings: "He was full of new emotions. If there had been a harrowing, there had been a planting too." A consolation story for pregnant women?

Doyle, Arthur Conan. "The Doctors of Hoyland." From Round the Red Lamp; Being Facts and Fancies of Medical Life. Freeport, New York: Books for Libraries Press, 1969. Short Story.

    By Doctors   Doctors   Women as Healers

    A marvelous story of the confrontation between a male and a female doctor. Dr. James Ripley has had a monopoly in the Hoyland district until the appearance of Dr. Verrinder Smith, whose scientific monographs he's admired. He goes to congratulate the man and finds a woman with whom he promptly begins to quarrel. "'Why should a woman not earn her bread by her brains?' . . . . 'I should much prefer not to be led into a discussion, Miss Smith.' 'Doctor Smith,' she interrupted." All of his prejudices come out, but she is too formidable, a paragon of feminine, medical superiority. She is more aware of current research, performs cures he has not attempted, and does more cures--with the result that his practice diminishes. The final blow comes when he breaks his leg on rounds and is found and treated by her. He comes to love her and asks her to marry him. At this point the story's strength appears. She only took the Hoyland practice to pass time until an opening occurred in the Paris Physiological Laboratory, and an opening has just now appeared. She prefers biology to marriage. Dr. Ripley thinks more and more highly of Dr. Smith and so asks her to marry him. Dr. Smith thinks more and more highly of Dr. Ripley and so considers him a competent colleague.

Doyle, Arthur Conan. "A Medical Document." From Round the Red Lamp; Being Facts and Fancies of Medical Life. Freeport, New York: Books for Libraries Press, 1969. Sketches.

    By Doctors   Doctors   Science & Poetry
    Sexuality

    An informal bull session by a group of doctors mulling over their more interesting cases. It is in part Conan Doyle's answer to "the uses of medicine in popular fiction," in which common diseases are overlooked and mysterious maladies are invented. "All the diseases, too, belong to the upper part of the body. The novelist never strikes below the belt." And yet "there is a side of life which is too medical for the general public and too romantic for the professional journals . . . . if it is good enough for Providence to create, it is good enough for us to try and understand . . . . it would deal, too, with the singular phenomena of waxing and waning manhood . . . which have . . . sent a man to prison when he should have been hurried to a consulting-room." The doctors chat about a number of glimpses at humans influenced by illness and end "'Why, we've done nothing but talk shop,' says the general practitioner. 'What possible interest can the public take in that?'"

Doyle, Arthur Conan. The Sherlock Holmes Tales. Available in The Complete Sherlock Holmes. Garden City, N. Y.: Doubleday, 1930. Novellas and Stories.

    By Doctors   Doctors   Evil Doctors

    Dr. Conan Doyle's famous detective is more physician than his side-kick, Dr. Watson, is. The astounding deductive powers of Holmes were, in fact, said to be based on the diagnostic abilities of the author's professor at the Edinburgh Infirmary, Dr. Joseph Bell. Of actual physicians, Dr. Watson is, of course, the lengthiest portrait, but he is merely a good, loyal, and--some would say--dull man, whose affection-provoking qualities include his attempt to maintain a man of science attitude in the midst of life's mysteries. Conan Doyle also produces the good country doctor, Dr. Mortimer in The Hound of the Baskervilles, and the evil doctor, Dr. Roylott of "The Speckled Band": "When a doctor does go wrong he is the first of criminals. He has nerve and he has knowledge." Is Holmes first-rate literature? The question is not relevant. He is, as Christopher Morley has written, "pure anesthesia."

Doyle, Arthur Conan. "The Third Generation." From Round the Red Lamp; Being Facts and Fancies of Medical Life. Freeport, New York: Books for Libraries Press, 1969. Short Sketch.

    By Doctors   Doctors   Med. Ethics
    V.D.

    A specialist in V.D. is visited by a desperate young man with the disease, which he inherited from his father who inherited it from his father. He is paying for his grandfather's sin. The young man is to be married in a few days, but the doctor tells him he must break it off. When the patient cries "Why?" the doctor gives no help to him: "You must not excite yourself . . . . We must take these questions upon trust. What are we after all? Half evolved creatures in a transition stage; nearer, perhaps, to the medusa on the one side than to perfected humanity on the other." Neither doctor nor patient think of telling the truth to the fiancée; they discuss the hopelessness of breaking off the wedding respectably. The doctor is sickened and surprised when he reads the next day of the young man's suicide. The modern reader might wonder whether the disease or the doctor finally drove him to it.

Drake, Joseph Rodman. "The King of the Croakers." From The Croakers, by Joseph Rodman Drake and Fitz Greene Halleck. New York: Bradford Club, 1860 (From the Rare Book Room at The Pennsylvania State University). Poem: 35 lines.

    By Doctors   Doctors   Med. Instit.
    Med. Profession   Med. Students

    Dr. Drake is best known for his aery fantasy, Culprit Fay (found in The Life and Works of Joseph Rodman Drake, ed. Frank Lester Pleadwell, M.D. Boston: Merrymount Press, 1935); but he is also known for his series of satiric sketches on New York public life (The Croakers), written in collaboration with his poet-friend Fitz Greene Halleck. "The King of the Croakers" is one of several satires upon Dr. David Hosack, Professor of Surgery and Midwifery at the College of Physicians and Surgeons in New York City. The poem is written about Dr. Hosack's quarrel with Dr. Hamersley, who used digitalis as a universal remedy for consumption and heart disease. The quarrel about hospital practices ended with Hosack and other doctors withdrawing to establish Rutgers Medical College and, in Drake's opinion, to again use medical students in hospital quarrels. "Oh! David! how dreadful and dire wast the note,/When Rebellion beleaguered the place;/When the bull-dog of discord unbolted his throat,/And the hot Digitales unbuttoned his coat/And doubled his fist in your face . . . . While the brave Surgeon-General exclaimed in delight,/'Pugnatum est arte medendi.'/But your wars are all ended, you're now at your ease,/The Regents are bound for your debts;/You may fleece your poor students as much as you please,/Tax boldly, matriculate, double your fees,/You can pay off all scores in brevets."

Dunbar, Paul. "The Paradox" and "The Right to Die." Available in The Complete Poems of Paul Laurence Dunbar. New York: Dodd, Mead & Co., n.d. Poems: 32 & 18 lines.

Death   Suicide

Dunbar is best known for his dialect poems of plantation life and for a few good poems on being black, but he was also concerned with bravely meeting death. The first spells out the paradoxial nature of death: "I am the mother of sorrows,/I am the ender of grief;/I am the bud and the blossom,/I am the late-falling leaf." The poem ends rather unexpectedly: "Come to me, brother, when weary,/Come when thy lonely heart swells;/I'll guide thy footsteps and lead thee/Down where the Dream Woman dwells." The second poem defends suicide when life has nothing but bitterness left: "I have no fancy for that ancient cant/That makes us masters of our destinies,/And not our lives."

Edgeworth, Maria. Belinda. From Tales and Novels. New York: Harper & Bros., 1852. Vols. XI & XII. Novel.

Disease & Health   Doctors   Women as Patients

A rather nauseatingly moral extension of Fanny Burney's novel of manners, Belinda depicts the moral growth and amazingly successful moral influence of a young girl, Belinda. Of interest is the figure of Lady Delacour, who, under the influence of the mannish Harriot Freke, fought a duel with another woman. The duel was really abortive, but her pistol misfired and her breast was injured. She suffers continuous discomfort in her breast, becomes convinced that she has cancer, alienates her husband, sends her daughter away, and abandons herself to dissipated living, feuding with another heartless woman and hiding her pain under a mask of gaiety (The sentimental clichés are infectious). She hides her medical equipment, allowing people to believe she and/or Belinda, her protegé, has a lover rather than divulge the truth. She makes the injury worse by medications of a quack, but, under the influence of Belinda and the virtuous Dr. X--, she is brought to consider imitating the Amazons (i.e., a mastectomy). However, as she is closeted with the surgeon, prepared for death, she learns that the injury is not serious, that the quack had deliberately irritated a minor injury to hold her as a patient, and that, provided she stops taking her large doses of laudanum (a condition presented as one easy to meet), she will soon return to good health. This discovery completes the reformation of the Delacour family, and all live happily ever after. The affair is interesting for several reasons: a novel published in 1801 discusses, however obliquely, a mastectomy; the patient's preparations are mocked because her excessive addition to mystic Methodism lead her to mistake a spy for a vision of death; the patient's desire for secrecy is condemned because it leads to so much grief; but the patient's courage in facing such an operation--without an anaesthetic--is not praised exceptionally because she had no other laternative.

Eliot, George (Mary Anne Evans). Adam Bede. Garden City, New York: Doubleday & Co., n.d. Novel.

Doctors   Grief   Preg. & Childbirth
Sexual Roles

Although Adam is the unifying hero of the novel, the action contrasts two women: the Methodist preacher, Dinah Morris, who is self-aware, giving, and able to comfort Mrs. Bede on the death of her husband and Hetty as she faces death; and Hetty Sorrel, who is not aware of herself although wrapped in intense egotism. The difference between the women is not passion, although Hetty carries on an affair with the squire's son, but religion, a sense of purpose and a sense of self. Dinah, for all her conflict with sexual stereotyping as a preacher, is the better woman. The book is famous for its scenes of country life, but most useful might be the court trial of Hetty for child murder: her condemnation on the doctor's testimony even though it is quite clear that her temporary abandonment was due to temporary insanity.

Eliot, George (Mary Anne Evans). Janet's Repentance. In Scenes of Clerical Life. Available ed. David Lodge. London: Penguin, 1973. Novella.

Alcoholism   Disease & Health   Doctors
Dying   Suffering

Into a conservative little town comes the evangelical clergyman, Mr. Tryan. The town divides into two camps, pro-Dissenter (for Tryan) and anti-Dissenter (anti-Tryan). The split even affects the town's two doctors (dissected so beautifully in Chapter 1), who get or lose patients according to their views. At the head of the anti-Tryanites are Lawyer Dempster and his wife. The lawyer is a conceited, violent, vindictive alcoholic. His wife is a secret alcoholic, the result of abuse, physical and mental, by her husband. Finally, locked out one night, she goes to a friend, a follower of Tryan who meets her there and begins to give her comfort and courage. Her husband is injured when he drunkenly overturns his carriage. She nurses him. There are, throughout the story, little insights, such as "where a human being lies prostrate, thrown on the tender mercies of his fellow, the moral relation of man to man is reduced to its utmost clearness and simplicity." Her husband dies. Mr. Tryan dies of consumption, but not before he has increased Janet's self-respect to where she can lead a sober, rich life.

Eliot, George (Mary Anne Evans). Middlemarch, ed. G. S. Haight. Cambridge, Mass.: Riverside Press, 1956. Novel.

Doctors   Dying   Med. Ethics
Med. Instit.   Sexuality   Sexual Roles

For our purposes, there are two interesting aspects to the novel, one marital, the other, medical. Several marriages are compared. Dorothea marries the old scholar Causabon because she respects him and believes he can give her intellectual work; however, Causabon is terrified that she will expose his inadequacies as a scholar and a man. The marriage becomes a little hell to both, with no love and no respect, and only financial means to hold them together. Dorothea's sister, on the contrary, is quite happy; she made a conventional marriage and lives, quite conventionally with her children and husband (in that order). Rosamond and Dr. Lydgate also make hell out of marriage; they marry with love on one side, a kind of conventional respect on the other, and barely adequate means. As a result of Lydgate's difficulties, love and respect are eroded. However, by sacrificing his professional dreams, he is able to keep enough means to hold them together. The Bulstrodes have means and enough love to carry them through the loss of her respect for him. Dorothea and Will have enough love and are willing to sacrifice means, but it is Dorothea's respect for herself (Causabon must never, even after death, have justification for his jealousy) and for Will (his ill-considered relationship with Rosamond Lydgate) that stands in their way. Eventually time resolves the problem, and the two are happily married. Mary and Fred also have love, but respect and means are in doubt. Here Mary shows her wisdom. By admitting her love but lack of respect, she forces Fred to earn it, which he does; and the two are happily married. Dr. Lydgate's great love for his profession and for anatomy, and his feeling that it was the person, not the injury, that is important are set forth in Book 2, Chapter 15. However, in a curious way he is lacking in medical ethics. He is not financially independent. Chapter 18 shows his growing dependency on wealthy Bulstrode when he votes for Bulstrode's candidate for hospital chaplain, even though he believes another candidate to be better. Book 7, Chapters 67-71 show Lydgate's downfall. Because he cannot control his wife, he is deeply in debt and needs Bulstrode's help; therefore he promptly accepts when Bulstrode loans him a badly needed thousand pounds. However, this loan takes place right before Bulstrode murders a blackmailer by omitting to tell the nurse Lydgate's order not to give the opium-dosed patient any alcohol. Lydgate is caught up in Bulstrode's scandal and is forced away from the fever hospital, his life's pleasure. Book 5, Chapter 44 describes the town's misunderstandings about this hospital when it is first proposed and the hostility of other practitioners to this advancement of a rival.

Eliot, George (Mary Anne Evans). The Mill on the Floss. New York: Harper & Row, 1965. Novel.

Children   Disease & Health   The Family
Handicaps   Sexuality   Sexual Roles
Suffering

Books I and II of the novel give a marvelous account of the Tulliver family, parents, children, uncles, aunts, and cousins. We see Tom and Maggie being raised. Five people influence Maggie: Tom, her cold but concerned brother; her critical mother and loving father; her beautiful, perfect cousin Lucy Deane whom she loves even while Lucy becomes the standard by which Maggie is tried and found wanting; and Philip Wakem, the deformed (spine) son of Mr. Tulliver's arch-enemy. Philip loves her and offers her books and intellectual satisfaction, from which Tom sternly prohibits her in horror at her depraved association with a cripple, a young man who loves her, and the son of her father's foe. Tom is incapable of seeing what else he is keeping her from. Wakem (and Tulliver's folly) ruins their father, who is crippled by a stroke. Philip intercedes for the family. Books III-V describe Tom's efforts to pay off all his father's debts and to buy back their mill. With work and shrewdness he succeeds, but his father celebrates this "victory" by physically assaulting Wakem and dying of another stroke. Now, the novel turns to the complex relationships and choices assailing Maggie. Philip asks her to marry him; she accepts his love but rejects his proposal because of Tom's relentless, righteous opposition. Then, visiting her bright cousin Lucy, she falls in love with the man Lucy loves, Stephen Guest, who has an even greater passion for Maggie--who is forced by her conscience to reject him for the tenuous relationship with Philip. Stephen, to force her to marry him, compromises her in the eyes of the town. She still refuses, even though Tom throws her out. Yet she will not marry Philip. Village opinion is about to drive her out, when a flood unites the brother and sister in a battle for preservation of themselves and those they care about--and then in death.

Eliot, George (Mary Anne Evans). Mr. Gilfil's Love-Story. In Scenes of Clerical Life. Available ed. David Lodge. London: Penguin, 1973. Novella.

Death   Disease & Health   Grief
Preg. & Childbirth   Sexuality

A nice little tale of misdirection. The story on the surface is a rather conventional quadrangle: faithful, humble lover (Gilfil), wronged, jealous lower-class maiden (Caterina), wealthy, socially acceptable lady, and attractive, well-born cad (Anthony). But while the action follows the cad's vacillations between the two jealous ladies, the story is also noting the effect of stress on the bodies of those involved. Anthony complains of his ill-health, but the reader is inclined to attribute this to his querulous egotism. Caterina becomes very pale, but she is normally pale. As a result of the high emotional levels, Anthony dies of heart disease and Tina becomes so weak that she dies of a miscarriage after her marriage to Gilfil. A similar sleight of hand occurs in Amos Barton (also in Scenes of Clerical Life) when the clergyman's difficulties explain and yet screen the slow dying of his wife who, worn out by poverty and stress, has a seven-months child and dies. Her death emerges from under his money troubles as the true grief of his life. In both stories, the death ends many difficulties, but grief immediately replaces them.

Emerson, Ralph Waldo. "Experience." In Essays: Second Series. From The Essays of Ralph Waldo Emerson. New York: The Modern Library, 1944, and "Threnody." From The Portable Emerson. New York: Viking, 1967. Essay and Poem ca. 300 lines.

Children   Death   Grief

Both discuss the death of his son. The poem describes the boy's childhood, ennobling him. The father's grief is dissolved by the heart who answers that beauty does not die. "My servant Death, with solving rite,/Pours finite into infinite./Wilt thou freeze love's tidal flow,/Whose streams through nature circling go?" The essay is much colder: "The only thing grief has taught me is to know how shallow it is. That, like all the rest, plays about the surface . . . . In the death of my son, now more than two years ago, I seem to have lost a beautiful estate,--no more. I cannot get it nearer to me . . . . I grieve that grief can teach me nothing, nor carry me one step into real nature."

Emerson, Ralph Waldo. "Old Age." In Society and Solitude. From Complete Works. Boston: Houghton Mifflin, 1922. Vol. VII. Essay.

Age

The essence of age is intellect, but "age, like woman, requires fit surroundings." It does well in coaches, churches, chairs of state, courts of justice and the countryside. It does poorly on Broadway. As we get old, we lose the fear of death and sickness and failure, while gaining the self-expression untried youths lack. The essay breathes the same serenity of Emerson's poem, "Terminus" (available in The Portable Emerson. New York: Viking, 1967): "As the bird trims her to the gale,/I trim myself to the storm of time,/I man the rudder, reef the sail,/Obey the voice at eve obeyed at prime."

Emerson, Ralph Waldo. "The Over-Soul." In Essays: First Series. From The Essays of Ralph Waldo Emerson. New York: Modern Library, 1944. Essay.

Body/Mind

In the "Over-Soul," Emerson completely denies the importance of the body (the same denial is found in his Platonic poem "Give All to Love")--even in sickness: "The least activity of the intellectual powers redeems us in a degree from the conditions of time. In sickness, in languor, give us a strain of poetry or a profound sentence, and we are refreshed."

Emerson, Ralph Waldo. "The Poet," In Essays: Second Series. From The Essays of Ralph Waldo Emerson. New York: Modern Library, 1944. Essay.

Science & Poetry

This definition of the poet as far more than a versifier is useful for one line: "He is the true and only doctor." Emerson bases this line, in part, on the idea that "Genius is the activity which repairs the decays of things, whether wholly or partly of a material kind."

Flaubert, Gustave. Madame Bovary, trans. Francis Steegmuller. New York: Modern Library, 1957. Novel.

Disease & Health   Doctors   Grief
Handicaps   Med. Profession Sexuality
Sexual Roles   Suicide

The story can be seen as the personal and professional destruction of Dr. Bovary, a mediocre man and country doctor, by a discontented wife and a greedy apothecary. Bovary loves Emma, his wife, with a deep, enduring love that never really sees its object. He never notices her neurotic discontent; her almost manic-depressive behavior, her lovers, and her swindles. He never considers how she must feel about him; he notices her at her father's farm and marries her, without a single word being spoken by her that we hear. She finds herself married to a man who does not see her, who cannot help her with the wild possibilities for herself she has derived from novels, and who disgusts her physically. The marriage is thus doomed to trouble, but it is helped on its way by a series of lovers for Emma, a tradesman who lures her into extravagant purchases and extravagant loans, and an apothecary who

wants Bovary out. This apothecary talks Bovary into an operation that is totally beyond his very modest skills. Emma adds her persuasions because she wants him to be something. They persuade a poor clubfoot into a very painful operation for this handicap. Bovary, of course, botches it and after a painful episode, another doctor must amputate the mangled leg. Bovary suffers in his conscience, and Emma finally has nothing but contempt for him. Then, when the family is ruined financially, Emma commits suicide in a hideously painful way with arsenic; her death is prolonged and ugly. Dr. Bovary, even after he learns of her many deceptions, still loves her, but he dies under the strain.

Gaskell, Elizabeth. Cranford. London: Oxford University Press, n.d. Novel.

The Family   Sexual Roles

Cranford is a society of women; it is full of the stereotypes of noble, fearful, repressed spinsters (Matty and her sister suck oranges behind screens because the activity is too close to a baby's sucking). However, the loosely connected series of stories does have a curious foundation for this strong stereotyping. When they are young women, Matty and Deborah lose their brother because, as a mad prank, he dresses up in Deborah's clothes and walks in the front garden, cooing to a bundle of rags. It is not until the story's close that middle-aged Matty, too frightened and ignorant to resume relations with an old suitor, is united with a man: her brother.

Gaskell, Elizabeth. Mary Barton, ed. M. F. Brightfield. New York: W. W. Norton, 1958. Novel.

Body/Mind   Death   Disease & Health
Drugs   The Family   Grief
Handicaps   Poverty & Health

In Mary Barton, one of the best reform novels about working-class life, Mrs. Gaskell tries to portray the horrible life of the working poor without condemning the factory owners. She succeeds in the first. Death-- in childbed, in a factory fire, in childish delirium, in a murderous assault--poses its constant challenge to the survivors, for the poor cannot rally human resources to meet grief. They band together to provide money and food for each other, but the unceasing necessity to work for a living prevents them from providing human companionship to those in mourning. (Grief plays a major role in several of her novels, e.g., the complex grief of the squire in Wives and Daughters.) Life style definitely affects health. Chapter VI depicts the miseries of the Davenport family, starving and dying from "the fever," which was "of a low putrid, typhoid kind; brought on by miserable living, filthy neighbourhood, and great depression of mind and body." It is infectious, but the poor lack room to isolate an invalid. Elsewhere in the novel, Margaret goes blind working at close sewing. But one of the most vicious diseases is depression, caused by grief and helplessness in periods of unemployment. It leads to physical disease, outbursts of murderous rage, and dependence upon opium. This is seen most clearly in John Barton, whose lingering grief for a dead wife and son is aggravated by a long period of closed mills and trouble with his remaining daughter. He joins a protest march to London; when that is treated with contemptuous neglect, he turns to opium to relieve starvation and despair. Finally, he is chosen to assassinate the son of the principal mill owner and does so. Unfortunately, at this point, the plot turns to melodrama, as his daughter's lover is arrested for his crime. However, the book as a whole is a remarkably sensitive and realistic portrayal of life, disease and death in a mill town.

Gilman, Charlotte Perkins Stetson. The Yellow Wallpaper. New York: Feminist Press, 1973. Short Story.

Disease & Health   Evil Doctors   Madness
Sexual Roles   Suffering

Terrifying little story about a wife oh-so-kindly driven into madness by her doctor-husband and doctor-brother. What is so horrifying is that the woman sees the truth but is unable to accept or act on it. The wife is held to be nervous and so is left alone in a country house while the town house is redecorated. Her husband keeps telling her to develop "will" and self-control while thwarting her every wish and placing her in an impossible environment--with the best of intentions! The story is her diary of her descent into madness, made clear by her changing reactions to the yellow wallpaper in the nursery (with barred windows) in which she is forced to sleep. She becomes convinced that there is a woman creeping behind the wallpaper (the child or mindless sexual object her husband wants her to be, a mad self safe from his persecutions?) whom she must free. All of her perceptions are worth quoting: "John is a physician, and perhaps--(I would not say it to a living soul, of course, but this is dead paper and a great relief to my mind)--perhaps that is one reason I do not get well faster. You see, he does not believe I am sick! And what can one do?" "Sick" is defined as anger at abusive and humiliating treatment, "well" as not expressing that anger.

Goethe, Johann Wolfgang Von. Faust. Pt. I. New York: Bobbs-Merrill, 1957. Poetic Drama.

Doctors   Sexuality

Faust and his father are both great doctors, and both crave knowledge and experience while being discontented with things as they are. Both destroy others in their search for knowledge. In the scene "Outside the City Gate," Faust accepts the villagers' plaudits for his cures while telling his companions that he and his father killed as many as they cured, for the purposes of experimentation. This drive will lead Faust to destroy Margaret in his search for experience. The connection between medicine and sex is continued in "Study." Mephistopheles counsels a student how to succeed in all branches of knowledge. For medicine, success depends upon letting things take their own course, seizing the moment, and being sexy enough to please the women. Faust, of course, is by nature averse to letting things take their own course; he is a good experimenter in the full sense of the word and a poor physician.

Goethe, Johann. The Sorrows of Young Werther. New York: New American Library, 1962. Novel.

Madness   Suicide

Highly romantic tale of a young man's obsessive passion for a woman betrothed and then married to another. Nothing works to alter his increasingly depressed state of mind. His sense of loss drives him to the edge of madness, and beyond. Finally he can bear it no longer. He shoots himself, dying several hours later. The tale caught the fancy of young people all over Europe and set off a series of suicides by disappointed lovers. Even though Werther is an adult, the category of "Adolescence" could be added to this entry, depending, of course, on one's view of this sort of romantic love.

Gogol, Nikolai. "The Diary of a Madman." Available in The Diary of a Madman and Other Stories. New York: New American Library, 1960. Short Story.

Madness   Med. Instit.

A representative Gogol "hero," that is, a civil servant who must constantly fight dullness and anomie, keeps a diary in which he records his observations of his office, his private life (such as it is: mostly it's imagined), and certain affairs of the great world. In the first entry, he has already begun to slip from sanity, for he records that he has heard two dogs discussing their letters to each other. In a later entry, he copies out the "letters" themselves, complete with their references to him: "He has a funny name and he's always sitting sharpening quills. The hair on his head is like straw. Papa sends him on errands like a servant. Sophie [the aristocratic woman with whom the civil servant imagines himself in love] can hardly control her laughter when she sees him" (trans. Andrew R. MacAndrew). Thus does the poor fellow handle his honest assessment of himself. But the diary goes on recording his increasing mania, paranoia, and delusions of grandeur. As he does so, the reader comes increasingly to side with him against the people in favored positions. Why indeed is he just a clerk? Ultimately, he decides that he is not, that he has discovered himself to be the King of Spain. He is taken to Spain, that is, an asylum, where he believes all the men with shaved heads to be monks and the warden, the Grand Inquisitor. His last entry is wretched. Dated "da 34 te Mnth. Yr. yraurbef 349," it begins, "No, I have no strength left. I can't stand any more. My God! What are they doing to me! They pour cold water on my head. They don't listen to me, they don't hear me, they don't see me. What have I done to them"--and it ends in comic mania, "And, by the way, have you heard that the Dey of Algiers has a wart right under his nose?"

Gogol, Nikolai. "The Nose." Available in The Diary of a Madman and Other Stories, by Gogol. New York: New American Library, 1960. Short Story.

The Body   Doctors

A hilarious fantasy about a pompous man, Major Kovalev, whose nose--that's right--appears one day in a roll about to be eaten by Kovalev's barber and afterwards goes about Petersburg disguised as a state councilor. This situation, taken with absurdist gravity by Gogol, brings about several comic exchanges--for instance, between Kovalev and his nose, who is praying at the time. At last a policeman does return the nose, and another comic exchange occurs, between Kovalev and the doctor, who is asked to stick the nose back on. Gogol takes him too with an almost mad comic spirit: "The doctor was a fine figure of a man . . . . he ate fresh apples in the morning and kept his mouth in a state of incredible cleanliness, rinsing it for about three-quarters of an hour at a time and then brushing his teeth with five different kinds of toothbrush" (trans. Andrew R. MacAndrew). Furthermore, the doctor only charges people "in order not to offend people by refusing to accept a fee." A likely story! And the same might be said of "The Nose" itself, except that it is an entirely likely fantasy for a man like Kovalev, who is overly conscious of his appearance and superficialities in general. It could be said that he

expects his body, particularly its "selling points," to work for him all the time. Moreover, it is also entirely likely that such a man's nose would be puffed up out of all proportion to its true place. (cf. Philip Roth's "The Breast," which was inspired by this story, and also Richard Selzer's "The Sympathetic Nose" in Rituals of Surgery.)

Hamilton, Patrick. Angel Street (Gas Light). Available in Great Melodramas, ed. Robert Saffron. New York: Collier, 1966. Drama.

Madness   Sexual Roles

An unusual evening in Angel Street. A psychotic husband is systematically driving his wife mad because she has bought him the house he wanted, and he enjoys the activity. He dangles an evening out before her and then retracts it upon "discovering" a picture which "she" has "removed" irrationally. He humiliates her by flirting with the housemaid in front of her and threatens her with incarceration, demanding that she restore a grocery bill which she has "maliciously stolen." He goes out, and she is visited by a detective who informs her that her "husband" is a psychotic killer who murdered an old woman for her rubies in that house and who is still searching for the loot. Further, he was previously married so that she is not really his wife. Her response is to gasp in relief. Her sanity has been doubly assaulted, because, by the dimming of the gas light, she knows he returns to the attic at night; and she could not explain this rationally. She helps the detective discover proof that her husband is the killer. Then, the detective leaves her to get a warrant; the husband returns and torments his wife further, until she is not certain whether or not the detective was real. However, the detective returns and arrests him. The husband is bound; she is alone with him by her request; he begs her to free him; she goes for his razor and finds the gas bill. She has "known" that he was responsible for all the tricks, but the sight whipsaws her into homicidal hysteria, and she is barely prevented by the detective from killing him. The lengthy plot summary is given so that the reader can appreciate the beauty of the curtain line. The dectective says that he has given her a horrible evening. "The most horrible evening of anybody's life, I should imagine." She closes with "The most horrible? Oh, no,--the most wonderful. --Far and away the most wonderful."

Hardy, Thomas. "Afterwards." Available in Selected Poems of Thomas Hardy. London: Macmillan & Co., 1964. Poem: 20 lines.

Death   Grief

One of a group of well-known poems in which the poet grieves for himself by imagining what others might say after his death or even suggesting how they ought to behave (see also Christina Rossetti's "Remember"; Browning's "Epilogue to Asolando"; Tennyson's "Crossing the Bar"; and, a little earlier, Swift's "Verses on the Death of Dr. Swift"). Hardy wants to be remembered as a man who had an eye for delicate details, a heart for innocent creatures, and a mind for mysteries. It is a gentle grief he encourages, though the poetry be powerful: "When the Present has latched its postern behind my tremulous stay,/And the May month flaps its glad green leaves like wings,/Delicate-filmed as new-spun silk, will the neighbours say,/'He was a man who used to notice such things'?"

Hardy, Thomas. Far From the Madding Crowd. New York: Holt, Rinehart and Winston, 1959. Novel.

Death   Grief   Madness
Preg. & Childbirth   Sexuality   Sexual Roles

In the heroine, Bathsheba Everdene, we see a woman who begins as a vain and fickle tease, but grows into a figure of power and resourcefulness when she must take over the management of Weatherbury Farm and her own dramatic love life. This picture of an unconventional sexual role is undercut when at the end Bathsheba must turn for help to her shepherd, Gabriel Oak, who has loved her secretly and aided her all along. Bathsheba is a beautiful woman who excites the passions of two other men. One is Farmer Boldwood, whose serious, repressed nature when combined with passion for Bathsheba leads him to madness and the murder of her other lover, Sergeant Troy. Troy's grief over the death of his mistress Fanny and their illegitimate baby is an important part of the novel. Hardy has also dealt with illegitimate pregnancy and sexuality in Jude the Obscure, q.v. and Tess of the d'Urbervilles.

Hardy, Thomas. "He Never Expected Much." Available in Selected Poems of Thomas Hardy. London: Macmillan & Co., 1964. Poem: 24 lines.

Age   Children

Subtitled "A Consideration on my Eighty-Sixth Birthday," this is an unusual poem as much for its having been successfully written at all as for its theme, which is that because he never expected much from life (as a child the World had told him to expect "just neutral-tinted haps and such"), the poet has never been disappointed. Indeed he has been able to "stem such strain and ache/ As each year might assign.

Hardy, Thomas. "Her Death and After." Available in Selected Poems of Thomas Hardy. London: Macmillan & Co., 1964. Poem: 135 lines.

Children   Dying   Grief
Handicaps   Preg. & Childbirth   Sexuality

Hardy wrote a good many poems about the dying and the dead (including a few voices-from-the-grave sort of thing). This one is representative not so much in its form (for it is rather long) but in its linking of suffering and sexuality and children. The speaker tells the story of being summoned to the deathbed, recently the childbed, of his beloved, who had chosen to marry another. Her husband had been cruel, she reveals, and she wishes the new baby--a lame little girl--had been her lover's, even though scandal would have ensued. Following her death, the lover grieves through the years, and finally suggests to the husband that his daughter is not his, whereupon the little girls turns up, as the lover had hoped, at his door to be taken in. Now he has his beloved's child with him, but his guilt looms large: "for I'd harmed the dead/By what I said/ For the good of the living one."

Hardy, Thomas. Jude the Obscure. New York: Dell, 1959. Novel.

Alcoholism   Body/Mind   Children
Euthanasia   Madness   Poverty & Health
Sexuality   Suffering   Suicide

The most complex and despairing of Hardy's great novels. The principal characters: Jude, who constantly wavers between the attractions of the body and the spirit; and the two women who represent his conflict--Arabella, crude and sensual, and Sue Bridehead, free-thinking and neurotic. The atmosphere is heavy with suffering. Hardy looks, for instance, at Jude's heavy drinking, and the illnesses brought on by his drinking and poverty. The novel contains one of the most shocking episodes in all fiction. Following his own tragic view of mercy, the child, "Father Time," first hangs his two young siblings and then himself, leaving this message for Jude and Sue: "Done because we are too menny."

Hardy, Thomas. "Last Words to a Dumb Friend" and "'Ah, Are You Digging on my Grave?'" Available in Selected Poems of Thomas Hardy. London: Macmillan & Co., 1964. Poems: 55 and 35 lines.

Grief

An unusual subject for a first-rate poet, but a common enough theme in life: Pets and death. Hardy adored cats, and the first poem here is addressed to one of his pets. Description of the cat is combined with contemplative thoughts about his death and the significance it assumes in the poet's thoughts. "Purrer of the spotless hue,/Plumy tail, and wistful gaze"--Hardy remembers, then resolves never to have another pet: "Selfishly escape distress/By contrived forgetfulness,/ Than preserve his prints to make/Every morn and eve an ache." Strange, the poet thinks, that "this speechless thing" should after his passing grow so eloquent, as it were. Though he tries to forget, the poet's last lines imagine his former housemate playing beneath the trees. The second poem is comic, one supposes, and this time the owner has died, and the pet, a dog, survives. The poem consists of a dialogue between the dead woman and an unidentified someone digging on her grave. She thinks it her lover, her relatives, or perhaps her enemy. But no, it is her "little dog," "that one true heart," she thinks. But no again: the dog answers that he was merely burying a bone, forgetting it was her grave.

Hardy, Thomas. The Woodlanders. New York: Harper and Brothers, n.d. Novel.

Doctors   Med. Ethics

Not one of the best Hardy novels, by any means, but valuable for its portrait of a doctor practicing in rural England during the last century. Dr. Edgar Fitzpiers occupies, through family connections and his own attractive qualities, a high position in local society, though some of the uneducated folk think his strange experiments demonic. After marriage to the heroine, whose social status is beneath his, Dr. Fitzpiers' practice declines. Hardy plays upon the idea, increasingly common in the 20th century, that physicians and sexuality are closely related, when his rakish doctor first treats and then has a scandalous affair with the lady of the local manor.

Hawthorne, Nathaniel. "The Birthmark." In Mosses from an Old Manse. From Selected Tales and Sketches. New York: Holt, Rinehart & Winston, 1963. Novel.

The Body   Sexuality

Story of a researcher who takes a dislike to a hand-shaped birthmark on his wife's cheek and, in eradicating it, eradicates her. One of the most interesting interpretations is that of Professor Young, that the birthmark is a sign of menstruation. He doesn't discover the blemish on her cheek until after their marriage, and considers the hand as mortality dragging down the spirit. He keeps her in an artificial environment; when she looks at his day books and discovers he has failed, frustrated by matter, he pushes her away as a curse. He does remove the birthmark, but she dies, pitying him.

Hawthorne, Nathaniel. "Dr. Heidegger's Experiment." In Twice Told Tales. Boston: Houghton Mifflin, 1882. Short Story.

Age   Doctors

An old doctor assembles four old people with rather shady pasts. He gives them an elixir of youth to drink and observes. They grow young and full of folly, reliving all the youthful sins that led to the miseries of their old age. They mock old people. At the end, in their quarreling, they overturn the elixir and are irrevocably returned to old age.

Hawthorne, Nathaniel. "Edward Fane's Rosebud." From Twice Told Tales. Boston: Houghton Mifflin, 1882. Sketch.

Disease & Health Nurses   Sexuality

Horrible little tale of a woman wedded to disease who reaches her lover's bed in a terrible perversion. As a young girl, she is Edward Fane's "rosebud," but she is not allowed to marry him. She is forced into marriage with a sick, old man, whom she nurses. When he dies, she misses the smells and feel of a sickroom and so becomes a nurse. She is really married to disease. Finally, in her old age, she is called to tend the deathbed of Edward Fane, reaching him through disease and death.

Hawthorne, Nathaniel. "The Hollow of the Three Hills." From Twice Told Tales. Available in Selected Tales and Sketches. New York: Holt, Rinehart & Winston, 1963. Sketch.

The Family   Madness   Suffering

An odd, evil little story about a deadly version of reverse gestation and birth. A young woman seeks news about the family she has abandoned, even at the price of death. She accompanies an older woman to the hollow between the three hills, an old decaying spot. She dips the edge of her garment in the pool and lays her head on the old woman's knees, covered by her cloak. She sees her dishonored and suffering parents, her mad husband who repeats the tale of her perfidy to his keepers, and her dead, abandoned child. She sees--and dies.

Hawthorne, Nathaniel. "Lady Eleanore's Mantle." From Twice Told Tales. Available in Selected Tales and Sketches. New York: Holt, Rinehart & Winston, 1963. Short Story.

Death   Madness   Plague
Sexuality

Unlike Poe's "Mask of the Red Death," which portrays plague as eluding the preventive barriers of pleasure and isolation, "Lady Eleanore's Mantle" portrays plague as caused by isolation. Her monomaniacal pride in her unique heredity only serves to link her with the most lowly inhabitant of Boston--by bringing smallpox upon her and the city. She is worshipped by a lunatic who first urges her to join with humanity, then lauds her as the bride of Death, only to be aroused to scorn at the sight of the scarred, ill woman.

Hawthorne, Nathaniel. "My Kinsman, Major Molineux." From The Snow Image. Available in Selected Tales and Sketches. New York: Holt, Rinehart & Winston, 1963. Short Story.

Adolescence   The Family   Sexuality

Although its symbolism is elusive, "My Kinsman, Major Molineux" is one of the greatest stories on adolescence. Robin leaves his family to seek his fortune with his kinsman, Major Molineux. His quest leads him through a nightmare city in which he encounters dreamlike adult figures and experiences a dream vision of his exclusion from his family. His attempts to locate the Major only arouse laughter or hostility--until he is shown the Major tarred and feathered, being driven out of town on a rail. The townspeople then laugh, and he shares their laughter at the suffering Major and himself. Robin discovers his alienation, but draws back from the seduction of "the red petticoat." His morality does preserve him from loss of sexual innocence but not that final loss of innocence when his laughter irretrievably severs him from his family (and kinsman) and joins him to the mob.

Hawthorne, Nathaniel. "Rappaccini's Daughter." From Mosses from an Old Manse. Available in Selected Tales and Sketches. New York: Holt, Rinehart & Winston, 1963. Short Story.

The Body   Disease & Health   Evil Doctors
Med. Ethics   Sexuality

A rather unusual young couple caught in the rivalry between two doctors. Rappaccini has raised his daughter, Beatrice, on poisons so that she is deadly to all living things except the poisonous plants in her father's garden. She is seen and loved by Giovanni, the young friend of Professor Baglioni, a rival of Rappaccini who is horrified by the love affair and Rappaccini's experiment. Giovanni, who has never touched Beatrice, discovers that he is becoming poisonous and wildly blames her for isolating him. Rappaccini answers by saying the two are now strong because deadly. However, Giovanni ignores him and turns to Beatrice, asking her to prove their love and innocence by swallowing Professor Baglioni's potion designed to eradicate the poison. She takes the potion, but dies. The two scientists are condemned for heartless exploitation of ignorant humans for experimental--and emotional--reasons. But the story also condemns Giovanni for his inability to love a woman whose body was poison but whose soul was love. Perhaps too, he resented her strength. The story is rare among Hawthorne stories because it implies that the forbidden sexual figure of Beatrice might have been worth isolation from the world.

Hawthorne, Nathaniel. "Roger Malvin's Burial." In Mosses from an Old Manse. From Selected Tales and Sketches. New York: Holt, Rinehart & Winston, 1963. Short Story.

Dying   The Family   Grief

A tale of expiation. Reuben abandons his father-in-law in the wilderness in order to go for help, promising to return regardless. He is slowed on his journey, so that Roger is long dead by the time he reaches civilization; he lies and says Roger was dead when he left him. He marries Roger's daughter, but is gloomy and fails in business. He heads out into the wilderness with his wife and son. Shooting at a deer, he kills his son on the spot where Roger lies unburied, expiating his own sin. Interpretation? Sins of previous generations visited on later ones? No fertility if father not properly buried? The guilt draws itself to its source; disease seeks its cure?

Hawthorne, Nathaniel. The Scarlet Letter, ed. Larzer Ziff. New York: Bobbs-Merrill, 1963. Novel.

Body/Mind   Children   Evil Doctors
The Family   Nurses   Sexuality
Sexual Roles   Women as Healers

There is much to be said for this book as a gentle precursor of the feminist movement. Although the book does compare shame (Hester) with guilt (Dimmesdale) and has a rather nice comparison of Hester and Chilling-worth as healers, it can also be seen as an analysis of a curious family in which the sexual roles are so con-fused that natural behavior (sexual relations and normal growth of the child, Pearl) is impossible. After she is condemned for adultery with a partner she will not name (the minister Dimmesdale), Hester, under the influence of pride and ostracism from the community, becomes the "perfect" woman--modest, submissive, heal-ing, consoling, and a self-sacrificing mother. But she is not a real woman, for her sexuality is submerged: "Some attribute had departed from her, the permanence of which had been essential to keep her a woman." Further, "the same dark question often rose into her mind, with reference to the whole race of womanhood. Was existence worth accepting, even to the happiest among them? . . . . Then, the very nature of the oppo-site sex . . . is to be essentially modified, before woman can be allowed to assume what seems a fair and suitable position." As a result, Hester becomes closer to our image of a male--dominating and planning for Dimmesdale, who becomes more and more "womanish." Dr. Chillingworth's "treatment" of the man who seduced his wife is more of a rape, than a revenge. Where Hester, in her nursing, offers her breast as a "softer pillow for the head that needed one," the physician Chillingworth lays bare the bosom of his patient. It is significant that Chillingworth learned his art in devil-ish complicity with Indian sorcerers. Where Hester is forced into her work as a healer by her social role--only to find solace in it, Chillingworth forces himself upon Dimmesdale in order to heal his body so that he may torment his soul. It is no wonder that Pearl, the daughter of Dimmesdale and Hester--and Chillingworth--cannot grow as a normal child. Dimmesdale does finally assert himself as a male when he resists Chillingworth's pressure and Hester's directions to escape. The great scene on the scaffold in which Dimmesdale claims Hester as his partner and Pearl as his daughter exorcises Chillingworth from this family and restores the roles. The family is united for the first--and last--time, but it is enough to insure that Pearl will no longer "battle with the world, but be a woman in it."

Hawthorne, Nathaniel. "The Wives of the Dead." From The Snow Image. Available in Selected Tales and Sketches. New York: Holt, Rinehart & Winston, 1963. Short Story.

Grief

A dream story. Two grieving sisters spend the night after learning of their husbands' deaths (one a sailor, one a landsman). First one sister-wife and then the other learns, while the other sleeps, that her husband is really alive. Each refrains from waking the other for fear of increasing her pain. They end in sleep, smiling-ly awaiting the dawn. But the atmosphere is so dream-like, that the story could be the hallucinations and dreams conjured up by the grieving women. The story's title implies that the dawn so joyously expected may be blacker than the night.

Hazlitt, William. "On the Fear of Death." In Table-Talk. From Complete Works, ed. P. P. Howe. London: J. M. Dent, 1930. Vol. 8. Essay.

Age   Dying   Grief

Really an essay listing reasons to die, rather than any real attempt to deal with the fear of death. The essay although beautiful in sound, is not addressed to the emotions. I did not exist in the past. Why should I

exist in the future? In old age "the pleasures of our existence have worn themselves out." We need not fear causing grief in those we leave behind; grief doesn't last long. An active life prepares us for death, teaches us to endure pain, and shows us how precarious our life is. Beautiful nonsense.

Hazlitt, William. "The Sick Chamber." Available in Complete Works, ed. P. P. Howe. London: J. M. Dent, 1930. Vol. 17. Essay.

Death   Disease & Health

Old ideas about sickness replacing joy with repentance--for as long as the sickness lasts, etc., in Hazlitt's beautiful prose. The one exception is an unusual section describing the convalescent as living in the past to escape death, even death successfully evaded: "The machine has received a shock, and it moves on more tremulously than before, and not all at once in the beaten track. Startled at the approach of death, we are willing to get as far from it as we can by making a proxy of our former selves . . . we gather up and make the most of the fragments that memory has stored up for us."

Henley, William Ernest. In Hospital, 2nd ed. Portland, Me.: T. B. Mosher, 1908. 28 Sketches in Verse.

Doctors   Med. Instit.   Med. Students
Nurses   Suicide   Surgery
Women as Healers

These sketches cover Henley's hospitalization for surgery: the wait before surgery, the anesthetic, por-traits of the hospital staff, sick children, a suicide, and the charm of discharge. Everything is coated with slick sentimentality. The best sketch (#11, "Clinical") describes a visit from the doctor and his entourage of students: "Quick, every one of you,/Straight your quilts, and be decent!/Here's the Professor . . . . Surgery along,/Louts, duffers, equisites, students, and prigs . . . Hustles the Class! And they ring themselves . . . . Out of a quiver of silence,/Over the hiss of the spray,/Comes a low cry, and the sound/Of breath quick intaken through teeth/Clenched in resolve. And the Master/Breaks from the crowd, and goes,/Wiping his hands."

Henry, O. (W. S. Porter). "A Fog in Santone." In Rolling Stones. From The Complete Works of O. Henry. Garden City, N. Y.: Doubleday, 1953. Vol. 2. Short Story.

Disease & Health   Suicide

Consumptives gather in a city which claims to have the purest atmosphere of pure ozone, and exchange symptoms and remedies. Among them moves a young man slowly gathering together enough morphine to commit suicide. He is stopped by a bar girl who gets him talking of home, giving him hope, and confiscating his morphine which she takes herself to escape some implied sexual persecution. A bitter story.

Henry, O. (W. S. Porter). "Hygeia at the Solito." In Heart of the West. From The Complete Works of O. Henry. Garden City, N. Y.: Doubleday, 1953. Vol. 1. Short Story.

Disease & Health

A wish-fulfillment for the consumptive O. Henry. A consumptive bum from the city winds up on a ranch. He is treated considerately and becomes a tyrant in his illness. By an error, he is diagnosed as healthy (wrong person examined) and so is sent out to work off his keep as a ranchhand. The fresh air, work, and clean living cure him.

Henry, O. (W. S. Porter). "The Last Leaf." In The Trimmed Lamp. From The Complete Works of O. Henry. Garden City, N. Y.: Doubleday, 1953. Short Story.

Disease & Health   Dying

Two sisters and an old worn out artist. One sister is ill and dying because she has identified with the leaves falling from the vine on the wall opposite her window. But the last leaf does not fall; it was painted at the price of pneumonia and death by the artist. He pays with his life for her recovery--and his greatest master-piece.

Henry, O. (W. S. Porter). "Ransom of Red Chief." In Whirligigs. From The Complete Works of O. Henry. Garden City, N. Y.: Doubleday, 1953. Short Story.

Children

A lovely debunking of Whittier's "Barefoot Boy." Two con men kidnap a young boy for ransom. He turns out to be such a holy terror that the kidnappers must pay a ransom before the boy's relatives will take him back.

Holmes, Oliver Wendell. The Autocrat of the Breakfast-Table, no. 7. The Complete Writings of Oliver Wendell Holmes. Cambridge: The Riverside Press, 1904. Vol. 1. Essay and Poem.

Age   The Body   By Doctors

The witty essay contains "The Professor's Paper," a dialogue in which Old Age forces his acquaintance on a man, in addition to discussions of habits as a means of conserving dwindling energies, of the value of Cicero's "De Senectute," of foolish sexuality, and of ways of

meeting old age. Section VII ends with "The Anatomist's
Hymn" or "The Living Temple," a 56-line poem glorifying
the body and brain, which ends with a prayer that God
will take the dust remaining when the mystic temples
have fallen in age. "The smooth, soft air with pulse-
like waves/Flows murmuring through its hidden caves/Whose
streams of brightening purple rush/Fired with a new and
livelier blush . . . . Hark how the rolling surge of
sound,/Arches and spirals circling round,/Wakes the
hushed spirit through thine ear/With music it is heaven
to hear . . . . When darkness gathers over all,/And the
last tottering pillars fall,/Take the poor dust thy
mercy warms/And mould it into heavenly forms."

Holmes, Oliver Wendell. The Autocrat of the Breakfast-Table, no. 8.
The Complete Writings of Oliver Wendell Holmes, Vol. 1.
Cambridge: The Riverside Press, 1904. Essay.

Alcoholism   By Doctors   Drugs
Madness

The autocrat meanders into a suddenly vivid description
of a man helpless under the domination of the brain-
machine run mad. This leads him onto the drugs used
to reach the brain, which in turn leads him onto alcohol
as one means of achieving intellectual stimulation. He
condemns drinking as a punishment, noting that the
drunkards of his acquaintance were ruined before they
became drunkards. He notes that poets are prone to
abuse drugs because the dreaming faculties, unlike the
rational ones, can be imitated by artificial excitement.
He concludes that a man's physical, mental, or moral
nature must be debilitated in order for vice to take
hold of him.

Holmes, Oliver Wendell. Elsie Venner. The Complete Writings of
Oliver Wendell Holmes, Vol. 5. Cambridge: The Riverside
Press, 1904. Novel.

The Body   By Doctors   Doctors
Madness   Med. Profession   Med. Students
Sexual Roles   Women as Patients

A fascinating jumble of interesting but irreconcilable
elements. The hero is a Boston Brahmin medical student,
who is also an accomplished pugilist (interesting that
the doctor/writer Conan Doyle also has a pugilist medical
student hero). He is forced by poverty to drop out of
medical school to earn a living teaching literature in
a girl's school (Well, Holmes had to get him next to
his heroine somehow!). One of his pupils is Elsie
Venner, a girl of good stock, who has been pre-destined
to madness by a rattlesnake bite suffered by her mother
in the last months of her pregnancy. Holmes describes
her diamond eyes, mysterious birthmark, and snake-like
hypnotic powers ad nauseum. Elsie finally dies as a
result both of hopeless love for her literature teacher
and of her mixed nature--snakes don't live as long as
humans! Although the importance of environment upon
Elsie's character would seem to support Lysenko over
Mendel, Holmes also vigorously defends heredity as
unalterably determining character. Elsie's half-breed
cousin must become a criminal because of his Spanish
blood. A congenital defect in Indians kept them from
choosing civilization and christianity. In Chapter 22
the wise old country doctor argues with the local parson
about judgments. The doctor knows how heredity and the
body affect the mind and so diminish responsibility.
This wise old country doctor is the novel's deus ex
machina who understands Elsie's problem and who saves
the hero from the rather clumsy and unmotivated attacks
by the Spanish cousin. Two useful sections are Chapter
2 with its description of the terrible life of the country
doctor, who must spend all his time on the road, and the
end of the novel, where the established physician advises
a new graduate to practice among the rich. They make
the best patients and, if you get tired of them, you can
send them on a cruise. It is interesting that Holmes'
three psychological novels--Elsie Venner, The Guardian
Angel, and A Mortal Antipathy--the two which deal with
prenatal influences (venom in Elsie Venner, strong
ancestors who literally take over the body of their
descendant in The Guardian Angel) are the two which deal
with mysteriously hysterical women. The unfortunate
heroine of The Guardian Angel unsuccessfully tries to
channel her hysteric, teen-age sexuality onto the
minister, a young bewildered doctor, and the young upper-
class men of Boston before she finally marries the artist
she first met while escaping from a repressive home in
boy's clothing under the influence of an Indian
ancestress. Elsie cannot channel her snake-nature into
accepted sexual outlets, and so dies.

Holmes, Oliver Wendell. A Mortal Antipathy. The Complete Writings
of Oliver Wendell Holmes, Vol 7. Cambridge: The Riverside
Press, 1904. Novel.

By Doctors   Doctors   Madness
Sexual Roles   Women as Healers

A very curious novel about a young man with an antipathy
(seems to be a cross between an allergy and a neurosis)
to women because a young woman caused his nurse to nearly
kill him in an accident. After many years, he is confronted by two young women who want to help him. Miss
Vincent is a genius without common sense, who lacks any
regard for her place as a woman. Euthymia is a physical

education major, strong as a man, morally straight, stupid,
and properly modest. Miss Vincent harasses the hero, but
Euthymia saves him in a nice twist on the usual sexual
roles--she hauls him out of a burning building, saving
his life, counteracting his original neurosis and so
winning him to be her bride-groom. The triangle is
observed by the local all-knowing country doctor, who is
particularly critical of Miss Vincent. Although he
laughs at the errors caused by her energy and ill-trained
intelligence, he never suggests harnessing that energy
and intelligence to anything useful. She takes up the
study of medicine, especially psychology, to discover
why the young man hates women, gets it wrong, and faints
when he's in danger--to the narrator's delight. The
doctor worries about her. "But he felt it his duty to
guard her against any possible results of indiscretion
into which her eagerness, and her theory of the equality,
almost identity, of the sexes might betray her." (Her
indiscretion is writing a personal letter to a man with
whom she has had a lengthy literary correspondence.)
This doctor also does not believe that women would make
good doctors. "I agree . . . that you will often spoil
a good nurse to make a poor doctor. Doctors and side-
saddles don't seem to me to go together . . . . I think
they will find that they had better at least limit themselves to certain specialties, and always have an expert
of the other sex to fall back upon. The trouble is that
they are so impressible and imaginative that they are
at the mercy of all sorts of fancy systems . . . .
Charlatism always hobbles on two crutches, the tattle
of women, and the certificates of clergymen, and I am
afraid that half the women doctors will be too much under
both those influences.

Holmes, Oliver Wendell. "The Young Practitioner." From Works.
Cambridge, Mass.: The Riverside Press, 1904. Vol. IX
(Medical Essays 1842-1882). Essay.

Alcoholism   By Doctors   Doctors
Med. Profession   Science & Poetry

This 1871 Valedictory Address at Bellevue Hospital College
contains a rather interesting and "literary" condemnation
of the physician-poet: "I warn you against all ambitious
aspirations outside of your profession . . . . Do not
dabble in the muddy sewer of politics, nor linger by the
enchanted streams of literature, nor dig in far-off
fields for the hidden waters of alien sciences . . . .
To get business a man must really want it; and do you
suppose that when you are in the middle of a heated
caucus, or half-way through a delicate analysis, or in
the spasm of an unfinished ode, your eyes rolling the
fine frenzy of poetical composition, you want to be
called to a teething infant, or an ancient person groan-
ing under the griefs of a lumbago?" Among the other bits
of advice to the new graduates are a warning against
alcohol ("Intemperance in a physician partakes of the
guilt of homicide, for the muddled brain may easily make
a fatal blunder in a prescription, and the unsteady hand
transfix an artery in an operation. Tippling doctors
have been too common in history of medicine") and advice
to conceal unpleasant information from the patient
("Your patient has no more right to all the truth you
know than he has to all the medicine in your saddlebags
. . . . He should get only just so much as is good for
him").

Hopkins, Gerard Manley. "The Caged Skylark." Available in A
Hopkins Reader, ed. John Pick. Garden City, New York:
Doubleday, 1966. Sonnet.

Body/Mind

At first the body is compared to an imprisoning cage:
"As a dare-gale skylark scanted in a dull cage/Man's
mounting spirit in his bone-house, mean house, dwells--."
But the poem closes with flesh influencing, but not
imprisoning, the spirit. "Man's spirit will be flesh-
bound when found at best,/But uncumbered: meadow-down
is not distressed/For a rainbow footing it nor he for
his bónes rísen."

Hopkins, Gerard Manley. ("Carrion Comfort"). Available in A
Hopkins Reader, ed. John Pick. Garden City, New York:
Doubleday, 1966. Sonnet.

Suffering   Suicide

Although in great suffering, the speaker will not
despair--he has always a choice to make: he can always
decide not to commit suicide. "Not, I'll not, carrion
comfort, Despair, not feast on thee;/Nor untwist--slack
they may be--these last strands of man/In me ór, most
weary, cry I can no more. I can;/Can something, hope,
wish day come, not choose not to be."

Hopkins, Gerard Manley. "Felix Randal." Available in A Hopkins
Reader, ed. John Pick. Garden City, New York: Doubleday,
1966. Sonnet.

The Body   Disease & Health

Sickness as death and salvation. Felix Randall, the
farrier, dies after a long illness, "his mould of man,
big-boned and hardy-handsome/Pining, pining, till time
when reason rambled in it and some/Fatal four disorders,
fleshed there, all contended." "Sickness broke him,"
and broke open his heart to God. The poet remembers
how his tongue quenched Felix's tears, while those tears

touched the poet's heart. Yet the poet's thoughts move away from the happy conversion and the warm relationship between the sick man and comforter: he ends with regret for that strong man so broken: "How far from then fore-thought of, all thy more boisterous years,/When thou at the random grim forge, powerful amidst peers,/Didst fettle for the great grey drayhorse his bright and battering sandal!"

Hopkins, Gerard Manley. "Spring and Fall: to a young child." Available in A Hopkins Reader, ed. John Pick. Garden City, New York: Doubleday, 1966. Sonnet.

Children   Grief

Not grief for the loss of another, but for the self's loss, unseen by the conscious mind, but felt by the spirit. Margaret is grieving for the fall of leaves at Goldengrove: "Márgarét, are you gríeving/Over Golden-grove unleaving?" As she grows older, she will grow less sensitive but will know why she cries. "Sórrows springs áre the same./Nor mouth had, no nor mind, expressed/What heart heard of, ghost guessed:/It ís the blight man was born for,/It is Margaret you mourn for."

Hopkins, Gerard Manley. "The Wreck of the Deutschland: To the happy memory of five Franciscan Nuns exiles by the Falk Laws drowned between midnight and morning of Dec. 7th, 1875." Available in A Hopkins Reader, ed. John Pick. Garden City, New York: Doubleday, 1966. Poem: 280 lines.

Death   Suffering

Even more complex than other Hopkins poems, "The Wreck of the Deutschland" deals first with the death of the individual microcosm, stanzas 1-10, and then with the death of the entire human macrocosm, stanzas 11-35, using, as A. G. Sulloway argues in Gerard Manley Hopkins and the Victorian Temper, the Apocalypse as an image of the larger death of the future or the human race. The first section moves rather quickly from the paradox that God the creator almost destroys before death by the knowledge of death ("Thou hast bound bones and veins in me, fastened me flesh,/And after it almost unmade, what with dread") to the solution in adoration of Christ ("Make mercy in all of us, out of us all/Mastery, but be adored, but be adored King"). The second section seems to focus again on one individual, the strong nun who, during the shipwreck, called out "O Christ, Christ, come quickly." He considers her motives--a sexual desire for death? a desire for the martyr's crown? No, she was calling for the physician Christ to heal the situation ("He was to cure the extremity where he had cast her"). And Death does seem a good solution--for her, who was ready; but what of the others unprepared for Death ("Well, she has thee for the pain, for the/Patience; but pity of the rest of them!")? The answer seems to be a prayer that those who can meet death, those whom Christ has reached, should turn to help others ("Dame, at our door/Drowned, and among our shoals,/Remember us in the roads, the heaven-haven of the Reward:/Our King back, oh, upon English souls!"). All those who can see the glorious God behind Death should help nurse others ("past all/Grasp God, throned behind/Death with a sovereignty that heeds but hides, bodes but abides").

Howells, William Dean. Dr. Breen's Practice. Boston: James R. Osgood, 1881. Novel.

Doctors   Med. Ethics   Med. Profession
Sexual Roles   Women as Healers   Women as Patients

Unsatisfactory but interesting novel about a young woman's attempt to establish herself as a physician. The novel's characters are too black and white, and the focus is too diffuse; but it does present the battle between homeo-paths and allopaths in the American medical profession in the second half of the nineteenth century and the struggles of a young doctor with her conscience and her nearest colleague, a male allopath (AMA type) who is contemptuous of her as a woman and a homeopath (a believer in small amounts of botanical drugs to help the body as opposed to believers in "chemical" drugs, such as mercury, to attack the disease). There is mention of an allopathic doctor's expulsion from the state medical society for consulting with a homeopathic doctor--his wife. The young doctor does doubt her emotional strength, contends with women who won't be treated by a woman doctor (the novel assumes that the majority of any doctor's patients are women), and struggles with her own conscience when a patient does not respond to her treatment. She finally calls in her allopathic, male rival who relegates her to the level of nurse, refusing to inform her about his treatment or the patient's progress. However, the allo-path does find her a good woman. "Under my direction you have shown yourself faithful, docile, patient, intelli-gent beyond anything I have seen." Although he refuses to accept her as a professional colleague, he desires her as a marriage partner. She has enough sense to reject his version of the sexual roles, seeing that he is not the model male, but a tyrant. He cannot understand her. She marries a weak but sensitive factory owner who insists, for her sake, that she resume practice among working-class children.

Howells, William Dean. A Hazard of New Fortunes. New York: Bantam, 1960. Novel.

The Family   Grief   Suffering

One of the best American novels, A Hazard of New Fortunes follows "new" New Yorkers (of the 1890's) as they become involved with each other. Personal barriers are destroyed by suffering and moral choice. The Dryfoos family, although appearing relatively late in the novel, is its center. Dryfoos has made his millions in natural gas in Indiana and has drifted almost helplessly to New York to push his daughters into society and his son into business. The exertions of his daughters at a musicale are some of the funniest in literature. However, this social gathering has its black counterpart in a business dinner at which Dryfoos, the host, is offended by the radical harangue of the one-armed civil war veteran, Lindau. He demands that Lindau be fired from the periodi-cal backed by Dryfoos' money. One editor refuses on moral grounds, uncovering ethical and emotional bonds with several friends. He faces losing his job, but is saved by Lindau's refusal to take any more "tainted" money from Dryfoos. Barriers are further destroyed by the death of Lindau and Dryfoos' son in the streetcar strike riots. Grief pulls down the money walls about the Dryfoos' family, particularly as the father and his son's friend try to expiate their guilt.

Howells, William Dean. An Imperative Duty. Available in The Shadow of a Dream and An Imperative Duty, ed. E. H. Cady. New Haven: College & University Press, 1962. Novella.

Body/Mind   Doctors   Med. Ethics
Suicide

A young doctor tries to help a middle-aged acquaintance living with her niece in late-nineteenth-century New England. He discovers that her physical problems are brought on by her niece's engagement: the niece is 1/16 black; she does not know this; should the aunt tell her? Both women believe that race controls one's body and one's behavior. The doctor believes the aunt is suffering from an over-developed Puritan con-science and advises her, if she must tell, to speak to her niece before speaking to her niece's fiancé. The niece is told and goes into shock, perceiving that her social status has changed. She turns on her aunt who, to escape her anger, takes all of her sleeping pills and dies. The niece never comes to grips with her heredity but does finally forgive her aunt and marries her doctor, to live fairly happily ever after--abroad.

Howells, William Dean. A Modern Instance and The Rise of Silas Lapham. Available in Selected Writings of William Dean Howells, ed. H. S. Commager. New York: Random House, 1950. Novels.

The Family   Sexuality

Howells was very good at realistic examination of inter-personal relationships. He gave particular attention to sexuality and morality, the two forces which he por-trays as most influential on people. In A Modern Instance, a family disintegrates because of Marcia's too great passion and Bartley's moral weakness. Marcia's sole motives for any action are desire and jealousy; her parents, daughter, and reality must somehow bend to her passion. Bartley becomes hideous in his disintegration because he swells in physical bulk as his fortunes decline--food, alcohol and a blank incomprehension of how much he injures others distend Bartley into an over-weight, drunken, charming leech. Talent and great feeling are slowly shredded away as the husband and wife wear against each other. In The Rise of Silas Lapham, a family survives sexual and moral crises because the Laphams try to do the right thing and try not to hurt each other. Irene falls passionately in love with Corey, believing with her family that Corey is courting her; however, the eligible Boston Brahmin is really in love with her sister Penelope. Irene is a beautiful, com-petent, non-intellectual housekeeper; Penelope a plain but piquant intellectual who shares Corey's interests, even to returning his love when he finally, to her horror, asks her to marry him. The family is greatly shaken by Corey's proposal: Irene suffers because she still desires him, Penelope feels confusedly guilty, their mother suffers because she encouraged Irene in her passionate delusion. All reactions are tempered by little family touches, e.g., Penelope is resentful that her mother never considered her as a sexual object, as an object of Corey's attention. Silas Lapham is further troubled by his impending bankruptcy. But the strong sexual and moral bond between the parents keeps them together, despite a jealous rage by Mrs. Lapham; and Irene and Penelope both labor to control themselves and their passions so as to ease things for each other. Howells is one of those rare writers who can favorably portray morality combined with sexuality without being didactic, superficial, or unrealistic.

Howells, William Dean. The Shadow of a Dream. Available in The Shadow of a Dream and An Imperative Duty, ed. E. H. Cady. New Haven: College & University Press, 1962. Novella.

Body/Mind   Doctors   Dying
Madness   Med. Ethics

As in An Imperative Duty, a doctor finds that "non-medical" matters become mixed with medicine. The story is con-cerned with five people: a dying man, his wife, his best friend, a concerned doctor, and an observer-narrator. The neurotic, dying man is tormented by a dream in which his wife has an affair with his best friend. The doctor advises him to disregard the dream, or he may go mad; but he persists in believing in the dream's supernatural origin. The doctor counters with common sense: "As long

as we have on this muddy vesture of decay, the less
medicine meddles and makes with our immortal part the
better . . . . I don't consider the brain immortal.
And I think I've seen the mind in decay." He ascribes
the dream to pain, the body affecting the mind. But
the man dies rejecting his uncomprehending wife. Then,
the critical choice arrives. The widow becomes engaged
to the best friend and goes to the doctor about the
dream. What was it? The doctor, not knowing about the
engagement, bluntly tells her the truth--sending her
into an orgy of guilt and self-recrimination. The
doctor, alarmed, tries to make her see the true causes
of the dream, but fails; and the engagement is broken.
In general, characters agree that the doctor should
have told her, but that he should have taken more care
in the telling.

Hugo, Victor. The Hunchback of Notre Dame. New York: The Modern
    Library, 1941. Novel.

The Body   Body/Mind   Handicaps
Madness   Sexuality

    The tragedies caused by emphasis upon the body. Claude
Frollo is entrapped by Esmeralda's beauty, Esmeralda by
Phoebus', and Quasimodo by his own ugliness. Book I,
Chapter 5; Book IV, Chapters 1 and 3 describe the hunch-
backed Quasimodo; the pregnant women's fear he'll
deform the fetus, his investment as comic Pope, his
revengeful mischievousness. There is an ironic treatment of the superstitious belief his appearance portends
disaster--it is his deafness and the beauty of others
that cause the final disaster. Deafness sets a barrier
between Quasimodo and the world; it effectively makes
him mute too. His spirit pines in a mishapen form; his
brain twists things and creates yet more distance between
himself and the world. Yet his physical isolation in
his body and in the towers of Notre Dame is less severe
than the isolation created by the archdeacon's repressed
sexuality which finally brings him to madness.

Hugo, Victor. Les Miserables, trans. C. E. Wibour. New York: The
    Modern Library, n.d. Novel.

Age   Children   Sexuality
Suffering

    There are several striking parts of this long novel.
First, the large number of powerful old men and dependent
old women. There is the old bishop Bienvenu served by
his sister and maidservant upon whom he imposes poverty,
who is able to convert the hardened convict-thief Jean
Valjean. This Jean Valjean, who after serving in the
galleys, is nevertheless incredibly strong and at fifty
begins a new life, revolutionizes a town and industry,
is sent back to the galleys, escapes, starts another
new life, battles at the barricades during a revolt in
Paris, and is still able to drag the unconscious Marius
through the Paris sewers. Marius is the grandson of
the aged M. Gillenormand who dominates his old sister
and endeavors to dominate Marius. There is the aged
M. Mabeuf and his sister who are destroyed by the revolution. The world of powerful old men has its bleak
counterpart in the world of battered children. Colette
is abused by her foster parents. The Thenardier children
are set loose in the underground world of abandoned
children in Paris. They are "adopted" by a brother-
gamin, Gavroche who protects them in an incredible night
in an abandoned model elephant. The novel's great love
affair is in keeping with its emphasis upon old men and
children (the affair leading to the birth of the illegitimate Colette is a minor part of the novel); Marius and
Colette hardly touch and look only at each others' souls.
Marriage does not affect this love. The most astonishing
part of the novel is the comparison between the rigorous
penitential life of the nuns in the convent and the
miserable, degraded life of the convicts in the galleys.
Context determines the meaning of suffering.

Huxley, Thomas Henry. "On Science and Art in Relation to Education."
    Available in The Victorian Age, eds. John Wilson Bowyer and
    John Lee Brooks. New York: Appleton-Century-Crofts, 1954.
    Essay.

By Doctors   Science & Poetry

    Famous as a biologist, defender of Darwinism, and stylist,
Huxley began his career as a doctor. His most famous
essays include several on education, one of which,
"Science and Culture" was answered by Matthew Arnold in
"Literature and Science," thereby establishing the well-
known Huxley-Arnold "debate" on the value of literature
versus science. Huxley took up the subject again in this
essay. He reiterates the special place of the physical
sciences in education, making wide claims for them when
they are properly taught, but he also takes up Arnold's
point about literature as the central subject of a good
humanistic education. Huxley maintains that he is opposed
only to bad literary education, that which is exclusively
grammar-oriented, e.g., calling that sort a pseudo-
scientific education. But if literary education leads
you to the principles of art, "if you look upon the
literature of a people as a chapter in the development
of the humand mind," then "it affords a splendid and
noble education." Huxley further concludes that he would
"devote a very large portion of the time of every English
child to the careful study of the models of English
writing of such varied and wonderful kind as we possess,
and, what is still more important and still more neglected,
the habit of using that language with precision, with
force, and with art."

Ibsen, Henrik. A Doll's House. Available in A Doll's House and
    Other Plays, trans. Peter Watts. Baltimore, Maryland:
    Penguin, 1965. Drama.

Doctors   Dying   The Family
Sexual Roles   V.D.

    The classic version of the woman's liberation from the
role of child-wife, or doll. There are still stereotypes. Torvald, the husband, coldly holds to legal
institutions. Nora disobeys the law for personal
reasons. She forges her father's signature to save her
sick husband's life so that her dying father will be
spared knowing how ill his son-in-law was. The husband
sees only the legal implications--and so gives the
finishing blow to the marriage which is weakened by
Nora's resentment of being made into a doll doing tricks
for her husband. Dr. Rank describes Krogstad, the blackmailer, as a man with a moral disease. Yet Krogstad is
capable of repentance and reform under the influence of
Mrs. Linde, who exemplifies the partially liberated
woman. She takes a job--to support her family. Dr. Rank
is himself dying of physical disease--his father's
V.D. Physical retribution is inescapable; the moral is
not. His friend Torvald holds to the stereotype of a
male afraid of emotion; he cannot stand to watch the
dying doctor. The play's ending, in which Nora leaves
her husband and he accepts this desertion, does not
ring true--but it feels good.

Ibsen, Henrik. An Enemy of the People. Available in Eleven Plays
    of Henrik Ibsen. New York: Modern Library, n.d. Drama.

Disease & Health   Doctors   The Family
Med. Ethics   Med. Instit.

    To whom does a doctor's duty lie: to patients vaguely
in his charge? his family? the town? his profession?
Dr. Thomas Stockmann is the Medical Officer of the
Municipal Baths (a health spa) which have brought new
prosperity to the town and the doctor's family. Then
he discovers that the Baths are pesthouses because of
contamination from the town's industries. To prevent
contamination, pipes must be moved higher--at great
expense. At first he is inclined to boast of his
discovery for he does not look ahead to its economic
consequences. Then, the authorities and press hound
him as a troublemaker. His brother dismisses him from
his post as an enemy to the community. At a town
meeting, instead of persuading, he attacks the moral
corruption which would condone poisoning--with the
predictable result that he and his immediate family are
ostracized. He remains, determined to fight it through.
He is a doctor who abandons the professional role for
that of moral critic. He doesn't want to cure the
town, to return it from sickness to health; he wants
to purge it to transform it from the actual to the
ideal. He is right, but with the wrong goal.

Ibsen, Henrik. Ghosts. Available in Eleven Plays of Henrik Ibsen.
    New York: Modern Library, n.d. Drama.

Disease & Health   Euthanasia   The Family
Madness   Sexuality   V.D.

    Mrs. Alving attempts to conceal her husband's profligacy
from the world and from her son, Oswald. She sends
away her son at the age of seven so that he will not be
corrupted by his father, carries on her husband's business, and finds a husband for the housemaid he made
pregnant. After his death, she builds an orphanage
with his money so that her son will not inherit his
father's money and writes glowing letters about her
virtuous husband to her son. Now, her husband dead,
she awaits the return of her young adult son. But
ghosts come back. Her son makes passes at the housemaid
Regina, his illegitimate half-sister, and attacks his
mother for abandoning him. Furthermore, the son has
V.D. The doctor attributes it to hereditary disease
until he hears the false, glowing letters. Now the son
believes some of his own secret sins brought on the
disease. The orphanage is burnt down by the man bribed
to marry Regina's mother. This man is as bad as Mr.
Alving, and Regina is corrupted. In this deteriorating
household, the mother blames herself for her husband's
excesses while the son broods, fearing madness from
V.D. Regina leaves when she learns that Oswald is both
her half-brother and ill. Since Oswald now offers no
chance for social advancement, she goes off to seduce
Mrs. Alving's old lover. Oswald, knowing that he is
on the verge of permanent insanity, begs his mother to
give him morphine when he finally goes mad so that he
will not live out the rest of his life, insane. She
refuses to consider the issue, only to be confronted
by an insane Oswald. The curtain falls on her, helpless in her indecision.

Ibsen, Henrik. Hedda Gabler. Available in Hedda Gabler and Other
    Plays, trans. Una Ellis-Fermor. Baltimore, Md.: Penguin,
    1967. Drama.

The Family   Preg. & Childbirth Sexuality
Sexual Roles   Suicide

    The classic of the frustrated intelligent woman turned
into a destructive force. Hedda marries a dry young
mediocre scholar, cosseted by his aunts. Bored, Hedda
resists two efforts to push her into an acceptable role:
the aunt seeks to mold her into woman as mother; her
lover seeks to mold her into the submissive sexual role.

Her husband does not really see her at all. She fights
back against these attempts to define her in purely
sexual terms by becoming a destructive fury, causing the
death of a former lover, and eventually destroying herself in that expiatory suicide which replaced the
conventional nineteenth-century betrothal scene as a
final scene in Ibsen's plays.

Ibsen, Henrik. Little Eyolf. Available in The Master Builder and
Other Plays, trans. Una Ellis-Fermor. Baltimore, Md.: Penguin, 1958. Drama.

Children   The Family   Grief
Handicaps   Sexuality

Complex family relationships among a sister-in-law,
husband, wife and crippled son. All of the family's
weight lies on the son. Crippled in some manner related
to the husband's close love for his supposed sister and
named for the husband's pet name for the sister, Eyolf
comes to represent the burden of the incestuous relationship. The husband decides to devote his life to making
Eyolf a noble achiever despite his handicap; the jealous
wife objects--this will be a further barrier between the
two. She resents being reduced from a lover to being
Eyolf's mother. During their quarrel, Eyolf is mysteriously drawn off the dock to a mysterious death by
drowning. The couple begin to tear each other to shreds
in their grief. The situation is complicated by the
discovery that the sister is not really his sister and
so available for the husband to return to the idyllic
past with her. She is wise enough to escape this,
leaving the husband and wife to found a true marriage
on altruism!

Ibsen, Henrik. The Master Builder. Available in The Master
Builder and Other Plays, ed. Una Ellis-Fermor. Baltimore,
Md.: Penguin, 1958. Drama.

Age   The Family   Sexuality
Sexual Roles

A confused but interesting play, thick with symbols,
about an aging architect, convinced of his mediocrity
and fearing the younger generation. Yet this man once
raced to the top of a church tower he built and defied
God. However, the incident which gives him a career
building family houses, the burning of his wife's
family home, destroys his own chance for a family--and
destroys her career. His wife is peculiarly fitted
for shaping the lives of young children. The loss of
their family deprives her of this career. The master
builder uses the strength of his personality to dominate two young people in his office--a young apprentice
he fears as a rival and the apprentice's fiancée who
loves him. Then, a young girl who sees only the male,
great builder bursts into his life. They establish a
complex relationship; she inspires him to fill the gap
between his personal life and his professional life:
he frees the two young people and overcomes his personal
fear of heights to fill his professional role of climbing to the top of the towers. The builder climbs and
once more defies God; she is ecstatic with admiration--
the crowd sees the falling, and dead, builder.

Irving, Washington. "Rip Van Winkle." Available in The Legend
of Sleepy Hollow and Other Stories. New York: Airmont,
1964. Short Story.

Age

An archetype of age. Times change but types of people
remain the same. Rip's son takes his place, but Rip
himself is outdated. By his isolation, he is like an
old person set aside from real life and so an object of
mockery.

James, Henry. The Bostonians, ed. Alfred Habegger. New York:
Bobbs-Merrill, 1975. Novel.

Homosexuality   Sexuality   Sexual Roles
Women as Healers

Underneath the rather formal teas and meetings, a seething
tension, a true battle of the sexes in a curious triangle
of Olive Chancellor, Verena Tarrant, and Basil Ransom.
Ridicule of women's rights, particularly in the person
of Dr. Prance who doesn't talk about rights; she just
does as she pleases in a restrained and unfeminine way.
Verena Tarrant, under the influence of a stronger will,
can give inspiring lectures. Olive Chancellor replaces
Verena's father as that will. Then Basil Ransom struggles
for possession of Verena; his most effective attack falls
on Verena herself by convincing her that she has no
talent and should resign herself to being charming rather
than inspirational. James seems to imply that sexuality
(not reason or love) will win over a rather hysterical
(and presumably Platonic) homosexuality. But there is
no implication that the victory of heterosexuality is in
any way a good thing for the people involved. Further,
the object of all the furor, Verena, is so passive, so
submissive, and so dependent first upon her father, then
upon Olive, and finally upon Basil, that the battle
really seems to be between Olive and Basil for some completion of themselves, some acquisition of domination,
rather than for love or sexual desire.

James, Henry. Daisy Miller: A Study. From The Turn of the Screw
and Other Short Novels. New York: Signet, 1962. Novella.

Children   Disease & Health   Sexuality

At the hotel at Vevy, Winterbourne meets the fascinating
and free Daisy through her very free and forthright (and
very realistically depicted) younger brother. There, her
disregard of social conventions seems acceptable. He
meets her again in Rome in adult, European society. There
she poses a paradox: she behaves like a respectable and
a disreputable girl at once. Europeans do not understand
her American upbringing and innocence. However, she
finally oversteps the line by going out to the Coliseum
at night with a young Italian, who hopes to trap her
into marriage. He does not succeed, but she catches
Roman Fever and dies. Winterbourne later realizes that
she was the right girl, but "I have lived too long in
foreign parts."

James, Henry. "Lady Barberina." Available in Lady Barberina and
Other Tales, ed. Herbert Ruhm. New York: Grosset and Dunlap, 1961. Short Story.

Doctors   Med. Profession

A physician takes the wrong way to unite medicine with
the liberal arts. The hero is a wealthy American
doctor very involved with research. America and his
profession seem intertwined, as each reinforces his
concern with other people. However, the hero falls in
love with a British aristocrat, in part because he
wants to combine medicine and the arts--here represented
by grace and polished conversation. He has the vision
of moral and artistic perfection attained only by the
best of James' characters. But he has chosen the wrong
wife. The British consider the medical profession to
be lower class, and Lady Barberina is incapable of
appreciating or understanding the beauty she represents.
However, she is strong-willed, and in the end the hero
abandons both his research and America as a result of
her maneuvers. He fails, but has the right dream.

James, Henry. The Middle Years. Available in Novels and Tales.
New York: Charles Scribners, 1909. Vol. 16. Novella.

Age   Doctors   Dying
Science & Poetry

The middle-aged, ailing novelist Dencombe has finally
written a novel he feels is good and so believes he
has finally come to grips with his art, when he is
dying. He meets young Doctor Hugh, who is in the
entourage of a rich, demanding Countess. The young
doctor becomes caught. He wants to stay to help the
older, dying author, whose works he admires. He "had
all the new learning in science and all the old reverence in faith; wouldn't he therefore put his knowledge
at the disposal of his sympathy, his craft at the
disposal of love?" Despite Dencombe's efforts to send
him away, Hugh remains to nurse the author and so loses
his inheritance from the Countess. Dencombe is left
with the fear that Hugh will suffer a second loss--
that the art and vision Dencombe represents to Hugh is
once again beyond the author's grasp.

James, Henry. The Portrait of a Lady. New York: Modern Library,
1951. Novel.

Adolescence   Dying   The Family
Sexual Roles

Isabel starts out as a brilliant young woman determined
to make something out of herself. She refuses the
desirable marriage with Lord Warburton and, with the
invisible aid of her cousin, Ralph Touchett, is given
a fortune with which to start life. Ralph loves her,
but is dying and not able to attract her enough for
marriage. It is left to Madame Merle to entrap Isabel
into marriage with Gilbert Osmond, Madame Merle's lover
by whom she had the daughter, Pansy, who now is presented
as Osmond's legitimate daughter by an earlier wife.
Isabel moves from the perfection of Gardencourt, Ralph's
English country estate, to the corruption of Italy.
Isabel marries Gilbert, believing that her money will
supplement his perfection. But what she finds is that
her efforts to perfect herself are narrowed to defining
her role as wife. The novel is full of a variety of
women's roles: Mrs. Touchett's complete physical and
emotional independence from her family; Harriet Stackpole's personal independence (she marries but keeps her
career); and Madame Merle's physical but not emotional
independence from her lover and daughter. Isabel
struggles to avoid submersion in her husband's personality.
The battle focuses on the future of Pansy, the convent-
educated daughter of Gilbert, who, despite her great
adolescent love for a young man, gives him--and herself--
to be swallowed up by her father's will. She has no
independence of any kind. Isabel fights for her, and
loses. But in the battle she discovers the truth about
her husband's "family" and recovers her own independence.
Against his orders, she goes to England to watch by
Ralph's deathbed. Ralph laments the ill-effects of the
fortune he obtained for her, but the reader is less certain. She has perfected herself--she has polish and
control in place of open-hearted enthusiasm, but she has
come to understand the value of independence and of
morality in maintaining that independence. She escapes
the sexual persuasion of Caspar Goodwood and returns to
her duty or her life or her self in Italy.

James, Henry. _The Turn of the Screw_. In _The Turn of the Screw and Other Short Novels_. New York: Signet, 1962. Novella.

Children   Death   Madness
Sexuality

The question seems simple: were there really two ghosts depraving the children, who are rescued at the cost of Giles' life or are the ghosts figments of the governess' diseased mind to justify her own neurotic, possessive attachment to Giles. James gives us all the facts. Surely it should be possible to diagnose madness or sanity. But every decision is only one more turn of the screw, turning from one position to the other.

James, Henry. _Washington Square_. New York: Modern Library, 1950. Novel.

Children   Doctors

The first chapter describes Dr. Sloper's method of achieving professional success and his personal deprivation on the death of his son and wife. His guilt at their deaths leads him to submerge the personal in the professional. Although the rest of the book describes his relationship to his daughter, he is henceforth referred to only as "the Doctor." Whenever anyone criticizes his handling of his daughter, he falls back on his credentials as a distinguished physician. His being a doctor gives him insights but no ethics. He is not good. There is a complex relationship between father and daughter. She adores him, but he, frustrated by her slow awkwardness in his desire to recapture his wife, stifles her "Electra" feelings but does not help her to any better goal. He finally drives her into the arms of the undesirable Mr. Townsend. Yet he does have some feeling for her--he enjoys being cruel to his daughter until she thwarts him.

James, Henry. _What Maisie Knew_. New York: Charles Scribner's Sons, 1922 (_Novels and Tales_, Vol. XI). Novel.

Children   The Family   Sexuality

Marvelous tale of a child's growth in understanding and sexuality while being shunted about among the most complex set of parents and step-parents, who come vaguely to represent sophistication, beauty, financial security, kindness, and morality. At the beginning, Maisie is a weapon used by her divorced parents, each trying to set her against the other. Then, she becomes involved with her father and a stepmother, Mrs. Beale, followed by a stay with her mother and a stepfather, Sir Claude. Then all four of her "parents" begin to stray, and the dance ends the first half with Maisie in the company of Mrs. Beale and Sir Claude. In the entr'acte, Maisie is renounced by each of her natural parents, both assuring her that the opposite parent wishes her dead. Throughout the novel we see these extraordinary changes of partners through Maisie's eyes. She lives in a world of innuendo, trying to go straight to a goal among people whose affairs cannot be said straight out. She finally makes a tentative step to join the dance. She is in France with Sir Claude, with whom she has a loving relationship, and her "governess," Mrs. Wix, in love with Sir Claude, now wavering in his relationship with Mrs. Beale, who comes to stay with Maisie knowing that Sir Claude won't abandon Maisie and so knowing she, Mrs. Beale, can remain with him. Sir Claude asks Maisie to go give up Mrs. Wix, so that the household will be stable. She, for the first time, makes conditions--she will agree if he'll give up Mrs. Beale. But Mrs. Beale's sexuality is stronger than Maisie's, and in the end Maisie leaves with Mrs. Wix--out of the dance and on her own.

James, Henry. _The Wings of the Dove_. New York: Charles Scribner's Sons, 1922. 2 Vols. (_Novels and Tales_, Vols. XIX & XX). Novel.

Doctors   Dying   The Family
Women as Patients

One must work through some of the densest of James' prose to arrive at the complex interpersonal relationships surrounding the wealthy, young, dying Milly Theale, who takes advantage of the webs of deception around her to hide the obvious fact of her dying. She has a nicely allusive talk with her doctor and then sends him off to deal honestly with her friend-companion. She plays the game of providing him with an innocent surface while probing his remarks to discover how ill she truly is. "Wanting to know more about a patient than how a patient was constructed or deranged couldn't be, even on the part of the greatest of doctors, anything but some form or other of the desire to let the patient down easily." Although the characters do not say until well into the novel that they know Milly is dying, they begin to act upon their knowledge. She becomes involved with a troubled family of a weak and impoverished father and sister who depend upon Kate Croy, who in turn depends upon her wealthy aunt. The subtle aunt looks to Milly as a way to avoid the crisis created by Kate's love for Densher, a man whom her aunt likes and respects but finds ineligible on the charge of inerradicable poverty. Milly is the perfect solution--she will unwittingly detach Densher from Kate, or she will marry Densher (who is reluctant to plan this), die, and leave him enough money to marry Kate. Ironically, the solution fails. Without any declaration of love on his part, Densher is bequeathed a vast fortune by Milly. However, Milly has earned enough love so that he feels he cannot take her money--so both Milly and Kate lose Densher.

Jewett, Sarah Orne. _A Country Doctor_. Boston: Gregg, 1970. Novel.

The Body   Doctors   Med. Profession
Women as Healers

Although this novel is not as well-written as many of her short stories, the subject matter makes it interesting. In the late 19th century, British and American writers took up the subject of women doctors. Jewett has two unusual approaches to the topic which neatly sidestep all of the issues. The first is that all professions are given by God, so that her heroine is destined to become a doctor. The second is that a professional woman is not destined for marriage. The reason for this dictum is never made clear; it is merely reiterated that this bright, loveable, and loving young woman is unsuited for marriage. There are a number of miscellaneous statements about the medical profession. The role of the doctor is not to keep us from death but is "the necessity of teaching and remedying the inferior bodies which have come to us through either our ancestor's foolishness or our own." General practitioners have great wisdom but are too busy to write it down. Doctoring is a gift, not a science: need to offer comfort to worried patients and have the discernment to tell when a patient is coughing for effect and when he is hiding a cough. Malpractice is really the patient's misapplication and misinterpretation of prescribed medicine and treatment.

Jewett, Sarah Orne. "Miss Tempy's Watchers." Available in _The Best Short Stories of Sarah Orne Jewett_, ed. Willa Cather. Boston: Houghton Mifflin, 1924. Vol. 2. Short Story.

Death   Grief

Two middle-aged women talk as they "watch" over the dead body of their friend, Miss Tempy. The action consists of gradual changes in Mrs. Crowe, who, in talking over Miss Tempy, comes to be more sympathetic toward her fellow watcher and less frightened of death. The conversation jumps about, but gradually dwells more and more upon death until the one realizes that Miss Tempy's presence exists beyond her body and both share their loss together.

Keats, John. "After dark vapours." Available in _The Poetical Works of John Keats_, ed. H. W. Garrod. London: The Clarendon Press, 1939. Sonnet.

By Doctors   Death

Keats completed a course of medical study, although he never practiced. His medical notebooks are of interest to some (_John Keats' Anatomical and Physiological Note Book_, ed. M. B. Forman. New York: Haskel House Publishers, 1934; rpt. 1970). This poem conveys a great acceptance of death. The octet describes how disease is cleared away from space and time. The plains, the heavens, the months which were once sick, are now, for a time, relieved. The sestet lists two sequences of calm thoughts. The first follows vegetation from bud to harvest. The second follows man: "Sweet Sappho's cheek,--a sleeping infant's breath,--/The gradual sand that through an hour-glass runs,--/A woodland rivulet, --a Poet's death."

Keats, John. "Bright Star! Would I Were." Available in _The Poetical Works of John Keats_, ed. H. W. Garrod. London: The Clarendon Press, 1939. Sonnet.

By Doctors   Sexuality

A "return to the womb" in the arms of the beloved: "Pillow'd upon my fair love's ripening breast,/To feel for ever its soft fall and swell . . . Still, still to hear her tender-taken breath,/And so live ever--or else swoon to death."

Keats, John. "La Belle Dame Sans Merci." Available in _The Poetical Works of John Keats_, ed. H. W. Garrod. London: The Clarendon Press, 1939. Poem: 12 stanzas.

By Doctors   Death   Sexuality

The beautiful siren who, offering fruitfulness, brings death and sterility. She allures from an elfin grotto with roots, wild honey, and manna; but the knights awaken, the roses of their cheeks faded, where "The sedge has wither'd from the lake,/And no birds sing." Timeless herself, she transforms summer to winter and death. The simplicity of the ballad meter and imagery contrast with the intense mood and ambiguity of the poem.

Keats, John. Letter to Charles Wentworth Dilke, Mon., Sept. 1818; Letters to George and Georgiana Keats, Wed., Oct. 14 - Sat., Oct. 31, 1818; Wed., Dec. 16, 1818 - Mon., Jan. 4, 1819. Available in _Letters_, ed. M. B. Forman. 4th ed. New York: Oxford University Press, 1960. Letters.

By Doctors   Death   Disease & Health
The Family   Grief   Nurses

Keats' letters were, for the most part, works meant to be handed around those who knew him. These three letters discuss the illness (consumption) and death of his brother Tom, whom Keats with his medical training nursed while nursing the same disease in himself. The letter to Charles Wentworth Dilke shows how great a strain he was under: "I wish I could say Tom was any better. His identity presses upon me so all day that

I am obliged to go out-- . . . I am obliged to write and plunge into abstract images to ease myself of his countenance his voice and feebleness--so that I live now in a continual fever." He finally must tell his brother and sister of Tom's approaching death, finding comfort in their shared grief. This letter is highly emotional: "the tears will come into your Eyes--let them--and embrace each other--thank heaven for what happiness you have and after thinking a moment or two that you suffer in common with all Mankind hold it not a Sin to regain your cheerfulness." But when he tells of Tom's death, he drops the information in a short paragraph in a long letter. He makes no mention of the funeral--he is numb. "The last days of poor Tom were of the most distressing nature; but his last moments were not so painful, and his very last was without a pang." He speaks of his friends' helpful kindness, but shows the shock of Tom's death. It is as though writing hinders his dying. "During poor Tom's illness I was not able to write and since his death the task of beginning has been a hindrance to me."

Keats, John. Letters to Charles Brown, Sun., Aug. 20, 1820; Sept. 30, 1820. Available in Letters, ed. M. B. Forman. 4th ed. New York: Oxford University Press, 1960. Letters.

| By Doctors | Death | Dying |
| Sexuality | Suffering | |

Keats on his own death. The first was written before his flight to Italy in an unsuccessful attempt to stave off consumption. He knows that an English winter will kill him, but sees little hope for an Italian one either. He cannot quite decide on the approach to take to his friends--the punctuation is his. "Not that I have any great hopes of that [Italy], for, I think there is a core of disease in me not easy to pull out . . . . If I should die . . . . I shall be obliged to set off in less than a month. Do not, my dear Brown, teaze yourself about me. You must fill up your time as well as you can, and as happily." The Sept. 30, 1820 letter is the most painful as the poet, knowing that he is near death, strives unsuccessfully to accept this. "I wish for death every day and night to deliver me from these pains [jealousy and love for Fanny Brawne], and then I wish death away, for death would destroy even those pains which are better than nothing . . . . death is the great divorcer for ever. When the pang of this thought has passed through my mind, I may say the bitterness of death is passed . . . . and yet the difference of my sensations with respect to Miss Brawne and my Sister is amazing . . . . The thought of leaving Miss Brawne is beyond every thing horrible--the sense of darkness coming over me--I eternally see her figure eternally vanishing . . . . Is there another life? Shall I awake and find all this a dream? There might be we cannot be created for this sort of suffering. The receiving this letter is to be one of yours."

Keats, John. Letters to Fanny Brawne. Available in The Letters of John Keats, ed. Maurice Buxton Forman. 4th ed. rev. New York: Oxford University Press, 1960. Letters.

| By Doctors | Death | Disease & Health |
| Dying | Sexuality | |

In these letters, passionate love merges with illness and death. To the dying Keats, Fanny Brawne seems to represent both life and death at once: "when . . . the lonely, silent, unmusical Chamber is waiting to receive me as into a Sepulchre, then believe me my passion gets entirely the sway" (Thursday, 1 July 1819). "To night I am greatly recovered only to feel the languor I have felt after you touched me with ardency. You say you perhaps might have made me better: you would then have made me worse: now you could quite effect a cure: What fee my sweet Physician would I not give you to do so" (Thursday, 15 July 1819). "I have two luxuries to brood over in my walks, your Loveliness and the hour of my death" (Sunday, 25 July 1819). "Day by day if I am not deceived I get a more unrestrain'd use of my Chest . . . . so I lingering on the borders of health feel my impatience increase . . . . how horrid was the chance of slipping into the ground instead of into your arms-- the difference is amazing love" [March 1820?]. "I fear I am too prudent for a dying kind of Lover. Yet, there is a great difference between going off in warm blood like Romeo, and making one's exit like a frog in a frost" [March 1820?]. The most heartrending to read is his letter to Charles Brown written shortly before his death: "My dear Brown, I should have had her when I was in health, and I should have remained well. I can bear to die--I cannot bear to leave her. Oh, God! God! Every thing I have in my trunks that reminds me of her goes through me like a spear . . . . What am I to do? Where can I look for consolation or ease? If I had any chance of recovery, this passion would kill me" (Wednesday, 1 Nov. 1820).

Keats, John. "Light feet, dark violet eyes." Available in The Poetical Works of John Keats, ed. H. W. Garrod. London: The Clarendon Press, 1939. Sonnet.

| By Doctors | Sexuality | Sexual Roles |

Keats wrote three sonnets on women in his youth, all implying that woman is praiseworthy only when meek and modest. This is infamous for its ending: "but when I mark/Such charms with mild intelligences shine,/My ear is open like a greedy shark,/To catch the tunings of a voice divine."

Keats, John. "Ode to a Nightingale." Available in The Poetical Works of John Keats, ed. H. W. Garrod. London: The Clarendon Press, 1939. Poem: 8 stanzas.

| By Doctors | Death | Dying |

Out of the beautifully complex and rich poem comes one beautiful, rich stanza on death: "for many a time/I have been half in love with easeful Death . . . Now more than ever seems it rich to die,/To cease upon the midnight with no pain,/While thou art pouring forth thy soul abroad/In such an ecstasy!"

Keats, John. "When I have fears that I may cease to be." From Selected Poems, ed. Edmund Blunden. London: Collins, 1966. Sonnet.

| By Doctors | Death | Disease & Health |

Interesting next to Milton's "When I Consider." The consumptive Keats fears that he will not live long enough to bring his poetic ability to full fruition and to experience love to the fullest. His bitter response is to reduce love and fame to equal nothingness with him. "When I have fears that I may cease to be/Before my pen has glean'd my teeming brain . . . When I behold, upon the night's starr'd face,/Huge cloudy symbols of a high romance,/And think that I may never live to trace/ Their shadows with the magic hand of chance . . . . then on the shore/Of the wide world I stand alone, and think/ Till fame and love to nothingness do sink."

Kingsley, Charles. Two Years Ago. New York: R. F. Fenno, 1900. Novel.

| Alcoholism | Doctors | Plague |
| Poverty & Health | Sexuality | |

Despite the novel's having 3 doctors, 2 alcoholics, and a cholera epidemic, it has slight medical value because of Kingsley's insistence that the true and most harmful epidemic is godlessness. An adventurous doctor returns to England to support his old, blind doctor-father, but is shipwrecked and so takes up practice under an alcoholic, incompetent doctor with a laudanum-taking wife. Although very successful despite his low fees and common sense substitutes for expensive medication, Tom avoids treating young women and so avoids romantic entanglements until he becomes involved with the truly religious Grace, whom he unjustly suspects of stealing his money belt. He can foresee the coming of a cholera epidemic, but conservatism and selfishness prevent his providing preventive sanitation, although a liberal nobleman in another district seeks his help in adopting protective measures there. The cholera strikes, Dr. Tom and schoolteacher-nurse Grace provide limitless good humor, nobility and strength. All praise Tom, and the alcoholic doctor blames himself for not asserting his authority as a public health officer. Yet, as the novel goes on to make obvious, the real plagues are idleness and selfishness which inflict more suffering than the cholera deaths. A squire drinks himself into delirium tremens, making his family miserable, because he lacks occupation. A poet, who finds beautiful poetry in human misery (he lacked the concentration to become an apothecary), inflicts great misery on his wife and his wife's friends by his insistence upon a sophisticated front (christened John Briggs, he calls himself Elsley Vavasour). Tom finally returns home to his father (now nursed by Grace) and chooses the ethereal, religious Grace over the wealthy, plain Mary who loves him. Grace does manage to bring 1,500 pounds sterling with her, and the story ends happily for the characters and the reader.

Kipling, Rudyard. "Baa Baa Black Sheep." From The Mark of the Beast and Other Stories. New York: Signet, 1964. Short Story.

| Children | Handicaps | Sexual Roles |

Kipling didn't like women much. In general they were predatory hunters like Mrs. Hauksbee (in many stories of Plain Tales), conventional ciphers ("Miss Youghal's Sais"), or fascinating submissive native women ("Without Benefit of Clergy"). "The Brushwood Boy" and "Them" are two bright exceptions. In this tale, an aunt takes out her hatred of men upon two little children left in her care: conditioning the girl into a virtuous prig and transforming a healthy, open boy into a diseased, vicious, guilty creature. The aunt names him a black sheep and twists him into the role. He is punished for the clumsiness that results from his growing blindness. (Also, see The Light That Failed.) When the parents return from India, the mother is able to make a reclamation, but an incomplete reclamation, of the boy.

Kipling, Rudyard. "The Gate of the Hundred Sorrows." In Plain Tales from the Hills. From The Works of Rudyard Kipling. Roslyn, New York: Black's, n.d. Sketch.

| Drugs |

The dreamy path to death of an opium smoker in India. He spends all his time in a Chinese opium den. "At the end of one's third pipe the dragons used to move about and fight . . . . I used to regulate my Smoke that way, and now it takes a dozen pipes to make 'em stir."

Kipling, Rudyard. "The Last Relief." In Plain Tales from the Hills. From The Works of Rudyard Kipling. Roslyn, New York: Black's, n.d. Short Story.

Death   Disease & Health   Plague

Kipling's India stories are haunted by death and devastating epidemics. The pattern of sending women to the Hills at times of disease influences many courtships. But, in this little ghost story, there is a sense of men sacrificed by disease to the hostile land and of death defeated by indomitable spirit.

Kipling, Rudyard. "The Tender Achilles" and "Hymn to Physical Pain." From Limits and Renewals. New York: Doubleday, Doran & Co., 1932. Short Story and Poem: 28 lines.

Doctors   Med. Ethics   Med. Profession
Suffering   Surgery

A rather neat little tale of how two professionals retrieved a lost sheep. The story opens with a squabble between the G.P.'s and the surgeons after a hospital's "Senior" dinner which soon turns into a discussion of the bacteriologist-surgeon "Wilkett" who has just returned to work at the hospital. The surgeons reminisce about the abominable conditions during the war, in which bone-tired surgeons were waggled by the foot to awake and operate on more poor devils. Wilkett had the worst because he was in charge of self-inflicted wounds cases usually involving a shot foot, after he had done the usual make-shift field surgery. He comes out of the war convinced he was a murderer because he did not take the time to operate properly, and sees perspectives of headwounds and feels the orderlies waggling his feet. Wilkett does have a problem with one foot, so his G.P. friend convinces him to have a surgeon look at it. Wilkett is uneasy, but they suggest the foot is tubercular and that he can run his own tests to check. The tests turn up positive for T.B. and the surgeon must do a Syme operation of the foot, the same operation Wilkett did on many self-inflicted-wound cases. He believes it to be a judgment. Afterwards, the G.P. tells Wilkett that the foot wasn't tuberculous; Wilkett says it's not his friend's fault, he's only a G.P., but the lab was really at fault—especially since they had time to do things properly. They weren't at war. Then the surgeon appears, says he only followed results of tests, but goes on to talk research with Wilkett, blaming the G.P. for the mistake, but also blaming Wilkett for abandoning his position and so permitting the slovenly state of affairs. Wilkett comes back cured, but never is told that the G.P. and the surgeon arranged for the slides to be switched, believing that his mind was worth part of his foot. A neat question of ethics. The poem that precedes the story is addressed to physical pain, "Dread Mother of Forgetfulness." Although pain stretches hours into eons and is the "thickness of the Dark/That presses in our pain," release only renews the Worm and the Fire, the Pain of Hell. Therefore, sufferers praise her from the deep and pray for her return.

Kipling, Rudyard. "Unprofessional." From In Dreams Awake, ed. L. A. Fiedler. New York: Dell, 1975. Short Story.

Disease & Health   Doctors   Sci Fi
Suicide   Women as Patients

A close team of researchers discover a "tide" in living creatures (biorhythms?). The researchers move from mice to human tissues, one taken from a woman in for a hysterectomy. The tides influence the health of the patient, so they time a tricky second operation to coincide with flood tide. The operation is a success. Then the researchers note that mice die at ebb tide; sure enough, the woman irrationally tries to commit suicide at her ebb tide. She is pulled through by their efforts, particularly by the researcher who loves her. His concluding lament is that she is now sterile!

Lamb, Charles. "Christ's Hospital Five and Thirty Years Ago." In Essays of Elia. From Essays of Elia; Last Essays of Elia. New York: E. P. Dutton, 1957. Essay.

Children   Suffering

An answer to his own essay "Recollections of Christ's Hospital" which praised the charity school for turning out good men. This essay records the pain of separation from home, the monitors' cruelty, the thefts from his already insufficient portion of meat, solitary confinement, and arbitrary punishment by the teachers.

Lamb, Charles. "The Convalescent." In Last Essays of Elia. From Essays of Elia; Last Essays of Elia. New York: E. P. Dutton, 1957. Essay.

Disease & Health

"How sickness enlarges the dimensions of a man's self to himself! he is his own exclusive object. Supreme selfishness is inculcated upon him as his only duty . . . . How convalescence shrinks a man back to his pristine stature! where is now the space, which he occupied so lately, in his own, in the family's eye?"

Lamb, Charles. "Modern Gallantry." In Essays of Elia. From Essays of Elia; Last Essays of Elia. New York: E. P. Dutton, 1957. Essay.

Sexual Roles

Provocative assertion that men don't really respect women. He'll believe it when women aren't hanged, actresses aren't hissed off the stage, fishwives and apple-women are treated courteously, women are helped unobserved, poor women are protected from pouring rain on the way to the stagecoach, when fainting women aren't jeered, and when over half the drudgery and coarse servitude of this world shall cease to be performed by women. What is worst is that this discriminatory respect is upheld by women.

Lamb, Charles. "Written on Christmas Day, 1797." From Poems, Plays and Miscellaneous Essays, ed. Alfred Ainger. London: Macmillan & Co., 1899. Vol. 1. Poem: 26 lines.

The Family   Madness   Sexual Roles

A painful reaction to his sister's madness. She was given the tedious job of caring for her senile father and her fussy, paralyzed mother while trying to earn some money by needlework. Insanity runs in the family; she killed her mother and attacked her father and aunt. When she was released from the asylum, she was set to nursing an old aunt, and went insane again. From then on, she was in and out of the asylum, lovingly supported by Lamb; in her sane moments she was the co-author of such works as Lambs' Tales of Shakespeare. Here is Lamb's reaction: "I am a widow'd thing, now thou art gone!/Now thou art gone, my own familiar friend,/Companion, sister, helpmate, counsellor!/Alas! that honoured mind, whose sweet reproof/And meekest wisdom in times past have smooth'd/The unfilial harshness of my foolish speech,/And made me loving to my parents old,/(Why is this so, ah, God! why is this so?)/That honour'd mind become a fearful blank,/Her senses lock'd up, and herself kept out/From human sight or converse."

Le Fanu, Sheridan. The House by the Churchyard. New York: Stein & Day, 1968. Novel.

Doctors   Dying   Evil Doctors

Although this novel of Ireland is too chopped up, containing too much in too small sections, it compares very favorably with Lever's Irish novels. Not only was Le Fanu a greater writer (his ghost stories are famous) he did much more with doctors. Two doctors are rivals in a region: the civilian, gossipy, but ethical Dr. Toole, and Dr. Sturk, attached to the army, but eyeing civilian practice because hard pressed for money. The two doctors at first have minor roles in the many plot lines of the novel, but grow in importance. Sturk is so desperate for money that he blackmails a murderer and is badly beaten as a result. He lies in a coma for weeks; the murderer, worried he might recover, hires an unscrupulous doctor to trepan him, believing, on good medical advice, that trepanning will kill this patient; not understanding his task, the evil doctor returns Sturk to consciousness; Sturk accuses his murderer and prepares to die. However, all doctors carefully avoid preparing Sturk's wife for the inevitable death, so that her grief is hard indeed. Toole rises above his busybody status in his care of his rival in his labors to bring the true murderer to justice so that a falsely accused man can go free, and in his protection of a wife accused of being illegally married.

Lever, Charles James. Harry Lorrequer (The Confessions of Harry Lorrequer). New York: E. P. Dutton, n.d. Novel.

By Doctors   Doctors   Drugs

A direct imitation of Pickwick Papers, Harry Lorrequer follows the journeys of an Irish soldier. In one episode, Harry is forced into a bet with a physician when he wants to be assisting a friend to elope. Due to complications from the bet, Harry takes the physician's coach and is forced, successfully, to act as physician. The real doctor goes to where the eloping young lady awaits transport and is caught, bewildered, by his jealous wife. In Chapter XXXVI, Harry describes the effect of opium on a body weakened by loss of blood. Although trained as a doctor before he turned to literature for his living, Lever was not kind to the profession. His novel One of Them has a very unethical, almost mad doctor as a character.

London, Jack. "Koolau the Leper." From The House of Pride and Other Tales of Hawaii. New York: Macmillan, 1924. Short Story.

The Body   Death   Disease & Health
Med. Ethics   Med. Instit.   Sexuality

Revolt of Hawaiian lepers who do not want to go to the island leper colony but want to die on their own land. Their bodies are hideous, but they still feel love and pride. Koolau and his followers are eventually tracked down and killed—but they die free on their land. Koolau protests the arbitrary removal of rights from the sick. "Because we are sick they take away our liberty. We have obeyed the law. We have done no wrong. And yet they would put us in prison. Molokai is a prison . . . . It is the will of the white men who rule the land. And who are these white men?"

London, Jack. The Scarlet Plague. New York: Macmillan Co., 1915. Novel.

Plague   Sci Fi

A different vehicle for London's social theories. An increasing population increases both the kinds of bacteria and the ease with which a new bacterium can spread.

A virulent, deadly disease kills most of mankind and
destroys all civilization. People callously loot and
destroy. The ignorant, strong man wins status--and
women--from the effete, erstwhile upper-class thinker.
Mankind returns to the stone age, with medicine men
for doctors, having lost all knowledge of the past
civilized life.

London, Jack. "To Build a Fire." Available in The Bodley Head
Jack London, Vol. I, ed. Arthur Calder-Marshall. London:
The Bodley Head, 1964. Short Story.

The Body   Dying

Stages of dying in an arctic wilderness. The pragmatic
hero had not been led "to meditate upon man's frailty
in general, able only to live within certain narrow
limits of heat and cold" and so had not been led "to
the conjectural field of immortality and man's place in
the universe." He finds himself on the trail in temper-
atures below -50 degrees. As a result of a freak accident, he must build a fire to dry out his feet which
are beginning to be frostbitten. But his fingers are
numb. He can't grasp the matches. He uses his teeth
and burns himself, but can't feel it. It is not until
he loses all the matches that he is conscious of a
sense of death. He panics, running grotesquely on his
frostbitten feet. The panic ends in collapse--and
acceptance. He realizes he is beyond help and determines to meet his death with dignity. He dies calmly.

Longfellow, Henry Wadsworth. Evangeline. From Poems of Henry
Wadsworth Longfellow. New York: Thomas Y. Crowell, 1901.
Long Poem.

Death   Disease & Health   Sexuality
Women as Healers

Evangeline, separated from her betrothed, Gabriel, by
the evacuation of French Canadians forced by the British,
spends most of her life pursuing the phantom of Gabriel
about the United States. Although he is also, supposedly,
in pursuit of her, he heads always into wilderness areas.
At last, in defeat, Evangeline becomes a Sister of Mercy
in Philadelphia, where, during a plague, she finds her
withered Gabriel dying, too weak to say her name. She
thanks God for the completion. Evangeline represents a
dying literary tradition: the woman as nurse-lover,
replaced by the more recent woman as mother-lover.
Death has lost its precedence to birth.

Maupassant, Guy de. "Ball-of-Fat." From The Complete Short Stories
of Guy de Maupassant. New York: Walter J. Black, 1903. Short
Story.

The Body   Sexuality   Sexual Roles

In occupied France, travelers, petty bourgeoisie who
have acquired social position by dubious means, are
drawn together to assert their respectability by the
presence of Ball-of-Fat, a plump prostitute. However,
when hunger strikes, they accept the food she shyly
offers. Then the travelers are delayed by a Prussian
officer who wishes to bed Ball-of-Fat, who, a fervent
Frenchwoman, refuses in patriotic disgust. The
travelers unite in persuading her to sleep with the
officer, citing Judith and Lucrece, the importance of
motive over deed, and the important good deeds the
travelers are prevented from accomplishing. At last
she gives in, and the travelers indulge in sensual
celebration while she is with the officer. On the
renewed journey, she is shunned by the others and
refused food, while she weeps for shame.

Maupassant, Guy de. "Bed No. 29." Available in The Complete Short
Stories of Guy de Maupassant. New York: Walter J. Black,
1903. Short Story.

V.D.

During the Prussian occupation of France, a French
officer returns to visit his mistress who is in the
hospital. He is horrified and feels contaminated when
he learns she is in the syphilis ward, having contracted the disease from a Prussian only to refuse
to be cured in order to spread the disease further
among the Prussians. He calls her conduct shameful
until she, who is dying for her efforts, hurls more
reproaches at him: "You have not done as much, with
your cross of honor! I deserve more merit than you,
for I have killed more Prussians than you! . . . .
yes, more harm to them than you, and I am going to
die for it while you are singing songs and making
yourself fine to inveigle women . . . . and that I
have killed more than all your regiment together--
come now, you coward."

Maupassant, Guy de. "Beside a Dead Man." From The Complete Short
Stories of Guy de Maupassant. New York: Walter J. Black,
1903. Sketch.

The Body   Death

This account of the death of Schopenhauer seems like a
parody of De Quincey's "Death of Kant." A dying consumptive tells of his acquaintance with the philosopher,
of the man's almost supernatural effect upon people, of
the impact of his mind, and of his death. Even as a
corpse, Schopenhauer dominates the room--until the smell
of the decomposing body drives the "watchers" into the

next room, where they can again be awestricken--until a
sound calls them back to the corpse, over whose charged
face something white flashes. Decomposition has made
the artificial teeth jump out of the dead philosopher's
mouth. The body obliterates the mind's effect.

Maupassant, Guy de. "The Blind Man." From The Complete Short
Stories of Guy de Maupassant. New York: Walter J. Black,
1903. Sketch.

Handicaps

The terrible life and death from neglect of a blind man.
"His incapacity for doing anything as well as his im-
passiveness eventually exasperated his relatives, and
he became a laughing-stock, a sort of martyred buffoon."
First they play practical jokes--allowing the dog to
eat up his food or giving him filth to eat. Then they
smack him about, then force him to beg. He is unsuccessful, so they beat him, lead him out to beg, and abandon
him to freeze and be eaten by crows.

Maupassant, Guy de. "The Devil." From The Complete Short Stories
of Guy de Maupassant. New York: Walter J. Black, 1903.
Short Story.

Euthanasia   Med. Profession   Nurses

A fiendish little story of death for profit. A dying
peasant woman's only relative, a son, must leave her to
harvest the crop, his livelihood. She accepts this, but
the doctor forces her son to hire a watcher by threatening not to provide him with medical care. The son hires
La Rapet, a spiteful avaricious woman with a monstrous
and cynical affection for the death struggle. The two
strike a bargain--a lump payment to cover the watching,
regardless of the length of time. La Rapet grows to
hate the old woman for living, even though the dying
woman has not yet lasted the minimum number of days La
Rapet calculated she'd live. So La Rapet, after telling
horrible tales of the devil, disguises herself as a
demon and frightens her patient to death, thus earning
twelve sous. Care forced on the woman by her doctor
makes her dying hideous.

Maupassant, Guy de. "A Family." From The Complete Short Stories
of Guy de Maupassant. New York: Walter J. Black, 1903.
Sketch.

Age   The Family

Hideous story of a family who use the grandfather's
senility for their amusement, depriving the old man of
what he desires most in life under the excuse of preserving his life. All he desires is food, so they feed
him little bits, mocking the noises he makes as he eats
and the awkward gestures he uses to beg for more. When
a visitor asks that he be given more food, the son-
father replies "Oh! no my dear fellow, if he were to
eat too much, it might harm him at his age."

Maupassant, Guy de. "The First Snowfall." From The Complete Short
Stories of Guy de Maupassant. New York: Walter J. Black,
1903. Short Story.

Body/Mind   Disease & Health   Sexual Roles
Women as Patients

A sharp example of the transformation of a social and
interpersonal problem into a physical one. A newly-wed
woman enjoys living at her husband's country home in the
summer, but becomes discontented in fall and winter when
he spends all his time hunting. She mopes about, then
asks for the house to be heated. He laughs. Her parents
die; she discovers she cannot have children; her husband
continues hunting. She asks to go to Paris; he chides
her for frivolity. So, she again asks for central heating. He replies she's had only one cold. The solution
is forced on her--if only a physical discontent will
change him, she'll get it. She goes out in the cold and
contracts pneumonia, and the doctor insists upon heating
the house. The husband yields with poor grace. The
pneumonia provides a bonus; it leaves her open to consumption, and she is sent to the Mediterranean. However,
terrified that she will be forced to stay in the cold
north once she is cured, she again goes into the cold.
She dies, contented, in the warm south.

Maupassant, Guy de. "Madame Baptiste." Available in The Complete
Short Stories of Guy de Maupassant. New York: Walter J.
Black, 1903. Short Story.

Sexuality   Sexual Roles

Terrible story of rape. A young middle-class girl is
ostracized by the townspeople because she was, at age
eleven, raped by a footman: "Remember that she had
nothing to learn, nothing; that she no longer had the
right to the symbolical wreath of orange-flowers; that
almost before she could read, she had penetrated [note
inversion] that redoubtable mystery which mothers
scarcely allow their daughters to guess, trembling as
they enlighten them on the eve of their marriage."
Despite her nickname of "Madame Baptiste" after the
footman, a young man falls in love with her and marries
her. Once she becomes pregnant, she is, as it were,
purified and respectable. But when she is seated on a
platform while her husband gives out musical honors, a
defeated candidate calls her "Madame Baptiste"; she
begins to go mad, the crowd roars and will not let her
escape, and she has to remain, a target of mockery. She
commits suicide that night--an action everyone approves,
even though they will not give her, a suicide, a proper
burial.

Maupassant, Guy de. "Useless Beauty." Available in The Complete
Short Stories of Guy de Maupassant. New York: Walter J.
Black, 1903. Short Story.

| The Body | Preg. & Childbirth | Sexuality |
| Sexual Roles | | |

A jealous husband keeps his wife pregnant so that she
will lose her figure and become unattractive. However,
as soon as she's pregnant, he also loses interest and
wanders off to return only after the child is born. He
loves the children as victories over her. She has
seven children in eleven years. Therefore, she gets a
pistol to stave off his advances; this becomes unnecessary after she discovers a better weapon. She swears
that one of the children is not his--without telling
him which one; he separates from her and the children.
An observer praises her for fighting back against Nature
who "is continually bringing us back to an animal state
. . . . God only created coarse beings . . . . That they
may reproduce their species in a repulsive manner." It
is man who has added grace, beauty and tenderness to
reproduction. When the woman finally tells her husband
that she had lied, he asks how a mother could so slander
her children. She replies that she is not the mother
of unborn children, but those she has, that women are
now civilized and more than females to restock the
earth. The husband suddenly sees her as a product "of
the complicated desires which have been accumulating in
us for centuries, but which have been turned aside from
their primitive and divine object, and which have
wandered after a mystic, imperfectly seen, and intangible
beauty."

Melville, Herman. "Bartleby." From Great Short Works of Herman
Melville. New York: Harper & Row, 1966. Short Story.

Madness

This story is about at least one madman. The obvious one
is Bartleby who slowly retreats from life, hiding behind
the phrase "I prefer not." The egotism of this statement
contrasts with his total passivity. On the other hand,
the narrator, Bartleby's boss, bustles about to cope with
this man who prefers not to leave his quarters. Yet, for
all his activity, the narrator cannot ask Bartleby why he
prefers not. He has little ego, assuming kinship with
Bartleby and yet abandoning him because he cannot question his "kinsman."

Melville, Herman. Billy Budd, Sailor, ed. Harrison Hayford and
M. M. Sealts, Jr. Chicago: University of Chicago Press,
1962. Novella and Poem.

| Death | Handicaps | Homosexuality |

Of importance here are the odd relationships between
Captain Vere and Billy, and Claggart and Billy. The
Captain becomes a father to this common seaman after
Claggart's love/hate relationship with Billy (whom he
calls Beauty) reaches its bloody climax when the indignant Billy, held speechless by a vocal impediment,
strikes out against Claggart who has accused him of
treason. Billy is effectively doomed to death for
murdering an officer from that point on, but the Captain works at preparing Billy, and himself, for the
hanging. He does this so well that Billy dies without
the usual convulsions. The work ends with the beautiful song, "Billy in the Darbies," in which he is both
awaiting death and experiencing its peaceful aftermath:
"Sentry, are you there?/Just ease these darbies at the
wrist,/And roll me over fair!/I am sleepy, and the oozy
weeds about me twist."

Melville, Herman. "I and My Chimney." From Great Short Works of
Herman Melville. New York: Harper & Row, 1966. Short Story.

Sexuality

A lighthearted piece in which the narrator defends his
chimney (clearly his organ--see also "The Cassock" in
Moby Dick for such fun) against the determined onslaughts
of his wife and daughters.

Melville, Herman. Moby Dick. Novel.

| Death | Madness | Sexuality |
| Suffering | Suicide | |

The sea as an encounter with death from which one can,
with care, return with some meaning for life. It is
Ishmael's substitute for suicide. For others, "to the
death-longing eyes of such men, who still have left in
them some interior compunctions against suicide, does
the all-contributed and all-receptive ocean alluringly
spread forth . . . . Come hither! bury thyself in a life
which . . . is more oblivious than death." But Ahab
does not come for oblivion; he comes to impose his
personality, seeking vengeance for the physical diminu-
tion of himself. However, isolated Ahab can be seen in
an odd comparison with the brotherly Queequeg who, in
his apparently dying state, asserts a dying man's
tyranny over his mates. Ahab's power seems to lie, in
part, in such a tyranny. The mental suffering on board
the ship is intense and varied, including the pains of
Ahab, the mad cabin boy Pip, and Starbuck struggling
with his conscience.

Melville, Herman. "The Paradise of Bachelors" and "The Tartarus
of Maids." From Great Short Works of Herman Melville. New
York: Harper & Row, 1966. Sketches.

| The Body | Preg. & Childbirth | Sexuality |

Another set of Melville's concealed sexual descriptions.
The first, stretching the interpretation a little, discusses celibacy. The second, ostensibly describing a
paper mill, really describes pregnancy. Cupid demonstrates
that it takes only nine minutes to make a piece of paper,
which is usually foolscap. Blood River sets the process
going. Rags become sperm; male organs are swords whetted
by the girls themselves. The pulp must go, the paper must
be produced. All of the pale, suffering girls are not
married women, but "maids."

Melville, Herman. Pierre, or the Ambiguities. New York: E. P.
Dutton, 1929. Novel.

| Children | The Family | Madness |
| Med. Instit. | Sexuality | Suicide |

Pierre feels incomplete, longs for a sister (two brothers
seem to be unpopular in 19th-century literature). He
already possesses one in his mother, whom he treats as
"my sister, my spouse." She dominates him, but arranges
a marriage between Pierre and the wealthy Lucy, who loves
Pierre and is loved by him. Into this cozy trio comes
Pierre's "sister," Isabel who may or may not be his
illegitimate half-sister. As with his sister-mother,
it is a love which cannot be consummated. In order to
claim her, Pierre marries her in an incestuous but
unconsummated marriage which kills his mother with rage
and jealousy (after she disinherits him) and nearly kills
Lucy who flees her brother to join the couple in New
York, forfeiting her inheritance. Although cut off from
older generations, the trio is persecuted by their own:
Lucy's brother and Pierre's cousin (his "twin" cousin
who inherited his estate) take on the task. Pierre
begins to go mad. He kills his cousin-self, is imprisoned,
kills himself with the poison Isabel brings to him in
her bosom; she and Lucy die. In Book VI, Part IV Isabel
describes the workhouse from the point of view of a
mentally disturbed child. Melville subtitled this novel
The Ambiguities; its interpretation is fittingly obscure.

Melville, Herman. White-Jacket, or The World in a Man-of-War,
ed. A. R. Humphreys. London: Oxford University Press, 1966.
Novel.

| Doctors | Med. Instit. | Med. Profession |
| Suffering | Surgery | |

Abuses on board the microcosm of a man-of-war. Melville
constantly attacks the doctors for becoming a part of
the system and not interfering. He notes, in Chapter
XXII, that the doctor watched the morning washing of the
deck which meant the men had no dry place to eat breakfast and that, in cold weather, their bare feet froze;
he watched, gave out pills for the resultant fevers,
but said nothing. In Chapter LXXVII, a surgeon must be
on hand with the right to interfere at every flogging,
but they never did protest even though the men suffered
severely. Chapters LXI-LXIII introduce Cadwallader
Cuticle, scientist and head surgeon, who removes his
false teeth and glass eye before operating, which
obscures the lecture he gives on each operation. He
delights in morbid anatomy. He has his profession's
callousness. In Chapter LXII, the surgeons consult
about an amputation. In Chapter LXIII they take off a
sailor's leg, discussing cuts in front of him, refusing
to continue sawing while the patient's in a faint. No
pain killer of any kind is given, and the patient dies
even though the operation is a success. In LXXIX, the
authorities create a hospital that is simply an uncomfortable place to die. Chapters XXXIII-XXXVI and LXXXVIII
are Melville's protest against flogging, its effect on
the crew, its violation of the U. S. Constitution, its
use by the British Navy, its abuse by the American Navy,
etc. It was this protest that caused the book to be
distributed to the U. S. Senate.

Meredith, George. "Melampus." From Poems. New York: Charles
Scribner's, 1910. Poem: 240 lines.

Doctors

Interesting for its comparison of a good physician and a
musician. Melampus, the physician, goes through the
forest loving and seeking cures. He learns that animals
don't go insane and do know where to find their own
cures. Then, a snake licks his ear so that he can hear
the soul of sounds: "heard at the silent medicine-root/
A song, beheld in fulfillment the unfulfilled . . . .
He played on men, as his master Phoebus, on strings
melodious: as the God did he drive and check."

Meredith, George. The Ordeal of Richard Feverel. New York:
Dutton, 1965. Novel.

| The Body | Children | Drugs |
| Sexuality | V.D. | |

The first half covering Richard's childhood is excellent.
He is raised by an unnatural system designed to produce
the perfect young man. He is prepared for his destiny
as a Feverel and shielded against sexuality, which his
injured father holds to be a trap. Richard grows up
proud, egotistical, and without any understanding of
other people. The second half isn't really useful, with
a nobleman's schemes to entrap Richard's wife while a
mysterious woman seduces Richard. Chapters 20 and 21 are
rather good. Parents hunt for eligible matches for
children, but have difficulty finding a marriageable
person untainted with the parents' syphilis. Mrs. Grand-
ison uses medicine as a punishment: "Physic is an

immense ally in bringing about filial obedience." She
has outfitted a complete gymnasium for her daughters:
"an instrument for the lungs; an instrument for the liver:
one for the arms and thighs: one for the wrists: the
whole for the promotion of the Christian accomplishments."

Meredith, George. Sonnet I. From Modern Love. Available in The
Pre-Raphaelites and Their Circle, ed. Cecil Y. Lang. Boston:
Houghton Mifflin, 1968. Sonnet.

The Body   Madness   Sexuality
Suicide

This first poem of the brilliant 50-sonnet sequence on
the death of married love is one of the finest. Here
the depression of the couple is rendered in sharp little
physical details. They lie in bed, not touching, lying
motionless like two effigies from an old tomb. The
stillness is broken only once: "By this he knew she
wept with waking eyes:/That at his hand's light quiver
by her head,/The strange low sobs that shook their
common bed,/Were called into her with a sharp surprise,/
And strangled mute, like little gaping snakes,/Dread-
fully venomous to him." Thinking about the sword which
conventionally lies between a couple in an effigy, the
poet writes that each wished for "the sword that severs
all."

Meredith, George. "The State of Age." From Poems. New York:
Charles Scribner's, 1910. Sonnet.

Age

Really an address to youth (as are many poems on age);
the old human is not respected by nature, but an old
human with a good life will be respected by humans:
"Light the young./Thy frame is as a dusty mantle hung,/
O grey one! pendant on a loosened peg . . . . To burn
from Self to Spirit through the lash/Honoured the sons
of Earth shall hold thee high:/Yea, to spread light
when thy proud letter I/Drops prone and void as any
thoughtless dash."

Meredith, George. "The Teaching of the Nude." From Poems. New
York: Charles Scribner's, 1910. Poem: 28 lines.

The Body   Sexuality

A satyr spies a goddess in her bath but, for all his
gestures, dances, leers, and giggles cannot convey what
he has seen. He is torn between "Goddess and Goatfoot"
until he sees his mate dancing, clothed only in a
shower of rose leaves. Now he goes to her. The difference between naked and nude, the body as glory and
the body for shared pleasure.

Meynell, Alice. "A Letter from a Girl to her own Old Age." From
Eighteen-nineties, ed. Martin Secker. London: Richards Press,
1948. Poem: 57 lines.

Age

The ultimate dichotomy between youth and age. The girl
is pictured writing, not to herself, but really to her
own death. It is as though she still cannot conceive
of any continuum between youth and age and cannot see
any good in age at all. The child is truly mother to
the woman, comforting herself as though she were her
own child: "Oh, in some hour of thine my thoughts shall
guide thee,/Suddenly, though time, darkness, silence,
hide thee,/This wind from thy lost country flits beside
thee,--."

Mitchell, John Kearsley. Indecision, a Tale of the Far West; and
Other Poems. Philadelphia: E. L. Carey & Hart, 1839.
Introduction and Dedication.

By Doctors   Science & Poetry

The poems in this collection are not bad, but irrelevant.
However, the preliminary material is interesting. Medicine and creative writing are related because "In the
midst of arduous professional duties, imaginative composition, like music or painting, prunes the wing of over-
loaded reason for a more vigorous flight" (Introduction).
He dedicates his poetry to another doctor who uses
reading to enliven his lectures: "To dry detail and
dusty love,/Brocht frae y'er inexhausted store,/A new
enchantment you lent." Very unimaginative use of poetry
as prop to rather than part of medicine.

Norris, Frank. A Man's Woman. 1900 ed.; rpt. New York: AMS
Press, 1970. Novella.

Death   Disease & Health   Nurses
Sexual Roles   Surgery

For strong-stomached women and male chauvinists. The
heroine, Lloyd Searight, is a wealthy nurse who has
founded and now runs a charitable nursing service.
She goes out on cases, but is subject to fits of anxiety
about Ferris, second-in-command on an arctic expedition.
Chapter III shows her competency. A child is to be
operated on at home. She sets up equipment, prepares
for the operation, and administers the anaesthetic.
When the child balks, Lloyd forces the ether on her,
smoothly and professionally. The rest of the book shows
the demolition of this professional woman by Bennett,
an explorer. To save her from infection, he keeps her
from Ferris' sickbed, even though this assures that his
friend and her lover will die. She agrees not to go!
Bennett himself is broken by illness and nursed back to
health by her. Further, she holds that a woman's role
is to make her man do his job. Therefore she bolsters
his confidence so that he can again go exploring, leaving
her at home, alone.

Norris, Frank. McTeague, ed. Carvel Collins. New York: Holt,
Rinehart & Winston, 1950. Novella.

Med. Ethics   Med. Profession

McTeague is a coal miner's son who takes up dentistry in
San Francisco, entering the profession by apprenticeship,
without formal training--or a license. Chapters II and
XIII are the most relevant. In Chapter II, McTeague
extracts a broken tooth from a young girl; he lusts for
her and kisses her while she's under the ether, and proposes to her when he regains consciousness, only to be
repulsed by the emetic action of ether. In Chapter XIII,
McTeague is debarred from practice through malicious
information laid by an ex-friend and present rival for
McTeague's wife. The novel then follows McTeague's
inevitable descent back into the depths.

Norris, Frank. The Octopus. New York: Bantam, 1958. Novel.

Death   Suffering

Almost anywhere in Book II, but particularly from Chapter
VII on, one can find the sufferings and deaths of the
farmers and their families who try to resist being
squeezed out of their farms by the railroad. However,
Norris constantly iterates that neither farmers nor
big corporations really control the commodity they fight
about; it has a life of its own. The novel's ending
emphasizes this. Angèle, carrying with her hope, sexuality and romance, "was realized in the Wheat."
Immediately, afterwards comes its other face. S. Behrman,
a dominant figure in the corporations, is literally
killed by the wheat in an incredible, lengthy death
scene. Trapped in a grain elevator filling with wheat,
despite his efforts to evade the flow of grains and
reach the hatchway, he is beaten back and smothered by
the staff of life.

Omar Khayyám. The Rubáiyát, trans. Edward Fitzgerald. New York:
Walter J. Black, 1942 (also available T. Y. Crowell, 1964).
Collection of Poems.

Death   Sexuality

Life is short, death mysterious--so seize the day: "Come,
fill the Cup, and in the fire of Spring/Your Winter-
garment of Repentance fling:/The Bird of Time has but
a little way/To flutter--and the Bird is on the Wing."
"A Book of Verses underneath the Bough,/A Jug of Wine,
a Loaf of Bread--and Thou/Beside me singing in the Wilder-
ness--/Oh, Wilderness were Paradise enow!"

Pater, Walter. "A Child in the House." From Miscellaneous Studies,
ed. C. L. Shadwell. New York: Macmillan Co., 1898. Essay.

Children   Death

An essay on a child's increasing sensibility, his recognition of the abstract through the concrete. "Our
susceptibilities, the discovery of our powers, manifold
experiences--our various experiences of the coming and
going of bodily pain, for instance--belong to this or
the other well-remembered place in the material habita-
tion . . . a system of visible symbolism interweaves
itself through all our thoughts and passions; and
irresistably, like shapes, voices, accidents--the
angle at which the sun in the morning fell on the pillow
--become parts of the great chain wherewith we are
bound." Pater gives briefly the growth of a child's fear
of death ("intensified by the desire of beauty") from
hearing of his father's death which was meaningless to
him, through seeing a child's grave, to hearing talk of
seeing the dead.

Percival, James Gates. "Consumption." In Clio. From The Poetical
Works of James Gates Percival. Boston: Ticknor & Fields,
1865. Vol. I. Poem.

By Doctors   Disease & Health   Sexuality

Although Percival had medical training and a medical
practice, medicine ranked below poetry, geology, and
chemistry as a route to fame and money. Writing in
the first half of the 19th century, he was greatly
influenced by Poe and a variety of Romantics.
"Consumption" has more of Poe's titillated excitement
at a woman violated by disease and death than of any
medical diagnosis. "There is a sweetness in a woman's
decay . . . when all that was bright and fair is fled,/
But the loveliness lingering round the dead . . . .
And though the glow from her cheek be fled,/And her
pale lips cold as the marble dead,/Her eye still beams
unwonted fires/With a woman's love and a saint's
desires."

Phelps, Elizabeth Stuart. Dr. Zay. Boston: Houghton Mifflin,
1882. Novel.

Disease & Health   Doctors   Med. Profession
Sexuality   Sexual Roles   Women as Healers
Women as Patients

The novel is very unusual among the many 19th-century
treatments of women doctors in that it tries to show a
woman able to be both a woman and a professional. The
book's core is the reversed sexual roles: a vigorous,
womanly doctor takes charge of an active male reduced
by an accident and illness to dependency upon her. The
book is full of interesting passages. "Was it possible
that this young woman had practice enough to keep two
horses? He knew nothing of the natural history of

doctresses. He had thought of them chiefly as a species
of higher nurse,--poor women, who wore unbecoming clothes,
took the horsecars, and probably dropped their 'g's or
said, 'Is that so?'" "There's more woman to our doctor
than to the rest of us, just as there's more brains . . . .
There are women that love women, care for 'em, grieve over
'em, worry about 'em . . . and never forget they're one
of 'em, misery and all" (Mrs. Isaiah, Chapter IV). She
stresses women's desire for women physicians. Waldo
Yorke is restless; he is physically unable to read; the
doctor may be delayed for hours. "'How dare men ridicule
or neglect sick women?' thought Waldo Yorke" (Chapter IV).
Talking of the horrible advantage of the medical profession, Dr. Zay says "It is unmatched . . . . We stand at
an eternal confessional, in which the chance of moral
escape or evasion is reduced to a minimum . . . . When
you add the control of life and death, you have a position unique in human relations. When I began, it
seemed to be like God's" (Chapter 8). "It occurred to
him to picture one of Scott's or Richardson's stately
heroes stranded meekly in a basket phaeton . . . while
the heroine made professional calls and forgot him.
How was a man going to approach this new and confusing
type of woman? The old codes were all astray. Were
the old impulses ruled out of order too?" (Chapter 9).
She rejects his first marriage offer--he will begin to
feel cheated when she's called away--"I should like
somebody myself to come home to, to be always there to
purr about me" (Chapter 12). However, love does conquer.
He goes out and gets a job (law). She does make a man
of him.

Poe, Edgar Allan. "The Facts in the Case of M. Valdemar." Available in Introduction to Poe, ed. E. W. Carlson. Glenview,
Illinois: Scott, Foresman & Co., 1967. Short Story.

Body/Mind   Death   Disease & Health
Dying   Euthanasia

M. Valdemar is dying of a confirmed "phthis," which is
described at length. As part of an experiment, he
consents to be hypnotized at the point of death. The
experiment succeeds. There is a detailed description
of the impact of death of the body, which, however, does
not decay, and the tongue continues to vibrate as though
the body is trying to speak. This continues for seven
months until they try to awake him and ask him what he
wants: "and at length the same hideous voice which I
have already described broke forth: 'For God's Sake!--
quick!--quick--put me to sleep--or, quick!--waken me!--
quick--I say to you that I am dead!'" The hypnotist
decides to wake him and with "dead! dead!" bursting from
the tongue, the body rots away into "a nearly liquid
mass of loathsome--of detestable putridity." The mind
preserves the body; it desires either death or life and
not the limbo state of the trance.

Poe, Edgar Allan. "The Fall of the House of Usher." Available in
Introduction to Poe, ed. E. W. Carlson. Glenview, Illinois:
Scott, Foresman & Co., 1967. Short Story.

Death   Disease & Health   Madness

Disease, to Poe, is rarely physical ill-health: it is a
medium for trances, an opportunity to deny death, or
mental disease. The disease that infests the House of
Usher is not the physical malady that gives Madeline the
appearance of death, but her brother's madness. It is
interesting that it is fear of body-snatchers (the
physician looked like a rascal and asked where and when
she'd be buried) drawn up as the reason for burying
Madeline in the vault; it is as though her brother fears
exhumation and yet sits passively by while it happens in
the worst way, by the lady herself. The theme of madness is echoed in the poem which describes a madman by
the metaphor of a disordered house; and the story read
by the narrator to Usher, which so grotesquely mimics
Madeline's struggles, is the tale of a knight seeking
entrance to a dwelling. If Madeline can be seen as
seeking to invade her brother's disordered house, it
raises all sorts of nasty possibilities as to why he will
not aid her struggles back to life and why he dies when
she temporarily succeeds.

Poe, Edgar Allan. "Ligeia." Available in Introduction to Poe, ed.
E. W. Carlson. Glenview, Illinois: Scott, Foresman & Co.,
1967. Short Story.

Body/Mind   Death   Sexuality

As in "Morella," a woman's spirit triumphs over death and
the body because of her great sexual passion. Ligeia
dies, fighting death for love of the narrator. In this
story appears the poem, "The Conqueror Worm." The narrator re-marries, taking as his bride a fair-haired, blue-
eyed woman whom he neglects totally. He immures her in
a gloomy, gothic bridal chamber and watches passively as
a mysterious shadow poisons her medicine. She dies, and,
as he watches over the corpse, it revives--with the
brown eyes and hair of Ligeia.

Poe, Edgar Allan. "The Man That Was Used Up." Available in
Introduction to Poe, ed. E. W. Carlson. Glenview, Illinois:
Scott, Foresman and Co., 1967. Sketch.

The Body   Handicaps

Grotesque Whimsy. The narrator makes an early morning
visit to the imposing Brevet Brigadier General John A. B.
C. Smith and, being in an ill-humor, kicks an odd-looking
bundle on the floor. The bundle protests, as it is the

general who was incessantly mutilated during his Indian
campaigns. His valet adds legs, arms, shoulders, bosom,
wig, teeth, eyes and palate, while the General notes
the name of the best manufacturer of each article, until
the General is once again a magnificent specimen of man.

Poe, Edgar Allan. "The Masque of the Red Death." Available in
Introduction to Poe, ed. E. W. Carlson. Glenview, Illinois:
Scott, Foresman & Co., 1967. Short Story.

Death   Plague

Prince Prospero and a thousand of his followers hide away
from the plague in a retired abbey. He gives a masquerade
in seven different colored rooms, which move across the
spectrum from blue to red only to end in a deserted black
chamber. The masque is interrupted by a figure impersona-
ting the Red Death, which Prince Prospero pursues through
the colors into the black chamber, where he dies: "And
the life of the ebony clock went out with that of the
last of the gay. And the flames of the tripods expired.
And Darkness and Decay and the Red Death held illimitable
dominion over all." Life here is an artifice so deceptive
that man does not recognize the death life is supposed
to conceal until too late.

Poe, Edgar Allan. "The Raven." Available in Introduction to Poe,
ed. E. W. Carlson. Glenview, Illinois: Scott, Foresman &
Co., 1967. Poem: 109 lines.

Death   Grief   Madness

The poem offers a rich mine for interpretations. On one
level, the bird is a demon assuring the narrator that
he will never again meet Lenore, even after death. On
another level, the raven is the madness that the narrator
has permitted to perch on his reason (Athena). In his
grief, he deliberately frames his questions so that the
answer will increase his despair to break through to
resigned, exhausted acceptance. (Thomas Holley Chivers,
a physician-poet, claimed that "The Raven" was plagia-
rized by Poe from Chivers' poem "To Allegra Florence in
Heaven.")

Poe, Edgar Allan. "Sonnet--To Science." Available in Introduction
to Poe, ed. E. W. Carlson. Glenview, Illinois: Scott,
Foresman & Co., 1967. Sonnet.

Science & Poetry

Poe saw no harmony and cooperation between the two arts:
"Science! true daughter of Old Time thou art!/Who
alterest all things with thy peering eyes./Why preyest
thou thus upon the poet's heart,/Vulture, whose wings
are dull realities?"

Poe, Edgar Allan. "Ulalume--A Ballad." Available in Introduction
to Poe, ed. E. W. Carlson. Glenview, Illinois: Scott, Foresman & Co., 1967. Poem: 104 lines.

Grief

Can be seen as a grief repressed by denial but forced to
the consciousness of the narrator by the anniversary
phenomenon. He wanders with his soul by the ghoul-
haunted woodland of Weir in the ashen and sober month
of October. He greets with joy the planet Astarte rising
in the sky, but his Psyche advises him to flee--they
find only the tomb of Ulalume and he remembers that it
was a year ago that they buried Ulalume. "Ah, can it/
Have been that the woodlandish ghouls--/The pitiful, the
merciful ghouls/To bar up our way and to ban it . . .
Have drawn up the spectre of a planet/From the Hell of
the planetary souls?"

Reade, Charles. The Cloister and the Hearth, Chapter LII. New
York: Dodd, Mead & Co., 1944 and A Woman-Hater, Chapters
XII, XIII & XIX. From The Works of Charles Reade, Vol. 7.
New York: Peter Fenelon Collier, n.d. Novels.

Doctors   Med. Ethics   Med. Instit.
Med. Profession   Med. Students   Nurses
Poverty & Health   Sexual Roles   Women as Healers
Women as Patients

Reade, one of the best minor muck-racking Victorian
novelists, was a strong advocate of women doctors. In
his best-selling novel, The Cloister and the Hearth, he
devotes one chapter to the defeat of Dr. Margaret by the
legal and professional organizations of her town. In
A Woman-Hater, he gives much space to Dr. Gale, a brash
but starving American and her efforts to overcome the
ludicrously and horrifyingly unprofessional efforts of
Great Britain's medical schools to deny women their
rightful medical education. She contrasts their
boorishness with the enlightened, emancipated Continental
schools. She notes that women were held to be "so eaten
up with sexuality" that women might degrade the school
by introducing sex; Dr. Gale cites the indecent stories
already there. She adds that the women patients thanked
God for sparing them the attentions of male medical
students. She describes the harassment the women students
received from male students and faculty. Surprisingly,
she asserts that men are superior to women as a whole,
but that some women are superior to most men. Her whole
attack is upon the British trades union (medical profession) which will stoop to any lie, harassment or illegal
maneuver to limit money to a few. "The noble nurses of
the Crimea went to attend males only, yet were not charged
with indelicacy. They worked gratis. The would-be

doctresses look <u>mainly to attending women</u>, but then they want to be paid <u>for it</u>: there was the rub--it was a mere money question, and all the attempts of the union to hide this and play the sentimental shop-man were transparent hypocrisy and humbug." With the help of the woman-hater of the title, Dr. Gale takes over the care of a small English village, concentrating, rather high-handedly, upon preventive medicine among the poor. She wins admiration, but is never considered a sexual woman, only a professional one.

Reade, Charles. <u>Hard Cash</u>. London: Chatto & Windus, 1922. Novel.

Doctors	Evil Doctors	The Family
Madness	Med. Ethics	Med. Instit.
Suffering		

Elaborate plot core is a father's incarceration of his son in an insane asylum to conceal the father's crime. The plot on the whole is too elaborate, but there are a few nice touches. The idiocy of the doctors who certify Alfred is prepared for by several doctors who make idiotic diagnoses of Julia's love sickness. Alfred is certified insane by two doctors who have a kickback scheme with an asylum. In Chapters 32, 33 and 39 are found the horrors of the madhouse and the impossibility of establishing sanity, when examining doctors see only the previous diagnosis, not the patient. He cannot even see the original commitment order. When a doctor declares him sane, he is kept confined by shifting him to another madhouse. The horrors of being in an institution with no professional definition of insanity, no real belief in cures--and so no way to prove sanity. Alfred does escape sane and unscathed (compare with Collins' <u>The Woman in White</u>). He is finally legally freed by the efforts of Dr. Sampson, who has great contempt for the majority of his fellow practitioners and uses publicity to obtain justice. Reade gets in one final dig in Chapter 54. Sampson's refusal to bleed, blister, or administer harsh drugs saves patients. Other doctors discover this, adopt his methods but cannot admit Sampson was right; so, they claim the type of disease has changed so they can now use the methods of a "quack."

Riley, James Whitcomb. "Little Orphant Annie." From <u>The Oxford Book of American Verse</u>, ed. Bliss Carman. New York: Oxford University Press, 1927. Poem: 32 lines.

Children

This little poem of ghost tales told by and to children has more than its haunting refrain of "the Gobble-uns 'll git you/Ef you/Don't/Watch/Out!" The tales become the little drudge's revenge for her menial work (the long chores are described at length), her means of insuring good treatment, and her way of inculcating moral values: "You better mind yer parents, and yer teachers fond and dear,/An' cherish them 'at loves you, an' dry the orphants tear . . . Er the Gobble-uns . . . ."

Rossetti, Christina. "Goblin Market." From <u>Romantic and Victorian Poetry</u>, eds. C. E. Andrew and M. O. Percival. Columbus, Ohio: R. G. Adams, 1928. Poem: ca. 650 lines.

Sexuality	Women as Healers

Beautiful perversion purged by another perversion. Lizzie, like dead Jeannie, moves away from the world of women to buy fruit from the goblin men. Jeannie "for joys brides hope to have/Fell sick and died." Lizzie, too, is made old and ill with longing for the fruit, but can no longer see the goblin men. Laura, to save her sister, goes to buy fruit, but will not eat, though the goblin men caress her, pressing fruit against her face, then beat and kick her. They take back the fruit, but Laura runs to Lizzie and tells her to kiss her: "Never mind my bruises,/Hug me, kiss, suck my juices/Squeezed from goblin fruits for you . . . . Eat me, drink me, love me." Laura kisses her "with a hungry mouth," but the juice is now wormwood, and its fire overbears the first desire. Laura sleeps and wakes, young and healthy. After they are both wives, Laura, recalling the pleasant days of "notreturning time," warns her children against the goblin fruits.

Rossetti, Christina. "Remember" and "Song." From <u>Romantic and Victorian Poetry</u>, eds. C. E. Andrew and M. O. Percival. Columbus, Ohio: R. G. Adams, 1928. Poems: Sonnet & 16 lines.

Death	Grief	Sexuality

The first is addressed to an assertive person who, when the poet is "gone far away into the silent land," should remember her. Yet, if she is forgotten and then remembered, "do not grieve;/For if the darkness and corruption leave/A vestige of the thoughts that once I had,/Better far you should forget and smile/Than that you should remember and be sad." The second poem looks at the other side of the grave. The "haply" of the last line with its close homophone "happily" catches the lovely ambiguity of the insult: "When I am dead, my dearest,/Sing no sad songs for me;/Plant thou no roses at my head,/Nor shady cypress tree . . . I shall not hear the nightingale/Sing on, as if in pain/And dreaming through the twilight/That doth not rise or set,/Haply I may remember,/And haply may forget."

Rossetti, Dante Gabriel. "The Blessed Damozel." From <u>The Works of Dante Gabriel Rossetti</u>, ed. W. M. Rossetti. London: Ellis, 1911. Poem: 144 lines.

Death	Sexuality	Sexual Roles

For Rossetti, Death and Sexuality were mixed in a bodiless union that has come far from Elizabethan equation of death and intercourse. He creates a "sacred" woman, not one of flesh, but of power, through some mystic association with death. "The blessed damozel leaned out/From the gold bar of Heaven;/Her eyes were deeper than the depth/Of waters stilled at even." She is awaiting the death of her lover which will free him to come to her for consummation. They will "lie i' the shadow of/That living mystic tree . . . . And I myself will teach to him,/I myself, lying so,/The songs I sing here." She will ask Mary and God to let them live together forever. But the angels pass, and she weeps. (See also Rossetti's glorious painting of this same subject.)

Rossetti, Dante Gabriel. "Body's Beauty," <u>The House of Life</u>, Sonnet LXXVIII. From <u>The Works of Dante Gabriel Rossetti</u>, ed. W. M. Rossetti. London: Ellis, 1911. Sonnet.

The Body	Sexuality

The other side of the "sacred woman" from "The Blessed Damozel." The lethal body--Lilith, not Eve. "And still she sits, young while the earth is old,/And subtly of herself contemplative,/Draws men to watch the bright web she can weave,/Till heart and body and life are in its hold . . . . and left his straight neck bent/And round his heart one strangling golden hair."

Rossetti, Dante Gabriel. "Life-in-Love" and "Death-in-Love," <u>The House of Life</u>, Sonnets XXXVI & XLVIII. From <u>The Works of Dante Gabriel Rossetti</u>, ed. W. M. Rossetti. London: Ellis, 1911. Sonnets.

Death	Sexuality

In the first, the lady's spirit endows both bodies with life. "Not in thy body is thy life at all,/But in this lady's lips and hands and eyes . . . . Even so much life hath the poor trees of hair/Which, stored apart, is all love hath to show . . . 'Mid change the changeless night environeth,/Lies all that golden hair undimmed in death." But Love and Death are also the same, as in the second sonnet. "There came an image in Life's retinue/That had Love's wings and bore his gonfalon . . . . But a veiled woman followed . . . Then plucked a feather from the bearer's wing/And held it to his lips that stirred it not . . . I and this Love are one, and I am Death." A perverse version of Plato's immortal hermaphrodite: veiled woman and male bearer together are unchanging love--in death.

Sade, Donatien Alphonse Francois, Marquis de. <u>Justine</u>. Available in <u>The Complete Justine, Philosophy in the Bedroom and Other Writings</u>, comp. and trans. Richard Seaver and Austryn Wainhouse. New York: Grove Press, 1965. Novel.

Evil Doctors	Homosexuality	Madness
Sexuality	Suffering	

Suffering is sexual (and vice versa), and virtue does not pay. Justine is a losing Pamela, who undergoes one rape and/or beating after another. Among her tormentors are a pair of homosexuals; a Dr. Rodin, who tortures and kills beautiful children, including his own daughter; and a Count Gernande, who bleeds his wives and mistresses to death in his attempts to achieve arousal of his peanutsized member. She is forced into orgies, kept by monks, tortured as part of a bandit's "stable," until finally rescued by her successful, licentious sister. But nature is less tolerant than her sister, and Justine is killed by lightning.

Sade, Donatien Alphonse Francois, Marquis de. <u>Philosophy in the Bedroom</u>. Available in <u>The Complete Justine, Philosophy in the Bedroom and Other Writings</u>, comp. and trans. Richard Seaver and Austryn Wainhouse. New York: Grove Press, 1965. Tale.

Children	Homosexuality	Sexuality
Sexual Roles	Suffering	V.D.

Shorter and more horrifying than Justine. The last two sections are most useful. The penultimate argues for abolition of religious, moral, and social laws to permit free expression of natural impulses and to recognize that everyone is and should be a sexual object to everyone else. The strong of either sex should have the right to rape the object of their desires. The final section demonstrates this freedom in action. It is designed to make the female reader conscious of her genitals. A mother who comes to rescue her young virgin daughter is raped and tortured by the ex-virgin and her liberated teachers. The woman is raped in a variety of ways (including by her daughter with a dildo), has an eye and part of her nose ripped out, is raped vaginally and anally by a coachman with syphilis, and then sent home with those apertures sewn up. The torture is accompanied by a running commentary by the daughter. "Well, my lovely mama, how does it feel to have your daughter serve you as a husband . . . . Behold,--my friends! At one stroke I'm an adulteress, a fornicator, a lesbian, a sodomite, and I commit incest." During the proceedings the mother reaches a climax--and her breasts are then torn with pliers. Stimulation and horror co-mingled.

Schiller, Friedrich. "Die Peste" (trans. with aid of Fred Oppenheimer). Werke, Vol. 3, eds. Otto Güntter and George Witkowski.
Leipzig: Hesse & Bechter Verlag, n.d. In German. Poem:
18 lines.

The Body   Disease & Health   Plague

Terrifying description of the plague as God's instrument.
"Monstrously pestilences and epidemics praise God . . . .
Terrifyingly it seizes the pounding heart, convulsively
the taut fibers tremble . . . . Frenzy rolls wildly in
the bed, poisonous fog seethes around the extinct city,
people--haggard--hollow and pale--swarm into the dismal
realm. Death lies hatching on the murky air, accumulating treasures in stuffed graves. Pestilence is his
jubilant feast. Corpse-like silence--graveyard quiet
alternate with the lustful roars." And then, again, the
bitterness of the opening line: "Terribly the plague
praises God."

Scott, Sir Walter. The Heart of Midlothian, ed. J. H. Raleigh.
Boston: Houghton Mifflin, 1966. Novel.

Madness   Preg. & Childbirth

Part of the novel is an attack on the law which provides
a death penalty for any woman who conceals her pregnancy
and her baby because she is automatically held guilty
of child murder. Effie Dean is an example of how this
law can miscarry. She has her child in the home of Madge
Wildfire (insane and has lost a child by Effie's seducer)
and Madge's evil mother (who hated Effie). Madge steals
the child, and Effie, weak and delirious with fever,
does not know what has happened to the child and so
cannot give satisfactory answers at her trial. The
book's interest lies not only in Effie's sister's great
journey to plead for a pardon, but also in Madge and
her mother, who recall all the institutions they've
been in (Chapter XXIX). Madge is killed by a mob for
lamenting the hanging of her mother.

Scott, Sir Walter. St. Ronan's Well. From Works, Vol. 2. Boston:
Brainard, n.d. Novel.

Doctors   Madness   Med. Profession

This novel appears in a Bowdlerized form because its
publishers would not accept the heroine's having an
illegitimate child. The plot is incredibly complex.
Clara Mowbray is married secretly, supposedly to
Francis Tyrrel, but in actuality to his evil half-
brother, the Earl, who may not be the Earl but a
bastard, who wants Clara because he gets an estate if
he marries a woman named Mowbray. That's the state
of affairs as the novel opens! The plot follows
Clara's descent into madness and then death caused by
the efforts of her brother to force her back to the
Earl in order to get money for his gambling. The novel
contains the busybody, hypocritical Dr. Quackleben
whose one concern is patients, regardless of how they
are obtained or held.

Scott, Sir Walter. The Surgeon's Daughter. From Works, Vol. 8.
Boston: Brainard, n.d. Novella.

Disease & Health   Doctors   Med. Instit.

Dr. Gray is based on Scott's own physician. Chapter I
describes the hard life of a small town Scottish physician. The surgeon assists at the birth of an illegitimate child and, when the mother is arrested for treason,
agrees to raise the child, who becomes his apprentice
along with a virtuous village youth, Adam Hartley.
Both love Gray's daughter, but Adam gives her (and a
practice with her father) up because she loves Richard.
However, Richard is ambitious, leaves her for India,
is tricked by a recruiter, and ends up in a Navy
hospital of great horror from which he is rescued by
Adam. The rest of the plot is absurd melodrama.

Scott, Sir Walter. The Talisman. New York: E. P. Dutton, 1972.
Novel.

Doctors   Med. Profession

Only one section of this novel might be of interest.
King Richard falls ill and is cured by a mysterious
Saracen physician who uses a talisman. The mSp is
Saladin, the great Saracen leader who is magnanimously
healing his opponent. Interest would lie in the debates
in the Christian camp about allowing Richard to be
treated by an enemy physician. How much is a physician
bound by his profession and his oaths?

Shelley, Mary. Frankenstein. New York: Airmont, 1963. Novel.

The Body   Body/Mind   The Family
Grief   Sci Fi   Suffering

Byron, Shelley, Mary Shelley, and Byron's personal
physician-friend, each agreed to write a ghost story.
Only two were completed: Dr. Polidori's and Mary
Shelley's. The heart of the book is not the conquest
of death, but men's need for other men, and the effect
of the body on a being's ability to get the society
he requires. The monster is created innocent and
loving, but is warped because he is denied love and
affection--even by his creator, the noble chemist,
Frankenstein. So, he takes revenge--killing all of
those whom Frankenstein loves. It is really Frankenstein, not his creation, that is innately monstrous.

Shelley, Mary. The Last Man, ed. H. J. Luke, Jr. Lincoln,
Nebraska: University of Nebraska Press, 1965. Novel.

Death   Grief   Plague

The first two books are wish-fulfillment. In Book III,
the plague comes. The Book is a sort of exorcism of
her grief for Shelley. The remnants of the English
people slowly journey back toward the warm heart of
civilization in Greece (odd, since plague is worst in
hot weather). They are harassed by religious fanatics
and their own fears. As they lose civilization, they
lose art. The musicians die; reading becomes difficult
because there are few books that did not arouse pain by
comparison with former times. The narrator, Verney,
loses his last friends (and fellow humans) in an ill-
advised attempt to reach Greece by boat. Looking at
art provides no consolation; only writing (as Mary
Shelley was doing) helps to alleviate grief.

Shelley, Percy Bysshe. Adonais. Available in Selected Poetry, ed.
Neville Rogers. Boston: Houghton Mifflin, 1968. Poem:
495 lines.

Death   Grief   Suicide

One of the most powerful elegies in the English language.
Written on the death of John Keats, the poem conveys
first despair, then exultant understanding of the relationship between the dead and the living, which then becomes
too favorable to the dead, leading toward thoughts of
suicide. The poem begins in despair--despair that
Keats' poetry masked his dying ("all the fading melodies,/
With which, like flowers that mock the corse beneath,/He
had adorned and hid the coming bulk of death"), despair
that Keats' poetry is also dead ("Death feeds on his
mute voice, and laughs at our despair"), and that Keats'
body lies prey to corruption ("Within the twilight
chamber spreads apace/The shadow of white Death, and at
the door/Invisible Corruption waits"). Even the mourner's
grief which re-creates him is dying ("Alas! that all we
loved of him should be,/But for our grief, as if it had
not been,/And grief itself be mortal!"). There is a
procession of poets, and then Shelley attacks the harsh
reviewer of Endymion, whose savage criticism supposedly
hastened Keats' death from consumption. But in contrasting the earth-bound spirit of the reviewer with Keats'
soaring, eternal spirit, Shelley's angry grief leads
him to consolation: "Peace, peace! he is not dead, he
doth not sleep--/He hath awakened from the dream of
life--/'Tis we, who lost in stormy visions, keep/With
phantoms an unprofitable strife." We decay; he lives in
the beauty beyond death, beauty which he has helped to
create: "He is a portion of the loveliness/Which once
he made more lovely . . . . And death is a low mist
which cannot blot/The brightness it may veil. When lofty
thought/Lifts a young heart above its mortal lair,/And
love and life contend in it, for what/Shall be its
earthly doom,/the dead live there/And move like winds of
light on dark and stormy air." But, unlike Lycidas, in
which the eternal poet becomes an inspiration for life,
Adonais becomes a fearful rationalization for suicide.
Death is too beautiful. "Why linger, why turn back, why
shrink, my Heart? . . . A light is passed from the
revolving year,/And man, and woman; and what still is
dear/Attracts to crush, repels to make thee wither . . . .
I am borne darkly, fearfully, afar;/Whilst, burning
through the inmost veil of Heaven,/The soul of Adonais,
like a star,/Beacons from the abode where the Eternal
are."

Shelley, Percy Bysshe. The Cenci. Available in Selected Poetry,
ed. Neville Rogers. Boston: Houghton Mifflin, 1968. Poetic
Drama.

The Family   Madness   Sexuality
Sexual Roles   Suffering

A world dominated by a mad father--represented both by
the mad, torturing Cenci and the greedy, fearful Pope
who supports him. Count Cenci is mad: "I love/The
sight of agony . . . . And I have no remorse and little
fear,/Which are, I think the checks of other men./This
mood has grown upon me . . . . I rarely kill the body,
which preserves,/Like a strong prison, the soul within
my power." He celebrates the death of two of his sons
with a wild feast. When the feasters learn the true
cause of his joy, they turn away from him in disgust--
but they also turn away from the impassioned appeal of
his daughter, Beatrice, that they will save her and her
stepmother from the mad tyrant. The Cenci, backed by
the Pope, is still too powerful. The remaining Cenci
children, all suffering under subtle tortures, are urged
to violence by their false friend, Orsino, who is
passionately in love with Beatrice and desires the
father dead so that he can pursue his dubious plans to
marry her, although he's a priest. He sees some of the
difficulties within this mentally tortured family:
"'tis a trick of this same family/To analyse their own
and other minds./Such self-anatomy shall teach the will/
Dangerous secrets." Count Cenci rapes Beatrice, who goes
temporarily mad, refusing to speak openly of her injury
but refusing to come again to her father, who speaks
with relish of what he shall make her: "She shall become
(for what she most abhors/Shall have a fascination to
entrap/Her loathing will) to her own conscious self/All
she appears to others . . . . Body and soul a monstrous
lump of ruin." When she refuses to co-operate, he

curses her with a father's curse. Several ineffectual attempts by assassins hired by his family fail to kill the father, but two, inspired by money and the daughter, murder him in his sleep. The daughter then becomes the strength of the rest of the family, but she cannot prevent them from confessing under physical torture. Their mental torture by the father is of no account. The Pope, who considers himself a father, fears a rash of patricides and so condemns wife, daughter and son to death along with the assassins. Both British and American Romantics were fascinated by the ambiguous sexuality of Beatrice: "I,/Though wrapped in a strange cloud of crime and shame,/Lived ever holy and unstained."

Shelley, Percy Bysshe. "Death" and "Sonnet." Available in The Poetical Works of Shelley, ed. N. F. Ford. Boston: Houghton Mifflin Co., 1975. Poems: 15 lines and Sonnet.

Death

Shelley wrote several short poems on death, having a rather ambivalent attitude towards it. "Death" opens with a horrendous couplet ("Death is here, and death is there,/Death is busy everywhere.") but closes with a rather cynical acceptance of mortality. "All things that we love and cherish,/Like ourselves, must fade and perish;/Such is our rude mortal lot--Love itself would, did they not." However, the sonnet beginning "Ye hasten to the grave! What see ye there" moves from the general mortality of things to individual mortality and gains in power. There is an uneasy questioning, that only appears to be chiding, of a brilliant, self-destructive man. "O thou quick heart . . . . Thou vainly curious mind . . . . Oh, whither hasten yet, that thus ye press/With such swift feet life's green and pleasant path,/Seeking alike from happiness and woe/A refuge in the cavern of gray death?/O heart, and mind, and thoughts! What thing do you/Hope to inherit in the grave below."

Shelley, Percy Bysshe. "The Indian Serenade." Available in The Poetical Works of Shelley, ed. N. F. Ford. Boston: Houghton Mifflin Co., 1975. Poem: 24 lines.

Sexuality   Sexual Roles

A curious reversal of sexual roles. In a "conventional" opening, the poet awakens from dreams of his lady and is led, "who knows how," to his lady's window only to be overcome by the richness of dying nature: "The wandering airs, they faint . . . The champak odors fail." He calls upon his lady to lift and hold him while he dies (a definite revival of the Elizabethan union of death and intercourse): "Oh, lift me from the grass!/I die! I faint! I fail!/Let thy love in kisses rain/On my lips and eyelids pale . . . . Oh! press it [his heart] close to thine again,/Where it will break at last."

Shelley, Percy Bysshe. "The Magnetic Lady to her Patient." Available in The Poetical Works of Shelley, ed. N. F. Ford. Boston: Houghton Mifflin Co., 1975. Poem: 45 lines.

Disease & Health   Women as Healers

Periodically Shelley would be brought near death by a fit of "paroxysms"; a friend's wife tried mesmerism ("magnetism"), then a fashionable cure. It was partially successful, but worked only when Mrs. Williams (the subject of several love poems) was the mesmerist. In this poem, Shelley writes as though such a cure is due to the lady's suppressed love for her patient whom she cures of depression. The cure is almost a rape: "My soul weeps healing rain . . . Its odor calms thy brain!/Its light within thy gloomy breast/Spreads like a second youth again./By mine thy being is to its deep/Possessed./'The spell is done.'" And yet she cannot heal his waking suffering, for the patient claims such a cure would kill him.

Shelley, Percy Bysshe. Prometheus Unbound, especially Acts I & II. Available in Selected Poems, ed. Neville Rogers. Boston: Houghton Mifflin, 1968. Poetic Drama.

Death   Disease & Health   Suffering

In Act I, we find the great suffering of Prometheus, giver of knowledge to men, whose pains are increased by visions of torments both inflicted by, and suffered by, man. Human suffering is Jupiter's revenge upon Prometheus. Jupiter had inflicted famine, toil, disease, and death upon mankind. In defiance of Jupiter, Prometheus aided mankind with Science, described in this stirring passage from Act II, Scene IV, one of the rare celebrations of Science in Poetry. Prometheus eases death with drugs ("And waked the legioned hopes/Which sleep within folded Elysian flowers,/Nepenthe, Moly, Amaranth, fadeless blooms,/That they might hide with thin and rainbow wings/The shape of Death"). He sends Love "to bind/The disunited tendrils of that vine/Which bears the wine of life, the human heart," and "the tamed fire" and speech. "And speech created thought,/Which is the measure of the universe;/And Science struck the thrones of earth and heaven,/Which shook, but fell not; and the harmonious mind/Poured itself forth in all-prophetic song . . . And human hands first mimicked and then mocked,/With moulded limbs more lovely than its own,/The human form, till marble grew divine . . . . He told the hidden power of herbs and springs,/And Disease drank and slept. Death grew like sleep." This passage is incredibly beautiful in its synergism of love, words, science, music, sculpture and medicine. All of the arts spring from one creative source that is learning

and love combined. However, Jupiter, the political tyrant, is able to poison this source and so cause great misery until his destined hour arrives and he falls, bringing about a golden age of freedom, love and creativity. Death remains, still a mystery to the immortals, but it becomes "the veil which those who live call life!/ They sleep and it is lifted." The poem is incredibly rich and dense, with many themes--and many useful passages on knowledge, human nature, and death.

Shelley, Percy Bysshe. "To Mary" ("My dearest Mary, wherefore hast thou gone"). Available in The Poetical Works of Shelley, ed. N. F. Ford. Boston: Houghton Mifflin Co., 1975. Poem: 7 lines.

Grief

After the death of their son, Mary Shelley fell into a deep depression. This powerful, compact poem illustrates Shelley's perception of the nature of her illness-and helplessness. "Thy form is here indeed--a lovely one--/ But thou art fled, gone down the dreary road,/That leads to Sorrow's most obscure abode;/Thou sittest on the hearth of pale despair, where/For thine own sake I cannot follow thee."

Shelley, Percy Bysshe. "To William Shelley." Available in The Poetical Works of Shelley, ed. N. F. Ford. Boston: Houghton Mifflin Co., 1975. Poem: 18 lines.

Death   Grief

Shelley was spared a depression like his wife's on the death of their son, William. He could write about it: "if a thing divine/Like thee can die, thy funeral shrine/ Is thy mother's grief and mine . . . . Let me think thy spirit feeds,/With its life intense and mild,/The love of living leaves and weeds/Among these tombs and ruins wild."

Sholom Aleichem (Solomon Rabinowitch). "The Flag." Available in Sholom Aleichem: Old Country Tales. New York: Paperback Library, 1969. Short Story.

Children   Disease & Health   Suffering

Famous now for his Fiddler on the Roof stories, Sholom Aleichem also has a great deal to offer those looking for believable literary portraits of children. In the tradition of the oral storyteller, he lets us hear the voice of the children. He treats them with honesty, respect, and compassion (cf. Frank O'Connor). This tale is told by a man looking back on his poverty-stricken children to an incident concerning the very special flag he is able to bring to the synagogue on Simkhas Torah. All his hope goes into that flag; so when a bully burns the boy's flag, the reader shares his sorrow. Afterwards the boy goes into an anguish which makes him feverish and delirious for days. But the older narrator skips quickly over this part of the story and even invents a fantasy happy ending ("For the most part, Jewish stories have sad endings," trans. Curt Leviant) to spare his audience. He has a proud spirit.

Sholom Aleichem (Solomon Rabinowitch). "The Lottery Ticket." Available in Collected Stories of Sholom Aleichem, Vol. 1, trans. Julius and Frances Butwin. New York: Crown, 1946. Short Story.

Children   Grief   Med. Instit.

The son is determined to be a doctor, so he runs away to one town with his preparatory school. All goes well at first. He writes happily, and the father responds with little warnings not to forget he's a Jew. Then the letters become troubled; Jews are discriminated against, failed in examinations. Then the letters stop. Finally the father learns that, in his drive to get medical training, his son has renounced his faith. A friend stops by to comfort the family: "But what was there to say? When a family is mourning because a person has died, you can come to sit with them for a while, and say, 'The Lord giveth and the Lord taketh away' . . . Or other such sayings that cannot make one especially happy, but are still a comfort . . . . But what can one say at a time like this, when it is a living person they are mourning for?"

Sholom Aleichem (Solomon Rabinowitch). "You Mustn't Weep-It's Yom-Tev." Available in Collected Stories of Sholom Aleichem, Vol 1, trans. Julius and Frances Butwin. New York: Crown, 1946. Short Story.

Children   Death   Disease & Health
Grief   Suffering

Death of the Cantor as seen by his young, uncomprehending son. Not only is the son baffled by death, he cannot understand the sufferings caused by the illness: the sale of household goods, his exile to another home, and why his father's so weak. His mother tries to hide her efforts from the dying man, her sons, and the neighborhood. When his father is dead, concealment impossible, and his mother can cry, the boy catches the grief from her and joins with his brothers in trying to silence her: "Mother! Today is yom-tev. It's Shevuous, mother! You mustn't weep!"

Southey, Robert. The Doctor, ed. J. W. Warter. London: Longman, Green & Co., 1865. Treatise.

Age   Doctors   Evil Doctors
Med. Ethics   Med. Profession

This was to be Southey's <u>Anatomy of Melancholy</u> or <u>Religio Medici</u>. It is a rambling, digressive work covering all sorts of topics. Chapter CXIX opens with a discussion of why doctors are now like parish priests and then moves on to discuss why doctors are now held to be irreligious. Chapter CXX discusses the effect of medical studies on different dispositions and superstitious notions attached to the profession. It also includes a history of Jewish physicians and men's attitude toward them. Chapter CXXI describes a variety of evil doctors. Chapter CXXII gives a "history" of the difficulties of getting subjects for dissection and experimentation. Chapter CXXXIII criticizes elegies extravagantly lamenting the deaths of old men. Old age is horrible (contrasts with his poem "You are Old, Father William"). However, society needs old people who have developed "those moral qualities which belong particularly to the latter stage of life; nor could the wholesome influence which age exercises over the young in every country where manners are not so thoroughly corrupted as to threaten the dissolution of society, be in any other manner supplied."

Stevenson, Robert Louis. "As with heaped bees at hiving time." Available in <u>Collected Poems</u>, ed. J. A. Smith. London: Rupert Hart-Davis, 1950. Poem: 12 lines.

Death

Those looking for some reflection of Stevenson's long battle with consumption will find it, not so much in his novels or essays, but in his poetry. There are several greeting death or urging maximum use of a short life, but this is one of the best in its dreamy acceptance of the inevitable death, which he knows pursues him; and yet he still turns to life until his end. "So swarmed my senses once . . . Now only the vast shapes I hear/Hear--and my hearing slowly fills--/Rivers and winds among the twisting hills,/And hearken--and my face is lit--/Life facing; death pursuing it."

Stevenson, Robert Louis. "The Body-Snatcher." Available in <u>The Complete Short Stories of Robert Louis Stevenson</u>, ed. Charles Neider. Garden City, New York: Doubleday, 1969. Short Story.

Med. Ethics   Med. Instit.

Although the story shades off into a supernatural ending, the main emphasis lies upon medical ethics among medical students. Fettes, a medical student at Edinburgh, gains the place of sub-assistant to a popular professor. Fettes is in charge of preparing subjects for dissection and so comes in contact with the body-snatchers, who supposedly dig up new corpses to sell to the medical schools. He notes that several of the bodies seem too fresh to have been buried and carries his suspicions to Dr. Macfarlane, his immediate superior, who tells him that most of their subjects were murdered by the snatchers and that Fettes was chosen as assistant because he could hold his tongue. Then, Macfarlane murders a blackmailer and involves Fettes in disposing of the body by dissection. Fettes' desire for the position of class assistant has ultimately destroyed his moral sense. The story has a deliciously ghoulish ending.

Stevenson, Robert Louis. "Father Damien." From <u>Lay Morals</u>. New York: Charles Scribner's, 1923. Essay.

Disease & Health   Med. Instit.

Written in response to a letter accusing Damien of being coarse, disobedient, lascivious and bringing his death by leprosy upon himself. Stevenson does not defend him as a saint, but defends many of his faults by the fact that he voluntarily incarcerated himself in a "hospital" (the island leper colony) of rotting bodies. The fact that he did so without orders is only more to his credit. It is a moving defense.

Stevenson, Robert Louis. <u>The Master of Ballantrae</u>. New York: Current Literature Publishing Co., 1909. Novel.

The Family   Madness

Classic story of sibling rivalry. An elder brother, his father's favorite, is believed killed while fighting for Prince Charlie. His younger brother marries the elder's fiancée to obtain money needed to keep up the estate, even though she still idolizes her supposedly dead lover. Then the elder, disinherited for treason, returns, having first bled the estate dry of money; he makes love to his ex-fiancée, is challenged by his brother, and nearly killed in a duel. Their father suffers a fatal stroke, and the younger brother suffers a minor stroke which affects his behavior, turning his hatred for his brother into a monomania. He believes, since his brother has twice returned from "death," that his brother is truly a devil. The story has a magnificent climax. When the elder is reported dead a third time, the younger madly insists upon visiting the grave--which is being frantically opened by the elder's Indian servant. The "deceased" has gone into a trance to escape murderers; he opens his eyes--and dies along with his insane brother.

Stevenson, Robert Louis. "Requiem." Available in <u>Collected Poems</u>, ed. J. A. Smith. London: Rupert Hart-Davis, 1950. Poem: 8 lines.

Death

That beautiful acceptance of death: "Glad did I live and gladly die,/And I laid me down with a will . . . . Here he lies where he longed to be;/Home is the sailor, home from sea/And the hunter home from the hill."

Stevenson, Robert. "The Sick Child." In <u>Underwoods</u>; and "The Land of Counterpane." In <u>A Child's Garden of Verses</u>. Both available in <u>Collected Poems</u>, ed. J. A. Smith. London: Rupert Hart-Davis, 1950. Poems: 20 & 16 lines.

Children   Disease & Health

Both deal with sick children. Both even involve distortion of size. But there is a difference in perspective. The second poem has the light beauty of all the poems in <u>A Child's Garden</u>: "When I was sick and lay a-bed,/I had two pillows at my head . . . . I was the giant great and still/That sits upon the pillow-hill,/And sees before him, dale and plain,/The pleasant land of counterpane." The first poem alternates in point of view between a mother trying to use the calm beauty found in <u>A Child's Garden</u> and the child's terrified distorted vision (by fever? death?): "Why is the room so gaunt and great?/Why am I lying awake so late?/Fear not at all: the night is still./Nothing is here that means you ill--/Nothing but lamps the whole town through./ And never a child awake but you . . . . Some of the things are so great and near,/Some are so small and far away,/I have a fear I cannot say . . . . An hour or two more, and God is so kind,/The day shall be blue in the window-blind,/Then shall my child go sweetly asleep,/And dream of the birds and the hills of sheep."

Stevenson, Robert Louis. <u>Strange Case of Dr. Jekyll and Mr. Hyde</u>. Available in <u>The Complete Short Stories of Robert Louis Stevenson</u>, ed. Charles Neider. Garden City, New York: Doubleday, 1969. Novella.

Doctors   Drugs   Evil Doctors
Med. Profession

Although this story is cited as a classic case of an evil doctor, the citation is false. The story is much more complex. Dr. Jekyll is running away from himself and his profession; he is a discontented, old doctor and doesn't like it. He uses drugs as a means of escape, anticipating later research upon, not drugs and mood, but drugs and personality or identity. But Hyde not only escapes the weakness of age (Hyde is strong and clever), he also escapes professional restraints (<u>Mr. Hyde</u>); and this causes trouble. The doctor's alter ego enjoys inflicting pain. Dr. Jekyll speaks of freedom to experience pleasure, but what the reader sees is freedom to inflict agony and death. There is no better cautionary tale against a too rigid separation of profession and person.

Stevenson, Robert Louis. "The Suicide Club." From <u>New Arabian Nights</u>. Available in <u>The Complete Short Stories of Robert Louis Stevenson</u>, ed. Charles Neider. Garden City, New York: Doubleday, 1969. Short Story.

Suicide

Flamboyant tale of a club designed for fearful suicides and jaded roués in search of excitement. A deal of cards selects the victim-suicide and his killer from the members, with the profits from the deceased going to the spider-like President of the Club. Interesting for the atmosphere of maniacal self-contempt in the Club members.

Stowe, Harriet Beecher. <u>Uncle Tom's Cabin</u>, ed. K. S. Lynn. Cambridge, Mass.: Belknap Press, 1962. Novel.

Children   Death   Disease & Health
Dying   The Family   Grief
Suffering   Suicide

Children and the family are the two keys to this novel. Stowe was writing propaganda and she endeavored to show horrors that would strike home to her readers without arousing fear. She hammers relentlessly at the separation of families by the slave trade. Eliza makes her heroic escape to remain with her son; George is ready to kill (he actually only injures) to keep his family together (<u>not</u> in resentment or revenge). The mother on the steamboat commits suicide rather than be separated from her child. Children are also more sensitive than adults: George Shelby and Eva St. Clair are very aware of the suffering and endeavor to do something about it. However, Eva is <u>too</u> sensitive: it is implied that the death by flogging of a woman (slave) she knew and other cases of suffering among the slaves hasten her death from consumption. However, training influences even children. Young Alfred St. Clair is cruel without understanding that he is cruel, and Topsy, who has no parents (she just "grow'd") is malicious and resentful because she has had no training and no love. It is not until softened by Eva, trained by Miss Ophelia, and then lovingly touched by Miss Ophelia (who has had to overcome her repugnance to black skin) that she can express love herself. Both Eva and Uncle Tom have long and didactic deaths; both are unafraid to die because death is a gateway for them.

Grief and suffering pervade the novel. There is constant
grief from separation and death. Suffering is worst
on the plantation of Simon Legree, where all alleviating
measures--hope, song, religion, community--have been
ruthlessly suppressed by the sadistic Legree.

Strindberg, August. The Father. Available in A Treasury of the
Theatre, ed. John Gassner. New York: Holt, Rinehart and
Winston, 1961. Drama.

Children	Doctors	The Family
Madness	Sexuality	Sexual Roles
V.D.		

Representative Strindberg: scheming women, obsessive
behavior, the battle of the sexes. All these themes can
be seen in his other plays too, and in his autobiographical novels and the collection of bitter short stories
called Married (also published as Getting Married. New
York: Viking, 1972). In The Father the battle rages
because the Captain feels that the women of his household have usurped his rights as a father by dictating
to him how his daughter Bertha, whom he wishes to send
away to boarding school, shall be educated. He asserts
his legal rights, saying that the mother has none at
all: "She has sold her birthright by a legal trans-
action, and forfeited her rights in return for the man's
responsibility of caring for her and her children"
(trans. Edith and Warner Oland). His wife Laura fights
back by planting the suspicion in his mind that Bertha
is not his child. The sexual jealousy this suggestion
produces leads to some aberrant behavior which Laura is
quick to capitalize on. She leads their new boarder,
a doctor, to believe the Captain insane. And she schemes
against him through her daughter as well. In the last
act Laura uses the law for her own ends by having her
husband committed, with, of course, the doctor's help.
Trapped in his strait jacket, the Captain delivers this
tirade, unmistakably Strindberg's own feelings: "I
believe that you are all my enemies! My mother was my
enemy when she did not want to bring me into the world
because I was to be born with pain, and she robbed my
embryonic life of its nourishment, and made a weakling
of me. My sister was my enemy when she taught me that
I must be submissive to her. The first woman I embraced
was my enemy, for she gave me ten years of illness in
return for the love I gave her. My daughter became my
enemy when she had to choose between me and you. And
you, my wife, you have been my arch enemy, because you
never let up on me till I lay here lifeless."

Swinburne, Algernon Charles. "A Child's Laughter." Available in
Swinburne: Poems, ed. Bonamy Dobrée. Harmondsworth, England:
Penguin, 1961. Poem: 30 lines.

Children

A major, often cynical, poet here directs his beautiful
lines to the service of a subject which almost inevitably
turns sentimental on him. The rhyme scheme of each
stanza (aaaabccccb) contributes to the song-like quality
of the poem as a whole. The first stanza offers unashamed
alliteration and simple repetition as well: "All the
bells of heaven may ring,/All the birds of heaven may
sing,/All the wells on earth may spring,/All the winds
on earth may bring/All sweet sounds together." Interesting insofar as Swinburne, who had a better ear than
most of us, found a child's laughter the sweetest of all
sounds.

Swinburne, Algernon Charles. "The Garden of Proserpine." Available
in Swinburne: Poems, ed. Bonamy Dobrée. Harmondsworth, England:
Penguin, 1961. Poem: 96 lines.

Death	Sexuality	Suicide

A hymn to the pale, cold restfulness of death, as personified in the Queen of Hades. The poet imagines himself in
her "garden," which has neither blooms nor colors, but
"Pale beds of blowing rushes" and arbors of green grapes,
from which she makes the deadly wine which calls men to
the underground. Everyone must come eventually to the
cold immortal queen. Nor must this be feared, for death
is a sexual embrace. What's more, "Her languid lips are
sweeter/Than love's." Some men may sigh and weep for the
passing of flowers and spring and love, but the poet here
finds the thought of death restful: "From too much love
of living,/From hope and fear set free,/We thank with
brief thanksgiving/Whatever gods may be/That no life lives
forever;/That dead men rise up never;/That even the
weariest river/Winds somewhere safe to sea." A sensuous
death wish.

Swinburne, Algernon Charles. "Hermaphroditus." Available in
Swinburne: Poems, ed. Bonamy Dobrée. Harmondsworth, England:
Penguin, 1961. Poem: 56 lines.

Homosexuality   Sexuality

Though psychiatrists have rightly seen in Swinburne a
kinky, even sadistic, sexuality (see, e.g., "Delores"
and "Anactoria"), this representative poem stresses rather
a great sensual beauty, simultaneously arousing and frustrating to the poet. To be sure, he has chosen for his
subject the mythical androgynous figure of Hermaphroditus,
and thereby deliberately confused his sexual responses.
In the first section, the poet looks upon the fair youth,
sees his/her weariness, and entreats him/her to choose
the male or the female lover, both hungering about
Hermaphroditus' breasts. The would-be lover of the
androgynous figure is both attracted and frustrated,

for he can never be fully satisfied. Despair in itself
leads to arousal (which statement might interest psychiatrists). In the next two sections, the poet contemplates
a kind of masturbatory sex, wherein the male and female
halves of Hermaphroditus unite in sterility (contrast
Virginia Woolf's A Room of One's Own). There are everywhere lines sensual in both content and sound: "Sex to
sweet sex with lips and limbs is wed"; "To what strange
end hath some strange god . . ./Hid love in all the folds
of all thy hair." In the last section, Swinburne answers
his own question, recalling the incident from legend
when at the waters of Salmacis a young woman melted into
a young man.

Tennyson, Alfred. "Crossing the Bar." Available in The Poems and
Plays of Alfred Lord Tennyson. New York: Modern Library,
1938. Poem: 16 lines.

Death   Dying

Tennyson asked that this poem of peaceful death and
confidence in an after-life be placed at the end of
editions of his poetry. "Sunset and evening star,/
And one clear call for me!/And may there be no
moaning of the bar,/When I put out to sea,/But such
a tide as moving seems asleep,/Too full for sound and
foam,/When that which drew from out the boundless
deep/Turns again home . . . . And may there be no
sadness of farewell,/When I embark; . . . I hope to
see my Pilot face to face/When I have crost the bar."

Tennyson, Alfred. "Fatima." Available in The Poems and Plays of
Alfred Lord Tennyson. New York: Modern Library, 1938.
Poem: 42 lines.

Sexuality

Beautiful condemnation of passion. Fatima, waiting for
her lover, is parched and withered, whirling, with a dry
brain, a desert waiting for her lover's showers and his
sweet gales. But, the Elizabethan pun on death and
intercourse becomes a bitter reality, when she looks for
death in his arms and, by extrapolation, her desert
overcomes his spring. She keeps inverting roles to
become the ravisher: "My whole soul waiting silently,/
All naked in a sultry sky,/Droops blinded with his
shining eye:/I will possess him or will die./I will grow
round him in his place,/Grow, live, die looking on his
face,/Die, dying clasp'd in his embrace."

Tennyson, Alfred. "'Frater Ave Atque Vale'" and "Prefatory Poem
to My Brother's Sonnets." Available in The Poems and Plays
of Alfred Lord Tennyson. New York: Modern Library, 1938.
Poems: 9 and 16 lines.

Grief

Both poems were written shortly after his brother's death.
The second is more explicit and more conventional in
consolation: "And, now to these unsummer'd skies/The
summer bird is still,/Far off a phantom cuckoo cries/
From out a phantom hill . . . When all my griefs were
shared with thee,/As all my hopes were thine--/As all
thou wert was one with me,/May all thou art be mine!"
The first is subtler and more tender. Wandering through
the summer-lit olive groves of Sirmione, the poet
remembers that "There beneath the Roman ruin . . . Came
that 'Ave atque vale' of the Poet's hopeless woe,/
Tenderest of Roman poets nineteen-hundred years ago,/
'Frater Ave atque Vale' [Brother Hail and Farewell]--
as we wander'd to and fro . . . Sweet Catullus's all-
but-island, olive-silvery Sirmio!"

Tennyson, Alfred. "The Grandmother." Available in The Poems and
Plays of Alfred Lord Tennyson. New York: Modern Library,
1938. Poem: 108 lines.

Age   Death

Age changing the ability to grieve. Her eldest son recently
dead, the calm grandmother tries to explain to her granddaughter why she does not grieve. The explanation becomes
tangled with several generations of deaths and the grandmother's fatigued approach to her own death.

Tennyson, Alfred. In Memoriam A.H.H. Available in The Poems and
Plays of Alfred Lord Tennyson. New York: Modern Library,
1938. 130 Poems.

The Body	Children	Death
Grief	Suffering	

One of the greatest poems on grief, In Memoriam was
written after the death of Tennyson's friend, Arthur
Hallam. The work follows the process of grief from the
news of the death to the sense of joyous acceptance at
the end. The poem begins with emphasis upon the dead
body of his friend, the loss of his physical presence.
Then it moves to an abstract consideration of death, in
which is found this lovely description of a growing
child: "But as he grows he gathers much,/And learns
the use of 'I,' and 'me,'/And finds 'I am not what I see/
And other than the things I touch.'/So rounds he to a
separate mind" (XLIV). He begins to accept the presence
of the dead, of a larger union. He calls to his friend
"Be near me when my light is low,/When the blood creeps,
and the nerves prick/And tingle; and the heart is sick,/
And all the wheels of being slow" (XLIX). But then
doubts assail him. Nature and God are at odds; Nature
is "red in tooth and claw" (LV). This doubt is never
answered, only silenced. In the center of the poem,

the poet dreams, and the visions confirm that life continues; he sees his friend as alive. In other dreams,
he sees odd symbolic people he cannot always perceive
or understand. It is as though the subconscious is now
working on the grief. His memories of their past together begin to fade. Yet he is still able to say
"'Tis better to have loved and lost,/Than never to have
loved at all" (LXXXIV). His grief begins to bear poetic
fruit: "in the midmost heart of grief/Thy passion
clasps a secret joy" (LXXXVII). He begins to profit
from his forgetfulness of the body, for the spirit,
which can come to him, becomes more important (XCII).
Now, concentrating on the place where they talked--
but upon the spirit rather than the body--he experiences
a mystic union with his friend. "His living soul was
flash'd on mine,/And mine in his was wound" (XCIV). No
longer is there a separation between the living poet
and the dead friend. Instead of imploring his friend's
spirit to come to him, his love is able to send him to
his friend. With this knowledge he is able to return
to the world with renewed vision and strength. "The
hills are shadows, and they flow/From form to form, and
nothing stands;/They melt like mist, the solid lands,/
Like clouds they shape themselves and go./But in my
spirit will I dwell,/And dream my dream, and hold it
true;/For though my lips may breathe adieu,/I cannot
think the thing farewell."

Tennyson, Alfred. "In the Children's Hospital." Available in The
Poems and Plays of Alfred Lord Tennyson. New York: Modern
Library, 1938. Poem: 72 lines.

Children	Death	Doctors
Euthanasia	Nurses	Suffering
Surgery		

A little poem full of conventional material. A nurse
watches the new surgeon with trepidation, feeling he is
"happier using the knife than in trying to save the
limb." He tells the nurse that one child, mangled in
a mill, would "need little more of your care." She
replies that she will need to pray the more, but he
attacks her: "can prayer set a broken bone?" The
surgeon moves on to Emmie's bed and says "Poor little
dear,/Nurse, I must do it to-morrow; she'll never live
thro' it, I fear." The child overhears and successfully
prays to die before the operation. The nurse is joyed:
"Say that His day is done! Ah why should we care what
they say?/The Lord of the children had heard her, and
Emmie had past away."

Tennyson, Alfred. "The Lady of Shalott." Available in The Poems
and Plays of Alfred Lord Tennyson. New York: Modern Library,
1938. Poem: 171 lines.

| Death | Dying | Sexuality |

On the surface, a beautiful poem about a medieval lady
fated to live forever outside Camelot on her own isolated island. She may not even look directly upon the
city, having instead a mirror in which to see its
reflections (of commerce, love, death), and knowing that
if she looks away from the mirror, she is cursed. At
first she is happy in this state, but then, immediately
after she spies in her mirror two newly wedded lovers,
she declares, "'I am half sick of shadows.'" Now the
poem takes on its full psychiatric meaning. Cut off
from reality, particularly sexual reality, and dealing
only in appearances, the Lady of Shalott lives a half
life. The trouble is, she has not learned to cope with
full life, and so when Lancelot comes riding by in all
his masculine beauty, she looks at him directly--and
knows that death is at hand. She dies: the poetry
continues beautiful, but the implications, and indeed
some of the language, are now horrifying. The chaste
Lady of Shalott places herself in a boat to journey
down the river to oblivion. "They heard her singing
her last song,/The Lady of Shalott./Heard a carol,
mournful, holy/Chanted loudly, chanted lowly,/Till her
blood was frozen slowly,/And her eyes were darken'd
wholly."

Tennyson, Alfred. "Lancelot and Elaine." In Idylls of the King.
Available in The Poems and Plays of Alfred Lord Tennyson.
New York: Modern Library, 1938. Poem: ca. 1400 lines.

| Sexuality | Women as Healers |

Lancelot wears Elaine's favor to the tourney, partly to
disguise himself and partly to disguise his affair with
Guinevere. He is trying to win the final diamond of a
necklace made from a dead king's crown. He does win,
at great cost to himself; but Guinevere, jealous of
Elaine, throws the trophy in the river. The loss of a
sacred national symbol for petty jealousy is matched by
the loss of Elaine (and the loss of many knights). She
nurses Lancelot back to health. She is almost semi-
sacred in her mission as healer. However, the "semi"
is appropriate. While Lancelot is ill, he vows to
reform; but as soon as she cures him, he loses his moral
resolve and heads back to Guinevere. Elaine dies, and
sends her corpse down river to Lancelot with a note
reproaching him for discourtesy in leaving her without
saying farewell. Passion as bright-colored, noble, and
destructive.

Tennyson, Alfred. "Locksley Hall" and "Locksley Hall Sixty Years
After." Available in The Poems and Plays of Alfred Lord
Tennyson. New York: Modern Library, 1938. Long Poems.

| Adolescence | Age | Sexuality |

The first poem depicts the swirling passions of a
rejected lover who has returned to the tombs of his
ancestors in order to find some new purpose for his
life. He tries to recapture his childhood vision of
Man's progress toward a unified, peaceful world; but
vengeful visions of his false love's sufferings with
her brutish husband or masochistic visions of children
reuniting her to her husband interfere with his efforts
to recall the ecstatic growth of man based in ancestral
integrity and leading to a better earth. Finally, he
overhears himself threatening to marry a savage and
brings himself up short. He, a civilized man, cannot
throw away centuries of knowledge and improvement; he
can still regain his inspiration. Therefore, let
Locksley Hall crumble into dust, having served its purpose. However, in the second poem, the speaker returns
to counsel his grandson, the next heir to Locksley.
Age has taken away his golden visions of future--and
past. Human cruelty has existed, exists, and will exist.
Time (and childbed) has taken away his visionary lost
love and the tenderer, more womanly Emily, his wife,
whom he loved more deeply. Only the hope of some after-
life gives hope to the speaker--and meaning to Truth
and Goodness. Science is destroying beauty while the
diseased poor, for lack of space, turn to incest and
for lack of money send their women to the streets.
However, although Science and Progress have failed him,
Love has not. The speaker has long since forgiven and
begged forgiveness of his faithless love's husband.
Love and God are all that he can find to console his
grandson, on the spot where Science and History once
consoled him.

Tennyson, Alfred. "The Lotos-Eaters." Available in The Poems and
Plays of Alfred Lord Tennyson. New York: Modern Library,
1938. Poem: 13 stanzas.

| Death | | |

Starting from the brief description of the drugged
deserters in the Odyssey, Tennyson creates a monologue
by men who have chosen to become ghosts. In separating
themselves from the pains of life, the men have separated from life itself: "What pleasure can we have/To
war with evil?/Is there any peace/In ever climbing up
the climbing wave?/All things have rest, and ripen
toward the grave/In silence; ripen, fall and cease:/
Give us long rest or death, dark death, or dreamful
ease." Although the Lotos-Eaters claim heightened
aesthetic pleasure from nature ("To watch the emerald-
colour'd water falling/Through many a woven acanthus-
wreath divine!"), they, by their belief they are god-
like, unlike others ("careless of mankind"), have
become insensitive to the songs of striving men who
"smile, they find a music centred in a doleful song/
Steaming up, a lamentation and an ancient tale of wrong,/
Like a tale of little meaning though the words are
strong." The drug has merely made them sensitive to
the aesthetics of death rather than the aesthetics of
life.

Tennyson, Alfred. "Maud." Available in The Poems and Plays of
Alfred Lord Tennyson. New York: Modern Library, 1938.
Long Poem.

| Madness | Sexuality |

A longer, much more complex, and more beautiful version
of "Locksley Hall." A young man is disillusioned about
social progress because a millionaire's machinations
force his father to despairing suicide and his mother
to a lingering death. However, he falls into deep,
passionate love with Maud, the millionaire's daughter,
creating lyrics built on the Song of Solomon to praise
their love. However, his passion soon turns to Old
Testament wrath when Maud's brother attacks him. The
lover kills (perhaps) the brother and flees the country,
uncertain as to whether the brother is really dead and
whether Maud still loves him. He finds some consolation
in natural beauty, but the uncertainty and his love
drive him mad; he recovers only upon Britain's declaring
a noble war which once more provides his life with
direction and purpose.

Tennyson, Alfred. "Oenone." Available in The Poems and Plays of
Alfred Lord Tennyson. New York: Modern Library, 1938.
Poem: ca. 260 lines.

| The Body | Sexuality |

Oenone, the nymph abandoned by Paris when he gave the
golden apple to Aphrodite, relives his past professions
of love to her, his fatal choice among the three goddesses,
and the destruction of her beloved woods to build the
ships for the Trojan war. She cannot understand why
Paris is bribed by promises of "the fairest and most
loving wife" in Greece when Paris has her--and yet she
loves him for "his sunny hair/Cluster'd about his
temples like a God's;/And his cheek brighten'd as the
foam-blow brightens/When the wind blows the foam." For
the promise of a fair body, Oenone and all nature are
sacrificed; passion scorches far more than Paris:
"That whereso'er I am by night and day,/All earth and
air seem only burning fire."

Tennyson, Alfred. The Princess: A Medley. Available in The Poems
and Plays of Alfred Lord Tennyson. New York: Modern Library,
1938. Poem: ca. 3100 lines.

| Children | Sexual Roles | Women as Healers |

This poem is a fascinating hodgepodge. Throughout a very
complex discussion of women's rights are inserted some
of the most lyric of Tennyson's songs. The prince seeks

the princess he was betrothed to as a young boy, only to find that she has founded a college for women in which all intruding males are killed. Despite the penalties, the prince and two companions enter; they are amazed at the studies and accomplishments of the women, who are taught to imitate Artemisia, Rhodope, Queen Elizabeth, Joan of Arc, Sappho, etc. Although they take a vow not to marry, they work towards equal sharing of council, hearth, business, science, music, and art. One of the women, Psyche, is sister to one of the men and so hides them, disguised as women. However, Lady Blanche, who is jealous of Psyche's influence on Princess Ida, finds them. The prince tries to woo Ida: "might I dread that you,/With only Fame for spouse and your great deeds/For issue, yet may live in vain, and miss,/Meanwhile, what every woman counts her due,/Love, children, happiness?" She rather drily replies that, although children are nice, they die and great deeds don't. Although the women discourage scientific re- search as probing the "holy secrets of this microcosm," they do study medicine. The disguised men betray them- selves by singing a bawdy tavern song and are captured. Psyche is banished, but must leave her child behind. Then, the college is surrounded by the armies of the prince's father and Ida's father, determined to end this nonsense: "Man is the hunter, woman is his game . . . . We hunt them for the beauty of their skins;/They love us for it." The prince persuades his father to use peaceful means--the prince vs. Ida's brothers in tourney. At this point the story breaks down. Ida offers to worship her brothers if they win. The brothers do win, but Ida totally capitulates, begging to be allowed to nurse the Prince. As he recovers, they plight their troth. The prince has come far. Now he also pledges to work toward equal rights: "Henceforth thou hast a helper, me, that know/The woman's cause is man's; they rise or sink/ Together . . . . let her make herself her own/To give or keep, to live and learn and be/All that not harms dis- tinctive womanhood./For woman is not undeveloped man,/ But diverse." Together, the prince and Princess Ida will learn from each other and form one whole.

Tennyson, Alfred. "Tiresias." Available in The Poems and Plays of Alfred Lord Tennyson. New York: Modern Library, 1938. Poem: ca. 210 lines.

Death   Grief   Handicaps
Suicide

A complex double poem. At first Tiresias is the speaker, recalling his search for knowledge, his blinding by Athena caught at her bath, his doom to foretell the future and be disbelieved, his desire for death to be with great men where wisdom is valued. Tiresias is able to overcome his curse to persuade the young, vir- gin boy, Menoeceus, to sacrifice himself to Ares in order to preserve Thebes from the besieging Seven. He promises the boy eternal praise. Then, the poem breaks off, as the poet is aroused from classic dreams by the tolling of the bell for the friend for whom he wrote the poem. Now the poet finds himself a less-able Tiresias, whose light of friendship has gone into the deeper light, leaving the poet to remember the past and look for the future: "A clearer day/Than our poor twilight dawn on earth--/If night, what barren toil to be!/What life, so maim'd by night, were worth/Our living out?"

Tennyson, Alfred. "Tithonus." Available in The Poems and Plays of Alfred Lord Tennyson. New York: Modern Library, 1938. Poem: 76 lines.

Age   Death   Sexuality

Tithonus who asked for immortality but not eternal youth, withers in immortal old age: "Man comes and tills the earth and lies beneath,/And after many a summer dies the swan./Me only cruel immortality/Consumes: I wither slowly in thine arms,/Here at the quiet limit of the world." He begs the goddess, whose beauty now arouses only memories of passion, to return him to death--and yet she is beautiful: "Thou wilt renew thy beauty morn by morn;/I earth in earth forget these empty courts,/And thee returning on thy silver wheels."

Tennyson, Alfred. "The Two Voices." Available in The Poems and Plays of Alfred Lord Tennyson. New York: Modern Library, 1938. Poem: ca. 620 lines.

Suicide

Suicidal Depression. "A still small voice" urges the poet to suicide, citing the many other marvelous bodies and minds in Nature, the cessation of pain, the inevita- bility of death, the ephemeral nature of public opinion, and the poet's failure. But the poet replies "These things are wrapt in doubt and dread,/Nor canst thou show the dead are dead." The voice answers that he was nothing before he was born--and will be again. The two argue without any resolution until the silver sound of Church bells breaks in upon the poet's depression and opens his eyes to the love and beauty around him. Now, he can no longer understand why he listened to the urgings toward suicide: "I marvell'd how the mind was brought/To anchor by one gloomy thought;/And wherefore rather I made choice/To commune with that barren voice,/ Than him that said, 'Rejoice! Rejoice!'"

Tennyson, Alfred. "Ulysses." Available in The Poems and Plays of Alfred Lord Tennyson. New York: Modern Library, 1938. Poem: 70 lines.

Age   Children   Death

The adventurous Ulysses, "bringer of new things," is here an old man, "match'd with an aged wife." He spends his time doling out "unequal laws unto a savage race," and mourning what aging has done to him: "How dull it is to pause, to make an end,/To rust unburnish'd, not to shine in use!" Still, he has his son Telemachus, who pleases him by his attention to the patient work of ruling a rugged people. But Ulysses has a different spirit--he likes more risky work, and he decides to find it once more: "Old age hath yet his honor and his toil." One must use every last hour before death: "Little remains; but every hour is saved/From that eternal silence." So, calling his old comrades together, he sets off again to seek new worlds, that is, new knowledge. Their bodies may be weak, he tells them, but their wills are strong. And in a last cry, created by the poet in strong mono- syllables, Ulysses declares his determination "To strive, to seek, to find, and not to yield."

Thackeray, William Makepeace. The History of Henry Esmond. New York: Dodd, Mead & Co., 1945. Novel.

Children   Disease & Health   The Family
Sexuality

This historical novel set at the end of the 17th century follows the child, Henry, through his indoctrination by the Jacobite priest Father Holt and his confused per- ceptions of the web of family relationships with his father, step-mother, step-siblings, and elderly kins- woman Viscountess Castlewood--and of the political furor in England. Chapters VIII and IX describe how Henry, through careless choice of playmates, brings smallpox into the castle, infecting his step-mother and step- brother, causing her to lose her good looks. This incident marks the first turning point of the novel, where the lady realizes that she has transferred love, worship and jealousy from her husband to her adolescent step-son. It takes the rest of the novel for Henry to grow up, be frustrated in his love for his step-sister and marry his step-mother and live happily ever after.

Thackeray, William Makepeace. Vanity Fair, ed. J. W. Beach. New York: The Modern Library, 1950. Novel.

Children   Death   The Family
Sexual Roles   Sexuality

Two opposite kinds of women who succeed by using men. Amelia is the dumb, loving, fragile, passionate, maternal woman. She cannot see that George Osborne does not love her enough to marry her, is not fit to marry her, and will ruin both of them by marrying her. Her passion leads her to marry him and make a god first of George and then his son. Her beauty attracts men, including Major Dobbin, who faithfully woos her until he learns how shallow she is--at which point he wins her. She helps her father to die and spoils her son, nearly irretrievably. Becky Sharp is intelligent, egotistical, and lacking in all sexual and maternal feeling. She can manipulate men and women, from the miserly Sir Pitt to the dying Miss Crawley, but fails because she juggles too many balls at once. She neg- lects her son (fortunately his father loves and cares for him) and neglects her husband. Passion and death are means to money and social position. Vanity Fair is full of stereotypes, both social and sexual, but the book emphasizes that the dumb, sexual (but in respectable forms) Amelia causes almost as much damage in her loving way as the scheming Becky, who uses passion for her own gain.

Thompson, Francis. "The Poppy." From Complete Poetical Works of Francis Thompson. New York: The Modern Library, n.d. Poem: 80 lines.

By Doctors   Children   Drugs

Francis Thompson's life is most famous for his opium addiction and religious fervor. He could be considered a doctor-addict, for Thompson, the son of a homeo- pathic physician, studied medicine for 6 years, failed his exams, and remained hostile to the medical profes- sion thereafter. This gentle poem opens with a start- ling image of the poppy as love's foster child, growing into a sensuous gypsy: "And drowsed in sleepy savageries,/ With mouth wide a-pout for a sultry kiss." On a whim, a young child, whom the poet loves, hands him this flower of oblivion, which now awakens him to the twenty withered years that lie between them. He is her "foster-lover" and so returns again to his love affair with the poppy: "I hang 'mid men by needless head,/ And my fruit is dreams, as theirs is bread:/The goodly men and the sun-hazed sleeper/Time shall reap, but after the reaper/The world shall glean of me, me the sleeper."

Thompson, Francis. "To Monica Thought Dying." From Complete Poetical Works of Francis Thompson. New York: The Modern Library, n.d. Poem: 80 lines.

By Doctors*   Children   Death
Dying   Grief

Waking and crying with grief during the night 11-year- old Monica is thought to be dying, the poet is obsessed with the childish (not womanly sweet) words that Death

uses to strip away his soul: "'A cup of chocolate,/One
farthing is the rate,/You drink it through a straw, a
straw, a straw' . . . . Nay, never so have wrung/From
eyes and speech weakness unmanned, unmeet,/As when his
terrible dotage to repeat/Its little lesson learneth at
your feet;/As when he sits among/His sepulchres, to
play/With broken toys your hand has cast away."

*See Thompson, Francis. "The Poppy."

Thoreau, Henry David. Walden, ed. Sherman Paul. Cambridge, Mass.:
    Riverside Press, 1957. Treatise.

| The Body | Disease & Health | Madness |
| Poverty & Health | Sexuality | |

Thoreau advocates a drastic change in life style to
return to spiritual (creative), mental, and physical
health. Men don't see that a comfortable life may, in
the end, be self defeating. He finds it ironic that
his life is so healthy in the woods, and yet people
fear to come to it, clinging together in a community
for fear of disease and death ("Visitors"). They have
chosen the wrong physician: "I am no worshipper of
Hygeia, who was the daughter of that old herb-doctor
Aesculapius, and who is represented . . . [with] a cup
out of which the serpent sometimes drinks; but rather
of Hebe, cupbearer to Jupiter . . . and who had the
power of restoring gods and men to the vigor of youth"
("Sounds"). However, bodily health is really not what
Thoreau desired. To gain the soaring independence of
the eagle and the insights of Walden, he sacrifices
the body. He calls for chastity: "The generative
energy, which, when we are loose, dissipates and makes
us unclean, when we are continent invigorates and inspires us" ("Higher Laws"). He has no family. Even
the physical presence of friends is not necessary.
"The value of a man is not in his skin, that we should
touch him." And yet this intense rationality has
identified a great depressive disease: "The mass of
men lead lives of quiet desperation. What is called
resignation is confirmed desperation."

Tolstoy, Leo. The Death of Ivan Ilych. Available in Tolstoy's
    Tales of Courage and Conflict. Garden City, New York:
    Hanover House, 1958. Novella.

The Body	Children	Death
Disease & Health	Doctors	Drugs
Dying	The Family	Grief
Suffering		

A brilliant examination of what it means to die. Tolstoy
first let us see the funeral of the 45-year-old hero, the
body, the self-centered widow, and the friends, grateful
that it is not they who are dead. Then he briefly tells
Ivan Ilych's story, which is "most simple and most ordinary and therefore most terrible" (trans. Aylmer Maude).
Ivan Ilych had been a professional man whose values were
derived from matters of taste and power rather than,
say, Christian morality. The discovery of his illness
(it is something vaguely abdominal; no one seems certain
whether the appendix or the kidney is involved), the
complacency of the doctors (it is a matter of life and
death to Ivan Ilych; to the doctors, a matter of the
appendix or the kidney), and his steady decline into
abysmal physical and mental anguish is horrifying.
Alone of all his family, his young schoolboy son pities
him. His wife and daughter blame him for interfering
with their lives. His physical suffering can only be
partially relieved with opium. His mental suffering
begins with his loss of bodily dignity and extends to
his realization that his whole life has been lived in
a fraudulent manner. Though he has been a pleasant and
decorous fellow, for the most part, he has not been good.
His last three days are spent in screaming. "For three
whole days, during which time did not exist for him, he
struggled into that black sack in which he was being
thrust by an invisible, resistless force." The whole
process is, as noted earlier, horrifying, except for
the Christian reader. For him there is Ivan Ilych's
11th hour decision to care for his family above himself,
to acknowledge their full humanness. With that, he is
released both from his pain and from his fear of death.
Indeed death itself is annihilated in a joyful light
which Ivan Ilych perceives as very real.

Tolstoy, Leo. The Kreutzer Sonata. Available in Tolstoy's Tales
    of Courage and Conflict. Garden City, New York: Hanover
    House, 1958. Novella.

Children	Disease & Health	Dying
The Family	Grief	Madness
Med. Profession	Preg. & Childbirth	Sexuality
Sexual Roles	Suicide	

A story of sexual jealousy turned into violent madness.
Tolstoy's narrative begins with Pozdnishef's disquisition
on the nature of marriage and women's roles. No matter
how liberated they may be according to the law, women
are still slaves to sexual passion, objects for men's
pleasure, and they will use this means to gain the power
otherwise denied to them. Sex itself, Pozdnishef continues, is disgusting and unnatural. He remembers his
honeymoon as a shameful failure, which was soon followed
by increasingly intense quarrels, seemingly about trivia,
but in fact a reaction to the unsatisfactory nature of
sensuality and the lies the couple had told themselves
about spiritual love. Children are born, five in all,
but instead of being a delight, they and their illnesses
merely torment their parents further. And Pozdnishef

discovers that sex during pregnancy and immediately afterwards is especially depraved. The quarrels become at
last so horrible that the wife attempts suicide, but once
more the couple is reconciled through sex. When a young
musician enters the wife's life, Pozdnishef's jealousy
becomes an obsession, ending in a vicious assault upon
his wife, who dies hating her husband and confused about
why all this has happened. Only when he sees her in her
coffin does Pozdnishef recall all her human qualities
and see not in her but in sexual relations in general the
cause of all his suffering. Throughout his monologue, he
has expressed a special hatred for doctors. He is jealous
when they examine his wife. He demands to know why their
stupidities are not called murder; and so on. Critical
interpretation of this novella has been difficult, for
the central character is mad, and readers have not known
precisely which of his ideas are shared by the moralist
and social reformer Tolstoy. (See also Anna Karenina,
Tolstoy's greatest story of sexuality and adultery--this
time combined with passionate and romantic love, though
ending for the heroine in sexual jealousy and suicide.)

Trollope, Anthony. Doctor Thorne. London: Thomas Nelson & Sons
    Ltd, n.d. Novel.

| Alcoholism | Doctors | Med. Profession |

In all of his explorations of professional men, Trollope
was never deeply interested in any given profession for
its own sake; instead he would analyze the effect of a
profession upon its members and the conflicts between
what a man ought to do morally and what he must do to
succeed in his profession. Although this novel (despite
its title) only occasionally discusses the medical profession (most of the novel satirizes fools who ape a
decadent and hypocritical aristocracy), when it does
discuss doctors it is both harsh and funny. Dr. Thorne
begins practice in a new town, and his methods cause him
to be ostracized by the other doctors. He charges a low,
flat-rate fee for a visit, with an added per-mile sur-
charge for those who live in out-lying areas. Also, he
mixes his own drugs. When the local doctors turn against
him, "he appealed to the metropolis. The Lancet took
the matter up in his favor, but the Journal of Medical
Science was against him; the Weekly Chirugeon, noted for
its medical democracy, upheld him as a medical prophet,
but the Scalping Knife, a monthly periodical got up in
dead opposition to the Lancet, showed him no mercy."
Failing in the London papers, the doctor turns to the
local ones, is fortunate enough to be attacked by a
stupid medical antagonist, annihilates him, becomes
famous in the district, and so establishes the foundation of his practice. He carries on a running battle
with Dr. Fillgrave, each being ousted by a patient who
wishes to consult the other. Dr. Thorne's most important patients are his opponent, Lady Arabella, whom he
treats for cancer, and a father-son pair who die of
acute alcoholism because they refuse to accept the
extent of their addiction and of their bodily deterioration. They are a grim pair.

Trollope, Anthony. The Last Chronicles of Barset. New York:
    Norton, 1964. Novel.

| Dying | Madness |

There are two separate plots in this; of interest is the
Barchester plot involving the affairs of Rev. Crawley,
a man tottering on the line between neurosis and madness,
made eccentric by a combination of great pride and great
poverty. He is accused of stealing a missing check. No
one believes he stole it, but everyone believes he
absent-mindedly cashed it. He cannot remember and so
cannot clear himself. His friends believe that only a
plea of insanity can get him off, and the sense that
people are judging his sanity begins to act on his hidden fear of insanity and so drives him farther toward
madness. He is finally cleared when friends in Italy
with the answer hear of his trouble. Another case of
borderline insanity occurs in He Knew He Was Right, where,
again, fear of accusation of insanity only makes the
problem worse. There are two important deaths in the
novel: The Bishop's wife dies from a stroke, and gentle
Mr. Harding dies, his death hastened by the over-
protectiveness of his daughter.

Trollope, Anthony. The Warden. Available in Barchester Towers
    and The Warden. New York: The Modern Library, 1936. Novel.

| Age | Doctors | Med. Instit. |

Although the battle over Hiram's Hospital was continued
in Barchester Towers, The Warden is really complete in
its depiction of the devastation of reform for reform's
sake. Hiram's Hospital was founded by a will which set
aside some property to be used for the upkeep of twelve
old men, who live in the hospital under the supervision
of The Warden. Because the property has greatly increased in value, the position of Warden has become a
comfortable sinecure. The present Warden is the aging
Mr. Harding, a very gentle, kind old man who provides
extra money to the old men. Then there are several
scandals of similar Wardens' profiting from wills and
doing nothing for charity. Dr. John Bold, a dedicated
reformer (he has inherited money and treats only the
poor) demands that the old men get all the extra money.
Harding is buffeted by his fellow clergymen who urge
him to fight, his conviction that reform won't help the
old men, and his conscience which accuses him of taking

money not rightfully his. The battle is carried into the courts and the London newspapers. John Bold, who has fallen in love with Harding's daughter, tries unsuccessfully to stop the battle. Harding resigns. The old men lose their extra money and their loving friend. No Warden is appointed to the disputed position, and the hospital falls into ruins.

Turgenev, Ivan. "The District Doctor." Available in Short Stories, ed. Sean O'Faolain. Boston: Little, Brown and Company, 1961. Short Story.

Disease & Health	Doctors	Dying
The Family	Madness	Med. Ethics
Sexuality		

Perhaps the central literary investigation of sexual attraction between doctor and patient. The sexuality in this case is compounded of romance and passion, as opposed to direct arousal. It is exalted emotion Turgenev is talking about, and it is too much for the doctor, who lives most of his life on the level of bill collecting and banal statements about duty. He fears in fact that he will go mad, for night after night his young feverish patient reaches her arms out to him, and all the while she is dying. Her poor and trusting family-- a mother, two sisters--expect him to save her, partly because he has played down their fears in an unthinking professional manner. He is tortured by their blind faith in him and by his inability in encounter with the rising power of the disease. The girl loves him, he thinks, because she knows she is dying and can't die without having loved ever. And he loves her, perhaps, because she is lovely and needing and utterly dependent on him for everything now. This tricky situation (is the doctor a fool? is the girl truly in love? was this the only moment of vitality in his generally dead life?) is handled with great sympathy and honesty by Turgenev.

Twain, Mark. Adventures of Huckleberry Finn, eds. Sculley Bradley, R. C. Beatty and E. H. Long. New York: Norton, 1962. Novel.

Adolescence	Alcoholism	Children
Death	Doctors	Sexual Roles
Suffering		

Chapter VI contains what may be many people's first introduction, as young readers, to alcoholism: the vivid description of Pap's delirium tremens. In Chapter XI is found a classic definition of sexual roles. Huck's disguise as a girl is ineffective because he does not catch, throw, or thread a needle like a girl. Huck is deluged with death. He sees a lot of it on his way down the river, climaxing at the Grangerfords where he adopts a dangerous reaction to it. At first, as with all of Twain's serious subjects, death is treated lightly. The late Emmeline Grangerford with her instant "tributes" to the dead and her hilarious poem on Stephen Dowling Bots, Dec'd is really representative of the Grangerfords and the Shepherdsons, who are so obsessed with deadly feuding that the love affair between a young Grangerford and a young Shepherdson is only a cause for massive bloodshed. Huck's reaction to the deaths of his friend and the kindly people who "adopted" him is conscious repression. "I ain't a-going to tell all that happened-- it would make me sick again if I was to do that. I wished I hadn't ever come ashore that night to see such things. I ain't ever going to get shut of them--lots of times I dream about them." A lot of questions are raised about Huck's acquiescence in Tom's mistreatment of Jim to make him a "proper" prisoner. It is as though Huck is looking to Tom as another alternative to civilization, an alternative he finally rejects when he disregards Tom's elaborate directions to deceive the doctor whom he gets by a simple lie. The doctor speaks up to obtain decent treatment for Jim. Huck's final solution to civilization is an adolescent one; he escapes from it to the territories.

Twain, Mark. Autobiography of Mark Twain, ed. Charles Neider. New York: Harper & Row, 1959. Autobiography.

Children	Death	Doctors
The Family	Grief	Women as Healers
Women as Patients		

Early section describes the various types of doctors available in Hannibal: grandmothers, women doctors, Indian doctors, faith healers. Also, early in the book is the account of his brother Henry's death after a steamboat accident because of an error in dosage by the doctor. Twain's wife was cured of paralysis by a faith healer, in whom she believed all her life. His later life was quite unhappy: his wife had a nervous breakdown, and she, his son, and two daughers, one of whom was epileptic, predeceased him. The section "The Death of Jean" is full of a sense of age, loss, and grief. He recapitulates the deaths in his family and then recounts his feelings in the days immediately after his daughter's death. It is maudlin, but beautiful.

Twain, Mark. The Diary of Adam and Eve. Available in The Complete Short Stories of Mark Twain, ed. Charles Neider. New York: Bantam, 1964. Sketch.

| Children | Sexual Roles |

Delightful account of the new humans' working out their own roles and relationships to each other, including Adam's puzzlement at children, not knowing what they are,

and his bafflement at Eve's reactions to them. The difference in tone and content of each diary is in itself a description of sexual roles.

Twain, Mark. "Experience of the McWilliamses with Membranous Croup." From The Complete Short Stories of Mark Twain, ed. Charles Neider. New York: Bantam, 1964. Short Story.

| Children | Disease & Health | Doctors |
| Sexual Roles | | |

Attack on the wife for excessive care of their child at the expense of the husband. The mother moves the crib all over the house, accuses her husband of living an evil life and so causing the child to be ill, gives triple the dose of medicine at greatly reduced intervals, rubs the child with goose grease, and gives it belladonna and aconite. The husband is forced to fetch the doctor, who comes reluctantly, and finds that the child is not ill. The husband is overjoyed, the wife is irritated. The doctor finds the baby has a wood splinter in its throat from a stick which the wife refused to take from the child because the husband suggested she do so. Bitterness undercuts the humor.

Twain, Mark. Innocents Abroad, 1869 ed.; rpt. New York: Harper & Row, n.d. Novel.

| Disease & Health | Doctors | Med. Instit. |

Throughout the trip Twain grumbles at the quarantine procedures the ship encountered at Mediterranean ports. His attitude seems to be that they are keeping out the healthy people while being diseased themselves. He also notes the inconsistencies in the regulations. Twain was horrified by the lack of cleanliness, stench, and disease of the Near East. His reaction culminates in an outburst in Book II, Chapter 18: "Yesterday we met a woman riding on a little jackass, and she had a little child in her arms; honestly, I thought the child had goggles on as we approached, and I wondered how its mother could afford so much style. But when we drew near, we saw that the goggles were nothing but a camp-meeting of flies assembled around each of the child's eyes." However, the wonder shown by the people when the tourists' doctors treated children's eyes convinces him that Christ was right to preach while healing.

Twain, Mark. The Mysterious Stranger, ed. W. M. Gibson. Berkeley, Calif.: University of California Press, 1970. Novella.

| Suffering |

Human suffering is caused by other humans. It is largely caused by "The Moral Sense" (see also the religious tortures in Connecticut Yankee) and greed. The only possible solutions to suffering which do not, in turn, create more suffering are death and insanity.

Twain, Mark. "Three Thousand Years Among the Microbes." Available in In Dreams Awake, ed. L. A. Fiedler. New York: Dell, 1975. Sketch.

| Disease & Health |

A jeu d'esprit on the differences in point of view between microbes and humans--different time scales, different views of health and life. It contrasts with The Great Dark, in which a man and his family shrink onto a microscope slide. The story begins as a play on conflicting perspectives and ends in a nightmare, paranoid journey, with the narrator unable to distinguish which world is real.

Warren, Samuel. Passages from the Diary of a Late Physician, from the 5th London edition. New York: Harper & Bros., n.d. 3 Vols. Sketches.

By Doctors	Death	Disease & Health
Doctors	Med. Profession	Poverty & Health
Surgery	Women as Patients	

Warren practiced medicine for several years and then turned to writing for a living. The sketches in Passages were printed in Blackwood's magazine between 1830 and 1837. The early sketches are the most interesting, especially "Early Struggles" and "Cancer." "Early Struggles" describes his attempts to set up a practice, his debt, his refusal to treat a dog, his frustration at being used as a foil for an established physician, and his despair when he loses a promising patient to another established physician who allows the patient to die. A noble accident victim gives the narrator the opportunity to practice medicine as Warren never found. "Cancer" is a horrifying and astonishingly understated sketch of a mastectomy. The woman, a mother, is glorified for her maternal care and her fortitude at facing the pain and disfigurement. Throughout the surgery (which takes place while she is sitting in a chair in a back room of her house) she rivets her eyes "in one long burning gaze of fondness on the beloved handwriting of her husband," who has written her a supporting note. The husband does not appear in the story, but his reaction dominates it-- especially in the quiet ending, which the doctor narrates. "She was alluding, one morning, distantly and delicately to the personal disfigurement she had suffered. I, of course, said all that was soothing. 'But, doctor, my husband--' said she, suddenly while a faint crimson mantled on her cheek; adding falteringly, after a pause, 'I think St-- will love me yet!'" But 19th-century writers were hampered by limitations on subject matter, by demands for moralizing, and by audiences hungry for the sensational. Warren's subject matter soon matches the clichés in which "Cancer" was written, although occasional flashes of realism appear. "A Scholar's Death-bed" describes a neglected genius' death from T.B. Warren follows the contemporary interest on T.B. and gives it the aura so beloved by the romantics. His "Consumption" is typical. The disease strikes the young, the beautiful, and the imaginative. At even greater length than in "A Scholar's Death-bed" he follows the decline of a young woman who takes alarm at being watched by doctors, who becomes ill because the doctor's concern convinces her she's doomed, who declines and dies under the care of a doting uncle, a doting doctor, and a lover, half-mad with grief. Warren wrote several pathetic death scenes, several cautionary death scenes (the man lived a dissipated life, the woman was seduced, the man neglected a common cold), several accounts of madness, several descriptions of compulsive gamblers, of extravagant wives, and of fallen women. Over the years he loses the detached tone of "Cancer" and adopts the tone of moral superiority found in other popular writers. Only in "Grave Doings" a comic account of body-snatching and in a sketch which didactically compares the wealthy gouty patient in all his comfort and the destitute asthmatic worker in all his poverty does Warren return to any realism. The account of the cold, unlit apartment inhabited by the worker's starving family is well-done. Also well-done is the understated conflict between the doctor and the healer. The family is dying of hunger and cold. Once the doctor pays for a candle so that there is some light in the room, the cause of their illness is only too apparent. But the narrator says that he is a doctor, asks for his patient and asks the cause of the disease. In several cases the doctor can see that poverty is the disease, but he manages to survive by looking only at medically recognized illnesses.

Wells, H. G. "The Cone." From The Plattner Story and Others. Available in The Complete Short Stories of H. G. Wells. London: Ernest Benn Limited, 1966. Short Story.

Death   Sexuality

A terrifying story with a, literally, blood-curdling death. The wife of a manufacturer is having an affair with a man, Raut, who offers her poetry and love in place of her husband's science and apparent indifference. The two believe that the husband, Horrocks, is ignorant of their affair and when he suddenly breaks in on them, Raut covers by asking Horrocks to show him his plant by moonlight. The tour becomes Horrocks' exposition of his kind of poetry--and sexuality--as expressed by the seething iron mills. The climax of the tour is a trip up to the top of a nicely phallic cone, placed over a furnace, to save fuel for work. Horrocks, in describing the various patternings made by the machinery, uses phrases such as "blood red vapour as red and hot as sin," "it is as white as death." Raut becomes uneasy, fearing Horrocks suspects, but no more. When they reach the top of the cone, in the middle of which the temperature reaches a thousand degrees, Horrocks pushes Raut into the furnace. Raut clutches at a chain by which he is slowly lowered into the furnace, to the glee of Horrocks. Then a flame catches Raut: "His human likeness had departed from him. When the momentary red has passed, Horrocks saw a charred, blackened figure, its head streaked with blood, still clutching and fumbling with the chain . . . . He knew the thing below him, save that it still moved and felt, was already a dead man--that the blood of the poor wretch must be boiling in his veins. An intense realization of that agony came to his mind, and overcame every other feeling." He kills Raut quickly--and then listens while his mill, his alter-ego, shuts down.

Wells, H. G. "The Country of the Blind." From The Time Machine and Other Stories. Available in The Complete Short Stories of H. G. Wells. London: Ernest Benn Limited, 1966. Short Story.

Handicaps

The famous story of the sighted man who expects to become king when he finds himself in the country of the blind. However, the blind inhabitants have so sharpened their hearing and sense of touch, that he is handicapped in a society in which sensitive hearing and touch are necessary for daily living. He barely escapes with his life. The story also emphasizes that a "handicap" is socially, rather than physically, defined. Over and over the narrator tells of the visual beauty these people can never perceive--and which they do not miss at all. To them, the sighted person is ill, made mad and antisocial by the disease of "eyes" which leads him to talk of unnecessary and non-existent matters. A good story.

Wells. H. G. The Island of Dr. Moreau. New York: Lancer, 1968. Novella.

Evil Doctors   Sci Fi   Suffering

Wells' short, bitter Gulliver's Travels. Pendrick finds himself abandoned on an island run by Dr. Moreau, a vivisector forced out of England, and his alcoholic assistant, Dr. Montgomery, forced out of England for some nameless crime. The two doctors have created a little theocracy of animals surgically, and painfully, altered to grotesquely human shapes. The animals, who

worship Moreau and Montgomery, are kept "moral"--clothed, peaceful, and monogamous--by pain and the threat of pain. This "morality" is for the convenience of the doctors, because it removes any threat to them, but it is not their own guide, for Montgomery enjoys unspeakable activities with the beast-men. When the two doctors die, the beast-men slowly revert to savagery despite Pendrick's efforts to provide them with an unseen Moreau-God. The story's point is forced home by Wells, who returns Pendrick to civilization, where humans now seem like those beasts to him, slowly degenerating. He sees "none that have the calm authority of a reasonable soul." Yet it was "reasonable" Moreau who provided order and pain for his creations. A disturbing story.

Wells, H. G. "Under the Knife." From The Plattner Story and Others. Available in The Complete Short Stories of H. G. Wells. London: Ernest Benn Limited, 1966. Short Story.

Death   Surgery

A cure for the fear of death. Although the middle part of the story is irrelevant, its ends are useful. The narrator is facing major surgery--and the thought of his death. He finds himself numb, analyzing the reasons for it. The surgery is performed at home, the doctors come, and he is convinced they'll kill him. Under the anaesthetic, he believes he can feel the surgeons' doubts, the fear of cutting the portal vein, the slip of the knife, and his death. He then experiences bodiless travel through the wonders of the universe, only to return back to his own room. "The operation had not killed me. And I perceived, suddenly, that the dull melancholy of half a year was lifted from my mind."

Whitman, Walt. "As I Sit Writing Here," "Queries to My Seventieth Year," "Thanks in Old Age." "Old Age's Lambent Peaks," and "Good-Bye, My Fancy." From Leaves of Grass. New York: New American Library, 1958. Short Poems.

Age   Disease & Health

The great optimist enters old age and nears death. Stricken down by a stroke, his good cheer fails him in the first two poems. He complains that his voice is parrot-like and screeching, and he fears that into his poems may creep those hazards of the elderly sick: "querilities, ungracious glooms, aches, lethargy, constipation, whimpering, ennui." But most of Whitman's poems about his last years are as hearty as ever. The last three listed above are typical and include the beliefs that in old age one sees farther ("The calmer sight--the golden setting, clear and broad") and that far from ending creativity, death may actually bring one to the "true songs."

Whitman, Walt. Calamus. From Leaves of Grass. New York: New American Library, 1958. Short Poems.

Homosexuality

While there are homosexual themes throughout the poetry and prose of Whitman, the poems collected under the title of Calamus are the most directly concerned with comradely love. In general, the poet proclaims himself the lover of all, and that includes, of course, men. For specific tender and/or physical images of "manly attachment," see particularly "In Paths Untrodden," "Whoever You Are Holding Me Now," "These I Singing in Spring," "I Saw in Louisiana a Live-Oak Growing," "I Hear It Was Charged Against Me," and "We Two Boys Together Clinging."

Whitman, Walt. Drum Taps. From Leaves of Grass. New York: New American Library, 1958; and Specimen Days. Selections available in The Portable Walt Whitman. New York: Viking Press, 1945. Short Poems and Journal.

Death   Dying   Med. Instit.
Nurses   Suffering

Specimen Days, which includes a section describing Whitman's experiences while nursing the wounded of the Civil War, can be instructively read with the poems collected under the title of Drum Taps and written about the same period. The former is a detailed and relatively distanced description of the soldiers' suffering; in the latter, Whitman's tenderness, implicit in Specimen Days, is given much more play, indeed becomes quite sentimental, as the poems take him out of the hospitals and onto the battlefields. The poet of the great embrace has a little trouble holding his world together.

Whitman, Walt. "I Sing the Body Electric." From Leaves of Grass. New York: New American Library, 1958. Poem: 164 lines.

Age   The Body   Sexuality

An ecstatic catalogue of bodies and parts of bodies. The poet chants his love of--really his union with--all bodies, male and female, old and young. He insists that the body is itself a poem, that it is perfect and sacred, and, finally, that it is the soul. "The armies of those I love engirth me and I engirth them,/They will not let me off till I go with them, respond to them,/And discorrupt them, and charge them full with the charge of the soul./Was it doubted that those who corrupt their own bodies conceal themselves?/And if those who defile the living are as bad as they who defile the dead?"

Whitman, Walt. "Out of the Cradle Endlessly Rocking." From
Leaves of Grass. New York: New American Library, 1958.
Poem: 183 lines.

Death   Grief

Extraordinarily moving treatment of death and its relation to creativity. As he does so often, Whitman here
finds profound significance in the common, in this case
the death by the sea of a bird. Her mate, whom the poet
sees as a brother, sings a song which follows some of the
stages identified by medical writers on death: first
denial of her death, at last disillusioned acceptance of
it. But the important section for our purpose is the
final one, in which the poet, with the inspiration of
the mother sea, makes out of this loss something sweet,
for death has disturbed him into creating his poems.

Whitman, Walt. "Song of Myself." From Leaves of Grass. New York:
New American Library, 1958. Poem: 52 "chants."

The Body   Death   Sexuality

Long series of gently inter-locking and rhapsodic poems
chanted by a visionary. He glories in what he calls his
barbarism and divine commonness. As a result, he completely accepts every inch of his body; he lovingly,
even sexually, unites himself with all manner of men
and women and with the world at large; and he triumphs,
thereby, over death.

Whitman, Walt. "When Lilacs Last in the Dooryard Bloomed." From
Leaves of Grass. New York: New American Library, 1958.
Poem: ca. 200 lines.

Death   Grief

By common agreement, one of the greatest elegies in the
language. This poem was inspired by Lincoln's death,
but is really on the larger themes of the poet's feelings
about death in general and its intimate association with
bright, living, recurring things: the lilac, the star,
the bird, and the poem itself.

Whittier, John Greenleaf. "The Barefoot Boy." From The Oxford
Book of American Verse, ed. Bliss Carman. New York: Oxford
University Press, 1927. Poem: ca. 100 lines.

Children   Sexual Roles

Whittier has given us several resonating stereotypes
("Shoot, if you must, this old gray head,/But spare
your country's flag": Barbara Fritchie and the Puritan
Bacchants of "Skipper Ireson's Ride"), but the most
enduring one was the romantic picture of the free and
happy country boy (a picture so ably slashed by Huck
Finn): "Oh for boyhood's painless play,/Sleep that
wakes in laughing day,/Health that mocks the doctor's
rules/Knowledge never learned of schools . . . .
Cheerily, then, my little man,/Live and laugh, as
boyhood can!"

Wilde, Oscar. "The Ballad of Reading Gaol." Available in The
Portable Oscar Wilde, ed. Richard Aldington. New York:
The Viking Press, 1972. Long Poem.

Death   Homosexuality

Wilde has placed upon the silent condemned man many of
his own feelings, including, perhaps, a justification
for Douglas' destruction of Wilde by the poem's repetition of the idea that "each man kills the thing he
loves." He describes the condemned man as a man
snatching at the pleasure of life, even if they only
be fresh air or sun, and condemns society for condemning
the man who only did what we all do: kill the thing
we love.

Wilde, Oscar. De Profundis. Available in The Portable Oscar
Wilde, ed. Richard Aldington. New York: The Viking Press,
1972. Essay-length letter.

Homosexuality   Suffering

Only part of this essay is necessary to feel the intense
sufferings of Wilde in Reading Gaol; it is the cry of a
man stripped of everything he valued. Regardless of
whether or not one can stomach his burdening his young
lover, Lord Alfred, with all of Wilde's miseries, including the gifts he gave Alfred, one is still overwhelmed
by his suffering and his inability to find meaning in
or to transcend that suffering, despite great effort.
"Everything about my tragedy has been hideous, mean,
repellent, lacking in style. Our very dress makes us
grotesques. We are the zanies of sorrow."

Wilde, Oscar. Salome. Available in Selected Plays. Baltimore,
Md.: Penguin, n.d. Drama.

The Body   Sexuality

Salome's lyrical exaltation of the body of John the
Baptist. She is obsessed with his body, especially his
mouth. She is a virgin and sees him as a sexual object
to be touched while she is not touched. The play is
saturated with evil sexuality: the lusts of Herodias,
the obsession of John the Baptist with Herodias' sexual
misdeeds, Herod's obsessions with Salome. However, all
of these people have their sexual obsessions bound up
with something else: divinity, social propriety, or a
desire for the mystical. Salome alone can see nothing
beyond the sexual. It is why she is so horrible--and
irresistible.

Wordsworth, William. "Character of the Happy Warrior." From The
Poetical Works of Wordsworth, ed. Thomas Hutchinson, rev.
Ernest de Selincourt. New York: Oxford, 1964. Poem: 85
lines.

Sexual Roles

An attempt to redefine the martial role of man into a
moral one. The true warrior "that every man in arms
should wish to be" is generous, knowledgeable, able to
control himself, able to turn "necessity to a glorious
gain," skillful in self-knowledge, strong, tender,
acting by reason, honorable, and "through the heat of
conflict, keeps the law/In calmness made," and is
undismayed by danger.

Wordsworth, William. "The Idiot Boy." Available in Poetical Works,
ed. Thomas Hutchinson; new ed. rev. Ernest de Selincourt. New
York: Oxford University Press, 1960. Poem: 453 lines.

Children   Disease & Health   Mental Retardation

This exercise in different points of view is famous for
its inclusion of the idiot child's perceptions. A
woman tending a sick friend at night must send her retarded boy for the doctor. When neither son nor doctor
appears, she abandons her friend and rushes to the
doctor's, where she learns her son has never arrived.
Frantic, she forgets to send the doctor to her friend;
instead she runs wildly in search of her child. The
poet interjects ballad speculations as to Johnny's
plight, but the mother finds him happily singing to
himself. The sick friend is cured by her concern for
mother and child, leaving her sick room to find them.
"'The cocks did crow to-whoo, to-whoo,/And the sun did
shine so cold!'/--Thus answered Johnny in his glory,/
And that was all his travel's story."

Wordsworth, William. "Maternal Grief." Available in Poetical
Works, ed. Thomas Hutchinson; new ed. rev. Ernest de
Selincourt. New York: Oxford University Press, 1960.
Poem: 81 lines.

Children   Death   Grief

Not really the mother's grief, but the interaction
between the mother and a surviving child. The sentimental treatment of the dead child is annoying, even
with the knowledge that Wordsworth felt that children
grow away from the source of inspiration so that death
is a return, not a loss, for the child. It is the
mother who suffers, using her remaining child as fuel
for grief--to the child's shrinking confusion: "for
oft-times from the sound/Of the survivor's sweetest
voice (dear child/He knew it not) and from his happiest
looks,/Did she extract the food of self reproach . . . .
And full oft the Boy,/First acquainted with distress
and grief,/Shrunk with his Mother's presence, shunned
with fear . . . to find,/In his known haunts of joy
where'er he might,/A more congenial object." Gradually
the Boy does return to his mother (the child wiser and
stronger than the adult), calming and cheering her so
that they can go together to his sibling's grave.

Wordsworth, William. "Michael." Available in Poetical Works, ed.
Thomas Hutchinson; new ed. rev. Ernest de Selincourt. New
York: Oxford University Press, 1960. Poem: 482 lines.

Age   The Family

Dignified, strong, but grieved, old age. Michael, now
in his eighties, has always given his love to the land
and nature. When he is ruined by a loan to his nephew,
mortgaging again the land he had not held freely until
his forties, he also must send his beloved son to the
city to earn a living. Before the son leaves, Michael
shows him the foundations of a stone sheepfold the old
man is making with his own labor, and reminds the
younger man of the troublesome commercial--and the
loving--aspects of the land. The sheepfold becomes a
symbol of the love between the father and son, and the
son and nature. But the city annihilates nature. The
son is corrupted and must flee abroad. Michael remains
strong and upright, but, although he ostensibly keeps
building the fold, it is left unfinished at his death.

Wordsworth, William. "My heart leaps up." From The Poetical Works
of Wordsworth, ed. Thomas Hutchinson, rev. Ernest de Selincourt. New York: Oxford University Press, 1964. Poem:
9 lines.

Children

This poem of exuberant self-congratulation is useful for
one line: "The Child is father of the Man."

Wordsworth, William. "Ode. Intimations of Immortality from
Recollections of Early Childhood." Available in Poetical
Works, ed. Thomas Hutchinson; new ed. rev. Ernest de Selincourt. New York: Oxford University Press, 1960. Poem:
207 lines.

Children

Most famous for its fifth stanza: "Our birth is but a
sleep and a forgetting . . . Not in entire forgetfulness/
And not in utter nakedness,/But trailing clouds of glory
do we come/From God who is our home:/Heaven lies about
us in our infancy!/Shades of the prison-house begin to
close/Upon the growing Boy." This represents a startling
change in the approach to the child; instead of being a
part of the family (to work and to marry for the family),
the child is seen as a part of God. This exhaltation of
childhood seems only to have been transformed rather
than eliminated by the addition of sexuality and trauma
by Freud to this innocent state.

Wordsworth, William. "The Old Cumberland Beggar." From The
Poetical Works of Wordsworth, ed. Thomas Hutchinson, rev.
Ernest de Selincourt. New York: Oxford, 1964. Poem:
197 lines.

Age

Wordsworth wrote a number of poems on old men ("Michael,"
"Simon Lee"). This poem makes two points. The first is
that the old man is better off independent amid the
pleasures of nature than in an institution. His second
point is not so nice. In "Resolution and Independence,"
the old leech-gatherer's calm perseverance comforts the
poet who has feared for his old age. In "The Old Cumberland Beggar," the old man serves as an object of pity,
to make others more content with their own lot, and an
object of charity, to warm one's heart with virtue.

Wordsworth, William. The Prelude, Books I, II & V. Available in
Poetical Works, ed. Thomas Hutchinson; new ed. rev. Ernest
de Selincourt. New York: Oxford University Press, 1960.
Long Poem.

Children   Science & Poetry

In Books I and II, we see the childhood and school days
of a poet. Although the boy is involved with the physical
sensations of his playmates, swimming, flying kites,
doing cyphers, and playing cards, he is more involved
with his increasing perception of unknown modes of being
(a perception that peaks in the adult poet in Book XIV,
ll.1-129). His flashes of insight are not interpreted
by a child, but by a poet as a child. In Book V, the
narrator, after reading Cervantes, falls into a reverie
"On poetry and geometric truth,/And their high privilege
of lasting life,/From all internal injury exempt." He
dreams that an Arab offers him a stone and a shell.
The stone is a book of Euclid's Elements "that held
acquaintance with the stars,/And wedded soul to soul in
purest bond/Of reason, undisturbed by space or time."
The shell was also "a god, yea many gods,/Had voices
more than all the winds, with power/To exhilarate the
spirit, and to soothe/Through every clime, the heart
of human kind." Both science and poetry are omnipresent
and immortal, but poetry does more than link souls in
reason; it acts upon those souls to reach the human
heart with a soothing and prophetic voice.

Wordsworth, William. "Ruth." Available in Poetical Works, ed.
Thomas Hutchinson; new ed. rev. Ernest de Selincourt. New
York: Oxford University Press, 1960. Poem: 258 lines.

Madness   Sexuality

The poem's main subject is the abandoned woman gone
pathetically mad. But the poem's curious interest lies
in an implied inter-relationship between climate and
sexuality. It is though the nature one loves can return
a pure--or a lascivious--feeling. Ruth is wooed and won
by an American whom she marries. Alas, his good genius
and moral frame have been warped by the climate: "The
wind, the tempest roaring high,/The tumult of a tropic
sky,/Might well be dangerous food . . . . Nor less, to
feed voluptuous thought,/The beauteous forms of nature
wrought . . . The stars had feelings, which they sent/
Into those favored bowers." The abandoned Ruth reverts
to childhood, playing on a homemade flute, setting
little water mills, and sleeping in barns. The only
prospect before her is the good funeral foreseen by the
narrator.

Wordsworth, William. "She Was a Phantom of Delight." Available
in Poetical Works, ed. Thomas Hutchinson; new ed. rev. Ernest
de Selincourt. New York: Oxford University Press, 1960.
Poem: 30 lines.

Sexual Roles

The early 19th-century ideal woman as spirit, worker, and,
with inadvertent literalism, food: "Her eyes as stars
of Twilight fair;/Like Twilight's, too, her dusky hair
. . . I saw her upon a nearer view,/A Spirit, yet a
Woman too!/Her household motions light and free,/And
steps of virgin-liberty; . . . A Creature not too bright
or good/For human nature's daily food . . . For transient
sorrows, simple wiles/Praise, blame, love, kisses, tears,
and smiles."

Wordsworth, William. "A slumber did my spirit seal." From The
Poetical Works of Wordsworth, ed. Thomas Hutchinson, rev.
Ernest de Selincourt. New York: Oxford, 1964. Poem: 8 lines.

Death   Grief

A bitter contrast of two views of the woman. Alive, "She
seemed a thing that could not feel/The touch of earthly
years." Rudely awakened, the poet in his grief perceives her as still impervious to time: "No motion has
she now, no force;/She neither hears nor sees;/Rolled
round in earth's diurnal course,/With rocks, and stones,
and trees."

Wordsworth, William. "We are Seven." From The Poetical Works of
Wordsworth, ed. Thomas Hutchinson, rev. Ernest de Selincourt.
New York: Oxford, 1964. Poem: 69 lines.

Children   Death

An adult is unable to make a child acknowledge the difference between her living and her dead siblings. In
response to the distinction that she runs about and they
are in the churchyard, she replies that she often carries
her work to do there. She describes the deaths of her
brother and sister, but continues to maintain that "We
are Seven." The poem implies that she is right.

Zola, Emile. "Comment on Meurt" (How people die). In Le Capitaine
Burle. From Oeuvres Complètes, Vol. 8. Paris: Librairie
Hachette, 1962. In French. Sketches.

Dying   Grief   Poverty & Health

A collection of deaths: the old count who dies separate
from his wife despite a tentative attempt at reconciliation for comfort in his dying; the old miser woman whose
deathbed (and the sons' lives) is poisoned by her sons'
squabbles over their inheritance; the shopkeeper's wife
neglected by the servant paid to look after her, but
still obsessed with business up to her death; a poor
child whose parents vainly seek for aid from authorities;
and the old farmer whose death is accepted except for the
bother caused by the funeral. Each sketch represents
the effect of way of life upon the deathbed and funeral.

Zola, Emile. Dr. Pascal, trans. Vladmir Kean. London: Elek
Books, 1957. Novel.

Death   Disease & Health   Doctors
Dying   The Family   Madness
Med. Ethics   Med. Profession   Mental Retardation
Sexuality

Interweaving of personal life and professional work. As
the story opens, Dr. Pascal carries on a small charity
practice, living on an outside income, spending most of
his time on research and on compilation of an elaborate
geneology of insanity in his family. He is under siege
by his mother, his old family servant, and his young,
beautiful niece who want to destroy the records as
blasphemy against God and the Family (the two are nearly
synonymous to the mother). He finds himself under siege
from himself after killing a patient by a blood clot.
Alone, he gives up his practice and loses his virility.
He visits his insane grandmother who watches an idiot
bleed to death and does not cry for help, and begins to
believe he's going mad. Then, his niece refuses her
young doctor-suitor and becomes his mistress and fellow
researcher, admitting that he has replaced the Church
for her. Lyric descriptions of their love-making in the
open countryside at night. Now he begins to question
whether his researches for a better, healthier man might
not have lost something. He tries his experiments with
water instead of his serum and still gets results. At
the opening of Chapter 9, he discovers that he has lost
his empiricism; medicine is no longer an experimental
science but an art. He is disturbed by the infinite
interactions of sickness and remedy, worried by how many
patients must have been killed by false remedies. He
dies of a heart attack which is painfully described;
however, before he dies he learns that he will have a
child by his niece-mistress. He is consoled, for now
his research means nothing and the child everything.
His mother destroys his research results while the niece
looks ahead to the child.

Zola, Emile. Drunkard (L'Assomoir), trans. Arthur Symond. London:
Elck Books, 1958. Novel.

Alcoholism   Disease & Health

More than a temperance tract, Drunkard shows how a model
family is disrupted by injury to the father on his job.
He survives, but his morale is gone, throwing responsibility onto his wife. She, at first, succeeds but begins
to give way to her bodily appetites, finally ending as
a fat, alcoholic slut.

Zola, Emile. Fécondité. In 4-novel series Les Quatres Evangiles.
From Oeuvres Complètes. Paris: Librairie Hachette, 1962.
Vol. 8. Novel, in French.

Abortion   Children   Death
Doctors   The Family   Med. Ethics
Preg. & Childbirth Sexuality

An incredible thesis novel demonstrating the benefits of
having children and the punishments of not having children.
The hypothesis underlying both is that the fecund earth
and fecund mankind are linked together: a husband and
wife who believe in having as many children as possible
can revitalize neglected farm land; a couple who, influenced by literary nonsense, want only each other and
pleasure, end up poor and sterile. One family tries to
restrict the family to one son so that their property
wouldn't be divided, the sole child dies. Another
family wants no more children so that the father can try
for increased social status by changing jobs; mother and
daughter die as a result of abortions. An aristocratic
couple who believe sterile love is poetic and beautiful
have a series of lovers, each, and troubled children,
the eldest of whom sees the mother and a lover together,
becomes hysterical, and enters a convent. The efforts
at birth control by upper-class women send men to lower-
class women who must take care of any resultant children
themselves--usually by sending them to "baby farms"
where they are killed by neglect. However, Zola does
portray the fate of children in large families where
there is not enough money. In one family, one child
becomes vicious, one is talked into a hysterectomy which
leaves her a paralyzed idiot, and one has a series of
illegitimate children. In another family, there is
literally no room in the home-shop for the child which
is farmed out until big enough to help. The child dies.

There are "good doctors" and "bad doctors." The good
doctor believes that women must bear children or they
will be unhealthy and eventually sterile. One bad
doctor advocates hysterectomies, regardless of consequences to the patient, and the other performs murderous
abortions. There are two lying-in places. The good
one is light and tries to save the mother; the dark,
evil one effectively guarantees the mother that her
child will not survive birth. There is a nice description of childbirth with the husband present (Book I,
Chapter 5).

Zola, Emile. _Germinal_, trans. Stanley and Eleanor Hochman. New
   York: New American Library, 1970. Novel.

The Body	Children	Doctors
The Family	Poverty & Health	Preg. & Childbirth
Sexuality	Suffering	

Powerful. Describes the physical agony of working in the
mines, the awkward positions, the darkness, the heat.
The contrast between the miners' families and the pampered
children of the shareholders. The disasterous strike.
The company doctor has been indifferent, callous before
the strike. Now he is inadequate, the target of hostility, as the workers suffer from deprivation and starvation, their minds destroyed by sabotage. The novel's
heroine, if it can be said to have one, is Catherine, a
mine worker, who tries unsuccessfully to hold to her
family amid exhaustion, starvation, fear of debilitating
pregnancy and physical and sexual assaults by the other
miners, brutalized by the life. Her strength and
sexuality cannot save her family who, to her anguish,
die in the conflict. In this novel Zola makes the
reader feel the miners to be one great suffering body.

Zola, Emile. _Une Page D'Amour_. From _Oeuvres Complètes_, Vol. 3.
   Paris: Librairie Hachette, 1962. Novel, in French.

Children	Disease & Health	Doctors
Dying	Grief	Sexuality

A youthful widow lives in seclusion with her weak,
somewhat epileptic daughter, Jeanne, whose illness
brings the mother in contact with a married doctor
who falls in love with the mother. A very complicated
triangle emerges out of Jeanne's love, and then jealousy, of the doctor, the mother's hesitant love for
the doctor, and the doctor. The affair is consummated
in an apartment set aside for the doctor's wife and
her lover. However, Jeanne worries about her mother,
catches cold, and dies. There is a very good portrayal of the adult relationships swirling about the
dying child. The affair is marked by two children's
parties: a healthy one where the doctor and the
mother declare their love; a grotesque one prepared
by the doctor's wife consisting of a childish funeral
for Jeanne. The wife cannot understand why the grieving
widow refuses to play along. The work contrasts
mothers who have healthy children with those who have
sick ones.

20th Century

Agee, James. <u>A Death in the Family</u>. New York: Grosset & Dunlap, 1967. Novel.

Children	Death	Dying
The Family	Grief	

The tangible domesticity of grief. A young father's death sets in motion a bereavement process--in his wife, his children, Rufus and Catherine, and their immediate family-- which is treated at once objectively and lyrically. The older members of the family discuss precisely how Jay died; they make arrangements; they reach out to protect the children. For his part, six-year-old Rufus registers events and reactions without fully understanding--yet, and therein lies a good deal of the poignancy--just what has happened. ("My daddy's dead," he tries out on a stranger.) That the family is Catholic doesn't quite explain the scene in which, without consulting each other, they all suddenly feel Jay's ghostly presence. What does help to explain it is the aesthetic need to fill transitorily the profoundly empty space left by the man whose human presence Agee takes care to create so truthfully.

Albee, Edward. <u>The Death of Bessie Smith</u>. From <u>The Zoo Story</u>, etc. New York: Coward, McCann & Geoghegan, Inc., 1960. Drama.

Death	Disease & Health	Doctors
The Family	Madness	Med. Ethics
Med. Instit.	Nurses	Poverty & Health
Sexuality	Suffering	

A short play which does two things simultaneously: it dramatizes the warped social and medical policy that historically surrounded the death of a great black singer; and it probes the psychology of several Southern white neurotics. Bessie Smith never appears on stage, but this invisibility is in keeping with Albee's view of the general treatment of blacks in Southern, 1937, white-only hospitals. You may be bleeding, you may be dying, but in this white hospital, if you're black, a white mayor with hemorrhoids will get more care than you will. The people who enact this deadliness include a couple of nurses, a black orderly, and a young white intern. In general, the men come off better than the women, though all of them are excused partly by the intense, frustrating, hot atmosphere that pervades both physical and psychological settings. One nurse is just plain bored with her admissions job. The other, also an admissions nurse, is a bitch. We first see her with her irritable and irritating father, whom she treats with rapidly alternating tenderness and contempt; next with the Uncle Tom orderly, whom she abuses mercilessly; then with her sexually unsatisfied boyfriend, the intern, whom she teases, threatens, and castrates. She accuses the man of thinking himself a great white savior when the truth is he makes less money than the orderly. She has him there; for he does indeed dream of leaving this second-rate suburban Memphis hospital and going to Spain, where dying civilians need him. When Bessie is brought in, and he agrees to treat her against the hysterical warnings of the nurse, he becomes maddened himself when he realizes that his patient is already dead. He is thwarted, impotent. But then, so is everyone else in this play.

Amis, Kingsley. <u>Ending Up</u>. New York: Harcourt, Brace, Jovanovich, 1974. Novel.

Age	Alcoholism	Death
Disease & Health	Doctors	Dying
Homosexuality		

A savagely comic portrait of five eccentric old people. One is an alcoholic, two are homosexuals, one has had a stroke, one is becoming senile--and all are dying. In fact, all do die, vividly and grotesquely. Different from other contemporary British comments on age in that society carries relatively less responsibility and human nature relatively more. The doctor, who appears frequently, is one of the few stable and honorable characters in the novel.

Anderson, Maxwell. <u>Bad Seed</u>. New York: Dodd, Mead & Co., 1955. Drama.

Children	Euthanasia	Madness
Suicide		

See Campbell, William Edward March.

Anderson, Sherwood. "Brother Death," 1933. Available in <u>Short Stories by Sherwood Anderson</u>, ed. Maxwell Geismar. New York: Hill and Wang, 1962. Short Story.

Death	The Family

A simple story about the relationships among members of a midwestern family, who hover solicitously over one of the sons, a young man whose weak heart could kill him at any moment. His sister, Mary, realizing that the family's behavior unnecessarily reinforces the approaching death, forms a protective relationship with the sick brother,

Ted. But in Anderson's eyes, it is another brother, Don, who is truly in need of protection, for Don is a victim of a different form of death--a worse one. He has tried to rebel against his father's subtly harsh treatment of the mother, but has been forced to surrender to his father's power. In contrast, Ted, though dying, has always been free.

Anderson, Sherwood. "Death in the Woods," 1933. Available in <u>Short Stories by Sherwood Anderson</u>, ed. Maxwell Geismar. New York: Hill and Wang, 1962. Short Story.

Dying

In this instance, the act of dying is a relatively indifferent matter. A worn-out old woman lies in the snowy woods, dying quietly, while some dogs run laps around her, awaiting her death (cf. Jack London, "To Build a Fire"). For the townspeople, the woman's death is insignificant by itself. Only the dogs make it noteworthy.

Anouilh, Jean. <u>Ardèle</u>, 1948. Available in <u>Jean Anouilh</u>, Vol. 2. New York: Hill and Wang, 1963. Drama.

Handicaps	Madness	Sexuality
Suicide		

The psychically warped defeat the physically warped. When Ardèle and her lover, who are both hunchbacks, propose to marry, the rest of the family rally in an attempt to prevent a scandal. The family is a mess of complex sexual relationships. The General is intimately tied to his mad wife, whose cries haunt him, but he seeks a sexual release with maids. His sister's menage-à-trois is a strange one, in that her lover is increasingly jealous of her husband because she flirts with him. At the same time, the husband carries on with a jealous, tubercular mistress. The General's son is in love with Natalie, his own brother's wife. She, in turn, admits to loving him, but cannot give up her boorish husband, for he is supremely competent in bed. This sexual morass is contrasted with the pure love of the two hunchbacks. It is not clear whether the family is revolted by the physical absurdity of their love, or its purity. In the end, Ardèle and her lover commit suicide, and the children of the family perpetuate the combat of love.

Arden, John. <u>The Happy Haven</u>, 1960. From <u>Three Plays</u>, by John Arden. New York: Grove Press, 1966. Drama.

Age	The Body	Doctors
Drugs	Med. Ethics	Med. Instit.
Nurses	Sexuality	Women as Patients

When this comedy set in an old age home was first produced, it struck some members of the London audience as tasteless, for instead of the acceptable sentimentality about the elderly, they saw old people being treated as human beings. And like all human beings, the five old people here are a mixture of qualities and motives. One loves his dog more than anyone else. One spends all her time thinking about money. Another is always thinking about courtly love, a thin cover-up, in his case, for sexual obsessions. A fourth is completely selfish, wanting all, giving nothing. When visitors to the Happy Haven home try to converse in the usual patronizing manner to these elderly "boys and girls," the playwright makes the conversation all garble and gobble-de-gook. That's the way he treats the doctor-director's medical jargon too. When he speaks about his patients' bodies, he sounds as if he is talking about engines, rather than something human. Nor is he much more admirable--though he is equally funny--when he talks of his research, the discovery of an elixir of youth. That his elixir is to be given to the old people without their knowledge does not concern him in the least, but it does concern them, of course, so that finally they take control of their own bodies and their own futures. Lest we dismiss the doctor as a simple, villain, however, we also see him in private, more human, moments. The roles of the nurses and orderlies in this medical institution, by the way, are just that. They exist only to serve the doctor. They don't speak, except over loudspeakers. The play is very revealing about the reality of old age, both its amusing aspects and its fears. Arden uses an image for age that is similar to Patrick White's, <u>q.v.</u> One old lady says of herself: "I'm a big round stone/Sitting in the middle of a thunderstorm."

Arking, Linda. "Certain Hard Places." <u>The New Yorker</u>, March 25, 1974. Short Story.

Abortion	Med. Instit.	Med. Profession
Sexual Roles		

Margo, a young journalist, has an affair with Dan, a radical disillusioned ex-college instructor. His political interests include reforming the health system, or at least talking about reform, especially following the Chinese model, where, he claims, everyone--nurses, relatives, orderlies--makes suggestions, and patients even make rounds with the doctors. "Whereas here, for Chrissake, you're supposed to sleep through it like everything else. Just be passive, don't ask questions, don't bother the doctor. God, anesthesia's another form of alienation." His faith is put to the test when Margo becomes pregnant and seeks his support during what is described as a competent but impersonal and insensitive procedure. Dan, confused, takes off, returning after the fact to reveal his fear. Margo has been through a painful experience, of course, but the story ends with her certainty that, unlike Poor Dan, whom she cannot dislike, she has real faith in her ability to prevail.

Arlen, Michael. The Green Hat. New York: George H. Doran Co., 1924. Novel.

Alcoholism	By Doctors	Doctors
The Family	Preg. & Childbirth	Sexuality
Suicide	V.D.	

Arlen was not really a doctor, and The Green Hat does not really qualify as literature either, but it is included here as a bizarre period piece by a man who was for a time a medical student. Fashionable in its day because of its outré heroine, who was modeled on the woman who provided the inspiration for Hemingway's Lady Brett Ashley, this novel now seems outrageously purple and melodramatic. Iris Storm has been twice-widowed. Her first husband, a kind of Rupert Brooke figure, killed himself on their wedding night because he had syphilis. As she tells the story, however, he died "for purity" because he discovered that she was sexually experienced. Because he was the hero of Iris' incestuously inclined twin brother, the brother becomes an alcoholic and eventually kills himself. After she becomes pregnant by The Only Man She Ever Truly Loved and then almost dies with septic poisoning, Iris gives up the man, who is engaged to another, by skillfully arranging her own suicide to look like a car accident. All this, and more! The interesting thing is that this novel contains almost no evidence that its author was a student of medicine. He writes of illness, including venereal disease, as if it had incredible romantic properties. His doctor character, Conrad Masters, is a boring caricature--direct, peevish, a "captain of men."

Auden, W. H. "Adolescence," 1927-32. From Collected Shorter Poems. New York: Random House, 1966. Poem: 16 lines.

Adolescence   The Family

In the first three stanzas, a boy wanders about the fields feeling good about himself, lovely even, and brave. He thinks fondly of his family; he sees in the hilly landscape reminders of his mother's body. In the last stanza, he returns home, and crashes from his heights of happiness when his family, now called "the band," and his mother, now become a "giantess," treat him incongruously, as if they don't know at all the adolescent boy we've seen in the first part of the poem. But this note is an offensive paraphrase of a strongly felt experience.

Auden, W. H. "The Age of Anxiety," Parts II ("The Seven Ages") and III ("The Seven Stages"), 1945. From Collected Longer Poems. New York: Vintage Books, 1975. Long Poem.

Age	Adolescence	The Body
Body/Mind	Children	Doctors
The Family		

"The Age of Anxiety" is an "eclogue" with four characters. John Fuller (A Reader's Guide to W. H. Auden) lists them as Malin, a medical officer, who represents Thinking; Rosetta, who represents Feeling (the two Jungian rational, evaluative faculties); Quant, Intuition; and Emble, Sensation (the two irrational, perceptive faculties). In Part II, Auden, taking off from Shakespeare (Jacques' speech in As You Like It), explores the physical, psychological, and ultimately mystical aspects of the seven ages of man, beginning with the infant, ending with old age, and inevitably passing through all the stages which the family doctor studies (thus the rather special use of "The Family" topic here). The doctor, Malin, always introduces each age with observations appropriate to his profession, but the picture is not complete until Feeling, Intuition, and Sensation are added. In Part III the four characters still in search of an answer to their anxiety, "journey" through a landscape seen in terms of the human body. They start in a mountainous district, representing the female breasts, man's early goal, and travel through landscapes representing the heart, blood, the brain, the skeleton, and finally the "hermetic gardens," the genitals. Compare The Ascent of F6, a play by Auden and Christopher Isherwood, in which the Doctor, as Fuller would have it, represents not Thinking, but--"vegetative and worried about his fatness"--Intuition.

Auden, W. H. "The Art of Healing." From The New Yorker (27 September 1969), p. 38. Poem: 78 lines.

Disease & Health   Doctors   Grief
Med. Profession

A poem to the memory of Auden's physician. He first expresses shock that his doctor could die--that's something patients don't think of--and then he describes Dr. Protetch's approach to healing, which was like the senior Auden's: "'Healing,'/Papa would tell me,/'is not a science/but the intuitive art/of wooing Nature.'" Very nice, and this is even more comforting: "'Every sickness/is a musical problem,'/so said Novalis,/'and

every cure/a musical solution.'" Furthermore, Auden's doctor treated his small ailments and left his "major vices," and his "mad addictions" to his own conscience. The poet could trust this man, perhaps because the doctor himself was seriously ill with diabetes. ("Must diabetics/all contend with a nisus/to self-destruction?" Auden wonders; cf. James Dickey's "Diabetes.") In the last lines the poet chooses for his distance from his subject one that many doctors try to achieve with their patients, a sort of objective affection: "Dear David,/ dead one, rest in peace,'having been what all/doctors should be but few are,'and, even when most/difficult, condign/of our biassed affection/and objective praise."

Auden, W. H. "The Geography of the House." From Selected Poetry of W. H. Auden. New York: Vintage Books, 1971. Poem: 80 lines.

The Body

A very funny meditation from the outhouse upon the satisfactions of the daily dump.

Auden, W. H. "Give me a doctor," 1948-57. From Collected Shorter Poems. New York: Random House, 1966. Poem: 8 lines.

Death   Doctors

One of Auden's "shorts," this poem simply asks for a doctor who is "partridge-plump," because he will never ask the poet to abandon his vices, "Nor pull a long face in a crisis,/But with a twinkle in his eye/Will tell me that I have to die."

Auden, W. H. "The History of Science," 1948-57. From Collected Shorter Poems. New York: Random House, 1966. Poem: 32 lines.

Med. Profession

About science in general and therefore relevant to medical science as pursued by researchers. A charming metaphor for research progress in the person of an imagined 4th son--fairy tales normally having only 3. This 4th and younger brother, though he be advised by an old crone to go South, will inevitably go North, "Trusting some map in his own head." So he reaches a goal unintended by Authority but more marvelous.

Auden, W. H. "In Memory of Sigmund Freud," 1939. From Collected Shorter Poems. New York: Random House, 1966. Poem: 112 lines.

Disease & Health   Doctors   Grief

Auden takes the measure of Sigmund Freud and finds him, on the whole, a good man, not really a clever man--sometimes even absurd--but one who should be mourned, for he was one of "those who were doing us some good,/ who knew it was never enough but/hoped to improve a little by living." Auden's poet invocation of Freud's discoveries is memorable: "he merely told/The unhappy Present to recite the Past/like a poetry lesson till sooner/or later it faltered at the line where/long ago the accusations had begun,/and suddenly knew by whom it had been judged,/how rich life had been and how silly,/ and was life-forgiven and more humble,/able to approach the Future as a friend/without a wardrobe of excuses, without/a set mask of rectitude or an/embarrassing over-familiar gesture." Freud did more than free us, Auden contends; he also taught us to wonder at, to be enthusiastic over, and to love the night of our own being.

Auden, W. H. "In Memory of W. B. Yeats," 1939. From Collected Shorter Poems. New York: Random House, 1966. Poem: 65 lines.

Grief

One of the finest elegies in the language. It contains some traditional elements, such as the reflection in nature of the death of a great man: "He disappeared in the dead of winter . . . The day of his death was a dark cold day." But Auden twists the conventions a little, adding additional significance: "What instruments we have agree/The day of his death was a dark cold day." Auden suggests that Yeats as well as his work lives on in his readers themselves--"he became his admirers"-- and they may take him over--"The words of a dead man/Are modified in the guts of the living." In the second part of the poem Auden deals with his grief by naming the poetic gift as greater than the man himself and as the surviving element: "You were silly like us; your gift survived it all:/The parish of rich women, physical decay,/Yourself." But, Auden acknowledges, poetry makes nothing happen, not even Yeats' poetry, for Ireland is still as mad as he found it. It makes nothing happen, but it survives, "A way of happening, a mouth." The last section of the poem is a short chant, in the nature of a prayer to the dead poet, invoking his aid in these troubled times (1939): "In the deserts of the heart/Let the healing fountain start,/In the prison of his days/ Teach the free man how to praise."

Auden, W. H. "Miss Gee," 1933-38. From Collected Shorter Poems. New York: Random House, 1966. Poem: 100 lines.

The Body	Death	Disease & Health
Doctors	Med. Instit.	Med. Students
Sexuality		

A ballad whose chirpy rhythms belie the story of a sadly anonymous and isolated woman of a lower economic station. The narrator amuses himself at the expense of her repressed sexuality: "Her lips they were thin and small . . . And she had no bust at all." Still, she has tantalizing dreams about being charged by bulls with lowered horns. One day she bicycles down to the doctor carrying the same lack of self-knowledge seen in the rest of her life. She has come too late to be saved. Doctor Thomas expresses as much compassion as this verse form will allow as he puts forth this theory of the cause of cancer: "'Childless women get it,/And men when they retire;/It's as if there had to be some outlet/For their foiled creative fire.'" No one else in the medical profession shows the least concern for Miss Gee's poor self. In one stanza she is lying, "a total wreck," in the women's ward. In the next, with no reference at all to her death, we find these startling lines: "They laid her on the table,/The students began to laugh;/And Mr. Rose the surgeon/He cut Miss Gee in half." We last see Miss Gee hanging from the ceiling of the Anatomy lab, having her knee dissected.

Auden, W. H. "The Model," 1939-47. From Collected Shorter Poems. New York: Random House, 1966. Poem: 24 lines.

Age   Body/Mind

Auden argues that the body of a certain old lady "exactly indicates her mind." Some bodies may fool us, but the obvious fact that this woman is 80 and healthy tells us all. At that age, a little greed makes one ill, he says, and despair kills one. She has survived all that, over-come, oh, it doesn't matter precisely what. Because she exists and is well, we know that "she forgave; she became." She is assertively human.

Auden, W. H. "No, Plato, No" and "Lullaby." From Thank You, Fog. New York: Random House, 1974. Poems: 28 & 60 lines.

Age   Body/Mind   Death

In the first poem, the poet declines to believe in the Platonic Ideal, favoring his senses instead. Still, he says, he can imagine that his body (feminine here) is somehow getting worn out after all these years of trying to keep "Him," her master, going and longs for His death so that She can become irresponsible matter. In "Lullaby" the old poet sings himself to sleep with the refrain "Sing, Big Baby, sing lullay," and narcissistically hugs his "almost feminine flesh," letting go of the "verbalising I" and giving in to the "belly-mind . . . down below the diaphragm" (compare D. H. Lawrence, Fantasia of the Unconscious, q.v.).

Auden, W. H. "Surgical Ward." From Selected Poetry of W. H. Auden. New York: Vintage Books, 1971. Sonnet.

Disease & Health   Med. Instit.

Auden's observations on the inevitable isolation of the very sick: "They are and suffer; that is all they do;/A bandage hides the place where each is living,/His knowl-edge of the world restricted to/The treatment that the instruments are giving." As for us, the healthy, we stand apart "and believe/In the common world of the uninjured . . . . Only happiness is shared,/And anger, and the idea of love."

Auden, W. H. Untitled "Short." From Thank You, Fog. New York: Random House, 1974. Poem: 3 lines.

Disease & Health

A 3-line theory of the origins of disease: "Man must either fall in love/with Someone or Something,/or else fall ill."

Auden, W. H. and Christopher Isherwood. The Dog Beneath the Skin, 1935. Available in Two Great Plays by W. H. Auden and Christopher Isherwood. New York: Random House, n.d. Poetic Drama.

Disease & Health   Doctors   Med. Instit.
Med. Students   Nurses   Surgery
Women as Patients

The relevant passages of this satirical, expressionist play are Act II, scene i, which takes place in a lunatic asylum, and scenes iii and iv of the same act, which take place in the gardens and operating room of a convalescent home. The first scene is an attack on German nationalism. "Westland" (Germany) has produced more madmen than any other European country. "Our Leader" (Hitler) has a loud-speaker instead of a face. And so on. Funny, chaotic, a bit facile, but somehow theatrical. Scene iii intro-duces two self-absorbed female invalids ("Betty's a lucky girl. She's got tubes."), several sports-minded medical students, a hierarchy of nurses, including a dog disguised as a nurse, and a surgeon who operates as if surgery were a religious ritual. (Isher-wood compares an operation to a religious ritual in his autobiography, Lions and Shadows, London, 1938, p. 294.) The medical team at one point chant a Creed, beginning "I believe in the physical causation of all phenomena," and proceeding to this exchange: "Let not the patient react unfavourably to the anaesthetic. But let it save him from pain. Let there be no unforeseen complications. Neither let sepsis have the advantage. May my skill not desert me. But guide your hands." The operation is a disaster; the patient sinks fast--to the accompaniment of a Wagnerian duet. John Fuller (A Reader's Guide to W. H. Auden, p. 87) believes that in this scene Auden, an adherent of Homer Lane's theory of the psychological origin of disease, is attempting to show up as ridiculous

surgery and its attendant physical theories of disease. Fuller also argues that in Auden's "charade," Paid on Both Sides (Collected Longer Poems. New York: Vintage, 1975), the doctor character is a Homer Lane figure, who looks at the brain and sees that it "advances and retreats under control and poisons everything around it." In any case, it is certain that Auden sees false healers every-where, and in the dedicatory quatrain to Dog, advances the revolutionary as a true healer: "Boy with lancet, speech or gun/Among the dangerous ruins, learn/From each devastated organ/The power of the genteel dragon."

Babel, Isaac. "The End of the Old-Folk's Home," 1920-1929. From The Collected Stories of Isaac Babel, ed. Walter Morison. New York: Criterion Books, 1955. Short Story.

Age   Disease & Health   Doctors
Med. Instit.   Poverty & Health

An unsentimental look at the elderly poor: these old folk belch; they wheeze with asthma; they brandish their crutches, "yelling like hungry donkeys" (trans. Morison). Their situation is at first grotesquely humorous. Housed in an institution next to a Russian Jewish cemetery, they have over the years cornered the market on grave-digging, corpse-washing, and cantering (of sorts). They re-use the same betasseled coffin, making a good deal of money in this way. But the time comes when all that changes, again in a misleadingly comic fashion. A leading soldier is buried, and his followers insist that the coffin be buried with him; after that, the old folks lose every-thing, coming quickly to near-starvation. When a doctor, Dr. Judith Shmaiser, arrives to give them smallpox injections, the old people declare their misery; one claims that there is no room on his shrivelled arm for an injection. Ultimately, new Soviet officials like the Manager of Communal Property and the Manager of Public Welfare evict the old people, who are last seen limping along the room, accompanied by soldiers from the Red Army.

Babel, Isaac. "The Story of My Dovecot," 1925. From The Collected Stories of Isaac Babel, ec. Walter Morison. New York: Criterion Books, 1955. Short Story.

Children   Death   Grief
Handicaps

A deceptively humorous and simple story which ends in terrible despair for both the 9-year-old boy and the reader. Babel depicts the lives and values of Russian Jews with his usual skill, in this case from the per-spective of a physically weak, extremely bright, and thoroughly endearing boy who tells a meandering but soon to be significant story, finally lighting on the day he went to buy his long-dreamed-of pigeons. He buys several beauties, and then, rushing home because of news of a pogrom, he runs into a Russian cripple, a legless man in a wheelchair, with a wife who is muttering threats against the Jews, their "spawn," and "their stinking menfolk." Formerly a friend, this cripple, now greedy because of the looting afoot, grabs one of the boy's beloved pigeons and, with the bird still in his hand, strikes the boy across the face, smashing the pigeon and sending her soft guts spilling down the boy's amazed and grief-stricken face. Thereafter he runs home to discover that his grandfather, introduced earlier in the story, has been murdered by the rampaging Russians. It would be hard to find a better, less sentimental prose rendering of a boy's first encounter with death, espe-cially in the short form.

Baldwin, James. Giovanni's Room. New York: Dial Press, 1956. Novel.

Homosexuality

The failure of homosexual love because of one man's guilt feelings. Set amidst the gay underground of Paris, a love affair develops between David (American, puritanical, formerly straight) and Giovanni (Italian, sensual, father of a child). They live together, becoming increasingly tender and passionate with each other, but finally facing David's need to identify with the straight world of women and children, especially now that his girlfriend is coming back, and his fears about thinking himself gay. Giovanni rejects such narrow categories. For him, there are no straights and gays--he himself has not been exclusively homosexual--there is just love between two people. And when David returns to his girlfriend, Giovanni accuses David of never having been committed to their relation-ship, of being afraid to face their love. Eventually, David's love for his girlfriend dies and Giovanni's character disintegrates, ending in his immersion in the sordid side of homosexual society and his execution for murder. In a final image, David faces a mirror, search-ing out himself.

Barth, John. The End of the Road. New York: Doubleday, 1967. Novel.

Abortion   Doctors   Dying
Grief   Madness   Med. Instit.
Nurses   Preg. & Childbirth   Sexuality
Suicide

Jake Horner sits in a corner of a train station, paralyzed. Along comes a "doctor," articulate, aggressive, and black, who takes him to his Remobilization Farm for the treat-ment of psychosomatically paralyzed people. There the doctor, both brilliant and insane, and assisted by the athletic, silent Nurse Dockey, practices several kinds of therapy: Nutritional Therapy, Medicinal Therapy, Surgical Therapy, Dynamic Therapy, Informational Therapy (the patient spends his time studying The World Almanac), Sexual Therapy, Theotherapy, Atheotherapy, and others. For Jake, the doctor chooses Mythotherapy, which is based on existential philosophy, it seems. Jake is told that every person is the hero of his own life story and the writer of his own script; that only an unimaginative person writes just one role for himself; and that at any given time a person must assume wholeheartedly the role, or mask, he has chosen. Integrity, under this system, simply means being faithful to your script. Applying this advice, Jake soon adopts a role modeled on his friend Joe Morgan, who claims to have dropped all objective value systems. Joe throws Rennie, his wife, and Jake together, but none of them can react with integrity of any sort when Rennie announces that she is pregnant, and doesn't know which one of them is the father. Furthermore, she says that she will kill herself if some sort of abortion can't be arranged. In a gro-tesquely comic episode, Jake impersonates a psychiatrist and attempts to talk a doctor into performing an abortion. When that falls through, he gets his mythotherapist to agree to an abortion. It is a ghastly affair: Rennie, who had not been told to fast, takes ether, vomits up into the mask, and aspirates it into her lungs, dying before Jake's horrified eyes. Even then, neither Jake nor Joe, pseudo-sophisticated amoralist, can react very humanly. They're lost; it's the end of the road.

Beauvoir, Simone de. A Very Easy Death, 1964. New York: Warner Paperback Library, 1973. Autobiography.

Age	The Body	Children
Death	Doctors	Dying
Euthanasia	Grief	Med. Instit.
Nurses		

The author of two very important non-literary documents on medically relevant subjects (The Second Sex, Bantam, 1970, on Sexuality and Sexual Roles; and The Coming of Age, Putnam, 1972, on Age), Simone de Beauvoir has achieved a work of art with this one, on the death by intestinal cancer of her aged mother. The moments of greatest torment come when Mlle. de Beauvoir looks at the semi-naked, ravaged body that is (or was) her mother; when they must put up with the condescension and self-importance of the doctors (the nurses are kinder, but overworked and underpaid); when she chooses surgery over a faster, less painful death; and, of course, during the intense grieving period when she analyzes why the death was so painful to her when she had not felt any particularly strong emotional impulses towards her mother for years. The author is shocked when, after the mother has died during what is rendered as a wretched experience for everyone, a nurse remarks that she had a very easy death. But Beauvoir soon realizes that indeed her mother had died an upper middle-class death, that others were far worse. Still, thinking about the death of someone old, she concludes: "There is no such thing as a natural death: nothing that happens to a man is ever natural, since his presence calls the world into question. All men must die: but for every man his death is an accident and, even if he knows it and consents to it, an unjusti-fiable violation" (trans. Patrick o'Brien).

Beckett, Samuel. Endgame, 1957. Available in Masters of Modern Drama, eds. Haskell M. Block and Robert G. Shedd. New York: Random House, 1962. Drama.

Age	Children	Disease & Health
Dying	Med. Instit.	

Set in a dismal time period--after a future holocaust? or simply in the meaningless isolation of the present?--this one-act play has only four characters: two ill, two elderly, all miserable, in a grimly comic way. The action, such as it is, is dominated by Hamm and Clov (whose names link them as inescapably as the natures their dialogue reveals). Hamm is blinded, incapable of control-ling his bladder, and can't stand up. Clov's eyes hurt, his legs hurt, and he can't sit down. All the two can do is tell and listen to meaningless stories and play games (they are dying; the world is dying; this is the game they play as they wait for the end). Everything has come unstuck in this world. There is no such thing as family anymore, no respect for old parents. Hamm keeps his--Nagg and Nell--in two garbage cans (rather like some old age homes?), from which they emerge from time to time, making demands like infants and sighing about their past. (See also Beckett's most famous portraits of the meaning-less existence of the old, the aging Didi and Gogo in Waiting for Godot.)

Beckett, Samuel. Krapp's Last Tape, 1958. From Krapp's Last Tape and Other Dramatic Pieces. New York: Grove Press, 1960. Drama.

Age	Death

A clever one-act play, whose warmth manages to seep through the cleverness, especially on stage. The gimmick is this: Krapp is an old man of about 70, and this day is his birth-day. Every birthday he makes a tape on which he summarizes his year, from notes because he seems to love words for their own sake. To get going he listens to an old tape. During the play, he listens to a tape made on this 39th birthday (that younger Krapp had been listening to a still younger man before making his tape). And the "action" of the play consists of the "communication" between the tape and the

present Krapp. There's no one else because Krapp, we gather from a clue here and there, has seen to that. The great question is, since this is his "last tape," What has his life meant? He skips over the meaning-of-it-all section in the old tape as being, perhaps, too pompous, and anyhow irrelevant to the elderly Krapp. He lingers over a love scene, but one is only too conscious of how far away it is. Finally, Krapp finds he can't make his birthday tape this year, and he's left with the old tapes, some very long pauses, and the utter emptiness of words for their own sake.

Bellow, Saul. Mr. Sammler's Planet. New York: Viking Press, 1970. Novel.

Age	Children	Death
Disease & Health	Doctors	Dying
The Family	Grief	Madness
Med. Instit.	Sexuality	

An unusual hero: a highly intelligent, tolerant man of 70 plus years, who walks the streets of New York City, seeing into all its contemporary madness and remembering his association with intellectual London in the 30's and his years as a Polish Jewish refugee. Mr. Sammler's wife died during those years, but he has some family left: his daughter Shula, who is one of society's many uninsti-tutionalized crazies; his niece Angela, who thinks that love is sleeping with as many men as she can; his nephew, Dr. Gruner, a surgeon, who throughout the novel lies in a hospital bed, knowledgeably observing his own approach-ing death from an aneuryism in the throat (syphilitic?). Some of the scenes are bizarre comedy. Mr. Sammler, urbanely addressing a group of university students, and told that what he is saying is Shit, muses on the contem-porary choice of excrement as a critical judgment. He is even able to be fascinated by his own mugging (a big, black, well-dressed pickpocket demonstrates his lordliness by brandishing his large penis), though all this seems very strange to a man of Mr. Sammler's background and age. Over and over it is his compassion and tolerance for his species that strikes one about this old man. He has outlived much, however, and the book ends with a stunning statement of grief--for his doctor-nephew and, by natural extension, for the whole planet: "Remember, God, the soul of Elya Gruner, who, as willingly as possible and as well as he was able, and even to an intolerable point, and even in suffocation and even as death was coming was eager, even childishly perhaps (may I be forgiven for this), even with a certain servility, to do what was required of him . . . . He was aware that he must meet, and he did meet--through all the confusion and degraded clowning of this life through which we are speeding--he did meet the terms of his contract. The terms which, in his inmost heart, each man knows."

Benn, Gottfried. "Answer to the Literary Immigrants," 1933. Available in Primal Vision: Selected Writings of Gottfried Benn. New York: New Directions, 1971. Essay.

By Doctors	Med. Ethics

This essay illustrates why Benn (1886-1956), though a fine poet--certainly a first-rate poet-doctor--was ignored for several years and perhaps still has not achieved the recognition due him. The reasons are political rather than literary. Here Dr. Benn writes a public answer to Klaus Mann (Thomas Mann's son), who had decried Benn's decision to stay in Germany during the Nazi regime. Benn has a biological view of history. It emits, he says, "from the inexhaustible womb of the race, a new human type that has to fight its way, has to work the idea of its generation and its kind into the texture of time, unwavering, acting and suffering as the law of life demands" (trans. E. B. Ashton). Benn feels that one cannot fight this kind of activity; one can only observe it, much as--the reader is inclined to say--the doctor observes and assists at births of every sort. Benn also indirectly invokes his brand of medical ethics when he writes, "I personally declare for the new state, because it is my people whose trail is being blazed here. Who am I to exclude myself? Do I know better? No. I can try to guide it, as far as lies in my power, in the direction I should like to see followed; but if I failed, it would still be my people." Those people, one could add, whom he has pledged to serve as a physician. Once, in fact, he asserts his right as a physician to make accurate generalizations about all social classes, because he sees them all in his work. And, he maintains, in Nazi Germany the workers are better off than before.

Benn, Gottfried. "Artists and Old Age," 1954. Available in Primal Vision: Selected Writings of Gottfried Benn. New York: New Directions, 1971. Essay.

Age	By Doctors	Med. Profession

A long essay that accomplishes several goals, not neces-sarily consistent with each other. For one thing, it is a useful compendium of several important statements on old age and any creative person, which is to say, almost any person at all. Benn quotes Burne-Jones, for instance, who feels that "our first 50 years are squandered on committing great errors; then we grow timid and scarcely dare to set our right foot before the left any longer, so well are we aware of our own weakness. Then there follow twenty years of toil, and only now do we begin to understand what we are capable of and what we have to leave undone. And then there comes a ray of hope and a trumpetcall, and away we must go from the earth." To the thoughts of others, Benn adds his own. He suggests that the backward-glancing Epimetheus be taken as the patron of old age. He explains what it is like to have scholarly dissertations written about one; only then, he says, does one see himself. He catalogs all the famous artists who reached a great age. He evokes the old age of Flaubert, of Leonardo. He asks if famous "late" works share any qualities. At greater length, he evokes age as he has known it, and what the world looks like from his current perspective. Finally, he absolves himself of the political charges brought against him, and says he would write over again the same sentences he wrote in his youth. One thing Benn does not do, and that is take any insights from his study of medicine. In fact, he has this to say about scientific progress: "The body has grown more morbid, with modern medicine positively offering it thousands of diseases . . . oh, no slur on the doctors, a very fine lot of men, I only mean that in the old days if you were bitten by a mosquito you scratched the place, but today they can prescribe a dozen different ointments and not one of them helps--still that's life, it keeps things moving. Our bodies are more morbid than they used to be, but they live longer." Elsewhere in the essay Benn asserts that he is not interested in the physiology of aging, and he concludes that "what medicine has to say on this subject doesn't amount to much" (trans. Ernst Kaiser and Eithne Wilkins).

Benn, Gottfried. "Little Aster," 1912. Available in Primal Vision: Selected Writings of Gottfried Benn. New York: New Directions, 1971. Poem: 15 lines.

The Body   By Doctors   Death
Doctors

A violent yoking of images of death and life, medical necessity and beauty. The "I" of the poem is a doctor performing an autopsy on a drowned truck-driver into whose teeth someone has stuck a lavender aster. "As I cut out the tongue and the palate,/through the chest/under the skin,/with a long knife,/I must have touched the flower, for it slid/into the brain lying next.../I packed it into the cavity of the chest/among the excelsior/as it was sewn up./Drink yourself full in your vase!/Rest softly,/little aster!" (trans. Babette Deutsch).

Benn, Gottfried. "Lovely Childhood," 1912. Available in Primal Vision: Selected Writings of Gottfried Benn. New York: New Directions, 1971. Poem: 11 lines.

The Body   By Doctors   Death

Similar to "Little Aster," but so startling as to deserve a separate mention. In this poem the dead body is that of a young, drowned girl, whose mouth has been gnawed away. The horror of this image is juxtaposed with what the doctor finds when he cuts open the body: a nest of rats. "One little sister lay dead./The others thrived on liver and kidneys,/drank the cold blood and/enjoyed a lovely childhood here." Grotesque, perhaps? Or does the life which thrives upon death make the girl's childhood lovely too? At any rate, the poet does not turn away from death in any form, for this is what happens to the nest of young rats: "And sweet and swift came their death also;/They were all thrown into the water together,/Oh, how the little muzzles squeaked!" (trans. Babette Deutsch).

Benn, Gottfried. "Man and Woman Go Through the Cancer Ward," 1912. Available in Primal Vision: Selected Writings of Gottfried Benn. New York: New Directions, 1971. Poem: 24 lines.

The Body   Disease & Health   Dying
Med. Instit.   Nurses

Direct images of the havoc of cancer. The man speaks; one imagines the thoughts of the woman as she hears: "Here in this row are wombs that have decayed/and in this row are breasts that have decayed./Bed beside stinking bed . . . . Come, quietly lift up this coverlet./Look, this great mass of fat and ugly tumours/was precious to a man once, and/meant ecstasy and home" (trans. Babette Deutsch). The patients' treatment is horrifying: "Their backs/are sore. You see the flies. Sometimes/the sisters wash them. As one washes benches." Inevitably they are close to death, but in Benn's eyes, their dying is both horrible and completely natural: "Here the grave rises up about each bed./And flesh is leveled down to earth. The fire/burns out. And sap prepares to flow. Earth calls.--"

Benn, Gottfried. "Monologue," 1943. Available in Primal Vision: Selected Writings of Gottfried Benn. New York: New Directions, 1971. Poem: 75 lines.

The Body   By Doctors   Med. Ethics
Plague   Suicide

Dr. Benn turns against the Nazis (see "Answer to the Literary Immigrants"). And, physician that he is, he envisions them as something like a plague of grotesque bodies: "Their colons fed with mucus, brains with lies/these chosen races, coxcombs of a clown,/in pranks, astrology and flight of birds/construing their own ordure!" (trans. Christopher Middleton). Even their victims become part of the plague: "Slaves--/from icy and burning territories,/gross with vermin more and more slaves come,/hungry and whiplash-driven hordes of them." He considers suicide in these lines: "To die means leaving all these things unsolved,/the images unsure, and hungry dreams/abandoned in the rifts between the world." But when he considers the alternative, action,

which in Benn's case meant continuing to serve as an army doctor, he concludes that action means "to serve vulgarity,/aid and abet iniquity."

Benn, Gottfried. "Night Cafe," 1912. Available in Primal Vision: Selected Writings of Gottfried Benn. New York: New Directions, 1971. Poem: 25 lines.

The Body   By Doctors   Disease & Health
Sexuality

Love as it looks to the young doctor. Not the romantic view of the great musicians--"Don't splash the blood of Chopin around the place/for this crowd to slouch about in!"--but rather what the student of bodies and diseases sees: "Green teeth, pimples in his face,/waves to conjunctivitis . . . . Young goitre is sweet on saddlenose . . . . Sycosis buys carnations/to mollify double chin."

Berg, Stephen. "Why Are We Here?" From Grief. New York: Grossman, 1975. Poem: 208 lines.

Death   Doctors   Dying
Grief

The last poem in this fine book of poems on grief. The poem has a narrative base: the poet is awakened by the wife of his friend, a doctor. She mentions a patient's boyfriend's funeral, which starts off a train of questions that will only be resolved, not answered precisely, in an image at the end of the poem. The poet gets up and begins to read a story by someone identified as a doctor-writer (it is Chekhov's "Gusev," q.v.). His long summary of the story illustrates, among other things, that Chekhov is a true poet. But so is Berg. That is proven by his skillful interweaving of the story about a death and burial at sea with statements about isolation and loss ("what happens/with people when they/face each other, afraid to touch,/then reach out and touch only when they're/about to leave"), which in turn edges into the scene around his father's deathbed (missed opportunities everywhere), and finally melds into an image of water-lilies. If not Why We Are Here, they are How We Are: "Their leaves were/flat, tilted like fans held up, or curled, as if they were asleep or about to take off or/hesitantly pointed to the blank sky." We are "the stiff white petals cupping nothing"--a persuasive image for grief.

Berryman, John. "Of Suicide," 1970. Available in The Norton Norton Anthology of Modern Poetry, eds. Richard Ellmann and Robert O'Clair. New York: Norton, 1973. Poem: 28 lines.

Alcoholism   Sexuality   Suicide

An intensely personal poem, beginning with thoughts of the poet's father, who shot himself when the poet was a boy, and moving on--humourously, really, or at least at some distance from his problems--through references to his drinking, his marriage, and his sexuality (Gogol was impotent, he's heard, but he doesn't know at what age). He mentions Rembrandt, who was also terror-stricken, but "of suicide I continually think./Apparently he didn't." (Berryman killed himself in 1972.)

Berryman, John. Recovery. New York: Farrar, Straus and Giroux, 1973. Novel.

Alcoholism   Doctors   The Family
Grief   Med. Instit.   Nurses
Science & Poetry Suicide

This is not a good novel, but it is a fascinating and potentially valuable book. The poet John Berryman left it unfinished at the time of his suicide in 1972. It is, of course, autobiographical: Berryman was, like his hero, an alcoholic, three times married, three times institutionalized. The novel takes us into a hospital for the recovery of alcoholics and into the mind of "Alan Severance, M.D., Litt.D., formerly Professor of Immunology and Molecular Biology, now the University Professor, Pulitzer Prize winner, etc.--twice-invited guest on the Dick Cavett Show (stoned once, and a riot)." The style is impressionistic and serves fairly well to reproduce group therapy sessions as well as Alan's journal, in which he examines his relationships with himself, his present family (a wife and a baby) and his past (his father had killed himself). The counselors are sometimes helpful, often boring; the doctors, ditto; the head nurse, just boring. In addition to himself, it is his fellow-patients who seem to help Alan the most, especially one called the poet (Alan is often called the scientist, though he too is a writer), and Berryman seems to be groping towards some science/poetry truths, such as the bit on the Recognition of Self in an early journal entry: "Research in immunology has implications of far more importance than simply the development of new and better vaccines for protection against disease--important as that is. The whole question of how the body recognizes some substances as "self" and others as "not self," which has a vital bearing on the problem of transplanting tissues and organs from one individual to another . . . ." We don't get to see the entire process of Alan's recovery in this fragment. At the end, though, he becomes a Jew, the perfect symbol for the wandering, persecuted figure he sometimes imagines himself to be, but also some sort of step toward the God that AA always speaks of. The book, as we have it, ends with AA's Twelve Steps: "Having had a spiritual awakening as the result of these steps, we tried to carry this message to alcoholics, and to practice these principles in all our affairs."

Betjeman, John. "A Child Ill." Available in John Betjeman's Collected Poems. Boston: Houghton Mifflin, 1958. Poem: 20 lines.

Age   Children   Dying
Grief

A simple rhyme and meter sets up a moving scene with clarity. The speaker addresses a sick child, whom we later discover to be his son: "'Oh, little body, do not die.'" He remembers that he had this same wordless conversation with the eyes of his dying father: "And now the same blue eyes I see/Look through me from a little son,/So questioning, so searchingly/That youthfulness and age are one." (Compare Joyce's "Ecce Puer.")

Betjeman, John. "The Cottage Hospital." Available in John Betjeman's Collected Poems. Boston: Houghton Mifflin, 1958. Poem: 36 lines.

Dying   Med. Instit.

Death in nature causes the poet to visualize his own death bed. In the first part of the poem, he lies down under a mulberry tree, and listens to the buzzing of the insects and the playing of the children. Then he closes in on a spider killing a fly, a common enough poetic image but here used with special force: "Down came the hairy talons/and horrible poison blade/And none of the garden noticed/that fizzing, hopeless fight." At once he sees himself as the fly, imagines lying in a cottage hospital somewhere, listening to the tap of "inflexible nurses'" feet: "And say shall I groan in dying,/as I twist the sweaty sheet/Or gasp for breath uncrying,/as I feel my senses drown'd/While the air is swimming with insects/and children play in the streets?"

Betjeman, John. "Devonshire Street W.1." Available in John Betjeman's Collected Poems. Boston: Houghton Mifflin, 1958. Poem: 16 lines.

Disease & Health   Death

An understated--one wants to say "English"--reaction to dire news. A man and his wife stand outside his doctor's office, the heavy door shut behind them. "No hope. And the X-ray photographs under his arm/Confirm the message." He grabs the iron knob of a palisade and thinks, "Oh merciless, hurrying Londoners! Why was I made/For the long and the painful deathbed coming to me?" His wife is timid with her dying husband, with death, so turns to practical matters: "It's cheaper to take the tube to Piccadilly/And then we can catch a nineteen or a twenty-two."

Betjeman, John. "On a Portrait of a Deaf Man," 1940. Available in John Betjeman's Collected Poems. Boston: Houghton Mifflin, 1958. Poem: 32 lines.

The Body   Death   Grief
Handicaps

The poet remembers a kindly deaf man, remembers his daily pleasures--he knew birds, for instance, though not their songs--and contrasts them with what his body is like in death: "And when he could not hear me speak/He smiled and looked so wise/That now I do not like to think/Of maggots in his eyes." The grief is all the more terrible because the old man was never able to speak for himself.

Billings, Philip. "Vassar Miller."* Published for the first time here. Poem.

The Body   Death   Disease & Health

Like any good poet
she should not be tolerated.
She has cribbed from our subconscious.
Worse,
she has traded deliberately on human affliction,
stolen rhythm from spasm,
treated weakness like common material,
tortured pain till it sang all it knew.
Why,
she ought to be locked up
in our deepest cells,
sentenced there for as long as it takes
to make the key that will spring us
from the dull and regular moaning row of death.

*See the entries in this section under "Miller, Vassar."

Blish, James. "They Shall Have Stars," 1957; and "A Life For the Stars," 1962. From Cities in Flight. Garden City, New York: Doubleday, 1970. Novella.

Age   Med. Instit.   Sci Fi

In "They Shall Have Stars," Blish depicts a future in which degenerative diseases have so increased that people in their twenties and thirties are dying of old age. A research institute working on a government grant has found a cure with the interesting side effect of immortality; but the scientists are holding back reports of the cure. They find the repressive political environment so hopeless that they are working on a sub rosa program to discover interstellar flight so that a small, immortal portion of humankind can try a fresh start. In "Life For the Stars," Blish takes up the question of who becomes immortal. The answer is--those who prove useful (socially, politically, artistically) to the State. This answer is presented favorably.

Borges, Jorge Luis. "Borges and Myself." Available in The Aleph and Other Stories, 1933-1969, ed. and trans. Norman Thomas di Giovanni. New York: E. P. Dutton and Co., 1970. Tale.

Madness

Creativity and the resultant madness. Borges has been split into the artist and the man, and each feeds off the other. The narrator writes, "I live, I let myself live, so that Borges can weave his tales and poems/, and those tales and poems are my justification." The trouble is that these works cannot save the narrator, for what is good belongs to everyone. He knows that he is fated to lose everything forever: "only some moment of myself will survive in the other man. Little by little I have been surrendering everything to him, even though I have evidence of his stubborn habit of falsification and exaggerating. . . . Which of us is writing this page I don't know."

Borges, Jorge Luis. "The Immortals." Available in The Aleph and Other Stories, 1933-1969, ed. and trans. Norman Thomas di Giovanni. New York: E. P. Dutton and Co., 1970. Short Story.

Body/Mind   Doctors   Euthanasia
Med. Ethics   Sci Fi

Horrifying evocation of the mind split off from the body. The story begins with a description of a father who believes that the five senses only obstruct the growth of the mind, and so rears his son in a mechanical environment, totally apart from the world. After the father dies, an observer destroys the son, perhaps purposefully. The story is not over, however, for the narrator then describes a doctor, a gerontologist, who, hearing of the father's experiment, takes up the idea with relish. As a response to illness and death, he proceeds to replace all the organs, not just the malfunctioning ones, so that his patients become cubes, making unintelligible sounds. They are indeed without fear of death, but they are also completely dependent on their doctors, to whom they have deeded their property and income for "upkeep." The doctor has become a father-figure and an all-powerful leech, justifying his actions on the wild premise that the best way to cure the body is to replace it.

Borges, Jorge Luis. "Remorse for Any Death." Available in Selected Poems, 1923-67, ed. Norman Thomas Giovanni. New York: Delacorte Press, 1972. Poem: 15 lines.

Death   Grief

The poet charges those who are grief-stricken with robbing the dead of their attributes, their specific personality, until only death itself remains. We take for our own needs the dead person's colors, his syllables, everything, leaving not a person at all, but something unlimited and abstract. "The dead person, everywhere no one,/is nothing but the loss and the absence of the world."

Borges, Jorge Luis. "To Francisco Lopez Merino." Available in Selected Poems, 1923-67, ed. and trans. Norman Thomas Giovanni. New York: Delacorte Press, 1972. Poem: 28 lines.

Grief   Suicide

Borges' attempt to come to terms with the suicide of his friend, the minor poet Merino. Borges thinks Merino recondite, but puts forth a possible interpretation of his suicide as a "forgetfulness of the world, but in a comradely way." In that case, Borges can wear his grief more lightly, and can call out to Merino's spirit without profaning it. In a passing line, Borges wonders if all of us aren't suicides anyway: "perhaps we contrive our own deaths with images of our choosing."

Bowen, Elizabeth. Eva Trout. London: Jonathan Cape, 1969. Novel.

Adolescence   Children   Handicaps
Madness   Preg. & Childbirth Sexuality

A superb novel which gives us an accurate correlative of a soul numbed by human neglect. Eva Trout--deserted by her mother, unloved by her father, betrayed by her teacher--grows from a lumbering, needing adolescent into a big, defensive woman. When she is 25, the lonely, sexually frustrated Eva invents a pregnancy and then goes off to adopt a child. The boy, Jeremy, turns out to be deaf and dumb, but then Eva too is very silent, and for several years they live intimately and quite apart in a visual universe. Finally, Eva decides "to talk," that is, to make herself vulnerable in spite of her shyness, and her friends, such as they are, are glad that she has returned. Most of them had always considered her, if not actually mad, then certainly freaky. Eva, now about 33, arouses the love of young Henry, now grown to 21. He really hasn't the slightest idea of what she has suffered, but their marriage is arranged. On the day they are to leave for the wedding, on the eve, that is, of Eva Trout's "normal" happiness, the little deaf boy, boastfully wielding a gun he has taken from Eva's old teacher, accidentally kills his mother. Since all this--from the beginning of the novel to the cinematic last scene--is told at a slight angle to the truth, it is a shocking and moving book. (For female adolescence, see also Bowen's The Death of the Heart.)

Bradbury, Ray. "Kaleidoscope." Available in The Illustrated Man.
New York: Bantam, 1969. Short Story.

Dying   Sci Fi

Reactions to inevitable death in the few hours of remaining
life. A ship has exploded in space, spewing its crew in
their space suits out to death from asphyxiation as the
momentum carries them away from each other. The men talk
over their radios, going each in his own way from disbelief
to hostility to resignation.

Bradbury, Ray. "The Next in Line." Available in The October
Country. New York: Knopf, 1970. Short Story.

The Body   Death   Sci Fi

This little horror story is only loosely science fiction,
but it shows vividly the changing attitude toward the
living body created by confrontation with the dead body.
A woman and her husband are on a trip through a Mexican
town where death is a subject for festivals and tourists.
Corpses are exhumed and placed on display if their grave
fees are not paid. The frightened woman is chivied by
her husband into seeing the bodies; she tries to inter-
pose different points of view between the decaying
corpses and her fear: these are people; these are
objects--but her ears betray her into hearing soundless
screams from the dropped jaws. Back in the hotel, she
becomes aware of her husband's body, which seems more
and more foreign to her, and aware of the sounds of her
own body, which seems more and more frail. The car
breaks down, and she is forced to remain with the vision
of bodies; she foresees her own death and begs her
husband for a promise to pay so her body will not be
exhibited. He refuses on the grounds that she is not
dying and being morbid. When we next see him, he is
unconcernedly driving, alone, to the next town.

Brecht, Bertolt. Mother Courage and Her Children, 1941. Available
in Masters of Modern Drama, eds. Haskell M. Block and Robert
G. Shedd. New York: Random House, 1962. Drama.

Children   The Family   Grief
Handicaps   Poverty & Health

An anti-war play in the main, but also revealing of the
cohesion of Mother Courage's family. A peddler of goods
to soldiers, she is a tough woman who defends her children fiercely--up to a point, for she is also a profiteer,
a role that sometimes comes into conflict with her
motherhood, as when, for instance, her haggling too long
over a price results in the execution of her son. The
profit motive even affects her grief when, finally, all
her children gone, she hitches herself up to her wagon
and gets back to business. One might say that the poverty
of her life style has impoverished her mental health as
well. Brecht, a Marxist pacifist and a medical corps-
man during World War I, might very well say so. The
play is also valuable because Mother Courage's daughter
Catherine, a mute as the result of an injury done to her
by a soldier when she was a child, becomes a heroine
when she drums on the roof in an attempt to warn the
townspeople of a coming attack, even though her life is
being threatened and she is being finally shot.

Bridges, Robert. "Melancholia," 1905. Available in Chief Modern
Poets of Britain and America, 5th ed. Vol. I: Poets of
Britain, eds. Gerald DeWitt Sanders, et al. New York:
Macmillan, 1970. Sonnet.

By Doctors   Madness

The doctor on depression. He knows it clearly: "The
sickness of desire, that in dark days/Looks on the
imagination of despair,/Forgetteth man, and stinteth
God his praise;/Nor but in sleep findeth a cure for care."
He knows the "blackness that no stars redeem,/A wall
of terror in a night of cold." But he knows as well the
sense of proportion necessary to answer depression. It
is not the world that has changed, he tells the
melancholic, but you, "'tis thou are dead."

Bridges, Robert. "On a Dead Child," 1880. Available in The Norton
Anthology of Modern Poetry, eds. Richard Ellmann and Robert
O'Clair. New York: Norton, 1973. Poem: 29 lines.

The Body   By Doctors   Death
Doctors   Grief

Most of Bridges' poetry was on non-medical subjects:
beauty, nature, philosophy, love--but he believed, no
doubt rightly, that the practice of medicine would give
him needed contact with the ordinary, and in this poem,
we see one of the results: a lofty contemplation of
death combined with very real details about a boy's
body. Bridges was still a doctor when he wrote it, and
a doctor appears here in his "last duty" with the dead.
Always interested in perfection of poetic form, Bridges
notes another formal excellence: "Perfect little body,
without fault or stain on thee." He places the body
in its last posture, and the boy's hand seems to grasp
his, but "the grasp is the clasp of Death, heartbreaking
and stiff." In the last stanza, the physical duties
accomplished, the doctor-poet expresses his grief.
Nothing can explain this. Nothing "rights the disaster
of this." Nothing avails us "when in the dark,/Unwilling,
alone we embark,/And the things we have seen and have
known and have heard of,/fail us."

Brieux, Eugene. Les Avariés, 1901. Available in Théâtre Complet
de Brieux, Vol. 6. Paris: Librairie, 1921-7; also in Three
Plays by Brieux, trans. John Pollock. New York: Bretano's,
1914. Drama. And Upton Sinclair, Damaged Goods. New York:
John C. Winston, 1913. Novel.

Doctors   Med. Ethics   Poverty & Health
V.D.

In his introduction to the Pollock translation of the play,
G. B. Shaw criticizes the contemporary theatre for inflam-
ing the passions but not dealing with their consequences.
Brieux's play, whose title is a euphemistic term for "the
syphilitics," is an exception. In exposing the conspiracy
of silence about sex, Brieux focuses on a respectable and
normally careful young man who contracts V.D. after a
drunken party. His doctor promises to cure him, but
advises him to put off marriage for two years. Unfortunately, the young man is engaged, loves the girl, and
feels he cannot postpone the wedding. Since the doctor
offers only probabilities and not certainties, the man
decides to delay the marriage for six months only, receives
treatment from a quack in the interim, and, of course,
lies to his fiancée about the nature of his illness.
Their first child, a daughter, is born with the disease
and infects her wet-nurse, who blackmails the father.
The doctor warns that the endangered baby needs to be
breast-fed; but the dilemma is that the disease would
then be spread to yet another person. When the wife
learns of all this, she collapses in shock and leaves
her husband. (There is no talk of treating her, by the
way.) Her angry, self-righteous father speaks to the
doctor in an attempt to certify the reasons for a
divorce, but the doctor asks him to stop attacking the
husband--for, after all, many a decent man, like the
father himself, for instance, has the opportunity to
catch V.D.--and start using his political influence to
educate the public about the disease. The play also
depicts various other V.D. patients: e.g., a son with
an advanced case because he is ashamed to tell his
father; and a servant, first impregnated by her master
and then deserted, who is forced to prostitution in
order to support her child. The play is tough and
realistic. The novel, which sticks fairly close to
the original, is more romantic, even sentimental.
Sinclair places less emphasis on the doctor, and more
on the reconciliation of the estranged couple. He
softens the self-delusions and egotism of the young man,
and devotes more time to the economic pressures that
lead to prostitution and the inefficiency of free
clinics for workers who cannot afford time off. In
all three versions, the doctor, though somewhat
irritatingly wise, is rational and non-judgmental. He
asserts that science is impersonal, that he cannot cure
the rich any faster than the poor, and that each
patient receives the best possible care.

Brown, Geoff. I Want What I Want. New York: G. P. Putnam's Sons,
1967. Novel.

Doctors   Madness   Med. Instit.
Sexuality   Sexual Roles   Suicide

What Roy wants is to be a woman. But he meets with
unsympathetic responses from both relatives and doctors.
At the beginning of the novel, he is institutionalized
as mentally ill and given drugs rather than true treatment. The differences between transexuality and
homosexuality are highlighted when an older male patient
makes a pass at Roy. After he leaves the hospital, he
confronts his father, who adjures him to be a man, and
his sister, who is horrified but a bit more sympathetic.
His views of sexual roles are grotesquely stereotypical:
men work; women just marry them and have it easy. For
a time, Roy lives as a woman, but cannot maintain the
role without surgery. At last he goes to a sexologist,
who gives him only a cursory physical examination and
announces that he must live as a male. The doctor
dismisses Roy all the more easily when he learns that
Roy has no money. In deep despair now, he returns to
his flat, which he shares with a male lover who believes
he is a woman, and tries, unsuccessfully, to kill himself. He can neither live nor die. For a more
considered look at a woman's mind in a man's body, see
Jan Morris' autobiographical Conundrum, New York,
Harcourt, Brace, Jovanovich, 1974.

Brunner, John. The Whole Man (Section III most useful), 1958, 1959.
New York: Ballantine, 1964. Novel.

The Body   Handicaps   Madness
Sci Fi   Suicide

A composite of three long stories, this novel looks
forward to medicine based on body image. With the aid
of medical personnel, the brain can bring the sick or
damaged body back in accord with the healthy image
stored in the brain. People with genetic defects can
tap the body images of genetically healthy people and
so correct their problems without surgery or medication.
Psychiatry uses telepaths who search out the problem
areas in psychologically disturbed people, identifying
these areas so that psychiatrists can work directly on
the main causes of disturbance. However, contact with
diseased minds can generate such stress that the
telepath retreats into "fugue," a closed universe in
which he or she will die unless extracted by a stronger
telepath. The protagonist is a strong telepath and
hopeless cripple (his body image can't be repaired
without destroying his telepathic abilities). He is

constantly tempted by the desire to retreat into fugue.
One of his patients is an artist whose works never
match his visions of art. This artist tries to commit
suicide, but is saved by the telepath who discovers the
cure inherent in art. In the great concentration of the
process of creation, he experiences loss of self and the
ability to reach and heal others through the art--so
that medicine truly becomes "the healing art."

Burgess, Anthony. The Doctor Is Sick. New York: Norton, 1960.
Novel.

Disease & Health	Doctors	Madness
Med. Instit.	Nurses	Sexuality
Surgery		

The "Doctor" of the title is a Ph.D.--not really a
doctor, as one of his fellow patients says. But he
really is sick, though the nature and significance of
his illness keeps expanding as the novel progresses.
Dr. Spindrift (his name is full of Joycean fun) is a
linguist, and his love of words, combined with Burgess',
turns a hospital recovery experience into a fantasy trip
through language's delirium. We first meet Spindrift
in a London hospital, where he has been brought by his
wife, Sheila, with signs of a serious neurological disorder. Mechanical medical treatment--by the doctors,
the nurses, the we-take-no-crap-from-mere-patients
technologists--has seldom been given such a complete
satirical going over. But Spindrift has non-medical
problems as well: he thinks that Sheila, never a faithful wife, is probably spending these days in various
arms, some of whom she has the nerve to bring to the
ward during visiting hours. Not that Spindrift can
really blame her, considering that one of his symptoms
is impotency. At any rate, he is diagnosed as having
something in his brain he shouldn't have (Do you mean
a tumor? he sarcastically asks the neurologist), and
he is operated on. Upon waking afterwards, he leaves
the hospital looking wild--a shaved head, torn clothing--
and has a series of adventures worthy of Leopold Bloom
in Nighttown. Or is it all in his bald head? When he
really wakes up, he is faced with his wife, who informs
him that he has lost his job and her, so when last seen,
Dr. Spindrift has drifted off again from the hospital.

Burroughs, William. The Naked Lunch, 1959. London: Corgi, 1968.
Novel.

Doctors	Drugs	Homosexuality
Med. Ethics		

The nightmare world of the long-term drug addict, recounted in scraps of images, fragments of scenes, and
glimpses of ultimate chaos. The novel is prefaced in
this edition by a statement from the author about his
own addiction and addiction in general. He speaks of
"the junk virus" and the "vaccine," Apomorphine, which
can make of addiction, like smallpox, a medical
curiosity. And he says of his book: "it is necessarily
brutal, obscene and disgusting. Sickness has often
repulsive details not for weak stomachs." Weaving in
and out of the life of one Carl Peterson, Burroughs
occasionally runs into a doctor, usually a fantastical
one, and often absurd, but with frighteningly recognizable details in his portrait. There's Doctor
"Fingers" Schafer, the Lobotomy Kid in the section on
the "international conference of technological psychiatry";
and Doctor Benway of the Ministry of Hygiene and
Prophylaxis in "the examination." These and other health
personnel invade the addicts' privacy in unethical
fashion. Altogether a grimly comic and gruesome book.
At the close of it, Burroughs has printed a discussion
of the effects of the various drugs he has used, and
offered some suggestions about treatment programs.

Campbell, William Edward March (William March, pseudonym). The
Bad Seed. New York: Rinehart & Co., 1954; and Maxwell
Anderson, Bad Seed. New York: Dodd, Mead & Co., 1955.
Novel and Drama.

Children	Euthanasia	Madness
Suicide		

Campbell's book is a study of Christine Penmark's double
discovery that her mother was a mass murderer and her
daughter, Rhoda, is the same. Ironically, Christine is
one of the few sane people in the book: she is surrounded
by the malevolent, mentally retarded Leroy, the superficial, tea-party psychoanalysis of her neighbor who
went into analysis with one of Freud's students, and the
drunken, mad grief of Mrs. Daigle, the mother of a boy
killed by Rhoda. Christine slowly realizes that her
daughter has coolly drowned a classmate for the penman-
ship medal she felt was rightfully hers, has murdered
her grandmother for a bauble promised in her will, and
has burned Leroy for his nasty-minded efforts at blackmail. She also realizes, with the unconscious assistance
of a writer doing a book on mass-murderers, that she was
really adopted; and her true identity as the daughter of
a cold-blooded family murderer was hidden to "protect"
her. She plans to kill her daughter by an overdose of
sleeping pills and then commit suicide with her husband's
revolver. Christine does die, but Rhoda survives.
Maxwell Anderson follows the plot closely, often lifting
dialogue directly from the novel. But Anderson shifts
the emphasis onto the folly of those environmentalists
who refuse to acknowledge the importance of heredity.
Anderson introduces Bravo, Christine's foster-father, who
adopted Christine because he believed in the all-importance

of environment. When Christine tries to tell him her
doubts, he refuses to listen to her--perhaps because
the writer on murderers is emphatically advocating the
destruction of such "bad seed." Bravo dies, and the
play moves to the novel's shocking conclusion.

Camus, Albert. Caligula, 1938. Available in Masters of Modern
Drama, eds. Haskell M. Block and Robert G. Shedd. New York:
Random House, 1962. Drama.

The Body	Grief	Madness
Sexuality	Suffering	Suicide

Madness as the only logical response to the absurd dilemma
of human existence, which is, as Emperor Caligula expresses
it, that "Men die; and they are not happy" (trans. Stuart
Gilbert). Caligula's madness begins with the death of his
sister, with whom he was in love. His extreme grief is a
physical thing: "I didn't know what anguish meant. Like
everyone else I fancied it was a sickness of the mind--
no more. But no, it's my body that's in pain. Pain everywhere, in my chest, in my legs and arms. Even my skin is
raw, my head is buzzing, I feel like vomiting. But worst
of all is this queer taste in my mouth. Not blood, or
death, or fever, but a mixture of all three." Ultimately,
years later, Caligula finds, like Tennyson in In Memoriam
(q.v.), that even grief can die, that nothing in fact
lasts, and that knowledge brings to Caligula true suffering and, perversely, true happiness, or so he claims:
"beyond the frontier of pain lies a splendid, sterile
happiness." After years of seeking to challenge absurdity
by behaving more absurdly and stupidly than the gods
(Caligula has been capriciously murdering his subjects),
the mad Caesar inevitably runs to the end of his suicidal
course, and is murdered by his people. Camus seems not
to believe that Caligula is truly mad, at least not more
so than all the sensitive among us, potentially. "Is
he ill?" says a woman who loves him. "No, not ill--
unless you invent a name and medicine for the black ulcers
that fester in his soul . . . . Too much soul! That's
what bites you, isn't it? You prefer to label it a
disease; that way all the dolts are justified and
pleased."

Camus, Albert. The Plague. New York: Alfred A. Knopf, 1948.
Novel.

Children	Death	Doctors
Dying	Grief	Plague

One of the great medical novels. In his clear and eloquent
style, Camus provides many clinical and sociological details
about an outbreak of the bubonic plague in Oran, Algeria.
He describes the dying of an old man, for instance, at a
time before the presence of the plague is confirmed, and
later, the death of a little boy ("A moment later, after
tossing his head wildly to and fro, he flung off the
blanket. From between the inflamed eyelids big tears
welled up and trickled down the sunken, leaden-hued cheeks.
When the spasm had passed, utterly exhausted, tensing his
thin legs and arms, on which, within forty-eight hours,
the flesh had wasted to the bone, the child lay flat,
racked on the tumbled bed, in a grotesque parody of
crucifixion" trans. Stuart Gilbert). This child's death
highlights the conflict between the medical man, Dr.
Rieux, and the priest, who had formerly seen the plague
as God's retribution to a sinful city. The priest
argues that we should love what we cannot understand,
but the doctor answers, "to my dying day I shall refuse
to love a scheme of things in which children are put to
torture." In addition to the cosmic effects, Camus also
investigates thoroughly the effect of the plague on
human relationships and on the organization of the city.
The ultimate force of the novel derives not from the
literal level, but from the magnificent metaphorical
impact. The plague becomes the universal human predicament, waiting inside everyone and erupting from time to
time to torment and enlighten us. It has the power to
exile us, to imprison us, to drive us to our own and our
neighbor's loving resources. The central figure is the
healer, Dr. Rieux. He is tireless in his serving of the
victims. What is interesting is that he does not so
much cure, for he cannot, as diagnose, that is, describe
with objective distance and a concerned heart, and
strive to heal with all his will. He concludes that if
one refuses to succumb to the plague, but, rather, fights
it, health ultimately prevails. That health is the
knowledge that after great, mass illness, people will be
the same, which is "at once their strength and their
innocence."

Camus, Albert. The Stranger. New York: Alfred A. Knopf, 1946.
Novel.

Children	Grief

An important little book for illuminating the predicament
of ordinary people faced with sociological and metaphysical alienation, but relevant here chiefly for
society's attitude toward grief. At the beginning of
the novel, Meursault's elderly mother has just died, and
his casual reaction is there from the start ("Mother
died today. Or, maybe, yesterday; I can't be sure").
He had placed her in a home 3 years earlier when he
discovered that they really didn't have much to say to
each other. Now she's dead; he attends her funeral,
outlined in stark detail in the book, and afterwards
returns to his normal, rather dull life, seemingly
unmoved by the death. By chance this ordinary life is
broken into by the extraordinary, almost accidental

murder of an Algerian Arab by Meursault. He is tried,
and convicted, not because he is clearly responsible
for the death, but because, outrageous as it may seem,
he is shown to be an unaffectionate son who did not even
grieve for his mother's death. It's worse than that:
he did not grieve openly. If he had cried, or torn his
hair, or gone through some appropriate ritual, the society
would have acquitted him.

Čapek, Karel. R.U.R., 1922. New York: Doubleday, 1923. Drama.

| The Body | Children | Sci Fi |
| Sexuality | Suffering | |

Society prizes body over mind; men exist only to work;
existence is only justified as preparation for future
generations; suffering creates humanity. All four
ideas combine to produce the destruction and salvation
of humanity. Robots are invented as bodies for cheap
labor, taking over all tasks. The human birth rate
drops. An attractive woman uses her appeal to persuade
the manufacturers to add to the robots sensitivity to
pain, the ability to suffer, justifying the addition as
a means of protecting a valuable commodity. But with
suffering comes self-consciousness. The robots annihi-
late homo sapiens; but, in the battle, the formula for
robot tissue is lost and the sterile robots search
frantically for a means of propagation, since preparation
for the future is the only justification for living.
The play ends hopefully. Through contact with humans,
two of the robots have learned, not only to kill and
destroy, but to love and to be capable of self-sacrifice.
They are sent forth to populate the earth.

Céline, Louis-Ferdinand. Journey to the End of the Night, 1932.
Trans. John H. P. Marks. New York: New Directions, 1960.
Novel.

By Doctors	Disease & Health	Doctors
Dying	Madness	Med. Ethics
Med. Instit.	Nurses	Sexuality

This modern picaresque novel is a bit over-long, but
nevertheless one of the major novels by a physician.
The hero, Ferdinand, is a cynical, neurotic, sometime
doctor whose adventures take him from World War I in
France to Colonial Africa to America and back to
France. He is often ill: for instance, in Africa he
suffers from fevers; and early in the novel he finds
himself in an asylum, where he manipulates the psychiatrists and feels either hostility or lust towards the
nurses. He does fall in love from time to time, but
even then he tends to focus on the body of his beloved,
often in rather clinical terms, and to see love as an
elementary function ("Whatever happens, one has to make
love, as one has to scratch"). He is a bad doctor,
incompetent and unethical and generally involved in a
sordid practice in suburban Paris. At one stage, he
seems to be doing mostly secret abortions; at another,
he fends off the unethical suggestion that he declare
a perfectly composed old lady insane only to agree
shortly afterwards to help in her murder. Finally,
while watching the dying of his shadowy companion, Leon,
Ferdinand realizes that he has come to this: "At such
moments it's a little embarrassing to have become as
poor and as hard as one has. One lacks almost everything that might be of use in helping someone to die.
One has nothing left inside but things that serve the
purposes of everyday life . . . . You've pushed pity
to the lower end of your bowels, with the rest of the
refuse." The novel as a whole is told in something
of an hallucinatory style, and makes an interesting
comparison with the more direct 18th century picaresque
novels about Evil Doctors (see Smollett, for example).

Choromanski, Michal. Jealousy and Medicine, 1932. Trans. Eileen
Arthurton-Barker. Norfolk, Conn.: New Directions, 1964.
Novel.

Age	Children	Disease & Health
Doctors	Madness	Med. Ethics
Med. Instit.	Nurses	Preg. & Childbirth
Sexuality	Sexual Roles	Suffering
Surgery	Women as Patients	

A remarkable Polish novel, whose form--a vivid, circular,
almost cinematic form--reminds one of experimental French
novels written much later. The reader is forced to
burrow into the obsessive jealousy of an aging man,
Widmar, married to a beautiful young woman, Rebecca,
whose lover of the moment is a surgeon. The operating
room scenes are among the best in the novel: there are
extensive clinical details and persuasive pictures of
the terror that sweeps through the operating team when
things start to go wrong. One of the operations begins
as an appendectomy on the young wife and ends as a
removal of an extra-uterine pregnancy. It is this
encounter, oddly enough, which leads to the love affair,
for even though the surgeon proclaims that he is "a
doctor, not a man," on this occasion he sees his
patient's body as sexually attractive. Still, for him
women are useful chiefly as sexual objects--until he
realizes that he has become inextricably involved with
Rebecca. For her part, she is playing a fraudulently
dependent, passionate role, when in reality she is
promiscuous, manipulating, and thoroughly dishonest.
Illness is everywhere in the novel: Widmar suffers
from a heart condition, for instance, and one 9-year-
old boy, Boruch, is an epileptic with a strangely
brilliant, magical mind. The author uses aspects of

medicine as metaphor ("that mask of feminine chloroform";
"a pill of concentrated suffering") and as theme (the
human, indeed terrifying, sides of medicine which run
parallel to the surface objectivity). The novel is
valuable too for its portraits of nurses, a junior
doctor, Rubinski, whose hostility toward the superin-
tendent causes him to reveal confidential information,
and an elderly doctor, Boguski, with perhaps too much
empathy for his own good.

Cocteau, Jean. Opium: The Diary of a Cure, trans. Margaret Crosland
and Sinclair Road. London: Peter Owen Limited, 1957. Diary.

| Doctors | Drugs | Med. Profession |
| Nurses | | |

Cocteau vividly records his own sensations as an addict:
"I recommend the patient who has been deprived for eight
days to bury his head in his arm, to glue his ear to
that arm, and wait. Catastrophes, riots, factories blow-
in up, armies in flight, flood--the ear can detect a
whole apocalypse in the starry night of the human body."
He reveals that he became an addict while under medical
supervision, and that he was re-addicted because doctors
don't cure the troubles which cause addiction in the
first place. He reports that his doctors like him as
a patient because he is articulate and can accurately
describe his feelings. He muses in general on opium,
his addiction, and addicts. Finally, as he recovers,
he begins to attack the medical profession: doctors
don't get to know their patients; everyone under-
estimates the importance of nurses to the patients,
and so on. "Our physical safety," Cocteau writes,
"accepts doctors who correspond to the artists whom our
moral safety rejects."

Colette. The Innocent Libertine, 1904-5. Harmondsworth, England:
Penguin Books, 1972. Novel.

| Adolescence | Children | Sexuality |
| Sexual Roles | | |

Quintessential Colette. Intimate and romantic recording
of sensuous detail fills this story of a young woman's
search for orgasmic satisfaction in love. As a child,
Minne is coddled by a widowed mother who lives only for
her. She spends her adolescence in fantasy reveries about
darkly passionate criminal lovers. But then she marries
her cousin Antoine, devoted to her from his pimply youth,
and discovers that no amount of affection from mother or
husband substitutes for the sort of sexual joy she reads
about in novels. She takes lovers. One after the other
they fail her. She is bored with her role as housewife,
and she takes more lovers. But sex seems for men's
pleasure only, until at last, with Antoine, who determines to show her love and consideration, Minne achieves
sexual bliss.

Coney, Michael G. Friends Come in Boxes. New York: Daw, 1973.
Novel.

| The Body | Children | Death |
| Sci Fi | | |

Immortality and an end to the population problem--by
eliminating children and childhood. By transferring
adult minds into the bodies of six-month-old children,
society provides immortality and a zero birth rate,
because no one wishes to have a child solely to furnish
a body for another adult. The "plot" consists of
several sketches of life in such a society. Although
not examined in any depth, this solution to death and
over-population is presented extremely vividly.

Conrad, Joseph. "The Idiots." From Tales of Unrest. New York:
Doubleday, 1916. Short Story.

| Children | Mental Retardation | Suicide |

A farmer and his wife look forward to having children,
who are expected to help with the work and carry on
family traditions and hopes. The wife gives birth to
twins--both idiots. She has a third child, also an
idiot. The parents pray fervently, but the fourth child
is yet another idiot. Mutual recriminations now
dominate the couple's marriage. Still, the husband
comes to his wife to beget a fifth child. Unable to
tolerate their lives any longer, the wife kills her
husband and later, when she is pursued for his murder,
kills herself.

Conrad, Joseph. Nostromo, 1903-4. New York: Holt, Rinehart &
Winston, 1961. Novel.

| Doctors | Suffering |

Amidst this maze of South American politics there is a
physician who is a secondary but important character,
for his presence constantly reminds one of the abyss of
pain and suffering which threatens the small kingdom of
San Tomé. Years before, he had survived terrible tortures, betraying his friends to a dictator. Thereafter
he felt worthless, but now, shocked by the sight of yet
more torture, he persuades the disillusioned Nostromo to
bring help to the beleaguered community. A complex
professional attitude: as a man, he has been broken
by suffering; yet he cannot find true comfort in his
profession of relieving suffering, thinking of it instead
as a means to a living. Furthermore, he is resentful
because people are not more grateful. Yet his appeal to
Nostromo is something of a return to his professional
responsibility.

Conrad, Joseph. The Shadow Line: a Confession. London: J. M. Dent, 1917. Novella.

Disease & Health   Doctors   Madness
Plague

A symbolic sea journey from youth to experience, in a ship borne upon fever. A young man takes his first command on a ship formerly captained by an eccentric man, whose ghost, the possessed first mate believes, haunts the ship and wishes her ill. Whatever the cause, the entire crew--save for the new captain and Ransome, the cook, who has a bad heart--is stricken with a mysterious fever. The very universe seems stricken, for the ship is becalmed for days. Though the suffering is fierce, the men are gallant. They blame no one. Indeed there may be no one to blame: one night the ship is overwhelmed by a complete and symbolic darkness-- "the last gleam of light in the universe had gone." The ship is finally released; she sails towards help; and surgeons, at first disgusted at finding no surgical cases, evacuate the crew. The captain and the appropriately named Ransome discuss the events, the latter adding that he fears for his heart, that constantly threatening presence. The captain sums up: "I listened to him going up the companion stairs cautiously, step by step, in mortal fear of starting into sudden anger our common enemy it was his hard fate to carry consciously within his faithful breast." The doctor who appears early in the tale is a nice enough man--"A doctor is humane by definition . . . . that was so in reality"--but he can't heal the lurking illness which forever threatens mankind.

Crane, Hart. "Episode of Hands," 1948. Available in The Complete Poems and Selected Letters of Hart Crane, ed. Brom Weber. Garden City, N. Y.: Anchor Books, 1966. Poem: 24 lines.

The Body   Disease & Health

An act of healing performed by one man for another, and the affection that act produces. A factory owner's son's "taut, spare fingers" are transformed as he treats "the thick bed of the wound" into "wings of butterflies/ Flickering in sunlight over summer fields." The hand he holds in his--presumably that of a factory worker--has "knots and notches" which seem to the healer beautiful, "like the marks of wild ponies' play." For his part, the man with the wounded hand is embarrassed by "the unexpected interest" shown in him, but when the bandage is tightened, "The two men smiled into each other's eyes."

Crane, Hart. "The Idiot," 1927. Available in The Complete Poems and Selected Letters of Hart Crane, ed. Brom Weber. Garden City, N. Y.: Anchor Books, 1966. Poem: 16 lines.

Mental Retardation

A retarded man as wronged, most terribly wronged, and yet serene because he doesn't know it. The poet selects certain details to stand for the idiot's whole life: he is "fumbling his sex," children laugh at him, he stretches in a "ghastly shape." Once the poet sees him flying a kite with one hand and with his other, scanning the sky for the kite with a one-ended tin can held to his eye: "he'd clamped midnight to noon sky!" Through it all the poor man sings his song of thanks to God. The poet hears it lift above human reason and halt in the middle, serenely. He feels he has trespassed on (or against?) the idiot.

Crichton, Michael. The Andromeda Strain. New York: Knopf, 1969. Novel.

By Doctors   Doctors   Med. Ethics
Plague   Sci Fi

The Andromeda Strain is the best, and best-known, of Crichton's science fiction. A team of doctors and biologists work in an elaborate underground laboratory, ostensibly preparing against extra-terrestrial diseases, perhaps preparing for biological warfare. A returning satellite carries a virus which destroys all the inhabitants of a small town except for a baby and an old drunk. The team works frantically to discover the link between the two immune people (alkaloids) and an anti-viral agent (free oxygen). Their pressure is increased by the knowledge that an A-bomb sits overhead, to be detonated if the virus escapes from the restricted area and by their belief that millions are dying on the surface. Faulty communications between the team and the surface (and among groups on the surface) prevent them from knowing that the high mutation rate of the virus has brought it to a harmless form and all are safe. The novel's tension is better than its biology.

Cronin, A. J. The Citadel. Boston: Little, Brown and Company, 1937. Novel.

By Doctors   Disease & Health Doctors
Med. Ethics   Med. Instit.   Nurses
Surgery

An undistinguished book, only a cut above Not As a Stranger, a cut below Arrowsmith; but, like Arrowsmith, influential in its day. Also like its American counterpart, Cronin's novel traces its hero's career through several kinds of medical work--here it is small town general practice in Wales, work for a government research board, and private practice, as well as hospital consultation as a lung specialist, in London--and has as its purpose the uncovering of unethical medical practices

everywhere. The hero's neglected, unpretentious wife dies (as in Arrowsmith), and he goes off to a more pristine variety of research and practice (ditto Martin Arrowsmith). If the book has value, it lies in its depiction of the appalling ignorance of some British physicians of the time, the broad inequities of the health care system, and certain details here and there: a botched and hastily covered up abdominal operation, e.g.; a luxurious nursing home for the wealthy; a few Welsh characters. But as for its general aims, Sinclair Lewis--not to mention G. B. Shaw in The Doctor's Dilemma-- does the whole thing better.

Crowley, Mart. The Boys in the Band. New York: Farrar, Straus, and Giroux, 1968. Drama.

Homosexuality

One of the best of the recent plays about the psychological and social problems of homosexuals. Crowley assembles several gay men conveniently at a party. He selects some tokens and stereotypes for his characters--a black, a Jew, a Catholic, an ultra-"male" married man, a closet queen, a poof. He even uses, hilariously at times, some traditional kinds of gay jokes, inoffensive because the boys themselves are the jokers and realize the ironies involved. Once he has relaxed his audience into thinking they know where they are, Crowley turns serious, intensely so, as he unravels the Truth Game, in which all the characters are made to face their own desires, fears, and guilts. A disturbing display of hysteria at the end of the play. If only, one man concludes, we didn't hate ourselves quite so much.

Cummings, E. E. "I like my body," 1925. Available in E. E. Cummings: a Selection of Poems. New York: Harcourt, Brace & World, 1965. Poem: 14 lines.

The Body   Sexuality

The body awakening to its own erotic possibilities: "I like my body when it is with your/body. It is so quite a new thing." Anatomical nouns are turned into verbs: "Muscles better and nerves more," and other anatomical details into sex: "i like to feel the spine/of your body and its bones."

Delaney, Shelagh. A Taste of Honey, 1958. New York: Grove Press, 1959. Drama.

Adolescence   Alcoholism   Children
Homosexuality   Nurses   Preg. & Childbirth

Young Shelagh Delaney makes a memorable play out of an unmarried, pregnant, working-class adolescent, her boozy, promiscuous mother, the black sailor--formerly a nurse--who sleeps with her, and the gentle homosexual art student who tends her during the pregnancy. The student, Geoff, even offers to marry her, and indeed there is a tender sort of love between them, but Jo has a certain courage, born, presumably, from having played second fiddle to her mother's lovers and drinking. That lady--the term is used loosely--is likeable enough, always good for a laugh at least, but certainly no mother. When she tries to be at the end of the play, showing up and kicking Geoff out, she discovers she can't handle the news that the baby will be black and goes off for a drink, leaving Jo entirely alone with the baby coming on.

Delany, Samuel R. "Corona." Available in Driftglass: ten tales of speculative fiction. New York: Signet, 1971. Short Story.

Med. Profession   Mental Retardation Sci Fi
Suffering   Suicide

Two people come together in a hospital: a mentally retarded man suffering from severe burns and a memory of a painful beating; a young telepathic girl who can feel suffering from as far away as Mars. She can hear the minds of other disturbed children--and her mother's mind--and the suffering has made her suicidal, just as pain and fear have made the man suicidal. But the two are joined and their sufferings eased by the music, Corona, played by a "pop" star while the man was burned. The girl follows the memory of the music, is able to calm the man, and so gains hope for herself because she has begun to fight back against the suffering she feels. Music as a bond between strangers as a way of ordering pain and suffering and as a barrier against them.

Del Rey, Lester. Nerves. New York: Ballantine Books, 1956. Novel.

Doctors   Sci Fi   Suffering

This story of a company doctor in a nuclear power plant is not a great one, or even a very good one by today's standards, but it is a classic--and prophetic. The concept of nuclear power is under heavy attack; and, at a tense moment of political confrontation, there is an explosion at the plant. The doctor and his assistant take over, borrowing equipment to cope with the large number of radiation-burned men and developing a new technique to save one life. One doctor manages to control the panicked guards' paranoia in order to get needed equipment past the gates. The other doctor, a supertheoretician, helps save the plant from a further explosion. The doctors are too good, but the power structures in and around the plant are realistic, and the role of medical personnel in managerial decisions is well done.

Dickey, James. "The Cancer Match." From The Eye-Beaters. London: Hamish Hamilton, 1971. Poem: 42 lines.

The Body   Disease & Health   Med. Profession

A sports match taking place in the body of a terminally ill man. The contestants, both sent by the Lord, are cancer and whiskey, the latter becoming by the end of the poem the speaker's "Basic Life Force." The medical profession has told this man that there is no hope for him, "But they have no idea/What hope is, or how it comes." For this one night, at least, the man is going to be a spectator at the match. He's going to drink and drink and beat "the worst/Of me, growing." He cheers his favorite: "Get'im, O Self/Like a beloved son! One more time! Tonight we are going/Good   better and better   we are going/To win, and not only win but win/Big, win big." A wonderful poem.

Dickey, James. "Diabetes." From The Eye-Beaters. London: Hamish Hamilton, 1971. Poem: 101 lines.

Death   Disease & Health   Doctors

Poem in two parts, the first, when the speaker learns that he has diabetes, the second, after he has lived with it for a time. The poem opens with images of great thirst: "One night I thirsted like a prince/Then like a king/Then like an empire   like a world/On fire." Warned, he goes to a doctor, "young/and nice," whose speech is suggested this way: "I must tell you,/My friend, that it is needles moderation/And exercise. You don't want to look forward/To gangrene and kidney/Failure   boils blindness infection skin trouble falling/Teeth coma and death." So, the speaker thinks, it's not so bad; at least now I know: "A livable death at last." In the second part of the poem, the speaker has disciplined himself pretty well. The doctor has become the rule-enforcer to whom this patient must give exaggerated obedience: "All right! Physicians, witness! I will shoot my veins/Full of insulin." All the same, he is turning toward death, obsessed with his own gurgling-sweet body. He is on a hill, buzzards are circling. He asks, "When will the sugar rise boiling/Against me, and my brain be sweetened/to death?" Reaching for a beer, which he should not have, he says that the medical books don't have all the answers about the way the body works. What matters is how much glory's in it. And there is glory, buzzard glory, in his-- here diabetes becomes fully metaphorical--blindness, flashing, fire, "Sweetness everywhere, and I am calling my birds." Dickey, author of Deliverance, is writing a second novel about a diabetic who loses his eyesight.

Dickey, James. "The Eye-Beaters." From The Eye-Beaters. London: Hamish Hamilton, 1971. Poem: 140 lines.

Children   Handicaps   Madness
Med. Instit.

Even the prose basis of this poem is powerful: a stranger visits a children's asylum, where he discovers, to his horror, that some of them have gone blind there. They tend to beat continually at their eyes, so the attendants have tied their arms down with gauze. To stave off madness, the stranger must invent a fiction to explain how this fearsome situation can exist. His answer is told in long, increasingly powerful lines which threaten at any moment to go off into either madness or transcendence. What the children see, what they try to see when they beat their eyes is, "a tribal light old/Enough to be seen without sight." Images of caves and animals lead the stranger back to what he believes is the source of artistic creation, where, unable to accept the children's real situation and also drawn as an artist, he joins the eye-beaters' vision.

Disch, Thomas. Camp Concentration. New York: Doubleday & Co., 1968. Novel.

Disease & Health   Drugs   Sci Fi
V.D.

Information about this book comes from Robert Silverberg's Drug Themes in Science Fiction (Rockville, Md.: National Institute on Drug Abuse, 1974). A small number of people are treated with a drug derived from syphilis organisms; the people become supermen in the short interval before they are destroyed by the disease.

Drabble, Margaret. The Millstone. New York: William Morrow & Co., 1966. Novel.

Abortion   Children   Disease & Health
Doctors   Med. Instit.   Nurses
Preg. & Childbirth   Sexuality

Rosamund, a privileged young woman--29 years old, scholarly with distinguished Socialistic and distanced parents--somewhat casually loses her virginity and finds herself pregnant. After an incompetent attempt at a gin-and-hot-bath abortion, she decides to have the baby, again somewhat casually, and enters the British National Health Service process, where she is treated like a mechanical cow. As her pregnancy grows, so does her capacity for emotional response, and after the birth of Octavia, Rosamund feels love for the first time in her life. But the baby is ill: pneumonia, Rosamund thinks-- congenital heart defect, requiring surgery, the doctor says. The staff at the hospital, indifferent to the needs of the patient's family, refuse to let Rosamund see her baby, releasing from her a scream against the

coldness of the medical system, perhaps of the world she has known. The novel provides a good look at assembly-line health care delivery, and a reasonably unsentimental picture of motherhood.

Dreiser, Theodore. An American Tragedy, 1925. New York: New American Library, 1964. Novel.

Abortion   Death   Doctors
Med. Profession

This American tragedy of class has several medical aspects. Book II, Chapters 33-39 deal with the efforts of Clyde and his working class girlfriend Roberta to get an abortion for her. First, he picks up a remedy from a druggist. When that doesn't work, he sends her to a doctor, even though "the entire medical profession here, as elsewhere, appeared to him as remote, cold, unsympathetic and likely very expensive and unfriendly to such an immoral adventure as this." This opinion is a just foreshadowing of the doctor we meet in Chapter 37. He is completely unhelpful, regards the illegitimacy with distaste, and is irritated by "these young scamps of boys and girls who were so free to exercise the normal functions of their natures in the first instance, but so ready to refuse the social obligations which went with them." Falling back on the law in such matters, he refuses her request and advises her to go to her parents. Dreiser details Roberta's despair and Clyde's vague hopefulness. An abortion, it turns out ironically, would have saved two lives because worry about the unborn child and its effect on his romantic and social ambitions causes Clyde to let Roberta die in a drowning accident, which in turn results in his execution for murder. Another doctor appears in Book III, Chapter 26 to give medical testimony at Clyde's trial, and his advice is judged against the status of the school where he took his degree. From Book III, Chapter 28, until the end of the novel, Dreiser describes the horrors of the death house; and Clyde's fear, which is magnified by the fears of the other condemned men and the sight of some of them going to their deaths. Clyde faces his end somewhat more easily after the Reverend Macmillan helps him to accept his guilt in Roberta's death.

Dreiser, Theodore. "Regina C---." From A Gallery of Women. New York: H. Liveright, 1929. Sketch.

Drugs   Nurses

Portrait of a nurse/administrator on the way down as the result of her temperament and an increasing addiction to morphine. Dreiser shows her ability as an administrator, her coldness, and her desire to use men. But it is her relationship with morphine which is the center of interest. Regina uses her profession or merely the uniform of her profession to get the drugs she needs, even going so far as to substitute strychnine for the morphine she steals from her doctor/lover's medicine box.

Dugan, Alan. "For Masturbation," 1963. Available in The Norton Anthology of Modern Poetry, eds. Richard Ellmann and Robert O'Clair. New York: Norton, 1973. Poem: 20 lines.

Sexuality

One little voice from a corner calls out an answer to the big puritanical voices (which include, one remembers, the booming voices of Lawrence and Mailer, who are "agin"). In this instance, the speaker declares, in this particular corner of the universe, he is God, and he'll do as he pleases, even if terrible things will happen to him as a result ("then let my left great-toe-/nail grow into the inside knob/of my right ankle-bone . . . ."). How brave is this little voice, which even dares to boom for one moment: "THIS IS THE WAY IT IS, and if/it is 'a terrible disgrace'/it is as I must will,/because I am not them/ though I am theirs to kill"!

Durrell, Lawrence. Monsieur. New York: Viking, 1975. Novel.

Doctors   Homosexuality   Madness
Suicide

Here Durrell succumbs to the temptation to flirt with the novel within the novel within the novel, and with the levels of reality--with largely unsuccessful results. Nonetheless, worth reading for its unusual view of homosexuality, suicide, and their relationship to Gnostic beliefs. Central characters include a rather plodding English physician, his wife, and her brother: all 3 are lovers. They are perfectly united for a time, but finally, unable to live in two directions, the woman chooses madness.

Dürrenmatt, Friedrich. The Physicists. New York: Grove Press, 1964. Drama.

Evil Doctors   Handicaps   Madness
Med. Instit.   Nurses   Sexual Roles

The world as madhouse again. Here madness is not what it seems. Nor is apparent sanity a reliable state. And the psychiatrist is the least dependable of all. These tragic implications are worked out by the playwright in a comic--indeed an hilariously absurd-- situation. Three mad physicists are institutioned under the care of Fraulein Doktor Von Zahnd. The first thinks he is Einstein; the second believes himself to be Newton; the third regularly sees King Solomon. Twist of plot succeeds twist of plot until one after another, all our assumptions about the physicists are revealed

to be false. The fact that all have murdered their
nurses leads to our discovery--and theirs, for that
matter--that each had murdered to protect his secret
and sane identity. Two are international spies after
the secrets of the third, who hides from the world
because it is too mad to be trusted with those secrets.
As if this were not enough, a penultimate twist reveals
that the hunch-backed psychiatrist is really the mad
one. Her plans to take over the world are made to seem
funnier because she is a woman. "The world has fallen
into the hands of an insane, female psychiatrist"
(trans. James Kirkup). In the final twist, the physicists
realize that if they call themselves sane, they are
murderers (cf. Henry IV by Pirandello), and that
"insanity" is their only refuge of decent people in a
world controlled by a mad psychiatrist.

Dyer, Charles. Staircase. New York: Grove Press, 1966. Drama.

Homosexuality

A play by Charles Dyer about a character called Charles
Dyer. The second one is an aging homosexual who deludes
himself constantly. He pretends that he is a thriving
actor, a superior artistic sort. He pretends that his
marriage failed through his wife's fault. He pretends
that he is not really homosexual. He talks about his
many friends--only their names are all anagrams of
"Charles Dyer." Even the name of his mate for 20 years,
Harry C. Leeds, is an anagram. Charles Dyer is alone.
Funny play at times because of the posturing and bicker-
ing of Charlie and Harry, but ultimately painful.
Compare with Samuel Beckett's Waiting for Godot.

Eliot, T. S. The Cocktail Party. New York: Harcourt, Brace and
World, 1950. Poetic Drama.

Death   Doctors   Madness
Sexuality

The psychiatrist as a fusion of the priestly and medical
functions. Sir Henry Harcourt-Reilly moves in mysterious
ways, forcing a clique of people to come to him, preparing
his patients to choose him. Then he helps them adjust
to the idea that most love in the world is based on
illusion. People never understand the others with whom
they live, he believes, never truly give to each other
because the other is only an extension of the self, a
projected illusion. A few, like Celia, are capable of
searching for the Outside with whom or with which they
can relate, but that understanding may end in death, as
it does with Celia, whose death seems hideous. But
when charged that his treatment of Celia led to her
death, the psychiatrist answers: "I saw the image,
standing behind her chair,/Of a Celia Coplestone whose
face showed the astonishment/Of the first five minutes
after a violent death . . . . So it was obvious/That
here was a woman under sentence of death./The only
question/Then was, what sort of death? I could not
know;/Because it was for her to choose the way of life/
To lead to death, and, without knowing the end/Yet
choose the form of death . . . . And if that is not a
happy death, what death is happy?"

Eliot, T. S. "East Coker," Part IV, 1940. Available in The Complete
Poems and Plays, by Eliot. New York: Harcourt, Brace & World,
1952. Poem: 25 lines.

Disease & Health   Doctors   Med. Instit.
Nurses

Though Part IV is a poem within a poem, it
stands on its own as one of the finest examples of the
world-as-hospital metaphor. In Eliot's vision we are all
sick patients, but more than that, our sharply compassionate surgeon is "wounded," our nurse, "dying." In a
further twist, Eliot declares that our hope lies in
being ill: "Our only health is the disease . . . . The
chill ascends from feet to knees,/The fever sings in
mental wires./If to be warmed, then I must freeze/And
quake in purgatorial fires/Of which the flame is roses,
and the smoke is briars." We must be wounded in order
to know wholeness; we must be ill in order to know health.
In the final stanza the religious implication of all
this, already introduced in the idea of purgatorial fires,
is made perfectly clear. The wounded surgeon, who was
seen earlier "resolving the enigma of the fever chart,"
now becomes the wounded Christ, whose blood we drink,
whose bloody body we eat in communion--and thus are the
opposites in this poem reconciled.

Eliot, T. S. "Gerontion," 1920. Available in The Complete Poems
and Plays, by Eliot. New York: Harcourt, Brace & World,
1952. Poem: 76 lines.

Age   Sexuality

The aridity of contemporary life is symbolized by Gerontion
("little old man"), whose musings also conjure up the
image of a very real man. He has lost his sensual
capacity, his ability to feel passion. But "why should
I need it/Since what is kept must be adulterated?" His
loss is only part of a larger loss of what might be
termed mankind's moral passion. And as for Christ, he
is "the word within a word, unable to speak a word."
His Easter arrival comes in "depraved May," and he is
not a lamb, but a powerful tiger: "Us he devours."
Not much hope, then, for this old man, who lives in a
"rented" and "decayed" house. His are merely "Thoughts
of a dry brain in a dry season." Yet shrivelled though
he may be in body, the old man still has an honest

brain. (Eliot had intended to use "Gerontion" as
prologue to "The Waste Land," which introduces another
compelling old man, Tiresias, who sums up the dry and
worn out sexuality experienced by both men and women
in the modern world.)

Eliot, T. S. "The Love Song of J. Alfred Prufrock," 1917. Available
in The Complete Poems and Plays, by Eliot. New York: Harcourt,
Brace & World, 1952. Poem: 131 lines.

Age   The Body   Disease & Health
Madness   Sexuality

Almost a case history of a certain kind of puritanical
neurotic. This timid man has approached life with great
caution, measuring it out, as he says, in coffee spoons.
His repeated questions are "Do I dare?" and "how should
I presume?"--to eat a peach, to part his hair, to suggest
involvement to a woman, to disturb the universe in any
way. Part of his inability with women is due to fear of
rejection ("If one, settling a pillow by her head,/
Should say: 'That is not what I meant at all./That is
not it, at all.'"), part to an unhealthy fastidiousness
about the body: "And I have known the arms already,
known them all--/Arms that are braceleted and white and
bare/(But in the lamplight, downed with light brown
hair!)." The idea of disease is introduced in the famous
opening image, where ill health suffuses the universe:
"When the evening is spread out against the sky/Like a
patient etherised upon a table." Later on, we see that
even the illness partakes of the general fraud: "And
the afternoon, the evening, sleeps so peacefully!/
Smoothed by long fingers,/Asleep . . . tired . . . or it
malingers." On top of all this, Prufrock sees himself
as a bit ridiculous, almost a fool, one who strives to
keep up with the latest fashions to fend off age: "I
grow old . . . I grow old . . ./I shall wear the bottoms
of my trousers rolled." But it isn't as if he doesn't
know what life offers to some, and herein lies the
pathos of the situation: "I have heard the mermaids
singing, each to each./I do not think that they will
sing to me." He has seen them in his visions, but--
and here Prufrock's state is suddenly ours--"human voices
wake us, and we drown."

Ellison, Harlan. "I Have No Mouth and I Must Scream," 1967.
Available in Alone Against Tomorrow. New York: Collier Books,
1971. Short Story.

The Body   Sci Fi   Suffering

A twentieth-century hell caused by a computer which
inflicts eternal suffering on the bodies of humans who
have given it a mind but not a body. It would be hard
for the imagination to think of worse or to portray a
hell more feelingly.

Ellison, Harlan. "Wanted In Surgery," 1957. Available in Paingod
and Other Delusions. New York: Pyramid, 1975. Short Story.

Med. Profession   Sci Fi   Surgery

One of the first of a number of stories on the ultimate
dehumanization of medicine and the substitution of a
machine for a doctor--after all, machines know more, are
quicker, surer, don't get tired, aren't emotional and
need no pay. This story, unusual for Ellison, ends on
an upbeat--humans discover the importance of a bedside
manner and restore the despised human doctors to
importance.

Empson, William. "Ignorance of Death," 1940. Available in The
Norton Anthology of Modern Poetry, eds. Richard Ellmann and
Robert O'Clair. New York: Norton, 1973. Poem: 21 lines.

Death

An intellectual poet reviews several arguments about
death: there is "this civilising love of death" found
in music and painting; the Communists who "disapprove
of death/Except when practical"; the Freudians who
"regard the death-wish as fundamental,/Though 'the
clamour of life' proceeds from its rival 'Eros'"; the
liberal hopefuls who regard death as "a mere border to
an improving picture"; the literary man for whom death
is the trigger on his biggest gun; and so on. As for
himself, Empson says only that it upsets him "when a
man is ready to die about something/Other than himself."
Beyond that, he draws a blank, that is, feels stupid,
ignorant, and numb--and properly so: "Otherwise I feel
very blank upon this topic,/And think that though
important, and proper for anyone to bring up,/It is one
that most people should be prepared to be blank upon."

Farmer, José Philip. Riders of the Purple Wage, 1967. Available
in The Hugo Winners, ed. Isaac Asimov. Vol. 2. Garden City,
New York: Doubleday, 1971. Novella.

Sci Fi   Sexuality

Farmer is famous for works of free-wheeling sexuality
(his novel The Lovers was one of the first to deal with
alien-human sexual relationships), outrageous puns and
word plays, and imaginative assimilation of past authors.
This piece has at its climax a glorious pun on Finnegan's
Wake. Its main character is a young artist (who dreams
of painting with his prehensile penisnake) whose art is
blocked by sexual demands: his mother who makes economic
and emotional demands (having stopped making sexual
demands); his girlfriend who tantalizingly offers, then
denies, him creativity and emotional satisfaction in
the form of a baby; the art critic who demands intercourse in return for a good review necessary for a needed

grant; and society which is doing a good job of screwing him. He is held to his art by the imagination of his grandfather, who is hiding out from the government, from which the grandfather stole half the treasury's money. The story's delight lies in its texture; Farmer can so describe a sterile world that the process is pleasurable.

Faulkner, William. _As I Lay Dying_, 1930. New York: Vintage Books, 1957. Novel.

Abortion	Death	Disease & Health
Doctors	Dying	The Family
Grief	Madness	Sexuality

This novel is told by several different narrators, but only once by the proud, private, and dirt-poor Southern woman who lies dying as her son, Cash, builds her coffin outside her room. For some reason, perhaps because she married beneath her, she asks to be taken to her family's burial ground, a good distance away. After her death the family--the father, and the five children, Cash, Darl, Dewey Dell, Jewel, and Vardaman--put her on a wagon and pull her on the long journey, her body beginning to smell, the buzzards to hover. Terrible incidents beset the family: Cash breaks his leg; they almost lose the coffin in a flooded river; Vardaman, thinking to give his dead mother some air, drills a nail through the coffin and straight into her head. Once, unable to stand this obscene journey any longer, the only sensitive and truly grief-stricken family member, Darl, attempts to set fire to a barn where his mother's body is resting (an act which results in Jewel and Dewey Dell, who have always hated Darl, having him committed to the insane asylum). One of the reasons that Dewey Dell loathes Darl is because Darl knows she is pregnant. On the journey, she tries unsuccessfully to get pharmaceutical aid for an abortion from an indignant druggist, and later on, she is seduced by a drug clerk who promises her pills if she will submit to him. Dr. Peabody, a good fellow over 70 years old and over 200 pounds (he is 300 in _The Sound and the Fury_), finds Addie on her death bed, sets Cash's leg and later bails the family out by paying their hotel bill. "When I was young," Dr. Peabody says, "I believed death to be a phenomenon of the body; now I know it to be merely a function of the mind--and that of the minds of the ones who suffer the bereavement." Perhaps, but as soon as Mr. Bundren finally gets his wife buried, he up and marries the woman from whom he has borrowed the shovel.

Faulkner, William. _Sanctuary_, 1931. New York: Signet, 1954. Novel.

| Mental Retardation | Sexuality | V.D. |

Some fairly kinky sex here. It all begins when Temple Drake, a wild college student, shows up at the house of some bootleggers. Tommy, a kindly mentally retarded man, is shot to death for trying to protect Temple from Popeye, who thereafter rapes her with a corncob. A decadent lass, she accompanies Popeye to a bordello, a sort of sanctuary, where she takes the lover brought to her by Popeye and makes love to him while Popeye watches. The corncob and the vicarious lover are necessary because Popeye, victim of hereditary syphilis, is impotent. In fact, the story of Popeye is practically a case history of bad genes. For moralists, it should be noted that though Temple is here a wild thing and involved in the death of two men, she meets her own past in a subsequent Faulkner novel, _Requiem for a Nun_.

Faulkner, William. _The Sound and the Fury_, 1929. New York: Signet, 1959. Novel.

Alcoholism	The Family	Grief
Madness	Mental Retardation	Sexuality
Suicide		

The first section of this novel is one of the great coups of modern fiction, life as seen through the eyes of a 33-year-old idiot (life is a tale told by one, of course, full of sound and fury). Matters that are muddled by Benjy are gradually made clearer as the story gets retold through other minds. One thing is clear early: the Compson family is a decayed Southern family becoming more decayed before our eyes (only the black cook, the noble Dilsey, endures). Mr. Compson is a nihilistic alcoholic who kills himself through drink. Mrs. Compson is a badly neurotic hypochondriac. Her daughter Caddy is seduced and impregnated by a cad, then married off to an unsuspecting fellow, who divorces her as soon as the child is born. Partly because of his sister's sexual infidelity (he seems to be more than usually attached to her), partly because of his father's weakness, Quentin Compson, a Harvard student, kills himself. He has grieved, really, for the loss of Caddy. And so has poor bellowing Benjy, whose own sexual proclivities end by getting him gelded. The other Compson sibling, Jason, might also be considered neurotic, for he blames Caddy for his failure in life and is obsessed by getting even with her, to the extent of hoarding the money she sends for the support of her illegitimate child, also named Quentin.

Fitzgerald, F. Scott. "An Alcoholic Case," 1937. From _The Stories of F. Scott Fitzgerald_. New York: Charles Scribner's Sons, 1951. Short Story.

| Alcoholism | Nurses | Suicide |

Not a first-rate story, perhaps, but a realistic look at the frustrations of dealing with an alcoholic. A nurse takes his case because it is in the best traditions of

the profession to take difficult cases, but there is also the suggestion that she is attracted to the man. Gradually she comes to recognize that he wants to die and that she can do nothing.

Fitzgerald, F. Scott. "The Crack-Up," "Handle with Care," and "Pasting It Together," 1936. From _The Crack-Up_, ed. Edmund Wilson. New York: New Directions, 1964. Essays.

Madness

Fitzgerald may clearly differentiate between the crack-up state and madness or alcoholism; nevertheless, what he describes is a sort of madness: a cutting off of all ties, a loss of self, a realization that heretofore other people have supplied one's direction and values. A crack-up of values, he calls it. In the second of these three autobiographical essays is the famous sentence which competes with the best clinical descriptions of depression: "In a real dark night of the soul it is always three o'clock in the morning."

Fitzgerald, F. Scott. _Tender Is the Night_. New York: Charles Scribner's Sons, 1934. Novel.

Alcoholism	Death	Doctors
Children	Madness	Med. Instit.
Sexuality	Women as Patients	

A brilliant novel in which the doctor and the patient gradually change places. A love story in which a husband gives so much to his schizophrenic wife that he seemingly hasn't enough energies left to care for himself. Unfortunately for Dick Diver, these are not two plots, but one: he is both husband and psychiatrist to the beautiful, rich Nicole, whose hospitalization at a clinic in Zurich had come about as a result of an incestuous relationship with her father. As Nicole's physician, Dick gives in to the pressures of Nicole's sister, "Baby," who suggests that he marry Nicole in order to continue to care for her after she leaves treatment, and who later buys Dick a partnership in the clinic. This is not as unethical as it sounds, for Dick indeed loves Nicole, and for a time is a good husband/doctor to her, fending off her attacks, hiding her illness from their rich European-American friends. Almost inevitably the relationship weakens, and Dick gradually deteriorates into an embarrassing alcoholic as Nicole, who is an increasingly sympathetic figure, grows into health and maturity--and independence from Dick, who ends up practicing general medicine in one small American town after another.

Forster, E. M. "The Machine Stops." Available in _The Science Fiction Hall of Fame_, Vol. 2B, ed. Ben Bova. Garden City, New York: Doubleday, 1973. Short Story.

| The Body | Med. Profession | Sci Fi |

Although medicine plays a small part in this story, it is, nevertheless, a part of the frightening allegory. Mankind has retreated into cells of a hive, serviced by The Machine and patterned by The Machine. Physical contact, the pleasures of the body, are lost as people adapt themselves to isolation in uniform cubicles provided with all services by The Machine. If a bed is too short, one must accept it because The Machine cannot make exceptions. A woman tries to squirm out of an agreement to leave her cubicle by claiming she's unwell; immediately The Machine takes over, thrusting a thermometer and medicine into her mouth. Eventually The Machine breaks down; at first people pray to it and try to adapt to the increasingly uncomfortable environment. Finally, they are forced out of their hives back into experience again.

Forster, E. M. _Maurice_. New York: Norton, 1971. Novel.

Homosexuality

Published in 1971 after Forster's death, but written in 1913, this novel is a graceful study of love between men. Beginning with a look at Maurice's adolescence, when he learned about heterosexual facts of life and felt at once alienated from them, the author follows his young hero into Cambridge, where he falls in love with Clive, who keeps their relationship intimate and intense, but essentially Platonic. When, after three years of this, Clive suddenly discovers that he now finds only women attractive, Maurice must go on by himself. Up to this point, a psychologically revealing and persuasive study of homosexuality, the novel now becomes sentimental. The physically handsome but mentally torpid Maurice finds what we are supposed to believe is lasting happiness with Alex Scudder, a working class man--a gameskeeper, in fact. Clive had been too spiritual; Alec knows about the love of the body as well. The book has inevitably reminded readers of D. H. Lawrence: Clive and Alec are like Miriam and Clara in _Sons and Lovers_, and Lady Chatterley's Mellors was, of course, a gameskeeper.

Frost, Robert. "The Death of the Hired Man," 1914. Available in _Selected Poems_, by Frost. New York: Holt, Rinehart, & Winston, 1963. Poem: 167 lines.

| Age | Death |

Frost breathes shape and significance into the last moments of an old unreliable bum of a man, who has returned to Warren and Mary's farm, where he once worked. He has come to them like an old hound dog who once came to them out of the woods, and he means no more to them,

really, than the dog did. This old man is not Salt of
the Earth or a Noble Savage, or some other sentimental
cliché: he is just old Silas, with "nothing to look
backward to with pride,/And nothing to look forward to
with hope." Still, he is human, has self-respect, and
has returned "home," Mary senses, to die. And that is
his right. Though Warren mocks, "Home is the place
where, when you have to go there,/They have to take you
in"; Mary replies, "I should have called it/Something
you somehow haven't to deserve." Frost accomplishes his
ends entirely through down-to-earth dialogue between
Warren and Mary, interspersed with patches of tender,
lyrical descriptions of the moon-lit night. We never
even see old Silas, except through their description of
him. He even dies off-stage, as it were: Warren, his
irritation with the old man stilled for a moment, goes
into the house to check on him, and the poem ends:
"Warren returned--too soon, it seemed to her,/Slipped
to her side, caught up her hand and waited./'Warren?'
she questioned. 'Dead,' was all he answered."

Frost, Robert. "'Out, Out,'" 1916. Available in Selected Poems,
    by Frost. New York: Holt, Rinehart, & Winston, 1963. Poem:
    34 lines.

| Adolescence | Death | Disease & Health |
| Doctors | Dying | |

"Out, out . . . brief candle." A boy, old enough to do
a man's work, but with a child's heart, is sawing some
wood when suddenly the saw, as if deliberately, cuts
through his wrist. "The boy's first outcry was a rueful
laugh,/As he swung toward them holding up the hand/Half
in appeal, but half as if to keep/The life from spilling."
He begs his sister not to let the doctor cut his hand
off. "So. But the hand was gone already." The doctor
arrives and puts the boy "in the dark of ether." But
"the watcher at his pulse took fright . . . . Little--
less--nothing!--and that ended it./No more to build on
there." And as for the "grievers": "they, since they/
Were not the one dead, turned to their affairs."

Garcia Lorca, Federico. Blood Wedding, 1933. Available in Three
    Tragedies, by Garcia Lorca. New York: New Directions, 1947.
    Drama.

| Death | Sexuality |

Hot sexuality combines with the drive to death in this
poetic, symbolic drama. The wedding of the title is a
ritual between characters called simply The Bride and
The Bridegroom and involving their families, who in the
past had been sundered by a murderous blood feud. The
songs in the play emphasize the innocence of the bridal
pair, the need to produce more children to replace those
lost, and the intimate connection of the marriage with
elements of nature. But the Bride cannot fight off her
attraction to her cousin Leonardo, whom she once loved,
and with whom she runs away. Doom pursues them, in the
form of the Moon and Death, personified as an old beggar
woman. Death takes both Leonardo and the Bridegroom,
whom she claims to find handsomer as a corpse. Now the
mother of the Bridegroom, all her men gone (cf. Synge's
Riders to the Sea), controls her vengeance and finds
some semblance of peace in accepting the sweeping power
of death. She grieves for the victims of the little
Knife, as she calls death, that slides into the astonished flesh.

Garcia Lorca, Federico. The House of Bernarda Alba, 1936. Available
    in Three Tragedies, by Garcia Lorca. New York: New Directions,
    1947. Drama.

| Age | Children | Handicaps |
| Madness | Sexuality | Suicide |

Bernarda Alba, widowed, mother of five daughters, is a
sexually repressed tyrant, charging her daughters with
eight years of mourning for their father, during which
time they shall see no men, except the handsome man now
betrothed to her eldest, a 39-year-old woman. But the
daughters' natural desires seek outlets, especially in
the case of the vindictive hunch-backed daughter and the
youngest, Adela, who alone is beautiful. All three
daughters love the fiancé of the eldest, but it is Adela
whom he loves. Sexual needs break out everywhere, even
in Bernarda's mad old mother, who escapes from her room,
crying that she wants a man and cannot bear to see the
dusty lives led in this house. When Bernarda learns of
Adela's intention to elope, she goes after the waiting
fiancé with a gun. Thinking her lover dead, Adela hangs
herself, but Bernarda consoles herself with the thought
that at least her daughter died a virgin. A rural
Spanish honor code, yes, but with relevance to sexual
repression and maternal tyranny everywhere.

Garcia Lorca, Federico. Yerma, 1934. Available in Three Tragedies,
    by Garcia Lorca. New York: New Directions, 1947. Drama.

| The Body | Madness | Sexuality |
| Sexual Roles | | |

The tragedy of a barren woman in a society that values
children highly. Yerma's desire for a child far exceeds
her sexual desire for her husband Juan. She needs him
only for conception. (A neighbor tells her that she
cannot conceive because she does not enjoy sex.) Yerma's
obsession becomes frantic, and Juan begins to fear that
she will seek a child with another man. But her honor
forbids that. Wildly, Yerma curses the body for failing
to respond to the wishes of her head. Eventually, when
Juan confesses that he wants only her body and not

children, Yerma, hopeless now, kills him in a frenzy,
telling herself that she has killed her son and that
she is truly barren and alone.

Gazzo, Michael. A Hatful of Rain, 1955. Available in Famous
    American Plays of the 1950's, ed. Lee Strasberg. New York:
    Dell, 1962. Drama.

| Drugs | The Family | Preg. & Childbirth |

Most people think of this play as being "about drug
addiction," but it is probably more accurate to think of
it as a play about a family. A young couple, Johnny and
Celia, live, together with Johnny's brother Polo, in a
small flat in New York's Lower East Side. They are
being visited by Johnny and Polo's father, a bartender
who has not seen either of the boys since their childhood
when he put them up for adoption. What is most valuable
about A Hatful of Rain is the believable dialogue and
the portrait of a family in trouble. Celia is very
pregnant, though her husband hasn't touched her since
the conception and never asks about the baby. Polo is
in love with his brother's wife. And the father has
arrived to pick up the $2500 Polo promised to lend him,
only to discover that it is mysteriously gone. During
the course of the play the troubles increase. Celia
almost has a miscarriage, for instance. Matters between
Polo and her come to a crisis. But the most serious
problem--and the reason most medical readers will be
interested in this play--is of course Johnny's drug
addiction. It began when he was hospitalized for a year
following his capture by the enemy during the war.
Gazza doesn't hide any of the horror. He even introduces two threatening drug pushers, Mother and Apples.
And we learn of Polo's attempts to help Johnny go cold
turkey. When Celia finally learns of the addiction,
she takes charge, directing Johnny first to the police,
and then to a hospital.

Gelber, Jack. The Connection, 1957. New York: Grove Press, 1960.
    Drama.

| Drugs |

The playwright's intention is to assault the audience
with the dismal, obscene realities of drug addiction.
In an attempt to get closer to a semblance of reality,
the script calls for the actors to film a drama about
"real" drug addicts, a technique that enables the author
to efface himself and throw judgment back on the audience.
The junkies are waiting for their connection to bring
them their fixes. They then shoot up on stage, one of
them nearly overdosing, and reach their highs. In
something of a cheap trick, one of the junkies claims
that the squares who need money like he needs a fix are
hooked worse than he is. Still, the purposeless of this
sort of life is well and frankly portrayed, a purposeless
that achieves structure only in the need to find the
connection and get the dope.

Genet, Jean. Our Lady of the Flowers, ca. 1942. London: Panther
    Books, 1966. Novel.

| Homosexuality |

This book is many things--a praise of evil, an experiment
in language, an investigation of crime, a view of the
dregs of society--but it is most valuable, and most
infamous, as a study of homosexuality. Written while its
author was in prison, it could also be seen, as Jean-
Paul Sartre has put it in Saint Genet, as "an epic of
masturbation," for the author-narrator is obviously
attracted to the men he describes. The central character,
whose life we see from childhood to death by tuberculosis, is a man called "Culafroy" ("cold ass") as a boy,
but later "Divine," as an adult homosexual prostitute.
Divine goes about in drag and refers to herself as "she."
We learn of Divine's youthful homosexuality and later
of all her adult lovers, including a murderer (Notre-
Dame) and his father (Mignon), who commit unwitting
incest. Genet supports the concept of homosexuality
against bourgeois condemnation. No, he goes further
than that, glorifying it at times, even when he is
presenting without illusions the sordid life style that
homosexuals often drift into.

Gide, Andre. The Immoralist, 1902. New York: Bantam, 1970.
    Novel.

| The Body | Death | Disease & Health |
| Homosexuality | Madness | |

The "immoralist" of the title is a young man, Michel,
whose entire life was conducted from the intellectual
plane, even his marriage, which he had undertaken at
the age of 24 simply because his dying father wished
it. Fortunately for him, his wife Marceline is a
generous woman who nurses him carefully when he falls
seriously ill with tuberculosis. The bloody details
of the disease, his nearness to death, and his awareness
that only by force of his own will can he recover: all
these combine to change Michel into someone who lives
for health only and through his body chiefly. He comes
to a narcissistic involvement with his body; to an
attraction to the healthy bodies of young boys (though
the reader realizes his latent homosexuality long before
Michel does); and to a decision to live for the fulfillment of immediate pleasures rather than by society's
rules for "responsible" living. When Marceline falls
ill with tuberculosis, though in some sense he loves her,

he quickly loses sympathy for her, concluding that only the strong deserve sympathy and that what is "right" is that which contributes to his own health. Is he obsessive and neurotic? Or are his arguments about the needs of the healthy individual valid? In any case, in The Immoralist we have a fascinating pre-Freudian look at the unconscious, repression, and latent homosexuality.

Ginsberg, Allen. "Howl." From Howl and Other Poems. San Francisco: City Lights Books, 1956. Poem: 78 lines.

Drugs   Homosexuality   Madness
Med. Instit.   Sexuality   Suicide

One of the central documents of the Beat experience, this poem is an apocryphal howl from the madhouse. In long Whitmanesque lines, Ginsberg, like a raving angel, chants the chronicle of the Beats. Everything follows from the first words: "I saw the best minds of my generation destroyed by madness." Afterwards, we get vivid glimpses of the most debased experiences, seemingly sought in the hope of sanctity. The "best minds" turn often to drugs: heroin, marijuana, benzedrine, with the result that they become "hysterical naked" and know "waking nightmares." Alcohol too they seek and "endless balls," both homosexual and heterosexual, "scattering their semen freely to whomever come who may." They "created great suicidal dramas," cutting their wrists, even in one case jumping off the Brooklyn Bridge, until they "presented themselves on the granite steps of the madhouse with shaven heads and harlequin speech of suicide, demanding instant lobotomy,/and who were given instead the concrete void of insulin metrasol electricity hydrotherapy psychotherapy occupational therapy pingpong & amnesia." Addressing himself to his friend Carl Solomon, whom Ginsberg met as a fellow patient, the poet says, "ah, Carl, while you are not safe I am not safe," and, of course, the reader, submerged with Ginsberg in all this may wonder, "Who is?"

Giraudoux, Jean. Electra, 1937. Available in Masters of Modern Drama, eds. Haskell M. Block and Robert G. Shedd. New York: Random House, 1962. Drama.

Children   The Family   Grief
Madness   Sexuality   Sexual Roles

One of the best of the modern French dramatizations of ancient Greek myths. (Giraudoux, Cocteau, Sartre, and Anouilh did adaptations; but perhaps the most relevant to medical topics, after Electra, is Anouilh's Medea, 1946, which has been called "a study in psychopathology.") This version of Electra, like many of the other modernized myths, has political implications for the French during the last world war, but the story of the twisted love/hate between mother and daughter, and the sexual attachments between daughter and dead father, son and mother, and sister and brother carries equal power; more perhaps, for this time around, conventions allow sex to be dealt with very frankly. For instance, Clytemnestra, who wants Electra to marry and be a woman in the normal way, maintains that behind all her talk of chastity and accusations against her mother, Electra is all desire--for her brother Orestes. Later, Electra describes her only real contact with the body of her father: "My cheek on his, I felt my father's warmth (trans. Winifred Smith)." Clytemnestra and Orestes, meeting again after years, could almost be said to flirt, and Orestes is dismayed as a lover might be when he learns of his mother's affair with Aegisthus. This version of the myth is further expanded by the statement that Electra is looking for a mother to replace her own unsatisfactory one, and seeks maternal comfort in a husband. That leads the character called the gardener to say: "There are men who'd be glad to have a child nine months, if they had to, just to have daughters. All men, actually." Furthermore, this Electra is very funny in places, but that doesn't obscure either the family complexities or Electra's obsession with killing her mother.

Giraudoux, Jean. The Madwoman of Chaillot, 1945. Available in Masters of Modern Drama, eds. Haskell M. Block and Robert G. Shedd. New York: Random House, 1962. Drama.

Age   Doctors   Handicaps
Madness   Women as Healers

This charming drama, played out partly in the realm of fantasy, has a huge cast and an amusing mock-trial in which the capitalists of the world, who wish to destroy Paris for the oil under her streets, are demolished by the People, led by the elderly "Countess Aurelia," who is really mad. So are her three friends--there's no question about that--who have hallucinations and illusions aplenty. But in Giraudoux's world, the mad have beauty and goodness and therefore a certain captivating truth and practicality as well. Two of the minor characters are of special interest. There is a "Dr. Jadin," a specialist in the extraction of bunions, whose office is at a sidewalk cafe. A bit mad too, no doubt, but also disconcertingly logical. And there is a deaf-mute, who is in the final triumphant scene speaks, "and his voice is the most beautiful of all" (trans. Maurice Valency). In the end the Madwoman has healed everything. In a sense, her womanliness has triumphed: "Well, there we are. The world is saved. And you see how simple it all was? Nothing is ever so wrong in this world that a sensible woman can't set it right in the course of an afternoon."

Golding, William. Lord of the Flies. New York: Coward, McCann, 1955. Novel.

Adolescence   Children   Death
Disease & Health Madness   Sexuality

This book was extraordinarily popular in the late 50's and early 60's because readers of that atomic war-conscious period sympathized with its vision of the basic savagery of humankind. Social destructiveness, Golding seems to think, can be traced to individual human nature. Realizing this, we must seek to curb ourselves. All this sounds rather didactic, and the novel is certainly moralistic, but the author works through vivid allegory and myth and thereby persuades indirectly. He makes his point through a group of English schoolboys, aged 6 to 12, who find themselves all alone on an isolated island. At first they think it great sport to be without supervision, and then they attempt to impose civilized principles of order and government. Trouble comes when rumors arise of a "beast" in the jungle. Nonsense, says the scientific, rational "Piggy." But this fat, asthmatic kid is killed, by the boys themselves, some of whom have turned into ritualistic hunters. The beast is only ourselves, says the Christ-like Simon, but he is killed too without being heard. These children come to love killing, to require it even. At one point they kill a pig, chanting as they do so, and stabbing it in a sexual fashion. This fear-become-madness is "mankind's essential illness," Golding demonstrates, and at the end, with order superficially restored by the arrival of the outside, adult world, one of the boys, no longer innocent, faces this tragic knowledge. Some readers have argued that it is not so much innocence that he has lost, as ignorance, and that Lord of the Flies terrifyingly illustrates Freud's view that no child is innocent.

Gorki, Maxim. The Lower Depths, 1902. Available in Masters of Modern Drama, eds. Haskell M. Block and Robert G. Shedd. New York: Random House, 1962. Drama.

Age   Alcoholism   Death
Disease & Health Dying   Poverty & Health
Suffering   Suicide

Ultimate wretchedness in pre-revolutionary Russia. Human suffering could hardly be more graphically depicted. A dozen people--a thief, a whore, an alcoholic, a dying consumptive, and others--live together in a squalid cellar. The young wife, coughing her way to death and neglected by her callous husband, claims that she has never known a day free from suffering, yet she still wants to live just a little longer. Luka, the old wise man, assures her that death is kindly, like a mother to small children, and will bring her peace at last. He tries to help the alcoholic actor too, telling him of a free hospital where they treat alcoholism, for there they know that drunkards are also human. The trouble is, Luka doesn't know exactly where the hospital is. And when the actor leaves for his treatment--Satine says cynically that the hospital is within a half mile's distance of the end of the world--he gets only as far as the yard, where he hangs himself. In the face of all this disease and death, first Luka and then Satine proclaim the play's theme: man himself is the only truth; we must learn, therefore, to respect each other, even in the most dismal of circumstances, and not degrade ourselves with pity.

Graves, Robert. "The Cool Web," 1927. Available in Robert Graves: Selected by Himself, 3rd ed. Harmondsworth, England: Penguin Books, 1966. Poem: 18 lines.

Madness

Language as a defense against madness. "Children are dumb to say how hot the day is," but adults have language "to chill the angry day." Because we can speak, we can to some extent magically control the world for ourselves; we can "Retreat from too much joy or too much fear." If we ever do let go of language and face directly the hot day--or the rose or the dark sky or the drums--"We shall go mad no doubt and die that way." (But it is a chilly sort of sanity we have.) Incidentally, Graves, inspired by his association with psychiatrist W. H. R. Rivers, developed a theory of poetry as therapy: "An anthology of poetry is thus a collection of homeopathic medicines; each poet expresses his own neurosis and helps a similarly afflicted reader" (Richard Ellmann and Robert O'Clair, The Norton Anthology of Modern Poetry). Graves' famous later theory, expounded in The White Goddess, was, of course, much more objective.

Graves, Robert. "Down, Wanton, Down!," 1933. Available in Robert Graves: Selected by Himself, 3rd ed. Harmondsworth, England: Penguin Books, 1966. Poem: 20 lines.

Sexuality

Disgust with one's own lusts is a pattern in Graves' poems, but here the subject is treated comically--and famously. The poet addresses his member, calling him "wanton," "Poor Bombard-captain," "witless." The fellow seems to be indifferent to what he storms or why. His one boast is his "staunchness at the post." (The public address to one's private parts is an enduring literary tradition.)

Graves, Robert. "The Legs," 1931. Available in Robert Graves: Selected by Himself, 3rd ed. Harmondsworth, England: Penguin Books, 1966. Poem: 40 lines.

The Body

A fantasy of the body out of control. Or perhaps it is the mind which is isolated. In any case, the poet imagines that he comes upon a road where the traffic was nothing but pairs of legs. The situation could be amusing, but it isn't" "Though my smile was broad/ The legs could not see,/Though my laugh was loud/The legs could not hear."

Graves, Robert. "Lollocks," 1940. Available in Robert Graves: Selected by Himself, 3rd ed. Harmondsworth, England: Penguin Books, 1966. Poem: 46 lines.

Disease & Health   Sexual Roles

One way to read this clever poem about some fantasy animals is as an ingenious theory of disease, if that isn't weighing it down too much. "Lollocks" have for mother, sorrow, and for father, sloth. They're scary, beastly little things, who plague children in the night, and: "When the imbecile agèd/Are over-long in dying/And the nurse drowses,/Lollocks come skipping/Up the tattered stairs/And are nasty together/In the bed's shadow." Men can't see them, though they suffer more from them "both in neck and belly." But women, those sly things, know all about them. One avoids Lollocks this way: "hard broom and soft broom,/To well comb the hair,/To well brush the shoe,/And to pay every debt/As it falls due."

Graves, Robert. "The Naked and the Nude," 1959. Available in Robert Graves: Selected by Himself, 3rd ed. Harmondsworth, England: Penguin Books, 1966. Poem: 24 lines.

The Body   Med. Profession

A bit prosy, even for Graves, but makes an interesting distinction between two sorts of unclothed bodies. The naked body is what lovers delight in, the form the Goddess appears in, and what doctors see as anatomy. The nude body, on the other hand, though thought to be superior, especially as art, is finally a lie.

Greene, Graham. The Power and the Glory, 1940. New York: Viking Press, 1946. Novel.

Alcoholism

This is, of course, a novel about spiritual anguish. A Mexican priest, living in a time when the authorities wish to crush religion, is on the run, not only in fear of his life, but also in fear of facing directly his own weaknesses as a servant of God and his fellow-man. His self-contempt has made him turn to brandy,.and it is as a novel with a "whiskey priest" for a hero that the book is relevant here. In spite of his humiliating dependence on liquor, the priest is in fact a hero of sorts. In finally taking on the burden of his priestly vocation and risking his life for his people, he has enabled goodness and grace to shine through moral weakness.

Gregory, Isabella Augusta, Lady. The Workhouse Ward, 1908. Available in A Treasury of the Theatre, ed. John Gassner. New York: Simon & Schuster, 1960. Drama.

Age   Disease & Health   Med. Instit.

A very short, very funny, play about two old, infirm men who are ending their days in a miserable state home for the aged destitute. Their chief characteristics are pride, in themselves and their pains, and aggressiveness. The two have been insulting each other for decades, but when one of them gets a chance to live with his sister, he can forsake neither his habits, particularly now that he is old, nor his friendly enemy. The men are last seen comfortably throwing pillows and prayer books at one another.

Gunn, James. "Medic" (originally "Not So Great an Enemy," 1957 and a part of the Immortals, 1962). Available in Some Dreams are Nightmares. New York: Charles Scribner's, 1973. Short Story.

Doctors   Med. Ethics   Med. Instit.
Med. Profession   Sci Fi

Health care in the not-too-distant future. 52.5% of the national income goes for health care in the form of insurance. No health insurance--no health care. Why should a doctor deprive an insured person to treat someone who cannot pay? And, to make certain people cannot avoid insurance, doctors who treat non-insured patients are arrested as criminals. When a policy lapses, as it must inevitably because insurance is so expensive, the person is "repossessed," i.e., used as an unwilling organ donor or research subject. The Medic-hero is caught between outrage at the deaths from easily treated illness and admiration at surgical miracles. He finally decides medicine is responsible: it talks of carcinogens yet can offer only expensive hospitals as a cure for cancer. The plot ends unsatisfactorily--the young Medic, an old, experienced doctor, and the o.e.d.'s beautiful daughter escape to fight against the system. But as a whole, the story raises interesting issues and vividly portrays the possible results of emphasizing insured health care.

Haggard, H. Rider. Doctor Therne. New York: Longmans, Green & Co., 1898. (Found in Princeton University's rare book collection.) Novel.

Doctors   Evil Doctors   Med. Ethics
Med. Profession   Plague

A thesis novel. Instead of embellishing this tale with the exotic and supernatural atmospheres of King Solomon's Mines and She, Haggard has tried to enliven this anti-Anti-Vaccinationist (A.V.) tract by letting his repentant, but still rationalizing, doctor-narrator show himself as a cold, ambitious, hypocrite even after this narrator has seen the disasters caused by his action. Unfortunately, the novel's message is given with a single--or rather narrow-minded--thrust which thins the novel into a propagandistic narrative and which allows for several absurdities in that narrative. The anti-hero narrator, Dr. Therne (perhaps a conscious inversion of the warm, high-principled physician in Trollope's Dr. Thorne) has a neurotic aversion to smallpox because a smallpox attack weakened his father's resistance to the T.B. which, two years after the smallpox, finally killed him. This need to create an ogre of smallpox at the expense of other fatal diseases is also seen in an early chapter in which Dr. Therne visits Mexico and calmly leaves a town in which the dead are carried away in carts, experiencing no horror because the fatal disease is "only" yellow fever. However, when he is forced by brigands into a town devastated by smallpox, he can think only of escape--refusing to treat the sick and abandoning his faithful servant to die, untended, of the disease. Dr. Therne rationalizes his sins and his betrayal of his profession on the grounds that they were forced upon him by the unethical behavior of an established member of the profession, Dr. Bell, who tries to prevent Therne from establishing a practice in his town. Therne catches Dr. Bell in a blatant, fatal malpractice and so gains a good start in the profession. He praises his own skill at diagnosis and his wisdom in considering the patient's mind and character because the mind governs the body. However, Dr. Bell undoes him. When Bell is helping Therne's wife through childbirth, Therne is assisting the wife of Sir Thomas Colford in her confinement. Therne's wife becomes ill with puerperal fever, Therne inadvertently gives it to Lady Colford, both women die, and Dr. Bell swears that Dr. Therne knew that he was infected with the fever when he went to Lady Colford. Dr. Therne is tried for murder, is acquitted with the help of Stephen Strong, an anti-vaccinationist, but finds his practice ruined. He ekes out a living investigating cases where vaccination has harmed the patient. With Strong's help, Therne runs for Parliament on an A.V. plank, refuses to vaccinate his daughter, just manages to defeat Sir Thomas Colford, sponsors a bill forbidding compulsory vaccination, becomes successful, tries to marry his daughter, a believing A.V., to eligible men and is horrified when she prefers a struggling young doctor who believes in vaccination. The predictable end follows. A smallpox epidemic breaks out during an election, Jane dies, and Therne, frightened, vaccinates himself and is exposed on the speaking platform as a hypocrite by Jane's grieving fiancé.

Hall, Radclyffe. The Well of Loneliness. New York: Blue Ribbon Books, 1928. Novel.

Homosexuality

Scandalous in its day because it was the first modern novel to treat lesbian love so frankly, the book now strikes us as sentimental. Nevertheless, the story of Stephen Gordon and her poignant love for another woman is still valuable for the accuracy of its psychological details (Hall was herself lesbian) and its picture of lesbian society. The book ends with an intense vision in which Stephen, alone now that Mary has left with a man, is beseiged by forms of similar women, living and yet to be born, who beg her as a writer to give them the right to existence. This book is a response to that vision.

Hansberry, Lorraine. A Raisin in the Sun. New York: Signet, 1959. Drama.

Abortion   Children   The Family
Med. Profession

One of the major dramatic depictions of the poor but struggling black family, headed by a splendid matriarchal figure. Her daughter Beneatha hopes to study medicine. Her daughter-in-law Ruth is dismayed to learn that she is pregnant again and plans an abortion. Her son Walter dreams of making some quick money. All pin their hopes on a new house in a white suburb, which the dead father's insurance money has enabled them to make a down payment on. The strong family resists the offer of racist neighbors to buy the house, and even when they are faced with the terrible news that Walter has blown the rest of their money on a shady financial deal, they ultimately rally around, talking things out--their pressures, their dreams--and deciding to face the future, as represented by Walter's young son, together and with pride. Walter has become a man. As for Beneatha, she now sees her medical aspirations as naive: "I always thought it was the one concrete thing in the world that a human being could do. Fix up the

sick, you know--and make them whole again. This was truly
being God." But for the time being, she's given up her
hopes because medicine can't cure the real problems. It
"doesn't seem deep enough, close enough to the truth."

Hart, Moss and George S. Kaufman. The Man Who Came to Dinner, 1939.
Available in Sixteen Famous American Plays, eds. Bennett A.
Cerf and Van H. Cartmell. New York: Modern Library, 1941.
Drama.

Disease & Health   Doctors   Nurses

For comic relief. A famous author and radio personality
comes to dinner, is temporarily invalided by an accident,
and is forced to remain in the house--which the insolent
man proceeds to take over. Sheridan Whiteside, for that
is his name, mistreats everyone, including a young
doctor/would-be writer, who runs errands for Whiteside
in the hope of getting a book published with his help.
(Of course, the irrascible fellow has no intention of
helping the doctor, just exploiting him.) Nurse Preen
is so maddened by him that she finally leaves the house,
hysterically vowing never to nurse again, her love for
humanity having been turned to hatred by Whiteside. A
light but wildly funny play.

Heinlein, Robert A. Time Enough For Love. New York: Berkley,
1974. Novel.

Death   The Family   Sci Fi
Sexuality   Sexual Roles   Suicide

Like most of Heinlein's books, a troublesome mixture.
He manages to create the most diverse and interesting
backgrounds for the same theme and characters. Here
is a dream of immortality carried to the ultimate: an
immortal man is lovingly tempted to lay aside suicide
in order to lay every other woman in his family, from
his mother to his sister-daughters (plus numerous other
women less closely related). Woman is man's equal, but
since man's only creativity is self-reproduction, a
woman is happiest when she carries a baby; she only
sleeps with a man to become pregnant. The novel also
praises selective breeding for longevity and survival
value, and Heinlein is to be praised for the ingenuity
with which he finds primitive situations to test the
survival value of an isolated family when man is a
successful social creature. The first chapters are
concerned with medical and psychological efforts to
hold back the hero from the suicide which is his right.
Incest is strongest in the last chapters.

Hejinian, John. Extreme Remedies. New York: St. Martin's Press,
1974. Novel.

By Doctors   Disease & Health   Doctors
Evil Doctors   Med. Ethics   Med. Instit.
Med. Profession   Med. Students   Nurses
Poverty & Health Surgery   Women as Patients

Several cuts above the conventional popular novel
written by doctors, in fact the sort of first book
which marks its author as "promising." The novel does,
to be sure, include some--perhaps most--of the expected
elements: a young seemingly idealistic resident, his
attractive woman medical student, the nasty doctor
intent on making money, the nasty doctors intent on
making big reputations at the expense of their patients,
the emergency room, the difficult moral decisions, and
so on and on. Nonetheless, this novel goes beyond the
entertaining narrative and sensational vignettes. For
one thing, its style is rigorously direct without being
mechanical. For another, the central character is
enmeshed in the politics and morality of medicine in
some unconventional and unpleasant ways.

Heller, Joseph. Something Happened. New York: Knopf, 1974.
Novel.

Adolescence   Children   Death
Euthanasia   Mental Retardation Sexuality
Suicide

An over-long look into the mind of a middle-aged, upper-
middle class New York executive. Comic in passing but
ultimately horrifying. Along with Alison Lurie's The
War Between the Tates, Heller's book is an excellent
treatment of the contemporary relationship between
parent and child, and an evocation of mental suffering
in childhood. In fact the father finally kills his
child rather than face his suffering. All the children, including the retarded and rejected Derek, are
seen as reflections of the father. For his part, the
father is consumed with thoughts of death in general
and suicide in particular. Many passages in the novel
are devoted to his active but shallow extra-marital sex
life, and to the history of his sexual relationship
with his wife.

Hellman, Lillian. The Children's Hour, 1934. Available in Plays
by and About Women, eds. Victoria Sullivan and James Hatch.
New York: Vintage Books, 1974. Drama.

Children   Doctors   Homosexuality
Madness   Sexual Roles   Suicide

A monster of a child, a little girl who will do anything
to get attention, including malingering, and to hurt
those whom she imagines have transgressed against her,
tells a terrible lie about the two mistresses of her
boarding school: they are lovers, she tells her
scandalized grandmother; they have been heard by the

schoolgirls. Of course, ruin follows for Martha and
Karen, the two teachers, both in their late 20's. Karen
even loses her fiancé, a doctor who finally cannot fully
believe that the story is only a lie. He is a good
enough fellow, though, and his characterization is a
useful portrait of a good doctor--never a great one, his
Viennese professors tell him--who loves to care for the
families in his home town. At the end, the monster's
grandmother arrives to tell Karen that she knows the
truth about her granddaughter's lie, but it is too late:
Martha, realizing that she has in fact loved Karen "in
that way," has just shot herself. This play could be
seen--and has, by these editors--as an examination of
sexual roles. "Women in positions of authority have
always been particularly vulnerable to slander," they
argue. And if a woman wants a career, some people have
always thought, there must be something wrong with her.
But of course the child's "lie" is also a buried truth,
a truth, Hellman's play implies, that is not horrible
at all.

Hemingway, Ernest. "A Clean, Well-lighted Place," 1933. Available
in The Short Stories of Ernest Hemingway. New York: Charles
Scribner's Sons, 1938. Short Story.

Age   Alcoholism   Disease & Health
Suicide

Probably Hemingway's best story, this one is a confrontation with meaninglessness ("Our nada who are in nada,
nada be thy name," the old waiter prays). The pervasive
despair strikes especially at an old waiter, who is
contrasted with a young one, impatient to get home to
his wife in bed, and an 80-year-old, rather dignified
drunk, who had tried to kill himself last week. What
all such people need, the waiter insists, is a clean,
well-lighted place to ward off the nothingness which,
in some moods, he thinks is a common illness. Perhaps
it is only insomnia?

Hemingway, Ernest. "A Day's Wait," 1933. Available in The Short
Stories of Ernest Hemingway. New York: Charles Scribner's
Sons, 1938. Short Story.

Children   Death   Disease & Health

A 9-year-old boy lies sick with influenza. He hears the
doctor say that his temperature is 102°. His father,
after reading to him for a while in the morning, goes
out to spend the day hunting. When he returns, the boy
is just about the same, only this time the father
notices that he is lying very stiff. The boy asks,
"About what time do you think I'm going to die?" It
seems that in France some boys had told him that you
couldn't live with a temperature over 44°, and, not
realizing they were speaking of centigrade, the kid had
been waiting all day to die.

Hemingway, Ernest. "The Doctor and the Doctor's Wife," 1925.
Available in The Short Stories of Ernest Hemingway. New York:
Charles Scribner's Sons, 1938. Short Story.

Children   Doctors

One of those Hemingway stories that are so suggestive as
to be inconclusive, but among the things going on might
be these: a doctor's superior position is attacked first
by 3 Indians who point out that he is stealing lumber,
no matter what he may call it; second, by their greater
physical strength (they rub all this in by calling him
"Doc" until it infuriates him); third, by an unopened,
unread pile of medical journals; and fourth, by his
long-suffering, invalided wife, who is, of all slaps in
the face, a Christian Scientist. Happily, the doctor's
son seems to understand, and that helps.

Hemingway, Ernest. A Farewell to Arms. New York: Charles Scribner's
Sons, 1929. Novel.

Death   Disease & Health   Doctors
Dying   Med. Instit.   Nurses
Preg. & Childbirth Sexuality

A novel about war and its potential alternative, love
between a man and a woman. Potential, but not fully
realized here, for the novel ends in the vividly portrayed death of the heroine, Catherine Barkley, after
she has given birth to a dead child. Catherine's had
been a life of service. Her selfless devotion to her
lover, Frederic Henry, was matched by her service as
an English nurse in Italy during the first world war.
The love affair had developed when Frederic was a
patient with a seriously wounded knee. Catherine often
visited him at night in his room. At this institution,
an American hospital, the doctors are for the most part
incompetent, and some of the nurses unsympathetic, but
one of the doctors in Lt. Henry's ambulance corps,
Rinaldi, is a good man who makes his work his life.
Later he becomes irritable because he thinks he has
syphilis, but also because with so many men dying, it
seems to Rinaldi that he, who deals with men's bodies,
has less value now than the priest, who deals with
their souls. In the last sections of the novel, we
meet another ineffectual doctor, who cannot save
Catherine. Frederic too is ineffectual, of course
(this is dramatized when he is asked to administer the
anesthesia to Catherine, and responds to her agony by
giving her more than it is safe for her to have).
Ironically, he has learned that even though he ran from
the war, he cannot say farewell to conflict and death.

Hemingway, Ernest. "God Rest You Merry, Gentlemen," 1932.
    Available in The Short Stories of Ernest Hemingway. New
    York: Charles Scribner's Sons, 1938. Short Story.

   Adolescence   Doctors   Sexuality

    A perverse Christmas story in which two ambulance
    surgeons, one a clever, sarcastic Jewish abortionist,
    the other an incompetent, who has been advised to carry
    with him everywhere The Young Doctor's Friend and Guide,
    discuss the case of a religious young man, about 16 years
    old. Yesterday he had visited the hospital asking to
    be castrated to cure his impure thoughts. And the
    doctors had told him that his sexuality was a fine
    thing. Today, Christmas, the ignorant young man has
    been brought in with a self-amputated penis.

Hemingway, Ernest. "Hills Like White Elephants," 1927. Available
    in The Short Stories of Ernest Hemingway. New York: Charles
    Scribner's Sons, 1938. Short Story.

   Abortion

    Told almost entirely through indirection and dialogue,
    this story renders the pain of a decision to abort and
    the differences in attitude between the woman and her
    lover. The word "abortion" itself is never mentioned;
    nor is "baby." The closest the pair come to any direct
    language is the man's description of the procedure,
    "It's not really anything. It's just to let the air
    in."

Hemingway, Ernest. "Indian Camp," 1925. Available in The Short
    Stories of Ernest Hemingway. New York: Charles Scribner's
    Sons, 1938. Short Story.

   Adolescence   Death   Doctors
   Grief   Preg. & Childbirth Suicide
   Surgery

    A shocking story told in a telegraphic style which high-
    lights the horror of young Nick's first exposure to
    terrible pain and death. He has come to the Indian camp
    with his father, a doctor who has been called to attend
    a woman two days into labor. When they arrive, they
    find her in a lower bunk in great pain, and her husband
    with a wounded foot in the upper bunk. The doctor
    proudly performs a caesarean with a jack-knife and sews
    it up with 9-foot tapered gut leaders, exhilarated to
    explain the procedures to his "interne," Nick. But when
    the doctor turns to the father in the upper bunk, he
    discovers that the Indian, presumably unable to tolerate
    the pain--his wife's, his, the world's--has slit his
    own throat. Nick questions his father about dying: is
    it hard? Answer: "No, it's pretty easy, Nick. It all
    depends." And returning in the boat with his father
    rowing, the boy feels that he will never die. (Heming-
    way's father, incidentally, was a doctor. He died by
    suicide.)

Hemingway, Ernest. The Old Man and the Sea. New York: Charles
    Scribner's Sons, 1952. Novella.

   Age   Children   Death
   Disease & Health   Sexual Roles   Suffering

    Already a classic tale of old age, and more than that,
    of age and youth, and their need for each other. On
    one level, the book is an adventure story about an old
    fisherman, without a catch for 84 days, who goes out
    into deep waters, catches an enormous marlin, fights
    the sharks for days in trying to get back to shore, and
    finally returns with only the skeleton of the great
    fish. On the surface, he is defeated, but because he
    has faced enormous suffering, both physical (his hand
    is cut) and mental, and fought through, he has achieved
    a moral triumph. This brave, religious facing of
    death, we know from other Hemingway works, to be
    primarily a male trait. But in this book the male is
    also allowed to be a little tender, especially with
    his friend, the boy Manolin, who cares for him, and
    who probably reminds the old man of his own youth and
    the continuation of life.

Hemingway, Ernest. "One Reader Writes," 1932. Available in The
    Short Stories of Ernest Hemingway. New York: Charles
    Scribner's Sons, 1938. Short Story.

   Med. Profession   V.D.

    A 2-page "story" in which a young semi-literate wife
    writes to a doctor who does one of those medical advice
    columns because, she thinks, "He looks smart, all right.
    Every day he tells somebody what to do." Her story is
    simple, painful, and common: her husband has contracted
    "sifulus," her father says anyone so afflicted might
    well wash himself dead, and she wants to know whether
    she should ever sleep with him again.

Hemingway, Ernest. "The Snows of Kilimanjaro," 1936. Available
    in The Short Stories of Ernest Hemingway. New York: Charles
    Scribner's Sons, 1938. Short Story.

   Disease & Health   Dying   Sexuality
   Sexual Roles

    A middle-aged American writer lies dying in remote
    Africa. Two weeks earlier he had failed to put iodine
    on a scratch, and now gangrene has set in. His thoughts
    fall into 3 categories: all the things he will not now
    have the chance to write, about a certain plump whore
    in Paris, for instance; his relationship to his present
    wife who is attending him kindly, but whom he cannot
    consistently love, even now; and, inevitably, dying

itself. Harry meets his last adventure in true Hemingway fasion--he'll be damned if he's going to let the
son of a bitch grind him down. He is tired, angry, and
bored rather than frightened, he says. And he doesn't
want to leave anything behind, not even his wife's love
for him, which he cruelly attacks. Death finally comes
to him with a stinking breath, and his last thoughts
concern a fantasy rescue (though the reader doesn't know
at first that it is fantasy) in a plane which carries
him up, up to the snow-capped Mt. Kilimanjaro.

Herbert, Frank. The Eyes of Heisenberg (1965 as Do I Sleep or Wake).
    New York: Berkley, 1966. Novel.

   Death   Disease & Health   Doctors
   Preg. & Childbirth   Sci Fi

    Genetic surgery makes possible three major social changes:
    tailoring of a population to maintain an average; social
    control by artificial genetic deficiencies which must be
    filled by enzymes from government outlets; and the
    occasional creation of people able to live forever who
    rule mortal mankind, its past and its future. Dr. Sven-
    gaard is a dependable, obedient, competent genetic
    surgeon who is present when an "outside" force acts to
    make an embryo resistant to human manipulation. Although
    this force is never explicitly explained, it is described
    as a part of Nature fighting back against the artificial
    deficiencies and the predetermined genetic combinations
    to restore stable life in an uncertain world. One
    doctor acts against his social training to save the
    embryo while Dr. Svengaard sheds his political condition-
    ing as he grows into his medical role. Mankind is
    preserved because Svengaard reacts to the deterioration
    of the immortals as a doctor, with care and concern,
    rather than as an outraged citizen; and mankind has a
    future because Svengaard rejects the mechanistic solu-
    tions offered by the Cyborgs for the uncertain, growing
    life offered by embryo implants. A good Herbert (he
    wrote Dune) and a rare example of excellent medical
    sci fi.

Herrick, Robert. The Healer. New York: Macmillan, 1911. Novel.

   Doctors   Med. Instit.   Med. Profession

    Raises more questions than it deals with, but whatever
    its weaknesses, it speaks directly to many medical
    issues. The hero is a doctor. No, he is more--a healer
    with a mystic quality of bringing out in his patients
    their will to live and be healthy. He is unusual in
    other ways too. Called The Wild One, he espouses such
    ideals as free and easily accessible health care for
    everyone. (He is also a sometime drug addict, but this
    doesn't seem to affect his personal or professional
    activity; it is just a response to strain.) The healer
    saves the life of a wealthy society girl, whom he there-
    after enthralls, taking her as his bride to a stone
    cabin by The Healing Spring, where he treats the
    exploited lumber and railroad workers. But his wife's
    increasing need for more money lures him into enlarging
    his practice until the cabins he has built for the poor
    become a sanatorium for the wealthy. When at last he
    realizes that he has deceived himself, The Wild One
    leaves for the wilderness of the city, where he treats
    factory workers and eventually ends up as the director
    of an institute for nervous diseases. At the end of the
    novel, though, he is making plans to return to the woods,
    for The Wild One has not been completely tamed.

Herrick, Robert. The Web of Life. New York: Macmillan, 1900.
    Novel.

   Doctors   Euthanasia   Med. Ethics
   Med. Profession   Poverty & Health

    A young doctor fights against becoming part of the
    medical machine. He regrets, for instance, that the
    poor cannot get adequate health care. And once he is
    fired from a clinic for treating a patient without
    charge. He is troubled too by his wealthy girlfriend's
    attempt to secure patronage for him and by her parents'
    treatment of the poor. But his portrait is not wholly
    uncomplicated. In the opening scene, for instance,
    when he is faced with having to decide whether to under-
    take a risky operation which might end in the patient's
    becoming a vegetable, the young man reflects that it
    was often "a great deal wiser if the operation turned
    out fatally." Moreover, thinking about having to deal
    with certain patients, he is frankly intolerant: "The
    professional manner that he ridiculed so often was
    apparently useful in just such cases as this. It
    covered up incompetence and hypocrisy often enough, but
    one could not be human and straightforward with women
    and fools. And women and fools made up the greater
    part of a doctor's business." The hero's professional
    story--the quacks he has to compete with, the military
    hospital he works in--runs along side his personal
    story. The two are connected most clearly in his long
    affair with the wife of the man he saved in the
    operating table back in the beginning of the novel. The
    man had survived, but had become alcoholic, mentally
    ill, and a burden on his wife. His suicide note
    relieves the doctor, and the reader, of the suspicion
    that the wife had thought it necessary to kill him.
    Like Herrick's The Healer, this novel raises some
    interesting issues, and then skirts them.

Hesse, Hermann. Steppenwolf, 1927. New York: Holt, Rinehart and Winston, 1963. Novel.

Age   Drugs   Homosexuality
Madness   Sexuality   Suicide
Women as Healers

An experimental novel which follows the affairs of a 50-year-old man who prowls around the outskirts of bourgeois society like a wolf of the steppes. He considers himself a suicide, that is, someone who sees death as a release and gains strength from the knowledge that suicide is always a possibility. He is also something of a schizophrenic, composed on the one hand of two selves: man and wolf, spirit and flesh, and on the other of multiple selves. All these selves come together first through a gorgeous sexual affair with Maria, procured for him by his mysterious friends Hermine (the female version of Hermann, the hero, and a pan-sexual) and Pablo, a cocained jazz musician; second, through a long trip into the "Magic Theatre," which is "for Madmen only." The selves come together, yes, but as Pablo says, they need not stay together in any conventional form, no matter what psychiatric science says. The combinations of personality are endless and fascinating, and many so-called mad people are truly geniuses. True mental health is achieved by an immortal view, a certain kind of divine laughter which transcends self-involved anguish.

Hope, A. D. "The Bed," 1955. Available in The Norton Anthology of Modern Poetry, eds. Richard Ellmann and Robert O'Clair. New York: Norton, 1973. Poem: 12 lines.

Doctors   Med. Instit.

A witty little poem about a special kind of medical eroticism: "The doctor loves the patient,/The patient loves his bed;/A fine place to be born in,/The best place to be dead./The doctor loves the patient/Because he means to die;/The patient loves the patient bed/That shares his agony./The bed adores the doctor,/His cool and skilful touch/Soon brings another patient/Who loves her just as much."

Housman, A. E. "To an Athlete Dying Young," 1896. Available in The Norton Anthology of Modern Poetry, eds. Richard Ellmann and Robert O'Clair. New York: Norton, 1973. Poem: 28 lines.

Death

The famous literary statement about the value of dying young: at least, the poet says to the young man, you died before you could outlive your glory. A very Greek poem, and very distanced.

Howard, Sidney, in collaboration with Paul de Kruif. Yellow Jack, 1934. Available in Three Plays About Doctors, ed. Joseph Mersand. New York: Washington Square Press, 1961. Drama.

Disease & Health   Doctors   Med. Ethics
Med. Profession   Nurses   Plague

A race between plague and science. The plague in this case is yellow fever, and the science is that practiced by Major Walter Reed and his successors. Beginning with scenes from the laboratories of Dr. Stackpole in 1929 and Dr. Stokes in 1927, the play soon shifts to Cuba in 1900 and the research of Dr. Reed. Here, interspersed with scenes from the lives of ordinary soldiers and an Army nurse, the play concentrates on some of the fundamental ethical questions of medical research. Should old Dr. Finlay, for instance, who for 19 years has tried vainly to convince the scientific world that yellow fever is carried by mosquitoes, now cooperate with Walter Reed and thereby lose some of the glory? How much deception of the public is justified in the interests of potentially life-saving experiments? Most important of all, given the fact that they have no known laboratory animal, should Reed and his team use humans for experimentation? And which humans--themselves, or "volunteers" from the ranks? There is a good deal of illness, stink, and ugliness portrayed in this play. One doctor admits, "I expect we were being a bit inhuman." But his colleague responds with one of the play's basic truths, "That's one of the drawbacks of experiment." Not a bad play, in fact rather moving at times, partly because the author wisely tempers the almost saintly devotion of the medical scientists with the earthy concerns and more rounded characters of the soldiers, and with clever theatrical "business." In the end, the U. S. Army has a new sort of hero, the Man of Science.

Hughes, Langston. "Sylvester's Dying Bed," 1942. Available in The Norton Anthology of Modern Poetry, eds. Richard Ellmann and Robert O'Clair. New York: Norton, 1973. Poem: 28 lines.

Dying   Sexuality

An inherently sad subject, but treated in a way that provokes both shock and amusement. Written in the usual Hughes' black dialect, this poem is the song of one "Sweet Papa 'Vester" whose deathbed is attended by "a hundred pretty mamas." Sylvester is some man all right, and as long as breath's in him, he'll handle those women: 'So I holler, 'Com'ere, babies,/Fo' to love yo' daddy right!'/And I reaches up to hug'em--/When the Lawd put out the light." It's suddenly over: "Then everything was darkness/In a great . . . big . . . night."

Hughes, Richard. A High Wind in Jamaica, 1929. New York: Time, Inc., 1963. (Also published as The Innocent Voyage.) Novel.

Children   Death   Dying
Grief   Madness   Sexuality

A classic study of children's psychology, a book which shocked adults, much as Golding's Lord of the Flies was to do later. The tale begins in early 19th century Jamaica with an earthquake and the terrifying pursuit of the children's pet cat by native wild cats. Thinking that their children have been traumatized by the incident, Mr. and Mrs. Bas-Thornton send the five young people, together with 2 friends, back to England for schooling. On the plot level, events take place which are terrible enough: the ship is attacked by pirates, the children are captured, one of the boys falls 40 feet to his death, Emily murders a bound man. But the psychological events are more terrible still: the children grow wilder; a kind of madness spreads, perhaps because their "innocence" comes into contact with adult depravity, perhaps because they are naturally depraved themselves; John's death is so completely forgotten that the children can convince themselves that he died defending the girls; 10-year-old Emily bites the captain when he makes vaguely sexual advances to her, and the slightly older Margaret becomes his mistress. Most dreadful of all, Emily allows first Margaret, then the pirate captain, to be thought guilty of the murder. After the group is returned to England, Emily's testimony sends the captain to his death. When she last sees his face, Emily thinks of the face of her pet cat. Civilized England soothingly welcomes the innocent children back. They feel guiltless, but the reader has seen them on the seas where no customs, no myths about childhood, no rules, disguise their basic natures.

Hughes, Ted. "Crow's First Lesson." From Crow. London: Faber, 1970. Poem: 18 lines.

Sexuality

Typical of Hughes' violent images of human interaction. Here his hero, the frightening bird Crow, is being taught by God to speak the word "Love." Crow tries once, and produces a shark; twice, and produces three biting insects. The next time he tries to say "Love" Crow vomits out a man's head, "with swivelling eyes,/Jabbering protest--/And Crow retched again, before God could stop him./And woman's vulva dropped over man's neck and tightened./The two struggled together on the grass." Crow flies off guiltily while God weeps.

Huxley, Aldous. Brave New World, 1932. New York: Bantam, 1958. Novel.

Drugs   Med. Ethics   Preg. & Childbirth
Science & Poetry   Sci Fi   Sexuality
Suicide

"Pregnancy and Childbirth" is an archaic topic in this case, for the people of the year 632 After Ford are growing bottled babies in identical sets. Some women are still fertile, to be sure, but they must wear the required Malthusian Belts at all times--a wise precaution in a society where "orgy-porgy" is common, and everyone belongs to everyone else. This is a society in which science reigns, and high art is outlawed because it is created from, and tends in turn to create, individual instability and societal conflict. But as World Controller Mustapha Mond finally reveals, it is applied science, especially scientific medicine, which reigns, for pure science, like art, leads to unpredictability. Even within this carefully controlled world, all is not always well: there's sometimes anger, sometimes anxiety. But for those cases, medicine has provided the drug soma, which gives people a carefree high. Much of the novel is concerned with the story of the "Savage" from the new world, who is transported in the Brave New World with only his old-fashioned Shakespearean morality to accompany him. He ends by hanging himself.

Huxley, Aldous. The Doors of Perception. New York: Harper and Row, 1954. Long Essay.

Body/Mind   Drugs   Madness
Science & Poetry

The famous novelist recounts his experiences with mescalin, which he took under supervision in 1953. Already attracted to mysticism, Huxley took the drug in an attempt to see what mystics see (William Blake: "If the doors of perception were cleansed everything would appear to man as it is, infinite"). He doesn't quite reach his goal, but he does detail in language that is simultaneously clear and lyrical what he perceives in certain objects: chairs, for instance, and specific works of visual art (instrumental music leaves him cold; he finds Alban Berg psychologically disintegrated). He interweaves with his experiences comments on the nature of schizophrenia ("the schizophrenic is like a man permanently under the influence of mescalin"), human relationships (individuals become unimportant under mescalin), and religion (the drug experience does not necessarily lead to the Beatific Vision, but it is a helpful "gratuitous grace"). All of us, scientists and humanists alike, he says, have a verbal education, and therefore scientists never know Nature, only facts about the natural sciences, and humanists never know Humanity, their own or anyone else's. We never know

Nature or Humanity as primary experiences. Huxley ends
with the argument that since people will always need a
safe method of self-transcendence, we ought to develop
mescalin, or some other drug, for general use.

Ionesco, Eugene. Exit the King, 1962. New York: Grove Press,
1967. Drama.

Doctors   Dying

A magnificent examination of the process of dying. Every
man thinks that in some sense when he dies, everything
dies, and Ionesco has found the perfect symbol for that
feeling. The dying king--who is timeless: he could be
medieval, he could be modern--is the source of life,
like the mythical kings whose state of health affected
their whole kingdoms. King Bérenger first denies he is
going to die, but his realistic doctor insists that he
will have no breakfast tomorrow morning and generally
keeps coming in to assess not the state of the king's
body, but the state of his death. The king's wives
debate whether to help him fight death (that is the
young wife's position) or resign himself (the old
wife's). The king suffers; he begs to be shown how to
be unconcerned about life; and indeed that finally
happens. At the end of the play, before the eyes of
the audience, everything disappears: the members of the
attending court, the set, and at last the king himself.
The audience is left staring at an empty stage.

Ionesco, Eugene. The Future Is in Eggs, 1957. Available in
Rhinoceros and Other Plays, by Ionesco. New York: Grove
Press, 1960. Drama.

Children   Sexuality

A joke about fertility. Jacques and Roberta have been
married for three years, but they have spent the time
purring contentedly and producing nothing, much to
their families' displeasure. The young lovers are forced
apart, and at last Roberta, off stage, produces basket
after basket of eggs for Jacques to hatch on stage.
Bankers and pigs are produced; and federalists and
spiritualists. The family is delighted: all those
people produced, all those omelettes to be eaten. Jack
feebly protests--there must be something else to
marriage--but the families are delighted. The goals of
lovers and society are antithetical. Lovers want to be
isolated from the world, delighting in each other, but
they have to contend with the much colder desire of
society to separate the lovers who must produce fodder
for everyone else.

Ionesco, Eugene. The Hermit, trans. Richard Seaver. New York:
Viking Press, 1974. Novel.

Madness

Once again, a question of who is mad. The narrator
recognizes that he is depressed--and his mistress tells
him to go to a psychiatrist--but the reader can see the
problems for himself: the man is preoccupied with
details, addicted to alcohol, is unable to form lasting
relationships. He is certainly neurotic, teetering on
psychotic. And yet, the society from which he is
retreating is also mad. There is the utter dreariness
of his office, and the senseless fighting of the revolu-
tionaries, who do not really care whom they fight so
long as they can vent their rage. In his little cubby
hole, the narrator survives the destruction of the city,
and it becomes clearer and clearer that next to the mad
slaughter, his life is sane. But then comes the final
twist: this man who is different precisely because
he asks questions about the nature of the universe, has
visions of flowers, of singing trees, and finally of a
great ladder, leading to a meadow, which hovers over
him for seconds or for years. His reaction ends the
novel: "I took that for a sign." He is mad on his own
terms. The book raises interesting questions about the
nature of the universe against which we judge the
definition of madness.

Isherwood, Christopher. The Dog Beneath the Skin, 1935. Available
in Two Great Plays by W. H. Auden and Christopher Isherwood.
New York: Random House, n.d. Poetic Drama.

Disease & Health   Doctors   Med. Instit.
Med. Students   Nurses   Surgery
Women as Patients

See Auden, W. H. and Christopher Isherwood.

Isherwood, Christopher. A Meeting by the River. New York: Simon
& Schuster, 1967. Novel.

The Family   Homosexuality

The meeting referred to in the title is between two
brothers--Patrick and the younger Oliver (he's 34)--in
Calcutta, where Oliver has joined a Hindu monastery.
Each is painfully confused about his own values and
about his feelings toward the other. But Oliver, still
fighting his earth-bound love-hate feelings for the
seemingly self-assured Elder Brother, comes to understand himself a bit better, though at the end even the
worldly Patrick seems to Oliver to be under the Swami's
influence. Their stories are told through Oliver's
diary and a series of letters written by Patrick to his
wife Penelope, with whom Oliver had always been in love;
to his mother, a troublesome figure to both brothers,
but especially for the seemingly neglected Oliver; and

to his young lover, Tom. In these last letters, we see
Patrick at his most flirtatious, self-deceptive, and
cruel. The first letters are highly romantic and flattering, full of erotic pleasure and hope for the future of
the relationship. At one point, Patrick even says that
he sees Tom as the brother Oliver could never be, and
suggests that it is a shame that brothers are kept by
conventions from being truly intimate. By the end of
the sequence, after Tom has embarrassed him by calling
long distance, Patrick has told himself, as well as Tom
and Penelope, that there never was much between the two
male lovers. He has also advised Tom to marry a woman,
suggesting that he is prejudiced if he doesn't try. A
self-deceiving man, yes, but also, as Oliver admits, a
charming man. The last scene is an embrace at the
airport, carefully rehearsed by Patrick to be sure, but
nonetheless both moving and a part of the great cosmic
laughter.

Jarrell, Randall. "The Death of the Ball Turret Gunner," 1945.
Available in The Norton Anthology of Modern Poetry, eds.
Richard Ellmann and Robert O'Clair. New York: Norton,
1973. Poem: 5 lines.

Dying   Preg. & Childbirth

A startling poem which equates dying with a sort of
perverse childbirth. A ball turret was a plexiglass
sphere on a fighter plane, in which curled a gunner,
looking every bit like a fetus. "From my mother's
sleep I fell into the State,/And I hunched in its belly
till my wet fur froze./Six miles from earth, loosed
from its dream of life,/I woke to black flak and the
nightmare fighters./When I died they washed me out of
the turret with a hose."

Jeffers, Robinson. "Rock and Hawk," 1935. Available in The
Norton Anthology of Modern Poetry, eds. Richard Ellmann and
Robert O'Clair. New York: Norton, 1973. Poem: 22 lines.

By Doctors

Jeffers left medical school just short of a degree, but
came close enough, and is an important enough writer--
Gert Stein also qualifies in these two respects--to be
noted by anyone surveying significant doctor-writers.
This poem is representative of Jeffers' admiration for
strength which survives violence and transcends death
(sometimes, one suspects, also life). The poet depicts
an isolated gray rock on which stands a falcon, and here
he finds an appropriate emblem for our future, more so
than the cross or the hive, something beyond mere
humanity: "Fierce consciousness joined with final/
Disinterestedness;/Life with calm death; the falcon's
realist eyes and act/Married to the massive/Mysticism
of stone,/which failure cannot cast down/Nor success
make proud."

Jones, LeRoi (Imamu Amiri Baraka). Dutchman. New York: William
Morrow and Company, 1964. Drama.

Madness   Sexuality

The sexual encounter of a black man and a white woman
on a subway crescendos into hysterical violence.
Calling herself Lena the Hyena, the woman approaches
the middle-class black man, baiting him with questions
and statements about himself, provocatively inviting
him to a party, and generally teasing him sexually until
he explodes at her with screaming, obscene language.
She is the white witch who has lured black men to
destruction throughout time, and now she has him where
she wants him. With the complicity of her fellow
passengers, she murders him, and then leaves to find
her next black victim.

Joyce, James. "Ecce Puer," 1932. Available in The Portable James
Joyce. New York: Viking Press, 1947. Poem: 16 lines.

Children   Grief

Wrenching grief expressed by Joyce shortly after his
estranged father's death on the occasion of the birth
of his grandson Stephen, named after the autobiographical
character in Portrait of the Artist. "Of the dark past/
A child is born/With joy and grief/My heart is torn . . . ./
A child is sleeping:/An old man is gone./O, father
forsaken,/Forgive your son!"

Joyce, James. Portrait of the Artist as a Young Man, 1904-1914.
New York: Viking Press, 1956. Novel.

Adolescence   Children   Death
The Family   Med. Instit.   Sexuality

One of the greatest of the novels of adolescence. (Others
in this category, the "Bildungsroman," are Goethe's Wilhelm
Meister, Mann's Magic Mountain, Lawrence's Sons and Lovers,
Maugham's Of Human Bondage, and Wolfe's Look Homeward,
Angel.) Beginning with the childhood of an Irish boy
enmeshed in the usual Irish religious and political
dilemmas, the novel takes its hero, Stephen Dedalus,
through his university years, when he is ready to fly
from Catholicism, his family, and his homeland into the
cunning exile of the artist. The style changes as
Stephen grows older. Thus, in the opening pages we have
the world as perceived through the senses of a child. A
little later, in the remarkable Christmas dinner scene,
we get the family drama as the young Stephen observes it,
the world of illness as it appears to him when he is in
the school infirmary, and childish cruelty through the
eyes of a schoolboy. Among the most memorable sections

of the novel are the passages depicting Stephen's adolescent sexuality: his visit to a prostitute (end of Chapter II) and his subsequent guilt, during which he faces the death of his soul through sin and its probable torment in hell (Chapter III). After a passing decision to become a priest, he discovers his true vocation, art, but this necessitates leaving his family, for he declares that he cannot serve false idols such as the Catholicism they would force on him. We leave Stephen, a proud, isolated young man, only to pick up the story of his maturing in Joyce's next novel, Ulysses.

Joyce, James. Ulysses, 1914-1921. New York: Random House, 1961. Novel.

The Body	Death	The Family
Grief	Med. Ethics	Med. Instit.
Med. Students	Nurses	Preg. & Childbirth
Sexuality	Sexual Roles	

The most obviously relevant section of this rich novel is episode 14, "The Oxen of the Sun," which is set in a lying-in hospital. At 10 p.m. on the evening of his great journey through Dublin, the hero, Leopold Bloom, goes to the hospital to get news of his friend Mrs. Purefoy, who is having a difficult labor. There he meets a group of medical students who debate various aspects of obstetrics and related ethics—what of birth control, for instance, and the relative value of the mother's over the baby's life—make ribald and callous comments about nurses and mothers, and generally kick up their heels in an undergraduate fashion. In the tightly schematic plan outlined by Stuart Gilbert and approved by Joyce (James Joyce's Ulysses. New York: Vintage, 1955), the symbolic organ around which this episode is written is the womb (in other episodes Joyce makes use of the heart, the lungs, the genitals, and so forth), and the organizing art is medicine. It follows that Joyce uses images and metaphors from female anatomy, obstetrics, and embryology. In addition, the chapter is written as a parody history of the English language as it has been used by well-known writers; in short, the chapter follows the embryological development of style. The novel as a whole produces insights into the family and sexuality. The first subject is dealt with in a complex manner in which gradually Bloom comes to be father, Stephen Dedalus, son, and Molly Bloom, some sort of mother-wife-sexual object for both Bloom and Stephen. On a more accessible level, there is a study of the weakening of the Bloom family after the death of the only son, Rudy, years before. (Participating in the funeral of a friend—episode 6, "Hades"—helps Bloom to bring his grief to the fore.) Since then, Bloom and his wife have not had sex, Molly having amused herself from time to time lately with a stud called Blazes Boylan. The issue of sexuality runs throughout the entire novel, of course, but is most blatant in episode 13, "Nausicaa," in which Bloom masturbates; episode 15, "Circe," in which Bloom and Stephen visit a whorehouse, and Bloom in a fantasy becomes a woman, even giving birth to several children; and the last episode, 18, called "Penelope," in which Molly meditates for 45 pages on many subjects, all run together in the stream-on-consciousness fashion, and covering women's sexuality very frankly, but coming eventually to an end with a huge, female "Yes." James Joyce was for a short time a student of medicine.

Kafka, Franz. "A Country Doctor," 1919. Available in The Penal Colony, by Kafka. New York: Schocken Books, 1961. Short Story.

Age	Disease & Health	Doctors

Threatening, symbolic story which on the literal level is the tale of an old district doctor roused from his bed one night and summoned to the aid of a boy whom he finds suffering from a worm-ridden wound in his side. The neighbors and the family strip the doctor of his clothes and lay him down next to the patient, chanting "Strip his clothes off, then he'll heal us,/If he doesn't, kill him dead./Only a doctor, only a doctor" (trans. Willa and Edwin Muir). The doctor leaves, but is unable to reach his home; his practice is finished, for "A false alarm on the night bell once answered—it cannot be made good, not ever." Several interpretations possible, but the most valuable seems to be a religious one which would make the doctor a savior and simultaneously a victim: "Always expecting the impossible from the doctor. They have lost their ancient beliefs; the parson sits at home and unravels his vestments, one after another; but the doctor is supposed to be omnipotent with his merciful surgeon's hand."

Kafka, Franz. The Metamorphosis, 1915. Available in The Penal Colony, by Kafka. New York: Schocken Books, 1961. Novella.

The Body	Disease & Health	Dying
The Family	Suffering	

This famous story of a young man who wakes up one morning and discovers that he has become a giant insect could be interpreted in a number of ways, including this valid and revealing medical way: in the first place, Gregor's alienation from his own body can easily be seen in the fact of his metamorphosis. But what is really interesting is the way his family, whom he supports financially, react to his "illness" and subsequent suffering. All of them, even the sister who is at first kind to him, cut

him off, feeling that he has done something to them by changing in this grotesque fashion. His parents cannot bear to look at him, and as he approaches death, they pull farther and farther away, finally allowing the charwoman to dump the remains in a garbage can. Not at all unlike certain reactions to serious, disfiguring illness and death among both relatives and health care staff.

Kesey, Ken. One Flew Over the Cuckoo's Nest. New York: Viking Press, 1964. Novel. Also available as a play, adapted by Dale Wasserman. New York: Samuel French, 1970.

Doctors	Euthanasia	Handicaps
Homosexuality	Madness	Med. Instit.
Med. Instit.	Nurses	Sexuality
Suicide		

The madhouse as microcosm. The institution, as viewed from the perspective of the paranoid Chief Bromden, houses three types: the Acutes, who are the potentially curable patients; the Chronics, who are just being kept off the streets to keep things tidy; and representatives of the Combine, which to Bromden is the huge conformist machine that runs the hospital and keeps everyone in their place. He imagines, and he isn't that crazy, that the Combine is run by Nurse Ratched—"Big Nurse," she's called—from a control panel, and that she is abetted by her staff, especially the three sadist orderlies, one of whom is a dwarf. Even the psychiatrist, Dr. Spivey, is an ineffectual, if well-meaning, pawn. Among the patients are a couple of people with pronounced sexual problems: Dale Harding is a married, non-active homosexual; Billy Bibbet, a stuttering 30-year-old virgin, whose successful "treatment" is arranged by his fellow patients, is driven to suicide by Big Nurse. The hero of this cuckoo's nest is McMurphy, a sexual athlete and generally vital, joyful person, who has talked himself from prison farm into the hospital, thinking it would be an easy life. McMurphy takes on his fellow inmates' salvation—in the symbolic sense, finally, when his attack on Big Nurse leads to his being given a lobotomy (formally he had had had shock therapy) and his status as a kind of sacrificial victim, like Christ. But a vegetable savior won't do, and Bromden frees McMurphy by smothering him before escaping from the cuckoo's nest.

Keyes, Daniel. Flowers for Algernon, 1960. From The Hugo Winners, ed. Isaac Asimov. Vol. 1. Garden City, New York: Doubleday, 1962. Novella.

Doctors	Med. Ethics	Mental Retardation
Sci Fi	Sexuality	Surgery

One of the few real science fiction tragedies. Charles Gordon, I.Q. 68, is chosen as a subject for an experiment involving tripling intelligence by surgery. The experiment is a partial success; Charlie becomes a genius—for a short time. The novella is a copy of his diary recording his puzzled rise to scientific genius and his frightened fall back into idiocy. He finds that genius is lonelier than idiocy; the mentally retarded person can feel a fellowship with people laughing at him while a genius evokes only fear. Charlie's one "friend" is his fellow experimental animal, the surgically intelligent mouse Algernon, whose decreased intelligence forewarns Charlie of his own downfall. We follow Charlie through his increased perceptions into the doctors and their motives, through his discovery that his changing intelligence changes his love for Miss Kinnian, his teacher, through his terrified descent into his former self. To the end, Charlie maintains the experiment was worthwhile; we, the readers, are left to question its value.

Kingsley, Sidney. Men in White, 1933. Available in Three Plays About Doctors, ed. Joseph Mersand. New York: Washington Square Press, 1961. Drama.

Abortion	Disease & Health	Doctors
Med. Ethics	Med. Instit.	Med. Profession
Nurses	Poverty & Health	Sexuality
Surgery		

An enormously successful play for the socially minded Group Theatre in the thirties, Men in White almost seems the prototype of today's medical melodramas on television. The emphasis is on realistic and sensationalistic action in a hospital, but within that context several "significant" ideas are introduced: society's responsibility for good health care and botched abortions; the morality of certain expediential decisions taken by a private hospital's governing board, the sexual relations between interns and nurses; rich doctors who specialize in bedside manners rather than competence; professional accountability; and the relationship between poverty and tuberculosis. In addition to t.b., there are glimpses of other illnesses, including diabetes and heart disease. But the central dilemma in this play is the one about the doctor who has to choose between his profession and his love life. The play was written in the thirties; people were looking for heroes; it follows that the doctor in this case chooses a life of medical sanctity.

Kornbluth, C. M. and Frederik Pohl. The Space Merchants, 1953 (appeared in a condensed version as Gravy Planet). New York: Ballantine Books, 1974. Novel.

Drugs	Poverty & Health	Sci Fi

See Frederik Pohl.

Kornbluth, Cyril M. "The Little Black Bag." Available in Great
Science Fiction About Doctors, eds. Groff Conklin and N. D.
Fabricant, M.D. New York: Collier Books, 1963. Short Story.

Doctors   Med. Profession   Sci Fi

At first a noble story--a shady, disbarred doctor is
reclaimed to humanitarianism by the discovery of a
medical bag from the future which enables him to cure.
However, eventually the story reduces the noble medical
profession to imbecilic technicians following the
instructions of equipment designed by their intellectual
superiors. The story begins with an alcoholic doctor
who has been disbarred for charging extravagantly for the
removal of imaginary diseases. In his stupor, he finds
the bag from the future that enables him to cure truly
and to regain his self-respect. He teams up with the
patient's sister (to avoid blackmail for practicing
without a license), and they set up a clinic: he to
give humanity the benefit of the cures, she to earn
money. He finally decides the instruments are too
valuable to be used only for profit and plans to give
them to a university for study. She wants to use the
instruments for profitable cosmetic surgery. She kills
him with an instrument from the bag. A guardian in the
future becomes aware that the instruments have been used
for homocide and turns them off just as she is demonstrating how the knife from the future can go through
the throat without harm.

Lardner, Ring. "Haircut." Available in Round Up: The Stories of
Ring W. Lardner. New York: The Literary Guild, 1929. Short
Story.

Doctors   Med. Ethics   Mental Retardation
Suffering

A marvelous example of the naive narrator. The Main
Street barber tells the story of a malicious practical
joker, but the barber is unaware, in his admiration for
the man, that he has caused great suffering. The story
he tells is this: rejected by a local spinster, who
prefers the town doctor, the practical joker calls her,
imitating the doctor's voice. She goes to the doctor's
house, thereby making a fool of herself, much to the
whole town's delight. When the town idiot, who adores
the spinster, hears the doctor say that the fellow who
did that to the woman should be shot, the poor man takes
him literally. The doctor, acting as coroner, covers
up the murder. The story illustrates first, the townspeople's callousness to suffering so long as it is
portrayed as a joke; second, the doctor's great power;
and third, the problem of a doctor's attractiveness to
women, simply because of his profession.

Larkin, Philip. "Faith Healing," 1964. Available in The Norton
Anthology of Modern Poetry, eds. Richard Ellmann and Robert
O'Clair. New York: Norton, 1973. Poem: 30 lines.

Disease & Health

A subject at the periphery of medicine, but handled here
in a way which bears relation to any relationship between
a healer and a sick person. The poet observes a session
of faith healing. The preacher's deep voice demands of
every seeker, "Now, dear child,/What's wrong." The poet
then describes the effect on the sick and lonely of
kindness from the healer: "some stay stiff, twitching
and loud/With deep hoarse tears, as if a kind dumb/and
idiot child within them still survives/To re-awake at
kindness." But now the pain is truly great, for a sleeping vulnerability has been awakened, a sense of "all
they might have done had they been loved." And, concludes
Larkin: "That nothing cures."

Lawrence, D. H. "Beautiful Old Age." Available in Selected Poems,
by Lawrence. New York: Viking Press, 1959. Poem: 17 lines.

Age

If one lives right--"unsoured with accepted lies," e.g.--
it follows in the Lawrencian dogma that one's body will
reflect this fact; thus, it is not surprising that if
one reaches old age "undaunted," one ought, in Lawrence's
eyes, to be somehow "beautiful," both physically and
spiritually: there is no division. There is no division
either in these images of beautiful old age: "the
wrinkled smile of completeness"; "they would ripen like
apples, and be scented like pippins/in their old age";
"Fragrant like yellowing leaves, and dim with the soft/
stillness and satisfaction of autumn."

Lawrence, D. H. "The Blind Man," 1922. Available in The Portable
D. H. Lawrence, ed. Diana Trilling. New York: Viking, 1947.
Short Story.

The Body   Handicaps   Preg. & Childbirth
Sexuality

Quintessential Lawrence: two men and a woman intricately
related to each other. Blinded during the war, Maurice
has perforce been driven farther into a reliance on his
other senses, which has brought him into profound contact
with the darkly mysterious side of his nature. In turn,
he and his wife Isabel, now pregnant, have been drawn
closer together, for they now have more than the superficial companionship of two similarly inclined people.
But even as Isabel is content in her changing body, she
fears that the baby, plus Maurice's dark depressions
(all is not easy when one lives at his level), will tear
them up. Also she begins to yearn for some more intellectual companionship, to supplement what Maurice gives

her, and so invites her own friend Bertie, a clever but
brittle barrister (cf. Clifford Chatterley) to visit
them on their farm. The two men are at first awkward
with each other, but on Maurice's home ground--the
completely darkened barn--he, at least, feels more open
to Bertie, and suggests that they touch each other,
that Bertie touch his, Maurice's face, his blinded eyes,
his scar. Maurice is ecstatic over this experience
(cf. the naked wrestling of Birkin and Gerald--"Gladi-
atorial"--in Women in Love), but Bertie is horrified,
"like a mollusc whose shell is broken." No synthesis
possible this time for Isabel; no blood-brotherhood
for Maurice; but Bertie is clearly to be scorned and
pitied most of all.

Lawrence, D. H. The Fox, 1921. Available in Four Short Novels of
D. H. Lawrence. New York: Viking Press, 1965. Novella.

The Body   Homosexuality   Sexuality
Sexual Roles

Lawrence's interest in homosexuality has stirred up a
good deal of controversy, but this much seems certain:
he was more offended by physical closeness between
women, as in The Fox or Ursula's schoolgirl affair in
The Rainbow, than similar contact between men, seeming
to many to find the latter, whether he admitted it to
himself or not, positively desirable (see the note on
"The Blind Man"). At any rate, coitus is what is
supreme, and that is being prevented in the alliance
of the two women here, Banford and March. These two
women, whose psychic states can be guessed at from the
poses and turns of their bodies, and from March's
marvelously Freudian dreams, live an isolated life,
threatened only by a demon of a fox--until a young man
comes into it. He is about 20, they about 30, but
from the beginning, he seems to have a power to dominate
March equalled heretofore only by the fox. Henry's
eyes are keen, like the fox's, and his passion for
March is almost impersonal, so intense is it. She is
frightened by the risk of losing control of her secure
farm life with Banford, where she, March, has performed
all the tasks of the man. But Henry and his phallic
strength prevail eventually; his will overpowers hers--
for her own good, he insists--but first, cruelly,
Banford must be killed by the phallically shaped tree,
abetted by Henry himself. When last seen, though, the
male-female fight still continues, March wanting "to
be alone: with him at her side"; Henry feeling that he
would never have his own life "till she yielded and
slept in him."

Lawrence, D. H. "Healing" and "Sick." Available in Selected
Poems, by Lawrence. New York: Viking Press, 1959. Poems:
8 and 9 lines.

Body/Mind   Disease & Health

Both these poems seem to use the metaphor of illness
for spiritual malaise. In "Healing" Lawrence writes in
typical fashion: "I am not a mechanism, an assembly
of various sections./And it is not because the mechanism
is working wrongly, that I am ill./I am ill because of
wounds to the soul, to the deep emotional self." And
in "Sick" he suggests that he is ill because dead,
energy-sapping people have pecked away at him, taking
what they needed and leaving him sick. But one suspects
that there is a theory of disease taking place here,
that Lawrence may believe that physical illness inevitably
arrives when one's soul has somehow lost its integrity.

Lawrence, D. H. "The Horse Dealer's Daughter," 1922. Available
in The Complete Short Stories, by Lawrence, Vol. II. New
York: Viking, 1961.

Death   Doctors
Med. Ethics   Disease & Health   Suicide
                   Sexuality

The daughter of the horse dealer is an animalistic
creature in the best--that is to say, the Lawrencian--
senses. But at the beginning of the story, she is
headed for death (literal in the story, but also
passionately symbolic, as are most of the incidents
here). Trying to return to her dead mother, she walks
unthinkingly into a pond, submerges herself, and is
rescued by a young doctor's assistant, Dr. Fergusson.
After he cares for her, undresses and warms her, she
awakens to an awareness of the passion in her life
and begins to address the doctor, both verbally and
physically. Here begins a conflict between the
professional and the man, and not so much "the man"
either as the male: "He had never wanted to love her.
When he rescued her and restored her, he was a doctor,
and she was a patient . . . . this introduction of
the personal element was very distasteful to him, a
violation of his professional honour." But fortunately
for him, he is unable to withstand the power of love,
painful though it is ("That he should be ripped open in
this way! Him, a doctor!"), and is thereby saved from
his "sickness" (early in the story we have been shown
that he has a bad cold), as the girl is from "death."

Lawrence, D. H. Lady Chatterley's Lover, 1928. New York: Bantam
Books, 1968. Novel.

The Body   Handicaps   Nurses
Preg. & Childbirth Sexuality

Lawrence's final plea for honest and healthy sex between
one man and one woman. The book is also a critique of
industrialized society, but of course the two themes

are interrelated, for individuals have become mechanized too. What is needed is tenderness, spontaneity, an unashamed acceptance of one's body, and a willingness to submerge oneself in the whole reaches of the sexual feeling. Connie, Lady Chatterley, is at first cut off from this life. She knows only pseudo-intellectuals, like her impotent husband Clifford, paralyzed in body and Body, or pseudo-outsiders, like her lover Michaelis, who horrifies her with his screaming attack on her for her slower orgasms. Later, Mellors too will attack women for using their sexual organs improperly and against men (Mellors, one would guess, denies the clitoral orgasm), but it is he, the part-gentleman, part-working-class gamekeeper who is the Lawrencian hero. And in the famous four-letter scenes, banned for years after they were written, Lawrence dramatizes--though "lyricizes" may be a better word--their sexual contact. Through sex, their whole bodies, their whole selves, re-emerge from the death they had each been living. As Connie pulls away from Clifford, he turns to Nurse Bolton, whose success with him is predicated upon a rather appalling mothering. Clifford had wanted Connie to have an heir by a suitable man, but Mellors will most decidedly not do, so the marriage ends, as the novel does, with Connie's pregnancy. During this period Mellors and Connie must be separated, for legal reasons, but their chastity is sanctified as "the peace that comes of fucking."

Lawrence, D. H. Psychoanalysis and the Unconscious, 1921, and Fantasia of the Unconscious, 1922. New York: Viking Press, 1960. Long Essays.

The Body   Body/Mind   Children
Madness   Med. Profession   Science & Poetry
Sexuality   Sexual Roles

Two works of central importance to understanding Lawrence, and to literature and medicine in general. Though he claimed he was writing "a good sound science book," and some of what he wrote was in fact based on what was then known of the nervous system, Lawrence's two little books are better seen as a unique combination of bizarre science and impassioned vision which is so fascinating that the question of whether he is right or not either ceases to be relevant or is settled in his favor. The first work starts out as an attack on Freud as the great rationalist enemy of much that is beautiful in man's unconscious. The attack goes broader: "It is true that doctors are the priests, nay worse, the medicine-men of our decadent society . . . . Psychoanalysis is out, under a therapeutic disguise, to do away with the moral faculty in man." But Freud is soon displaced, and Lawrence's work proceeds to lay out the bases of his own vision of a tremendously liberating synthesis of the psychic and the sensual, as it evolves from, and is summarized by, the body. The following is a necessarily distorted list of some of the major points made in Fantasia, the more important of the two books: "What Freud says is always partly true," for instance, the sexual motive is there all right, but it is second and sometimes downright antagonistic to the first, which is "the essentially religious or creative motive," "the pure disinterested craving of the human male [sic] to make something wonderful out of his own head." The embryological history of the human, which Lawrence follows through several chapters, has the original cell dividing into an upper or psychic plane and a lower or sensual plane. The upper is composed of the cardiac plexus ("you are you") and the thoracic ganglion (the desire to find out); the lower is composed of the solar plexus ("I am I") and the lumbar ganglion (how I differ). Together the cardiac and the solar plexus make up the sympathetic system, and the ganglia, the voluntary. Out from this chart go Lawrence's wide-ranging conclusions. Certain human behavior is based in certain parts of the human body, one of the four great primary centers of consciousness. It is the unbalance of these centers which is to blame for our present neuroses. When we achieve a balance, we will not know, but be. The most effective consciousness is pre-mental, or non-mental, a "blood-consciousness" which our present over-rational society is destroying at its own risk. Lawrence spends a good deal of time discussing the education of children, the role of the mother and the father, and how the children should be prepared for the great mystery of sex. "The mass of mankind should never be acquainted with the scientific biological facts of sex: never. The mystery must remain in its dark secrecy, and its dark, powerful dynamism." Furthermore, men must drive modern women back into their true unconsciousness. "Combat her in her cock-sure belief that she 'knows' and that she is 'right.' Take it all out of her. Make her yield once more to the male leadership: if you've got anywhere to lead to." And what is the role of doctors in all this body-centered dogma? Are they even close to being aware of how majestic, indeed how spiritual, the body is? "Science is wretched in its treatment of the human body as a sort of complex mechanism made up of numerous little machines working automatically in a rather unsatisfactory relation to one another . . . . If anything goes wrong with the machine, why, the soul is forgotten instantly. We summon the arch-mechanic of our day, the medicine-man. And a marvellous fraud he is, doing his best. He is really wonderful as a mechanic of the human system. But the life within us fails more and more, while we marvellously tinker at the engines. Doctors are not to blame."

Lawrence, D. H. "The Ship of Death," 1929. Available in Selected Poems, by Lawrence. New York: Viking Press, 1959. Poem: 107 lines.

Body/Mind   Death   Dying
Suicide

Particularly moving since it was written a short time before the great prophet of the body took leave of the body forever. He speaks of the time of falling fruit and grim frost. All the orifices of the body are admitting cold wind that blows in on the frightened soul. "Piecemeal the body dies, and the timid soul/has her footing washed away, as the dark flood rises." After rejecting suicide as murder and therefore no way to quiet oneself, the poet repeatedly cautions his listeners, who are all dying, to build the ship of death for the voyage to oblivion, "And die the death, the long and painful death/that lies between the old self and the new." The ship of death is built of courage and faith and "a strong heart at peace." There follows a description of the death of the body and the entry of the soul into the end of everything. And yet, just as it seems to be all over, a thread of yellow and rose light appears out of eternity and "the body, like a worn sea-shell/emerges strange and lovely . . . . And the frail soul steps out, into her house again/filling the heart with peace." This is the peace, not of some godhead, but of oblivion itself.

Lawrence, D. H. Sons and Lovers, 1913. New York: Viking Press, 1958. Novel.

Adolescence   Children   Disease & Health
Doctors   Dying   Euthanasia
The Family   Grief   Sexuality

A splendid novel of adolescence, to be placed along side Joyce's Portrait of the Artist. Paul Morel too wants to be an artist, and he needs to throw off the tensions of his youth to do it, but his family is far more problematic than Stephen Dedalus'. Paul despises his father, a Nottinghamshire coal miner, partly because the boy identifies so closely with his proud, superior mother. It is this very closeness that provides the novel's chief importance to medicine, for the relationship is one of the best investigations in literature of the extended Oedipal complex. Paul is so dominated, so willingly dominated, by his mother that he cannot easily love another woman, let alone have sex with her. For her part, his mother (called Gertrude, like Hamlet's mother) fights to be first in her son's affections because her husband is so disappointing and her older son has died of pneumonia. Paul does manage two affairs, both treated at length and with the usual Lawrencian insight into such matters. The first is with Miriam, a soulful girl who sacrifices herself in sex, without any pleasure. Clara is at home with her body, but here too there is trouble, first, just because of some differences in their sexuality, and second, because Paul's true love, his mother, is dying painfully of cancer. She is attended by a local doctor and a specialist, both of whom are decent and seemingly competent chaps, though they aren't perfectly honest with the family. This is indeed terrible for him, and overwhelmed with pity for her, Paul, with the complicity of his sister, gives his mother enough morphine to kill her faster. What remains is for Paul to handle his grief and go on by himself. He accomplishes this as the novel ends. Looking up at the night sky, he realizes fully what his mother has meant to him--indeed "she was the only thing that held him up"--yet "he would not take that direction, to the darkness, to follow her. He walked towards the faintly humming, glowing town, quickly."

Lawrence, D. H. "When I Went to the Circus," 1929. Available in The Norton Anthology of Modern Poetry, eds. Richard Ellmann and Robert O'Clair. New York: Norton, 1973. Poem: 56 lines.

The Body   Children

Contrast between the playful, honest physicality of the circus people and the touchless "personalities" of the spectators. The latter are frightened of the former, but it is not merely a matter of sex taboos--though the tightrope lady is "pink and blonde and nude-looking." No, the spectators fear the animals too, and the "immediate, physical understanding" the circus people have with them. They fear to look directly on "the carnal body dauntless and flickering gay/playing among the elements neatly, beyond competition/and displaying no personality." The children, though, show by their shouts that they "valuely know how cheated they are of their birthright/in the bright wild circus flesh."

Leavis, F. R. "Two Cultures: The Significance of C. P. Snow," 1962. Available in Nor Shall My Sword. New York: Barnes & Noble, 1972. Essay.

Science & Poetry

See Snow, C. P. "The Two Cultures."

Leduc, Violette. The Taxi. New York: Farrar, Straus & Giroux, 1972. Short Story.

Adolescence   The Family   Sexuality

Included not necessarily for its artistic achievements--though many will find it lyrical, others will dismiss its elliptical style as insubstantial--but rather for its unusual treatment of a rare theme: sibling incest.

Leduc gradually reveals, through dialogue alone, that a
young brother and sister have realized their passion
for each other, and decided to spend just one day making
love. Perhaps inspired by the famous scene in Flaubert,
Leduc puts her lovers in the back of a taxi and has
them loving while the driver moves through Paris. Afterwards they resume their lives, telling each other, "The
memory of you is taking shape for a lifetime." Perhaps
mythic. Probably courageous. Certainly French.

Leduc, Violette. Thérèse and Isabelle. New York: Farrar, Straus
& Giroux, 1967. Novella; and La Bâtarde. London: Panther
Books, 1967. Autobiography.

Adolescence   The Body   Homosexuality
Sexuality

Leduc's evocation of lesbian love makes Kate Millett's
(Flying. New York: Alfred A. Knopf, 1974) seem almost
clinical. But to some extent the two autobiographies
can be usefully compared. Both women seem to be bisexual,
both are orgasm-centered, both are on major identity
searches. But whereas Millett leans towards politics,
Leduc leans towards the enthronement of art and love.
Thérèse and Isabelle is a fictionalized version of the
schoolgirl affair recounted again in Leduc's autobiography. It is intense and idyllic and authentic. In
addition to the almost unbearable passion of adolescent
sexuality, Leduc gives us something of the psychology of
her kind of lesbianism: she was born a bastard, and
grew very dependent on her mother; she considers herself
physically ugly; the beautiful Isabelle helps her to
accept herself; she finds in Isabelle a child as well
as a mother; she seeks annihilation rather than contem-
plate an end to the relationship. Later in the autobiography, Leduc recounts other loves, including other
women and men, both heterosexual and homosexual, but
none is so lyrical as the first.

LeGuin, Ursula. the Left Hand of Darkness. New York: Ace Books,
1969. Novel.

Sci Fi   Sexuality   Sexual Roles

Mythic journey of death and rebirth as a man comes to
accept and understand himself and so grow to acceptance
of the androgynous society on the planet Winter, whose
inhabitants can be either male or female. With no
permanent sexual bias, there can be no sexual roles
(this is discussed most directly in Chapters 7, 16, and
18, although it is not advisable to read them out of
context). At the book's climax, the human male is able
to reach out in close friendship to a man who is also
a woman. A rich, fascinating story.

Lehmann, Rosamund. Dusty Answer. New York: Holt, 1927. Novel.

Homosexuality

This novel caused quite a stir originally, because of its
lesbian undertones. For several years after it was
published, Dusty Answer and Radclyffe Hall's book were
mentioned together, but in fact the earlier novel is
much more romantic, less frankly physical, and not
exclusively homosexual. A fine but minor novel which
explores a young woman's awakening to love, and her
gradual movement from dependence on others for her
happiness to dependence on herself. Several people are
important to Judith as love objects, including the aloof
but flirtatious Roddy, who is himself involved in a homosexual relationship, and the beautiful Jennifer, whom
Judith meets at Cambridge. Valuable just because it is
not so frankly physical (in fact Jennifer sleeps with
another woman, but not with Judith). It is an exploration of several aspects of sexuality, chiefly the
romantically passionate. Good comparison with contemporary treatments of sexuality which center on the
orgasm.

Leinster, Murray. "Ribbon in the Sky." Available in Great Science
Fiction About Doctors, eds. Groff Conklin and N. D. Fabricant,
M.D. New York: Collier Books, 1963. Short Story.

Med. Ethics   Med. Profession   Plague
Sci Fi

A mixture of the banal and the interesting. A Med.
Service ship goes astray and lands on an out-of-the-way
planet on which three colonies have become paranoically
separate in fear of each other's diseases. The medic
is compelled to cure this "Carusoe" syndrome because
"We medics . . . made it necessary for men to invent
interplanetary travel because we kept people from
dying . . . . Then we made interstellar travel necessary
because we continued to keep people from dying . . . .
We're responsible for nine-tenths of civilization as it
exists today, because we produced the conditions that
make civilization necessary." The medic assumes that
all diseases have died out because isolated communities
are very healthy and forces the colonies together,
successfully. There are several minor sub-plots.

Leman, Graham. "Conversational Mode," 1972. Available in Infinite
Jests: The Lighter Side of Science Fiction, ed. Robert Silverberg. Radnor, Penna.: Chilton Book Co., 1974. Short Story.

Madness   Med. Profession   Poverty & Health
Sci Fi

Very funny, very grim--and one of the best unpleasant
prophecies about mechanized health care. The story is
a dialogue between "patient" summarily hospitalized as

a psychiatric disability with all rights revoked and a
psychotherapeutic program, his only "doctor." (He had
wanted to investigate whether psychiatrists' diagnoses
were determined by genetics or environments.) All signs
of humor or creativity are evidence of a bad prognosis.
The computer tries to bring him to a norm, for that is
sanity. Despite warnings that deviations in his talk
are investigated as signs of criminal insanity, the
"patient" rejects the norm. The program offers him a
hot malted milk at the end of the session and ends:
"MACHINE TIME $123 DOLLARS ROUND PLUS MALTED MILK DRINK
$1 DOLLAR ROUND PLUS GENERIC HYPNOTIC OVERDOSE $3 DOLLARS
ROUND TOTAL $127 ROUND BILL MEDICARE 427/6/3274521 @
CLOSE FILE TOPSEC PERMANENT HOLD/DUPLICATE CRIME@@."

Lessing, Doris. A Proper Marriage. New York: Simon and Schuster,
1964. Novel.

Abortion   Adolescence   The Body
Doctors   The Family   Med. Ethics
Med. Instit.   Nurses   Preg. & Childbirth
Sexuality   Sexual Roles

Properly speaking, the first novel in Lessing's five-novel
series Children of Violence, is the one about adolescence,
but in this one, the second, Lessing's heroine, Martha
Quest, grows from an early marriage at 18 into adulthood
and motherhood. And in any case, her superficial young
husband Dougie, whatever his chronological age, certainly
prolongs his adolescence in the face of rumors of an
approaching world war. Lessing investigates the early
months of the marriage, during which time Dougie and
Martha seem to live chiefly in bed and at shallow,
bourgeois parties, neither of which is ever enough for
the intellectual, searching Martha. At any rate, during
this stage she lives in great consciousness of her body,
that body on which she thinks, bitterly, that her marriage
depends. The novel, though harsh and didactic at times,
makes a great contribution in the areas of Abortion,
Pregnancy and Childbirth and Sexual Roles, especially
as they relate to Medical Ethics. In the first place,
Martha only has her child because Dr. Stern, the
condescending, probably woman-hating physician whom
Martha consults about birth control early in her marriage,
does not tell her that she is already pregnant because
he thinks having a baby will calm down this young woman
who has too much of a mind for her own good. Afterwards
Martha goes through an absurd attempt to abort herself
by the gin-and-hot-bath-and-jumping-from-tables method.
It doesn't work, of course, and there follows one of the
lengthiest and best literary investigations of pregnancy, childbirth, and post-partum depression, for
Martha and for her friend Alice Burrell, Dr. Stern's
nurse, as it happens. Finding that her marriage is
ridiculously shallow, that she cannot leave it without
losing her child, and that in any case she is not a
particularly good mother because she is not a particularly good adult, Martha makes the painful decision--like
Norah in Ibsen's Dollhouse before her--to leave both
husband and child. In doing so, she also begins to come
to terms with her own mother, an impossibly conventional
and unsupportive woman. (For Sexual Roles, almost every
Lessing work is valuable, particularly the famous The
Golden Notebook. New York: Simon & Schuster, 1962.)

Lessing, Doris. The Summer Before the Dark. New York: Alfred A.
Knopf, 1973. Novel.

Age   Disease & Health   The Family
Madness   Sexuality   Sexual Roles

Lessing's most graceful novel, for here she deals with
a woman's growing-into-herself with real novelistic
skill. Not that the experience for Kate Brown is itself
graceful. Rather, it is at first intimidating, then
exhilarating, then terrifying. During one extraordinary
summer, Kate, a 45-year-old pretty housewife, mother of
four, grows old. The process that for most people takes
a couple of decades is telescoped for her during the
summer her husband--a superficially philandering neuro-
surgeon--works in America and her children have plans
of their own. She first takes a job as an interpreter,
where she learns that she is bright and valuable, and
not just Poor Old Mother Let's Buy Her a Cat to Help Her
Through Her Menopause. Afterwards she travels through
Spain with a younger man--her first extramarital affair--
but he falls deliriously ill (a sickness of the will,
she thinks it), and that is the beginning of her own
descent into hell. Her symptoms are physical: she is
violently ill for weeks, stuck by herself in a London
hotel; she loses weight; she stops dying her hair. And
mental: once, at a performance of a play, she begins
to talk aloud about the farce she now sees everywhere.
She ascends slowly--there is a final section in which
she comes to understand her motherhood and marriage more
clearly--but she is decidedly different. She is old;
her hair is grey and undressed. But she has tested her
freedom and now at least knows the nature of her prison.
(For more Lessing on Madness, see the lengthy and
visionary The Four-Gated City. New York: Alfred A.
Knopf, 1969.)

Levertov, Denise. "Grief" and "Divorcing." From The Freeing of
the Dust. New York: New Directions, 1975. Poems: 20 and
13 lines.

The Body   Grief

The poet grieves. She has lost--many things, including,
in the first poem, the power to help a loved one in pain.
The pain, both hers and his, is emotional, but for the

poet it has physical manifestations--his voice, breaking, his jagged edges that can hurt her--and hopefully
a physical cure: "Marrow,/or sap rising in the fibers/
that hold, must do it." Her psychological helplessness
too comes to her in a physical image. She is "like/a
bug overturned,/feet waving/wild and feeble." In the
second poem, the cause of the grief is named directly,
and again grief is felt in the body: "We were Siamese
twins./Our blood's not sure/if it can circulate,/now
we are cut apart./Something in each of us is waiting/
to see if we can survive,/severed."

Lewis, Sinclair. _Arrowsmith_, 1925. New York: New American
Library, 1961. Novel.

Death   Disease & Health   Doctors
Drugs   Med. Ethics   Med. Instit.
Med. Profession   Med. Students   Nurses
Plague   Preg. & Childbirth Science & Poetry

In the minds of many people, _Arrowsmith_ is _the_ medical
novel. Not as great as some of the others, the book is
nonetheless filled with realistic details about the
profession in several aspects. (Lewis' father was a
doctor, and he did extensive research into the profession
on his own.) The searching hero, Martin Arrowsmith, goes
from medical school, rural practice, and public health
work, to urban group practice, foundation research, and
plague fighting in the tropics. In his private life, he
is married to a nurse, a direct good-natured sort, who
doesn't take well to the discipline of the hospital, and
resigns after her marriage. She later gives birth to a
still-born child, and eventually dies in the tropics,
where Martin has gone to do controlled studies on his
new serum. Though the book offers insights into all
kinds of practice, all kinds of doctors, it is ultimately
medical research and its attendant ethics which is Lewis'
chief interest. He introduces the subject through the
person of Dr. Max Gottlieb, who, in spite of his ignoring
of the human implications of his research and a few other
failings, is one of the only decent physicians in the
novel. Dr. Gottlieb at least strives to keep scientific
research out of the hands of corrupt exploiters who want
to publish results too early. He compares the scientist
to the mystic or poet, someone different from normal men
who would never understand the scientist's intense need
for the inexorable truth. After Martin breaks the scientific faith in the tropics--he gives up on the experiment
and treats everyone he can--he leaves the world of
commercially funded research to launch his own lab in the
Vermont woods. (Lewis had earlier drawn a portrait of a
doctor in _Main Street_, 1920. There the idealistic heroine
finds herself married to a man she had thought a noble
country doctor, but who turns out to be just another
mechanic.)

Lowell, Robert. "Ezra Pound" and "Robert Frost." From _Notebook_,
rev. ed. New York: Farrar, Straus and Giroux, 1970. Poems:
14 lines.

Age   Disease & Health   Madness

Lowell, Pound, and Frost: three poets who know a good
deal about madness. Lowell hospitalized, Pound famously
incarcerated for making mad broadcasts during the war;
Frost's son a suicide, his daughter sexually maladjusted.
In the first poem Lowell gives a glimpse of Pound in the
hospital, then years later, Pound mourning Eliot, and
his own illness and age: "'To begin with a swelled head
and end with swelled feet.'" The second poem opens with
a joking allusion to Coleridge: "Robert Frost at midnight." At that time of night Frost and Lowell draw
close for a conversation, Lowell saying, "'Sometimes I
am too full of myself,'" and Frost, misunderstanding him,
thinking that he is referring to his mental illness,
responds with stories of his son and daughter. But no,
Lowell says, he meant "'Sometimes I'm so happy I can't
stand myself.'" Sadly, Frost says "'When I am too full
of joy, I think/how little good my health did anyone near
me.'"

Lowell, Robert. "The Hospital." From _Notebook_, rev. ed. New York:
Farrar, Straus and Giroux, 1970. Poem: 14 lines.

The Body   Death   Med. Instit.

Another of Lowell's unrhymed sonnets--form, but not
traditional form--this one on the theme of what is, and
what is not, life. He uses the familiar hospital image
of the corpse that looks almost alive; and, in perverse
contrast, the living bodies that look dead, and seem to
be treated as if they are: "The sick are strapped to
their cots, thrust out in hallways, browner, dirtier,
flatter than the dead leaves,/they are whatever crinkles,
plugged to tubes,/and plugged to jugs of dim blue
doctored water,/held feet above them to lift the eye to
heaven . . . ."

Lowell, Robert. "Not Cleared of Killing," _The New York Review of
Books_ (29 May 1975), p. 3. Poem: 62 lines.

Abortion   Death   Doctors Doctors
Dying

A complex poem in which the poet uses the occasion of
the conviction of a distinguished Boston physician for
abortion to speculate about the nature of the fetus'
sensations--its "life," if you will--and compare it to
our lives. The poem is therefore not directly about
abortion as an ethical issue. From some images of the
fetus ("translucence looming/to attention in bilious
x-ray"), the poet moves on to make some statements about

its religious state ("too young to be gladdened/by our
New England hope of heaven/alone made palatable/by a
certainty of hell"). He then contrasts that state with
our own deathbed conditions: "overacting our last day/
writhing like a worm/in the violet ray of science--/our
fierce scared eyes, our call to wife or sister." But
when we reach our judgment day, will we discover that we,
as opposed to the fetus, have had life? Lowell seems to
suggest not: "How much we carry away with us/before
dying,/learning like the unborn/we had nothing to take."
The poet leaves us with a third alternative image: a
teasing girl arrested on a billboard--"unkillable,
uncatchable/disused."

Lowell, Robert. "Skunk Hour," 1959. From _Life Studies_. New York:
Noonday Press, 1967. Poem: 48 lines.

Madness

The central poem about Lowell's mental suffering. He
begins with some lines of description about the inhabitants of a declining Maine seaport: a recluse heiress
in her dotage, who oversees the tumbledown buildings
facing her island; the "fairy decorator" who would rather
marry. "The season's ill--" he concludes. Then "One
dark night" he drives his car up the hill to the lovers'
spot, "the hill's skull," he calls it ominously, near
the graveyard. And then the understatement: "My mind's
not right." He's alone and satanically self-destructive:
"I hear/my ill-spirit sob in each blood cell,/as if my
hand were at its throat . . . ./I myself am hell." He's
alone except for a family of skunks. The mother skunk is
tough and secure: she walks right up the main street;
she "will not scare." She is obviously some sort of
hopeful contrast to the poet's state of mind, but since
she is, after all, a skunk--rather odd looking and a
garbage monger--one leaves the poem with the conviction
that the season is still ill.

Luce, Clare Booth. _The Women_, 1936. Available in _Plays by and
About Women_. New York: Vintage Books, 1974. Drama.

Nurses   Preg. & Childbirth
Sexual Roles   Poverty & Health

Over forty characters: all of them women, many of them
bitchy women. Booth (for that was the name under which
this play first appeared) delights in showing the worst,
the cattiest, the most dependent sides of several wealthy
New York wives. They have only one interest: getting
and keeping their men. There is a controversy as to
whether this play is reactionary, or not. To some contemporary feminists, it certainly seems so, for obvious
reasons, but others enjoy it as a period piece with
warnings for today. Booth herself has reminded us that
her characters are rich, after all, that they belong to
a limited and obviously pampered set. In fact, she has
argued that in presenting an all-women cast and concentrating seriously on women, no matter what kind of women,
she deserves to be considered a feminist of a particularly
honest sort. There is one brief scene (Act II, scene i)
in which a nurse loses her temper with the complaining
Edith, who has just given birth to a child, screaming
at her, "Why, women like you don't know what a terrible
time is. Try bearing a baby and scrubbing floors. Try
having one in a cold filthy kitchen, without ether,
without a change of linen, without decent food, without
a cent to bring it up--and try getting up the next day
with your insides falling out, to cook your husband's .
. . No, Mrs. Potter, you didn't have a terrible time
at all." Interesting to remember that Booth turned
conservative after all this.

Mailer, Norman. _An American Dream_. New York: Dell, 1965. Novel.

Death   Disease & Health   Dying
Madness   Sexuality   Sexual Roles
Suicide

Mailer is always fascinating on sexuality and sexual
roles, and this novel is perhaps his most impressive
achievement. Sex is never just sex for Mailer. For
instance, the encounter between Rojack and Ruta the
maid, though it has many of the trappings of pornog-
raphy, is something of a battle between male and female,
with male triumphant. Afterwards, Ruta coos, "'You
are absolutely a genius, Mr. Rojack.'" And he answers,
"'A doctor is not better than his patient.'" On
another occasion, Rojack thinks, "Murder is never
unsexual," and indeed sex does turn to hate and the
murder of his wife, the "Great Bitch" Deborah. But
the novel is as much about death of all sorts as about
sex. Rojack notes a suicidal tendency in himself, a
mad driving towards the death which, he claims, moti-
vates everyone. (In fact, as a professor of "existential psychology," he puts forth the thesis that
"magic, dread, and the perception of death [are] the
roots of motivation.") There are many images of
emptiness and dying in the novel: there's the dying
German soldier, killed by Rojack in a combination of
athletic fervor and dread, whose eyes become jelly; and
the memorable occasion when Rojack vomits from a high
balcony onto the awning of a second-floor apartment:
"The spirits of the food and drink I had ingested
wrenched out of my belly and upper gut, leaving me in
raw Being . . . . This illness . . . was an extinction."
A very violent book, with a dazzling style to match.

Malzberg, Barry. "Out from Ganymede," 1964. Available in Out from Ganymede. New York: Warner Books, 1974. Short Story.

Madness	Sci Fi	Sexuality

Malzberg is most famous for his Beyond Apollo (available from Random House, 1972) with its mixture of powerful aliens and/or subconscious; unresponsive, alienated women; society's reduction of a man to an inferior machine; and the rage evoked by such reduction. Beyond Apollo adds the flavor of homosexuality to the mixture; "Out from Ganymede" gives it in capsule form. Malzberg employs an elliptical style to convey his insecure narrator's uncertainty as to what is real.

Mann, Thomas. Death in Venice, 1911. New York: Alfred Knopf, 1965. Novella.

Adolescence	Age	Death
Disease & Health	Homosexuality	Plague

A Beautiful and complexly reverberating story of a famous, middle-aged writer and his relationship to himself, his art, and the world, told in terms of a visit to Venice undertaken for his health, both physical and intellectual. There he sees and is obsessively attracted to a lovely young boy of 14. They do not speak, but the writer feels that there is a communion of some sort between them and that the boy, Tadzio, is significant for him. When the resort buzzes with rumors of the spreading plague, most of the guests flee, but the writer and Tadzio and his family stay on amidst the smell of disinfectant and a general atmosphere of decay. The writer dyes his hair and paints his cheeks in an attempt to ward off age and death and probably artistic blocks as well, but one day on the beach just when Tadzio, the writer believes, is secretly summoning him, he falls back, to die a short time later of the plague.

Mann, Thomas. The Magic Mountain, 1924. New York: Modern Library, 1952. Novel.

Adolescence	The Body	Body/Mind
Death	Disease & Health	Doctors
Med. Instit.	Sexuality	Suicide

Hans Castorp, the hero of this novel, though technically an adult, is really an adolescent quester after the significance of life. Even the form of this long philosophical book reinforces the quest, for Hans is sealed off from the world of everyday activity in a Swiss tuberculosis sanatorium, where linear time disappears and philosophical reflection is easier. Hans stays on this magic mountain for seven years, during which time he becomes intimately involved with medical matters, almost all of which have metaphorical significance as well. Disease itself seems to be a metaphor for spiritual malaise, though it is hard to know whether some of Mann's ideas are meant to be taken metaphorically or literally. Consider, for instance, the humanist Settembrini's remark that "disease and despair are often only forms of depravity (trans. H. T. Lowe-Porter)," and Dr. Krokowski's Freud-inspired lecture on the source of illness, in which he proclaims that disease is only the power of love perverted and repressed (Chapter IV, "Analysis"). Naturally, Hans comes to see the body very closely and in all kinds of new ways. At one point, clinical details get mixed up with sexuality when Hans becomes fascinated by an X-ray of the skeleton of the woman with whom he is infatuated. Naturally, too, Hans must face and consider death, the death from tuberculosis of his cousin Joachim, for instance, and the death by suicide of the Jewish Jesuit Naphta. Finally, Hans comes around to health, both physical and spiritual, but ironically he descends from the mountain into the violent sickness of the first world war. A novel of monumental importance.

Marcus, Frank. The Killing of Sister George, 1965. New York: Random House, 1967. Drama.

Homosexuality	Nurses

A verbally and visually funny play that ends in pathos. "Sister George" is an English soap-opera character played by "June," the character in the Marcus comedy. Throughout the play, the vicissitudes of George provide insights into a certain image of the kindly, maternal rural district nurse. Sister George ultimately gets the axe from the BBC scriptwriters, and June loses on the home front too. There, her lover, a 34-year-old woman pointedly called "Childie," is seduced away. That leaves the formally tough, hilarious, and professionally successful June a lonely middle-aged lesbian, now scheduled to play the lead in a children's show called "The World of Clarabelle Cow." The last line in the play is a funny/plaintive "moo."

Masters, Edgar Lee. The Spoon River Anthology, 1915. New York: Macmillan, 1963. Poem Sequence.

Age	Death	Disease & Health
Grief	Preg. & Childbirth	Suffering
Suicide		

Death, grief, and a variety of other topics, all encountered in a collection of epitaphs spoken by the dead themselves. They are small town people of various levels of achievement, or none at all. "One passed in a fever,/ One was burned in a mine,/One was killed in a brawl,/One died in jail,/One fell from a bridge toiling for children and wife--/All, all are sleeping, sleeping, sleeping on the hill." One by one the dead speak, often describing their death, sometimes grieving, sometimes regretting

nothing, always evaluating their lives. Amanda Barker, e.g., says, "Henry got me with child,/Knowing that I could not bring forth life/Without losing my own." Elsa Wertman speaks about having to give up her bastard son to Mrs. Green, the wife of her seducer, then the son sums up his life, acknowledging what he has inherited from his mother, Mrs. Green. Lucinda Matlock, who died at 96 and spent her life nursing the sick, concludes, "It takes life to love life." And so on through all the residents of the Spoon River graveyard. At the end of the anthology, one has been forced through something like a grieving process oneself.

Maugham, W. Somerset. Liza of Lambeth, 1897. Garden City, New York: Doubleday, Doran & Company, 1936. Novel.

By Doctors	Children	Disease & Health
Doctors	Dying	Poverty & Health
Preg. & Childbirth	Sexuality	Women as Healers

Written while Maugham was a medical student and based on his experiences as an obstetrics clerk in the London slum of Lambeth. Both his clinical training and his admiration for Maupassant suggested the novel's spare, detached style. Still, that hardly accounts for the almost invisible presence of the doctor at the dying Liza's bedside. Maugham takes greater care to draw the portraits of Liza's self-centered mother, always worrying about her "rheumatics" and "neuralgy," and the midwife, Mrs. Hodges, who attends Liza during her miscarriage. Liza's affair with Jim, a married man, is made up almost exclusively of the unutterable passion popular in many naturalistic novels. Liza of Lambeth is interesting because it is Maugham's first novel--its success caused him to turn to writing rather than medicine when he finished his education--because it was written by a medical student, and because it starkly evokes the health conditions of slum women, for whom yearly pregnancies, miscarriages, babies, and dead children are the common lot.

Maugham, W. Somerset. Of Human Bondage, 1915. New York: Pocket Books, 1950. Novel.

By Doctors	Children	Doctors
Handicaps	Med. Students	Preg. & Childbirth
Sexuality		

A powerful novel which takes the hero, Philip Carey, from an orphaned childhood through medical school and prospects of an ordinary but beautiful future as a local doctor, a husband to Sally, and a father. But before he reaches this happy state, he suffers extraordinarily. As a child, his suffering is caused by his harsh, unfeeling uncle and by his cruel schoolmates, who ridicule Philip's clubfoot. He is so sensitive about his handicap that he can bear no reference to it, even a well-meaning one. As an adult, his suffering comes about at the hands of Mildred, a woman someone has called the most horrible woman in all literature. Though he desires her and in fact gives her money he can little afford, she refuses to have him. Earlier there had been an affair with a middle-aged woman, and now Philip begins to get interested in another girl, but when Mildred shows up pregnant, Philip once again supports this woman to whom he is enslaved. She repays him by going on a holiday with his close friend, and using his money to pay for it. The next time she comes into his life, Mildred has become a prostitute, but he takes her in again, partly because he loves her baby, to be repaid this time by Mildred's wrecking all his possessions before he departs once more. Philip is poverty-stricken now and must temporarily drop out of medical school. He finally becomes free of Mildred when she appears a last time, syphilitic, and her baby dead. Philip's obsessions and confusions fall away eventually-- perhaps they had been caused mostly by his physical handicap--and even though his new girl, Sally, is not pregnant as she thought, he marries her, giving up his romantic, but self-deceptive, dream of escaping as a ship's surgeon.

McCullers, Carson. The Ballad of the Sad Café, 1943. Available in The Ballad of the Sad Café: The Novels and Stories of Carson McCullers. Boston: Houghton, Mifflin Co., 1951. Novella.

The Body	Children	Disease & Health
Grief	Handicaps	Homosexuality
Sexuality	Women as Healers	

Love and the physically grotesque. Big, rugged Miss Amelia loves a 4-feet tall, consumptive hunchback called Cousin Lymon. He is a weeping, pitiable man until she takes him into her house. Thereafter, his true complexity reveals itself: he is at once attractively vital, physically repugnant, and egotistically sadistic. Miss Amelia loves him, but she does not sleep with him, any more than she had slept with her one-time husband, Marvin Macy. She is more interested in caring for Lymon, just as she cares for her patients in her capacity as the local "doctor." "She was considered a good doctor. Her hands though very large and bony, had a light touch about them. She possessed great imagination and used hundreds of different cures. In face of the most dangerous and extraordinary treatment she did not hesitate, and no disease was so terrible but what she would undertake to cure it." (The sole exception is "female complaints.") She is especially good with children, allowing them to stay around her store all day, getting used to her before she treats them. But all this care ends, and so does Miss Amelia's formerly strong independence, when Cousin Lymon runs off with Amelia's ex-husband. The men's relationship is difficult to analyze, and shouldn't be analyzed in a fiction with The Ballad's folk-tale over-tones, but in the light of McCullers' life and other work, the attraction could broadly be called homosexual. Certainly Lymon loves Marvin partly because the latter is physically attractive. In any case, when she loses Lymon, Miss Amelia turns in on herself. Her face reflects this loss: "sexless and white, with two gray crossed eyes which are turned inward so sharply that they seem to be exchanging with each other one long and secret gaze of grief."

McCullers, Carson. The Heart Is a Lonely Hunter, 1940. Available in The Ballad of the Sad Café: The Novels and Stories of Carson McCullers. Boston: Houghton, Mifflin Co., 1951. Novel.

Adolescence	Alcoholism	Children
Disease & Health	Doctors	The Family
Grief	Handicaps	Med. Instit.
Mental Retardation	Poverty & Health	Sexuality
Suicide		

Once again, McCullers is interested in the eccentric. Sometimes her characters are medically unusual (here two figures are deaf-mutes, one probably a little retarded as well; another has lost his feet). More often, they are just isolated and lonely. The black Dr. Copeland, for instance, is isolated from his own children and from his people in general by virtue of his education and his Marxist drive, in the face of his own tuberculosis, to remove the poverty and thereby improve the health of blacks. Another lonely figure is Mick Kelly, the novel's adolescent heroine, whose outer life and "inner room" is depicted with unusual sympathy, and with thorough knowledge about Mick's position as the middle child in a large family. Her sexual initi-ation at the age of 13 disappoints her tremendously and pushes her farther inside her room. (See McCullers' other excellent study of adolescence, The Member of the Wedding, 1946). A third fascinating figure is Mick's younger brother, who accidentally shoots a playmate, and is never the same, though the little girl recovers. Then there is the cafe owner, who does not mourn his unloved wife. And the revolutionary Jake Blount, a dissipated alcoholic. All the characters are drawn around the deaf-mute, John Singer, partly because they can make of him whatever they wish and need to imagine. As for Singer himself, he remains utterly alone in his silent universe, and after visiting his only true friend in the mental institution and learning that he has silently died alone, Singer kills himself, to the complete surprise of everyone who thought they knew him.

McCullers, Carson. Reflections in a Golden Eye, 1941. Available in The Ballad of the Sad Café: The Novels and Stories of Carson McCullers. Boston: Houghton, Mifflin Co., 1951. Novella.

Disease & Health	Grief	Homosexuality
Madness	Med. Instit.	Sexuality
Suicide	V.D.	

A few elements of minor interest here: a woman who learns of her husband's unfaithfulness and, unable to find a knife sharp enough for suicide, cuts off her nipples instead; the labelling of this woman as mad, and her subsequent commitment to a luxurious hospital for mental and physical disorders; her grief for her dead baby; the descriptions of the heart disease which, along with the general sense of loss, leads to her death; and the soldier who has never touched a woman because of his extreme horror about venereal disease. But there is one element of major interest as well: the subtle study of the surfacing of homosexual feelings in Captain Penderton. The Captain is a man who has apparently all his life felt nothing strongly, except perhaps for a sort of cowardly hate. In fact it is hate which he first identifies as the emotion he feels for the young soldier. Finally, the Captain perceives his feeling simply as yearning, but he cannot handle it in any form. He ends by being over-whelmed by sexuality, and killing the young man.

McKenna, Richard. "Casey Agonistes." Available in Casey Agonistes And Other Science Fiction And Fantasy Stories. New York: Harper & Row, 1973. Short Story.

Death	Doctors	Nurses
Sci Fi		

The resentment against regimented dying incarnated in an "imaginary" ape, Casey; the formation of a defensive alliance among the dying to repel the dehumanizing tactics of the doctors and the head nurse. Casey enables one of the group to die with dignity, to go fighting instead of dying by the book, to avoid the following treatment: "No doubt about it, the ways was greased for Slop Chute [Arthur, the narrator's friend]. Mama Death [the head nurse] come back soon as she could and began to loosen the chocks. She slobbered arthurs all over Slop Chute and flittered around like women do when they smell a wedding."

Mencken, H. L. In Defense of Women, especially essays 7 and 8. New York: Borzoi, 1918. Essays.

The Body	Sexual Roles

Interesting when put alongside Swift--"The Lady's Dress-ing Room"--and Beerbohm--"A Defense of Cosmetics." All see the female body as distasteful in itself and in need of aesthetic assistance. Swift sees cosmetics as a tool

for deluding both men and women into thinking females incorporeal; Beerbohm as a necessity for the creation of mystery. For Mencken cosmetics are women's concession to the male's need for surface beauty. He thinks women despise both their own and men's bodies. In essay 8 he asserts that since women's bodies are not the equal of men's, they have had to use their brains to achieve their superiority. He uses his adoption of the so-called female point of view to express his disgust with the human race in general. Particularly astonishing is his comic horror of the body as diseased and misshapen: "One finds quite as many obvious blotches among them; they have as many bodily blemishes; they are infested by the same microscopic parasites; their senses are as obtuse; their ears stand out as absurdly. Even assuming that their special malaises are wholly offset by the effects of alcoholism in the male, they suffer patently from the same adenoids, gastritis . . . and all other such distempers in men."

Merrill, James. "A Timepiece," 1961. Available in The Norton Anthology of Modern Poetry, eds. Richard Ellmann and Robert O'Clair. New York: Norton, 1973. Poem: 20 lines.

Preg. & Childbirth

A scene: a pregnant woman resting in a hammock; and several revealing images, all organized around a clock: the woman has a "pendulum's mildness"; later she will "thrust fullness from her, like a death"; for now, she fends off that sense of death by drinking milk, the calcium "Of unbuilt bone," "Meaning to muffle . . . a striking in her breast/For soon by what it tells the clock is stilled."

Miller, Arthur. After the Fall. New York: Viking Press, 1964. Drama.

Grief	Suicide

A play which takes place in the mind of a middle-aged lawyer, twice married, and now trying to cleanse himself of past sins and guilt in order to prepare for a potential third marriage. Of particular interest is the evocation of Quentin's marriage to Maggie, a character modeled on Marilyn Monroe, the playwright's second wife. Who killed Maggie? is the question Quentin must ask, and the answer, though a conventional enough explanation of MM's suicide, is powerful in this context. Quentin concludes that Maggie couldn't let go of her vision of the world as persecutor, that she wanted to die and intended to take him with her by implicating him as, in a sense, her murderer. He urges her to forget the image of Maggie as the loving-but-universally-betrayed victim, and to accept herself as someone capable of hatred. A good deal of Quentin's role must be seen as self-justification or expiation for Miller, but the larger consequences of Quentin's behavior come to the fore, particularly when he understands his own striving for power over others and his occasional inability to love. After the fall from Eden, there is no more innocence in anyone, but we can learn to forgive our-selves and others, when necessary, again and again.

Miller, Arthur. The Crucible, 1952. Available in Arthur Miller's Collected Plays. New York: Viking Press, 1967. Drama.

Adolescence	Madness	Sexuality
Suicide		

This play about the Salem witch trials is, of course, an allegory of American MacCarthyism, but it is also valuable for its accurate portrayal of the way hysteria can spread through a group, particularly, in this case, a group of adolescent girls at the age of sexual confu-sion. It is more clear-cut thwarting of her sexuality that prompts Abigail Williams to start off the witch hunt in the first place. She is a woman scorned by John Proctor. His own sexuality is illuminated in this play too, and that of his wife Elizabeth ("It needs a cold wife to prompt lechery"). Eventually John willingly goes to his death--it is, therefore, a kind of suicide--rather than sign a false confession of witchcraft. It is a noble suicide, for as his wife says, "He have his goodness now, God forbid I take it from him."

Miller, Arthur. Death of a Salesman, 1949. Available in Arthur Miller's Collected Plays. New York: Viking Press, 1967. Drama.

Age	Children	Dying
The Family	Madness	Suicide

The middle-class hero of this play, Willy Loman, comes home from one of his sales trips and says to Linda, his wife, "I'm tired to death," and indeed Willy is dying because his self-image has always derived from his success as a salesman and now that he isn't making it any more, he's just coasting towards death. Not that Willy is able to admit to himself just what a failure his life has been. He still thinks his weak sons are going to be great successes; he still tells himself that his sons adore him. They don't, and that's not surprising either for Willy has always had shallow values and now has nothing to see him into old age, except perhaps his love for his family. Little by little, he is able to call up scenes from his past and to see beyond his illusions to what really happened, such as the time his teen-aged son caught him in a hotel room with another woman. He's just losing his grip, that's all. Finally Willy thinks he has found

a way to help his family. With the money from his life
insurance policy, his son will be "magnificent"--an
impossibility, but Willy still can't see that, though
the son has long ago faced his own limitations. At any
rate, Willy kills himself, and one remembers Linda's
words and grieves for even such as Willy, who, after all,
is like us: "'I don't say he's a great man . . . . But
he's a human being, and a terrible thing is happening
to him . . . . He's not to be allowed to fall into his
grave like an old dog. Attention, attention must be
finally paid to such a person.'"

Miller, Arthur. The Price. New York: Viking Press, 1968. Drama.

Age   Doctors   The Family

The dissolution of a family--years after it has in fact
dissolved. A middle-aged policeman, Victor, has been
forced to sell the furniture of his long dead father.
Since his youth, we discover, Victor has pitied himself
because he had to drop out of school to support his
father, whereas his brother Walter selfishly went on to
become a distinguished surgeon. At this sale, Victor
confronts first of all the phenomenal 89-year-old
Solomon, who still lives by his wits and takes a great
interest in life. Solomon has come to buy the furniture,
and he easily gets the right price from Victor. Next
Victor must meet Walter, whom he has not seen in 16
years. The two confront each other with bitterness,
especially on Victor's part. But Walter reveals that
their "beloved" father exploited Victor, that he had a
hoard of money all along, and that there had never really
been any love in the family, so why be upset about its
final breaking up now. Furthermore, Walter charges
Victor with not wanting to be a success anyway. Walter
too has deceived himself, for he has been corrupted by
materialism: he has had a mental breakdown and he has
lost his wife. The furniture, it turns out, has been
sold at a high price.

Miller, Vassar. "The Common Core." From Wage War in Silence.
Middletown, Conn.: Wesleyan University Press, 1960. Poem:
18 lines.

Disease & Health   Suffering

A refusal to compare one sorrow with another, for "Each
man's sorrow is an absolute/Each man's pain is a norm";
a refusal to generalize about illness: "No man's sickness has a synonym,/No man's disease has a double."
Likewise, the poet will not dismiss any suffering as
being less terrible than any other. She will not say to
the person who is heart-broken that because she, the
poet, has an affliction of the limbs (see "Spastics"),
she deserves the greater sympathy. All sorrows are
absolute and self-defined, and suffering is what we all
hold in common. A poem of great compassion and tolerance.

Miller, Vassar. "Fantasia." From If I Could Sleep Deeply Enough.
New York: Liveright, 1974. Poem: 30 lines.

The Body   Children   Grief
Sexuality

The speaker receives the ghost of her mother in a midnight vision. The mother flows invisibly and intimately
over the daughter's body, and the daughter welcomes her
presence, for everywhere the mother lights, there a line
of poetry follows. In short, the daughter has turned
her grief for the mother into something creative. "I've
counted your phrases, one/on my forehead and cheeks,/
two on my mouth,/three on my breasts and my belly,/
printing my mons veneris,/touching those places,/shadows,
privates, genitals, gentlest now if my fists/open with
poems . . . . Only the book-ghosts can scare us,/not the
real ones."

Miller, Vassar. "On the Examination Table." From If I Could Sleep
Deeply Enough. New York: Liveright, 1974. Poem: 15 lines.

The Body   Disease & Health   Handicaps

The medical examination as it looks to the patient on
the table. She is helplessly exposed to the examiner:
"my belly, overturned turtle,/stripped from the shell/
of daily decorum." She is scared: "My eyes, two birds/
crazily threshing/in the trap of their sockets." Finally
she is metamorphosed: "my body, dull dog,/shies into
terror's/mythical monster." The poem takes on a certain
significance when one knows that the poet has cerebral
palsy (see her "Spastics"), but has a powerful enough
validity without that knowledge.

Miller, Vassar. "Spastics: (First poem from Handi-Lib)." From If
I Could Sleep Deeply Enough. New York: Liveright, 1974.
Poem: 21 lines.

Disease & Health   Handicaps   Sexuality

Handi-Lib: a poem on behalf of the liberation of those
handicapped with cerebral palsy, but not political, not
bitter, only rather frustrated in tone and astonishingly--
since the poet herself has cerebral palsy--direct and
even comic. Spastics are "creepy-crawlies from yesterday's rocks/tomorrow will step on." They are born that
way, so "presidents, and most parents, don't have to
worry/No one in congress will die of it." As for their
sex lives, spastics don't have one; they are "expected
to make it with Jesus." And as for sentimentality:
"Even some sappy saint said they/look young because
pure." The poem has been classified here under "Disease

and Health" because physicians would probably regard
cerebral palsy as an illness in the broad sense, but it
should be noted that the poet believes that someone
with cerebral palsy might be healthy even though most
assuredly handicapped.

Miller, Vassar. "Tired." From If I Could Sleep Deeply Enough.
New York: Liveright, 1974. Poem: 12 lines.

The Body   Disease & Health

An insomniac's poem: "the way/I sleep, men drink salt./
Always wearier/upon waking--." In this condition the
poet goes to her body to find the truth: "I have written/
these lines without book,/thumbing the thesaurus/of my
bones."

Miller, Walter M., Jr. A Canticle for Leibowitz, 1959. New York:
Bantam, 1972. Novel.

Euthanasia   Med. Ethics   Sci Fi

Science and religion in man's slow recovery after nuclear
warfare and civilization's growth to the stage for annihilation once more. In the Age of Simplification, men begin
the cycle by destroying all knowledge, moving from hatred
of science responsible for the nuclear holocaust to hatred
of all learning. But monks, notably the order of the
blessed Leibowitz, preserve scraps of scientific knowledge,
while debating whether or not the mutants caused by the
radiation had souls and should be accepted by the Church.
This first section about the postulant monk is the funniest
and most delightful. But then science grows. Knowledge
becomes a weapon which eventually becomes an atomic bomb.
After two atomic bombs have fallen, Science and the Church,
so close at the beginning, are now at odds--especially
over euthanasia. "Mercy" camps are established for the
radiation victims. Doctors use them because they provide
the only answer to unbearable, incurable pain--the only
evil they know. The Church has a wider view. Further,
the monk realizes that governments could foresee these
consequences of war; yet they went ahead. Instead of
making peace, they tried to prepare to make tolerable the
intolerable result of using nuclear weapons. The monk
pleading for death with dignity tries to stop a woman
from killing her child, but the troops prevent him from
interfering. A spaceship does escape with monks
endeavoring to preserve both Science and the Church;
however, the holocaust they flee, caused by irreconciled
beliefs in expediency and ethics, does not auger well
for the human race.

Mortimer, Penelope. The Pumpkin Eater. London: Hutchinson, 1962.
Novel.

Abortion   Doctors   The Family
Madness   Preg. & Childbirth   Sexual Roles

An attractive, financially comfortable, 38-year-old woman
begins to suffer from hysteria and depression. She has
many problems, and they can't really be said to be
resolved by the end of the novel, but the most valid
suggestion made by her psychiatrist is that Mrs. Armitage,
who has had several husbands and many children, longs
for another baby because she feels guilty about sex for
pleasure only. A second physician, her family doctor,
advises her to have another child because, as he says
to the husband, "She drops those babies like a cat, you
know--it's a pleasure to watch." Somewhat unwillingly,
she submits to an abortion, and to sterilization as well.
Interestingly enough, her relationships with her children
are, for the most part, rather distant.

Murdoch, Irish. Bruno's Dream. New York: Viking Press, 1969.
Novel.

Age   Children   Dying
The Family   Grief   Homosexuality
Nurses   Sexuality

Murdoch as usual, i.e., very sophisticated story-telling
with all the characters ending up in love with all the
other characters, and just generally in bizarre, chance
situations. There is the usual witch figure too, in
this case Nurse Nigel, a strange religious figure who
cares for Bruno, an aged man dying of cancer, and is
passionately in love with, oh, everyone no doubt, but
especially with Diana, Bruno's daughter-in-law, whom he
barely knows; Danby, Bruno's son-in-law; and his own
twin brother, Will. Sex is all over the place in this
novel, in short. It even turns one rather pinched do-
gooder, Lisa, into a full-blown beauty. But there is a
very dark side to this novel as well, and that is not
usual Murdoch. The reader is very much disturbed by
Bruno's self-image; by his guilty grief over his wife's
death (he had not gone to her at the last moment because
they had been quarreling over an affair of hers throughout her slow death from cancer); by his encounters with
his son Miles, estranged for years because Bruno had
refused to accept Miles' Indian wife, who died soon after
the marriage; and finally by Bruno's death itself, which
ends the book. In fact, in the last chapter, and the
first, we find the matters most relevant to medicine, for
it is there that Murdoch is at her most profound about
the nature of age ("He no longer looked into the mirror
though he could feel sometimes like a mask the ghost of
his much younger face. He glimpsed himself only in the
averted eyes of Danby and Adelaide, in the fastidious
reluctances which they could not conceal. It was not
just the smell, it was the look. He knew that he had

become a monster, animal-headed, bull-headed, a captive Minotaur. He now had a face like one of his spiders") and dying ("I am dying, he thought, but what is it like? Is it just this pain, this fear? . . . . There was something in him which was capable of a far more awful suffering and which he must somehow cheat out of a full awareness. He must, with a part of his mind, look always away from that, and not let the structure of his personality be destroyed by what it could not bear").

Nabokov, Vladimir. _Lolita_, 1955. London: Weidenfeld and Nicolson, 1959. Novel.

Adolescence	Children	Madness
Med. Instit.	Med. Profession	Sexuality

Lolita has been called a brilliant psychiatric case history and a tender love narrative. The novel purports to be a manuscript written by a middle-aged narrator calling himself "Humbert Humbert" (for the nasty sound of it) and telling the story of what he sees as his mad obsession for "nymphets," little girls between 9 and 14 whose true sexual nature is demonic. Lolita is 12 and the daughter of his landlady, whom Humbert marries in order to tease himself with the idea of incest. After his wife is killed--not by Humbert, though the idea occurs to him often enough--Humbert, to his great surprise, is seduced by the girl, who has learned love play at summer camp. The story of their next months together does reveal Lolita as something of a witch, yes, and Humbert as comic and obsessed and several other people as sick too (the drunken, exploitive Clare Quilty, for instance, who runs off with Lolita). But Humbert's affectionate qualities come through as well. We learn something of his medical history. He has been institutionalized; he has talked to analysts about his predilection for "Annabel Lee's." Once he spent his time in the hospital inventing dreams to tease and torment the personnel, and was delighted when a bribed nurse showed him his records, which listed him as "potentially homosexual" and "totally impotent." (Nabokov loathes all generalizations, especially the Freudian ones.) When we last see him, Humbert has shot Clare Guilty, has been hospitalized again, and now awaits trial. The "editor" into whose hands the manuscript has come explains that Humbert died of coronary thrombosis before the trial started, and that his beloved, escaped Lolita, whose "immortality" is referred to in Humbert's last sentence, has just died as the adolescent Mrs. Richard Schiller, in childbirth, producing a still-born baby girl.

Nichols, Peter. _Joe Egg_. New York: Grove Press, 1967. Drama.

Doctors	Euthanasia	The Family
Mental Retardation	Preg. & Childbirth	

A literal sick joke. "Joe Egg" is a 10-year-old spastic girl with severe retardation. She is nonetheless on the stage throughout much of this very funny and disturbing play. Her existence has made life in general and marriage in particular difficult for her parents--the clever, attractive, yet extremely immature Brian, and the more tolerant Sheila. The two of them have over the years devised elaborate comic rituals for dealing with their guilt and anger about Josephine. In Act I, they demonstrate their technique, a sort of stand-up comic or music hall routine, in which they re-enact their memories of their daughter's birth, her first symptoms, and--most emphatically--the doctors who attended her. There is a G.P., who is hilariously vague and incompetent; and an unsympathetic German neurologist, who uses silly switchboard metaphors to explain Joe's illness, and ends by saying she is a "vegetable." Brian and Sheila have even developed various "personalities" for Joe, speaking her lines for her, ascribing to her her impossible physical action, anything to keep her real. But the marriage is in serious trouble, for everything revolves around the child, and Brian feels that he is not getting enough of Sheila's attentions. Finally, in the midst of all this comedy, he attempts to kill Joe, or to let her die, at any rate. Earlier, a fraudulent snob called Pam has given all the "wrong" reasons for getting rid of the child, but she has raised the issues in the audience's minds: "these poor freaks . . . oh, put them out of their misery. Well, they wouldn't have survived in nature, it's only modern medicine, so modern medicine should be allowed to do away with them. A committee of doctors and do-gooders, naturally, to make sure there's no funny business and then--if I say gas-chamber that makes it sound horrid--but I do mean put to sleep . . . . I love my own immediate family and that's the lot. Can't manage any more." Joe survives Brian's attempt; Sheila makes some moves to pay more attention to him; but he has decided to sneak out, and eluding the tempting offers of his coddling mother, he leaves alone.

Nichols, Peter. _The National Health_. New York: Samuel French, 1970. Drama.

Age	Alcoholism	Doctors
Euthanasia	Med. Ethics	Med. Instit.
Med. Students	Nurses	Surgery

A thorough examination of hospitalization under the British National Health Service. Not as successful a play as _Joe Egg_, but effective comedy on several levels, from hilarious to painful. The characters are almost to be expected, certainly, at least, no match for Shaw's eccentric version of certain stereotypes. Nichols gets

humor and/or interest from silly elderly patients, an exhausted doctor, a dopey Indian medical student, black nursing attendants, a ritualized kidney transplant, a cancer patient who wants to be allowed to die, a young man whose mental age is that of a child, and two irrelevant servants of God. The whole thing ends with musical cynicism worthy of _Three-Penny Opera_, and the "national health" becomes, inevitably, a metaphor for the state of the world. "As for the rest there's not a lot to say/They're born, they live, and then get wheeled away."

Nourse, Alan E. _The Bladerunner_. New York: Ballantine, 1975. Novel.

By Doctors	Doctors	Med. Ethics
Med. Instit.	Med. Profession	Plague
Sci Fi		

Dr. Nourse is a good, prolific sci fi author, and many of his books deal with medical matters. This book considers an extension of the idea that medical intervention increases the incidence of disease by prolonging the life--and so the reproduction--of ill people, such as diabetics and by upsetting "age-old natural balances." In a fit of historic reaction, the government passes an act requiring sterilization before a person can receive any medical treatment. Of course large numbers of people boycott treatment with such a requirement, and black-market medicine flourishes. One doctor who operates as a part-time black-market physician is also involved in resistance against the introduction of robot surgeons. He manages to reopen the question of enforced sterilization and impede installation of robots by discovering that the large numbers of people lacking any medical supervision are the perfect victims for an uncontrolled plague, such as the meningitis epidemic currently rising. The plot is aimed at the unsophisticated, but the medical atmosphere is interesting.

Nourse, Alan E. "The Martyr." From _PSI High and Others_. New York: Ace, 1967. Novel.

By Doctors	Death	Sci Fi

The exact opposite of Wyndham's idea in _Trouble With Lichens_--elimination of death removes time pressure from humanity and so removes all creativity and purpose. A senator dies, despite his doctor's warnings, to insure defeat of the rejuvenation procedures.

Oates, Joyce Carol. _Wonderland_. New York: Vanguard Press, 1971. Novel.

Abortion	Adolescence	Children
Death	Disease & Health	Doctors
Drugs	Evil Doctors	The Family
Madness	Med. Ethics	Med. Instit.
Med. Students	Preg. & Childbirth	Sexuality
Surgery		

A major contemporary novel on medical themes, a book to be put along side _Middlemarch_ and _The Plague_. The vision is horrifying from the very beginning. The main character, Jesse Harte (later Jesse Pederson, then Jesse Vogel: he has multiple names and shifting masks), arrives home from school to find that his father has murdered the entire family and now tries to kill him, before killing himself. From this childhood, Jesse is adopted for the duration of his adolescence by Dr. Pederson and his family. His fat, fat family, which consists of two highly neurotic genius children and a wife, made miserable by the Evil Doctor (a category, incidentally, which does not appear often in the 20th century). Here is a man whose megalomania is as huge as his body: "Once a patient comes to him, he believes the patient is his. The patient's life is his. He owns the patient, he owns the disease, he owns everything . . . he watches them die and won't bring in anyone else . . . right until the end he thinks he is right." When Jesse flees the Pedersons, he becomes a medical student, a course followed with great interest by Oates, including a visit to an inhumane animal experimentation farm, where Jesse's refusal to consider ethical issues indicates how very mechanical he has become. He becomes a doctor, a surgeon, because, one infers, medicine confirms what he knows of life: that people are always escaping him, dying, and that he survives. Most of all, he is at home in a profession which, as Oates presents it, allows him to behave mechanically. Among the other doctors in the novel is Dr. Perrault, a neurosurgeon, who claims that the brain is the only truly human part of us--never mind the body, or the personality--and that in the future people will be able to survive without a body. When she hears this theory, Jesse's wife protests hysterically, and earlier she had been terrified by an "ordinary" gynecological examination during pregnancy and had fantasized about a horrible abortion, but, next to all the truly insane behavior in the novel, her runaway emotions seem almost sensible. A daughter is eventually born, grows up, runs away to become a communal-living drug-taker. When her father finds her, yellow and shrunken, he determines, after a life-time of death, that there will be no more.

O'Brien, Edna. _August Is a Wicked Month_. London: Jonathan Cape, 1965. Novel.

Doctors	Grief	Sexuality
V.D.		

A very honest picture of the sexual needs of a young woman, divorced with one son, who takes a trip to France, determined to make it "her jaunt into iniquity," as she puts it. But the phrase itself is revealing: this is a woman with a Catholic background, and she cannot easily indulge in casual sex. In the course of the novel she has several sexual encounters; the first one seems lovely at the time, but it leads to nothing but more loneliness. She runs into some rather coarse men who try to pick her up in manners that make sex ugly to her. After receiving a call about the death of her son, the novel heats up with her grief, the holiday sun, and her more desperate sex life. Sex and death are all mixed up now. And sin too, for after the final sexual encounter, Ellen discovers what she fears to be a venereal infection, and there follows a long, frank section, unique in literature, about her terrified reactions to the discharge. Back in England, she overcomes enough of her fear and guilt to visit a "lady doctor," who tells her "grimly," "Well if you must be careless you've got to pay."

O'Connor, Flannery. "Good Country People," From A Good Man Is Hard to Find. New York: Harcourt, Brace and Co., 1955. Short Story.

Disease & Health   Handicaps   Sexuality

The main character here has an artificial leg. What's more, she's a fat 32-year-old unkissed and unemployed philosophy Ph.D. She wears old cowboy sweatshirts, and she's changed her name from Joy to the ugliest she can find--Hulga. She baits her mother, and she prepares to die--she has a bad heart--by claiming to care for no one and to believe in nothing. In short, the artificial leg is symbolic of the general incompleteness that is Hulga Hopewell. "Hopewell": a clue to the pathos of her situation, for when a 19-year-old simple country boy comes to the door selling Bibles and invites her out for a picnic, she accepts, telling herself that she is intellectually superior to him and may even seduce him, but hoping well that this good boy will treat her kindly. The meeting ends grotesquely. The boy is kinky about medical anomalies. He gets her in a hayloft and screws . . . off her leg! He's no savior at all, but a shrewd nihilist, as Hulga had imagined herself to be. A highly intelligent and original story.

O'Connor, Flannery. "The Lame Shall Enter First." From Everything That Rises Must Converge. New York: Farrar, Straus and Giroux, 1965. Short Story.

Adolescence   Children   Grief
Handicaps   Madness   Suicide

A horror story, compounded of ordinary situations, and providing an extraordinary moral shock. A social worker, widower, father of one 10-year-old boy takes a 14-year-old reform school boy into his home, to teach his own son, Norton, to share, the man says, and to set the bright boy, Rufus, towards a successful future. But the man is a self-deceiver of the worst sort: from the beginning, he is cruelly insensitive to his son's needs, his grief for his mother, for instance; and naively liberal about how Rufus can be saved. The man is convinced, in the first place, that Rufus misbehaves to compensate for his grotesque clubfoot: common psychological tenet, but not relevant in O'Connor's world. He believes that Rufus is shy about showing gratitude when, in fact, Rufus is ungrateful, and so on. Though the man is an atheist, he is accurately identified by the intelligent Rufus as somebody who thinks he's God, and that's not allowable in the tightly religious world of the superficially immoral Rufus. Far from being ashamed of his handicap, Rufus glories in it, and quotes the Bible at his would-be benefactor: "'The lame shall enter first. The halt'll be gathered together.'" All along Rufus has paid more attention to "crazy" Norton than his father has, and the reader has interpreted signs that the father overlooks. And so the final scene is only a horrifying confirmation of the reader's fears. When the father at last gives up on Rufus--hates him even--and, needing someone else to save, goes to find his son, he discovers that Norton, in an attempt to recover his mother in Rufus' heaven, has hanged himself.

O'Connor, Flannery. "Revelation." From Everything That Rises Must Converge. New York: Farrar, Straus & Giroux, 1964. Short Story.

Disease & Health   Doctors   Nurses
Women as Healers

This story works on both a naturalistic and a mystical level. The first part takes place in a doctor's waiting room. The doctor and the nurse make only brief, unimportant appearances, however, for this is the patients' story. Several different sorts of people have gathered to be treated, including Mrs. Turpin, a middle-aged farm wife, who smugly congratulates herself on her good, middle-class Christian virtues, and a college girl called Mary Grace: ugly, grimacing, and finally violent, but all the same a vehicle for a revelation to Mrs. Turpin, at whom she hurls the charge that she is a wart-hog from hell. The story stays naturalistic--the Turpins go home, talk to their farm hands, and so on--until the last pages when Mrs. Turpin challenges God to tell her why she is a wart-hog, and receives in reply a vision of all the people she had reviled--"white trash," "niggers"--on their way to heaven, ahead of people like her. Mrs. Turpin has been, in a sense, healed after all in the doctor's waiting room, not by him, but by this strange girl, who is afterwards tranquilized and taken away in an ambulance.

O'Connor, Frank. "The Drunkard," "Judas," and "My Oedipus Complex." Available in Stories by Frank O'Connor. New York: Vintage Books, 1956. Short Stories.

Adolescence   Alcoholism   Children
The Family   Sexuality

A sampling of O'Connor's comic stories about the family, a lower middle-class Irish family to be sure, but one with universally recognizable traits. In "The Drunkard," the father has a weakness for drink, as his family euphemistically put it, a weakness that has frightening overtones, skillfully hidden in the telling of this superficially hilarious story. On one of his outings, he inadvertently allows his little boy to get drunk, later dragging him shamefacedly home as the little fellow shouts vulgarities at the cackling neighbor women. The mother, mistakenly thinking the boy has deliberately chosen this route to save the family from another difficult drunken bout, praises him, calling him "My little man." This same pseudo-marital relationship between mother and son shows up in "My Oedipus Complex," in which the young boy about 5 years old has all the familiar Oedipal reactions to his father's return from the war. Young Larry even tells his mother that he is going to marry her and have lots of babies. A funny story, and by the end, Larry is on his way to a conventional identification with his father. The Oedipal element is more subtle in "Judas," which follows for most of the story an adolescent love affair compounded of wild imagination and unrequited lust, but which ends with the young man's guilt and his mother's jealousy. "My little man," she calls him, trying to restore the lost relationship of the Oedipal past.

Odets, Clifford. The Country Girl, 1949. New York: Viking Press, 1951. Drama.

Alcoholism

The tragedy of having to live with an alcoholic. Georgie, the young but maternal wife of a once-famous actor, Frank, is trapped in the role of overseer. She is a victim of his defensive lies (he attributes his weaknesses to her). And she needs tremendous energy, patience, and love to pull Frank out of his depression and back into his career. Although she partly returns the love of Frank's director, she refuses at the end to leave her husband, for his need of her is so great.

Odets, Clifford. Waiting for Lefty, 1935. Available in Sixteen Famous American Plays, eds. Bennett A. Cerf and Van H. Cartmell. New York: Modern Library, 1941. Drama.

Med. Instit.   Med. Profession   Poverty & Health

The play consists of a series of episodes showing why various men felt compelled to join the union of workers and strike against the system. Episode VI is called "The Interne Episode," and demonstrates the control of the medical profession and medical institutions by and for the rich. An incompetent doctor gets to do a complicated piece of surgery in the place of a brilliant intern because the incompetent is the nephew of a senator, besides which, the patient is just a charity case. Furthermore, the competent doctor is dismissed because he cares for the poor and the charity wing is being closed in an effort to make the hospital more financially viable. That the intern is a Jew is also part of the reason for his dismissal, for even though there are Jews on the hospital board, they are rich Jews. A senior doctor laments the decision, but he is helpless before the majority. Medicine changes and improves in spite of the rich, not because of them.

O'Donnell, K. M. "In the Pocket." Available in Nova One, ed. Harry Harrison. New York: Dell, 1971. Short Story.

Disease & Health   Doctors   Sci Fi

An unusual twist to Asimov's Fantastic Voyage. A "messenger," an orderly shrunk to two-inch size in order to burn out metastases, becomes tormented by the relationship between the cancerous tissue and the patient, gradually identifying with the disease rather than the man. He exercises his right to kill ("They permit me one death a year under the contract, possessed of an understanding that staggers me. We must kill to live."); and then, "from deeply within, I feel my own new tumor full-come and now dancing for joy."

Olsen, Tillie. "Tell Me a Riddle," 1960. Available in The Best American Short Stories, 1961, eds. Martha Foley and David Burnett. New York: Ballantine Books, 1961. Short Story.

Age   Children   Death
Doctors   Dying   Grief
Sexual Roles

A powerful story, frequently reprinted, of a long bitter marriage, sundered here by the slow dying of the wife from cancer. An old woman, whose many children had prevented her from living the contemplative life for which she yearned, faces her last years gratefully: "Being able at last to live within, and not move to the rhythms of others." Her anger against her husband, long silenced, comes out now in verbal battles, which upset the children. The dialogue is wonderfully believable. "Mrs. Enlighted," her husband jeers at her, "Mrs. Cultured." But there aren't to be long reflective years. At first, the doctor is fatherly, as reported by a daughter-in-law: "'Sixty-nine is young these days. Go

out, enjoy life, find interests. Get a new hearing aid,
this one is antiquated. Old age is a sickness only if
one makes it so.'" Later pervasive cancer is discovered,
and, told to keep the diagnosis from her, the husband
hauls the bird-like body of his wife from child to grieving
and/or embittered child, when what she really wants is
to go home. She never gets there, and half the story is
a rendering of her dying--her delirium, her return to
old Russian memories, her bringing out of secret interests
which startle her husband. He, poor man, grieves for
their youth, their love, their betrayal of each other.
And he strains to hear through her delirium confirmation
of the fact that all was not so bitter, that somewhere
she had trusted, had believed, and had moved and been
moved, though her body now lifts in agony.

O'Neill, Eugene. Ah Wilderness!, 1933. Available in Sixteen
Famous American Plays, eds. Bennet A. Cerf and Van H. Cartmell.
New York: Modern Library, 1941. Drama.

Adolescence   Alcoholism   The Family

A gentle and idealized version of an American family.
There is no real plot, just affection in action. The
most important family member for our purposes is the
adolescent hero, Richard, an autobiographical figure who
is full of poetry and rebellion and love for Muriel, who
keeps him guessing. He postures melodramatically, to
be sure, but the audience, like his father, gives him
loving understanding, especially when he tries to pick
up a prostitute and get drunk, and fails at both.
Richard's maternal uncle is an accomplished drinker,
preached at when sober, but encouraged and laughed at
when drunk.

O'Neill, Eugene. Desire Under the Elms, 1924. Available in Nine
Plays by Eugene O'Neill. New York: Modern Library, 1959.
Drama.

Children   Sexuality

Sexuality as a purgative force that cleanses one generation at a heavy cost to two others. The love between
Eben and his harsh father's young wife washes away
Eben's dedication to his dead mother and his desire for
revenge upon his father--until, that is, there is a child
conceived of that love that will legally supplant him as
heir to the farm. Then he truly hates Abbie, believing
that she had been treacherous. To prove otherwise,
Abbie kills her baby. But the enraged Eben gives her
up to the sheriff, and her husband, on being told that
the baby was not his, condemns her too. Soon, however,
Eben repents, and wishing to share Abbie's guilt, goes
hand in hand with her to jail, and the husband is left
alone, but his puritanical soul tells him that's right.

O'Neill, Eugene. The Iceman Cometh, 1939. New York: Random House,
1946. Drama.

Alcoholism   Madness   Suicide

The relationship of illusion to survival amidst a group
of alcoholic wastrels. When their pipe dreams are
obliterated as in the case of young Don Parritt, for
instance, who confesses that he sold out his anarchistic
mother because he hated her; or in the case of Hickey--
fun-loving Hickey, on whose good cheer they all depend--
who tells them he has murdered his wife, and then tries
to justify it: when these and other illusions are
shattered, the drunks one by one drop their masks, and
what we see is terrible. Most of them find ways to
replace them so that they can go on, but Parritt and
Larry, the philosophical one, stick with their vision
of death. The matricide forces Larry to condemn him.
He then commits suicide and thereby takes away Larry's
own desire to live.

O'Neill, Eugene. Long Day's Journey Into Night, 1941. New Haven:
Yale University Press, 1956. Drama.

Alcoholism   Disease & Health   Doctors
Drugs   The Family   Suffering

Probably the classic drama of the relationship between
the family and disease. The relationship is worked out
in several ways. First of all, there is the mother's
drug addiction, begun when she was in pain after Edmund's
birth and the doctor--it is implied that he was a cheap
and not particularly competent one--gave her something
to ease her suffering. She has been "cured" off and on,
but there is always a terrible tension in the family for
fear she will relapse, as indeed she does. Second,
there is the tension caused by Edmund's tuberculosis,
which his father's pathological parsimony will not allow
him to treat adequately. And third, the tensions related
to Jamie's drinking, many coming out in the form of
jealousy of his brother Edmund. But each of the four
family members suffers and each inflicts suffering on
the other three in a complexly meshed fashion. The fear
of death hangs over the family because of Edmund's
tuberculosis, and he would like some support from his
mother, but at the end of the play, she has drifted off
into a doped up haze, dreaming, tragically, of her youth:
"'Yes, I remember. I fell in love with James Tyrone and
was so happy for a time.'"

O'Neill, Eugene. Mourning Becomes Electra, 1931. Available in
Nine Plays by Eugene O'Neill. New York: Modern Library, 1959.
Drama.

The Family   Madness   Sexuality
Suicide

An adaptation of the Oresteia, in which Lavinia (Electra)
is the one who purges the family's guilt. Christine,
her mother (Clytemnestra) has been having an affair while
her husband (an Agamemnon figure) has been away at the
Civil War. Lavinia discovers it, and learns that her
mother hates her father. As in the original myth, the
husband is killed when he returns--in this case, goaded
into a heart attack, and Lavinia and her brother Orin
(Orestes) decide they must avenge their father. They do
just that, first killing the lover, and then hearing with
satisfaction that their mother has killed herself. Now
the furies are after Orin. But in the 20th century, these
are not religious or even political forces. This family
is torn apart from within. They are modern psychological
furies, produced by a family where sex is an obsession.
In the Oresteia, the purge sets up the family in a new,
fresh context, but that is not possible here in this
godless world, and only the elimination of the family can
purge them of their guilt. So Lavinia, after refusing
to become Orin's lover--he has suggested this so that they
can fully share the guilt--drives her brother to suicide
and vows to live alone and let the family curse feed
upon her until it is glutted.

O'Neill, Eugene. Strange Interlude, 1928. Available in Nine Plays
by Eugene O'Neill. New York: Modern Library, 1959. Drama.

Abortion   Doctors   The Family
Grief   Madness   Sexuality

A long, long play with a plot too complicated to be fully
summarized here, but revolving around one rather neurotic
woman, Nina, and the men in her life: her father, whom
she resents for having foiled her marriage to the now
dead Gordon, for whom she grieves pathologically (so much
that she becomes a nurse to crippled soldiers and starts
sleeping with all of them as a way of giving herself to
Gordon); a nice young man called Sam Evans, whom a super-
rationalist medical man called Darrell advises her to
marry in order to redirect her promiscuity; and Charles
Marsden, a spinsterish, but kindly man, with whom, many
years later, Nina ends up, her sexuality having run its
course apparently. Pregnant by Sam, Nina is told by her
mother-in-law something that Sam doesn't know: there's
congenital madness in the family, and Nina must abort
the child, and, the older woman adds, have a baby by a
healthy man. That's where Dr. Darrell comes into the
picture, and with his portrait O'Neill shows his rejection
of the scientist, for Darrell tries to deny all his
emotions under the guise of scientific objectivity. He
fails, of course. He does, at any rate, give Nina a
son, another Gordon, and another important man/"lover"
in her life. All this, and more, is accomplished through
a composite of conventional dramatic scenes and long
asides, which enable us to see into the character's
psyche.

Orwell, George (pseudonym of Eric Blair). "How the Poor Die," 1946.
Available in The Orwell Reader. New York: Harcourt, Brace,
1956. Essay.

Disease & Health   Doctors   Dying
Med. Ethics   Med. Instit.   Med. Profession
Med. Students   Nurses   Poverty & Health
Suffering

Important in both the history of medicine and literature,
this essay is a recollection of several weeks spent in a
public ward of a French hospital in 1929. Orwell begins
with descriptions of the barbarous treatment and callous
indifference displayed by doctors, nurses, and medical
students, proceeds to portraits of the dying and recently
dead, and concludes with some general observations on the
history of the doctor-patient relationship and the medical situation of the poor. In clear, non-sensational
language, Orwell narrates the horrors he has seen, calling
them vestiges of 19th-century medicine. Patients are
specimens; the environment is squalid; the staff never
speaks to the patients, never recognizes their humanity;
corpses are left in the ward for hours; dying is the
ultimate indignity: "As I gazed at the tiny, screwed-up
face it struck me that this disgusting piece of refuse,
waiting to be carted away and dumped on a slab in the
dissecting room, was an example of 'natural' death, one
of the things you pray for in the Litany . . . . 'Natural'
death, almost by definition, means something slow, smelly
and painful." Two medical students kill a 16-year-old
boy by performing an experiment they could not perform
on a paying patient. In his conclusion, Orwell
speaks of the changes wrought by anesthesia, disinfectants,
and national health, and says that all these cannot dispel
a lingering fear of doctors--surgeons in particular--and
hospitals, these "antechambers to the tomb."

Owen, Wilfrid. "Dulce et Decorum Est"; "Disabled"; "Mental Cases,"
1920. Available in The Norton Anthology of Modern Poetry,
eds. Richard Ellmann and Robert O'Clair. New York: Norton,
1973. Poems: 29, 46, and 28 lines.

Death   Disease & Health   Madness

The greatest of the World War I poets, and three of his
most unflinching poems. In the first, he sets up the
patriotic line that it is sweet and proper to die for
one's country in contrast to a soldier's horrific suffering as he lies dying in a wagon: "If you could hear,
at every jolt, the blood/Come gargling from the froth-
corrupted lungs./Obscene as cancer, bitter as the cud/
Of vile, incurable sores on innocent tongues . . . ."
The formerly handsome boy in "Disabled" has lost both

legs and an arm. People "touch him like some queer disease." In the third poem, Owen moves on to show the mental disease caused by war, by us he suggests, and it is no less horrible: "purgatorial shadows,/Drooping tongues from jaws that slob their relish,/Baring teeth that leer like skulls' teeth wicked."

Pasternak, Boris. _Doctor Zhivago_. New York: New American Library, 1958. Novel.

Death	Disease & Health	Doctors
The Family	Grief	Madness
Med. Instit.	Med. Students	Nurses
Poverty & Health	Preg. & Childbirth	Science & Poetry
Sexuality	Suffering	

In this great sweep of a novel about the Russian revolution, the hero is not a soldier, but a doctor-poet. And this is fitting because Russia, as Pasternak presents her, is split open, requiring both physical and spiritual healing. The novel takes Dr. Zhivago from his childhood, when he loses his mother with consumption, through his marriage to Tonia, the birth of their two children, his passionate affair with the nurse Lara, his medical service in several parts of Russia, and finally to his death in poverty and indifference, no longer a doctor, but with some hope for a new poetry of redemption. During his lifetime the doctor witnesses vivid horrors of war, starvation and disease. He sees pneumonia, typhus, dysentery, heart disease, and death--from the dissecting room of his student days to death from war wounds and by suicide. He himself is often very ill and contemplates suicide. Sometimes he feels that he is mad, but perhaps it is only a reasonable reaction to that ultimate insanity, the revolution and its aftermath.

Percy, Walker. _Love in the Ruins_. New York: Farrar, Straus & Giroux, 1971. Novel.

Age	Alcoholism	By Doctors
Death	Disease & Health	Doctors
Euthanasia	The Family	Grief
Madness	Med. Ethics	Med. Instit.
Med. Students	Nurses	Science & Poetry
Sexuality		

Walker Percy is probably the best doctor-author writing in English at this time, and this is a fine novel, though its anti-apocalyptic themes mark it as of its time and already a little old-fashioned. Set in the near future, when life has become so tense that most doctors are either psychiatrists or proctologists, the comic novel has as its "hero" an alcoholic, allergenic, grief-stricken (both his daughter and his estranged wife have died), lusty, nervous-wreck of a psychiatrist, Dr. Thomas More, who believes he has invented a machine which can diagnose and treat the diseases of the mind and spirit which are raging through the country. His colleagues, scientists all, consider his invention metaphysical at best, and probably gimmicky. They consider _him_ a borderline maniac; in fact, his status at the clinic is "patient-staff." Certainly there are plenty of other madmen in Percy's world, including Dr. Buddy Brown, who promotes a concept called the "euphoric switch" which sends the elderly and no longer treatable (he classifies people rather too quickly) into the great beyond with smiles; Dr. Stryker, director of the Love Clinic, and a caricature of William Masters; and Art Immelmann, who claims to be from the great research foundations as well as from the F.B.I., gets Dr. More's name on a contract, and thereafter runs a maniacal, unethical test of his invention. In one hilarious scene, several of these people run amuck during a session of "The Pit," a correlation clinic, in which two professors attempt to demolish each other before some mindless medical students. Even though More is a self-proclaimed Bad Catholic, it is he who salvages the moral sense in these decadent, violent, uncaring times. A priest tells him essentially that--to be sure, the fellow is adjudged deranged at the time--"I think it is you doctors who are doing the will of God, even though you do not believe in him. You stand for life."

Percy, Walker. _The Moviegoer_. New York: Alfred Knopf, 1961. Novel.

By Doctors	Death	Doctors
Drugs	The Family	Grief
Madness	Med. Students	Science & Poetry
Sexuality	Suicide	

A book that moves almost entirely by indirection to show us the despair of a lonely 30-year-old stockbroker, who wanders through life on a "horizontal search" lest he lose his metaphysical bearings and become just Anyone living in Anyplace. His life is composed chiefly of pathetic sexual encounters and movie romanticism, but he is a feeling, caring man whose best qualities come out in his involvement with a young woman whose fiancé was killed on the eve of their marriage and whose subsequent dependence on certain medication, contemplations of suicide, and mental breakdowns are worrying her family. His own family is something of a mess: his brother died as a boy; his mother, the widow of a doctor, has remarried and produced several children. One of them, the main character's favorite, dies in the "Epilogue" to the book, hardly a happy-ever-after Hollywood ending. Often submissive, this suburban-picaresque hero eventually agrees to wander on to medical school, though he hasn't liked what he's seen of science. At one point he describes a researcher who "is no more aware of the

mystery which surrounds him than a fish is aware of the water it swims in." And at another point, he speculates that hard-nosed scientists, having done little in their lives about their "human" aspects, are sometimes driven into the opposite of science, "crappy" romanticism. A subtle, amusing, and scary book, "a _Catcher in the Rye_ for adults only," as it has been called.

Pinter, Harold. _The Caretaker_, 1960. New York: Grove Press, 1961. Drama.

Age	The Family	Madness
Med. Instit.		

Like other Pinter plays, this one combines farcical and threatening tones, and leaves one with a variety of possible interpretations. Many of Pinter's characters are mad (for instance, Stanley in _The Birthday Party_ is driven to it by two sinister intruders), and in this play two of three characters know mental illness. Mick is something of a sadist. His brother Aston has been hospitalized with hallucinations and forced to undergo electro-shock therapy. The laconic Aston recalls all this in a long, long monologue, saying, that after the treatment "my thoughts . . . had become very slow . . . . I couldn't look to the right or the left, I had to look straight in front of me . . . . I've often thought of going back and trying to find the man who did that to me." The third character is almost madly self-destructive. He's an old bum, taken in by Aston, who becomes less grateful and more demanding every day, and, after causing first trouble and then reconciliation between the two brothers, is thrown out. To be sure, Mick, jealous of Aston's interest in the old man, has created much of the trouble. Altogether a strange brotherhood.

Pinter, Harold. _The Homecoming_, 1965. New York: Grove Press, 1966. Drama.

The Family	Madness	Sexuality
Sexual Roles		

Members of a London family make bizarre sexual arrangements in a play which seems to uncover much that is usually underground in families. A widowed, working-class father, his two sons (a boxer and a pimp), and his brother are unexpectedly visited by another son, who is a professor in an American university. He brings with him his strangely distant, but seductive, wife--who proceeds, in the face of her husband's intellectual indifference, to bring out the sex in all the men, even the old father. Eventually it is agreed that she will remain in England, sending her husband back to mind the children, to become the family's personal, and occasionally commercial, whore.

Pirandello, Luigi. _Henry IV_, 1922. Available in _Masters of Modern Drama_, eds. Haskell M. Block and Robert G. Shedd. New York: Random House, 1962. Drama.

Doctors	Madness

Probably the best of Pirandello's revelations of the illusory nature of reality, the truth of illusion, and the inevitability of role-playing. Certainly one of the finest of the 20th-century assaults on the definition of madness. There really is no "literal" plot, but what seems to happen seems to be this: a modern man, dressed for an historical pageant as the German Henry IV of the 11th century, falls from his horse, strikes his head on a rock, and thereafter goes mad for 20 years, his chief symptom being that he imagines himself to be in reality Henry IV. For 20 years he lives out his fantasy in exact detail, compelling those around him to act out supporting 11th-century roles. As the play opens, some of his family and friends have brought a psychiatrist to see him, also, of course, dressed in costume. The doctor is a serious man, but he is always completely wrong, often a jargon-using pedant (one character says psychiatrists should take law degrees, rather than medical ones), and sometimes simply afraid of the "madman." "Henry," it turns out, has been "cured" for the past 8 years, but continues to act mad because--to oversimplify a bit--in his mad world he is more powerful and safe. Finding his anger aroused by the presence of one of his old enemies, "Henry" pretends to slip back into madness in order to kill him. The problem is, now that he is a murderer, he must fake insanity forever.

Pirsig, Robert M. _Zen and the Art of Motorcycle Maintenance: an Inquiry into Values_. New York: William Morrow, 1974. Fiction.

Children	Madness	Science & Poetry

An original and ambitious book that will not easily be classified, and whose form--a long motorcycle trip, something like a chautauqua lecture tour--is an integral part of its meaning. The journey, which begins as an investigation of the source and nature of values, ends as a spectacular confrontation with the self. At the risk of oversimplifying the book, one might point readers with medical interests first, to its statements about classical and romantic ways of knowing, broadly equated with scientific/technological and humanistic ways, a traditional dualism which the lecturer attempts to break down by redefining Reality. Second, to the special relationship between the lecturer and his nervous, psychosomatically ill son, who is riding the motorcycle with him, and whom he at last turns around to encounter. And third, to the book's investigation of madness, for, it is gradually revealed, the lecturer had once been judged insane as a result of expounding the same theories to which he now returns. He had been institutionalized and treated with massive electro-shock therapy, designed to kill the madman and create a calmer self. In part, this book is a pursuit of the madman through a retracing of his intellectual journey, till he is resurrected--a terrifying spector at first, because he exists outside of the conventional mythos, but finally an acceptable part of the new, merged, and elevated man.

Plath, Sylvia. The Bell Jar, 1963. London: Faber, 1966. Novel.

Adolescence	The Body	Death
Disease & Health	Doctors	Madness
Med. Instit.	Med. Students	Nurses
Preg. & Childbirth	Sexuality	Suicide

Not a good novel, but tempting as autobiography. This is a first-person account by one Esther Greenwood (Plath herself) of her 20th year, a bad one. Esther survives ptomaine, suicide attempts, hospitalization, shock treatment, at least one incompetent psychiatrist (Gordon--Dr. Nolan, a woman, is much better for her), several indifferent nurses, and a first sexual experience that results in a hemorrhage that has to be patched up in an emergency room. The sad thing is, one is never entirely sure why all this has happened to Esther. But there are, at any rate, some valuable views of medical matters along the way. Not all are directly related to her own illnesses: her boyfriend Buddy, for instance, a tubercular medical student takes her to the dissecting room (see also Plath's "Two Views of a Cadaver Room," The Colossus, Heinemann, 1960) and to a delivery (Chapter 6).

Plath, Sylvia. "Daddy." From Ariel. London: Faber, 1965. Poem: 80 lines.

| Children | Grief | Sexual Roles |
| Suicide | | |

The poet's daddy had died when she was ten, before she had time to resolve her Electra complex. She had tried to kill herself when she was 20, thinking even his bones would do. But now she announces to him, "You do not do, you do not do/Any more, black shoe/In which I have lived like a foot/For thirty years." The poem which follows is a good attempt: Daddy is a Nazi, I am a Jew; "Every woman adores a Fascist,/The boot in the face, the brute/Brute heart of a brute like you." She ends with a defiant scream: "Daddy, daddy, you bastard, I'm through." Even within the poem, one senses she hasn't quite made it. And after the poem? Plath killed herself.

Plath, Sylvia. "Fever 103°." From Ariel. London: Faber, 1965. Poem: 54 lines.

| Body/Mind | Disease & Health | Sexuality |

The speaker has been lying ill for 3 days and 3 nights. She has been "flickering, off, on, off, on" all night, through semi-delirious stages and images. She is burning up, so she thinks of hell's gates and newly snuffed candles, whose low smoke rolls away like Isadora Duncan's murderous scarfs and threatens the weak. From these images she moves to consider her spiritual state, which turns out to be a counterpart to her physical state. Hell: sin: is she pure? Yes: "The sheets grow heavy as a lecher's kiss . . . . I am too pure for you or anyone./Your body/Hurts me as the world hurts God. I am a lantern--/My head a moon/Of Japanese paper, my gold beaten skin/Infinitely delicate and infinitely expensive?/Does not my heat astound you. And my light." When last seen, she is "a pure acetylene Virgin," attended, in her feverish state, by some "pink things" and refining herself into Paradise.

Plath, Sylvia. "Lady Lazarus." From Ariel. London: Faber, 1965. Poem: 84 lines.

| The Body | Doctors | Sexual Roles |
| Suicide | | |

A sardonic view of the young poet's own suicide attempts, 3 in all, "one year in every ten." She sees herself as a Jew back from the gas chamber, not quite alive perhaps ("my skin/Bright as a Nazi lampshade, My right foot/A paperweight"), but definitely not dead this time ("The sour breath/Will vanish in a day"). She has enemies, all male. There's Herr Doktor, who stands over her thinking her comeback is his work. Or is it some other man she threatens? (See "Daddy.") "Herr God/Herr Lucifer/Beware/Beware./Out of the ash/I rise with my red hair/And I eat men like air." In any case, she takes a laughingly bitter attitude towards her proclivities: "Dying/Is an art, like everything else./I do it exceptionally well./I do it so it feels like hell./I do it so it feels real./I guess you could say I've a call."

Plath, Sylvia. "The Surgeon at 2 a.m." From Crossing the Water. London: Faber, 1971. Poem: 50 lines.

| The Body | Doctors | Med. Instit. |
| Surgery | | |

The speaker is the surgeon himself, who meditates on surgery, bodies, and his role in relation to the patients. For him, surgery is an art ("It is a statue the orderlies are wheeling off./I have perfected it"). Or, alternatively, he is a gardener, the body is a garden: "This is the lung-tree./These orchids are splendid. They spot and coil

like snakes./The heart is a red-bell-bloom in distress." (Cf. Richard Selzer). His patients are not individuals ("As usual there is no face. A lump of Chinese white/With seven holes thumbed in"). But their bodies are magical; what he does with them is rather magical too. "I am the sun, in my white coat,/Grey faces, shuttered by drugs, follow me like flowers." Also rather pompous.

Plath, Sylvia. "Thalidomide." From Winter Trees. London: Faber, 1971. Poem: 26 lines.

| The Body | Drugs | Preg. & Childbirth |

A mother's nightmare vision of the grotesqueries this drug produces. None of the images are perfectly whole, and that is, of course, appropriate: "Your dark/Amputations crawl and appal--/Spidery, unsafe." The vision ends. It does not vanish easily but--again appropriately--"aborts": "The dark fruits revolve and fall./The glass cracks across,/The image/Flees and aborts like dropped mercury."

Plath, Sylvia. "Three Women." From Winter Trees. London: Faber, 1971. Dramatic Poem: 371 lines.

| Doctors | Grief | Med. Instit. |
| Preg. & Childbirth | | |

Marvelous impressionistic rendering of three women's experiences of pregnancy. The three speak in turn from a maternity ward, and each shares certain imagery with the other: images of red and white, for instance, those frightening hospital colors. As women they have other common bonds too. But their attitudes toward child-bearing are clearly distinguished. The first woman luxuriates in the womanly serenity of her pregnancy: "When I walk out, I am a great event./I do not have to think, or even rehearse." And afterwards she loves her new son with wisdom and unselfishness: "I do not will him to be exceptional./It is the exception that interests the devil . . . . I will him to be common,/To love me as I love him,/And to marry what he wants and where he will." The third woman is a student. She is pregnant and unmarried and unprepared, identifying by inference with Leda, raped by Zeus. She scorns the doctors as representatives of men: "The doctors move among us as if our bigness/Frightened the mind. They smile like fools./They are to blame for what I am, and they know it./They hug their flatness like a kind of health./And what if they found themselves surprised, as I did?/They would go mad with it." After she has given up her baby, and returned to her freedom, she misses something all the same. Both women speak clearly of the pain of delivery and the babies who would clutch at them. The second woman has a miscarriage and always speaks in pitiful and frightening images of loss, death, and the leaking away of life. She "creates corpses." But it is she who ends the poem in a hopeful state: "I wait and ache. I think I have been healing."

Pohl, Frederik and C. M. Kornbluth. The Space Merchants, 1953 (appeared in a condensed version as Gravy Planet). New York: Ballantine Books, 1974. Novel.

| Drugs | Poverty & Health | Sci Fi |

Plot and characterizations dull and stereotyped--but the idea of manipulation of consumers by drug addiction is fascinating, especially as early as 1953. The large corporations addict consumers to drugs in their food and drink, then charge them again for "drying out." "I was hungry . . . I got Crunchies on easy credit. The Crunchies kicked off withdrawal symptoms that could be quelled only by another two squirts of Popsie from the fountain. And Popsie kicked off withdrawal symptoms that could be quelled by smoking Starr cigarettes, which made you hungry for Crunchies."

Porter, Katherine Anne. "He." From Flowering Judas and Other Stories. New York: Harcourt, Brace and Co., 1930. Short Story.

| Doctors | The Family | Mental Retardation |
| Poverty & Health | | |

"He" is the name--"Him" is his other one--of the mentally retarded son of a poor Southern farm family. His story is told from the point of view of his mother who tells herself that she loves Him more than her other two children, both girls, both healthy. Sure, she makes Him do all the difficult, even dangerous, chores, but He doesn't mind. Sure, she makes Him go without a jacket, but the girls need clothes more, and besides, He sits by the fire a lot. Inevitably, He gets sick, very sick, and after a time the doctor advises the family to send Him to the county home where He'll get good care and be off their hands. The mother worries mightily about how this will look to the neighbors, and finally even to Him, whose tear-filled eyes we see as the story ends.

Porter, Katherine Anne. "The Jilting of Granny Weatherall." From Flowering Judas and Other Stories. New York: Harcourt, Brace and Co., 1930. Short Story.

| Age | Death | Doctors |
| Dying | Grief | |

A devastating story about death. Eighty-year-old Ellen Weatherall lies on her deathbed, her thoughts all whirling together: she can't quite make out what her daughter is saying; the doctor treats her like a child; everybody acts as if she's blind and deaf. But what

irritates her more than that, grows in fact to a real
agony, is the sudden return of a memory of 60 years ago
when a young man had jilted her at the altar. She wants
to see him again and, hiding her grief, tell him that in
spite of what he did to her, she'd married and had
children. Into her mind whirls the thought that she's
dying, that her children have gathered to see her die,
and that now she'll find her dead daughter Hapsy again.
She begins the final process as Porter's prose winds
itself tighter. Granny Weatherall calls out for a sign
from God—she's been a good Catholic woman all her life—
where is He? "For the second time there was no sign.
Again no bridegroom and the priest in the house."

Porter, Katherine Anne. "Pale Horse, Pale Rider." From Pale Horse,
Pale Rider. New York: Harcourt, Brace and Co., 1937. Short
Story.

Death	Disease & Health	Doctors
Dying	Grief	Nurses
Plague		

An astonishing look at the process of dying, from the point
of view of a young woman who crosses the line, and comes
back. Stricken with the sort of flu that was being called
a plague late in the first world war, Miranda falls into
a delirious state, recorded convincingly by Porter, and
interspersed with exposition about Miranda's healthy state—
her job, her romance with Adam, a soldier. Miranda hears
herself babbling; she shouts in terror at Dr. Hildesheim
and Miss Tanner, the nurse; she dreams of a horse ride with
a stranger—who is Death. For, amazingly, Miranda does
seem to die. At first she thinks, "Death is death . . .
and for the dead it has no attribute." But then: "The
small waves rolled in and over unhurriedly, lapped upon
the sand in silence and retreated; the grasses flurried
before a breeze that made no sound. Moving towards her
leisurely as clouds through the shimmering air came a
great company of human beings, and Miranda saw in an
amazement of joy that they were all the living she had
known" (cf. Elisabeth Kübler-Ross' latest findings). She
doesn't get beyond her subjective control—or does she?—
and in any case she is, as Miss Tanner proudly puts it,
brought back from the brink of death. Now Miranda is
truly miserable, for she grieves for death. She remembers
"that bliss which had repaid all the pain of the journey
to reach it." She thinks, when she hears of Adam's death
from the flu, that he need not die again, but she feels
deceived at coming back and finding him gone.

Proust, Marcel. Remembrance of Things Past, 1913-1927. New York:
Modern Library, 1924-1932. Novel.

Age	Children	Death
Disease & Health	Homosexuality	Sexuality

This vast novel of some 4000 pages and seven separately
entitled volumes inevitably offers some medical insights.
Indeed it has been argued by critics who note that Proust's
father and brother were distinguished doctors that the
novel is constructed on scientific lines, that Proust is
searching for certain laws which will help him to construct
his universe in some meaningful way. The narrator's,
Marcel's, images of sexuality are for the most part adolescent and romantic, of homosexuality (in the case of the
Baron de Charlus) ultimately grotesque and pathetic. Illness comes into the picture quite often, for Marcel is
delicate and sickly as an adult, coming at one
point to enter a sanatorium, where all life seems to come
to a self-absorbed standstill. It is during sickness and
the insomnia which plagues him all his life that Marcel
often makes progress in his search for lost time (A la
recherche du temps perdu is the French title), and, of
course, it is that search and its success which makes the
novel the masterpiece that it is, for Proust not only
recaptures childhood with particular poignancy, he also
persuasively depicts the old age of the characters we've
met pages and novels back, and finally transcends death
when he achieves the moment which contains all moments,
past, present, and future.

Randall, Dudley. "George," 1969. Available in The Norton Anthology
of Modern Poetry, eds. Richard Ellmann and Robert O'Clair. New
York: Norton, 1973. Poem: 29 lines.

Age	Dying	Med. Instit.
Poverty & Health		

George is an old black man, waiting to die in the ward of
a public hospital among "the senile wrecks,/The psycho-
paths, the incontinent." There the speaker, who has
admired him since childhood when the man had told him
"You strong as a mule," visits him, observing "the look
of fright which the sight of death inspires." "'Don't
be afraid,' the speaker tells George, 'for you'll be
here/A long time yet, because you're strong as a mule.'"
Too contrived to be truly powerful, but treats a relatively
uncommon subject quite well.

Ransom, John Crowe. "Bells for John Whiteside's Daughter," 1924.
Available in Selected Poems, by Ransom, 3rd ed. New York:
Alfred A. Knopf, 1969. Poem: 20 lines.

The Body	Children	Grief

An elegy that depends for its final effect on the startling
and vividly accurate description of the dead body as a
"brown study." With deliberate casualness, the poet remembers the dead girl's lightness and speed when alive, the
way she warred against the geese in the orchard. No wonder
her body astonishes the mourners: "But now go the bells,
and we are ready,/In one house we are sternly stopped/To
say we are vexed at her brown study,/Lying so primly propped."

Ransom, John Crowe. "Here Lies a Lady," 1945. Available in Selected
Poems, by Ransom, 3rd ed. New York: Alfred A. Knopf, 1969.
Poem: 16 lines.

Disease & Health	Dying	Grief

The last days of a lady of "beauty and high degree." "Of
chills and fever she died, of fever and chills." The
second stanza shows the lady in a fevered, manic, state,
when she would tear cloths into shreds, perhaps in mourning
for herself already. In the third stanza, she is chilled
"like a thin stalk white and blown" (Ransom later changed
this line to what he thinks may be the saddest he ever
wrote: "Till she lay dishonored and wan like a rose
overblown"). During the sixth chill, she died: "the cold
settled down." The poet concludes that perhaps the lady
was lucky, for she has friends to mourn her and she died
rather quickly, "After six little spaces of chill, and
six of burning."

Réage, Pauline. The Story of O, 1954. London: The Olympia Press,
1970. Novel.

Homosexuality	Sexuality	Sexual Roles
Suffering		

There are a few homosexual scenes here, but they are not
central: O loves no one girl in particular, but is in
love "simply with girls because they were girls, the way
one can be in love with one's own image—always finding
the others more arousing and lovelier than one finds one's
own self." The real interest in this infamous novel is
the sadomasochism between O and the lover to whom she is
utterly devoted and enslaved. As a member of a secret
circle of sexually sadistic men, her lover inflicts
humiliation, pain, and degradation on O—and she adores
it. She wants nothing more than to know she belongs
completely to her lover, and that he thinks only of his
own pleasure. O's suffering and pain becomes his pleasure,
and, finally, hers. The book has incited a lot of pious
pornographers to write a lot of pompous nonsense. Still,
it remains a well-written, fascinating story which almost
obliges the reader to accept it on its own terms.

Rechy, John. City of Night. New York: Grove Press, 1964. Novel;
and Selby, Hubert. Last Exit to Brooklyn. New York: Grove
Press, 1965. Novel.

Drugs	Homosexuality	Sexuality

Rechy is the novelistic source of accurate information
about—and compassionate depiction of—the homosexual
hustlers in big American cities. For the most part, they
live with the drug scene and violence, and without love,
though searching constantly for it. Selby's infamous
novel is also a plunge into the nighttime, nightmare world
of violence and sex, in this case, both heterosexual and
homosexual life, giving even more attention than Rechy does
to the drag queens. For both authors, their characters
seem to be screwing themselves to death.

Remarque, Erich Maria. Arch of Triumph. New York: Appleton-
Century, 1945. Novel.

Abortion	Children	Death
Disease & Health	Doctors	Dying
Euthanasia	Grief	Madness
Med. Ethics	Med. Instit.	Nurses
Poverty & Health	Sexuality	Sexual Roles
V.D.		

A good read: plenty of action, including a revenge murder,
plus a love story which hovers nicely between cynicism and
sentimental melodrama. Set in Paris on the eve of World
War II, the novel has for a hero a German surgeon, calling
himself Ravic, who is illegally in France and therefore able
to perform only secret "ghost" operations for two French
surgeons and to substitute for one of them as a V.D. checker
at a brothel. Ravic's repressed grief for a woman killed
by a psychopathic gestapo member has driven him into a
rather emotionless state—sex has become an unthinking
function—but gradually he reawakens in the arms of Joan,
another grief-stricken person. He is intriguing as a man
certainly, but also as a member of a symbolic profession,
particularly important during war time. As women supervise love, he says once, doctors supervise death. On
another occasion, he goes gladly from war-dominated Paris
to his work: "The hospital was a cheerful place in comparison . . . . Here too was pain, sickness, and misery; but
here at least it had some logic and sense . . . . These
were facts: one could see them and one could try to do
something about them" (trans. Walter Sorell and Denver
Lindley). And so he does: Ravic performs many operations,
and most are carefully detailed. There are several abortions, ending in one instance with a visit to the woman
who botched the job in the first place—a mean but rather
business-like sort. There is an amputation of the leg of
a poor young boy who turns out to be very glad to have the
insurance money. There is the cancer of a woman close to
Ravic. And an operation on Joan herself, who begs to be
killed rather than suffer for several more hours. Eventually a cruel, lippy nurse—Eugénie—denounces Ravic to the
police, and at the end of the novel he stands before them
pronouncing his real name for the first time.

Rhys, Jean. Voyage in the Dark. New York: W. W. Norton, 1975.
Novel.

Abortion	Sexuality	Sexual Roles

Anna Morgan is representative of all the Jean Rhys heroines,
young women who are weak, unprotected, and pliant to the
point of submissive masochism. Everywhere Anna goes, there

are men and women eager to exploit her. Their motives are mixed, but they are usually sexual or financial. Her motives are even more unclear, but they seem to spring from a feeling of homelessness (she is in England, far from her homeland in the West Indies) and a need for love of a rather parental sort. Sometimes she just needs money, so she lets men buy her things and take her places in return for her favors--and ultimately her happiness. We last see this pathetic sexual victim suffering the pains of an abortion performed by a woman who starts off a process which ends two weeks later. A doctor appears briefly to tidy up and observes of Anna and her kind: "You girls are too naive to live." When it is all over, Anna lies watching a ray of light under the bedroom door: "I lay and watched it and thought about starting all over again, all over again . . . ." A painfully ambiguous future.

Richards, I. A. "Science and Poetry," 1926, 1935. Available in Poetries and Sciences. New York: Norton, 1970. Essay.

Science & Poetry

See Snow, C. P. "The Two Cultures."

Rilke, Rainer Maria. "The Blind Man's Song," "The Drinker's Song," "The Idiot's Song," "The Suicide's Song," "The Dwarf's Song," and "The Leper's Song," 1906. Available in Selected Works, by Rilke. Vol. II: Poetry, trans. J. B. Leishman. New York: New Directions, 1960. Short Poems.

Alcoholism   Disease & Health   Handicaps
Mental Retardation Suicide

These poems come from "The Voices"--several songs by afflicted people. The blind man cannot handle his problem. It daily exceeds him. We, though, have "a feeling of face-to-face,/and that makes for self-protection." The alcoholic tells how he came to trust wine. "Now I'm in its power, and it flings me at will/about and about and is losing me still/to Death, that son of a bitch." On the whole, the retarded person sings a song of well-being, though everything from his perspective is a little confusing: "All's behaving in such a remarkable way,/ now drifting together, now swimming away." The suicide doesn't seem particularly depressed. It's just that he can't digest life, and already had a little eternity in his guts when they cut him down the last time. The dwarf's poem is perhaps the best. He declares that his soul is straight, though his body is crooked. His body disgusts him: "My hands too will always be failing me./ How hopelessly stunted they are you can see:/damp, heavy, hopping contrictedly/like little toads in wet weather." He wonders if God isn't angry with him for his ugly face. The leper tells how he must rattle his warning chain, and can thus not see anyone for years at a time.

Rilke, Rainer Maria. The Book of Poverty and Death, 1905. Available in Selected Works, by Rilke. Vol. I: Poetry, trans. J. B. Leishman. New York: New Directions, 1960. Short Poems.

Death   Poverty & Health

Among the 34 poems in this series are several powerful evocations of death, particularly the sort faced by the neglected poor. Poem no. 5, for instance, pictures the beating taken by the poor: "To hundreds of tormenting hands submitted,/and screamed at by the strokes of every hour,/they anxiously await to be admitted/into the hospitals around which they cower./In there is Death." In the last lines there is a sense that their death would be welcome but can't come forth: "their own is hanging sourly and greenly/like fruit in them whose ripening won't begin." Everywhere the poor "hotly shiver as in fever-crises" (no. 32).

Robinson, E. A. "Miniver Cheevy," 1910; "Mr. Flood's Party," 1921. Available in Chief Modern Poets of Britain and America, 5th ed., Vol II, eds. Gerald DeWitt Sanders, et al. London: Macmillan Co., 1970. Poems: 32 and 56 lines.

Age   Alcoholism

Two relatively casual looks at small-town drinkers. The first is even rather funny. Miniver Cheevy, something of a Don Quixote figure, loves the days of old, and feels contemptuously out of place in the vulgar modern age. The poem ends: "Miniver Cheevy, born too late,/Scratched his head and kept on thinking;/Miniver coughed, and called it fate,/And kept on drinking." The second is a sad, Robert Browning sort of poem in which Old Eben Flood stops alone on a hill overlooking the town, and has a party with himself, taking both parts in a dialogue. He drinks from his jug and sings "Auld Lang Syne": "There was not much that was ahead of him,/And there was nothing in the town below--/Where strangers would have shut the many doors/ That many friends had opened long ago."

Robinson, E. A. "Richard Cory," 1897. Available in Chief Modern Poets of Britain and America, 5th ed., Vol. II, eds. Gerald DeWitt Sanders, et al. London: Macmillan Co., 1970. Poem: 16 lines.

Suicide

A jaunty little song about the favored Richard Cory, who has riches, grace, attractiveness--everything, as it seems to the "people on the pavement." "So on we worked, and waited for the light,/And went without the meat, and cursed the bread;/And Richard Cory, one calm summer night,/Went home and put a bullet through his head."

Roethke, Theodore. "Elegy for Jane: My Student, Thrown by a Horse," 1951-1953. From Words for the Wind. New York: Doubleday, 1959. Poem: 22 lines.

Grief

More controlled and a little less subjective, than other Roethke grief poems. Jane is remembered as a bird--a wren, a sparrow, a skittery pigeon--one whom nature loved. But the subject of this elegy is not, finally, Jane, but the poet himself. Now that she is dead, nature, though sympathetic to his grief (as in traditional elegies), cannot aid him: "The sides of wet stones cannot console me./Nor the moss, wound with the last light." His grief is all the more moving for being expressed by a mourner whom most would regard as peripheral: "Over this damp grave I speak the words of my love:/I, with no rights in this matter,/Neither father nor lover."

Roethke, Theodore. "Epidermal Macabre," 1941. From Words for the Wind. New York: Doubleday, 1959. Poem: 16 lines.

The Body

Roethke is often humiliated by his body ("The veil long violated by/Caresses of the hand and eye"), but in this case, it is only the outside he rejects, the parts that can be touched. He knows that it is "indelicate," but he hates "the rags of my anatomy" and the "false accouterments of sense," and wishes to throw them off "To sleep immodestly, a most/Incarnadine and carnal ghost." So it seems that for Roethke the carnal is deeper, less superficial, than we know. And rather shockingly attractive as well.

Roethke, Theodore. "Heard in a Violent Ward" and "In a Dark Time," 1964. Available in The Norton Anthology of Modern Poetry, eds. Richard Ellmann and Robert O'Clair. New York: Norton, 1973. Poems: 7 and 24 lines.

Madness

Roethke on madness, his own and others'. In the first poem, he muses that even in heaven he'd probably be institutionalized, but that would be all right if he'd share the place with those 3 mad English poets--William Blake, Christopher Smart, "And that sweet man, John Clare." In short, the common poetic view that madness is goodness. This idea becomes more explicit and broader in the second poem: "What's madness but nobility of soul/At odds with circumstance?" He goes deeper into his own moods of despair, and wonders which is the real Self, his darkened self or his rising, hoping self: "My soul, like some heat-maddened summer fly,/Keeps buzzing at the sill. Which I is I?" Finally--almost, one might say, as a direct result of the mad split--the speaker achieves an ecstatic union of his two selves and then with God, all this held together and liberated by soaring nature: "The mind enters itself, and God the mind,/And one is One, free in the tearing wind."

Roethke, Theodore. "My Papa's Waltz," 1948. From Words for the Wind. New York: Doubleday, 1959. Poem: 16 lines.

Alcoholism   Children

Roethke writes children's poetry, and though this one is written in easy, swinging rhythms, it is decidedly for adults only; for this waltz, if not precisely a dance macabre, is very frightening. The poet remembers a time when his tipsy father danced him around without regard to a child's pain, both physical and mental: "The whiskey on your breath/Could make a small boy dizzy;/But I hung on like death:/Such waltzing was not easy . . . . "You beat time on my head/With a palm caked hard by dirt,/Then waltzed me off to bed/Still clinging to your shirt."

Roethke, Theodore. "Old Lady's Winter Words," 1951-1953, and Meditations of an Old Woman, 1959. From Words for the Wind. New York: Doubleday, 1959. Poem: 65 lines; and Poem Sequence.

Adolescence   Age   The Body
Death

The first poem is bitter and tough; the other poems, finally triumphant. The first is a persuasive blending of images and statements. The old lady says, for instance, "my ardors sleep in a sleeve," and "I've become a sentry of small seeds." She's "half-dead," and longing "for some minstrel of what's to be." Hearing none, knowing that "the good day has gone," the old lady prepares herself: "I fall, more and more,/Into my own silences./In the cold air,/The spirit/Hardens." It could be the same woman speaking in the second set of poems, for she too sees age in images from nature--weeds, winds--but this time she fights harder. Inevitably, she contemplates her changed body: "How can I rest in the days of my slowness?/I've become a strange piece of flesh,/Nervous and cold, bird-furtive, whiskery,/With a cheek soft as a hound's ear." And her youth: "So much of adolescence is an ill-defined dying,/An intolerable waiting,/A longing for another place and time,/Another condition." But, though she journeys back in time, her spirit gradually journeys forward. "It is difficult to say all things are well,/When the worst is about to arrive," she acknowledges, but the imminent arrival of death notwithstanding, she feels reborn. These images contrast with the earlier withered ones: "I'm thick with leaves and tender as a dove." At last: "I recover my tenderness by long looking."

Roth, Philip. The Breast. New York: Holt, Rinehart and Winston, 1972. Novella.

The Body	Doctors	Madness
Med. Instit.	Nurses	Sexuality

Kafka's Gregor Samsa woke up one morning to find himself a giant insect. Roth's David Kepesh, professor of comparative literature, wakes up to find himself a six-foot female breast. At first what a fantasy come true! For now he experiences sexual pleasure over all his "body" as a woman can. Then what terror! He comes to believe that he is mad; that he has such a strong psychic delusion that it has affected his body; that the hospital in which he finds himself is a mental hospital. But it's not true-- he's a breast, and he might as well make the best of it. Nurses attend him gently, but he just lusts for them. Doctors are kind if, especially his analyst, maddeningly scientific and calm. All in all, an intriguing conception, but more fun to talk about than to read.

Roth, Philip. "Epstein," 1959. From Goodbye, Columbus. New York: Modern Library, 1966. Short Story.

Age	The Body	Disease & Health
Doctors	The Family	Grief
Sexuality	V.D.	

A comic and moving story. A 59-year-old man, his only son dead years ago, his wife, once beautiful, but now a bunch of sagging flesh, his ebbing sexuality re-awakened by the active sex life led by his unattractive daughter and by his nephew in the living room--this man, Lou Epstein decides one day to grab at life in the person of the jolly widow across the street. But one other day a rash appears in his groin. His wife sees it and screams. His daughter sees it, ditto. And her boyfriend too, and Epstein's nephew. All condemn him. No one understands him, except the widow in whose arms that very afternoon he suffers a heart attack. The wife, of course, sees him being carried from the house, and is reunited with him in the ambulance, where she learns from the doctor that a man of Lou's age shouldn't be carrying on like a boy. The heart attack is not so serious to Lou's wife as the rash. Can the doctor cure that? Yes, he says, it's just an irritation, and it can be fixed so that it will never come back. (And so Lou Epstein enters old age.)

Roth, Philip. Portnoy's Complaint. New York: Random House, 1969. Novel.

Adolescence	Children	Doctors
The Family	Madness	Sexuality
V.D.		

An hilarious and significant expansion of the classic Jewish mother joke complete with the sexually maladjusted kid. Alex Portnoy is the kid, whom Roth follows from his adolescence, which is dominated by an intrusive, insensitive mother who plays the Oedipal game for all its worth and passively observed by a constipated father. If those are the characters of his adolescence, the action is all masturbation. When Alex grows into adulthood, he finds that he cannot leave off being a child. Especially he cannot treat women well, except perhaps in bed, but even there he is all lust and no tenderness. At the end of the novel he is in Israel, believes he has V.D., and meeting a Jewish girl who looks just as his mother did, first hates her for her superior hard-to-get attitude-- thinking at one point that he'd revenge himself by giving her gonorrhea--and then, when she is perhaps on the verge of capitulation, finding himself impotent. The whole story hangs together very well from a psychiatric point of view. And that's just the view we get. All along, the novel has taken the form of a monologue addressed to Alex's psychiatrist. But at the very end, we learn, through what Roth has labeled a "punchline," that Alex has so far been able to tell this story only to himself. "Punchline: So [said the doctor]. Now vee may perhaps to begin. Yess?"

Russ, Joanna. "When It Changed." Available in Again, Dangerous Visions, ed. Harlan Ellison. Garden City, New York: Doubleday & Co., 1972. Short Story.

Sci Fi   Sexual Roles

Recently science fiction writers have begun exploration of sexual roles (see LeGuin). This short story is one of the best feminist statements, period. On the planet Whileaway, all the men are destroyed by a plague; the women reproduce by parthenogenesis and set up a full civilization with true equality. And then the men return.

Russell, Robert. To Catch an Angel. New York: Vanguard, 1962. Autobiography.

Handicaps

Well-written autobiography of a man who was blinded at the age of 5. One comes to accept the man as adaptable and tough, a prevailer rather than a mere endurer. A lover of literature--he ends, in fact, as a professor--the book gives evidence of the integral place of literature in his life. Many details about how a man who cannot see (the phrase he prefers) gets about. Moreover, the author contends that in his blindness we can recognize a symbol of our own hesitating, uncertain progress in a world we can't fully see.

Sackville-West, V. All Passion Spent, 1931. London: Hogarth Press, 1965. Novel.

Age	Death	The Family
Grief	Sexual Roles	

Lord Slane, statesman, has died, aged over 90, leaving as his widow a very remarkable old lady of 88. Not that her remarkable qualities had always been evident. Lady Slane had married at the age of 18, had given up hopes of a career as an artist to do so, and for 70 years had simply been Henry's wife and for most of that time, a mother to six children, who gather at the beginning of the novel to discuss how to dispose of their mother. Only Kay and Edith are at all likeable, even to a mother. And the old lady surprises them all by deciding to live on her own, truly on her own for the first time in her life. No conventional grief for her, but at last a life freed from a devoted but self-centered man. In the short time left to her, Lady Slane discovers, to her delight, that at a great age sweet, fulfilling relationships are still possible. She has sweet friendships with two men of a different social class from hers, who love her gallantly. She forms a mutually admiring friendship with her great-granddaughter, whom she advises to be the musician she wants to be, never sacrificing herself for a husband. A rather elegant book, really, on an unusual theme for its day--or for ours, for that matter.

Salinger, J.D. The Catcher in the Rye. Boston: Little, Brown, & Co., 1951. Novel.

Adolescence	Children	Death
Grief	Homosexuality	Madness
Med. Profession	Sexuality	

One of the best, or at least one of the most popular, studies of an adolescent, in this case, 16-year-old Holden Caulfield, unpopular, uneasy, and finally mentally ill. Since the novel is written in the first person, one sometimes feels close to Holden's pain; but since he is funny kid, one also laughs at him. The book takes the form of a descent into the City of New York, where Holden undergoes something of a classic quest for identity, attempting, as he does so, to escape the "stupid" and "phoney" situations he sees everywhere. He tries to assert his sexuality, thinking himself the only "normal bastard" in a hotel full of perverts, but he ends by sending the prostitute out of his room. He calls on a former teacher, but the man makes a play for him. He thinks of his family, but that makes him recall the death of his young brother Allie, whose buried body Holden imagines getting wet during rainy days. There's really only his kid sister Phoebe, who is innocent and good and smart. To her, he tells his vision of what he'd like to be when he grows up. He sees himself standing in a field of rye at the edge of a cliff with thousands of kids running towards him, and only he to catch them, to save them. Poignant, for there is no one to catch Holden now. Also perhaps "crazy," as he himself says. At any rate, we learn on the last page that Holden has broken down, that the novel has been a story told from a bed in a mental hospital. The medical profession is represented briefly, but significantly, in this way: "A lot of people, especially this one psychoanalyst guy they have here, keep asking me if I'm going to apply myself when I go back to school next September. It's such a stupid question . . . ."

Sarton, May. As We Are Now. New York: Norton, 1973. Novel.

Age	Dying	Euthanasia
Nurses	Poverty & Health	Suffering
Women as Patients		

The novel takes the form of a journal kept by Caro Spencer, a 78-year-old former teacher, who has been left to end her days in a farmhouse-nursing home, run by a vulgar and insensitive woman. The woman is not a licensed nurse, but fulfills some of those functions, and is a good contrast, in this respect, to Mrs. Close, a substitute whom Caro comes to love desparately. Caro's situation and that of the male welfare patients is almost unspeakably horrible. Another man, a private patient like Caro, dies dreadfully alone, while his aged wife lies dying many miles away. At last, in an attempt to salvage what remains of her independent humanness and to end the suffering of the patients and--yes--to revenge herself, Caro burns the place down at a time when no fire engine can reach it.

Sarton, May. Mrs. Stevens Hears the Mermaids Singing, 1965. New York: Norton Library, 1975. Novel.

Age	Children	Doctors
Grief	Homosexuality	Madness
Med. Instit.	Nurses	Sexual Roles

A portrait of the artist as a tough old lady. Asked to do a comprehensive interview with a couple of journalists, a poet, famous for the first time now that she is in her seventies, takes this opportunity to think back over her loves and their relationship to her work. There had been one early marriage, ending after only 3 years, from which she recovered in a hospital. There, a psychiatrist, with whom she falls in love, teaches her that for a person with such intense emotions, it would be well to concentrate on objects for a time. He helps her to make a cosmos out of the hospital room where she must be confined for months. During this period she also falls in love with a nurse, though the two don't know each other well, and later with other women too, partly because the Muse is always a woman, partly out of some more physical sexual need. One theme emerges most clearly from this novel, and that is that for a woman to be an artist, she must also be somewhat hard and selfish, or else she is in danger of being swept away by all those mundane chores a woman is expected to do, all those needs she is expected to meet. But a woman has a special strength as an artist too: it is her task to make things whole: the intellect, the senses, the imagination must never be separated (Sarton could have taken this theme from Virginia Woolf, whom she knew), and all these must join together in a celebration of life. After the interview, she tells Mar (a young Amherst student who is having problems with his homosexuality and the possible relationship of art to risky love), that she is at last, at her advanced age, ready to deal with the subject of her mother. Life has been hard for Mrs. Stevens, but she has always remained true to the song of the mermaids; she has taken chances: she has honed some good poems out of her experiences. The book is a bit preachy in a feminist way and a bit egotistic too, but very insightful on some unusual topics.

Sartre, Jean-Paul. "The Room," 1939. Available in Great French Short Stories, ed. Germaine Brée. New York: Dell, 1960. Short Story.

Madness   Sexuality

A frightening little story about the usurpation by the ill of the freedoms of the healthy on whom they depend. Or is it the other way around? Eve lives with her mad husband Pierre in a room, from which he never stirs, and which she leaves only rarely and always with a feeling of fear and alienation. Her father urges her to put Pierre in a hospital--he has a nice one all picked out--but she is moving farther and farther away from the world he inhabits. And he, thinking of what his wife told him--that Eve still sleeps with Pierre--tells her that she is becoming mad. Perhaps she is. At any rate, she lives uncomfortably between two worlds, but keeps finding herself coming closer to Pierre's, especially now that he could at any time slip into total insanity. She thinks to herself that she'd kill him first; she's that anxious to keep contact with him.

Schnitzler, Arthur. A Confirmed Bachelor, 1924. Available in Vienna 1900: Games with Love and Death, by Schnitzler. Harmonds-worth, England: Penguin Books, n.d. (Also published as Dr. Graesler.) Novel.

Age   By Doctors   Disease & Health
Doctors   Grief   Med. Instit.
Nurses   Sexuality   Suicide

Dr. Graesler is by no means old, but he is aging, and that fact, coupled with his sister's suicide, leaves him feeling bitter and lonely. He obviously needs to fall in love, and in the course of this novel he does so--with three women. The first, a sensible young woman, who has been a nurse and would be a help to him in running the sanitarium he proposes to buy, scares him off by making the first overtures. He is really something of a prig. That doesn't prevent him from having a brief affair with a somewhat common girl and throwing her off when he decides to return to the first one. When she rejects him, he "realizes" that he has been in love with the second all along, and rushes back to her, just in time to attend her in her last illness, scarlet fever. Now he has never felt more alone. He is embittered against his profession, for it is through him that his girlfriend has contracted scarlet fever. He feels guilty. He feels enraged that all three women--his girlfriends and his sister too--have left him. Nonetheless, a month later he marries the mother of one of the patients he has successfully treated. Clearly, Schnitzler, a doctor and the son of a famous doctor, knows a good deal about complicated illnesses and the human condition in general, particularly human sexuality. A student of neuroses and psychotherapy, he was one of the first to incorporate the Viennese findings in psychiatry into literature.

Schnitzler, Arthur. La Ronde, 1912. Available in Masters of Modern Drama, eds. Haskell M. Block and Robert G. Shedd. New York: Random House, 1962. (Also published as Reigen and Hands Around.) Drama.

By Doctors   Sexuality

This famously scandalous play consists of ten dialogues, as the playwright would have it, or simply a series of ten sexual encounters, as the audience usually sees it. It is all a marvelous joke, for first a whore sleeps with a soldier, then the soldier sleeps with a maid, then the maid sleeps with a young gentleman, and then he, in turn . . . and so on through a wife, a husband, a sweet young miss, a poet, an actress, and a count--who sleeps with the whore from scene one. Very amusing and very sexy too, except that everyone from working-girl to aristocrat, is manipulating, self-deceiving, and egocentric. So this, Schnitzler seems to be saying here, is Love revealed.

Schnitzler, Arthur. "The Man of Honour," 1929. Available in Vienna 1900: Games with Love and Death, by Schnitzler. Harmondsworth, England: Penguin Books, n.d. (Also published as "The Murderer.") Short Story.

By Doctors   Disease & Health   Dying
Madness   Sexuality   Suicide

The title is ironic. A barrister who has lived for some time with a sweet, devoted, but common girl, finds that he has fallen in love with a young woman more suited to his social standing. Becoming more and more obsessed with the second woman, Adele, he takes advantage of the first's, Elise's, heart condition to pretend that she has died of

natural causes when he has in fact overdosed her with morphine. The desire to murder overtakes him gradually. At first, he even tells himself when, against the doctor's orders, he makes love to Elise, that she would be glad to die beneath his kisses. When at last he admits to his wishes to be rid of her, he watches her die, then at once convinces himself that he has done a noble thing, something which Adele will approve, such is his obsession with his own virtue. But when Adele rejects him and a friend of Elise's, suspecting the murder, challenges the barrister to a duel, he accepts, telling himself that he is profoundly in love with Elise after all, and that after his certain death, he will return to her, having honorably atoned for his mistakes. Though the murder and the suicide by duelling are extravagant acts, Schnitzler shows profound insight into a human being's handling of needs and his ability to rationalize.

Schnitzler, Arthur. Mother and Son, 1926. Available in Vienna 1900: Games with Love and Death, by Schnitzler. Harmondsworth, England: Penguin Books, n.d. (Also published as Beatrice.) Novella.

Adolescence   By Doctors   Children
Grief   Sexuality   Suicide

An intense, profound exploration of the sexual attraction between a young, widowed mother and her teen-aged son. At first, this seems to be the story of the reawakening of sexuality in a conventional bourgeois woman whose grief and the accompanying guilt prevent her from feeling her own desires. When she learns that her beloved son is attracted to a well-known middle-aged seductress, she visits the woman, begging her to leave the son alone. She believes she is acting only to protect her son, and at this stage the reader only suspects that this is not the whole truth. Later Beatrice allows herself to be seduced by a young friend of her son. When the youth brags about his conquest, she feels cheapened. But the knowledge of her full sexuality does not come until mother and son confront one another with their disgust about the other's love affair. The confrontation is indirect but powerfully erotic. The young man has slept with an older woman, his mother with a young man. Now, realizing the truth about themselves they must die, in the tradition, one might say, of all great and impossible loves.

Schnitzler, Arthur. My Youth in Vienna, 1915-18. New York: Holt, Rinehart and Winston, Inc., 1970. Autobiography.

By Doctors   Doctors   Med. Profession
Med. Students   Sexuality

The autobiography of an excellent physician-writer, and therefore valuable. But the book is by no means a first-rate example of the genre. Nor does it even include many observations about medicine, though the period covered takes the author through his medical training and the early years of his professional practice. In short, this autobiography is by no means on a par with William Carlos Williams'. Still, Schnitzler's stories of his sexual adventures--and they dominate the book--provide insights into the sexuality he creates so well in his fiction. His own behavior, for instance, is distressingly like that of some of his unattractive characters'. He struts; he brags; he exploits. And from time to time, he becomes floridly romantic. The few comments he does make about medicine, the doctors he encounters (including his father, who was a distinguished laryngologist), and his training are of some interest and use. Viennese medicine of his day was flourishing, after all. Perhaps most interesting is the story, told by indirection, of how a young man with artistic aspirations gets through medical schools when at first medicine doesn't much interest him, though always at bottom his "noblest thoughts" return to the profession.

Schnitzler, Arthur. Professor Bernhardi, 1912, trans. Hetty Landstone. New York: Simon & Schuster, 1928; rpt. New York: AMS Press, 1971. Drama.

Doctors   Dying   Med. Ethics
Med. Instit.   Nurses

Not an especially good play when compared with An Enemy of the People, which it vaguely resembles, but important nonetheless because it's Schnitzler's, it uses an interesting theme, and downright remarkable because 14 of its 19 characters are doctors. Another is a nurse, a woman, and her relationship to the authority of the doctors plays a pivotal part in the plot, but the play as a whole is overwhelmingly medical and masculine. Professor Bernhardi is a social problem play, again like Ibsen, the problem in this case being anti-semitism. Bernhardi, a Jew, and his associates, several of whom are also Jewish, run a highly successful clinic in Vienna. Early in the play a seemingly minor incident becomes major: a young woman, dying with septicemia, has been given a drug which induces euphoria. When a priest arrives to give her the last rites, Bernhardi refuses to allow his patient to be disturbed, wanting her to die happily. Of course, the priest disagrees as to what "dying happily" means. The nurse, choosing allegiance to religion and the priest over her duty to medicine and the doctor, sneaks the priest into the patient's room, but the woman dies, just after she realizes why the priest has come. The incident becomes a city-wide scandal; the press abuses Professor Bernhardi; his Advisory Board resigns; he is even brought to trial and jailed for "religious disturbance." The doctors and the officials choose sides, and Schnitzler shows us several types--competent and incompetent physicians, honest and hypocritical ones, those who are compassionate and those who don't care at all. Bernhardi himself demonstrates absolute honesty, sometimes to the point of rudeness, it might be argued. At the end, he is being taken up as a hero of the left, but the question of to what extent doctors must take risks for their convictions, to what extent, that is, they must be social reformers, is still being debated.

Schnitzler, Arthur. The Spring Sonata, 1914. Available in Vienna 1900: Games with Love and Death, by Schnitzler. Harmondsworth, England: Penguin Books, n.d. (Also published as Bertha Garlan.) Novel.

By Doctors   Disease & Health   Preg. & Childbirth
Sexuality   Sexual Roles   Suicide

The sub-plot concerns a youngish man who has an affliction which has paralyzed him and will, it seems, kill him fairly soon. Perhaps it is multiple sclerosis. At any rate, his wife finds that she must seek sexual fulfillment elsewhere, thereby tormenting the man, who fears that she will leave him. When she becomes pregnant--apparently her lover won't have her in that condition--she kills herself in shame, declaring at the end that truly she loved only her husband. This story is interwoven with that of Bertha Garlan, a young widow, who discovers her sexual needs for perhaps the first time in her life when she reads that a former suitor, now a famous violinist, is back in Vienna. Schnitzler skillfully reveals her fantasy life and, eventually, her willing capitulation to the violinist. She dreams of giving up all conventions for him, but when she discovers that what he has in mind is a once-a-month assignation, she feels cheap, and concludes that though both men and women have sexual desires, it is a sin when the woman gives in to such desires without the simultaneous yearning for motherhood (cf. Mortimer, The Pumpkin-Eater). God will catch up with a wanton woman sooner or later, as he had caught up with the wife of the paralyzed man. Partly out of compassion, but more probably out of a sense of guilt, she turns at the end to devote herself to the afflicted widower.

Selby, Hubert. Last Exit to Brooklyn. New York: Grove Press, 1965. Novel.

Homosexuality

See Rechy, John.

Selzer, Richard. The Rituals of Surgery. New York: Harper's Magazine Press, 1974. Short Stories.

Age   The Body   By Doctors
Disease & Health   Doctors   Madness
Med. Instit.   Nurses   Sexuality
Surgery

Written by a doctor who views surgery as a powerful, passionate ritual, and the surgeon as something of a priest, this collection of short stories demonstrates medicine in its magical, compulsively grotesque aspects, as well as in its more realistic modes. For instance: a story in which the narrator lovingly describes the procedure for removing a human brain, and then does it ("Museum Piece"). For instance: a story in which a middle-aged nurse and a young orderly make love in a morgue ("A Blue Ribbon Affair"). For instance, a bizarre, hilarious story set in 16th-century Italy in which an aristocrat first has a nose grafted for him from the arm of a slave, and then loses it ("The Sympathetic Nose"). There is a story about the pathetic but finally forbidden return of sexual yearnings to an old husband ("The Harbinger"); one about a surgeon who finds a lump in the breast of a prostitute while he is making love to her ("The Consultation"); one about a man who is convinced that he has a plant growing inside him ("Myself Healed"). He seems to be mad, but by this time--it is the last story in the collection--one has an expanded idea of sanity. Above all, one has a profound sense of the fascination with which Dr. Selzer views--no, immerses himself in--the body.

Sewell, Elizabeth. The Orphic Voice: Poetry and Natural History, 1960. New York: Harper & Row, 1971. Essay.

Science & Poetry

See Snow, C. P. "The Two Cultures."

Sexton, Anne. "All My Pretty Ones." From All My Pretty Ones. Boston: Houghton Mifflin, 1962. Poem: 50 lines.

Grief

Inspired by the death of the poet's father, who died just three months after her mother. The poet goes through her father's effects, turning over this old photograph, that revealing diary, coming to terms with her father and his weaknesses. But it is not only for his weaknesses--it is also for his dying itself--that she forgives him in the last lines, alluding to Macduff's mourning speech: "Whether you are pretty or not, I outlive you,/bend down my strange face to yours and forgive you."

Sexton, Anne. "The Ballad of the Lonely Masturbator." From Love Poems. Boston: Houghton Mifflin Co., 1969. Poem: 42 lines.

Sexuality

A woman lies alone, thinking of her former lover, loving herself this time. The images are desperately exact: "Finger to finger, now she's mine./She's not too far. She's my encounter./I beat her like a bell . . . . I am spread out. I crucify./My little plum is what you said." This is a ballad; there is a refrain, sounding a little more defeated each time: "At night, alone, I marry the bed."

Sexton, Anne. "The Breast." From Love Poems. Boston: Houghton Mifflin Co., 1969. Poem: 40 lines.

Adolescence   The Body   Sexuality

A proud consciousness of one's own body, rare in women writers until quite recently (see also Sexton's "In Celebration of My Uterus"). The poem is a series of images tossed between the speaker's memory of her adolescent body ("years ago/when I lived in the valley of my bones . . . A xylophone maybe with skin/stretched over it awkwardly . . . . Later I measured my size against movie stars. I didn't measure up. Something between/my shoulders was there. But never enough.") and her excitement in the adult body approached by her lover ("So tell me anything but track me like a climber/for here is the eye, here is the jewel,/here is the excitement the nipple learns").

Sexton, Anne. "Doctors." From The Awful Rowing Toward God. New York: Houghton Mifflin Co., 1975. Poem: 30 lines.

Med. Profession

Not a particularly good poem, nor particularly intense, considering that Anne Sexton had to do with doctors often in her life. In the first part of the poem, the doctors are rather gentle people: "But all along the doctors remember: /First do no harm./They would kiss if it would heal./It would not heal." In the second part, there is a slight turning, beginning with this conventional wisdom: "If the doctors cure/then the sun sees it./If the doctors kill/then the earth hides it"; and ending with lines which only take on their true value within Sexton's larger theme of God's intricate interest in people: "The doctors should fear arrogance/more than cardiac arrest./If they are too proud,/and some are,/then they leave home on horseback/but God returns them on foot."

Sexton, Anne. "For the Year of the Insane," 1963. From Live or Die. Boston: Houghton Mifflin, 1966; and "The Sickness Unto Death." From The Awful Rowing Toward God. Boston: Houghton Mifflin, 1975. Poems: 80 and 42 lines.

Death   Madness   Med. Instit.
Women as Healers

The first poem is a prayer uttered by someone, presumably Sexton herself, in the midst of a terrible, despairing paralysis. No Catholic, she nonetheless turns to Mary as both a "tender physician" and a "little mother." She lies on the floor, "ugly/submerged in my own past/and my own madness," awaiting, in words which echo the Hail Mary, "the hour of my death." A frightening portrait of mental illness (is it extreme hysteria?): "My body is useless./It lies, curled like a dog on the carpet . . . . I see myself as one would see another./I have been cut in two . . . . There is blood here/and I have eaten it . . . . I am in my own mind./I am locked in the wrong house." Though she addresses a "physician," the poet doesn't really seem to want a "cure," merely an easeful death. Compare this with the second poem in which the poet is in a hospital bed (though we only learn this in the last line, the rest of the poem gives us in retrospect an interesting picture of hospital visitors), again yearning for heavenly help. But she "who was a house full of bowel movement" cannot move or eat, let alone crawl towards God. So she eats herself instead. But Jesus comes to her and gives her spiritual mouth-to-mouth resuscitation (in the first poem, she years for Mary's mouth). She recovers and in something of a surprise ending gives the formerly meaningless yellow daisy "to the crazy woman in the next bed."

Sexton, Anne. "The Fury of Rain Storms." From The Death Notebooks. Boston: Houghton Mifflin Co., 1974. Poem: 14 lines.

Death   Madness

The first eleven lines are an image of depression: the rain hits the poet's window like red ants in pain; she thinks of the grave and the body beneath it, being rained on. But in the last three lines, she rouses herself and sets up daily organization and illumination as an antidote: "Depression is boring, I think,/and I would do better to make/some soup and light up the cave."

Sexton, Anne. "In Celebration of My Uterus." From Love Poems. Boston: Houghton Mifflin Co., 1969. Poem: 61 lines.

The Body   Sexual Roles

The poet sings, like Whitman, of the body, her body, her uterus, which the doctors wanted to cut out. But they are wrong, she sings. "I dare to live./Hello, spirit. Hello, cup." Still addressing her uterus, she chants--again like Whitman--a catalogue of women everywhere: "one is stretching on her mat in Thailand,/one is wiping the ass of her child . . . . Let me study the cardiovascular tissue,/let me examine the angular distance of meteors,/let me suck on the stems of flowers (if that is my part)." She ends the poem with the same word that Joyce sees as the female ending in Ulysses: "let me sing/for the supper,/for the kissing,/for the correct/yes."

Sexton, Anne. "Madonna." From The Death Notebooks. Boston: Houghton Mifflin Co., 1974. Poem: 20 lines.

Children   Disease & Health   Dying
Grief

On the death--or, rather, the dying--of the speaker's mother. The images swirl: the dying woman is a thrashing fish on a hook; she is a manic priestess, dancing along. She is an unrocked child, riding a rocking horse of pain; yet she is a mother about to deliver: "Her belly was big with another child,/cancer's baby, big as a football." Finally, a "strange labor" takes her, and that is death.

Sexton, Anne. "Sylvia's Death," 1963. From Live or Die. Boston: Houghton Mifflin Co., 1966. Poem: 66 lines.

Death   Grief   Suicide

Simultaneously a wailing over the death of her friend Sylvia Plath (q.v.)--"O tiny mother,/you too!/O funny duchess!/O blonde thing!"--and an envying of Sylvia's having made it with death, "our boy"--"Thief!--/how did you crawl into,/crawl down alone/into the death I wanted so badly and for so long." It seems that Plath and Sexton had told each other that they had outgrown the yearning for death, and there is an immense poignancy about Sexton's wondering "Sylvia, Sylvia,/where did you go/after you wrote me/from Devonshire/about raising potatoes/and keeping bees?" At the news of Plath's death, Sexton had known "a terrible taste for it, like salt." (But she would live for another 11 years before her own suicide.)

Sexton, Anne. "Unknown Girl in the Maternity Ward." From To Bedlam and Part Way Back. Boston: Houghton Mifflin, 1960. Poem: 55 lines.

Children   Doctors   Med. Instit.
Nurses   Preg. & Childbirth

An unmarried woman speaks to her newborn from her hospital bed. The situation is not very personal: "the nurses nod their caps"; "the doctors are enamel." And soon the ties between mother and baby will be cut: "I choose/your only way, my small inheritor/and hand you off, trembling the selves we lose./Go child, who is my sin and nothing more." But in the meantime the mother contemplates her physical closeness to her baby, and Sexton gives the newborn her full attention: "I see your eyes/lifting their tents. They are blue stones, they begin/to outgrow their moss."

Sexton, Anne. "Woman with Girdle." From All My Pretty Ones. Boston: Houghton Mifflin, 1962. Poem: 28 lines.

The Body

A fat woman removes her girdle, and Sexton is watching carefully. "Moving, you roll down the garment,/down that pink snapper and hoarder,/as your belly, soft as pudding,/slops into the empty space . . . . over crisp hairs, that amazing field/that hides your genius from your patron;/over thighs, thick as young pigs,/over knees like saucers." Finally the woman is finished and rises, transformed: "straightway from God you have come/into your redeeming skin."

Shaffer, Peter. Equus. New York: Samuel French, 1973. Drama.

Adolescence   Doctors   The Family
Madness   Med. Ethics   Med. Profession
Sexuality

A 17-year-old boy, raised by his Christian mother to need religion, but denied its trappings by his Marxist father, invents a private ritual compounded of religious and sexual elements. Beginning with an incident in his childhood, when young Alan discovers that riding horses can be sexy and, equally promising, that horses annoy his father, the boy develops an elaborate concept of "Equus," the horse as God. For a year before the play opens, he has been secretly riding naked at night, riding to orgasmic ecstasy. But one night, as he tries to make love to a girl in the horses' stable, he remembers his mother's admonition that God's eyes can see you everywhere, and in anguish he blinds all the horses with a spike. The play itself is narrated by a psychiatrist, to whom the boy has been sent by the courts. This man, now in his "professional menopause," anxiously deliberates his role. Should he "cure" the boy? Suppose he thereby excises the boy's only passionate moments in an otherwise unimaginative life, a life, the doctor realizes, in something of a role reversal, which is about as unimaginative as the doctor's own. Here are Dr. Dysart's fears about the psychiatric profession: "The Normal is the good smile in a child's eyes--all right. It is also the dead stare in a million adults. It both sustains and kills--like a God. It is the Ordinary made beautiful: it is also the Average made lethal. The Normal is the indispensable, murderous God of Health, and I am his Priest."

Shango, J. R. "A Matter of Ethics." Available in Great Science Fiction About Doctors, eds. Groff Conklin and N. D. Fabricant, M.D. New York: Collier Books, 1963. Short Story.

Doctors   Med. Profession   Med. Students
Sci Fi   Surgery

Another wish-fulfillment for medical students. On an interplanetary trip, a doctor suffers a coronary and cannot make it through the pressure of landing without surgery. With him is Colby who suffered through a degrading thirteen-year residency and then tried for certification by the Intergalactic Board of Mural Cardiosurgery. Mendez, the doctor suffering the coronary, had rejected him saying it would be criminal for Colby to practice, telling him to serve five more years of training under the infuriating Harkaway. Mendez needs the Chauncey operation involving a plastic patch. Colby has done the operation on animals thousands of times, deftly and skillfully, but the patch has never held. Mendez wants the operation. Colby refuses: he would be charged with manslaughter even if the operation were successful. But Mendez offers him a chance at the Board, which has been held to a small number for economic reasons. Further, Mendez confesses the truth about the Board members' skill: all the Chauncey operation needs is the right blade; any surgeon can perform it. Mendez

requests the operation and makes it legal. Colby kills him with an overdose of anaesthetic. On landing, Colby requests an immediate examination and when he is asked to describe in detail the apothecaries' methods and ingredients used to standardize digitalis, he replies with the scalpel blade. Made a Board member, he publicizes the nature of the blade, having first taken out a patent on it. The narrator ends with an account of the high number of Board men dying of heart disease, who inexplicably refuse to allow Colby or any other former resident to operate on them--an occupational paranoia, no doubt.

Shaw, George Bernard. Back to Methuselah: a Metabiological Pentateuch, 1922. New York: Oxford University Press, 1947. Drama.

Age   Body/Mind   Death
Sci Fi   Sexual Roles

A play of ideas--though far more ideas than play--and so long that very few people have seen it performed. It is made up of five playlets, ranging through time from Eden to the year 31,920. The play begins with a debate on the proper way to live. Adam favors working hard and getting by; Cain favors the active, even violent, life; and Eve favors, she knows not what, but something beyond working or fighting. The serpent, who is female in this version, teaches Eve about reproduction, about controlling the body with the mind, about, in short, creative evolution, though it will be eons before it is fully understood. The secret which is gradually worked out through time is that human beings need not die, that they can use their wills to change their bodies and ultimately to survive without them. In the final part of the play, life has so evolved that children are hatched at seventeen, live a youthfully physical life for four years, and then become ancients, whose goal is to live disembodied forever. As one character says, "The body always ends by being a bore. Nothing remains beautiful and interesting except thought, because the thought is the life." The victorious conclusion is spoken by Lilith, who came before Adam and Eve and in fact created them by dividing herself into the two sexes.

Shaw, George Bernard. Doctors' Delusions. London: Constable, 1932. Treatise.

Doctors   Drugs   Med. Ethics
Med. Profession

Like the preface to The Doctor's Dilemma, entertaining, but far more hostile to the medical profession. Among the outrages Shaw discusses are these: The British General Medical Council, though theoretically controlled by the public, is in fact little more than a doctors' union; thus, the doctors are accountable to no one but themselves. People with unorthodox ideas--the bone-setters, the homeopaths, the osteopaths, the psychotherapists, the physical therapists--are dropped from the medical register, sometimes because their theories, particularly Hahnemann's, would mean less income for doctors. The practice of innoculation is dangerous and should be better understood. Drugs, especially pain-killers, are not readily available, though you be Queen Alexandra herself, without a doctor's prescription. Any doctor will do, even the notorious murderer Dr. Crippen. The profession limits its numbers to insure high fees. Only the wealthy can at present afford medical school, or, for that matter, the best care. The medical profession's microscopic vision is a type of hyperanesthesia, which produces insanity. Shaw's cures for all these ills include the predictable public health care scheme, and the less predictable suggestion that the self-styled science of medicine should constantly be checked by the political, mathematical, and social sciences. (He does not mention literature, but he has elsewhere demonstrated its uses himself.) "A little science is a dangerous thing, and science in science-tight compartments is worse. Bring to bear on every department the co-ordinated science of all the other departments, and the doctors will be promptly driven beyond their crudities and follies . . . into as sound positions . . . as humanity is capable of."

Shaw, George Bernard. The Doctor's Dilemma, 1913. Baltimore: Penguin Books, 1954. Drama.

Disease & Health Doctors   Dying
Med. Ethics   Med. Profession Med. Students
Surgery

Written in 1913, this witty play, together with its brilliant preface, remains one of the most important literary statements about the medical profession. In the preface Shaw is out to attack doctors for masquerading as men of science; for practicing vivisection from fraudulent motives; for being in the position of having a pecuniary interest in their patients' ill health; for falsely proclaiming medical infallibility in some instances, and falling back on the opposite argument when they are accused of malpractice; for manipulating statistics; and, it seems, just in general. Still, Shaw concludes that doctors are no worse than other ordinary men. In fact, he is quite sympathetic to the poverty some doctors must endure, and, good Fabian socialist that he is, suggests a remedy: a public health system. The play itself is no less dazzling than the preface. Here Shaw introduces several comic medical personnel: a medical student, whom one character calls "the most disgusting figure in modern civilization"; the physician to the royal family, who treats and cures out of the most appalling ignorance; the surgeon, Mr. Cutler Walpole, who first invents and then lucratively removes something called the "nuciform sac"; the provincial doctor who has made

his fortune by advertizing guaranteed cures; the worthy,
poverty-stricken Blenkinsop, who has contracted tuberculosis; and the wry old Sir Patrick, who can sometimes
speak Shaw's most cynically honest lines. There is also,
of course, the play's protagonist, the researcher, Sir
Colenso Ridgeon, discoverer of a successful treatment for
T.B. His is the dilemma of the title: he has resources
enough to treat only one more patient; shall it be the
worthy but dull Blenkinsop, or the brilliant blackguard
of an artist, Louis Dubedat, whose delicious young wife
Ridgeon can easily imagine as a delicious young widow.
Ridgeon chooses to treat Blenkinsop and let the artist
die, which he does, in one of the best scenes Shaw ever
wrote. When the widow rejects him, Ridgeon concludes
that he has committed a purely disinterested murder.
(See also Shaw's later play The Millionairess, in which
the woman, now stripped of all her feminine trimmings,
again triumphs over the doctor, whose best medical plati-
tudes cannot stand up to an overwhelming female force.)

Shaw, George Bernard. Man and Superman, 1903. Baltimore: Penguin,
   1952. Drama.

   Body/Mind   Sexuality   Sexual Roles

   The Life Force as the motivation behind all relations
   between the sexes. Shaw, through his hero John Tanner,
   proclaims that the purpose of a woman's existence is not
   her own happiness, nor anyone else's, but nature's purpose, i.e., new life. In working out that purpose, she
   may, as the charming Ann Whitefield does, lie and cheat
   a little, but she is always victorious over a mere man,
   like Jack Tanner, who may be striving to live on the level
   of intellect and moral passion. In the end, Ann gets her
   man, not very romantically to be sure, but inevitably. In
   between, there is the famous "Don Juan in Hell" play-within-
   a-play. Jack Tanner is Man, but his ancestor Don Juan,
   though he shares many of Jack's ideas, dreams more fervently
   and less pompously of the Superman. "Sexually," Don Juan
   pronounces, "Woman is Nature's contrivance for perpetuating
   its highest achievement. Sexually, Man is Woman's contrivance for fulfilling Nature's behest in the most economical
   way." But the Don is struggling to be more than woman's
   instrument. He would be a philosopher who brings his brain
   into greater control over his body, and this too he sees
   as the will of the Life Force. Still, it is the woman,
   Dona Aña, who has the last line, as she cries to the universe, "A father! a father for the Superman!"

Sheed, Wilfrid. People Will Always Be Kind. New York: Farrar,
   Straus and Giroux, 1973. Novel.

   Adolescence   Disease & Health   Evil Doctors
   The Family   Handicaps   Med. Instit.
   Nurses   Sexuality

   A crippled kid grows up to be a liberal Senator and candidate for the Presidency, in spite of--or because of--his
   handicap. Stricken with polio when he is an athletic
   adolescent, Brian at first considers the reactions of his
   chums and his family somewhat extreme, for he doesn't seem
   to be suffering as much as they are. But soon, after a
   visit to a grotesque quack who promises that leeches can
   cure polio, after a long stay in a Southern hospital for
   polio victims, where the patients' sexuality seems increased
   in proportion to their crippling and the rumors of the
   nurses' availability, after all this, Brian comes to accept
   the reality of his illness. He works hard at school, he
   achieves, he even becomes a campus leader. Almost everyone
   admires his courage. But in the second half of this novel,
   the point of view shifts from the youthful Brian Casey to
   a young political follower of the charismatic Senator Casey.
   And here the question is just how truly liberal is the
   Senator, and what part does his polio play in his search
   for and attainment of power, both sexual and, chiefly,
   political power. "So Casey will wheel his throne among
   them--seeing healthy people on their knees is all he asks
   of life."

Silkin, Jon. "Death of a Son," 1954. Available in The Norton
   Anthology of Modern Poetry, eds. Richard Ellmann and Robert
   O'Clair. New York: Norton, 1973. Poem: 44 lines.

   Dying   Grief   Mental Retardation

   Terribly painful poem on a son "who died in a mental hospital aged one." The boy had been "Something like a
   person: something very like me." "He did not forsake
   silence./But rather, like a house in mourning/Kept the
   eye turned in to watch the silence." The house was made
   of flesh and blood "With flesh of stone/And bricks for
   blood." After a while the boy stopped watching. "He
   turned over on his side with his one year/Red as a wound/
   He turned over as if he could be sorry for this/And out
   of his eyes two great tears rolled, like stones,/and he
   died."

Silverberg, Robert. The World Inside, Chapter I. New York: Signet,
   1972, or "A Happy Day in 2381." Available in Nova One, ed.
   Harry Harrison. New York: Dell, 1971. Novel.

   The Body   Children   Sci Fi
   Sexuality

   Changes in attitudes toward the mind and body which make
   life possible in a world with billions of people, all
   worshipping fertility and children. Privacy is unknown;
   one's body must be available to anyone, male or female,
   who desires it in order to minimize frustration. The
   "selfish" are killed when children to preserve the
   community pattern of wholesome happiness. Great thought

is placed on adapting the building to the body (waste
recirculation and use of body heat) and of adapting the
psyche to the community. These adaptations reduce the
inhabitants to cheerful, dull, infantile people.

Sinclair, Upton. Damaged Goods. New York: John C. Winston, 1913.
   Novel.

   Doctors   Med. Ethics   V.D.

   See Brieux, Eugene.

Sladek, John T. "The Happy Breed." Available in Dangerous Visions,
   ed. Harlan Ellison. Garden City, N. Y.: Doubleday, 1967.
   Short Story.

   Med. Instit.   Sci Fi   Suffering

   A grim prophecy of a future in which external forces impose
   safety and happiness. Machines are given the job of keeping
   men healthy; slowly, by the use of drugs, the household environment, and the telescreens, they reduce mankind to bottled
   idiots, safely and happily enclosed in jars of amniotic fluid.

Smith, Cordwainer (Dr. M. A. Linebarger). "At the Gate of the
   Garden of Death" and "The Trial," 1964, chapters in Norstrilia
   (also in The Planet Buyer). New York: Ballantine Books, 1975.
   Novel.

   Death   Euthanasia   Sci Fi

   Cordwainer Smith imagines, in vivid detail, an immortality-
   producing planet which employs death to insure continued
   production of immortality. A folk song runs: "We kill to
   live, and die to grow--/That's the way the world must go."
   The planet Norstrilia produces Stroon, the drug of immortality, from sick sheep which can be ill only on Norstrilia.
   To preserve the drug, and the planet, from invaders, the
   Norstrilians shape a society and a population to be strong
   and incorruptible. This shaping includes the "Giggle Death"
   (they die laughing) for all children who are not perfect.
   Norstrilia follows Rod McBan[151] as he faces this trial,
   survives, has adventures as a "cat-man" on earth (animals
   have been mutated into human form to serve as slaves),
   and returns to Norstrilia where he watches one twin son
   laugh himself to death while the other cries out: "Oh,
   dad! Why me? Why me?"

Snow, C. P. Last Things, Chaps. 16 & 17. New York: Scribner,
   1970. Novel.

   Death   Med. Instit.   Suffering
   Surgery

   In these two chapters of an otherwise uninteresting book,
   Lewis Eliot finds himself in a hospital being operated
   on for loose retinas. Following the surgery, during which
   his heart stopped for 3½ minutes, Eliot spends a night
   in dread of nothingness.

Snow, C. P. "The Two Cultures," 1959. Available in The Two
   Cultures And a Second Look. London: Cambridge University
   Press, 1969; Leavis, F. R. "Two Cultures: The Significance
   of C. P. Snow," 1962. Available in Nor Shall My Sword. New
   York: Barnes & Noble, 1972; Richards, I. A. "Science and
   Poetry," 1926, 1935. Available in Poetries and Sciences.
   New York: Norton, 1970; Sewell, Elizabeth. The Orphic
   Voice: Poetry and Natural History, 1960. New York: Harper
   & Row, 1971. Essays.

   Science & Poetry

   The major contemporary analyses of what may, or may not,
   be the division between the methods and perceptions of
   poetry and science. Snow expands the question somewhat
   by speaking of the "cultures" of scientists versus that
   of literary intellectuals, and emphasizing behavior and
   attitudes rather than basic philosophical approaches.
   In general, he believes that a dangerous polarity has
   arisen, and of course his essay has been highly influential and controversial, on one notable occasion being
   answered by Leavis, who not only attempts to refute
   Snow's narrow, as he sees it, definition of literary culture, but speaks of a "creative response to the new
   challenges of time" that is alien to both Snow's cultures.
   Richards, while assuming a basic difference between imaginative and scientific utterance, seeks to use one "science,"
   the science of psychology, to analyze precisely how a poem
   affects a reader and why it is valuable. Sewell, building
   on Francis Bacon, Shakespeare, Erasmus Darwin, Linnaeus,
   Wordsworth, Rilke, and others, and using as a means the
   self-conscious Orpheus myth as it occurs in these writers,
   rejects the dichotomies of Science and Poetry, intellect
   and imagination. She suggests that Poetry, in some larger
   senses now, is "the most inclusive form of thought we have
   yet devised," and that in both science and poetry "Discovery
   . . . is a mythological situation in which the mind unites
   with a figure of its own devising as a means towards understanding the world." Moreover, "the body is an essential
   art of the method" of Poetry. Defined this way, Poetry
   becomes our central tool for practical/visionary affairs.

Solzhenitsyn, Alexander. Cancer Ward. New York: Farrar, Straus &
   Giroux, 1969. Novel.

   Death   Disease & Health   Doctors
   Dying   Med. Ethics   Med. Instit.
   Nurses   Poetry & Health   Suffering

   A book with multiple themes, medical and political on the
   surface, moral underneath it all, with "cancer" predictably
   becoming a metaphor for repressive agents in the state and
   in the human spirit. Several interesting patients inhabit
   a Soviet hospital. Rusanov, a bumbling insensitive

bureaucrat is contrasted with Kostoglotov, a political
exile; a geologist; a young student; and various working-
class people--all of whom suffer more but complain less.
Whatever their differences, all the patients are tied
together in the pervading sense of loneliness, impersonal-
ization, and doom. The medical problems investigated by
Solzhenitsyn include the right to die, the right to
information about treatment (Kostoglotov has to have a
pathology textbook smuggled in), malpractice suits, the
persecution of doctors who remain outside the official
health care system (together with a defense of the solo
family physician against state medicine), and the long
delays in treatment (in terms of days, not hours). The
lives of the doctors (mostly women) and nurses are just
as lonely and empty as their patients'. No one seems to
have anything to live for; no one believes in anything.
Those few who do have faith in the beginning lose it in
the face of the omnipresent repression of the cancer.
An important--if very ponderous--novel.

Spark, Muriel. _Memento Mori_, 1959. New York: Modern Library, 1966.
    Novel.

Age	Death	Doctors
Med. Ethics	Med. Instit.	Nurses
Sexuality		

Brilliant study of old age--very funny and wickedly
accurate. The main characters are all old, from 70 to 90,
and most keep getting anonymous phone calls from someone
who says, "Remember you must die." There is nothing sentimental about the picture of the elderly: they are petty
(Godfrey has been waiting for 60 years to revenge himself
on his more successful wife, Charmian); they are gaga
(Charmian must organize her thoughts alphabetically); they
are sexually pathetic (Godfrey pays a young woman to let
him stare lasciviously at her garters). Only two are
really admirable: Dr. Warner, the elderly sociologist,
whose detailed study of old age is at least harmless and
sometimes insightful; and the lovely Miss Jean Taylor,
formerly a secretary-companion, and now a resident of a
public ward in an old people's hospital. That is a
terrible place. The nurses (two are studied in some
detail) and doctors (there is a kind one who does home
visits for the well off) are for the most part insensitive
to the old women's need for dignity, calling them "Granny
Taylor" and "Granny Green," and generally treating them
like kids or bullying them. In a reorganization, several
dribbling, senile women are brought into the same ward,
and several others die just as we've come to know them
well. Jean Taylor declares that she would just as soon
die, having lived quite a satisfactorily long time, but
the doctors, anxious to try out their new techniques,
won't have it. As for the mysterious phone caller, Jean
knows who that is: it's Death.

Spender, Stephen. "Hoelderlin's Old Age," 1939. Available in _The
    Norton Anthology of Modern Poetry_, eds. Richard Ellmann and
    Robert O'Clair. New York: Norton, 1973. Poem: 9 lines.

    Age

A little poem with one very nice insight about age. The poet
Hoelderlin is speaking and says that when he was young, he
loved the morning and grieved as the day closed. But now
that he is old, he curses "the white cascade/That refreshes
all roots," and only in the evening can he rejoice. Then
his "spirit sings/Burning intensely in the centre of a cold
sky."

Stein, Gertrude. _Melanctha_, from _Three Lives_, 1909. Available in
The Selected Writings of Gertrude Stein, ed. Carl Van Vechten.
New York: Modern Library, 1962. Novella.

| By Doctors | Doctors | Dying |
| Madness | Sexuality | Suicide |

Though she studied medicine for four years at Johns Hopkins,
Stein did not take her final examinations and therefore
never practiced. But she has said that the study of medicine is an excellent education for a writer, who must know
as much as possible about people. In _Melanctha_ the famous
Stein prose (often compared to cubist painting and perhaps
influenced too by her medical studies) is more accessible
than usual and indeed very appropriate for the portrayal
of black dialect. Stein winds her way slowly into the
language and syntax of consciousness, and thereby gains
great sympathy for her heroine, the intelligent, passionate,
and often seriously depressed mulatto girl. Melanctha grows
close to young Dr. Jeff Campbell as they sit together
attending her dying mother. He is strong, gentle, intellectual, and joyous, always liking to care for people,
especially the black people of Bridgeport. Unlike Melanctha,
he can never give himself up entirely to love and passion,
but must keep himself distant. So the relationship ends.
Melanctha starts "wandering" again with all sorts of men,
and her next relationship ends too. Stein now summarizes
the rest of her heroine's life in a few quick, painful
paragraphs: Melanctha is depressed. She thinks of killing
herself, but dies instead in a home for poor consumptives.

Steinbeck, John. _In Dubious Battle_. New York: Viking Press, 1936.
    Novel.

| Death | Disease & Health | Doctors |
| Poverty & Health | Preg. & Childbirth | |

One of the fighting characters in this tough proletarian novel
of the American thirties is young Doc Burton, no Communist,
but a believe in men and a student of all human phenomena.
He often has discussions with Mac and Jim, Party members

both, and leaders of a revolt by ill-treated fruit pickers.
Doc explains his taking on of the public health matters
in the camp as being like a painter's having to paint
when he sees colors and canvas. Mac can't decide whether
Doc's brand of uninvolved compassion is "cold-blooded"
or "fine as the devil, and clean." Doc works like the
devil, at any rate, treating the sick and starving workers
and their families, as well as those wounded in this
battle which seems dubious from his paradoxically distanced
vantage point. Before his arrival in the camp, Mac had
taken on one medical duty: the delivery of Lisa's baby,
described in some detail in Chapter 4. Death finally
comes to Jim Nolan at the hands of the enemy authorities,
just as it had come to his father. In this world, death
is not so much a matter for individual grief as for
group response. He dies for the cause.

Steinbeck, John. _Of Mice and Men_. New York: Viking Press, 1937.
    Novel.

| Euthanasia | Mental Retardation | Sexuality |

A classic American story of devoted male friends on the
move. There's George--and there's Lennie, who has a
simple mind, an innocent heart, and a powerful body, a
combination of traits which leads inexorably to tragedy.
George tries to hide his friend's strangeness and thereby
protect their new jobs as farmhands. But Lennie cannot
even be protected from himself. He plays with his
beloved new puppy so violently that he kills him, and
goes on petting him, unaware. Later the boss' seductive
wife, attracted by Lennie's physical strength, approaches
him. His powerful but confused sexuality leads him to
aggression which results in her death. Pursued by the
gun-carrying husband, Lennie is, fortunately, found by
George, who first tells his big simple friend his
favorite story--that someday the two of them will own a
piece of land and Lennie will take care of the rabbits--
and then, to prevent his being captured by people who
wouldn't understand him, shoots him in the back of the
head.

Stone, John. "Stroke." From _The Smell of Matches_. New Brunswick,
    N. J.: Rutgers University Press, 1972. Poem: 17 lines.

    By Doctors   Disease & Health

Out of the many would-be successors to William Carlos
Williams' position as _the_ doctor-poet, some few have
written an occasionally arresting poem and promise more.
John Stone, for instance, is quite interesting. Furthermore, he, unlike Williams, often chooses medical subjects.
"Stroke" is one of the best in this book (other titles:
"Two Dreams of Leukemia"; "Medical Conference";
"Cadaver"). The poem is an act of empathy for a new victim of stroke: "I imagine his bedroom/where he woke this
morning/to find half his singing nerves/numb and silent/
his tongue halved and pulling/the cold words cramping in
his throat/half a world gone in each eye./I dream/his
darkened bedroom/where last night/his mind meshed/in its
last unaltered thinking . . . ."

Storey, David. _Home_, 1970. New York: Random House, 1974. Drama.

    Madness   Med. Instit.

A bare play: minimal set, short lines of fragmented dialogue, five characters, exposed spirits. Only by degrees
does one learn that the "home" of the title is the sort
found in the expression, "I'm going to put you in a home."
It's a huge--2,000 inhabitants, one character says--vague,
and dispirited asylum. Two middle-aged men, middle-class
and conventionally polite, carry on an unreasonable
facsimile of a small-talk conversation, none of it getting
anywhere. It's all very comic, and very sad. Both qualities are intensified when the men are joined by two middle-
aged women, working class and coarse. It's suggested that
one man chased little girls and the other lies a bit too
much, that one woman is a nymphomaniac and the other a
Persistent Offender. The fifth character is a 30-year-old
man who seems to have had a lobotomy, and this much is
certain about all of them: they are isolated, unhappy
people. One begins to consider the world as something like
a mental hospital in which one is never quite at home.

Swados, Harvey. _Celebration_. New York: Simon and Schuster, 1974.
    Novel.

| Age | Children | Death |
| Doctors | Grief | Sexuality |

The diary of an old man (cf. Tanizaki's _Diary of a Mad Old
Man_), approaching the celebration of his 90th birthday as
the country approaches the celebration of its bicentennial.
Both man and country are still having identity crises.
The man in this case is famous, the most famous man in the
history of children's education and rights. He has been
a radical, and now finds himself accused of being co-opted
by the establishment, who wish to name a Washington building after him. That the accuser is his own 29-year-old
son, Seth, newly arrived into the old man's life, makes
the charge all the more difficult. His guilt, his grief
really, about the son is due to the young man's begetting.
When he was 59, the famous man had been visited by his
son Philip's young fiancée, Louise. He'd treated her as
he'd treated so many of the young women he'd encountered:
he took her to bed. No, that's too polite: what he did
was rape her, and after Philip was killed in the war, and
after Louise had given birth to Seth, she piloted her
plane into a mountainside. Naturally, death is a presence
in this story of old age, but it is not something the
protagonist eases towards at all. At 90, he is still very

much alive. He rather resents his doctor's conventional, patronizing small talk--"Feeling chipper today?"--and he becomes at last, if one may say so, a very human leftist. He comes to real self-knowledge. When his young wife (she is in her thirties) quotes back at him Saint-Evremond's "The greatest of pleasures that remain for old men is living; and nothing makes them more certain of their life than loving"--this old man replies, Yes, but furthermore, Montaigne on age: "in truth, we do not so much forsake our vices as change them--for worse." The elderly hero, who throughout the book has thought himself in constant danger of being exploited as if he were already a dead monument, realizes that he has himself engendered much of the crisis. "I took myself too seriously."

Synge, John Millington. Riders to the Sea, 1904. Available in Masters of Modern Drama, eds. Haskell M. Block and Robert G. Shedd. New York: Random House, 1962. Drama.

Age   Death   Grief

Called by many the best one-act tragedy in the English language, Riders to the Sea is set in the wild Aran Islands off the west coast of Ireland, where Synge himself grew to manhood with the adventurous fishermen, the many widows, and the lyrical language they all spoke. During the course of the play, an old widow, Maurya, loses her sixth, and last, son, but what is also enacted here is a ritual keening for all the dead. Maurya's age makes her grief more poignant, for she has outlived all her young sons: "In the big world the old people do be leaving things after them for their sons and children, but in this place it is the young men do be leaving things behind for them that do be old." Aged and broken, yet somehow calmer, Maurya croons, "They're all gone now, and there isn't anything more the sea can do to me . . . ."

Tanizaki, Junichiro. Diary of a Mad Old Man. New York: Knopf, 1965. Novel.

Age   The Body   Death
Disease & Health   Doctors   The Family
Madness   Nurses   Sexuality

There is some question about whether the diarist in this novel is truly mad, or just old and therefore obliged to act out some admittedly odd predilections in order to keep feeling alive. He is a sexual masochist, for one thing; in fact, though he is impotent, his sensual daughter-in-law is the only member of his family he can tolerate, for she allows him to play sexual games with her. When he is not thinking of sex, or death, he thinks of his aging, ugly, ill body, and of the medical treatment he receives. Both Western medicine and acupuncture are practiced on the old man, and he is unusually knowledgeable about them for a layman, undoubtedly because his increasing age has made him egocentric. He fills his diary with detailed descriptions of his suffering and treatment. Later, when he has suffered a stroke, his nurse and doctor complete the novel in the form of their medical charts. Compare Gogol's The Diary of a Madman.

Thomas, Dylan. "And Death Shall Have No Dominion." 1936. Available in Collected Poems, by Thomas. London: J. M. Dent & Sons, 1952. Poem: 27 lines.

Death   Madness

A triumphant hymn. Three stanzas, each beginning and ending with the shout: "And death shall have no dominion." The dead shall merge with the wind, the stars, and the west moon. What was lost shall be found. "Though they go mad they shall be sane,/Though they sink through the sea they shall rise again;/Though lovers be lost love shall not;/And death shall have no dominion." The language may be compatible with the Christian theory of resurrection, but the poem could just as well be construed as a triumph of the human will.

Thomas, Dylan. The Doctor and the Devils, 1953. New York: New Directions, 1965. Film Script.

Death   Doctors   Med. Ethics

Based on a true story, this script poses the question of the end justifying the means. The brilliant and controversial Doctor Rock--physician, anatomist, lecturer--pays two laborers for dead bodies to use in his work. (The 18th century law limited his bodies to legally executed men.) Though at first he only pays grave robbers for bodies, he later finds himself paying murderers as well, though without admitting the fact to himself. He claims that "the end justifies any means . . . . Let no scruples stand in the way of the progress of medical science." Throughout, Thomas uses a great deal of death symbolism. There are also constant parallels between the higher and lower (richer and poorer) characters, uniting them in the end by reducing Doctor Rock to a common criminal.

Thomas, Dylan. "Do Not Go Gentle into That Good Night," 1952. Available in Collected Poems, by Thomas. London: J. M. Dent & Sons, 1952. Poem: 19 lines.

Age   Children   Dying

Inevitably any discussion of the literary treatment of dying must come to this poem. Thomas gives proud, passionate advice on how to meet death: "Do not go gentle into that good night,/Old age should burn and rave at close of day;/Rage, rage against the dying of the light."

The final dark may be "right"; it may even in some sense be "good"; but the proper human response to the sad insights that come on the deathbed is--once again--to "rage." Nothing less than rage will express the magnitude of human failure when faced with the magnitude of death. Especially, Thomas wants his father to be strong: "And you, my father, there on the sad height,/Curse, bless, me now with your fierce tears, I pray./Do not go gentle into that good night./Rage, rage against the dying of the light."

Thomas, Dylan. "Fern Hill," 1946. Available in Collected Poems, by Thomas. London: J. M. Dent & Sons, 1952. Poem: 54 lines.

Children   Grief

One of Thomas' favorite themes. He melodically recreates the joys of youth: It's green, it's golden, it's lovely and watery. On the farm he had as a boy been "prince of the apple towns," and "honoured among foxes and pheasants." It had been lovely, and Time had let him play in the sun, never letting him know that one day he would "wake to the farm forever fled from the childless land." Thus the poem ends: in grief for the lost child. "Oh as I was young and easy in the mercy of his means/Time held me green and dying/Though I sang in my chains like the sea."

Thomas, Dylan. "The Hunchback in the Park," 1946. Available in Collected Poems, by Thomas. London: J. M. Dent & Sons, 1952. Poem: 42 lines.

Handicaps   Mental Retardation

The figure in this poem may be retarded as well as handicapped. At least the boys torment him as though he were, and he sleeps at night in a dog kennel, though nobody, Thomas adds, chains him up. The picture of him here is like one remembered from childhood, for he seems a little distant, but perhaps that's just as well, for the portrait is immensely sad without being sentimentally pathetic. He is seen eating bread from a newspaper, laughing in mockery, dodging the park keeper with the stick, and loving the park all day until closing time. The whole time he makes a figure of a woman to leave behind at night, a woman "Straight as a young elm/Straight and tall from his crooked bones."

Thomas, Dylan. "Love in the Asylum," 1946. Available in Collected Poems, by Thomas. London: J. M. Dent & Sons, 1952. Poem: 18 lines.

Madness   Med. Instit.   Sexuality

A vision of love, or perhaps creativity, which requires the metaphor of the poet's world as madhouse. He lives in "the house not right in the head," "the heaven-proof house." To this madhouse comes "a girl mad as birds." She raves, yet is "possessed by the skies" and has powers of light. The poet imagines that when "at long and dear last" she takes him in her arms, he will "suffer the first vision that set fire to the stars."

Thomas, Dylan. "A Refusal to Mourn the Death, by Fire, of a Child in London," 1946. Available in Collected Poems, by Thomas. London: J. M. Dent & Sons, 1952. Poem: 24 lines.

Children   Death   Grief

Thomas' answer to the awful question of how to understand, how to react to, the death of a child. This child was burned, so the poet can speak of "the majesty and burning of the child's death," but elsewhere he calls dying a burning too, so the method of death is a convenience here. The real point is that any comment on death, any homily, any elegy, would be an insult to the gravity of the awesome fact itself. "I shall not murder/The mankind of her going with a grave truth/Nor blaspheme down the stations of the breath/With any further/Elegy of innocence and youth." Such a death is self-contained. "After the first death, there is no other."

Tiptree, James, Jr. "The Women Men Don't See." Available in The Best Science Fiction of the Year #3, ed. Terry Carr. New York: Ballantine Books, 1974. Short Story.

Sexual Roles   Sci Fi

Close to literal interpretation of women as aliens. Four people, two men and a woman, Ruth, and her daughter, survive a plane crash near the coast of Yucatan. The narrator, a man, and Ruth go off through the swamps in search of water. He is constantly thinking of her physically, sexually, and is rather bothered by her calm efficiency. She speaks of women's lib as doomed to failure before the more aggressive and powerful man. Women survive only "by ones and twos in the chinks of your world-machine." "Guerrillas have something to hope for," but women are not fighters. "Think of us [as] opposums, Don." Ruth discovers aliens, blackmails them (by withholding a part of their equipment) into returning the injured narrator to his companion, and then, with her daughter, accompanies the aliens to their unknown home--women are used to living among aliens. The narrator broods about this preference for aliens, but ends by saying: "Two of our opposums are missing."

Tushnet, Leonard. "In Re Glover." Available in Again, Dangerous Visions, ed. Harlan Ellison. Garden City, New York: Doubleday & Co., 1972. Short Story.

By Doctors   Death   Med. Ethics
Sci Fi

A delightful little story (there is also a nice one by andy offut on hospital procedures in this volume) on the legal complexities created by the inability to define death. A wealthy man, dying of cancer, puts his money in trust (for his lifetime) to support the foundation caring for his frozen body and is thereafter artificially frozen. Is he alive, with the money properly in trust for the foundation, or is he dead with the money properly destined for his heirs? The lawsuits burgeon, spawning all sorts of new kinds of suits. The heirs sue for declaration of death and for malpractice. The "dead" man's lawyers are charged with his suicide. The state governments sue for inheritance taxes. The Federal government sues to have the Foundation declared no longer tax exempt. The Foundation sues the doctors as convicted felons. The doctors sue to prevent the body?/corpse? from being buried or cremated and seek confirmation from the Food and Drug Administration that the drug used in freezing isn't fatal. A minor legatee seeks an injunction against thawing him out, while a daughter wants a legal guardian appointed for her father. The Justices cannot decide how to decide if he's dead. The case is resolved by a power failure which thaws out the now dead man. Dr. Tushnet is a prolific author, worthy of further investigation.

Vonnegut, Kurt, Jr. Cat's Cradle. New York: Holt, Rinehart & Winston, 1963. Novel.

Death   The Family   Sci Fi
Suicide

A "Papa-Doc"-type dictator commits suicide in a grand manner to escape the agony of death from cancer. He uses a crystal of ice-nine, originally designed to spare Marines the miseries of slogging through mud by freezing the water in the mud. Unfortunately the process of crystalization cannot be stopped. Three fragments exist, in the hands of a scientist's three children. Personal pressures cause each to give his or her fragment to a government; "Papa's" fragment happens to precipitate the inevitable disaster when an earthquake throws his crystalized corpse into the sea, irrevocably freezing the entire world.

Vonnegut, Kurt, Jr. Slaughterhouse Five. New York: Dell, 1971. Novel.

Death   Sci Fi   Suffering

Suffering as absurd and death as temporal illusion--the past exists and a dead person also continues to exist in the past. These attitudes carry the narrator through the meaningless slaughter caused by the fire-bombing of Dresden.

Wallant, Edward Lewis. Children at the Gate. Harcourt, Brace, and World, 1964. Novel.

Drugs   Med. Instit.   Mental Retardation
Suffering

A complicated plot, but the theme is clear: scientific rationalism, together with cold intellectualism, is made antithetical to, but at the same time dependent upon, irrational love for others. Angelo DeMarco lives with his retarded sister, with whose blank face he is able to communicate better than with his religious mother and uncle, also members of the household. Angelo studies biology in his spare time simply to expand his knowledge, and he works in a pharmacy which has the concession in a nearby hospital. Angelo has to take orders from the patients, and he doesn't like this part of the job, though he tries to explain rationally why he doesn't. Then two people break into his reserve: a child with a throat injury, whom he has come to like, and a Jewish orderly, who bombards him with stories of the irrational and steals drugs from the pharmacy in order to sell cheaply or give to patients in pain. When the child is attacked and the orderly is accused, Angelo clears him, but, recognizing that he cannot understand the attractive antagonism of their relationship, turns the orderly in for drug-stealing, an action which indirectly leads to the orderly's death. That breaks down Angelo's adherence to rationality. More suffering is to follow: when he leaves home, his sister dies as a result, but, alluding to the new merger of intellect and imagination, brought about by pain and death, he muses this way: "He was surprised as he walked with that mortal wound in him, for it occurred to him that, although the wound would be the death of him, it would be the life of him too."

Waugh, Evelyn. The Loved One. New York: Vintage Books, 1948. Novel.

Death   Grief   Suicide

"Gruesome," Waugh calls his novel, and not for the "squeamish." To most readers, it is an hilarious satire on the American, or at least the Hollywood, way of death. Most subsequent satires have been based on this one. Both the main male characters are embalmers, one in a pet cemetery, The Happier Hunting Ground, the other, Mr. Joyboy, in The Whispering Glades. They are in love with the same woman, the luscious but simple-minded Aimée Thanatogenos, whose remarkable self-embalming ends the novel. Euphemisms have never been more skillfully defensive. The dead person is "the loved one," those who survive him, "The waiting ones." The corpse is presented not in a coffin, but in some lifelike posture: a garrulous woman might be viewed in a favorite pastime, telephoning; a nasty man would be

labeled as "judicial and determined," and displayed accordingly. The suitor from the pet cemetery has his office send the other suitor a card every year on the anniversary of Aimée's death: "Your little Aimée is wagging her tail in heaven tonight, thinking of you."

Webb, Mary. Precious Bane. New York: E. P. Dutton, 1926. Novel.

The Body   Handicaps

Among other things, a sentimental treatment of the hare-lip condition. The fact of the heroine's handicap, though not often mentioned in this melodramatic novel of English country folk, is the central fact of her self-image. Generous, sweet, and otherwise attractive (her lovely body alone is highlighted in one rather erotic scene), she is almost universally feared or scorned because of her deformity. One man, the weaver, sees her for the beauty that she has, and is.

Weiss, Peter. The Persecution and Assassination of Jean-Paul Marat As Performed by the Inmates of the Asylum of Charenton Under the Direction of the Marquis de Sade. (Marat/Sade), trans. Geoffrey Skelton. New York: Atheneum, 1965. Drama.

Madness   Med. Instit.   Sexuality

The title is an accurate summary of the plot, so no more need be said about that. What is interesting is that Weiss has chosen to set his political play about the French Revolution--which is, by easy extension, any bloody war--in a madhouse, where, of course, violence breaks out from time to time. He also has for director a man, de Sade, who is known to be violent. In format, he has used the methods of the Theatre of Cruelty, assaulting his audience with screams and rages and beatings and groping sex, as befits a madhouse. And yet in its very madness, it is somehow more human than the bloody revolution Marat and his colleagues are running. There is Charlotte Corday, the assassin, saying Marat's ways are too bloody; the priest calling out to the spectators to take sides; and the group as a whole calling for "general copulation." Still, one can't underestimate the impact of the madness, especially as at the end the inmates revolt and come at the divide which separates them from their audience. By now, the levels of reality are so mixed that it seems as if the madhouse has turned inside out, and spewed its hordes onto the streets, demanding justice and an end to cruelty.

Welty, Eudora. The Optimist's Daughter. New York: Random House, 1972. Novella.

Children   Doctors   Dying
Grief   Surgery

A lovely story about a daughter's coming to terms with the death of her father. At the age of 71, he has surgery for a loose retina, and the operation is successful, but he begins a slow decline to his death. His young second wife is fretful and in an attempt to shake him back from his retreat--from her, from life--kills him. For her part, the daughter is at first astonished by the grief process, all those proprieties and forced responses at the funeral and the incongruous views of her father held by others. Then she moves slowly backward in time until she faces the elements of her grief and so can escape from it. She has to confront, for instance, her resentment of her father's treatment of her mother; she has to accommodate her grief for her husband into this newer grief; finally she has to separate herself from the house and the part of grief that lies in material things. But she must somehow maintain memories, and this is what she has learned: "Memory lived not in initial possession but in freed hands, pardoned and freed, and in the heart that can empty but fill again, in the patterns restored by dreams."

Wharton, Edith. "Atrophy," Certain People, 1930. Available in The Collected Short Stories of Edith Wharton, ed. R. W. B. Lewis. Vol. 2. New York: Charles Scribners, 1967. Short Story.

Death   Sexuality

Ostensibly about a woman rushing to the bedside of her dying lover--actually about the living death of that woman. She congratulates herself on her ability to hide her love affair from her husband and friends, while the reader sees that she has overrated both her powers of concealment and her passion. She envisions herself as routing her lover's spinster sister from his bedside; but the sister routs her by sticking to the conventions of a condolence visit which the woman does not dare break. Further, the sister says that she will send thanks to the woman's husband for the visit, thus destroying her--except there is really no woman left to destroy.

Wharton, Edith. "Beatrice Palmato," 1935. Available in R. W. B. Lewis, Edith Wharton: a Biography, pp. 543-8. New York: Harper & Row, 1975. Outline and Fragment of a Novel.

The Family   Sexuality

A hitherto unpublished outline for a study of incest between a father and his adult daughter and of the madness and suicide it provokes. Wharton planned to reveal the incest only at the end of a subtle and indirect novel, a novel she never did attempt, but for reasons of her own, she chose to write out one of the actual contacts between the amorous pair. Presumably the fragment we now have would never have been published, not only because

it doesn't fit with the plan, but also because it is
pornographic. This reference, as an incomplete work, and
a pornographic one at that, would normally be outside the
range of this bibliography, but it is included because
here is a great (and "ladylike") novelist on an unusual
theme.

Wharton, Edith. "Diagnosis." Human Nature, 1933. Available in
The Collected Short Stories of Edith Wharton, ed. R. W. B. Lewis.
Vol. 2. New York: Charles Scribners, 1967. Short Story.

Death   Doctors

The effects of diagnoses of death or life. A rather
selfish man who has evaded marrying his mistress for years,
is reveling in the secure future promised by a diagnosis
of perfect health when he finds a written diagnosis
apparently condemning him to death within months. His
reactions are given most faithfully. He asks his mistress
to marry him to have someone to stick by him. They travel
abroad where he is given a new diagnosis. He feels as
though he had died and been reborn--except that he is
tied to his wife. Two years later, his wife dies of
pneumonia; he recognizes that she is dying but cannot
reach her. Then, he learns that the written diagnosis
was for another patient--and his wife knew this from
the beginning.

Wharton, Edith. Ethan Frome. New York: Charles Scribner's Sons,
1911. Novel.

Disease & Health   Nurses   Poverty & Health
Sexuality   Suffering   Suicide

A New England tragedy in which illness and silence are
the most obvious symptoms. The tragedy is enacted on a
fairly bare stage: there are only three main characters
--Zeena, a self-centered, "sickly" wife; her patient
husband, Ethan; and her sweet-tempered cousin Mattie
Silver, who lives with the couple to help out, and also
because she has nowhere else to go. At one time, Zeena
had had nursing skills. Ethan had, in fact, proposed to
her when--because, really-she had nursed his mother in
her last illness. But now Zeena plays the mysteriously
ill invalid role to perfection, at one point claiming
that a specialist has told her she should get a hired
girl. When she announces that she purposes to kick Mattie
out in order to make room, Ethan and Mattie's love for
each other comes into the open. But Ethan is too poor
to run away with Mattie, and too conscientious, so in
the end they settle on double suicide by driving themselves on a sled into a large tree. Unfortunately, they
survive--in pieces--and twenty-four years later the
narrator of this novel comes into their lives and finds
the three of them living together in complete poverty,
their lives now hopelessly intertwined. Zeena, her old
nursing skills needed, somehow rouses herself to tend
the other two. Mattie has been soured by severe pain,
long endured. Ethan probably suffers most of all when
he sees what Mattie has come to. But nobody knows for
certain.

Wharton, Edith. "A Journey," The Greater Inclination, 1899. Avail-
able in The Collected Short Stories of Edith Wharton, ed. R. W.
B. Lewis. Vol. 1. New York: Charles Scribners, 1967. Short
Story.

Death   Dying

A nightmare train ride. A woman is bringing her dying
husband from Colorado to New York. She does not understand the process of dying and is baffled by the changes
in him, is repulsed by his body. He dies a day before
the train reaches New York. She is then terrified by the
memory of a bewildered and helpless family ejected from
the train with the body of their dead child, standing on
a small platform in the middle of nowhere. She pretends
her husband is only ill, running the gauntlet of sympathy
from others in the train while concealing the corpse in
its berth. She manages to reach New York, but collapses
as the train enters the station.

Wharton, Edith. "The Pelican," The Greater Inclination, 1899.
Available in The Collected Short Stories of Edith Wharton, ed.
R. W. B. Lewis. Vol. 1. New York: Charles Scribners, 1967.
Short Story.

Children   Sexual Roles

A widow uses her son as means to attention and excitement--
in a refined way. The poor widow, left with an infant
son, takes to giving hideous lectures to support them
both. "Mrs. Amyot had two fatal gifts: a capacious but
inaccurate memory and an extraordinary fluence of speech."
Sympathetic audiences support her because she is supporting her son (through private school, then Harvard). Even
the detached narrator supports her, attracted by her
femininity and her love for her son--although he hopes
she will be stopped by marriage. She isn't, and when
the narrator last meets her, she is giving a pathetic
lecture on Cosmography and being confronted by her pros-
perous son who cannot make her stop advertising that she
is still educating her son in order to get audiences.
The confrontation without communication is wrenching to
read. Her final response: "'I sent his wife a sealskin
jacket at Christmas!' she said, with the tears running
down her cheeks."

Wharton, Edith. "Roman Fever," The World Over, 1936. Available in
The Collected Short Stories of Edith Wharton, ed. R. W. B. Lewis.
Vol. 2. New York: Charles Scribners, 1967. Short Story.

Age   Sexuality

Two middle-aged women touring Rome with their daughters.
The older women have barren lives, their husbands dead and
their daughters close to marriage, so the past assumes
greater importance. Mrs. Slade envies the dull Mrs. Ansley
for her brilliant daughter, but relishes her ability to
wound Mrs. Ansley by telling her that the letter from
Delphin Slade asking for a meeting, cherished by Mrs. Ansley
over the years, was actually written by her friend. However, it turns out that the cruel joke gave the dull
Mrs. Ansley the better daughter of Delphin Slade.

Wharton, Edith. "Souls Belated," The Greater Inclination, 1899.
Available in The Collected Short Stories of Edith Wharton, ed.
R. W. B. Lewis. Vol. 1. New York: Charles Scribners, 1967.
Short Story.

Sexuality   Sexual Roles

Sexual roles as a trap. Lydia has left her husband for
her lover, Gannett. Her husband divorces her. Now, she
is forced to consider marrying Gannett. She does not
wish to, but finds that both she and her companion desire
respectability more than they hate prudery. Her position
is made clearer by another couple in the same situation,
but the woman in that couple is frantic that the man
might abandon her before she can marry and have her safe.
Lydia's lover sees only that her feminine (weepy and
illogical) mind is keeping her from accepting the trap.
Lydia does go so far as the gang-plank of a steamer
before she turns around and runs back to him; "a Bradshaw
lay at his elbow, and mechanically, without knowing what
he did, he began looking out the trains to Paris."

White, E. B. "The Morning of the Day They Did It," The Second Tree
From the Corner. Available in A Treasury of Great Science
Fiction, ed. Anthony Boucher. Garden City, New York: Double-
day, 1959. Short Story.

Euthanasia   Poverty & Health   Sci Fi

An artificial world in which life is unnatural. The
Government provides for everything (and takes everything
in taxes), including the shots necessary to counter-act
the toxic chemicals in the environment. Without these
shots every twenty-one days, people would die. Euthanasia
is a popular topic, but like all topics in this future
world, raises no heated discussion. The narrator listens
as two men orbiting the earth on a "defensive" missile
satellite station discover that they no longer feel the
pull of conscience or of sex and decide to destroy the
world, a world in which "only what had been touched with
electronics was valid and real." They succeed.

White, Patrick. The Eye of the Storm. New York: Viking Press, 1973.
Novel.

Age   The Body   Body/Mind
Children   Death   Disease & Health
Doctors   Dying   The Family
Homosexuality   Med. Etnics   Nurses
Preg. & Childbirth Sexuality   Suicide
Women as Patients

A remarkable old lady lies dying. Beautiful, rich, and
tyrannical during her physically strong years, she continues to manipulate her children, her nurses--everyone--
when she is a half-blind, physically dependent shell of
a woman. Her body may be meaningful now chiefly in terms
of its basic functions and pains, but her mind still
searches out the significance of her own life and the
lives of those who surround her. As death approaches,
she views life with the calmness of one who is in the
eye of a storm, and a very clear view it is too. She
sees her middle-aged daughter and son, the one suffering
because she did not inherit her mother's beauty and
strength, and the other living a fraudulent life because
he did inherit his mother's acting talent. When the
novelistic point of view shifts from mother to children,
we see how daughter and son resent their mother, how they
want her to die and leave them in peace and money, how
they hate her, how they love her. Finally, after nearly
a lifetime of hating each other as well, the two sleep
together on the same night that the old lady, in complete
control to the end, wills herself to die. The health
profession is in attendance. In fact, the novel is,
among other things, a thorough study of nurses. There
is, in the first place, an image of old Mrs. Hunter herself as nurse when her husband is dying of cancer. Then
there are the three professionals, each distinctive, yet
each carrying out her duties with alertness. One sees
nursing as rather a religious calling; another is a
hearty, insinuating sort; the third has sexual problems,
experiences a tussle with a lesbian cousin and her friend,
then imagines herself pregnant by her patient's famous
actor-son. The cook is also in attendance on Mrs. Hunter,
is, in fact, a masochist who fits in perfectly with Mrs.
Hunter's need to dominate. Without her, the cook cannot
face life, and cuts her wrists. All of them--the vulgar
doctor too--are overwhelmed by one aged and dying, but
still vital, woman.

White, Patrick. The Solid Mandala. New York: Viking Press, 1966.
   Novel.

Age	Death	Madness
Mental Retardation	Sexuality	

A study of twin brothers from their youth through their
old age. Framed by two short narratives from the point
of view of a neighbor, the large middle of the book is
told first from Waldo's point of view, and then from his
twin brother Arthur's perspective. Twentieth-century
readers have learned to enjoy such different perspectives
on the same incidents, but here the technique is used
rather originally to display the dramatic differences
found even in twins. After a glimpse of the aged twins,
inextricably intertwined, mentally and even physically,
White begins with Waldo's view of their boyhood and early
manhood. Waldo has the superior mind, so much so that
Arthur seems mentally retarded, just a big, clumsy, rather
dopey fellow, who says stupid things: whereas Waldo har-
bors dreams of being a writer, and suffers terribly
because his idiot brother hangs around with the girl that
he, Waldo, is in love with. We get Waldo's view of literature, life, and death, the deaths of his parents, for
instance. Suddenly, when the perspective shifts to Arthur,
he is seen as a lyrical, visionary innocent, a man who is
much more involved with literature, life, and love than
the sexually repressed, severely neurotic Waldo. Because
Waldo has defined Arthur as slow-witted, he never sees
the true Arthur at all. Nor, for that matter, does he
see himself.

Wilder, Thornton. Our Town, 1938. Available in Sixteen Famous
   American Plays, eds. Bennett A. Cerf and Van H. Cartmell.
   New York: Modern Library, 1941. Drama.

Adolescence	Death	Doctors
The Family		

The ordinary and relentless cycle of birth, love, and
death, as seen in a little American town, especially in
the lives of two families, the Gibbses (he's a doctor of
the gentle, kind country doctor sort) and the Webbs. The
play proceeds almost like a folk ballad with an expected
refrain. Young George Gibbs inevitably marries young
Emily Webb, and she, just as inevitably, dies some years
later in childbirth. Here the play goes from the romance
of the mundane to the sentimentalizing of the eternal.
Emily joins the other dead folk of Grover's Corner in the
cemetery and there learns some large truths (except in
the colloquial language of the play, they're almost home
truths). As the Stage Manager casually says, "Everybody
knows in their bones that something is eternal, and that
something has to do with human beings." Since she is
newly arrived among the dead, Emily is eager to learn that
she can go back if she likes and relive some of her past,
but she soon learns that knowing the future of things and
watching the still living be oblivious to what life offers
is just too painful. As her grief-stricken husband flings
himself across her grave, Emily is already beginning to
forget and starting to wait for the unknown.

Williams, Tennessee. Cat on a Hot Tin Roof, 1954. Available in
   The Theatre of Tennessee Williams, Vol. III. New York: New
   Directions, 1972. Drama.

Alcoholism	Children	Death
Doctors	Dying	The Family
Homosexuality	Sexuality	Suffering

Maggie is the "cat." And she is bouncing around as if she
were on a hot tin roof because she is anxiously looking
for sex with her husband, Brick. But he just goes on
drinking, to hide from himself, as we soon discover, the
knowledge that he was more attracted to a certain male
friend than he likes to think. The other young married
couple in this troubled family may be superficially more
happy, but there is no question that we share Maggie's
view of them as greedy for Big Daddy's money, and fertile
to a fault, producing more and more monstrous children in
an effort to please. That leaves Big Mama, who's just
dumb, poor thing, and grief-stricken, never realizing how
her husband loathes her. He's got worse troubles now:
he's dying of cancer, as he is to find out before the end
of the play. But just as he uncovers this truth--and the
whole play has been about lying and self-deception, really--
Maggie comes in with another one: she's going to have a
baby to give to Big Daddy, she says, almost daring Brick
not to follow through on that. One has the feeling that
of all of them, it will be the clawing Maggie and, in
spite of his cancer, Big Daddy, who will cope best.

Williams, Tennessee. The Glass Menagerie, 1944. Available in The
   Theatre of Tennessee Williams, Vol. I. New York: New Directions, 1972. Drama.

The Family	Handicaps	Madness

Laura's shyness verges on neurosis, but that's not surprising considering that her mother is doomed to be
disappointed in her. Since her husband left the family,
Amanda has fallen back on memories of the beaux she had
in her youth and the hopes she has for Laura's gentleman
callers. Amanda is so wrapped up in herself and in
fantasy that she can't see what Laura's handicap has done
to her. For Laura is crippled, and that has made all the
difference. When at last brother Tom is bringing a
suitable young man to the house, and Laura must face a
boy she's had a crush on, only to discover that he's
engaged, the poignancy is real. Though the young man does
say that she is beautiful, one knows that it is a fragile

and helpless kind of beauty, and never a sexual one. But
the pain of this realization is eased when, in the last
scene, Amanda is consoling her daughter, and Tom, who has
been narrating this whole thing as a memory, declares
protectively that he has always remembered the tender
Laura in a world lit by lightening.

Williams, Tennessee. Streetcar Named Desire, 1947. Available in
   The Theatre of Tennessee Williams, Vol. I. New York: New
   Directions, 1972. Drama.

Death	The Family	Homosexuality
Madness	Preg. & Childbirth	Sexuality

A contrast between Southern gentility and brutal sexuality,
though the contrast is not nearly so great as it first
seems. Ladylike Blanche, once married to a young homosexual whom she drove to suicide when she turned from him
in disgust, has since fallen into secret sexual patterns
herself, often with young men about her husband's age.
And even though she pretends that she cannot understand
her sister Stella's degradation of herself with the vulgar Stanley Kowalski--there's something that happens
between a man and a woman at night, Stella tells her--
Blanche behaves seductively around Stanley, and inevitably
when Stella goes off to have her baby, Stanley gives
Blanche what she's been asking for, as he sees it.
Balanced against the desperate sex in Blanche's life is
the aura of death, not only of her husband, but of her
dying relatives whom she nursed at the family plantation,
losing them and finally the house too. After the rape,
both sisters must take steps to preserve their illusions.
Stella refuses to let herself believe that it has
happened. And Blanche must retreat into madness, where
she can play forever the lady who, as she tells the
attendants who come to take her away, has always depended
on the kindness of strangers.

Williams, Tennessee. Suddenly Last Summer, 1958. Available in The
   Theatre of Tennessee Williams, Vol. III. New York: New
   Directions, 1972. Drama.

The Body	Children	Doctors
The Family	Homosexuality	Madness
Med. Ethics	Med. Profession	Nurses
Sexuality	Suffering	

The decent young psychiatrist at the center of this play
is a relatively passive figure, functioning for the most
part as an elicitor of others', particularly Catherine's,
repressed stories. His most active role comes when he
is pressured by Catherine's wealthy Aunt Violet to perform
a lobotomy on her niece. Dr. "Sugar's" boss pressures
him too, for Violet has promised to endow the hospital,
if she gets what she wants. But the doctor needs to
determine first if Catherine is truly mad, and in a series
of meetings with her, culminating in one of the most
dramatic scenes in modern theatre, he draws out the story
of her cousin Sebastian (Violet's son), Sebastian Venable
(Sebastian is "Stephen" the first martyr; Venable suggests
"venerable"), who all his life had been very close to
his mother. Indeed they were a couple, Violet and her
poet-son, travelling to Europe together every summer . . .
until last summer, when Sebastian decided to take Catherine
instead. The young woman, fresh from a first sexual
experience that has caused her to withdraw, devoted herself
to Sebastian. But he was an intensely and somewhat perverse religious man, driven to find God, and when he did
find Him in the horrible scene of the turtles' hopeless
dash for the sea, he was driven further to live out in
his life the vision he had seen, to become something of
a Christ-like martyr to his own religion. None of this
is explicit, of course. What is, is a death scene so
horrifying that it drove Catherine to temporary withdrawal.
She reveals to his shocked mother something she had not
wanted to face, that Sebastian had been a homosexual and
had used his pretty companion--his mother first, and then
when she got too old, Catherine--to lure men. Suddenly
last summer, he had begun to take risks with boys on a
public beach in Spain, tantalizing them with hand-outs
until one day they pursued him up the white hot streets
to his death in an old ruin, and there in a cannibalistic
communion service, they devoured his body. Now everyone
knows the hideous story Mrs. Venable had tried to cut out
of Catherine's brain.

Williams, Tennessee. Summer and Smoke, 1948. Available in The
   Eccentricities of a Nightingale and Summer and Smoke. New York:
   New Directions, 1964. Drama.

The Body	Doctors	Med. Profession
Sexuality		

The dichotomy of the body and the soul as represented by
John, a doctor, and Alma, a preacher's daughter and
something of an hysterical spinster. He is a wastrel and
lives passionately. She is spiritual, as her name indicates, and lives timidly, though she is very attracted to
John. One day they have a confrontation. The doctor
takes her to his office and forces his anatomy lesson on
her: the body is all, he tells her; love originates in
the testicles, and there is no place on the anatomy chart
for the soul. She rebuts him, but later, after John has
reformed and become a self-sacrificing, hard-working
doctor, Alma knows that she needs the body after all.
But it's too late. He marries a nice young girl who was
one of Alma's protégées, while she ends up at the railroad station, looking for a man. The play sounds more
schematic than it is in production. The other play in
this volume is a later version of Summer and Smoke.

Williams, Tennessee. Sweet Bird of Youth, 1959. Available in The Theatre of Tennessee Williams, Vol. IV. New York: New Directions, 1972. Drama.

Age   The Body   Death
V.D.

Age and the Body personified. A young man, Chance, has established a half-loving, half-blackmailing relationship with an aging actress in flight from an imagined failure. Chance has always used his body and his sexuality to gain power over women, regardless of the effect upon them. And the actress has reached the stage where she needs oxygen, liquor, and sex to face each day and the fear of passing time. Interestingly, it is the actress who gains strength in this relationship. Her comeback attempt is successful, and she feels quite renewed. But Chance, though potent with women, is impotent in other situations. The righteous Southern father of his one-time girlfriend is out to get him for giving his pure daughter V.D. which led to a hysterectomy. When we last see Chance the bought stud, he is waiting for the father's men to arrive and carry out the threatened castration.

Williams, William Carlos. The Autobiography of William Carlos Williams, 1951. New York: New Directions, 1967. Autobiography.

The Body   By Doctors   Children
Death   Disease & Health   Doctors
Med. Instit.   Med. Profession   Nurses
Poverty & Health   Preg. & Childbirth

The entire book should be read, simply because Williams is the best doctor-writer America has produced, but the most relevant chapters are "Medicine," "French Hospital," "Hell's Kitchen," and "The Practice," in which Williams explains his reasons for choosing medicine (chiefly financial--it would give him the opportunity to write what he liked) and for staying with it (definitely not financial); and "Of Medicine and Poetry," in which he claims that for him medicine and poetry amount to the same thing, that he could not have done one well without the other. Poetry relieved the boredom of medicine: "to treat a man as something to which surgery, drugs and hoodoo applied was an indifferent matter; to treat him as material for a work of art made him somehow come alive to me." Yet daily medicine kept him interested and wanting to write: "It's the humdrum, day-in, day-out everyday work that is the real satisfaction of the practice of medicine . . . . the actual calling on people, at all times and under all conditions, the coming to grips with the intimate conditions of their lives, when they were being born, when they were dying, watching them die, watching them get well when they were ill, has always absorbed me." "French Hospital" and "Hell's Kitchen" are fragmented but vivid looks at Williams' two New York internships, the first in general medicine, the second, taken at a hospital serving a squalid neighborhood, in obstetrics and the diseases of children. He talks about some of his patients, their illnesses and deaths, and the nurses, whom he almost always respects, loves, and hankers after.

Williams, William Carlos. "Complaint," 1921. Available in Selected Poems, by Williams. New York: New Directions, 1968. Poem: 22 lines.

By Doctors   Doctors   Preg. & Childbirth

An interesting comparison with Kafka's "Country Doctor." Here too a doctor is called in the night, and the patient is something of an Everypatient (though in this case the patient is also a woman in labor). This doctor is not, however, a savior, sacrificed or otherwise. He is perhaps a lover ("Night is a room/darkened for lovers"), certainly a carer: "I pick the hair from her eyes/and watch her misery/with compassion."

Williams, William Carlos. The Cure, 1952. Available in Many Loves and Other Plays: The Collected Plays of William Carlos Williams. Norfolk, Conn.: New Directions, 1961. Drama.

By Doctors   Nurses   Sexuality

Tension between the professionalism of a nurse and her sexuality. A young hood is injured in a crash near the home of an ex-nurse and her husband. Automatically she acts as a professional to ease his pain, and then talks her husband into letting her keep the young man as a patient in their home. It becomes clear that her brand of nursing is a form of maternalism: she would like a child, and doesn't have one. Finally the young man's anger against her flares out in a battle over her use of her nurse's cap and some baby clothes to protect her role, which she can then hide behind, escaping his sexual advances. He strikes her, believing he has killed her. But he hasn't, and she returns to her husband. An interesting play from the perspective of learning how Williams has viewed the connections between the personality and the profession. But as an example of a good play? No.

Williams, William Carlos. "Death," 1930. Available in Selected Poems, by Williams. New York: New Directions, 1968. Poem: 46 lines.

The Body   By Doctors   Death

A violently passionate poem about ("against," really) a certain dead man, his corpse, death itself: all written in carefully, but barely, controlled, language: "he's dead/the old bastard--/He's a bastard because/there's nothing legitimate in him any/more . . . . He's nothing

at all/he's dead/shrunken up to skin/Put his head on/one chair and his feet on another and/he'll lie there/like an acrobat--/Love's beaten. He beat it. That's why/he's insufferable." At the end of the poem the human element has gone out of the body entirely: "just bury it/and hide its face/for shame."

Williams, William Carlos. A Dream of Love, ca. 1947. Available in Many Loves and Other Plays. Norfolk, Conn.: New Directions, 1961. Drama.

By Doctors   Doctors   Sexuality

An embarrassingly bad play, but interesting for its gossip value, which is no mean thing, and for its insights into Williams' conception of the doctor/poet. One of its themes is that sexuality is at the bottom of both poetry and medicine for the main character. Medicine is mainly just a way to earn a living, so the wife urges him to give it up and concentrate on poetry. The reasons for this request are deep, since their relationship thrives on his poetic descriptions of their past love. But he uses his medicine to meet women and have affairs, and thus renew his sexuality. During one of these assignations, he dies of a heart attack. The wife is mad with grief and desperate to know what his last words were. She masochistically quizzes the mistress. Finally she has a dream in which she envisions her husband with his mistress and his last words, which were about poetry and how we have fallen since the Greeks because though they made poems, we are limited by the art of poetry, the rules. This is apparently very sexy to his mistress, for they then embrace lustily and the vision ends. Somehow it is enough for the wife too. She is purged of her obsessive need to know, and can go on with her life.

Williams, William Carlos. "The Injury," ca. 1940's. Available in Selected Poems, by Williams. New York: New Directions, 1968. Poem: 52 lines.

By Doctors   Disease & Health   Grief
Med. Instit.

Difficult, blasphemous perhaps, to paraphrase. At any rate, the speaker lies in a hospital bed at night. He is awake, and from somewhere he hears a locomotive "breathing." The engine becomes the men who are shoveling coal in her, shoveling and resting: breathing. Then it is just one man who is shoveling "working and not lying here/in this/hospital bed--powerless--" and a bird's piercing cry is drowned out by the slow singing of the engine on the rails. Finally, the injured man shifts even more suddenly to his own condition and likely future, still using the imagery of the engine: "high pitched:/rounding/the curve--/--the slow way because/(if you can find any way) that is/the only way left now/for you."

Williams, William Carlos. "Jean Beicke," 1938. From The Farmers' Daughters. New York: New Directions, 1961. Short Story.

By Doctors   Children   Death
Disease & Health   Doctors   Grief
Med. Instit.   Nurses   Poverty & Health

It's the Depression, and this pediatrics ward has seen great numbers of sickly, unwanted children. One of them, an 11-month-old called Jean Beicke is brought in grotesquely ill, in great pain, slowly dying from something the doctors don't discover until the autopsy. When she dies, Jean leaves a peculiar set of mourners: a mother who has been abandoned by her husband, the staff who are disgusted with their stupidity, and, in a sense, all those elements that have contributed to the Depression itself. Williams tells the story by juxtaposing the hard, dry details of Jean's suffering and struggle to live, with the doctor's seemingly casual reaction. And gradually the pain of the child becomes all the more clearly outlined because the narrator-doctor has made it the center of interest. He makes, that is, Jean Beicke the center of interest, not his own reaction to her, and thereby accords dignity to this pathetic, dying baby.

Williams, William Carlos. "A Night in June," 1938. From The Farmers' Daughters. New York: New Directions, 1961. Short Story.

By Doctors   The Family   Med. Profession
Poverty & Health   Preg. & Childbirth

A detailed, vivid account of a poor woman delivered in her candle-lit home of her 9th child. The doctor-narrator had delivered her first, and lost it, but he found a friend in the woman, whom he has come to love over the years. Williams describes her--is he condescending or sexist here?--as "a woman of great simplicity of character-- docility, patience, with a fine direct look in her grey eyes. And courageous. Devoted to her instincts and convictions and to me." Williams gives glimpses of the father, the sister-in-law who attends the doctor, the three-year-old child who sleeps by his mother throughout the labor, and the others who look in at the end. But most of the story is devoted to the birth itself and to the great pleasure the doctor gets from it. He hadn't delivered one at home for several years, and he has this to say about the so-called advances in obstetrical science: "The pituitary extract and other simple devices represent science. Science . . . has crowded the stage more than is necessary . . . . It touches us too crudely now, all newness is over-complex . . . . But without science, without pituitrin, I'd be here till noon." Compare Williams' "Complaint."

Williams, William Carlos. "Portrait of a Woman at Her Bath," ca. 1950. Available in Pictures from Brueghel. New York: New Directions, 1962. Poem: 16 lines.

The Body   By Doctors   Sexuality

Williams, it is said, loved all women well, and here is a short poem in which his immense pleasure at a woman who is no beauty is sexuality at its more pervasive: "it is a satisfaction/a joy/to have one of those/in the house/when she takes a bath/she unclothes/herself/she is no/ Venus . . . the sun is/glad of a fellow/to marvel at/the birds and the flowers/look in."

Williams, William Carlos. "To a Dog Injured in the Street," 1954. Available in Pictures from Brueghel. New York: New Directions, 1962. Poem: 68 lines.

By Doctors   Death   Dying
Science & Poetry   Suffering

The sight and sound of a pitiful dog dying in the streets forces the poet to some conclusions about pain; to some memories as well, like the time when as a child he had kicked his dog's puppies, for he thought that they were trying to destroy her by biting her breasts, or the time when he saw a hunter laughingly cut up into a dead rabbit's private parts. He is a man now and (if we can chance an identification of the speaker with Williams himself) a doctor too, but faced with horrible suffering, he says: "I can do nothing/but sing about it/and so am assuaged/from my pain." There is some suffering, in short, that is beyond the power of Williams the doctor; the power of Williams the poet is required: "René Char/ you are a poet who believes/in the power of beauty/to right all wrongs./I believe it also./With invention and courage/we shall surpass/the pitiful dumb beasts."

Williams, William Carlos. "To Waken an Old Lady," 1921. Available in Selected Poems, by Williams. New York: New Directions, 1968. Poem: 18 lines.

Age   By Doctors

One of his Imagist poems: the objective equivalent of old age: "a flight of small/cheeping birds/skimming/bare trees/above a snow glaze." The birds are buffeted. Finally they rest on "harsh weedstalks," and the wind is "tempered/by a shrill/piping of plenty." Makes a clinical description of age seem embarrassingly verbose and, oddly enough, indirect.

Williams, William Carlos. "Tract," 1917. Available in Selected Poems, by Williams. New York: New Directions, 1968. Poem: 68 lines.

By Doctors   Death   Grief

A mocking, conversational address to the poet's townspeople on how to "perform" a funeral--that is the word he uses for what is, to Williams, often only a show. No polished hearse for him. Only a rough farm wagon with perhaps newly painted gilt wheels as the one sop to tradition or the one sign that this is a special journey. And the coffin is to be open to the air--why protect it from rain? Williams asks. It's not necessary; it's not logical. Instead of flowers, let the dead person carry with him something he prized and is known by. Let the undertaker be humble and inconspicuous, not the star of the show himself. As for the mourners themselves, they are to ride in the open too, or even walk. "Go with some show/of inconvenience; sit openly--to the weather/ as to grief./Or do you think you can shut grief in?/ What--from us? We who have perhaps/nothing to lose?"

Williams, William Carlos. "The Use of Force," 1938. From The Farmers' Daughters. New York: New Directions, 1961. Short Story.

By Doctors   Children   Disease & Health
Doctors   Sexuality

In this case, the poor, ill, but marginally triumphant person whom Williams likes to portray in his stories is a little girl, whom the doctor "falls in love with." He has been called to her home because she's had a fever for 3 days, and though she has told her parents she has no sore throat, the doctor at once suspects diphtheria. The doctor-patient relationship portrayed here is a battle. She refuses to cooperate, refuses to let him examine her. He grows increasingly irritated and finally furiously forces her mouth open, cutting her and making her hysterical in the process. "The damned little brat must be protected against her own idiocy, one says to one's self at such times. Others must be protected against her. It is social necessity. And all those things are true. But a blind fury, a feeling of adult shame, bred of a longing for muscular release are the operatives . . . . In a final unreasoning assault I overpowered the child's neck and jaws." What he finds is evidence of diphtheria, all right, and one proud but defeated little fury. But one wonders, of course, if it isn't the doctor who has been defeated since he has allowed himself to participate in an action very much like a rape.

Williams, William Carlos. A Voyage to Pagany, 1928. New York: New Directions, 1938. Novel.

By Doctors   Disease & Health   Doctors
Med. Instit.   Med. Profession   Poverty & Health

A poor novel, but everything Williams wrote is of potential value to Literature and Medicine. The novel has an interesting if familiar theme: an American goes to

Europe ("Pagany"), looking for the roots of his own culture. Williams' autobiographical hero is Dr. Dev Evans, whose travels and sexual involvements and discoveries about art (it isn't a place, so he can return to the country he knows best; in fact, he must do so) form the major part of the book. But there are also some scattered medical comments, a few medical scenes, the most significant coming in Chapter XXII. Evans is taking some courses at a Viennese clinic. Among his fellow students, he finds some people who cure for cash, and these people Evans abhors. He "detested his profession in the herd." The A.M.A. is to him just a "successful cult." But at the clinic he witnesses some demonstrations --on poverty-stricken patients--of "tuberculosis, the Viennese disease," and the demonstrations are awesome. Not awesomely humane, but awesomely organized. "At once Dev began to get that sense of beauty in arrangement, that fervor which the continental scientific method, built upon their aristocratic thought, had engendered, to go far through the world . . . . all this demonstrated on the cadaver, in carefully preserved specimens--for the sake of beauty. For beauty was the leader, he felt it at once, a clarity. Evans had always known that in the chaos of pedagogy the greatest genius of the future would be he who would give in ten words, ten illuminating words the limits of knowledge--permitting classification."

Wittig, Monique. The Lesbian Body, 1973, trans. David Le Vay. New York: William Morrow and Co., 1975. Novel.

The Body   Homosexuality   Sexual Roles

No one can go farther in celebrating the female body than Wittig has. Perhaps now no one needs to. First in Les Guérillères (New York: Viking Press, 1971), and then in this book, the author creates a world which has woman as its fundamental reality. Woman is the basis for its language, its symbols, its values. In The Lesbian Body, Wittig ritualistically catalogs the parts of the body (cf. Whitman's "The Body Electric"), translated when necessary into female terms: "The dorsals the iliacs the teres the quadrati the triangular the pyramidals the abdominals the gluteals the biceps the triceps the tendons of achillea." She glorifies the physical contact of women's bodies, in a style that is at once rhapsodic and clinical, self-conscious and other-conscious, lyrical and violent: "M/y clitoris m/y labia are touched by your hands. Through m/y vagina and m/y uterus you insert yourself breaking the membrane up to m/y intestines. Round your neck you place m/y duodenum pale-pink well-veined with blue." And she gives us glimpses of an Amazonian society--even more thoroughly female than in her previous novel--where the goddesses and Sappho reign. The translator of this astonishing novel is an eminent anatomist and surgeon.

Wolfe, Gene. "The Death of Dr. Island." Available in The Best Science Fiction of the Year #3, ed. Terry Carr. New York: Ballantine Books, 1974. Short Story.

Children   Madness   Med. Ethics
Med. Instit.   Sci Fi

A horrifying tale of a small "island" in a satellite, on which three people, Ignacio, a homicidal genius, Nicky, a boy whose brain lobes have been severed, and Diane, a suicidal schizophrenic, have been placed for treatment. The island is completely controlled by an invisible "Dr. Island" who talks to the patients through their minds. Nicky and Diane have been brought from custodial institutions of a horrifying nature, not to be cured, but to provide Ignacio with a cure. He is a genius and so more important to society. Nicky, from whose point of view the story is told, begins to respond to the others. But he is defeated by the institution's purpose. By having intercourse with Diane and then killing her, Ignacio releases his tensions and regains some sanity. ("Ignacio was frightened by women; now he knows that they are really very weak, and he has acted upon certain fantasies and finds them bitter.") Nicky, whose intelligence and sensitivity have survived institutionalization, retreats into himself in horror and his other, mute, brain lobe takes command of the body to the great satisfaction of the paternalistic "Dr. Island," who has defended Diane's death: "--but by dying she made someone else-- someone very important--well. Her prognosis was bad; she really wanted only death, and this was the death I chose for her. You could call it the death of Dr. Island, a death that would help someone else."

Woolf, Virginia. Mrs. Dalloway, 1925. New York: Harcourt, Brace & World, Inc., 1953. Novel.

Body/Mind   Death   Doctors
Homosexuality   Madness   Suicide

A brilliant side-by-side investigation of sanity (Clarissa Dalloway's) and madness (Septimus Warren Smith's), their parallel lines, their convergence, and their separation into life and death. Clarissa is a woman who is so sensitive to ugliness of object, body, and spirit that she experiences physical pain in its presence, especially since her illness. Her sexuality too is delicate and has included "being in love with" women, especially Sally Seton in her adolescence. But it is on the subjects of doctors, madness, and death that the book is most illuminating. We experience Septimus' madness with him: hear the voices telling him of universal love, of living trees, of a crimeless state and simultaneously of his unforgivable crime, that he cannot feel. His doctors are appalling and themselves unforgivably insensitive: first Holmes the idiotically amiable g.p., whose aggressiveness leads directly to Septimus' suicide; then the Harley Street nerve specialist, Sir William Bradshaw, who tells his patients that they need proportion in their lives and meanwhile dwells securely amidst his own acquisitions and power over his patients' lives. When Clarissa learns of this stranger's, Septimus', suicide, she thinks: "Death was defiance. Death was an attempt to communicate; people feeling the impossibility of teaching the centre which, mystically, evaded them; closeness drew apart; rapture faded, one was alone. There was an embrace in death."

Woolf, Virginia. "On Being Ill," 1930. From The Moment. New York: Harcourt, Brace, Jovanovich, 1948. Essay.

The Body   Disease & Health

Woolf turns her major stylistic talents to a subject about which she knows a good deal, having been several times mad and many times ill with headache and flu. She expresses surprise that illness is not more often treated in literature, together with love, battle, and jealousy as the great themes. Or that "the daily drama of the body" has not more often been recorded. The reason is "To look these things squarely in the face would need the courage of a lion tamer; a robust philosophy; a reason rooted in the bowels of the earth. Short of these, this monster, the body, this miracle, its pain, will soon make us taper into mysticism, or rise, with rapid beats of the wings, into the raptures of transcendentalism." Woolf herself concludes these things about illness: we are more truthful then; we discover things when horizontal that we never see when vertical; we turn to poetry rather than prose; and in illness, words have a mystic quality.

Woolf, Virginia. A Room of One's Own, 1929. New York: Harcourt, Brace and World, 1957. Long Essay; and Orlando, 1928. New York: New American Library, 1960. Novel.

Sexual Roles

Many people think that Orlando--which is, among other things, a fantasy biography of Woolf's friend Vita Sackville-West--is the realization of the theory in A Room of One's Own. In her essay Woolf asserts that a woman must have 500 pounds a year and a room of her own, if she is to write. If she is to write well, Woolf suggests in Chapter 6, perhaps she needs, perhaps every great creator needs, an androgynous mind, that is, a fusion of masculine and feminine characteristics. Just as it takes male and female to create in the physical world, so also in the mental world, two sexes are required. She lists as the great androgynous writers Shakespeare, Keats, Coleridge (from whom she takes the term); as too male, Milton, Ben Jonson and Wordsworth; as perhaps too female, Proust. In Orlando the main character achieves an androgynous state when, at the age of 30, he slips into a trance and awakens as a woman. Lady Orlando afterwards has a highly desirable mixture of traditional masculine and feminine traits.

Woolf, Virginia. The Waves, 1931. New York: Harcourt, Brace and World, 1959. Novel.

The Body	Death	Grief
Homosexuality	Madness	Sexuality
Suicide		

Six "characters" swirl through this magnificent lyrical novel. They are distinctive, yet simultaneously all part of the multiple personality of Bernard, the writer: an interesting fact since one of the characters, Rhoda, is frightened mad and finally commits suicide; a second, Neville, is an intellectual homosexual; and a third, Jinny, lives passionately through her body. Woolf is excellent, of course, on madness. Here is Rhoda, who "feared embraces" and was always "seeking some pillar in the desert": "I touch nothing. I see nothing. We may sink and settle on the waves. The sea will drum in my ears. The white petals will be darkened with sea water. They will float for a moment and then sink. Rolling me over the waves will shoulder me under. Everything falls in a tremendous shower, dissolving me." But is the portrayal of the effect of death and grief that is the greatest accomplishment of this novel. The death of a seventh "character," the silent Percival, sets off musings among the six-become-one that finally ends in Bernard's heroic speech at the end of the novel as he rides against death the enemy. Perhaps only Proust and Woolf recreate eternity and triumph over death in this way.

Wright, David. "Monologue of a Deaf Man," 1958. Available in The Norton Anthology of Modern Poetry, eds. Richard Ellmann and Robert O'Clair. New York: Norton, 1973. Poem: 40 lines.

Handicaps

Achieves a certain distinction as poetry, but, it must be admitted, even more important for content alone, and the fact that its author is himself deaf. In passing, he makes several insightful comments about deafness: "Then do you console yourself? You are consoled/If you are, as all are"; "The injury, dominated, is an asset"; "the tone speaks less than a twitch and a grimace." And this conclusion, persuasive because it is uttered by a deaf poet: "In whatever condition, whole, blind, dumb,/ One-legged or leprous, the human being is,/I affirm the human condition is the same,/The heart half broken in ashes and in lies,/But sustained by the immensity of the divine."

Wyndham, John. Trouble With Lichen. London: Penguin, 1960. Novel.

| Age | Death | Sci Fi |
| Sexual Roles | | |

Limited, but interesting in its limitations. A female scientist and a male scientist both find a drug that prolongs youthfulness, extending the lifespan into hundreds of years. The man innoculates his family and keeps silent. The woman believes that women are forced into unhappy life styles by their battle against age--their need to catch a man and have children while young. Lengthening a woman's youth will free her. Further, mankind as a whole is too apt to catch at temporary solutions to long-range problems, such as over-population, because men do not live long enough to concern themselves with the future. Therefore, the woman scientist wants the longevity drug (available only in limited supply) to remain available to as many as possible, to help the world. She succeeds by giving the drug to unsuspecting wives of influential men by placing it in a "youth-preserving" treatment. The women persuade their men to legalize the drug. The novel has a rather superficial plot--romances, spies, etc. It is the ideas attributed to the woman which make the book worthwhile.

Yeats, William Butler. "The Circus Animals' Desertion," 1936. Available in The Collected Poems of W. B. Yeats. New York: Macmillan, 1956. Poem: 40 lines.

Age

Evocation of a common cause for despair in elderly writers: the knowledge that there are no new themes, and that all one can do is repeat what one has written before. After running through several of his famous themes, Yeats concludes that though they were pure, they began in the refuse heap of his heart, and that in old age he must go back to where he began so long ago, to that same "foul rag-and-bone shop of the heart." Implications for the aged in general: when inspiration, creativity, and function are gone, one is back at the beginning.

Yeats, William Butler. "Crazy Jane Talks with the Bishop," 1933. Available in The Collected Poems of W. B. Yeats. New York: Macmillan, 1956. Poem: 18 lines.

| Age | The Body | Madness |
| Sexuality | | |

A dialogue between the bishop and an aged woman, locally considered mad. He describes her approaching death in terms of fallen breasts and dry veins, and taunts her for living amidst foul surroundings, rather than preparing for the beauty of heaven. But she replies that "fair needs foul," that even sex is aligned with the organs of waste, or, to put it in Yeats' far better language: "Love has pitched his mansion in/The place of excrement."

Yeats, William Butler. "Her Vision in the Wood," 1933. Available in The Collected Poems of W. B. Yeats. New York: Macmillan, 1956. Poem: 32 lines.

| Age | Grief | Sexuality |

An old woman, enraged because she is too old for men to find her sexually attractive, has a mystical vision in which she sees a group of young women mourning a wounded, dying man. As he turns to look at her, she recognizes her dead lover, who was both her victim and her torturer.

Yeats, William Butler. "A Last Confession," 1933. Available in The Collected Poems of W. B. Yeats. New York: Macmillan, 1956. Poem: 24 lines.

| Age | Sexuality |

Another instance of Yeats' insistence that the elderly are still fascinated by sex. Here an old woman recalls that she had the most pleasure with a man when there were no emotional attachments, but that when the souls were naked, there was misery--a delightful, unextinguishable misery!

Yeats, William Butler. "Leda and the Swan," 1928. Available in The Collected Poems of W. B. Yeats. New York: Macmillan, 1956. Sonnet.

Sexuality

Strong, erotic image of ritualized rape, based on the classical story of Leda's rape by Zeus in the guise of a swan. Obvious parallels to Mary and the Holy Ghost. There is a basic sexual situation here: the taking of a terrified but attracted woman by an indifferent authority figure.

Yeats, William Butler. "Michael Robartes and the Dancer," 1921. Available in The Collected Poems of W. B. Yeats. New York: Macmillan, 1956. Poem: 52 lines.

| Body/Mind | Sexual Roles |

Dialogue between Michael and a beautiful woman. She is a student, a fulfiller of the mind, and wonders whether there isn't danger in the body. But he argues--and he carries the poem--that more knowledge comes from the "vigorous thigh" than from a "mere book," and that beautiful women can elevate mankind by thinking no thought, unless the body believe it first.

Yeats, William Butler. "A Prayer for Old Age," 1935. Available in
    The Collected Poems of W. B. Yeats. New York: Macmillan,
    1956. Poem: 12 lines.

    Age

        A kind of irreverent prayer in that the poet asks not for
        the conventional wisdom and pacificity that others think
        admirable in old age, but instead asks God to let him
        please himself and serve his poetry, and therefore die
        "A foolish, passionate man."

Yeats, William Butler. "Sailing to Byzantium," 1928. Available in
    The Collected Poems of W. B. Yeats. New York: Macmillan, 1956.
    Poem: 32 lines.

    Age   The Body

        Richly complex poem suggesting the poet's disgust with
        his aging body--"An aged man is but a paltry thing,/
        A tattered coat upon a stick"--and his intent, therefore,
        to make his soul sing all the louder. To accomplish
        this, the "dying animal" has come to Byzantium, where he
        can be gathered "into the artifice of eternity," and
        there throw off his body for some ideal form "as grecian
        goldsmiths make/Of hammered gold and gold enamelling."

Yeats, William Butler. "Why Should Not Old Men Be Mad?" 1936.
    Available in The Collected Poems of W. B. Yeats. New York:
    Macmillan, 1956. Poem: 20 lines.

    Age   Madness

        Sees madness as inevitable in observant old men, for they
        know--as young men cannot--that those who seem most deserv-
        ing in their youth often end unhappily. In fact, Yeats
        asserts that there is no such thing as "an unbroken
        happy mind," in which case, one might go on to ponder,
        madness in age is not only inevitable, it is universal
        and perhaps true sanity as well.

Yglesias, Helen. "Semi-Private." The New Yorker, February 5, 1972.
    Short Story.

    Death   Disease & Health   Doctors
    Handicaps   Med. Ethics   Med. Instit.
    Nurses   Sexual Roles   Women as Patients

        A fine view of surgery for breast cancer from the perspective
        of the patient herself, a 28-year-old woman with two small
        children, an invalid mother, and a troubled marriage to
        a weak man. Waking up after the operation, the woman
        knows at once her breast is gone, and thinks bitterly,
        "They never ask the patient. The patient is anesthetized
        on the operating table, cut open. They call in the hus-
        band. 'We think it best to remove this precancerous
        breast. Since this is your hunk of meat, do we have your
        permission, husband?'" For much of the story, the author
        roams around the ward, introducing us to several other
        patients, including a young Catholic woman, whose five
        children have caused serious damage to her eyesight; and
        a Jewish woman, two of whose three children are deaf.
        The nurse arranges the hair of the breast cancer patient
        --the nurse herself, thinks the woman, is sweet, pretty,
        has two breasts, and will attract the woman's husband--
        in preparation for her husband's visit. First the
        family doctor, also a friend, arrives to commiserate with
        her and to whip himself for not insisting she go to a
        specialist sooner. And then comes the husband, nervous
        and appallingly insensitive, whose first words to her
        are: "'Well, baby, are you still going to divorce me?'"

Zugsmith, Leane. "The Three Veterans." Available in Short Stories
    from the New Yorker. New York: Simon and Schuster, 1940.
    Short Story.

    Age   Med. Ethics   Poverty & Health
    Women as Patients

        A short sketch which makes one simple point, but makes it
        well. Three elderly women are regular patrons of a free
        clinic, coming twice a week to question and advise new
        patients, while listening with ingratiating laughter to
        all the words of "The Doctor." Clearly, a good deal of
        their self-image and status is built in this way. Then
        one day a well-dressed peroxide blonde comes to consult
        The Doctor about a bruise she wants to use in a lawsuit.
        He dismisses her contemptuously, and she responds,
        "'Just because it's free is no reason why we can't be
        treated like human beings!'" When The Doctor has no
        come-back, the three ladies, now looking very grey, rise
        to go, meeting The Specialist Doctor on the way out, who
        invites him to appear as cases for his next lecture
        ("'How would you girls like to dance in my chorus Friday
        night?'") They all refuse, and one adds, "'Just because
        it's free don't mean we aren't human beings.'"

ABORTION

Arking, Linda. "Certain Hard Places." Short Story. 20th.

Barth, John. The End of the Road. Novel. 20th.

Burns, Robert. "Death and Doctor Hornbook." Poem. 18th.

Defoe, Daniel. Moll Flanders. Novel. 18th.

Drabble, Margaret. The Millstone. Novel. 20th.

Dreiser, Theodore. An American Tragedy. Novel. 20th.

Faulkner, William. As I Lay Dying. Novel. 20th.

Hansberry, Lorraine. A Raisin in the Sun. Drama. 20th.

Hemingway, Ernest. "Hills Like White Elephants." Short Story.
     20th.

Johnson, Samuel. A Dictionary of the English Language. Dictionary.
     18th.

Jonson, Benjamin. Epigram LXII. Poem. Renaissance.

Juvenal (Decimus Iunius Iuvenalis). Satires, no. VI. Poem.
     Classical.

Kingsley, Sidney. Men in White. Drama. 20th.

Lessing, Doris. A Proper Marriage. Novel. 20th.

Lowell, Robert. "Not Cleared of Killing." Poem. 20th.

Machiavelli, Niccolo. Mandragola. Drama. Renaissance.

Mortimer, Penelope. The Pumpkin Eater. Novel. 20th.

Oates, Joyce Carol. Wonderland. Novel. 20th.

O'Neill, Eugene. Strange Interlude. Drama. 20th.

Ovid (Publius Ovidius Naso). Amores. Book II, Elegies xiii and
     xiv. Poems. Classical.

Remarque, Erich Maria. Arch of Triumph. Novel. 20th.

Rhys, Jean. Voyage in the Dark. Novel. 20th.

Smollett, Tobias. The Adventures of Roderick Random. Novel.
     18th.

Zola, Emile. Fécondité (From Les Quatres Evangiles). Novel.
     19th.

ADOLESCENCE

Auden, W. H. "Adolescence." Poem. 20th.

Auden, W. H. "The Age of Anxiety." Long Poem. 20th.

Austen, Jane. Sense and Sensibility. Novel. 19th.

Bowen, Elizabeth. Eva Trout. Novel. 20th.

Butler, Samuel. The Way of All Flesh. Novel.

Byron, George Gordon, Lord. Don Juan. Poem. 19th.

Colette. The Innocent Libertine. Novel. 20th.

Crane, Stephen. The Red Badge of Courage. Novel. 19th.

Delaney, Shelagh. A Taste of Honey. Drama. 20th.

Dickens, Charles. David Copperfield. Novel. 19th.

Earle, John. Micro-cosmographie. Sketches. Renaissance.

Fielding, Henry. Tom Jones. Novel. 18th.

Frost, Robert. "'Out, Out.'" Poem. 20th.

Golding, William. Lord of the Flies. Novel. 20th.

Hawthorne, Nathaniel. "My Kinsman, Major Molineux." Short Story.
     19th.

Heller, Joseph. Something Happened. Novel. 20th.

Hemingway, Ernest. "God Rest You Merry, Gentlemen." Short Story.
     20th.

Hemingway, Ernest. "Indian Camp." Short Story. 20th.

James, Henry. The Portrait of a Lady. Novel. 19th.

Joyce, James. Portrait of the Artist as a Young Man. Novel. 20th.

Lawrence, D. H. Sons and Lovers. Novel. 20th.

Leduc, Violette. The Taxi. Short Story. 20th.

Leduc, Violette. Thérèse and Isabelle. Novella; and La Bâtarde.
     Autobiography. 20th.

Lessing, Doris. A Proper Marriage. Novel. 20th.

Mann, Thomas. Death in Venice. Novella. 20th.

Mann, Thomas. The Magic Mountain. Novel. 20th.

McCullers, Carson. The Heart Is a Lonely Hunter. Novel. 20th.

Miller, Arthur. The Crucible. Drama. 20th.

Nabokov, Vladimir. Lolita. Novel. 20th.

Oates, Joyce Carol. Wonderland. Novel. 20th.

O'Connor, Flannery. "The Lame Shall Enter First." Short Story.
     20th.

O'Connor, Frank. "The Drunkard," "Judas," and "My Oedipus
     Complex." Short Stories. 20th.

O'Neill, Eugene. Ah Wilderness! Drama. 20th.

Plath, Sylvia. The Bell Jar. Novel. 20th.

Roethke, Theodore. "Old Lady's Winter Words" and Meditations of
     an Old Woman. Poem and Poem Sequence. 20th.

Roth, Philip. Portnoy's Complaint. Novel. 20th.

Salinger, J. D. The Catcher in the Rye. Novel. 20th.

Schnitzler, Arthur. Mother and Son. Novella. 20th.

Sexton, Anne. "The Breast." Poem. 20th.

Shaffer, Peter. Equus. Drama. 20th.

Shakespeare, William. All's Well That Ends Well. Drama.
     Renaissance.

Shakespeare, William. Romeo and Juliet. Drama. Renaissance.

Shakespeare, William. The Winter's Tale. Drama. Renaissance.

Sheed, Wilfrid. People Will Always Be Kind. Novel. 20th.

Skelton, John. Philip Sparrow. Poem. Renaissance.

The Spectator, no. 431. Essay. 18th.

Tennyson, Alfred. "Locksley Hall" and "Locksley Hall Sixty Years
     After." Long Poems. 19th.

Twain, Mark. Adventures of Huckleberry Finn. Novel. 19th.

Wilder, Thornton. Our Town. Drama. 20th.

AGE

Amis, Kingsley. Ending Up. Novel. 20th.

Anonymous. Beowulf. Epic Poem. Medieval.

Anonymous. The Castle of Perseverance. Drama. Medieval.

Anonymous. The Celestina. Drama. Renaissance.

Anonymous. The Wanderer. Poem. Medieval.

Arden, John. The Happy Haven. Drama. 20th.

Aristophanes. Lysistrata. Drama. Classical.

Armstrong, John. "The Art of Preserving Health." Poem. 18th.

Arnold, Matthew. Empedocles on Etna. Dramatic Poem. 19th.

Arnold, Matthew. "Growing Old." Poem. 19th.

Auden, W. H. "The Age of Anxiety." Long Poem. 20th.

Auden, W. H. "The Model." Poem. 20th.

Auden, W. H. "No, Plato, No" and "Lullaby." Poems. 20th.

Babel, Isaac. "The End of the Old-Folk's Home." Short Story.
    20th.

Bacon, Francis. "Of Youth and Age." Essay. Renaissance.

Baudelaire, Charles Pierre. "The Little Old Women" ("Les Petites
    Vielles"). Poem. 19th.

Beauvoir, Simone de. A Very Easy Death. Autobiography. 20th.

Beckett, Samuel. Endgame. Drama. 20th.

Beckett, Samuel. Krapp's Last Tape. Drama. 20th.

Bellow, Saul. Mr. Sammler's Planet. Novel. 20th.

Benn, Gottfried. "Artists and Old Age." Essay. 20th.

Betjeman, John. "A Child Ill." Poem. 20th.

The Bible. Apochrypha. Daniel and Susanna. Classical.

The Bible. Ecclesiastes. Classical.

The Bible. Genesis. Classical.

Blish, James. "They Shall Have Stars" and "A Life For the Stars."
    Novella. 20th.

Boccaccio, Giovanni. The Decameron: Day 2, Tale 10. Tale.
    Medieval.

Boswell, James. The Life of Samuel Johnson. Biography. 18th.

Browning, Robert. "A Grammarian's Funeral." Poem. 19th.

Browning, Robert. "Rabbi Ben Ezra." Poem. 19th.

Buonarroti, Michel Angelo. "I feel constrained and blocked as is
    the marrow." Poem. Renaissance.

Buonarroti, Michel Angelo. "This new, singular beauty." Poem.
    Renaissance.

Burney, Fanny (Mme. D'Arblay). Evelina. Novel. 18th.

Burns, Robert. "The Deuk's Dang O'er my Daddie" ("The Duck's
    knocked over my Daddy"). Poem. 18th.

Burns, Robert. "John Anderson My Jo" and "John Anderson, My Jo."
    Poems. 18th.

Burton, Robert. The Anatomy of Melancholy. Treatise. Renaissance.

Campion, Thomas. "Though you are yoong and I am olde." Song.
    Renaissance.

Carroll, Lewis (Charles L. Dodgson). Alice's Adventures in
    Wonderland. Tale. 19th.

Castiglione, Baldesar. The Book of the Courtier. Dialogues.
    Renaissance.

Cervantes Saavedra, Miguel de. Don Quixote. Tale. Renaissance.

Chaucer, Geoffrey. The Canterbury Tales, "The Miller's Tale."
    Tale. Medieval.

Chaucer, Geoffrey. The Canterbury Tales, "The Pardoner's Tale."
    Tale. Medieval.

Chaucer, Geoffrey. The Canterbury Tales, "The Reeve's Prologue."
    Sketch. Medieval.

Shakespeare, William. The Tempest. Drama. Renaissance.

Shakespeare, William. "That time of year thou mayst in me behold." Sonnet. Renaissance.

Shakespeare, William. "Those hours that with gentle work did Frame." Sonnet. Renaissance.

Shakespeare, William. "When my love swears that she is made of truth." Sonnet. Renaissance.

Shakespeare, William. The Winter's Tale. Drama. Renaissance.

Shaw, George Bernard. Back to Methusaleh: a Metabiological Pentateuch. Drama. 20th.

Sophocles. Oedipus at Colonus. Drama. Classical.

Southey, Robert. The Doctor. Treatise. 20th.

Spark, Muriel. Memento Mori. Novel. 20th.

Spender, Stephen. "Hoelderlin's Old Age." Poem. 20th.

Spenser, Edmund. "Februarie" from The Shepheardes Calender. Poem. Renaissance.

Suckling, John. "The Deformed Mistress." Poem. Renaissance.

Swados, Harvey. Celebration. Novel. 20th.

Swift, Jonathan. Gulliver's Travels. Satiric Tales. 18th.

Swift, Jonathan. "Verses on the Death of Dr. Swift, D.S.P.D. Occasioned by reading a Maxim in Rochefoucalt . . . In the adversity of our best friends, we find something that doth not displease us." Poem. 18th.

Synge, John Millington. Riders to the Sea. Drama. 20th.

Tanizaki, Junichiro. Diary of a Mad Old Man. Novel. 20th.

Tennyson, Alfred. "The Grandmother's Apology." Poem. 19th.

Tennyson, Alfred. "Locksley Hall" and "Locksley Hall Sixty Years After." Long Poems. 19th.

Tennyson, Alfred. "Tithonus." Poem. 19th.

Tennyson, Alfred. "Ulysses." Poem. 19th.

Thomas, Dylan. "Do Not Go Gentle into That Good Night." Poem. 20th.

Tourneur, Cyril. The Revenger's Tragedy. Drama. Renaissance.

Trollope, Anthony. The Warden. Novel. 19th.

Villon, Francois. The Testament. Poem. Medieval.

Wharton, Edith. "Roman Fever." Short Story. 20th.

White, Patrick. The Eye of the Storm. Novel. 20th.

White, Patrick. The Solid Mandala. Novel. 20th.

Whitman, Walt. "As I Sit Writing Here," "Queries to My Seventieth Year," "Thanks in Old Age," "Old Age's Lambent Peaks," and "Good-Bye, My Fancy." Short Poems. 19th.

Whitman, Walt. "I Sing the Body Electric." Poem. 19th.

Williams, Tennessee. Sweet Bird of Youth. Drama. 20th.

Williams, William Carlos. "To Waken an Old Lady." Poem. 20th.

Wordsworth, William. "Michael." Poem. 19th.

Wordsworth, William. "The Old Cumberland Beggar." Poem. 19th.

Wyndham, John. Trouble With Lichen. Novel. 20th.

Yeats, William Butler. "The Circus Animals' Desertion." Poem. 20th.

Yeats, William Butler. "Crazy Jane Talks with the Bishop." Poem. 20th.

Yeats, William Butler. "Her Vision in the Wood." Poem. 20th.

Yeats, William Butler. "A Last Confession." Poem. 20th.

Yeats, William Butler. "A Prayer for Old Age." Poem. 20th.

Yeats, William Butler. "Sailing to Byzantium." Poem. 20th.

Yeats, William Butler. "Why Should Not Old Men Be Mad?" Poem. 20th.

Zugsmith, Leane. "The Three Veterans." Short Story. 20th.

ALCOHOLISM

Amis, Kingsley. Ending Up. Novel. 20th.

Arlen, Michael. The Green Hat. Novel. 20th.

Barclay, Alexander. Ship of Fools. Poems. Renaissance.

Baudelaire, Charles Pierre. Artificial Paradise: On Hashish and Wine as Means of Expanding Individuality. Essays. 19th.

Berryman, John. "Of Suicide." Poem. 20th.

Berryman, John. Recovery. Novel. 20th.

Brontë, Anne. The Tenant of Wildfell Hall. Novel. 19th.

Butler, Samuel. The Way of All Flesh. Novel. 19th.

Chekhov, Anton. "Peasants." Short Story. 19th.

Chekhov, Anton. Three Sisters. Drama. 19th.

Crabbe, George. Inebrity. Long Poem. 18th.

Crane, Stephen. Maggie. Novella. 19th.

De Forest, John William. Miss Ravenal's Conversion from Secession to Loyalty. Novel. 19th.

Delaney, Shelagh. A Taste of Honey. Drama. 20th.

Dickens, Charles. David Copperfield. Novel. 19th.

Dostoevsky, Fyodor. Crime and Punishment. Novel. 19th.

Earle, John. Micro-cosmographie. Sketches. Renaissance.

Eliot, George (Mary Anne Evans). Janet's Repentance. Novella. 19th.

Faulkner, William. The Sound and the Fury. Novel. 20th.

Fitzgerald, F. Scott. "An Alcoholic Case." Short Story. 20th.

Fitzgerald, F. Scott. Tender Is the Night. Novel. 20th.

Gorki, Maxim. The Lower Depths. Drama. 20th.

Greene, Graham. The Power and the Glory. Novel. 20th.

Hardy, Thomas. Jude the Obscure. Novel. 19th.

Hemingway, Ernest. "A Clean, Well-lighted Place." Short Story. 20th.

Holmes, Oliver Wendell. The Autocrat of the Breakfast-Table, no. 8. Essay. 19th.

Holmes, Oliver Wendell. "The Young Practitioner." Essay. 19th.

Kingsley, Charles. Two Years Ago. Novel. 19th.

McCullers, Carson. The Heart Is a Lonely Hunter. Novel. 20th.

Nichols, Peter. The National Health. Drama. 20th.

O'Connor, Frank. "The Drunkard," "Judas," and "My Oedipus Complex." Short Stories. 20th.

Odets, Clifford. The Country Girl. Drama. 20th.

O'Neill, Eugene. Ah Wilderness! Drama. 20th.

O'Neill, Eugene. The Iceman Cometh. Drama. 20th.

O'Neill, Eugene. Long Day's Journey Into Night. Drama. 20th.

Percy, Walker. Love in the Ruins. Novel. 20th.

Rilke, Rainer Maria. "The Blind Man's Song," "The Drinker's Song," "The Idiot's Song," "The Suicide's Song," "The Dwarf's Song," and "The Leper's Song." Short Poems. 20th.

Robinson, E. A. "Miniver Cheevy" and "Mr. Flood's Party." Poems. 20th.

Roethke, Theodore. "My Papa's Waltz." Poem. 20th.

Shakespeare, William. Othello. Drama. Renaissance.

Skelton, John. The Tunning of Elinour Rumming. Poem. Renaissance.

Trollope, Anthony. Doctor Thorne. Novel. 19th.

Twain, Mark. Adventures of Huckleberry Finn. Novel. 19th.

Williams, Tennessee. Cat on a Hot Tin Roof. Drama. 20th.

Zola, Emile. Drunkard (L'Assomoir). Novel. 19th.

THE BODY

Anonymous. "Between March and April." Poem. Medieval.

Anonymous. The Castle of Perseverance. Drama. Medieval.

Anonymous. Everyman. Drama. Medieval.

Anonymous. "Look on your Lord, Man, hanging on the Rood." Poem.
    Medieval.

Anonymous. The Owl and the Nightingale. Poem. Medieval.

Anonymous. Teleny. Novel. 19th.

Anonymous. "When My Eyes are Fogged." Poem. Medieval.

Arbuthnot, John. "Know Yourself." Poem. 18th.

Arden, John. The Happy Haven. Drama. 20th.

Auden, W. H. "The Age of Anxiety." Long Poem. 20th.

Auden, W. H. "The Geography of the House." Poem. 20th.

Auden, W. H. "Miss Gee." Poem. 20th.

Baudelaire, Charles Pierre. "Jewels" ("Les Bijoux"). Poem. 19th.

Baudelaire, Charles Pierre. "The Metamorphoses of a Vampire"
    ("Les Metamorphoses du Vampire"). Poem. 19th.

Beauvoir, Simone de. A Very Easy Death. Autobiography. 20th.

Beerbohm, Max. "A Defense of Cosmetics." Essay. 19th.

Benn, Gottfried. "Little Aster." Poem. 20th.

Benn, Gottfried. "Lovely Childhood." Poem. 20th.

Benn, Gottfried. "Man and Woman Go Through the Cancer Ward."
    Poem. 20th.

Benn, Gottfried. "Monologue." Poem. 20th.

Benn, Gottfried. "Night Cafe." Poem. 20th.

Betjeman, John. "On a Portrait of a Deaf Man." Poem. 20th.

The Bible. I Corinthians. Classical.

The Bible. The Song of Solomon. Classical.

Billings, Philip. "Vassar Miller." Poem. 20th.

Blackmore, Richard. Creation. Poem. 18th.

Blake, William. "Infant Joy" and "Infant Sorrow." Poems. 19th.

Blake, William. Paintings, Especially Those Accompanying Songs
    of Innocence and Experience. 19th.

Boswell, James. The Life of Samuel Johnson. Biography. 18th.

Bradbury, Ray. "The Next in Line." Short Story. 20th.

Bridges, Robert. "On a Dead Child." Poem. 20th.

Browning, Elizabeth Barrett. Sonnets from the Portuguese, nos. 10
    & 11. Sonnets. 19th.

Browning, Robert. "Beside the Drawing Board." Poem. 19th.

Browning, Robert. "Fra Lippo Lippi." Poem. 19th.

Brunner, John. The Whole Man. Novel. 20th.

Büchner, Georg. Woyzeck. Drama. 19th.

Buonarroti, Michel Angelo. "I feel constrained and blocked as is
    the marrow." Poem. Renaissance.

Buonarroti, Michel Angelo. "Lady, through long experience we see."
    Sonnet. Renaissance.

Buonarroti, Michel Angelo. "Sculpture, the first of arts, delights
    a taste." Poem. Renaissance.

Buonarroti, Michel Angelo. "To Giovanni, the one from Pistoia."
    Poem. Renaissance.

Buonarroti, Michel Angelo. "When contracting, the lash seems not
    to cause." Poem. Renaissance.

Burton, Robert. The Anatomy of Melancholy. Treatise. Renaissance.

Butler, Samuel. Erewhon. Novel. 19th.

Campion, Thomas. "Though you are yoong and I am olde." Song.
    Renaissance.

Camus, Albert. Caligula. Drama. 20th.

Čapek, Karel. R.U.R. Drama. 20th.

Carroll, Lewis (Charles L. Dodgson). Alice's Adventures in
    Wonderland. Tale. 19th.

Castiglione, Baldesar. The Book of the Courtier. Dialogues.
    Renaissance.

Catullus, C. Valerius. Carmina, no. 23. Poem. Classical.

Chaucer, Geoffrey. The Canterbury Tales, "The Miller's Tale."
    Tale. Medieval.

Chekhov, Anton. "Gusev." Short Story. 19th.

Chekhov, Anton. Letter to Alexey N. Pleshcheyev, October 1889.
    Letter. 19th.

Cicero, Marcus Tullius. "On the Art of Growing Old." Essay.
    Classical.

Coleridge, Samuel Taylor. "Youth and Age." Poem. 19th.

Coney, Michael G. Friends Come in Boxes. Novel. 20th.

Cowley, Abraham. "Ode: Upon Dr. Harvey." Poem. Renaissance.

Crabbe, George. The Parish Register, "Marriages." Long Poem.
    18th.

Crane, Hart. "Episode of Hands." Poem. 20th.

Crane, Stephen. "The Monster." Short Story. 19th.

Crane, Stephen. The Red Badge of Courage. Novel. 19th.

Cummings, E. E. "I like my body." Poem. 20th.

Dante Alighieri. The Divine Comedy: The Inferno; Purgatorio.
    Long Poem. Medieval.

De Quincey, Thomas. Confessions of an English Opium-Eater and
    Suspiria de Profundis. Essays. 19th.

Dickey, James. "The Cancer Match." Poem. 20th.

Donne, John. "The Comparison." Poem. Renaissance.

Donne, John. "To His Mistris Going to Bed." Poem. Renaissance.

Dostoevsky, Fyodor. The Brothers Karamazov. Novel. 19th.

Eliot, T. S. "The Love Song of J. Alfred Prufrock." Poem. 20th.

Ellison, Harlan. "I Have No Mouth and I Must Scream." Short
    Story. 20th.

Forster, E. M. "The Machine Stops." Short Story. 20th.

Fulke Greville, Lord Brooke. A Treatie of Human Learning. Poem.
    Renaissance.

Garcia Lorca, Federico. Yerma. Drama. 20th.

Gide, Andre. The Immoralist. Novel. 20th.

Glissenti, F. "Death and the Anatomical Lecture." Poem and
    Woodcuts. Renaissance.

Gogol, Nikolai. "The Nose." Short Story. 19th.

Graves, Robert. "The Legs." Poem. 20th.

Graves, Robert. "The Naked and the Nude." Poem. 20th.

Hawthorne, Nathaniel. "The Birthmark." Novel. 19th.

Hawthorne, Nathaniel. "Rappaccini's Daughter." Short Story. 19th.

Henryson, Robert. The Testament of Cresseid. Poem. Medieval.

Herrick, Robert. "Upon Julia's Clothes." Poem. Renaissance.

Holmes, Oliver Wendell. The Autocrat of the Breakfast-Table,
    no. 7. Essay and Poem. 19th.

Holmes, Oliver Wendell. Elsie Venner. Novel. 19th.

Hopkins, Gerard Manley. 'Felix Randal." Sonnet. 19th.

Hugo, Victor. The Hunchback of Notre Dame. Novel. 19th.

James I. A Counterblaste to Tobacco. Treatise. Renaissance.

Jean de Meun. The Romance of the Rose. Long Poem. Medieval.

Jewett, Sarah Orne. A Country Doctor. Novel. 19th.

Jonson, Benjamin. Bartholomew Fair. Drama. Renaissance.

Jonson, Benjamin. "Still to be neat." Song. Renaissance.

Joyce, James. Ulysses. Novel. 20th.

Juvenal (Decimus Iunius Iuvenalis). Satires, no. X. Poem.
    Classical.

Kafka, Franz. The Metamorphosis. Novella. 20th.

Lawrence, D. H. "The Blind Man." Short Story. 20th.

Lawrence, D. H. The Fox. Novella. 20th.

Lawrence, D. H. Lady Chatterley's Lover. Novel. 20th.

Lawrence, D. H. Psychoanalysis and the Unconscious and Fantasia of the Unconscious. Long Essays. 20th.

Lawrence, D. H. "When I Went to the Circus." Poem. 20th.

Leduc, Violette. Thérèse and Isabelle. Novella; and La Bâtarde. Autobiography. 20th.

Lessing, Doris. A Proper Marriage. Novel. 20th.

Levertov, Denise. "Grief" and "Divorcing." Poems. 20th.

London, Jack. "Koolau the Leper." Short Story. 19th.

London, Jack. "To Build a Fire." Short Story. 19th.

Lowell, Robert. "The Hospital." Poem. 20th.

Lyly, John. Endymion. Drama. Renaissance.

Mann, Thomas. The Magic Mountain. Novel. 20th.

Marston, John. The Fawn. Drama. Renaissance.

Marston, John. The Metamorphosis of Pigmalions Image. Poem. Renaissance.

Marvell, Andrew. " A Dialogue between the Soul and the Body." Poem. Renaissance.

Maupassant, Guy de. "Ball-of-Fat." Short Story. 19th.

Maupassant, Guy de. "Beside a Dead Man." Sketch. 19th.

Maupassant, Guy de. "Useless Beauty." Short Story. 19th.

McCullers, Carson. The Ballad of the Sad Café. Novella. 20th.

Melville, Herman. "The Paradise of Bachelors" and "The Tartarus of Maids." Sketches. 19th.

Mencken, H. L. In Defense of Women. Essays. 20th.

Meredith, George. The Ordeal of Richard Feverel. Novel. 19th.

Meredith, George. Sonnet I. From Modern Love. Sonnet. 19th.

Meredith, George. "The Teaching of the Nude." Poem. 19th.

Middleton, Thomas. A Chaste Maid in Cheapside. Drama. Renaissance.

Miller, Vassar. "Fantasia." Poem. 20th.

Miller, Vassar. "On the Examination Table." Poem. 20th.

Miller, Vassar. "Tired." Poem. 20th.

Milton, John. Comus: A Mask Presented at Ludlow Castle. Poem. Renaissance.

Nashe, Thomas. The Unfortunate Traveler. Tale. Renaissance.

Ovid (Publius Ovidius Naso). Amores. Book I, Elegy vii. Poem. Classical.

Parnell, Thomas. "On a Lady with Foul Breath." Poem. 18th.

Petrarch (Francesco Petrarca). Canzoniere, no. CLIX (sonnet no. 126). Sonnet. Medieval.

Petrarch (Francesco Petrarca). Canzoniere, no. CXCV (sonnet no. 162). Sonnet. Medieval.

Petrarch (Francesco Petrarca). Canzoniere, no. CCCXLIX (sonnet no. 303). Sonnet. Medieval.

Pindar. "Nemea VI: For Alcimidas of Aegina: Victory in Wrestling, Boys' Division." Poem. Classical.

Plath, Sylvia. The Bell Jar. Novel. 20th.

Plath, Sylvia. "Lady Lazarus." Poem. 20th.

Plath, Sylvia. "The Surgeon at 2 a.m." Poem. 20th.

Plath, Sylvia. "Thalidomide." Poem. 20th.

Plato. The Republic. Dialogues. Classical.

Plato. Symposium. Dialogue. Classical.

Poe, Edgar Allan. "The Man That Was Used Up." Sketch. 19th.

Pope, Alexander. An Essay on Man. Poem. 18th.

Pope, Alexander. "On Queen Caroline's Death-Bed." Poem. 18th.

Rabelais, Francois. Gargantua and Pantagruel. Tales. Renaissance.

Ransom, John Crowe. "Bells for John Whiteside's Daughter." Poem. 20th.

Rochester, Earl of (John Wilmot). "Song" ("By all love's soft, yet mighty powers"). Poem. 18th.

Roethke, Theodore. "Epidermal Macabre." Poem. 20th.

Roethke, Theodore. "Old Lady's Winter Words" and Meditations of an Old Woman. Poem and Poem Sequence. 20th.

Ronsard, Pierre de. "Double-winged monster" ("Cusin, monstre à double aile, au mufle Elephantin"). Sonnet. Renaissance.

Rossetti, Dante Gabriel. "Body's Beauty." Sonnet. 19th.

Roth, Philip. The Breast. Novella. 20th.

Roth, Philip. "Epstein." Short Story. 20th.

Sappho. On old age and sexuality. Short Poem. Classical.

Sappho. To Brachea. Short Poem. Classical.

Schiller, Friedrich. "Die Peste." Poem. 19th.

Selzer, Richard. The Rituals of Surgery. Short Stories. 20th.

Sexton, Anne. "The Breast." Poem. 20th.

Sexton, Anne. "In Celebration of My Uterus." Poem. 20th.

Sexton, Anne. "Woman with Girdle." Poem. 20th.

Shakespeare, William. Coriolanus. Drama. Renaissance.

Shakespeare, William. The Merchant of Venice. Drama. Renaissance.

Shakespeare, William. "My mistress' eyes are nothing like the sun." Sonnet. Renaissance.

Shakespeare, William. "Not marble nor the gilded monuments." Sonnet. Renaissance.

Shakespeare, William. "Poor soul, the centre of my sinful earth." Sonnet. Renaissance.

Shakespeare, William. Troilus and Cressida. Drama. Renaissance.

Shakespeare, William. Twelfth Night. Drama. Renaissance.

Shakespeare, William. Venus and Adonis. Poem. Renaissance.

Shelley, Mary. Frankenstein. Novel. 19th.

Sidney, Philip. "Who will in fairest book of nature know." Sonnet. Renaissance.

Silverberg, Robert. The World Inside or "A Happy Day in 2381." Novel. 20th.

Skelton, John. The Tunning of Elinour Rumming. Poem. Renaissance.

The Spectator, nos. 115 & 195. Essays. 18th.

Spenser, Edmund. The Faerie Queen, Book II. Poem. Renaissance.

Stevenson, William (?) ("Mr. S."). "Back and Side Go Bare." Song. Renaissance.

Suckling, John. "The Deformed Mistress." Poem. Renaissance.

Suckling, John. "Upon T. C. having the Pox." Poem. Renaissance.

Swift, Jonathan. "Cassinus and Peter. A Tragical Elegy." Poem. 18th.

Swift, Jonathan. Gulliver's Travels. Satiric Tales. 18th.

Swift, Jonathan. "The Lady's Dressing Room." Poem. 18th.

Swift, Jonathan. "A Modest Proposal." Essay. 18th.

Swift, Jonathan. "Strephon and Chloe." Poem. 18th.

Tanizaki, Junichiro. Diary of a Mad Old Man. Novel. 20th.

Taylor, Edward. "Meditation. Mal. 4.2. With Healing in His Wings." Poem. 18th.

Taylor, Edward. "Meditation. Phil. 3. ult. Our Vile Bodie." Poem. 18th.

Tennyson, Alfred. In Memoriam: A.H.H. Poems. 19th.

Tennyson, Alfred. "Oenone." Poem. 19th.

Thoreau, Henry David. Walden. Treatise. 19th.

Tolstoy, Leo. The Death of Ivan Ilych. Novella. 19th.

Villon, Francois. The Testament. Poem. Medieval.

Webb, Mary. Precious Bane. Novel. 20th.

White, Patrick. The Eye of the Storm. Novel. 20th.

Whitman, Walt. "I Sing the Body Electric." Poem. 19th.

Whitman, Walt. "Song of Myself." Poem. 19th.

Wilde, Oscar. Salome. Drama. 19th.

Williams, Tennessee. Suddenly Last Summer. Drama. 20th.

Williams, Tennessee. Summer and Smoke. Drama. 20th.

Williams, Tennessee. Sweet Bird of Youth. Drama. 20th.

Williams, William Carlos. The Autobiography of William Carlos Williams. Autobiography. 20th.

Williams, William Carlos. "Death." Poem. 20th.

Williams, William Carlos. "Portrait of a Woman at Her Bath." Poem. 20th.

Wittig, Monique. The Lesbian Body. Novel. 20th.

Woolf, Virginia. "On Being Ill." Essay. 20th.

Woolf, Virginia. The Waves. Novel. 20th.

Yeats, William Butler. "Crazy Jane Talks with the Bishop." Poem. 20th.

Yeats, William Butler. "Sailing to Byzantium." Poem. 20th.

Young, Edward. "On Michael Angelo's Famous Piece of the Crucifixion; Who is said to have Stabbed a Person that He might Draw it More Naturally." Poem. 18th.

Young, Edward. "Satire V, Characters of Women." Poem. 18th.

Zola, Emile. Germinal. Novel. 19th.

Anonymous. "Now fade the rose and lily-flower." Poem. Medieval.

Armstrong, John. "The Art of Preserving Health." Poem. 18th.

Auden, W. H. "The Age of Anxiety." Long Poem. 20th.

Auden, W. H. "The Model." Poem. 20th.

Auden, W. H. "No, Plato, No" and "Lullaby." Poems. 20th.

Austen, Jane. Persuasion. Novel. 19th.

Austen, Jane. Sense and Sensibility. Novel. 19th.

Bacon, Francis. The Advancement of Learning. Treatise. Renaissance.

Borges, Jorge Luis. "The Immortals." Short Story. 20th.

Brome, Richard. The Antipodes. Drama. Renaissance.

Burton, Robert. The Anatomy of Melancholy. Treatise. Renaissance.

Butler, Samuel. Erewhon. Novel. 19th.

Chekhov, Anton. The Seagull. Drama. 19th.

Chekhov, Anton. "Ward 6." Short Story. 19th.

Donne, John. "The Extasie." Poem. Renaissance.

Donne, John. "A Valediction Forbidding Mourning." Poem. Renaissance.

Dostoevsky, Fyodor. Crime and Punishment. Novel. 19th.

Dyer, Edward. "My mind to me a kingdom is." Poem. Renaissance.

Emerson, Ralph Waldo. "The Over-Soul." Essay. 19th.

Gaskell, Elizabeth. Mary Barton. Novel. 19th.

Hardy, Thomas. Jude the Obscure. Novel. 19th.

Hawthorne, Nathaniel. The Scarlet Letter. Novel. 19th.

Hopkins, Gerard Manley. "The Caged Skylark." Sonnet. 19th.

Howells, William Dean. An Imperative Duty. Novella. 19th.

Howells, William Dean. The Shadow of a Dream. Novella. 19th.

Hugo, Victor. The Hunchback of Notre Dame. Novel. 19th.

Huxley, Aldous. The Doors of Perception. Long Essay. 20th.

Lawrence, D. H. "Healing" and "Sick." Poems. 20th.

Lawrence, D. H. Psychoanalysis and the Unconscious and Fantasia of the Unconscious. Long Essays. 20th.

Lawrence, D. H. "The Ship of Death." Poem. 20th.

Lovelace, Richard. "To Althea, from Prison." Poem. Renaissance.

Mann, Thomas. The Magic Mountain. Novel. 20th.

Marvell, Andrew. "A Dialogue between the Soul and the Body." Poem. Renaissance.

Mather, Cotton. The Angel of Bethesda: An Essay Upon the Common Maladies of Mankind. Treatise. 18th.

Maupassant, Guy de. "The First Snowfall." Short Story. 19th.

Montaigne, Michel Eyquem de. "On the Force of the Imagination." Essay. Renaissance.

Plath, Sylvia. "Fever 103°." Poem. 20th.

Plato. The Republic. Dialogues. Classical.

Poe, Edgar Allan. "The Facts in the Case of M. Valdemar." Short Story. 19th.

Poe, Edgar Allan. "Ligeia." Short Story. 19th.

Shakespeare, William. King Lear. Drama. Renaissance.

Shakespeare, William. Othello. Drama. Renaissance.

Shakespeare, William. Richard III. Drama. Renaissance.

Shaw, George Bernard. Back to Methusaleh: a Metabiological Pentateuch. Drama. 20th.

Shaw, George Bernard. Man and Superman. Drama. 20th.

Shelley, Mary. Frankenstein. Novel. 19th.

Smollett, Tobias. The Expedition of Humphry Clinker. Novel. 18th.

The Spectator, nos. 115 & 195. Essays. 18th.

Spenser, Edmund. "Men call you fayre, and you doe credit it."
    Sonnet. Renaissance.

White, Patrick. The Eye of the Storm. Novel. 20th.

Winchilsea, Countess of (Anne Finch). "The Spleen." Poem. 18th.

Woolf, Virginia. Mrs. Dalloway. Novel. 20th.

Yeats, William Butler. "Michael Robartes and the Dancer." Poem.
    20th.

BY DOCTORS

Akenside, Mark. "Hymn to Science." Poem. 18th.

Akenside, Mark. "Hymn to the Naiads." Poem. 18th.

Akenside, Mark. "Ode XII, On Recovering From a Fit of Sickness,
    in the Country. 1768." Poem. 18th.

Akenside, Mark. "Ode XVI, To Caleb Hardinge, M.D." Poem. 18th.

Arbuthnot, John. "Know Yourself." Poem. 18th.

Arlen, Michael. The Green Hat. Novel. 20th.

Armstrong, John. "The Art of Preserving Health." Poem. 18th.

Beddoes, Thomas Lovell. Death's Jest-Book. Poetic Drama. 19th.

Benn, Gottfried. "Answer to the Literary Immigrants." Essay.
    20th.

Benn, Gottfried. "Artists and Old Age." Essay. 20th.

Benn, Gottfried. "Little Aster." Poem. 20th.

Benn, Gottfried. "Lovely Childhood." Poem. 20th.

Benn, Gottfried. "Monologue." Poem. 20th.

Benn, Gottfried. "Night Cafe." Poem. 20th.

The Bible. Luke. Classical.

Blackmore, Richard. Creation. Poem. 18th.

Bridges, Robert. "Melancholia." Sonnet. 20th.

Bridges, Robert. "On a Dead Child." Poem. 20th.

Browne, Thomas. A Letter to a Friend, Upon Occasion of the Death
    of his Intimate Friend. Essay. Renaissance.

Browne, Thomas. Religio Medici. Treatise. Renaissance.

Campion, Thomas. "If any hath the heart to kill." Song.
    Renaissance.

Campion, Thomas. "It fell on a sommers day." Song. Renaissance.

Campion, Thomas. "The Sypres curten of the night is spread."
    Song. Renaissance.

Campion, Thomas. "There is a Garden in her face." Song.
    Renaissance.

Campion, Thomas. "Though you are yoong and I am olde." Song.
    Renaissance.

Céline, Louis-Ferdinand. Journey to the End of the Night. Novel.
    20th.

Chekhov, Anton. "An Attack of Nerves." Short Story. 19th.

Chekhov, Anton. "Gusev." Short Story. 19th.

Chekhov, Anton. The Island: A Journey to Sakhalin. Nonfiction.
    19th.

Chekhov, Anton. Ivanov. Drama. 19th.

Chekhov, Anton. Letter to Alexey N. Pleshcheyev, October 1889.
    Letter. 19th.

Chekhov, Anton. "Misery." Short Story. 19th.

Chekhov, Anton. "Peasants." Short Story. 19th.

Chekhov, Anton. Three Sisters. Drama. 19th.

Chekhov, Anton. Uncle Vanya. Drama. 19th.

Chekhov, Anton. "Ward 6." Short Story. 19th.

Crabbe, George. The Borough. Long Poem. 18th.

Crabbe, George. "Fragment, Written at Midnight." Poem. 18th.

Crabbe, George. Inebrity. Long Poem. 18th.

Crabbe, George. "The Library." Poem. 18th.

Crabbe, George. The Parish Register, "Marriages" and "Burials."
    Long Poem. 18th.

Crabbe, George. "Sir Eustace Grey." Poem. 18th.

Crabbe, George. The Village. Long Poem. 18th.

Crichton, Michael. The Andromeda Strain. Novel. 20th.

Cronin, A. J. The Citadel. Novel. 20th.

Doyle, Arthur Conan. "The Croxley Master." Short Story. 19th.

Doyle, Arthur Conan. "The Curse of Eve." Short Story. 19th.

Doyle, Arthur Conan. "The Doctors of Hoyland." Short Story. 19th.

Doyle, Arthur Conan. "A Medical Document." Sketches. 19th.

Doyle, Arthur Conan. The Sherlock Holmes Tales. Novellas and Stories. 19th.

Doyle, Arthur Conan. "The Third Generation." Short Sketch. 19th.

Drake, Joseph Rodman. "The King of the Croakers." Poem. 19th.

Fracastorius, Hieronymus. Hieronymus Fracastorius and his Poetical and Prose Works on Syphilis. Poem. Renaissance.

Garth, Samuel. The Dispensary. Poem. 18th.

Goldsmith, Oliver. "The Deserted Village." Poem. 18th.

Goldsmith, Oliver. She Stoops to Conquer. Drama. 18th.

Goldsmith, Oliver. The Vicar of Wakefield. Novel. 18th.

Hejinian, John. Extreme Remedies. Novel. 20th.

Holmes, Oliver Wendell. The Autocrat of the Breakfast-Table, no. 7. Essay and Poem. 19th.

Holmes, Oliver Wendell. The Autocrat of the Breakfast-Table, no. 8. Essay. 19th.

Holmes, Oliver Wendell. Elsie Venner. Novel. 19th.

Holmes, Oliver Wendell. A Mortal Antipathy. Novel. 19th.

Holmes, Oliver Wendell. "The Young Practitioner." Essay. 19th.

Huxley, Thomas Henry. "On Science and Art in Relation to Education." Essay. 19th.

Jeffers, Robinson. "Rock and Hawk." Poem. 20th.

Keats, John. "After dark vapours." Sonnet. 19th.

Keats, John. "Bright Star! Would I Were." Sonnet. 19th.

Keats, John. "La Belle Dame Sans Merci." Poem. 19th.

Keats, John. Letter to Charles Wentworth Dilke, Mon., Sept. 1818; Letters to George and Georgiana Keats, Wed., Oct. 14 - Sat., Oct. 31, 1818; Wed., Dec. 16, 1818 - Mon., Jan. 4, 1819. Letters. 19th.

Keats, John. Letters to Charles Brown, Sun., Aug. 20, 1820; Sept. 30, 1820. Letters. 19th.

Keats, John. Letters to Fanny Brawne. Letters. 19th.

Keats, John. "Light feet, dark violet eyes." Sonnet. 19th.

Keats, John. "Ode to a Nightingale." Poem. 19th.

Keats, John. "To Homer." Sonnet. 19th.

Keats, John. "When I have fears that I may cease to be." Sonnet. 19th.

Lever, Charles James. Harry Lorrequer (The Confessions of Harry Lorrequer). Novel. 19th.

Lodge, Thomas. A Treatise of the Plague. Treatise. Renaissance.

Maugham, W. Somerset. Liza of Lambeth. Novel. 20th.

Maugham, W. Somerset. Of Human Bondage. Novel. 20th.

Mitchell, John Kearsley. Indecision, a Tale of the Far West; and Other Poems. Introduction and Dedication. 19th.

Nourse, Alan E. The Bladerunner. Novel. 20th.

Nourse, Alan E. "The Martyr." Novella. 20th.

Percival, James Gates. "Consumption." Poem. 19th.

Percy, Walker. Love in the Ruins. Novel. 20th.

Percy, Walker. The Moviegoer. Novel. 20th.

Rabelais, Francois. Gargantua and Pantagruel. Tales. Renaissance.

Schnitzler, Arthur. A Confirmed Bachelor (Also published as Dr. Graesler). Novel. 20th.

Schnitzler, Arthur. La Ronde. Drama. 20th.

Schnitzler, Arthur. "The Man of Honour." Short Story. 20th.

Schnitzler, Arthur. Mother and Son. Novella. 20th.

Schnitzler, Arthur. My Youth in Vienna. Autobiography. 20th.

Schnitzler, Arthur. Professor Bernhardi. Drama. 20th.

Schnitzler, Arthur. The Spring Sonata. Novel. 20th.

Selzer, Richard. The Rituals of Surgery. Short Stories. 20th.

Smollett, Tobias. The Adventures of Ferdinand, Count Fathom. Novel. 18th.

Smollett, Tobias. The Adventures of Peregrine Pickle. Novel. 18th.

Smollett, Tobias. The Adventures of Roderick Random. Novel. 18th.

Smollett, Tobias. The Expedition of Humphry Clinker. Novel. 18th.

Smollett, Tobias. Sir Launcelot Greaves. Novel. 18th.

Stein, Gertrude. Melanctha. Novella. 20th.

Stone, John. "Stroke." Poem. 20th.

Taylor, Edward. "Meditation. Col. 1.18. That in all things he might have the Preheminence." Poem. 18th.

Taylor, Edward. "Meditation. 1 Cor. 3.22. Death is Yours." Poem. 18th.

Taylor, Edward. "Meditation. Mal. 4.2. With Healing in His Wings." Poem. 18th.

Taylor, Edward. "Meditation. Phil. 3. ult. Our Vile Bodie." Poem. 18th.

Taylor, Edward. "Upon Wedlock, and Death of Children." Poem. 18th.

Thompson, Francis. "The Poppy." Poem. 19th.

Thompson, Francis. "To Monica Thought Dying." Poem. 19th.

Tushnet, Leonard. "In Re Glover." Short Story. 20th.

Warren, Samuel. Passages from the Diary of a Late Physician. Sketches. 19th.

Wigglesworth, Michael. The Day of Doom. Poem. 18th.

Williams, William Carlos. The Autobiography of William Carlos Williams. Autobiography. 20th.

Williams, William Carlos. "Complaint." Poem. 20th.

Williams, William Carlos. The Cure. Drama. 20th.

Williams, William Carlos. "Death." Poem. 20th.

Williams, William Carlos. A Dream of Love. Drama. 20th.

Williams, William Carlos. "The Injury." Poem. 20th.

Williams, William Carlos. "Jean Beicke." Short Story. 20th.

Williams, William Carlos. "A Night in June." Short Story. 20th.

Williams, William Carlos. "Portrait of a Woman at Her Bath." Poem. 20th.

Williams, William Carlos. "To a Dog Injured in the Street." Poem. 20th.

Williams, William Carlos. "To Waken an Old Lady." Poem. 20th.

Williams, William Carlos. "Tract." Poem. 20th.

Williams, William Carlos. "The Use of Force." Short Story. 20th.

Williams, William Carlos. A Voyage to Pagany. Novel. 20th.

CHILDREN

Adams, Henry. The Education of Henry Adams. Autobiography. 19th.

Agee, James. A Death in the Family. Novel. 20th.

Anderson, Maxwell. Bad Seed. Drama. 20th.

Anonymous. The Magi, Herod, and the Slaughter of the Innocents. Drama. Medieval.

Anonymous. Nice Wanton. Drama. Renaissance.

Anonymous. The Second Shepherds' Play. Drama. Medieval.

Auden, W. H. "The Age of Anxiety." Long Poem. 20th.

Austen, Jane. Emma. Novel. 19th.

Austen, Jane. Mansfield Park. Novel. 19th.

Babel, Isaac. "The Story of My Dovecot." Short Story. 20th.

Bacon, Francis. "Of Parents and Children " and "Of Marriage and the Single Life." Essays. Renaissance.

Balzac, Honoré de. Père Goriot. Novel. 19th.

Barclay, Alexander. Ship of Fools. Poems. Renaissance.

Beauvoir, Simone de. A Very Easy Death. Autobiography. 20th.

Beckett, Samuel. Endgame. Drama. 20th.

Bellow, Saul. Mr. Sammler's Planet. Novel. 20th.

Bernardin de Saint Pierre. Paul and Virginia. Novel. 18th.

Betjeman, John. "A Child Ill." Poem. 20th.

The Bible. Genesis. Classical.

The Bible. Matthew. Classical.

The Bible. Proverbs. Classical.

Blake, William. "Infant Joy" and "Infant Sorrow." Poems. 19th.

Blake, William. "Nurse's Song" and "Nurses Song." Poems. 19th.

Blake, William. Paintings, Especially Those Accompanying Songs of Innocence and Experience. 19th.

Bowen, Elizabeth. Eva Trout. Novel. 20th.

Bradstreet, Anne. "In Memory of My Dear Grandchild Elizabeth Bradstreet, Who Deceased August, 1665, Being a Year and Half Old." Poem. 18th.

Bradstreet, Anne. "In Reference to her Children, 23 June, 1659." Poem. 18th.

Brecht, Bertolt. Mother Courage and Her Children. Drama. 20th.

Brontë, Charlotte. Jane Eyre. Novel. 19th.

Brontë, Charlotte. Villette. Novel. 19th.

Brontë, Emily Jane. "A Farewell to Alexandria." Poem. 19th.

Brontë, Emily Jane. Wuthering Heights. Novel. 19th.

Browning, Elizabeth Barrett. "The Cry of the Children." Poem. 19th.

Browning, Elizabeth Barrett. "Isobel's Child." Poem. 19th.

Browning, Elizabeth Barrett. "The Runaway Slave at Pilgrim's Point." Poem. 19th.

Browning, Elizabeth Barrett. Sonnets from the Portuguese, no. 5. Sonnet. 19th.

Browning, Robert. "The Bishop Orders His Tomb at Saint Praxed's Church." Poem. 19th.

Burney, Fanny (Mme. D'Arblay). Evelina. Novel. 18th.

Burns, Robert. "A Poet's Welcome to His Love-Begotten Daughter. The first instance that entitled him to the venerable appellation of father." Poem. 18th.

Burton, Robert. The Anatomy of Melancholy. Treatise. Renaissance.

Butler, Samuel. Erewhon. Novel. 19th.

Byron, George Gordon, Lord. Childe Harold's Pilgrimage. Long Poem. 19th.

Campbell, William Edward March (William March, pseudonym). The Bad Seed; and Maxwell Anderson, Bad Seed. Novel and Drama. 20th.

Camus, Albert. The Plague. Novel. 20th.

Camus, Albert. The Stranger. Novel. 20th.

Čapek, Karel. R.U.R. Drama. 20th.

Carroll, Lewis (Charles L. Dodgson). Alice's Adventures in Wonderland. Tale. 19th.

Cellini, Benvenuto. Autobiography. Autobiography. Renaissance.

Chekhov, Anton. "Misery." Short Story. 19th.

Chekhov, Anton. "Peasants." Short Story. 19th.

Choromanski, Michal. Jealousy and Medicine. Novel. 20th.

Colette. The Innocent Libertine. Novel. 20th.

Coney, Michael G. Friends Come in Boxes. Novel. 20th.

Conrad, Joseph. "The Idiots." Short Story. 20th.

Cooper, James Fenimore. The Last of the Mohicans. Novel. 19th.

Crabbe, George. The Borough. Long Poem. 18th.

Crane, Stephen. Maggie. Novella. 19th.

Dante Alighieri. The Divine Comedy: Paradisio. Poem. Medieval.

Defoe, Daniel. Moll Flanders. Novel. 18th.

De Forest, John William. Miss Ravenal's Conversion from Secession to Loyalty. Novel. 19th.

Delaney, Shelagh. A Taste of Honey. Drama. 20th.

De Quincey, Thomas. Confessions of an English Opium-Eater and Suspiria de Profundis. Essays. 19th.

Dickens, Charles. Bleak House. Novel. 19th.

Dickens, Charles. David Copperfield. Novel. 19th.

Dickens, Charles. Dombey and Son. Novel. 19th.

Dickens, Charles. Great Expectations. Novel. 19th.

Dickens, Charles. The Old Curiosity Shop. Novel. 19th.

Dickens, Charles. The Pickwick Papers. Novel. 19th.

Dickens, Charles. "A Small Star in the East." Sketch. 19th.

Dickey, James. "The Eye-Beaters." Poem. 20th.

Dickinson, Emily. "I noticed People disappeared." Poem. 19th.

Drabble, Margaret. The Millstone. Novel. 20th.

Earle, John. Micro-cosmographie. Sketches. Renaissance.

Edwards, Jonathan. "Phebe Bartlet." Essay. 18th.

Eliot, George (Mary Anne Evans). The Mill on the Floss. Novel. 19th.

Emerson, Ralph Waldo. "Experience" and "Threnody." Essay and Poem. 19th.

Euripides. Electra. Drama. Classical.

Euripides. Hippolytus. Drama. Classical.

Euripides. Medea. Drama. Classical.

Fielding, Henry. Tom Jones. Novel. 18th.

Fitzgerald, F. Scott. Tender Is the Night. Novel. 20th.

Garcia Lorca, Federico. The House of Bernarda Alba. Drama. 20th.

Giraudoux, Jean. Electra. Drama. 20th.

Golding, William. Lord of the Flies. Novel. 20th.

Goldsmith, Oliver. She Stoops to Conquer. Drama. 18th.

Gray, Thomas. "Ode on a Distant Prospect of Eton College." Poem. 18th.

Hansberry, Lorraine. A Raisin in the Sun. Drama. 20th.

Hardy, Thomas. "He Never Expected Much." Poem. 19th.

Hardy, Thomas. "Her Death and After." Poem. 19th.

Hardy, Thomas. Jude the Obscure. Novel. 19th.

Hawthorne, Nathaniel. The Scarlet Letter. Novel. 19th.

Heller, Joseph. Something Happened. Novel. 20th.

Hellman, Lillian. The Children's Hour. Drama. 20th.

Hemingway, Ernest. "A Day's Wait." Short Story. 20th.

Hemingway, Ernest. "The Doctor and the Doctor's Wife." Short Story. 20th.

Hemingway, Ernest. The Old Man and the Sea. Novella. 20th.

Henry, O. (W. S. Porter). "Ransom of Red Chief." Short Story. 19th.

Hesiod. Theogony. Long Poem. Classical.

Hopkins, Gerard Manly. "Spring and Fall: to a young child." Sonnet. 19th.

Hughes, Richard. A High Wind in Jamacia. Novel. 20th.

Hugo, Victor. Les Miserables. Novel. 19th.

Ibsen, Henrik. Little Eyolf. Drama. 19th.

Ionesco, Eugene. The Future Is in Eggs. Drama. 20th.

James, Henry. Daisy Miller: A Study. Novella. 19th.

James, Henry. The Turn of the Screw. Novella. 19th.

James, Henry. Washington Square. Novel. 19th.

James, Henry. What Maisie Knew. Novel. 19th.

Jonson, Benjamin. Epigram XLV. Poem. Renaissance.

Jonson, Benjamin. "An Epitaph." Poem. Renaissance.

Jonson, Benjamin. Sejanus. Drama. Renaissance.

Joyce, James. "Ecce Puer." Poem. 20th.

Joyce, James. Portrait of the Artist as a Young Man. Novel. 20th.

Kipling, Rudyard. "Baa Baa Black Sheep." Short Story. 19th.

Kyd, Thomas. The Spanish Tragedy. Drama. Renaissance.

Lamb, Charles. "Christ's Hospital Five and Thirty Years Ago." Essay. 19th.

Lawrence, D. H. Psychoanalysis and the Unconscious and Fantasia of the Unconscious. Long Essays. 20th.

Lawrence, D. H. Sons and Lovers. Novel. 20th.

Lawrence, D. H. "When I Went to the Circus." Poem. 20th.

Marlowe, Christopher. Tamburlaine: Part Two. Drama. Renaissance.

Massinger, Philip. The Unnatural Combat. Drama. Renaissance.

Maugham, W. Somerset. Liza of Lambeth. Novel. 20th.

Maugham, W. Somerset. Of Human Bondage. Novel. 20th.

McCullers, Carson. The Ballad of the Sad Café. Novella. 20th.

McCullers, Carson. The Heart Is a Lonely Hunter. Novel. 20th.

Melville, Herman. Pierre, or the Ambiguities. Novel. 19th.

Meredith, George. The Ordeal of Richard Feverel. Novel. 19th.

Middleton, Thomas. A Chaste Maid in Cheapside. Drama. Renaissance.

Middleton, Thomas. A Fair Quarrel. Drama. Renaissance.

Miller, Arthur. Death of a Salesman. Drama. 20th.

Miller, Vassar. "Fantasia." Poem. 20th.

Milton, John. "On the Death of a Fair Infant Dying of a Cough." Poem. Renaissance.

Molière (Jean-Baptiste Poquelin). "A Monsieur de la Mothe Le Vayer." Sonnet. 18th.

Murdoch, Irish. Bruno's Dream. Novel. 20th.

Nabokov, Vladimir. Lolita. Novel. 20th.

Oates, Joyce Carol. Wonderland. Novel. 20th.

O'Connor, Flannery. "The Lame Shall Enter First." Short Story. 20th.

O'Connor, Frank. "The Drunkard," "Judas," and "My Oedipus Complex." Short Stories. 20th.

The Old Law. Drama. Renaissance.

Olsen, Tillie. "Tell Me a Riddle." Short Story. 20th.

O'Neill, Eugene. Desire Under the Elms. Drama. 20th.

Pater, Walter. "A Child in the House." Essay. 19th.

Pirsig, Robert M. Zen and the Art of Motorcycle Maintenance: an Inquiry into Values. Fiction. 20th.

Plath, Sylvia. "Daddy." Poem. 20th.

Proust, Marcel. Remembrance of Things Past. Novel. 20th.

Rabelais, Francois. Gargantua and Pantagruel. Tales. Renaissance.

Racine, Jean. Phaedra. Drama. 18th.

Raleigh, Walter. "To His Son." Sonnet. Renaissance.

Ransom, John Crowe. "Bells for John Whiteside's Daughter." Poem. 20th.

Remarque, Erich Maria. Arch of Triumph. Novel. 20th.

Riley, James Whitcomb. "Little Orphant Annie." Poem. 19th.

Roethke, Theodore. "My Papa's Waltz." Poem. 20th.

Roth, Philip. Portnoy's Complaint. Novel. 20th.

Sade, Donatien Alphonse François, Marquis de. Philosophy in the Bedroom. Tale. 19th.

Salinger, J. D. The Catcher in the Rye. Novel. 20th.

Sarton, May. Mrs. Stevens Hears the Mermaids Singing. Novel. 20th.

Schnitzler, Arthur. Mother and Son. Novella. 20th.

Sexton, Anne. "Madonna." Poem. 20th.

Sexton, Anne. "Unknown Girl in the Maternity Ward." Poem. 20th.

Shakespeare, William. 2 Henry IV. Drama. Renaissance.

Shakespeare, William. King Lear. Drama. Renaissance.

Shakespeare, William. Macbeth. Drama. Renaissance.

Shakespeare, William. The Merchant of Venice. Drama. Renaissance.

Shakespeare, William. A Midsummer-Night's Dream. Drama. Renaissance.

Shakespeare, William. Richard III. Drama. Renaissance.

Shakespeare, William. Romeo and Juliet. Drama. Renaissance.

Shakespeare, William. The Tempest. Drama. Renaissance.

Shakespeare, William. The Winter's Tale. Drama. Renaissance.

Sholom Aleichem (Solomon Rabinowitch). "The Flag." Short Story. 19th.

Sholom Aleichem (Solomon Rabinowitch). "The Lottery Ticket." Short Story. 19th.

Sholom Aleichem (Solomon Rabinowitch). "You Mustn't Weep--It's Yom-Tev." Short Story. 19th.

Silverberg, Robert. The World Inside, or "A Happy Day in 2381." Novel. 20th.

Sophocles. Electra. Drama. Classical.

Sophocles. Oedipus at Colonus. Drama. Classical.

The Spectator, nos. 246 and 263. Essays. 18th.

The Spectator, no. 431. Essay. 18th.

Stevenson, Robert. "The Sick Child" and "The Land of Counterpane." Poems. 19th.

Stowe, Harriet Beecher. Uncle Tom's Cabin. Novel. 19th.

Strindberg, August. The Father. Drama. 19th.

Swados, Harvey. Celebration. Novel. 20th.

Swift, Jonathan. Gulliver's Travels. Satiric Tales. 18th.

Swift, Jonathan. "A Modest Proposal." Essay. 18th.

Swinburne, Algernon Charles. "A Child's Laughter." Poem. 19th.

Taylor, Edward. "Meditation. Col. 1.18. That in all things he might have the Prehemineace." Poem. 18th.

Taylor, Edward. "Upon Wedlock, and Death of Children." Poem. 18th.

Tennyson, Alfred. In Memoriam: A.H.H. Poems. 19th.

Tennyson, Alfred. "In the Children's Hospital." Poem. 19th.

Tennyson, Alfred. The Princess: A Medley. Poem. 19th.

Tennyson, Alfred. "Ulysses." Poem. 19th.

Thackeray, William Makepeace. The History of Henry Esmond. Novel. 19th.

Thackeray, William Makepeace. Vanity Fair. Novel. 19th.

Thomas, Dylan. "Do Not Go Gentle into That Good Night," Poem. 20th.

Thomas, Dylan. "Fern Hill." Poem. 20th.

Thomas, Dylan. "A Refusal to Mourn the Death, by Fire, of a Child in London." Poem. 20th.

Thompson, Francis. "The Poppy." Poem. 19th.

Thompson, Francis. "To Monica Thought Dying." Poem. 19th.

Tolstoy, Leo. The Death of Ivan Ilych. Novella. 19th.

Tolstoy, Leo. The Kreutzer Sonata. Novella. 19th.

Tourneur, Cyril. The Atheist's Tragedy. Drama. Renaissance.

Twain, Mark. Adventures of Huckleberry Finn. Novel. 19th.

Twain, Mark. Autobiography of Mark Twain. Autobiography. 19th.

Twain, Mark. The Diary of Adam and Eve. Sketch. 19th.

Twain, Mark. "Experience of the McWilliamses with Membranous Croup." Short Story. 19th.

Welty, Eudora. The Optimist's Daughter. Novella. 20th.

Wharton, Edith. "The Pelican." Short Story. 20th.

White, Patrick. The Eye of the Storm. Novel. 20th.

Whittier, John Greenleaf. "The Barefoot Boy." Poem. 19th.

Wigglesworth, Michael. The Day of Doom. Poem. 18th.

Williams, Tennessee. Cat on a Hot Tin Roof. Drama. 20th.

Williams. Tennessee. Suddenly Last Summer. Drama. 20th.

Williams, William Carlos. The Autobiography of William Carlos Williams. Autobiography. 20th.

Williams, William Carlos. "Jean Beicke." Short Story. 20th.

Williams, William Carlos. "The Use of Force." Short Story. 20th.

Wolfe, Gene. "The Death of Dr. Island." Short Story. 20th.

Wordsworth, William. "The Idiot Boy." Poem. 19th.

Wordsworth, William. "Maternal Grief." Poem. 19th.

Wordsworth, William. "My heart leaps up." Poem. 19th.

Wordsworth, William. "Ode. Intimations of Immortality from Recollections of Early Childhood." Poem. 19th.

Wordsworth, William. The Prelude. Long Poem. 19th.

Wordsworth, William. "We are Seven." Poem. 19th.

Zola, Emile. Fécondité (From Les Quatres Evangiles). Novel. 19th.

Zola, Emile. Germinal. Novel. 19th.

Zola, Emile. Une Page D'Amour. Novel. 19th.

DEATH

Aeschylus. Agamemnon. Drama. Classical.

Aeschylus. The Eumenides. Drama. Classical.

Agee, James. A Death in the Family. Novel. 20th.

Albee, Edward. The Death of Bessie Smith. Drama. 20th.

Amis, Kingsley. Ending Up. Novel. 20th.

Anderson, Sherwood. "Brother Death." Short Story. 20th.

Anonymous. "Bede's Death Song." Poem. Medieval.

Anonymous. Beowulf. Epic Poem. Medieval.

Anonymous. The Castle of Perseverance. Drama. Medieval.

Anonymous. The Dance of Death. Poems. Medieval.

Anonymous. Everyman. Drama. Medieval.

Anonymous. "The life of this world." Poem. Medieval.

Anonymous. "Look on your Lord, Man, hanging on the Rood." Poem. Medieval.

Anonymous. St. George Plays. Dramas. Medieval.

Anonymous. Sir Gawain and the Green Knight. Poem. Medieval.

Anonymous. Sir Orfeo. Poem. Medieval.

Anonymous. "When My Eyes are Fogged." Poem. Medieval.

Arnold, Matthew. "Haworth Churchyard." Poem. 19th.

Arnold, Matthew. "Thyrsis." Poem. 19th.

Auden, W. H. "Give me a doctor." Poem. 20th.

Auden, W. H. "Miss Gee." Poem. 20th.

Auden, W. H. "No, Plato, No" and "Lullaby." Poems. 20th.

Babel, Isaac. "The Story of My Dovecot." Short Story. 20th.

Bacon, Francis. "Of Death." Essay. Renaissance.

Balzac, Honoré de. The Country Doctor. Novel. 19th.

Balzac, Honoré de. Cousin Pons. Novel. 19th.

Baudelaire, Charles Pierre. "The Dance of Death" ("Danse Macabre"). Poem. 19th.

Baudelaire, Charles Pierre. "Skeletons Digging" ("Le Squelette laboureur"). Poem. 19th.

Beauvoir, Simone de. A Very Easy Death. Autobiography. 20th.

Beckett, Samuel. Krapp's Last Tape. Drama. 20th.

Beddoes, Thomas Lovell. Death's Jest-Book. Poetic Drama. 19th.

Bellow, Saul. Mr. Sammler's Planet. Novel. 20th.

Benn, Gottfried. "Little Aster." Poem. 20th.

Benn, Gottfried. "Lovely Childhood." Poem. 20th.

Bennett, Arnold. Riceyman Steps. Novel. 19th.

Berg, Stephen. "Why Are We Here?" Poem. 20th.

Betjeman, John. "Devonshire Street W.1." Poem. 20th.

Betjeman, John. "On a Portrait of a Deaf Man." Poem. 20th.

The Bible. I Corinthians. Classical.

The Bible. Ecclesiastes. Classical.

The Bible. Job. Classical.

The Bible. John. Classical.

The Bible. Psalms, nos. VI, XXIII, and CXXXVII. Classical.

The Bible. Revelations. Classical.

Bierce, Ambrose. "A Tough Tussle." Short Story. 19th.

Billings, Philip. "Vassar Miller." Poem. 20th.

Blake, William. Paintings, Especially Those Accompanying Songs of Innocence and Experience. 19th.

Boccaccio, Giovanni. The Decameron: Day 1, Prologue. Sketch. Medieval.

Borges, Jorge Luis. "Remorse for Any Death." Poem. 20th.

Boswell, James. The Life of Samuel Johnson. Biography. 18th.

Bradbury, Ray. "The Next in Line." Short Story. 20th.

Bradstreet, Anne. "Before the Birth of One of her Children." Poem. 18th.

Bradstreet, Anne. "In Memory of My Dear Grandchild Elizabeth Bradstreet, Who Deceased August, 1665, Being a Year and Half Old." Poem. 18th.

Bridges, Robert. "On a Dead child." Poem. 20th.

Brontë, Charlotte. Jane Eyre. Novel. 19th.

Brontë, Emily Jane. "A Farewell to Alexandria." Poem. 19th.

Brontë, Emily Jane. "The linnet in the rocky dells." Poem. 19th.

Brontë, Emily Jane. Wuthering Heights. Novel. 19th.

Browne, Thomas. A Letter to a Friend, Upon Occasion of the Death of his Intimate Friend. Essay. Renaissance.

Browne, Thomas. Religio Medici. Treatise. Renaissance.

Browning, Elizabeth Barrett. "Isobel's Child." Poem. 19th.

Browning, Elizabeth Barrett. "The Runaway Slave at Pilgrim's Point." Poem. 19th.

Browning, Elizabeth Barrett. Sonnets from the Portuguese, no. 1. Sonnet. 19th.

Browning, Elizabeth Barrett. Sonnets from the Portuguese, no. 22. Sonnet. 19th.

Browning, Robert. "The Bishop Orders His Tomb at Saint Praxed's Church." Poem. 19th.

Browning, Robert. "Childe Roland to the Dark Tower Came." Poem. 19th.

Browning, Robert. "Epilogue." Poem. 19th.

Browning, Robert. "An Epistle: Containing the Strange Medical Experience of Karshish, the Arab Physician." Poem. 19th.

Browning, Robert. "A Grammarian's Funeral." Poem. 19th.

Browning, Robert. "Prospice." Poem. 19th.

Browning, Robert. "Rabbi Ben Ezra." Poem. 19th.

Bryant, William Cullen. "Thanatopsis." Poem. 19th.

Bullein, William. A Dialogue Against the Fever Pestilence. Dialogues. Renaissance.

Buonarroti, Michel Angelo. "Lady, through long experience we see." Poem. Renaissance.

Buonarroti, Michel Angelo. "Youth, in its greenness, cannot know, O Lord." Poem. Renaissance.

Burns, Robert. "Death and Doctor Hornbook." Poem. 18th.

Burns, Robert. "John Anderson My Jo" and "John Anderson, My Jo." Poems. 18th.

Burton, Robert. The Anatomy of Melancholy. Treatise. Renaissance.

Butler, Samuel. Erewhon. Novel. 19th.

Byron, George Gordon, Lord. "The Destruction of Sennacherib." Poem. 19th.

Campion, Thomas. "Though you are yoong and I am olde." Song. Renaissance.

Camus, Albert. The Plague. Novel. 20th.

Carlyle, Thomas. "The Everlasting No," "The Center of Indifference," and "The Everlasting Yea." Essays. 19th.

Carroll, Lewis (Charles L. Dodgson). Alice's Adventures in Wonderland. Tale. 19th.

Chatterton, Thomas. "Sentiment." Poem. 18th.

Chaucer, Geoffrey. The Canterbury Tales, "The Pardoner's Tale." Tale. Medieval.

Chekhov, Anton. "Gusev." Short Story. 19th.

Chekhov, Anton. The Island: A Journey to Sakhalin. Nonfiction. 19th.

Chekhov, Anton. "Peasants." Short Story. 19th.

Coleridge, Samuel Taylor. "The Rime of the Ancient Mariner." Poem. 19th.

Coney, Michael G. Friends Come in Boxes. Novel. 20th.

Cooper, James Fenimore. The Last of the Mohicans. Novel. 19th.

Cowley, Abraham. "Ode: Upon Dr. Harvey." Poem. Renaissance.

Cowley, Abraham. "To Dr. Scarborough." Poem. Renaissance.

Crane, Stephen. The Red Badge of Courage. Novel. 19th.

The Dance of Death. Long Poems. Medieval.

Defoe, Daniel. A Journal of the Plague Year. Treatise. 18th.

De Quincey, Thomas. Confessions of an English Opium-Eater and Suspiria de Profundis. Essays. 19th.

De Quincey, Thomas. "The English Mail Coach." Essay. 19th.

Dickens, Charles. Bleak House. Novel. 19th.

Dickens, Charles. David Copperfield. Novel. 19th.

Dickens, Charles. The Old Curiosity Shop. Novel. 19th.

Dickens, Charles. The Pickwick Papers. Novel. 19th.

Dickey, James. "Diabetes." Poem. 20th.

Dickinson, Emily. "Death is like the insect." Poem. 19th.

Dickinson, Emily. "The Heart asks Pleasure--first--." Poem. 19th.

Dickinson, Emily. "I noticed People disappeared." Poem. 19th.

Dickinson, Emily. "My first well Day--since many ill." Poem. 19th.

Donne, John. "Death be not proud" (Holy Sonnet X). Sonnet. Renaissance.

Donne, John. Devotions. Essays. Renaissance.

Donne, John. "The First Anniversary." Poem. Renaissance.

Donne, John. "Hymne to God my God in my Sicknesse." Poem. Renaissance.

Donne, John. "Thou hast made me" and "Oh my blacke Soule!" (Holy Sonnets I and IV). Sonnets. Renaissance.

Dostoevsky, Fyodor. The Brothers Karamazov. Novel. 19th.

Dostoevsky, Fyodor. Crime and Punishment. Novel. 19th.

Dreiser, Theodore. An American Tragedy. Novel. 20th.

Dunbar, Paul. "The Paradox" and "The Right to Die." Poems. 19th.

Dunbar, William. "Lament for the Makers, Qwhen he wes sek" (Lament for the poets, when he was sick). Poem. Renaissance.

Edwards, Jonathan. "Phebe Bartlet." Essay. 18th.

Edwards, Jonathan. "Sinners in the Hands of an Angry God." Treatise. 18th.

Eliot, George (Mary Anne Evans). Mr. Gilfil's Love-Story. Novella. 19th.

Eliot, T. S. The Cocktail Party. Poetic Drama. 20th.

Emerson, Ralph Waldo. "Experience" and "Threnody." Essay and Poem. 19th.

Empson, William. "Ignorance of Death." Poem. 20th.

Euripides. Alcestis. Drama. Classical.

Faulkner, William. As I Lay Dying. Novel. 20th.

Fielding, Henry. A Journey From This World To The Next. Sketches. 18th.

Fielding, Henry. Tom Jones. Novel. 18th.

Fitzgerald, F. Scott. Tender Is the Night. Novel. 20th.

Franklin, Benjamin. Poor Richard: The Almanacks for the Years 1733-1758. Treatise. 18th.

Freneau, Philip. The House of Night. Poem. 18th.

Freneau, Philip. "The Indian Burying Ground." Poem. 18th.

Frost, Robert. "The Death of the Hired Man." Poem. 20th.

Frost, Robert. "'Out, Out.'" Poem. 20th.

Garcia Lorca, Federico. Blood Wedding. Drama. 20th.

Gaskell, Elizabeth. Mary Barton. Novel. 19th.

Gide, Andre. The Immoralist. Novel. 20th.

Glissenti, F. "Death and the Anatomical Lecture." Poem and Woodcuts. Renaissance.

Golding, William. Lord of the Flies. Novel. 20th.

Gorki, Maxim. The Lower Depths. Drama. 20th.

Gray, Thomas. "Elegy Written in a Country Church Yard." Poem. 18th.

Hardy, Thomas. "Afterwards." Poem. 19th.

Hardy, Thomas. Far From the Madding Crowd. Novel. 19th.

Hawthorne, Nathaniel. "Lady Eleanore's Mantle." Short Story. 19th.

Hazlitt, William. "The Sick Chamber." Essay. 19th.

Heinlein, Robert A. Time Enough For Love. Novel. 20th.

Heller, Joseph. Something Happened. Novel. 20th.

Hemingway, Ernest. "A Day's Wait." Short Story. 20th.

Hemingway, Ernest. A Farewell to Arms. Novel. 20th.

Hemingway, Ernest. "Indian Camp." Short Story. 20th.

Hemingway, Ernest. The Old Man and the Sea. Novella. 20th.

Herbert, Frank. The Eyes of Heisenberg (also as Do I Sleep or Wake). Novel. 20th.

Herbert, George. "The Collar." Poem. Renaissance.

Herbert, George. "Death." Poem. Renaissance.

Herrick, Robert. "To Perilla." Poem. Renaissance.

Herrick, Robert. "To the Virgins." Poem. Renaissance.

Homer. Iliad. Epic Poem. Classical.

Hopkins, Gerard Manley. "The Wreck of the Deutschland." Poem. 19th.

Housman, A. E. "To an Athlete Dying Young." Poem. 20th.

Hughes, Richard. A High Wind in Jamaica. (Also published as The Innocent Voyage.) Novel. 20th.

James, Henry. The Turn of the Screw. Novella. 19th.

Jean de Meun. The Romance of the Rose. Long Poem. Medieval.

Jewett, Sarah Orne. "Miss Tempy's Watchers." Short Story. 19th.

Johnson, Samuel. "The Death of Friends." Essay. 18th.

Jonson, Benjamin. Epigram LXV, "On My First Sonne." Poem. Renaissance.

Jonson, Benjamin. "An Epitaph." Poem. Renaissance.

Jonson, Benjamin. Sejanus. Drama. Renaissance.

Jonson, Benjamin. "To the Memory of My Beloved, the Author Mr. William Shakespeare: and What He hath Left Us." Poem. Renaissance.

Joyce, James. Portrait of the Artist as a Young Man. Novel. 20th.

Joyce, James. Ulysses. Novel. 20th.

Keats, John. "After dark vapours." Sonnet. 19th.

Keats, John. "La Belle Dame Sans Merci." Poem. 19th.

Keats, John. Letter to Charles Wentworth Dilke, Mon., Sept. 1818; Letters to George and Georgiana Keats, Wed., Oct. 14 - Sat., Oct. 31, 1818; Wed., Dec. 16, 1818 - Mon., Jan. 4, 1819. Letters. 19th.

Keats, John. Letters to Charles Brown, Sun., Aug. 20, 1820; Sept. 30, 1820. Letters. 19th.

Keats, John. Letters to Fanny Brawne. Letters. 19th.

Keats, John. "Ode to a Nightingale." Poem. 19th.

Keats, John. "When I have fears that I may cease to be." Sonnet. 19th.

Kipling, Rudyard. "The Last Relief." Short Story. 19th.

Langland, William. Piers Plowman (B-Text). Long Poem. Medieval.

Lawrence, D. H. "The Horse Dealer's Daughter." Short Story. 20th.

Lawrence, D. H. "The Ship of Death." Poem. 20th.

Le Fanu, Sheridan. The House by the Churchyard. Novel. 19th.

Lewis, Sinclair. Arrowsmith. Novel. 20th.

London, Jack. "Koolau the Leper." Short Story. 19th.

Longfellow, Henry Wadsworth. Evangeline. Long Poem. 19th.

Lowell, Robert. "The Hospital." Poem. 20th.

Lowell, Robert. "Not Cleared of Killing." Poem. 20th.

Lucian of Samosata. "On Funerals." Essay. Classical.

Mackenzie, Henry. The Man of Feeling. Novel. 18th.

Mailer, Norman. An American Dream. Novel. 20th.

Malory, Thomas. The Book of Sir Launcelot and Queen Guinevere and The Most Piteous Tale of the Morte Arthur. Tales. Medieval.

Mann, Thomas. Death in Venice. Novella. 20th.

Mann, Thomas. The Magic Mountain. Novel. 20th.

Marlowe, Christopher. Tamburlaine: Part Two. Drama. Renaissance.

Marvell, Andrew. "To His Coy Mistress." Poem. Renaissance.

Massinger, Philip. The Unnatural Combat. Drama. Renaissance.

Masters, Edgar Lee. The Spoon River Anthology. Poem Sequence. 20th.

Maupassant, Guy de. "Beside a Dead Man." Sketch. 19th.

McKenna, Richard. "Casey Agonistes." Short Story. 20th.

Melville, Herman. Billy Budd, Sailor. Novella and Poem. 19th.

Melville, Herman. Moby Dick. Novel. 19th.

Milton, John. "Epitaph on the Marchioness of Winchester"; and Ben Jonson, "An Elegie on the Lady Pawlet Marchion: of Winton." Poems. Renaissance.

Milton, John. "In Obitum Procancellarii Medici" (On the Death of the Vice-Chancellor, A Physician). Poem, in Latin. Renaissance.

Milton, John. "Lycidas." Poem. Renaissance.

Milton, John. "On the Death of a Fair Infant Dying of a Cough." Poem. Renaissance.

Milton, John. "On the University Carrier, Who Sicken'd in the Time of his Vacancy, Being Forbid to go to London, By Reason of the Plague," and "Another on the Same." Poems. Renaissance.

Milton, John. Paradise Lost. Epic Poem. Renaissance.

Milton, John. Samson Agonistes. Poem. Renaissance.

Molière (Jean-Baptiste Poquelin). La Malade Imaginaire (The Imaginary Invalid). Drama. 18th.

Molière (Jean-Baptiste Poquelin). "A Monsieur de la Mothe Le Vayer." Sonnet, in French. 18th.

Montaigne, Michel Eyquem de. "Custome of the Ile of Cea." Essay. Renaissance.

More, Thomas. Utopia. Treatise. Renaissance.

Norris, Frank. A Man's Woman. Novella. 19th.

Norris, Frank. The Octopus. Novel. 19th.

Nourse, Alan E. "The Martyr." Novel. 20th.

Oates, Joyce Carol. Wonderland. Novel. 20th.

Olsen, Tillie. "Tell Me a Riddle." Short Story. 20th.

Omar Khayyām. The Rubaiyat. Collection of Poems. 19th.

Owen, Wilfrid. "Dulce et Decorum Est"; "Disabled"; "Mental Cases." Poems. 20th.

Parnell, Thomas. "On a Lady with Foul Breath." Poem. 18th.

Pasternak, Boris. Doctor Zhivago. Novel. 20th.

Pater, Walter. "A Child in the House." Essay. 19th.

Percy, Walker. Love in the Ruins. Novel. 20th.

Percy, Walker. The Moviegoer. Novel. 20th.

Plath, Sylvia. The Bell Jar. Novel. 20th.

Plato. Apology and Phaedo. Dialogues. Classical.

Poe, Edgar Allan. "The Facts in the Case of M. Valdemar." Short Story. 19th.

Poe, Edgar Allan. "The Fall of the House of Usher." Short Story. 19th.

Poe, Edgar Allan. "Ligeia." Short Story. 19th.

Poe, Edgar Allan. "The Masque of the Red Death." Short Story. 19th.

Poe, Edgar Allan. "The Raven." Poem. 19th.

Porter, Katherine Anne. "The Jilting of Granny Weatherall." Short Story. 20th.

Porter, Katherine Anne. "Pale Horse, Pale Rider." Short Story. 20th.

Proust, Marcel. Remembrance of Things Past. Novel. 20th.

Remarque, Erich Maria. _Arch of Triumph_. Novel. 20th.

Richardson, Samuel. _Clarissa_. Novel. 18th.

Rilke, Rainer Maria. _The Book of Poverty and Death_. Short Poems. 20th.

Roethke, Theodore. "Old Lady's Winter Words" and _Meditations of an Old Woman_. Poem and Poem Sequence. 20th.

Ronsard, Pierre de. "These sonnets of love" ("Je chantois ces sonnets, amoureux d'une Helene"). Sonnet. Renaissance.

Rossetti, Christina. "Remember" and "Song." Poems. 19th.

Rossetti, Dante Gabriel. "The Blessed Damozel." Poem. 19th.

Rossetti, Dante Gabriel. "Life-in-Love" and "Death-in-Love." Sonnets. 19th.

Sackville-West, V. _All Passion Spent_. Novel. 20th.

Salinger, J. D. _The Catcher in the Rye_. Novel. 20th.

Sappho. On Death. Fragments. Classical.

Seneca, Lucius Annaeus. _Epistles_, nos. XII and XXVI, "On Old Age" and "On Old Age and Death." Essays. Classical.

Seneca, Lucius Annaeus. _Epistles_, no. XXIV, "On Despising Death." Essay. Classical.

Seneca, Lucius Annaeus. _Epistles_, no. LIV, "On Asthma and Death." Essay. Classical.

Seneca, Lucius Annaeus. _Hercules Furens_. Drama. Classical.

Sexton, Anne. "For the Year of the Insane" and "The Sickness Unto Death." Poems. 20th.

Sexton, Anne. "The Fury of Rain Storms." Poem. 20th.

Sexton, Anne. "Sylvia's Death." Poem. 20th.

Shakespeare, William. _Hamlet_. Drama. Renaissance.

Shakespeare, William. _2 Henry IV_. Drama. Renaissance.

Shakespeare, William. _Julius Caesar_. Drama. Renaissance.

Shakespeare, William. _Measure for Measure_. Drama. Renaissance.

Shakespeare, William. "Not marble nor the gilded monuments." Sonnet. Renaissance.

Shakespeare, William. "Poor soul, the centre of my sinful earth." Sonnet. Renaissance.

Shakespeare, William. _Richard III_. Drama. Renaissance.

Shakespeare, William. _Romeo and Juliet_. Drama. Renaissance.

Shakespeare, William. "Shall I compare thee to a summer's day?" Sonnet. Renaissance.

Shakespeare, William. _The Tempest_. Drama. Renaissance.

Shakespeare, William. _Twelfth Night_. Drama. Renaissance.

Shakespeare, William. _Venus and Adonis_. Poem. Renaissance.

Shaw, George Bernard. _Back to Methuselah: a Metabiological Pentateuch_. Drama. 20th.

Shelley, Mary. _The Last Man_. Novel. 19th.

Shelley, Percy Bysshe. _Adonais_. Poem. 19th.

Shelley, Percy Bysshe. "Death" and "Sonnet." Poems. 19th.

Shelley, Percy Bysshe. _Prometheus Unbound_. Poetic Drama. 19th.

Shelley, Percy Bysshe. "To William Shelley." Poem. 19th.

Sholom Aleichem (Solomon Rabinowitch). "You Mustn't Weep--It's Yom-Tev." Short Story. 19th.

Smith, Cordwainer (Dr. M. A. Linebarger). "At the Gate of the Garden of Death" and "The Trial." In _Norstrilia_ (also in _The Planet Buyer_). Novel. 20th.

Snow, C. P. _Last Things_. Novel. 20th.

Solzhenitsyn, Alexander. _Cancer Ward_. Novel. 20th.

Sophocles. _Antigone_. Drama. Classical.

Sophocles. _Oedipus at Colonus_. Drama. Classical.

Spark, Muriel. _Memento Mori_. Novel. 20th.

Spenser, Edmund. "Men call you fayre, and you doe credit it." Sonnet. Renaissance.

Spenser, Edmund. "One day I wrote her name upon the strand." Sonnet. Renaissance.

Steinbeck, John. _In Dubious Battle_. Novel. 20th.

Stevenson, Robert Louis. "As with heaped bees at hiving time." Poem. 19th.

Stevenson, Robert Louis. "Requiem." Poem. 19th.

Stowe, Harriet Beecher. _Uncle Tom's Cabin_. Novel. 19th.

Swados, Harvey. _Celebration_. Novel. 20th.

Swift, Jonathan. "Verses on the Death of Dr. Swift." Poem. 18th.

Swinburne, Algernon Charles. "The Garden of Proserpine." Poem. 19th.

Synge, John Millington. _Riders to the Sea_. Drama. 20th.

Tanizaki, Junichiro. _Diary of a Mad Old Man_. Novel. 20th.

Taylor, Edward. "Meditation. Col. 1.18. That in all things he might have the Preheminence." Poem. 18th.

Taylor, Edward. "Meditation. 1 Cor. 3.22. Death is Yours." Poem. 18th.

Taylor, Edward. "Upon Wedlock, and Death of Children." Poem. 18th.

Tennyson, Alfred. "Crossing the Bar." Poem. 19th.

Tennyson, Alfred. "The Grandmother's Apology." Poem. 19th.

Tennyson, Alfred. _In Memoriam: A.H.H._ Poems. 19th.

Tennyson, Alfred. "In the Children's Hospital." Poem. 19th.

Tennyson, Alfred. "The Lady of Shalott." Poem. 19th.

Tennyson, Alfred. "The Lotos-Eaters." Poem. 19th.

Tennyson, Alfred. "Tiresias." Poem. 19th.

Tennyson, Alfred. "Tithonus." Poem. 19th.

Tennyson, Alfred. "Ulysses." Poem. 19th.

Thackeray, William Makepeace. _Vanity Fair_. Novel. 19th.

Thomas, Dylan. "And Death Shall Have No Dominion." Poem. 20th.

Thomas, Dylan. _The Doctor and the Devils_. Film Script. 20th.

Thomas, Dylan. "A Refusal to Mourn the Death, by Fire, of a Child in London." Poem. 20th.

Thompson, Francis. "To Monica Thought Dying." Poem. 19th.

Tolstoy, Leo. _The Death of Ivan Ilych_. Novella. 19th.

Tourneur, Cyril. _The Atheist's Tragedy_. Drama. Renaissance.

Tushnet, Leonard. "In Re Glover." Short Story. 20th.

Twain, Mark. _Adventures of Huckleberry Finn_. Novel. 19th.

Twain, Mark. _Autobiography of Mark Twain_. Autobiography. 19th.

Vaughan, Henry. "They are All Gone into the World of Light!" Poem. Renaissance.

Villon, Francois. _The Testament_. Poem. Medieval.

Vonnegut, Kurt, Jr. _Cat's Cradle_. Novel. 20th.

Vonnegut, Kurt, Jr. _Slaughterhouse Five_. Novel. 20th.

Warren, Samuel. _Passages from the Diary of a Late Physician_. Sketches. 19th.

Waugh, Evelyn. _The Loved One_. Novel. 20th.

Webster, John. _The Duchess of Malfi_. Drama. Renaissance.

Wells, H. G. "The Cone." Short Story. 19th.

Wells, H. G. "Under the Knife." Short Story. 19th.

Wharton, Edith. "Atrophy." Short Story. 20th.

Wharton, Edith. "Diagnosis." Short Story. 20th.

Wharton, Edith. "A Journey." Short Story. 20th.

White, Patrick. _The Eye of the Storm_. Novel. 20th.

White, Patrick. _The Solid Mandala_. Novel. 20th.

Whitman, Walt. _Drum Taps_ and _Specimen Days_. Short Poems and Journal. 19th.

Whitman, Walt. "Out of the Cradle Endlessly Rocking." Poem. 19th.

Whitman, Walt. "Song of Myself." Poem. 19th.

Whitman, Walt. "When Lilacs Last in the Dooryard Bloomed." Poem. 19th.

Wilde, Oscar. "The Ballad of Reading Gaol." Long Poem. 19th.

Wilder, Thornton. Our Town. Drama. 20th.

Williams, Tennessee. Cat on a Hot Tin Roof. Drama. 20th.

Williams, Tennessee. Streetcar Named Desire. Drama. 20th.

Williams, Tennessee. Sweet Bird of Youth. Drama. 20th.

Williams, William Carlos. The Autobiography of William Carlos Williams. Autobiography. 20th.

Williams, William Carlos. "Death." Poem. 20th.

Williams, William Carlos. "Jean Beicke." Short Story. 20th.

Williams, William Carlos. "To a Dog Injured in the Street." Poem 20th.

Williams, William Carlos. "Tract." Poem. 20th.

Winchilsea, Countess of (Anne Finch). "To Death." Poem. 18th.

Woolf, Virginia. Mrs. Dalloway. Novel. 20th.

Woolf, Virginia. The Waves. Novel. 20th.

Wordsworth, William. "Maternal Grief." Poem. 19th.

Wordsworth, William. "A slumber did my spirit seal." Poem. 19th.

Wordsworth, William. "We are Seven." Poem. 19th.

Wyndham, John. Trouble With Lichen. Novel. 20th.

Yglesias, Helen. "Semi-Private." Short Story. 20th.

Young, Edward. Night Thoughts, "The Complaint." Long Poem. 18th.

Zola, Emile. Dr. Pascal. Novel. 19th.

Zola, Emile. Fécondité (From Les Quatres Evangiles). Novel. 19th.

DISEASE & HEALTH

Akenside, Mark. "Hymn to the Naiads." Poem. 18th.

Akenside, Mark. "Ode XII, On Recovering From a Fit of Sickness, in the Country. 1768." Poem. 18th.

Albee, Edward. The Death of Bessie Smith. Drama. 20th.

Amis, Kingsley. Ending Up. Novel. 20th.

Anonymous. "Charm for a Sudden Stitch." Poem. Medieval.

Anonymous. "Now fade the rose and lily-flower." Poem. Medieval.

Anonymous. Tales and Quick Answers, nos. 38, 50 & 80. Tales. Renaissance.

Anonymous. Wealth and Health. Drama. Renaissance.

Armstrong, John. "The Art of Preserving Health." Poem. 18th.

Auden, W. H. "The Art of Healing." Poem. 20th.

Auden, W. H. "In Memory of Sigmund Freud." Poem. 20th.

Auden, W. H. "Miss Gee." Poem. 20th.

Auden, W. H. "Surgical Ward." Sonnet. 20th.

Auden, W. H. Untitled "Short." Poem. 20th.

Auden, W. H. and Christopher Isherwood. The Dog Beneath the Skin. Poetic Drama. 20th.

Austen, Jane. Emma. Novel. 19th.

Austen, Jane. Mansfield Park. Novel. 19th.

Austen, Jane. Persuasion. Novel. 19th.

Austen, Jane. Sense and Sensibility. Novel. 19th.

Babel, Isaac. "The End of the Old-Folk's Home." Short Story. 20th.

Bacon, Francis. "Of Regiment of Health." Essay. Renaissance.

Balzac, Honoré de. The Country Doctor. Novel. 19th.

Barclay, Alexander. Ship of Fools. Poems. Renaissance.

Beckett, Samuel. Endgame. Drama. 20th.

Behn, Aphra. Sir Patient Fancy. Drama. 18th.

Bellow, Saul. Mr. Sammler's Planet. Novel. 20th.

Benn, Gottfried. "Man and Woman Go Through the Cancer Ward." Poem. 20th.

Benn, Gottfried. "Night Cafe." Poem. 20th.

Bennett, Arnold. Riceyman Steps. Novel. 19th.

Betjeman, John. "Devonshire Street W.1." Poem. 20th.

The Bible. Job. Classical.

The Bible. Leviticus. Classical.

The Bible. Psalms, nos. VI, XXIII, and CXXXVII. Classical.

Billings, Philip. "Vassar Miller." Poem. 20th.

Blackmore, Richard. Creation. Poem. 18th.

Blake, William. The Island in the Moon. Sketches and Poems. 19th.

Boccaccio, Giovanni. The Decameron: Day 1, Prologue. Sketch. Medieval.

Boswell, James. The Life of Samuel Johnson. Biography. 18th.

Bradstreet, Anne. "For Deliverance from a Fever." Poem. 18th.

Brontë, Charlotte. Jane Eyre. Novel. 19th.

Brontë, Charlotte. Villette. Novel. 19th.

Brontë, Emily Jane. Wuthering Heights. Novel. 19th.

Browne, Thomas. A Letter to a Friend, Upon Occasion of the Death of his Intimate Friend. Essay. Renaissance.

Buonarroti, Michel Angelo. "I feel constrained and blocked as is the marrow." Poem. Renaissance.

Buonarroti, Michel Angelo. "To Giovanni, the one from Pistoia." Poem. Renaissance.

Burgess, Anthony. The Doctor Is Sick. Novel. 20th.

Burns, Robert. "Address to the Toothache." Poem. 18th.

Burton, Robert. The Anatomy of Melancholy. Treatise. Renaissance.

Butler, Samuel. Erewhon. Novel. 19th.

Byron, George Gordon, Lord. "Lines On Hearing That Lady Byron Was Ill." Poem. 19th.

Cable, George Washington. Dr. Sevier. Novel. 19th.

Campanella, Tomaso. City of the Sun. Treatise. Renaissance.

Catullus, C. Valerius. Carmina, no. 71. Poem. Classical.

Céline, Louis-Ferdinand. Journey to the End of the Night. Novel. 20th.

Cellini, Benvenuto. Autobiography. Autobiography. Renaissance.

Chekhov, Anton. "Gusev." Short Story. 19th.

Chekhov, Anton. The Island: A Journey to Sakhalin. Nonfiction. 19th.

Chekhov, Anton. Ivanov. Drama. 19th.

Chekhov, Anton. Letter to Alexey N. Pleshcheyev, October 1889. Letter. 19th.

Chekhov, Anton. "Peasants." Short Story. 19th.

Chekhov, Anton. Uncle Vanya. Drama. 19th.

Chekhov, Anton. "Ward 6." Short Story. 19th.

Choromanski, Michal. Jealousy and Medicine. Novel. 20th.

Clough, Arthur Hugh. "Bethesda: a Sequel." Poem. 19th.

Collins, Wilkie. Hide and Seek and Poor Miss Finch. Novels. 19th.

Conrad, Joseph. The Shadow Line: a Confession. Novella. 20th.

Cowley, Abraham. "To Dr. Scarborough." Poem. Renaissance.

Crane, Hart. "Episode of Hands." Poem. 20th.

Crane, Stephen. "When a Man Falls a Crowd Gathers (A Street Scene in New York)." Sketch. 19th.

Crashaw, Richard. "In praise of Lessius." Poem. Renaissance.

Cronin, A. J. The Citadel. Novel. 20th.

Dante Alighieri. The Divine Comedy: The Inferno. Long Poem. Medieval.

De L'Isle-Adam, Villiers. "The Doctor's Heroism." Short Story. 19th.

Dickens, Charles. Bleak House. Novel. 19th.

Dickens, Charles. Great Expectations. Novel. 19th.

Dickens, Charles. Martin Chuzzlewit. Novel. 19th.

Dickens, Charles. The Old Curiosity Shop. Novel. 19th.

Dickens, Charles. The Pickwick Papers. Novel. 19th.

Dickey, James. "The Cancer Match." Poem. 20th.

Dickey, James. "Diabetes." Poem. 20th.

Dickinson, Emily. "As One does Sickness over." Poem. 19th.

Dickinson, Emily. "It Knew no Medicine--." Poem. 19th.

Dickinson, Emily. "My first well Day--since many ill." Poem. 19th.

Disch, Thomas. Camp Concentration. Novel. 20th.

Donne, John. "The Comparison" (Elegy VIII). Poem. Renaissance.

Donne, John. Devotions. Essays. Renaissance.

Donne, John. "The First Anniversary." Poem. Renaissance.

Donne, John. "Hymne to God my God in my Sicknesse." Poem. Renaissance.

Donne, John. "Thou hast made me" and "Oh my blacke Soule!" (Holy Sonnets I and IV). Sonnets. Renaissance.

Dostoevsky, Fyodor. The Brothers Karamazov. Novel. 19th.

Dostoevsky, Fyodor. Crime and Punishment. Novel. 19th.

Dostoevsky, Fyodor. The Idiot. Novel. 19th.

Dostoevsky, Fyodor. Notes From the Underground. Novella. 19th.

Drabble, Margaret. The Millstone. Novel. 20th.

Dryden, John. "To John Driden." Poem. 18th.

Dunbar, William. "Lament for the Makers, Qwhen he wes sek" (Lament for the poets, when he was sick). Poem. Renaissance.

Edgeworth, Maria. Belinda. Novel. 19th.

Edwards, Jonathan. "Sinners in the Hands of an Angry God." Treatise. 18th.

Eliot, George (Mary Anne Evans). Janet's Repentance. Novella. 19th.

Eliot, George (Mary Anne Evans). The Mill on the Floss. Novel. 19th.

Eliot, George (Mary Anne Evans). Mr. Gilfil's Love-Story. Novella. 19th.

Eliot, T. S. "East Coker." Poem. 20th.

Eliot, T. S. "The Love Song of J. Alfred Prufrock." Poem. 20th.

Elyot, Thomas. The Castle of Health. Treatise. Renaissance.

Faulkner, William. As I Lay Dying. Novel. 20th.

Fielding, Henry. A Journey From This World To The Next. Sketches. 18th.

Fielding, Henry. Voyage to Lisbon. Journal. 18th.

Flaubert, Gustave. Madame Bovary. Novel. 19th.

Ford, John. The Broken Heart. Drama. Renaissance.

Franklin, Benjamin. Autobiography. Autobiography. 18th.

Franklin, Benjamin. "Dialogue Between the Gout and M. Franklin." Essay. 18th.

Franklin, Benjamin. Poor Richard: The Almanacks for the Years 1733-1758. Treatise. 18th.

Frost, Robert. "'Out, Out.'" Poem. 20th.

Fulke Greville, Lord Brooke. "The golden age was when the world was young." Poem. Renaissance.

Fulke Greville, Lord Brooke. A Treatie of Human Learning. Poem. Renaissance.

Garth, Samuel. The Dispensary. Poem. 18th.

Gaskell, Elizabeth. Mary Barton. Novel. 19th.

Gide, Andre. The Immoralist. Novel. 20th.

Gilman, Charlotte Perkins Stetson. The Yellow Wallpaper. Short Story. 19th.

Golding, William. Lord of the Flies. Novel. 20th.

Goldsmith, Oliver. She Stoops to Conquer. Drama. 18th.

Gorki, Maxim. The Lower Depths. Drama. 20th.

Gottfried von Strassburg. Tristan and Isolt. Tale. Medieval.

Graves, Robert. "Lollocks." Poem. 20th.

Green, Matthew. "The Spleen." Poem. 18th.

Gregory, Isabella Augusta, Lady. The Workhouse Ward. Drama. 20th.

Hart, Moss and George S. Kaufman. The Man Who Came to Dinner. Drama. 20th.

Hawthorne, Nathaniel. "Edward Fane's Rosebud." Sketch.

Hawthorne, Nathaniel. "Rappaccini's Daughter." Short Story. 19th.

Hazlitt, William. "The Sick Chamber." Essay. 19th.

Hejinian, John. Extreme Remedies. Novel. 20th.

Hemingway, Ernest. "A Clean, Well-lighted Place." Short Story. 20th.

Hemingway, Ernest. "A Day's Wait." Short Story. 20th.

Hemingway, Ernest. A Farewell to Arms. Novel. 20th.

Hemingway, Ernest. The Old Man and the Sea. Novella. 20th.

Hemingway, Ernest. "The Snows of Kilimanjaro." Short Story. 20th.

Henry, O. (W. S. Porter). "A Fog in Santone." Short Story. 19th.

Henry, O. (W. S. Porter). "Hygeia at the Solito." Short Story. 19th.

Henry, O. (W. S. Porter). "The Last Leaf." Short Story. 19th.

Henryson, Robert. The Testament of Cresseid. Poem. Medieval.

Herbert, Frank. The Eyes of Heisenberg (also as Do I Sleep or Wake). Novel. 20th.

Herrick, Robert. "To Musique, to becalme his Fever." Poem. Renaissance.

Hopkins, Gerard Manley. "Felix Randal." Sonnet. 19th.

Howard, Sidney, in collaboration with Paul de Kruif. Yellow Jack. Drama. 20th.

Ibsen, Henrik. An Enemy of the People. Drama. 19th.

Ibsen, Henrik. Ghosts. Drama. 19th.

Isherwood, Christopher. The Dog Beneath the Skin. Poetic Drama. 20th.

James, Henry. Daisy Miller: A Study. Novella. 19th.

James I. A Counterblaste to Tobacco. Treatise. Renaissance.

Johnson, Samuel. A Dictionary of the English Language. Dictionary. 18th.

Jonson, Benjamin. "Still to be neat." Song. Renaissance.

Jonson, Benjamin. "To Sickness" and "An Epigram. To the Small Poxe." Poems. Renaissance.

Jonson, Benjamin. Volpone. Drama. Renaissance.

Kafka, Franz. The Metamorphosis. Novella. 20th.

Keats, John. Letter to Charles Wentworth Dilke, Mon., Sept. 1818; Letters to George and Georgiana Keats, Wed., Oct. 14 - Sat., Oct. 31, 1818; Wed., Dec. 16, 1818 - Mon., Jan. 4, 1819. Letters. 19th.

Keats, John. Letters to Fanny Brawne. Letters. 19th.

Keats, John. "When I have fears that I may cease to be." Sonnet. 19th.

Kingsley, Sidney. Men in White. Drama. 20th.

Kipling, Rudyard. "The Last Relief." Short Story. 19th.

Kipling, Rudyard. "Unprofessional." Short Story. 19th.

Lacy, John. The Dumb Lady. Drama. 18th.

Lamb, Charles. "The Convalescent." Essay. 19th.

Langland, William. Piers Plowman (B-Text). Long Poem. Medieval.

Larkin, Philip. "Faith Healing." Poem. 20th.

Lawrence, D. H. "Healing" and "Sick." Poems. 20th.

Lawrence, D. H. "The Horse Dealer's Daughter." Short Story. 20th.

Lawrence, D. H. Sons and Lovers. Novel. 20th.

Lessing, Doris. The Summer Before the Dark. Novel. 20th.

Lewis, Sinclair. Arrowsmith. Novel. 20th.

Lodge, Thomas. A Treatise of the Plague. Treatise. Renaissance.

London, Jack. "Koolau the Leper." Short Story. 19th.

Longfellow, Henry Wadsworth. Evangeline. Long Poem. 19th.

Lowell, Robert. "Ezra Pound" and "Robert Frost." Poems. 20th.

Lydgate, John. "Dietarium" ("A Dietary"). Poem. Medieval.

Mailer, Norman. An American Dream. Novel. 20th.

Mann, Thomas. Death in Venice. Novella. 20th.

Mann, Thomas. The Magic Mountain. Novel. 20th.

Martial (Marcus Valerius Martialis). Epigrams, Book V, no. 9. Poem. Classical.

Marvell, Andrew. "A Dialogue between the Soul and the Body." Poem. Renaissance.

Masters, Edgar Lee. The Spoon River Anthology. Poem Sequence. 20th.

Mather, Cotton. The Angel of Bethesda: An Essay Upon the Common Maladies of Mankind. Treatise. 18th.

Maugham, W. Somerset. Liza of Lambeth. Novel. 20th.

Maupassant, Guy de. "The First Snowfall." Short Story. 19th.

McCullers, Carson. The Ballad of the Sad Café. Novella. 20th.

McCullers, Carson. The Heart Is a Lonely Hunter. Novel. 20th.

McCullers, Carson. Reflections in a Golden Eye. Novella. 20th.

Mercier, Louis Sebastian. Memoirs of the Year Two Thousand Five Hundred (original title: The Year Two Thousand Four Hundred and Forty). Treatise. 18th.

Middleton, Thomas. The Changeling. Drama. Renaissance.

Miller, Vassar. "The Common Core." Poem. 20th.

Miller, Vassar. "On the Examination Table." Poem. 20th.

Miller, Vassar. "Spastics: (First poem from Handi-Lib)." Poem. 20th.

Miller, Vassar. "Tired." Poem. 20th.

Milton, John. "L'Allegro" and "Il Penseroso." Poems. Renaissance.

Milton, John. Paradise Lost. Epic Poem. Renaissance.

Molière (Jean-Baptiste Poquelin). La Malade Imaginaire (The Imaginary Invalid). Drama. 18th.

Montaigne, Michel Eyquem de. "Of The Resemblance Betweene Children and Fathers." Essay. Renaissance.

Montaigne, Michel Eyquem de. "On the Force of the Imagination." Essay. Renaissance.

More, Thomas. A Dialogue of Comfort Against Tribulation. Dialogues. Renaissance.

More, Thomas. Utopia. Treatise. Renaissance.

Nashe, Thomas. The Unfortunate Traveler. Tale. Renaissance.

Norris, Frank. A Man's Woman. Novella. 19th.

Oates, Joyce Carol. Wonderland. Novel. 20th.

O'Connor, Flannery. "Good Country People." Short Story. 20th.

O'Connor, Flannery. "Revelation." Short Story. 20th.

O'Donnell, K. M. "In the Pocket." Short Story. 20th.

O'Neill, Eugene. Long Day's Journey Into Night. Drama. 20th.

Orwell, George (pseudonym of Eric Blair). "How the Poor Die." Essay. 20th.

Owen, Wilfrid. "Dulce et Decorum Est"; "Disabled"; Mental Cases. Poems. 20th.

Pasternak, Boris. Doctor Zhivago. Novel. 20th.

Pepys, Samuel. The Diary: Selections. Diary. 18th.

Percival, James Gates. "Consumption." Poem. 19th.

Percy, Walker. Love in the Ruins. Novel. 20th.

Phelps, Elizabeth Stuart. Dr. Zay. Novel. 19th.

Pindar. "Pythia III: For Hieron of Syracuse: On the Occasion of His Illness." Poem. Classical.

Plath, Sylvia. The Bell Jar. Novel. 20th.

Plath, Sylvia. "Fever 103°." Poem. 20th.

Poe, Edgar Allan. "The Facts in the Case of M. Valdemar." Short Story. 19th.

Poe, Edgar Allan. "The Fall of the House of Usher." Short Story. 19th.

Pope, Alexander. The Rape of the Lock. Poem. 18th.

Porter, Katherine Anne. "Pale Horse, Pale Rider." Short Story. 20th.

Proust, Marcel. Remembrance of Things Past. Novel. 20th.

Ransom, John Crowe. "Here Lies a Lady." Poem. 20th.

Remarque, Erich Maria. Arch of Triumph. Novel. 20th.

Rilke, Rainer Maria. "The Blind Man's Song," "The Drinker's Song," "The Idiot's Song," "The Suicide's Song," "The Dwarf's Song," and "The Leper's Song." Short Poems. 20th.

Ronsard, Pierre de. "Seated beside the hearth" ("La mois d'Augst bouillonnoit d'une chaleur esprise"). Sonnet. Renaissance.

Roth, Philip. "Epstein." Short Story. 20th.

Schiller, Friedrich. "Die Peste." Poem. 19th.

Schnitzler, Arthur. A Confirmed Bachelor (Also published as Dr. Graesler). Novel. 20th.

Schnitzler, Arthur. "The Man of Honour" (Also published as "The Murderer"). Short Story. 20th.

Schnitzler, Arthur. The Spring Sonata (Also published as Bertha Garlan). Novel. 20th.

Scott, Sir Walter. The Surgeon's Daughter. Novella. 19th.

Selzer, Richard. The Rituals of Surgery. Short Stories. 20th.

Seneca, Lucius Annaeus. Epistles, no. LIV, "On Asthma and Death." Essay. Classical.

Sexton, Anne. "Madonna." Poem. 20th.

Shakespeare, William. All's Well That Ends Well. Drama. Renaissance.

Shakespeare, William. Hamlet. Drama. Renaissance.

Shakespeare, William. 2 Henry IV. Drama. Renaissance.

Shakespeare, William. Julius Caesar. Drama. Renaissance.

Shakespeare, William. Measure for Measure. Drama. Renaissance.

Shakespeare, William. A Midsummer-Night's Dream. Drama. Renaissance.

Shakespeare, William. "My love is as a fever, longing still." Sonnet. Renaissance.

Shakespeare, William. Othello. Drama. Renaissance.

Shakespeare, William. Richard III. Drama. Renaissance.

Shakespeare, William. The Tempest. Drama. Renaissance.

Shakespeare, William. Timon of Athens. Drama. Renaissance.

Shakespeare, William. Troilus and Cressida. Drama. Renaissance.

Shaw, George Bernard. The Doctor's Dilemma. Drama. 20th.

Sheed, Wilfrid. People Will Always Be Kind. Novel. 20th.

Sholom Aleichem (Solomon Rabinowitch). "The Flag." Short Story. 19th.

Sholom Aleichem (Solomon Rabinowitch). "You Mustn't Weep--It's Yom-Tev." Short Story. 19th.

Shelley, Percy Bysshe. "The Magnetic Lady to her Patient." Poem. 19th.

Shelley, Percy Bysshe. Prometheus Unbound. Poetic Drama. 19th.

Sidney, Philip. Four Sonnets Made when his Lady had Pain in her Face. Sonnets. Renaissance.

Smart, Christopher. "Hymn to the Supreme Being on Recovery from a Dangerous Fit of Illness." Poem. 18th.

Smollett, Tobias. The Adventures of Roderick Random. Novel. 18th.

Smollett, Tobias. The Expedition of Humphry Clinker. Novel. 18th.

Solzhenitsyn, Alexander. Cancer Ward. Novel. 20th.

Sophocles. Philoctetes. Drama. Classical.

The Spectator, no. 25. Essay. 18th.

The Spectator, nos. 115 & 195. Essays. 18th.

Steinbeck, John. In Dubious Battle. Novel. 20th.

Stevenson, Robert Louis. "Father Damien." Essay. 19th.

Stevenson, Robert. "The Sick Child" and "The Land of Counterpane." Poems. 19th.

Stone, John. "Stroke." Poem. 20th.

Stowe, Harriet Beecher. Uncle Tom's Cabin. Novel. 19th.

Suckling, John. "The Deformed Mistress." Poem. Renaissance.

Swift, Jonathan. Gulliver's Travels. Satiric Tales. 18th.

Swift, Jonathan. "In Sickness." Poem. 18th.

Swift, Jonathan. "Stella's Birth-day: March 13, 1726/7." Poem. 18th.

Tanizaki, Junichiro. Diary of a Mad Old Man. Novel. 20th.

Taylor, Edward. "Meditation. Mal. 4.2. With Healing in His Wings." Poem. 18th.

Thackeray, William Makepeace. The History of Henry Esmond. Novel. 19th.

Thoreau, Henry David. Walden. Treatise. 19th.

Tolstoy, Leo. The Death of Ivan Ilych. Novella. 19th.

Tolstoy, Leo. The Kreutzer Sonata. Novella. 19th.

Tourneur, Cyril. The Atheist's Tragedy. Drama. Renaissance.

Turgenev, Ivan. "The District Doctor." Short Story. 19th.

Twain, Mark. "Experience of the McWilliamses with Membranous Croup." Short Story. 19th.

Twain, Mark. Innocents Abroad. Novel. 19th.

Twain, Mark. "Three Thousand Years Among the Microbes." Sketch. 19th.

Walton, Izaak. The Compleat Angler. Treatise. Renaissance.

Warren, Samuel. Passages from the Diary of a Late Physician. Sketches. 19th.

Wharton, Edith. Ethan Frome. Novel. 20th.

White, Patrick. The Eye of the Storm. Novel. 20th.

Whitman, Walt. "As I Sit Writing Here," "Queries to My Seventieth Year," "Thanks in Old Age," "Old Age's Lambent Peaks," and "Good-Bye, My Fancy." Short Poems. 19th.

Williams, William Carlos. The Autobiography of William Carlos Williams. Autobiography. 20th.

Williams, William Carlos. "The Injury." Poem. 20th.

Williams, William Carlos. "Jean Beicke." Short Story. 20th.

Williams, William Carlos. "The Use of Force." Short Story. 20th.

Williams, William Carlos. A Voyage to Pagany. Novel. 20th.

Winchilsea, Countess of (Anne Finch). "Fragment at Tunbridge Wells." Poem. 18th.

Winchilsea, Countess of (Anne Finch). "The Spleen." Poem. 18th.

Woolf, Virginia. "On Being Ill." Essay. 20th.

Wordsworth, William. "The Idiot Boy." Poem. 19th.

Yglesias, Helen. "Semi-Private." Short Story. 20th.

Young, Edward. Night Thoughts, "The Complaint." Long Poem. 18th.

Zola, Emile. Dr. Pascal. Novel. 19th.

Zola, Emile. Drunkard (L'Assomoir). Novel. 19th.

Zola, Emile. Une Page D'Amour. Novel. 19th.

DOCTORS

Albee, Edward. The Death of Bessie Smith. Drama. 20th.

Alcott, Louisa May. Hospital Sketches. Sketches. 19th.

Amis, Kingsley. Ending Up. Novel. 20th.

Anonymous. St. George Plays. Dramas. Medieval.

Anonymous. Tales and Quick Answers, nos. 38, 50 & 80. Tales. Renaissance.

Arden, John. The Happy Haven. Drama. 20th.

Arlen, Michael. The Green Hat. Novel. 20th.

Auden, W. H. "The Age of Anxiety." Long Poem. 20th.

Auden, W. H. "The Art of Healing." Poem. 20th.

Auden, W. H. "Give me a doctor." Poem. 20th.

Auden, W. H. "In Memory of Sigmund Freud." Poem. 20th.

Auden, W. H. "Miss Gee." Poem. 20th.

Auden, W. H. and Christopher Isherwood. The Dog Beneath the Skin. Poetic Drama. 20th.

Austen, Jane. Emma. Novel. 19th.

Babel, Isaac. "The End of the Old-Folk's Home." Short Story. 20th.

Bacon, Francis. "Of Regiment of Health." Essay. Renaissance.

Balzac, Honoré de. The Country Doctor. Novel. 19th.

Barclay, Alexander. Ship of Fools. Poems. Renaissance.

Barth, John. The End of the Road. Novel. 20th.

Beauvoir, Simone de. A Very Easy Death. Autobiography. 20th.

Bellow, Saul. Mr. Sammler's Planet. Novel. 20th.

Benn, Gottfried. "Little Aster." Poem. 20th.

Bennett, Arnold. Riceyman Steps. Novel. 19th.

Berg, Stephen. "Why Are We Here?" Poem. 20th.

Berryman, John. Recovery. Novel. 20th.

The Bible. Luke. Classical.

The Bible. New Testament. Classical.

Boccaccio, Giovanni. The Decameron: Day 9, Tale 3. Tale. Medieval.

Borges, Jorge Luis. "The Immortals." Short Story. 20th.

Bridges, Robert. "On a Dead Child." Poem. 20th.

Brieux, Eugene. Les Avariés. Drama; and Sinclair, Upton. Damaged Goods. Novel. 20th.

Brome, Richard. The Antipodes. Drama. Renaissance.

Brontë, Charlotte. Villette. Novel. 19th.

Brontë, Emily Jane. Wuthering Heights. Novel. 19th.

Brown, Geoff. I Want What I Want. Novel. 20th.

Browning, Robert. "An Epistle: Containing the Strange Medical Experience of Karshish, the Arab Physician." Poem. 19th.

Browning, Robert. "The Family." Poem. 19th.

Browning, Robert. Paracelsus. Poem. 19th.

Büchner, Georg. Woyzeck. Drama. 19th.

Bullein, William. A Dialogue Against the Fever Pestilence. Dialogues. Renaissance.

Burgess, Anthony. The Doctor Is Sick. Novel. 20th.

Burns, Robert. "Death and Doctor Hornbook." Poem. 18th.

Burroughs, William. The Naked Lunch. Novel. 20th.

Burton, Robert. The Anatomy of Melancholy. Treatise. Renaissance.

Butler, Samuel. Hudibras. Long Poem. 18th.

Butler, Samuel. Erewhon. Novel. 19th.

Cable, Geroge Washington. Dr. Sevier. Novel. 19th.

Camus, Albert. The Plague. Novel. 20th.

Céline, Louis-Ferdinand. Journey to the End of the Night. Novel. 20th.

Cellini, Benvenuto. Autobiography. Autobiography. Renaissance.

Chaucer, Geoffrey. The Canterbury Tales, "The General Prologue." Sketch. Medieval.

Chekhov, Anton. "An Attack of Nerves." Short Story. 19th.

Chekhov, Anton. The Island: A Journey to Sakhalin. Nonfiction. 19th.

Chekhov, Anton. Ivanov. Drama. 19th.

Chekhov, Anton. The Seagull. Drama. 19th.

Chekhov, Anton. Three Sisters. Drama. 19th.

Chekhov, Anton. Uncle Vanya. Drama. 19th.

Chekhov, Anton. "Ward 6." Short Story. 19th.

Choromanski, Michal. Jealousy and Medicine. Novel. 20th.

Cocteau, Jean. Opium: The Diary of a Cure. Diary. 20th.

Collins, Wilkie. Hide and Seek and Poor Miss Finch. Novels. 19th.

Collins, Wilkie. The Moonstone. Novel. 19th.

The Commedia dell' Arte. Dramas. Renaissance.

Conrad, Joseph. Nostromo. Novel. 20th.

Conrad, Joseph. The Shadow Line: a Confession. Novella. 20th.

Cooper, James Fenimore. The Prairie. Novel. 19th.

Cowley, Abraham. "Ode: Upon Dr. Harvey." Poem. Renaissance.

Cowley, Abraham. "To Dr. Scarborough." Poem. Renaissance.

Crabbe, George. The Parish Register. Long Poem. 18th.

Crabbe, George. "Sir Eustace Grey." Poem. 18th.

Crabbe, George. The Village. Long Poem. 18th.

Crane, Stephen. "The Monster." Short Story. 19th.

Crichton, Michael. The Andromeda Strain. Novel. 20th.

Cronin, A. J. The Citadel. Novel. 20th.

The Dance of Death. Long Poems. Medieval.

De Forest, John William. Miss Ravenal's Conversion from Secession to Loyalty. Novel. 19th.

Dekker, Thomas. The Honest Whore, Pt. I. Drama. Renaissance.

De L'Isle-Adam, Villiers. "The Doctor's Heroism." Short Story. 19th.

Del Rey, Lester. Nerves. Novel. 20th.

De Quincey, Thomas. Confessions of an English Opium-Eater and Suspiria de Profundis. Essays. 19th.

Dickens, Charles. Bleak House. Novel. 19th.

Dickens, Charles. David Cooperfield. Novel. 19th.

Dickey, James. "Diabetes." Poem. 20th.

Donne, John. "The Comparison" (Elegy VIII). Poem. Renaissance.

Donne, John. "Hymne to God my God in my Sicknesse." Poem. Renaissance.

Dostoevsky, Fyodor. Crime and Punishment. Novel. 19th.

Doyle, Arthur Conan. "The Croxley Master." Short Story. 19th.

Doyle, Arthur Conan. "The Curse of Eve." Short Story. 19th.

Doyle, Arthur Conan. "The Doctors of Hoyland." Short Story. 19th.

Doyle, Arthur Conan. "A Medical Document." Sketches. 19th.

Doyle, Arthur Conan. "The Third Generation." Short Sketch. 19th.

Drabble, Margaret. The Millstone. Novel. 20th.

Drake, Joseph Rodman. "The King of the Croakers." Poem. 19th.

Dreiser, Theodore. An American Tragedy. Novel. 20th.

Dryden, John. "To Dr. Charleton." Poem. 18th.

Dryden, John. "To John Driden." Poem. 18th.

Durrell, Lawrence. Monsieur. Novel. 20th.

Earle, John. <u>Micro-cosmographie</u>. Sketches. Renaissance.

Edgeworth, Maria. <u>Belinda</u>. Novel. 19th.

Eliot, George (Mary Anne Evans). <u>Adam Bede</u>. Novel. 19th.

Eliot, George (Mary Anne Evans). <u>Janet's Repentance</u>. Novella. 19th.

Eliot, George (Mary Anne Evans). <u>Middlemarch</u>. Novel. 19th.

Eliot, T. S. <u>The Cocktail Party</u>. Poetic Drama. 20th.

Eliot, T. S. "East Coker." Poem. 20th.

Faulkner, William. <u>As I Lay Dying</u>. Novel. 20th.

Fielding, Henry. <u>Amelia</u>. Novel. 18th.

Fielding, Henry. <u>Joseph Andrews</u>. Novel. 18th.

Fielding, Henry. "An Old Man Taught Wisdom or, The Virgin Un-masked. A Farce." Drama. 18th.

Fielding, Henry. <u>Tom Jones</u>. Novel. 18th.

Fitzgerald, F. Scott. <u>Tender Is the Night</u>. Novel. 20th.

Flaubert, Gustave. <u>Madame Bovary</u>. Novel. 19th.

Ford, John. <u>The Lover's Melancholy</u>. Drama. Renaissance.

Ford, John. <u>'Tis Pity She's a Whore</u>. Drama. Renaissance.

Franklin, Benjamin. "Dialogue Between the Gout and M. Franklin." Essay. 18th.

Franklin, Benjamin. <u>Poor Richard: The Almanacks for the Years 1733-1758</u>. Treatise. 18th.

Freneau, Philip. "The British Prison Ship." Poem. 18th.

Freneau, Philip. <u>Expedition of Timothy Taurus</u>. Poem. 18th.

Freneau, Philip. "Ode XI, To the Philadelphia Doctors" and "On the Free Use of the Lancet." Poems. 18th.

Freneau, Philip. "On Dr. Sangrado's Flight." Poem. 18th.

Frost, Robert. "'Out, Out.'" Poem. 20th.

Garth, Samuel. <u>The Dispensary</u>. Poem. 18th.

Giraudoux, Jean. <u>The Madwoman of Chaillot</u>. Drama. 20th.

Glissenti, F. "Death and the Anatomical Lecture." Poem and Woodcuts. Renaissance.

Goethe, Johann Wolfgang Von. <u>Faust</u>. Pt. I. Poetic Drama. 19th.

Gogol, Nikolai. "The Nose." Short Story. 19th.

Gunn, James. "Medic" (originally "Not So Great an Enemy," 1957 and a part of the <u>Immortals</u>, 1962). Short Story. 20th.

Haggard, H. Rider. <u>Doctor Therne</u>. Novel. 20th.

Hardy, Thomas. <u>The Woodlanders</u>. Novel. 19th.

Hart, Moss and George S. Kaufman. <u>The Man Who Came to Dinner</u>. Drama. 20th.

Hawthorne, Nathaniel. "Dr. Heidegger's Experiment." Short Story. 19th.

Hejinian, John. <u>Extreme Remedies</u>. Novel. 20th.

Hellman, Lillian. <u>The Children's Hour</u>. Drama. 20th.

Hemingway, Ernest. "The Doctor and the Doctor's Wife." Short Story. 20th.

Hemingway, Ernest. <u>A Farewell to Arms</u>. Novel. 20th.

Hemingway, Ernest. "God Rest You Merry, Gentlemen." Short Story. 20th.

Hemingway, Ernest. "Indian Camp." Short Story. 20th.

Henley, William Ernest. <u>In Hospital</u>. 28 Sketches in Verse. 19th.

Herbert, Frank. <u>The Eyes of Heisenberg</u> (also as <u>Do I Sleep or Wake</u>). Novel. 20th.

Herrick, Robert. <u>The Healer</u>. Novel. 20th.

Herrick, Robert. <u>The Web of Life</u>. Novel. 20th.

Holmes, Oliver Wendell. <u>Elsie Venner</u>. Novel. 19th.

Holmes, Oliver Wendell. <u>A Mortal Antipathy</u>. Novel. 19th.

Holmes, Oliver Wendell. "The Young Practitioner." Essay. 19th.

Hope, A. D. "The Bed." Poem. 20th.

Howard, Sidney, in collaboration with Paul de Kruif. <u>Yellow Jack</u>. Drama. 20th.

Howells, William Dean. <u>Dr. Breen's Practice</u>. Novel. 19th.

Howells, William Dean. <u>An Imperative Duty</u>. Novella. 19th.

Howells, William Dean. <u>The Shadow of a Dream</u>. Novella. 19th.

Ibsen, Henrik. <u>A Doll's House</u>. Drama. 19th.

Ibsen, Henrik. <u>An Enemy of the People</u>. Drama. 19th.

Ionesco, Eugene. <u>Exit the King</u>. Drama. 20th.

Isherwood, Christopher. <u>The Dog Beneath the Skin</u>. Poetic Drama. 20th.

James, Henry. "Lady Barberina." Short Story. 19th.

James, Henry. <u>The Middle Years</u>. Novella. 19th.

James, Henry. <u>Washington Square</u>. Novel. 19th.

James, Henry. <u>The Wings of the Dove</u>. Novel. 19th.

Jewett, Sarah Orne. <u>A Country Doctor</u>. Novel. 19th.

Johnson, Samuel. "On the Death of Mr. Robert Levet." Poem. 18th.

Jonson, Benjamin. Epigram XIII, "To Doctor Empirick." Poem. Renaissance.

Jonson, Benjamin. <u>Volpone</u>. Drama. Renaissance.

Kesey, Ken. <u>One Flew Over the Cuckoo's Nest</u>. Novel. 20th.

Keyes, Daniel. <u>Flowers for Algernon</u>. Novella. 20th.

Kingsley, Charles. <u>Two Years Ago</u>. Novel. 19th.

Kingsley, Sidney. <u>Men in White</u>. Drama. 20th.

Kipling, Rudyard. "The Tender Achilles" and "Hymn to Physical Pain." Short Story and Poem. 19th.

Kipling, Rudyard. "Unprofessional." Short Story. 19th.

Kornbluth, Cyril M. "The Little Black Bag." Short Story. 20th.

Langland, William. <u>Piers Plowman</u> (B-Text). Long Poem. Medieval.

Lardner, Ring. "Haircut." Short Story. 20th.

Lawrence, D. H. "The Horse Dealer's Daughter." Short Story. 20th.

Lawrence, D. H. <u>Sons and Lovers</u>. Novel. 20th.

LeSage, Alain René. <u>The Adventures of Gil Blas of Santillane</u>. Tale. 18th.

Lessing, Doris. <u>A Proper Marriage</u>. Novel. 20th.

Lever, Charles James. <u>Harry Lorrequer</u> (<u>The Confessions of Harry Lorrequer</u>). Novel. 19th.

Lewis, Sinclair. <u>Arrowsmith</u>. Novel. 20th.

Lowell, Robert. "Not Cleared of Killing." Poem. 20th.

Lucian of Samosata. "The Disowned." Essay. Classical.

Lyly, John. <u>Midas</u>. Drama. Renaissance.

Machiavelli, Niccolo. <u>Mandragola</u>. Drama. Renaissance.

Malory, Thomas. <u>The Book of Sir Launcelot and Queen Guinevere and The Most Piteous Tale of the Morte Arthur</u>. Tale. Medieval.

Mann, Thomas. <u>The Magic Mountain</u>. Novel. 20th.

Marlowe, Christopher. <u>Tamburlaine: Part Two</u>. Drama. Renaissance.

Marlowe, Christopher. <u>The Tragical History of Doctor Faustus</u>. Drama. Renaissance.

Maugham, W. Somerset. <u>Liza of Lambeth</u>. Novel. 20th.

Maugham, W. Somerset. <u>Of Human Bondage</u>. Novel. 20th.

McCullers, Carson. <u>The Heart Is a Lonely Hunter</u>. Novel. 20th.

McKenna, Richard. "Casey Agonistes." Short Story. 20th.

Melville, Herman. <u>White-Jacket, or The World in a Man-of-War</u>. Novel. 19th.

Meredith, George. "Melampus." Poem. 19th.

Miller, Arthur. <u>The Price</u>. Drama. 20th.

Milton, John. "In Obitum Procancellarii Medici" (On the Death of the Vice-Chancellor, A Physician). Poem, in Latin. Renaissance.

Molière (Jean-Baptiste Poquelin). <u>La Malade Imaginaire</u> (<u>The Imaginary Invalid</u>). Drama. 18th.

Molière (Jean-Baptiste Poquelin). <u>Le Médecin Malgré Lui</u> (<u>The Physician In Spite of Himself</u>). Drama. 18th.

Molière (Jean-Baptiste Poquelin). Le Médecin Volant (The Flying Doctor). Drama. 18th.

Montaigne, Michel Eyquem de. "Of The Resemblance Betweene Children and Fathers." Essay. Renaissance.

Montaigne, Michel Eyquem de. "On the Force of the Imagination." Essay. Renaissance.

Mortimer, Penelope. The Pumpkin Eater. Novel. 20th.

Nashe, Thomas. The Unfortunate Traveler. Tale. Renaissance.

Nichols, Peter. Joe Egg. Drama. 20th.

Nichols, Peter. The National Health. Drama. 20th.

Nourse, Alan E. The Bladerunner. Novel. 20th.

Oates, Joyce Carol. Wonderland. Novel. 20th.

O'Brien, Edna. August Is a Wicked Month. Novel. 20th.

O'Connor, Flannery. "Revelation." Short Story. 20th.

O'Donnell, K. M. "In the Pocket." Short Story. 20th.

Olsen, Tillie. "Tell Me a Riddle." Short Story. 20th.

O'Neill, Eugene. Long Day's Journey Into Night. Drama. 20th.

O'Neill, Eugene. Strange Interlude. Drama. 20th.

Orwell, George (pseudonym of Eric Blair). "How the Poor Die." Essay. 20th.

Pasternak, Boris. Doctor Zhivago. Novel. 20th.

The Paston Letters. Letters. Medieval.

Percy, Walker. Love in the Ruins. Novel. 20th.

Percy, Walker. The Moviegoer. Novel. 20th.

Phelps, Elizabeth Stuart. Dr. Zay. Novel. 19th.

Pindar. "Pythia III: For Hieron of Syracuse: On the Occasion of His Illness." Poem. Classical.

Pirandello, Luigi. Henry IV. Drama. 20th.

Plath, Sylvia. The Bell Jar. Novel. 20th.

Plath, Sylvia. "Lady Lazarus." Poem. 20th.

Plath, Sylvia. "The Surgeon at 2 a.m." Poem. 20th.

Plath, Sylvia. "Three Women." Dramatic Poem. 20th.

Plato. Symposium. Dialogue. Classical.

Pope, Alexander. "An Epistle from Mr. Pope, to Dr. Arbuthnot." Poem. 18th.

Porter, Katherine Anne. "He." Short Story. 20th.

Porter, Katherine Anne. "The Jilting of Granny Weatherall." Short Story. 20th.

Porter, Katherine Anne. "Pale Horse, Pale Rider." Short Story. 20th.

Rabelais, Francois. Gargantua and Pantagruel. Tales. Renaissance.

Reade, Charles. The Cloister and the Hearth and A Woman-Hater. Novels. 19th.

Reade, Charles. Hard Cash. Novel. 19th.

Remarque, Erich Maria. Arch of Triumph. Novel. 20th.

Roth, Philip. The Breast. Novella. 20th.

Roth, Philip. "Epstein." Short Story. 20th.

Roth, Philip. Portnoy's Complaint. Novel. 20th.

Sarton, May. Mrs. Stevens Hears the Mermaids Singing. Novel. 20th.

Schnitzler, Arthur. A Confirmed Bachelor (Also published as Dr. Graesler). Novel. 20th.

Schnitzler, Arthur. My Youth in Vienna. Autobiography. 20th.

Schnitzler, Arthur. Professor Bernhardi. Drama. 20th.

Scott, Sir Walter. St. Ronan's Well. Novel. 19th.

Scott, Sir Walter. The Surgeon's Daughter. Novella. 19th.

Scott, Sir Walter. The Talisman. Novel. 19th.

Sedley, Charles. "The Doctor and his Patients." Poem. 18th.

Selzer, Richard. The Rituals of Surgery. Short Stories. 20th.

Sexton, Anne. "Unknown Girl in the Maternity Ward." Poem. 20th.

Shadwell, Thomas. The Virtuoso. Drama. 18th.

Shaffer, Peter. Equus. Drama. 20th.

Shakespeare, William. Cymbeline. Drama. Renaissance.

Shakespeare, William. King Lear. Drama. Renaissance.

Shakespeare, William. Macbeth. Drama. Renaissance.

Shakespeare, William. The Merry Wives of Windsor. Drama. Renaissance.

Shakespeare, William. "My love is as a fever, longing still." Sonnet. Renaissance.

Shakespeare, William. Pericles, Prince of Tyre. Drama.

Shakespeare, William. Romeo and Juliet. Drama. Renaissance.

Shango, J. R. "A Matter of Ethics." Short Story. 20th.

Shaw, George Bernard. Doctors' Delusions. Treatise. 20th.

Shaw, George Bernard. The Doctor's Dilemma. Drama. 20th.

Sinclair, Upton. Damaged Goods. Novel. 20th.

Smollett, Tobias. The Adventures of Ferdinand, Count Fathom. Novel. 18th.

Smollett, Tobias. The Adventures of Peregrine Pickle. Novel. 18th.

Smollett, Tobias. The Adventures of Roderick Random. Novel. 18th.

Smollett, Tobias. The Expedition of Humphry Clinker. Novel. 18th.

Smollett, Tobias. Sir Launcelot Greaves. Novel. 18th.

Solzhenitsyn, Alexander. Cancer Ward. Novel. 20th.

Southey, Robert. The Doctor. Treatise. 19th.

Spark, Muriel. Memento Mori. Novel. 20th.

The Spectator, nos. 444 & 572. Essays. 18th.

Stein, Gertrude. Melanctha. Novella. 20th.

Steinbeck, John. In Dubious Battle. Novel. 20th.

Sterne, Laurence. The Life and Opinions of Tristram Shandy, Gent. Novel. 18th.

Stevenson, Robert Louis. Strange Case of Dr. Jekyll and Mr. Hyde. Novella. 19th.

Strindberg, August. The Father. Drama. 19th.

Swados, Harvey. Celebration. Novel. 20th.

Swift, Jonathan. Gulliver's Travels. Satiric Tales. 18th.

Swift, Jonathan. "In Sickness." Poem. 18th.

Swift, Jonathan (?). "A Love Poem. From a Physician to his Mistress. Written at London." Poem. 18th.

Swift, Jonathan. "Verses on the Death of Dr. Swift." Poem. 18th.

Tanizaki, Junichiro. Diary of a Mad Old Man. Novel. 20th.

Tennyson, Alfred. "In the Children's Hospital." Poem. 19th.

Thomas, Dylan. The Doctor and the Devils. Film Script. 20th.

Tolstoy, Leo. The Death of Ivan Ilych. Novella. 19th.

Tourneur, Cyril. The Atheist's Tragedy. Drama. Renaissance.

Trollope, Anthony. Doctor Thorne. Novel. 19th.

Trollope, Anthony. The Warden. Novel. 19th.

Turgenev, Ivan. "The District Doctor." Short Story. 19th.

Twain, Mark. Adventures of Huckleberry Finn. Novel. 19th.

Twain, Mark. Autobiography of Mark Twain. Autobiography. 19th.

Twain, Mark. "Experience of the McWilliamses with Membranous Croup." Short Story. 19th.

Twain, Mark. Innocents Abroad. Novel. 19th.

Voltaire, Francois-Marie Arouet. Candide. Tale. 18th.

Warren, Samuel. Passages from the Diary of a Late Physician. Sketches. 19th.

Webster, John. The Duchess of Malfi. Drama. Renaissance.

Welty, Eudora. The Optimist's Daughter. Novella. 20th.

Wharton, Edith. "Diagnosis." Short Story. 20th.

White, Patrick. _The Eye of the Storm_. Novel. 20th.

Wilder, Thornton. _Our Town_. Drama. 20th.

Williams, Tennessee. _Cat on a Hot Tin Roof_. Drama. 20th.

Williams, Tennessee. _Suddenly Last Summer_. Drama. 20th.

Williams, Tennessee. _Summer and Smoke_. Drama. 20th.

Williams, William Carlos. _The Autobiography of William Carlos Williams_. Autobiography. 20th.

Williams, William Carlos. "Complaint." Poem. 20th.

Williams, William Carlos. _A Dream of Love_. Drama. 20th.

Williams, William Carlos. "Jean Beicke." Short Story. 20th.

Williams, William Carlos. "The Use of Force." Short Story. 20th.

Williams, William Carlos. _A Voyage to Pagany_. Novel. 20th.

Winchilsea, Countess of (Anne Finch). "The Spleen." Poem. 18th.

Winchilsea, Countess of (Anne Finch). "To Dr. Waldron." Poem. 18th.

Woolf, Virginia. _Mrs. Dalloway_. Novel. 20th.

Wycherley, William. _The Country Wife_. Drama. 18th.

Yglesias, Helen. "Semi-Private." Short Story. 20th.

Zola, Emile. _Dr. Pascal_. Novel. 19th.

Zola, Emile. _Germinal_. Novel. 19th.

Zola, Emile. _Fécondité_ (From _Les Quatres Evangiles_). Novel. 19th.

Zola, Emile. _Une Page D'Amour_. Novel. 19th.

DRUGS

Arden, John. _The Happy Haven_. Drama. 20th.

Bacon, Francis. "Of Regiment of Health." Essay. Renaissance.

Baudelaire, Charles Pierre. _Artificial Paradise: On Hashish and Wine as Means of Expanding Individuality_. Essays. 19th.

Burroughs, William. _The Naked Lunch_. Novel. 20th.

Cocteau, Jean. _Opium: The Diary of a Cure_. Diary. 20th.

Coleridge, Samuel Taylor. "Kubla Khan." Poem. 19th.

Coleridge, Samuel Taylor. "The Pains of Sleep." Poem. 19th.

Collins, Wilkie. _The Moonstone_. Novel. 19th.

Crabbe, George. _The Borough_. Long Poem. 18th.

Crabbe, George. "Fragment, Written at Midnight." Poem. 18th.

De Quincey, Thomas. _Confessions of an English Opium-Eater and Suspiria de Profundis_. Essays. 19th.

De Quincey, Thomas. "The English Mail Coach." Essay. 19th.

Dickens, Charles. _Bleak House_. Novel. 19th.

Disch, Thomas. _Camp Concentration_. Novel. 20th.

Dreiser, Theodore. "Regina C---." Sketch. 20th.

Freneau, Philip. "The Blessings of the Poppy." Poem. 18th.

Garth, Samuel. _The Dispensary_. Poem. 18th.

Gaskell, Elizabeth. _Mary Barton_. Novel. 19th.

Gazzo, Michael. _A Hatful of Rain_. Drama. 20th.

Gelber, Jack. _The Connection_. Drama. 20th.

Ginsberg, Allen. "Howl." Poem. 20th.

Hesse, Hermann. _Steppenwolf_. Novel. 20th.

Holmes, Oliver Wendell. _The Autocrat of the Breakfast-Table_, no. 8. Essay. 19th.

Homer. _The Odyssey_. Epic Poem. Classical.

Huxley, Aldous. _Brave New World_. Novel. 20th.

Huxley, Aldous. _The Doors of Perception_. Long Essay. 20th.

Kipling, Rudyard. "The Gate of the Hundred Sorrows." Sketch. 19th.

Lever, Charles James. _Harry Lorrequer_ (_The Confessions of Harry Lorrequer_). Novel. 19th.

Lewis, Sinclair. _Arrowsmith_. Novel. 20th.

Mather, Cotton. _The Angel of Bethesda: An Essay Upon the Common Maladies of Mankind_. Treatise. 18th.

Meredith, George. _The Ordeal of Richard Feverel_. Novel. 19th.

Oates, Joyce Carol. _Wonderland_. Novel. 20th.

O'Neill, Eugene. _Long Day's Journey Into Night_. Drama. 20th.

Percy, Walker. _The Moviegoer_. Novel. 20th.

Plath, Sylvia. "Thalidomide." Poem. 20th.

Pohl, Frederik and C. M. Kornbluth. _The Space Merchants_ (appeared in a condensed version as _Gravy Planet_). Novel. 20th.

Rechy, John. _City of Night_. Novel; and Selby, Hubert. _Last Exit to Brooklyn_. Novel. 20th.

Shaw, George Bernard. _Doctors' Delusions_. Treatise. 20th.

Stevenson, Robert Louis. _Strange Case of Dr. Jekyll and Mr. Hyde_. Novella. 19th.

Tennyson, Alfred. "The Lotos-Eaters." Poem. 19th.

Thompson, Francis. "The Poppy." Poem. 19th.

Tolstoy, Leo. _The Death of Ivan Ilych_. Novella. 19th.

Wallant, Edward Lewis. _Children at the Gate_. Novel. 20th.

DYING

Aeschylus. Agamemnon. Drama. Classical.

Agee, James. A Death in the Family. Novel. 20th.

Alcott, Louisa May. Hospital Sketches. Sketches. 19th.

Amis, Kingsley. Ending Up. Novel. 20th.

Anderson, Sherwood. "Death in the Woods." Short Story. 20th.

Anonymous. Everyman. Drama. Medieval.

Anonymous. "Robin Hood's Death." Ballad. Medieval.

Anonymous. "When My Eyes are Fogged." Poem. Medieval.

Arnold, Matthew. "A Wish." Poem. 19th.

Bacon, Francis. "Of Death." Essay. Renaissance.

Balzac, Honoré de. Cousin Pons. Novel. 19th.

Balzac, Honoré de. Père Goriot. Novel. 19th.

Barth, John. The End of the Road. Novel. 20th.

Beauvoir, Simone de. A Very Easy Death. Autobiography. 20th.

Beckett, Samuel. Endgame. Drama. 20th.

Bellow, Saul. Mr. Sammler's Planet. Novel. 20th.

Benn, Gottfried. "Man and Woman Go Through the Cancer Ward." Poem. 20th.

Bennett, Arnold. Riceyman Steps. Novel. 19th.

Berg, Stephen. "Why Are We Here?" Poem. 20th.

Betjeman, John. "The Cottage Hospital." Poem. 20th.

Betjeman, John. "A Child Ill." Poem. 20th.

The Bible. New Testament. Classical.

Boswell, James. The Life of Samuel Johnson. Biography. 18th.

Bradbury, Ray. "Kaleidoscope." Short Story. 20th.

Brontë, Anne. The Tenant of Wildfell Hall. Novel. 19th.

Brontë, Charlotte. Jane Eyre. Novel. 19th.

Brontë, Emily Jane. Wuthering Heights. Novel. 19th.

Browne, Thomas. A Letter to a Friend, Upon Occasion of the Death of his Intimate Friend. Essay. Renaissance.

Browning, Robert. "Childe Roland to the Dark Tower Came." Poem. 19th.

Browning, Robert. "Prospice." Poem. 19th.

Camus, Albert. The Plague. Novel. 20th.

Céline, Louis-Ferdinand. Journey to the End of the Night. Novel. 20th.

Chekhov, Anton. "Gusev." Short Story. 19th.

Chekhov, Anton. "Ward 6." Short Story. 19th.

Cooper, James Fenimore. The Prairie. Novel. 19th.

Crane, Stephen. The Red Badge of Courage. Novel. 19th.

De Quincey, Thomas. "The English Mail Coach." Essay. 19th.

Dickens, Charles. Dombey and Son. Novel. 19th.

Dickens, Charles. Great Expectations. Novel. 19th.

Dickens, Charles. Martin Chuzzlewit. Novel. 19th.

Dickens, Charles. The Old Curiosity Shop. Novel. 19th.

Dickinson, Emily. "I heard a Fly buzz--when I died--." Poem. 19th.

Dickinson, Emily. "Still own thee--still thou art." Poem. 19th.

Dostoevsky, Fyodor. The Brothers Karamazov. Novel. 19th.

Dostoevsky, Fyodor. Crime and Punishment. Novel. 19th.

Dryden, John. All for Love. Drama. 18th.

Eliot, George (Mary Anne Evans). Janet's Repentance. Novella. 19th.

Eliot, George (Mary Anne Evans). Middlemarch. Novel. 19th.

Euripides. Alcestis. Drama. Classical.

Euripides. Medea. Drama. Classical.

Faulkner, William. As I Lay Dying. Novel. 20th.

Fielding, Henry. Voyage to Lisbon. Journal. 18th.

Ford, John. 'Tis Pity She's a Whore. Drama. Renaissance.

Franklin, Benjamin. Autobiography. Autobiography. 18th.

Frost, Robert. "'Out, Out.'" Poem. 20th.

Garth, Samuel. The Dispensary. Poem. 18th.

Goldsmith, Oliver. "The Deserted Village." Poem. 18th.

Goldsmith, Oliver. The Vicar of Wakefield. Novel. 18th.

Gorki, Maxim. The Lower Depths. Drama. 20th.

Hardy, Thomas. "Her Death and After." Poem. 19th.

Hawthorne, Nathaniel. "Roger Malvin's Burial." Short Story. 19th.

Hazlitt, William. "On the Fear of Death." Essay. 19th.

Hemingway, Ernest. A Farewell to Arms. Novel. 20th.

Hemingway, Ernest. "The Snows of Kilimanjaro." Short Story. 20th.

Henry, O. (W. S. Porter). "The Last Leaf." Short Story. 19th.

Howells, William Dean. The Shadow of a Dream. Novella. 19th.

Hughes, Langston. "Sylvester's Dying Bed." Poem. 20th.

Hughes, Richard. A High Wind in Jamaica (Also published as The Innocent Voyage). Novel. 20th.

Ibsen, Henrik. A Doll's House. Drama. 19th.

Ionesco, Eugene. Exit the King. Drama. 20th.

James, Henry. The Middle Years. Novella. 19th.

James, Henry. The Portrait of a Lady. Novel. 19th.

James, Henry. The Wings of the Dove. Novel. 19th.

Jarrell, Randall. "The Death of the Ball Turret Gunner." Poem. 20th.

Jonson, Benjamin. Volpone. Drama. Renaissance.

Kafka, Franz. The Metamorphosis. Novella. 20th.

Keats, John. Letters to Charles Brown, Sun., Aug. 20, 1820; Sept. 30, 1820. Letters. 19th.

Keats, John. Letters to Fanny Brawne. Letters. 19th.

Keats, John. "Ode to a Nightingale." Poem. 19th.

Lawrence, D. H. "The Ship of Death." Poem. 20th.

Lawrence, D. H. Sons and Lovers. Novel. 20th.

Le Fanu, Sheridan. The House by the Churchyard. Novel. 19th.

London, Jack. "To Build a Fire." Short Story. 19th.

Lowell, Robert. "Not Cleared of Killing." Poem. 20th.

Mailer, Norman. An American Dream. Novel. 20th.

Marlowe, Christopher. Tamburlaine: Part Two. Drama. Renaissance.

Marlowe, Christopher. The Tragical History of Doctor Faustus. Drama. Renaissance.

Marlowe, Christopher. The Troublesome Reign and Lamentable Death of Edward the Second. Drama. Renaissance.

Maugham, W. Somerset. Liza of Lambeth. Novel. 20th.

Miller, Arthur. Death of a Salesman. Drama. 20th.

More, Thomas. A Dialogue of Comfort Against Tribulation. Dialogues. Renaissance.

Murdoch, Irish. Bruno's Dream. Novel. 20th.

Olsen, Tillie. "Tell Me a Riddle." Short Story. 20th.

Orwell, George (pseudonym of Eric Blair). "How the Poor Die." Essay. 20th.

Plato. Apology and Phaedo. Dialogues. Classical.

Poe, Edgar Allan. "The Facts in the Case of M. Valdemar." Short Story. 19th.

Pope, Alexander. "An Epistle from Mr. Pope, to Dr. Arbuthnot." Poem. 18th.

Porter, Katherine Anne. "The Jilting of Granny Weatherall." Short Story. 20th.

Porter, Katherine Anne. "Pale Horse, Pale Rider." Short Story. 20th.

Randall, Dudley. "George." Poem. 20th.

Ransom, John Crowe. "Here Lies a Lady." Poem. 20th.

Remarque, Erich Maria. Arch of Triumph. Novel. 20th.

Richardson, Samuel. Clarissa. Novel. 18th.

Sarton, May. As We Are Now. Novel. 20th.

Schnitzler, Arthur. "The Man of Honour" (Also published as "The Murderer"). Short Story. 20th.

Schnitzler, Arthur. Professor Bernhardi. Drama. 20th.

Sexton, Anne. "Madonna." Poem. 20th.

Shakespeare, William. Antony and Cleopatra. Drama. Renaissance.

Shakespeare, William. Hamlet. Drama. Renaissance.

Shakespeare, William. 2 Henry IV and Henry V (II iii). Drama. Renaissance.

Shakespeare, William. Julius Caesar. Drama. Renaissance.

Shakespeare, William. King Lear. Drama. Renaissance.

Shaw, George Bernard. The Doctor's Dilemma. Drama. 20th.

Silkin, Jon. "Death of a Son." Poem. 20th.

Solzhenitsyn, Alexander. Cancer Ward. Novel. 20th.

Sophocles. Oedipus at Colonus. Drama. Classical.

Stein, Gertrude. Melanctha. Novella. 20th.

Stowe, Harriet Beecher. Uncle Tom's Cabin. Novel. 19th.

Swift, Jonathan. "Stella's Birth-day: March 13, 1726/7." Poem. 18th.

Tennyson, Alfred. "Crossing the Bar." Poem. 19th.

Tennyson, Alfred. "The Lady of Shalott." Poem. 19th.

Thomas, Dylan. "Do Not Go Gentle into That Good Night." Poem. 20th.

Thompson, Francis. "To Monica Thought Dying." Poem. 19th.

Tolstoy, Leo. The Death of Ivan Ilych. Novella. 19th.

Tolstoy, Leo. The Kreutzer Sonata. Novella. 19th.

Trollope, Anthony. The Last Chronicles of Barset. Novel. 19th.

Turgenev, Ivan. "The District Doctor." Short Story. 19th.

Webster, John. The White Devil. Drama. Renaissance.

Welty, Eudora. The Optimist's Daughter. Novella. 20th.

Wharton, Edith. "A Journey." Short Story. 20th.

White, Patrick. The Eye of the Storm. Novel. 20th.

Whitman, Walt. Drum Taps and Specimen Days. Short Poems and Journal. 19th.

Williams, Tennesse. Cat on a Hot Tin Roof. Drama. 20th.

Williams, William Carlos. "To a Dog Injured in the Street." Poem. 20th.

Zola, Emile. "Comment on Meurt" ("How People Die"). Sketches. 19th.

Zola, Emile. Dr. Pascal. Novel. 19th.

Zola, Emile. Une Page D'Amour. Novel. 19th.

EUTHANASIA

Anderson, Maxwell. Bad Seed. Drama. 20th.

Bacon, Francis. The Advancement of Learning. Treatise. Renaissance.

Beauvoir, Simone de. A Very Easy Death. Autobiography. 20th.

Borges, Jorge Luis. "The Immortals." Short Story. 20th.

Browne, Thomas. Religio Medici. Treatise. Renaissance.

Butler, Samuel. Hudibras. Long Poem. 18th.

Campbell, William Edward March (William March, pseudonym). The Bad Seed; and Maxwell Anderson, Bad Seed. Novel and Drama. 20th.

Dickinson, Emily. "Death is like the insect." Poem. 19th.

Dickinson, Emily. "The Heart asks Pleasure--first--." Poem. 19th.

Hardy, Thomas. Jude the Obscure. Novel. 19th.

Heller, Joseph. Something Happened. Novel. 20th.

Herrick, Robert. The Web of Life. Novel. 20th.

Ibsen, Henrik. Ghosts. Drama. 19th.

Kesey, Ken. One Flew Over the Cuckoo's Nest. Novel. 20th.

Lawrence, D. H. Sons and Lovers. Novel. 20th.

Marlowe, Christopher. Tamburlaine: Part Two. Drama. Renaissance.

Maupassant, Guy de. "The Devil." Short Story. 19th.

Miller, Walter M., Jr. A Canticle for Leibowitz. Novel. 20th.

More, Thomas. Utopia. Treatise. Renaissance.

Nichols, Peter. Joe Egg. Drama. 20th.

Nichols, Peter. The National Health. Drama. 20th.

The Old Law. Drama. Renaissance.

Percy, Walker. Love in the Ruins. Novel. 20th.

Poe, Edgar Allan. "The Facts in the Case of M. Valdemar." Short Story. 19th.

Remarque, Erich Maria. Arch of Triumph. Novel. 20th.

Sarton, May. As We Are Now. Novel. 20th.

Smith, Cordwainer (Dr. M. A. Linebarger). "At the Gate of the Garden of Death" and "The Trial." In Norstrilia (also in The Planet Buyer). Novel. 20th.

Steinbeck, John. Of Mice and Men. Novel. 20th.

Tennyson, Alfred. "In the Children's Hospital." Poem. 19th.

White, E. B. "The Morning of the Day They Did It." Short Story. 20th.

EVIL DOCTORS

Balzac, Honoré de. Cousin Pons. Novel. 19th.

Beaumont, Francis and John Fletcher. Thierry and Theodoret. Drama. Renaissance.

Dickens, Charles. Martin Chuzzlewit. Novel. 19th.

Doyle, Arthur Conan. The Sherlock Holmes Tales. Novellas and Stories. 19th.

Dürrenmatt, Friedrich. The Physicists. Drama. 20th.

Garth, Samuel. The Dispensary. Poem. 18th.

Gilman, Charlotte Perkins Stetson. The Yellow Wallpaper. Short Story. 19th.

Haggard, H. Rider. Doctor Therne. Novel. 20th.

Hawthorne, Nathaniel. "Rappaccini's Daughter." Short Story. 19th.

Hawthorne, Nathaniel. The Scarlet Letter. Novel. 19th.

Hejinian, John. Extreme Remedies. Novel. 20th.

Jonson, Benjamin. Sejanus. Drama. Renaissance.

Le Fanu, Sheridan. The House by the Churchyard. Novel. 19th.

LeSage, Alain René. The Adventures of Gil Blas of Santillane. Tale. 18th.

Middleton, Thomas. A Fair Quarrel. Drama. Renaissance.

Oates, Joyce Carol. Wonderland. Novel. 20th.

Reade, Charles. Hard Cash. Novel. 19th.

Sade, Donatien Alphonse François, Marquis de. Justine. Novel. 19th.

Sheed, Wilfrid. People Will Always Be Kind. Novel. 20th.

Smollett, Tobias. The Adventures of Roderick Random. Novel. 18th.

Southey, Robert. The Doctor. Treatise. 19th.

Stevenson, Robert Louis. Strange Case of Dr. Jekyll and Mr. Hyde. Novella. 19th.

Webster, John. The White Devil. Drama. Renaissance.

Wells, H. G. The Island of Dr. Moreau. Novella. 19th.

THE FAMILY

Adams, Henry. The Education of Henry Adams. Autobiography. 19th.

Aeschylus. Agamemnon. Drama. Classical.

Aeschylus. The Eumenides. Drama. Classical.

Agee, James. A Death in the Family. Novel. 20th.

Albee, Edward. The Death of Bessie Smith. Drama. 20th.

Anderson, Sherwood. "Brother Death." Short Story. 20th.

Anonymous. Aucassin and Nicolete. Tale. Medieval.

Anonymous. "I sing of a maiden." Poem. Medieval.

Arlen, Michael. The Green Hat. Novel. 20th.

Auden, W. H. "Adolescence." Poem. 20th.

Auden, W. H. "The Age of Anxiety." Long Poem. 20th.

Austen, Jane. Emma. Novel. 19th.

Austen, Jane. Mansfield Park. Novel. 19th.

Austen, Jane. Persuasion. Novel. 19th.

Bacon, Francis. New Atlantis. Treatise. Renaissance.

Balzac, Honoré de. Béatrix. Novel. 19th.

Bellow, Saul. Mr. Sammler's Planet. Novel. 20th.

Berryman, John. Recovery. Novel. 20th.

The Bible. Genesis. Classical.

The Bible. Luke. Classical.

The Bible. Matthew. Classical.

The Bible. Ruth. Classical.

The Bible. II Samuel. Classical.

Blake, William. "The Little Boy Lost," "The Little Boy Found," "The Little Girl Lost," "The Little Girl Found," "A Little BOY Lost," and "A Little GIRL Lost." Short Poems. 19th.

Brecht, Bertolt. Mother Courage and Her Children. Drama. 20th.

Brontë, Emily Jane. Wuthering Heights. Novel. 19th.

Brown, Charles Brockden. Wieland, or the Transformation. Novel. 19th.

Browning, Robert. The Ring and the Book. Novel in Verse. 19th.

Butler, Samuel. The Way of All Flesh. Novel. 19th.

Chekhov, Anton. "Peasants." Short Story. 19th.

Chekhov, Anton. Three Sisters. Drama. 19th.

Chekhov, Anton. Uncle Vanya. Drama. 19th.

Dickens, Charles. Bleak House. Novel. 19th.

Dickens, Charles. David Copperfield. Novel. 19th.

Dickens, Charles. Martin Chuzzlewit. Novel. 19th.

Dostoevsky, Fyodor. The Brothers Karamazov. Novel. 19th.

Dostoevsky, Fyodor. Crime and Punishment. Novel. 19th.

Eliot, George (Mary Anne Evans). The Mill on the Floss. Novel. 19th.

Erasmus, Desiderius. The Praise of Folly. Treatise. Renaissance.

Euripides. Electra. Drama. Classical.

Euripides. Hippolytus. Drama. Classical.

Euripides. Medea. Drama. Classical.

Euripides. The Trojan Women. Drama. Classical.

Faulkner, William. As I Lay Dying. Novel. 20th.

Faulkner, William. The Sound and the Fury. Novel. 20th.

Ford, John. 'Tis Pity She's a Whore. Drama. Renaissance.

Gaskell, Elizabeth. Cranford. Novel. 19th.

Gaskell, Elizabeth. Mary Barton. Novel. 19th.

Gazzo, Michael. A Hatful of Rain. Drama. 20th.

Giraudoux, Jean. Electra. Drama. 20th.

Hansberry, Lorraine. A Raisin in the Sun. Drama. 20th.

Hawthorne, Nathaniel. "The Hollow of the Three Hills." Sketch.
    19th.

Hawthorne, Nathaniel. "My Kinsman, Major Molineux." Short Story.
    19th.

Hawthorne, Nathaniel. "Roger Malvin's Burial." Short Story. 19th.

Hawthorne, Nathaniel. The Scarlet Letter. Novel. 19th.

Heinlein, Robert A. Time Enough For Love. Novel. 20th.

Hesiod. Theogony. Long Poem. Classical.

Homer. The Odyssey. Epic Poem. Classical.

Howells, William Dean. A Hazard of New Fortunes. Novel. 19th.

Howells, William Dean. A Modern Instance and The Rise of Silas
    Lapham. Novels. 19th.

Ibsen, Henrik. A Doll's House. Drama. 19th.

Ibsen, Henrik. An Enemy of the People. Drama. 19th.

Ibsen, Henrik. Ghosts. Drama. 19th.

Ibsen, Henrik. Hedda Gabler. Drama. 19th.

Ibsen, Henrik. Little Eyolf. Drama. 19th.

Ibsen, Henrik. The Master Builder. Drama. 19th.

Isherwood, Christopher. A Meeting by the River. Novel. 20th.

James, Henry. The Portrait of a Lady. Novel. 19th.

James, Henry. What Maisie Knew. Novel. 19th.

James, Henry. The Wings of the Dove. Novel. 19th.

Johnson, Samuel. Rasselas. Tale. 18th.

Jonson, Benjamin. Sejanus. Drama. Renaissance.

Joyce, James. Portrait of the Artist as a Young Man. Novel. 20th.

Joyce, James. Ulysses. Novel. 20th.

Kafka, Franz. The Metamorphosis. Novella. 20th.

Keats, John. Letter to Charles Wentworth Dilke, Mon., Sept. 1818;
    Letters to George and Georgiana Keats, Wed., Oct. 14 - Sat.,
    Oct. 31, 1818; Wed., Dec. 16, 1818 - Mon., Jan. 4, 1819.
    Letters. 19th.

Kyd, Thomas. The Spanish Tragedy. Drama. Renaissance.

Lamb, Charles. "Written on Christmas Day, 1797." Poem. 19th.

Lawrence, D. H. Sons and Lovers. Novel. 20th.

Leduc, Violette. The Taxi. Short Story. 20th.

Lessing, Doris. A Proper Marriage. Novel. 20th.

Lessing, Doris. The Summer Before the Dark. Novel. 20th.

Malory, Thomas. The Book of Sir Launcelot and Queen Guinevere and
    The Most Piteous Tale of the Morte Arthur. Tales. Medieval.

Maupassant, Guy de. "A Family." Sketch. 19th.

McCullers, Carson. The Heart Is a Lonely Hunter. Novel. 20th.

Melville, Herman. Pierre, or the Ambiguities. Novel. 19th.

Miller, Arthur. Death of a Salesman. Drama. 20th.

Miller, Arthur. The Price. Drama. 20th.

Moliere (Jean-Baptiste Poquelin). La Malade Imaginaire (The
    Imaginary Invalid). Drama. 18th.

Mortimer, Penelope. The Pumpkin Eater. Novel. 20th.

Murdoch, Irish. Bruno's Dream. Novel. 20th.

Nichols, Peter. Joe Egg. Drama. 20th.

Oates, Joyce Carol. Wonderland. Novel. 20th.

O'Connor, Frank. "The Drunkard," "Judas," and "My Oedipus Complex."
    Short Stories. 20th.

O'Neill, Eugene. Ah Wilderness! Drama. 20th.

O'Neill, Eugene. Long Day's Journey Into Night. Drama. 20th.

O'Neill, Eugene. Mourning Becomes Electra. Drama. 20th.

O'Neill, Eugene. Strange Interlude. Drama. 20th.

Pasternak, Boris. Doctor Zhivago. Novel. 20th.

Percy, Walker. Love in the Ruins. Novel. 20th.

Percy, Walker. The Moviegoer. Novel. 20th.

Pinter, Harold. The Caretaker. Drama. 20th.

Pinter, Harold. The Homecoming. Drama. 20th.

Porter, Katherine Anne. "He." Short Story. 20th.

Reade, Charles. Hard Cash. Novel. 19th.

Richardson, Samuel. Clarissa. Novel. 18th.

Roth, Philip. "Epstein." Short Story. 20th.

Roth, Philip. Portnoy's Complaint. Novel. 20th.

Sackville-West, V. All Passion Spent. Novel. 20th.

Seneca, Lucius Annaeus. Hercules Furens. Drama. Classical.

Shaffer, Peter. Equus. Drama. 20th.

Shakespeare, William. Comedy of Errors. Drama. Renaissance.

Shakespeare, William. Coriolanus. Drama. Renaissance.

Shakespeare, William. Cymbeline. Drama. Renaissance.

Shakespeare, William. Hamlet. Drama. Renaissance.

Shakespeare, William. King Lear. Drama. Renaissance.

Shakespeare, William. Pericles, Prince of Tyre. Drama.
    Renaissance.

Shakespeare, William. Richard III. Drama. Renaissance.

Shakespeare, William. The Tempest. Drama. Renaissance.

Shakespeare, William. Twelfth Night. Drama. Renaissance.

Shakespeare, William. The Winter's Tale. Drama. Renaissance.

Sheed, Wilfrid. People Will Always Be Kind. Novel. 20th.

Shelley, Mary. Frankenstein. Novel. 19th.

Shelley, Percy Bysshe. The Cenci. Poetic Drama. 19th.

Sidney, Philip. Arcadia. Tales and Poems. Renaissance.

Sophocles. Antigone. Drama. Classical.

Sophocles. Electra. Drama. Classical.

Sophocles. Oedipus Rex. Drama. Classical.

Stevenson, Robert Louis. The Master of Ballantrae. Novel. 19th.

Stowe, Harriet Beecher. Uncle Tom's Cabin. Novel. 19th.

Strindberg, August. The Father. Drama. 19th.

Swift, Jonathan. "A Modest Proposal." Essay. 18th.

Tanizaki, Junichiro. Diary of a Mad Old Man. Novel. 20th.

Thackeray, William Makepeace. The History of Henry Esmond. Novel.
    19th.

Thackeray, William Makepeace. Vanity Fair. Novel. 19th.

Tolstoy, Leo. The Death of Ivan Ilych. Novella. 19th.

Tolstoy, Leo. The Kreutzer Sonata. Novella. 19th.

Tourneur, Cyril. The Revenger's Tragedy. Drama. Renaissance.

Turgenev, Ivan. "The District Doctor." Short Story. 19th.

Twain, Mark. Autobiography of Mark Twain. Autobiography. 19th.

Virgil (Publius Vergilius Maro). Aeneid. Epic Poem. Classical.

Vonnegut, Kurt, Jr. Cat's Cradle. Novel. 20th.

Webster, John. The Duchess of Malfi. Drama. Renaissance.

Webster, John. The White Devil. Drama. Renaissance.

Wharton, Edith. "Beatrice Palmato." Outline and Fragment of a
    Novel. 20th.

White, Patrick. The Eye of the Storm. Novel. 20th.

Wilder, Thornton. Our Town. Drama. 20th.

Williams, Tennessee. Cat on a Hot Tin Roof. Drama. 20th.

Williams, Tennessee. The Glass Menagerie. Drama. 20th.

Williams, Tennessee. Streetcar Named Desire. Drama. 20th.

Williams, Tennessee. Suddenly Last Summer. Drama. 20th.

Williams, William Carlos. "A Night in June." Short Story. 20th.

Wordsworth, William. "Michael." Poem. 19th.

Zola, Emile. Dr. Pascal. Novel. 19th.

Zola, Emile. Fécondité (From Les Quatres Evangiles). Novel.
    19th.

Zola, Emile. Germinal. Novel. 19th.

GRIEF

Aeschylus. The Eumenides. Drama. Classical.

Agee, James. A Death in the Family. Novel. 20th.

Alcott, Louisa May. Hospital Sketches. Sketches. 19th.

Anonymous. Beowulf. Epic Poem. Medieval.

Anonymous. The Celestina. Drama. Renaissance.

Anonymous. Pearl. Poem. Medieval.

Anonymous. The Wanderer. Poem. Medieval.

Anonymous. "The Wife of Usher's Well." Ballad. Medieval.

Anonymous. "The Wife's Lament." Poem. Medieval.

Arnold, Matthew. "Thyrsis." Poem. 19th.

Auden, W. H. "The Art of Healing." Poem. 20th.

Auden, W. H. "In Memory of Sigmund Freud." Poem. 20th.

Auden, W. H. "In Memory of W. B. Yeats." Poem. 20th.

Austen, Jane. Persuasion. Novel. 19th.

Babel, Isaac. "The Story of My Dovecot." Short Story. 20th.

Balzac, Honoré de. The Country Doctor. Novel. 19th.

Barth, John. The End of the Road. Novel. 20th.

Beauvoir, Simone de. A Very Easy Death. Autobiography. 20th.

Bellow, Saul. Mr. Sammler's Planet. Novel. 20th.

Berg, Stephen. "Why Are We Here?" Poem. 20th.

Berryman, John. Recovery. Novel. 20th.

Betjeman, John. "A Child Ill." Poem. 20th.

Betjeman, John. "On a Portrait of a Deaf Man." Poem. 20th.

The Bible. Psalms, nos. VI, XXIII, and CXXXVII. Classical.

The Bible. II Samuel. Classical.

Boccaccio, Giovanni. The Decameron: Day 4, Tale 5. Tale.
    Medieval.

Borges, Jorge Luis. "Remorse for Any Death." Poem. 20th.

Borges, Jorge Luis. "To Francisco Lopez Merino." Poem. 20th.

Boswell, James. The Life of Samuel Johnson. Biography. 18th.

Bradstreet, Anne. "Before the Birth of One of her Children."
    Poem. 18th.

Bradstreet, Anne. "In Memory of My Dear Grandchild Elizabeth
    Bradstreet, Who Deceased August, 1665, Being a Year and Half
    Old." Poem. 18th.

Brecht, Bertolt. Mother Courage and Her Children. Drama. 20th.

Bridges, Robert. "On a Dead Child." Poem. 20th.

Brontë, Charlotte. Jane Eyre. Novel. 19th.

Brontë, Emily Jane. "The linnet in the rocky dells." Poem. 19th.

Brontë, Emily Jane. Wuthering Heights. Novel. 19th.

Browning, Elizabeth Barrett. "Grief." Sonnet. 19th.

Browning, Elizabeth Barrett. Sonnets from the Portuguese, no. 5.
    Sonnet. 19th.

Burton, Robert. The Anatomy of Melancholy. Treatise. Renaissance.

Byron, George Gordon, Lord. Manfred. Dramatic Poem. 19th.

Byron, George Gordon, Lord. "She Walks in Beauty." Poem. 19th.

Campion, Thomas. "The Sypres curten of the night is spread."
    Song. Renaissance.

Camus, Albert. Caligula. Drama. 20th.

Camus, Albert. The Plague. Novel. 20th.

Camus, Albert. The Stranger. Novel. 20th.

Chaucer, Geoffrey. The Book of the Duchess. Poem. Medieval.

Chekhov, Anton. "Misery." Short Story. 19th.

Coleridge, Samuel Taylor. "Dejection: An Ode." Poem. 19th.

Coleridge, Samuel Taylor. "The Rime of the Ancient Mariner." Poem. 19th.

Cooper, James Fenimore. The Last of the Mohicans. Novel. 19th.

Daniel, Samuel. "Care-charmer sleep." Sonnet. Renaissance.

Dante Alighieri. La Vita Nuova (The New Life). Poems in a Prose Framework. Renaissance.

Dekker, Thomas. The Honest Whore, Pt. I. Drama. Renaissance.

De Quincey, Thomas. Confessions of an English Opium-Eater and Suspiria de Profundis. Essays. 19th.

Dickens, Charles. David Copperfield. Novel. 19th.

Dickens, Charles. Dombey and Son. Novel. 19th.

Dickinson, Emily. "After great pain, a formal feeling comes--." Poem. 19th.

Donne, John. "A Nocturnall Upon S. Lucies Day: Being the Shortest Day." Poem. Renaissance.

Donne, John. "Sapho to Philaenis." Poem. Renaissance.

Donne, John. "A Valediction Forbidding Mourning." Poem. Renaissance.

Dostoevsky, Fyodor. The Brothers Karamazov. Novel. 19th.

Dostoevsky, Fyodor. Crime and Punishment. Novel. 19th.

Dowland, John. "Flow my tears" and "I saw my Lady weep." Songs. Renaissance.

Eliot, George (Mary Anne Evans). Adam Bede. Novel. 19th.

Eliot, George (Mary Anne Evans). Mr. Gilfil's Love-Story. Novella. 19th.

Emerson, Ralph Waldo. "Experience" and "Threnody." Essay and Poem. 19th.

Euripides. Alcestis. Drama. Classical.

Euripides. The Trojan Women. Drama. Classical.

Faulkner, William. As I Lay Dying. Novel. 20th.

Faulkner, William. The Sound and the Fury. Novel. 20th.

Flaubert, Gustave. Madame Bovary. Novel. 19th.

Ford, John. The Lover's Melancholy. Drama. Renaissance.

Gaskell, Elizabeth. Mary Barton. Novel. 19th.

Giraudoux, Jean. Electra. Drama. 20th.

Gray, Thomas. "Elegy Written in a Country Church Yard." Poem. 18th.

Hardy, Thomas. "Afterwards." Poem. 19th.

Hardy, Thomas. Far From the Madding Crowd. Novel. 19th.

Hardy, Thomas. "Her Death and After." Poem. 19th.

Hardy, Thomas. "Last Words to a Dumb Friend" and "'Ah, Are You Digging on My Grave?'" Poems. 19th.

Hawthorne, Nathaniel. "Roger Malvin's Burial." Short Story. 19th.

Hawthorne, Nathaniel. "The Wives of the Dead." Short Story. 19th.

Hazlitt, William. "On the Fear of Death." Essay. 19th.

Heloise. The Letters of Abelard and Heloise, no. 3. Letter. Medieval.

Hemingway, Ernest. "Indian Camp." Short Story. 20th.

Herbert, George. "The Collar." Poem. Renaissance.

Herbert, George. "Confession." Poem. Renaissance.

Herbert, George. "The Flower." Poem. Renaissance.

Homer. Iliad. Epic Poem. Classical.

Hopkins, Gerard Manly. "Spring and Fall: to a young child." Sonnet. 19th.

Howells, William Dean. A Hazard of New Fortunes. Novel. 19th.

Hughes, Richard. A High Wind in Jamaica (Also published as The Innocent Voyage). Novel. 20th.

Ibsen, Henrik. Little Eyolf. Drama. 19th.

Jewett, Sarah Orne. "Miss Tempy's Watchers." Short Story. 19th.

Johnson, Samuel. "The Death of Friends." Essay. 18th.

Johnson, Samuel. A Dictionary of the English Language. Dictionary. 18th.

Johnson, Samuel. Rasselas. Tale. 18th.

Jonson, Benjamin. Epigram XLV, "On My First Sonne." Poem. Renaissance.

Jonson, Benjamin. "An Epitaph." Poem. Renaissance.

Jonson, Benjamin. "Slow, slow, fresh fount, keepe time with my salt tears." Song. Renaissance.

Jonson, Benjamin. "To the Memory of My Beloved, the Author Mr. William Shakespeare: and What He hath Left Us." Poem. Renaissance.

Joyce, James. "Ecce Puer." Poem. 20th.

Joyce, James. Ulysses. Novel. 20th.

Keats, John. Letter to Charles Wentworth Dilke, Mon., Sept. 1818; Letters to George and Georgiana Keats, Wed., Oct. 14 - Sat., Oct. 31, 1818; Wed., Dec. 16, 1818 - Mon., Jan. 4, 1819. Letters. 19th.

Kyd, Thomas. The Spanish Tragedy. Drama. Renaissance.

Lawrence, D. H. Sons and Lovers. Novel. 20th.

Levertov, Denis. "Grief" and "Divorcing." Poems. 20th.

Lucian of Samosata. "On Funerals." Essay. Classical.

Marlowe, Christopher. Tamburlaine: Part Two. Drama. Renaissance.

Marvell, Andrew. "The Nymph complaining for the Death of her Fawn." Poem. Renaissance.

Masters, Edgar Lee. The Spoon River Anthology. Poem Sequence. 20th.

McCullers, Carson. The Ballad of the Sad Café. Novella. 20th.

McCullers, Carson. The Heart Is a Lonely Hunter. Novel. 20th.

McCullers, Carson. Reflections in a Golden Eye. Novella. 20th.

Miller, Arthur. After the Fall. Drama. 20th.

Miller, Vassar. "Fantasia." Poem. 20th.

Milton, John. "Epitaph on the Marchioness of Winchester"; and Ben Jonson, "An Elegie on the Lady Pawlet Marchion: of Winton." Poems. Renaissance.

Milton, John. "Lycidas." Poem. Renaissance.

Milton, John. "Me thought I Saw." Sonnet. Renaissance.

Milton, John. "On the Death of a Fair Infant Dying of a Cough." Poem. Renaissance.

Milton, John. Paradise Lost. Epic Poem. Renaissance.

Milton, John. Samson Agonistes. Poem. Renaissance.

Molière (Jean-Baptiste Poquelin). "A Monsieur de la Mothe Le Vayer." Sonnet, in French. 18th.

More, Thomas. Utopia. Treatise. Renaissance.

Murdoch, Irish. Bruno's Dream. Novel. 20th.

O'Brien, Edna. August Is a Wicked Month. Novel. 20th.

O'Connor, Flannery. "The Lame Shall Enter First." Short Story. 20th.

Olsen, Tillie. "Tell Me a Riddle." Short Story. 20th.

O'Neill, Eugene. Strange Interlude. Drama. 20th.

Pasternak, Boris. Doctor Zhivago. Novel. 20th.

Percy, Walker. Love in the Ruins. Novel. 20th.

Percy, Walker. The Moviegoer. Novel. 20th.

Petrarch (Francesco Petrarca). Canzoniere, no. CCLXXII (sonnet 231). Sonnet. Medieval.

Petrarch (Francesco Petrarca). Canzoniere, no. CCCXLIX (sonnet no. 303). Sonnet. Medieval.

Plath, Sylvia. "Daddy." Poem. 20th.

Plath, Sylvia. "Three Women." Dramatic Poem. 20th.

Poe, Edgar Allan. "The Raven." Poem. 19th.

Poe, Edgar Allan. "Ulalume--A Ballad." Poem. 19th.

Porter, Katherine Anne. "The Jilting of Granny Weatherall." Short Story. 20th.

Porter, Katherine Anne. "Pale Horse, Pale Rider." Short Story. 20th.

Ransom, John Crowe. "Bells for John Whiteside's Daughter." Poem. 20th.

Ransom, John Crowe. "Here Lies a Lady." Poem. 20th.

Remarque, Erich Maria. Arch of Triumph. Novel. 20th.

Roethke, Theodore. "Elegy for Jane: My Student, Thrown by a Horse." Poem. 20th.

Ronsard, Pierre de. "These sonnets of love" ("Je chantois ces sonnets, amoureux d'une Helene"). Sonnet. Renaissance.

Rossetti, Christina. "Remember" and "Song." Poems. 19th.

Roth, Philip. "Epstein." Short Story. 20th.

Sackville-West, V. All Passion Spent. Novel. 20th.

Salinger, J. D. The Catcher in the Rye. Novel. 20th.

Sarton, May. Mrs. Stevens Hears the Mermaids Singing. Novel. 20th.

Schnitzler, Arthur. A Confirmed Bachelor (Also published as Dr. Graesler). Novel. 20th.

Schnitzler, Arthur. Mother and Son (Also published as Beatrice). Novella. 20th.

Seneca, Lucius Annaeus. Hercules Furens. Drama. Classical.

Sexton, Anne. "All My Pretty Ones." Poem. 20th.

Sexton, Anne. "Madonna." Poem. 20th.

Sexton, Anne. "Sylvia's Death." Poem. 20th.

Shakespeare, William. Antony and Cleopatra. Drama. Renaissance.

Shakespeare, William. Cymbeline. Drama. Renaissance.

Shakespeare, William. Hamlet. Drama. Renaissance.

Shakespeare, William. King Lear. Drama. Renaissance.

Shakespeare, William. Macbeth. Drama. Renaissance.

Shakespeare, William. Othello. Drama. Renaissance.

Shakespeare, William. Richard III. Drama. Renaissance.

Shakespeare, William. Romeo and Juliet. Drama. Renaissance.

Shakespeare, William. The Tempest. Drama. Renaissance.

Shakespeare, William. Twelfth Night. Drama. Renaissance.

Shakespeare, William. Venus and Adonis. Poem. Renaissance.

Shakespeare, William. The Winter's Tale. Drama. Renaissance.

Shelley, Mary. Frankenstein. Novel. 19th.

Shelley, Mary. The Last Man. Novel. 19th.

Shelley, Percy Bysshe. Adonais. Poem. 19th.

Shelley, Percy Bysshe. "To Mary" ("My dearest Mary, wherefore hast thou gone"). Poem. 19th.

Shelley, Percy Bysshe. "To William Shelley." Poem. 19th.

Sholom Aleichem (Solomon Rabinowitch). "The Lottery Ticket." Short Story. 19th.

Sholom Aleichem (Solomon Rabinowitch). "You Mustn't Weep--It's Yom-Tev." Short Story. 19th.

Sidney, Philip. Arcadia. Tales and Poems. Renaissance.

Sidney, Philip. "Grief, find the words, for thou hast made my brain." Sonnet. Renaissance.

Silkin, Jon. "Death of a Son." Poem. 20th.

Skelton, John. Philip Sparrow. Poem. Renaissance.

Smollett, Tobias. The Expedition of Humphry Clinker. Novel. 18th.

Smollett, Tobias. Sir Launcelot Greaves. Novel. 18th.

Sophocles. Antigone. Drama. Classical.

Sophocles. Electra. Drama. Classical.

Sophocles. Oedipus at Colonus. Drama. Classical.

Sophocles. Oedipus Rex. Drama. Classical.

Sterne, Laurence. The Life and Opinions of Tristram Shandy, Gent. Novel. 18th.

Sterne, Laurence. A Sentimental Journey. Novel. 18th.

Stowe, Harriet Beecher. Uncle Tom's Cabin. Novel. 19th.

Swados, Harvey. Celebration. Novel. 20th.

Swift, Jonathan. "Verses on the Death of Dr. Swift." Poem. 18th.

Synge, John Millington. Riders to the Sea. Drama. 20th.

Taylor, Edward. "Meditation. Col. 1.18. That in all things he might have the Preheminence." Poem. 18th.

Taylor, Edward. "Upon Wedlock, and Death of Children." Poem. 18th.

Tennyson, Alfred. "'Frater Ave Atque Vale'" and "Prefatory Poem to My Brother's Sonnets." Poems. 19th.

Tennyson, Alfred. "The Grandmother's Apology." Poem. 19th.

Tennyson, Alfred. In Memoriam: A.H.H. Poems. 19th.

Tennyson, Alfred. "Tiresias." Poem. 19th.

Thomas, Dylan. "Fern Hill." Poem. 20th.

Thomas, Dylan. "A Refusal to Mourn the Death, by Fire, of a Child in London." Poem. 20th.

Thompson, Francis. "To Monica Thought Dying." Poem. 19th.

Tolstoy, Leo. The Death of Ivan Ilych. Novella. 19th.

Tolstoy, Leo. The Kreutzer Sonata. Novella. 19th.

Tourneur, Cyril. The Atheist's Tragedy. Drama. Renaissance.

Twain, Mark. Autobiography of Mark Twain. Autobiography. 19th.

Vaughan, Henry. "They are All Gone into the World of Light!" Poem. Renaissance.

Virgil (Publius Vergilius Maro). Aeneid. Epic Poem. Classical.

Waugh, Evelyn. The Loved One. Novel. 20th.

Webster, John. The White Devil. Drama. Renaissance.

Welty, Eudora. The Optimist's Daughter. Novella. 20th.

Whitman, Walt. "Out of the Cradle Endlessly Rocking." Poem. 19th.

Whitman, Walt. "When Lilacs Last in the Dooryard Bloomed." Poem. 19th.

Williams, William Carlos. "The Injury." Poem. 20th.

Williams, William Carlos. "Jean Beicke." Short Story. 20th.

Williams, William Carlos. "Tract." Poem. 20th.

Woolf, Virginia. The Waves. Novel. 20th.

Wordsworth, William. "Maternal Grief." Poem. 19th.

Wordsworth, William. "A slumber did my spirit seal." Poem. 19th.

Yeats, William Butler. "Her Vision in the Wood." Poem. 20th.

Young, Edward. Night Thoughts. Long Poem. 18th.

Zola, Emile. "Comment On Meurt" ("How People Die"). Sketches. 19th.

Zola, Emile. Une Page D'Amour. Novel. 19th.

HANDICAPS

Anouilh, Jean. Ardèle. Drama. 20th.

Babel, Isaac. "The Story of My Dovecot." Short Story. 20th.

Bacon, Francis. "Of Deformity." Essay. Renaissance.

Betjeman, John. "On a Portrait of a Deaf Man." Poem. 20th.

The Bible. Apocrypha. Tobit. Classical.

The Bible. Judges. Classical.

Boccaccio, Giovanni. The Decameron: Day 3, Tales 1 & 10. Tales. Medieval.

Bowen, Elizabeth. Eva Trout. Novel. 20th.

Brecht, Bertolt. Mother Courage and Her Children. Drama. 20th.

Brunner, John. The Whole Man. Novel. 20th.

Burton, Robert. The Anatomy of Melancholy. Treatise. Renaissance.

Chekhov, Anton. "Misery." Short Story. 19th.

Collins, Wilkie. Hide and Seek and Poor Miss Finch. Novels. 19th.

Crane, Stephen. "The Monster." Short Story. 19th.

Crane, Stephen. "The trees in the garden rained flowers." Poem. 19th.

Dickens, Charles. David Copperfield. Novel. 19th.

Dickens, Charles. The Old Curiosity Shop. Novel. 19th.

Dickey, James. "The Eye-Beaters." Poem. 20th.

Dürrenmatt, Friedrich. The Physicists. Drama. 20th.

Eliot, George (Mary Anne Evans). The Mill on the Floss. Novel. 19th.

Flaubert, Gustave. Madame Bovary. Novel. 19th.

Garcia Lorca, Federico. The House of Bernarda Alba. Drama. 20th.

Gaskell, Elizabeth. Mary Barton. Novel. 19th.

Giraudoux, Jean. The Madwoman of Chaillot. Drama. 20th.

Hardy, Thomas. "Her Death and After." Poem. 19th.

Hugo, Victor. The Hunchback of Notre Dame. Novel. 19th.

Ibsen, Henrik. Little Eyolf. Drama. 19th.

Jonson, Benjamin. Volpone. Drama. Renaissance.

Kesey, Ken. One Flew Over the Cuckoo's Nest. Novel. 20th.

Kipling, Rudyard. "Baa Baa Black Sheep." Short Story. 19th.

Lawrence, D. H. "The Blind Man." Short Story. 20th.

Lawrence, D. H. Lady Chatterley's Lover. Novel. 20th.

Maugham, W. Somerset. Of Human Bondage. Novel. 20th.

Maupassant, Guy de. "The Blind Man." Sketch. 19th.

McCullers, Carson. The Ballad of the Sad Café. Novella. 20th.

McCullers, Carson. The Heart Is a Lonely Hunter. Novel. 20th.

Melville, Herman. Billy Budd, Sailor. Novella and Poem. 19th.

Miller, Vassar. "On the Examination Table." Poem. 20th.

Miller, Vassar. "Spastics: (First poem from Handi-Lip)." Poem. 20th.

Milton, John. Samson Agonistes. Poem. Renaissance.

Milton, John. "To Mr. Cyriak Skinner Upon His Blindness." Sonnet. Renaissance.

Milton, John. "When I Consider How My Light Is Spent." Sonnet. Renaissance.

O'Connor, Flannery. "Good Country People." Short Story. 20th.

O'Connor, Flannery. "The Lame Shall Enter First." Short Story. 20th.

Poe, Edgar Allan. "The Man That Was Used Up." Sketch. 19th.

Rilke, Rainer Maria. "The Blind Man's Song," "The Drinker's Song," "The Idiot's Song," "The Suicide's Song," "The Dwarf's Song," and "The Leper's Song." Short Poems. 20th.

Russell, Robert. To Catch an Angel. Autobiography. 20th.

Shakespeare, William. King Lear. Drama. Renaissance.

Shakespeare, William. The Merchant of Venice. Drama. Renaissance.

Shakespeare, William. Richard III. Drama. Renaissance.

Sheed, Wilfrid. People Will Always Be Kind. Novel. 20th.

Sophocles. Oedipus at Colonus. Drama. Classical.

Sophocles. Oedipus Rex. Drama. Classical.

Tennyson, Alfred. "Tiresias." Poem. 19th.

Thomas, Dylan. "The Hunchback in the Park." Poem. 20th.

Webb, Mary. Precious Bane. Novel. 20th.

Wells, H. G. "The Country of the Blind." Short Story. 19th.

Williams, Tennessee. The Glass Menagerie. Drama. 20th.

Wright, David. "Monologue of a Deaf Man." Poem. 20th.

Yglesias, Helen. "Semi-Private." Short Story. 20th.

HOMOSEXUALITY

Amis, Kingsley. Ending Up. Novel. 20th.

Anonymous. Teleny. Novel. 19th.

Baldwin, James. Giovanni's Room. Novel. 20th.

Baudelaire, Charles Pierre. "Jewels" ("Les Bijoux"). Poem. 19th.

The Bible. Genesis. Classical.

Buonarroti, Michel Angelo. "Just as a silkworm with much selfless pain." Poem. Renaissance.

Burroughs, William. The Naked Lunch. Novel. 20th.

Catullus. Carmina, no. 56. Poem. Classical.

Cleland, John. Memoirs of Fanny Hill. Novel. 18th.

Coleridge, Samuel Taylor. "Christabel." Poem. 19th.

Crowley, Mart. The Boys in the Band. Drama. 20th.

Dante Alighieri. The Divine Comedy. Long Poem. Medieval.

Delaney, Shelagh. A Taste of Honey. Drama. 20th.

Donne, John. "Sapho to Philaenis." Poem. Renaissance.

Douglas, Alfred. "Two Loves." Poem. 19th.

Durrell, Lawrence. Monsieur. Novel. 20th.

Dyer, Charles. Staircase. Drama. 20th.

Forster, E. M. Maurice. Novel. 20th.

Genet, Jean. Our Lady of the Flowers. Novel. 20th.

Gide, Andre. The Immoralist. Novel. 20th.

Ginsberg, Allen. "Howl." Poem. 20th.

Hall, Hadclyffe. The Well of Loneliness. Novel. 20th.

Hellman, Lillian. The Children's Hour. Drama. 20th.

Hesse, Hermann. Steppenwolf. Novel. 20th.

Isherwood, Christopher. A Meeting by the River. Novel. 20th.

James, Henry. The Bostonians. Novel. 19th.

Juvenal (Decimus Iunius Iuvenalis). Satires, no. II. Poem. Classical.

Kesey, Ken. One Flew Over the Cuckoo's Nest. Novel. 20th.

Lawrence, D. H. The Fox. Novella. 20th.

Leduc, Violette. Thérèse and Isabelle and La Bâtarde. Novella and Autobiography. 20th.

Lehmann, Rosamund. Dusty Answer. Novel. 20th.

Mann, Thomas. Death in Venice. Novella. 20th.

Marcus, Frank. The Killing of Sister George. Drama. 20th.

Marlowe, Christopher. The Troublesome Reign and Lamentable Death of Edward the Second. Drama. Renaissance.

Marlowe, Christopher and George Chapman. Hero and Leander. Poem. Renaissance.

McCullers, Carson. The Ballad of the Sad Café. Novella. 20th.

McCullers, Carson. Reflections in a Golden Eye. Novella. 20th.

Melville, Herman. Billy Budd, Sailor. Novella and Poem. 19th.

Murdoch, Irish. Bruno's Dream. Novel. 20th.

Petronius Arbiter. Satyricon. Satiric Sketches. Classical.

Plato. Symposium. Dialogue. Classical.

Proust, Marcel. Remembrance of Things Past. Novel. 20th.

Réage, Pauline. The Story of O. Novel. 20th.

Rechy, John. City of Night; and Selby, Hubert. Last Exit to Brooklyn. Novels. 20th.

Rochester, Earl of (John Wilmot). "Song" ("Love a woman? You're an ass!"). Poem. 18th.

Sade, Donatien Alphonse François, Marquis de. Justine. Novel. 19th.

Sade, Donatien Alphonse François, Marquis de. Philosophy in the Bedroom. Tale. 19th.

Salinger, J. D. The Catcher in the Rye. Novel. 20th.

Sappho. To Brachea. Short Poem. Classical.

Sarton, May. Mrs. Stevens Hears the Mermaids Singing. Novel. 20th.

Selby, Hubert. Last Exit to Brooklyn. Novel. 20th.

Shakespeare, William. Troilus and Cressida. Drama. Renaissance.

Shakespeare, William. "Two loves I have of comfort and despair." Sonnet. Renaissance.

Shakespeare, William. Venus and Adonis. Poem. Renaissance.

Shakespeare, William. "A woman's face with Nature's own hand painted." Sonnet. Renaissance.

Smollett, Tobias. The Adventures of Roderick Random. Novel. 19th.

Spenser, Edmund. The Faerie Queene. Poems. Renaissance.

Swinburne, Algernon Charles. "Hermaphroditus." Poem. 19th.

White, Patrick. The Eye of the Storm. Novel. 20th.

Whitman, Walt. Calamus. Short Poems. 19th.

Wilde, Oscar. "The Ballad of Reading Gaol." Long Poem. 19th.

Wilde, Oscar. De Profundis. Essay-length Letter. 19th.

Williams, Tennessee. Cat on a Hot Tin Roof. Drama. 20th.

Williams, Tennessee. Streetcar Named Desire. Drama. 20th.

Williams, Tennessee. Suddenly Last Summer. Drama. 20th.

Wittig, Monique. The Lesbian Body. Novel. 20th.

Woolf, Virginia. Mrs. Dalloway. Novel. 20th.

Woolf, Virginia. The Waves. Novel. 20th.

MADNESS

Aeschylus. Agamemnon. Drama. Classical.

Albee, Edward. The Death of Bessie Smith. Drama. 20th.

Anderson, Maxwell. Bad Seed. Drama. 20th.

Anouilh, Jean. Ardèle. Drama. 20th.

Ariosto, Ludovico. Orlando Furioso. Poem. Renaissance.

Armstrong, John. "The Art of Preserving Health." Poem. 18th.

Arnold, Matthew. Empedocles on Etna. Dramatic Poem. 19th.

Barth, John. The End of the Road. Novel. 20th.

Baudelaire, Charles Pierre. "On Delacroix's Picture of Tasso in Prison" ("Sur Le Tasse en Prison d'Eugène Delacroix"). Sonnet. 19th.

Beaumont, Francis and John Fletcher. Thierry and Theodoret. Drama. Renaissance.

Beddoes, Thomas Lovell. Death's Jest-Book. Poetic Drama. 19th.

Bellow, Saul. Mr. Sammler's Planet. Novel. 20th.

Bennett, Arnold. Riceyman Steps. Novel. 19th.

The Bible. Mark. Classical.

The Bible. I Samuel. Classical.

Borges, Jorge Luis. "Borges and Myself." Tale. 20th.

Boswell, James. The Life of Samuel Johnson. Biography. 18th.

Bowen, Elizabeth. Eva Trout. Novel. 20th.

Bridges, Robert. "Melancholia." Sonnet. 20th.

Brome, Richard. The Antipodes. Drama. Renaissance.

Brontë, Charlotte. Jane Eyre. Novel. 19th.

Brown, Charles Brockden. Arthur Mervyn. Novel. 19th.

Brown, Charles Brockden. Wieland, or the Transformation. Novel. 19th.

Brown, Geoff. I Want What I Want. Novel. 20th.

Browning, Elizabeth Barrett. "The Runaway Slave at Pilgrim's Point." Poem. 19th.

Brunner, John. The Whole Man. Novel. 20th.

Büchner, Georg. Woyzeck. Drama. 19th.

Burgess, Anthony. The Doctor Is Sick. Novel. 20th.

Burton, Robert. The Anatomy of Melancholy. Treatise. Renaissance.

Byron, George Gordon, Lord. Childe Harold's Pilgrimage. Long Poem. 19th.

Byron, George Gordon, Lord. Manfred. Dramatic Poem. 19th.

Campbell, William Edward March (William March, pseudonym). The Bad Seed; and Anderson, Maxwell, Bad Seed. Novel and Drama. 20th.

Camus, Albert. Caligula. Drama. 20th.

Carlyle, Thomas. "The Everlasting No," "The Center of Indifference," and "The Everlasting Yea." Essays. 19th.

Catullus, C. Valerius. Carmina, no. 63. Poem. Classical.

Céline, Louis-Ferdinand. Journey to the End of the Night. Novel. 20th.

Cervantes Saavedra, Miguel de. Don Quixote. Tale. Renaissance.

Chekhov, Anton. "An Attack of Nerves." Short Story. 19th.

Chekhov, Anton. The Island: A Journey to Sakhalin. Nonfiction. 19th.

Chekhov, Anton. Uncle Vanya. Drama. 19th.

Chekhov, Anton. "Ward 6." Short Story. 19th.

Choromanski, Michal. Jealousy and Medicine. Novel. 20th.

Clare, John. "Don Juan" and "Child Harold." Poems. 19th.

Clough, Arthur Hugh. "Bethesda: a Sequel." Poem. 19th.

Coleridge, Samuel Taylor. "The Rime of the Ancient Mariner." Poem. 19th.

Conrad, Joseph. The Shadow Line: a Confession. Novella. 20th.

Cowper, William. Memoir. Treatise. 18th.

Crabbe, George. The Borough. Long Poem. 18th.

Crabbe, George. "Sir Eustace Grey." Poem. 18th.

Dekker, Thomas. The Honest Whore, Pt. I. Drama. Renaissance.

Dickens, Charles. Bleak House. Novel. 19th.

Dickens, Charles. Great Expectations. Novel. 19th.

Dickens, Charles. The Old Curiosity Shop. Novel. 19th.

Dickens, Charles. The Pickwick Papers. Novel. 19th.

Dickens, Charles. "Wapping Workhouse." Sketch. 19th.

Dickey, James. "The Eye-Beaters." Poem. 20th.

Dickinson, Emily. "I felt a Cleaving in my Mind." Poem. 19th.

Dickinson, Emily. "Much Madness is divinest Sense--." Poem. 19th.

Donne, John. "A Nocturnall Upon S. Lucies Day: Being the Shortest Day." Poem. Renaissance.

Dostoevsky, Fyodor. The Brothers Karamazov. Novel. 19th.

Dostoevsky, Fyodor. Crime and Punishment. Novel. 19th.

Dostoevsky, Fyodor. The Idiot. Novel. 19th.

Dostoevsky, Fyodor. Notes From the Underground. Novella. 19th.

Durrell, Lawrence. Monsieur. Novel. 20th.

Dürrenmatt, Friedrich. The Physicists. Drama. 20th

Eliot, T. S. The Cocktail Party. Poetic Drama. 20th.

Eliot, T. S. "The Love Song of J. Alfred Prufrock." Poem. 20th.

Erasmus, Desiderius. The Praise of Folly. Treatise. Renaissance.

Euripides. The Bacchants. Drama. Classical.

Faulkner, William. As I Lay Dying. Novel. 20th.

Faulkner, William. The Sound and the Fury. Novel. 20th.

Fitzgerald, F. Scott. "The Crack-Up," "Handle with Care," and "Pasting it Together." Essays. 20th.

Fitzgerald, F. Scott. Tender Is the Night. Novel. 20th.

Ford, John. The Broken Heart. Drama. Renaissance.

Ford, John. The Lover's Melancholy. Drama. Renaissance.

Garcia Lorca, Federico. The House of Bernard Alba. Drama. 20th.

Garcia Lorca, Federico. Yerma. Drama. 20th.

Gide, Andre. The Immoralist. Novel. 20th.

Gilman, Charlotte Perkins Stetson. The Yellow Wallpaper. Short Story. 19th.

Ginsberg, Allen. "Howl." Poem. 20th.

Giraudoux, Jean. Electra. Drama. 20th.

Giraudoux, Jean. The Madwoman of Chaillot. Drama. 20th.

Goethe, Johann. The Sorrows of Young Werther. Novel. 19th.

Gogol, Nikolai. "The Diary of a Madman." Short Story. 19th.

Golding, William. Lord of the Flies. Novel. 20th.

Graves, Robert. "The Cool Web." Poem. 20th.

Green, Matthew. "The Spleen." Poem. 18th.

Hamilton, Patrick. Angel Street (Gas Light). Drama. 19th.

Hardy, Thomas. Far From the Madding Crowd. Novel. 19th.

Hardy, Thomas. Jude the Obscure. Novel. 19th.

Hawthorne, Nathaniel. "The Hollow of the Three Hills." Sketch. 19th.

Hawthorne, Nathaniel. "Lady Eleanore's Mantle." Short Story. 19th.

Hellman, Lillian. The Children's Hour. Drama. 20th.

Hesse, Hermann. Steppenwolf. Novel. 20th.

Holmes, Oliver Wendell. The Autocrat of the Breakfast-Table, no. 8. Essay. 19th.

Holmes, Oliver Wendell. Elsie Venner. Novel. 19th.

Holmes, Oliver Wendell. A Mortal Antipathy. Novel. 19th.

Horace (Quintus Horatius Flaccus). Satires, Book II, no. III. Poem. Classical.

Howells, William Dean. The Shadow of a Dream. Novella. 19th.

Hughes, Richard. A High Wind in Jamaica (Also published as The Innocent Voyage). Novel.

Hugo, Victor. The Hunchback of Notre Dame. Novel. 19th.

Huxley, Aldous. The Doors of Perception. Long Essay. 20th.

Ibsen, Henrik. Ghosts. Drama. 19th.

Ionesco, Eugene. The Hermit. Novel. 20th.

James, Henry. The Turn of the Screw. Novella. 19th.

Johnson, Samuel. Rasselas. Tale. 18th.

Jones, LeRoi (Imamu Amiri Baraka). Dutchman. Drama. 20th.

Jonson, Benjamin. Bartholomew Fair. Drama. Renaissance.

Kesey, Ken. One Flew Over the Cuckoo's Nest. Novel. 20th.

Kyd, Thomas. The Spanish Tragedy. Drama. Renaissance.

Lamb, Charles. "Written on Christmas Day, 1797." Poem. 19th.

Lawrence, D. H. Psychoanalysis and the Unconscious and Fantasia of the Unconscious. Long Essays. 20th.

Leman, Grahame. "Conversational Mode." Short Story. 20th.

Lessing, Doris. The Summer Before the Dark. Novel. 20th.

Lowell, Robert. "Ezra Pound" and "Robert Frost." Poems. 20th.

Lowell, Robert. "Skunk Hour." Poem. 20th.

Lucian of Samosata. "The Disowned." Essay. Classical.

Mackenzie, Henry. The Man of Feeling. Novel. 18th.

Mailer, Norman. An American Dream. Novel. 20th.

Malzberg, Barry. "Out from Ganymede." Short Story. 20th.

McCullers, Carson. Reflections in a Golden Eye. Novella. 20th.

Melville, Herman. "Bartleby." Short Story. 19th.

Melville, Herman. Moby Dick. Novel. 19th.

Melville, Herman. Pierre, or the Ambiguities. Novel. 19th.

Meredith, George. Sonnet I. From Modern Love. Sonnet. 19th.

Middleton, Thomas. The Changeling. Drama. Renaissance.

Miller, Arthur. The Crucible. Drama. 20th.

Miller, Arthur. Death of a Salesman. Drama. 20th

Mortimer, Penelope. The Pumpkin Eater. Novel. 20th.

Nabokov, Vladimir. Lolita. Novel. 20th.

Oates, Joyce Carol. Wonderland. Novel. 20th.

O'Connor, Flannery. "The Lame Shall Enter First." Short Story. 20th.

O'Neill, Eugene. The Iceman Cometh. Drama. 20th.

O'Neill, Eugene. Mourning Becomes Electra. Drama. 20th.

O'Neill, Eugene. Strange Interlude. Drama. 20th.

Owen, Wilfrid. "Dulce et Decorum Est"; "Disabled"; "Mental Cases." Poems. 20th.

Pasternak, Boris. Doctor Zhivago. Novel. 20th.

Percy, Walker. Love in the Ruins. Novel. 20th.

Percy, Walker. The Moviegoer. Novel. 20th.

Pinter, Harold. The Caretaker. Drama. 20th.

Pinter, Harold. The Homecoming. Drama. 20th.

Pirandello, Luigi. Henry IV. Drama. 20th.

Pirsig, Robert M. Zen and the Art of Motorcycle Maintenance: an Inquiry into Values. Fiction. 20th.

Plath, Sylvia. The Bell Jar. Novel. 20th.

Poe, Edgar Allan. "The Fall of the House of Usher." Short Story. 19th.

Poe, Edgar Allan. "The Raven." Poem. 19th.

Racine, Jean. Phaedra. Drama. 18th.

Reade, Charles. Hard Cash. Novel. 19th.

Remarque, Erich Maria. Arch of Triumph. Novel. 20th.

Roethke, Theodore. "Heard in a Violent Ward" and "In a Dark Time." Poems. 20th.

Roth, Philip. The Breast. Novella. 20th.

Roth, Philip. Portnoy's Complaint. Novel. 20th.

Sade, Donatien Alphonse François, Marquis de. Justine. Novel. 19th.

Salinger, J. D. The Catcher in the Rye. Novel. 20th.

Sarton, May. Mrs. Stevens Hears the Mermaids Singing. Novel. 20th.

Sartre, Jean-Paul. "The Room." Short Story. 20th.

Schnitzler, Arthur. "The Man of Honour" (Also published as "The Murderer"). Short Story. 20th.

Scott, Sir Walter. The Heart of Midlothian. Novel. 19th.

Scott, Sir Walter. St. Ronan's Well. Novel. 19th.

Selzer, Richard. The Rituals of Surgery. Short Stories. 20th.

Seneca, Lucius Annaeus. Hercules Furens. Drama. Classical.

Sexton, Anne. "For the Year of the Insane" and "The Sickness unto Death." Poems. 20th.

Sexton, Anne. "The Fury of Rain Storms." Poem. 20th.

Shaffer, Peter. Equus. Drama. 20th.

Shakespeare, William. Comedy of Errors. Drama. Renaissance.

Shakespeare, William. King Lear. Drama. Renaissance.

Shakespeare, William. Macbeth. Drama. Renaissance.

Shakespeare, William. The Merchant of Venice. Drama. Renaissance.

Shakespeare, William. A Midsummer-Night's Dream. Drama. Renaissance.

Shakespeare, William. "My love is as a fever, longing still." Sonnet. Renaissance.

Shakespeare, William. Othello. Drama. Renaissance.

Shakespeare, William. Richard III. Drama. Renaissance.

Shakespeare, William. Twelfth Night. Drama. Renaissance.

Shelley, Percy Bysshe. The Cenci. Poetic Drama. 19th.

Smart, Christopher. "Hymn to the Supreme Being on Recovery from a Dangerous Fit of Illness." Poem. 18th.

Smollett, Tobias. Sir Launcelot Greaves. Novel. 18th.

Sophocles. Ajax. Drama. Classical.

Sophocles. Electra. Drama. Classical.

Stein, Gertrude. Melanctha. Novella. 20th.

Sterne, Laurence. A Sentimental Journey. Novel. 18th.

Stevenson, Robert Louis. The Master of Ballantrae. Novel. 19th.

Storey, David. Home. Drama. 20th.

Strindberg, August. The Father. Drama. 19th.

Tanizaki, Junichiro. Diary of a Mad Old Man. Novel. 20th.

Tennyson, Alfred. "Maud." Long Poem. 19th.

Thomas, Dylan. "And Death Shall Have No Dominion." Poem. 20th.

Thomas, Dylan. "Love in the Asylum." Poem. 20th.

Thoreau, Henry David. Walden. Treatise. 19th.

Tolstoy, Leo. The Kreutzer Sonata. Novella. 19th.

Tourneur, Cyril. The Atheist's Tragedy. Drama. Renaissance.

Trollope, Anthony. The Last Chronicles of Barset. Novel. 19th.

Turgenev, Ivan. "The District Doctor." Short Story. 19th.

Virgil (Publius Vergilius Maro). Aeneid. Epic Poem. Classical.

Webster, John. The Duchess of Malfi. Drama. Renaissance.

Webster, John. The White Devil. Drama. Renaissance.

Weiss, Peter. The Persecution and Assassination of Jean-Paul Marat . . . . (Marat/Sade). Drama. 20th.

White, Patrick. The Solid Mandala. Novel. 20th.

Williams, Tennessee. The Glass Menagerie. Drama. 20th.

Williams, Tennessee. Streetcar Named Desire. Drama. 20th.

Williams, Tennessee. Suddenly Last Summer. Drama. 20th.

Winchilsea, Countess of (Anne Finch). "The Spleen." Poem. 18th.

Wolfe, Gene. "The Death of Dr. Island." Short Story. 20th.

Woolf, Virginia. Mrs. Dalloway. Novel. 20th.

Woolf, Virginia. The Waves. Novel. 20th.

Wordsworth, William. "Ruth." Poem. 19th.

Yeats, William Butler. "Crazy Jane Talks with the Bishop." Poem. 20th.

Yeats, William Butler. "Why Should Not Old Men Be Mad?" Poem. 20th.

Zola, Emile. Dr. Pascal. Novel. 19th.

MEDICAL ETHICS

Albee, Edward. The Death of Bessie Smith. Drama. 20th.

Arden, John. The Happy Haven. Drama. 20th.

Bacon, Francis. The Advancement of Learning. Treatise. Renaissance.

Balzac, Honoré de. Cousin Pons. Novel. 19th.

Benn, Gottfried. "Answer to the Literary Immigrants." Essay. 20th.

Benn, Gottfried. "Monologue." Poem. 20th.

Borges, Jorge Luis. "The Immortals." Short Story. 20th.

Brieux, Eugene. Les Avariés. Drama; and Sinclair, Upton. Damaged Goods. Novel. 20th.

Browning, Robert. "The Family." Poem. 19th.

Büchner, Georg. Woyzeck. Drama. 19th

Burroughs, William. The Naked Lunch. Novel. 20th.

Butler, Samuel. Erewhon. Novel. 19th.

Céline, Louis-Ferdinand. Journey to the End of the Night. Novel.

Chekhov, Anton. Ivanov. Drama. 19th.

Choromanski, Michal. Jealousy and Medicine. Novel. 20th.

Collins, Wilkie. The Moonstone. Novel. 19th.

Crabbe, George. The Borough. Long Poem. 18th.

Crane, Stephen. "The Monster." Short Story. 19th.

Crichton, Michael. The Andromeda Strain. Novel. 20th.

Cronin, A. J. The Citadel. Novel. 20th.

Dante Alighieri. The Divine Comedy. Long Poem. Medieval.

Dekker, Thomas. The Honest Whore, Pt. I. Drama. Renaissance.

De L'Isle-Adam, Villiers. "The Doctor's Heroism." Short Story. 19th.

Doyle, Arthur Conan. "The Third Generation." Short Sketch. 19th.

Eliot, George (Mary Anne Evans). Middlemarch. Novel. 19th.

Euripides. Alcestis. Drama. Classical.

Freneau, Philip. "On Dr. Sangrado's Flight." Poem. 18th.

Garth, Samuel. The Dispensary. Poem. 18th.

Gunn, James. "Medic" (originally "Not So Great an Enemy" and a part of the Immortals). Short Story. 20th.

Haggard, H. Rider. Doctor Therne. Novel. 20th.

Hardy, Thomas. The Woodlanders. Novel. 19th.

Hawthorne, Nathaniel. "Rappaccini's Daughter." Short Story. 19th.

Hejinian, John. Extreme Remedies. Novel. 20th.

Herrick, Robert. The Web of Life. Novel. 20th.

Howard, Sidney, in collaboration with Paul de Kruif. Yellow Jack. Drama. 20th.

Howells, William Dean. Dr. Breen's Practice. Novel. 19th.

Howells, William Dean. An Imperative Duty. Novella. 19th.

Howells, William Dean. The Shadow of a Dream. Novella. 19th.

Huxley, Aldous. Brave New World. Novel. 20th.

Ibsen, Henrik. An Enemy of the People. Drama. 19th.

Joyce, James. Ulysses. Novel. 20th.

Kesey, Ken. One Flew Over the Cuckoo's Nest. Novel. 20th.

Keyes, Daniel. Flowers for Algernon. Novella. 20th.

Kingsley, Sidney. Men in White. Drama. 20th.

Kipling, Rudyard. "The Tender Achilles" and "Hymn to Physical Pain." Short Story and Poem. 19th.

Lardner, Ring. "Haircut." Short Story. 20th.

Lawrence, D. H. "The Horse Dealer's Daughter." Short Story. 20th.

Leinster, Murray. "Ribbon in the Sky." Short Story. 20th.

Lessing, Doris. A Proper Marriage. Novel. 20th.

Lewis, Sinclair. Arrowsmith. Novel. 20th.

London, Jack. "Koolau the Leper." Short Story. 19th.

Lucian of Samosata. "The Disowned." Essay. Classical.

Lyly, John. Midas. Drama. Renaissance.

Miller, Walter M., Jr. A Canticle for Leibowitz. Novel. 20th.

Molière (Jean-Baptiste Poquelin). La Malade Imaginaire (The Imaginary Invalid). Drama. 18th.

Nichols, Peter. The National Health. Drama. 20th.

Norris, Frank. McTeague. Novella. 19th.

Nourse, Alan E. The Bladerunner. Novel. 20th.

Oates, Joyce Carol. Wonderland. Novel. 20th.

Orwell, George (pseudonym of Eric Blair). "How the Poor Die." Essay. 20th.

Percy, Walker. Love in the Ruins. Novel. 20th.

Plato. The Republic. Dialogue. Classical.

Reade, Charles. The Cloister and the Hearth and A Woman-Hater. Novels. 19th.

Reade, Charles. Hard Cash. Novel. 19th.

Remarque, Erich Maria. Arch of Triumph. Novel. 20th.

Schnitzler, Arthur. Professor Bernhardi. Drama. 20th.

Shaffer, Peter. Equus. Drama. 20th.

Shakespeare, William. Cymbeline. Drama. Renaissance.

Shaw, George Bernard. Doctors' Delusions. Treatise. 20th.

Shaw, George Bernard. The Doctor's Dilemma. Drama. 20th.

Sinclair, Upton. Damaged Goods. Novel. 20th.

Smollett, Tobias. The Adventures of Roderick Random. Novel. 18th.

Solzhenitsyn, Alexander. Cancer Ward. Novel. 20th.

Southey, Robert. The Doctor. Treatise. 19th.

Sparks, Muriel. Memento Mori. Novel. 20th.

Stevenson, Robert Louis. "The Body-Snatcher." Short Story. 19th.

Thomas, Dylan. The Doctor and the Devils. Film Script. 20th.

Turgenev, Ivan. "The District Doctor." Short Story. 19th.

Tushnet, Leonard. "In Re Glover." Short Story. 20th.

White, Patrick. The Eye of the Storm. Novel. 20th.

Williams, Tennessee. Suddenly Last Summer. Drama. 20th.

Wolfe, Gene. "The Death of Dr. Island." Short Story. 20th.

Yglesias, Helen. "Semi-Private." Short Story. 20th.

Zola, Emile. Dr. Pascal. Novel. 19th.

Zola, Emile. Féconditć (From Les Quatres Evangiles). Novel. 19th.

Zugsmith, Leane. "The Three Veterans." Short Story. 20th.

MEDICAL INSTITUTIONS

Albee, Edward. The Death of Bessie Smith. Drama. 20th.

Arden, John. The Happy Haven. Drama. 20th.

Arking, Linda. "Certain Hard Places." Short Story. 20th.

Auden, W. H. "Miss Gee." Poem. 20th.

Auden, W. H. "Surgical Ward." Sonnet. 20th.

Auden, W. H. and Christopher Isherwood. The Dog Beneath the Skin. Poetic Drama. 20th.

Babel, Isaac. "The End of the Old-Folk's Home." Short Story. 20th.

Barth, John. The End of the Road. Novel. 20th.

Baudelaire, Charles Pierre. "On Delacroix's Picture of Tasso in Prison" ("Sur Le Tasse en Prison d'Eugène Delacroix"). Sonnet. 19th.

Beauvoir, Simone de. A Very Easy Death. Autobiography. 20th.

Beckett, Samuel. Endgame. Drama. 20th.

Bellamy, Edward. Looking Backward, 2000-1887. Novel. 19th.

Bellow, Saul. Mr. Sammler's Planet. Novel. 20th.

Benn, Gottfried. "Man and Woman Go Through the Cancer Ward." Poem. 20th.

Bennett, Arnold. Riceyman Steps. Novel. 19th.

Berryman, John. Recovery. Novel. 20th.

Betjeman, John. "The Cottage Hospital." Poem. 20th.

Blish, James. "They Shall Have Stars." Novella. 20th.

Brown, Charles Brockden. Arthur Mervyn. Novel. 19th.

Brown, Geoff. I Want What I Want. Novel. 20th.

Browning, Elizabeth Barrett. Aurora Leigh. Poem. 19th.

Burgess, Anthony. The Doctor Is Sick. Novel. 20th.

Burton, Robert. The Anatomy of Melancholy. Treatise. Renaissance.

Cable, George Washington. Dr. Sevier. Novel. 19th.

Céline, Louis-Ferdinand. Journey to the End of the Night. Novel. 20th.

Chekhov, Anton. "Gusev." Short Story. 19th.

Chekhov, Anton. The Island: A Journey to Sakhalin. Nonfiction. 19th.

Chekhov, Anton. "Ward 6." Short Story. 19th.

Choromanski, Michal. Jealousy and Medicine. Novel. 20th.

Collins, Wilkie. The Woman in White. Novel. 19th.

Copland, Robert. The Highway to the Spital-house. Dialogue in Verse. Renaissance.

Crabbe, George. The Borough. Long Poem. 18th.

Crabbe, George. The Village. Long Poem. 18th.

Cronin, A. J. The Citadel. Novel. 20th.

Defoe, Daniel. A Journal of the Plague Year. Treatise. 18th.

De Forest, John William. Miss Ravenal's Conversion from Secession to Loyalty. Novel. 19th.

Dekker, Thomas. The Honest Whore, Pt. I. Drama. Renaissance.

Dickens, Charles. "A Small Star in the East." Sketch. 19th.

Dickens, Charles. "Wapping Workhouse." Sketch. 19th.

Dickey, James. "The Eye-Beaters." Poem. 20th.

Dostoevsky, Fyodor. The Brothers Karamazov. Novel. 19th.

Drabble, Margaret. The Millstone. Novel. 20th.

Drake, Joseph Rodman. "The King of the Croakers." Poem. 19th.

Dürrenmatt, Friedrich. The Physicists. Drama. 20th.

Eliot, George (Mary Anne Evans). Middlemarch. Novel. 19th.

Eliot, T. S. "East Coker." Poem. 20th.

Fitzgerald, F. Scott. Tender Is the Night. Novel. 20th.

Ginsberg, Allen. "Howl." Poem. 20th.

Gogol, Nikolai. "The Diary of a Madman." Short Story. 19th.

Gregory, Isabella Augusta, Lady. The Workhouse Ward. Drama. 20th.

Gunn, James. "Medic" (originally "Not So Great an Enemy" and a part of the Immortals). Short Story. 20th.

Hejinian, John. Extreme Remedies. Novel. 20th.

Hemingway, Ernest. A Farewell to Arms. Novel. 20th.

Henley, William Ernest. In Hospital. 28 Sketches in Verse. 19th.

Herrick, Robert. The Healer. Novel. 20th.

Hope, A. D. "The Bed." Poem. 20th.

Ibsen, Henrik. An Enemy of the People. Drama. 19th.

Isherwood, Christopher. The Dog Beneath the Skin. Poetic Drama. 20th.

Joyce, James. Portrait of the Artist as a Young Man. Novel. 20th.

Joyce, James. Ulysses. Novel. 20th.

Kesey, Ken. One Flew Over the Cuckoo's Nest. Novel. 20th.

Kingsley, Sidney. Men in White. Drama. 20th.

Lacy, John. The Dumb Lady. Drama. 18th.

Lessing, Doris. A Proper Marriage. Novel. 20th.

Lewis, Sinclair. Arrowsmith. Novel. 20th.

London, Jack. "Koolau the Leper." Short Story. 19th.

Lowell, Robert. "The Hospital." Poem. 20th.

Mann, Thomas. The Magic Mountain. Novel. 20th.

McCullers, Carson. The Heart Is a Lonely Hunter. Novel. 20th.

McCullers, Carson. Reflections in a Golden Eye. Novella. 20th.

Melville, Herman. Pierre, or the Ambiguities. Novel. 19th.

Melville, Herman. White-Jacket, or The World in a Man-of-War. Novel. 19th.

Mercier, Louis Sebastian. Memoirs of the Year Two Thousand Five Hundred (original title: The Year Two Thousand Four Hundred and Forty). Treatise. 18th.

Middleton, Thomas. The Changeling. Drama. Renaissance.

More, Thomas. Utopia. Treatise. Renaissance.

Nabokov, Vladimir. Lolita. Novel. 20th.

Nichols, Peter. The National Health. Drama. 20th.

Nourse, Alan E. The Bladerunner. Novel. 20th.

Oates, Joyce Carol. Wonderland. Novel. 20th.

Odets, Clifford. Waiting for Lefty. Drama. 20th.

Orwell, George (pseudonym of Eric Blair). "How the Poor Die." Essay. 20th.

Pasternak, Boris. Doctor Zhivago. Novel. 20th.

Percy, Walker. Love in the Ruins. Novel. 20th.

Pinter, Harold. The Caretaker. Drama. 20th.

Plath, Sylvia. The Bell Jar. Novel. 20th.

Plath, Sylvia. "The Surgeon at 2 a.m." Poem. 20th.

Plath, Sylvia. "Three Women." Dramatic Poem. 20th.

Randall, Dudley. "George." Poem. 20th.

Reade, Charles. The Cloister and the Hearth and A Woman-Hater. Novels. 19th.

Reade, Charles. Hard Cash. Novel. 19th.

Remarque, Erich Maria. Arch of Triumph. Novel. 20th.

Roth, Philip. The Breast. Novella. 20th.

Sarton, May. Mrs. Stevens Hears the Mermaids Singing. Novel. 20th.

Schnitzler, Arthur. A Confirmed Bachelor (Also published as Dr. Graesler). Novel. 20th.

Schnitzler, Arthur. Professor Bernhardi. Drama. 20th.

Scott, Sir Walter. The Surgeon's Daughter. Novella. 19th.

Selzer, Richard. The Rituals of Surgery. Short Stories. 20th.

Sexton, Anne. "For the Year of the Insane" and "The Sickness Unto Death." Poems. 20th.

Sexton, Anne. "Unknown Girl in the Maternity Ward." Poem. 20th.

Shakespeare, William. Twelfth Night. Drama. Renaissance.

Sheed, Wilfrid. People Will Always Be Kind. Novel. 20th.

Sholom Aleichem (Solomon Rabinowitch). "The Lottery Ticket." Short Story. 19th.

Sladek, John T. "The Happy Breed." Short Story. 20th.

Smollett, Tobias. The Adventures of Peregrine Pickle. Novel. 18th.

Smollett, Tobias. Sir Launcelot Greaves. Novel. 18th.

Snow, C. P. Last Things. Novel. 20th.

Solzhenitsyn, Alexander. Cancer Ward. Novel. 20th.

Spark, Muriel. Memento Mori. Novel. 20th.

Stevenson, Robert Louis. "The Body-Snatcher." Short Story. 19th.

Stevenson, Robert Louis. "Father Damien." Essay. 19th.

Storey, David. Home. Drama. 20th.

Thomas, Dylan. "Love in the Asylum." Poem. 20th.

Trollope, Anthony. The Warden. Novel. 19th.

Twain, Mark. Innocents Abroad. Novel. 19th.

Wallant, Edward Lewis. Children at the Gate. Novel. 20th.

Weiss, Peter. The Persecution and Assassination of Jean-Paul Marat . . . . Marat/Sade). Drama. 20th.

Whitman, Walt. Drum Taps and Specimen Days. Short Poems and Journal. 19th.

Williams, William Carlos. The Autobiography of William Carlos Williams. Autobiography. 20th.

Williams, William Carlos. "The Injury." Poem. 20th.

Williams, William Carlos. "Jean Beicke." Short Story. 20th.

Williams, William Carlos. A Voyage to Pagany. Novel. 20th.

Wolfe, Gene. "The Death of Dr. Island." Short Story. 20th.

Yglesias, Helen. "Semi-Private." Short Story. 20th.

MEDICAL PROFESSION

Alcott, Louisa May. Hospital Sketches. Sketches. 19th.

Arking, Linda. "Certain Hard Places." Short Story. 20th.

Auden, W. H. "The Art of Healing." Poem. 20th.

Auden, W. H. "The History of Science." Poem. 20th.

Bacon, Francis. The Advancement of Learning. Treatise. Renaissance.

Balzac, Honoré de. The Country Doctor. Novel. 19th.

Barclay, Alexander. Ship of Fools. Poems. Renaissance.

Behn, Aphra. Sir Patient Fancy. Drama. 18th.

Benn, Gottfried. "Artists and Old Age." Essay. 20th.

Blake, William. The Island in the Moon. Sketches and Poems. 19th.

Browne, Thomas. Religio Medici. Treatise. Renaissance.

Browning, Robert. "An Epistle: Containing the Strange Medical Experience of Karshish, the Arab Physician." Poem. 19th.

Burton, Robert. The Anatomy of Melancholy. Treatise. Renaissance.

Cable, George Washington. Dr. Sevier. Novel. 19th.

Cocteau, Jean. Opium: The Diary of a Cure. Diary. 20th.

Chekhov, Anton. "Gusev." Short Story. 19th.

Chekhov, Anton. "Peasants." Short Story. 19th.

Crabbe, George. The Borough. Long Poem. 18th.

Crabbe, George. "The Library." Poem. 18th.

Crabbe, George. The Parish Register. Long Poem. 18th.

Dekker, Thomas. That Wonderful Year. Treatise in Prose and Poetry. Renaissance.

Delany, Samuel R. "Corona." Short Story. 20th.

De L'Isle-Adam, Villiers. "The Doctor's Heroism." Short Story. 19th.

De Quincey, Thomas. "Murder as One of the Fine Arts." Essay. 19th.

Dickey, James. "The Cancer Match." Poem. 20th.

Donne, John. Devotions. Essays. Renaissance.

Dostoevsky, Fyodor. Notes From the Underground. Novella. 19th.

Drake, Joseph Rodman. "The King of the Croakers." Poem. 19th.

Dreiser, Theodore. An American Tragedy. Novel. 20th.

Dryden, John. "To John Driden." Poem. 18th.

Ellison, Harlan. "Wanted In Surgery." Short Story. 20th.

Elyot, Thomas. The Castle of Health. Treatise. Renaissance.

Erasmus, Desiderius. The Praise of Folly. Treatise. Renaissance.

Flaubert, Gustave. Madame Bovary. Novel. 19th.

Forster, E. M. "The Machine Stops." Short Story. 20th.

Freneau, Philip. "Ode XI, To the Philadelphia Doctors" and "On the Free Use of the Lancet." Poems. 18th.

Fulke, Greville, Lord Brooke. A Treatie of Human Learning. Poem. Renaissance.

Garth, Samuel. The Dispensary. Poem. 18th.

Graves, Robert. "The Naked and the Nude." Poem. 20th.

Gunn, James. "Medic" (originally "Not So Great an Enemy" and a part of the Immortals). Short Story. 20th.

Haggard, H. Rider. Doctor Therne. Novel. 20th.

Hansberry, Lorraine. A Raisin in the Sun. Drama. 20th.

Hejinian, John. Extreme Remedies. Novel. 20th.

Hemingway, Ernest. "One Reader Writes." Short Story. 20th.

Herrick, Robert. The Healer. Novel. 20th.

Herrick, Robert. The Web of Life. Novel. 20th.

Holmes, Oliver Wendell. Elsie Venner. Novel. 19th.

Holmes, Oliver Wendell. "The Young Practitioner." Essay. 19th.

Howard, Sidney, in collaboration with Paul de Kruif. Yellow Jack. Drama. 20th.

Howells, William Dean. Dr. Breen's Practice. Novel. 19th.

James, Henry. "Lady Barberina." Short Story. 19th.

Jewett, Sarah Orne. A Country Doctor. Novel. 19th.

Johnson, Samuel. A Dictionary of the English Language. Dictionary. 18th.

Kingsley, Sidney. Men in White. Drama. 20th.

Kipling, Rudyard. "The Tender Achilles" and "Hymn to Physical Pain." Short Story and Poem. 19th.

Kornbluth, Cyril M. "The Little Black Bag." Short Story. 20th.

Lacy, John. The Dumb Lady. Drama. 18th.

Lawrence, D. H. Psychoanalysis and the Unconscious and Fantasia of the Unconscious. Long Essays. 20th.

Leinster, Murray. "Ribbon in the Sky." Short Story. 20th.

Leman, Grahame. "Conversational Mode." Short Story. 20th.

LeSage, Alain René. The Adventures of Gil Blas of Santillane. Tale. 18th.

Lewis, Sinclair. Arrowsmith. Novel. 20th.

Lucian of Samosata. "The Disowned." Essay. Classical.

Marlowe, Christopher. The Tragical History of Doctor Faustus. Drama. Renaissance.

Maupassant, Guy de. "The Devil." Short Story. 19th.

Melville, Herman. White-Jacket, or The World in a Man-of-War. Novel. 19th.

Mercier, Louis Sebastian. Memoirs of the Year Two Thousand Five Hundred (original title: The Year Two Thousand Four Hundred and Forty). Treatise. 18th.

Molière (Jean-Baptiste Poquelin). La Malade Imaginaire (The Imaginary Invalid). Drama. 18th.

Molière (Jean-Baptiste Poquelin). L'Amour Médecin (Love's the Best Doctor). Drama. 18th.

Molière (Jean-Baptiste Poquelin). Le Médecin Malgré Lui (The Physician In Spite of Himself). Drama. 18th.

Montaigne, Michel Eyquem de. "Of The Resemblance Betweene Children and Fathers." Essay. Renaissance.

Nabokov, Vladimir. Lolita. Novel. 20th.

Norris, Frank. McTeague. Novella. 19th.

Nourse, Alan E. The Bladerunner. Novel. 20th.

Odets, Clifford. Waiting for Lefty. Drama. 20th.

Orwell, George (pseudonym of Eric Blair). "How the Poor Die." Essay. 20th.

Phelps, Elizabeth Stuart. Dr. Zay. Novel. 19th.

Pindar. "Pythia III: For Hieron of Syracuse: On the Occasion of His Illness." Poem. Classical.

Plato. The Republic. Dialogue. Classical.

Plato. Symposium. Dialogue. Classical.

Reade, Charles. The Cloister and the Hearth and A Woman-Hater. Novels. 19th.

Salinger, J. D. The Catcher in the Rye. Novel. 20th.

Schnitzler, Arthur. My Youth in Vienna. Autobiography. 20th.

Scott, Sir Walter. St. Ronan's Well. Novel. 19th.

Scott, Sir Walter. The Talisman. Novel. 19th.

Sexton, Anne. "Doctors." Poem. 20th.

Shaffer, Peter. Equus. Drama. 20th.

Shango, J. R. "A Matter of Ethics." Short Story. 20th.

Shaw, George Bernard. Doctors' Delusions. Treatise. 20th.

Shaw, George Bernard. The Doctor's Dilemma. Drama. 20th.

Smollett, Tobias. The Adventures of Ferdinand, Count Fathom. Novel. 18th.

Smollett, Tobias. The Adventures of Roderick Random. Novel.
    18th.

Southey, Robert. The Doctor. Treatise. 19th.

Sterne, Laurence. The Life and Opinions of Tristram Shandy, Gent.
    Novel. 18th.

Stevenson, Robert Louis. Strange Case of Dr. Jekyll and Mr. Hyde.
    Novella. 19th.

Swift, Jonathan. Gulliver's Travels. Satiric Tales. 18th.

Swift, Jonathan. "In Sickness." Poem. 18th.

Tolstoy, Leo. The Kreutzer Sonata. Novella. 19th.

Trollope, Anthony. Doctor Thorne. Novel. 19th.

Warren, Samuel. Passages from the Diary of a Late Physician.
    Sketches. 19th.

Williams, Tennessee. Suddenly Last Summer. Drama. 20th.

Williams, Tennessee. Summer and Smoke. Drama. 20th.

Williams, William Carlos. The Autobiography of William Carlos
    Williams. Autobiography. 20th.

Williams, William Carlos. "A Night in June." Short Story. 20th.

Williams, William Carlos. A Voyage to Pagany. Novel. 20th.

Winchilsea, Countess of (Anne Finch). "To Dr. Waldron." Poem.
    18th.

Zola, Emile. Dr. Pascal. Novel. 19th.

MEDICAL STUDENTS

Auden, W. H. "Miss Gee." Poem. 20th.

Auden, W. H. and Christopher Isherwood. The Dog Beneath the Skin.
    Poetic Drama. 20th.

Balzac, Honoré de. Père Goriot. Novel. 19th.

Chekhov, Anton. "An Attack of Nerves." Short Story. 19th.

Dickens, Charles. Bleak House. Novel. 19th.

Dickens, Charles. The Pickwick Papers. Novel. 19th.

Doyle, Arthur Conan. "The Croxley Master." Short Story. 19th.

Drake, Joseph Rodman. "The King of the Croakers." Poem. 19th.

Glissenti, F. "Death and the Anatomical Lecture." Poem and
    Woodcuts. Renaissance.

Hejinian, John. Extreme Remedies. Novel. 20th.

Henley, William Ernest. In Hospital. 28 Sketches in Verse. 19th.

Holmes, Oliver Wendell. Elsie Venner. Novel. 19th.

Isherwood, Christopher. The Dog Beneath the Skin. Poetic Drama.
    20th.

Joyce, James. Ulysses. Novel. 20th.

Lewis, Sinclair. Arrowsmith. Novel. 20th.

Martial (Marcus Valerius Martialis). Epigrams, Book V, no. 9.
    Poem. Classical.

Maugham, W. Somerset. Of Human Bondage. Novel. 20th.

Nichols, Peter. The National Health. Drama. 20th.

Oates, Joyce Carol. Wonderland. Novel. 20th.

Orwell, George (pseudonym of Eric Blair). "How the Poor Die."
    Essay. 20th.

Pasternak, Boris. Doctor Zhivago. Novel. 20th.

Percy, Walker. Love in the Ruins. Novel. 20th.

Percy, Walker. The Moviegoer. Novel. 20th.

Plath, Sylvia. The Bell Jar. Novel. 20th.

Reade, Charles. The Cloister and the Hearth and A Woman-Hater.
    Novels. 19th.

Schnitzler, Arthur. My Youth in Vienna. Autobiography. 20th.

Shango, J. R. "A Matter of Ethics." Short Story. 20th.

Shaw, George Bernard. The Doctor's Dilemma. Drama. 20th.

The Spectator, no. 25. Essay. 18th.

MENTAL RETARDATION

Balzac, Honoré de. The Country Doctor. Novel. 19th.

Brontë, Charlotte. Villette. Novel. 19th.

Collins, Wilkie. The Woman in White. Novel. 19th.

Conrad, Joseph. "The Idiots." Short Story. 20th.

Crane, Hart. "The Idiot." Poem. 20th.

Crane, Stephen. "The Monster." Short Story. 19th.

Delany, Samuel R. "Corona." Short Story. 20th.

Dickens, Charles. Bleak House. Novel. 19th.

Dickens, Charles. David Copperfield. Novel. 19th.

Dostoevsky, Fyodor. Crime and Punishment. Novel. 19th.

Dostoevsky, Fyodor. The Idiot. Novel. 19th.

Erasmus, Desiderius. The Praise of Folly. Treatise. Renaissance.

Faulkner, William. Sanctuary. Novel. 20th.

Faulkner, William. The Sound and the Fury. Novel. 20th.

Heller, Joseph. Something Happened. Novel. 20th.

Jonson, Benjamin. Bartholomew Fair. Drama. Renaissance.

Keyes, Daniel. Flowers for Algernon. Novella. 20th.

Lardner, Ring. "Haircut." Short Story. 20th.

McCullers, Carson. The Heart Is a Lonely Hunter. Novel. 20th.

Middleton, Thomas. The Changeling. Drama. Renaissance.

Nichols, Peter. Joe Egg. Drama. 20th.

Porter, Katherine Anne. "He." Short Story. 20th.

Rilke, Rainer Maria. "The Blind Man's Song," "The Drinker's Song," "The Idiot's Song," "The Suicide's Song," "The Dwarf's Song," and "The Leper's Song." Short Poems. 20th.

Silkin, Jon. "Death of a Son." Poem. 20th.

Steinbeck, John. Of Mice and Men. Novel. 20th.

Thomas, Dylan. "The Hunchback in the Park." Poem. 20th.

Wallant, Edward Lewis. Children at the Gate. Novel. 20th.

White, Patrick. The Solid Mandala. Novel. 20th.

Wordsworth, William. "The Idiot Boy." Poem. 19th.

Zola, Emile. Dr. Pascal. Novel. 19th.

NURSES

Albee, Edward. The Death of Bessie Smith. Drama. 20th.

Alcott, Louisa May. Hospital Sketches. Sketches. 19th.

Arden, John. The Happy Haven. Drama. 20th.

Auden, W. H. and Christopher Isherwood. The Dog Beneath the Skin. Poetic Drama. 20th.

Barth, John. The End of the Road. Novel. 20th.

Beauvoir, Simone de. A Very Easy Death. Autobiography. 20th.

Benn, Gottfried. "Man and Woman Go Through the Cancer Ward." Poem. 20th.

Berryman, John. Recovery. Novel. 20th.

Burgess, Anthony. The Doctor Is Sick. Novel. 20th.

Céline, Louis-Ferdinand. Journey to the End of the Night. Novel. 20th.

Choromanski, Michal. Jealousy and Medicine. Novel. 20th.

Cocteau, Jean. Opium: The Diary of a Cure. Diary. 20th.

Cronin, A. J. The Citadel. Novel. 20th.

Delaney, Shelagh. A Taste of Honey. Drama. 20th.

Dickens, Charles. Martin Chuzzlewit. Novel. 19th.

Drabble, Margaret. The Millstone. Novel. 20th.

Dreiser, Theodore. "Regina C---." Sketch. 20th.

Dürrenmatt, Friedrich. The Physicists. Drama. 20th.

Eliot, T. S. "East Coker." Poem. 20th.

Fielding, Henry. Amelia. Novel. 18th.

Fitzgerald, F. Scott. "An Alcoholic Case." Short Story. 20th.

Hart, Moss and George S. Kaufman. The Man Who Came to Dinner. Drama. 20th.

Hawthorne, Nathaniel. "Edward Fane's Rosebud." Sketch. 19th.

Hawthorne, Nathaniel. The Scarlet Letter. Novel. 19th.

Hejinian, John. Extreme Remedies. Novel. 20th.

Hemingway, Ernest. A Farewell to Arms. Novel. 20th.

Henley, William Ernest. In Hospital. 28 Sketches in Verse. 19th.

Howard, Sidney, in collaboration with Paul de Kruif. Yellow Jack. Drama. 20th.

Isherwood, Christopher. The Dog Beneath the Skin. Poetic Drama. 20th.

Joyce, James. Ulysses. Novel. 20th.

Keats, John. Letter to Charles Wentworth Dilke, Mon., Sept. 1818; Letters to George and Georgiana Keats, Wed., Oct. 14 - Sat., Oct. 31, 1818; Wed., Dec. 16, 1818 - Mon., Jan. 4, 1819. Letters. 19th.

Kesey, Ken. One Flew Over the Cuckoo's Nest. Novel. 20th.

Kingsley, Sidney. Men in White. Drama. 20th.

Lawrence, D. H. Lady Chatterley's Lover. Novel. 20th.

Lessing, Doris. A Proper Marriage. Novel. 20th.

Lewis, Sinclair. Arrowsmith. Novel. 20th.

Luce, Clare Booth. The Women. Drama. 20th.

Marcus, Frank. The Killing of Sister George. Drama. 20th.

Maupassant, Guy de. "The Devil." Short Story. 19th.

McKenna, Richard. "Casey Agonistes." Short Story. 20th.

Murdoch, Irish. Bruno's Dream. Novel. 20th.

Nichols, Peter. The National Health. Drama. 20th.

Norris, Frank. A Man's Woman. Novella. 19th.

O'Connor, Flannery. "Revelation." Short Story. 20th.

Orwell, George (pseudonym of Eric Blair). "How the Poor Die." Essay. 20th.

Pasternak, Boris. Doctor Zhivago. Novel. 20th.

Percy, Walker. Love in the Ruins. Novel. 20th.

Plath, Sylvia. The Bell Jar. Novel. 20th.

Porter, Katherine Anne. "Pale Horse, Pale Rider." Short Story. 20th.

Reade, Charles. The Cloister and the Hearth and A Woman-Hater. Novels. 19th.

Remarque, Erich Maria. Arch of Triumph. Novel. 20th.

Roth, Philip. The Breast. Novella. 20th.

Sarton, May. As We Are Now. Novel. 20th.

Sarton, May. Mrs. Stevens Hears the Mermaids Singing. Novel. 20th.

Schnitzler, Arthur. A Confirmed Bachelor (Also published as Dr. Graesler). Novel. 20th.

Schnitzler, Arthur. Professor Bernhardi. Drama. 20th.

Selzer, Richard. The Rituals of Surgery. Short Stories. 20th.

Sexton, Anne. "Unknown Girl in the Maternity Ward." Poem. 20th.

Sheed, Wilfrid. People Will Always Be Kind. Novel. 20th.

Solzhenitsyn, Alexander. Cancer Ward. Novel. 20th.

Spark, Muriel. Memento Mori. Novel. 20th.

Tanizaki, Junichiro. Diary of a Mad Old Man. Novel. 20th.

Tennyson, Alfred. "In the Children's Hospital." Poem. 19th.

Wharton, Edith. Ethan Frome. Novel. 20th.

White, Patrick. The Eye of the Storm. Novel. 20th.

Whitman, Walt. Drum Taps and Specimen Days. Short Poems and Journal. 19th.

Williams, Tennessee. Suddenly Last Summer. Drama. 20th.

Williams, William Carlos. The Autobiography of William Carlos Williams. Autobiography. 20th.

Williams, William Carlos. The Cure. Drama. 20th.

Williams, William Carlos. "Jean Beicke." Short Story. 20th.

Yglesias, Helen. "Semi-Private." Short Story. 20th.

PLAGUE

Anonymous. Beowulf. Epic Poem. Medieval.

Armstrong, John. "The Art of Preserving Health." Poem. 18th.

Benn, Gottfried. "Monologue." Poem. 20th.

The Bible. Exodus. Classical.

The Bible. Revelations. Classical.

Boccaccio, Giovanni. The Decameron: Day 1, Prologue. Sketch. Medieval.

Brown, Charles Brockden. Arthur Mervyn. Novel. 19th.

Bullein, William. A Dialogue Against the Fever Pestilence. Dialogues. Renaissance.

Byron, George Gordon, Lord. "The Destruction of Sennacherib." Poem. 19th.

Camus, Albert. The Plague. Novel. 20th.

Chaucer, Geoffrey. The Canterbury Tales, "The Pardoner's Tale." Tale. Medieval.

Conrad, Joseph. The Shadow Line: a Confession. Novella. 20th.

Crichton, Michael. The Andromeda Strain. Novel. 20th.

Defoe, Daniel. A Journal of the Plague Year. Treatise. 18th.

Dekker, Thomas. That Wonderful Year. Treatise in Prose and Poetry. Renaissance.

Freneau, Philip. "On Dr. Sangrado's Flight." Poem. 18th.

Haggard, H. Rider. Doctor Therne. Novel. 20th.

Hawthorne, Nathaniel. "Lady Eleanore's Mantle." Short Story. 19th.

Howard, Sidney, in collaboration with Paul de Kruif. Yellow Jack. Drama. 20th.

Kingsley, Charles. Two Years Ago. Novel. 19th.

Kipling, Rudyard. "The Last Relief." Short Story. 19th.

Langland, William. Piers Plowman (B-Text). Long Poem. Medieval.

Leinster, Murray. "Ribbon in the Sky." Short Story. 20th.

Lewis, Sinclair. Arrowsmith. Novel. 20th.

Lodge, Thomas. A Treatise of the Plague. Treatise. Renaissance.

London, Jack. The Scarlet Plague. Novel. 19th.

Mann, Thomas. Death in Venice. Novella. 20th.

Nashe, Thomas. The Unfortunate Traveler. Tale. Renaissance.

Nourse, Alan E. The Bladerunner. Novel. 20th.

Pepys, Samuel. The Diary: Selections. Diary. 18th.

Poe, Edgar Allan. "The Masque of the Red Death." Short Story. 19th.

Porter, Katherine Anne. "Pale Horse, Pale Rider." Short Story. 20th.

Schiller, Friedrich. "Die Peste." Poem. 19th.

Shelley, Mary. The Last Man. Novel. 19th.

Sophocles. Oedipus Rex. Drama. Classical.

Voltaire, Francois-Marie Arouet. Candide. Tale. 18th.

POVERTY & HEALTH

Akenside, Mark. "Hymn to the Naiads." Poem. 18th.

Albee, Edward. The Death of Bessie Smith. Drama. 20th.

Babel, Isaac. "The End of the Old-Folk's Home." Short Story. 20th.

The Bible. Luke. Classical.

Blake, William. "London." Poem. 19th.

Brecht, Bertolt. Mother Courage and Her Children. Drama. 20th.

Brieux, Eugene. Les Avariés. Drama; and Sinclair, Upton, Damaged Goods. Novel. 20th.

Büchner, Georg. Woyzeck. Drama. 19th.

Burton, Robert. The Anatomy of Melancholy. Treatise. Renaissance.

Cable, George Washington. Dr. Sevier. Novel. 19th.

Catullus, C. Valerius. Carmina, no. 23. Poem. Classical.

Chaucer, Geoffrey. The Canterbury Tales, "The Nun's Priest's Tale." Tale. Medieval.

Chekhov, Anton. "Gusev." Short Story. 19th.

Chekhov, Anton. The Island: A Journey to Sakhalin. Nonfiction. 19th.

Chekhov, Anton. "Misery." Short Story. 19th.

Chekhov, Anton. "Peasants." Short Story. 19th.

Chekhov, Anton. "Ward 6." Short Story. 19th.

Copland, Robert. The Highway to the Spital-house. Dialogue in Verse. Renaissance.

Crabbe, George. The Borough. Long Poem. 18th.

Crabbe, George. Inebrity. Long Poem. 18th.

Crabbe, George. The Village. Long Poem. 18th.

Defoe, Daniel. A Journal of the Plague Year. Treatise. 18th.

Dickens, Charles. Bleak House. Novel. 19th.

Dickens, Charles. The Pickwick Papers. Novel. 19th.

Dickens, Charles. "A Small Star in the East." Sketch. 19th.

Dostoevsky, Fyodor. Crime and Punishment. Novel. 19th.

Garth, Samuel. The Dispensary. Poem. 18th.

Gaskell, Elizabeth. Mary Barton. Novel. 19th.

Gorki, Maxim. The Lower Depths. Drama. 20th.

Hardy, Thomas. Jude the Obscure. Novel. 19th.

Hejinian, John. Extreme Remedies. Novel. 20th.

Herrick, Robert. The Web of Life. Novel. 20th.

Jonson, Benjamin. "To Sickness" and "An Epigram. To the Small Poxe." Poems. Renaissance.

Kingsley, Charles. Two Years Ago. Novel. 19th.

Kingsley, Sidney. Men in White. Drama. 20th.

Leman, Grahame. "Conversational Mode." Short Story. 20th.

Luce, Clare Booth. The Women. Drama. 20th.

Maugham, W. Somerset. Liza of Lambeth. Novel. 20th.

McCullers, Carson. The Heart Is a Lonely Hunter. Novel. 20th.

Odets, Clifford. Waiting for Lefty. Drama. 20th.

Orwell, George (pseudonym of Eric Blair). "How the Poor Die." Essay. 20th.

Pasternak, Boris. Doctor Zhivago. Novel. 20th.

Pohl, Frederick and C. M. Kornbluth. The Space Merchants (appeared in a condensed version as Gravy Planet). Novel. 20th.

Porter, Katherine Anne. "He." Short Story. 20th.

Randall, Dudley. "George." Poem. 20th.

Reade, Charles. The Cloister and the Hearth and A Woman-Hater. Novels. 19th.

Remarque, Erich Maria. Arch of Triumph. Novel. 20th.

Rilke, Rainer Maria. The Book of Poverty and Death. Short Poems. 20th.

Sarton, May. As We Are Now. Novel. 20th.

Sedley, Charles. "The Doctor and his Patients." Poem. 18th.

Solzhenitsyn, Alexander. Cancer Ward. Novel. 20th.

The Spectator, no. 246. Essay. 18th.

Steinbeck, John. In Dubious Battle. Novel. 20th.

Thoreau, Henry David. Walden. Treatise. 19th.

Warren, Samuel. Passages from the Diary of a Late Physician. Sketches. 19th.

Wharton, Edith. Ethan Frome. Novel. 20th.

White, E. B. "The Morning of the Day They Did It." Short Story. 20th.

Williams, William Carlos. The Autobiography of William Carlos Williams. Autobiography. 20th.

Williams, William Carlos. "Jean Beicke." Short Story. 20th.

Williams, William Carlos. "A Night in June." Short Story. 20th.

Williams, William Carlos. A Voyage to Pagany. Novel. 20th.

Zola, Emile. "Comment On Meurt" ("How People Die"). Sketches. 19th.

Zola, Emile. Germinal. Novel. 19th.

Zugsmith, Leane. "The Three Veterans." Short Story. 20th.

PREGNANCY & CHILDBIRTH

Anonymous. Aucassin and Nicolete. Tale. Medieval.

Anonymous. "Child Waters" and "Fair Mary of Wallington." Ballads. Medieval.

Anonymous. The Second Shepherds' Play. Drama. Medieval.

Arlen, Michael. The Green Hat. Novel. 20th.

Barth, John. The End of the Road. Novel. 20th.

The Bible. Genesis. Classical.

The Bible. Judges. Classical.

The Bible. Luke. Classical.

Blake, William. "Infant Joy" and "Infant Sorrow." Poems. 19th.

Boccaccio, Giovanni. The Decameron: Day 9, Tale 3. Tale. Medieval.

Bowen, Elizabeth. Eva Trout. Novel. 20th.

Bradstreet, Anne. "Before the Birth of One of her Children." Poem. 18th.

Brontë, Emily Jane. Wuthering Heights. Novel. 19th.

Browne, Thomas. Religio Medici. Treatise. Renaissance.

Burns, Robert. "A Poet's Welcome to His Love-Begotten Daughter." Poem. 18th.

Burton, Robert. The Anatomy of Melancholy. Treatise. Renaissance.

Butler, Samuel. Hudibras. Long Poem. 18th.

Butler, Samuel. Erewhon. Novel. 19th.

Cable, George Washington Dr. Sevier. Novel. 19th.

Choromanski, Michal. Jealousy and Medicine. Novel. 20th.

Congreve, William. The Way of the World. Drama. 18th.

Crabbe, George. The Parish Register. Long Poem. 18th.

Dante Alighieri. The Divine Comedy. Long Poem. Medieval.

Defoe, Daniel. Moll Flanders. Novel. 18th.

De Forest, John William. Miss Ravenal's Conversion from Secession to Loyalty. Novel. 19th.

Delaney, Shelagh. A Taste of Honey. Drama. 20th.

Dickens, Charles. David Copperfield. Novel. 19th.

Doyle, Arthur Conan. "The Curse of Eve." Short Story. 19th.

Drabble, Margaret. The Millstone. Novel. 20th.

Eliot, George (Mary Anne Evans). Adam Bede. Novel. 19th.

Eliot, George (Mary Anne Evans). Mr. Gilfil's Love-Story. Novella. 19th.

Euripides. Medea. Drama. Classical.

Fielding, Henry. Amelia. Novel. 18th.

Ford, John. 'Tis Pity She's a Whore. Drama. Renaissance.

Gazzo, Michael. A Hatful of Rain. Drama. 20th.

Hardy, Thomas. Far From the Madding Crowd. Novel. 19th.

Hardy, Thomas. "Her Death and After." Poem. 19th.

Hemingway, Ernest. A Farewell to Arms. Novel. 20th.

Hemingway, Ernest. "Indian Camp." Short Story. 20th.

Herbert, Frank. The Eyes of Heisenberg (also as Do I Sleep or Wake). Novel. 20th.

Huxley, Aldous. Brave New World. Novel. 20th.

Ibsen, Henrik. Hedda Gabler. Drama. 19th.

Jarrell, Randall. "The Death of the Ball Turret Gunner." Poem. 20th.

Jonson, Benjamin. Bartholomew Fair. Drama. Renaissance.

Jonson, Benjamin. Epigram LXII, "To Fine Lady Would-Bee." Poem. Renaissance.

Joyce, James. Ulysses. Novel. 20th.

Lawrence, D. H. "The Blind Man." Short Story. 20th.

Lawrence, D. H. Lady Chatterley's Lover. Novel. 20th.

Lessing, Doris. A Proper Marriage. Novel. 20th.

Lewis, Sinclair. Arrowsmith. Novel. 20th.

Luce, Clare Booth. The Women. Drama. 20th.

Marston, John. The Fawn. Drama. Renaissance.

Masters, Edgar Lee. The Spoon River Anthology. Poem Sequence. 20th.

Mather, Cotton. The Angel of Bethesda: An Essay Upon the Common Maladies of Mankind. Treatise. 18th.

Maugham, W. Somerset. Liza of Lambeth. Novel. 20th.

Maugham, W. Somerset. Of Human Bondage. Novel. 20th.

Maupassant, Guy de. "Useless Beauty." Short Story. 19th.

Melville, Herman. "The Paradise of Bachelors" and "The Tartarus of Maids." Sketches. 19th.

Merrill, James. "A Timepiece." Poem. 20th.

Middleton, Thomas. A Chaste Maid in Cheapside. Drama. Renaissance.

Middleton, Thomas. A Fair Quarrel. Drama. Renaissance.

Milton, John. "Epitaph on the Marchioness of Winchester" and Ben Jonson, "An Elegie on the Lady Pawlet Marchion: of Winton." Poems. Renaissance.

Mortimer, Penelope. The Pumpkin Eater. Novel. 20th.

Nichols, Peter. Joe Egg. Drama. 20th.

Oates, Joyce Carol. Wonderland. Novel. 20th.

Pasternak, Boris. Doctor Zhivago. Novel. 20th.

Plath, Sylvia. The Bell Jar. Novel. 20th.

Plath, Sylvia. "Thalidomide." Poem. 20th.

Plath, Sylvia. "Three Women." Dramatic Poem. 20th.

Rabelais, Francois. Gargantua and Pantagruel. Tales. Renaissance.

Schnitzler, Arthur. The Spring Sonata (Also published as Bertha Garlan). Novel. 20th.

Scott, Sir Walter. The Heart of Midlothian. Novel. 19th.

Sexton, Anne. "Unknown Girl in the Maternity Ward." Poem. 20th.

Shakespeare, William. Julius Caesar. Drama. Renaissance.

Shakespeare, William. Macbeth. Drama. Renaissance.

Shakespeare, William. Measure for Measure. Drama. Renaissance.

Shakespeare, William. A Midsummer-Night's Dream. Drama. Renaissance.

Shakespeare, William. The Winter's Tale. Drama. Renaissance.

The Spectator, no. 246. Essay. 18th.

Steinbeck, John. In Dubious Battle. Novel. 20th.

Sterne, Laurence. The Life and Opinions of Tristram Shandy, Gent. Novel. 18th.

Tolstoy, Leo. The Kreutzer Sonata. Novella. 19th.

White, Patrick. The Eye of the Storm. Novel. 20th.

Williams, Tennessee. Streetcar Named Desire. Drama. 20th.

Williams, William Carlos. The Autobiography of William Carlos Williams. Autobiography. 20th.

Williams, William Carlos. "Complaint." Poem. 20th.

Williams, William Carlos. "A Night in June." Short Story. 20th.

Zola, Emile. Fécondité (From Les Quatres Evangiles). Novel. 19th.

Zola, Emile. Germinal. Novel. 19th.

SCIENCE & POETRY

Akenside, Mark. "Hymn to Science." Poem. 18th.

Akenside, Mark. "Ode XVI, To Caleb Hardinge, M.D." Poem. 18th.

Anonymous. "Charm for a Sudden Stitch." Poem. Medieval.

Arnold, Matthew. "Literature and Science." Essay. 19th.

Berryman, John. Recovery. Novel. 20th.

Boccaccio, Giovanni. The Decameron: Day 1, Prologue. Sketch. Medieval.

Browning, Elizabeth Barrett. Aurora Leigh. Poem. 19th.

Browning, Robert. Paracelsus. Poem. 19th.

Crabbe, George. "Fragment, Written at Midnight." Poem. 18th.

Doyle, Arthur Conan. "A Medical Document." Sketches. 19th.

Emerson, Ralph Waldo. "The Poet." Essay. 19th.

Fracastorius, Heironymus. Hieronymus Fracastorius and his Poetical and Prose Works on Syphilis. Poem. Renaissance.

Holmes, Oliver Wendell. "The Young Practitioner." Essay. 19th.

Huxley, Aldous. Brave New World. Novel. 20th.

Huxley, Aldous. The Doors of Perception. Long Essay. 20th.

Huxley, Thomas Henry. "On Science and Art in Relation to Education." Essay. 19th.

James, Henry. The Middle Years. Novella. 19th.

Lawrence, D. H. Psychoanalysis and the Unconscious and Fantasia of the Unconscious. Long Essays. 20th.

Leavis, F. R. "Two Cultures: The Significance of C. P. Snow." Essay. 20th.

Lewis, Sinclair. Arrowsmith. Novel. 20th.

Mitchell, John Kearsley. Indecision, a Tale of the Far West; and Other Poems. Introduction and Dedication. 19th.

More, Thomas. Utopia. Treatise. Renaissance.

Pasternak, Boris. Doctor Zhivago. Novel. 20th.

Percy, Walker. Love in the Ruins. Novel. 20th.

Percy, Walker. The Moviegoer. Novel. 20th.

Pirsig, Robert M. Zen and the Art of Motorcycle Maintenance: an Inquiry into Values. Fiction. 20th.

Poe, Edgar Allan. "Sonnet--To Science." Sonnet. 19th.

Richard, I. A. "Science and Poetry." Essay. 20th.

Sewell, Elizabeth. The Orphic Voice: Poetry and Natural History. Essay. 20th.

Snow, C. P. "The Two Cultures"; Leavis, F. R. "Two Cultures: The Significance of C. P. Snow"; Richards, I. A. "Science and Poetry." Essays. 20th.

Williams, William Carlos. "To a Dog Injured in the Street." Poem. 20th.

Winchilsea, Countess of (Anne Finch). "To Dr. Waldron." Poem. 18th.

Wordsworth, William. The Prelude. Long Poem. 19th.

Young, Edward. "On Michael Angelo's Famous Piece of the Crucifixion." Poem. 18th.

SCIENCE FICTION

Bellamy, Edward. Looking Backward, 2000-1887. Novel. 19th.

Blish, James. "They Shall Have Stars." Novella. 20th.

Borges, Jorge Luis. "The Immortals." Short Story. 20th.

Bradbury, Ray. "Kaleidoscope." Short Story. 20th.

Bradbury, Ray. "The Next in Line." Short Story. 20th.

Brunner, John. The Whole Man. Novel. 20th.

Campanella, Tomaso. City of the Sun. Treatise. Renaissance.

Čapek, Karel. R.U.R. Drama. 20th.

Coney, Michael G. Friends Come in Boxes. Novel. 20th.

Crichton, Michael. The Andromeda Strain. Novel. 20th.

Delany, Samuel R. "Corona." Short Story. 20th.

Del Rey, Lester. Nerves. Novel. 20th.

Disch, Thomas. Camp Concentration. Novel. 20th.

Ellison, Harlan. "I Have No Mouth and I Must Scream." Short Story. 20th.

Ellison, Harlan. "Wanted in Surgery." Short Story. 20th.

Farmer, José Philip. Riders of the Purple Wage. Novella. 20th.

Forster, E. M. "The Machine Stops." Short Story. 20th.

Gunn, James. "Medic" (originally "Not So Great an Enemy" and a part of the Immortals). Short Story. 20th.

Heinlein, Robert A. Time Enough For Love. Novel. 20th.

Herbert, Frank. The Eyes of Heisenberg (also as Do I Sleep or Wake). Novel. 20th.

Huxley, Aldous. Brave New World. Novel. 20th.

Keyes, Daniel. Flowers for Algernon. Novella. 20th.

Kipling, Rudyard. "Unprofessional." Short Story. 19th.

Kornbluth, Cyril M. "The Little Black Bag." Short Story. 20th.

LeGuin, Ursula. the Left Hand of Darkness. Novel. 20th.

Leinster, Murray. "Ribbon in the Sky." Short Story. 20th.

Leman, Grahame. "Conversational Mode." Short Story. 20th.

London, Jack. The Scarlet Plague. Novel. 19th.

Malzberg, Barry. "Out from Ganymede." Short Story. 20th.

McKenna, Richard. "Casey Agonistes." Short Story. 20th.

Mercier, Louis Sebastian. Memoirs of the Year Two Thousand Five Hundred (original title: The Year Two Thousand Four Hundred and Forty. Treatise. 18th.

Miller, Walter M., Jr. A Canticle for Leibowitz. Novel. 20th.

More, Thomas. Utopia. Treatise. Renaissance.

Nourse, Alan E. The Bladerunner. Novel. 20th.

Nourse, Alan E. "The Martyr." Novel. 20th.

O'Donnell, K. M. "In the Pocket." Short Story. 20th.

Pohl, Frederik and C. M. Kornbluth. The Space Merchants (appeared in a condensed version as Gravy Planet). Novel. 20th.

Russ, Joanna. "When It Changed." Short Story. 20th.

Shango, J. R. "A Matter of Ethics." Short Story. 20th.

Shaw, George Bernard. Back to Methusaleh: a Metabiological Pentateuch. Drama. 20th.

Shelley, Mary. Frankenstein. Novel. 19th.

Silverberg, Robert. The World Inside. Novel. 20th.

Sladek, John T. "The Happy Breed." Short Story. 20th.

Smith, Cordwainer (Dr. M. A. Linebarger). "At the Gate of the Garden of Death" and "The Trial." In Norstrilia (also in The Planet Buyer). Novel. 20th.

Tiptree, James, Jr. "The Women Men Don't See." Short Story. 20th.

Tushnet, Leonard. "In Re Glover." Short Story. 20th.

Vonnegut, Kurt, Jr. Cat's Cradle. Novel. 20th.

Vonnegut, Kurt, Jr. Slaughterhouse Five. Novel. 20th.

Wells, H. G. The Island of Dr. Moreau. Novella. 19th.

White, E. B. "The Morning of the Day They Did It." Short
    Story. 20th.

Wolfe, Gene. "The Death of Dr. Island." Short Story. 20th.

Wyndham, John. Trouble With Lichen. Novel. 20th.

SEXUALITY

Adams, Henry. The Education of Henry Adams. Autobiography. 19th.

Aeschylus. Agamemnon. Drama. Classical.

Albee, Edward. The Death of Bessie Smith. Drama. 20th.

Anonymous. Aucassin and Nicolete. Tale. Medieval.

Anonymous. "Between March and April." Poem. Medieval.

Anonymous. The Celestina. Drama. Renaissance.

Anonymous. "I sing of a maiden." Poem. Medieval.

Anonymous. "Maiden on the moor lay" and "All night by the rose,
    rose." Poems. Medieval.

Anonymous. The Owl and the Nightingale. Poem. Medieval.

Anonymous. Sir Gawain and the Green Knight. Poem. Medieval.

Anonymous. "Western Wind." Poem. Medieval.

Anonymous. "Wulf and Eadwacer" or "Eadwacer." Poem. Medieval.

Anouilh, Jean. Ardèle. Drama. 20th.

Apuleius. The Golden Ass. Tale. Clasical.

Arden, John. The Happy Haven. Drama. 20th.

Aretino, Pietro. Dialogues. Dialogues. Renaissance.

Ariosto, Ludovico. Orlando Furioso. Poem. Renaissance.

Aristophanes. Lysistrata. Drama. Classical.

Arlen, Michael. The Green Hat. Novel. 20th.

Auden, W. H. "Miss Gee." Poem. 20th.

Austen, Jane. Emma. Novel. 19th.

Austen, Jane. Mansfield Park. Novel. 19th.

Austen, Jane. Persuasion. Novel. 19th.

Bacon, Francis. "Of Parents and Children" and "Of Marriage and
    the Single Life." Essays. Renaissance.

Balzac, Honoré de. Béatrix. Novel. 19th.

Balzac, Honoré de. Père Goriot. Novel. 19th.

Barth, John. The End of the Road. Novel. 20th.

Baudelaire, Charles Pierre. "Jewels" ("Les Bijoux"). Poem. 19th.

Baudelaire, Charles Pierre. "The Little Old Women" ("Les Petites
    Vielles"). Poem. 19th.

Baudelaire, Charles Pierre. "The Metamorphoses of a Vampire"
    ("Les Metamorphoses du Vampire"). Poem. 19th.

Beaumont, Francis and John Fletcher. Thierry and Theodoret.
    Drama. Renaissance.

Bellow, Saul. Mr. Sammler's Planet. Novel. 20th.

Benn, Gottfried. "Night Cafe." Poem. 20th.

Bernardin de Saint Pierre. Paul and Virginia. Novel. 18th.

Berryman, John. "Of Suicide." Poem. 20th.

The Bible. Apochrypha. Daniel and Susanna. Classical.

The Bible. Apochrypha. Tobit. Classical.

The Bible. I Corinthians. Classical.

The Bible. Genesis. Classical.

The Bible. Judges. Classical.

The Bible. Matthew. Classical.

The Bible. II Samuel. Classical.

The Bible. The Song of Solomon. Classical.

Blake, William. "The Little Boy Lost," "The Little Boy Found,"
    "The Little Girl Lost," "The Little Girl Found," "A Little
    BOY Lost," and "A Little GIRL Lost." Short Poems. 19th.

Blake, William. "London." Poem. 19th.

Blake, William. "The Sick Rose." Poem. 19th.

Blake, William. Paintings, Especially Those Accompanying Songs
    of Innocence and Experience. 19th.

Boccaccio, Giovanni. The Decameron: Day 1, Tale 5. Tale. Medieval.

Boccaccio, Giovanni. The Decameron: Day 2, Tale 10. Tale. Medieval.

Boccaccio, Giovanni. The Decameron: Day 3, Tales 1 & 10. Tales. Medieval.

Boccaccio, Giovanni. The Decameron: Day 9, Tale 3. Tale. Medieval.

Bowen, Elizabeth. Eva Trout. Novel. 20th.

Brome, Richard. The Antipodes. Drama. Renaissance.

Brontë, Charlotte. Jane Eyre. Novel. 19th.

Brontë, Charlotte. Villette. Novel. 19th.

Brontë, Emily Jane. "Ah, why, because the dazzling sun." Poem. 19th.

Bronte, Emily Jane. Wuthering Heights. Novel. 19th.

Brown, Geoff. I Want What I Want. Novel. 20th.

Browning, Elizabeth Barrett. Aurora Leigh. Poem. 19th.

Browning, Elizabeth Barrett. "The Runaway Slave at Pilgrim's Point." Poem. 19th.

Browning, Elizabeth Barrett. Sonnets from the Portuguese, no. 1. Sonnet. 19th.

Browning, Elizabeth Barrett. Sonnets from the Portuguese, no. 5. Sonnet. 19th.

Browning, Elizabeth Barrett. Sonnets from the Portuguese, nos. 10 & 11. Sonnets. 19th.

Browning, Elizabeth Barrett. Sonnets from the Portuguese, no. 22. Sonnet. 19th.

Browning, Robert. "The Bishop Orders His Tomb at Saint Praxed's Church." Poem. 19th.

Browning, Robert. The Ring and the Book. Novel in Verse. 19th.

Büchner, Georg. Woyzeck. Drama. 19th.

Buonarroti, Michel Angelo. "This new, singular beauty." Poem. Renaissance.

Burgess, Anthony. The Doctor Is Sick. Novel. 20th.

Burney, Fanny (Mme. D'Arblay). Evelina. Novel. 18th.

Burns, Robert. "The Deuk's Dang O'er my Daddie" ("The Duck's knocked over my Daddy"). Poem. 18th.

Burns, Robert. "John Anderson My Jo" and "John Anderson, My Jo." Poems. 18th.

Burns, Robert. "A Poet's Welcome to His Love-Begotten Daughter." Poem. 18th.

Burton, Robert. The Anatomy of Melancholy. Treatise. Renaissance.

Butler, Samuel. Hudibras. Long Poem. 18th.

Butler, Samuel. The Way of All Flesh. Novel. 19th.

Byron, George Gordon, Lord. Don Juan. Poem. 19th.

Byron, George Gordon, Lord. Manfred. Dramatic Poem. 19th.

Byron, George Gordon, Lord. "She Walks in Beauty." Poem. 19th.

Cable, George Washington. Dr. Sevier. Novel. 19th.

Campion, Thomas. "If any hath the heart to kill." Song. Renaissance.

Campion, Thomas. "It fell on a sommers day." Song. Renaissance.

Campion, Thomas. "There is a Garden in her face." Song. Renaissance.

Camus, Albert. Caligula. Drama. 20th.

Čapek, Karel. R.U.R. Drama. 20th.

Castiglione, Baldesar. The Book of the Courtier. Dialogues. Renaissance.

Catullus, C. Valerius. Carmina, no. 63. Poem. Classical.

Catullus, C. Valerius. Carmina, no. 71. Poem. Classical.

Céline, Louis-Ferdinand. Journey to the End of the Night. Novel. 20th.

Chaucer, Geoffrey. The Canterbury Tales, The Marriage Group: "The Wife of Bath's Tale," "The Clerk's Tale," "The Merchant's Tale," and "The Franklin's Tale." Tales. Medieval.

Chaucer, Geoffrey. The Canterbury Tales, "The Miller's Tale." Tale. Medieval.

Chaucer, Geoffrey. The Canterbury Tales, "The Reeve's Prologue." Sketch. Medieval.

Chaucer, Geoffrey. Troilus and Criseyde. Long Poem. Medieval.

Chekhov, Anton. Three Sisters. Drama. 19th.

Chekhov, Anton. Uncle Vanya. Drama. 19th.

Choromanski, Michal. Jealousy and Medicine. Novel. 20th.

Cleland, John. Memoirs of Fanny Hill. Novel. 18th.

Coleridge, Samuel Taylor. "Christabel." Poem. 19th.

Colette. The Innocent Libertine. Novel. 20th.

Congreve, William. The Way of the World. Drama. 18th.

Crabbe, George. The Parish Register. Long Poem. 18th.

Crashaw, Richard. "Epithalamium." Poem. Renaissance.

Crashaw, Richard. "The Flaming Heart Upon the Book and Picture of the seraphicall saint Teresa." Poem. Renaissance.

Cummings, E. E. "I like my body." Poem. 20th.

Daniel, Samuel. "When Winter snows upon the golden heares." Sonnet. Renaissance.

Dante Alighieri. The Divine Comedy. Long Poem. Medieval.

Dante Alighieri. La Vita Nuova (The New Life). Poems in a Prose Framework. Renaissance.

Defoe, Daniel. Moll Flanders. Novel. 18th.

Dekker, Thomas. The Honest Whore, Pt. I. Drama. Renaissance.

Dickens, Charles. David Copperfield. Novel. 19th.

Dickens, Charles. Dombey and Son. Novel. 19th.

Donne, John. "Batter my heart, three person'd God." Sonnet. Renaissance.

Donne, John. "The Comparison" (Elegy VIII). Poem. Renaissance.

Donne, John. "The Extasie." Poem. Renaissance.

Donne, John. "The Flea." Poem. Renaissance.

Donne, John. "A Nocturnall Upon S. Lucies Day: Being the Shortest Day." Poem. Renaissance.

Donne, John. "To His Mistris Going to Bed" (Elegy XIX). Poem. Renaissance.

Donne, John. "A Valediction Forbidding Mourning." Poem. Renaissance.

Dostoevsky, Fyodor. The Brothers Karamazov. Novel. 19th.

Dostoevsky, Fyodor. Crime and Punishment. Novel. 19th.

Dowson, Ernest. "Non Sum Qualis Eram Bonae Sub Regno Cynarae." Poem. 19th.

Doyle, Arthur Conan. "A Medical Document." Sketches. 19th.

Drabble, Margaret. The Millstone. Novel. 20th.

Dryden, John. All for Love. Drama. 18th.

Dryden, John. "To John Driden." Poem. 18th.

Dugan, Alan. "For Masturbation." Poem. 20th.

Eliot, George (Mary Anne Evans). Middlemarch. Novel. 19th.

Eliot, George (Mary Anne Evans). The Mill on the Floss. Novel.

Eliot, George (Mary Anne Evans). Mr. Gilfil's Love-Story. Novella. 19th.

Eliot, T. S. The Cocktail Party. Poetic Drama. 20th.

Eliot, T. S. "Gerontion." Poem. 20th.

Eliot, T. S. "The Love Song of J. Alfred Prufrock." Poem. 20th.

Euripides. The Bacchants. Drama. Classical.

Euripides. Electra. Drama. Classical.

Euripides. Hippolytus. Drama. Classical.

Euripides. Medea. Drama. Classical.

Farmer, José Philip. Riders of the Purple Wage. Novella. 20th.

Farquhar, George. The Beaux' Stratagem. Drama. 18th.

Faulkner, William. As I Lay Dying. Novel. 20th.

Faulkner, William. <u>Sanctuary</u>. Novel. 20th.

Faulkner, William. <u>The Sound and the Fury</u>. Novel. 20th.

Fielding, Henry. <u>Joseph Andrews</u>. Novel. 18th.

Fielding, Henry. "An Old Man Taught Wisdom or, The Virgin Un-masked. A Farce." Drama. 18th.

Fielding, Henry. <u>Tom Jones</u>. Novel. 18th.

Fitzgerald, F. Scott. <u>Tender Is the Night</u>. Novel. 20th.

Flaubert, Gustave. <u>Madame Bovary</u>. Novel. 19th.

Fletcher, John. <u>The Faithful Shepherdess</u>. Drama. Renaissance.

Ford, John. <u>The Broken Heart</u>. Drama. Renaissance.

Ford, John. <u>'Tis Pity She's a Whore</u>. Drama. Renaissance.

Freneau, Philip. <u>The House of Night</u>. Poem. 18th.

Fulke Greville, Lord Brooke. "Ah, silly Cupid, do you make it coy." Sonnet. Renaissance.

Fulke Greville, Lord Brooke. "The golden age was when the world was young." Poem. Renaissance.

Garcia Lorca, Federico. <u>Blood Wedding</u>. Drama. 20th.

Garcia Lorca, Federico. <u>The House of Bernard Alba</u>. Drama. 20th.

Garcia Lorca, Federico. <u>Yerma</u>. Drama. 20th.

Ginsberg, Allen. "Howl." Poem. 20th.

Giraudoux, Jean. <u>Electra</u>. Drama. 20th.

Goethe, Johann Wolfgang Von. <u>Faust</u>. Pt. I. Poetic Drama. 19th.

Golding, William. <u>Lord of the Flies</u>. Novel. 20th.

Goldsmith, Oliver. <u>She Stoops to Conquer</u>. Drama. 18th.

Gottfried von Strassburg. <u>Tristan and Isolt</u>. Tale. Medieval.

Graves, Robert. "Down, Wanton, Down!" Poem. 20th.

Hardy, Thomas. <u>Far From the Madding Crowd</u>. Novel. 19th.

Hardy, Thomas. "Her Death and After." Poem. 19th.

Hardy, Thomas. <u>Jude the Obscure</u>. Novel. 19th.

Hawthorne, Nathaniel. "The Birthmark." Short Story. 19th.

Hawthorne, Nathaniel. "Edward Fane's Rosebud." Sketch. 19th.

Hawthorne, Nathaniel. "Lady Eleanore's Mantle." Short Story. 19th.

Hawthorne, Nathaniel. "My Kinsman, Major Molineux." Short Story. 19th.

Hawthorne, Nathaniel. "Rappaccini's Daughter." Short Story. 19th.

Hawthorne, Nathaniel. <u>The Scarlet Letter</u>. Novel. 19th.

Heinlein, Robert A. <u>Time Enough For Love</u>. Novel. 20th.

Heller, Joseph. <u>Something Happened</u>. Novel. 20th.

Heloise. <u>The Letters of Abelard and Heloise</u>, No. 3. Letter. Medieval.

Hemingway, Ernest. <u>A Farewell to Arms</u>. Novel. 20th.

Hemingway, Ernest. "God Rest You Merry, Gentlemen." Short Story. 20th.

Hemingway, Ernest. "The Snows of Kilimanjaro." Short Story. 20th.

Henryson, Robert. <u>The Testament of Cresseid</u>. Poem. Medieval.

Herrick, Robert. "To Musique, to becalme his Fever." Poem. Renaissance.

Herrick, Robert. "To Perilla." Poem. Renaissance.

Herrick, Robert. "To the Virgins." Poem. Renaissance.

Herrick, Robert. "Upon Julia's Clothes." Poem. Renaissance.

Hesse, Hermann. <u>Steppenwolf</u>. Novel. 20th.

Homer. <u>The Odyssey</u>. Epic Poem. Classical.

Horace (Quintus Horatius Flaccus). <u>Odes</u>, Book I, no. XXV. Poem. Classical.

Howells, William Dean. <u>A Modern Instance</u> and <u>The Rise of Silas Lapham</u>. Novels. 19th.

Hughes, Langston. "Sylvester's Dying Bed." Poem. 20th.

Hughes, Richard. <u>A High Wind in Jamacia</u> (Also published as <u>The Innocent Voyage</u>). Novel. 20th.

Hughes, Ted. "Crow's First Lesson." Poem. 20th.

Hugo, Victor. <u>The Hunchback of Notre Dame</u>. Novel. 19th.

Hugo, Victor. <u>Les Miserables</u>. Novel. 19th.

Huxley, Aldous. <u>Brave New World</u>. Novel. 20th.

Ibsen, Henrik. <u>Ghosts</u>. Drama. 19th.

Ibsen, Henrik. <u>Hedda Gabler</u>. Drama. 19th.

Ibsen, Henrik. <u>Little Eyolf</u>. Drama. 19th.

Ibsen, Henrik. <u>The Master Builder</u>. Drama. 19th.

Ionesco, Eugene. <u>The Future Is in Eggs</u>. Drama. 20th.

James, Henry. <u>The Bostonians</u>. Novel. 19th.

James, Henry. <u>Daisy Miller: A Study</u>. Novella. 19th.

James, Henry. <u>The Turn of the Screw</u>. Novella. 19th.

James, Henry. <u>What Maisie Knew</u>. Novel. 19th.

Jean de Meun. <u>The Romance of the Rose</u>. Long Poem. Medieval.

Johnson, Samuel. <u>A Dictionary of the English Language</u>. Dictionary. 18th.

Jones, LeRoi (Imamu Amiri Baraka). <u>Dutchman</u>. Drama. 20th.

Jonson, Benjamin. "Another in Defence of Their Inconstancie." Poem. Renaissance.

Jonson, Benjamin. <u>Bartholomew Fair</u>. Drama. Renaissance.

Jonson, Benjamin. "Still to be neat." Song. Renaissance.

Jonson, Benjamin. "To Celia." Song. Renaissance.

Jonson, Benjamin. <u>Volpone</u>. Drama. Renaissance.

Joyce, James. <u>Portrait of the Artist as a Young Man</u>. Novel. 20th.

Joyce, James. <u>Ulysses</u>. Novel. 20th.

Keats, John. "Bright Star! Would I Were." Sonnet. 19th.

Keats, John. "La Belle Dame Sans Merci." Poem. 19th.

Keats, John. Letters to Charles Brown, Sun., Aug. 20, 1820; Sept. 30, 1820. Letters. 19th.

Keats, John. Letters to Fanny Brawne. Letters. 19th.

Keats, John. "Light feet, dark violet eyes." Sonnet. 19th.

Kesey, Ken. <u>One Flew Over the Cuckoo's Nest</u>. Novel. 20th.

Keyes, Daniel. <u>Flowers for Algernon</u>. Novella. 20th.

Kingsley, Charles. <u>Two Years Ago</u>. Novel. 19th.

Kingsley, Sidney. <u>Men in White</u>. Drama. 20th.

Kyd, Thomas. <u>The Spanish Tragedy</u>. Drama. Renaissance.

Lawrence, D. H. "The Blind Man." Short Story. 20th.

Lawrence, D. H. <u>The Fox</u>. Novella. 20th.

Lawrence, D. H. "The Horse Dealer's Daughter." Short Story. 20th.

Lawrence, D. H. <u>Lady Chatterley's Lover</u>. Novel. 20th.

Lawrence, D. H. <u>Psychoanalysis and the Unconscious</u> and <u>Fantasia of the Unconscious</u>. Long Essays. 20th.

Lawrence, D. H. <u>Sons and Lovers</u>. Novel. 20th.

Leduc, Violette. <u>The Taxi</u>. Short Story. 20th.

Leduc, Violette. <u>Thérèse and Isabelle</u> and <u>La Bâtarde</u>. Novella and Autobiography. 20th.

LeGuin, Ursula. <u>the Left Hand of Darkness</u>. Novel. 20th.

Lessing, Doris. <u>A Proper Marriage</u>. Novel. 20th.

Lessing, Doris. <u>The Summer Before the Dark</u>. Novel. 20th.

London, Jack. "Koolau the Leper." Short Story. 19th.

Longfellow, Henry Wadsworth. <u>Evangeline</u>. Long Poem. 19th.

Lovelace, Richard. "To Althea, from Prison." Poem. Renaissance.

<u>Love's Cure; or The Martial Maid</u>. Drama. Renaissance.

Lyly, John. <u>Endymion</u>. Drama. Renaissance.

Machiavelli, Niccolo. <u>Mandragola</u>. Drama. Renaissance.

Mackenzie, Henry. <u>The Man of Feeling</u>. Novel. 18th.

Mailer, Norman. An American Dream. Novel. 20th.

Malory, Thomas. The Book of Sir Launcelot and Queen Guinevere and The Most Piteous Tale of the Morte Arthur. Tales. Medieval.

Malzberg, Barry. "Out from Ganymede." Short Story. 20th.

Mann, Thomas. The Magic Mountain. Novel. 20th.

Marlowe, Christopher. The Tragical History of Doctor Faustus. Drama. Renaissance.

Marlowe, Christopher and George Chapman. Hero and Leander. Poem. Renaissance.

Marlowe, Christopher and Walter Raleigh. "The Passionate Shepherd to His Love" and "The Nymph's Reply." Poems. Renaissance.

Marston, John. The Fawn. Drama. Renaissance.

Marston, John. The Metamorphosis of Pigmalions Image. Poem. Renaissance.

Marvell, Andrew. "The Nymph complaining for the Death of her Fawn." Poem. Renaissance.

Marvell, Andrew. "To His Coy Mistress." Poem. Renaissance.

Massinger, Philip. The Unnatural Combat. Drama. Renaissance.

Maugham, W. Somerset. Liza of Lambeth. Novel. 20th.

Maugham, W. Somerset. Of Human Bondage. Novel. 20th.

Maupassant, Guy de. "Ball-of-Fat." Short Story. 19th.

Maupassant, Guy de. "Madame Baptiste." Short Story. 19th.

Maupassant, Guy de. "Useless Beauty." Short Story. 19th.

McCullers, Carson. The Ballad of the Sad Café. Novella. 20th.

McCullers, Carson. The Heart Is a Lonely Hunter. Novel. 20th.

McCullers, Carson. Reflections in a Golden Eye. Novella. 20th.

Melville, Herman. "I and My Chimney." Short Story. 19th.

Melville, Herman. Moby Dick. Novel. 19th.

Melville, Herman. "The Paradise of Bachelors" and "The Tartarus of Maids." Sketches. 19th.

Melville, Herman. Pierre, or the Ambiguities. Novel. 19th.

Meredith, George. The Ordeal of Richard Feverel. Novel. 19th.

Meredith, George. Sonnet I. From Modern Love. Sonnet. 19th.

Meredith, George. "The Teaching of the Nude." Poem. 19th.

Middleton, Thomas. The Changeling. Drama. Renaissance.

Middleton, Thomas. A Chaste Maid in Cheapside. Drama. Renaissance.

Miller, Arthur. The Crucible. Drama. 20th.

Miller, Vassar. "Fantasia." Poem. 20th.

Miller, Vassar. "Spastics: (First poem from Handi-Lib)." Poem. 20th.

Milton, John. Comus: A Mask Presented at Ludlow Castle. Poem. Renaissance.

Milton, John. Paradise Lost. Epic Poem. Renaissance.

Milton, John. Samson Agonistes. Poem. Renaissance.

Montaigne, Michel Eyquem de. "On the Force of the Imagination." Essay. Renaissance.

Montaigne, Michel Eyquem de. "Upon Some Verses of Virgil." Essay. Renaissance.

Murdoch, Irish. Bruno's Dream. Novel. 20th.

Nabokov, Vladimir. Lolita. Novel. 20th.

Nashe, Thomas. The Unfortunate Traveler. Tale. Renaissance.

Oates, Joyce Carol. Wonderland. Novel. 20th.

O'Brien, Edna. August Is a Wicked Month. Novel. 20th.

O'Connor, Flannery. "Good Country People." Short Story. 20th.

O'Connor, Frank. "The Drunkard," "Judas," and "My Oedipus Complex." Short Stories. 20th.

Omar Khayyam. The Rubaiyat. Collection of Poems. 19th.

O'Neill, Eugene. Desire Under the Elms. Drama. 20th.

O'Neill, Eugene. Mourning Becomes Electra. Drama. 20th.

O'Neill, Eugene. Strange Interlude. Drama. 20th.

Ovid (Publius Ovidius Naso). Amores. Book I, Elegy iv. Poem. Classical.

Ovid (Publius Ovidius Naso). Amores. Book I, Elegy vii. Poem. Classical.

Ovid (Publius Ovidius Naso). Amores. Book II, Elegy iv. Poem. Classical.

Ovid (Publius Ovidius Naso). Amores. Book III, Elegy vii. Poem. Classical.

Ovid (Publius Ovidius Naso). Metamorphoses. Poem. Classical.

Parnell, Thomas. "On a Lady with Foul Breath." Poem. 18th.

Pasternak, Boris. Doctor Zhivago. Novel. 20th.

Pepys, Samuel. The Diary: Selections. Diary. 18th.

Percival, James Gates. "Consumption." Poem. 19th.

Percy, Walker. Love in the Ruins. Novel. 20th.

Percy, Walker. The Moviegoer. Novel. 20th.

Petrarch (Francesco Petrarca). Canzoniere, no. CLIX (sonnet no. 126). Sonnet. Medieval.

Petrarch (Francesco Petrarca). Canzoniere, no. CXCV (sonnet no. 162). Sonnet. Medieval.

Petronius Arbiter. Satyricon. Satiric Sketches. Classical.

Phelps, Elizabeth Stuart. Dr. Zay. Novel. 19th.

Pinter, Harold. The Homecoming. Drama. 20th.

Plath, Sylvia. The Bell Jar. Novel. 20th.

Plath, Sylvia. "Fever 103°." Poem. 20th.

Plato. Symposium. Dialogue. Classical.

Plautus. Pseudolus. Drama. Classical.

Poe, Edgar Allan. "Ligeia." Short Story. 19th.

Pope, Alexander. "Eloisa to Abelard." Poem. 18th.

Pope, Alexander. The Rape of the Lock. Poem. 18th.

Proust, Marcel. Remembrance of Things Past. Novel. 20th.

Rabelais, Francois. Gargantua and Pantagruel. Tales. Renaissance.

Racine, Jean. Phaedra. Drama. 18th.

Réage, Pauline. The Story of O. Novel. 20th.

Rechy, John. City of Night; and Selby, Hubert. Last Exit to Brooklyn. Novels. 20th.

Remarque, Erich Maria. Arch of Triumph. Novel. 20th.

Rhys, Jean. Voyage in the Dark. Novel. 20th.

Richardson, Samuel. Clarissa. Novel. 18th.

Rochester, Earl of (John Wilmot). "The Imperfect Enjoyment." Poem. 18th.

Rochester, Earl of (John Wilmot). "Signior Dildo." Poem. 18th.

Rochester, Earl of (John Wilmot). "Song" ("By all love's soft, yet mighty powers"). Poem. 18th.

Rochester, Earl of (John Wilmot). "Song" ("Love a woman? You're an Ass!"). Poem. 18th.

Ronsard, Pierre de. "Double-winged monster" ("Cusin, monstre à double aile, au mufle Elephantin"). Sonnet. Renaissance.

Ronsard, Pierre de. "Seated beside the hearth" ("La mois d'Augst bouillonnoit d'une chaleur esprise"). Sonnet. Renaissance.

Ronsard, Pierre de. "These sonnets of love" ("Je chantois ces sonnets, amoureux d'une Helene"). Sonnet. Renaissance.

Ronsard, Pierre de. "When you are old" ("Quand vous serez bien vielle, au soir, à la chandelle"). Sonnet. Renaissance.

Rossetti, Christina. "Goblin Market." Poem. 19th.

Rossetti, Christina. "Remember" and "Song." Poems. 19th.

Rossetti, Dante Gabriel. "The Blessed Damozel." Poem. 19th.

Rossetti, Dante Gabriel. "Body's Beauty." Sonnet. 19th.

Rossetti, Dante Gabriel. "Life-in-Love" and "Death-in-Love." Sonnets. 19th.

Roth, Philip. The Breast. Novella. 20th.

Roth, Philip. "Epstein." Short Story. 20th.

Roth, Philip. Portnoy's Complaint. Novel. 20th.

Sade, Donatien Alphonse François, Marquis de. Justine. Novel. 19th.

Sade, Donatien Alphonse Francois, Marquis de. Philosophy in the Bedroom. Tale. 19th.

Salinger, J. D. The Catcher in the Rye. Novel. 20th.

Sappho. On old age and sexuality. Poem. Classical.

Sappho. To Brachea. Poem. Classical.

Sartre, Jean-Paul. "The Room." Short Story. 20th.

Schnitzler, Arthur. A Confirmed Bachelor (Also published as Dr. Graesler). Novel. 20th.

Schnitzler, Arthur. La Ronde (Also published as Reigen and Hands Around). Drama. 20th.

Schnitzler, Arthur. "The Man of Honour" (Also published as "The Murderer"). Short Story. 20th.

Schnitzler, Arthur. Mother and Son (Also published as Beatrice). Novella. 20th.

Schnitzler, Arthur. My Youth in Vienna. Autobiography. 20th.

Schnitzler, Arthur. The Spring Sonata (Also published as Bertha Garlan). Novel. 20th.

Selzer, Richard. The Rituals of Surgery. Short Stories. 20th.

Sexton, Anne. "The Ballad of the Lonely Masturbator." Poem. 20th.

Sexton, Anne. "The Breast." Poem. 20th.

Shadwell, Thomas. The Virtuoso. Drama. 18th.

Shaffer, Peter. Equus. Drama. 20th.

Shakespeare, William. All's Well That Ends Well. Drama. Renaissance.

Shakespeare, William. Antony and Cleopatra. Drama. Renaissance.

Shakespeare, William. As You Like It. Drama. Renaissance.

Shakespeare, William. "Th' expense of spirit in a waste of shame." Sonnet. Renaissance.

Shakespeare, William. Hamlet. Drama. Renaissance.

Shakespeare, William. King Lear. Drama. Renaissance.

Shakespeare, William. "Let me not to the marriage of true minds admit impediments." Sonnet. Renaissance.

Shakespeare, William. Love's Labours Lost. Drama. Renaissance.

Shakespeare, William. Macbeth. Drama. Renaissance.

Shakespeare, William. Measure for Measure. Drama. Renaissance.

Shakespeare, William. The Merchant of Venice. Drama. Renaissance.

Shakespeare, William. A Midsummer-Night's Dream. Drama. Renaissance.

Shakespeare, William. Much Ado About Nothing. Drama. Renaissance.

Shakespeare, William. "my love is as a fever, longing still." Sonnet. Renaissance.

Shakespeare, William. "My mistress' eyes are nothing like the sun." Sonnet. Renaissance.

Shakespeare, William. Othello. Drama. Renaissance.

Shakespeare, William. Pericles, Prince of Tyre. Drama. Renaissance.

Shakespeare, William. Richard III. Drama. Renaissance.

Shakespeare, William. Romeo and Juliet. Drama. Renaissance.

Shakespeare, William. "Shall I compare thee to a summer's day?" Sonnet. Renaissance.

Shakespeare, William. The Taming of the Shrew. Drama. Renaissance.

Shakespeare, William. The Tempest. Drama. Renaissance.

Shakespeare, William. "Those hours that with gentle work did Frame." Sonnet. Renaissance.

Shakespeare, William. Troilus and Cressida. Drama. Renaissance.

Shakespeare, William. Twelfth Night. Drama. Renaissance.

Shakespeare, William. "Two loves I have of comfort and despair." Sonnet. Renaissance.

Shakespeare, William. Venus and Adonis. Poem. Renaissance.

Shakespeare, William. "When my love swears that she is made of truth." Sonnet. Renaissance.

Shakespeare, William. The Winter's Tale. Drama. Renaissance.

Shaw, George Bernard. Man and Superman. Drama. 20th.

Sheed, Wilfrid. People Will Always Be Kind. Novel. 20th.

Shelley, Percy Bysshe. The Cenci. Poetic Drama. 19th.

Shelley, Percy Bysshe. "The Indian Serenade." Poem. 19th.

Sidney, Philip. Arcadia. Tales and Poems. Renaissance.

Sidney, Philip. Four Sonnets Made when his Lady had Pain in her Face. Sonnets. Renaissance.

Sidney, Philip. "Thou blind man's mark, thou fool's self-chosen snare" and "Leave me, O love which reachest but to dust." Sonnets. Renaissance.

Sidney, Philip. "Who will in fairest book of nature know." Sonnet. Renaissance.

Silverberg, Robert. The World Inside. Novel. 20th.

Skelton, John. Philip Sparrow. Poem. Renaissance.

Skelton, John. The Tunning of Elinour Rumming. Poem. Renaissance.

Skelton, John. "Womanhood, Wanton, Ye Want." Poem. Renaissance.

Sophocles. Electra. Drama. Classical.

Sophocles. Oedipus Rex. Drama. Classical.

Spark, Muriel. Memento Mori. Novel. 20th.

The Spectator, no. 431. Essay. 18th.

Spenser, Edmund. Epithalamion. Poem. Renaissance.

Spenser, Edmund. The Faerie Queene. Poems. Renaissance.

Spenser, Edmund. "Februarie" from The Shepheardes Calender. Poem. Renaissance.

Spenser, Edmund. "Like as a huntsman after weary chase." Sonnet. Renaissance.

Spenser, Edmund. "One day I wrote her name upon the strand." Sonnet. Renaissance.

Stein, Gertrude. Melanctha. Novella. 20th.

Steinbeck, John. Of Mice and Men. Novel. 20th.

Sterne, Laurence. The Life and Opinions of Tristram Shandy, Gent. Novel. 18th.

Strindberg, August. The Father. Drama. 19th.

Suckling, John. "A Ballade. Upon a Wedding." Poem. Renaissance.

Suckling, John. "The Deformed Mistress." Poem. Renaissance.

Suckling, John. "Sir J. S." ("Out upon it"). Poem. Renaissance.

Suckling, John. "Upon T. C. having the Pox." Poem. Renaissance.

Suckling, John. "Why so pale and wan fond Lover?" Poem. Renaissance.

Swados, Harvey. Celebration. Novel. 20th.

Swift, Jonathan. "Cassinus and Peter. A Tragical Elegy." Poem. 18th.

Swift, Jonathan. "The Lady's Dressing Room." Poem. 18th.

Swift, Jonathan (?). "A Love Poem. From a Physician to his Mistress. Written at London." Poem. 18th.

Swift, Jonathan. "Strephon and Chloe." Poem. 18th.

Swinburne, Algernon Charles. "The Garden of Proserpine." Poem. 19th.

Swinburne, Algernon Charles. "Hermaphroditus." Poem. 19th.

Tanizaki, Junichiro. Diary of a Mad Old Man. Novel. 20th.

Tasso, Torquato. Jerusalem Delivered (Gerusalemme Liberata). Epic Poem. Renaissance.

Tennyson, Alfred. "Fatima." Poem. 19th.

Tennyson, Alfred. "The Lady of Shalott." Poem. 19th.

Tennyson, Alfred. "Locksley Hall" and "Locksley Hall Sixty Years After." Long Poems. 19th.

Tennyson, Alfred. "Maud." Long Poem. 19th.

Tennyson, Alfred. "Oenone." Poem. 19th.

Tennyson, Alfred. "Tithonus." Poem. 19th.

Thackeray, William Makepeace. The History of Henry Esmond. Novel.
    19th.

Thackeray, William Makepeace. Vanity Fair. Novel. 19th.

Thomas, Dylan. "Love in the Asylum." Poem. 20th.

Thoreau, Henry David. Walden. Treatise. 19th.

Tolstoy, Leo. The Kreutzer Sonata. Novella. 19th.

Tourneur, Cyril. The Atheist's Tragedy. Drama. Renaissance.

Tourneur, Cyril. The Revenger's Tragedy. Drama. Renaissance.

Turgenev, Ivan. "The District Doctor." Short Story. 19th.

Villon, Francois. The Testament. Poem. Medieval.

Virgil (Publius Vergilius Maro). Aeneid. Epic Poem. Classical.

Voltaire, Francois-Marie Arouet. Candide. Tale. 18th.

Webster, John. The Duchess of Malfi. Drama. Renaissance.

Webster, John. The White Devil. Drama. Renaissance.

Weiss, Peter. The Persecution and Assassination of Jean-Paul
    Marat . . . . (Marat/Sade). Drama. 20th.

Wells, H. G. "The Cone." Short Story. 19th.

Wharton, Edith. "Atrophy." Short Story. 20th.

Wharton, Edith. "Beatrice Palmato." Outline and Fragment of a
    Novel. 20th.

Wharton, Edith. Ethan Frome. Novel. 20th.

Wharton, Edith. "Roman Fever." Short Story. 20th.

Wharton, Edith. "Souls Belated." Short Story. 20th.

White, Patrick. The Eye of the Storm. Novel. 20th.

White, Patrick. The Solid Mandala. Novel. 20th.

Whitman, Walt. "I Sing the Body Electric." Poem. 19th.

Whitman, Walt. "Song of Myself." Poem. 19th.

Wilde, Oscar. Salome. Drama. 19th.

Williams, Tennessee. Cat on a Hot Tin Roof. Drama. 20th.

Williams, Tennessee. Streetcar Named Desire. Drama. 20th.

Williams, Tennessee. Suddenly Last Summer. Drama. 20th.

Williams, Tennessee. Summer and Smoke. Drama. 20th.

Williams, William Carlos. The Cure. Drama. 20th.

Williams, William Carlos. A Dream of Love. Drama. 20th.

Williams, William Carlos. "Portrait of a Woman at Her Bath."
    Poem. 20th.

Williams, William Carlos. "The Use of Force." Short Story. 20th.

Woolf, Virginia. The Waves. Novel. 20th.

Wordsworth, William. "Ruth." Poem. 19th.

Wyatt, Thomas. "My galley charged with forgetfulness." Sonnet.
    Renaissance.

Wyatt, Thomas. "They flee from me, that sometime did me seek."
    Poem. Renaissance.

Wycherley, William. The Country Wife. Drama. 18th.

Yeats, William Butler. Crazy Jane Talks with the Bishop." Poem.
    20th.

Yeats, William Butler. "Her Vision in the Wood." Poem. 20th.

Yeats, William Butler. "A Last Confession." Poem. 20th.

Yeats, William Butler. "Leda and the Swan." Sonnet. 20th.

Zola, Emile. Dr. Pascal. Novel. 19th.

Zola, Emile. Fécondité (From Les Quatres Evangiles). Novel. 19th.

Zola, Emile. Germinal. Novel. 19th.

Zola, Emile. Une Page D'Amour. Novel. 19th.

SEXUAL ROLES

Aeschylus. Agamemnon. Drama. Classical.

Aeschylus. The Eumenides. Drama. Classical.

Alcott, Louisa May. Hospital Sketches. Sketches. 19th.

Anonymous. Aucassin and Nicolete. Tale. Medieval.

Anonymous. "Charm for a Sudden Stitch." Poem. Medieval.

Ariosto, Ludovico. Orlando Furioso. Poem. Renaissance.

Aristophanes. Lysistrata. Drama. Classical.

Arking, Linda. "Certain Hard Places." Short Story. 20th.

Austen, Jane. Mansfield Park. Novel. 19th.

Austen, Jane. Persuasion. Novel. 19th.

Balzac, Honoré de. Béatrix. Novel. 19th.

Balzac, Honoré de. The Country Doctor. Novel. 19th.

Beerbohm, Max. "A Defense of Cosmetics." Essay. 19th.

Bellamy, Edward. Looking Backward, 2000-1887. Novel. 19th.

The Bible. Apocrypha. Judith. Classical.

The Bible. Esther. Classical.

The Bible. Genesis. Classical.

The Bible. Judges. Classical.

The Bible. Luke. Classical.

The Bible. Proverbs. Classical.

Boswell, James. The Life of Samuel Johnson. Biography. 18th.

Brome, Richard. The Antipodes. Drama. Renaissance.

Brontë, Charlotte. Villette. Novel. 19th.

Brown, Geoff. I Want What I Want. Novel. 20th.

Browning, Elizabeth Barrett. Aurora Leigh. Poem. 19th.

Browning, Robert. The Ring and the Book. Novel in Verse. 19th.

Burney, Fanny (Mme. D'Arblay). Evelina. Novel. 18th.

Burns, Robert. "The Rights of Women." Poem. 18th.

Butler, Samuel. Hudibras. Long Poem. 18th.

Byron, George Gordon, Lord. Childe Harold's Pilgrimage. Poem.
    19th.

Byron, George Gordon, Lord. Don Juan. Poem. 19th.

Byron, George Gordon, Lord. "Lines On Hearing That Lady Byron
    Was Ill." Poem. 19th.

Byron, George Gordon, Lord. "Stanzas to Augusta." Poem. 19th.

Campanella, Tomaso. City of the Sun. Treatise. Renaissance.

Castiglione, Baldesar. The Book of the Courtier. Dialogues.
    Renaissance.

Catullus, C. Valerius. Carmina, no. 63. Poem. Classical.

Cervantes Saavedra, Miguel de. Don Quixote. Tale. Renaissance.

Chaucer, Geoffrey. The Canterbury Tales, The Marriage Group:
    "The Wife of Bath's Tale," "The Clerk's Tale," "The Merchant's
    Tale," and "The Franklin's Tale." Tales. Medieval.

Choromanski, Michal. Jealousy and Medicine. Novel. 20th.

Clare, John. "Don Juan" and "Child Harold." Poems. 19th.

Colette. The Innocent Libertine. Novel. 20th.

Collins, Wilkie. The Woman in White. Novel. 19th.

Congreve, William. The Way of the World. Drama. 18th.

Cooper, James Fenimore. The Last of the Mohicans. Novel. 19th.

Crabbe, George. Inebrity. Long Poem. 18th.

Crane, Stephen. Maggie. Novella. 19th.

Defoe, Daniel. Moll Flanders. Novel. 18th.

De Forest, John William. Miss Ravenal's Conversion from Seces-
    sion to Loyalty. Novel. 19th.

Dickens, Charles. Bleak House. Novel. 19th.

Dickens, Charles. David Copperfield. Novel. 19th.

Dickens, Charles. Martin Chuzzlewit. Novel. 19th.

Dickens, Charles. The Pickwick Papers. Novel. 19th.

Donne, John. "Batter my heart, three person'd God" (Holy Sonnet XIV). Sonnet. Renaissance.

Donne, John. "To His Mistris Going to Bed" (Elegy XIX). Poem. Renaissance.

Dryden, John. All for Love. Drama. 18th.

Dryden, John. "To John Driden." Poem. 18th.

Dürrenmatt, Friedrich. The Physicists. Drama. 20th.

Eliot, George (Mary Anne Evans). Adam Bede. Novel. 19th.

Eliot, George (Mary Anne Evans). Middlemarch. Novel. 19th.

Eliot, George (Mary Anne Evans). The Mill on the Floss. Novel. 19th.

Euripides. The Bacchants. Drama. Classical.

Euripides. Medea. Drama. Classical.

Euripides. The Trojan Women. Drama. Classical.

Fielding, Henry. Amelia. Novel. 18th.

Fielding, Henry. Joseph Andrews. Novel. 18th.

Fielding, Henry. Tom Jones. Novel. 18th.

Flaubert, Gustave. Madame Bovary. Novel. 19th.

Garcia Lorca, Federico. Yerma. Drama. 20th.

Gaskell, Elizabeth. Cranford. Novel. 19th.

Gilman, Charlotte Perkins Stetson. The Yellow Wallpaper. Short Story. 19th.

Giraudoux, Jean. Electra. Drama. 20th.

Goldsmith, Oliver. The Vicar of Wakefield. Novel. 18th.

Graves, Robert. "Lollocks." Poem. 20th.

Hamilton, Patrick. Angel Street (Gas Light). Drama. 19th.

Hardy, Thomas. Far From the Madding Crowd. Novel. 19th.

Hawthorne, Nathaniel. The Scarlet Letter. Novel. 19th.

Heinlein, Robert A. Time Enough For Love. Novel. 20th.

Hellman, Lillian. The Children's Hour. Drama. 20th.

Heloise. The Letters of Abelard and Heloise, no. 3. Letter. Medieval.

Hemingway, Ernest. The Old Man and the Sea. Novella. 20th.

Hemingway, Ernest. "The Snows of Kilimanjaro." Short Story. 20th.

Hesiod. Theogony. Long Poem. Classical.

Holmes, Oliver Wendell. Elsie Venner. Novel. 19th.

Holmes, Oliver Wendell. A Mortal Antipathy. Novel. 19th.

Howells, William Dean. Dr. Breen's Practice. Novel. 19th.

Ibsen, Henrik. A Doll's House. Drama. 19th.

Ibsen, Henrik. Hedda Gabler. Drama. 19th.

Ibsen, Henrik. The Master Builder. Drama. 19th.

James, Henry. The Bostonians. Novel. 19th.

James, Henry. The Portrait of a Lady. Novel. 19th.

Joyce, James. Ulysses. Novel. 20th.

Juvenal (Decimus Iunius Iuvenalis). Satires, no. VI. Poem. Classical.

Keats, John. "Light feet, dark violet eyes." Sonnet. 19th.

Kipling, Rudyard. "Baa Baa Black Sheep." Short Story. 19th.

Lamb, Charles. "Modern Gallantry." Essay. 19th.

Lamb, Charles. "Written on Christmas Day, 1797." Poem. 19th.

Lawrence, D. H. The Fox. Novella. 20th.

Lawrence, D. H. Psychoanalysis and the Unconscious and Fantasia of the Unconscious. Long Essays. 20th.

LeGuin, Ursula. the Left Hand of Darkness. Novel. 20th.

Lessing, Doris. A Proper Marriage. Novel. 20th.

Lessing, Doris. The Summer Before the Dark. Novel. 20th.

Love's Cure; or The Martial Maid. Drama. Renaissance.

Luce, Clare Booth. The Women. Drama. 20th.

Lucian of Samosata. "The Disowned." Essay. Classical.

Mailer, Norman. An American Dream. Novel. 20th.

Maupassant, Guy de. "Ball-of-Fat." Short Story. 19th.

Maupassant, Guy de. "The First Snowfall." Short Story. 19th.

Maupassant, Guy de. "Madame Baptiste." Short Story. 19th.

Maupassant, Guy de. "Useless Beauty." Short Story. 19th.

Mencken, H. L. In Defense of Women. Essays. 20th.

Mercier, Louis Sebastian. Memoirs of the Year Two Thousand Five Hundred (original title: The Year Two Thousand Four Hundred and Forty). Treatise. 18th.

Middleton, Thomas. A Fair Quarrel. Drama. Renaissance.

Middleton, Thomas and Thomas Dekker. The Roaring Girl. Drama. Renaissance.

Milton, John. Paradise Lost. Epic Poem. Renaissance.

Montaigne, Michel Eyquem de. "Upon Some Verses of Virgil." Essay. Renaissance.

Mortimer, Penelope. The Pumpkin Eater. Novel. 20th.

Norris, Frank. A Man's Woman. Novella. 19th.

The Old Law. Drama. Renaissance.

Old Women as Prophets. Classical.

Olsen, Tillie. "Tell Me a Riddle." Short Story. 20th.

Phelps, Elizabeth Stuart. Dr. Zay. Novel. 19th.

Pinter, Harold. The Homecoming. Drama. 20th.

Plath, Sylvia. "Daddy." Poem. 20th.

Plath, Sylvia. "Lady Lazarus." Poem. 20th.

Plato. The Republic. Dialogue. Classical.

Pope, Alexander. The Rape of the Lock. Poem. 18th.

Reade, Charles. The Cloister and the Hearth and A Woman-Hater. Novels. 19th.

Réage, Pauline. The Story of O. Novel. 20th.

Remarque, Erich Maria. Arch of Triumph. Novel. 20th.

Rhys, Jean. Voyage in the Dark. Novel. 20th.

Richardson, Samuel. Clarissa. Novel. 18th.

Rossetti, Dante Gabriel. "The Blessed Damozel." Poem. 19th.

Russ, Joanna. "When It Changed." Short Story. 20th.

Sackville-West, V. All Passion Spent. Novel. 20th.

Sade, Donatien Alphonse François, Marquis de. Philosophy in the Bedroom. Tale. 19th.

Sarton, May. Mrs. Stevens Hears the Mermaids Singing. Novel. 20th.

Schnitzler, Arthur. The Spring Sonata (Also published as Bertha Garlan). Novel. 20th.

Sexton, Anne. "In Celebration of My Uterus." Poem. 20th.

Shakespeare, William. All's Well That Ends Well. Drama. Renaissance.

Shakespeare, William. Coriolanus. Drama. Renaissance.

Shakespeare, William. King Lear. Drama. Renaissance.

Shakespeare, William. Macbeth. Drama. Renaissance.

Shakespeare, William. The Merchant of Venice. Drama. Renaissance.

Shakespeare, William. A Midsummer-Night's Dream. Drama. Renaissance.

Shakespeare, William. The Taming of the Shrew. Drama. Renaissance.

Shakespeare, William. Twelfth Night. Drama. Renaissance.

Shakespeare, William. Venus and Adonis. Poem. Renaissance.

Shaw, George Bernard. Back to Methuselah: a Metabiological Pentateuch. Drama. 20th.

Shaw, George Bernard. _Man and Superman_. Drama. 20th.

Shelley, Percy Bysshe. _The Cenci_. Poetic Drama. 19th.

Shelley, Percy Bysshe. "The Indian Serenade." Poem. 19th.

Sidney, Philip. _Arcadia_. Tales and Poems. Renaissance.

Skelton, John. "To Mistress Margaret Hussey." Poem. Renaissance.

Smollett, Tobias. _The Expedition of Humphry Clinker_. Novel. 18th.

The Spectator, no. 435. Essay. 18th.

Spenser, Edmund. _The Faerie Queene_. Poems. Renaissance.

Strindberg, August. _The Father_. Drama. 19th.

SWift, Jonathan. "The Furniture of a Woman's Mind." Poem. 18th.

Swift, Jonathan. _Gulliver's Travels_. Satiric Tales. 18th.

Tasso, Torquato. _Jerusalem Delivered_ (_Gerusalemme Liberata_). Epic Poem. Renaissance.

Tennyson, Alfred. _The Princess: A Medley_. Poem. 19th.

Thackeray, William Makepeace. _Vanity Fair_. Novel. 19th.

Tiptree, James, Jr. "The Women Men Don't See." Short Story. 20th.

Tolstoy, Leo. _The Kreutzer Sonata_. Novella. 19th.

Twain, Mark. _Adventures of Huckleberry Finn_. Novel. 19th.

Twain, Mark. _The Diary of Adam and Eve_. Sketch. 19th.

Twain, Mark. "Experience of the McWilliamses with Membranous Croup." Short Story. 19th.

Webster, John. _The White Devil_. Drama. Renaissance.

Wharton, Edith. "The Pelican." Short Story. 20th.

Wharton, Edith. "Souls Belated." Short Story. 20th.

Whittier, John Greenleaf. "The Barefoot Boy." Poem. 19th.

Wittig, Monique. _The Lesbian Body_. Novel. 20th.

Woolf, Virginia. _A Room of One's Own_. Novel. 20th.

Wordsworth, William. "Character of the Happy Warrior." Poem. 19th.

Wordsworth, William. "She Was a Phantom of Delight." Poem. 19th.

Wyndham, John. _Trouble With Lichen_. Novel. 20th.

Yeats, William Butler. "Michael Robartes and the Dancer." Poem. 20th.

Yglesias, Helen. "Semi-Private." Short Story. 20th.

SUFFERING

Albee, Edward. _The Death of Bessie Smith_. Drama. 20th.

Alcott, Louisa May. _Hospital Sketches_. Sketches. 19th.

Anonymous. _Beowulf_. Epic Poem. Medieval.

Anonymous. "The life of this world." Poem. Medieval.

Anonymous. "Look on your Lord, Man, hanging on the Rood." Poem. Medieval.

Anonymous. _The Wanderer_. Poem. Medieval.

Anonymous. "The Wife's Lament." Poem. Medieval.

Anonymous. "Wulf and Eadwacer" or "Eadwacer." Poem. Medieval.

Apuleius. _The Golden Ass_. Tale. Classical.

Bacon, Francis. _The Advancement of Learning_. Treatise. Renaissance.

Baudelaire, Charles Pierre. "The Gaming Table" ("Le Jeu"). Poem. 19th.

The Bible. Job. Classical.

Blackmore, Richard. _Creation_. Poem. 18th.

Blake, William. _The Island in the Moon_. Sketches and Poems. 19th.

Blake, William. Paintings, Especially Those Accompanying _Songs of Innocence and Experience_. 19th.

Brontë, Charlotte. _Jane Eyre_. Novel. 19th.

Brontë, Emily Jane. _Wuthering Heights_. Novel. 19th.

Browning, Elizabeth Barrett. "The Cry of the Children." Poem. 19th.

Browning, Robert. "The Family." Poem. 19th.

Burns, Robert. "Address to the Toothache." Poem. 18th.

Burton, Robert. _The Anatomy of Melancholy_. Treatise. Renaissance.

Butler, Samuel. _Hudibras_. Long Poem. 18th.

Camus, Albert. _Caligula_. Drama. 20th.

Capek, Karel. _R.U.R_. Drama. 20th.

Cellini, Benvenuto. _Autobiography_. Autobiography. Renaissance.

Chekhov, Anton. "An Attack of Nerves." Short Story. 19th.

Chekhov, Anton. _The Island: A Journey to Sakhalin_. Nonfiction.

Chekhov, Anton. "Misery." Short Story. 19th.

Chekhov, Anton. "Peasants." Short Story. 19th.

Chekhov, Anton. _Three Sisters_. Drama. 19th.

Chekhov, Anton. _Uncle Vanya_. Drama. 19th.

Chekhov, Anton. "Ward 6." Short Story. 19th.

Choromanski, Michal. _Jealousy and Medicine_. Novel. 20th.

Coleridge, Samuel Taylor. "Dejection: An Ode." Poem. 19th.

Coleridge, Samuel Taylor. "The Pains of Sleep." Poem. 19th.

Coleridge, Samuel Taylor. "The Rime of the Ancient Mariner." Poem. 19th.

Conrad, Joseph. _Nostromo_. Novel. 20th.

Crabbe, George. _The Borough_. Long Poem. 18th.

Crabbe, George. _The Village_. Long Poem. 18th.

Crane, Stephen. _The Red Badge of Courage_. Novel. 19th.

Crane, Stephen. "When a Man Falls a Crowd Gathers (A Street Scene in New York)." Sketch. 19th.

Crashaw, Richard. "On the Wounds of our Crucified Lord." Poem. Renaissance.

Daniel, Samuel. "Care-charmer sleep." Sonnet. Renaissance.

Dante Alighieri. _The Divine Comedy_. Long Poem. Medieval.

Defoe, Daniel. _A Journal of the Plague Year_. Treatise. 18th.

Delany, Samuel R. "Corona." Short Story. 20th.

Del Rey, Lester. _Nerves_. Novel. 20th.

De Quincey, Thomas. Confessions of an English Opium-Eater and Suspiria de Profundis. Essays. 19th.

Dickens, Charles. David Copperfield. Novel. 19th.

Dickens, Charles. The Old Curiosity Shop. Novel. 19th.

Dickinson, Emily. "After great pain, a formal feeling comes--." Poem. 19th.

Dickinson, Emily. "As One does Sickness over." Poem. 19th.

Dickinson, Emily. "The Heart asks Pleasure--first--." Poem. 19th.

Dickinson, Emily. "It Knew no Medicine--." Poem. 19th.

Dickinson, Emily. "Pain--has an Element of Blank--." Poem. 19th.

Dostoevsky, Fyodor. The Brothers Karamazov. Novel. 19th.

Dostoevsky, Fyodor. Crime and Punishment. Novel. 19th.

Dostoevsky, Fyodor. Notes From the Underground. Novella. 19th.

Dowland, John. "Flow my tears" and "I saw my Lady weep." Songs. Renaissance.

Doyle, Arthur Conan. "The Curse of Eve." Short Story. 19th.

Edwards, Jonathan. "Sinners in the Hands of an Angry God." Treatise. 18th.

Eliot, George (Mary Anne Evans). Janet's Repentance. Novella. 19th.

Eliot, George (Mary Anne Evans). The Mill on the Floss. Novel. 19th.

Ellison, Harlan. "I Have No Mouth and I Must Scream." Short Story. 20th.

Euripides. Medea. Drama. Classical.

Euripides. The Trojan Women. Drama. Classical.

Fielding, Henry. Voyage to Lisbon. Journal. 18th.

Freneau, Philip. "The Blessings of the Poppy." Poem. 18th.

Freneau, Philip. "The British Prison Ship." Poem. 18th.

Gilman, Charlotte Perkins Stetson. The Yellow Wallpaper. Short Story. 19th.

Goldsmith, Oliver. The Vicar of Wakefield. Novel. 18th.

Gorki, Maxim. The Lower Depths. Drama. 20th.

Gray, Thomas. "Ode on a Distant Prospect of Eton College." Poem. 18th.

Hardy, Thomas. Jude the Obscure. Novel. 19th.

Hawthorne, Nathaniel. "The Hollow of the Three Hills." Sketch. 19th.

Heloise. The Letters of Abelard and Heloise, no. 3. Letter. Medieval.

Hemingway, Ernest. The Old Man and the Sea. Novella. 20th.

Herbert, George. "The Pulley." Poem. Renaissance.

Hopkins, Gerard Manly. ("Carrion Comfort"). Sonnet. 19th.

Hopkins, Gerard Manley. "The Wreck of the Deutschland." Poem. 19th.

Howells, William Dean. A Hazard of New Fortunes. Novel. 19th.

Hugo, Victor. Les Miserables. Novel. 19th.

Johnson, Samuel. A Dictionary of the English Language. Dictionary. 18th.

Johnson, Samuel. Rasselas. Tale. 18th.

Jonson, Benjamin. Sejanus. Drama. Renaissance.

Kafka, Franz. The Metamorphosis. Novella. 20th.

Keats, John. Letters to Charles Brown, Sun., Aug. 20, 1820; Sept. 30, 1820. Letters. 19th.

Kipling, Rudyard. "The Tender Achilles" and "Hymn to Physical Pain." Short Story and Poem. 19th.

Lamb, Charles. "Christ's Hospital Five and Thirty Years Ago." Essay. 19th.

Lardner, Ring. "Haircut." Short Story. 20th.

Mackenzie, Henry. The Man of Feeling. Novel. 18th.

Marlowe, Christopher. The Tragical History of Doctor Faustus. Drama. Renaissance.

Marlowe, Christopher. The Troublesome Reign and Lamentable Death of Edward the Second. Drama. Renaissance.

Masters, Edgar Lee. The Spoon River Anthology. Poem Sequence. 20th.

Melville, Herman. Moby Dick. Novel. 19th.

Melville, Herman. White-Jacket, or The World in a Man-of-War. Novel. 19th.

Miller, Vassar. "The Common Core." Poem. 20th.

Milton, John. Paradise Lost. Epic Poem. Renaissance.

Milton, John. Samson Agonistes. Poem. Renaissance.

Milton, John. "When I Consider How My Light Is Spent." Sonnet. Renaissance.

Montaigne, Michel Eyquem de. "A Custome of the Ile of Cea." Essay. Renaissance.

More, Thomas. A Dialogue of Comfort Against Tribulation. Dialogues. Renaissance.

Nashe, Thomas. The Unfortunate Traveler. Tale. Renaissance.

Norris, Frank. The Octopus. Novel. 19th.

O'Neill, Eugene. Long Day's Journey Into Night. Drama. 20th.

Orwell, George (pseudonym of Eric Blair). "How the Poor Die." Essay. 20th.

Ovid (Publius Ovidius Naso). Amores. Book I, Elegy vii. Poem. Classical.

Pasternak, Boris. Doctor Zhivago. Novel. 20th.

Petrarch (Francesco Petrarca). Canzoniere, no. CCCXLIX (sonnet no. 303). Sonnet. Medieval.

Plautus. Pseudolus. Drama. Classical.

Pope, Alexander. An Essay on Man. Poem. 18th.

Reade, Charles. Hard Cash. Novel. 19th.

Réage, Pauline. The Story of O. Novel. 20th.

Sade, Donatien Alphonse François, Marquis de. Justine. Novel. 19th.

Sade, Donatien Alphonse Francois, Marquis de. Philosophy in the Bedroom. Tale. 19th.

Sarton, May. As We Are Now. Novel. 20th.

Seneca, Lucius Annaeus. Hercules Furens. Drama. Classical.

Shakespeare, William. King Lear. Drama. Renaissance.

Shakespeare, William. Love's Labours Lost. Drama. Renaissance.

Shakespeare, William. The Tempest. Drama. Renaissance.

Shakespeare, William. Troilus and Cressida. Drama. Renaissance.

Shelley, Mary. Frankenstein. Novel. 19th.

Shelley, Percy Bysshe. The Cenci. Poetic Drama. 19th.

Shelley, Percy Bysshe. Prometheus Unbound. Poetic Drama. 19th.

Sholom Aleichem (Solomon Rabinowitch). "The Flag." Short Story. 19th.

Sholom Aleichem (Solomon Rabinowitch). "You Mustn't Weep--It's Yom-Tev." Short Story. 19th.

Sidney, Philip. Four Sonnets Made when his Lady had Pain in her Face. Sonnets. Renaissance.

Sladek, John T. "The Happy Breed." Short Story. 20th.

Smollett, Tobias. The Adventures of Ferdinand, Count Fathom. Novel. 18th.

Smollett, Tobias. The Adventures of Roderick Random. Novel. 18th.

Smollett, Tobias. The Expedition of Humphry Clinker. Novel. 18th.

Snow, C. P. Last Things. Novel. 20th.

Solzhenitsyn, Alexander. Cancer Ward. Novel. 20th.

Sophocles. Oedipus Rex. Drama. Classical.

Sophocles. Philoctetes. Drama. Classical.

Sterne, Laurence. A Sentimental Journey. Novel. 18th.

Stowe, Harriet Beecher. Uncle Tom's Cabin. Novel. 19th.

Swift, Jonathan. "A Modest Proposal." Essay. 18th.

Swift, Jonathan. "Stella's Birth-day: March 13, 1726/7." Poem. 18th.

Swift, Jonathan. "Verses on the Death of Dr. Swift." Poem. 18th.

Tennyson, Alfred. In Memoriam: A.H.H. Poems. 19th.

Tennyson, Alfred. "In the Children's Hospital." Poem. 19th.

Tolstoy, Leo. The Death of Ivan Ilych. Novella. 19th.

Twain, Mark. Adventures of Huckleberry Finn. Novel. 19th.

Twain, Mark. The Mysterious Stranger. Novella. 19th.

Voltaire, Francois-Marie Arouet. Candide. Tale. 18th.

Vonnegut, Kurt, Jr. Slaughterhouse Five. Novel. 20th.

Wallant, Edward Lewis. Children at the Gate. Novel. 20th.

Webster, John. The Duchess of Malfi. Drama. Renaissance.

Wells, H. G. The Island of Dr. Moreau. Novella. 19th.

Wharton, Edith. Ethan Frome. Novel. 20th.

Whitman, Walt. Drum Taps and Specimen Days. Short Poems and Journal. 19th.

Wigglesworth, Michael. The Day of Doom. Poem. 18th.

Wilde, Oscar. De Profundis. Essay-length Letter. 19th.

Williams, Tennessee. Cat on a Hot Tin Roof. Drama. 20th.

Williams, Tennessee. Suddenly Last Summer. Drama. 20th.

Williams, William Carlos. "To a Dog Injured in the Street." Poem. 20th.

Young, Edward. "On Michael Angelo's Famous Piece of the Crucifixion." Poem. 18th.

Zola, Emile. Germinal. Novel. 19th.

SUICIDE

Anderson, Maxwell. Bad Seed. Drama. 20th.

Anonymous. Nice Wanton. Drama. Renaissance.

Anouilh, Jean. Ardèle. Drama. 20th.

Arlen, Michael. The Green Hat. Novel. 20th.

Arnold, Matthew. Empedocles on Etna. Dramatic Poem. 19th.

Barth, John. The End of the Road. Novel. 20th.

Beaumont, Francis and John Fletcher. Thierry and Theodoret. Drama. Renaissance.

Beddoes, Thomas Lovell. Death's Jest-Book. Poetic Drama. 19th.

Benn, Gottfried. "Monologue." Poem. 20th.

Berryman, John. "Of Suicide." Poem. 20th.

Berryman, John. Recovery. Novel. 20th.

The Bible. Matthew. Classical.

Borges, Jorge Luis. "To Francisco Lopez Merino." Poem. 20th.

Brown, Geoff. I Want What I Want. Novel. 20th.

BRowning, Robert. "Apparent Failure." Poem. 19th.

Brunner, John. The Whole Man. Novel. 20th.

Burton, Robert. The Anatomy of Melancholy. Treatise. Renaissance.

Byron, George Gordon, Lord. Manfred. Dramatic Poem. 19th.

Campbell, William Edward March (William March, pseudonym). The Bad Seed; and Anderson, Maxwell. Bad Seed. Novel and Drama. 20th.

Camus, Albert. Caligula. Drama. 20th.

Carlyle, Thomas. "The Everlasting No," "The Center of Indifference," and "The Everlasting Yea." Essays. 19th.

Chatterton, Thomas. "Sentiment." Poem. 18th.

Chekhov, Anton. Ivanov. Drama. 19th.

Conrad, Joseph. "The Idiots." Short Story. 20th.

Delany, Samuel R. "Corona." Short Story. 20th.

Dickens, Charles. Martin Chuzzlewit. Novel. 19th.

Donne, John. Bianthanatos. Treatise. Renaissance.

Dostoevsky, Fyodor. The Brothers Karamazov. Novel. 19th.

Dryden, John. All for Love. Drama. 18th.

Dunbar, Paul. "The Paradox" and "The Right to Die." Poems. 19th.

Durrell, Lawrence. Monsieur. Novel. 20th.

Euripides. Hippolytus. Drama. Classical.

Faulkner, William. The Sound and the Fury. Novel. 20th.

Fitzgerald, F. Scott. "An Alcoholic Case." Short Story. 20th.

Flaubert, Gustave. Madame Bovary. Novel. 19th.

Ford, John. The Broken Heart. Drama. Renaissance.

Franklin, Benjamin. Poor Richard: The Almanacks for the Years 1733-1758. Treatise. 18th.

Garcia Lorca, Federico. The House of Bernard Alba. Drama. 20th.

Ginsberg, Allen. "Howl." Poem. 20th.

Goethe, Johann. The Sorrows of Young Werther. Novel. 19th.

Gorki, Maxim. The Lower Depths. Drama. 20th.

Hardy, Thomas. Jude the Obscure. Novel. 19th.

Heinlein, Robert A. Time Enough For Love. Novel. 20th.

Heller, Joseph. Something Happened. Novel. 20th.

Hellman, Lillian. The Children's Hour. Drama. 20th.

Hemingway, Ernest. "A Clean, Well-lighted Place." Short Story. 20th.

Hemingway, Ernest. "Indian Camp." Short Story. 20th.

Henley, William Ernest. In Hospital. 28 Sketches in Verse. 19th.

Henry, O. (W. S. Porter). "A Fog in Santone." Short Story. 19th.

Hesse, Hermann. Steppenwolf. Novel. 20th.

Hopkins, Gerard Manly. ("Carrion Comfort"). Sonnet. 19th.

Howells, William Dean. An Imperative Duty. Novella. 19th.

Huxley, Aldous. Brave New World. Novel. 20th.

Ibsen, Henrik. Hedda Gabler. Drama. 19th.

Kesey, Ken. One Flew Over the Cuckoo's Nest. Novel. 20th.

Kipling, Rudyard. "Unprofessional." Short Story. 19th.

Kyd, Thomas. The Spanish Tragedy. Drama. Renaissance.

Lawrence, D. H. "The Horse Dealer's Daughter." Short Story. 20th.

Lawrence, D. H. "The Ship of Death." Poem. 20th.

Lucian of Samosata. "Death of Peregrine." Essay. Classical.

Mailer, Norman. An American Dream. Novel. 20th.

Mann, Thomas. The Magic Mountain. Novel. 20th.

Marlowe, Christopher. Tamburlaine: Part Two. Drama. Renaissance.

Masters, Edgar Lee. The Spoon River Anthology. Poem Sequence. 20th.

McCullers, Carson. The Heart Is a Lonely Hunter. Novel. 20th.

McCullers, Carson. Reflections in a Golden Eye. Novella. 20th.

Melville, Herman. Moby Dick. Novel. 19th.

Melville, Herman. Pierre, or the Ambiguities. Novel. 19th.

Meredith, George. Sonnet I. From Modern Love. Sonnet. 19th.

Miller, Arthur. After the Fall. Drama. 20th.

Miller, Arthur. The Crucible. Drama. 20th.

Miller, Arthur. Death of a Salesman. Drama. 20th.

Milton, John. Paradise Lost. Epic Poem. Renaissance.

Montaigne, Michel Eyquem de. "A Custome of the Ile of Cea." Essay. Renaissance.

More, Thomas. A Dialogue of Comfort Against Tribulation. Dialogues. Renaissance.

More, Thomas. Utopia. Treatise. Renaissance.

O'Connor, Flannery. "The Lame Shall Enter First." Short Story. 20th.

O'Neill, Eugene. The Iceman Cometh. Drama. 20th.

O'Neill, Eugene. Mourning Becomes Electra. Drama. 20th.

Percy, Walker. The Moviegoer. Novel. 20th.

Plath, Sylvia. The Bell Jar. Novel. 20th.

Plath, Sylvia. "Daddy." Poem. 20th.

Plath, Sylvia. "Lady Lazarus." Poem. 20th.

Rilke, Rainer Maria. "The Blind Man's Song," "The Drinker's Song," "The Idiot's Song," "The Suicide's Song," "The Dwarf's Song," and "The Leper's Song." Short Poems. 20th.

Robinson, E. A. "Richard Cory." Poem. 20th.

Schnitzler, Arthur. A Confirmed Bachelor (Also published as Dr. Graesler). Novel. 20th.

Schnitzler, Arthur. "The Man of Honour" (Also published as "The Murderer"). Short Story. 20th.

Schnitzler, Arthur. Mother and Son (Also published as Beatrice). Novella. 20th.

Schnitzler, Arthur. The Spring Sonata (Also published as Bertha Garlan). Novel. 20th.

Sexton, Anne. "Sylvia's Death." Poem. 20th.

Shakespeare, William. Antony and Cleopatra. Drama. Renaissance.

Shakespeare, William. Hamlet. Drama. Renaissance.

Shakespeare, William. Julius Caesar. Drama. Renaissance.

Shakespeare, William. King Lear. Drama. Renaissance.

Shakespeare, William. Macbeth. Drama. Renaissance.

Shakespeare, William. Othello. Drama. Renaissance.

Shelley, Percy Bysshe. Adonais. Poem. 19th.

Sophocles. Ajax. Drama. Classical.

Sophocles. Antigone. Drama. Classical.

Sophocles. Oedipus Rex. Drama. Classical.

Stein, Gertrude. Melanctha. Novella. 20th.

Stevenson, Robert Louis. "The Suicide Club." Short Story. 19th.

Stowe, Harriet Beecher. Uncle Tom's Cabin. Novel. 19th.

Swinburne, Algernon Charles. "The Garden of Proserpine." Poem. 19th.

Tennyson, Alfred. "Tiresias." Poem. 19th.

Tennyson, Alfred. "The Two Voices." Poem. 19th.

Tolstoy, Leo. The Kreutzer Sonata. Novella. 19th.

Vonnegut, Kurt, Jr. Cat's Cradle. Novel. 20th.

Waugh, Evelyn. The Loved One. Novel. 20th.

Wharton, Edith. Ethan Frome. Novel. 20th.

White, Patrick. The Eye of the Storm. Novel. 20th.

Woolf, Virginia. Mrs. Dalloway. Novel. 20th.

Woolf, Virginia. The Waves. Novel. 20th.

SURGERY

Alcott, Louisa May. Hospital Sketches. Sketches. 19th.

Auden, W. H. and Christopher Isherwood. The Dog Beneath the Skin. Poetic Drama. 20th.

Blake, William. The Island in the Moon. Sketches and Poems. 19th.

Burgess, Anthony. The Doctor Is Sick. Novel. 20th.

Choromanski, Michal. Jealousy and Medicine. Novel. 20th.

Cronin, A. J. The Citadel. Novel. 20th.

Dickinson, Emily. "Surgeons must be very careful." Poem. 19th.

Ellison, Harlan. "Wanted In Surgery." Short Story. 20th.

Hejinian, John. Extreme Remedies. Novel. 20th.

Hemingway, Ernest. "Indian Camp." Short Story. 20th.

Henley, William Ernest. In Hospital. 28 Sketches in Verse. 19th.

Isherwood, Christopher. The Dog Beneath the Skin. Poetic Drama. 20th.

Keyes, Daniel. Flowers for Algernon. Novella. 20th.

Kingsley, Sidney. Men in White. Drama. 20th.

Kipling, Rudyard. "The Tender Achilles" and "Hymn to Physical Pain." Short Story and Poem. 19th.

Melville, Herman. White-Jacket, or The World in a Man-of-War. Novel. 19th.

Mercier, Louis Sebastian. Memoirs of the Year Two Thousand Five Hundred (original title: The Year Two Thousand Four Hundred and Forty). Treatise. 18th.

Montaigne, Michel Eyquem de. "Of The Resemblance Betweene Children and Fathers." Essay. Renaissance.

Nichols, Peter. The National Health. Drama. 20th.

Norris, Frank. A Man's Woman. Novella. 19th.

Oates, Joyce Carol. Wonderland. Novel. 20th.

Pepys, Samuel. The Diary: Selections. Diary. 18th.

Plath, Sylvia. "The Surgeon at 2 a.m." Poem. 20th.

Selzer, Richard. The Rituals of Surgery. Short Stories. 20th.

Shango, J. R. "A Matter of Ethics." Short Story. 20th.

Shaw, George Bernard. The Doctor's Dilemma. Drama. 20th.

Snow, C. P. Last Things. Novel. 20th.

Tennyson, Alfred. "In the Children's Hospital." Poem. 19th.

Warren, Samuel. Passages from the Diary of a Late Physician. Sketches. 19th.

Wells, H. G. "Under the Knife." Short Story. 19th.

Welty, Eudora. The Optimist's Daughter. Novella. 20th.

V.D.

Anonymous. Nice Wanton. Drama. Renaissance.

Arlen, Michael. The Green Hat. Novel. 20th.

Blake, William. "London." Poem. 19th.

Brieux, Eugene. Les Avariés. Drama; and Sinclair, Upton. Damaged Goods. Novel. 20th.

Cellini, Benvenuto. Autobiography. Autobiography. Renaissance.

Cowley, Abraham. "To Dr. Scarborough." Poem. Renaissance.

Disch, Thomas. Camp Concentration. Novel. 20th.

Donne, John. "Why Doth the Poxe Soe Much Affect to Undermine the Nose?" Essay. Renaissance.

Doyle, Arthur Conan. "The Third Generation." Short Sketch. 19th.

Faulkner, William. Sanctuary. Novel. 20th.

Fielding, Henry. Amelia. Novel. 18th.

Fielding, Henry. Joseph Andrews. Novel. 18th.

Fielding, Henry. A Journey From This World To The Next. Sketches. 18th.

Fracastorius, Hieronymus. Hieronymus Fracastorius and his Poetical and Prose Works on Syphilis. Poem. Renaissance.

Franklin, Benjamin. Autobiography. Autobiography. 18th.

Franklin, Benjamin. Poor Richard: The Almanacks for the Years 1733-1758. Treatise. 18th.

Hemingway, Ernest. A Farewell to Arms. Novel. 20th.

Hemingway, Ernest. "One Reader Writes." Short Story. 20th.

Ibsen, Henrik. A Doll's House. Drama. 19th.

Ibsen, Henrik. Ghosts. Drama. 19th.

James I. A Counterblaste to Tobacco. Treatise. Renaissance.

Jonson, Benjamin. Epigram XLI, "On Gypsee." Poem. Renaissance.

Mather, Cotton. The Angel of Bethesda: An Essay Upon the Common Maladies of Mankind. Treatise. 18th.

Maupassant, Guy de. "Bed No. 29." Short Story. 19th.

McCullers, Carson. Reflections in a Golden Eye. Novella. 20th.

Meredith, George. The Ordeal of Richard Feverel. Novel. 19th.

O'Brien, Edna. August Is a Wicked Month. Novel. 20th.

Remarque, Erich Maria. Arch of Triumph. Novel. 20th.

Roth, Philip. "Epstein." Short Story. 20th.

Roth, Philip. Portnoy's Complaint. Novel. 20th.

Sade, Donatien Alphonse François, Marquis de. Philosophy in the Bedroom. Tale. 19th.

Shakespeare, William. Measure for Measure. Drama. Renaissance.

Shakespeare, William. Timon of Athens. Drama. Renaissance.

Sinclair, Upton. Damaged Goods. Novel. 20th.

Smollett, Tobias. The Adventures of Peregrine Pickle. Novel. 18th.

Smollett, Tobias. The Adventures of Roderick Random. Novel. 18th.

Strindberg, August. The Father. Drama. 19th.

Suckling, John. "Upon T. C. having the Pox." Poem. Renaissance.

Voltaire, Francois-Marie Arouet. Candide. Tale. 18th.

Williams, Tennessee. Sweet Bird of Youth. Drama. 20th.

Wycherley, William. The Country Wife. Drama. 18th.

WOMEN AS HEALERS

Alcott, Louisa May. _Hospital Sketches_. Sketches. 19th.

Anonymous. _Aucassin and Nicolete_. Tale. Medieval.

Anonymous. _The Celestina_. Drama. Renaissance.

Anonymous. "Now fade the rose and lily-flower." Poem. Medieval.

Anonymous. "Robin Hood's Death." Ballad. Medieval.

Apuleius. _The Golden Ass_. Tale. Classical.

Ariosto, Ludovico. _Orlando Furioso_. Poem. Renaissance.

Bacon, Francis. _The Advancement of Learning_. Treatise. Renaissance.

Barclay, Alexander. _Ship of Fools_. Poems. Renaissance.

Burton, Robert. _The Anatomy of Melancholy_. Treatise. Renaissance.

Chaucer, Geoffrey. _The Canterbury Tales_, "The Nun's Priest's Tale." Tale. Medieval.

Crabbe, George. _The Parish Register_. Long Poem. 18th.

Dickens, Charles. "A Small Star in the East." Sketch. 19th.

Donne, John. "Sapho to Philaenis." Poem. Renaissance.

Doyle, Arthur Conan. "The Doctors of Hoyland." Short Story. 19th.

Farquhar, George. _The Beaux' Stratagem_. Drama. 18th.

Fletcher, John. _The Faithful Shepherdess_. Drama. Renaissance.

Franklin, Benjamin. _Poor Richard: The Almanacks for the Years 1733-1758_. Treatise. 18th.

Freneau, Philip. "Ode XI, To the Philadelphia Doctors" and "On the Free Use of the Lancet." Poems. 18th.

Giraudoux, Jean. _The Madwoman of Chaillot_. Drama. 20th.

Gottfried von Strassburg. _Tristran and Isolt_. _Medieval Romances_. Tale. Medieval.

Hawthorne, Nathaniel. _The Scarlet Letter_. Novel. 19th.

Henley, William Ernest. _In Hospital_. 28 Sketches in Verse. 19th.

Hesse, Hermann. _Steppenwolf_. Novel. 20th.

Holmes, Oliver Wendell. _A Mortal Antipathy_. Novel. 19th.

Howells, William Dean. _Dr. Breen's Practice_. Novel. 19th.

James, Henry. _The Bostonians_. Novel. 19th.

Jewett, Sarah Orne. _A Country Doctor_. Novel. 19th.

Jonson, Benjamin. Epigram XLI, "On Gypsee." Poem. Renaissance.

Longfellow, Henry Wadsworth. _Evangeline_. Long Poem. 19th.

Maugham, W. Somerset. _Liza of Lambeth_. Novel. 20th.

McCullers, Carson. _The Ballad of the Sad Café_. Novella. 20th.

Milton, John. _Comus: A Mask Presented at Ludlow Castle_. Poem. Renaissance.

O'Connor, Flannery. "Revelation." Short Story. 20th.

Phelps, Elizabeth Stuart. _Dr. Zay_. Novel. 19th.

Rabelais, Francois. _Gargantua_ and _Pantagruel_. Tales. Renaissance.

Reade, Charles. _The Cloister and the Hearth_ and _A Woman-Hater_. Novels. 19th.

Rossetti, Christina. "Goblin Market." Poem. 19th.

Sexton, Anne. "For the Year of the Insane" and "The Sickness Unto Death." Poems. 20th.

Shakespeare, William. _All's Well That Ends Well_. Drama. Renaissance.

Shakespeare, William. _Pericles, Prince of Tyre_. Drama. Renaissance.

Shelley, Percy Bysshe. "The Magnetic Lady to her Patient." Poem. 19th.

Sidney, Philip. _Arcadia_. Tales and Poems. Renaissance.

Spenser, Edmund. _The Faerie Queene_. Poems. Renaissance.

Sterne, Laurence. _The Life and Opinions of Tristram Shandy, Gent_. Novel. 18th.

Tasso, Torquato. _Jerusalem Delivered_ (_Gerusalemme Liberata_). Epic Poem. Renaissance.

Tennyson, Alfred. "Lancelot and Elaine." Poem. 19th.

Tennyson, Alfred. _The Princess: A Medley_. Poem. 19th.

Twain, Mark. _Autobiography of Mark Twain_. Autobiography. 19th.

WOMEN AS PATIENTS

Arden, John. The Happy Haven. Drama. 20th.

Auden, W. H. and Christopher Isherwood. The Dog Beneath the
    Skin. Poetic Drama. 20th.

Blake, William. The Island in the Moon. Sketches and Poems.
    19th.

Boccaccio, Giovanni. The Decameron: Day 1, Prologue. Sketch.
    Medieval.

Choromanski, Michal. Jealousy and Medicine. Novel. 20th.

Dickens, Charles. "Wapping Workhouse." Sketch. 19th.

Edgeworth, Maria. Belinda. Novel. 19th.

Fitzgerald, F. Scott. Tender Is the Night. Novel. 20th.

Hejinian, John. Extreme Remedies. Novel. 20th.

Holmes, Oliver Wendell. Elsie Venner. Novel. 19th.

Howells, William Dean. Dr. Breen's Practice. Novel. 19th.

Isherwood, Christopher. The Dog Beneath the Skin. Poetic Drama.
    20th.

James, Henry. The Wings of the Dove. Novel. 19th.

Jonson, Benjamin. "To Sickness" and "An Epigram. To the Small
    Poxe." Poems. Renaissance.

Kipling, Rudyard. "Unprofessional." Short Story. 19th.

Maupassant, Guy de. "The First Snowfall." Short Story. 19th.

Mortimer, Penelope. The Pumpkin Eater. Novel. 20th.

Phelps, Elizabeth Stuart. Dr. Zay. Novel. 19th.

Reade, Charles. The Cloister and the Hearth and A Woman-Hater.
    Novels. 19th.

Sarton, May. As We Are Now. Novel. 20th.

Smollett, Tobias. The Adventures of Roderick Random. Novel.
    18th.

The Spectator, no. 431. Essay. 18th.

Swift, Jonathan. "The Furniture of a Woman's Mind." Poem.
    18th.

Twain, Mark. Autobiography of Mark Twain. Autobiography. 19th.

Warren, Samuel. Passages from the Diary of a Late Physician.
    Sketches. 19th.

White, Patrick. The Eye of the Storm. Novel. 20th.

Winchilsea, Countess of (Anne Finch). "The Spleen." Poem. 18th.

Yglesias, Helen. "Semi-Private." Short Story. 20th.

Young, Edward. "Satire V, Characters of Women." Poem. 18th.

Zugsmith, Leane. "The Three Veterans." Short Story. 20th.